CW01604667

The Book of DIY and HOME REPAIRS

© 1985, 1986 Orbis Publishing Ltd
© 1989 Macdonald & Co (Publishers) Ltd

This edition specially produced for CEEPI Ltd/Dealerfield Ltd in 1989

All rights reserved

No part of this publication may be reproduced, stored in a retrieval system, or transmitted, in any form or by any means without the prior permission in writing of the publishers, nor be otherwise circulated in any form of binding or cover other than that in which it is published without a similar condition including this condition being imposed on the subsequent purchaser.

ISBN 0 907305 32 6

Printed and bound in Yugoslavia by Mladinska Knjiga, Ljubljana

The Book of DIY and HOME REPAIRS

Edited by Mike Lawrence

CAXTON

CONTENTS

PART 1
PLUMBING

PART 2
ELECTRICS

PART 1

PLUMBING

WATER SUPPLY

Very few people are aware of what is involved in supplying clean, drinkable water to their homes. Yet beyond the taps is a vast network of underground pipes, pumping stations, reservoirs, water towers and treatment works, all designed to ensure an efficient and constant supply of fresh water.

UNDERSTANDING WATER SUPPLY

Each one of us uses about 160 litres (35 gallons) of water a day, and takes it for granted. Only in a long spell of dry weather comes an awareness that we should use it carefully. Our use is controlled by the supply system – this is how it works.

In the last 50 years the consumption of water has almost doubled. Rising standards of living have given rise to increased consumption, and a greater awareness of the need for hygiene has also played a large role in increasing the demand. Faced with this high demand, supply sources have been hard pressed to keep up.

Where it comes from

Water is supplied by the local water authority (or the 'Undertaking' as it is known in the plumbing trade). After falling as rain it is collected in reservoirs which are fed by streams and rivers, or is pumped from underground wells. Water varies a lot in its chemical makeup since it picks up minerals and gases as it flows. If it picks up calcium, magnesium and sodium salts it will be 'hard' – the menace of pipe systems. Before being distributed it is usually filtered through sand and pebble beds to remove solids and organisms, and may have chlorine added to it to ensure that it is 'potable' – drinkable. Fluoride is also sometimes added for the protection of teeth.

Distribution is carried out by a network of pipes starting with 'trunk mains' which may be as much as 610mm (24in) in diameter. These split into mains and sub-mains which run underneath streets and side streets. It is these sub-mains which are tapped by individual houses for their supply.

The house system may be 'direct' in which all cold water supplies are piped direct from the rising main, with the cistern only being used to supply the hot water tank. Or it may be an 'indirect' system in which all cold-water supplies are taken from the cistern, with the exception of a direct supply to the kitchen sink for drinking purposes.

For water to flow through the trunk mains – and eventually into your house – it must be under a certain amount of pressure. This pressure is assisted by pumps but it is vital that somewhere in the mains system the water should reach a height in a reservoir or water tower, higher than any domestic system it has to supply. The vertical distance through which the water 'falls' is known as the 'pressure head' and without it our cisterns would never fill up without a lot of expensive additional pumping. The storage cistern also provides a pressure head inside the house, which is why it's preferable to have it in the roof space.

The house system

The sub-main underneath the road is tapped by the 'communication pipe' which ends at the authority's stop-valve. This is usually situated under the pavement about 300mm (1ft) outside the boundary of your property. The stop-valve is located at the bottom of a vertical 'guard' pipe – about 1 metre (39in) deep – which is covered at the surface by a hinged metal cover. It should only be operated by the water authority and requires a special key to turn it. But in a real emergency you may be able to turn it yourself. In old houses it may be the only way of turning off the water supply. After this stop-valve the water enters the service pipe and from then on all pipes become your responsibility.

The service pipe continues under the wall of the property at a depth of at least 750mm (2ft 6in) to protect it from frost – though some water authorities insist that it should be 900mm (3ft) deep. As it travels under the house wall or foundation it usually goes through an earthenware pipe to protect it

Ready Reference

TURNING OFF THE WATER

It's essential you know where to turn off the mains water supply in case of an emergency. Check for stop-valves:

- under the kitchen sink
- in a utility room
- under the stairs
- just outside the boundary fence of your property. This one should only be turned off by the water authority, unless it's an emergency and you have no option
- in the front garden near the path and about a metre (39in) down. Look for a hinged metal cover. You might have to use a home-made wooden 'key' to reach the tap

INDIRECT COLD SUPPLY

The most common system of water supply in the UK is called 'indirect' because most taps take water from the storage cistern in the roof and not direct from the mains. The cistern is fed by the rising main which in turn is fed by the distribution pipe from the mains.

Water input to the cistern is controlled by a high pressure ball-valve. If this valve jams open the water level rises to flow out of the overflow or 'warning' pipe which should stick well out from the wall.

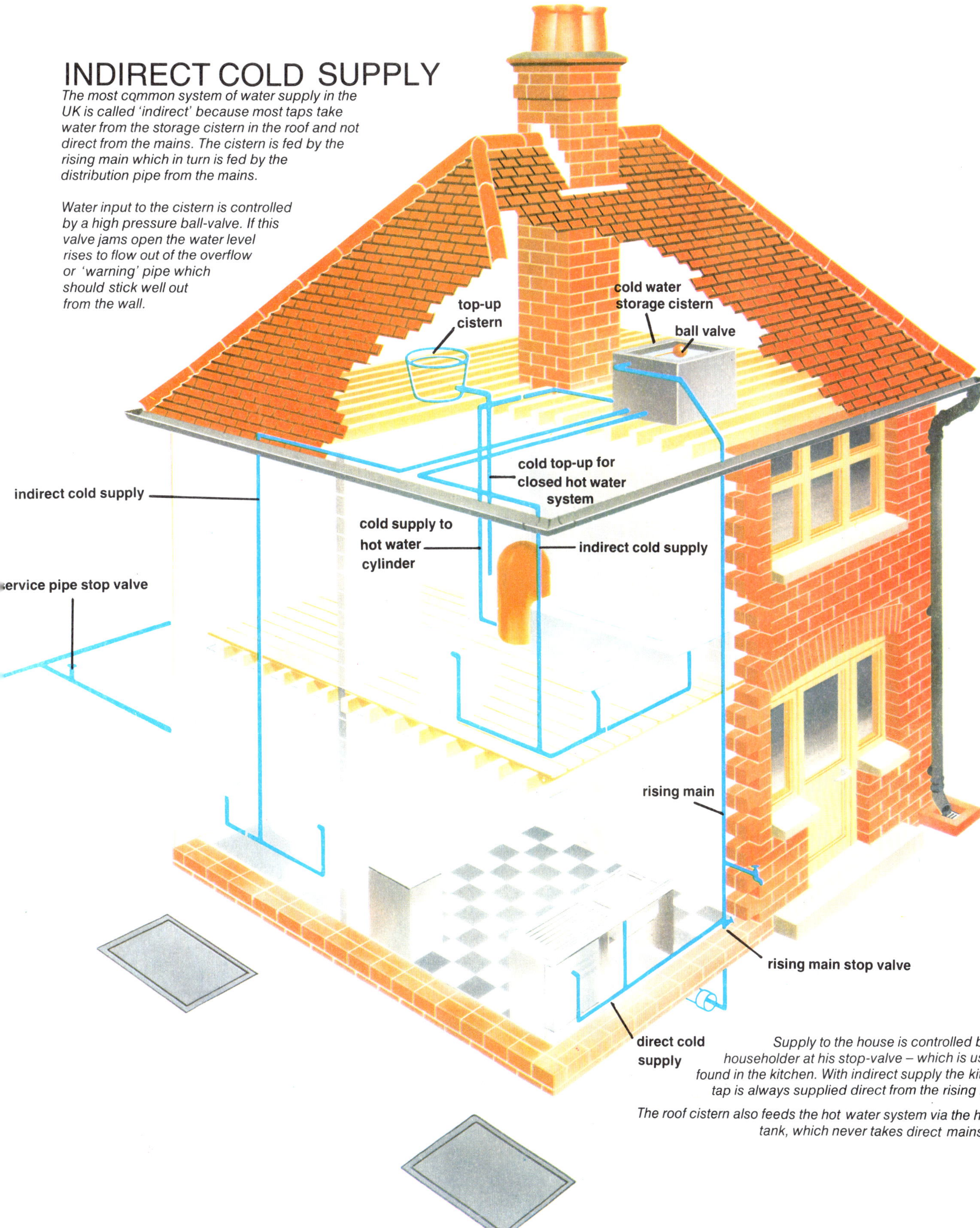

Supply to the house is controlled by the householder at his stop-valve – which is usually found in the kitchen. With indirect supply the kitchen tap is always supplied direct from the rising main.

The roof cistern also feeds the hot water system via the hot water tank, which never takes direct mains supply.

from possible settlement which might cause it to fracture. To prevent any risk of freezing in cold weather the service pipe should not emerge above ground level until it is at least 600mm (2ft) inside the inside wall surface.

Up to about 40 years ago, service pipes were usually made of lead (in fact the word plumbing originally stemmed from the Latin word for lead – *plumbum*). Today copper and polythene are used instead. The latter is particularly good as it is a poor conductor of heat and is less prone to freezing and fracture.

The service pipe

The service pipe continues under the wall near the kitchen sink, which means that it is often attached to the inner face of the outside wall. This is contrary to the recommendation that it should be attached to an inside wall, and so such a pipe should be lagged with insulation material. The pipe should also be insulated if it comes through any sub-ground floor cavity where it would be subjected to the icy blasts of winter from under-floor ventilation. Again these precautions are both intended to minimise the risk of frost damage.

When the service pipe rises above the ground floor it is called the 'rising main' and it eventually terminates in the supply cistern, which is usually in the roof cavity. The householder's main stop-valve is usually found on the rising main a little way above floor level. This is the most important 'tap' in the house. In any plumbing emergency – when bursts or leaks occur, for example, your first action should be to turn this tap off, thus isolating the house system from the mains water supply. The stop-valve should always be turned off when you go away if the house is going to be empty. In old houses the location of the stop-valve may vary considerably, it may be in the cellar, under the stairs, or even under a cover beneath the front path – or it may not exist at all, in which case the authority's stop-valve is the only control.

Branch supply pipes

At least one 'branch' supply pipe leaves the rising main close above the stop-valve and drain tap – this is to the tap over the kitchen sink. This tap must be supplied direct from the main supply as it is supposed to provide all drinking and cooking water. Water which has been in a storage cistern is no longer considered drinkable, sometimes termed 'potable', as it may be slightly contaminated by debris in the storage cistern.

Other branches may be taken at this point to an outside tap, or to a washing machine or dishwasher.

The rising main continues upwards and while its ultimate destination is the cold water storage cistern the pipework in between will vary from house to house, depending on

OTHER SYSTEMS

Other systems

There are other sorts of supply systems both for hot and cold water – and many variations. Systems reflect the design of buildings and the regulations.

Direct cold supply

The direct cold water system takes water direct from the main to all cold water taps. A roof storage cistern is still used but only as a supply reservoir for the hot water tank. Not only the main cistern but also all WC cisterns must have high pressure valves. The indirect system has the advantage of relieving the piping of high pressures and providing a temporary reserve in periods of drought when supplies may be restricted.

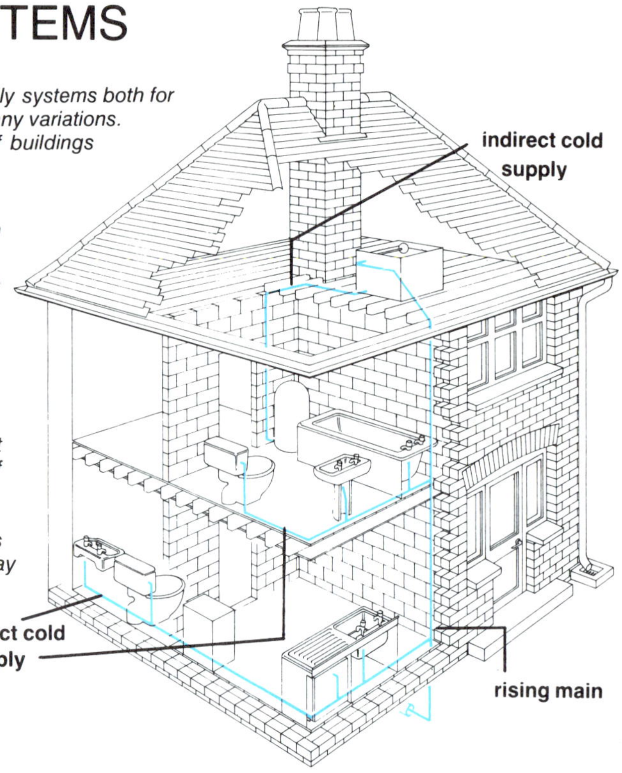

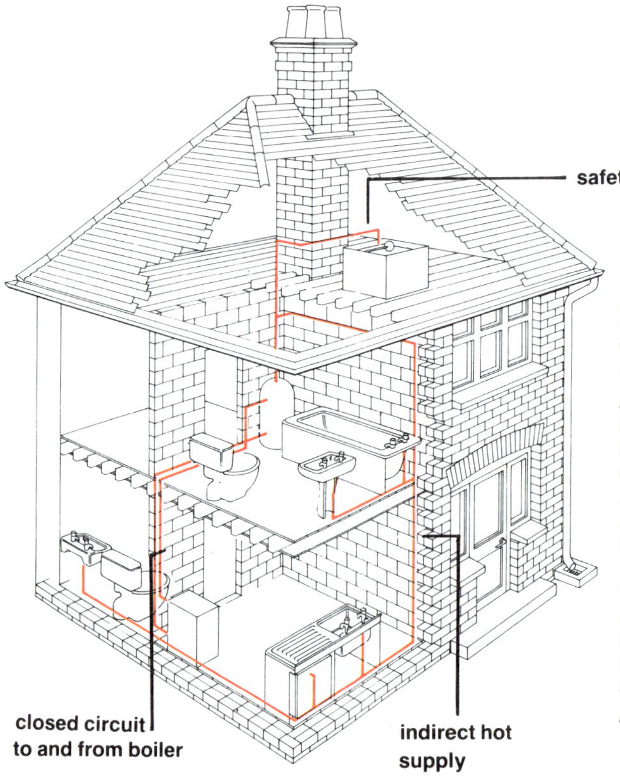

Hot supply from direct tank

The direct or 'open' system of hot water supply is based on the water being supplied to the hot water tank from the cold water cistern, passed to the boiler for heating, returned to the tank for storage and then piped to the supply taps.

The cold water cistern is always used to supply water to the hot water tank. Direct feed from the mains supply should never be used as the pressure would be too great.

INDIRECT HOT WATER SUPPLY

In an indirect or 'closed' hot water system a closed pipe runs from the boiler, through a heat exchanger in the hot water tank and back to the boiler again. This closed system contains water which never comes into contact with the hot water used by the household. The closed circuit between boiler and hot water cylinder loses water very slowly, and is topped up automatically by water from a small reservoir cistern in the loft. A safety pipe returns over-heated water to this or the main cistern.

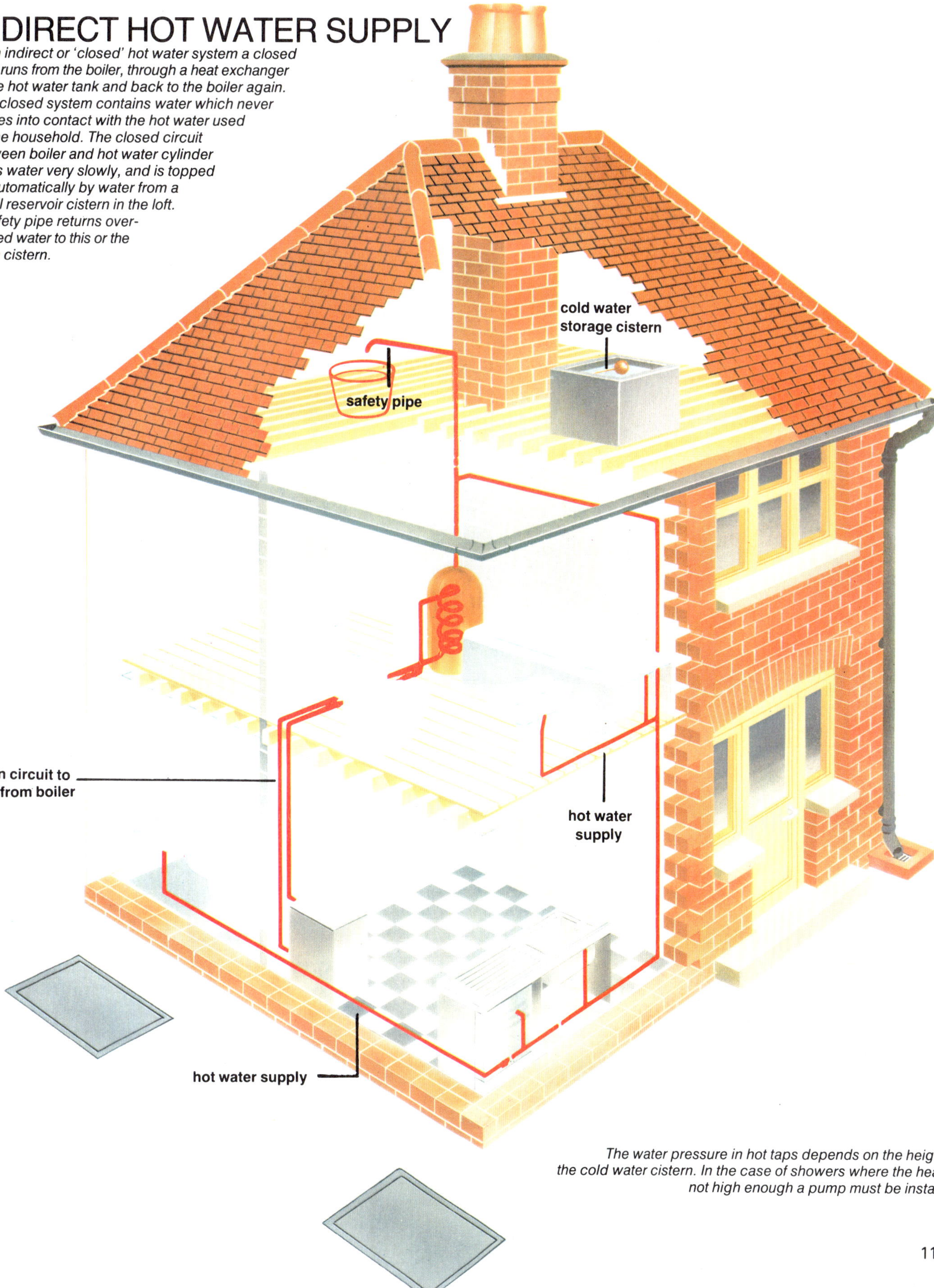

The water pressure in hot taps depends on the height of the cold water cistern. In the case of showers where the head is not high enough a pump must be installed.

whether a 'direct' or 'indirect' system has been installed.

In many areas indirect systems must be installed in new buildings, yet in Western Europe direct systems are the rule. Indirect systems have been encouraged because of the difficulty in maintaining constant mains pressure particularly at times of peak demand. Routing of most supplies through the storage cistern evens out fluctuations, and it also rules out the risk of 'back siphonage' whereby dirty water could be sucked back into the mains supply – though this rarely occurs. The 1976 drought in the UK provided good reason for indirect systems, since each house had an emergency supply in the storage cistern if the mains water had to be shut off.

Cisterns

The 'tank' in your loft or attic is in fact a 'cistern'. Cisterns are not sealed – though they should be covered – and so are subject to atmospheric pressure. Tanks are completely sealed – as with a hot water storage tank – and are not subject to atmospheric pressure.

Cold water cisterns ,have traditionally been made of galvanised mild steel and it is quite likely that you will find one like this in your loft. They are still available, but are not usually installed in new houses. Other materials used have been asbestos, cement, copper and glass fibre, but today the most common material is plastic, of which glass fibre reinforced polyester (GRP), polythene and polypropylene are the most common varieties.

The advantages plastics have over all other cistern materials are their lightness in weight, resistance to corrosion and flexibility. Galvanised steel is heavy and liable to corrode, while asbestos and cement are not only heavy but can become porous and are prone to accidental damage. Don't forget the capacity of a typical cistern is 227 litres (50 gallons), and this water alone weighs nearly 0.25 tonne (1/4 ton), so all cisterns must be fully supported on the joists. With rigid materials such as steel the cistern can rest across the joists, but with plastic and glass fibre a platform should be installed to support the whole area of the bottom, otherwise the material may develop local weaknesses.

Cisterns should be covered to prevent any contamination of the water. Where the underside of the roof is exposed dust and dirt are liable to fall in. The top and sides should also be insulated to minimise the risk of freezing. The bottom is left uncovered to allow rising warm air from rooms below to keep the water above freezing point, and so you shouldn't insulate the roof space under the cistern.

Cisterns were often installed before the roof was put on and if you want to replace yours, perhaps because it's made of steel and is corroding, you may not be able to get it through the trap door. While it is sometimes suggested that a cistern should be cut up to get it out this is in fact a very heavy and arduous job in such a confined space and it would be better to manoeuvre it to one side and leave it in the loft, installing a new cistern alongside. Modern plastic cisterns can literally be folded up so they can be passed through small loft hatches.

Pipes and taps

Water leaves the storage cistern in distribution pipes which are usually 22mm (3/4in) or 15mm (1/2in) in diameter. In a direct system, supply from the cistern will usually only be to the hot water tank, and in an indirect system this link must also be direct – but other distribution pipes are used with branches to supply the other appliances – basins, baths and WC cisterns. Distribution pipes usually end in taps but in the case of a WC a low pressure ball-valve controls the flow.

The WC in an indirect system has a low pressure ball-valve because when the water leaves the storage cistern it is no longer at mains pressure but at normal atmospheric pressure which is pressing down on the surface of the stored water. This means that the higher up the house a tap or other outlet is situated the lower will be the water pressure. In practice this means that you can't have a tap in an indirect system which is above the level of its distribution outlet from the cistern. Showers are particularly affected by this difference of pressure, and if there is not sufficient 'head' to 'drive' the shower a special pump may have to be installed.

Cold water supplied to the hot water tank is heated in two different ways again called indirect and direct systems – or, respectively, closed and open. In the latter the cold water is circulated through the boiler, where it is heated, and returned to the tank from where it flows to tapped outlets. In the indirect system the cold water supplied never actually goes to the boiler, instead it is heated in the tank by a coiled pipe or jacket containing hot water which is continuously circulating through the boiler. In either case a pump often helps the water flow through the boiler, and supplementary or alternative heat may come from an immersion heater. If there is no boiler but only an immersion heater in the tank the system is essentially direct with the heating of the water taking place in the tank rather than in the boiler.

Draining the system

Just above the rising main stop-valve should be a drain cock. With the stop-valve turned off the drain cock can be used to drain part of the cold water system when repairs are necessary – the hot water system has its own drain cock.

Ready Reference

PIPE SIZES AND THEIR USES

Distribution pipes

- 22mm (3/4in) pipe – water supply to bath and hot water cylinder
- 15m (1/2in) pipe – WC, basin, bidet and shower supplies
- 28mm (1in) pipe – for use with multiple appliances, but usually unnecessary.

Warning pipes (Overflows)

- these must have a diameter greater than that of the inlet pipe to prevent cold water cisterns and WC cisterns from overflowing.

CONNECTIONS AT COLD WATER CISTERN

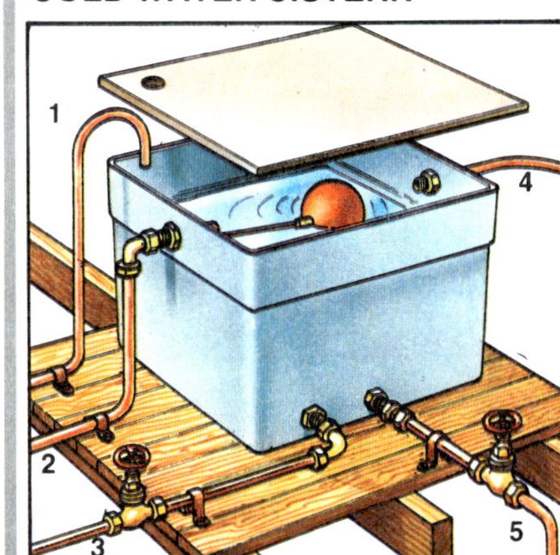

1 safety pipe **2 rising main** **3 cold supply to taps** **4 overflow** **5 cold supply to hot water tank**

DRAINING THE SYSTEM

To drain the system from the mains stop-valve to cistern, turn off the stop-valve and attach one end of the hose to the drain cock, which should be just above the stop-valve, and run the other end to a drain. Then open the drain cock.

Drain remainder of system by turning off

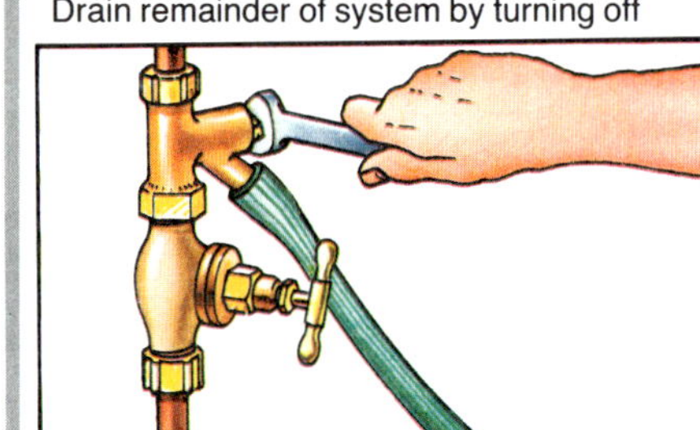

mains supply and opening cold water taps. The hot water system has its own drain cock, usually found close to the boiler.

BASIC SKILLS AND TOOLS

There is no doubt that a professional plumber is a highly skilled person and matching his expertise would take you many years of study and training. However, you can acquire sufficient skills without too much trouble, allowing you to carry out most of the plumbing jobs you will come up against, provided you take care in what you are doing.

JOINTS FOR COPPER PIPE

Joining copper pipe is one of the basic plumbing skills. Compression and capillary joints are easy to make and once you've mastered the techniques, you'll be prepared for a whole range of plumbing projects.

Connecting pipes effectively is the basis of all good plumbing as most leaks result from poorly constructed joints. For virtually all domestic plumbing purposes you will only have to use compression or capillary joints. Compression joints are easy to use but expensive, while capillary joints are cheap but need some care in fitting.

If you are making a join into an existing pipe system remember to make sure the water supply has been turned off at the relevant stop-valve (see EMERGENCY PIPE REPAIRS, pages 70 and 71) and the pipe completely drained.

Preparing the pipes

Before joining pipes together, check that the ends are circular and have not been distorted. If they have been dented, cut back to an undamaged section of the pipe using a hacksaw with a sharp blade or a wheel tube cutter (see pages 19–21).

The ends should also be square and a simple way of checking this is shown on page 17 (*see Ready Reference*). Use a file to make any correction and remove ragged burrs of metal. If you're using a capillary joint clean up the sides of the pipe with abrasive paper or steel wool.

Compression joints (friction joints)

A compression joint, as its name implies, is made by compressing two brass or copper rings (known as olives or thimbles) round the ends of the pipes to be joined, so forming a watertight seal. There are two main types of compression joint – the non-manipulative fitting and the manipulative fitting.

Although not the cheapest means of joining a pipe, a non-manipulative joint is the easiest to use and requires only the minimum of tools. It comprises a central body made of brass or gunmetal with a cap-nut at each end which, when rotated, squeezes the olive tightly between the pipe end and the casing. This is the most commonly used type of compression joint suitable for most internal domestic plumbing purposes.

A manipulative joint is now rarely used in indoor domestic water systems. Because it cannot be pulled apart it is sometimes used for underground pipework, but capillary joints will do equally well in these situations.

The joint usually comprises a male and a female union nut. These are slipped over the pipe ends which are then flared ('manipulated') using a special steel tool called a *drift*. Jointing compound is smeared on the inside of the flares and a copper cone is inserted between them. The nuts are then screwed together to complete the seal.

How a compression joint works

The olive (thimble) is the key part of a non-manipulative compression joint. When the cap-nut is rotated clockwise the olive is forced between the casing and the pipe and is considerably deformed in the process.

A watertight seal is dependent upon the pipe ends having been well prepared so they butt up exactly to the pipe stop in the casing. This forms a primary seal and ensures that the pipe is parallel to the movement of the rotating cap-nut. An even pressure is then applied to the olive so that it does not buckle under the strain of tightening.

What size of pipework and fittings?

Pipework is now sold in metric dimensions, but plumbing in your home may be in imperial sizes. The metric sizes are not exactly the same as their imperial equivalents – check the table *(Ready Reference,* right) which shows the different ways pipe can be bought.

These differences can cause problems. With capillary joints you have to use adaptors when converting pipe from one system to another. Adaptors are also needed for some compression joints although the 12mm, 15mm, 28mm and 54mm sizes are compatible with their imperial equivalents. This means if you already have imperial compression joints you can connect in new metric pipework, without replacing the joints.

Adaptors are made with different combinations of metric and imperial outlets to fit most requirements. A supplier will advise on what replacements to use.

HOW OLIVES MAKE A WATERTIGHT SEAL

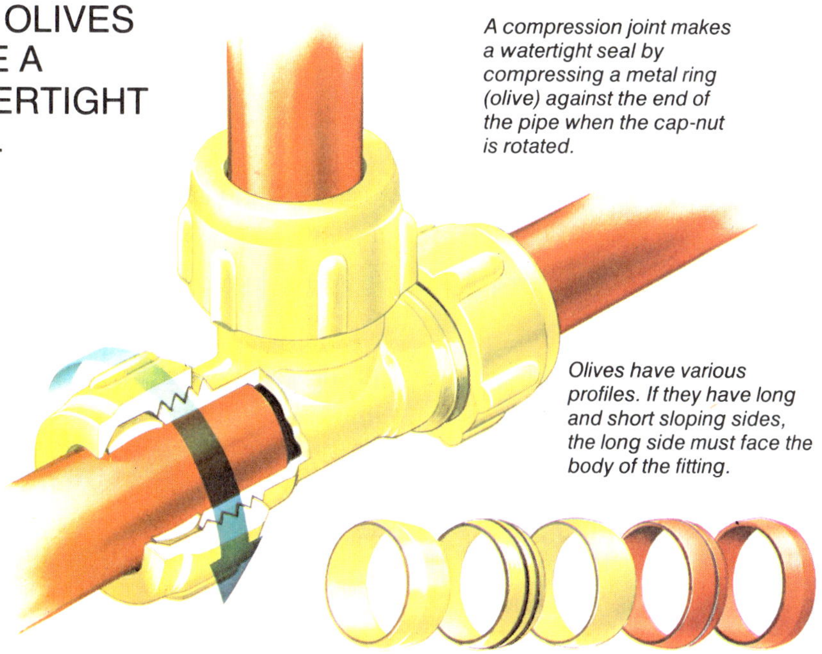

A compression joint makes a watertight seal by compressing a metal ring (olive) against the end of the pipe when the cap-nut is rotated.

Olives have various profiles. If they have long and short sloping sides, the long side must face the body of the fitting.

Capillary joints

A capillary joint is simply a copper sleeve with socket outlets into which the pipe ends are soldered. It is neater and smaller than a compression joint and forms a robust connection that will not readily pull apart.

Because it is considerably cheaper than a compression joint it is frequently used when a number of joints have to be made and is particularly useful in awkward positions where it is impossible to use wrenches.

Some people are put off using capillary fittings because of the need to use a blow-torch. But modern gas-canister torches have put paid to the fears associated with paraffin lamps and are not dangerous.

How a capillary joint works

If two pipes to be joined together were just soldered end to end the join would be very weak because the contact area between solder and copper would be small. A capillary fitting makes a secure join because the sleeve increases this contact area and also acts as a brace to strengthen the connection.

Molten solder is sucked into the space between the pipe and fitting by capillary action, and combines with a thin layer of copper at the contact surface thus bonding the pipe to the fitting. To help the solder to

What happens when solder melts

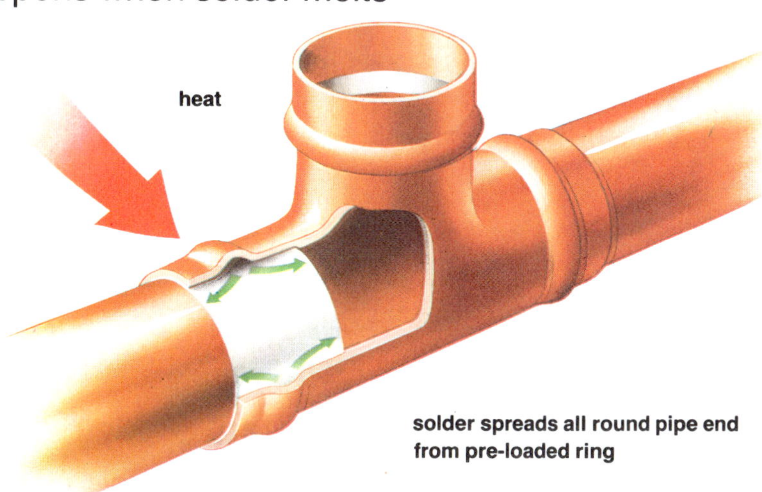

Ready Reference

WHICH TYPE OF FITTING?

Capillary fittings are
- cheap to buy
- unobtrusive when fitted
- useful in confined spaces
- very quick to install – and to unmake during alterations, BUT
- using them requires a blow-torch to melt the solder
- if the joint leaks you have to completely remake it.

Compression fittings are
- easy to assemble – you'll only need two wrenches or adjustable spanners – BUT
- they're much more expensive than capillary fittings
- they are much bulkier and obtrusive on exposed pipe runs
- in awkward places you may not be able to get wrenches in to tighten up the joint. Leaks can sometimes be cured by further tightening.

MATCHING UP PIPEWORK

Matching new pipe to old isn't always as easy as it sounds because even if your existing pipework is copper it may have been manufactured to imperial sizes – and all new copper pipe comes in metric sizes.
- metric/imperial equivalents for the most widely used sizes are given below

UK metric (external diameter)	Imperial (internal diameter)	Australian metric (internal diameter)
12mm	3/8in	–
15mm	1/2in	10mm
22mm	3/4in	20mm
28mm	1in	25mm
35mm	1 1/4in	32mm

- if you're using integral-ring capillary fittings (where the solder is pre-loaded into the fitting) you'll always need special adaptors to join new copper pipe to old – these adaptors are just ordinary fittings with one end slightly larger than the other
- end-feed capillary fittings can be made to work simply by adding more solder – but it requires more skill
- if you're making compression joints, the 12mm, 15mm and 28mm fittings will work with old 3/8in, 1/2in and 1in pipe. For other imperial pipe sizes, again you'll need special adaptors.

SAFETY TIPS

When using a blow-torch always
- wear thick heat-resistant gloves
- put down a lighted blow-torch on a firm flat surface with the flame pointing into space
- clear any flammable material from the area where you are working

MAKING A COMPRESSION JOINT

1 *Check that the end of the pipe is square using a file to make any correction and to remove burrs. Clean pipe end and olive with steel wool.*

2 *The olive goes on after the cap-nut. If it has both long and short sloping sides, make sure the long side faces the main body of the compression fitting.*

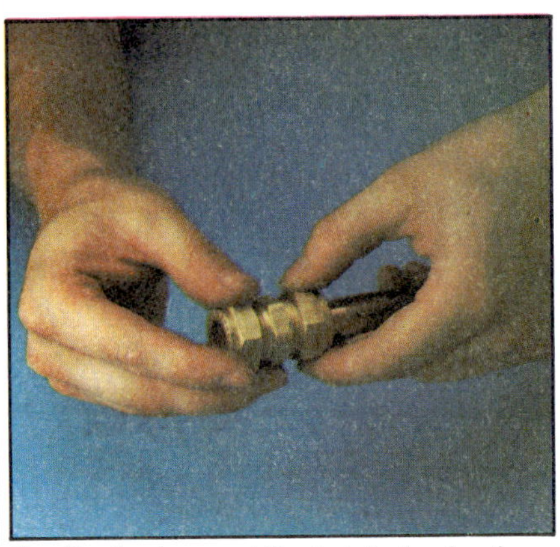

3 *Push pipe end firmly into body of fitting so that it rests squarely against pipe stop. Screw up cap-nut tightly with your fingers.*

4 *Make pencil mark on cap-nut and another aligning on body of fitting to act as guide when tightening cap-nut with wrench.*

5 *Use one wrench to secure body of fitting and the other to rotate the cap-nut clockwise. About 1½ turns is sufficient to give a watertight seal.*

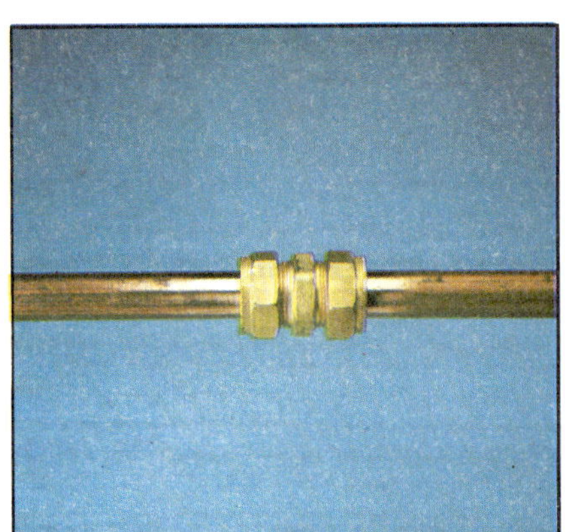

6 *Repeat operation to join other pipe to fitting. If water seeps through when supply is turned on, tighten cap-nut further by half a turn.*

'take' the copper needs to be clean and shining. Therefore flux is applied to prevent oxides forming which would impair the solder-copper bond.

Types of capillary joint

The most common type of capillary joint has a ring of solder pre-loaded into the sleeve. It is known as an integral ring or 'Yorkshire' fitting – the name of a leading brand.

The 'end feed' type of capillary joint is virtually the same as an integral ring fitting, but you have to add the solder in a separate operation. The sleeve is slightly larger than the pipe and liquid solder is drawn into the space between by capillary action.

Flux and solder

Essential in the soldering operation, flux is a chemical paste or liquid which cleans the metal surfaces and then protects them from the oxides produced when the blow-torch heats the copper so a good metal-solder bond is formed. Mild non-corrosive flux is easy to use as it can be smeared onto the pipe and fitting with a clean brush or a sliver of wood. Although it is best to remove any residue this will not corrode the metal. There is an acid-corrosive flux which dissolves oxides quickly, but this is mostly used with stainless steel. The corrosive residue must be scrubbed off with soapy water.

Solder is an alloy (mixture) of tin and lead and is bought as a reel of wire. Its advantage in making capillary joints is that it melts at relatively low temperatures and quickly hardens when the heat source (blow-torch) is removed.

Blow-torches

A blow-torch is an essential piece of equipment when making capillary joints. It is easy, clean and safe to use providing you handle it with care. Most modern torches operate off a gas canister which can be unscrewed and inexpensively replaced (larger cans are relatively cheaper than small). Sometimes a range of nozzles can be fitted to give different types of flame, but the standard nozzle is perfectly acceptable for capillary joint work.

Using a blow-torch

When using a blow-torch it's most convenient to work at a bench, but you'll find most jointing work has to be carried out where the pipes are to run. Pipework is usually concealed so this may mean working in an awkward place, such as a roof space, or stretching under floorboards. However, always make sure you are in a comfortable position and there's no danger of you dropping a lighted blow-torch.

MAKING A CAPILLARY FITTING

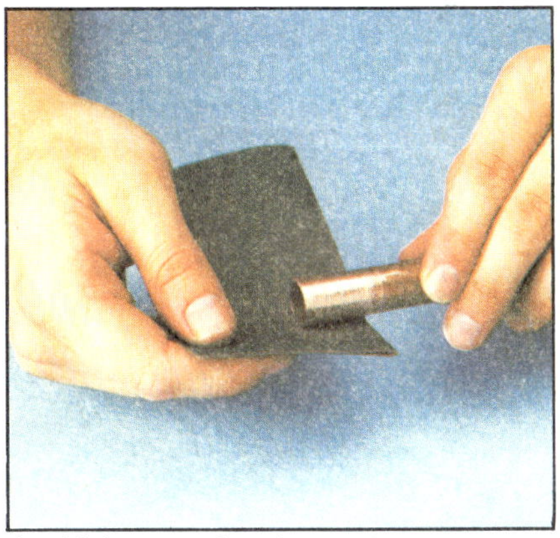

1 *Make sure the pipe end is square, then clean it and the inner rim of the fitting with steel wool or abrasive paper until shining.*

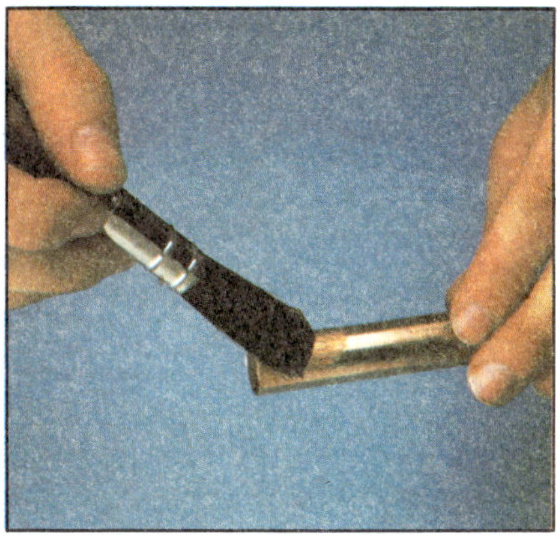

2 *Flux can be in liquid or paste form. Use a brush, rather than your finger, to smear it over the end of the pipe and the inner rim of the fitting.*

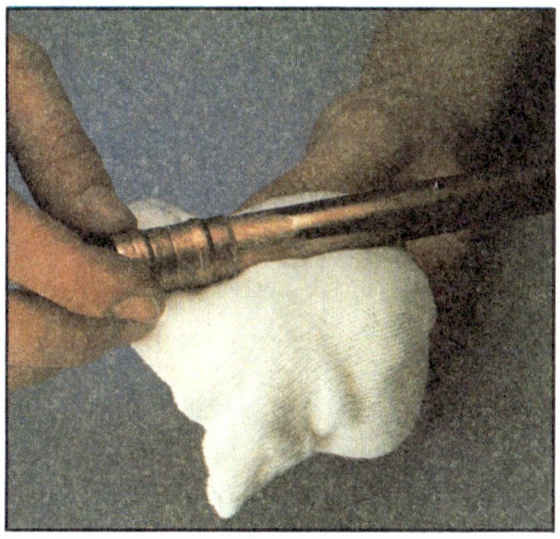

3 *Push pipe into fitting so that it rests against pipe stop, twisting a little to help spread the flux. Remove excess flux with a cloth.*

4 *When you're making up a whole pipe-run, it helps to make corresponding pencil marks on pipe ends and fittings as a guide for correct lining up.*

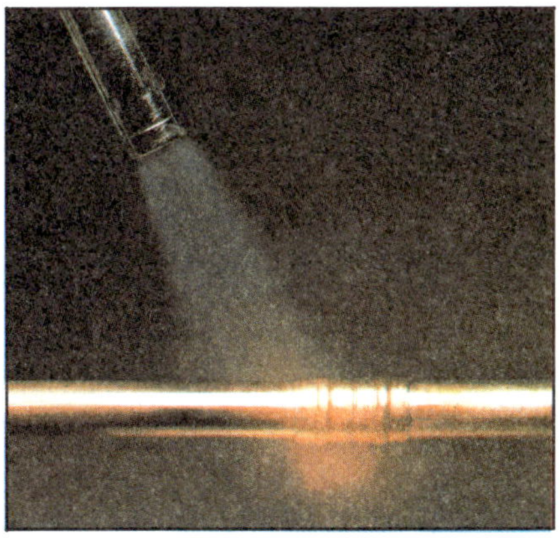

5 *Make other side of joint in same way, then apply blow-torch. Seal is complete when bright ring of solder is visible at ends of fitting.*

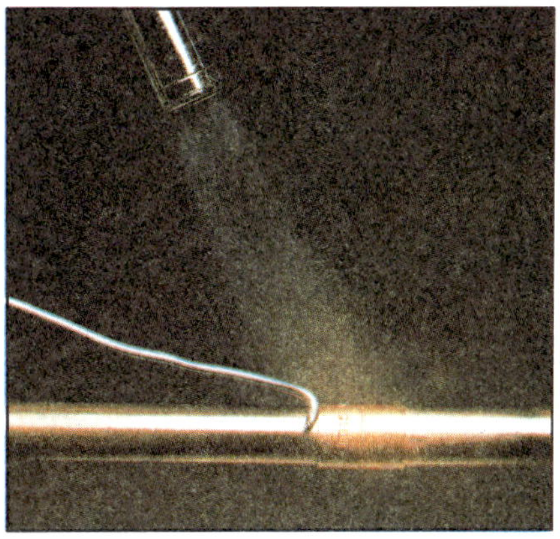

6 *For an end feed fitting, heat the pipe, then hold the solder to mouth of joint. A bright ring all the way round signifies a seal.*

Ready Reference

WHICH TOOLS?

For cutting pipe:

- hire a **wheel tube cutter** (which ensures perfectly square pipe ends)

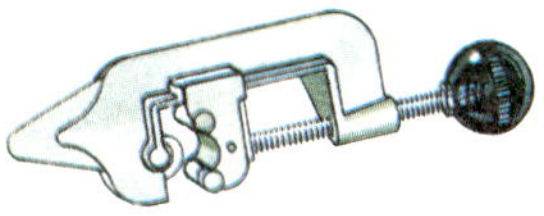

or use a **hacksaw**

- use a **metal file** for removing ragged burrs of metal and for squaring ends of pipe that have been cut with a hacksaw. A half-round 'second-cut' type is ideal.

For compression joints:

- use two adjustable **spanners** or **pipe wrenches** (one to hold the fitting, the other to tighten the cap-nut)

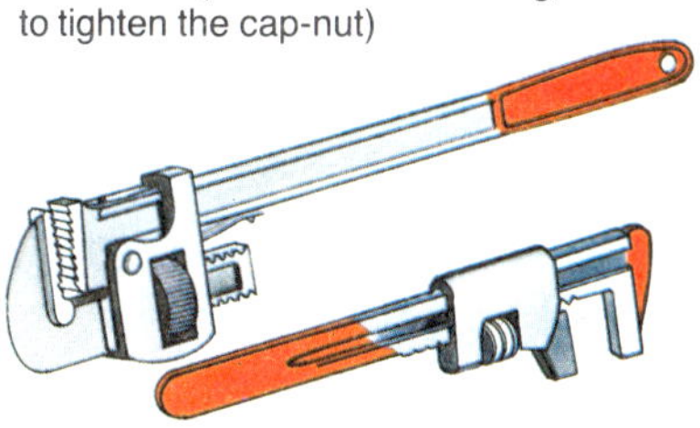

- **steel wool** to clean the surface of pipes before assembling a joint.

For capillary joints:

- a **blow-torch** to melt the solder
- **steel-wool** for cleaning pipe surfaces
- **flux** to ensure a good bond between the solder and copper
- **solder** because even if you're using integral ring fittings (which already have solder in them) you may need a bit extra
- **flame-proof glass fibre** (or a ceramic tile) to deflect the torch flame from nearby surfaces.

TIP: CUTTING PIPE SQUARELY

For a perfect fit, pipe ends must be cut square. If you're using a hacksaw, hold a strip of paper round the pipe so its edges align and saw parallel to the paper edge. Use the same trick if you have to file an inaccurately-cut end.

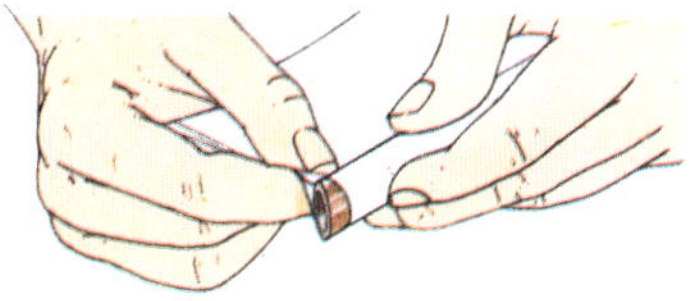

TIP: PROTECT NEARBY JOINTS

With capillary fittings, the heat you apply could melt the solder in nearby fittings. To help prevent this, wrap them in wet cloths.

When working near to joists and floorboards, glass, paintwork and other pipework with capillary joints it is important to shield these areas with flame-proof glass fibre matting.

Applying the heat

When making a capillary joint gradually build up the temperature of the copper by playing the flame up and down and round the pipe and then to the fitting. When the metal is hot enough the solder will melt and you can then take away the flame. The joint is complete when a bright ring of solder appears all round the mouth of the fitting. Stand the torch on a firm level surface and turn it off as soon as you have finished. Where two or more capillary joints are to be made with one fitting, for example the three ends of a tee, they should all be made at the same time. If this is not possible wrap a damp rag round any joints already made.

Repairing a compression joint

If a compression joint is leaking and tightening of the cap-nut doesn't produce a watertight seal you'll have to disconnect the fitting and look inside – after turning off the water supply. If a cap-nut is impossible to move, run a few drops of penetrating oil onto the thread. If that doesn't do the trick, you'll have to cut it out and replace the fitting and some piping.

Once you have unscrewed one of the cap-nuts there will be enough flexibility in the pipe run to pull the pipe from the casing. Usually the olive will be compressed against the pipe. First check that it is the right way round (see page 15) and if it isn't replace it with a new one making sure that it is correctly set.

Sometimes the olive is impossible to remove and needs to be cut off with a hacksaw – make the cut diagonally. Reassemble the joint following the procedure on page 16 and repeat the operation for the other end of the pipe. Turn on the water supply to check that the repair is watertight.

Repairing a capillary joint

Poor initial soldering is usually the reason why a capillary fitting leaks. You can try and rectify this by 'sweating' in some more solder but if this doesn't work you'll have to remake the joint.

Play the flame of the blow-torch over the fitting and pipe until the solder begins to run from the joint. At this stage you can pull the pipe ends out of the sockets with gloved hands. You can now reuse the fitting as an end feed joint or replace it with a new integral ring capillary connection.

If you reuse the fitting clean the interior surface and the pipe ends with abrasive paper or steel wool and smear them with flux. Then follow the procedure for making an end feed capillary joint.

REPAIRING A COMPRESSION JOINT

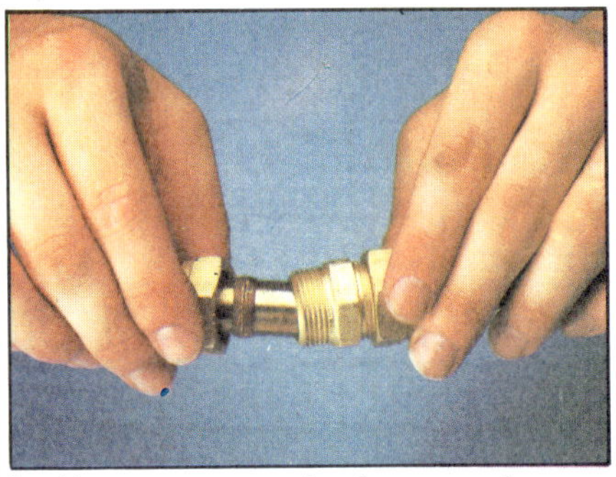

1 *Unscrew cap-nut using wrenches. There's enough flexibility in pipe run to pull pipe from casing. Check that olive fits, and isn't damaged.*

2 *A damaged olive must be removed. Use a hacksaw and to make it easier make the cut on the diagonal – but take care not to cut into the pipe itself.*

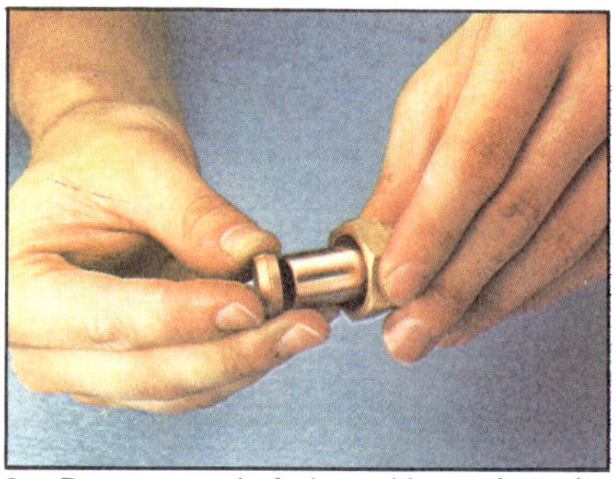

3 *Prepare end of pipe with steel wool or abrasive paper. Slip on new olive and finger tighten cap-nut. Rotate cap-nut 1½ turns using wrenches.*

REPAIRING A CAPILLARY JOINT

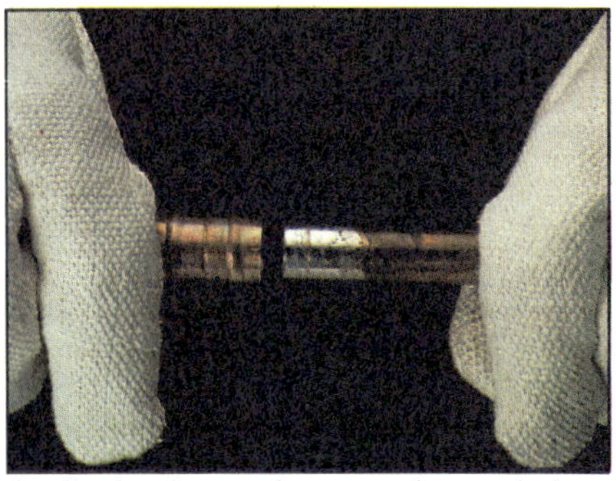

1 *Drain pipe and wrap a damp cloth round nearby joints. Play flame on fitting and pull pipe from rim using gloved hands.*

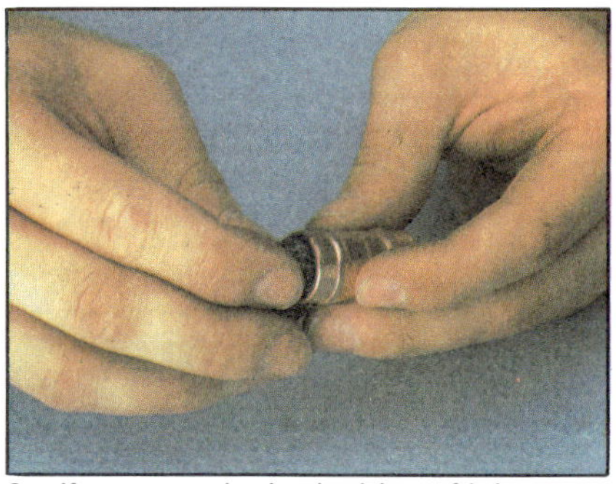

2 *If you remake both sides of joint use a new fitting. A spent integral ring fitting, thoroughly cleaned, can be used as an end feed joint.*

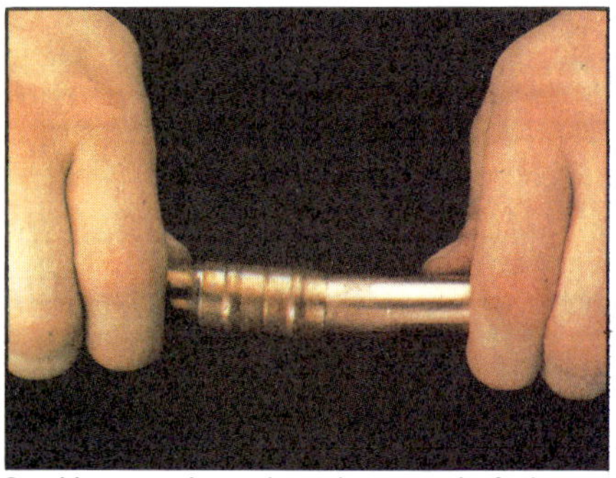

3 *Use steel wool to clean end of pipe and inside of fitting. Brush with flux and push pipe into socket. Apply blow-torch to melt solder.*

CUTTING & BENDING COPPER PIPE

One of the advantages of domestic copper pipe is that it's easy to cut and bend. Few tools are required and even if you've only a few bends to make in a pipe run, it makes sense to know how it's done. Making accurate bends may need some practice, but it's cheaper than buying specially-shaped fittings.

In all plumbing water has to be carried from a source to a fixture and often then to some type of exit where it can disperse as waste. Basic to all of this is that water must run smoothly with nothing causing resistance to the flow — an important factor when the pressure is low.

Generally the best plumbing practice is to make pipe runs as straight and direct as possible. But sometimes bends are unavoidable (like, for example, when pipe has to go around a room or to turn down into an area below) and if available fittings are neither right for the angle nor attractive to look at, then you'll have to bend the pipe to suit.

Copper piping, because it is both light and resistant to corrosion, is a popular choice for home plumbing work. It can be joined with either capillary or compression fittings (as described on pages 14–18) and when bends are needed you can create the angles in several ways.

The first essential is to accurately work out the pipe lengths you require. Once you've made the measurement double check it — it's quite easy to forget to allow for the pipe that will fit into the socket ends of the joints. You can make the actual marks on the pipe with pencil as this is clearly visible on copper and is a good guide when you come to cutting.

Cutting pipe accurately

For smaller pipe sizes, a sharp-bladed hacksaw is the best tool to use to make the cut. You'll need to hold the pipe firmly, but if you use a vice be careful not to over-tighten the jaws and crush the bore of the pipe (see *Ready Reference*, on page 21).

It's important to cut the pipe square so that it butts up exactly to the pipe stop in the joint. This will ensure the pipe is seated squarely in the fitting which is essential for making a watertight seal. It will also help to make that seal. It's surprising how near to square you can get the end just cutting by eye. But the best way to make a really accurate cut is to use a saw guide. This can be made very easily by placing a small rectangle of paper round the pipe with one long edge against the cut mark. By bringing the two short edges of the paper together and aligning them you effectively make a template that's square to the pipe. All you then have to do is hold the paper in place and keep the saw blade against it as you cut. Any burr that's left on the cut edges can be removed with a file.

If you intend to carry out a lot of plumbing, or are working mainly in the larger pipe sizes, it may be worthwhile buying (or hiring) a wheel tube cutter. Of course using one of these is never absolutely essential, but it does save time if you've more than, say, half a dozen cuts to make. And once you have one you'll use it for even the smallest jobs. It's quick to use and will ensure a square cut without trouble every time. You simply place the pipe in the cutter and tighten the control knob to hold it in place. The cutter is then rotated round the pipe and as it revolves it cuts cleanly into the copper. This circular action automatically removes burr from the outside of the pipe, but burr on the inside can be taken away with the reamer (a scraping edge) which is usually incorporated in the tool.

Bending copper pipe

If a lot of changes of direction are necessary in a pipe run it's cheaper and quicker to bend the pipe rather than use fittings. This also makes the neatest finish particularly if the pipework is going to be exposed. Under a pedestal wash-basin, for example, the hot and cold supply pipes rise parallel to each other in the pedestal before bending outwards and upwards to connect to the two tap tails.

Ready Reference

GETTING BENDS RIGHT

The trickiest part of bending copper pipe is getting the bends in the right place.
To avoid mistakes
- don't try to make too many bends in one pipe length
- mark the position for one bend at a time.

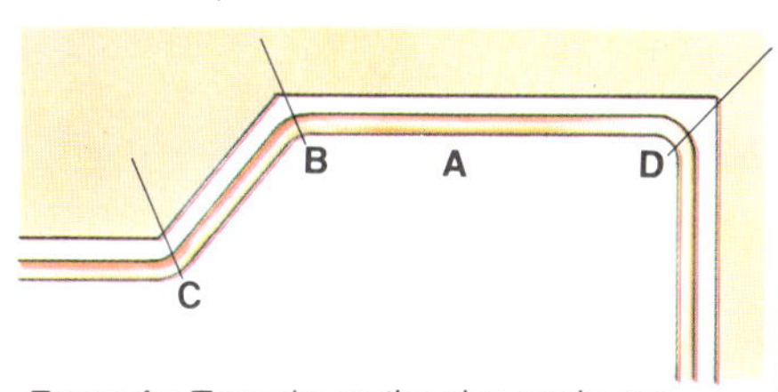

Example: To make up the pipe run in our sketch, plan to divide up the run at A; here two pipe lengths will be joined by a straight coupling after the bends have been formed.
- form bend B at approximately the right distance from point A
- offer up bend B to the wall, mark the start of bend C where the pipe touches the corner point
- form bend C and check for fit.

To get bend D in the right place on the second length of pipe
- measure the distance from A into the corner of the wall
- form bend D at this distance from the pipe end
- lay the two lengths in place, cut off any overlap and connect them with a straight coupling.

Using fittings in this situation would be more costly as well as possibly being unsightly, while the cheaper alternative, making bends, means the pipework is less conspicuous. The pipe can also be bent to the exact angle required so this method of changing direction is not limited by the angles of the fittings. And with fewer fittings in a pipe system there are fewer places where leaks can occur.

The smaller sizes of copper pipe, those most commonly used in domestic plumbing (15mm, 22mm and 28mm), can be bent quite easily by hand. The technique of annealing — heating the pipe to red heat in the vicinity of the bend to reduce its temper (strength) and so make bending easier — is unnecessary when working in these pipe sizes. But you will need to support the pipe wall, either internally or externally, as the bend is made. If you don't you'll flatten the profile of the pipe. Using it in this condition would reduce the flow of water at the outlet point.

For small jobs a bending spring is the ideal tool, supporting the pipe internally. It is a long hardened steel coil which you push into the pipe to the point where the bend will be made. It's best used for bends near the end of the pipe, since the spring can be easily pulled out after the bend is made. However, it can be used further down the pipe if it is attached to a length of stout wire (which helps to push it into place, and is vital for retrieving it afterwards).

Bending techniques

You actually bend the pipe over your knee, overbending slightly and bringing back to the required angle. The spring will now be fixed tightly in the pipe and you won't be able simply to pull it out. However, its removal is quite easy. All you have to do is to insert a bar — a screwdriver will do — through the ring at the end of the spring and twist it. This reduces the spring's diameter and will enable you to withdraw it. It's a good idea to grease the spring before you insert it as this will make pulling it out that much easier (also see *Ready Reference* page opposite).

Slight wrinkles may be found on the inside of the bend, but these can be tapped out by gentle hammering. It's wise not to attempt this before taking out the spring. If you do you'll never be able to remove it.

Bending springs are suitable for 15mm and 22mm diameter pipe. But although it is possible to bend 28mm pipe as well, it's advisable to use a bending machine instead. This is also preferable if you have a lot of bends to make. And if you don't want to go to the expense of buying one, you can probably hire a machine from a tool hire shop.

A bending machine consists of a semicircular former that supports the pipe externally during the bending operation and a roller that forces the pipe round the curve when the levers of the machine are brought together. The degree of bend depends on how far you move the handles.

Flexible pipe

This is a kind of corrugated copper pipe which can be bent easily by hand without any tools. You can buy it with two plain ends for connection to compression joints or with one end plain and one with a swivel tap connector for connection to a tap or ball-valve.

As it's the most expensive way of making a bend, it's not cost effective to use it when you have to make a number of changes of direction in a pipe run. It's not particularly attractive to look at so it is best used in places where it won't be seen. As such it's most commonly used for connecting the water supply pipes to the bath taps in the very confined space at the head of the bath. And it can make the job of fitting kitchen sink taps easier, particularly when the base unit has a back which restricts access to the supply pipes.

CUTTING COPPER PIPE

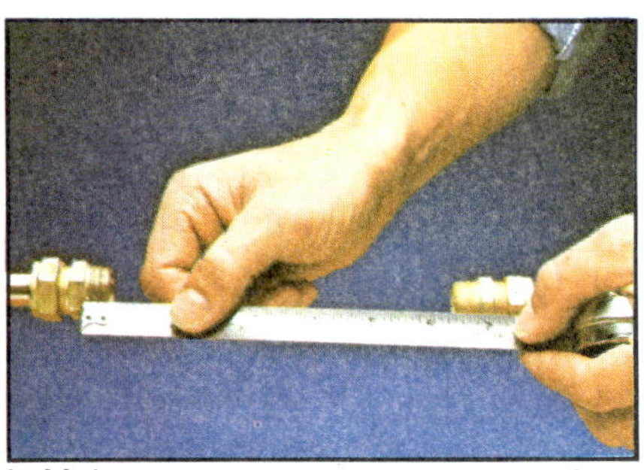

1 *Make an accurate measurement of the proposed pipe run. Don't forget to allow extra for the pipe that will fit inside the joints.*

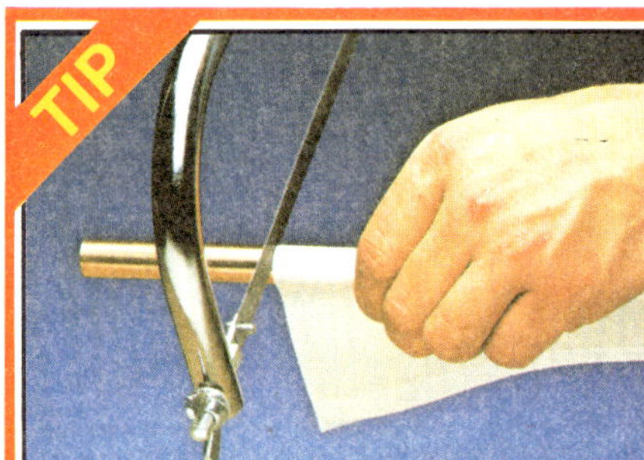

2 *Use a simple paper template to help you cut pipe squarely. Wrap the paper round the pipe and align the edges.*

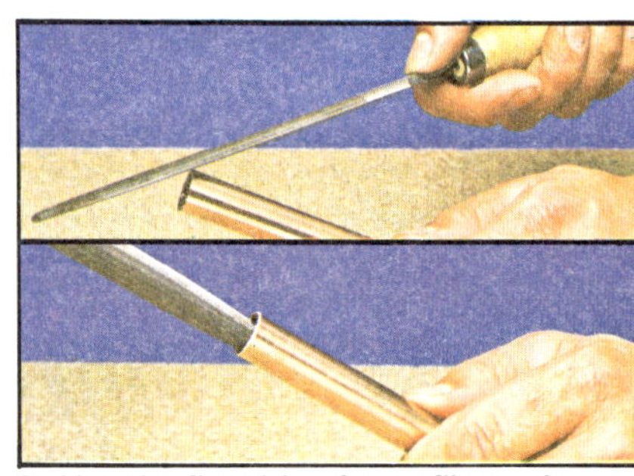

3 *Use the flat side of your file to clean any burr from the outside of the pipe. The curved side of the file can be used to clean the inside.*

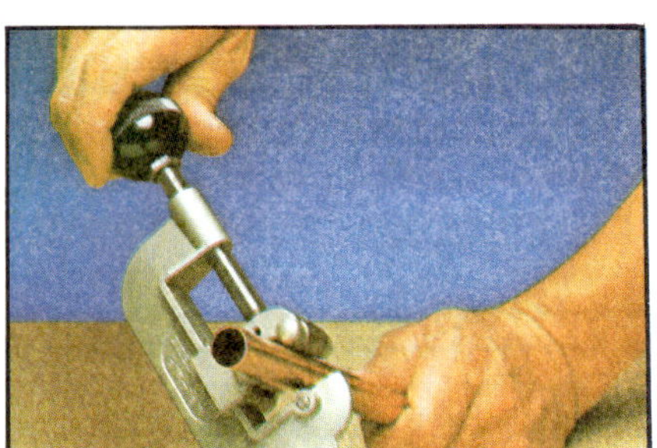

4 *When using a wheel tube cutter, position the cutting mark on the pipe against the edge of the cutting wheel, then tighten the control knob.*

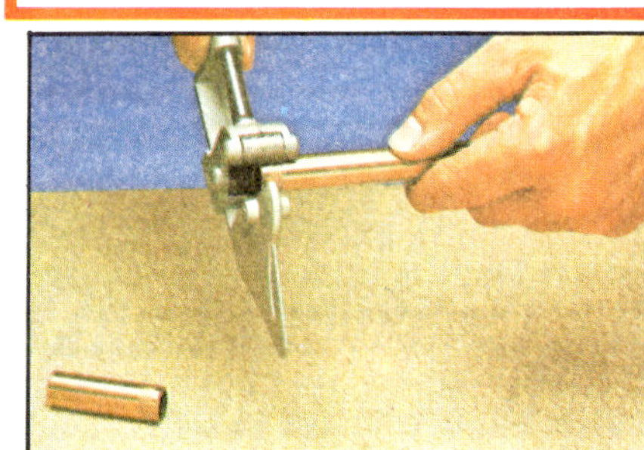

5 *Once the pipe is clamped in place, rotate the cutter so it makes an even cut. The rollers on the tool will keep the blade square to the pipe.*

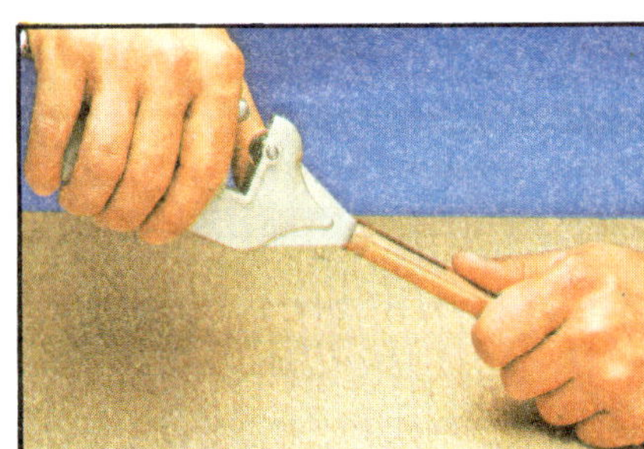

6 *A wheel tube cutter leaves a clean cut on the outside of the pipe, but any burr on the inside can be removed with the reamer (an attachment to the tool).*

BENDING COPPER PIPE

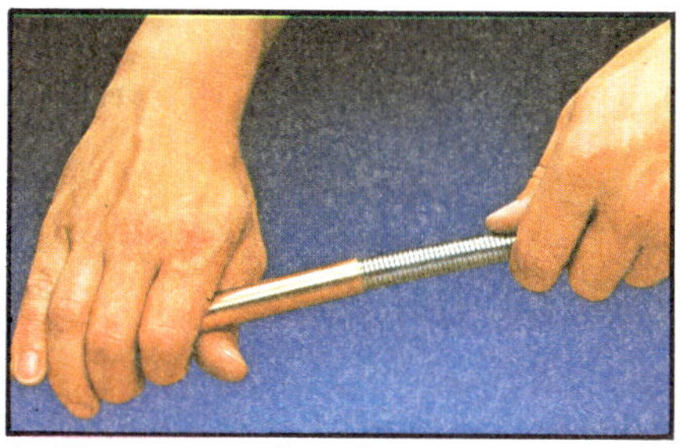

1 *Always use a bending spring which is compatible in size with the pipe. Smear it with petroleum jelly.*

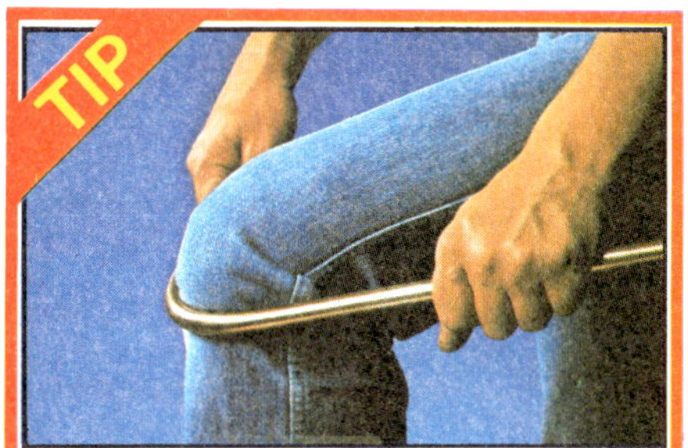

2 *Overbend the pipe slightly, and then bend it back to the required angle.*

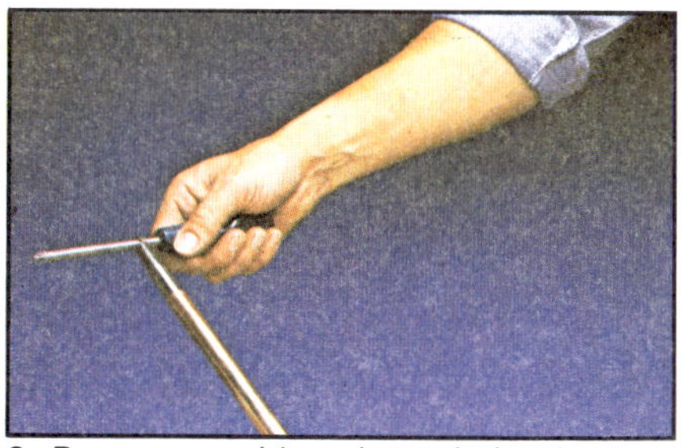

3 *Put a screwdriver through the ring at the end of the spring. Twist it, then pull the spring out.*

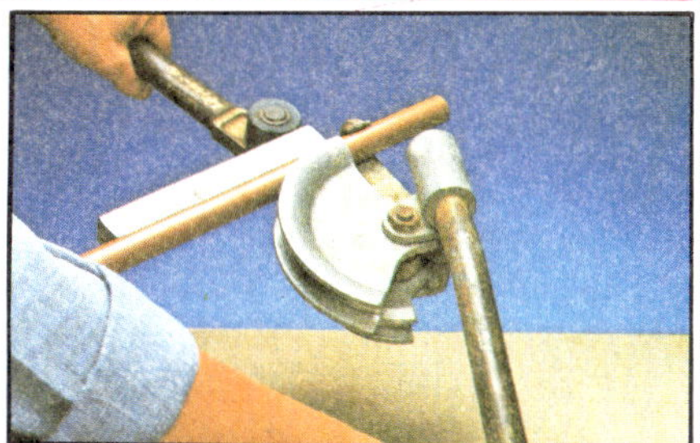

4 *To use a bending machine, open the levers and position the pipe as shown, then slide the straight former on top.*

5 *Raise the levers so the wheel runs along the straight edge and the pipe is forced round the circular former.*

6 *Bend the pipe to the required angle, then remove by opening the levers, and taking out the straight former.*

FLEXIBLE COPPER PIPE

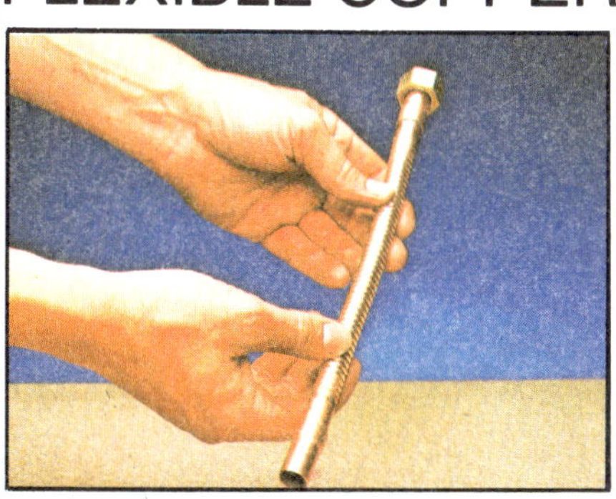

1 *Although relatively expensive, flexible pipe is ideal for making awkward bends in the pipe run to connect to taps.*

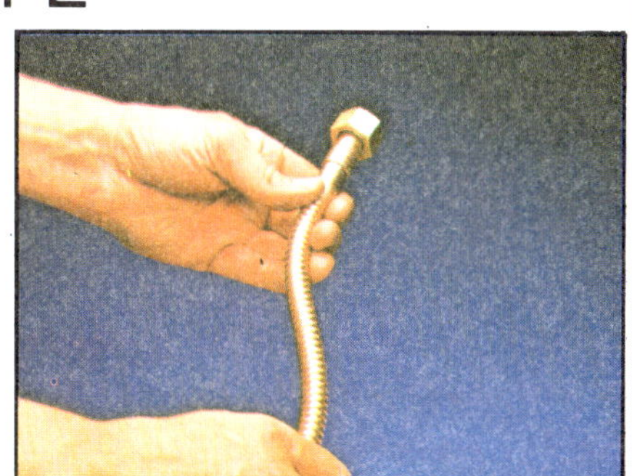

2 *It's easy to hand bend the pipe to the required shape, but don't continually flex it or the thin wall will split.*

Ready Reference

PIPE LENGTHS

Draw a rough sketch plan of the complete pipe run, then work out:

- how many 2 metre lengths you'll need
- where to join them in on the straight (not at a bend)
- how many fittings you'll need to connect the pipes to each other.

TIP: CUTTING PIPE

Copper pipe can be crushed in the jaws of a vice so use a bench hook when cutting with a hacksaw. Pin a scrap of wood beside it to hold the pipe snugly.

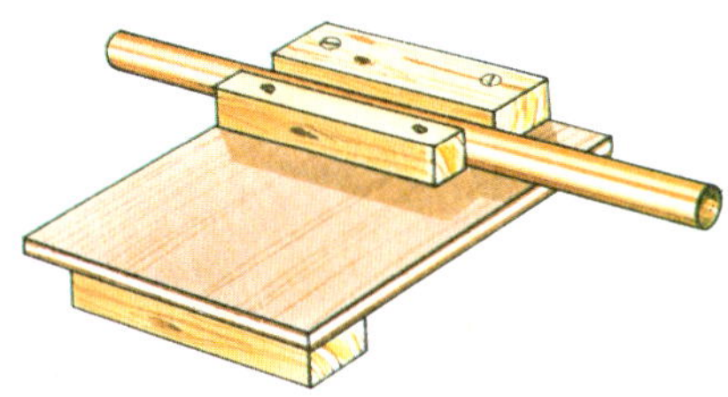

BENDING AIDS

For 15mm and 22mm pipe use a *bending spring* to match the pipe size. It's a flexible coil of hardened steel about 600mm (2ft) long.

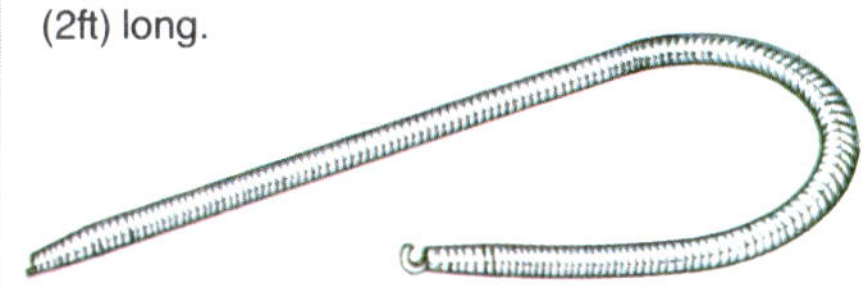

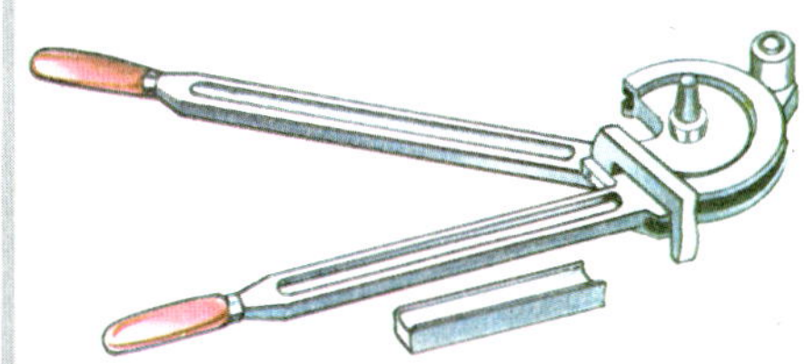

For 28mm pipe hire a *pipe bending machine* which supports the outside of the pipe wall as it bends.

TIP: REMOVING BENDING SPRINGS

For bends over 600mm (2ft) from the pipe end use a wire coathanger with a hooked end to turn and withdraw the spring.

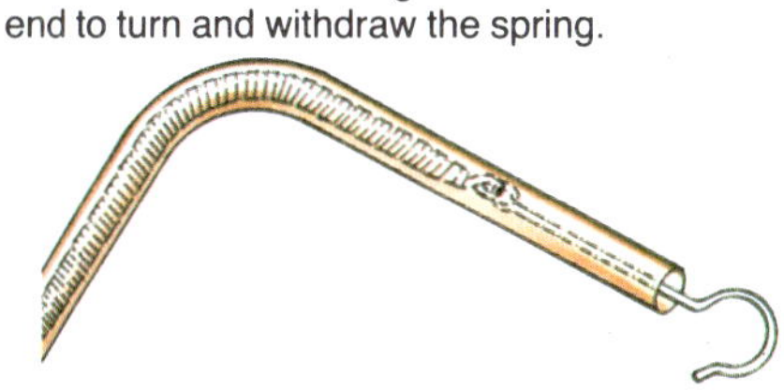

CONNECTING NEW PIPES TO OLD

Improvements or additions to a domestic plumbing system inevitably involve joining new pipework into old. How you do this depends largely upon whether the existing pipework is made of lead, iron or more modern materials – copper, polythene or even unplasticised PVC.

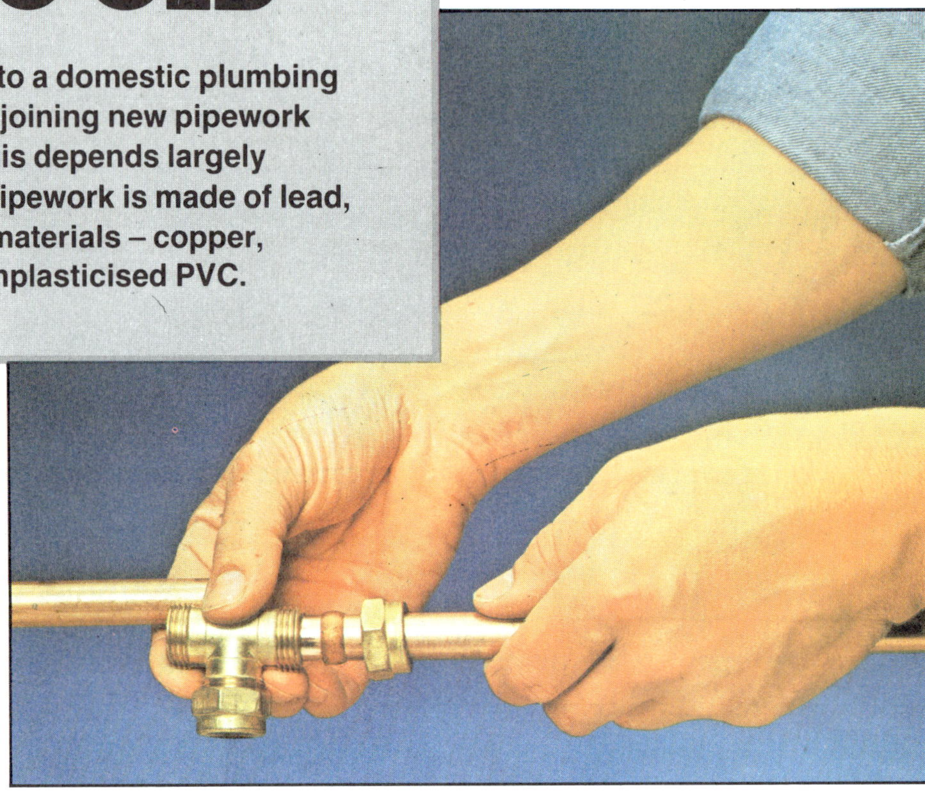

The principle of joining into existing pipework is quite straightforward. You decide where you will need your new water supply – at a bedroom basin or an outside tap, for example – and then pick a convenient point on the plumbing system to connect up your 'branch line'. At this point you have to cut out a small section of the old pipe and insert a tee junction into which the branch pipe will be fitted. That's all there is to it: laying the branch pipe will simply involve routine cutting, bending and joining of new pipe, and final connection to the new tap or appliance at the other end.

Before you can begin the job, however, you have to do some reconnaissance work to identify what sort of existing pipework you have. You might be tempted to relate the plumbing to the age of the house, thinking that an old house will have an old system with lead or iron pipework. But this isn't a reliable guide. Many old properties have been modernised and so may actually have a more up-to-date system than a house built relatively recently.

Until the 1950s the only types of pipe used in domestic plumbing were lead and iron, but then these were superseded by thin-walled copper piping. Today there are other alternatives too: stainless steel is sometimes used as an alternative to copper, and polythene and UPVC (unplasticised polyvinyl chloride) pipes can be installed for cold water supplies only.

Check the table (see *Ready Reference*, right) for the type of pipe you can use. While copper is the most common one for new work, it must *never* be joined to galvanised iron because of the severe risk of electrolytic corrosion of the iron if the galvanising is not in perfect condition.

First things first

Before cutting into a pipe run you'll first have to turn off the water supply to the pipe and then drain it by opening any taps or drain cocks connected to it (as described on pages 43–45). But this need not be too inconvenient if you make up the complete branch line before you turn the water off so you are without water only while you make the final branch connection.

Connecting into copper pipe

When taking a branch from a copper pipe it's probably easier to use a compression tee fitting rather than a capillary fitting. A compression fitting can be made even if there is some water in the pipe run – capillary joints need the pipe to be dry – and you won't have to worry about using a blow-torch and possibly damaging other capillary joints nearby (if they are heated up, their solder will soften and the joint will leak).

It's quite easy to work out how much pipe to cut out of the main run in order to insert a tee junction (of either compression or capillary fittings). Push a pencil or stick into the tee until it butts up against the pipe stop. Mark this length with your thumbs, then place the stick on top of the fitting so you can mark the outside to give a guide line. Next you have to cut the pipe at the place where the branch has to be made and prepare one of the cut ends (see the pictures on page 24). Now connect to the pipe the end of the tee that doesn't have the guide line marked on the casing and rest the tee back against the pipe. You will now be able to see where the pipe stop comes to and you can then mark the pipe to give you the second cutting point. Remove the section of pipe with a hacksaw and prepare the pipe end.

With a compression fitting put on the other cap-nut and olive. If you gently push the pipe and tee sideways to the pipe run this will give you more room to position the body before you allow the pipe end to spring into place. When this is done the cap-nut can be pushed up to the fitting and can be tightened with your fingers. Both sides of the tee can then be tightened using your wrenches to give the cap-nuts about one-and-a-half turns.

Remember that you must use a second wrench to grip the body of the fitting so it stays still as the cap-nut is tightened. If it should turn, other parts of the joint which have already been assembled will be loosened or forced out of position, and leaks will result. The connection into the main pipe run is now complete and you can connect up the branch pipe.

If you are using a capillary tee fitting there are a number of points to bear in mind. It's easiest to use one with integral rings of solder (this saves the bother of using solder wire) and after the pipe ends and the inside rims have been prepared and smeared with flux the fitting can be 'sprung' into place. The branch pipe should also be inserted at this stage so all the joints can be made at the same time.

When using the blow-torch, it is important to protect the surrounding area from the effects of the flame with a piece of flame-proof glass fibre matting or the back of a ceramic tile. It's also worthwhile wrapping damp cloths round any nearby capillary joints to protect them from accidental over-heating and thus 'sweating'

IDENTIFYING YOUR PIPEWORK

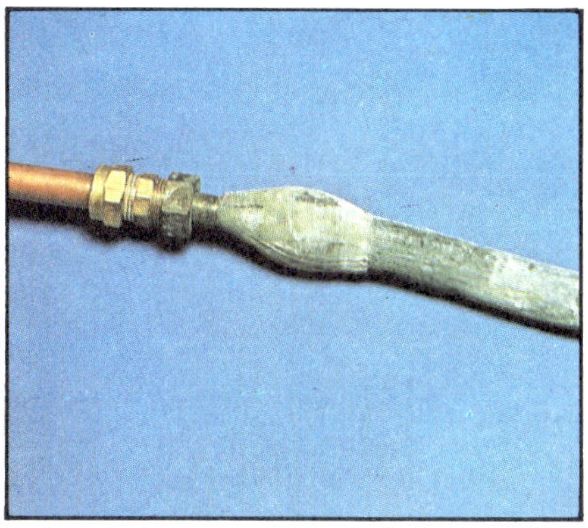

1 *Lead pipes are grey and give a dull thud when knocked. You can nick the surface with a knife. Look for smooth bends and neat even swellings – these are 'wiped' soldered joints. Repairs are often made using copper pipe.*

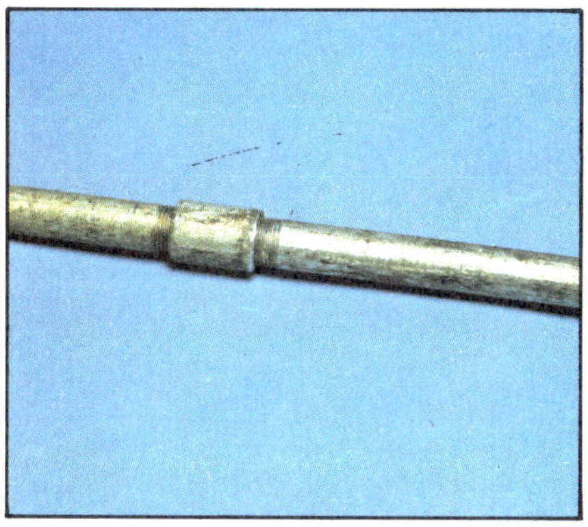

2 *Iron pipes have a grey galvanised or black finish and give a clanging sound when knocked. A knife will only scrape along the surface. Look for the large threaded joints which appear as a collar on the pipe or at a bend.*

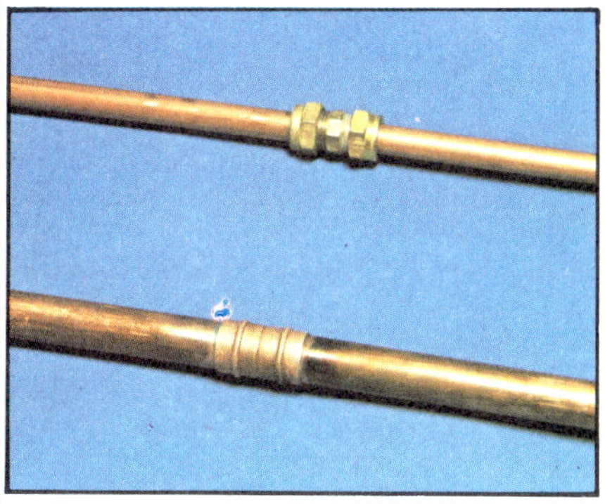

3 *Copper pipes are recognised by their familiar copper colour. Changes of direction are often made by bends in the pipe itself or by using angled fittings. The joints will be either the compression or capillary type.*

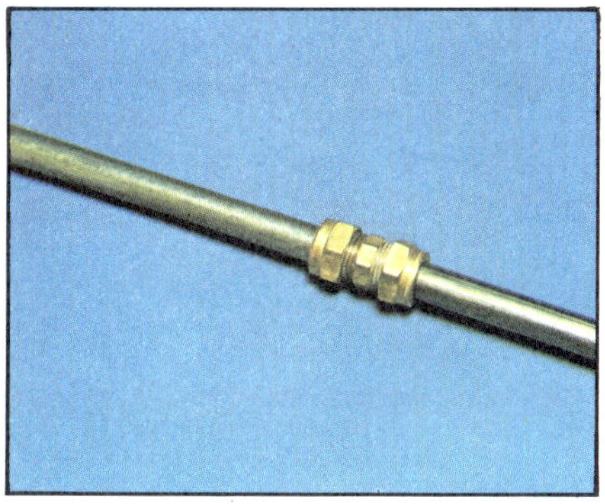

4 *Stainless steel pipes have a bright silvery surface. They come in the same sizes as copper and can be joined in the same way. Bends are only found in sizes up to 15mm. These pipes are not commonly used in the home.*

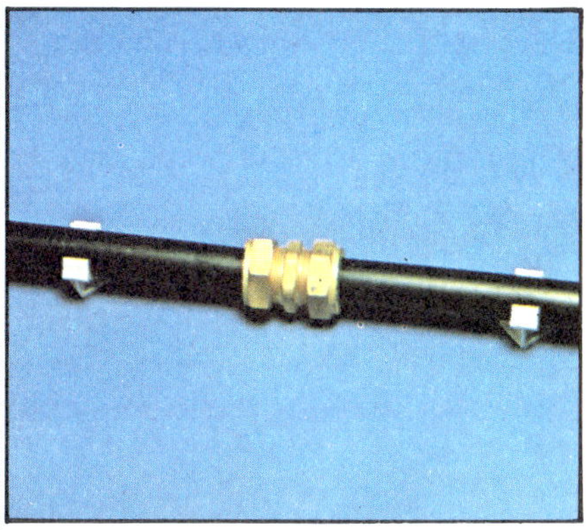

5 *Polythene pipes are usually black and are soft enough to be slightly compressed between the fingers. Joints are made with metal compression fittings which require special gunmetal olives and liners.*

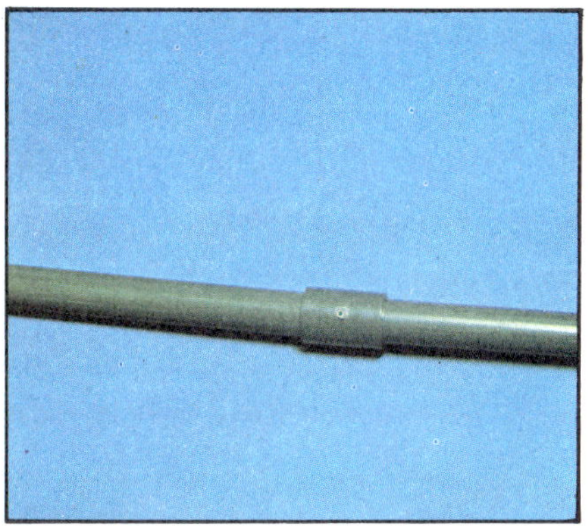

6 *UPVC pipes are grey and rigid. Connections and changes in direction are made by angled joints which fit like slim collars over the ends of the pipes. These are fixed in place using solvent weld cement.*

Ready Reference

WHAT JOINS TO WHAT?

Use this table as a guide to choosing new pipework – the first material mentioned is the best or most usual choice.

Existing pipe	New pipework
copper	copper, stainless steel, polythene
lead	copper, stainless steel, polythene
iron	iron, stainless steel, polythene
stainless steel	stainless steel, copper, polythene
polythene	polythene, copper, stainless steel
UPVC	copper, stainless steel, polythene

CONNECTING OLD TO NEW

Fitting metric to imperial pipework can be complicated by the slight differences in pipe diameters. The problem connections are:

copper to copper (compression fittings)
- some metric fittings can be used directly with imperial-sized pipes (eg, 15mm fittings with ½in pipe and 28mm fittings with 1in pipe)
- with other sizes you need to buy special adaptors or larger olives to replace those inside the fittings, so to connect a 15mm branch into existing ¾in pipe you'll need a tee 22 x 22 x 15mm with special olives for the 22mm ends of the tee.

copper to copper (capillary fittings)
- metric capillary fittings with integral solder rings are not compatible with imperial pipes, but straight adaptors are available to connect the two sizes of pipe
- use these to join in short lengths of metric pipe, the other ends of which are connected to opposite ends of the metric tee
- with end-feed type fittings, extra solder can be added to make a good joint with imperial-sized pipe.

copper to stainless steel – as for copper to copper connections, but usually compression fittings only.

stainless steel to copper – as above for copper to stainless steel.

stainless steel to stainless steel – as for copper to copper.

Connecting into lead pipe

Inserting a tee junction into lead pipe involves joining the run of the tee into two 'wiped' soldered joints. Join short lengths of new copper pipe into opposite ends of a compression tee. Measure the length of this assembly, and cut out 25mm (1in) less of lead pipe. Join the assembly in with wiped soldered joints – a job that takes a lot of practice, and one you may prefer to leave to a professional plumber until you have acquired the skill. You then connect the branch pipe to the third leg of the tee.

Connecting into iron

Existing iron pipework will be at least 25 years old, and likely to be showing signs of corrosion. Extending such a system is not advisable – you would have difficulty connecting into it, and any extension would have to be in stainless steel. The best course is to replace the piping completely with new copper piping.

Connecting into polythene pipe

If you have to fit a branch into a polythene pipe it's not a difficult job, especially if you use the same material. Polythene pipes are joined by compression fittings similar to those used for copper. Polythene hasn't yet been metricated in the UK and each nominal pipe size has a larger outside diameter than its copper equivalent. So you'll have to use either special gunmetal fittings for polythene pipe (still made to imperial sizes) or else an ordinary metric brass fitting a size larger than the pipe – 22mm for ½in polythene.

You also need to slip a special metal liner inside the end of the pipe before assembling each joint to prevent the pipe from collapsing as the cap-nuts are tightened. In addition, polythene rings are used instead of metal olives in brass fittings. Apart from these points, however, inserting a tee in a length of polythene pipework follows the same sequence as inserting one into copper.

Connecting into UPVC pipe

As with polythene it's an easy job to cut in a solvent weld tee – a simple collar fitting over the ends of the pipe and the branch. After you've cut the pipe run with a hacksaw you have to roughen the outsides of the cut ends and the insides of the tee sockets with abrasive paper and then clean the surfaces with a spirit cleaner and degreaser. Solvent weld cement is smeared on the pipe ends and the insides of the sockets, and the pipe ends are then 'sprung' into the sockets.

You have to work quickly as the solvent begins the welding action as soon as the pipes meet. Wipe surplus cement off immediately, and hold the joint securely for 15 seconds. After this you can fit your branch pipe to the outlet of the tee.

CUTTING INTO METRIC COPPER PIPE

1 On one side of the tee, push a pencil or piece of dowelling along the inside until it butts against the pipe stop. Mark this length with your thumb.

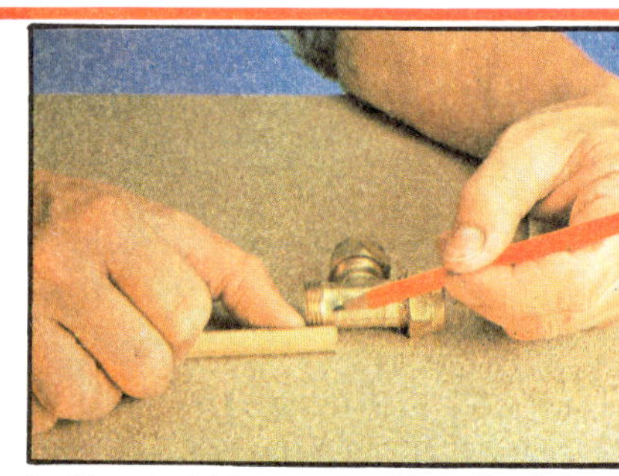

2 Now hold the marked length of dowel against the outside of the fitting so you can see exactly where the pipe stops. Mark this position on the fitting.

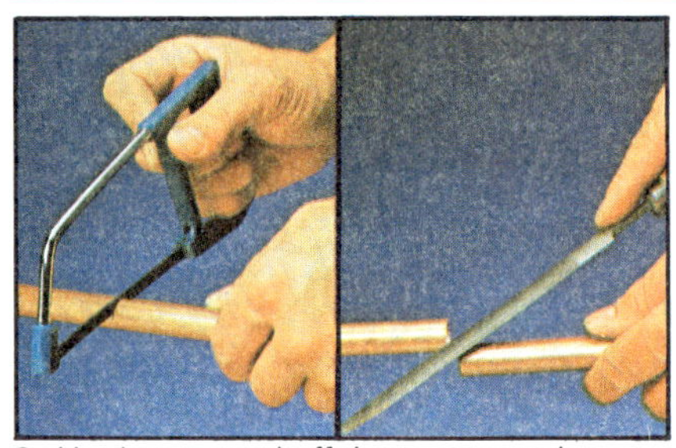

3 Having turned off the water and drained the supply pipe, cut it at the place where you want the branch to join in. Clean one of the ends with steel wool.

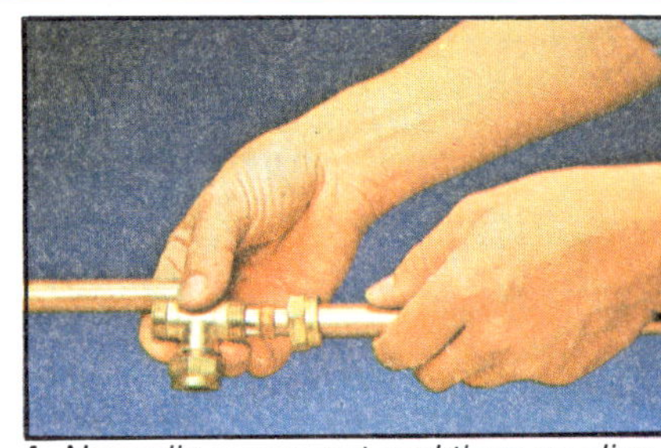

4 Now slip a cap-nut and then an olive over the cleaned pipe end and connect up the unmarked end of the tee fitting to the pipe.

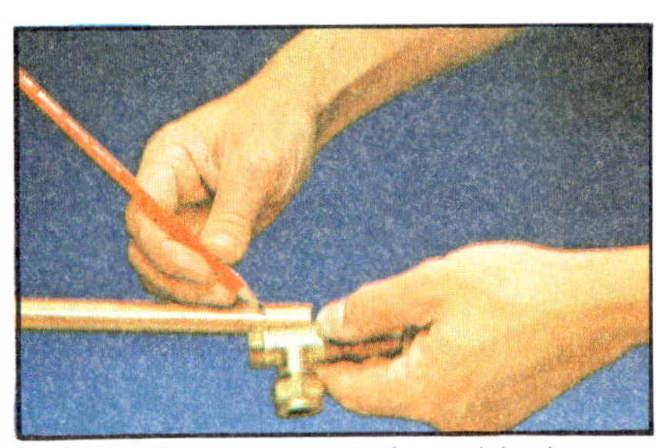

5 Allow the tee to rest alongside the pipe run. The mark on the front of the fitting is your guide to where the pipe has to be cut again.

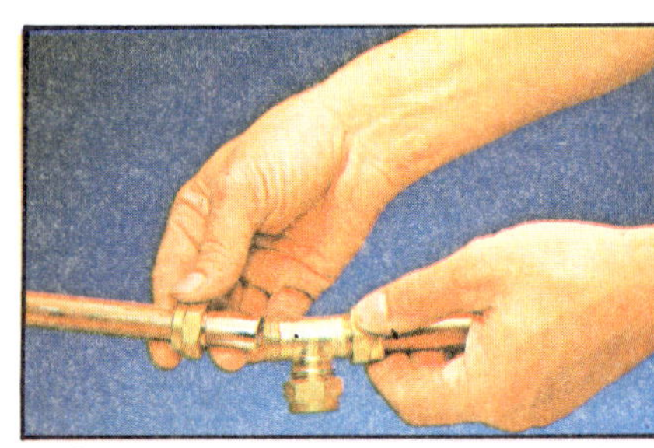

6 Cut the pipe at this mark, thus taking out a small section. Clean the end and slip a cap-nut and olive into place. Spring the pipe end into the tee.

7 Support the fitting with a wrench while tightening the cap-nuts on both ends of the tee with an adjustable spanner or wrench.

8 Insert the cleaned end of the branch pipe into the tee and tighten the cap-nut 1½ turns with a wrench, holding the fitting to stop it from twisting.

JOINING METRIC TO IMPERIAL PIPE

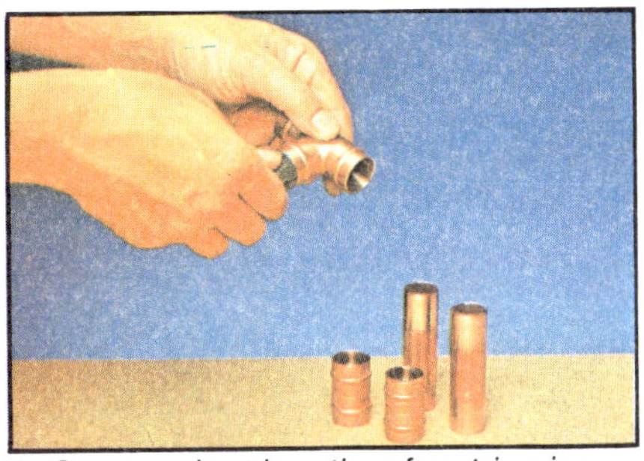

1 Cut two short lengths of metric pipe and prepare the pipe ends, the metric/imperial adaptors and also the tee junction.

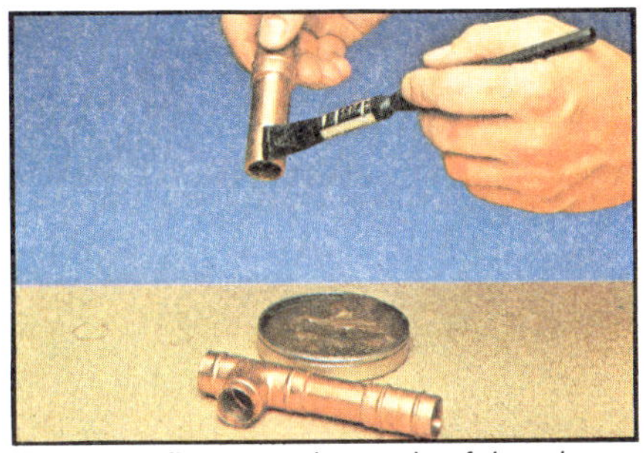

2 Smear flux over the ends of the pipe, inside the rims of the adaptors and each opening on the tee. Then assemble the fitting.

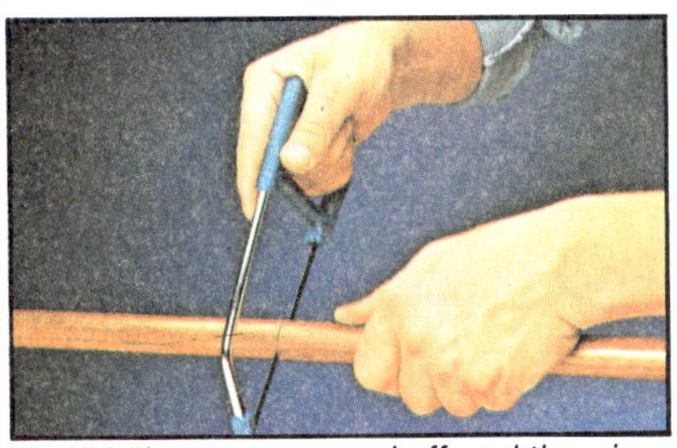

3 With the water turned off and the pipe drained, cut it where you want to make the connection. Prepare one of the ends with steel wool.

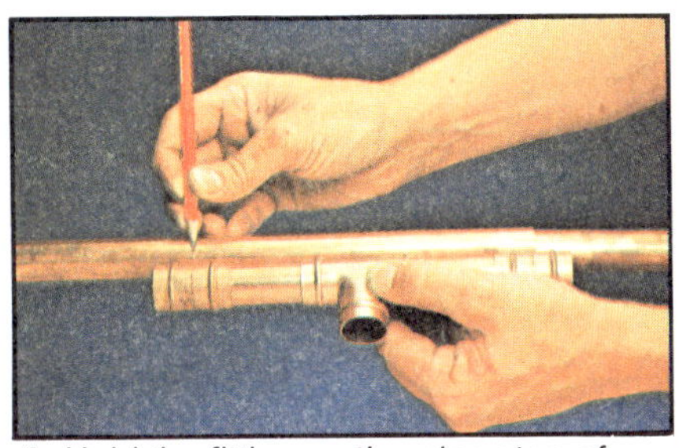

4 Hold the fitting so the pipe stop of one adaptor rests against the cut. Now you can mark the other pipe stop position on the pipe run.

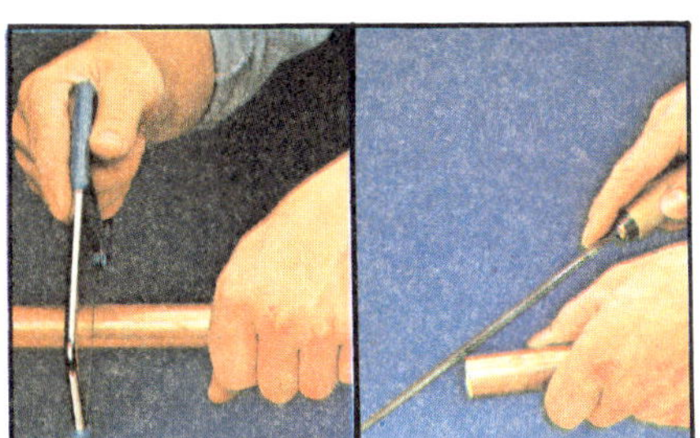

5 Cut out the section of pipe and prepare the newly-cut end. Don't forget to apply the flux, smearing it on the outside of both pipe ends.

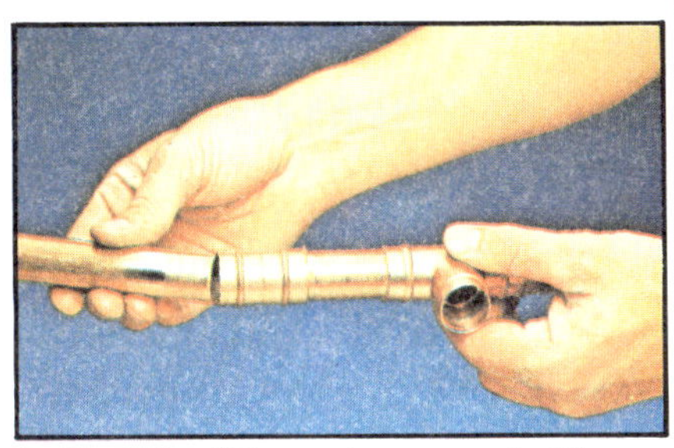

6 Push the fitting onto one end of the supply run, then gently spring the other end into place so that the tee junction is correctly positioned.

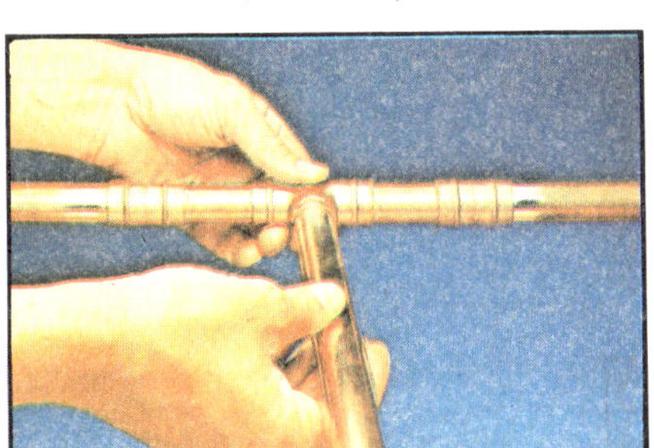

7 Prepare the end of the branch pipe and push it into the tee. Make sure that all the pipe ends are butting up fully against the pipe stops.

8 Make all the joints at the same time. Rings of solder round the mouths of the fittings indicate that sound, watertight connections have been made.

Ready Reference

CONVENIENT CUTTING

Try to join into existing pipework at a point where you have room to manoeuvre.
If space is very tight
- use a junior hacksaw instead of a full-sized one, or
- use a sawing wire for cutting pipes in corners

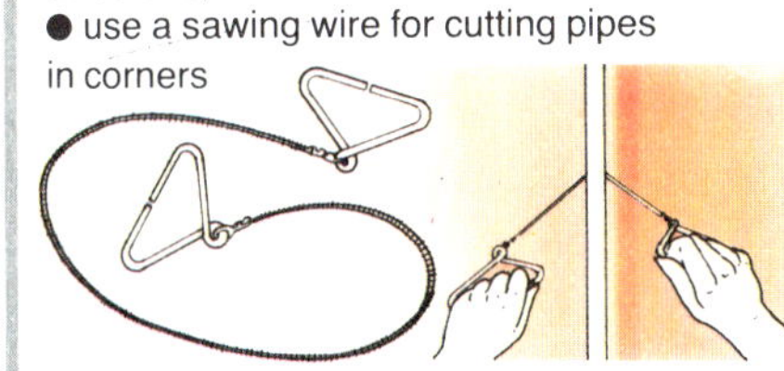

THE RIGHT TEE

Your branch line may be the same diameter as the main pipe, or smaller (it should never be larger). Tees are described as having all ends equal (eg, 15 x 15 x 15mm), or as having the branch reduced (eg, 22 x 22 x 15mm).

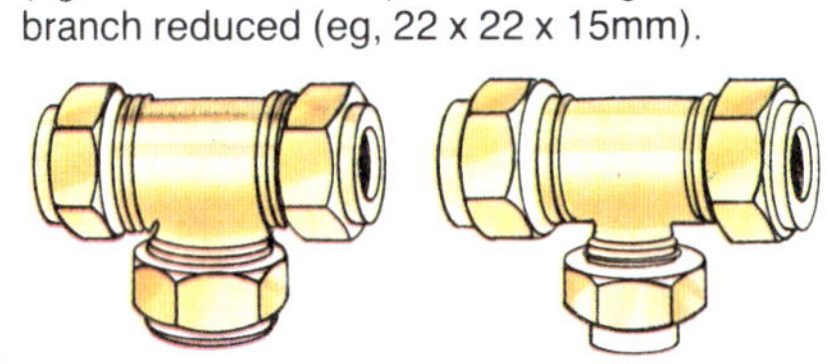

SUPPORTING THE PIPEWORK

All pipework needs supporting at intervals along its length with pipe clips (usually plastic or metal). Fit them at
- 1.2m (4ft) intervals on horizontal pipe runs
- 1.5m (5ft) intervals on vertical pipe runs.

TO SAVE TIME AND TROUBLE

- hold the body of a compression fitting securely with one wrench or spanner while doing up the cap-nut with another
- wrap nearby capillary fittings in damp cloths when soldering in new ones
- make up the entire branch line before cutting in the branch tee
- have cloths handy for mopping up when cutting into existing pipework
- if you're using compression fittings on a vertical pipe run, stop the lower cap-nut and olive from slipping down the pipe by clipping a clothes peg or bulldog clip to it
- keep a replacement cartridge for your blow-torch in your tool kit so you don't run out of gas in the middle of a job.

JOINING INTO PLASTIC PIPES

1 Polythene pipe is joined by a compression fitting with a larger olive than usual (right hand) and pipe liners to support the pipe walls.

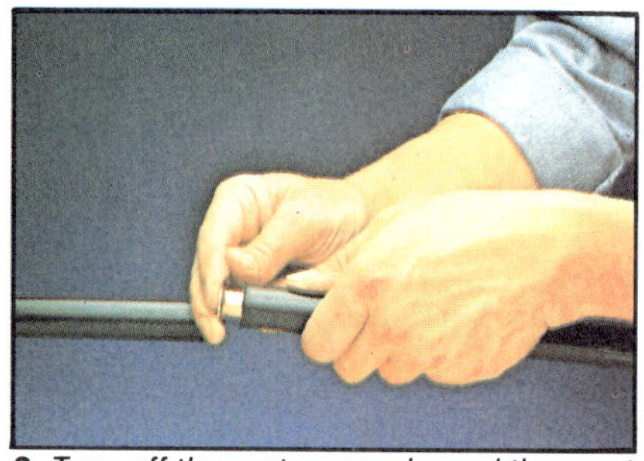

2 Turn off the water supply and then cut the pipe. Use a file to remove any rough edges and then insert a liner into one end of the pipe.

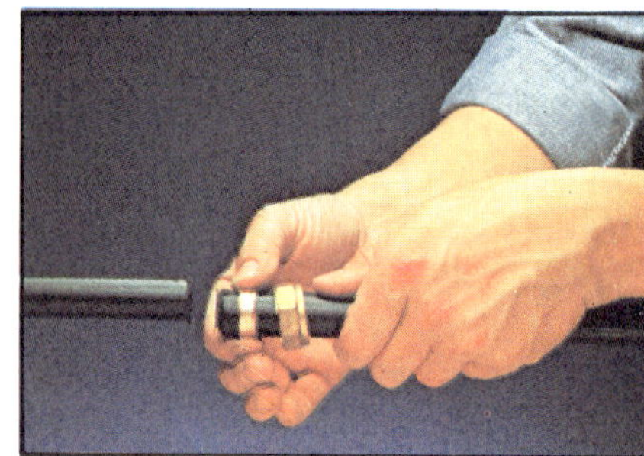

3 Undo the compression fittings and slip a cap-nut over the pipe end containing the liner; then slip on the olive.

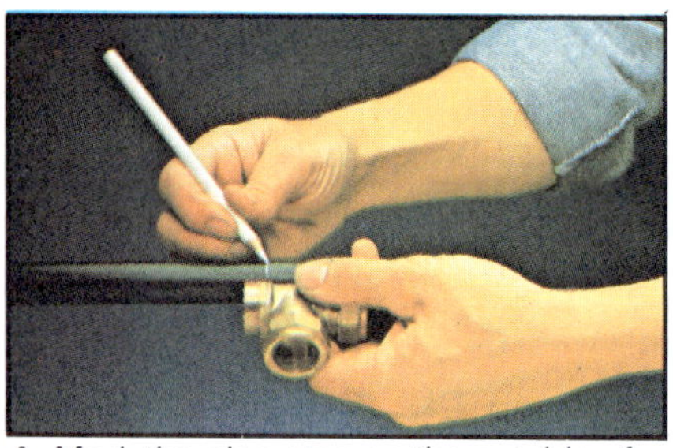

4 Mark the pipe stop on the outside of the tee, join the tee to the prepared end, then mark across the pipe stop to show where the pipe is to be cut.

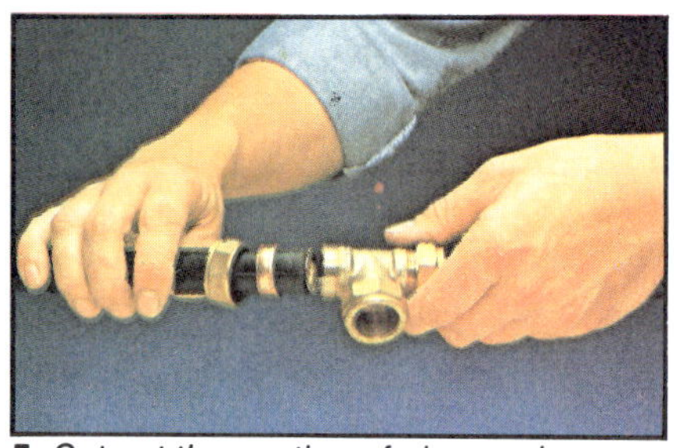

5 Cut out the section of pipe and connect the other end of the tee. Hold the fitting securely while you tighten the cap-nuts $1\frac{1}{2}$ turns.

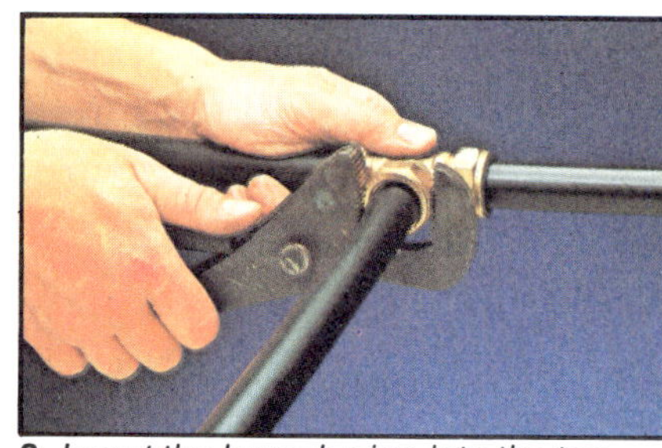

6 Insert the branch pipe into the tee fitting and again use a wrench or adjustable spanner to give the cap-nuts $1\frac{1}{2}$ turns.

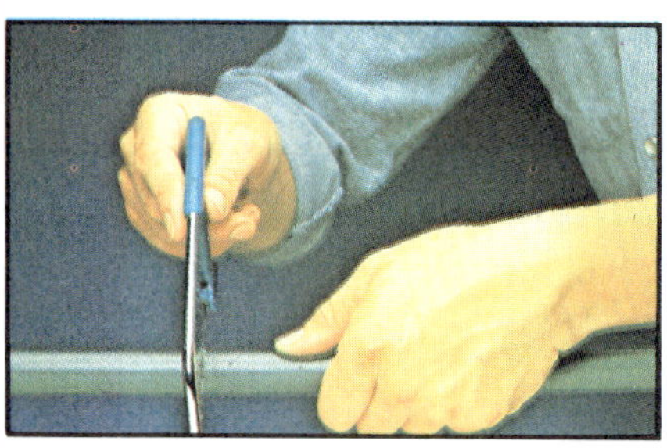

7 With UPVC pipe, mark the pipe stops on the outside of the tee. Use these as a gauge to cut out a small section of pipe with a hacksaw.

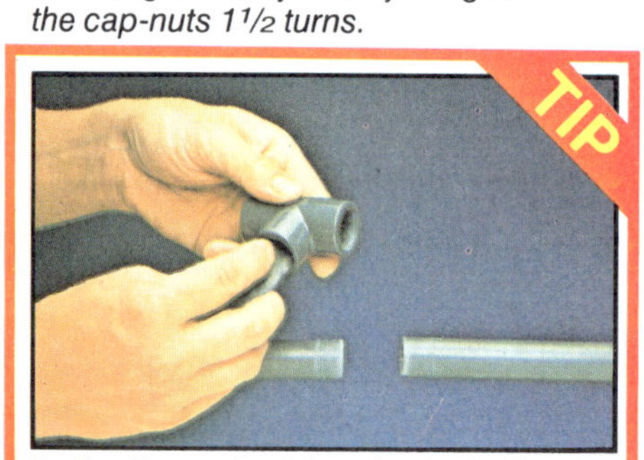

8 Key the ends of the pipe including the branch and the inside of the tee with abrasive paper. This is essential when using solvent-weld cement.

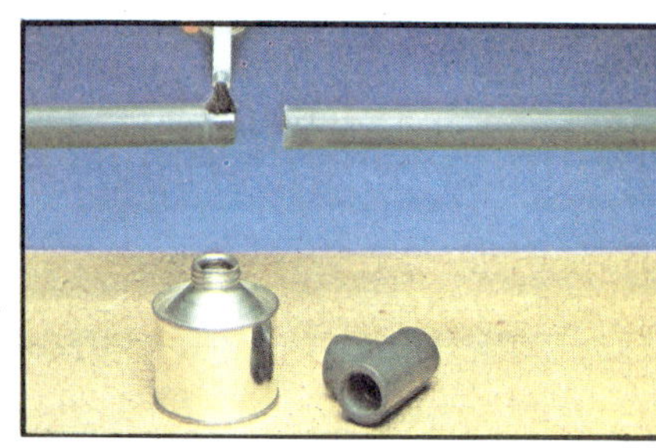

9 Thoroughly clean the ends of the pipes with a degreaser, which you apply with a brush, and leave until completely dry.

10 Once you've done this, spread solvent weld cement on the contact surfaces. Take care not to inhale the fumes as you work.

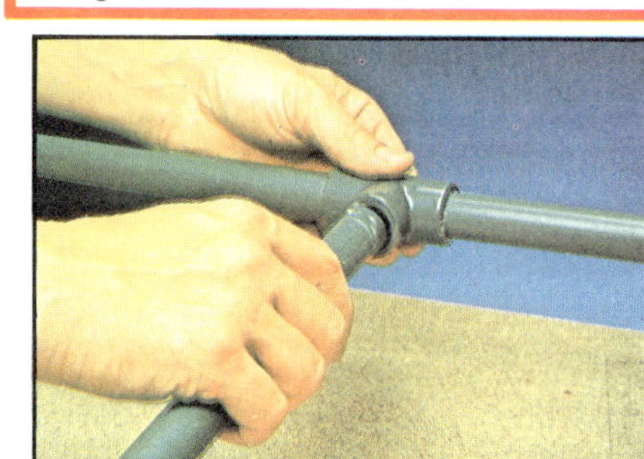

11 Make all the connections at the same time, and check to ensure that all the pipes are pushed right into the tee. Hold for 30 seconds.

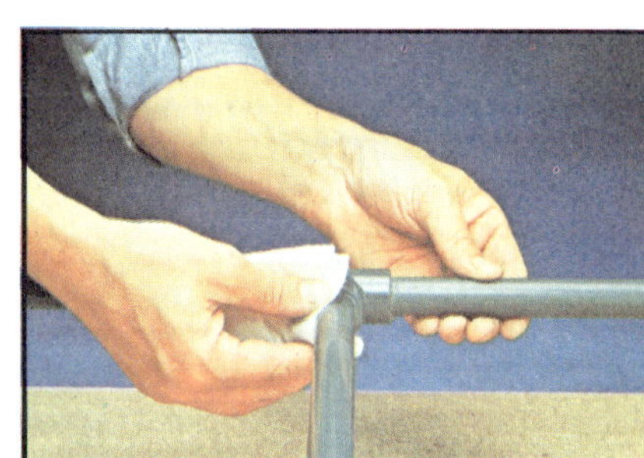

12 As soon as you've made all the connections, use a cloth to remove any surplus cement from the pipes. Water shouldn't be turned on for 24 hours.

USING PLASTIC PIPE AND FITTINGS

Plastic pipe and fittings can now be used for hot water supplies and central heating. They are easy to work with and allow the DIY plumber to tackle a wide range of jobs.

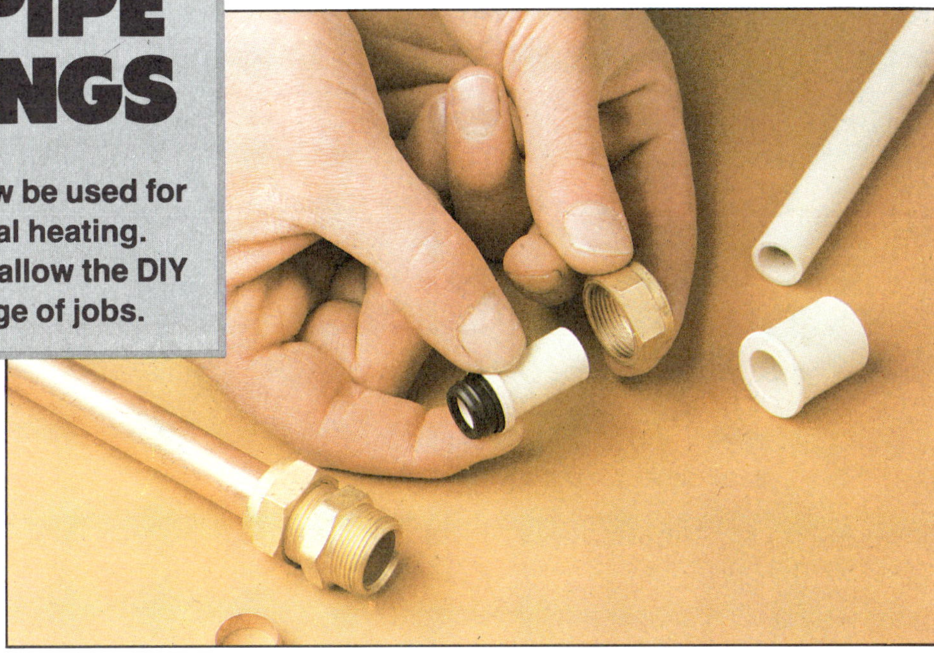

Over the last twenty years plastic has become the most popular plumbing material for above and below ground drainage, for rainwater collection and disposal, and for subsoil drainage. In the form of black polythene tubing it has also become a material widely used for water transportation on camping sites and farms. In the home, however, it has not proved popular. Although this lack of interest can partly be attributed to the conservatism of plumbers and householders, the main reason has been that up until now the plastic pipes that have been available have been suitable for cold water supplies only. This has meant that plumbers, who have had no choice but to use copper or some other metal for the hot water or central heating system, have almost always tended to use the same material when dealing with the cold water system. Householders have doubted the ability of plastic pipework to do a good, life-long job, and have also tended to resist its use on grounds of taste: quite simply, in places where pipework is exposed to view the combination of plastic and copper (or stainless steel or iron) is not one that is very pleasing to the eye.

Now, however, all this has changed. Recently the National Water Council (NWC) gave its approval to two proprietary systems of plastic plumbing, one made out of polybutylene and the other of chlorinated polyvinyl chloride (CPVC), both of which can now be used for cold *and* hot water supply as well as for wet central heating systems. These two rival plumbing systems should hold a special appeal for the DIY enthusiast and – now that they have gained the NWC's approval – there is nothing to prevent them gaining widespread acceptance.

The advantages of plastic pipework

The most obvious advantage is the lightness of the pipework, which makes for ease of handling, but the most important benefit is the ease with which plastic can be cut and joined. This means that the level of skill you require to undertake a particular plumbing task is greatly reduced, as is the amount of time you require to carry it out. Both systems are also strong and durable, more resistant to frost than a traditional plumbing system and, unlike the latter, not subject to corrosion. Last but not least, they are competitively priced.

Plastic pipes are less vulnerable to frost because plastic is a poor conductor of heat compared to metal (which means that, unlike metal, it provides a certain amount of insulation), and because it has greater elasticity. This means that plastic pipes are not only less likely to freeze than metal ones, but also that in the event of their doing so they are much less likely to burst. The greater degree of insulation that plastic provides also brings other benefits: it results in less heat being lost from pipe runs between radiators (or between the hot water cylinder and the hot taps), as well as meaning that less insulation is necessary for pipework that needs to be protected against the cold.

Plastic pipes aren't subject to corrosion for the simple reason that plastic isn't attacked by the water supply. Electrolytic corrosion, which results in the build up of hydrogen gas and black iron oxide sludge (magnetite) and can ultimately lead to leaky radiators and early pump failure, is therefore far less of a problem when a central heating system is fitted with plastic pipes.

This also means that plastic is a safer material to use for your drinking water supply pipes than metal, the use of which can, under some circumstances, present a health risk.

One final point to be borne in mind before you replace metal pipes with plastic ones is that plastic is a non-conductor of electricity. This means that all-plastic plumbing systems cannot be used to earth a domestic electricity supply (see *Ready Reference*).

You can obtain both polybutylene and CPVC tubing in the 15mm (½in), 22mm (¾in) and 28mm (1in) diameters commonly used in domestic hot and cold water supply and in small-bore central heating. However, in other respects – particularly as regards the flexibility of the two different types of tubing and methods of cutting and jointing – the two systems differ. So, before you undertake a plumbing task using plastic pipes and fittings, you'd do well to consider which system best suits your particular application.

Polybutylene tubing

Polybutylene tubing is brown in colour and naturally flexible; in this respect it differs from CPVC tubing, which is rigid. As well as being available in 3m (10ft) lengths in all three diameters, it is also obtainable as a 100m (325ft) coil in the 15mm (½in) size, and as a 50m (162ft) coil in the 22mm (¾in) size. This flexibility, and the long lengths in which the tubing is available, is particularly useful as it cuts down the time you need to spend on installation, and reduces the number of fittings necessary (which means less cost). You can thread polybutylene pipes under floors and between joists with minimal disturbance, their flexibility also allowing you to take them through apertures and round obstacles that would otherwise present serious difficulties. You can bend the tubing cold to easy bends with a minimum radius of eight times the pipe diameter; 15mm (½in) tube can therefore be bent to a minimum radius of 120mm (4¾in) and 22mm (¾in) to a minimum radius of 176mm (7in). You must, however, provide a clip on either side of the bend to secure it. The flexibility of polybutylene tubing means that

POLYBUTYLENE PIPE AND FITTINGS

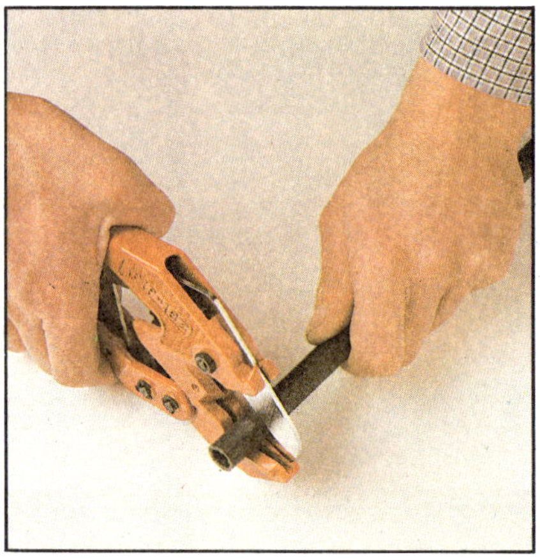

1 *The best way to cut polybutylene pipe is with the manufacturer's shears. These are easy to use and ensure that you get a square-cut pipe end every time.*

2 *Alternatively, you can cut polybutylene pipe with a hacksaw or a sharp knife. If you use this method don't forget to clean off any burr or swarf with a file.*

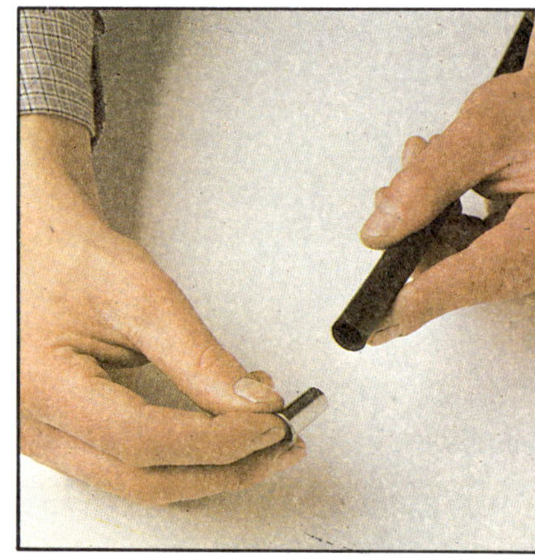

3 *Before jointing the pipe, insert a stainless steel support sleeve into the pipe end. This prevents the tube end getting crushed within the fitting.*

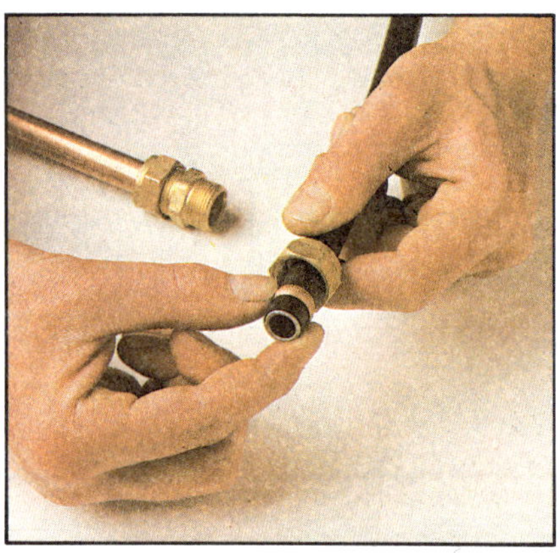

4 *Polybutylene pipe can be used with ordinary compression fittings. The joint is made in exactly the same way as one made using ordinary copper pipe.*

5 *Within a polybutylene fitting a grab ring holds the pipe in place, while an 'O' ring ensures a watertight seal. The two are separated by a spacer washer.*

TIP

6 *The witness lines on the body of the fitting indicate the length of pipe hidden within it when the joint is assembled. Remember to allow for this.*

7 *Before inserting polybutylene pipe into a polybutylene fitting, apply a special lubricant to both the pipe end and the interior of the socket.*

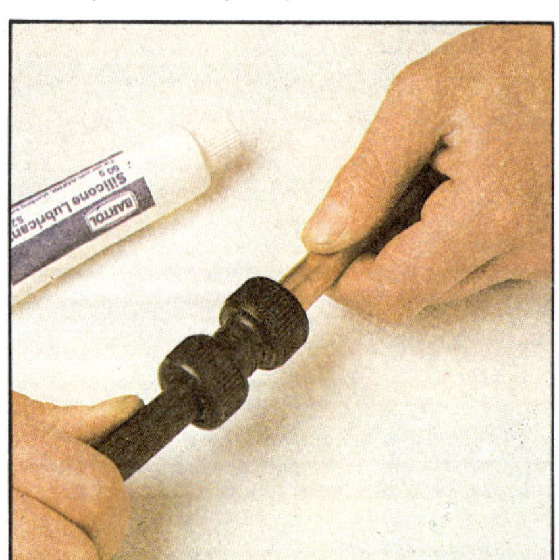

8 *Make the joint without unscrewing or even loosening the cap-nuts. Simply thrust the pipe end into the socket until it meets the pipe stop inside.*

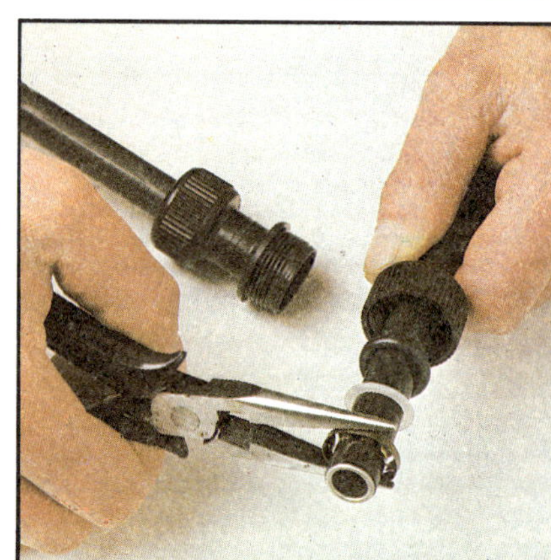

9 *The pipe can be withdrawn only if you unscrew the cap-nut. To re-use the joint, crush and discard the grab ring, and then replace it with a new one.*

CPVC PIPE AND FITTINGS

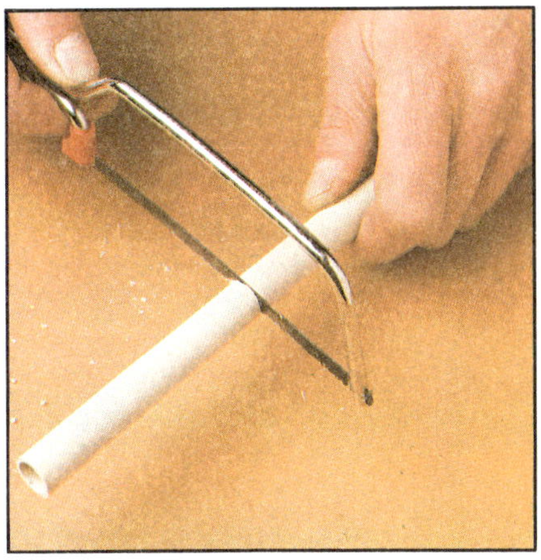

1 *You can cut CPVC pipe with either a fine-toothed saw or an ordinary pipe cutter. If using a saw, make sure that you hold it at right-angles to the pipe.*

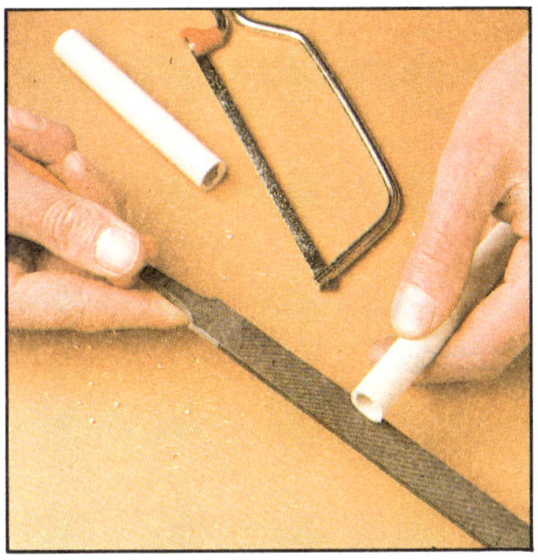

2 *Use a file or a knife to remove the swarf from the pipe end. Check that the pipe fits snugly in the socket, and that the fitting is free from imperfections.*

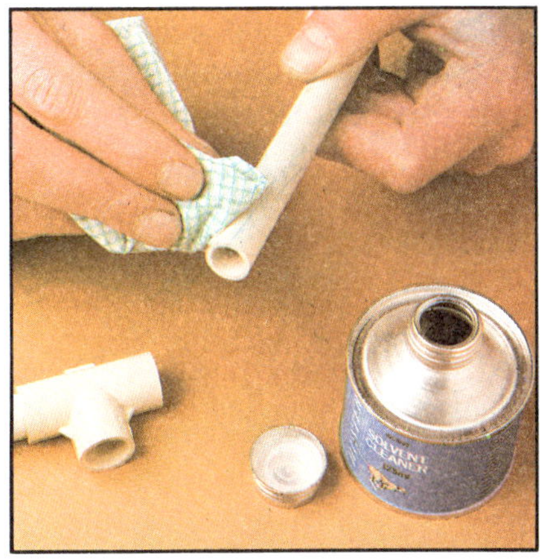

3 *Before making a joint with CPVC the surfaces to be solvent-welded must first be cleaned. Use the manufacturer's special solvent cleaner for this purpose.*

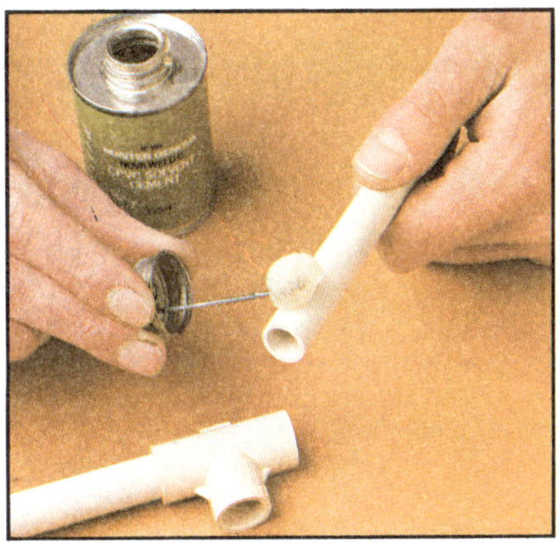

4 *Immediately afterwards, apply the solvent weld cement, brushing this liberally on the tube end and only sparingly in the interior of the fitting socket.*

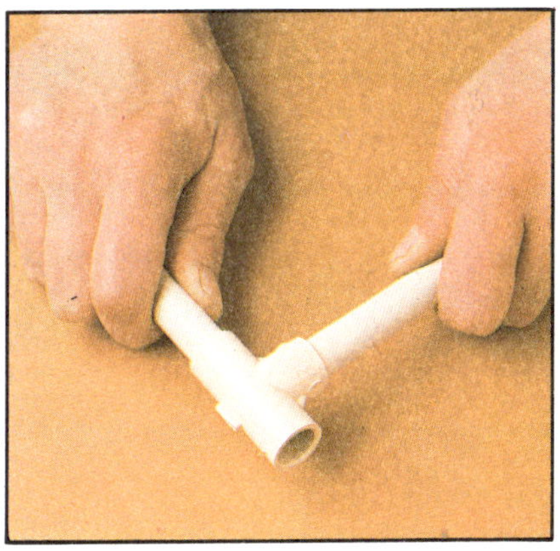

5 *The solvent-weld cement goes off fairly rapidly, so you must make the joint as soon as you've applied it. Push the pipe home with a slight twisting motion.*

TIP

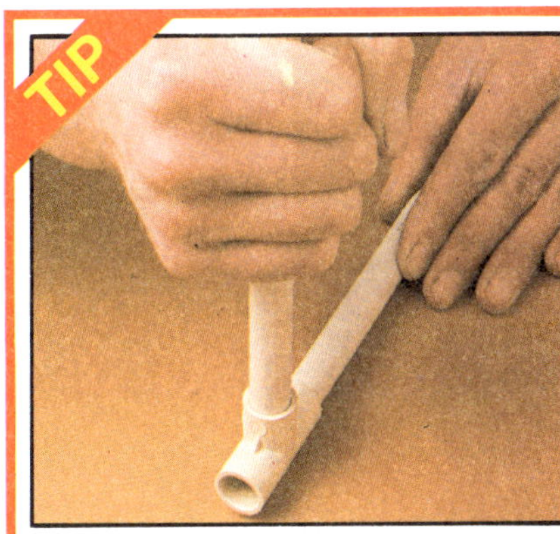

6 *The solvent-weld cement's rapid setting time also means you must make adjustment for alignment immediately. Do not remove surplus cement.*

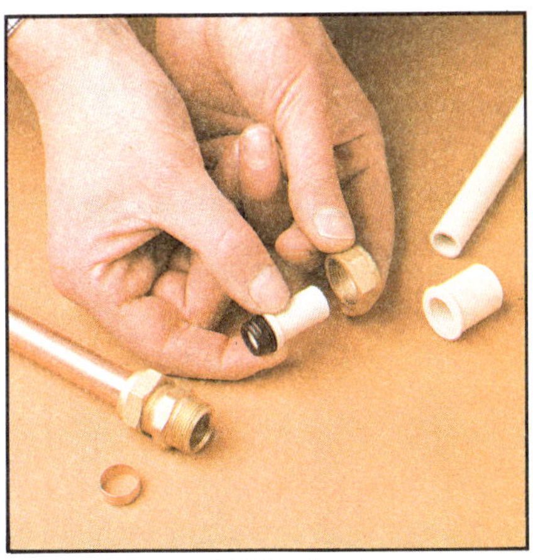

7 *You can join CPVC pipe to copper using a compression fitting and a two-part adaptor. Discard the olive as the first part of the adaptor is self-sealing.*

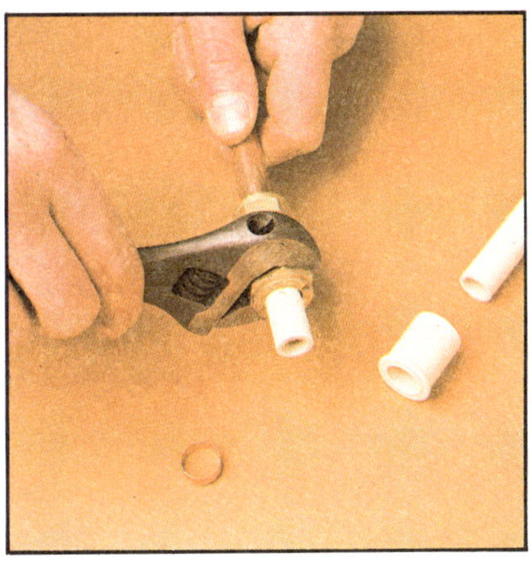

8 *Tighten up the compression fitting in the usual way. Use a second spanner to hold the body of the fitting before giving the coupling nut a final turn.*

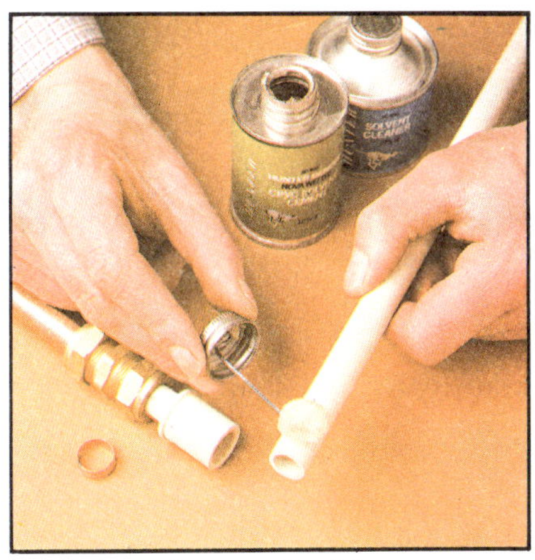

9 *Having solvent-welded the two parts of the adaptor together, complete the fitting by solvent-welding the CPVC pipe to the second part of the adaptor.*

you will have to give continuous support to any visible horizontal pipe runs in order to eliminate the possibility of unsightly sagging (see *Ready Reference*).

You can cut polybutylene tube with a sharp knife or a hacksaw. However, for speed of operation and to ensure an absolutely square cut pipe end every time, the manufacturers recommend that you use their specially designed pipe shears. It would certainly be worthwhile investing in a pair of these shears before embarking on a major project that involved the making of a large number of joints.

You can join polybutylene tubing by using either non-manipulative (Type 'A') compression joints (as used with copper), or else the manufacturer's own patent push-fit connectors. One of the advantages of being able to use Type 'A' compression joints with tubing is that it enables you to replace a length of copper pipe with polybutylene tubing using the existing compression tee or coupling.

When using polybutylene tubing with this type of joint the procedure you follow is identical to that which you adopt with copper pipe (as described on pages 20 to 24). But in order to prevent the collapse of the tube end when the cap-nut is tightened, you must insert a purpose-made stainless steel support sleeve into it. And if you use jointing compound to complete a threaded fitting connected to polybutylene pipe, make sure none comes into contact with the polybutylene.

The patent polybutylene joints and fittings are available in the usual range of straight couplings, tees, elbows, reducing fittings and tap and tank connectors, and in appearance they resemble their brass compression counterparts. But there is one important difference – you don't have to loosen or unscrew the cap-nuts to make a joint. To make a connection you simply have to push the prepared pipe end into the fitting (see step-by-step photographs). Polybutylene fittings have one further advantage in that they allow you to rotate a pipe that has been inserted into one of them, even when it is filled with water. This means, for example, that a polybutylene stop-valve can rest neatly against a wall until you need to use it. You then pull the handle away from the wall so you can open and close it easily.

CPVC tubing

CPVC tubing differs from the polybutylene type in two basic ways. First, it is rigid rather than flexible, which means that it is only available in relatively short lengths of 2m (6ft 6in) or 3m (9ft 9in). Secondly, it is joined by a process known as solvent welding, a slightly more involved procedure than making a push-fit or compression connection (see step-by-step photographs). Superficially, CPVC tubing can be distinguished from polybutylene by its off-white colour. An hour after the last joint has been made you can flush through the system and fill it with cold water; before filling with hot water you need to wait at least four hours.

CPVC pipe does expand when hot water passes through it, but this won't cause a problem in most domestic systems unless one of the pipe runs exceeds 10m (33ft), which is unlikely. In this case you will have to create an expansion loop using four 90° elbows and three 150mm (6in) lengths of pipe.

The manufacturers of CPVC tubing provide an exceptionally wide range of fittings to meet every eventuality. There are 90° and 45° elbows, equal and unequal tees, reducing pieces, tap and ball-valve connectors, stop-valves and gate-valves, and provision for connection to existing copper or screwed iron fittings. The connectors for copper tubing have a solvent-weld socket at one end and a conventional Type 'A' compression joint at the other. Those for iron fittings have a solvent-weld fitting at one end and either a male or female threaded joint at the other. If you are connecting a fitting to an existing iron socket, make sure that you render the screwed connection watertight by binding plastic PTFE tape round the male thread before screwing home.

What system to use

Neither system is 'better' than the other, and each has its merits and its drawbacks. The polybutylene tubing is flexible and available in extremely long lengths which reduce the number of joints you will have to use, as well as enabling you to get through or round obstacles that might prove difficult were you using the CPVC system. On the other hand the push-fit polybutylene joints are bulkier and more obtrusive than those used with the CPVC system.

Bearing in mind this, and the fact that the rigid CPVC pipes will be less prone to sagging than the flexible polybutylene tubing, the CPVC system is probably the more acceptable one in situations where plumbing is exposed to view. The more complex construction of the polybutylene joints – the cause of their bulkiness – also makes them relatively expensive: which means that the smaller number necessary for carrying out a given plumbing task won't always cost you less than the greater number necessary with CPVC. However, polybutylene joints, unlike CPVC ones, can be used more than once.

Lastly, in case your decision to opt for one system or the other is influenced by the colour of the material out of which it is made (dark brown for polybutylene and off-white for CPVC), you can paint both systems with ordinary household paints.

Ready Reference

TIP: CHECK EARTHING

Metal plumbing systems were often used to earth the domestic electricity supply. Since plastic pipework doesn't conduct electricity, it's vital that the house's earthing arrangements are checked by an electrician if you replace any part of the plumbing system with plastic.

BENDING POLYBUTYLENE PIPE

You can form bends in polybutylene pipe to a minimum radius of eight times the pipe diameter.

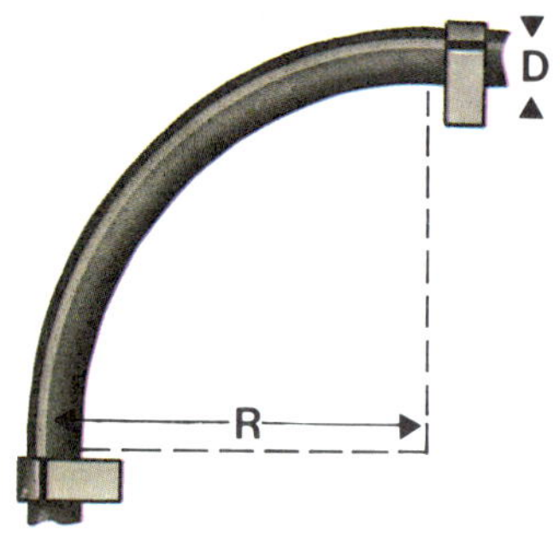

CONNECTING POLYBUTYLENE TO IMPERIAL COPPER PIPES

You can use 15mm (½in) polybutylene fittings with ½in imperial-sized copper pipe without adaptation. If you wish to use 22mm (¾in) fittings with ¾in imperial-sized copper pipe, you have to replace the sealing ring with a purpose-made one of larger size.

SUPPORTING PIPE RUNS

With CPVC pipe, space pipe brackets at 500mm (20in) intervals on horizontal pipe runs, at 1m (39in) intervals on vertical ones. With polybutylene pipe, use the following spacings:

Pipe size	Horizontal run	Vertical run
15mm (½in)	400mm (16in)	800mm (31in)
22mm (¾in)	600mm (24in)	1m (39in)

Reduce these by 25 per cent for pipes carrying water over 60°C (140°F), increase them by 25 per cent for cold pipe runs.

CONNECTIONS TO BOILERS

Although polybutylene and CPVC pipes are suitable for all other applications, you can't connect them directly to a boiler. Instead you should

- connect short lengths of copper pipe to the boiler flow and return tappings
- link the plastic pipe to the copper using the appropriate type of fitting. The copper pipe tails should be
- 380mm (15in) long with CPVC pipe
- 1m (39in) long with polybutylene pipe.

COMPARING THE SYSTEMS

To show how the two plastic systems look in use, here is the pipe run involved in teeing off a spur to a washing machine, assembled using the appropriate fittings in each case. For comparison the same run has been assembled using copper pipe with capillary and compression fittings too.

Key to fittings
1 *Male iron socket adaptor 22mm x 3/4in BSP*
2 *Straight connector 22x22mm*
3 *Socket reducer 22x15mm*
4 *Stop-valve 15x15mm*
5 *90° elbow 15x15mm*
6 *Polybutylene pipe clip 15mm*
7 *Equal tee 15x15x15mm*
8 *Straight coupling copper x male iron*
9 *Stop-valve 15x15mm*
10 *Elbow copper x copper 15x15mm*
11 *Tee for copper 15x15x15mm*
12 *Tank connector 15mm x 1/2in*
13 *Straight tap connector 15mm x 1/2in*
14 *Male iron socket adaptor 15mm x 1/2in BSP*
15 *Female iron socket adaptor 15mm x 1/2in BSP*
16 *Pipe clip for copper 15mm.*

Polybutylene pipe and fittings

Compression fittings with copper pipe

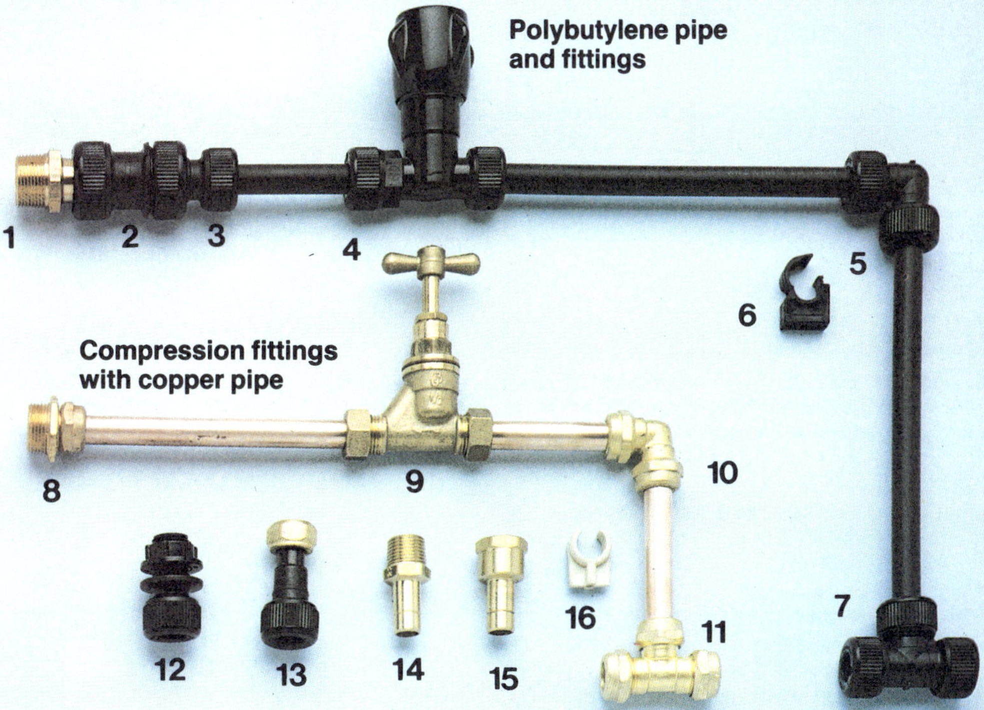

CPVC pipe and fittings

Capillary fittings with copper pipe

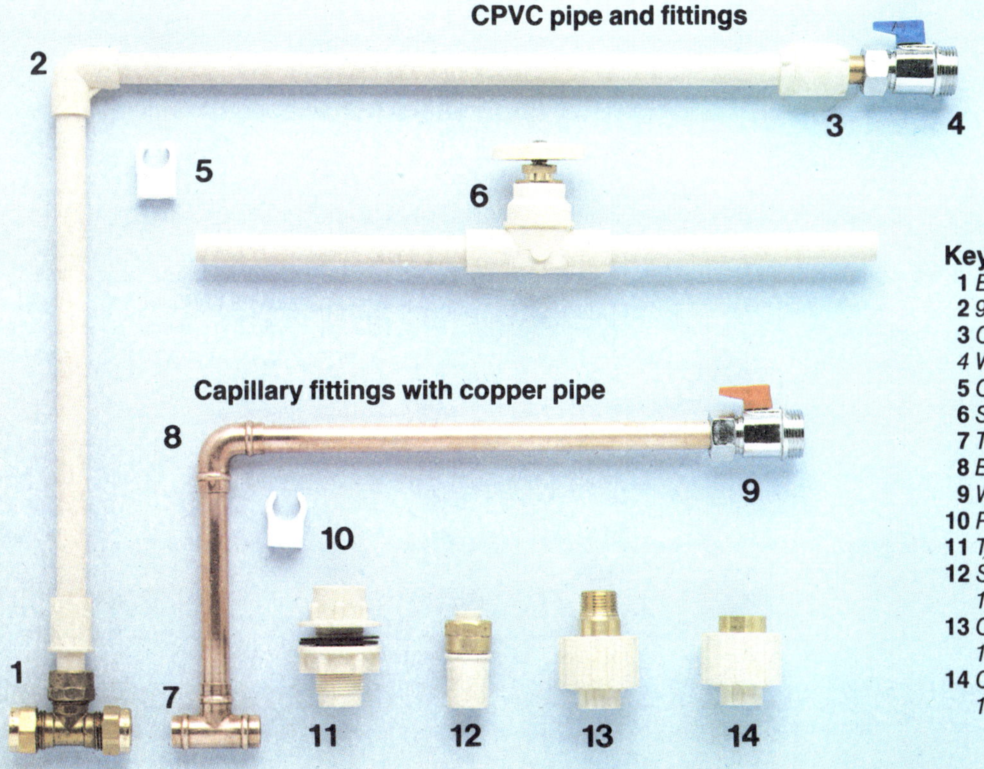

Key to fittings
1 *Equal tee adaptor 15x15x15mm*
2 *90° elbow 15x15mm*
3 *Coupler with copper spigot 15mm*
4 *Washing machine valve 15mm*
5 *CPVC pipe clip 15mm*
6 *Stop-valve 15mm (alternative to* **4**)
7 *Tee for copper 15x15x15mm*
8 *Elbow copper x copper 15x15mm*
9 *Washing machine valve 15mm*
10 *Pipe clip for copper 15mm*
11 *Tank connector 22mm x 3/4in*
12 *Straight tap connector 15mm x 1/2in*
13 *Connector to female iron 15mm x 1/2in BSP*
14 *Connector to male iron 15mm x 1/2in BSP*

JOINING PLASTIC WASTE PIPES

Most waste pipes installed today are made of plastic, which is cheap, lightweight and easy to work with. A little practice and careful measuring will enable you to replace all parts of your system. Here's how to join them together.

Waste systems draining baths, basins and sinks used to be made of lead, heavy galvanised steel with screwed joints, or copper. Soil pipes from WCs were traditionally cast iron, as was all the outside pipework for both waste and soil disposal. Nowadays waste and soil pipes are made of one or other of a variety of plastic materials, which may be used for repairs, extension work or complete replacement of an existing system.

These plastic pipes are lightweight and easily cut, handled and joined. They are made of materials usually known by the initials of their chemical names – UPVC (unplasticised polyvinyl chloride), MPVC (modified polyvinyl chloride), ABS (acrylonitrile butadiene styrene) and PP (polypropylene). CPVC (chlorinated polyvinyl chloride) is usually used for hot and cold water supply pipes. Pipes and fittings are available in white, grey or a copper colour, depending on type and manufacture.

All these materials are satisfactory for domestic waste systems and – with one exception – can all be joined in the same way: either by push-fit (ring-seal) jointing or by solvent welding.

The exception is PP pipe. This was first developed because of its good resistance to very hot water and chemical wastes, and was therefore extensively used in industry. Nowadays, however, it is frequently used in the home for waste or rainwater drainage. The big difference between PP and other plastic pipes used in waste drainage is that it cannot be solvent-welded. All joints must be push-fit. In most situations this is no great disadvantage but it does make it important to be able to distinguish PP from other plastics. It has a slightly greasy feel and, when cut with a fine toothed saw, leaves fine strands of fibrous material round the cut edges.

Sizes

When buying plastic pipe and components it is wise to stick to one brand only. Pipes and fittings from different makers, though of the same size, are not necessarily interchangeable. Most suppliers stock the systems of only one manufacturer, although the same

PREPARING THE PIPE ENDS

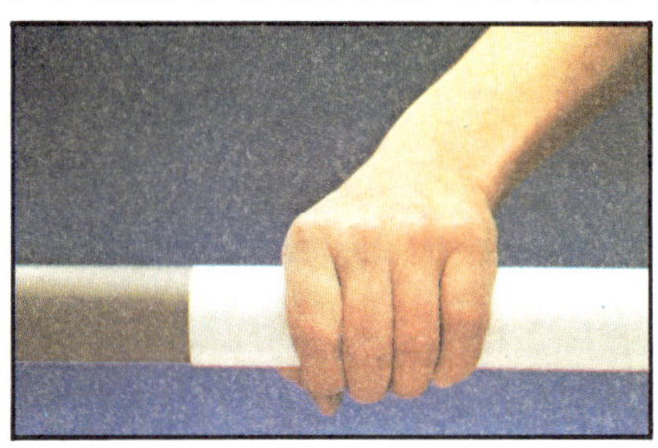

1 *To make sure that you cut the pipe squarely, hold a sheet of paper around it so that the edges meet and overlap each other. This is your cutting line.*

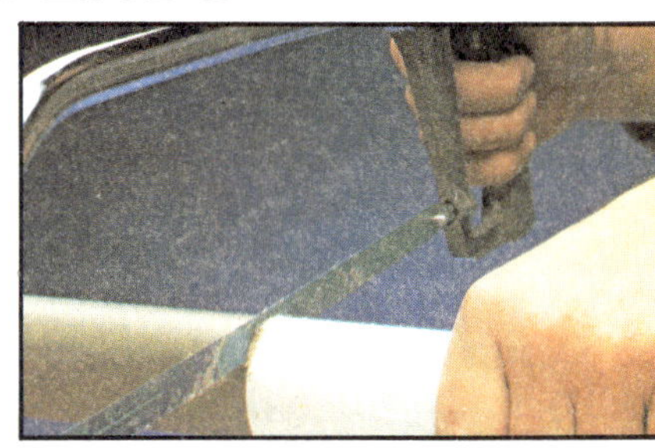

2 *Hold the pipe firmly and cut it with a hacksaw, using gentle strokes. You may find it easier to use a junior hacksaw, which gives a finer cut.*

3 *When you've cut the pipe, use a piece of fine glass paper to clean off the burr left by sawing.*

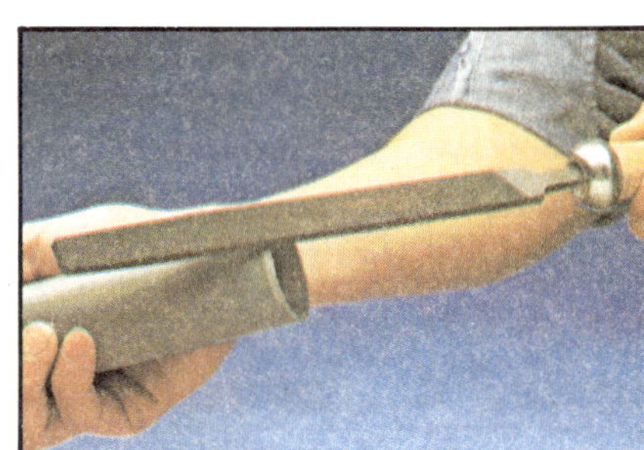

4 *Now take a file and chamfer the end of the pipe all round the edge to a 45° angle. Try to keep the chamfer even.*

SOLVENT-WELD JOINTING

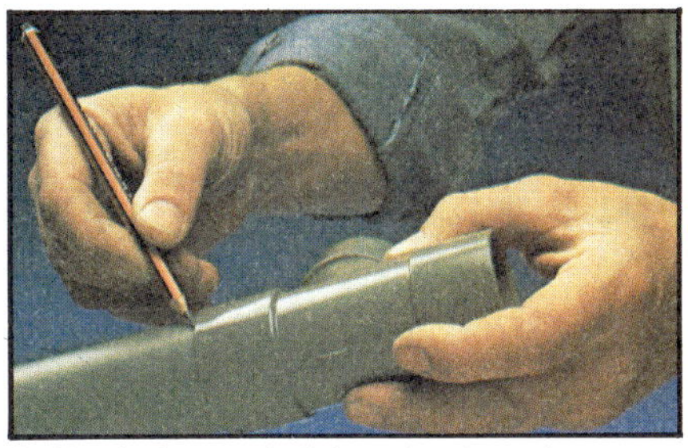

1 Push the end of the pipe into the socket of the fitting as far as it will go. Mark the pipe at this point with a pencil as a guide to the length within the joint.

2 Take the pipe out of the fitting and, with a file, roughen the whole of the end surface that will be inside the fitting up to the pencil mark.

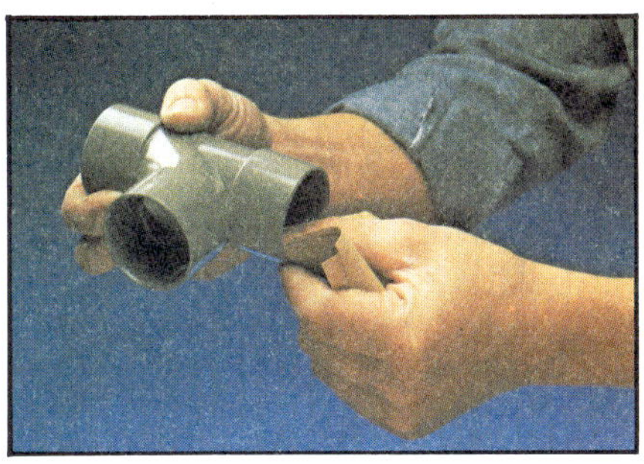

3 Take the fitting itself and roughen the inside of the socket with fine glass paper. This will provide a key for the solvent cement.

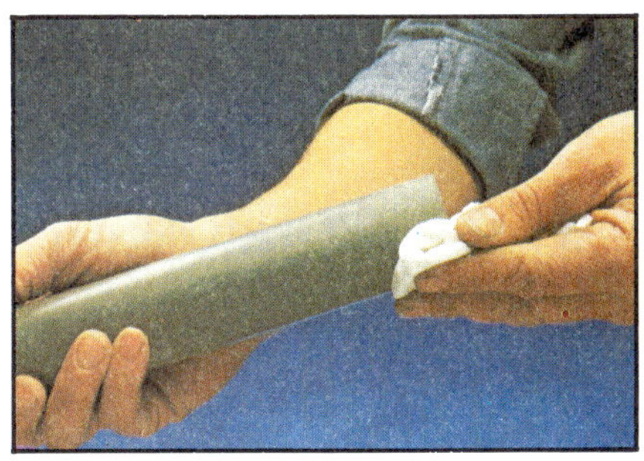

4 Now clean off the roughened surface of the pipe and socket with spirit as recommended by the manufacturer to remove all dust and debris.

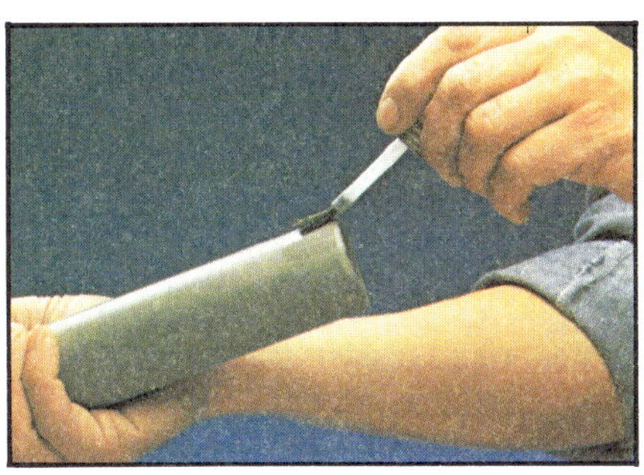

5 Apply the solvent cement to the roughened end of the pipe, making sure that the whole roughened area is covered. Try and keep it off your fingers.

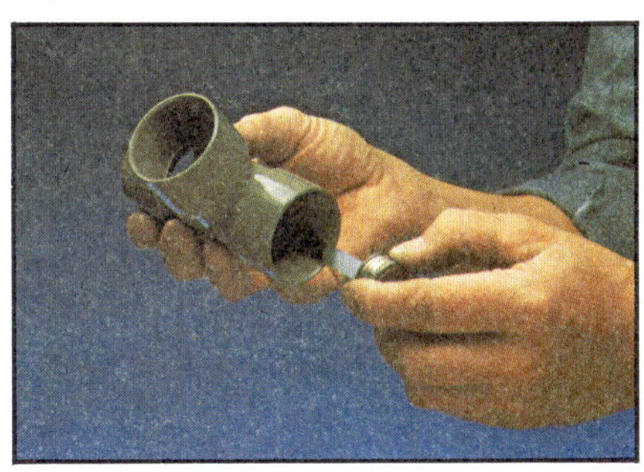

6 Also apply solvent cement to the socket of the fitting. Try to use brush strokes along the line of the pipe.

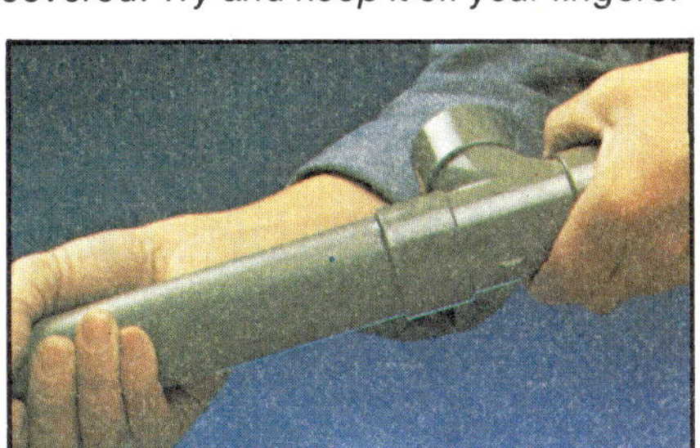

7 Gently push the pipe fully home into the socket. Some manufacturers suggest a slight twisting action in doing this but check their instructions first.

TIP

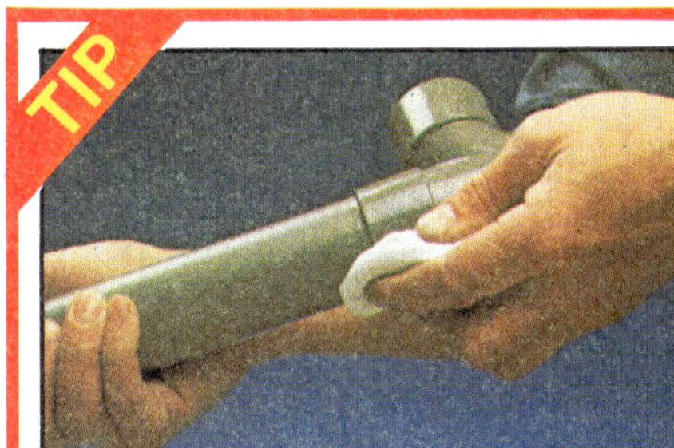

8 Remove any excess solvent at the edge of the socket with a clean cloth, hold the joint in position for 30 seconds.

Ready Reference

THE TOOLS YOU'LL NEED

- hacksaw – a junior or larger – for cutting the lengths of pipe as you need them
- piece of paper – to help cut the pipe truly square
- tape measure
- file – for chamfering the pipe ends
- fine glasspaper – to abrade pipes and sockets for solvent-welding, and for cleaning up the ends of pipes where you have cut them
- pencil – for marking the cutting points and socket depths to find the working area of the pipe.

VITAL ACCESSORIES

- solvent cement – for solvent-welding
- cleaning fluid – for cleaning the pipe ends and socket fittings when making solvent-weld joints
- petroleum jelly – for lubrication when inserting the pipe into the socket in push-fit joint assemblies
- tissues or rag for cleaning off excess solvent or petroleum jelly.

TYPES OF PIPE

Unplasticised PVC (UPVC) is used for all waste pipe applications.
Modified PVC (MPVC) has rubber or some other plasticiser added to make it more resistant to shock.
Chlorinated PVC (CPVC or MUPVC) is used where very hot water discharge occurs, such as washing machine out-flows.
Polypropylene (PP) is an alternative to PVC and can withstand hot water – but it expands a lot and is only suitable on short runs.
Acrylonitrile butadiene styrene (ABS) is stronger than UPVC and is used for waste connection mouldings.

SAFETY TIPS

- don't smoke when you are solvent-weld jointing – solvent cement and solvent cement cleaner become poisonous when combined with cigarette smoke
- don't inhale the fumes of solvent-weld cement or cleaning fluid – so avoid working in confined spaces
- don't get solvent-weld cement on any part of the pipe you're not joining as this can later lead to cracking and weaknesses, especially inside sockets where the solvent cement can easily trickle down
- hold all solvent-weld joints for 15 seconds after joining and then leave them undisturbed for at least 5 minutes – if hot water is going to flow through the pipe don't use it for 24 hours.

PUSH-FIT JOINTING

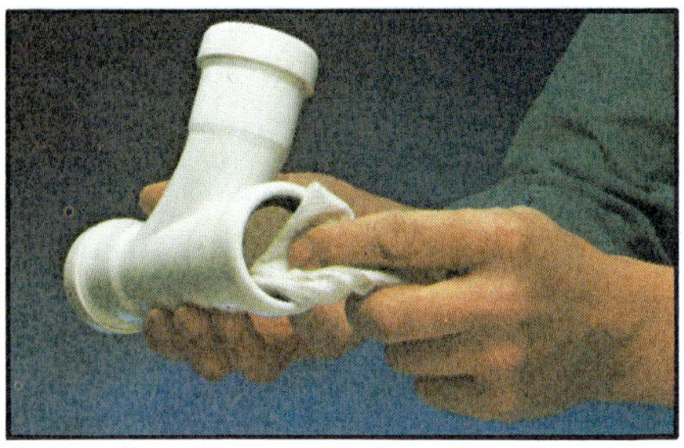

1 Cut the pipe squarely as in solvent-weld jointing and remove the burr, then take the fitting and clean the socket out with the recommended cleaner.

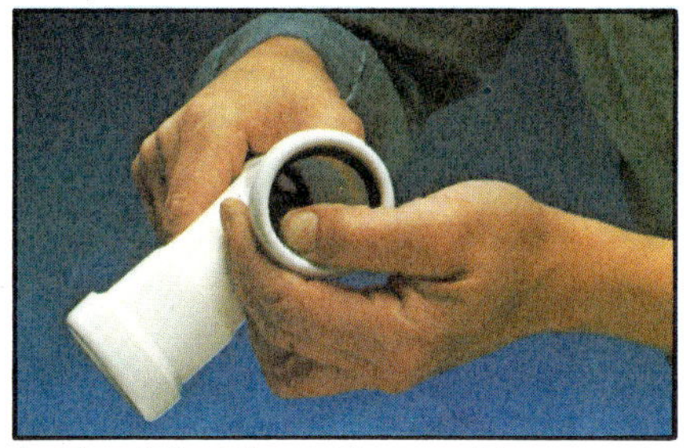

2 Check that the rubber seal is properly seated in the socket. You may find seals are supplied separately and you will have to insert them.

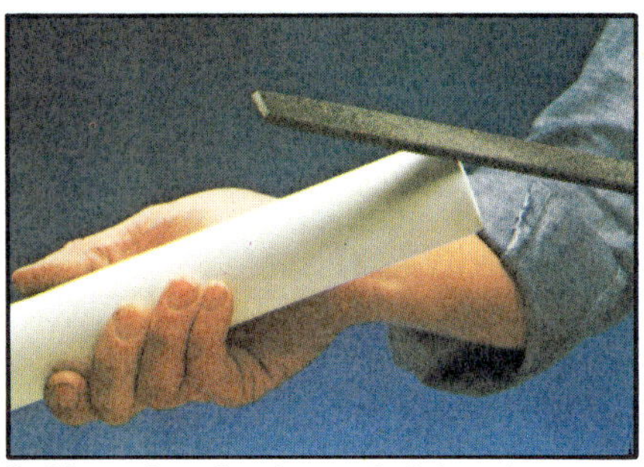

3 Now chamfer the end of the pipe to an angle of 45°, and smooth off the chamfer carefully with fine glass paper so that no rough edges remain.

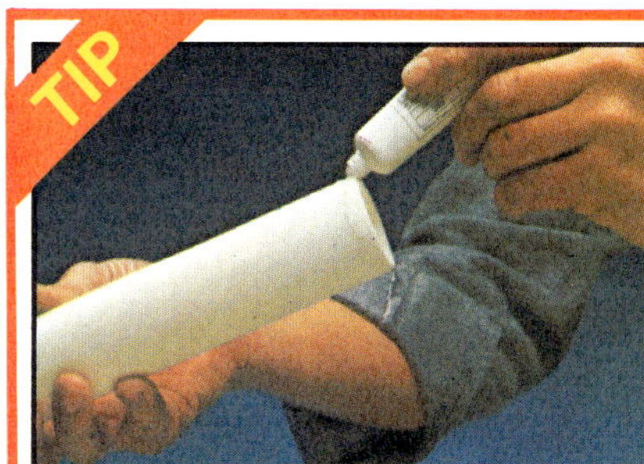

4 Lubricate the end of the pipe with petroleum jelly over a length of about 5mm (3/16in).

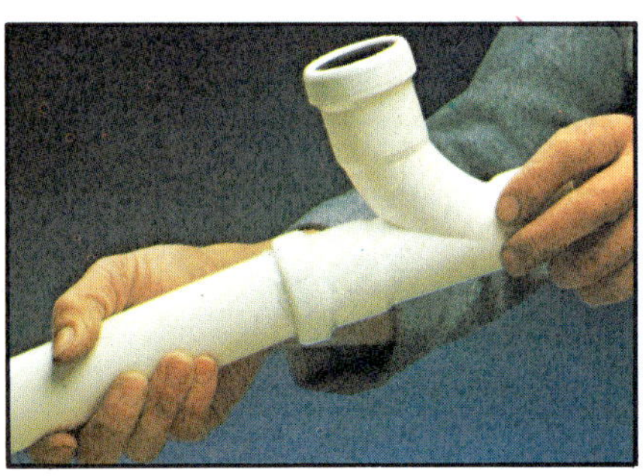

5 Push the pipe into the socket gently but firmly. Then push it fully home and check that all is square, otherwise you may damage the sealing ring.

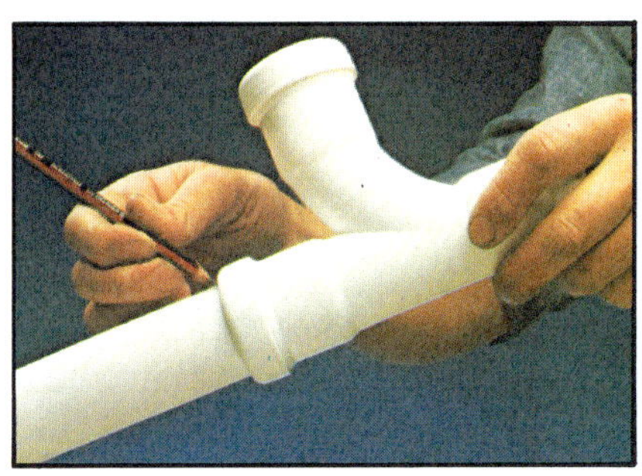

6 Now make a pencil mark on the pipe at the edge of the socket – you can easily rub it off later if you want to – to act as a guide in setting the expansion gap.

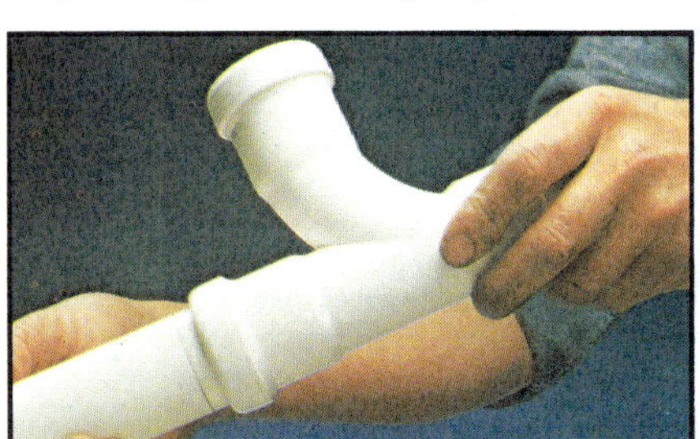

7 Gently pull the pipe out from the fitting so that your pencil mark is about 10mm (3/8in) away from the fitting to allow for expansion when hot water is flowing.

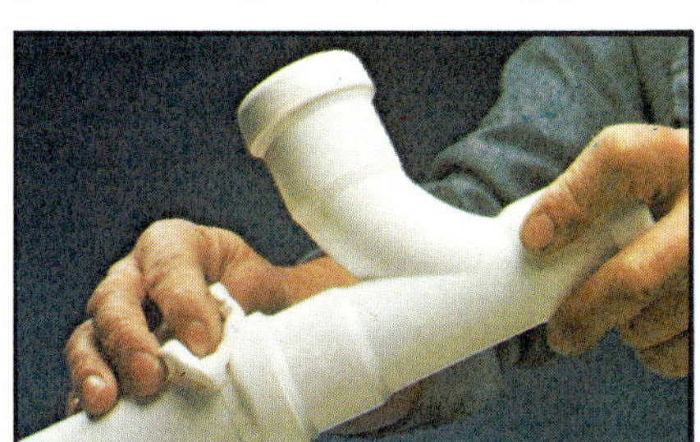

8 The joint is now complete. Wipe off any excess petroleum jelly. Don't lose the expansion allowance when joining the other side of the fitting.

manufacturer may make both PP and either PVC or ABS systems.

It is worth asking the supplier if there is an instruction leaflet supplied by the maker. There are slight variations in the methods of using each particular make of pipe and fitting. The manufacturer's instructions, if available, should be followed to the letter.

Buying new pipe

Existing waste pipe is likely to be imperial in size – 1½in internal diameter for a sink or bath and 1¼in internal diameter for a wash basin.

Metric sized plastic pipes are normally described – like thin-walled copper tubes – by their external diameter, though at least one well-known manufacturer adds to the confusion by using the internal diameter. Both internal and external diameters may vary slightly – usually by less than one millimetre between makes. This is yet another reason for sticking to one make of pipe for any single project.

The outside diameter of a plastic tube that is the equivalent of a 1¼in imperial sized metal tube is likely to be 36mm and the inside diameter 32mm. The outside diameter of the equivalent of a 1½in pipe is likely to be 43mm and the inside diameter 39mm. If in doubt, it is usually sufficient to ask the supplier for waste pipe fittings for a basin waste or – as the case may be – a bath or sink waste. Plain-ended plastic pipe is usually supplied in 3m (10ft) lengths, though a supplier will probably cut you off a shorter piece.

Joining solvent-weld types

Solvent-weld fittings are neater and less obtrusive than push-fit ones and they offer the facility of pre-fabrication before installation. However, making them does demand a little more skill and care and – unlike push-fit joints – they cannot accommodate the expansion (thermal movement) that takes place as hot wastes run through the pipe. A 4m (13ft) length of PVC pipe will expand by about 13mm (½in) when its temperature is raised above 20°C (70°F). For this reason, where a straight length of waste pipe exceeds 1.8m (6ft) in length, expansion couplings must be introduced at 1.8m intervals if other joints are to be solvent-welded. This rarely occurs in domestic design, however, and use of push-fit or solvent-weld is a matter of personal preference.

Although the instructions given by the different manufacturers vary slightly, the steps to making solvent-weld joints follow very similar lines. Of course, the first rule is to measure up all your pipe lengths carefully. Remember to allow for the end of the pipe overlapping the joint. When you've worked out pipe lengths cutting can start.

JOINING SOIL PIPES

These are joined in the same way as plastic waste pipes but are much bigger – about 100mm (4in) in diameter – so they take longer to fit. They also have some different fittings, such as a soil branch for use where the outlet pipe joins the stack, and access fittings with bolted removable plates for inspection. There are also special connectors to link to the WC pan, via a special gasket, and to link to the underground drainage system which is traditionally made of vitrified clay.

The accurate moulding of the fittings and the ease of assembly means that you can confidently tackle complete replacement of a soil system.that you can confidently tackle complete replacement of a soil system.

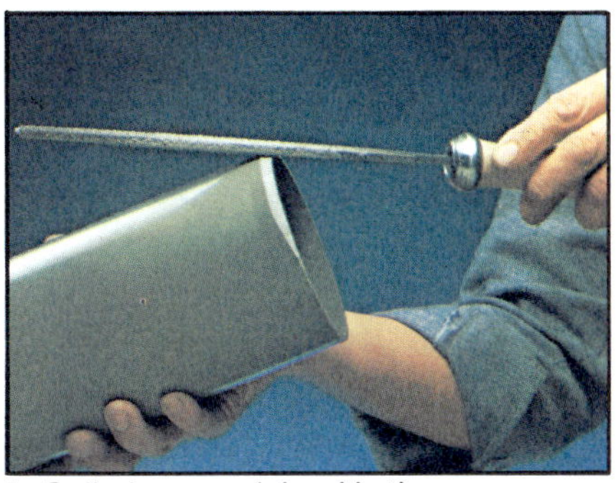

1 *Soil pipes are joined in the same way as their narrower waste counterparts, but as they're bigger take special care with cutting and chamfering.*

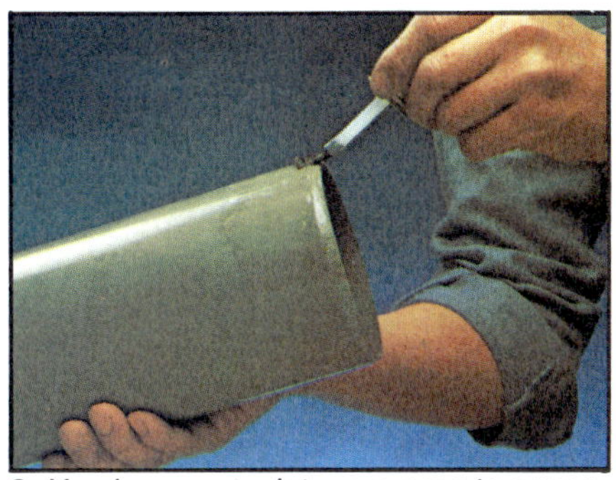

2 *You have got a lot more area to cover with the solvent cement so you must work speedily – but don't neglect accurate application.*

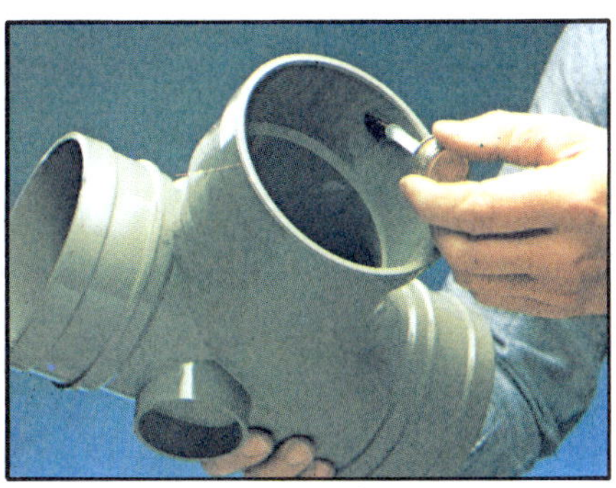

3 *The soil branch pipe has a swept entry into the main stack fitting. This is one of the most important joints in the system, so make sure you get it right.*

4 *When you finally push the pipe into the fitting socket make quite sure that it goes right home against the pipe stop inside the fitting.*

Cut the pipe clean and square with a hacksaw or other fine-toothed saw. A useful tip to ensure a square cut is to fold a piece of newspaper over the pipe and join the edges beneath it. The paper will then act as a template.

Remove all internal and external burrs or roughness at the end of the pipe, then use a file to chamfer the outside of the pipe end to about 45°. Not all manufacturers recommend this, but it does provide an extra key for the solvent.

Insert the pipe end into the fitting and mark the depth of insertion with a pencil. Using medium grade abrasive paper, or a light file, lightly roughen the end of the pipe, as far as the pencil mark, and also roughen the interior of the socket. Thoroughly clean the roughened surfaces of the socket and the pipe end using a clean rag moistened with a spirit cleaner recommended by the manufacturer of the fittings.

Select the correct solvent cement (PVC pipes need a different solvent cement from ABS ones; once again, buy all the materials needed at the same time from the same supplier). Read the label on the tin and stir only if instructed.

Using a clean paintbrush, apply the solvent cement to the pipe end and to the

Ready Reference

TYPES OF FITTINGS

A number of fittings are available in both solvent-weld and push-fit systems – here are just a few of them. Check the complete range before you plan a new system – special bends and branches may exist that will make the job much easier.

Solvent-weld 92½° bend

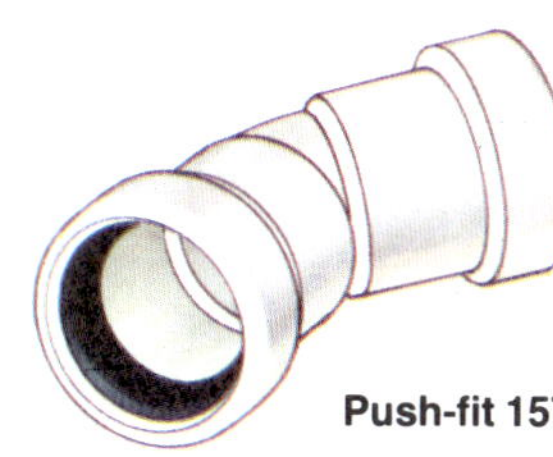

Push-fit 157½° bend

Expansion coupling solvent-weld/push-fit

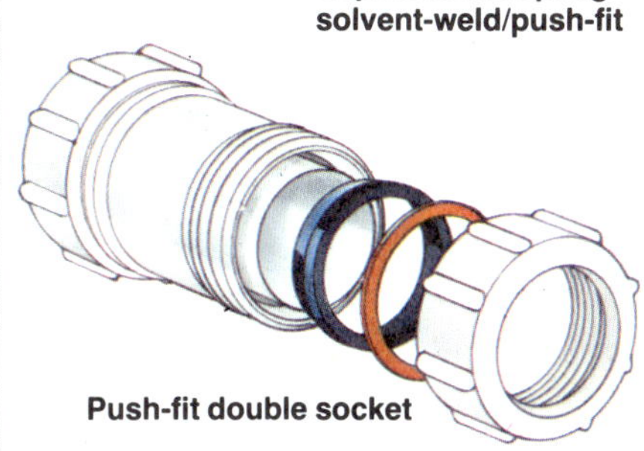

Push-fit double socket

Solvent-weld adaptor

inside of the fittings, brushing in the direction of the pipe. It is usually necessary to apply two coats to ABS pipes and fittings. The second coat should be brushed on quickly before the first has dried.

Push the pipe fully home into the fitting (some, but not all, manufacturers suggest that this should be done with a slight twisting action). Remove excess solvent cement and hold the assembled joint securely in position for about 30 seconds. If hot water will be flowing through the pipe, don't use it for 24 hours to give time for the joint to set completely.

Joining ring-seal types

Preparation for ring-seal or push-fit jointing is similar to that for solvent welding. The pipe end must be cut absolutely squarely and all the burr removed. You should draw a line round the cut end of the pipe 10mm from its end and chamfer back to this line with a rasp or shaping tool, then clean the recess within the push-fit connector's socket and check that the sealing ring is evenly seated. One manufacturer supplies sealing rings separately, and they should be inserted at this point. The pipe end should now be lubricated with a small amount of petroleum jelly and pushed firmly into the socket past the joint ring. Push it fully home and mark the insertion depth on the pipe with a pencil. Then withdraw it by 10mm (3/8in), which is the allowance made for expansion. The expansion joint that is inserted into long straight lengths of solvent-welded waste pipe consists of a coupling with a solvent-weld joint at one end and a push-fit joint at the other.

As with solvent-weld jointing, individual manufacturers may give varying instructions. Some, for instance, advise the use of their own silicone lubricating jelly. Where the manufacturer supplies instructions it is best to follow these exactly.

Fittings

PVC pipe can be bent by the application of gentle heat from a blow-torch, but this technique needs practice and it is best to rely on purpose-made fittings. Sockets are used for joining straight lengths of pipe, tees for right-angled branches, and both 90° and 45° elbows are usually available. If you need to reduce the diameters from one pipe to another you can use reducing sockets. These are really sockets within sockets which can be welded together, one taking the smaller diameter pipe and the other the larger. Soil outlet pipes from WCs are joined in the same way; they are merely bigger – usually 100mm (4in) – in diameter. Sockets work in the same way, but the branch-junction with the main soil stack must be of a specially 'swept' design.

HOW PLASTIC FITTINGS WORK

Solvent-weld joints

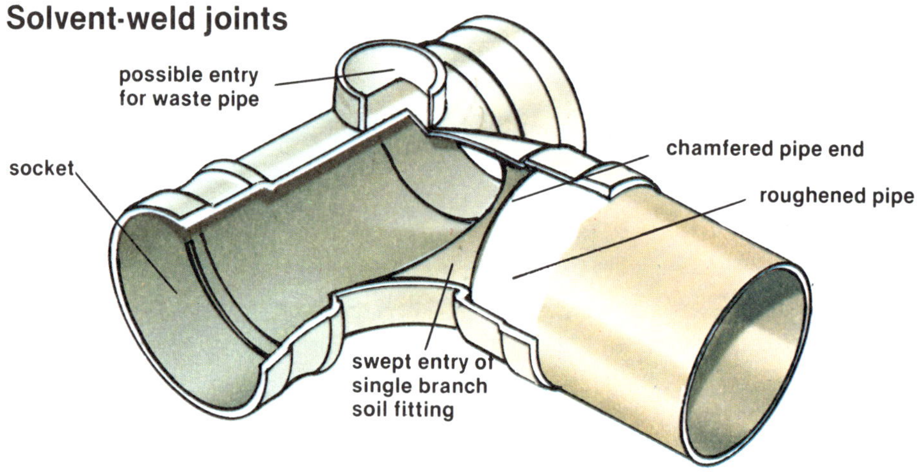

Push-fit joints

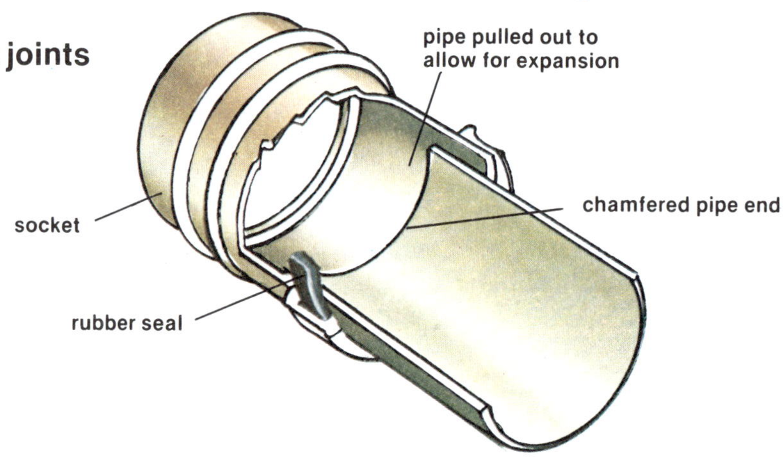

SPECIAL FITTINGS

Special fittings are available when pipe fitting is not straightforward. This is a reducing adaptor for push-fit fittings where you need to join a 32mm pipe to a 40mm pipe. You join the relevant pipe to the mating part of the adaptor and then join the two adaptor parts together.

TYPES OF PIPEWORK

Lead and iron are no longer used as plumbing materials, having been replaced by copper or stainless steel. Now plastic pipework is revolutionising domestic plumbing.

Virtually all **soil pipes** are now made from UPVC (1), which can be joined together using solvent welds or ring seals. Likewise, **overflow pipes** (2) are also made from UPVC, and lengths of these are connected with push-fit joins.

Waste pipes, made of UPVC and ABS plastic, are used for taking water away from baths, basins and sinks (3). Depending on the system they can be joined either by solvent welding or push-fit connections.

Plastic can also be used for water supply pipes. **Polybutylene pipes** (4) can take hot and cold water, the pipes being joined by compression fittings or special push-fit connectors. Similarly, **CPVC pipe** (5) can be used for hot and cold runs, but this is joined with solvent welds.

Black **polythene pipe** (6), the first plastic pipe to be used generally in domestic plumbing, is only suitable for cold water supplies, and consequently is mainly employed for garden and other outside water services.

Rainwater downpipes (7) are made from UPVC and have either circular or square profiles.

Half-hard temper **copper pipe** (8) is used for hot and cold distribution and central heating pipes, being easy to bend and join. **Stainless steel** (9) has also been used, mainly because it can be joined to copper and galvanised steel without causing electrolytic action.

Flexible copper pipe (10), which can be bent simply in the hands, is ideal for making the awkward connections between tap tails and the supply pipes without having to alter the existing runs.

PLUMBING FITTINGS

Putting in hot and cold pipes means you'll need a lot of different fittings at the pipe junctions, elbows, tees, valves and so on. Here is a basic selection to show you what's available.

The most important skill required in any plumbing project involving hot or cold water pipe installation is that of making sound, water-tight joints between lengths of copper tubing and other pieces of plumbing equipment such as taps, ball-valves, and cold water cylinders. You will be required, for example, to take branches from existing water pipes and to make changes of direction in a pipe run.

To do all this, you need plumbing fittings, which make compression or soldered capillary joints (see pages 20 to 24). They are easily assembled using only a small tool kit. Type 'A' or non-manipulative compression joints are by far the more common. The other sort, type 'B' or manipulative joints are usually only used where the water authorities insist on them for underground pipe work.

It is possible to make Type 'A' compression fittings with only a couple of adjustable wrenches, a hacksaw and a metal file, but for a major project involving a number of joints, the purchase or hire of a wheel tube cutter is advisable; and to make soldered capillary joints some kind of blow-torch is also necessary, together with a pad of flame-proof glass fibre.

Compression joints and fittings

Compression joints and fittings are made either of brass or gunmetal, although brass is the more common. As brass is an alloy of copper and zinc, impurities in the water supply in some areas may produce a phenomenon called dezincification. This is an electro-chemical reaction which results in the extraction of the zinc from the alloy, leaving the fitting unchanged in appearance but virtually without structural strength. Where dezincification is likely to occur, gunmetal fittings are traditionally used. Gunmetal is an alloy of copper and tin. However, a more economical alternative these days is to use one of the recently developed corrosion-resistant ranges of brass fittings.

Sizes of compression fittings

Compression fittings are available for use with a number of sizes of copper or stainless steel pipe, but the only sizes likely to be required in domestic plumbing are 15mm, 22mm and 28mm. An existing plumbing system may well have imperial-sized pipe, and the imperial equivalents of 15mm, 22mm and 28mm are ½in, ¾in and 1in. The apparent difference between metric sizes and their imperial equivalents is accounted for by the fact that imperial-sized pipe is described by its internal diameter, and metric-sized pipe by its external diameter. You can use metric 15mm and 28mm compression joints and fittings to make connections with ½in and 1in imperial-sized pipe. When 22mm fittings are used with ¾in pipe, an adaptor is needed.

Compression fitting range

The copper-to-copper coupling is the basic compression joint. There are reducing couplings to enable 28mm or 22mm tubing to be joined to tubes of smaller diameter. There are equal-ended and reducing T junctions (usually simply called 'tees') to enable branch supply pipes to be taken from existing pipes. There are elbow bends and 135° bends.

There are also fittings with one end a compression joint and the other a threaded outlet for direct connection to cisterns, cylinders or pipes of other materials. Male outlets are threaded on the outside, female ones on the inside. Threaded joints of this kind are made watertight by binding the thread with plumbers' PTFE tape.

Soldered capillary joints

Capillary joints, which are neater and cheaper than compression joints, consist of a copper sleeve that fits fairly tightly over the tube ends so that solder may be run between the outside of the tube ends and the interior of the sleeve. 'Integral ring' or 'solder ring' capillary joints contain within the fitting sufficient solder to make the joint. With the cheaper 'end feed' fittings, solder has to be fed in separately from a reel of solder wire.

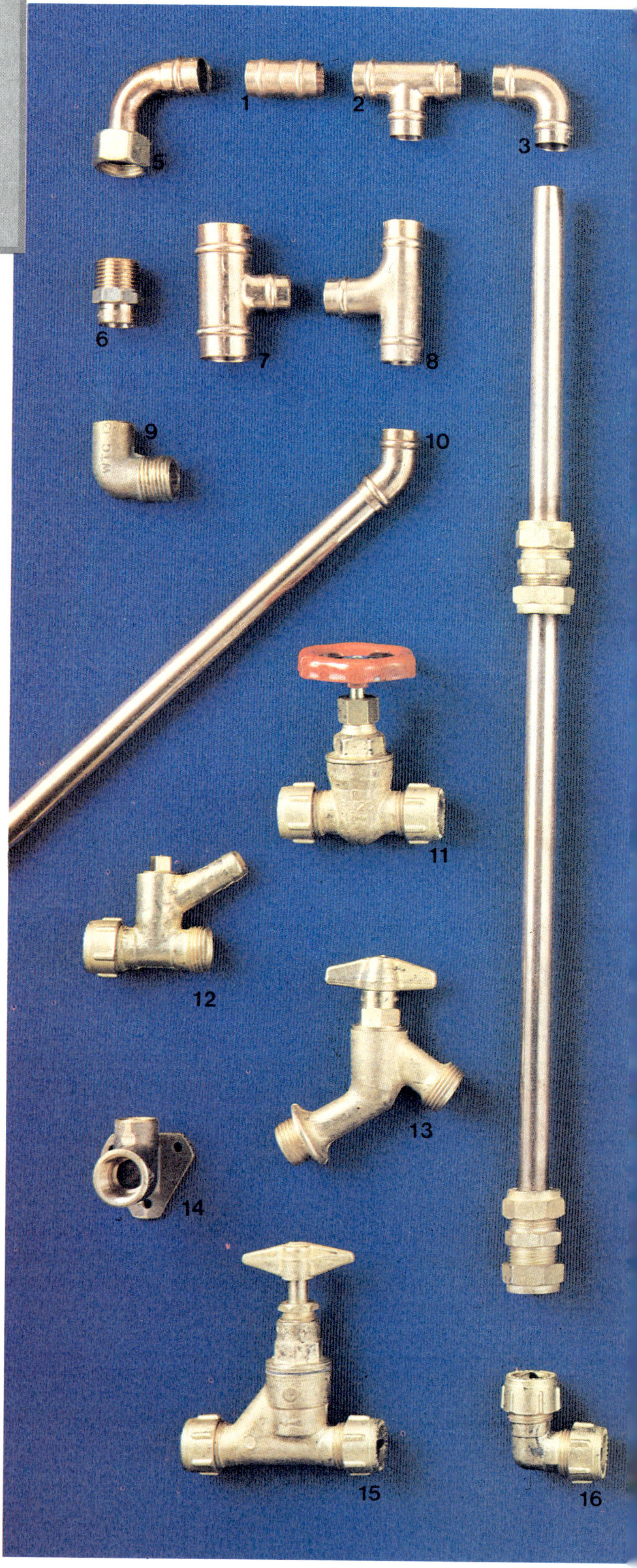

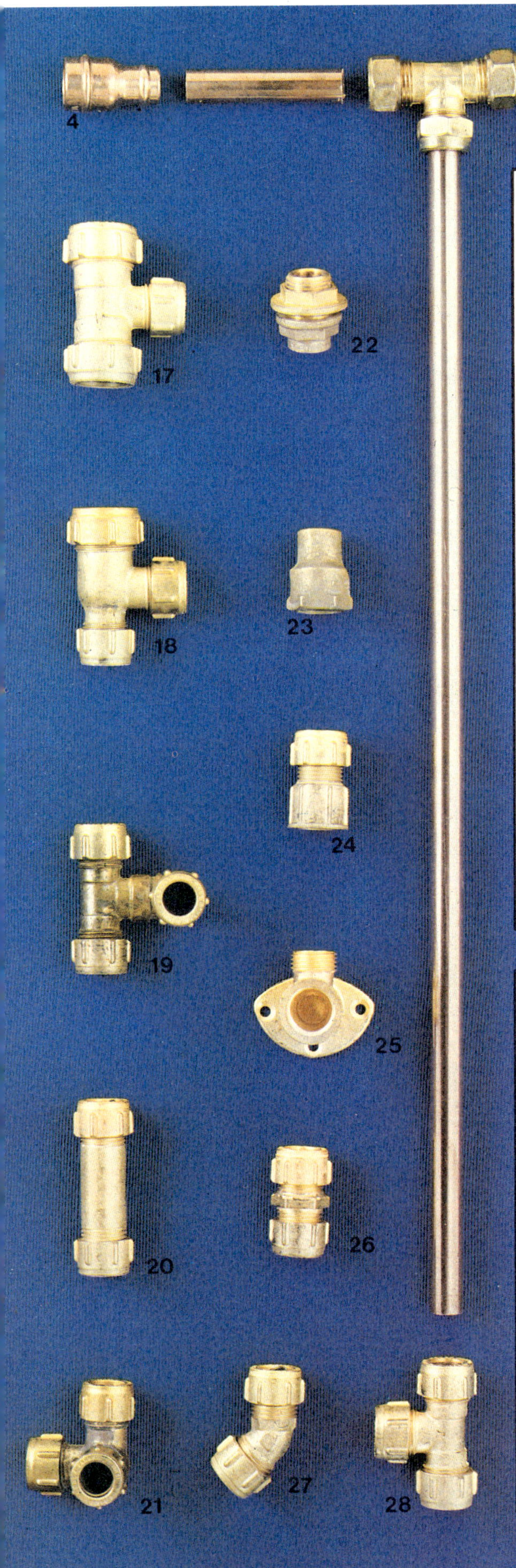

COMPRESSION FITTINGS

Joints are formed by screwing up a cap-nut, thus compressing the olive tightly between the fitting and the pipe. Although more expensive than capillary fittings, they are easier and quicker to use.

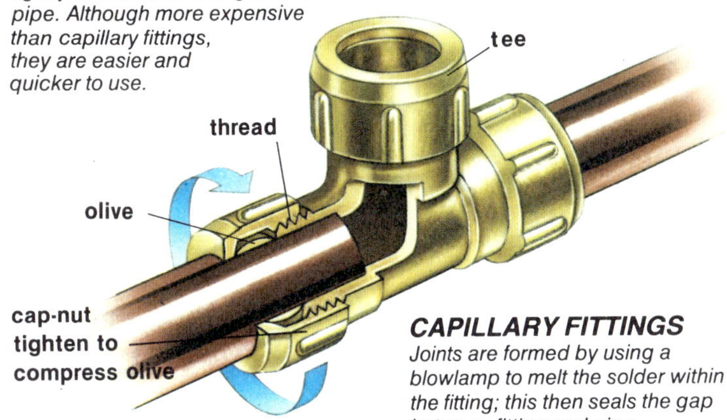

CAPILLARY FITTINGS

Joints are formed by using a blowlamp to melt the solder within the fitting; this then seals the gap between fitting and pipe.

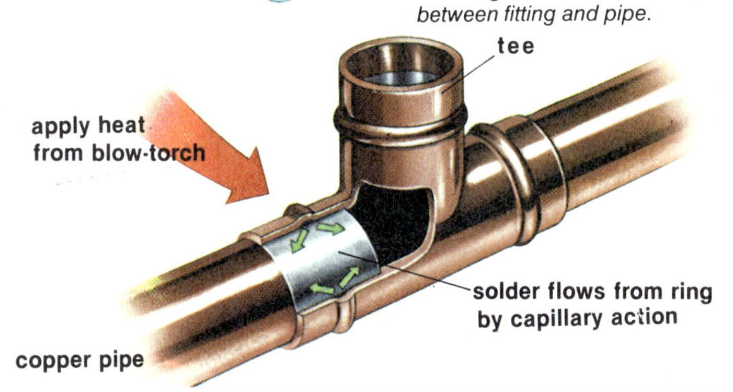

KEY TO FITTINGS

CAPILLARY FITTINGS

1 *– a 15mm straight coupling;*
2 *– a tee all ends 15mm;*
3 *– a 90° elbow;*
4 *– a 22x15mm reducer;*
5 *– a 15mm angled tap connector*
6 *– a male threaded adaptor;*
7 *– an unequal tee – 22x22x15mm;*
8 *– a swept 15mm tee commonly used in central heating for a smooth flow;*
9 *– a brass elbow connector between capillary and compression systems;*
10 *– a 135° elbow*

COMPRESSION FITTINGS

11 *– a gate-valve, commonly used at cistern and cylinder outlets;*
12 *– a drain cock;*
13 *– an angled bib-tap for outdoor supply, with threaded hose connection;*
14 *– a capillary-type bib-tap wall flange;*
15 *– a stop tap;*
16 *– a 15mm elbow;*
17 *– an unequal tee 22x22x15mm;*
18 *– a 22x15x15mm tee, with one end and branch reduced;*
19 *– a 15mm offset tee;*
20 *– an extended straight coupling;*
21 *– 15mm corner tee;*
22 *– a tank connector;*
23, 24 *– threaded copper to female connectors;*
25 *– a compression-type bib-tap wall flange, screwed for female thread;*
26 *– a straight connector;*
27 *– a 135° elbow;*
28 *– a plain 15mm tee;*
29 *– a stop end.*

TOOLS FOR PLUMBING JOBS

You should always check you've got the right tools to hand before starting any work, and plumbing is no exception. Here's a list of the ones you're most likely to need, plus some essential items to help you cope with emergencies.

Anyone living in a fairly modern – or modernised – house with copper or stainless steel water supply pipes and a plastic waste water system can carry out all routine plumbing maintenance and repair work with only a minimal tool kit. In fact, many of the tools required for plumbing work will already be part of the general household or car tool kit. But, if you plan to do a lot of plumbing work you'll need a few specialised tools.

Before buying any expensive new tool ask yourself how often you will need to use it. If the honest answer is 'not more than once a year' then you should seriously consider hiring it instead.

Spanners

You'll need a couple of adjustable spanners for tightening up compression fittings – one to hold the fitting steady while you use the other to tighten it up. You'll need them for many other types of fittings too.

A useful tool which can make life easier is the 'crows-foot' spanner. It's used to undo the virtually inaccessible back-nuts that secure bath and basin taps in position. Unless you have a lot of room beneath the taps you'll find it almost impossible to undo these nuts with an ordinary spanner.

Wrenches

Only wrenches are capable of gripping and turning round objects such as pipes. There are two types used in plumbing. The pipe wrench looks like an adjustable spanner but its lower jaw is able to pivot slightly, and both jaws are serrated. As you use it, the lower jaw is able to open just enough to grip the pipe, then, as you turn it, the serrations dig in, pull in the jaws and grip even tighter. The harder you turn, the tighter they grip, so they're suitable for really stubborn jobs. Wrenches will only work in one direction; if you turn them the wrong way the jaws won't grip and the pipe will slip round.

The lockable wrench is slightly different. You adjust the jaw separation with a screw, then close them round the pipe, squeezing the handles to lock them on tightly.

Pipe cutters

You can cut pipes with a hacksaw quite successfully, but if you plan to do a lot of plumbing work you should consider buying a pipe cutter. The pipe is placed between two hardened rollers and a thin cutting wheel; the tool is then rotated round the pipe while the cutting wheel is screwed down into the metal. A pipe cutter always produces a perfectly square and smooth cut – there is none of the rough metal burr that you'd get with a hacksaw. Yet it does round the end of the pipe inwards a little and the metal flange must be removed with a reamer which is usually incorporated in one end of the tool. Since pipe cutters need to be rotated round the rube they can't be used to cut existing pipes fitted close to a wall. So you will need a hacksaw as well.

Pipe benders

Sharp bends in pipes are easiest to make with capillary or compression fittings. But you can bend pipe by hand it you want, and you'll have to if you want shallow curves. Copper pipe with a diameter of 22mm (¾in) or less can be bent using bending springs or in a bending machine. The purpose of both springs and bending machine is to support the walls of the tube so that they don't flatten or wrinkle inside the curve as the bend is made. A bending spring supports the tube internally, while the bending machine supports it externally. As you're unlikely to want to bend copper pipe that often, these are tools it's best to hire when they're required.

Thread sealers

Jointing compound and PTFE tape are both used to make a watertight – and gas-tight – seal on screwed fittings. Jointing compound is a sticky paste which you smear round the thread, and PTFE thread sealing tape is wound anticlockwise round the male fitting before the joint is assembled.

Flame-proof gloves

If you're using a blowlamp and doing a lot of soldering then you'd be wise to invest in a pair of flame-proof gloves. Copper pipe conducts heat very efficiently so the gloves could prevent many burnt fingers.

Torch

Very often you'll need to work at the back of sinks and baths or in dark, awkward corners in the loft, so a torch is essential. Change the batteries as soon as the bulb dims.

Tape measure

You'll need a tape measure for accurate cutting of lengths of pipe and for positioning taps and fittings in the right place.

Files and steel wool

A file is essential for removing burrs left by a hacksaw. Emery paper and steel wool are both used to clean the ends of copper pipe ready for making soldered joints. They're also used to roughen plastic pipe to provide a key for adhesives.

Blowlamp

Unless you plan to use compression fittings for all your plumbing work you'll certainly need a blowlamp for making soldered joints. In most cases, a small blowlamp operating off a disposable canister of gas is easiest to use. Don't forget to keep a spare canister in your tool kit; they have a habit of running out at the most awkward moments.

Other tools

Apart from the tools described above, you'll also need a power drill for drilling holes for fixing screws and pipes, a set of screwdrivers and a pair of pliers.

TOOLS FOR MAJOR JOBS

KEY

Tools for major plumbing work

1 *crowsfoot spanner (one end for bath taps, the other for basins)*
2 *pipe bender and formers for 15 and 22mm pipe*
3 *retractable tape measure*
4 *wheeled pipe cutter*
5 *bending spring (available in 15 and 22mm sizes)*
6 *half-round file*
7 *screwdrivers for slotted and cross-head screws*
8 *flame-proof gloves*
9 *hacksaw with spare blades*
10 *lockable wrench*
11 *junior hacksaw*
12 *pliers*
13 *pipe wrench*
14 *adjustable spanners*
15 *flux paste for soldered capillary fittings*
16 *solder in coil form for end-feed capillary fittings*
17 *jointing compound (and/or PTFE tape) for threaded connections*
18 *wire wool pads*
19 *butane or propane blowlamp with replacement gas canisters.*

In addition to the tools and items of equipment mentioned above, you are also likely to need:

- *power drill with a selection of different sized masonry, twist drills and wood-boring bits*
- *pipe clips in 15 and 22mm sizes*
- *wallplugs (the stick type that you cut to length are the most economical)*
- *screws for mounting pipe clips, radiator brackets and so on*
- *a torch*
- *a bag to carry everything round the house in.*

AN EMERGENCY PLUMBING KIT

There's really no point in assembling a full plumbing tool kit if you never intend to do any plumbing work. But emergencies can always happen so it's wise to keep a small tool kit to hand to stop an accident turning into a disaster. This should include an adjustable spanner, a locking wrench, a screwdriver and a pair of pliers, plus equipment to cope with bursts and leaks.

If you hammer a nail into a pipe you can easily make a quick repair with a two-part pack of epoxy resin sold especially for plumbing repairs. The adhesive and hardener are worked together in the hands and the material is moulded round the hole. This makes a permanent repair for small holes or leaking joints, but a larger hole is repaired more securely by cutting out the damaged section of pipe and inserting a straight compression coupling. So keep at least two of these in your tool kit – one each for 15mm and 22mm pipe.

Keep some penetrating oil for freeing jammed stop-valves or corroded nuts and, of course, an adjustable spanner to undo the latter. You'll also need a selection of tap washers – one for each type of tap, and some O-rings for the ball-valve. A few spare olives are always handy – compression fittings can be reused but you need a new olive each time. For clearing blocked waste pipes you'll need a 'force cup' or sink waste plunger, and a piece of flexible wire for clearing out blocked pipes and drains. Finally, mini-hacksaws are so cheap it's worth keeping one specially for your emergency tool kit. For more information see the following chapter.

ROUTINE MAINTENANCE AND REPAIRS

Looking after your home's plumbing system is essential if you are to get the best from it, and every member of the family should know what to do in an emergency when the system springs a leak, so that it can be dealt with quickly and effectively.

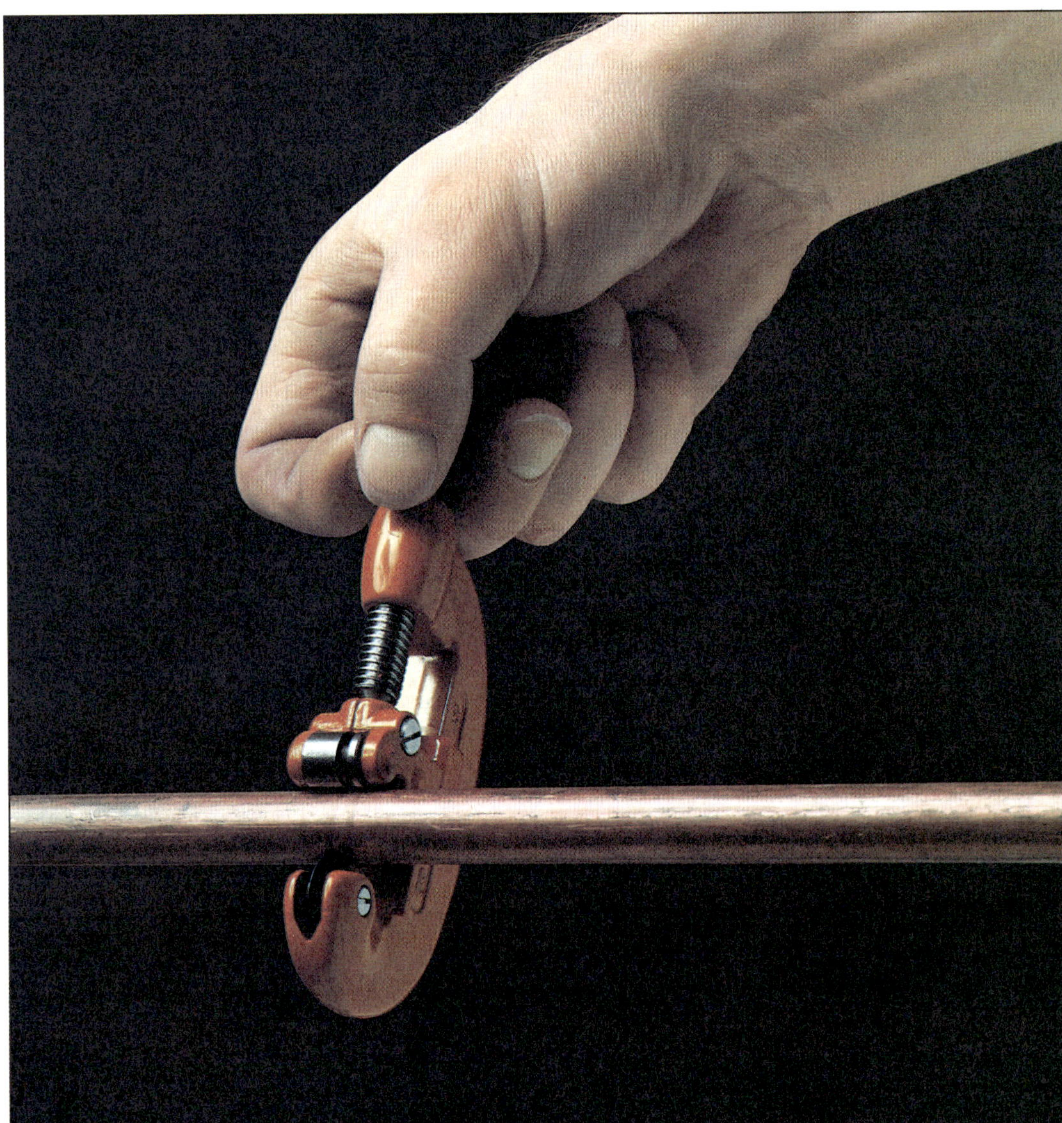

DRAINING PLUMBING SYSTEMS

When you are carrying out repairs or alterations to your plumbing or wet central heating system, you will usually have to drain water from the parts you are working on. Here's what you'll have to do.

Virtually all major and many minor plumbing operations demand the partial or total drainage of either the domestic hot or cold water supply. If you have a 'wet' central heating system you'll also have to drain that before carrying out repairs or alterations. Before attempting this – long before the need for drainage arises, in fact – you should make yourself thoroughly familiar with the design and layout of these systems in your home. Here are some questions to which you should know the answers:

- Are all cold water draw-off points supplied direct from the rising main, or are the bathroom cold taps and the WC cistern supplied with water from a main cold water storage cistern (probably situated in the roof space)?
- Is the hot water system 'direct' or 'indirect' (see pages 8–12).
- If the system is direct, is the domestic hot water heated solely by means of an electric immersion heater, solely by means of a domestic boiler (gas, oil or solid fuel), or are both means of heating available?
- If hot water is provided solely by means of an immersion heater, is there a drain-valve at the base of the cold supply pipe from the storage cistern to the hot water cylinder?
- If hot water is provided by means of a boiler, is there a drain-valve on the pipework beside the boiler, or possibly incorporated into the boiler itself?
- If the system is indirect, is it a conventional indirect system (indicated by the presence of a small feed-and-expansion tank in the roof space, feeding the primary circuit) or is it a self-priming indirect system such as the Primatic?
- Is there a 'wet' central heating system provided in conjunction with hot water supply?
- Where is the main stop-valve, and are there any other stop-valves or gate-valves fitted into distribution or circulating pipes in the system?
- Are there drain-valves at low points in the central heating circuit?

Draining down for simple repairs

Once you are thoroughly familiar with the contents and layout of your own plumbing and central heating systems, you will be able to work out for yourself how much draining-down will be necessary before you undertake any particular item of maintenance or any particular project. If, for instance, you wish to rewasher the cold tap over the kitchen sink (this is supplied direct from the rising main) or to tee into the rising main to provide a garden water supply, all that you need to do is to turn off the main stop-valve and to turn on the kitchen cold tap until water ceases to flow from it. You will then have drained the rising main to the level of the cold tap. In many modern homes a drain-valve is provided immediately above the main stop-valve to permit the rising main to be completely drained.

Rather more drainage is necessary when you wish to renew the washer on a hot tap, or on a cold tap supplied from a storage cistern, or to renew a ball-valve in a WC cistern that is supplied with water from a storage cistern. First of all, see if there are any stop-valves or gate-valves on the distribution pipes leading to the particular tap or ball-valve. There could be gate-valves on the main hot and cold distribution pipes just below the level of the main cold water storage cistern. There could even be a mini-stop-valve on the distribution pipe immediately before its connection to the tail of the tap or ball-valve.

In either of these circumstances you're in luck!. All you have to do is to turn off the appropriate gate-valve or mini-stop-valve and then to turn on the tap or flush the lavatory cistern. You can then carry out the necessary repairs.

Avoiding unnecessary drainage

The chances are, though, that the main stop-valve will be the only one in the system, and that you'll have to contemplate draining the main cold water storage cistern and the appropriate distribution pipes before you can get on with your task, by turning off the main stop-valve and draining the cistern and pipes from the taps supplied by the cistern. This, however, will mean that the whole of the plumbing system is out of action for as long as it takes you to complete the job. It is generally better to go up into the roof space and lay a slat of wood across the top of the cold water storage cistern. You can then tie the float arm of the ball-valve up to it, so that water cannot flow into the cistern. Then drain the cistern by opening the bathroom taps. In this way the cold tap over the sink will not be put out of action.

Here's another useful money-saving tip: even if you are draining down to rewasher a hot tap, there is no need to run to waste all that hot water stored in the hot water cylinder, *provided that your bathroom cold taps are supplied from the cold water storage cistern.* Having tied up the ball-valve, run the bathroom *cold* taps until they cease to flow and only then turn on the hot tap you want to work on. Because the hot water distribution pipe is taken from above the hot water storage cylinder, only a little hot water – from the pipe itself – will flow away to waste and the cylinder will remain full of hot water.

For the same reason, unless you expect to have the hot water system out of action for a

WHERE TO DRAIN THE SYSTEM

On a well-designed plumbing system you should find that drain-valves have been installed at several points, so that partial draining-down is possible.

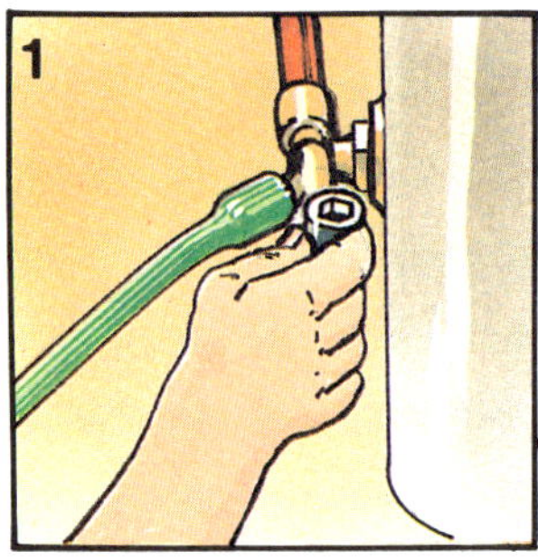

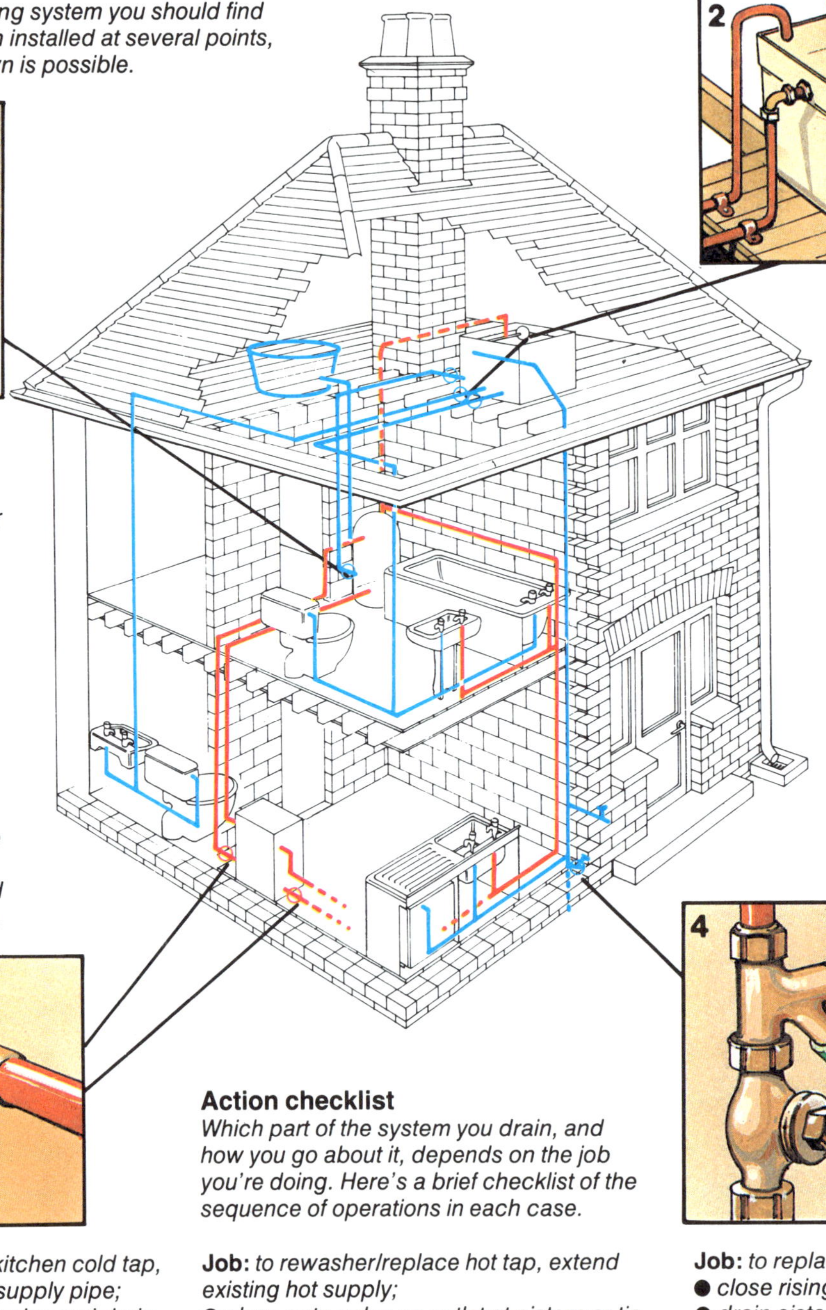

1 *A drain-valve at the point where the cold feed from the storage cistern in the loft enters the hot water cylinder means that you can empty the main body of the cylinder (at least, down to the level of the inlet pipe) in the event of it springing a leak. Here a T-shaped drain-valve spanner is being used to open the valve.*

2 *If gate-valves are fitted on the outlets from the cold water storage cistern, all you have to do to drain a pipe run is shut the appropriate valve and open the taps. If they are not fitted, you will have to drain the cistern too. To stop it filling, tie the float arm up to a piece of wood resting across the cistern.*

4 *A drain-valve fitted above the rising main stop-valve allows you to drain the main and connect tees to it. The stop-valve saves you from having to tie up the storage cistern ball-valve when draining the cold supply pipes.*

3 *Drain-valves fitted beside the boiler allow you to drain the primary circuit and the central heating system.*

Action checklist

Which part of the system you drain, and how you go about it, depends on the job you're doing. Here's a brief checklist of the sequence of operations in each case.

Job: *to rewasher/replace kitchen cold tap, tee off rising main for new supply pipe;*
- *turn off rising main stop-valve and drain rising main via drain-valve*
- *if no drain-valve fitted, open kitchen cold tap to drain main down to level of tee to kitchen sink.*

Job: *to rewasher/replace other cold tap, renew WC ball-valve, extend cold supply;*
- *if gate-valve fitted to outlet at cold cistern, close valve and open lowest appropriate cold tap; otherwise*
- *tie up arm of cold cistern ball-valve and drain cistern by opening cold taps.*

Job: *to rewasher/replace hot tap, extend existing hot supply;*
- *close gate-valve on outlet at cistern or tie up cistern ball-valve*
- *open cold tap until flow stops*
- *only then open hot tap.*

Job: *to replace hot cylinder;*
- *close gate-valve or tie up ball-valve arm*
- *turn off boiler or immersion heater*
- *empty cylinder via cylinder drain-valve*
- *close gate-valve on outlet from feed/ expansion tank, or tie up ball-valve*
- *drain primary circuit via drain-valve at boiler.*

Job: *to replace cold cistern;*
- *close rising main stop-valve*
- *drain cistern by opening cold taps (hot water will still run from cylinder).*

Job: *to replace boiler;*
- *on* ***direct systems,*** *turn off boiler or immersion heater and also heating system*
- *close rising main stop-valve*
- *open all taps, and drain boiler from drain-valve nearby*
- *on* ***indirect systems,*** *turn off boiler*
- *close feed/expansion tank gate-valve*
- *drain primary and central heating systems from drain-valves at boiler.*

prolonged period there is no need to switch off the immersion heater or to let out the boiler when carrying out a maintenance operation on the bathroom hot tap.

Problems with air locks

If your hot and cold water distribution systems are properly designed – with 'horizontal' runs of pipe actually having a slight fall away from the storage cistern or the vent pipe to permit air to escape – then the system should fill up with little or no trouble when you untie the ball-valve and permit water to flow into the cistern again. Should an air-lock prevent complete filling, try connecting one end of a length of hose to the cold tap over the kitchen sink and the other end to one of the taps giving trouble. Turn on first the tap giving trouble and then the one over the kitchen sink. Mains pressure from this cold tap should blow the air bubble out of the system.

Draining the whole system

Very occasionally – perhaps because of a major reconstruction of the system or because of that most traumatic of all plumbing emergencies, a leaking boiler – it may be necessary to drain the whole system. Let's assume, first of all, that you have either a direct hot water system or a self-priming indirect one.

Switch off the immersion heater and let out or switch off the boiler. Turn off the central heating system if this is operated from the self-priming cylinder. Close the main stop-valve and open up every tap in the house – hot as well as cold. Connect one end of a length of hose to the drain-valve beside the boiler or, if the cylinder is heated by an immersion heater only, at the base of the cold supply pipe entering the cylinder, and take the other end of the hose to an outside gully. Open up the drain-valve and allow the system to drain.

If you have an indirect system you should again turn off the boiler and central heating system. Then close the gate-valve leading from the feed-and-expansion tank, or tie up it's ball-valve, and drain the system from the boiler drain-valves.

How you proceed depends upon the reason for which you have carried out the draining-down. Your aim should be to get as much of the plumbing system as possible back into operation quickly.

Restoring partial supplies

The first step is to go up into the roof space and tie up the ball-valve on the main storage cistern as already described. Open up the main stop-valve and water supply will be restored to the cold tap over the kitchen sink.

It should also be possible to restore the bathroom cold water supplies. Trace the distribution pipe that takes water from the cold water storage cistern to the hot water cylinder.

COPING WITH AIRLOCKS

Clear supply-pipe airlocks by linking the affected tap to the kitchen cold tap with hose secured by worm-drive clips. Open the affected tap first, then the kitchen tap.

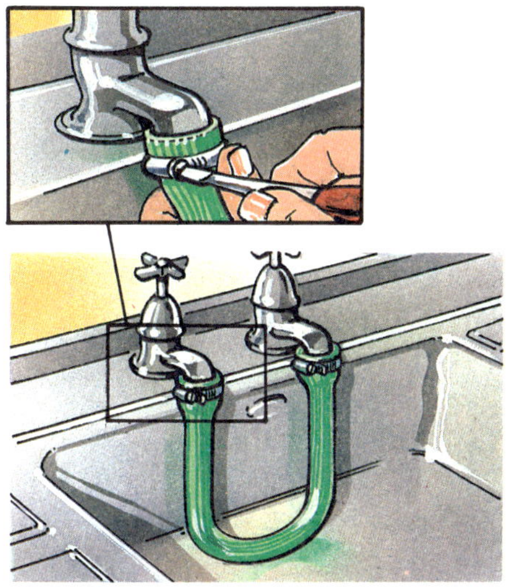

Avoid airlocks in primary or heating circuits by filling them upwards via a hose linking the kitchen cold tap and the boiler drain-valve. Close vents as radiators fill.

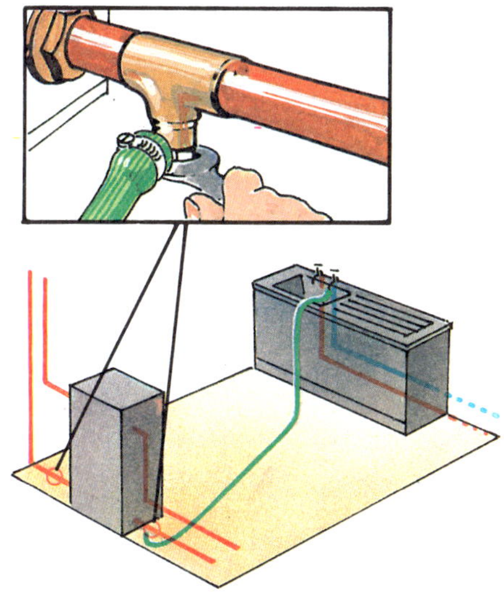

Find a cork of the correct size, lean into the cistern and push it into the pipe's inlet. Before doing so, it is a good idea to screw a substantial woodscrew part of the way into the cork to facilitate removal. You can then untie the ball-valve and allow the cistern to refill; no water will flow to the hot cylinder.

Draining heating systems

If you have a conventional indirect hot water system – perhaps installed in conjunction with a central heating system – you can drain the primary circuit, together with the radiator circuit if there is one, without draining the water from the outer part of the storage cylinder. Because of the increased risk of corrosion that arises from water and air coming into contact with steel surfaces, a radiator circuit should be drained only when absolutely essential. When this has to be done – to add additional radiators, perhaps – you should tie up the ball-valve serving the feed-and-expansion tank and drain from both the drain-valve beside the boiler and from any drain-valves provided at low points of the system. You must, of course, let out or switch off the boiler before attempting this.

When refilling the primary circuit (or when refilling a direct system with boiler) it may help to prevent the formation of air-locks if you connect one end of your garden hose to the boiler drain-valve and the other end to the cold tap over the kitchen sink. Open them both up and the system will fill upwards, with air being driven out in front of the rising water. As the central heating circuit refills, open up all the radiator vents – and any other air vents that there may be in the system – and leave them open until water begins to flow through them. It is a good idea, when refilling a central heating system, to introduce a reliable corrosion-proofer into the feed-and-expansion tank to prevent future internal corrosion, but you can do this only if you fill the system from the top, not from the bottom.

Winter precautions

One final point: if you are leaving your home empty during the winter months, you should drain the main cold water storage cistern and, if you have a direct hot water system and will be away for more than two or three days, you should drain the hot cylinder, the boiler and its circulation pipes as well. Human memory is fallible. Having done so, leave a conspicuous notice on the boiler and by the immersion heater switch saying 'SYSTEM DRAINED – DO NOT LIGHT BOILER OR SWITCH ON HEATER UNTIL IT HAS BEEN REFILLED'.

Because of the risk of corrosion already referred to, the primary circuit and any central heating system connected to it should not be drained in these circumstances. If you have a central heating system that is capable of automatic control, leave it switched on under the control of a frost-stat. This is a thermostatic control, usually positioned in a garage or in the roof space, that will bring the heating into operation when a predetermined, near-freezing-point temperature, is reached.

STOPPING TAPS LEAKING

Although taps are in frequent use, they rarely need maintenance. But if one starts to leak don't ignore it. Leaking taps are not only annoying and wasteful, but also, if they are hot taps, expensive — you've paid to heat the water going down the drain.

A tap is a device for controlling the flow of water at an outlet point, and is opened and closed by turning a handle. This may be a 'tee' or 'capstan' type (so called because of the shape) fitted onto a spindle rising from the body of the tap. Or it may be a 'shrouded head', covering all of the upper part of the tap.

Turning the handle clockwise forces a jumper unit down onto a valve seating in the waterway of the tap and stops the flow of water. Because metal against metal doesn't make a very tight seal, a synthetic rubber disc — a washer — is attached to the base of the jumper so that it beds firmly onto the seating.

Turning the handle anti-clockwise raises the jumper from the seating and allows water to flow. An exception to this is the Supatap where the nozzle is rotated to control the flow. When you open a tap water pressure will also force water round the jumper unit and, unless there is some way of preventing it, this would escape from round the spindle. To get round this problem some taps have 'O' ring seals fitted to the spindle while older taps have greased wool packed tightly in a gland around the spindle. More modern taps have rubber tube for packing.

Mixers work in exactly the same way as ordinary taps except that they have only one spout that combines the flow of water from the hot and cold supplies. On kitchen mixers particularly this spout can be swivelled so that it can be pushed to one side to give better access to the sink or can supply a double sink.

When a tap starts to leak, there's a strong temptation either to ignore it or to try to stop it by closing it as tightly as you can. Such action is invariably ineffective and could lead to the valve seating being permanently damaged.

Where leaks occur

Basically there are three places a tap can leak: at the spout, in which case the washer and perhaps the seating will need looking at; at the spindle when the tap is turned on, which means either the packing in the gland or the 'O' ring has failed; or at the swivel point at the spout of a mixer tap, which means that the 'O' ring is at fault. All these repairs are easy to deal with. But first you must know the type of tap and the terminology related to it.

How washers are replaced

Conventional pillar tap This is the basic type of tap design and provides a good example of the procedure to follow when replacing a washer. These taps are commonly used for the hot and cold water supply over the kitchen sink and in this position they are probably the most frequently used taps in the house. It's quite likely that sooner or later the washers will need replacing.

To do this you'll first have to turn off the water supply either at the mains or, if you're lucky, at isolating stop-valves under the sink which when shut cut off the supply either to the hot or cold tap without affecting the rest of the system (see previous section and pages 70–71). Turn on the tap fully so it is drained before you start work.

Usually with a pillar tap the spindle rises out of a dome-like easy-clean cover, which you should be able to unscrew by hand. If this proves too difficult, you can use a wrench, but pad the jaws thoroughly with rag to avoid damaging the finish on plated taps.

With the tap turned on fully you can then raise the cover sufficiently to slip the jaws of a wrench under it to grip the 'flats' of the headgear — the main body of the tap which has a nut-shaped section to it. If you can't do this you'll need to take off the tap handle and easy-clean cover. First you'll have to remove the tiny grub-screw in the side of the handle which can then be lifted off. If this proves difficult a good tip is to open the tap fully, unscrew, then raise the easy-clean cover and place pieces of wood (a spring-loaded clothes peg will do) between the bottom of the easy-clean cover and the body of the tap. By turning the tap handle as if you were trying to close it the upward pressure on the easy-clean cover will force it off the spindle. However, you then have to replace it over the spindle just sufficiently to enable you to turn the tap on. When this is done take it off again and remove the easy-clean cover. While you are doing all this make sure

Bib with capstan handle
Pillar with capstan handle
Supatap
Pillar with shrouded head

you hold the tap steady. If the headgear is stiff and the entire tap turns you could damage the part of the sink into which the tap fits.

You can now put the headgear to one side. You should be able to see the jumper, with the washer attached, resting on the valve seating within the body of the tap (though sometimes it gets stuck and lifts out with the headgear). Often the washer is held in position on the jumper by a tiny nut which has to be undone with pliers before the washer can be replaced. This may be easier said than done, and rather than waste time attempting the all-but-impossible, it's probably better to fit a new washer and jumper complete rather than just renewing the washer. Once this has been done the tap can be reassembled, and as you do this smear the screw threads with petroleum jelly.

Tap with shrouded head This is basically a pillar tap where the spindle is totally enclosed by an easy-clean cover that also acts as a handle to turn the tap on and off. Some shrouded heads are made of plastic and care is therefore needed when using wrenches. But the mystery of this tap is how to get to the inside — and methods vary with the make of tap.

Some shrouded heads can simply be pulled off, perhaps after opening the tap fully and then giving another half turn. Some are secured by a tiny grub-screw in the side. But the commonest method of attaching the head is by a screw beneath the plastic 'hot' or 'cold' indicator. Prise the plastic bit off with a small screwdriver to reveal the retaining screw (normally a cross-headed screw). When the shrouded head has been removed you'll find that you can unscrew the headgear to reach the interior of the tap in the same way as with an ordinary pillar tap. Rewashering can then be done in the same way.

If the jumper is not resting on the valve seating in the body of the tap, but is 'pegged' into the headgear so that it can be turned round and round but can't be withdrawn, it's slightly more of a problem to remove the washer-retaining nut. The easiest way is to fasten the jumper plate in a vice (although pliers will do) and turn the nut with a spanner. Some penetrating oil will help to free the thread. If after this you still can't loosen the nut, a good tip is to slip the blade of a screwdriver between the plate of the jumper and the tap headgear and lever it to break the pegging. A new jumper and washer can then be fitted complete, although the stem should be 'burred' or roughened with a file to give an 'interference fit' when it is slipped into the headgear.

Bib taps These taps are treated in exactly the same way as a conventional pillar tap. You might find with a garden tap that there's no easy-clean cover, so the headgear is already exposed.

TOOLS FOR TAP REPAIRS

- **thin screwdriver** is useful for prising off clipped on coverings, separating washer from jumper, removing 'O' rings, grub-screws
- **cross-headed screwdriver** might be needed for retaining-screw on some shrouded or mixer taps
- **adjustable wrench or spanner** is needed to remove the headgear.

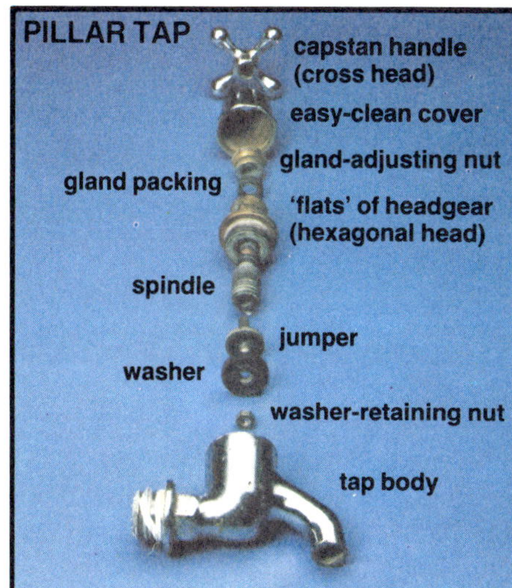

New taps rarely need repairs – and the actuality is more likely to be taps like these which won't be bright and clean inside. In hard-water areas lime scale will have accumulated which can cause the tap to jam so remove it with wire wool when the tap's dismantled. This will also help you identify the parts.

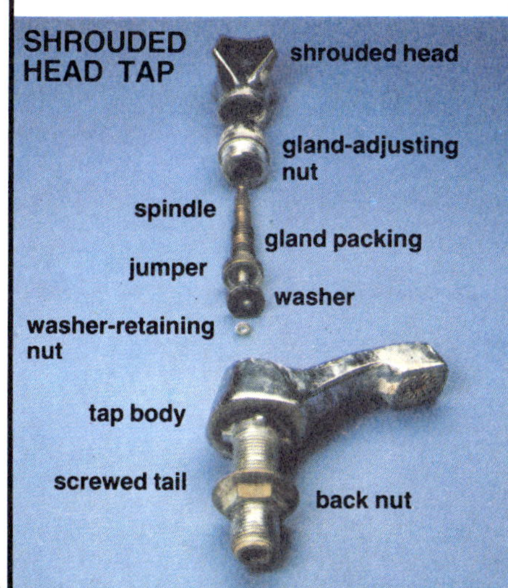

REPLACING A PILLAR TAP WASHER

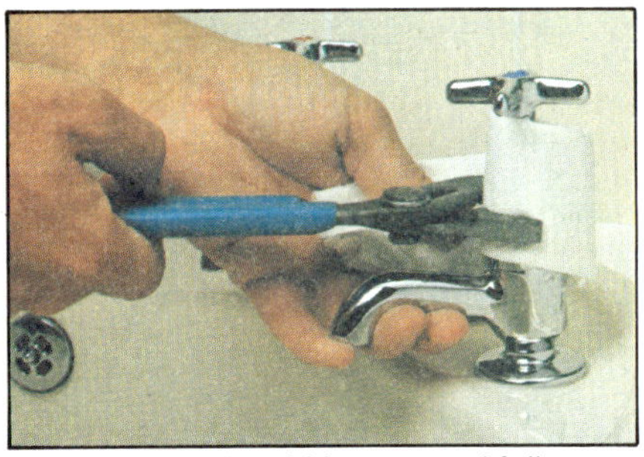

1 *Pillar taps should be opened fully after turning off the water supply. Now unscrew the easy-clean cover.*

2 *Lift up the easy-clean cover so you can slip an adjustable spanner or wrench in to undo the headgear.*

If there isn't enough space for the spanner or wrench, undo the grub-screw and then remove the handle.

If the handle won't come out, put a wedge under the cover and try to close the tap and force the cover up.

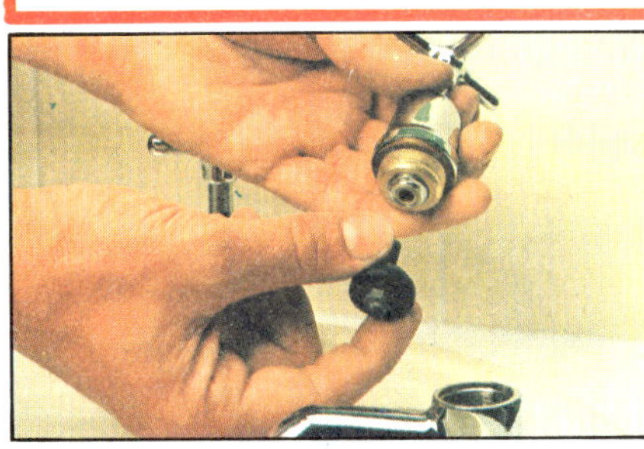

3 *With the handle fully opened, the headgear can be removed and the jumper unit pulled away.*

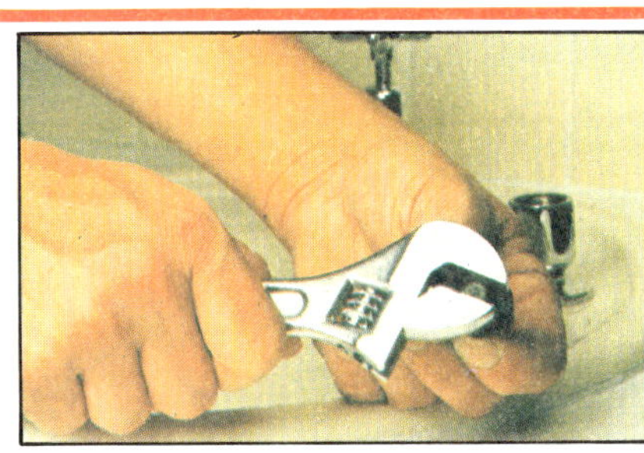

4 *Some taps have the washer fixed to the jumper unit by a nut; in others it has to be prised off.*

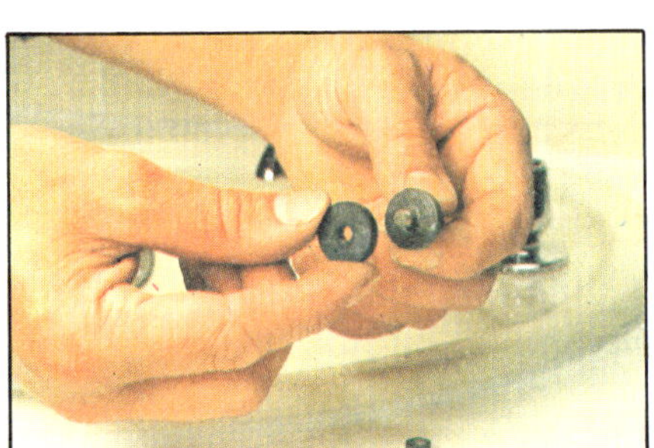

5 *Push a washer of the correct size over the end of the jumper unit. If held by a nut clean it with steel wool before replacing it.*

6 *Push the jumper unit back onto the headgear and replace in the tap. Turn the handle to half close the tap, then restore the mains supply.*

SHROUDED TAP

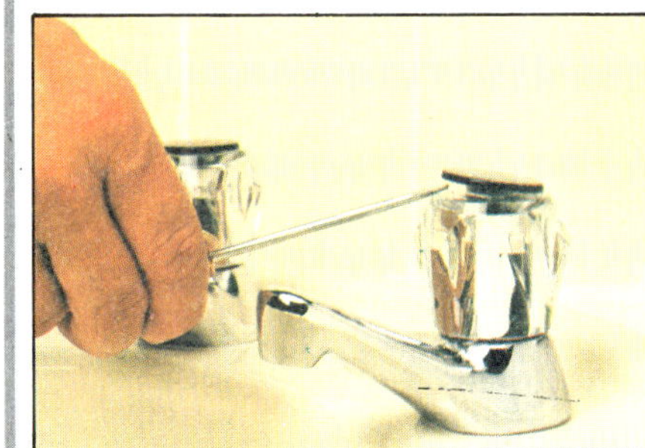

1 *With a shrouded head tap, you can either pull it off or prise off the indicator cap with a screwdriver after turning the water supply off and the tap on.*

2 *Undo the retaining screw (probably a cross-headed type so you'll need the right screwdriver) and then you will be able to pull off the head.*

3 *Hold the spout to prevent damaging the basin while you unscrew the headgear either using a spanner or an adjustable wrench.*

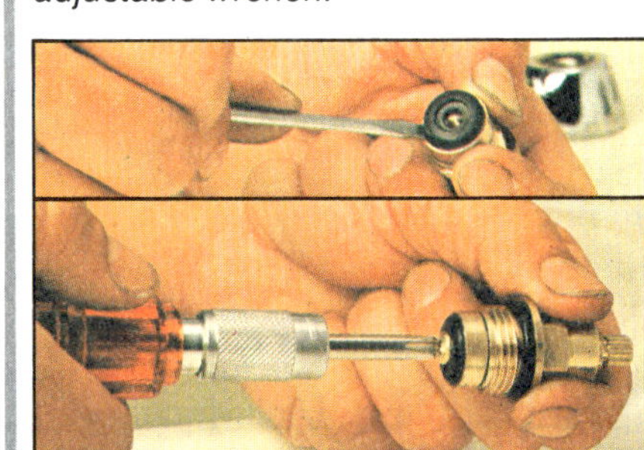

4 *Unscrew the retaining nut, remove the old washer and replace with one of the correct size. Reassemble the tap, then restore the water supply.*

Jem Grischotti

RE-WASHERING A SUPATAP

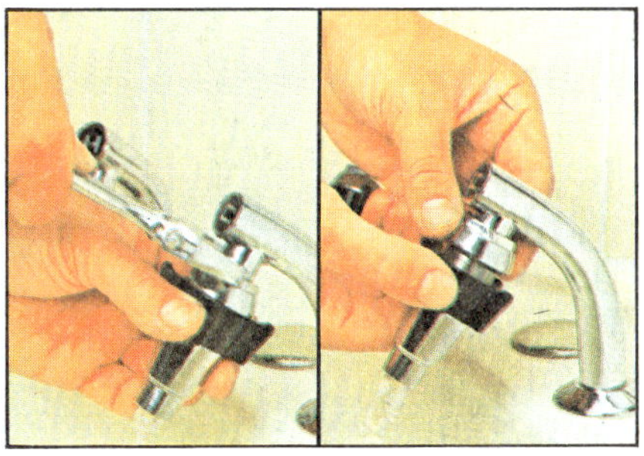

1 *Turn on the tap slightly and hold it while you undo the top nut. Open the tap fully, then turn the nozzle to unscrew it from the headgear.*

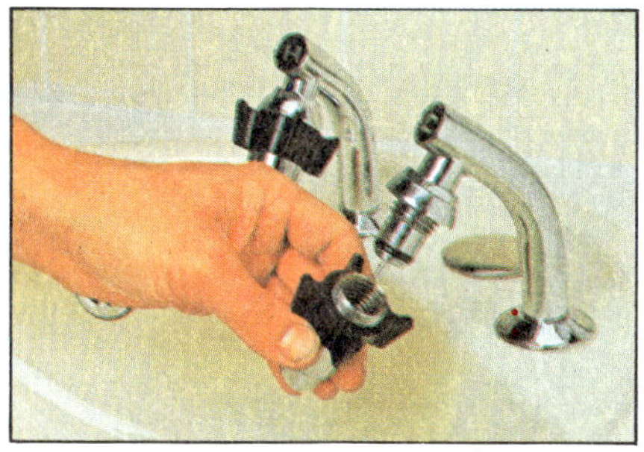

2 *As the nozzle comes away in your hand, a valve in the tap will automatically cut off the water so that you can make the repair.*

3 *Tap the nozzle on a hard surface so you can shake out the anti-splash device to which will be attached the jumper unit and the washer.*

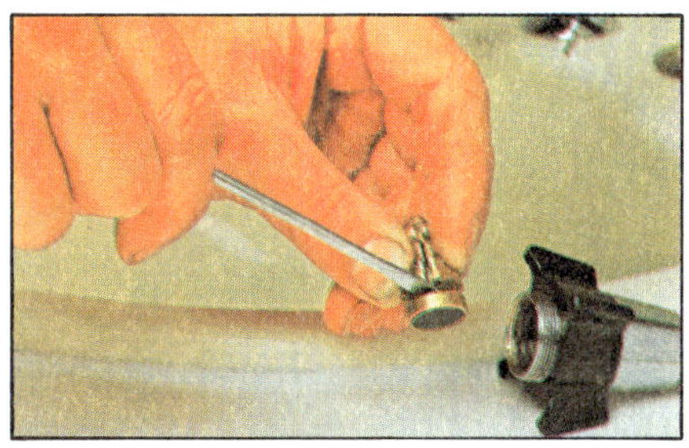

4 *Prise the old washer and jumper unit from the anti-splash device and press in a new complete unit. Now you can reassemble the tap.*

Supataps Changing the washer on this type of tap can be carried out in minutes, without the need to cut off the water supply first. Before you begin, check that you have a replacement Supatap washer and jumper unit. Once you've undone the retaining nut at the top of the nozzle you have to open up the tap fully — and then keep on turning. At first the flow will increase, but then, just before the nozzle comes off in your hand, a check-valve inside the tap will fall into position and stop the flow. You can separate the anti-splash device, (containing the washer and jumper unit) from the nozzle by turning it upside down and tapping the nozzle on a hard surface — not a ceramic sink or basin. The washer and jumper unit then need to be prised from the anti-splash device — you can use a knife blade or the edge of a coin to do this. A new washer and jumper unit can then be snapped in. When reassembling the tap it's necessary to remember that the nozzle has a left-hand thread and so has to be turned anti-clockwise to tighten it.

Repairing a poor seating

Sometimes a tap will continue to drip although you've changed the washer. This is usually because the valve seating has become scored and damaged by grit from the mains, so the washer can't make a watertight connection.

You can use a reseating tool to put the problem right. This entails removing the headgear after the water has been turned off, inserting the tool into the body of the tap and turning it to cut a new seating. It won't be worthwhile buying one of these tools for what is a once-in-a-lifetime job, but you may be able to hire one from a tool hire company.

An alternative method, and certainly one that's a lot easier, is to use a nylon 'washer and seating set'. Again with the water supply off, the headgear and the washer and jumper are removed from the tap end and the nylon liner is placed in position over the seating. The jumper and washer are then inserted into the headgear, which is screwed back onto the tap. The tap handle is then turned to the off position. This action will force the liner into and over the old seating to give a watertight joint.

You can't, of course, use one of these sets to reseat a Supatap. However, the makers (Deltaflow Ltd) will supply a reseating tool on request, but these taps very rarely need reseating.

You can also use a domed washer to cure a poor seating. It increases the surface area in contact with the waterway and so

Ready Reference

WHAT'S GONE WRONG?

Check out the problem first.

Washers may be worn or disintegrating. Replace with 12mm (½in) or 18mm (¾in) synthetic rubber washers, available from hardware stores. A good tip for a temporary repair is to reverse the old washer.

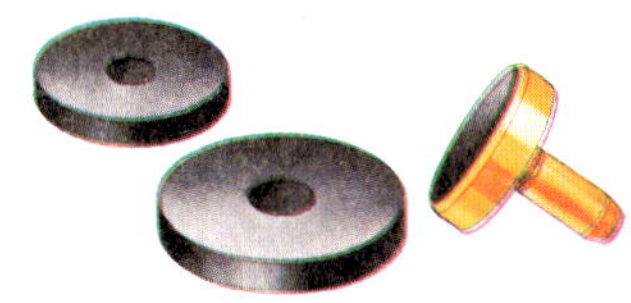

'O' rings that look worn may also cause leaks. Choose the same size so they fit snugly.

Valve seating is damaged if rough and uneven. You can:

- use a domed, not a flat, washer

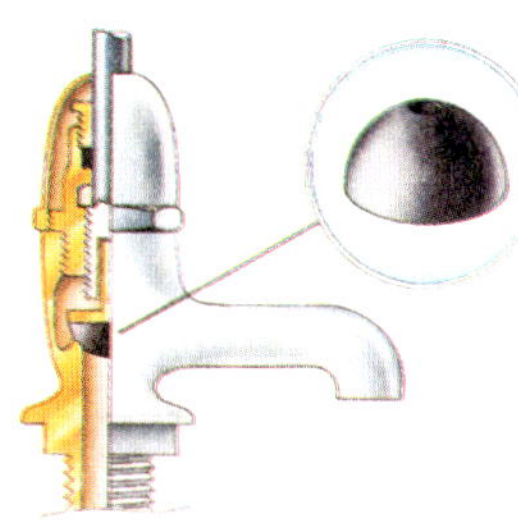

- fit a washer and seating set which covers up the damage
- buy or hire a reseating tool to grind the damaged seat smooth

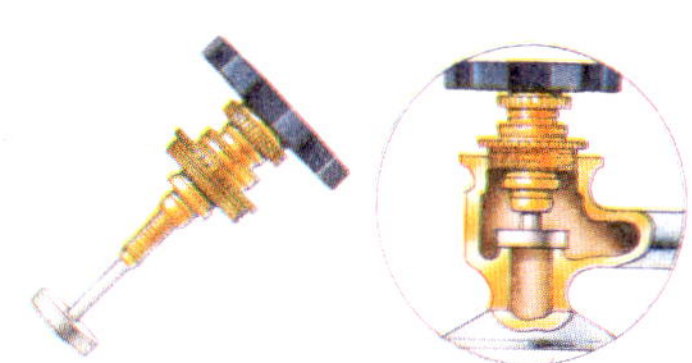

TIPS TO SAVE TIME AND TROUBLE

- If you can't undo the nut holding the washer to the jumper, buy an all-in-one jumper and washer set.

- If a metal easy-clean cover is stuck pour very hot water over it. It should then unscrew.
- After repairing a tap, leave the water to run gently for 15 minutes to remove any air trapped in the pipes.

LEAKAGE UP THE SPINDLE

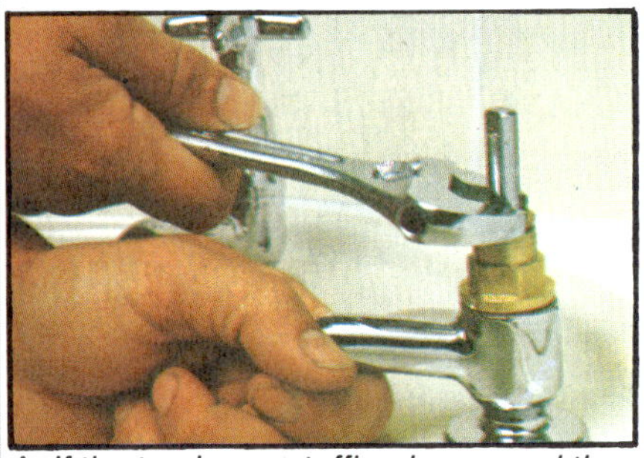

1 *If the tap has a stuffing box round the spindle, first try to tighten the gland-adjusting nut.*

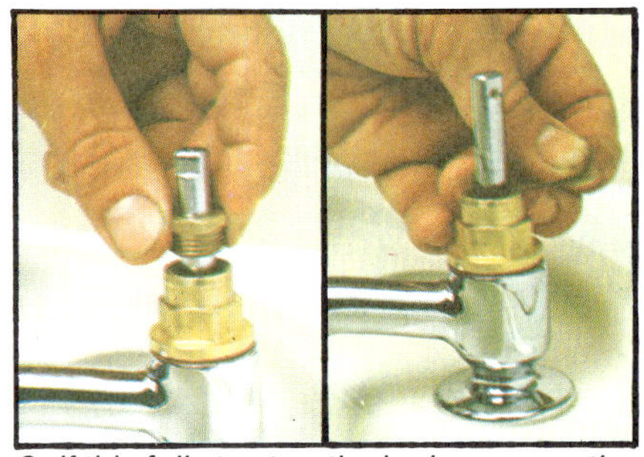

2 *If this fails to stop the leak, remove the nut and then pick out the old greased wool stuffing.*

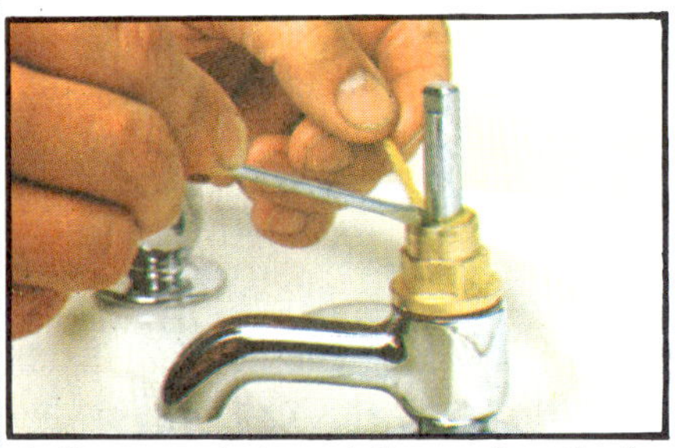

3 *Smear petroleum jelly on a length of knitting wool, then wind it around the spindle, packing it down tightly.*

4 *Alternatively you may be able to use a rubber packing washer which just has to be slipped on.*

Keith Morris

REPLACING 'O' RING SEALS

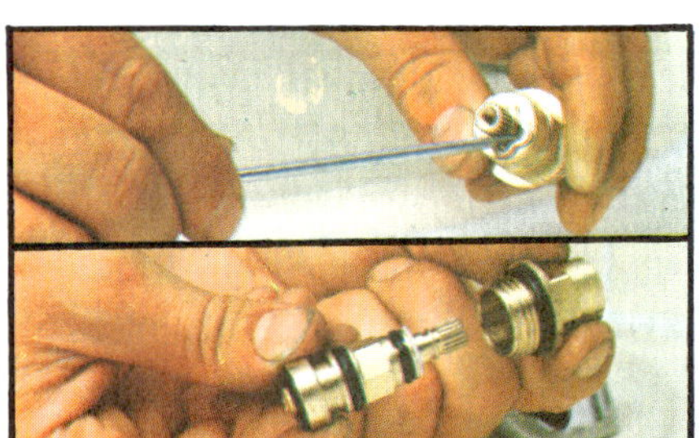

1 *To get to the seals on a tap, remove the headgear and prise off the circlip which holds the spindle in place.*

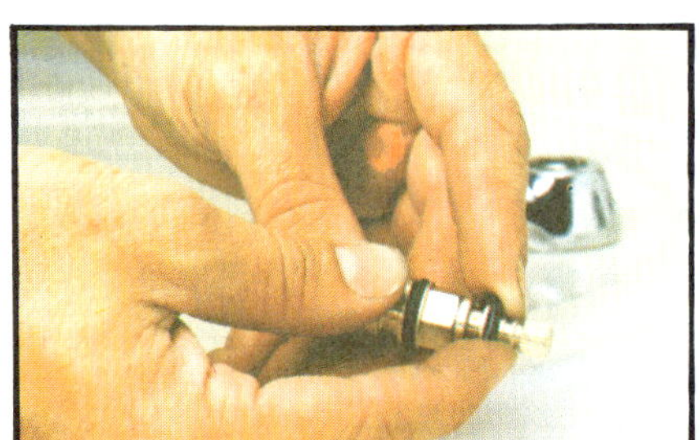

2 *Use a thin-bladed screwdriver to work off the worn 'O' rings and then replace them with new ones.*

3 *At the swivel point of a spout, first undo any grub-screw. Now twist the spout to one side and gently ease it from the mounting.*

4 *Prise off the worn seals with a screwdriver and then slip new ones into position. Replace the spout back in the mounting, restore water.*

effectively cuts off the flow when the tap is turned off even though the top of the valve seating may not be smooth.

Repacking a gland

This is necessary when you turn the tap on and water bubbles up the spindle towards the handle. At the same time the tap can be turned on and off far too easily — you might even be able to spin the handle with a flick of the fingers. This fault is a common cause of water hammer — heavy thudding following the closure of a tap or float-valve — that can result in damage to the plumbing system.

Leakage up the spindle is most likely to occur in rather old fashioned — but still very common — taps in which the spindle passes through a gland or 'stuffing box' filled with greased wool. It's inevitable that water containing detergent will be splashed onto the tap and this may result in the grease being washed out of the gland. The leakage can also be created if you run a garden or washing machine hose from the tap.

Fortunately, to make a repair you don't have to cut off the water supply to the tap, but you must be able to get at the gland-adjusting nut. This is the first nut through which the spindle passes.

Giving the gland-adjusting nut about half a turn may be enough to stop the leakage up the spindle, but eventually all the adjustment available will be taken up and you'll then have to repack the gland. When the gland-adjusting nut has been unscrewed and removed, the old gland packing material can be taken out and replaced with knitting wool saturated with petroleum jelly. The wool is wound round the spindle and packed down tightly before the gland-adjusting nut is put back and tightened until the tap handle can be turned fairly easily but without any leaks occurring.

Replacing an 'O' ring

Many modern taps have 'O' ring seals instead of a packed gland or stuffing box. If an 'O' ring fails the remedy is simply to undo the gland-adjusting nut, pick out the old 'O' ring and replace it with a new one. Leaks from taps with this fitting are rare. 'O' rings are also found at the swivel point of many mixer taps and if a leak occurs here you have to remove the spout to make the change – but this is usually only held with a grub-screw.

Older Supataps aren't fitted with an 'O' ring seal but if water leaks from the top of the nozzle you can fit a ring round the valve casing. Modern Supataps have an 'O' ring already fitted and if it needs replacing, it's a simple matter of slipping it off and pushing on another — but choose one that fits snugly and doesn't move about. If this doesn't cure the leak you'll have to replace the anti-splash device which could have become worn.

REPLACING TAPS

Changing the old taps on your basin is a bright and practical way of making your bathroom more attractive. It may also be a good idea if they are old and inefficient. Here's what is involved.

There may be a number of reasons why you wish to replace the taps supplying your sink, basin or bath. They may continually drip or leak, where new taps would give efficient, trouble-free service. Perhaps you want the advantages that mixers have over individual taps or perhaps it is simply that the chromium plating has worn off leaving the taps looking incurably shabby.

It is more likely, however, that appearance, rather than malfunction, will be your reason for changing. There are fashions in plumbing fittings as in clothing and furniture. Taps of the 1950s or 60s are instantly recognisable as out-of-date in a bathroom or kitchen of the 1980s. Fortunately, fashions in sinks, basins and baths have changed rather less dramatically over the past three decades. There is probably no more cost-effective way of improving bathroom and kitchen appearance than by the provision of sparkling new taps or mixers.

Choosing taps

When you come to select your new taps you may feel that you are faced with a bewildering choice. Tap size, appearance, the material of which the tap is made, whether to choose individual taps or mixers and – for the bath – whether to provide for an over-bath shower by fitting a bath/shower mixer: all these things need to be considered.

Size is easily enough dealt with. Taps and mixers are still in imperial sizes. Bath tap tails are ¾in in diameter, and basin and sink taps ½in in diameter. There are, however, a few suppliers who are beginning to designate taps by the metric size, not of the taps themselves, but of the copper supply pipes to which they will probably be connected. Such a supplier might refer to bath taps as 22mm and sink and basin taps as 15mm.

Most taps are made of chromium-plated brass, though there are also ranges of enamelled and even gold-plated taps and mixers. Although taps and mixers are still manufactured with conventional crutch or capstan handles, most people nowadays prefer to choose taps with 'shrouded' heads made of acrylic or other plastic. In effect, these combine the functions of handle and easy-clean cover, completely concealing the tap's headgear. A still popular alternative is the functional 'Supatap', nowadays provided with plastic rather than metal 'ears' for quick and comfortable turning on and off.

There is also a very competitively priced range of all-plastic taps. These usually give satisfactory enough service in the home, but they cannot be regarded as being as sturdy as conventional metal taps, and they can be damaged by very hot water.

So far as design is concerned the big difference is between 'bib taps' and 'pillar taps'. Bib taps have a horizontal inlet and are usually wall-mounted while pillar taps have a vertical inlet and are mounted on the bath, basin or sink they serve.

Taking out old basin taps

When replacing old taps with new ones the most difficult part of the job is likely to be – as with so many plumbing operations – removing the old fittings. Let's first consider wash basin taps.

You must, of course, cut off the hot and cold water supplies to the basin. The best way of doing this will usually be to tie up the float arm of the ball valve supplying the cold water storage cistern so as to prevent water flowing in. Then run the bathroom cold taps until water ceases to flow. Only then open up the hot taps. This will conserve most of the expensively heated water in the hot water storage cylinder.

If you look under the basin you will find that the tails of the taps are connected to the water supply pipes with small, fairly accessible nuts, and that a larger – often

REMOVING OLD TAPS

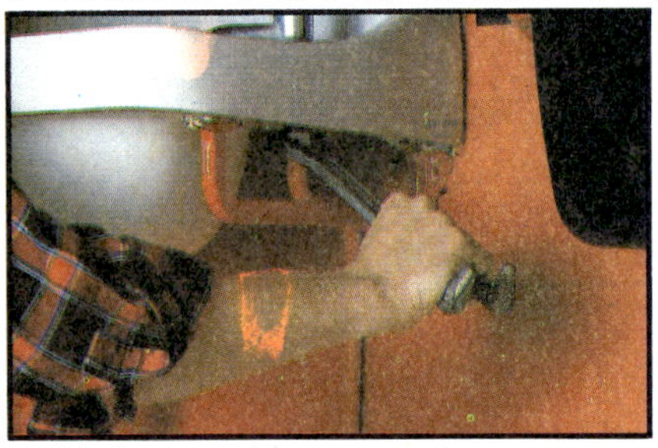

1 *It's best to change taps by removing the basin completely. Loosen the two tap connectors carefully with an adjustable spanner.*

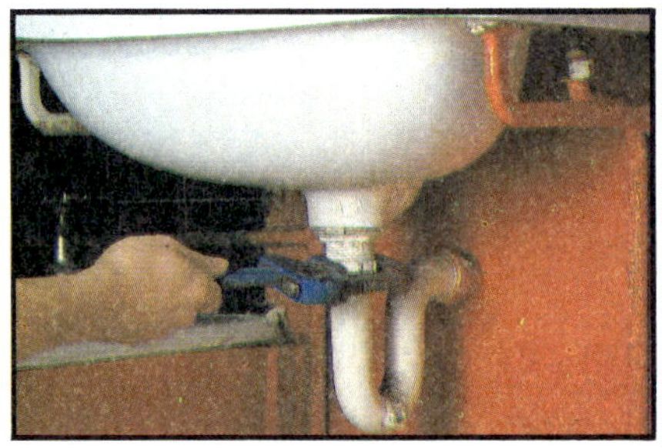

2 *Disconnect the waste trap connector using an adjustable wrench. Take care not to damage the trap, particularly if it is lead or copper.*

3 *Undo any screws holding the basin to its brackets on the wall, and lift it clear of the brackets before lowering it carefully to the floor.*

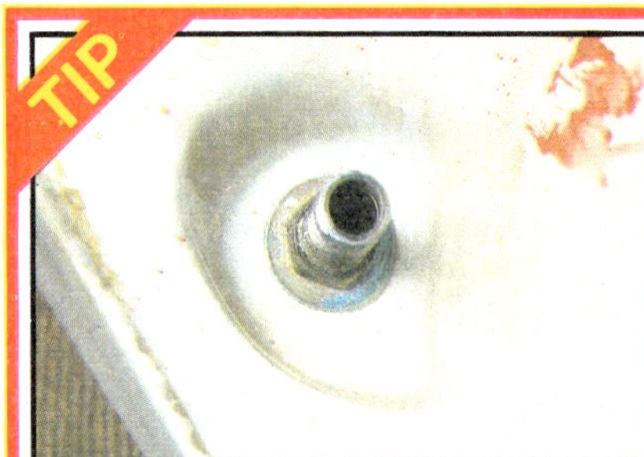

4 *Check the condition of the back-nuts, which may be badly corroded. It's a good idea to apply penetrating oil and leave this to work for a while.*

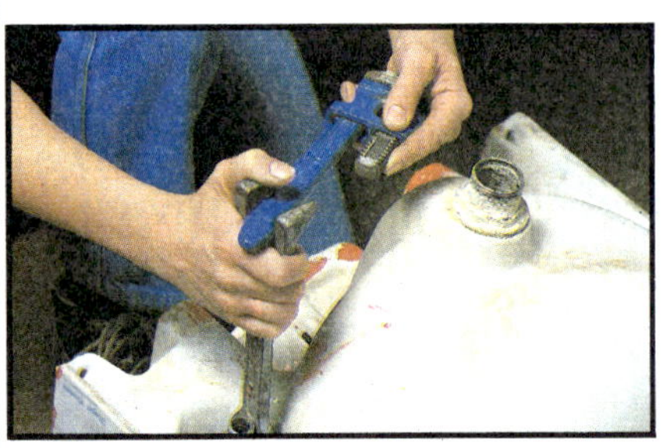

5 *Use the crowsfoot (with extra leverage if necessary) to undo the back-nut. If more force is needed, grip the tap itself with a wrench to stop it turning.*

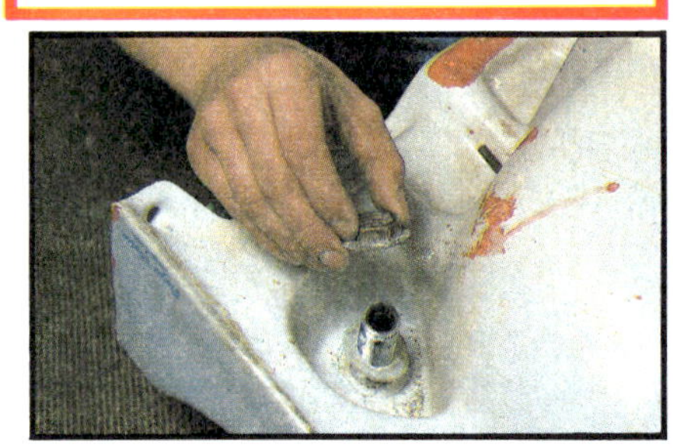

6 *Remove the back-nut and any washers between it and the basin. Old washers like these should always be replaced with new washers.*

inaccessible – back-nut secures the tap to the basin. The nuts of the swivel tap connectors joining the pipes to the taps are usually easily undone with a wrench or spanner of the appropriate size. The back-nuts can be extremely difficult – even for professional plumbers!

There are special wrenches and basin or crowsfoot spanners that may help, but they won't perform miracles and ceramic basins can be very easily damaged by heavy handedness. The best course of action is to disconnect the swivel tap connectors and to disconnect the trap from the waste outlet. These are secured by nuts and are easily undone. Then lift the basin off its brackets or hanger and place it upside down on the floor. Apply some penetrating oil to the tap tails and, after allowing a few minutes for it to soak in, tackle the nuts with your wrench or crowsfoot spanner. You'll find they are much more accessible. Hold the tap while you do this to stop it swivelling and damaging the basin.

Fitting the new taps

When fitting the new taps or mixer, unscrew the back-nuts, press some plumber's putty round the tail directly below the tap body or fit a plastic washer at the top of the tail.

Ready Reference

EQUIPMENT CHECKLIST

For replacing existing taps, you will need the following tools and equipment:

- new taps of the right type and size
- an adjustable spanner
- a basin wrench ('crowsfoot')
- an adjustable wrench
- penetrating oil
- plastic washers (see below)
- plumber's putty
- PTFE tape

You may also need tap tail adaptors (if the new taps have shorter tails than the old ones) and new tap connectors (if your new taps have metric tails instead of imperial ones).

WHAT ABOUT WASHERS?

With ceramic basins, use a plastic washer above and below the basin surface (A) so you don't crack the basin as you tighten the back-nut. You can use plumber's putty instead of the upper washer.

On thin basins, use a special top-hat washer between basin and back-nut (B).

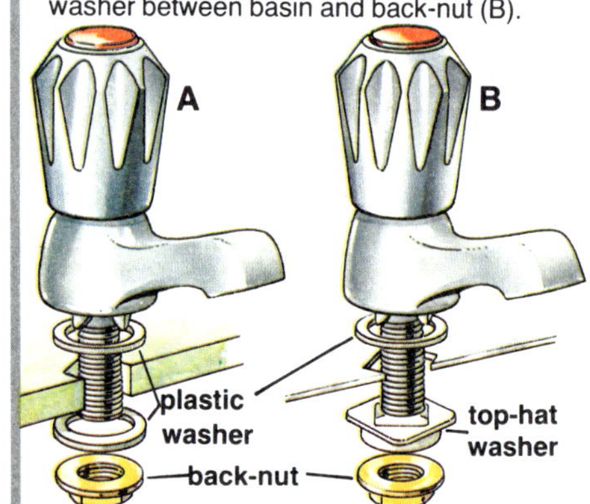

The lugs at the top of the tap tail are meant to stop it turning in square tap holes. Use special anti-rotation washers to stop new taps with smaller lugs from turning in old tap holes.

TIPS TO SAVE TROUBLE

- to undo stubborn back-nuts, add extra leverage to the crowsfoot by hooking a wrench handle into its other end
- if this fails, squirt penetrating oil around the back-nuts. Leave for a while and try again
- in really stubborn cases, remove the basin completely, and turn it upside down on the floor so you have more room to work
- grip the tap body with an adjustable spanner to stop it turning as you use the crowsfoot; otherwise the tap lugs could crack the basin

FITTING NEW TAPS

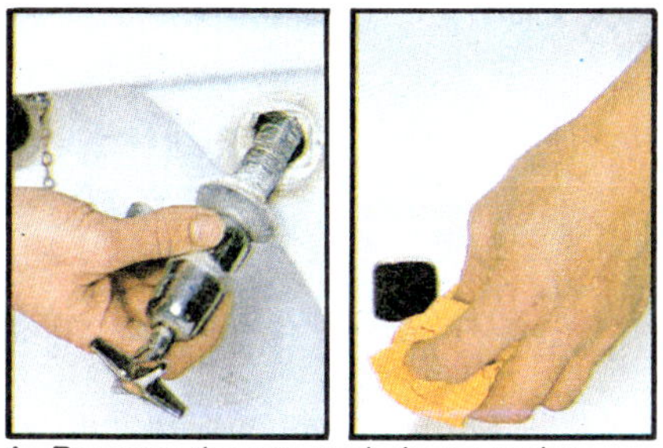

1 Remove the tap and clean up the basin surround, chipping away scale and any old putty remaining from when the tap was originally installed.

2 Now take one of the new taps and fit a washer or plumber's putty around the top of the tail before pushing it into the hole in the basin.

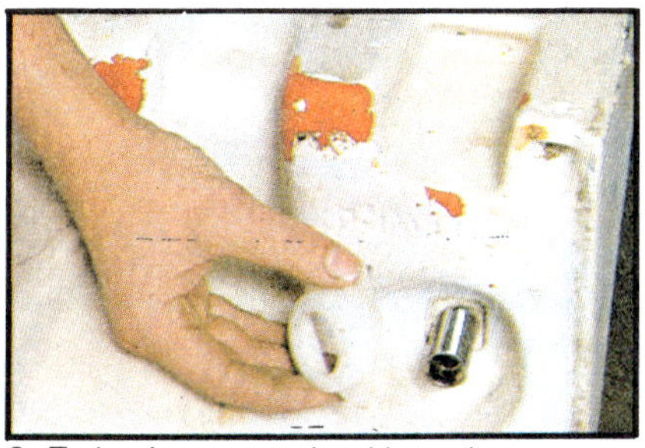

3 Twist the tap so that it's at the correct angle to the basin and is firmly bedded on the putty. Then push a top-hat washer onto the tail.

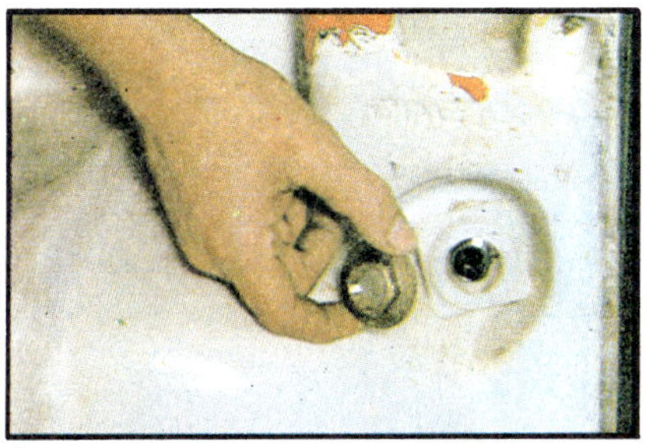

4 With the top-hat washer firmly in place, take the new back-nut and screw it up the tail of the tap by hand.

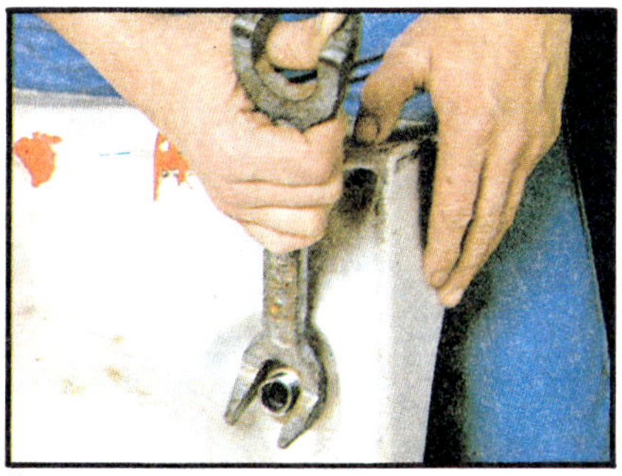

5 Tighten up the back-nut until the tap assembly is completely firm, using the crowsfoot or an adjustable spanner. Repeat the process for the other tap.

6 Reconnect all the pipework. Use tap-tail adaptors if the new taps have shorter tails than the old ones.

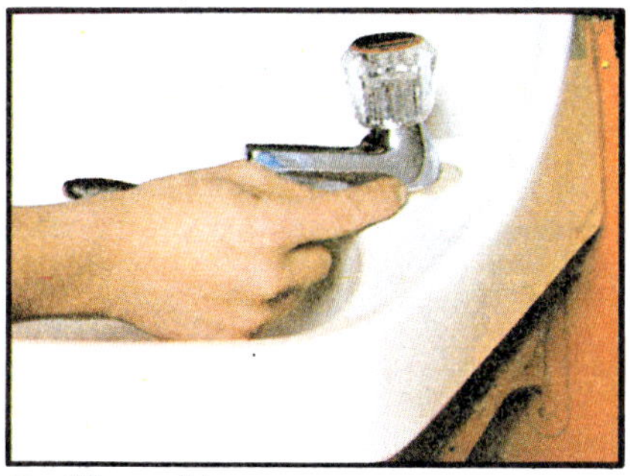

7 When all is secure, remove any surplus putty from around the base of the taps, wiping it over with a finger to leave a smooth, neat finish.

8 Turn the water back on. Check that the flow from the taps is regular and that the waste trap is not leaking. If it is, tighten up its connectors slightly.

Push the tails through the holes in the basin. Slip flat plastic washers over the tails where they protrude from beneath the basin, screw on the back-nuts and tighten them up. Make sure that the taps or mixer are secure, but don't overtighten them. To make tightening easier, (and undoing, if ever necessary) use top-hat washers.

All that remains to be done is to connect the swivel tap connectors to the tails of the new taps or mixer. You will see that a tap connector consists of a lining – with a flange – that is inserted into the tap tail and is then secured by the coupling nut. This nut is provided with a washer to ensure a watertight connection. When renewing taps you may well need to renew this small washer.

It is possible that when you come to connect the water supply pipes to the taps you will get an unpleasant surprise. The tails of modern taps are slightly shorter than those of older ones and the tap connectors may not reach. If the water supply pipes are of lead or of copper it is quite likely that they will have enough 'give' to enable you to make the connection but, if not, there are extension pieces specially made to bridge the gap.

Bib taps

If you're replacing existing bib taps with those of a more modern design, it's a relatively simple matter of disconnecting and unscrewing the old ones and fitting the new taps in their place. However, it's quite possible that you'll want to remove the bib taps altogether and fit a new sink with some pillar taps. This will involve a little more plumbing work. To start with, turn off the water supply and remove the taps and old sink. If the pipework comes up from the floor, you'll need to uncover the run in the wall to below where the new sink will go. You should then be able to ease the pipes away from the wall and cut off the exposed sections. This will allow you to join short lengths of new pipe, bent slightly if necessary, to link the pipe ends and the tap tails. Alternatively, if the pipes come down the wall you'll have to extend the run to below the level of the new sink and use elbow fittings to link the pipe to the tap tails. In either case it's a good idea to fit the taps to the new sink first and to make up the pipe-work runs slightly overlong, so that when the new sink is offered up to the wall you can measure up accurately and avoid the risk of cutting off too much pipe. Rather than having to make difficult bends you can use lengths of corrugated copper pipe. One end of the pipe is plain so that it can be fitted to the 15mm supply pipes with either a soldered capillary or compression fitting; the other end has a swivel tap connector.

STOP-VALVES AND BALL-VALVES

The valves that control your household water system aren't difficult to understand – or to fit or repair. So the next time one of yours goes wrong, be prepared to put it right yourself.

Stop-valves, gate-valves and ball-valves are all plumbing fittings that in different ways do precisely the same thing, which is to regulate the flow of water through pipes. Each of the three types of valve performs an important function in your water system, and it is therefore in your interest to know not only what they do and how they do it, but also how to put right any of the faults to which they are prone.

Stop-valves

Your main stop-valve is perhaps the single most important plumbing fitting in your house. In the event of almost any plumbing emergency the very first thing that you should do is turn it off. This will stop the flow of water into your house and reduce the extent of any damage. Looking like a very basic brass tap, your main stop-valve will be found set into the rising main not far from the point where this pipe enters your house. Often it will be located under the kitchen sink.

If your house is fairly old then it could be that it won't be provided with a main stop-valve. If this is the case, then you will have to use the local water authority's stop-valve instead. You will find it under a hinged metal flap set into your garden path or the pavement outside your property. This sort of stop-valve usually has a specially-shaped handle that can only be turned with one of the water authority's turnkeys. So that you can deal promptly with any emergency you should make sure that you either have one of these turnkeys, or at least that you have ready access to one. However, both for the sake of convenience and because specialist gadgets like turnkeys have a habit of disappearing when they're most needed, you may decide to install a main stop-valve yourself – not a difficult task if the rising main is made of copper pipe (see step-by-step photographs).

The internal construction of a stop-valve is identical to that of an ordinary tap, and so it is prone to the same types of faults (see *Ready Reference*). But one further trouble that may afflict your stop-valve – which doesn't crop up with ordinary taps – is that of jamming in the open position as a result of disuse. It's a problem cured simply by applying penetrating oil to the spindle. However, you can prevent this happening by closing and opening the stop-valve regularly, and by leaving it fractionally less than fully open – a quarter turn towards closure will do.

Gate-valves

Whereas stop-valves are always fitted to pipes that are under mains pressure, gate-valves are used on pipes that are only subject to low pressure. They are therefore found on hot and cold water distribution pipes and on those of the central heating system. Gate-valves differ from stop-valves in as much as they control the flow of water through them, not with a washered valve, but by means of a metal plate or 'gate'. You can distinguish them from stop-valves by the fact that their valve bodies are bigger, and by their wheel – as opposed to crutch – handles. Due to the simplicity of their internal construction gate-valves require little attention (see *Ready Reference*). Unlike stop-valves, which have to be fitted so that the water flowing through them follows the direction of an arrow stamped on the valve body, you can install a gate-valve either way round.

Mini stop-valves

Mini stop-valves are useful little fittings that you can insert into any pipe run. Their presence enables you to re-washer or renew a tap or ball-valve (see below) or repair a water-using appliance such as a washing machine without disrupting the rest of your water system. They can also be used to quieten an excessively noisy lavatory flushing cistern that is fed directly from the rising main, since by slowing down the flow of water to the ball-valve you can reduce the noise without materially affecting the cistern's rate of filling after flushing. You usually fit a mini stop-valve immediately before the appliance that it is to control; and they can be turned off and on either with a screwdriver, or by turning a small handle through 180°.

Ball-valves

Ball-valves are really just self-regulating taps designed to maintain a given volume of water in a cistern. While there are a number of different patterns they all have a float – not necessarily a ball these days – at one end of a rigid arm which opens or closes a valve as the water level in the cistern falls or rises. There are basically two types of ball-valve: the traditional type, generally made of brass, in which the water flow is controlled by a washered plug or piston; and the type that has been developed more recently in which the flow is controlled by a large rubber diaphragm housed within a plastic body.

Croydon and Portsmouth ball-valves

The oldest of the traditional types of ball-valve is the Croydon pattern. You can easily recognise one of these by the position of its piston, which operates vertically, and by the fact that it delivers water to the cistern in two insufferably noisy streams. Due to their noisi-

FITTING A STOP-VALVE

1 *When installing a main stop-valve use the type that has compression fittings. If it isn't combined with a drain-cock then fit one separately.*

2 *Make sure that you fit the stop-valve the right way round. The direction of the water flow is clearly indicated by an arrow stamped on the valve body.*

3 *Take care when marking off the rising main. The extent to which the pipe will penetrate the fitting is indicated by a shoulder; use this as your guide.*

4 *Turn off the water authority's stop-valve and cut it at the mark with a hacksaw. Some water will flow out as you do this; be prepared for it.*

5 *Spring the stop-valve into the cut pipe so that the two ends meet the pipe stops within the fitting. The valve handle should be angled away from the wall.*

6 *Tighten up the nuts, restore the water supply at the water authority's stop-valve, then turn on the stop-valve and check the fitting for leaks.*

Ready Reference

HOW A STOP-VALVE WORKS

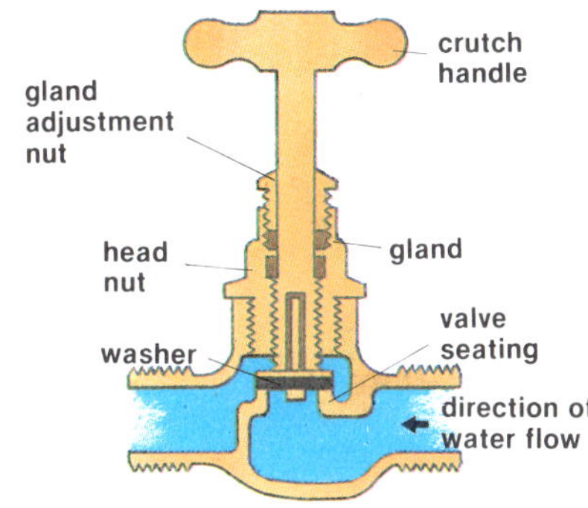

Because a stop-valve works in the same way as an ordinary tap its washer and gland are also subject to wear. You can:
- remove headgear to replace a worn washer (see pages 46–50), and
- deal with a worn gland by tightening the adjustment nut, or by re-packing the gland.

HOW A GATE-VALVE WORKS

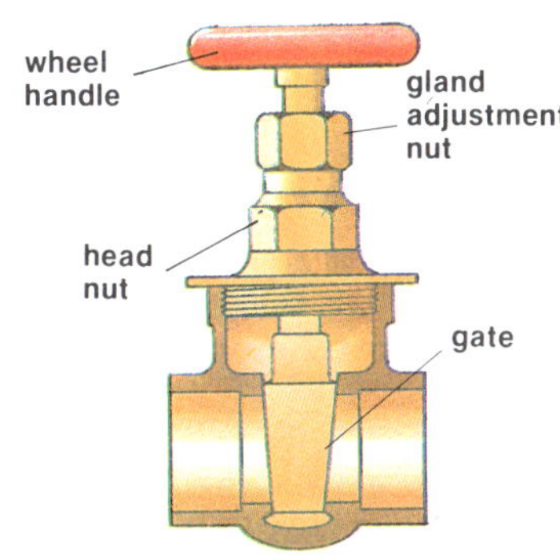

A gate-valve requires little attention. The only thing that may give trouble is the gland, which sometimes needs adjusting or renewing.

DEZINCIFICATION

In areas where the water supply is unusually acidic the zinc content of pipe fittings made of brass (an alloy of copper and zinc) can be dissolved by the water. This phenomenom is known as dezincification, and it results in the fittings losing their structural strength. When it presents a problem, fittings made of gunmetal (an alloy of copper and tin) are usually used though cheaper corrosion-resistant brass fittings are also available. These usually have CR stamped on the valve body.

For more information on household water supply see pages 8–12.

VALVE TYPES

Apart from the float arm the only moving part on a diaphragm-type valve is a small plunger. When prompted by the float arm this plunger presses a large rubber diaphragm against the valve nozzle to close it.

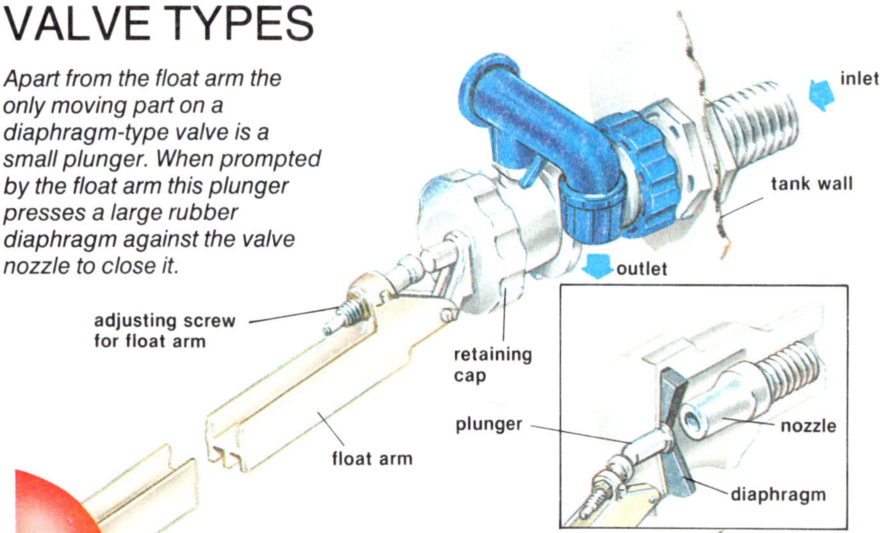

In the Portsmouth-type valve the flow of water is regulated by a washered piston rather than by a diaphragm.

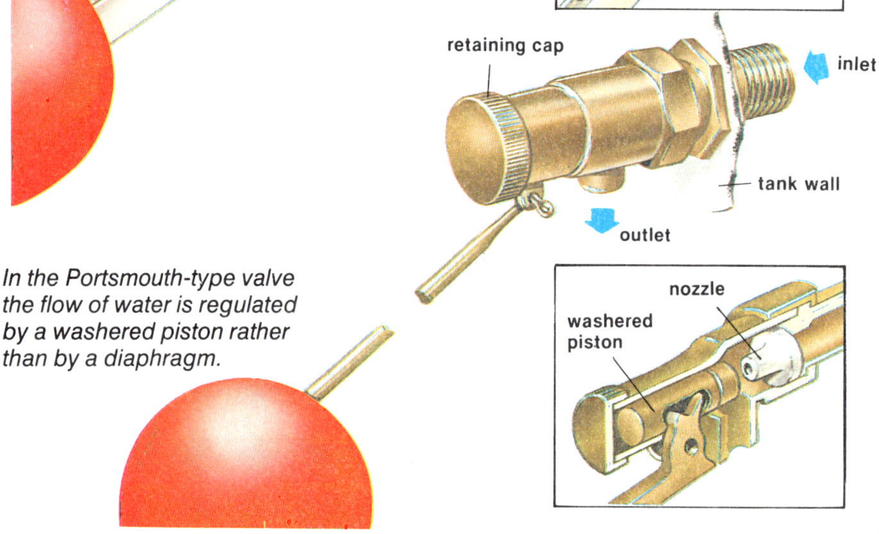

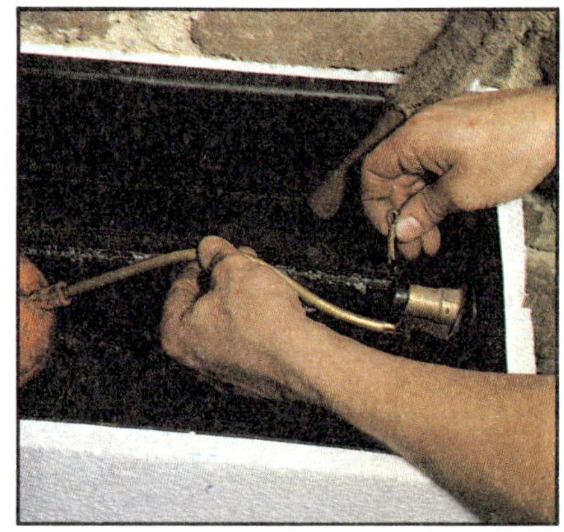

1 *The first thing you do when faced with a faulty Portsmouth valve is examine the piston. In order to get at it you will first have to remove the float arm.*

5 *A piston usually consists of two parts. If it's hard to unscrew, slip a screwdriver into the slot and turn the washer-retaining cap with a wrench.*

ness, Croydon valves are now by and large obsolete, and if you do come across one you will almost certainly want to replace it. The traditional type of valve that superseded the Croydon pattern was the Portsmouth valve (see illustration). You can distinguish it from the former type by the fact that its piston operates horizontally; and as it is still popular with plumbers despite the development of more sophisticated diaphragm type valves, it is a pattern that you may well find in your home.

When one of your ball-valves goes wrong the first thing you will notice is water dripping from an outside overflow pipe. If the valve is a Portsmouth pattern then it is likely to have developed one of three faults. First, it could have jammed partially open as a result of the build-up of scale or the presence of grit; or, secondly, it could need re-washering. In either of these cases this will necessitate you turning off the water supply so that you can either clean the ball-valve or fit a new washer to it (see step-by-step photographs). Lastly, the valve could have been incorrectly adjusted to maintain the proper water level in the cistern – which should be about 25mm (1in) below the overflow pipe. Even modern Portsmouth valves are rarely provided with any specific means of adjusting the water level, so if you need to do so you will have to resort to bending the float arm.

Noise can be a problem with Portsmouth valves. It is caused either by the inrush of water through the valve nozzle, or by vibration created by the float bouncing on ripples on the surface of the water ('water hammer'). As silencer tubes are now banned by water authorities, you will have to try other methods to deal with this problem. Reducing the mains pressure by closing the rising main stop-valve slightly may help, and as vibration can be magnified by a loose rising main it is worth making sure that this pipe is properly secured with pipe clips. Another measure you could take would be to improvise a stabiliser for the float using a submerged plastic flowerpot tied to the float arm with nylon cord. However, if all the above measures fail you will have to consider replacing the Portsmouth valve with one of the modern diaphragm types.

Diaphragm ball-valves

Diaphragm ball-valves, which are also referred to as BRS or Garston ball-valves, were specially developed to overcome the noisiness and inherent faults of the Croydon and Portsmouth valves. Since the moving parts of a diaphragm valve are protected from incoming water by the diaphragm (see illustration) there is no risk of them seizing as a result of scale deposits; and the problem of noisy water delivery is often overcome nowadays by an overhead sprinkler outlet which sprays rather than squirts the water into the cistern. Should you need to adjust the water

REPAIRING A BALL- VALVE

2 *Then unscrew the retaining cap and push out the piston. Do this by inserting a screwdriver into the slot in the underside of the valve body.*

3 *If you can't get the piston out or if you suspect that your ball-valve needs a clean rather than a new washer, then you will have to remove the whole valve body.*

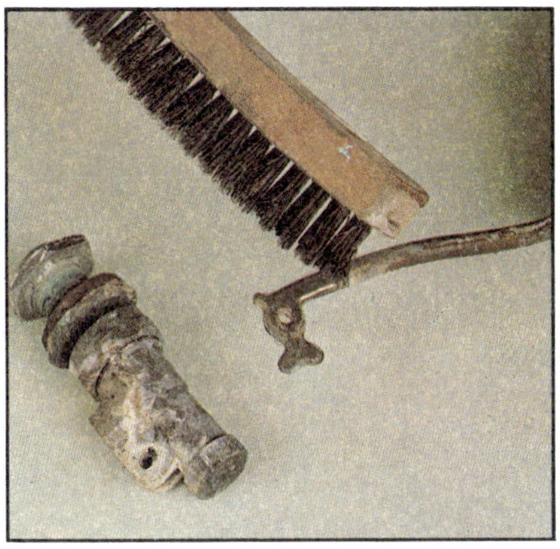

4 *If a build-up of scale does turn out to be the cause of your problem, clean the valve and the end of the float arm with a wire brush.*

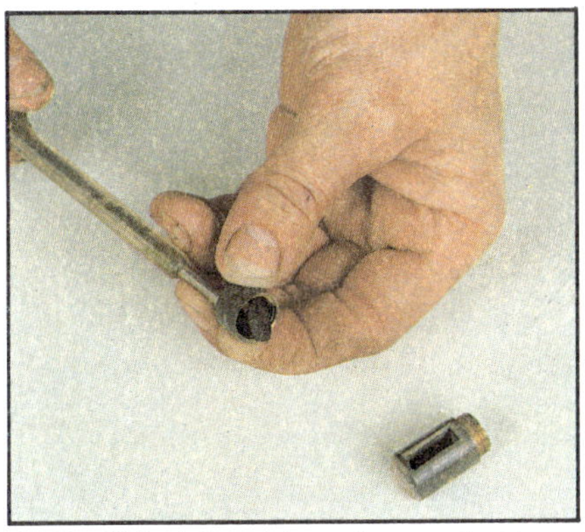

6 *You'll find the old washer seated in the cap. Poke it out and substitute a new one. Smear the piston with petroleum jelly before replacing it in the valve.*

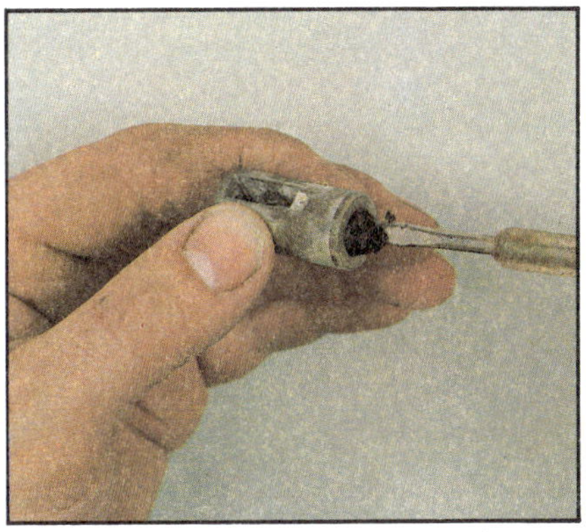

7 *Rather than risk damaging a piston that refuses to unscrew, pick out the old washer with a point and force a new one back in its place.*

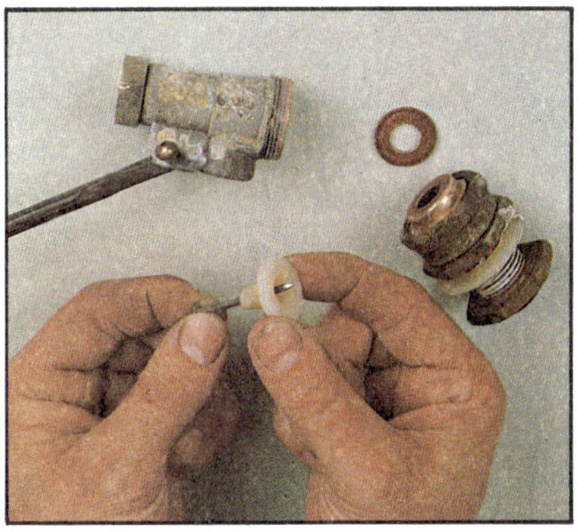

8 *Debris caught in the valve nozzle can interrupt the water flow. Cure this problem by dismantling the valve and removing the debris with a nail.*

level in a cistern fitted with a diaphragm valve, then invariably you can by means other than bending the float arm. The only problems you are likely to encounter with diaphragm valves are jamming of the diaphragm against the valve nozzle, and obstruction of the space between the nozzle and diaphragm with debris from the main. You remedy these problems by unscrewing the knurled retaining cap and either freeing the diaphragm with a pointed tool or removing the debris.

High and low pressure water supply

The water pressure under which a ball-valve operates is an important factor, as the size of the hole in the nozzle of the valve will be either smaller or larger according to whether it is under high pressure (ie, mains pressure) or low pressure (ie, supplied by water from a storage tank). Older Portsmouth valves have either HP (high pressure) or LP (low pressure) stamped on their bodies, and will only operate satisfactorily under the pressure for which they are designed. Modern valves, on the other hand, have interchangeable nozzles which allow you to convert them from low to high pressure or vice versa. If you fit a high-pressure valve (or nozzle) in a situation where a low-pressure one is required this will result in an agonisingly slow refill. A constantly dripping overflow may be the sign of a low-pressure valve that has been fitted to a cistern that is fed by the mains.

In some areas, mains pressure varies considerably throughout a 24-hour period. During the day, when demand is high, pressure will be low, whereas in the evening as demand falls off the pressure increases. These fluctuations in pressure don't affect low pressure valves but they do affect high pressure ones, which can perform erratically as a result. You can overcome this problem if it affects you by replacing your high pressure ball-valves with equilibrium valves.

Equilibrium ball-valves

You can buy Portsmouth and diaphragm equilibrium valves. These are both designed to allow a small quantity of water to pass through or round the washered piston (or diaphragm) into a watertight chamber beyond. Acting as it does on the rear of the piston, and being at the same pressure as the mains, the water in the chamber ensures that the piston is held in equilibrium. What this means in practice is that the valve is operated solely by the movement of the float arm, rather than by a combination of the movement of the float arm *and* the pressure of the incoming water as is the case in an ordinary high-pressure valve. In addition to refilling your cistern promptly regardless of any fluctuations in mains pressure, equilibrium valves also eliminate the 'bounce' as the valve closes – a common cause of water hammer. A diaphragm equilibrium valve will give you a particularly rapid and silent refill.

REPLACING A RADIATOR

If one of your existing radiators is malfunctioning in some way, or else just out of character with the decor of your home why not replace it with a brand new one? You'll find this job straightforward if you follow our instructions.

There are a number of reasons why you may want to replace an existing radiator in your home's central heating system. These can range from the aesthetic to the purely practical. At one time radiators were ugly and cumbersome, and if you have any still in use like this it's quite likely that they'll clash with the decor of your home. On the practical side, you may well find that a radiator in your system has developed leaks. This will mean both water and heat loss, as well as the inconvenience of cleaning up the mess. And, of course, you may simply feel that a modern radiator would produce more heat, and so improve the comfort in your home. Whatever your reasons for replacing a radiator, you'll have to choose a new one to go in its place, before actually removing the existing one.

Choosing a new radiator

Modern radiators are usually made of 1.25mm (about 1/16in) thick pressed steel, and are designed to be space-saving, neat and attractive. For a simple replacement job, size will be among the most important considerations. If the new radiator can be successfully connected to the existing fittings, you won't need to alter or modify the circulating pipes. Consequently, the job will be that much easier. Radiators are available in a wide variety of sizes, ranging in height from 300mm (12in) to 800mm (32in) and in length from 480mm (19in) to 3200mm (10ft 6in) – so you shouldn't have too much difficulty in finding one that will fit into the space left by the old one. Special low, finned radiators are also available. These are usually fitted along the skirting and are both neat and unobtrusive – yet can be turned into decorative features in their own right.

But size isn't the only important consideration. After all, a radiator's job is to provide heat, so you'll have to shop around and find the one which, for its size, will produce most heat. A radiator's heat output is measured in kW – kilowatts – so you should look for the one with the highest kW rating for its size. Remember, it's always possible to turn off a radiator that makes a room too warm; it's far less easy to increase heat output in a room which, with the radiator

THE FITTINGS

A typical panel radiator is fitted with a flow control valve (below), a lock-shield valve (bottom right), an air-bleed valve (right) and a blanking off plug (far right).

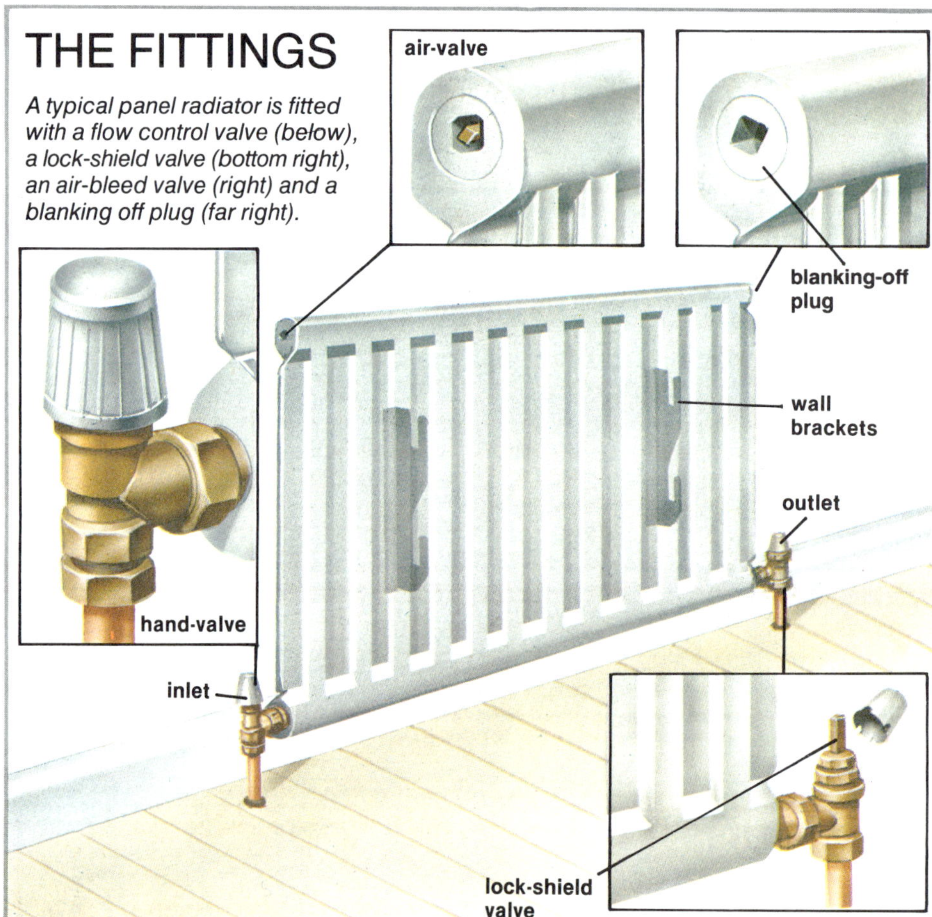

REMOVING THE OLD RADIATOR

1 *Turn off the flow control valve by hand, and the lock-shield valve by turning its spindle with pliers. Note how many turns are needed to close it completely.*

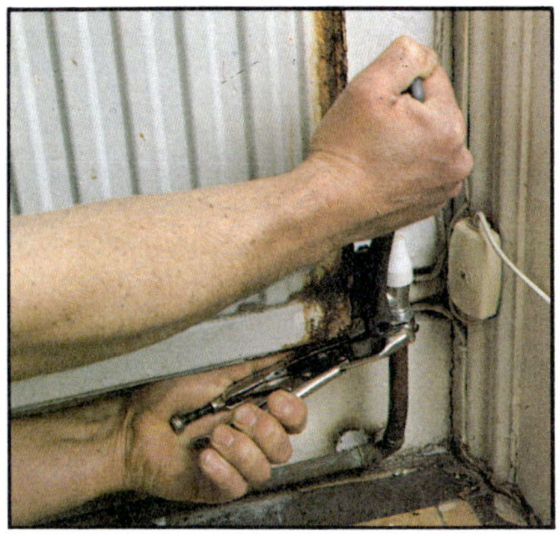

2 *Hold the lock-shield valve body with a wrench so you don't bend the pipework, and undo the valve coupling carefully with an adjustable spanner.*

3 *Open the air-bleed valve, pull the coupling away and allow the radiator to drain into a convenient container. Have rags and a larger bowl handy too.*

4 *Having drained most of the water, undo the other coupling, lift the radiator off its brackets and drain out the dregs. Then remove the old brackets.*

turned fully on, remains uncomfortably chilly.

However, one way of increasing heat output, while retaining the same sized radiator, is to install a double-panel radiator. This is, literally, an ordinary radiator with two panels for the hot water to fill instead of the usual one and therefore has virtually double the heat output. So, while a single panel radiator 675mm x 750mm (27in x 30in) will have a heat output of 0.68kW, a double panel one of the same size will be rated at 1.15kW.

Although modern radiators are likely to provide more heat than the older variety, they do have one drawback. Because of the thinness of their metal, they are more prone to internal corrosion and this will ultimately produce leaks.

Dealing with internal corrosion

Internal corrosion in modern radiators arises from an electrolytic reaction between the steel of the radiators and the copper circulating pipes of the central heating system. This results in the production of a corrosive black iron oxide sludge (magnetite) and hydrogen gas. In a similar fashion, if the original installation of your heating system was somewhat messily done, then copper swarf, produced when the pipes were cut, could have been retained within the circulating pipes. This will also corrode the steel at any point where the two come in contact – usually within a radiator. Because the raw material from which the sludge is produced is the metal of the radiators, eventually they will leak and need to be replaced. And as the sludge is also attracted by the magnetic field of the circulating pump, its abrasive qualities are a common cause of early pump failure.

Early indications of serious internal corrosion are a need to vent one or more radiators at regular intervals, and cold spots on their

Ready Reference

HOW RADIATORS WORK

A radiator works by convection. It heats up the air in direct contact with its surface. This becomes lighter, rises and is replaced by cooler, heavier air from floor level. So, gradually, the whole room is warmed.

POSITIONING A RADIATOR

A radiator is most effective if positioned under a window. That way it kills the convection down-draught produced when warm air comes into contact with the cooler glass, and so increases comfort.

CLEARING AIR LOCKS

You might find air locks in your existing radiators or your new one. In that case you'll have to vent the radiator. You should
- obtain a square-ended bleed key from a plumbing or hardware shop
- insert the key into the air-bleed valve and turn in an anti-clockwise direction
- hold a cloth or container under the valve to catch water
- tighten the valve once all the air is displaced and water emerges.

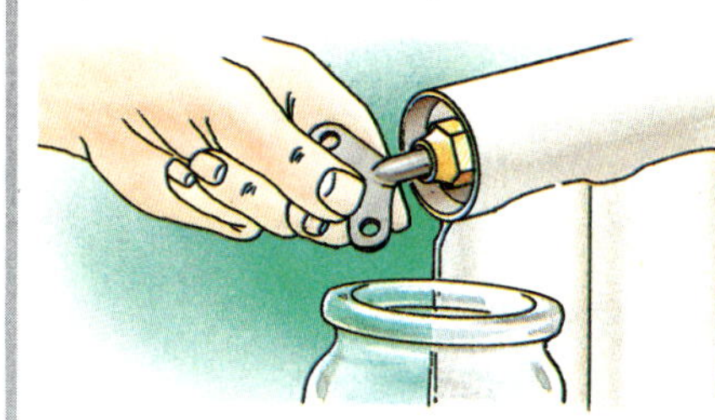

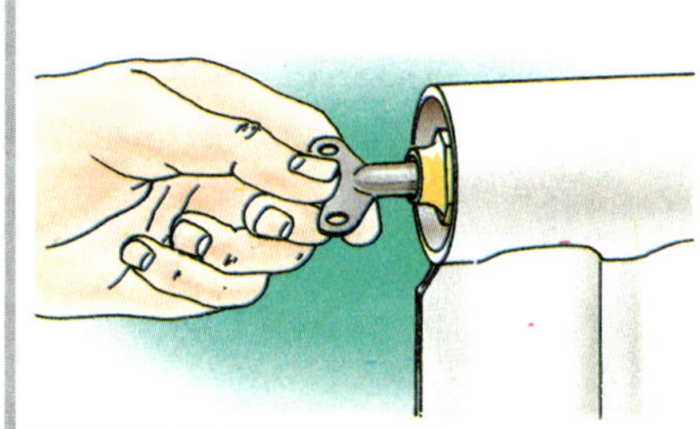

DECORATING YOUR RADIATORS

Your new radiator will be finished in white factory-applied primer. Paint it with special radiator paint or gloss before you fix it to the wall, otherwise you won't be able to reach the back. Once the radiator is in place you can touch up any parts scratched during installation.

TIP: FIXING A FOIL REFLECTOR

Before fitting a replacement radiator against an outside wall it's a good idea to fit reflective foil against the wall. That way you'll help to cut down on heat losses.

surfaces. If in doubt, the diagnosis can be confirmed by applying a flame to the escaping gas when the radiator is being vented. If it burns with a blue and yellow flame, you can be sure that hydrogen is in the system and will have been produced by the chemical reaction of the two metals. Once you've confirmed that corrosion is present within the system, you'll have to flush it through and introduce a reliable corrosion preventative chemical into the feed and expansion tank as you refill the system. That way you should be able to prevent further corrosion and so save your system.

Removing the old radiator

One of the great deterrents to anyone wanting to remove a radiator is the prospect of having to drain the whole system. However, this won't be necessary provided the radiator to be replaced has a valve at both the hot water inlet and the outlet. Once these are closed, you'll be able to keep virtually all the system's water isolated in other parts.

At the inlet end you're likely to find the hand-valve which is the control by which you open and close the radiator. At the outlet end you'll find what is termed the lock-shield valve. When you come to inspect your radiator, don't worry if their positions are reversed – they will still be equally effective.

The first thing to do when removing a radiator is to close these valves. The hand-valve is straightforward, but you'll have to remove the cover to get at the lock-shield valve. You'll be able to close this valve using a spanner or an adjustable wrench with which to grip its spindle.

As you turn it, it's a good idea to note carefully how many turns it takes to close. And you'll find this task slightly easier if you mark the turning nut with a piece of chalk before you begin. The reason for all this is to maintain the balance of the system. After it was first installed, your system would have been balanced. The lock-shield valves of all the radiators were adjusted to give an equal level of water through-flow so that they were all heating up equally. So, by noting the number of turns taken to close the lock-shield, when you come to fit the new radiator you can simply open it up by the same amount – so avoiding the somewhat tedious task of re-balancing the whole system.

Once you've closed both valves, you can unscrew the nuts which connect the valves to the radiator inlet and outlet. Do these one at a time after having placed a low dish under each end to collect the water and protect the floor. Use an adjustable wrench to undo the coupling nuts. It's wise to hold the circulating pipe securely in place with another wrench. Otherwise, if you apply too much pressure to the coupling nut you risk fracturing the flowpipe, and this would cause

FITTING THE NEW RADIATOR

1 *To ensure watertight connections to the new radiator, wrap PTFE tape round all threaded fittings and then smear on some jointing compound.*

2 *Screw in the valve couplings with a hexagonal radiator spanner. Use extension pieces if the new radiator is slightly narrower than the old one.*

5 *Mark the height taken in* **4** *on the wall above each valve, and join up the marks at each end with a pencil line. This marks the level of the new brackets.*

6 *Transfer the measurements taken in* **3** *to the wall to indicate the vertical position of each bracket. Accuracy is not so vital here as in* **5**.

9 *Lift the radiator into place on its brackets. You can move it slightly from side to side to align the valve couplings with the inlet and outlet valves.*

10 *Wrap the coupling threads in PTFE tape and jointing compound, and do up the couplings. Again, use a wrench to support the valve body and prevent strain.*

3 *Lay the radiator down in line with the two valves, and measure the distance from each valve coupling to the centre of the nearest bracket mounting.*

4 *Next, measure the height of the base of the radiator brackets from a line joining the centres of the inlet and outlet valves.*

7 *Hold the bracket against the wall in line with the vertical and horizontal marks you've made, and draw in the positions for the fixing screws.*

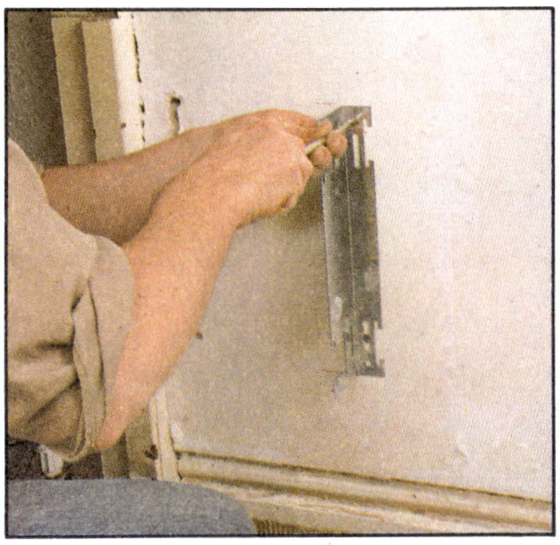

8 *Drill and plug the four holes – two to each bracket – and fix the brackets in position. Make sure the wallplug is well below the plaster to avoid cracking.*

11 *After connecting up the couplings, use a bleed key to open the air-bleed valve slightly so that air can escape as the radiator fills with water.*

12 *Open the inlet valve, allow the radiator to fill and then close the air-bleed valve. Finally open the lock-shield valve by as many turns as you took to close it.*

you a lot of extra work and expense to mend – as well as causing quite a mess. As you unscrew each nut, the water from the radiator will flow out. If the system has been previously treated with corrosion proofer, it's well worth saving the water. That way you can pour it back into the feed-and-expansion tank when the job is complete.

Once the water has drained out, remove the tail pieces and coupling nuts from each end. Then block up each hole with a rag and lift the radiator from the brackets that hold it to the wall. It's a good idea to get the radiator out of your home as soon as possible – just in case it leaks any remaining dirty water on to your carpet.

Fitting a new radiator

Your new radiator will probably have four holes or tappings – one at each corner – and each one will have a female screwed thread. How you connect the radiator up to your system depends on the way in which the old one was fitted. Nowadays it is usual for the flow and return connections to be made to the bottom two holes but, of course, if your system had the flow pipe at a higher level then you'll have to reconnect it in the same way.

Fit an air-valve into one of the top tappings. First wrap PTFE thread sealing tape anti-clockwise round the male thread of the valve and then use a radiator key that grips inside the body of the valve to screw it home. Unless your radiator has a top inlet the other top tapping must be plugged with a blanking off plug. This should also be wrapped with PTFE tape and screwed home in the same way as the air vent.

You'll then have to fit tail pieces and coupling screws (either new ones, or the ones from the original radiator if you can remove them) on to the new one. Again wrap each thread with PTFE tape before fitting them. It's a good idea to buy new wall brackets for your replacement radiator. After all, you can't be sure the old ones will be suitable. You should drill and plug the wall and then fix the brackets in place. Fit the radiator so that the air vent end is fractionally higher than the outlet valve. This will make venting easier. You can now fix the radiator in place and connect the coupling nuts to the hand-valve and lock-shield valve and screw them up tightly.

You'll have to open the air-valve at the top of the radiator so that the air in it can be displaced as it fills with water. All you do is slowly open the hand-valve and allow the radiator to fill. When water starts to flow from the air-valve you'll know all the air has been displaced and you should immediately close the valve. Finally, open the lock-shield valve by the same number of turns and part turns it took originally to close it.

INSULATING TANKS AND PIPEWORK

Worried by the thought of your next heating bill? Concerned by the prospect of your pipes freezing in winter? Proper insulation could well be the answer – and what's more it's cheap and easy to install.

Insulation is important because it reduces heat loss, and when properly applied to your water system it benefits you in a number of ways. Firstly, it saves you money by slowing down the rate at which heat is lost from the pipes and tanks of your hot water system. Secondly, by reducing the heat loss from your cold water system (and even the coldest water contains *some* heat) it tends to keep your cold water warmer in winter, thereby minimising the risk of frozen pipes. Warmer cold water in winter also means that it takes less energy to heat it up to the desired temperature when it enters your hot water tank. In this respect, too, insulation saves you money.

So for all the above reasons you should consider properly insulating your pipes and tanks. The cost of the materials you will need is small and the potential savings great. And if you have already insulated your loft floor then this is one job you really must attend to. It has to be done because the temperature of your loft in winter will now be only marginally higher than that of the air outside, which means that the danger of any exposed pipework freezing in cold weather is greatly increased. Ideally you should therefore insulate your pipes and tanks before you tackle the loft floor. And don't forget that the risk of frozen pipes also applies to pipes in the cellar, and anywhere else where they might be subject to extremes of cold.

Before purchasing the insulation material for your pipes and tanks, work out how much you are likely to need. Most tanks will have their capacity and/or their dimensions marked on them somewhere – if yours don't then measure them yourself. You will also need to calculate the combined length of the pipes you intend insulating and establish what their diameter is – though this last measurement is only important if you plan to use split sleeve insulation (see below). As you'll want the insulation on your tanks to overlap that which you fit to any pipes that run into them, it's best to start by insulating your pipework.

Insulating pipes

Two types of pipe insulation are commonly available. The first is made out of a glass fibre or mineral wool material similar to that used for insulating loft floors, but supplied in bandage form (75 to 100mm/3 to 4in wide and 10mm/⅜in thick) generally with a flimsy plastic backing. The second type comes in the form of split sleeves which are made from some sort of foamed material – usually plastic. Both types of pipe insulation have their advantages and disadvantages (see below) and both types are cheap. And since there is no reason why they can't be used side by side on the same pipe system, you'll almost certainly find that the easiest way to insulate your pipework is by using lengths of both.

Fitting bandage insulation

The bandage type is fitted by wrapping it around the pipe in a spiral, with each turn overlapping the previous one by at least 10mm (⅜in). It doesn't matter which way round the plastic backing goes. Make sure that the bandage is sufficiently tight to prevent air circulating between the turns, but don't pull it too tight or you will reduce its effectiveness. When starting or finishing each roll, and at regular intervals in between, hold it in place using plastic adhesive tape or string. Tape or tie the bandage, too, on vertical pipe runs and on bends as these are places where the turns are likely to separate. And don't forget to lag any stop-valves properly – only the handle should be left visible.

Apart from being rather more time consuming to install than split-sleeve insulation the main drawback with the bandage type is that it is difficult to wrap round pipes in awkward places, such as those that run under floorboards. For pipes like these you will generally find that sleeves are more suitable since once fitted they can be pushed into position.

Fitting split-sleeve insulation

Split-sleeve insulation normally comes in 1m (3ft 3in) or 2m (6ft 6in) lengths. It is available in a variety of sizes to fit piping from 15mm (½in) to 35mm (1½in) in diameter. The thickness of the insulating foam is generally around 12mm (½in). Make sure that you buy the right size sleeve for your pipes – if the sleeves don't fit snugly round your pipework they won't provide satisfactory insulation.

INSULATING PIPEWORK

1 *Start by wrapping the bandage twice round the end of the pipe next to the tank. Hold the turns in place securely with string or tape.*

2 *Wrap the bandage round the pipe in a spiral. Make sure that each turn overlaps the previous one by at least 10mm (3/8in). Don't pull the bandage too tight.*

3 *Whenever you finish a roll of bandage and start a new one allow a generous overlap to prevent air circulating between the turns of the join.*

4 *Finish off the pipe in the same way that you started, with an extra turn of bandage. Lastly, check the pipe to make sure all the insulation is secure.*

5 *Fitting split-sleeve insulation is simple. You just prise apart the split and slip the sleeve over the pipe. Use tape to keep the sleeve in place.*

6 *At bends, where the sleeve tends to come apart, tape the split lengthways. Tape the sleeves, too, whenever you join one to another.*

7 *At tees, first cut a 'notch' from the main pipe sleeve. Then shape the end of the branch pipe sleeve to fit and slot it into place. Tape the join.*

8 *Use split sleeve insulation on pipes that would be hard – or impossible – to fit with bandage. Slip the sleeve over the pipe and slide it into position.*

9 *Sleeve and bandage insulation can – and sometimes must – be used together. A stop-valve, for example, can only be properly lagged with bandage.*

INSULATING COLD TANKS

1 *Proprietary jackets will fit most cold water tanks. Start by flopping the jacket over the tank and pulling it roughly into position.*

2 *Rather than cut into the jacket's 'envelopes', try to accommodate a pipe by parting the seam between them. All cuts must be sealed with tape.*

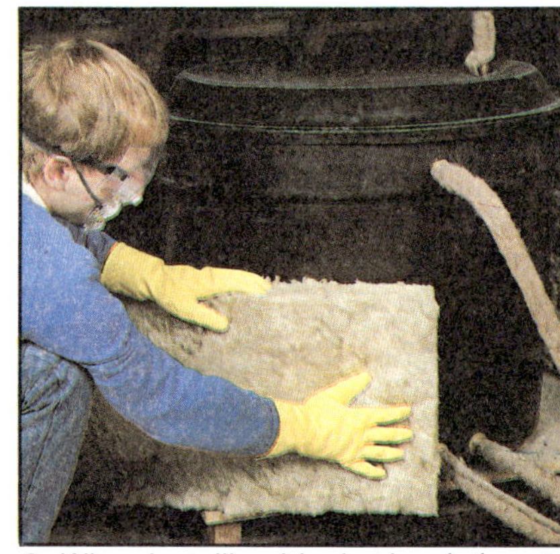

3 *When installing blanket insulation start with the side of the tank. If you're using glass fibre blanket wear gloves and a face mask.*

5 *The tank must have a firm lid to prevent the water inside being polluted. Don't tie the lagging to the lid in such a way that it is impossible to undo.*

6 *Expansion tanks need insulating too. If using sheet polystyrene, remember to cut the panels so that their ends overlap when fitted to the tank.*

7 *Use tape, string, or glue to hold the side panels together. Fill the gaps left as a result of making cut-outs with wedges of waste polystyrene.*

Both flexible and rigid sleeves are available, but as the rigid type isn't much use for pipework that bends frequently, you'd probably be better off using the flexible variety.

Fitting the sleeves is very straightforward. You simply prise apart the slit that runs along the length of the sleeve and slip the insulation over the pipe. It's advisable to tape the sleeve at intervals, and you must do so at joins. At bends, where the sleeves will tend to come apart, you should tape the split lengthways.

Once sleeve insulation has been fitted, it can easily be slid along a length of pipe to protect a part of it that may be hard to get at. However, you should bear in mind that it won't be able to get beyond any pipe clips, very sharp bends or bulky joints it may encounter. You'll find that most flexible sleeves will readily slide round curves and even 90° bends made using soldered fittings, but whenever you run up against problems in the form of bulky compression elbows or tee connectors the sleeves will have to be cut accordingly. However, in some circumstances you might well find that bandage insulation provides the better solution.

To fit round a 90° elbow the sleeve should be cut in two and the sleeve ends then cut at an angle of 45° before being slipped over the pipe. You should then tape over the resulting join. For the most convenient method of dealing with a tee fitting see the step-by-step photographs

Insulating cold water storage tanks

When it comes to insulating your cold water storage tank and central heating expansion tank (if you have one), there are a number of options open to you. If your tank is circular you could cover it with a proprietary jacket consisting of a number of polythene or plastic 'envelopes' filled with insulant; or you could simply wrap it up in a layer of mineral wool or glass fibre blanket similar to – or even the same as – that which is used to insulate loft floors. If, on the other hand, your cold water tank happens to be rectangular then you could construct a 'box' for it yourself out of expanded polystyrene, or buy a proprietary one ready-made.

A proprietary jacket couldn't be easier to fit: you simply pull it into position and then tie it in place – tapes are sometimes provided by the manufacturer. If you have to cut into the jacket to accommodate a pipe, make sure that you seal it up again with plastic adhesive tape to prevent moisture getting in and the insulating material from escaping.

Expanded polystyrene kits are also extremely easy to fit. Apart from having to fix the pieces of polystyrene together with tape, string or polystyrene cement, the only work you will have to do is to make cut-outs for the pipework. More work will be required should you decide to make your tank kit out of sheet polystyrene (see step-by-step photographs)

4 If the blanket isn't as wide as the tank is deep, a second layer, which should overlap the first, will be necessary. Use string to hold the blanket in place.

8 Make a lid for your tank by gluing together two panels of polystyrene. The smaller (inner) panel should just fit inside the tank.

HOT TANKS

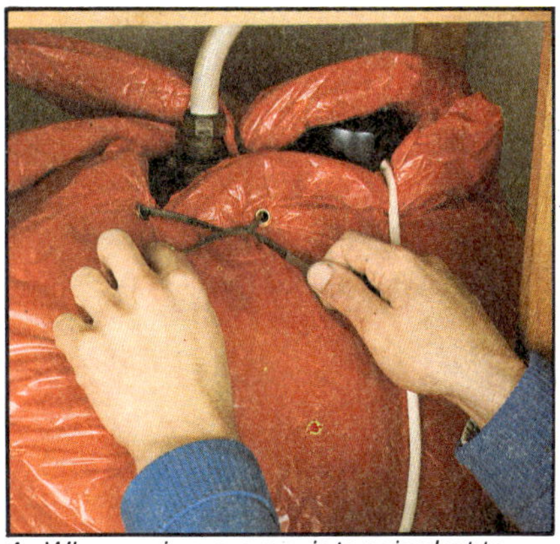

1 When using a proprietary jacket to insulate a hot water cylinder, start by securing the polythene 'envelopes' round the hot water supply pipe.

2 The sides of the jacket are held in place with straps. Take care not to cover the capping and wiring of any immersion heater.

Ready Reference

SLEEVING SIZES

To be effective, split-sleeve insulation must be the right size for your pipes. If they are modern – which usually means copper – most of your pipes will be 15mm (½in), though the main distribution ones are likely to be 22mm (¾in). Check any pipes that you aren't sure of.

TIP: PROBLEM PIPES

There are two areas where you must take extra care:

- when insulating a pipe that runs close to a wall – especially an outside wall – make sure that you protect the *whole* surface. To insulate only the more accessible side of the pipe would be worse than useless: the pipe would still be exposed to the cold wall but denied the heat of your house
- if the expansion pipe of the cold water tank you are insulating stops short of the lid then you'll have to devise some means of catching any outflow. The easiest way to do this is to use a plastic funnel. Bore a hole to accommodate the funnel through the lid and the insulation material, and fix it in place with plastic adhesive tape.

TIP: GOING AWAY

Insulation alone may not be sufficient to protect your pipes and tanks from the cold if you leave your house unoccupied for more than a few days in winter. So in your absence make sure that the heating is switched on briefly each day. If you can't trust your thermostat, ask a neighbour.

– but it would of course be a lot cheaper.

If you decide to use insulation blanket to lag your tank then try to buy the sort that is bonded with paper as you will find it much easier to handle. Buy a roll that is as wide as your tank is deep if you can, as this will save you the trouble of having to go round the side of your tank twice. The thickness of the blanket isn't critical, but blanket 50mm (2in) thick will give your tank adequate insulation and be easier to work with than a thicker one. However, it could well be that you have an odd roll or two of blanket left over from some previous insulation job; if you do, then use that rather than going to the expense of buying additional rolls.

The top of the tank to be insulated must have a firm covering to prevent the water inside being contaminated by fibres from the blanket you are fitting. So if it doesn't already have a lid, cut one out of hardboard, polystyrene or some other sheet material.

Lagging a tank with blanket insulation is simply a matter of common sense. You cut the blanket to size, drape it round the side of the tank, and having cut slits to enable the blanket to fit round the pipes, secure it with string. The lagging on the lid should overlap the side lagging by about 150mm (6in); and as you'll need to inspect the inside of your tank from time to time make sure it's easily removable.

Under normal circumstances the bottom of your tank should not be insulated, nor should the loft floor directly below. The reason for this is that it allows heat from the house to rise up through the floor and slightly increase the temperature of your cold water. The only circumstance in which you do insulate these places (and this applies regardless of what form of insulation you are using) is when, in order to increase the water pressure for a shower on the floor below, the tank has been raised more than a foot or so above the joists.

Insulating hot water tanks

Although you could in theory lag your hot water tank by adapting any of the methods that are used for cold water tanks, in practice you will nearly always find that you have no choice but to use a proprietary jacket. The fact that most hot water tanks are situated in airing cupboards means that blanket insulation is out of the question, and unless your tank is a rectangular one (which these days are very rare) you won't be able to use polystyrene.

Proprietary jackets for hot water tanks are made of the same materials as those used on cold water tanks and are just as easy to fit. The system used to fasten the jacket to the tank varies, but basically at the top you secure the 'envelopes' round the hot water supply pipe with a loop of cord, while further down you hold them in place with straps. The base of the tank is left uninsulated, as is the capping and wiring of any immersion heater.

CLEARING BLOCKAGES

There are few plumbing emergencies quite as unpleasant as a blocked drain or waste pipe. However, it's usually possible to cure the problem if you know what to do when you've tracked down the blockage and you have the right equipment.

Professional plumbers rarely relish being called out to deal with a blockage. There *are* specialist drain clearance firms, but they can't always be contacted quickly in an emergency – and their charges reflect what can sometimes be the unpleasantness of the job. Drain or waste-pipe clearance is usually well within the capacity of the householder, and there are certainly few more cost-effective do-it-yourself jobs about the house.

Coping with blocked sinks

The outlet of the sink, usually the trap immediately beneath the sink itself, is the commonest site of waste-pipe blockage. Usually the obstruction can be cleared quickly and easily by means of a sink-waste plunger or force cup. This is a very simple plumbing tool obtainable from any do-it-yourself shop, ironmongers or household store. It consists of a rubber or plastic hemisphere, usually mounted on a wooden or plastic handle. Every household should have one.

To use it to clear a sink waste blockage, first press a damp cloth firmly into the overflow outlet, holding it securely with one hand. Then pull out the plug and lower the plunger into the flooded sink so that the cup is positioned over the waste outlet. Plunge it up and down sharply half a dozen or more times. Since water cannot be compressed, the water in the waste between the cup and the obstruction is converted into a ram to clear the blockage. The overflow outlet is sealed to prevent the force being dissipated up the overflow.

If your first efforts at plunging are unsuccessful, persevere. Each thrust may be moving the obstruction a little further along the waste pipe until it is discharged into the drain gully or the main soil and waste stack.

Should plunging prove unsuccessful you'll have to gain access to the trap. Brass and lead U-shaped traps have a screwed-in plug at the base. With plastic U-shaped and bottle traps the lower part can be unscrewed and removed – see *Ready Reference*. Before attempting this, put the plug in the sink and place a bucket under the trap; it will probably be full of water unless the blockage is immediately below the sink

WHERE BLOCKAGES OCCUR

Blockages can occur in several different places around your home's waste and drain systems. The commonest sites are:

1. *traps under basins, baths and sinks;*
2. *WC traps;*
3. *waste pipes running to soil stacks, hoppers or gullies;*
4. *rainwater or yard gullies;*
5. *underground drain runs between house and manhole;*
6. *intercepting chambers (see* Ready Reference*);*
7. *underground drain runs between manhole and sewer.*

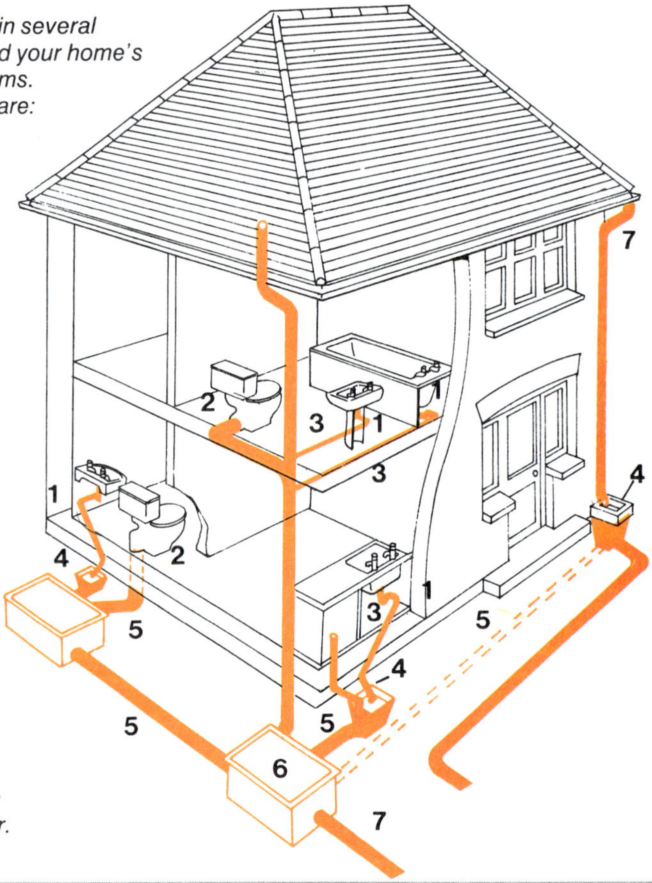

CLEARING BLOCKED TRAPS

1 Try using a plunger to clear blocked sinks, basins, baths or WCs. Cover the overflow with a damp cloth, then push the plunger down sharply several times.

2 If the blockage persists, you will have to open up the trap. Put the plug in the basin and have a bucket handy to catch the trap contents.

TIP

3 In a confined space like this, you may find it easier to remove the next push-fit elbow before tackling the connection to the waste outlet itself.

4 With the trap fully dismantled, wash each component thoroughly to remove the blockage and any scum clinging to the pipe sides. Leave the plug in.

5 Before reassembling the trap fully, check that the next section of the waste pipe is clear by poking a length of wire down it as far as you can reach.

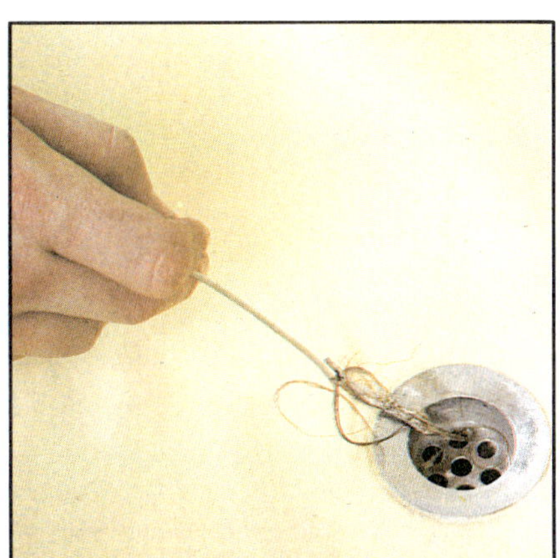

6 A build-up of hair and scum can often block basin wastes just below the outlet. Fish out as much as possible with a slim wire hook passed through the grating.

Ready Reference

TYPES OF TRAP

On old plumbing systems you may still come across lead traps, which have a removable rodding eye in the base. On more modern systems plastic traps will have been installed, and it is easy to unscrew part of the trap to clear a blockage.

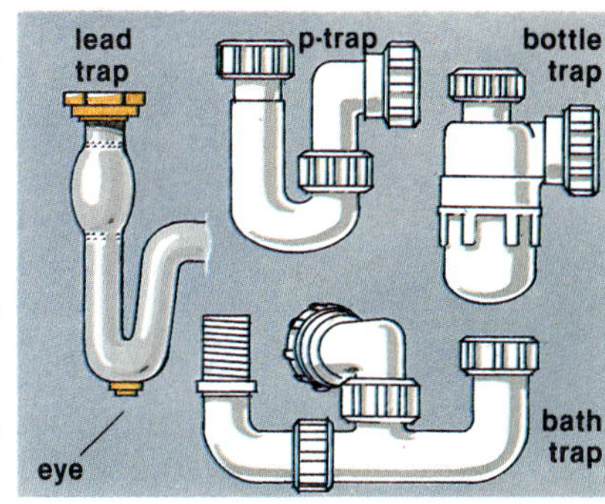

TIP: SUPPORT LEAD TRAPS

Lead traps are very soft, and may bend or split if you use force to open the rodding eye. To avoid this:

- insert a piece of scrap wood into the U-bend of the trap
- undo the rodding eye with a spanner, turning it in the direction shown while bracing the trap with the scrap wood
- reverse the procedure to replace it.

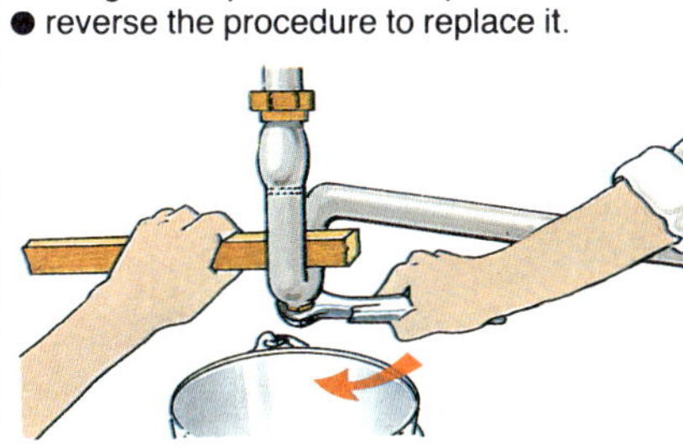

RODDING INTERCEPTING TRAPS

The manhole nearest the main sewer may be an intercepting trap, designed to keep sewer gases out of the house drains. To clear a blockage between it and the sewer,

feed your rods into the rodding arm. To prevent the stoneware plug from being dislodged and causing a blockage, cement a glass disc in its place.

outlet, and the chances are that opening the trap will release it. Having done so, probe into the trap, and into the waste pipe itself. You can buy purpose-made sink waste augers for this purpose, but you'll find that a piece of expanding curtain wire, with a hook on the end, can be equally effective.

Blocked baths and basins

Basin and bath wastes are less likely to be totally blocked than sink wastes but, when blockages do occur, they can usually be cleared in the same way. They are, however, very subject to partial blockage. The waste water is often found to run from the bath or basin ever more slowly. This may be due to a build-up of scum, scale and hair on the inside of the waste pipe, and the use of a proprietary drain-clearing chemical will usually clear it. These frequently have a caustic soda base, so they should be kept away from children and handled with care, strictly in accordance with the manufacturer's instructions. Before spooning them into the bath or basin waste outlet it is wise to smear petroleum jelly over the rim of the outlet to protect the chromium finish, especially with plastic baths or fittings.

Partial blockage of a wash basin waste may often be caused by hair suspended from the grid of the outlet. This may be all but invisible from above, but probing with a piece of wire (the old standby of a straightened-out wire coathanger is useful) can often produce festoons. If you can't clear the hair by this means, unscrew the nut that connects the threaded waste outlet to the trap and pull the trap to one side. Now use a pair of pliers to pull the hair away from beneath the grid.

Overflows from gullies

Where waste pipes and downpipes discharge into gullies, the first signs of trouble may be when the gully overflows and the surrounding area is flooded as a result. The gully trap has probably become blocked, either by blown leaves or other debris, or by a build-up of grease and scum on the sides of the trap. Raise the gully grid if one is fitted (and get a new one if it's broken or missing). Then scoop out any debris with a rubber-gloved hand or an improvised scoop, scrub the gully out with caustic soda and flush it through with plenty of clean water before replacing the grid.

Blockages below ground

A blockage in the underground drains may be shown up by a WC which, when flushed, fills with water almost to the rim and then very slowly subsides, or by dirty water seeping from under a manhole cover. You'll need a set of drain rods to clear any underground blockage. It is best to hire these from a local tool hire firm if and when the emergency arises. A drain that blocks sufficiently frequently to justify the purchase of a set of rods undoubtedly has a major defect that needs professional advice and attention.

Raising the manhole covers will give you an indication of the position of the blockage. If, for instance, the manhole near your front boundary is empty, but the one beside the house into which the soil pipe and yard gully discharges is flooded, then the blockage must be between these two manholes. Screw two or three lengths of drain-rod together, add the appropriate accessory to one end and then lower it into the flooded manhole. Feel for the drain half-channel at its base and push the rod end along it and into the drain towards the obstruction. Screw on extra rods as necessary until you reach and clear the blockage. You may find it easier to push the rods into the drain – and to extract them again – if you twist them as you do so. *Always* twist in a clockwise direction. If you twist anti-clockwise the rods will unscrew and one or more lengths will be left irretrievably in the drain.

Many older houses have intercepting traps. These traps, which were intended to keep sewer gases out of the house drains, are the commonest site of drain blockage. You can see if your drains have an intercepting trap by raising the cover of the manhole nearest to your property boundary before trouble occurs and looking inside. If there is an intercepting trap the half-channel of the gully will fall into what appears to be a hole at the end of the manhole; actually it is the inlet to the trap. Immediately above this hole will be a stoneware stopper. This closes the rodding arm giving access to the length of drain between the intercepting trap and the sewer.

A blockage in the intercepting trap is

CLEARING BLOCKED GULLIES

1 *Both surface-water and yard gullies are easily blocked by wind-blown debris such as waste paper and dead leaves. First lift off the gully grating.*

2 *Try to scoop out as much debris as possible from the gully trap, either by hand or with an improvised scoop such as an old tin can.*

3 *If the blockage is cleared and the water flows away, scrub out the sides of the gully with detergent or caustic soda. Clean the gully grating too.*

4 *Finally, hose the gully out thoroughly with running water. If you are unable to clear the blockage, you may have to rod the drain run from a nearby manhole.*

RODDING BLOCKED DRAINS

1 *Raise manhole covers carefully. If the hand grips are missing, use an old brick bolster to lift one edge, and then slide in a piece of wood.*

2 *With the wood supporting one end of the cover, grasp it securely and lift it to one side. Bend from the knees so you don't strain your back.*

3 *Select one of the drain rod heads (a rubber disc is being fitted here) and screw it securely onto the threaded end of the first drain rod.*

4 *Screw a second rod onto the end of the first, and lower the head into the half-channel in the bottom of the chamber. Push the rods towards the blockage.*

5 *Screw on further rods as necessary and work the head in and out to clear the blockage. Never turn the rods anticlockwise, or they may unscrew and be lost.*

6 *When you have cleared the blockage, hose down the sides and base of the manhole with running water, and let water run through the drain for a while.*

indicated when all the drain inspection chambers are flooded. It can usually be cleared quite easily by plunging. To do this, screw a drain plunger (a 100mm or 4in diameter rubber disc) onto the end of a drain rod. Screw on one or two other rods as necessary and lower the plunger into the flooded manhole. Feel for the half-channel at its base and move the plunger along until you reach the inlet of the intercepting trap. Plunge down sharply three or four times and, unless you are very unlucky, there will be a gurgle and the water level in the manhole will quickly fall.

Very occasionally, there may be a blockage between the intercepting trap and the sewer, and the point must be made that this length of drain is the householder's responsibility, even though much of it may lie under the public highway. To clear such a blockage the stoneware cap must be knocked out of the inlet to the rodding arm (this can be done with the drain rods but it isn't the easiest of jobs) and the rods passed down the rodding arm towards the sewer.

Intercepting traps are also subject to a kind of partial blockage that may go unnoticed for weeks or even months. An increase in pressure on the sewer side of the trap – due to a surge of storm water, for instance – may push the stopper out of the rodding arm. It will fall into the trap below and cause an almost immediate stoppage. However this will not be noticed because sewage will now be able to escape down the open rodding arm to the sewer. The householder usually becomes aware of a partial blockage of this kind as a result of an unpleasant smell, caused by the decomposition of the sewage in the base of the manhole.

The remedy is, of course, to remove the stopper and to replace it. Where the trouble recurs it is best to discard the stopper and to lightly cement a glass or slate disc in its place. In the very unusual event of a stoppage between the intercepting trap and the sewer, this disc can be broken with a crowbar and replaced after the drain has been cleared – see *Ready Reference*.

After any drain clearance the manhole walls should be washed down with a hot soda solution and a garden hose should be used to flush the drain through thoroughly.

Blocked gutters

Roof rainwater gutters may become obstructed by leaves or other objects. An overflowing gutter isn't an instant catastrophe but, if neglected, it will cause dampness to the house walls. An inspection, removal of debris and a hose down of gutters should be a routine part of every householder's preparations for winter.

EMERGENCY PIPE REPAIRS

A leaking pipe is no joke. First you have to stop the water – so you need to know where to turn if off – and then to make some kind of emergency repair, even if it's just a holding operation.

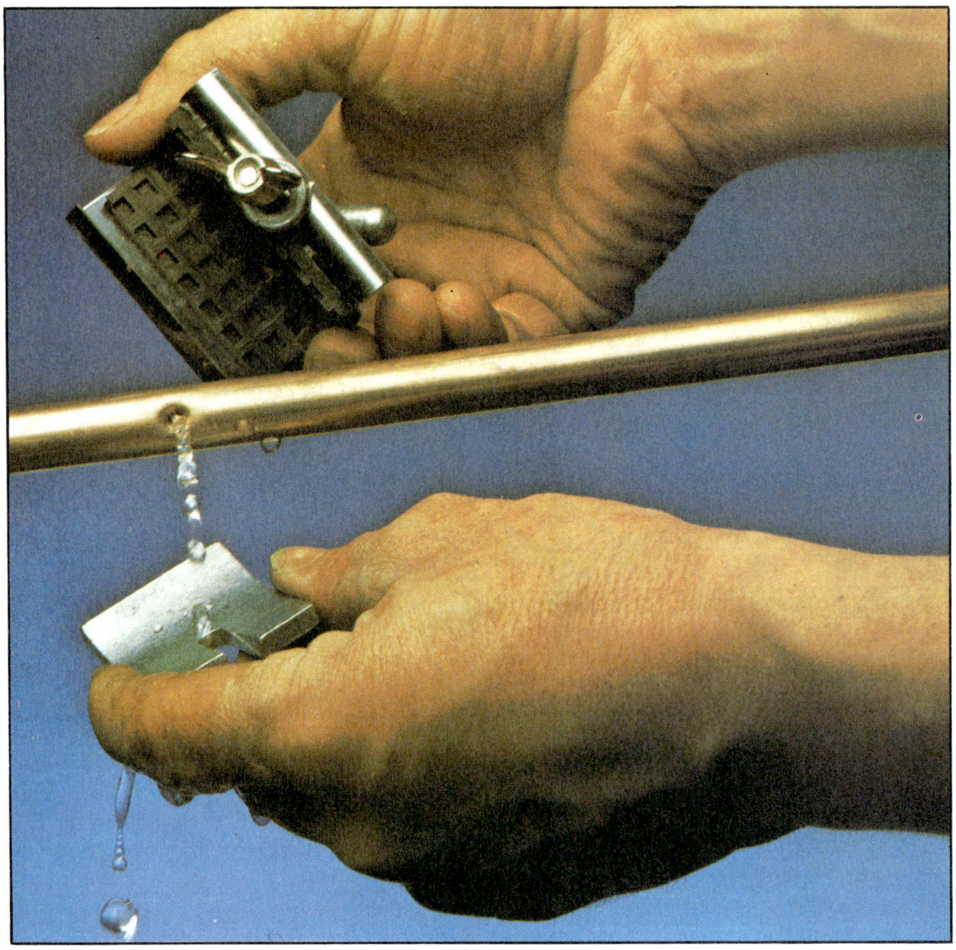

Leaks in domestic plumbing systems have a nasty habit of happening at the most inconvenient of times, often when it isn't possible to carry out a proper permanent repair. What you need is a plumbing emergency first aid kit, and there are now several proprietary products available that will at least enable you to make a temporary repair and get the water flowing again.

With any leak, the vital first step is to stop the flow of water. Even a small leak can create a surprisingly large pool of water in no time. Stopping the flow in any pipe is relatively easy provided that you know the locations of the various stop-taps or valves that isolate parts of your water system, or cut it off completely from the mains supply.

Water comes into the house through a pipe known as the rising main, and because water in this pipe (and others leading from it) is under mains pressure, leaks from it will be particularly serious. It enters the house underground, and from there leads either to all the cold taps and a water heating system, or to just the cold tap in the kitchen and to a cold water storage tank.

Leaks can result from a number of causes. Pipework may have been forced or strained at some point, resulting in a leak at one of the fittings connecting the lengths of pipe together, or in a fracture at a bend.

Corrosion within pipes may lead to pinholes in pipe lengths, while frost damage can lead to bursts and splits in pipes and to leaks at fittings caused by ice forcing the fitting open. Whatever the cause, cutting off the water supply to the affected pipe is the first vital step.

Where to turn off the water

1 Cold water supply pipes connected directly to the mains: in the UK these pipes usually only supply the kitchen cold tap, the cold water storage tank and sometimes instantaneous water heaters. In many other countries, the pipes may supply *all* cold water taps and the hot water storage cylinder. The simple way of deciding whether any pipe or tap is supplied directly by the mains is by the pressure – taps supplied from a tank are what's known as gravity-fed and the pressure of water is relatively low compared to mains pressure.

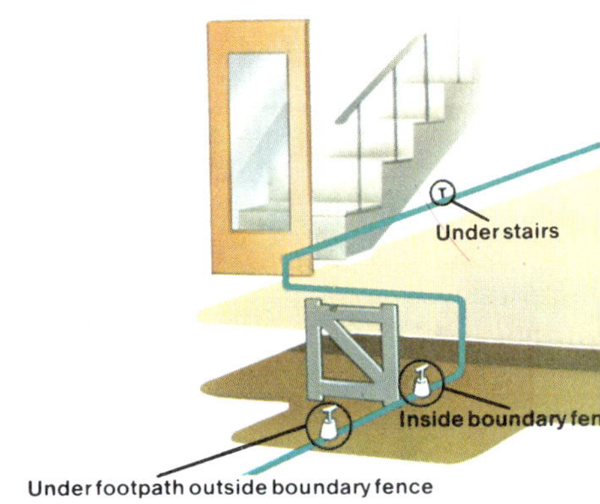

2 Cold water supply pipes from a cold water storage tank: in the UK these pipes usually supply the bathroom cold taps, the WC cistern and the hot water cylinder.

To close off the water supply in these pipes there's often a stop-valve immediately alongside the cold water tank where the pipe exits. Turn this off first and then open all cold water taps. They'll run dry almost immediately. If there isn't a stop-valve, you have to drain the whole tank. So first you stop water entering the tank by either turning off the mains (as above) or by tying up the ball-valve in the tank so that it remains closed. Then you open all the taps in the house.

3 Hot water pipes: these are all supplied from a hot water cylinder, which in turn gets its cold water either from the cold tank or from the mains.

Since hot water leaves the hot water storage cylinder from the top, it's only the pressure of water going in at the bottom of the cylinder that forces the water out. Turn off the supply of cold water (either at the cold water tank, or at the mains) and you stop the flow. In this sort of situation the hot water cylinder remains full. If for any reason you need to drain this as well, use the drain cock near the bottom. It's essential in this case to turn off either the immersion heater or boiler.

To turn off the water, look for the mains stop-valves. There may, in fact, be two: one inside the house where the mains pipe enters (under the kitchen sink, in the utility room, or even under the stairs); the other outside – either just inside the boundary of the property (near to a water meter, if you have one), or under the footpath outside the garden fence. Outdoor stop-valves may be set as much as a metre (3 ft) down beneath a hinged cover or metal plate, and you may need a special 'key' which is really just a long rod with a square socket on the end which fits over the tap to turn it. In most cases, however, it's simply a matter of reaching down to turn it off by hand or with a wrench. Some outdoor stop-valves also control a neighbour's water supply, so do warn them if you're turning it off.

The stop-valve inside will either be a wheel type or an ordinary T-shaped type. The only possible complication is if it hasn't been touched for years and is stuck fast. A little penetrating oil and tapping it with a hammer will usually loosen it sufficiently. (It's worth closing the stop-valve now and again to see that it doesn't get stuck.)

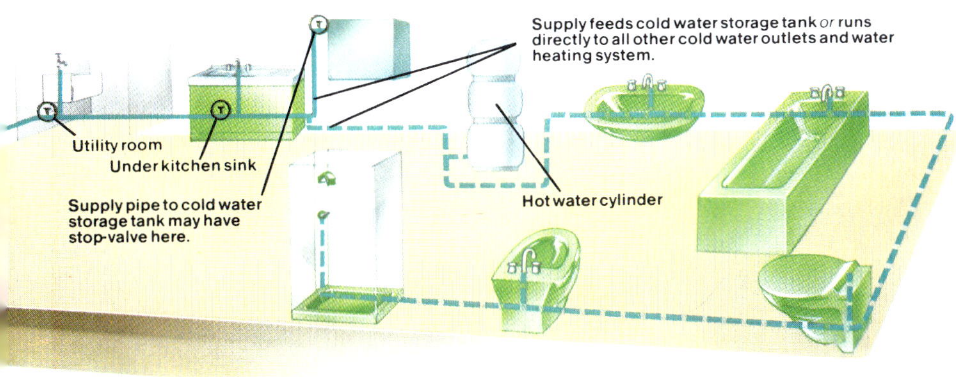

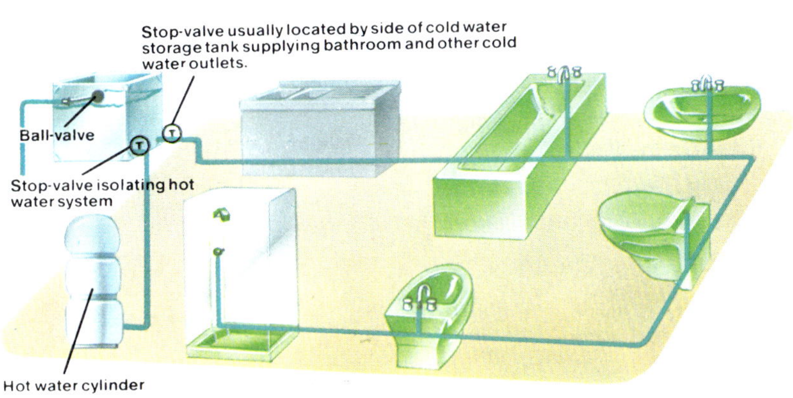

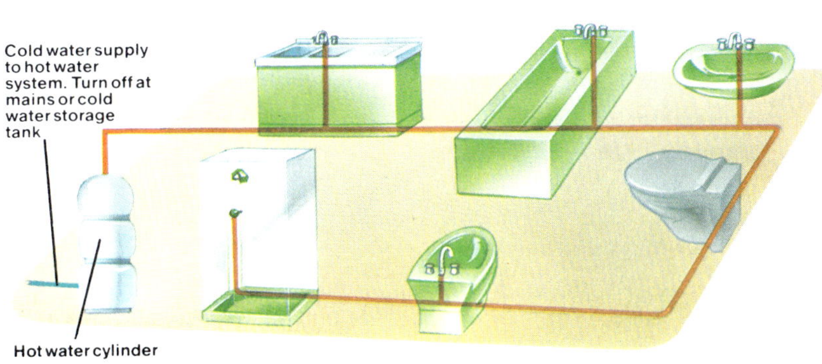

Ready Reference

TURNING OFF THE STOP TAP

Make sure the family knows where the mains stop tap is.

- do not force the handle if it has seized up – it could break off
- use a hammer or wrench to tap the fitting while pouring penetrating oil down spindle.
- if you can't free it call the water authority emergency service — they can turn the water off where your supply pipe leaves the mains.
- don't reopen stop valve fully when turning on the supply until a permanent pipe repair is made. This reduces water pressure on a temporary seal.

TIP: MAKESHIFT REPAIRS

If you don't have the right materials to hand (see next page) try this:

- bandage insulating tape round the pipe and hole
- cover with a 150mm (6in) piece of garden hosepipe slit along its length and tie with wire at each end, twisting ends of wire together with pliers
- wrap more tape tightly over this

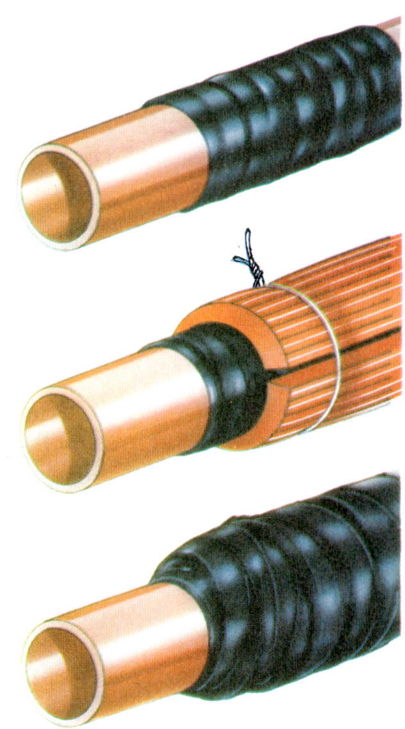

For permanent repairs of leaks at joints in copper pipe see pages 14–18.

EMERGENCY REPAIRS

● One type of repair kit is based on a two-part **epoxy resin plastic putty** supplied as two strips of differently-coloured putty in an airtight pack. When the strips are thoroughly kneaded together the putty is packed firmly round the pipe, where it will harden to form a seal. However, this hardening process takes up to 24 hours and the water supply will have to remain off for this period. (If you don't need to use all the pack in one go, reseal it immediately).

Equal amounts of putty should always be used and mixed together thoroughly until a uniform colour results, otherwise it won't harden properly. It's also essential that the pipe or joint is scrupulously rubbed down and cleaned with methylated spirit or nail polish remover. This will ensure a good bond between the putty and the metal.

● One of the most valuable aids is a multi-size **pipe repair clamp** which has the added advantage of being reusable. It consists of a rubber pad which fits over the hole (for this repair it's not necessary to turn off the water) and a metal clamp which draws the rubber tightly against the pipe when it is screwed in place.

Position the pad and one side of the clamp over the hole, and link the two parts of the clamp together, making sure that the pad is still in place. Tighten the wing nut fully. If the position of the hole makes this difficult, use blocks of wood to hold the pipe away from the wall. This method of repair cannot, of course, be used to mend leaks occurring at fittings.

● Another proprietary product uses a two-part **sticky tape** system which builds up waterproof layers over the leak — in the true sense this does form an instant repair. The area round the leak should be dried and cleaned and then the first of the tapes is wrapped tightly round the pipe, covering the leak and 25mm (1in) either side of it. Then 150mm (6in) strips of the second tape, with the backing film removed, are stuck to the pipe and stretched as they are wound round, each turn overlapping the previous one by about half the width of the tape. This covering should extend 25mm (1in) beyond either end of the first layer of tape. The job is completed by wrapping the first tape over all the repair.

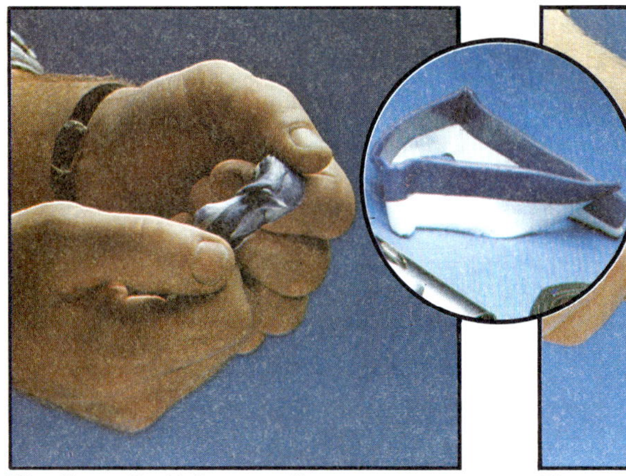

Plastic putty *Using your fingers, mix together equal amounts of the two putty strips. It's ready for use when the colour is even all through.*

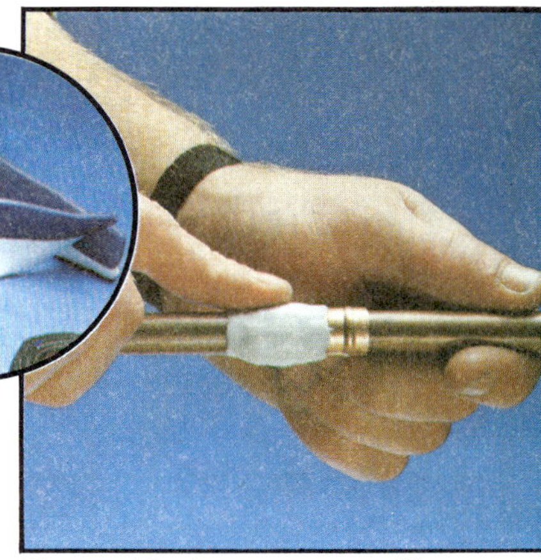

Thoroughly clean area round the leaking pipe, then pack putty round fitting. It can be sanded smooth when it's completely hard.

Pipe clamp *Place rubber pad and one side of metal clamp directly over leak in pipe. There's no need to turn off the water with this type of repair.*

Link the two parts of clamp together, being careful to keep it in position. Screw down wing nut to secure rubber pad against pipe.

Sticky tape *Start winding first tape round pipe about 25mm (1in) from the leaking fitting. Continue over the joint and for 25mm on other side.*

Stretch and overlap 150mm (6in) strips of second tape round pipe. Continue 25mm (1in) either side of first tape. Finish off with layer of first tape.

PLUMBING JOBS IN THE BATHROOM

There are many reasons why you might want to carry out plumbing work in the bathroom – to improve or increase the facilities offered or to make more efficient use of the available space by rearranging the position of fittings.

PLUMBING IN A BATH

Replacing a bath may seem to be an ambitious do-it-yourself project but it is well within the capabilities of the determined home handyman prepared to tackle the job carefully and logically. Here is what is involved.

As with many other plumbing projects the most difficult part is likely to be the removal of the old fitting rather than the installation of the new one.

The old bath will almost certainly be made of enamelled cast iron. The once-white enamel may be discoloured and wearing away, and may even reveal rusting bare metal underneath. Green or brown coloured stains beneath the taps indicate a long-neglected need for rewashering. The taps may look out of date and have worn chromium plating. The finish of the bath may be old and unattractive and the bath itself not panelled in.

Checking it out

First have a look at the existing bath. If there are side or end panels, strip them off and examine, with the aid of an electric torch, the water supply pipes and the waste and the overflow arrangements in the cramped and badly lit space between the foot of the bath and the wall. You will see that the water supply pipes connect the threaded tails of the taps by means of brass 'swivel tap connectors' or 'cap and lining joints'.

Check whether the water supply pipes are made of copper or lead by scraping their surface with the blade of a pocket knife. If this reveals the characteristic grey sheen of lead you should think of replacing the piping. If you *do* want to retain the lead piping you will have to call in a qualified plumber – it's not an easy task. If the pipes are of copper you should be able to tackle the entire project without professional aid.

The overflow from a modern bath is taken, by means of a flexible pipe, to the waste trap. In the past, the overflow pipe often simply led through the external wall, and was the source of incurable bathroom draughts. If your bath's overflow is like this, you'll have to cut it off flush with the wall.

If the bath has adjustable feet, apply some penetrating oil to the screws. Once they begin to move, lowering the level of the bath before you attempt to remove it can help to prevent damage to the wall tiling.

The alternatives

It is possible to replace your cast iron bath with a new one made of the same material, but more modern in styling. However, these baths are expensive and very heavy indeed. Carrying one into the bathroom and fitting it requires considerable strength (you'd need at least one strong helper) as well as care. There are other snags about enamelled cast iron baths. They normally have a slippery base that can make them dangerous to use – particularly by the very young and the elderly, though some are available with a non-slip surface. Furthermore, the material of which they are made rapidly conducts the heat away from the water and while this didn't matter too much in the days when energy was plentiful and cheap, large amounts of hot water cost rather more today.

One economical alternative is an enamelled pressed steel bath. This is lighter and cheaper than enamelled cast iron but can be more easily damaged in storage or installation.

For do-it-yourself installation a plastic bath is the obvious choice. These are made of acrylic plastic sheet, sometimes reinforced with glass fibre. They are available in a number of attractive colours and, as the colour extends right through the material of which they are made, any surface scratches can be easily polished out. They are light in weight and one man can quite easily carry one upstairs for installation. The plastic of which they are made is a poor conductor of heat which means that they are both comfortable and economical to use. Many of them have a non-slip base to make them safe.

But plastic baths do have their snags. They are easily damaged by extreme heat. You should be beware of using a blow torch in proximity to one and a lighted cigarette should never be rested, even momentarily, on the rim. A fault of early plastic baths was their tendency to creak and sag when filled with hot water and, sometimes, when you got into them. This has now been overcome by the manufacturers who provide substantial frames or cradles for support; but these frames must be assembled and fixed exactly as recommended. Some come already attached to the bath

A combined plastic waste and overflow assembly is likely to be the choice nowadays for any bath, and is obligatory with a plastic bath. If a rigid metal trap is used with a plastic bath, the material of the bath could be damaged as hot water causes unequal expansion.

You obviously won't want to re-use the old bath taps and will probably opt for either individual modern ¾in bath pillar taps or a bath mixer. A mixer should be chosen only if the cold water supply is taken from the same cold

REPOSITIONING A BATH

In many bathrooms, a new bath simply takes the place of an existing one; there's no room for manoeuvre. But in some cases moving the bath to another position in the room can lead to a more practical arrangement and better use of the available space. In this bathroom the new bath was installed at the other side of the room, so that the space it had formerly occupied could house a shower cubicle and a WC. Moving the bath to this position involved extending the existing hot and cold water supply pipes, but brought it nearer the soil stack on the outside wall and meant that the waste pipe was short and simple to connect up outside.

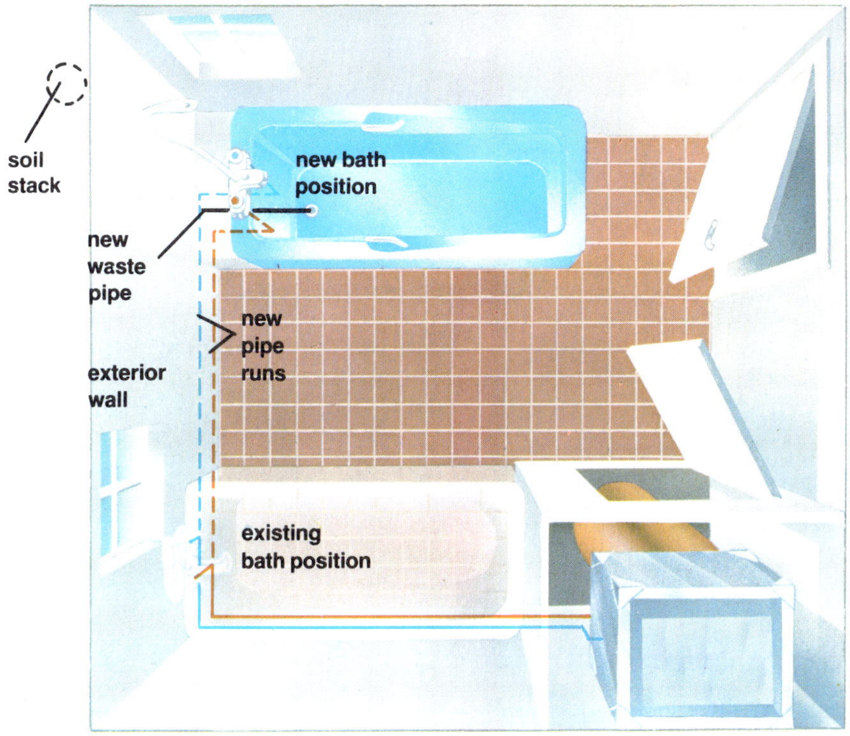

water storage cistern that supplies the hot water system. It should not be used where the cold water supply to the bathroom comes directly from the mains supply.

How to proceed

To avoid too long a disruption of the domestic hot and cold water supplies you can fit the taps, waste and trap into the new bath before removing the old one.

Slip a flat plastic washer over the tail of each tap and insert the tails through the holes provided for them. A mixer usually has one large flat washer or gasket with two holes — one for each tap tail. Beneath the rim of the bath, slip 'top hat' or 'spacer' washers over the tails to accommodate the protruding shanks of the taps. Screw on the back-nuts and tighten them. For details, see pages 51–53.

Bed the waste flange onto plumber's putty or non-setting mastic, secure the back-nut and connect up the trap. Then connect up the overflow pipe.

Removing the old bath may well be the most difficult part of the procedure. Turn off the hot and cold water supplies and drain the distribution pipes from the bath taps. If you haven't done so already, remove the bath panel to give access to the plumbing at the foot of the bath. You can try to unscrew the back-nuts holding the taps in position, but it's generally easier to undo the nuts that connect the distribution pipes to the tails of the taps. In order to reach the one nearest the wall you may have to dismantle the overflow, either by unscrewing it or, if it is taken through the wall, by cutting it off flush with the wall. Then undo the waste connection.

The bath is now disconnected from the water supply pipes and from the branch waste pipe and can be pulled away from the wall. Unless you particularly want to save the old bath and

Ready Reference

EQUIPMENT ROUND-UP

To replace a bath, you're likely to need the following tools:

- crowsfoot wrench
- adjustable spanner
- adjustable wrench
- hacksaw (possibly)
- spirit level

You'll also need:

- new bath — measure up carefully before you buy it to make sure it fits. It should come complete with supports, carcase and side panels, otherwise you'll need these as well
- new overflow connection, waste outlet and PVC trap
- taps/mixer and new inlet pipe if you are replacing them
- plumber's putty

KNOW YOUR BATH

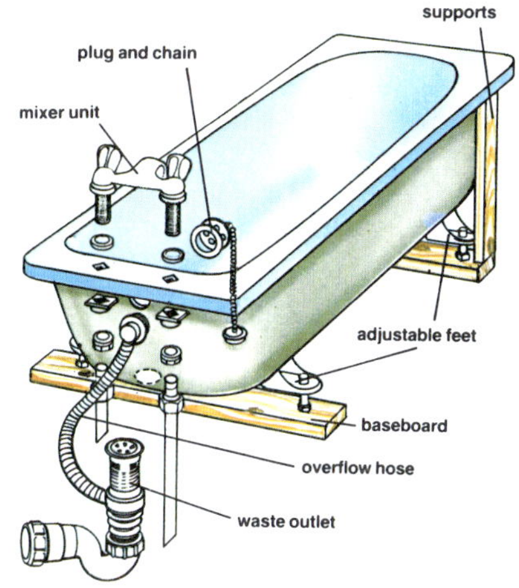

THE SPACE YOU NEED

You need a minimum amount of space around a bath (below) and also a minimum ceiling height above it (right).

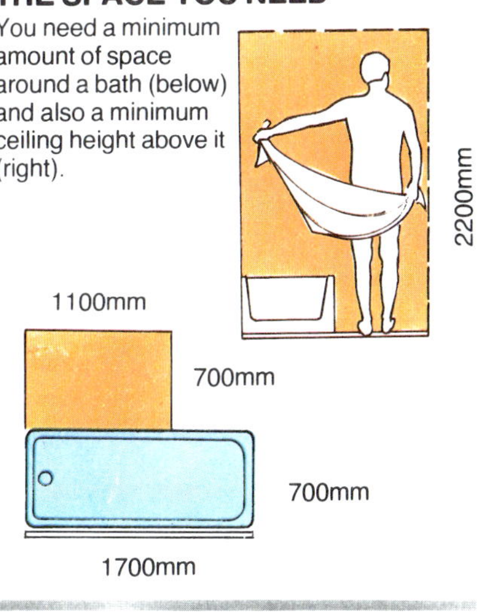

have some strong helpers, do not attempt to remove it from the room or the house in one piece. It is very heavy. The best course of action is to break it into manageable pieces. Drape an old blanket over it to prevent flying chips of enamel and wear goggles to protect the eyes. Then, with a club hammer, break the bath up into pieces that you can easily carry away.

Place the new plastic bath in position and assemble the cradle or other support exactly as recommended by the manufacturer. It is most unlikely that the tails of the new taps will coincide with the position of the tap connectors of the old distribution pipes. If they don't, the easiest way of making the connections is by means of bendable copper pipe. This is corrugated copper tubing – easily bent by hand. It is obtainable in 15mm and 22mm sizes and either with two plain ends for connection to soldered capillary or compression joints, or with one plain end and a swivel tap connector at the other. For this particular job two lengths of 22mm corrugated copper pipe will be required, each with one end plain and one end fitted with a swivel tap connector.

Offer the corrugated pipe lengths up to the tap tails and cut back the distribution pipes to the length required for connection to the plain ends. Leave these pipes slightly too long rather than too short. The corrugated pipe can be bent to accommodate a little extra length. Now connect the plain ends to the cut distribution pipes using either soldered capillary or Type 'A' compression couplings.

The chances are that the distribution pipes will be ¾in imperial size. If you use compression fittings an adaptor — probably simply a larger olive — will be needed for connection to a 22mm coupling. If you use soldered capillary fittings, special ¾in to 22mm couplings must be used. Remember to keep the blowtorch flame well away from the plastic of the bath. Connect up the swivel tap connectors of the corrugated pipe and the overflow of the bath. Do this in a logical order. First connect the tap connector to the further tap. A fibre washer inside the nut of the tap connector will ensure a watertight joint. Then connect up the flexible overflow pipe of the combined waste-and-overflow fitting to the bath's overflow outlet. Finally connect the nearer tap to the nearer tap connector.

If you have installed new pipework then you can install the entire trap, waste and water supply pipe spurs before moving the bath into position. Whatever you have decided upon, finish making all the connections, then reinstate the water supply and check for leaks.

The level of the positioned bath should now be checked using a spirit level, and adjustments made (you'll need a spanner to set the adjustable feet). When all is level, fit the side and end panels in position and the job is finished.

TAKING OUT THE OLD BATH

1 Think about how you're going to get the old bath out before you begin. The connections are likely to be inaccessible, old and corroded.

2 Start by trying to detach the waste trap using an adjustable wrench and, if necessary, penetrating oil.

3 Undo the back-nuts underneath the taps or mixer. These are likely to be more difficult to undo than the trap; use a crowsfoot wrench.

4 If the back-nuts won't undo you may have to detach the supply pipes at another joint. Use an adjustable spanner to undo the nut.

5 Unscrew the old overflow pipe. Alternatively you can simply saw off both supply and overflow pipes — but you'll need to install new ones.

6 When the bath is free, drag it out of position. You'll need at least one other person to help you get a cast iron bath out unless you break it up first.

ATTACHING THE NEW FITTINGS

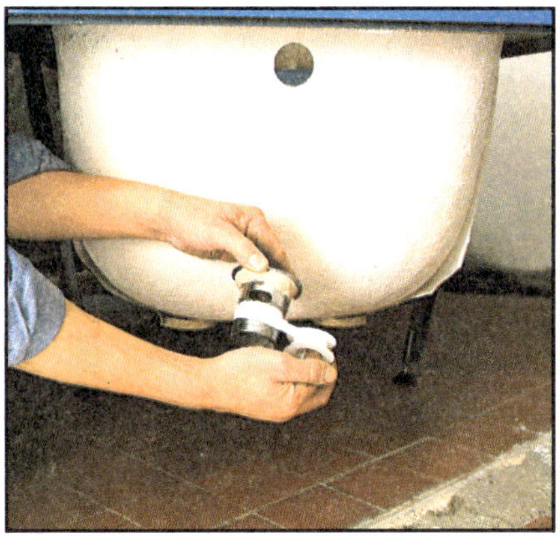

1 *Start to assemble the new plumbing. Wind PTFE tape around the screw thread of the waste outlet and spread some plumber's putty underneath the rim.*

2 *Put the waste outlet in position and make sure that it is firmly seated. These days the overflow will be made of plastic and connects to the waste outlet.*

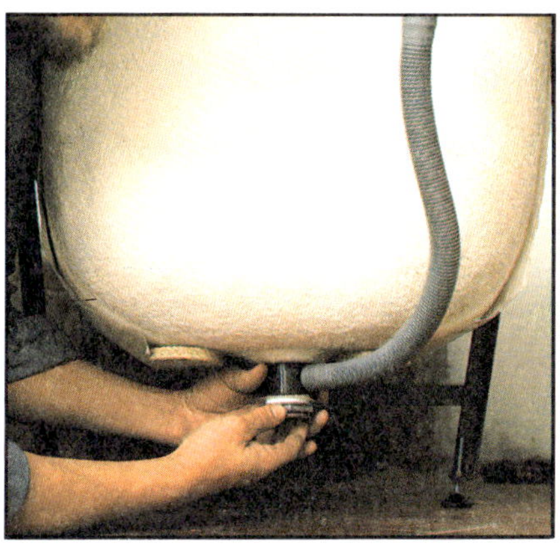

3 *Attach the overflow to the outlet with a locking nut and a plastic O ring, which is inserted between them. Screw up the nut and tighten gently.*

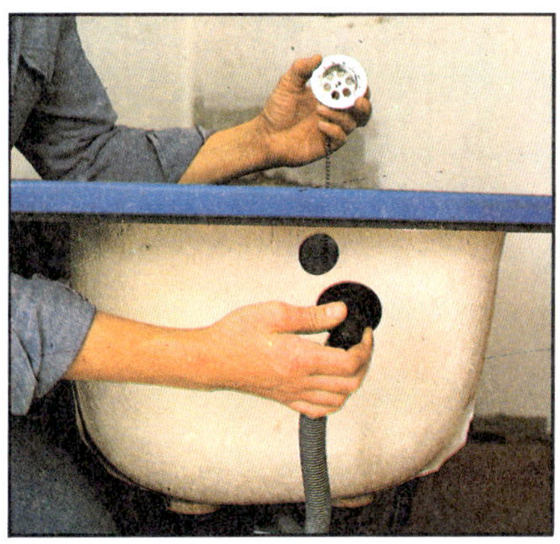

4 *Attach the inlet end of the overflow which will have the plug and chain attached to it. Screw it into the pipe connector and tighten it up.*

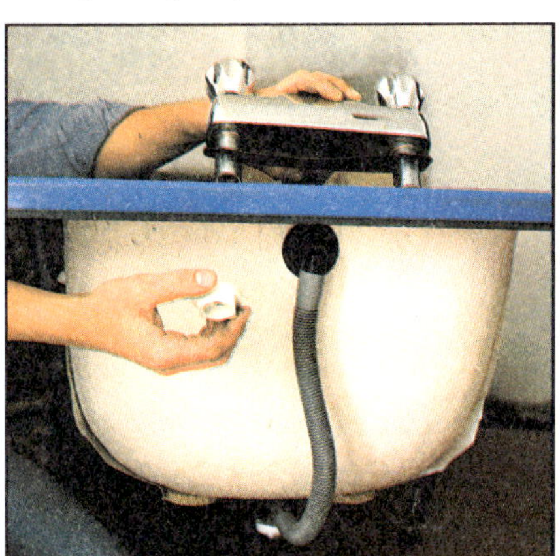

5 *Take the mixer and check that the rubber gasket is in position between the unit and the bath, and also that it is clean and free from bits of grit.*

6 *Screw the back-nuts up onto the trap and tighten them. Insert a flat plastic washer or top hat washer between the nut and the bath.*

Ready Reference

BATH TYPES

Most baths sold today have outside dimensions of about 1675mm (66in) long, 750mm (30in) wide, and 550mm (21in) high. Shorter baths are available for particularly small bathrooms and these are roughly 1525mm (60in) and 1375mm (54in) long. Other baths may be up to 1825mm (72in) long and 1100mm (43in) wide. They also come in different bottom mouldings to make them safe and often have handles to help the less active get in and out. Although most are basically rectangular inside and out some are oval-shaped and designed to fit into corners. There are also special baths for the disabled which are much shorter and formed in the shape of a seat.

Plain traditional rectangular

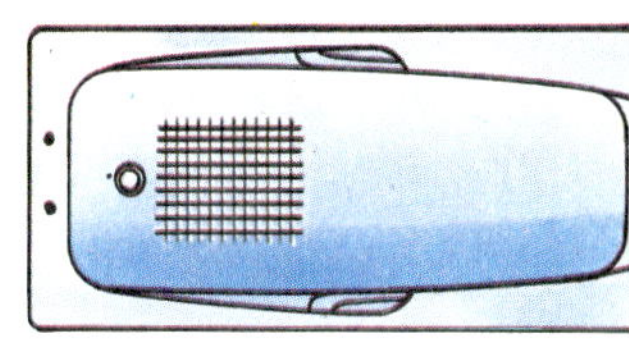

Off-rectangular with handles

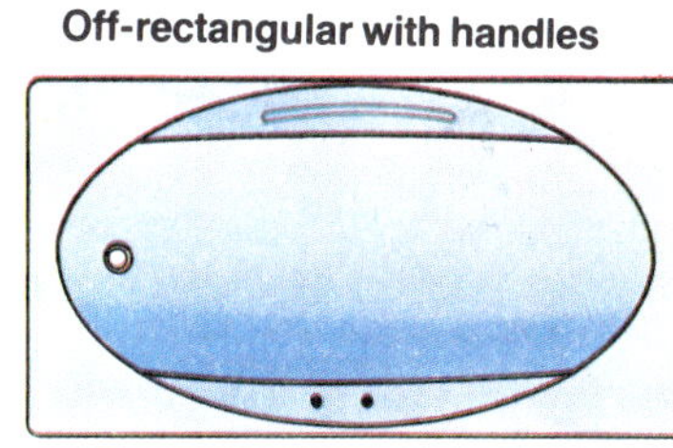

Large oval with side plumbing

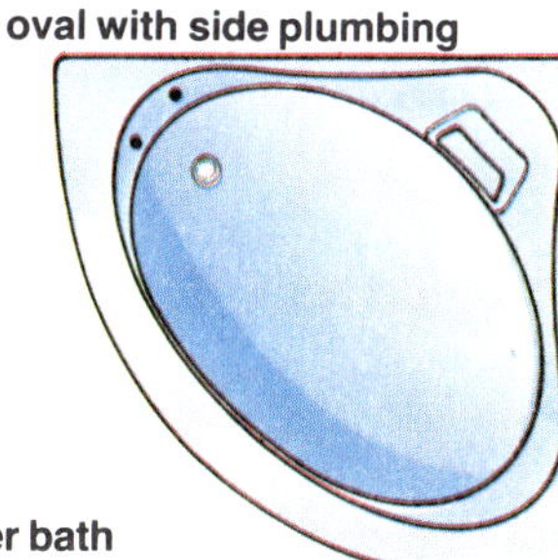

Corner bath

Disabled bath

INSTALLING THE NEW BATH

1 *If you have installed new pipework, you should attach inlet spurs to the taps before you have to install the bath in its final position.*

2 *Put the bath into position. You may want to stand it away from the wall at the front end so that you can build in a shelf. Connect the inlet pipes.*

3 *Fit the waste trap and attach it to the waste pipe. When all the pipework is connected up, turn on the water and check for leaks.*

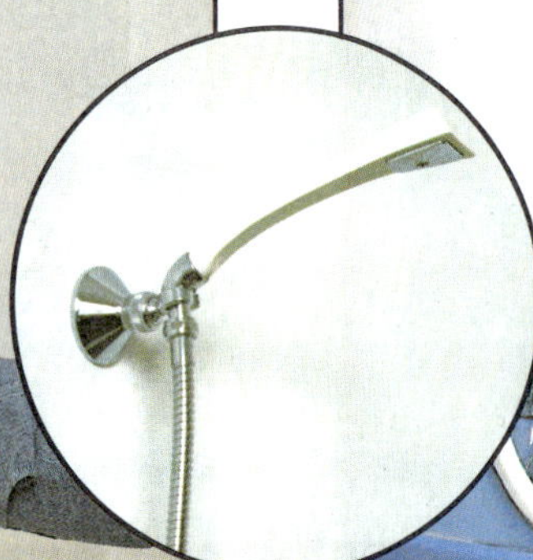

4 *When installing a mixer with a shower attachment, fix the shower head bracket to the wall and fit the shower head into the bracket (inset).*

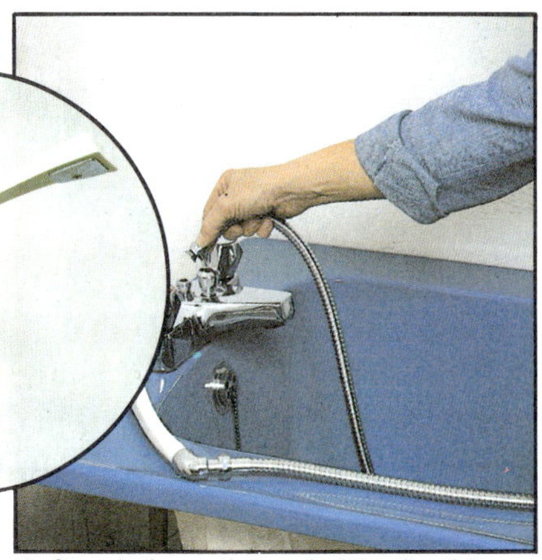

5 *Attach the outlet end of the flexible shower hose to central outlet on the mixer unit. It should plug in and click into position with a slight turn.*

6 *Check that the bath is level both lengthways and widthways with a spirit level. Adjust the screwed-on feet to get the level right.*

7 *Fix the bath panels in position by screwing them to the wooden carcase which surrounds the bath and is supplied by the manufacturer.*

8 *Screw the panels on carefully. They will usually be made of moulded high impact polystyrene which is easily chipped around the screw holes.*

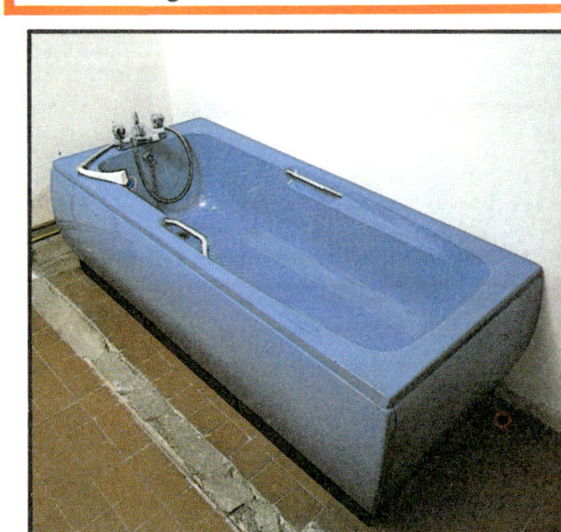

9 *When all the bath work is complete you will have to make good the décor. If possible tile around the bath and box in the pipework.*

INSTALLING A SHOWER

Showers have become a part of the modern home, whether fitted over the bath or in a separate cubicle. They save time, space and energy and are quite easy to install once the design is right.

It is possible for four or five members of a family to have showers in the same time – and with the same amount of hot water – that would be needed for just one of them to have a bath. Showers, if properly installed, are safer for use by the elderly and the very young than a sit-down bath and need less cleaning. They are also more hygienic to use than a bath, as the bather isn't sitting in his own soapy and dirty water, and can rinse thoroughly in fresh water.

Where a shower is provided in its own cubicle, as distinct from over a bath, it takes up very little extra space. One can be provided in any space which is at least 900mm (36in) square, and can be put in a variety of locations such as a bedroom, on a landing, in a lobby or even in the cupboard under the stairs.

Yet shower installation can all too often prove to be a disappointment. Poorly designed systems may provide only a trickle of water at the sprinkler, or may run icy cold until the cold tap is almost turned off, and will then run scalding hot.

So, although it is possible to provide a shower in virtually any household, it is important that you match the shower equipment and your existing hot and cold water systems. If you have a cylinder storage hot water system, which is by far the commonest kind of hot water supply to be found in British homes, a conventional shower connected to the household's hot and cold water supplies is likely to be the most satisfactory and the easiest to install. But the hot and cold water systems must comply with certain quite definite design requirements if the shower is to operate safely and satisfactorily.

Pressure

The most important requirement is that the hot and cold supply pipes to the shower must be under equal water pressure. With a cylinder storage hot water system, whether direct or indirect (described on pages 8–12), hot water pressure comes from the main cold water storage cistern supplying the cylinder with water. The cold water supply to the shower must therefore also come from this cistern (or perhaps from a separate cistern at the same level); it must not be taken direct from the cold water main. It is, in fact, illegal to mix, in any plumbing appliance, water which comes direct from the main and water coming from a storage cistern. However, quite apart from the question of legality, it is impossible to mix streams of water satisfactorily under such differing pressures. The shower will inevitably run either very hot or very cold, depending on which stream is the high-pressure one.

The cold water storage cistern must also be high enough above the shower sprinkler to provide a satisfactory operating pressure. Best results will be obtained if the base of the cold water storage cistern is 1.5m (5ft) or more above the sprinkler. However, provided that pipe runs are short and have only slight changes of direction, a reasonable shower can be obtained when the vertical distance between the base of the cistern and the shower sprinkler is as little as 1m (39in). The level of the hot water storage tank in relation to the shower doesn't matter in the least. It can be above, below or at the same level as the shower. It is the level of the cold water storage cistern that matters.

There is yet another design requirement for conventional shower installation which sometimes applies. This is that the cold water supply to the shower should be a separate 15mm (½in) branch direct from the cold water storage cistern, and not taken from the main bathroom distribution pipe. This is a safety precaution. If the cold supply were taken as a branch from a main distribution pipe, then flushing a lavatory cistern would reduce the pressure on the cold side of the shower causing it to run dangerously hot. For the same reason it is best for the hot supply to be taken direct from the vent pipe immediately above the hot water storage cylinder and not as a branch from another distribution pipe, though this is rather less important. A reduction in the hot water pressure would result in the shower running cold. This would be highly unpleasant, although not dangerous.

Mixers

Showers must have some kind of mixing valve to mix the streams of hot and cold water and thus to produce a shower at the required temperature. The two handles of the bath taps provide the very simplest mixing valve, and push-on shower attachments can be cheaply obtained. Opening the bath taps then mixes the two streams of water and diverts them upwards to a wall-hung shower rose. These very simple attachments work quite satisfactorily – provided that the design requirements already referred to are met. However, it isn't always easy to adjust the tap handles to provide water at exactly the temperature required.

A bath/shower mixer provides a slightly more sophisticated alternative operating on the same principle. With one of these, the tap handles are adjusted until water is flowing through the mixer spout into the bath at the required temperature. The water is then

CHOOSING THE RIGHT SHOWER TYPE

The type of shower you can install depends on the sort of water supply you have in your home. This chart will help you make the right selection.

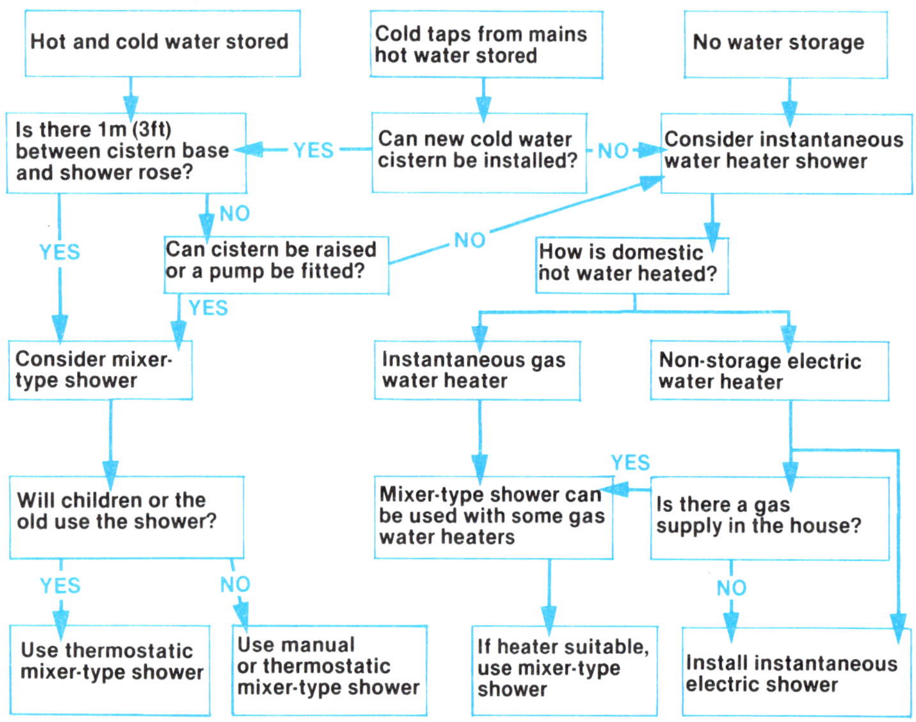

diverted up to the head by turning a valve.

Then there are manual shower mixers. These are standard equipment in independent shower cubicles and may also be used over a bath. With a manual mixer the hot and cold streams of water are mixed in a single valve. Temperature, and sometimes flow control, are obtained by turning large knurled control knobs.

Finally, there are thermostatic shower mixing valves. These may resemble manual mixers in appearance but are designed to accommodate small pressure fluctuations in either the hot or cold water supplies to the shower. They are thus very useful safety devices. But thermostatic valves cannot, even if it were legal, compensate for the very great difference of pressure between mains supply and a supply from a cold water storage cistern. Nor can they add pressure to either the hot or cold supply. If pressure falls on one side of the valve the thermostatic device will reduce flow on the other side to match it.

Thermostatic valves are more expensive but they eliminate the need to take an independent cold water supply pipe from the storage cistern to the shower and can possibly reduce the total cost of installation.

Where a shower is provided over an existing bath, steps must be taken to protect the bathroom floor from splashed water. A plastic shower curtain provides the cheapest means of doing this but a folding, glass shower screen has a much more attractive appearance and is more effective.

Electric showers

You can run your shower independently of the existing domestic hot water system by fitting an instantaneously heated electric one. There are a number of these on the market nowadays. They need only to be connected to the rising main and to a suitable source of electricity to provide an 'instant shower'. You'll find more information about these on pages 83–87.

Installing a bath/shower mixer

To install a shower above a bath, first disconnect the water supply, and drain the cistern (see pages 43–45). Remove the bath panel, if there is one, and disconnect the tap tails from the supply pipes. Then unscrew and remove the tap back-nuts and take the taps off.

You can now fix the new mixer in place (see pages 74–78). Finally, decide on the position for the shower spray bracket and fix it in place.

Ready Reference

WHY HAVE A SHOWER?

Showers have many advantages over baths:

- they are hygienic as you don't sit in dirty, soapy water and you get continually rinsed
- they are pleasant to use. Standing under jets of water can be immensely stimulating, especially first thing in the morning
- they use a lot less water per 'wash' than a bath, which saves energy and is also an advantage where water softeners are in use
- economy of hot water usage means that at peak traffic times there is more water to go round
- showers take less time, they don't have to be 'run', and users can't lay back and bask, monopolizing the bathroom
- easy temperature adjustment of a shower gives greater comfort for the user and lessens the risk of catching cold in a cold bathroom.

SHOWER LOCATION

You don't have to install a shower over a bath or even in the bathroom. A bedroom is one alternative site, but landings and utility rooms are another possibility. Provided a supply of water is available, the pressure head satisfactory, and the disposal of waste water possible, a shower can provide a compact and very useful house improvement in many parts of the home.

In a bathroom a shower will usually go over a bath, which is the easiest and most popular position. In a larger bathroom a cubicle is a good idea.

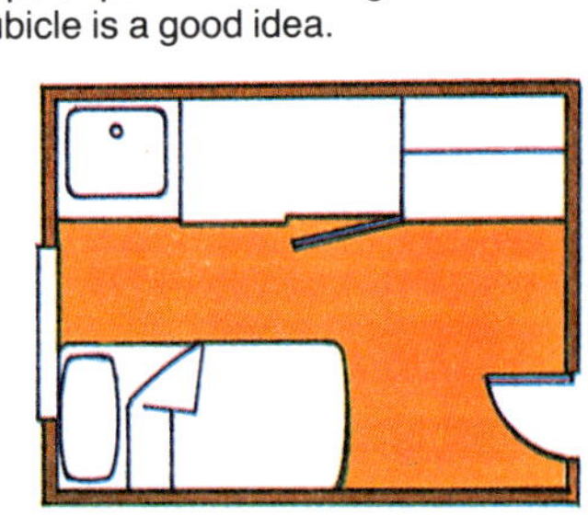

In a bedroom a shower can be easily fitted at the end of built-in wardrobes.

HOW TO ADAPT YOUR SYSTEM

1

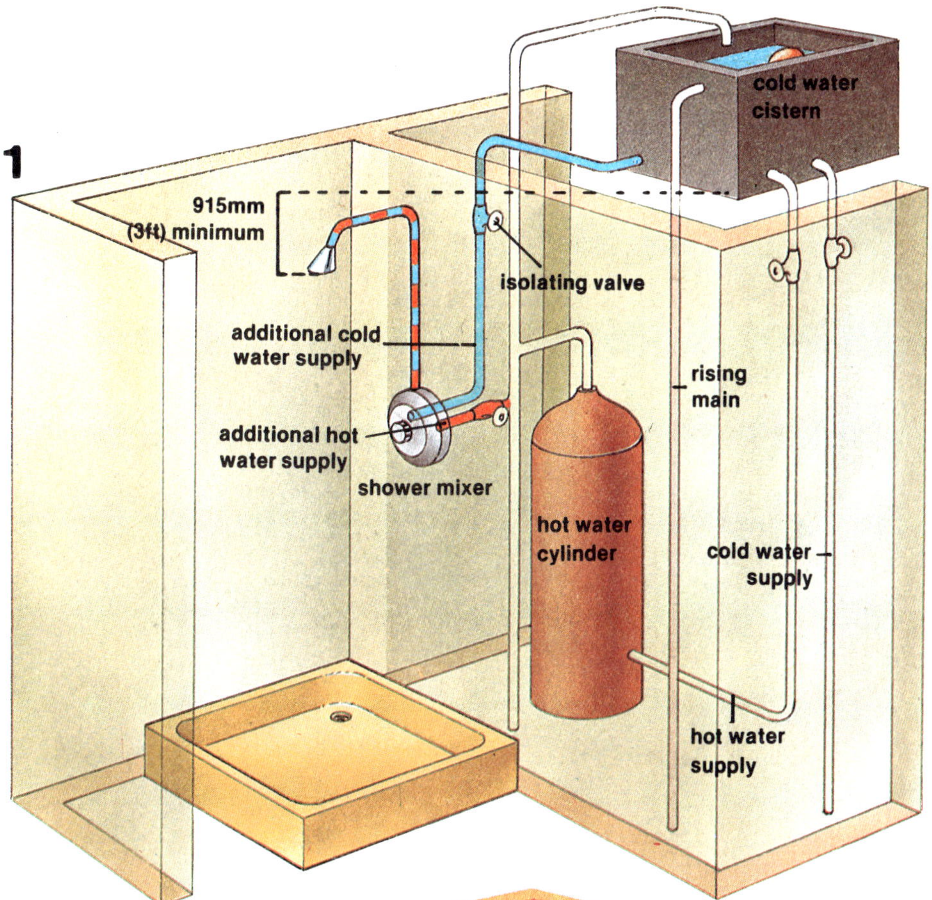

1 : Just add pipework

◁ *The most common domestic plumbing system has a cold water cistern in the loft which feeds a hot water tank. In this case you must check that the vertical distance from the bottom of the cold cistern to the shower outlet head is at least 915mm (3ft). To install a shower you must take a 15mm cold water supply direct from the cistern to the cold inlet of the mixer, and a 15mm (1/2in) hot water supply from the draw-off pipe, which emerges from the hot water tank, to the hot water inlet of the mixer.*

2 : Raise the cistern

▷ *In many older houses the cold water cistern may be in the airing cupboard immediately above the hot water tank, or in another position but still beneath ceiling height. This will usually mean that there is insufficient pressure for a mixer-type shower on the same floor. To get round this problem the cistern can be raised into the loft by extending the pipework upwards. Moving an old galvanised cistern will be rather arduous so this is a good opportunity to replace it with a modern plastic one, (see pages 156 to 159).*

3

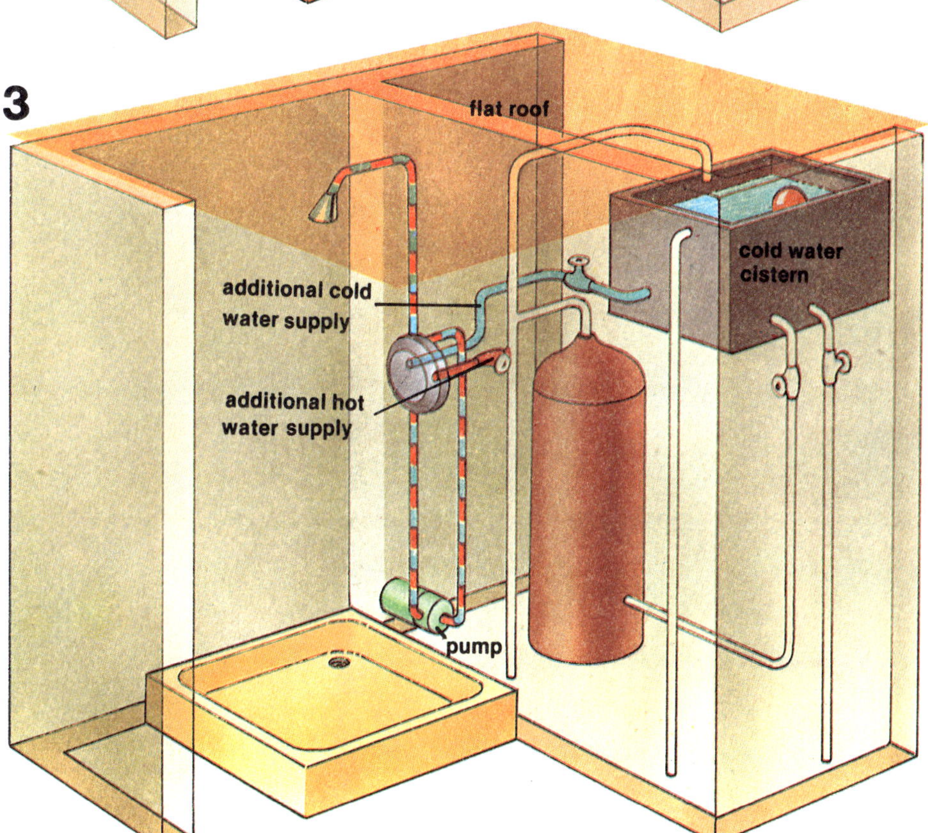

3 : Install a pump

◁ *In some homes which have flat roofs it is impossible to raise the cistern indoors to provide a sufficient pressure head for a shower on the same floor. While you could consider putting the cistern on top of the roof this would involve providing extensive insulation and is an unsatisfactory solution. Pump-assisted mixer showers are available which will artificially increase the pressure head when the shower is turned on and these are fairly simple to install. As they are electrically operated they should be situated outside the bathroom area.*

4 : Add a new cistern

▷ *Many modern houses have combination hot and cold water storage units which are supplied and installed as one unit. They have a disadvantage in that cold water capacity is about one-third of the hot water cylinder and would provide an insufficient supply for a shower. This problem can be overcome by installing a pump and a supplementary cold water storage cistern. To ensure similar hot and cold pressures at the shower the supplementary cistern must be at a comparable level with the combination unit's cold water storage.*

2

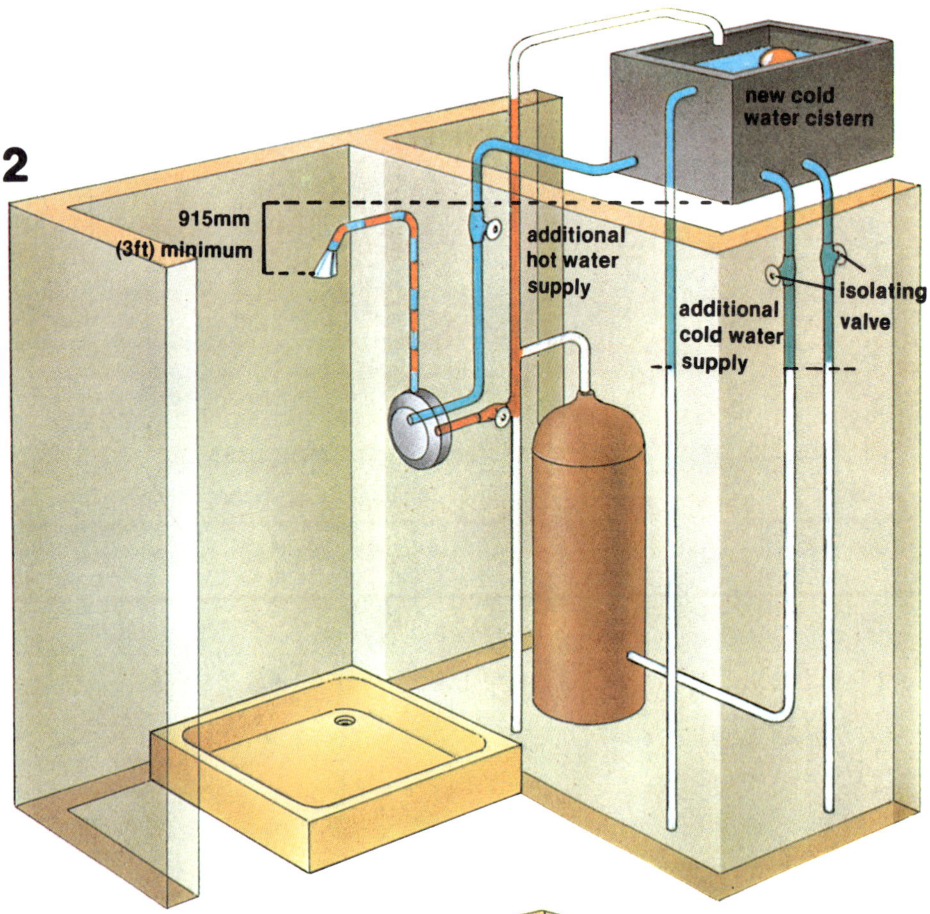

4

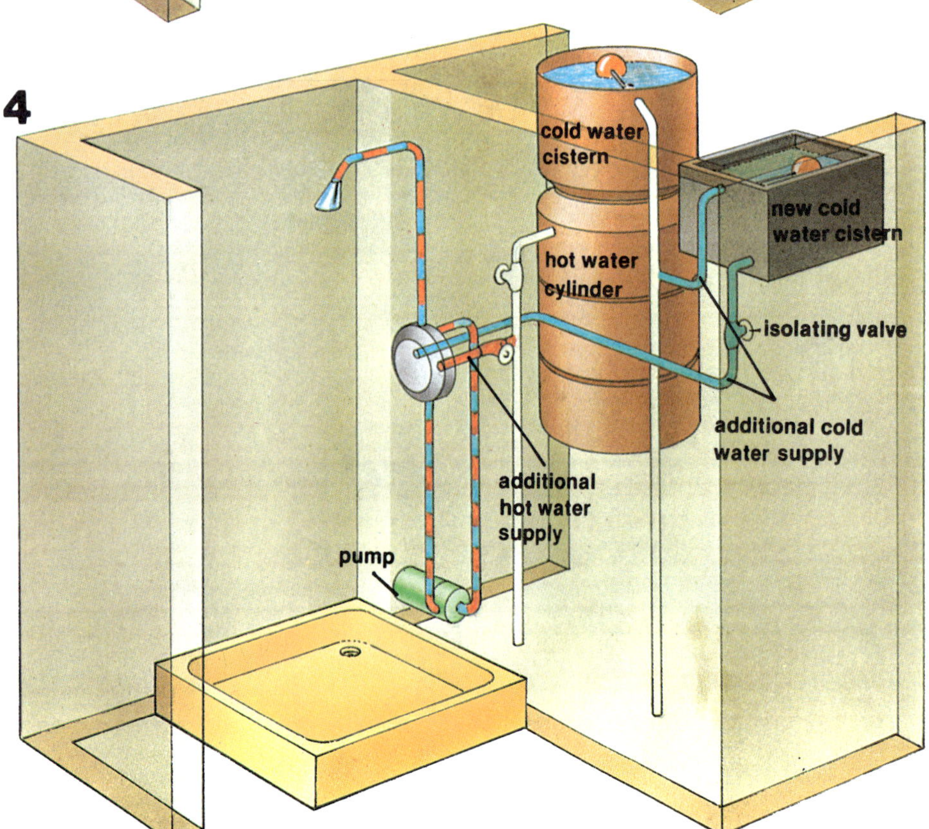

Ready Reference

TYPES OF SHOWER

There are two basic types of shower:

- those attached to a mixer on a bath
- those independent of the bath, discharging over their own bases, in their own cubicles.

Bath showers may be attached to a mixer head on which you have to adjust both taps, or they may simply fit over the tap outlets. The shower head in either case is detachable and may be mounted at whatever height you require.

Independent showers have fixed position heads or are adjustable. They may have a single control mixer, or a dual control which means that you can adjust the flow as well as the temperature. Thermostatic mixing valves are also available which can cope with small pressure fluctuations in the hot and cold water supply. These only reduce pressure on one side of the valve if that on the other side falls; they cannot increase the pressure unless they have already decreased it.

bath/shower mixer

single control mixer

dual control mixer with fixed head

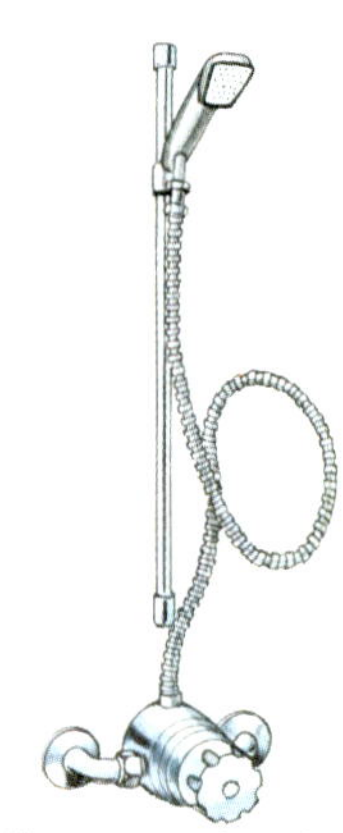

thermostatic mixer with adjustable head

PLUMBING IN AN ELECTRIC SHOWER

If you would like to install a shower but think you can't because there's insufficient water pressure, you might like to consider an instantaneous electric shower. It's connected directly to the mains cold water supply, so you are guaranteed a good jet of water. And as you heat only the water you use, it's very economical to run.

Until quite recently a properly functioning shower was all but an impossibility in many homes. Either it lacked the cylinder storage hot water system needed to supply a conventional shower, or the system that existed wouldn't permit a successful shower installation. For example, the main cold water storage cistern might have had insufficient capacity to supply the cold side of the shower mixer as well as feeding the hot water storage cylinder, or it may have been situated at too low a level to give adequate pressure at the shower rose. (For more information about the theory of shower design see previous section.)

The increasing popularity of showers has led to two new developments: the electric shower pump which increases pressure at the shower rose where this is inadequate; and the instantaneous electric shower.

Going back to geysers

There is nothing particularly new about appliances which heat water 'instantaneously' as it flows through them. The Edwardian geyser, installed over the bath in many a turn-of-the century middle-class home, was an early example. The modern single-point or multi-point instantaneous gas water heater – which can provide hot water for the whole house – is its direct descendant. Instantaneous water heaters were designed for connection directly to the rising main so they could operate under mains pressure. They needed no cold water storage cistern or storage cylinder and they had the advantage that heat energy was expended only to heat water that was actually to be used at that time.

However, until a couple of decades ago, the only instantaneous water heating appliances that were available were – like the early geysers – gas-operated. It just wasn't possible to devise an electric appliance that could 'instantaneously' heat a sufficiently large volume of water to fill a sit-down bath, a sink or even a wash basin. It still isn't. But manufacturers have now produced electric water heaters powerful enough to provide a steady flow of hot water for spray hand-washing over a washbasin in a WC compartment and for the provision of a shower. In neither case is very hot water needed in large volumes.

An instantaneous electric water heater is a relatively compact appliance that needs only to be connected – by means of a 15mm (½in) branch water supply pipe – to the main supply, and to a suitable supply of electricity. It is normally operated by a flow-switch which ensures that electricity is switched on only when water is flowing through the appliance. As it does so, it passes over powerful electrical heating elements.

Temperature control was originally obtained solely by controlling the volume of water flowing through the heater. Opening up the tap or control valve produced a heavy flow of cool water. As the control valve was closed down and the flow diminished, warmer and warmer water was obtained from the shower spray.

The crude, early models were something of a disaster and were frowned on by water authorities and electricity boards. They rarely provided a satisfactory shower. The flow was markedly less than that from a conventional, cylinder-supplied shower. Flushing the WC or opening up any other tap in the house would reduce the pressure of the water entering the heater, so reducing the flow and raising the water temperature from the shower spray. Such unpredictable temperature changes could cause serious scalding to an unsuspecting user. Other problems arose from the hard water scale that tended to form on the heating elements.

Instantaneous showers today

However, an unhappy experience a decade or so ago with one of the early instantaneous electric showers need not deter you from having a modern one installed today. There have been some tremendous advances in design and construction and you can be confident that a modern model will work

WHAT'S INSIDE THE CASING

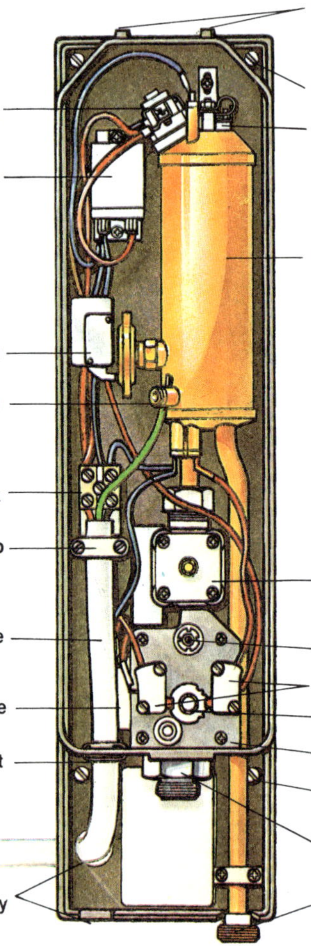

properly provided that it is properly installed according to the manufacturer's instructions.

Most instantaneous showers must be supplied with water at a minimum pressure of 1.05kg per sq cm (15lb per sq in). They are intended for connection direct to the mains supply, though they can be supplied by a cistern if it is at least 10.75m (35ft) above the level of the shower spray. In most cases mains water pressure will be adequate, but those who live in an area where mains pressure is low should check the actual pressure with their local water authority before incurring the expense of installation.

Modern electric showers usually have an electrical loading of 6kW to 7kW and it is often possible, for the sake of economy, to switch to a low setting of 3kW or 4kW during the summer months. Choose a model that incorporates a temperature stabiliser. This is an anti-scald device that maintains the water temperature at the level chosen by the user of the shower, despite any fluctuations in pressure which may result from water being drawn off from taps or by flushing the W.C. Should there be a drop in pressure beyond the capacity of the stabiliser, a safety sensor turns the shower off completely.

When choosing your instantaneous electric shower, look for evidence that it has been approved by such national safety committees as the B.E.A.B., the National Water Council and the A.N.T. (Assessment of Techniques) Committee of the Institute of Electrical Engineers.

Fitting a shower

Although instantaneous electric showers can be fitted over a sit-down bath, they are usually installed in a separate shower cubicle which may be in a bathroom, in a bedroom or even on a landing. The shower tray must have a trapped outlet and the branch waste pipe can discharge by the same route as basin or bath wastes.

Plumbing connections should be straightforward. It's best to connect the supply pipe to the shower heater first and then work backwards to the main supply, making this connection last of all. In this way you will interrupt the supply to the rest of the house as little as possible.

The connection to the shower may be a simple compression coupling (described on pages 14–18) or it may have a screwed male thread. In which case you'll need a compression fitting with a coupling at one end and a female screwed connector at the other. To connect into the rising main you should use a compression tee (as described on pages 22–26).

Obtaining the power

Instantaneous showers get their power from a separate radial circuit taken from the consumer unit. As most models of shower have a loading of either 6 or 7kW they can be supplied safely by a circuit that has a current rating of 30A and is run in $6mm^2$ two-core and earth cable. Recently, however, an 8kW shower has been introduced on the market by some manufacturers. This shouldn't pose extra problems for anyone intending to install it: provided the radial circuit originates at either a cartridge fuse or MCB – which both have the effect of uprating the circuit by one third – then a 30A circuit will be adequate. Should you decide to install one of these larger showers then it's still probably a good idea to check their requirements with the makers beforehand.

Showers should be controlled by a 30A double-pole cord-operated switch. From this a length of $6mm^2$ two-core and earth cable will run to the shower unit. There is one type that requires a slightly different method of connecting up. If you're going to fit a shower that has a control unit already connected to a length of three-core flex then you'll have to fix a flex outlet unit on the wall near the shower unit so you can connect the flex into the circuit.

Fitting the switch

Ceiling switches can either be surface or flush mounted. If you're going to surface mount one, you'll have to pierce a hole in the ceiling so the cables can be drawn through into a plastic mounting box. Before fixing this in position with No 8 wood screws, you should knock a thin section of plastic from the base to align with the hole in the ceiling. Ideally the box should be fitted against a joist, but if there isn't one suitably placed, you'll have to fix a support batten between the joists made from 75 x 25mm (3 x 1in) timber with a hole drilled in it big enough to let two lengths of

INSTALLING THE SHOWER UNIT

1 First take the shower spray support assembly and fix it to the wall. It is important to follow the manufacturer's recommendations as to height.

2 Remove the control knobs and any other fittings from the shower unit to enable the faceplate to be taken off before further installation takes place.

3 Carefully position the unit on the shower cubicle wall and mark the screw fitting holes, water and power channels; drill out the fixing holes.

TIP

4 Using a hole saw attachment for your drill, cut holes in the cubicle wall for the water and power supplies, then fix the unit to the wall.

5 Make a tee junction with the main, and run a length of pipe to the water access; then add an elbow and length of pipe to go through the wall.

6 Use a swivel tap connector to attach the cold water feed to the unit; this is linked to the inlet pipe by a soldered capillary joint.

7 Make sure the fibre washer in the connector is in place; then screw it up and tighten. Don't use any sealant on the nylon inlet.

8 Attach the shower hose to the screwed outlet, making sure that the rubber washer is in place. Then make the electrical connections (page 118).

9 Turn on the water supply and also the electricity to make sure that the unit works. Finally, replace the cover and control knobs.

6mm^2 cable pass through. When you're feeding the cables into the mounting box, it's a good idea to write 'mains' on the end of the circuit cable and 'shower' on the end of the shower feed cable. This could be surface mounted on the ceiling and wall, but it's neater to conceal it in the ceiling void and chase it into the wall, running it in plastic conduit.

You can now strip back the insulation and make the connections. The mains cable should go to the 'supply' side of the switch, with the red core going to the terminal marked L and the black to the one marked N, and the shower cable to the equivalent terminals on the 'load' side. Remember to sleeve the earth cores in green/yellow PVC and connect them to the earth terminal in the switch. Place the six cores neatly in the box and screw the switch to it.

If you're going to flush-mount the switch you'll have to mark the size of the mounting box on the ceiling and, using a pad saw, carefully cut out an equivalent size hole. Then cut a piece of timber to fit between the joists, lay it across the hole and mark the square on it. Knock out a blank from the base of the metal box and drill a hole in the corresponding spot in the timber. Then screw the box to the timber and fix the timber to the joists at a height above the ceiling that allows the box edge to sit flush with the ceiling surface. This can be checked by holding a straight edge across the hole in the ceiling. You should then thread in the two marked cables and make the connections. If you want to fix the switch at a point where there is a joist you can always cut away a section of it. This is best done by using a drill fitted with a 25mm (1in) wood bit to remove most of the wood and then chiselling the remainder away. That way you won't need access to the ceiling void as long as you can 'fish' the cable across the ceiling using a length of stiff wire.

Connecting into the shower

The cable to the shower can be run down the wall on the surface, using plastic cable clips or mini-trunking, or buried in a chase chopped in the plaster. The cover of the control unit must be removed to allow you access to the terminal block, but do read fully the manufacturer's instructions before going any further. Thread in the cable and strip off some of the sheathing and insulation before connecting the red core to the L terminal and the black to the N terminal. Before connecting the earth core to the earth terminal make sure you've sleeved it in green/yellow PVC. If the unit has a cable clamp, fix the cable in it, double checking that it's the whole, sheathed cable that is held by it and not just individual cores. This is very important as it serves to protect the connections. Finally, refit the unit cover, finish off the radial circuit connections at the consumer unit, switch on at the mains and test the shower.

CONNECTING THE POWER

1 *After fixing the shower unit to the bathroom wall and making the connection from the rising main, thread in the circuit cable.*

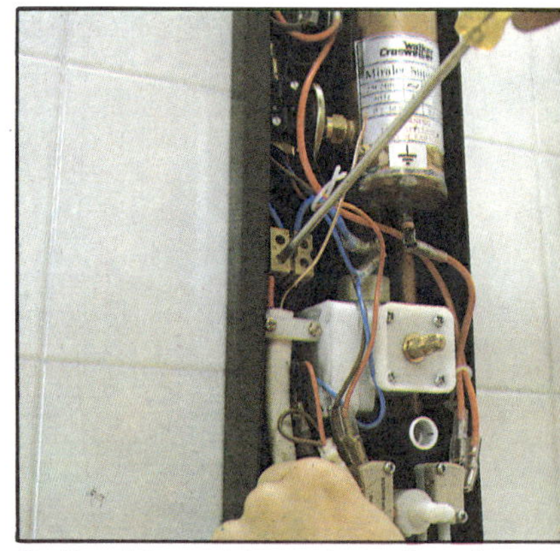

2 *Feed the cable up the unit and strip it before connecting the red and black cores to the L and N terminals respectively.*

3 *Remember to sleeve the bare earth core in green/yellow PVC before feeding it into the earth terminal and connecting it up.*

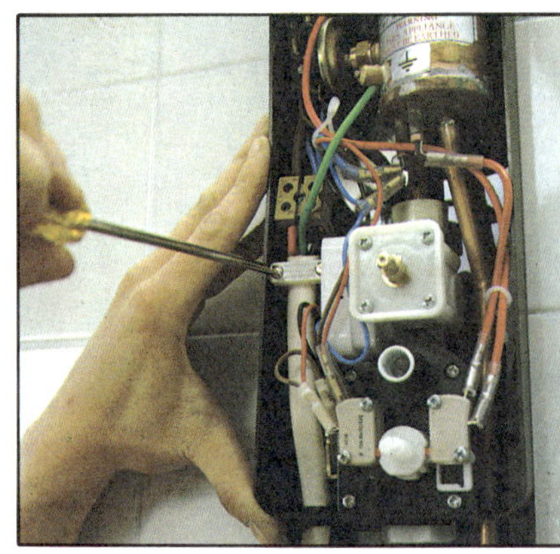

4 *Then make sure that the clamp plate will bear down on the cable sheathing before tightening it up to protect all the connections.*

Fitting a flex outlet plate

You'll have to use a flex outlet plate only if there is already a flex connected to the shower unit. This can be fitted on either a one-gang moulded plastic box for surface mounting, or else in a 35mm (1½in) metal box for flush mounting, in which case you'll have to chop a hole. After fixing one or other of the boxes to the wall, run the cable into it through a knockout hole, which, in the case of the metal box, should be fitted with a grommet. The unit has three banks of terminals with two terminal screws per bank and you should connect the green/yellow sleeved earth core to a terminal of the non-shielded bank marked 'E'. Then connect the red insulated core to a terminal of one of the shielded banks and the black to a terminal of the other bank.

Prepare the end of the flex by stripping off approximately 12mm (½in) of insulation from the end of each core. Remember to thread the flex through the hole in the unit's cover before you connect the flex to the unit as you won't be able to fit it after you've made the connections. Then connect the earth core, which should be already sleeved in green and yellow PVC, to the other terminal in the 'E' bank, the brown core to the bank containing the red core and the blue core to the bank containing the black circuit core. Tighten the cord clamp, again making sure that it's the flex sheath that it grips and not the unsheathed cores as this protects the connections. Lay the six cores neatly in the box and fix the unit to the box with the two screws supplied. You can then switch on the power and test the shower.

THE ELECTRICAL CONNECTIONS

Providing and controlling the power to an instantaneous shower is straightforward and making the connections is quite simple.

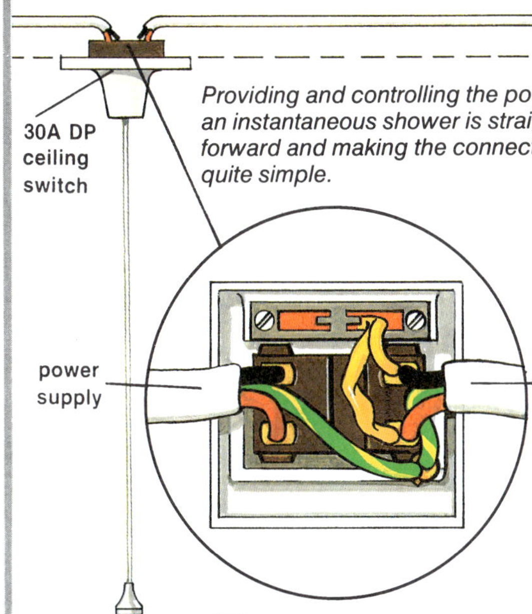

1 The ceiling switch: *feed in the two cables and mark the power supply cable 'mains' and the shower cable 'shower'. Connect the cores of the power cable to the terminals on the supply side and the shower cable to the load side of the switch.*

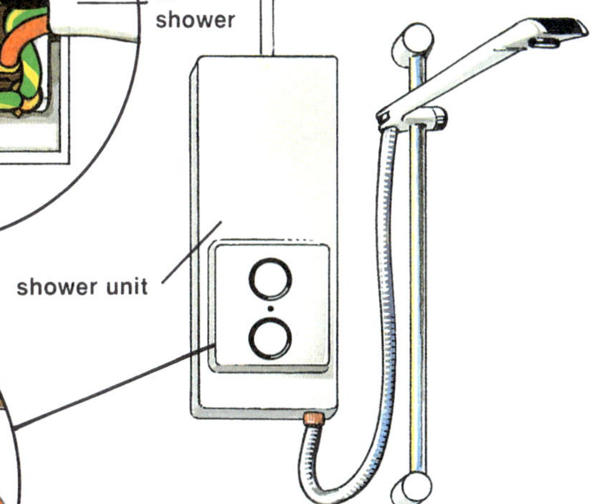

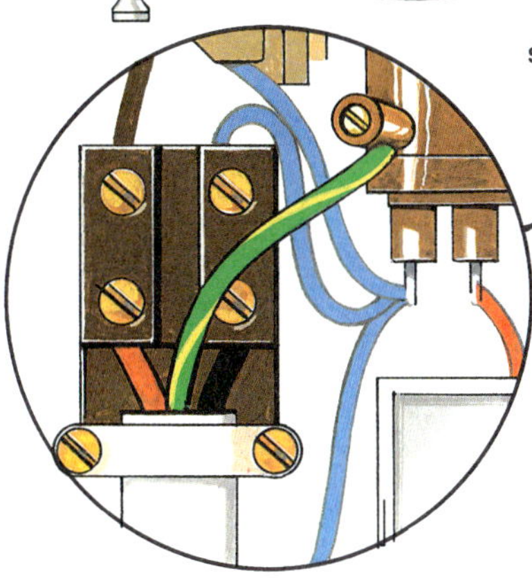

2 The terminal block: *feed the cable under the clamp and connect the red core to L, the black core to N and the green/yellow PVC sleeved earth core to the earth screw on the heater tank. Make sure you tighten the clamp on the cable and not individual cores.*

FITTING A CEILING SWITCH

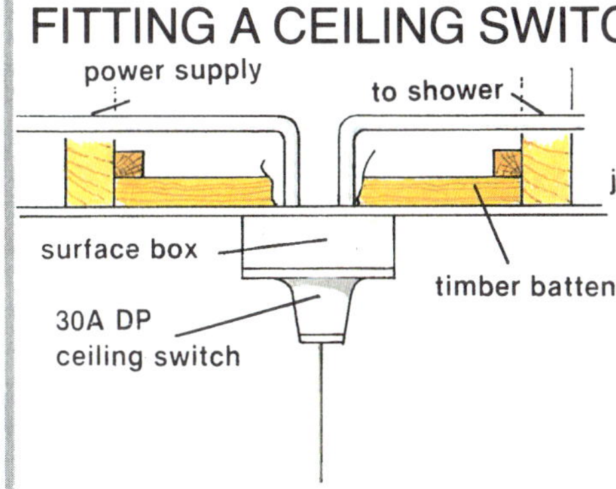

Surface mounted: *try to mount the switch on a joist. If you can't, fit a timber batten. Drill holes in the batten and ceiling to admit the cables and remove a knockout from the base of the box. Fix the box to the ceiling and make the connections.*

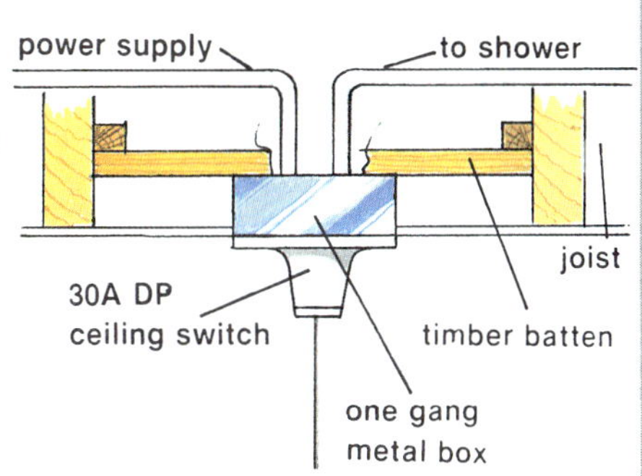

Flush mounted: *use a pad saw to cut a hole in the ceiling for the mounting box. Fix the box to a batten between the joists and set the batten so the box is flush with the ceiling. Feed the cables through and make the connections.*

Ready Reference

PLUMBING REQUIREMENTS

The shower unit should be connected directly to the cold water mains supply. If this isn't possible, a storage tank may be used to supply the unit; but it must be about 10.75m (35ft) above the shower spray head.

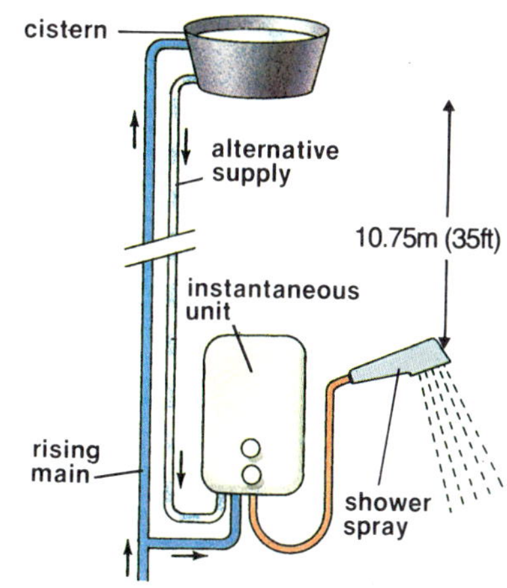

USING THE SHOWER

After turning on the unit, you'll have to wait a short while so the water retained in the heater tank and shower fittings from the last shower is drawn off. The water temperature is controlled by the rate of flow through the heater – the slower the flow rate, the higher the temperature, and vice versa. Because the cold water supply is likely to be comparatively colder in the winter than in summer, this means in winter you may have to put up with a slower flow rate in order to get the required temperature.

ELECTRICAL CONNECTION

When you're wiring up an instantaneous shower, you must ensure that:

- it is permanently connected to its own separate 30A power supply, and is properly earthed
- it is controlled by a 30A double-pole cord-operated switch mounted on the ceiling. An ordinary ceiling light switch is not suitable.

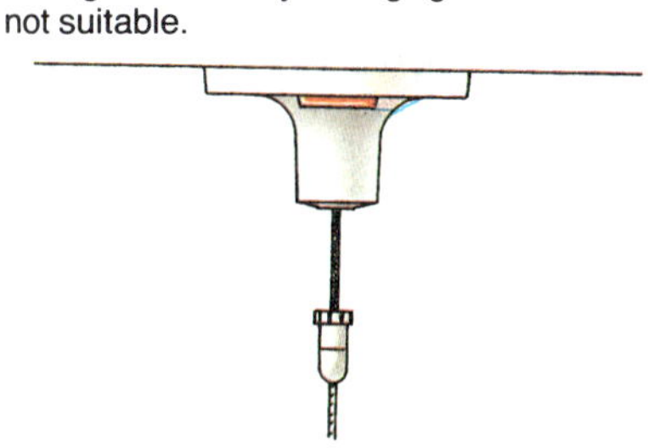

NEVER turn on the electricity supply until all the plumbing has been completed, including mounting the handset and hose, and the power supply and earthing connections are made.

CONNECTING SHOWER FITTINGS

Before you get to grips with installing a new shower cubicle, you ought to select the type of control fitting you're going to use. Your choice may affect the way you organise the plumbing.

Once you've decided where you're going to site your shower – over a bath or in a separate cubicle – you'll have to determine what type of fitting you're going to use to run it. In order for the shower to work effectively, you need to be able to control the rate of flow of water and also, more importantly, it's temperature. There's nothing worse than standing under a stuttering supply of water that's hot one minute and cold the next. So it's the job of the shower fitting to provide this control fast and effectively.

Some fittings work by having individual taps to control the hot and cold water supplies, while the more sophisticated types have a simple valve or a mixer. How they are connected up to the water supply depends primarily on their design. For example, instantaneous showers (see the previous section) need only to be connected to the mains cold water supply, as they heat all the hot water required just before it comes out of the shower rose. A hot water supply is therefore unnecessary. But for all other showers, the temperature of the water is controlled by mixing together separate supplies of hot and cold water which may also be at different pressures.

The simplest fittings

Before proper showers over a bath and separate shower cubicles became popular, it was quite common to find a rather make-shift device being used to supply a spray of water. This consisted of a length of rubber hose with a rose attached at one end and two connectors fitted at the other which slipped over the hot and cold taps on the bath. By adjusting these taps you could regulate the flow and temperature of the water. In fact the principle of this very basic mixing valve was used in early shower cubicles. Gate valves on the hot and cold distribution pipes were used to control the flow, and the two supplies were mixed at a 'tee' in the pipework before being fed in a single pipe to an overhead shower rose.

Mixer taps

An improvement on this very simple arrangement, as far as showers over baths are concerned, is the bath/shower mixer. This resembles an ordinary mixer tap on a bath, except that a flexible metal hose rises from the centre of the mixer to a spray head which can be fixed at varying heights on the wall above the bath. Again the water is mixed by adjusting the hot and cold taps, and at this stage it will be coming out of the spout of the tap. When the required temperature has been reached you pull up a lever on the body of the tap and this diverts the water upwards to the spray head.

Nowadays, showers in cubicles normally have what's known as a manual mixing valve. This has two inlets, one for the hot and another for the cold supply; but the temperature is regulated by turning just one mixer knob. The flow may also be adjusted by turning another knob which is set round the outside of the temperature control. In this way you can control the water more quickly and positively than you could do if you had to adjust two separate taps (which tends to be a bit of a juggling act).

Shower mixers are constantly being improved so that they are more convenient and safer to use. With one modern manual mixing valve, for example, the temperature of the water is controlled by turning a knurled knob, not unlike the handle of a tap. And the flow and on/off control is worked by pushing in or pulling out this knob. You can therefore control the flow and temperature of the water in one movement. Another advantage of this kind of control is that the shower can be stopped instantly if the pressure on the cold side falls (as a result of a toilet being flushed or cold water being drawn off elsewhere in the house, for example). If this happened the shower would suddenly run very hot, but by flicking the control knob downwards the flow ceases. It's not so serious if the pressure falls on the hot side, because the shower would just run cold. But again, to prevent discomfort the flow can be stopped quickly by flicking the control knob.

However, prevention is better than cure and there are ways of organising the plumbing so that this problem can't arise. To alleviate the danger it's best to run the 15mm (½in) cold water supply pipe to the shower direct from the cold water storage cistern and not as a branch from the 22mm (¾in) distribution pipe to the bathroom. This will supply a continuous volume of cold water provided the cistern is working properly.

Thermostatic valves

Of course it may mean too much of an upheaval to lay in a new pipe run, but instead you could install a special thermostatic mixing valve. This enables you to pre-set the temperature of the shower water and this will remain constant despite fluctuations of pressure in the hot and cold supplies. And apart from this, thermostatic mixers provide

INSTALLING A FIXED ROSE

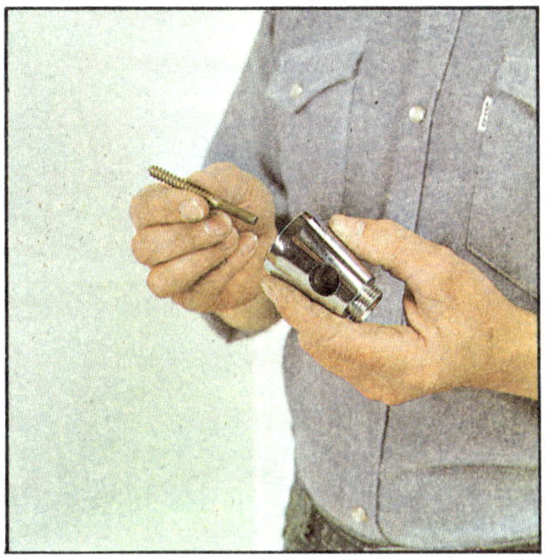

1 *To mount the wall fixing, thread one end of the double-ended screw supplied into the hole in the base of the casting.*

2 *With the flange in place, screw the fitting into the shower wall using a pre-drilled fixing hole. The inlet hole must point downwards.*

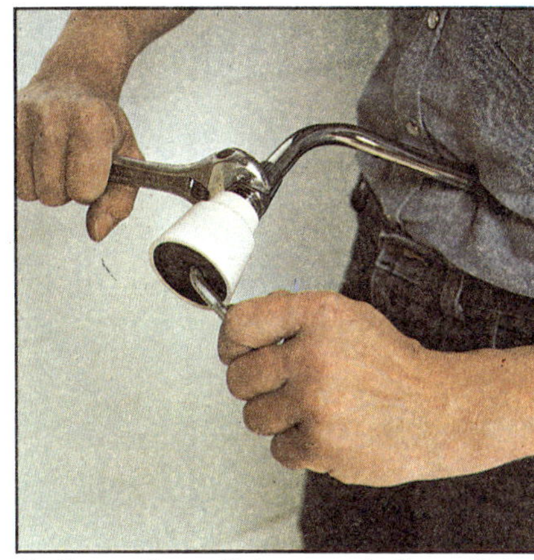

3 *Screw the outlet rose onto the outlet pipe by removing the rose and inserting an Allen key into the recess you will find inside.*

4 *Attach the outlet fitting to the wall fixing, by tightening the fixing nut on the rose so it crushes the olive. But don't chip the chrome.*

5 *Make sure that the outlet rose swivels firmly but freely on its ball bearing, and that it emerges at right angles to the wall.*

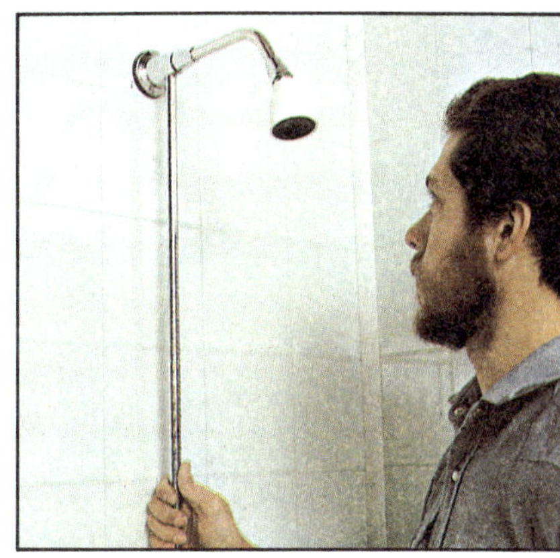

6 *Screw the supply pipe into the outlet supply until it is tight against the washer, and check that it is truly vertical.*

7 *Attach the supply pipe to the thermostatic control unit and mark the position of the supply pipe holes on the shower wall.*

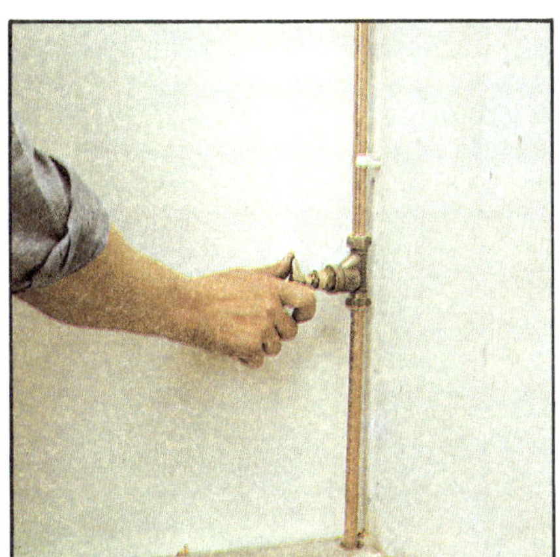

8 *Turn off the water supplies via stop-valves, if fitted, and tee off the supply pipes to feed the hot and cold inlets of the shower mixer.*

9 *Drill holes in the shower wall so that the supply pipes can be fed through from behind and connected up to the shower mixer.*

INSTALLING AN ADJUSTABLE ROSE

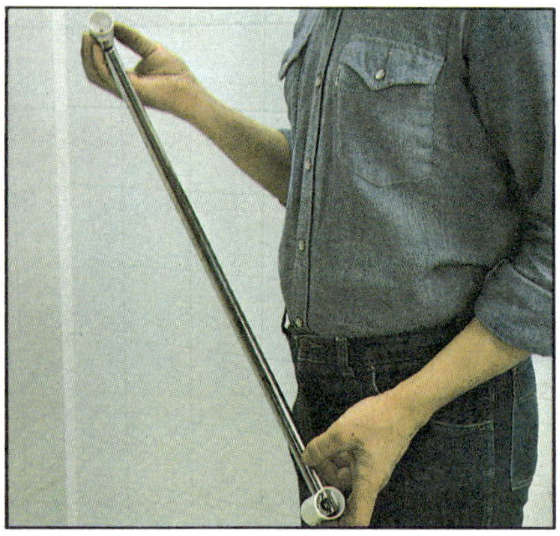

1 Fit the two wall fixing brackets to the end of the runner, and align them both so that they are pointing in the same direction.

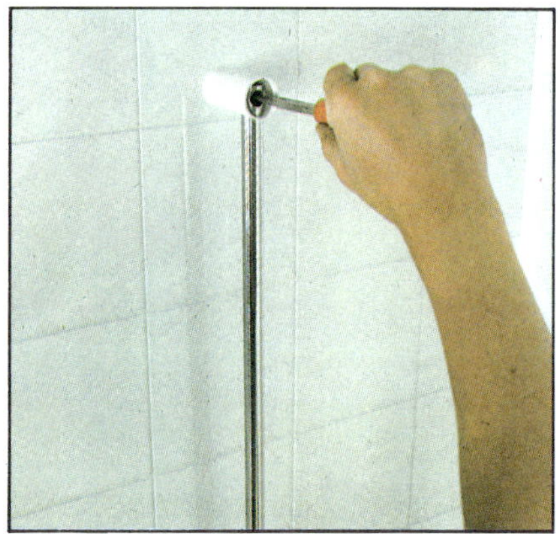

2 Mark the positions for the fixing screws on the shower wall, drill the holes and then proceed to screw on the uppermost bracket.

3 Slide on the movable rose support and fix the lower bracket to the wall. Cover the screw entry holes with plastic caps.

4 Take the one-piece shower head and rose and screw on the flexible hose, making sure that the fibre washer is correctly placed.

5 Hold the wall supply point fixing in place and mark the wall for drilling. Drill the hole, making sure you don't damage the tiled surround.

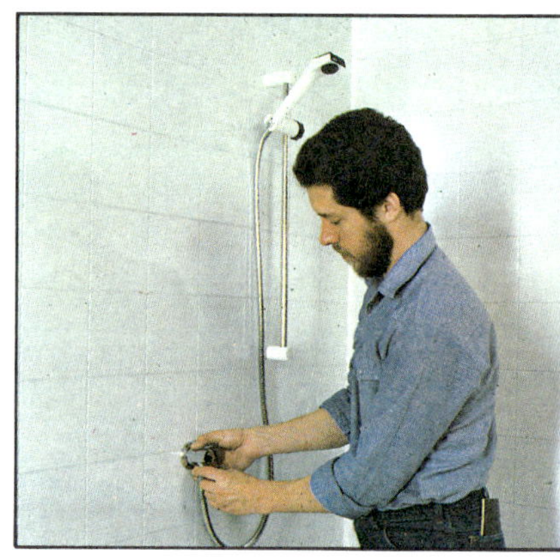

6 Insert the fixing and screw it up tight. Then take your chosen mixer, drill its fixing holes and plumb in the supply pipes.

just that extra margin of safety and assurance against discomfort.

Before buying a thermostatic mixing valve, it's important that you recognise its limitations as well as its advantages. These valves can deal with relatively minor fluctuations in pressure that can result from water being drawn off from one or other of the supply pipes. They can't accommodate the great differences in pressure between a hot water supply under pressure from a storage cylinder and a cold supply taken direct from the main (in any case, you should never arrange your shower plumbing in this way). Some thermostatic valves even require a greater working 'hydraulic head' (the vertical distance between the cold water cistern and the shower rose) than the 1m (3ft) minimum that is usual for manual mixers. So it's a good idea to check on these points and on the 'head' available before you buy one of them.

Shower pumps

An inadequate 'head' is, of course, one of the commonest reasons why a shower won't work properly. Although the minimum distance between the base of the cold water cistern and the shower rose must be 1m (3ft), for best results this distance ought to be 1.5m (5ft) or more.

However, all is not lost if you can't get this head because you can install a shower pump. They're expensive but they can make the difference between a stimulating shower and a miserable, low-pressure trickle, which isn't much good to anyone.

Different types of pump are controlled in different ways. Some have manual switches which are controlled by a pull-cord. In this case the pump is only switched on after the water has begun to flow, and is turned off before it has been stopped. Other pumps are operated automatically when the water is turned on at the shower by the movement of water in the pipes.

You can install a simple pump between the mixer and the shower rose outlet, but you may find it difficult to conceal. On the other hand, automatic pumps must be connected into the water supply before it reaches the mixer, so it's easier to choose a convenient site where the pump can be hidden from view or disguised.

Shower pumps need quite a lot of plumbing in, and if you're not careful about planning you may end up with a lot of exposed pipework. It's also worth remembering that when you wire up the electricity supply you have to connect the pump to a fused connection unit with a double-pole switch. And if the pump is situated inside the bathroom it must be protected from steam and water (except in the case of units specially designed to be inside the shower cubicle).

THREE TYPES OF SHOWER

There are several types of shower mixer available on the market. They fall into two types – those which simply mix the hot and cold flows, and those which make an effort to provide the mixed flows at a constant, pre-set, temperature. All of them are usually finished in chrome and the controls are made of a strong plastic which will resist most knocks and blows.

Surface-mounted mixer
Left: This is a surface-mounted mixer control with separate supply pipes emerging through the wall to supply the control which provides power over flow and temperature.

Built-in mixer
Right: This built-in control is supplied from behind the shower wall so that the supply pipes are hidden. These fittings are also available in a gold finish.

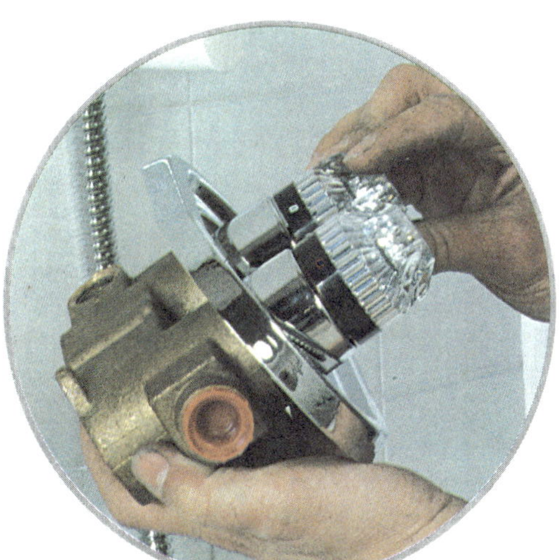

Thermostatic mixer
Left: This thermostatic mixer is also supplied from behind and provides two separate controls – one for pre-setting the temperature, and one for adjusting the flow of the water once the user is inside the shower.

Ready Reference

TYPES OF SUPPLY

Here is a summary of the various types of shower supply you could choose:

Rear supply – surface mounting
Both hot and cold supplies come through the wall behind the mixer, which is surface mounted on the cubicle wall.

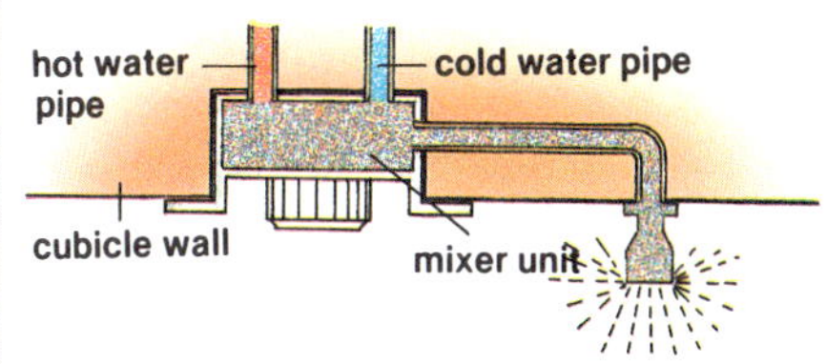

Surface supply – surface mixing
The hot and cold supplies come independently through the shower wall and can be seen entering the surface-mounted mixing unit.

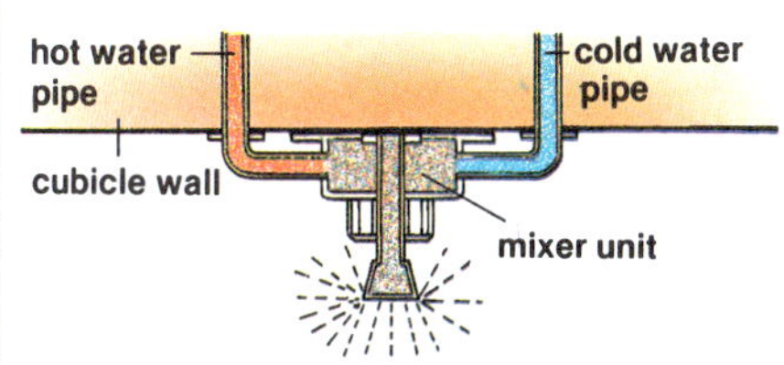

Surface supply – thermostatic mixing
Water supplies come through the wall into the surface-mounted unit, and then are regulated by sensitive flow and temperature controls.

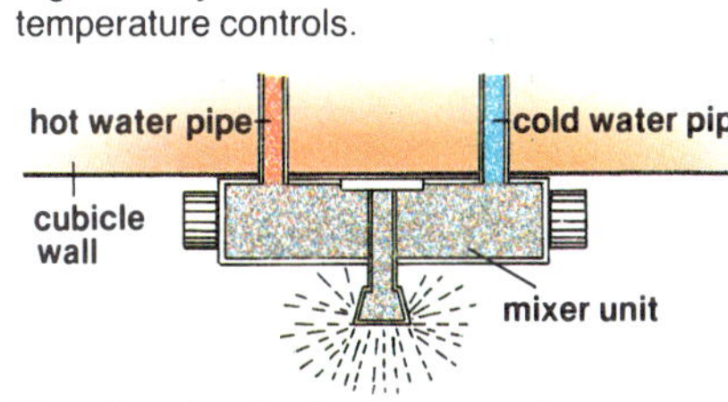

Rear supply – instantaneous shower
The mains (cold-water only) supply comes through or along the wall, and enters the unit for rapid heating and distribution through the rose.

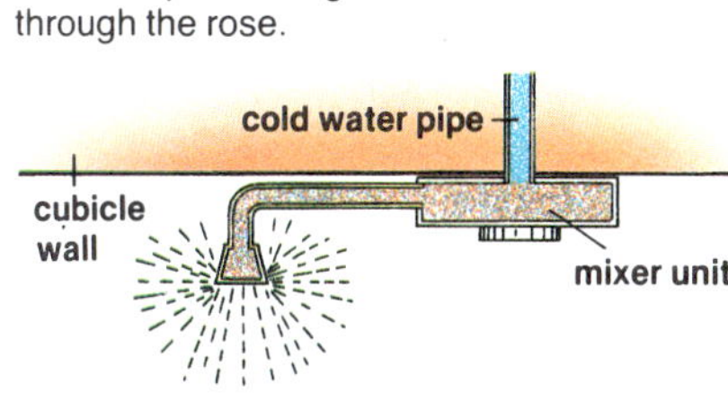

TIP: TEST YOUR SEALS

However much purpose-built shower surround you buy – or however much you build – it must all have a waterproof seal with the tray and any solid cubicle walls. Test all joints for leaks with a hand spray, and if they do leak, make sure they are filled with a flexible non-setting mastic.

BUILDING A SHOWER CUBICLE

The simplest way to add showering facilities to your bathroom is to install the shower over the bath. However, building a separate cubicle is a better solution.

When you come to install a shower in your home, the most obvious place for it is over the bath because you can make use of the bath's water supply and waste facilities. But this isn't the most advantageous site: putting a shower there does not increase your bathing facilities, it merely improves the existing ones. It's far better to have your shower as a separate cubicle, even if the cubicle is in the bathroom itself. If you can put the cubicle in another part of the home, you have as good as provided an extra bathroom.

You may think that you have no room in your home for a shower outside the bathroom, but that is not necessarily true. A shower does not require all that much space and you can make do with an area about 900mm (3ft) square. But you've got to think about how much space you need to get into and out of the shower. It isn't usually that easy or efficient to dry off inside, so you need some space to dry off at the point of exit. You will also have to take into consideration the relationship of the drying area with bathroom fittings.

You can buy a ready-made shower cubicle, or build your own from scratch. The latter course will save a lot of money, and is easier than you might think, but you've got to take care to ensure that it is properly waterproofed.

Putting in the tray

To build a shower cubicle you start with the shower tray. Many people attempt to make one of these themselves by building a box that they cover with some impervious material – usually tiles. However, the construction is not easy because making the box absolutely waterproof can present problems, and then it is difficult to get the right gradient from every part of the tray to carry water to the waste outlet. On the whole, you would do better to buy a tray.

Normally, trays are made in acrylic plastic or glazed ceramics. The latter are dearer, but much longer-lasting, as acrylics can crack. Both types are available in standard sanitary-ware colours, so if you have a modern coloured bathroom suite, you should be able to match it. Trays come in a range of sizes, so be sure to choose one to fit the space you have, since obviously the size of tray governs the area your installation will take up. Ceramic trays can also be very heavy so it's likely you'll need help to get one into position.

The tray will have a waste outlet, and this may be in one corner, or in the middle of one side. It must be sited so that its waste pipe can discharge conveniently into a hopper of a two-pipe system, or be connected up to an existing waste pipe, or to the main stack of a single-pipe system. The waste pipe must slope downwards all the way, and it is important to get the fall right in order to drain water away efficiently. In general, the fall should be between 6 and 50mm per 300mm run of pipe (¼ to 2in per ft) depending on the length of the run (measured from the actual waste outlet). Too steep a run can produce a siphonage effect that will drain the water out of the trap, thus depriving your home of its protection from drain smells (see pages 14 to 18). It's a good idea to set a fall of 25mm (1in) per 300mm for a short run of say 600 to 900mm (2 to 3ft), but only a 12mm (½in) fall where the run will be 3 to 4.5m (10 to 15ft).

Most shower trays are square, and obviously these can be turned round to place the outlet in the most convenient position. However, for installation in a corner, triangular shaped trays, or quadrants – with two straight sides at right angles and a curved front – are on sale, but they're quite expensive.

The outlet does not have a plug, because it is never the intention that the tray should be filled up. Since there is no plug, no overflow is required. However, like all your bathroom fittings, it must have a trap. This should be 38mm (1½in) in diameter but, like a bath, does not have to be of the deep-seal variety.

Some trays are designed to have enough depth to enable the trap to be installed above floor level. Others are quite shallow, and the trap must go under the floor, a point to bear in mind if you have a concrete floor. Yet another possibility is to mount the tray on supports, to raise its height, and some manufacturers sell special supports to raise the tray off the ground. Otherwise you can use bricks or timber, suitably disguised by a plinth. It's a good idea to provide an inspection panel should you ever want to get access to the plumbing. Whatever the case, you will never have good access to the outlet plumbing after it's been installed – so be sure to make a good job of it.

Providing a cubicle

A shower tray is best positioned in a corner, so that two sides of the shower enclosure are already provided by the shower tray itself; you can bridge the gap with timber covered with tiles set flush with the top of the tray.

INSTALLING THE SHOWER TRAY

1 *Press a sausage of plumber's putty around the underside of the outlet flange, then wind PTFE tape along the length of the thread.*

2 *Push the flange into the waste hole in the tray, press it home until the putty squeezes out round the edge, and put on the metal washer.*

3 *Screw on the back-nut by hand and tighten it with an adjustable wrench. This will squeeze more putty out; remove the excess neatly.*

4 *Take the special low-seal shower trap and screw it onto the outlet flange, after first making sure that the O ring is in place.*

5 *Measure up the position needed for the waste run, and install the plastic waste pipe in position ready to be connected up to the trap.*

6 *Lower the tray into place and connect up the trap to the waste pipe. Check that it is level on your prepared base.*

Ready Reference

WASTE OUTLET RUNS

You must provide sufficient depth underneath the shower tray to accommodate the waste trap and the outlet pipe. You can:

- support the tray on timber or bricks and face the elevation with panels

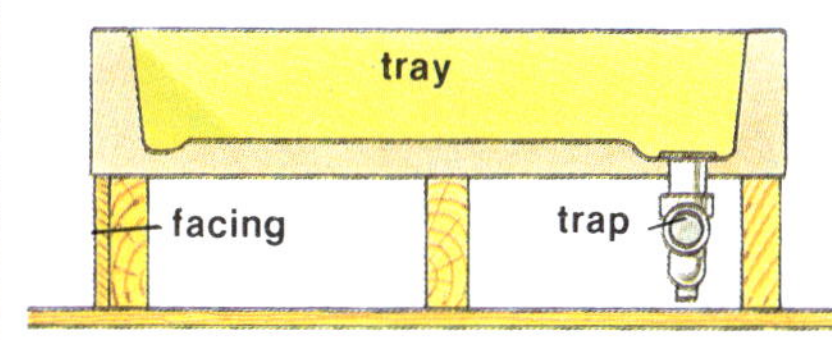

- support the tray with special supporting brackets which are usually available from shower tray manufacturers, and face the elevation with panels

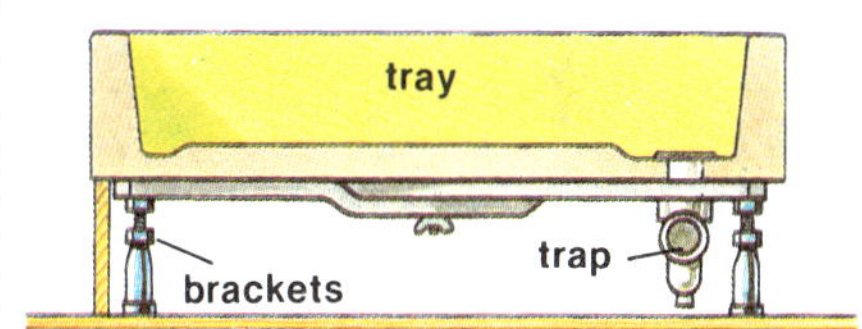

- cut a hole in the floor – if it's made of wood – and run the trap and waste above the ceiling of the room underneath. You can do this only if the joists run in the same direction as the waste pipe.

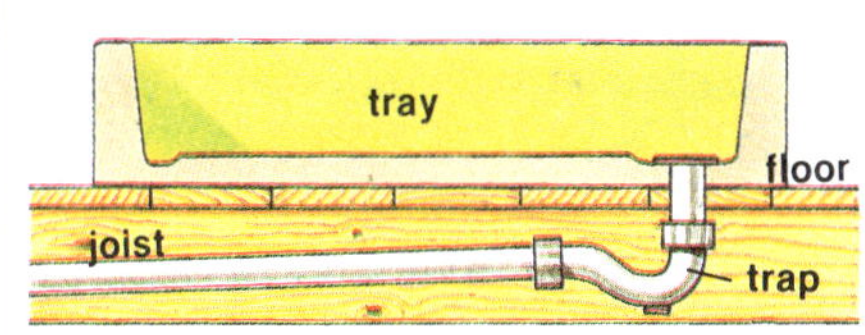

HOW MUCH SPACE?

It's very easy to think of a shower as only occupying the same space as the tray itself. But don't forget that you will usually step out of it soaking wet and so will need sufficient area in which to dry off. If the shower is enclosed on three sides you will need more space than if it's enclosed on one side and curtained on the others.

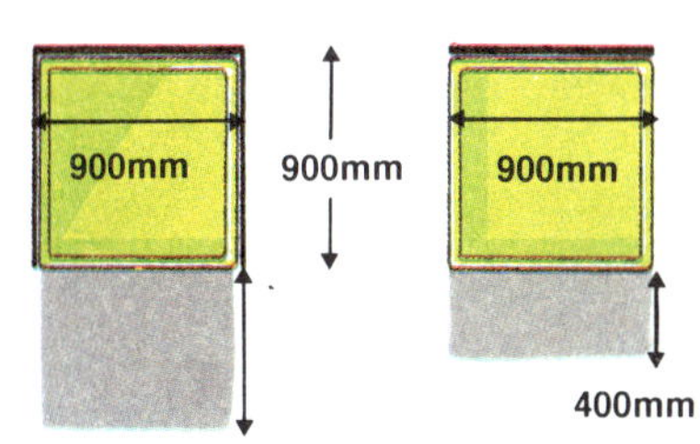

PUTTING UP A SURROUND KIT

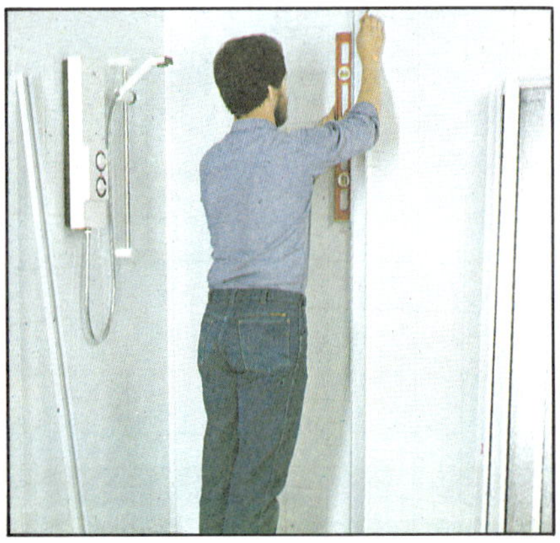

1 *Mark the position of the wall uprights; use a spirit level to make sure that they will be truly vertical when fixed in position.*

2 *Drill holes for the upright fixings, then plug them with plastic wall plugs and screw on the uprights with the screws supplied.*

3 *Slide the first panel into position on the wall upright and fix it; again check that the structure is in a properly vertical position.*

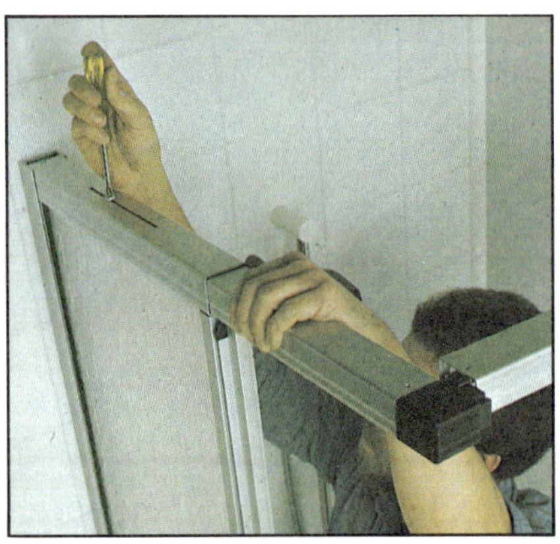

4 *Adjust the length of the panel to fit the size of the shower tray and tighten up the screws carefully. Attach the corner bracket.*

5 *Fix the other panel in position and adjust its length so that it mates up accurately and squarely with the corner bracket.*

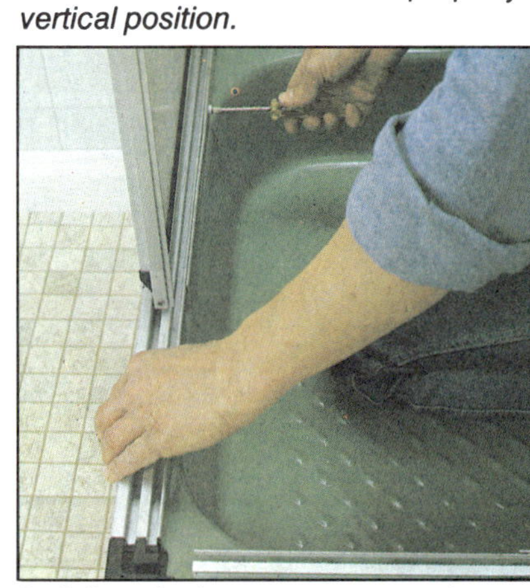

6 *Adjust the bottom runners to the correct size so that they match up with the bottom corner bracket; check they are square to the tray.*

7 *Screw up the bottom corner bracket, then check that the whole structure is firm and square and that the door opens and closes smoothly.*

8 *Loosen the wall upright fixings and wedge up each side in turn. Squeeze sealant between the frame and the tray and refix the frame.*

9 *Check again for alignment, then finish off the base by firmly fixing the supports in position and finally boarding in the sides of the shower.*

Existing walls forming part of the cubicle will also need tiling or covering with some laminated material – commonly waterproofed decorative wallboard, or even glass or sheet plastic over paint or wallpaper. It is obviously very important to make sure that all gaps are sealed, otherwise gradual water seepage will occur which will damage the fabric of your house.

The sides of the cubicle you have to install can be home-made or bought as kits. The simplest way to fill one or two sides is with a curtain rail and shower curtain. This works quite well with a shower in the bath, but the sides of a shower tray are much shallower than those of a bath and water is therefore quite likely to splash onto the floor. This means that curtains are really only at all suitable for the entry side of the cubicle where you might protect the floor with a bath mat, or where the floor of your bathroom is tiled and fully sealed.

You can construct any solid sides of the cubicle using a timber framework, but you will have to buy a suitable proprietary door unless you use a curtain. These doors are usually made of aluminium frames with opaque safety glass or plastic panels. They come in a wide variety of designs and colours. You can have, for example, a plain aluminium frame with clear glass, or a gold satin frame with dark smoked glass. If you plan to buy a door, check that you have calculated the size of your cubicle to fit it, and that the door comes with suitable rust-proof fittings to hang it.

The easiest (though most expensive) solution is to buy the complete surround, including a sliding or ordinary door, which will be supplied in kit form. These surrounds are made by the same manufacturers as shower doors and usually come complete with fixing instructions. They are usually adjustable to fit different shower tray sizes, and are simply fitted to the wall at each end to provide a rigid frame. Before finishing they have to be sealed where they meet the tray using a proprietary sealant, to ensure a waterproof joint. If this isn't done perfectly, water will gradually seep in and cause damp on the floor and walls of your bathroom.

Home-made surrounds

Making your own surround will save money, and it has the advantage that you can tailor it exactly to your needs. You might, for example, want a surround which is larger than the tray itself; in which case you can install a shelf or seat next to the tray.

Begin by making a framework of 50mm (2in) square timber. You need a length on every edge, plus extra horizontal ones at 450mm (18in) centres. All should be joined with halving joints. In addition, fit any extra length needed to provide a fixing point (for the shower rose, for instance). The inside face of the partition should then be clad with 6mm (1/4in) plywood. Use an exterior-grade board if the cubicle is to be tiled.

Another possibility is to use 10mm (3/8in) thick plasterboard. The framework for this should consist of a 50mm (2in) square batten on every edge, plus one extra vertical and horizontal in the middle, and any additional member needed to provide a fixing point. Fix the board with galvanised plasterboard nails driven in until the head slightly dimples the surface of the board, but without fracturing the paper liner. You can use 3mm (1/8in) hardboard to cover the outside of the cubicle framework.

Do not fix the exterior cladding for the time being. You should first clad the inside face, then fix the half-completed partition in place by driving screws through the frame members into the floor below, the wall behind and the ceiling too if it is to be a room height job.

The interior of this partition is a good place in which to conceal the supply pipes to the shower. You would then need an inspection panel, held by screws (not glued and nailed) to allow easy access to the pipework should maintenance ever be needed.

If the cubicle is not a floor-to-ceiling one, you will also need extra support at the top as you cannot leave the front top edge flapping free. This can take the form of a 75x25mm (3x1in) batten, decoratively moulded if you wish, spanning the two sides of the cubicle or fixed at one end to a block screwed to the wall, should there be only one side.

The whole interior of the shower cubicle needs to be clad with an impervious material to make sure it is waterproof. The most obvious choice is tiles, and these can be fixed to both the plywood or plasterboard cladding and the plaster of a wall. Make sure that the latter is clean and sound before tiling. Do not, however, fix the tiles direct to the timber part of the framing.

As an alternative to tiles you could use a special plastic-faced hardboard, with a tile pattern and a backing of plain hardboard. Fix the plastic-faced board by glueing and pinning with rustproof nails (if these can be lost somewhere in the pattern). Otherwise use a contact adhesive. This does not need to be spread all over the meeting surfaces. Apply it in a pattern similar to that detailed for the framework of the partitions. Adhesives applied by gun are available for this sort of work. The board on the back wall should be fixed in a similar manner.

Whatever material you use, all joins – where partitions meet the wall, or the tray – should be sealed with a silicone bath sealant. Any parts not clad with impervious material should be well painted with a three-coat system of primer, undercoat and one or two top coats.

Ready Reference

SHOWER SURROUNDS

Buying a ready-made shower surround and door in kit form is the easy, but expensive, solution to enclosing the shower tray. You can use a curtain, which is less efficient, but cheaper. Surrounds can fill one, two or three sides; some of the options are illustrated below.

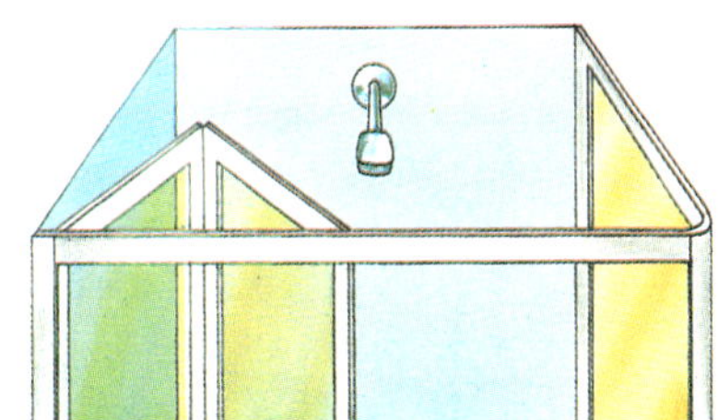

corner shower surround

free standing surround

built-in shower surround

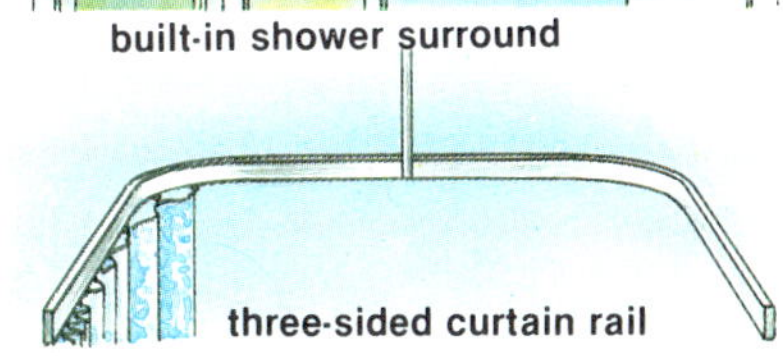

three-sided curtain rail

TIP: WATERPROOF SEALS

There's no point in fitting a surround if it's not watertight, and it is most likely to leak where the surround meets the tray. Fill this gap with non-setting mastic and then seal with any acrylic or silicone sealant to match the tray colour.

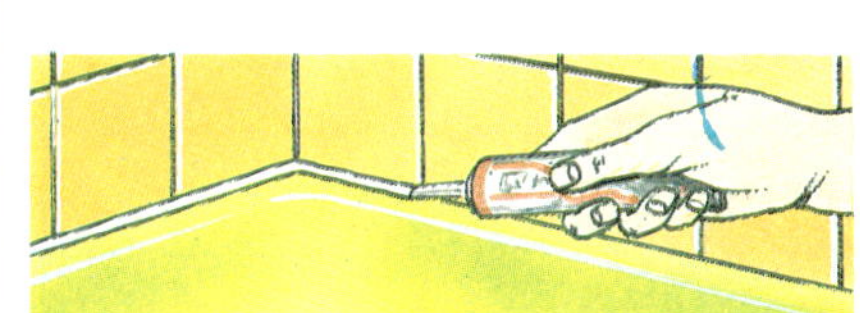

BUILDING A CUBICLE

If you are prepared to build one of the walls of the cubicle then the basic ingredients for the whole job are the tray itself, suitable shower fittings, a ready-made door, your other plumbing attachments and the materials for the partition.

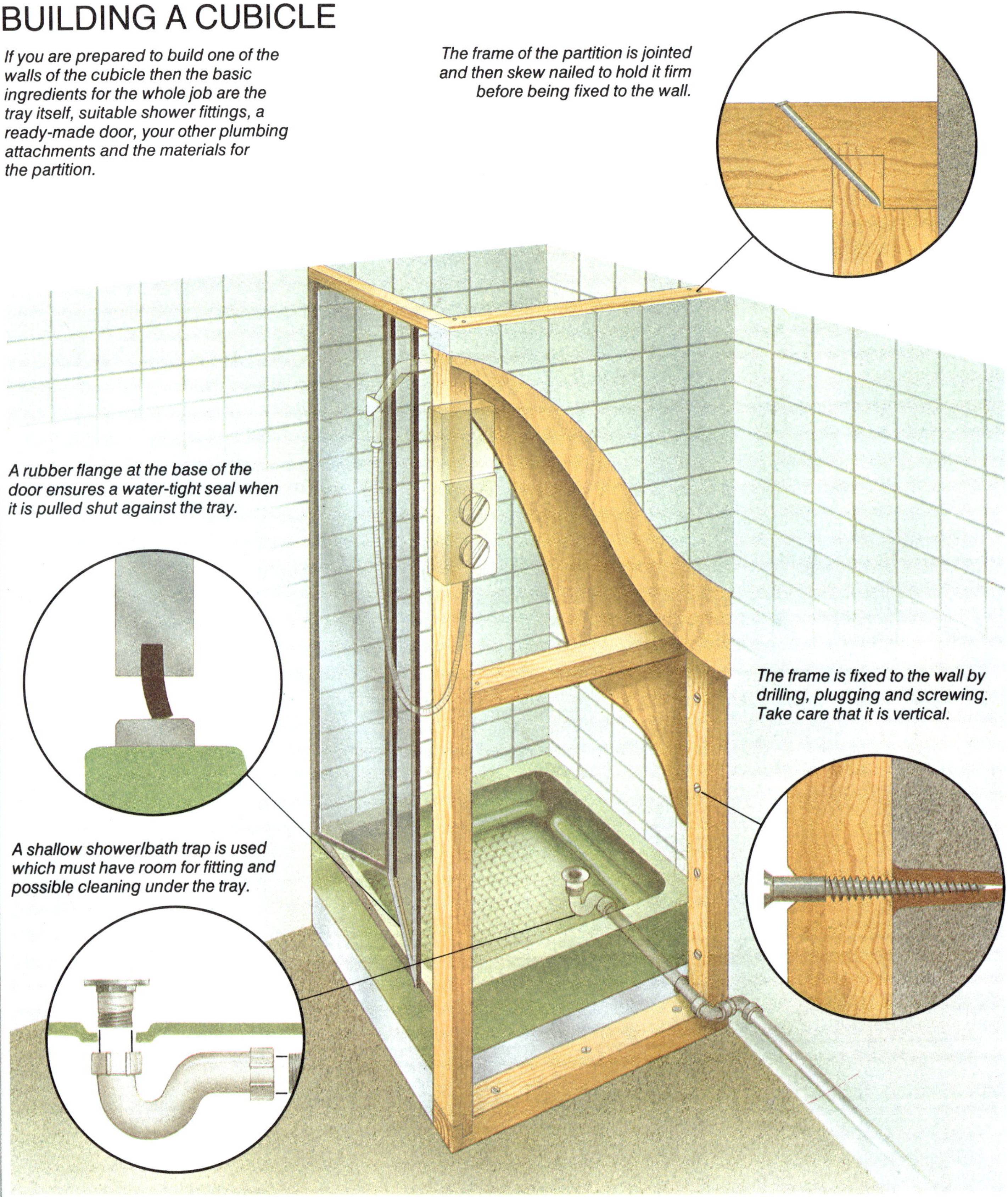

The frame of the partition is jointed and then skew nailed to hold it firm before being fixed to the wall.

A rubber flange at the base of the door ensures a water-tight seal when it is pulled shut against the tray.

The frame is fixed to the wall by drilling, plugging and screwing. Take care that it is vertical.

A shallow shower/bath trap is used which must have room for fitting and possible cleaning under the tray.

REPLACING A WASHBASIN

Replacing a washbasin is fairly straightforward. It's a job you'll have to undertake if the basin is cracked – but you may also want to change the basin if you're redesigning your bathroom and adding some up-to-date fittings.

Apart from replacing a cracked basin, which you should do immediately, the most common time to install a new basin is when you're improving a bathroom or decorating a separate WC. The chances are that the basin you'll be removing will be one of the older ceramic types, wall-hung, a pedestal model or built into a vanity unit.

The main advantage of a wall-hung basin is that it doesn't take up any floor space and because of this it is very useful in a small bathroom, WC or cloakroom. You can also set the basin at a comfortable height, unlike a pedestal basin the height of which is fixed by the height of the pedestal. However, it's usual to fit a wall-hung basin with the rim 800mm (32in) above the floor.

Vanity units are now increasing in popularity. In fact they're the descendents of the Edwardian wash-stand, with its marble top, bowl and large water jug. The unit is simply a storage cupboard with a ceramic, enamelled pressed steel or plastic basin set flush in the top. The advantage of vanity units is that you have a counter surface round the basin on which to stand toiletries. There is rarely, if ever, sufficient room for these items behind or above conventional wall-hung or pedestal basins. Usually the top has some form of plastic covering or can be tiled for easy cleaning.

Fittings for basins

It's a good idea to choose the taps and waste fittings at the same time you select the basin, so everything matches. You could perhaps re-use the taps from the old basin, but it's doubtful if these will be in keeping with the design of the new appliance. As an alternative to shrouded head or pillar taps, you could fit a mixer, provided the holes at the back of the basin are suitably spaced to take the tap tails. But remember that because of the design of most basin mixers, you shouldn't use them if the cold water supply is directly from the mains.

Ceramic basins normally have a built-in overflow channel which in most appliances connects into the main outlet above the trap. So if you accidentally let the basin overfill you reduce the risk of water spillage.

PUTTING IN A NEW BASIN

You should have little trouble installing a new washbasin in the same place as the old one. It's also a good opportunity to check the pipe runs. If they're made of lead it's a good idea to replace them.

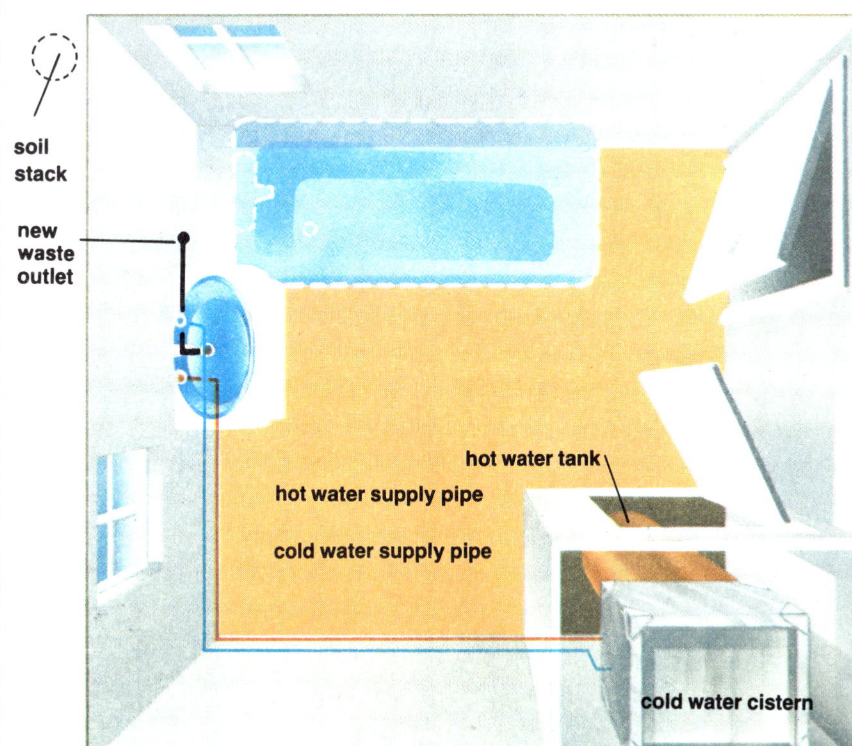

Vanity unit basins are usually sold complete with a waste and overflow unit which resembles that of a modern stainless steel sink. A flexible tube connects the overflow outlet of the basin with a sleeve or 'banjo' unit which fits tightly round a slotted waste fitting.

With both types of basin the flange of the waste outlet has to be bedded into the hole provided for it in the basin on a layer of plumber's putty. The thread of the screwed waste must also be smeared with jointing compound to ensure a watertight seal where the 'banjo' connects to it.

Traps

The outlet of the waste must, of course, connect to a trap and branch waste pipe. At one time it was the practice to use 'shallow seal' traps with a 50mm (2in) depth of seal for two-pipe drainage systems, and 'deep seal' traps with a 75mm (3in) depth of seal for single stack systems. Today, however, deep seal traps are always fitted.

Of course, the modern bottle trap is one of the most common types used. It's neater looking and requires less space than a traditional U-trap. Where it's concealed behind a pedestal or in a vanity unit you can use one made of plastic, but there are chromium-plated and brass types if you have a wall-hung basin where trap and waste will be clearly visible. The one drawback with bottle traps is that they discharge water more slowly than a U-trap. You can now also buy traps with telescopic inlets that make it easy to provide a push-fit connection to an existing copper or plastic branch waste pipe (see page 18).

Connecting up the water supply

It's unlikely that you'll be able to take out the old basin and install a new one without making some modification to the pipework. It's almost certain that the tap holes will be in a different position. To complicate matters further, taps are now made with shorter tails so you'll probably have to extend the supply pipes by a short length.

If you're installing new supply pipes, how you run them will depend on the type of basin you're putting in. With a wall-hung basin or the pedestal type, the hot and cold pipes are usually run neatly together up the back wall and then bent round to the tap tails. But as a vanity unit will conceal the plumbing there's no need to run the pipes together.

You might find it difficult to bend the required angles, so an easy way round the problem is to use flexible corrugated copper pipe which you can bend by hand to the shape you need. You can buy the pipe with a swivel tap connector at one end and a plain connector, on which you can use capillary or

FITTING A VANITY UNIT

1 *Cut a hole in the vanity unit with the help of the template provided or, if the hole is precut, check the measurement against that of the sink.*

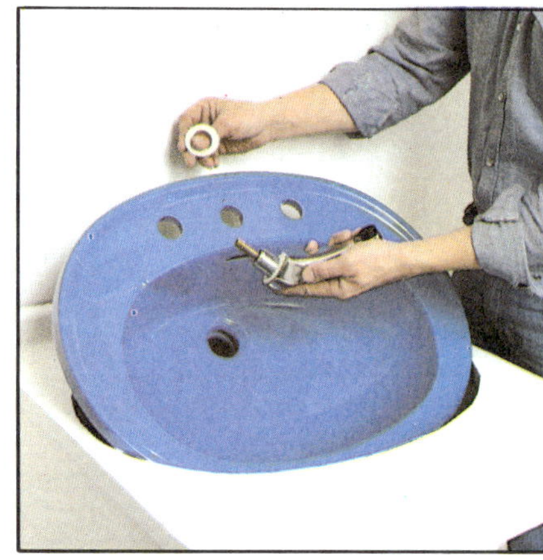

2 *Prop the basin up while you install the mixer unit. Start with the outlet spout which is fixed with a brass nut and packing washers.*

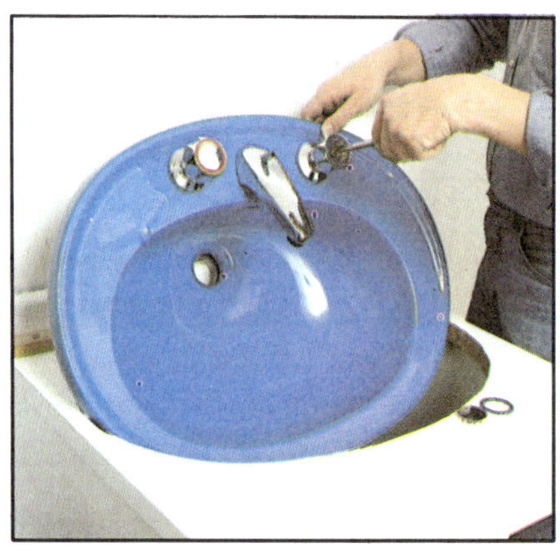

5 *Now complete the tap heads by first sliding on the flange which covers up the securing nut; next put on the headwork and tighten the retaining nut.*

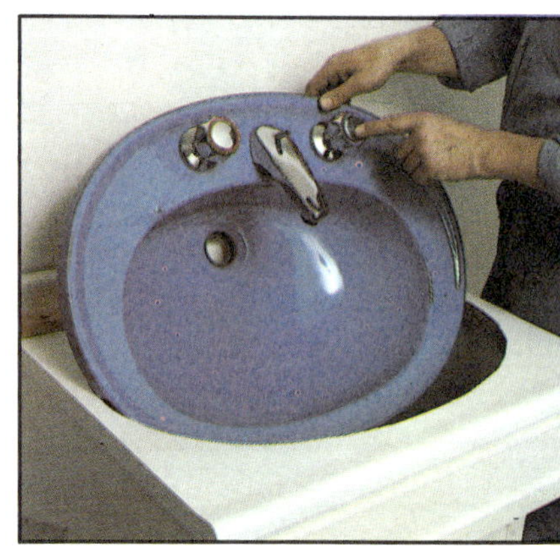

6 *Finish off the tap assembly by fitting the coloured markers into place (red for hot is usually on the left), and gently pressing home the chrome cap.*

9 *Before you put the basin into its final position put a strip of mastic around the opening in the vanity unit to ensure a watertight seal.*

10 *Press the basin gently into position and fix it to the underside of the top of the vanity unit. Attach the waste plug to its keeper.*

3 *Now take the water inlet assembly and check that the hot and cold spur pipes are the right length so that the tap sub-assemblies are correctly positioned.*

4 *Fix the assembly in position with the brass nuts supplied by the manufacturer. Make sure that all the washers are included otherwise the fitting won't be secure.*

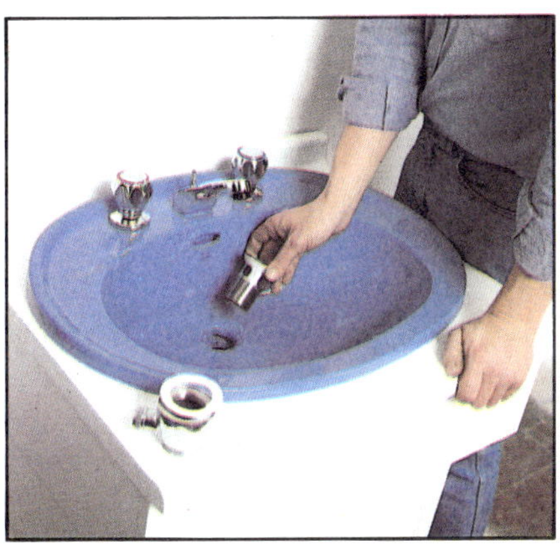

7 *Now insert the waste outlet. Make sure the rubber flange is fitted properly and seats comfortably into the basin surround.*

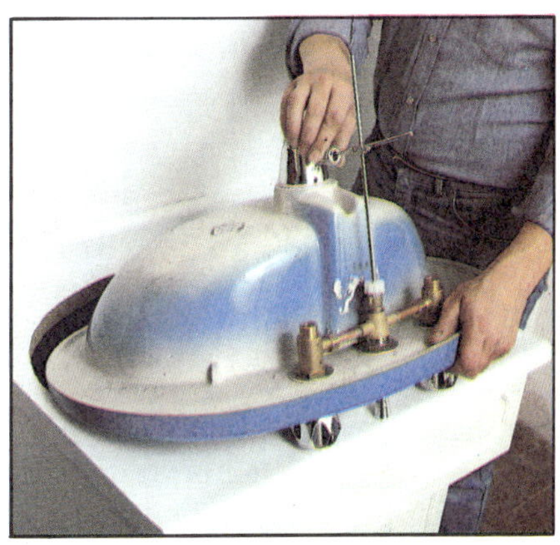

8 *Turn the basin over; secure the outlet and the pop-up waste control rods. These may need shortening depending on clearance inside the vanity unit.*

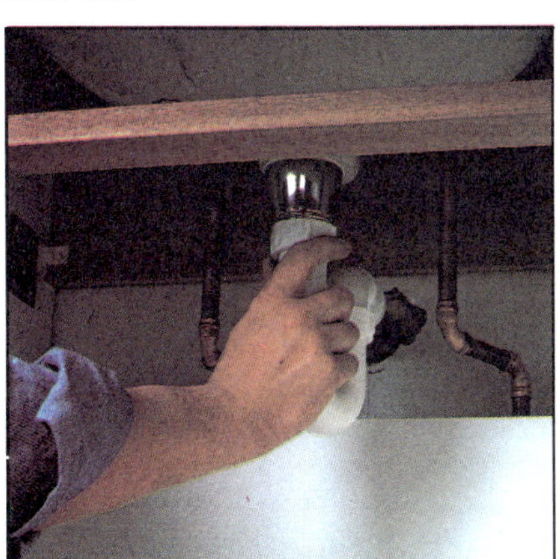

11 *Now fix the inlet pipes to the two mixer connections and screw on the waste trap. Take the doors off the vanity unit to make access easier.*

12 *Turn the water back on and check for leaks. Check the pop-up waste system works, then put the doors of the vanity unit back on.*

Ready Reference

BASIN SIZES

On basins, the dimension from side to side is specified as the length, and that from back to front as the width.

Most standard sized basins are between 550 and 700mm (22 and 28in) long, and 450 to 500mm (18 to 20in) wide.

BASIN COMPONENTS

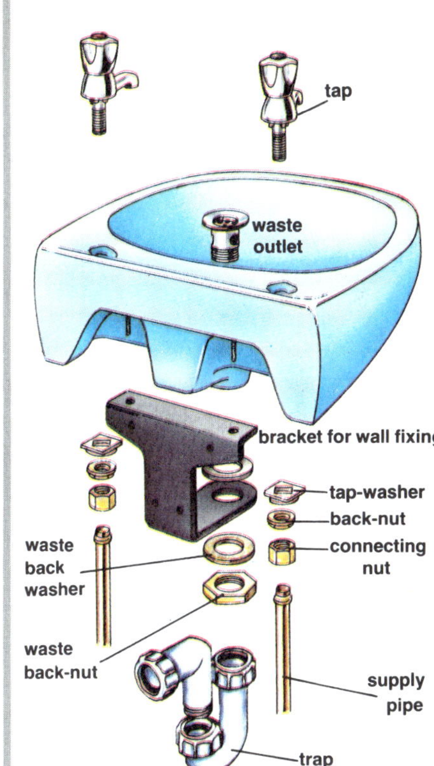

THE SPACE YOU'LL NEED

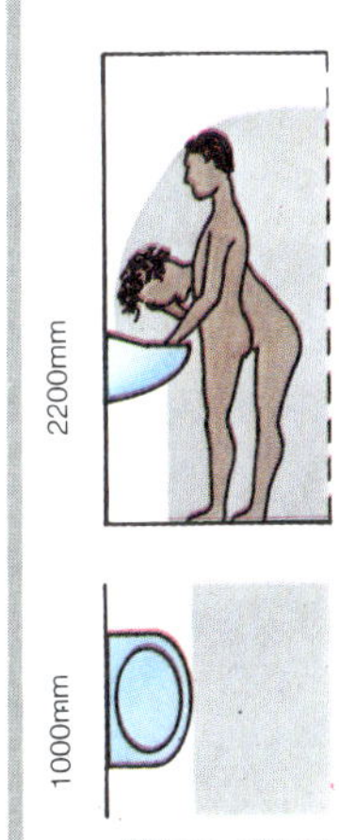

Think about the space around your basin particularly if you are installing a new one. You not only need elbow room when you are bending over it, such as when you are washing your hair, but also room in front to stand back – especially if you put a mirror above it. Here are the recommended dimensions for the area around your basin.

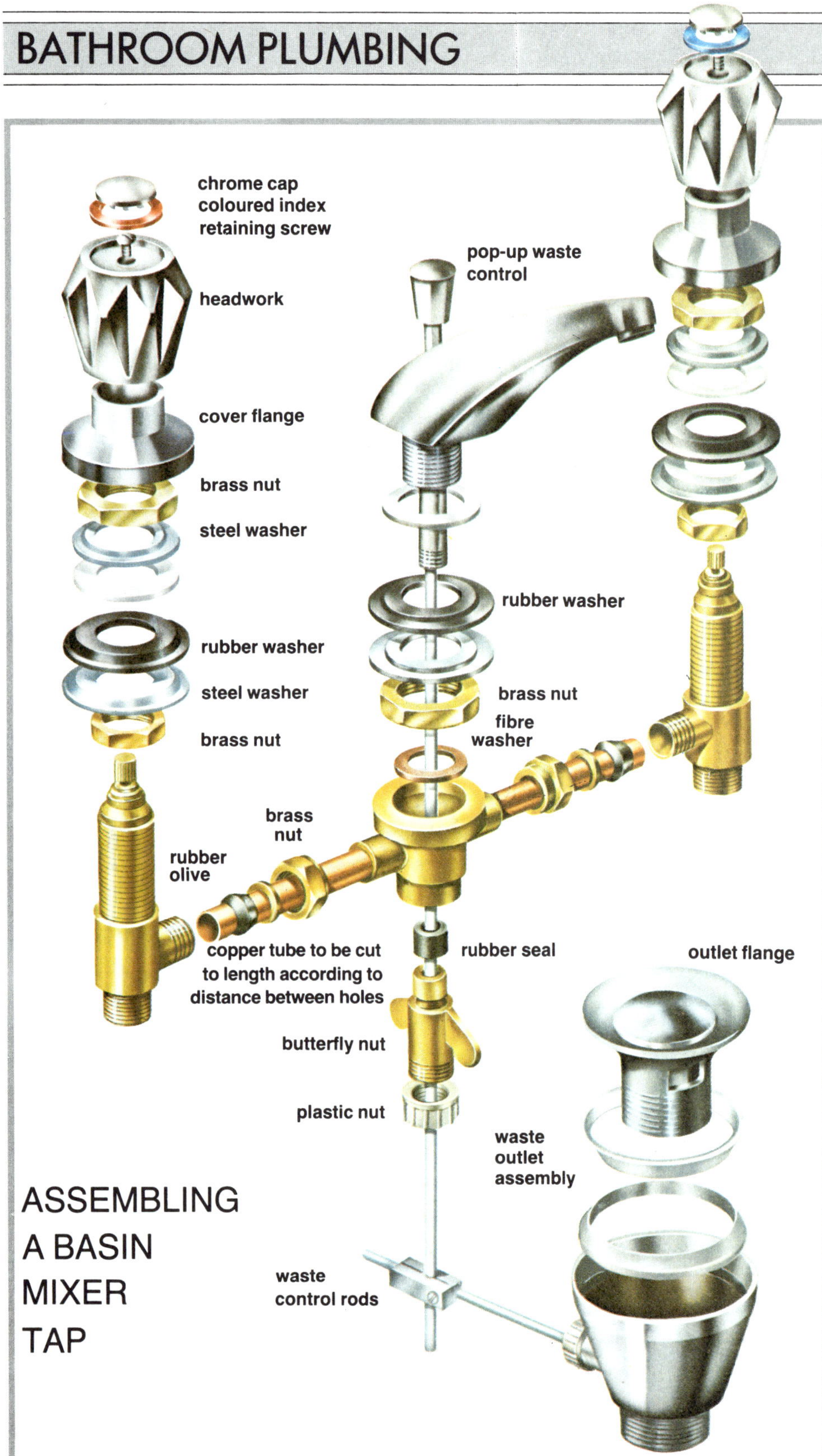

ASSEMBLING A BASIN MIXER TAP

When fitting the taps all you have to do is to remove the back-nuts and slip flat plastic washers over the tails (if they aren't there already). The taps can then be positioned in the holes in the basin. When this has been done more plastic washers (or top hat washers) have to be slipped over the tails before the back-nuts are replaced. It's important not to overtighten these as it's quite easy to damage a ceramic basin.

Because some vanity unit basins are made of a thinner material, you may find that the shanks of the taps fitted into them will protrude below the under-surface of the basin. The result is that when the back-nut is fully tightened, it still isn't tight against the underside of the basin. To get round the problem you have to fit a top hat washer over the shank so the back-nut can be screwed up against it.

Mixers usually have one large washer or gasket between the base of the mixer and the top of the basin and you fix them in exactly the same way.

When you've fitted the taps you can then fit the waste. With a ceramic basin you'll have to use a slotted waste to enable water from the overlfow to escape into the drainage pipe. Getting this in place means first removing the back-nut so you can slip it through the outlet hole in the basin – which itself should be coated with a generous layer of plumber's putty. It's essential to make sure that the slot in the waste fitting coincides with the outlet of the basin's built-in overflow. You'll then have to smear jointing compound on the protruding screw thread of the tail, slip on a plastic washer and replace and tighten the back-nut. As you do this the waste flange will probably try to turn on its seating, but you can prevent this by holding the grid with pliers as you tighten the back-nut.

Finally, any excess putty that is squeezed out as the flange is tightened against the basin should be wiped away.

A vanity unit will probably be supplied with a combined waste and overflow unit. This is a flexible hose that has to be fitted (unlike a ceramic basin, where it's an integral part of the appliance). The slotted waste is bedded in exactly the same way as a waste on a ceramic basin. You then have to fit one end of the overflow to the basin outlet and slip the 'banjo' outlet on the other end over the tail of the waste to cover the slot. It's held in position by a washer and back-nut.

compression fittings at the other. If you're using ordinary copper pipe, the easiest way to start is by bending the pipe to the correct angle first, and then cutting the pipe to the right length at each end afterwards. See pages 19–21.

Preparing the basin

Before you fix the basin in position, you'll need to fit the taps (or mixer) and the waste. It's much easier to do this at this stage than later when the basin is against the wall because you will have more room to manoeuvre in.

Fitting the basin

Once the taps and waste have been fixed in position on the new basin, you should be ready to remove the old basin and fit the new one in its place. First you need to cut off the water supply to the basin, either by turning off the main stop-valve (or any gate valve on the distribution pipes) or by tying up the ball-valve supplying the main cold water storage cistern. Then open the taps and leave them until the water ceases to flow. If the existing basin is a pedestal model you'll have to remove the pedestal which may be screwed to the floor. Take off the nut that connects the basin trap to the threaded waste outlet and unscrew the nuts that connect the water supply pipes to the tails of the taps. These will either be swivel tap connectors or cap and lining joints. You'll need to be able to lift the basin clear and then remove the brackets or hangers on which it rests.

You'll probably need some help when installing the new basin as it's much easier to mark the fixing holes if someone else is holding the basin against the wall. With a pedestal basin, the pedestal will determine the level of the basin. The same applies with a vanity unit. But if the basin is set on hangers or brackets, you can adjust the height for convenience.

Once the fixing holes have been drilled and plugged, the basin can be screwed into position and you can deal with the plumbing. Before you make the connections to the water supply pipes you may have to cut or lengthen them to meet the tap tails. If you need to lengthen them you'll find it easier to use corrugated copper pipe. The actual connection between pipe and tail is made with a swivel tap connector – a form of compression fitting.

Finally you have to connect the trap. You may be able to re-use the old one, but it's more likely you'll want to fit a new one. And if its position doesn't coincide with the old one, you can use a bottle trap with an adjustable telescopic inlet.

FITTING A PEDESTAL BASIN

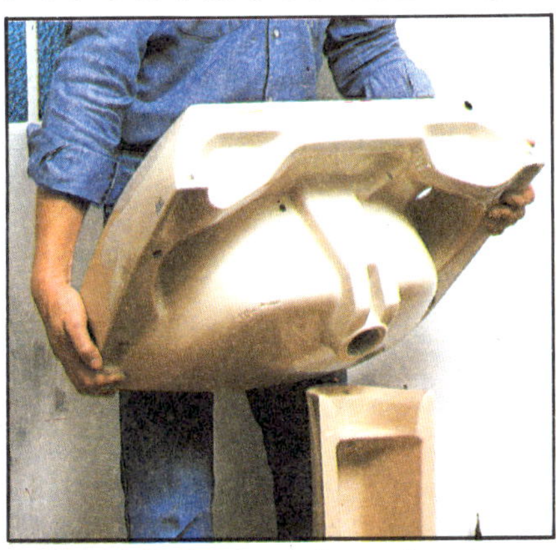

1 Stand the basin on the pedestal to check the height of the water supply pipe runs and the outlet. Measure the height of the wall fixing points.

2 When you're making up the pipe run to connect to the tap tails, plan it so the pipes are neatly concealed within the body of the pedestal.

3 Line up the piped waste outlet and fix the trap to the basin outlet. A telescopic trap may be useful here to adjust for a varying level.

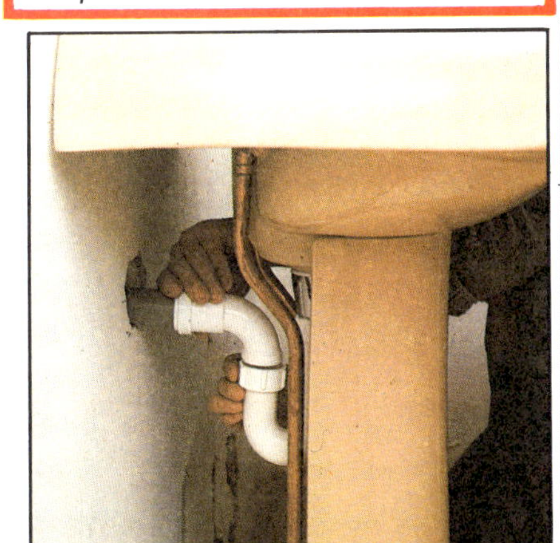

4 Move the whole unit into its final position, screw the basin to the wall, connect the waste trap to the outlet, and connect up the supply pipes.

Ready Reference

TYPES OF BASIN

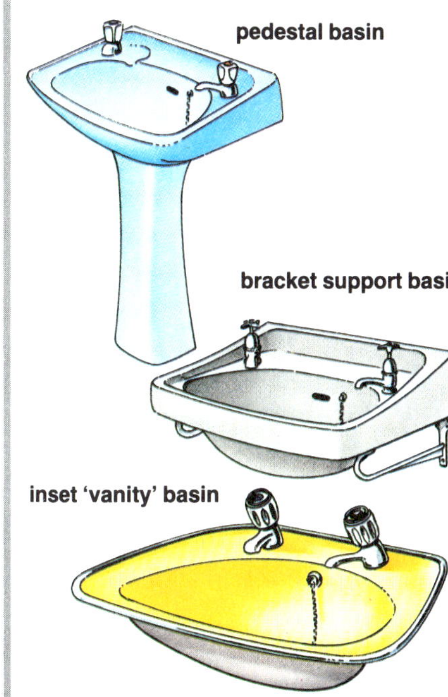

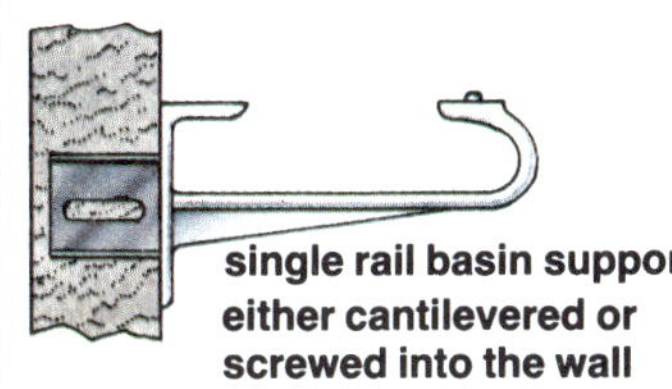

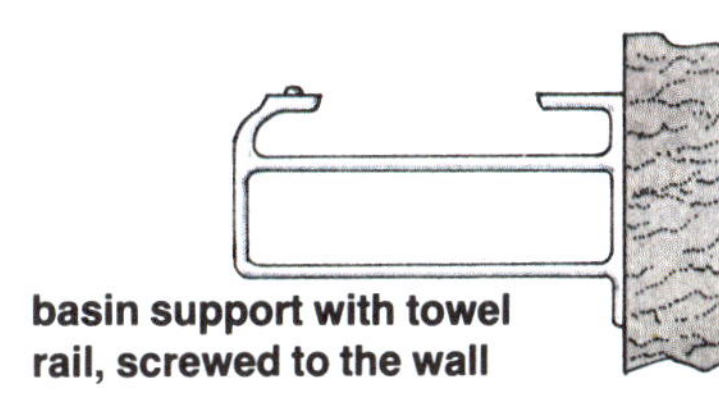

FITTING A VANITY BASIN

When you buy a vanity basin it should be supplied with a template to guide you in cutting your work surface or vanity unit. This should also include fitting instructions, and necessary fixing screws and mastic strip. It may look like this.

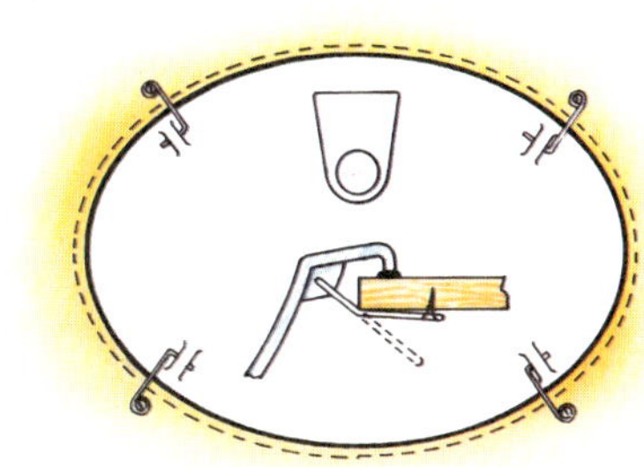

INSTALLING A BIDET

If you've got the room, a bidet can provide a useful addition to the bathroom. There are two types available, each of which is installed in a different way.

A bidet is a specially-shaped, low-level basin designed for washing between the legs – you squat on it facing the taps. In addition it can be used as a footbath, or even as a sink for soaking clothes, so it's a particularly useful appliance to have in the bathroom.

Strangely, in Britain, which has generally led in matters of hygiene and efficient plumbing, bidets are not that common. Until recently they were misguidedly seen as somewhat undesirable appliances found in the bathrooms of foreign hotels. Fortunately sense is now prevailing and the need to save space in buildings and to conserve energy means that the bidet (and the shower) are likely to increase in popularity at the expense of the traditional space-consuming bath which uses large quantities of water.

Types of bidet

When you're buying a bidet, it's important to understand that there are in fact two types, and how you install them depends on which type you choose.

Basically the difference between the two kinds lies in the way they are supplied with hot and cold water. The simpler, cheaper and easier-to-install version is the 'over rim' bidet', sometimes referred to as a 'washbasin bidet'. It's simply a low-level washbasin supplied with hot and cold water from two basin taps, or a basin mixer, fitted in holes in the rear of the appliance.

The other kind of bidet, which seems to be the more popular type, is known as a 'rim supply bidet with ascending spray'. But it's more expensive and can be more difficult to install. A bidet of this kind has a hollow rim – not unlike the flushing rim of a lavatory pan – round which warm water first flows before entering the pan. This has the effect of warming the rim and making it more comfortable to sit on. At the flick of a control knob the warm water is diverted from the rim to a spray which is set in the bottom of the pan. The water therefore rises vertically for washing.

Because of the position of the spray outlet, it means that the rose can be submerged in water when the bidet is in use. And it's this type of inlet that can cause a few problems when you're installing such a bidet. Submerged inlets are always regarded with suspicion by water authorities because of the risk of contaminating the water supply by back siphonage. And it's particularly important that this risk should be eliminated as far as bidets are concerned because of the use to which they are put.

Bidets are available in floor-standing and wall-mounted versions, in colours and styles that match other items of bathroom equipment.

Connecting an over-rim bidet

When you come to install any bidet, it's best to start at the appliance end and finish by breaking into the water supply pipes. If you do this the water supply to the rest of the home will be disrupted as little as possible.

Connecting the hot and cold water supplies to this type of bidet shouldn't present any real difficulties. Because you mustn't mix water from the mains and water from a storage cistern in the same appliance, you can use a mixer only if the bathroom cold water is taken from a cold water storage cistern. The hot water will come from the hot tank, fed in turn from the same cistern. If the bathroom cold water is piped from the mains – in a direct system – then the bidet must have separate hot and cold taps.

Bidets – made, like more conventional washbasins, of ceramic material – normally have a built-in overflow discharging into the waste outlet via a slot in the waste fitting.

Once all the fittings are in place you can stand the bidet in the position where it's to be fixed so you can work out where the supply pipes and the waste outlet pipes will run. If your bathroom has modern copper or stainless steel hot and cold water distribution pipes then the task of laying in the pipes to the bidet should be fairly straightforward. You should use 15mm (½in) pipe, and the connections to the tap or mixer tails can be made using a special fitting which has a compression or capillary joint inlet on one side and a swivel tap connector or 'cap and lining joint' on the other which attaches to the tap tail (see PLUMBING FITTINGS). But since the final lengths of the supply pipes to the bidet are likely to be concealed behind the appliance, this is where two short lengths of flexible corrugated pipe with a swivel tap connector at one end can make installation that much easier.

The main bathroom water supplies are usually run in 22mm pipe, so you'll need 22mm to 15mm branch reducing tees when you come to connect your branch pipe into them. If your bathroom was installed in pre-metrication days, you'll have imperial sized $\frac{3}{4}$in pipe in place of the 22mm pipe. As you can't use 22mm fittings with this size pipe, you'll have to use some form of adaptor.

Connecting a spray bidet

Before buying a spray bidet you should check on the regulations of your local Water Authority to make sure that the plumbing system of your home complies with these regulations, or can be made to do so. In all probability you'll need to run a separate cold water supply pipe from the cold water storage cistern to the bidet. You're not allowed to run this branch from another cold water distribution pipe, or to make a direct connection from the main. Similarly the hot water supply to the bidet must be taken by a separate distribution pipe from just above the hot water storage cylinder and not as a branch from the existing bathroom hot water supply pipe. A further requirement is likely to be that the base of the cold water storage cistern must be at least 2.75mm (9ft) above the level of the bidet inlet – a rule that could involve you in raising the position of your cistern.

While ordinary basin taps can be used for over-rim bidets, a special mixer with a diversion valve and a supply pipe to the spray must be fitted into a spray bidet. These mixers often incorporate a pop-up waste which enables the waste plug to be raised and the bidet emptied by pressing a control knob which is part of the mixer and diversion valve mechanism. This kind of bidet is normally sold with mixer, spray and pop-up waste already fitted.

Dealing with the waste water

The waste water from a bidet must run through a trap. If your house has a single stack drainage system this should have a deep seal of 75mm (3in). With the older two-pipe drainage system a shallow seal of 50mm (2in) is permissible.

If you've got a single stack system you'll have to run the branch waste from the bidet and connect it into the main stack. And you'll have to follow the district or borough council's requirements regarding the gradient of the branch waste pipe and how the possibility of it being fouled by the discharges from the WC can be averted.

If your house has a two-pipe drainage system, then it's important to remember that a bidet is a waste and not a soil appliance, so the waste water can be run into an open gully.

HOW TO RUN THE PIPEWORK

1 An over-rim supply bidet

With this sort of bidet the water supply can be teed directly off the nearest available hot and cold supplies – usually those supplying the basin or bath. The connections at the bidet end are the same as the tap connections at the basin. The waste can connect to the nearest waste pipe or can be run direct to a hopper head or soil stack.

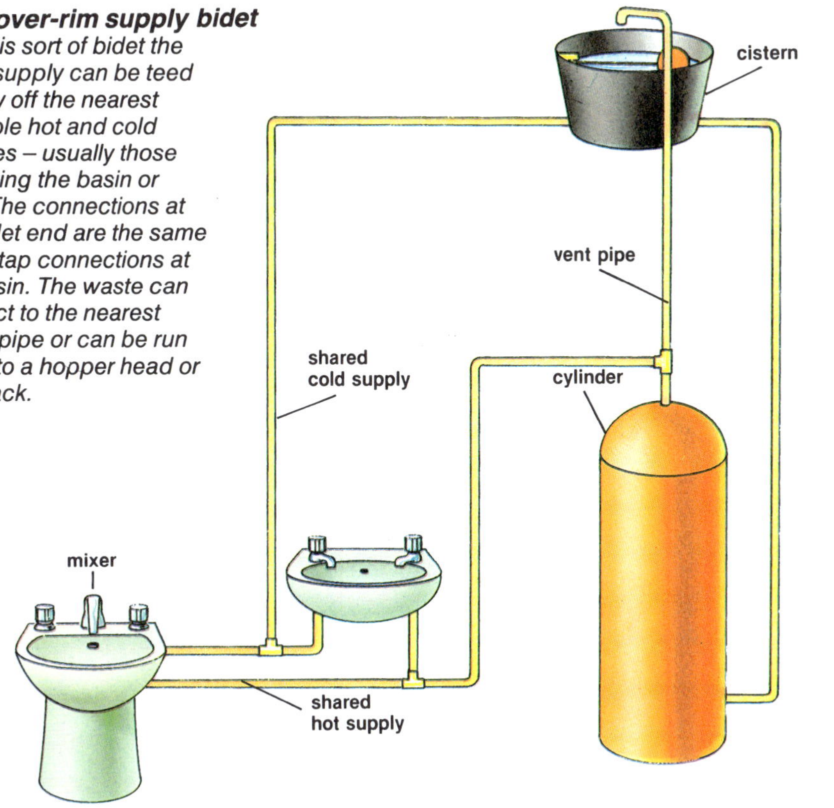

2 A spray-supply bidet

Here the supplies must be connected directly to the cold cistern and the hot cylinder outlet.

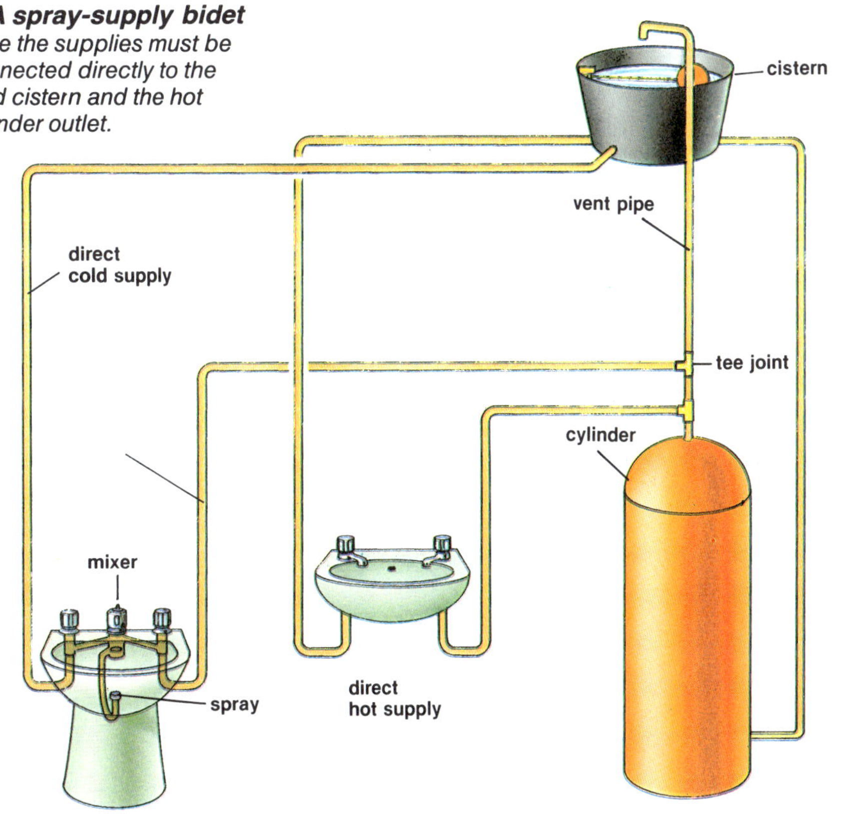

PLUMBING IN A SPRAY BIDET

1 *Take the rather complex plumbing assembly provided with the bidet and dismantle the central control mechanism with a screwdriver.*

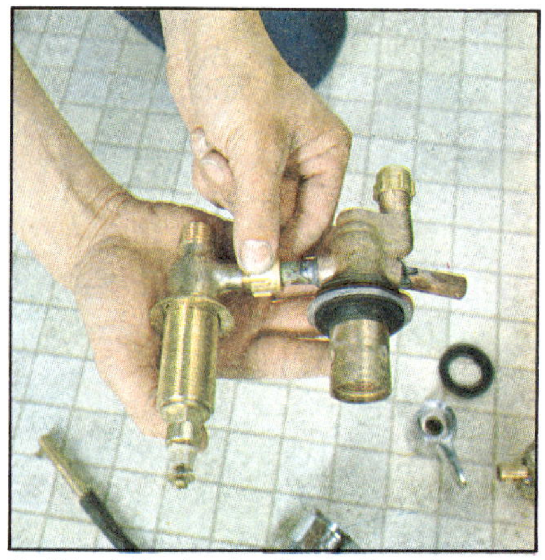

2 *Attach the tap bodies to the wing pipes of the central unit, fixing them in the usual way with the compression fittings which are supplied.*

3 *Place the back-nuts and washers over the tap bodies, insert them into the tap holes in the bidet and screw up the head nuts.*

6 *Tighten up the back-nuts on the tap tails. These may be rather inaccessible and you will have to use any spanner or wrench that fits.*

7 *Fix the spray outlet in position at the bottom of the bowl. Make sure the rubber washers are in place, then tighten the back-nut.*

TIP

8 *Make a seal round the underside of the outlet flange using a long sausage of plumber's putty, and bed the flange firmly into place.*

11 *Attach the waste linkage to the waste outlet, making the connection via a split pin. You may have to shorten the control rod.*

12 *Attach the plastic spray outlet pipe to the control unit and to the spray; both connections are made with compression fittings.*

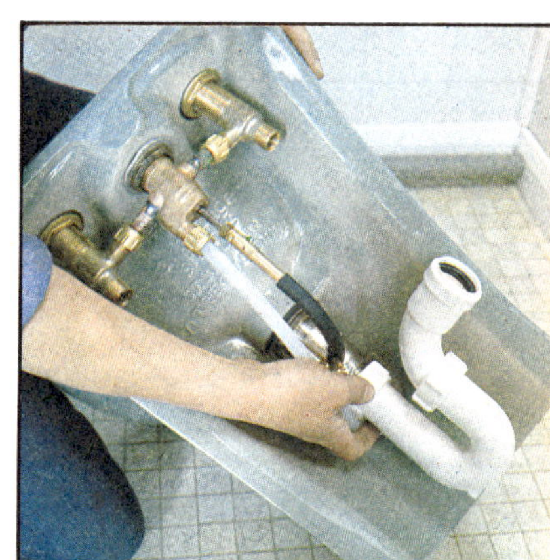

13 *Attach the waste trap to the waste outlet pipe and check all connections for tightness. Then place the bidet in position.*

4 *Fix the cover flanges in place over the tap heads, after putting a ring of plumber's putty round the underside of each one of them.*

5 *Put the central control column into position, making sure that the rubber gasket is correctly seated underneath it.*

9 *With all three washers in position, tighten the back-nut; this will squeeze out excess putty inside the bowl. Then remove the excess.*

10 *Screw on the waste outlet extension, slip the waste control rod in through the control unit and fix the control link to the waste.*

14 *Complete the tap head fittings by pushing on the shrouds, screwing up and pressing home the cap and index; fit the control knob too.*

15 *Attach the waste outlet and water inlet pipes, and check for leaks. Then screw the bidet to the floor using brass screws.*

Ready Reference

PLUMBING CONNECTIONS

Spray-supply bidets
These incorporate a switch to direct water to the rim or the spray.

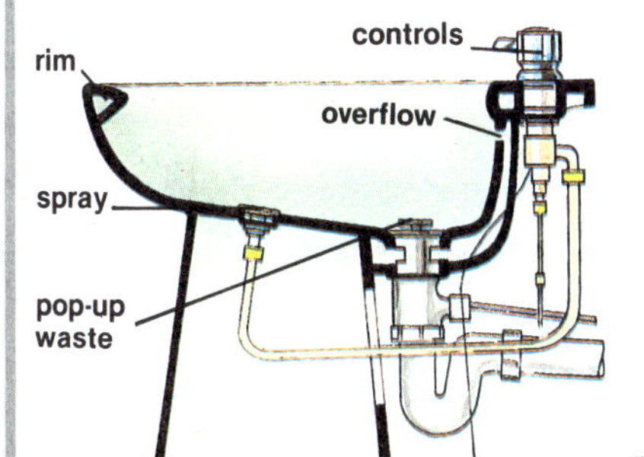

Over rim supply bidets
The water supply is through separate taps or a mixer unit, as for a washbasin.

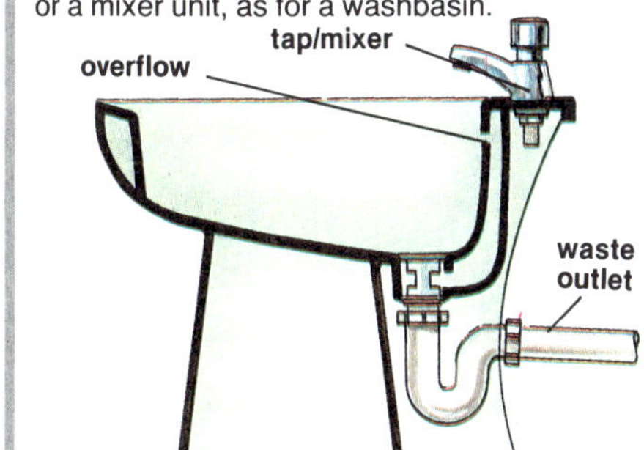

The components
Connecting up the supply and waste pipes simple involves assembling washers and back-nuts in the correct order to the tap tails and waste outlet. Check that you have all the necessary components before starting work.

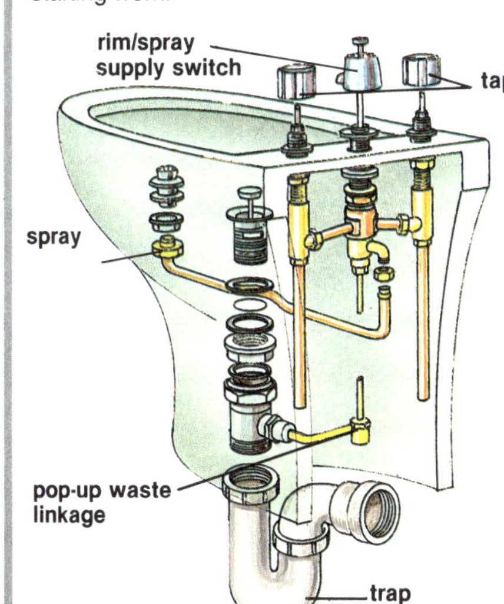

REPLACING YOUR WC

Replacing your WC need not be a frightening prospect provided you follow a few basic rules. It also gives you the opportunity to install a quieter and more efficient piece of equipment.

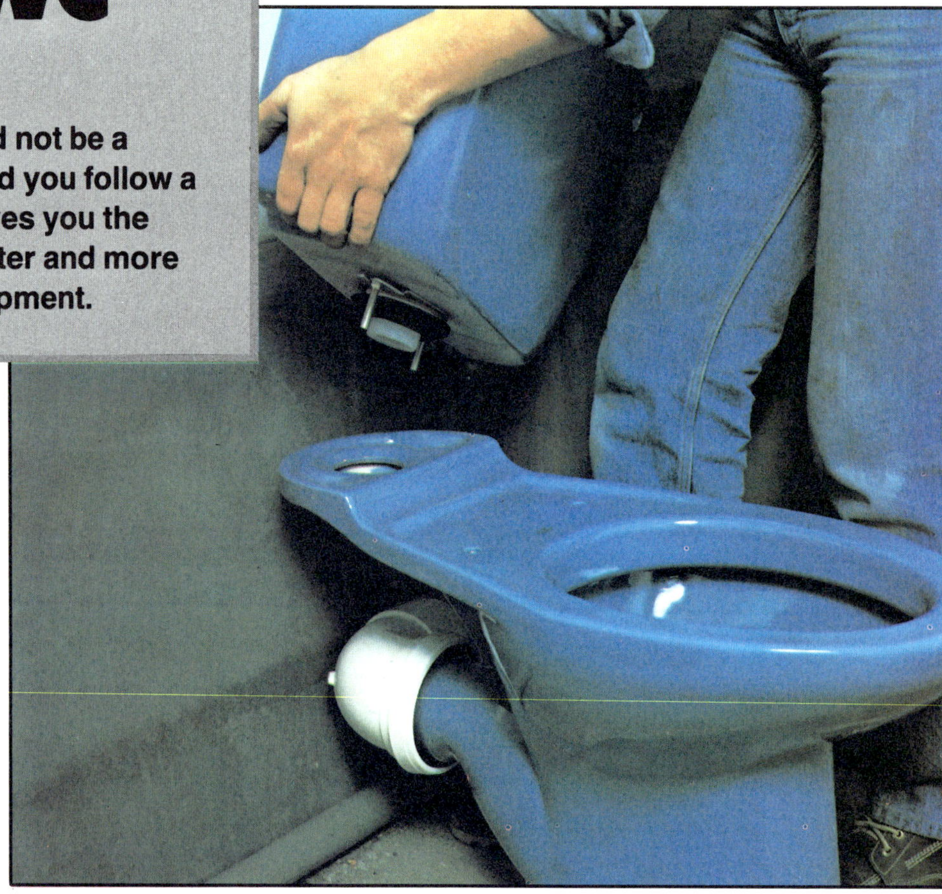

There are several reasons why you may wish to remove and replace your WC suite. The existing pan may be cracked, in which case replacement must not be delayed, and no attempt should be made to repair it. Or the porcelain may be crazed making it unsightly, and difficult to keep clean. Most likely, however, the reason will be that your existing WC is simply old fashioned and due for replacement as part of an overall improvement plan.

Pan or cistern?

If it's just the pan you find fault with then that's all you need to replace. Colours for sanitary-ware, as WCs are usually called by the manufacturers, are fairly standardised, and you should have no difficulty in obtaining a pan to match the existing cistern.

If, on the other hand, you want to convert an old-fashioned lavatory suite with a high-level cistern, it may be possible to replace only the flushing cistern and flush pipe (or 'flush bend' as it is often called) with a low level one, while keeping the existing pan.

However, in order to accommodate the flushing cistern, the pans of low level suites are usually positioned 25 to 50mm (1 to 2in) further from the wall behind the suite than are those of high level ones. If you overlook this point you are likely to find that the seat and cover of the pan cannot be raised properly when the new cistern is fitted.

Slim-line cisterns

In recent years manufacturers have developed slim-line flushing cisterns or 'flush panels' only about 115mm (4¼in) deep. These can, in most cases, be used to convert a WC from high level to low level operation without moving the pan. With such a cistern the flushing inlet to the pan can be as little as 130mm (5¼in) from the wall behind, instead of the 200 to 230 (8 to 9in) required by an ordinary low level cistern. To make room for the full 9 litres (2 gal) of water needed for an adequate flush, these slimline cisterns are rather wider from side to side than conventional ones. So make sure that there is sufficient unobstructed width of wall behind the suite to accommodate it.

PLANNING THE MOVE

The biggest problem concerns the position of the soil stack. In this bathroom the old soil pipe was disconnected, and a new soil pipe run was installed on the outside of the bathroom wall to link the new WC to the existing soil stack. This was much neater than running the new pipe inside the bathroom, where it would have had to be boxed in.

The other alteration to existing pipework involved cutting the cold feed to the cistern part-way along its run, and re-connecting it to the new cistern.

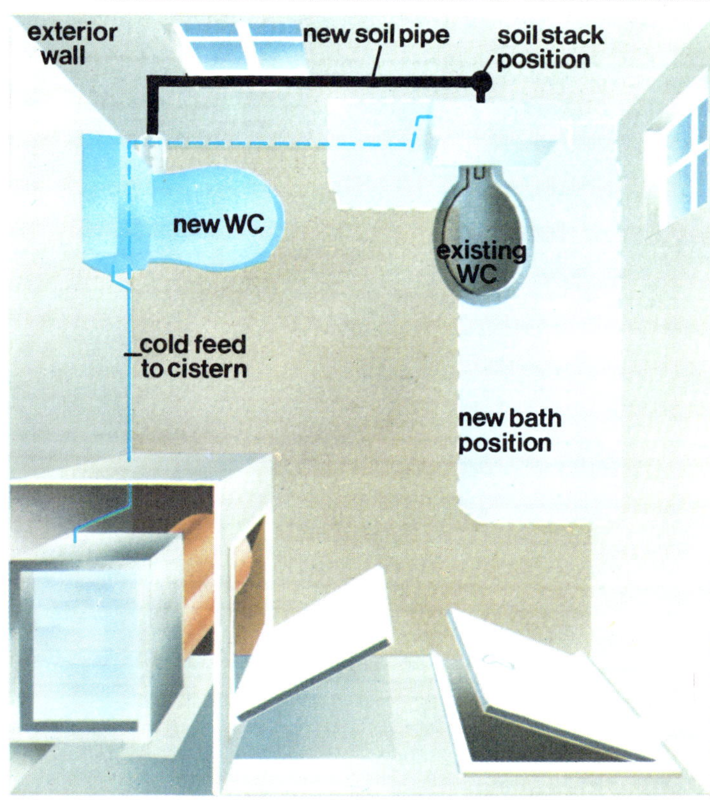

Siphonic suites

Close-coupled lavatory suites, in which the pan and cistern form one unit without even the short flush bend of a low level cistern, are neater in appearance than the other kinds. They are particularly silent and effective where they are flushed and cleansed by siphonic action, as distinct from the 'wash down' action in which flushing simply releases the full contents of the cistern into the pan, and the weight of water carries away its contents. They also provide a larger water surface area than older pans, an important factor in maintaining the cleanliness of the pan.

There are two kinds of siphonic suite, single-trap and double-trap. The single-trap pattern is the simpler and cheaper. The outlet is first constricted and then widened to connect to the branch drain or soil pipe. When the suite is flushed, water completely fills the restricted section of the outlet and passes on, taking air with it, to create a partial vacuum. Atmospheric pressure then pushes the contents of the pan into the drain. The siphonic action is broken, often with a gurgle, as air passes under the bend of the trap.

With a double-trap siphonic suite, a specially designed air pipe or 'pressure reducer' connects the air space between the two traps to the channel through which the flushing water passes. As this water flows past the pressure reducer it sucks up air from the space between the two traps, in the same way that the wind passing over the top of a chimney sucks up air from a room below. It's this that creates the partial vacuum on which siphonic action depends. Where a double-trap siphonic suite is working properly, you'll see the water level in the pan fall before the 'flush' water flows in. Although more expensive than other kinds, these suites are valuable where, as in an entrance lobby cloakroom for instance, silent operation is a prime consideration.

Just as low level WC suites normally project further from the wall behind them than high level ones, close-coupled suites project further than either. Don't forget this when considering the provision of such a suite in a small bathroom or cloakroom. You may have to change the position of the washbasin and this, in turn, could obstruct the door.

Pan fixings

Moving an existing WC pan isn't always easy. It's likely to depend largely upon whether it is installed upstairs or on the ground floor. Upstairs WCs usually have a P-trap outlet, which is almost horizontal and is connected to a branch soil pipe by means of a putty or mortar joint. This can easily be broken with a club hammer and cold chisel once you have disconnected the pan from the floor.

Downstairs WCs usually have their bases firmly cemented to a solid floor and usually have an S-trap outlet which is vertical. This connects via a cement joint to an earthenware drain socket protruding above floor level. To remove such a pan it's necessary to break the outlet. Use a cold chisel to detach the front part of the pan from the floor, then use a cold chisel and hammer again to clear the pan outlet and the joining material from the drain socket.

Nowadays it is usual to connect both ground floor and upstairs WCs to the soil pipe using a flexible joint, usually a patent plastic push-fit joint with a spigot that is inserted into the drain and a 'finned' socket that fits over the WC pan outlet.

Such patent joins are nowadays manufactured in a range that covers virtually any WC installation. Not only are they easy to use but they help reduce the noise of a flushing lavatory. It's not considered to be good practice today to cement the base of a WC to a solid floor, as the setting of the cement can create stresses resulting in a cracked pan. It is best to remove every trace of cement from the floor and, having achieved a dead-level base, to secure the WC pan with screws driven into plugs pushed into holes drilled in the floor.

How to start

After you have turned off the water supply and flushed the cistern to empty it, the next step is to disconnect the cistern's water supply, overflow and outlet pipes. So begin by unscrewing the cap-nut connecting the water-supply pipe to the cistern's ball-valve inlet. Then undo the back-nut retaining the cistern's overflow or warning pipe. Finally undo the large nut which secures the threaded outlet of the cistern to the flush pipe. It should now be possible to lift the old cistern off its supporting bracket or brackets.

If the WC suite is a very old one and screwed to a timber floor, unscrew and remove the pan's fixing screws. Then, taking the pan in both hands, pull it from side to side and away from the wall. If the connection to the soil pipe is made with a mastic or putty joint, the pan outlet should come easily out of its socket (which will have to be cleaned of all jointing material before the new unit is fitted). If a rigid cement joint has been used then there's usually no alternative but to use a bit of force. This means deliberately breaking the pan outlet, just behind the trap and above the pipe socket, with a club hammer. You can then prise the front part of the pan away from the floor using a cold chisel and hammer. This will separate the pan outlet from the pipe. At this point it's a

Ready Reference

PAN AND CISTERN POSITIONS

There are various WC suite arrangements you're likely to come across. The position of the pan in relation to the cistern is crucial, and if you're changing one without the other you must measure up carefully, to ensure that major changes of position can be avoided.

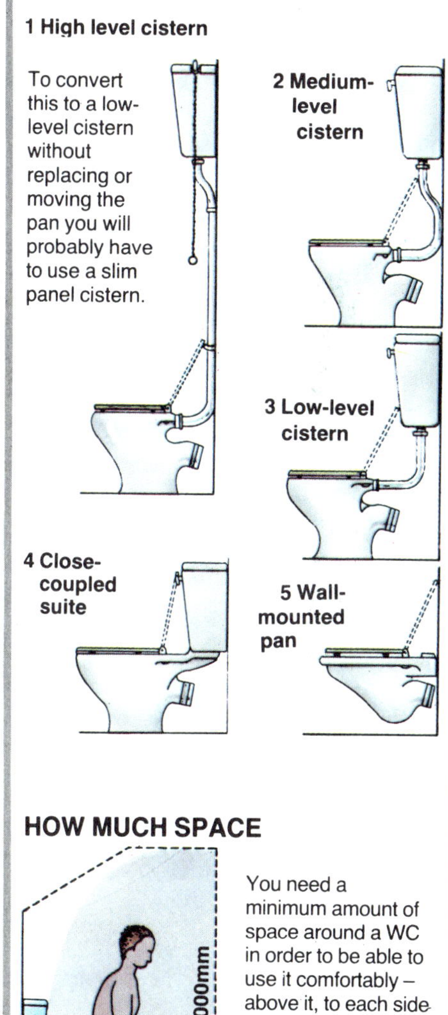

HOW MUCH SPACE

You need a minimum amount of space around a WC in order to be able to use it comfortably – above it, to each side of it and in front of it.

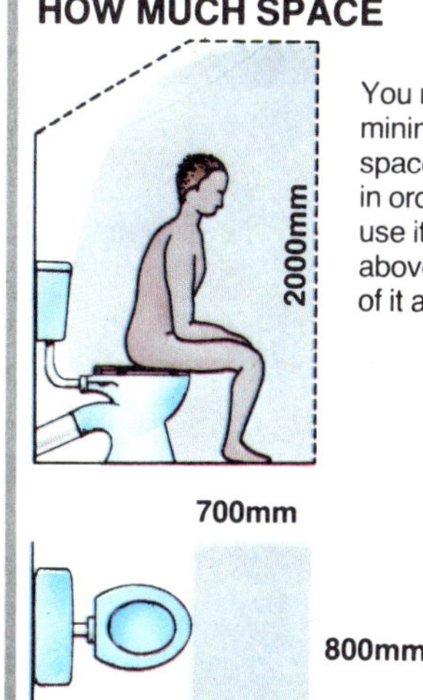

REMOVING THE OLD PAN

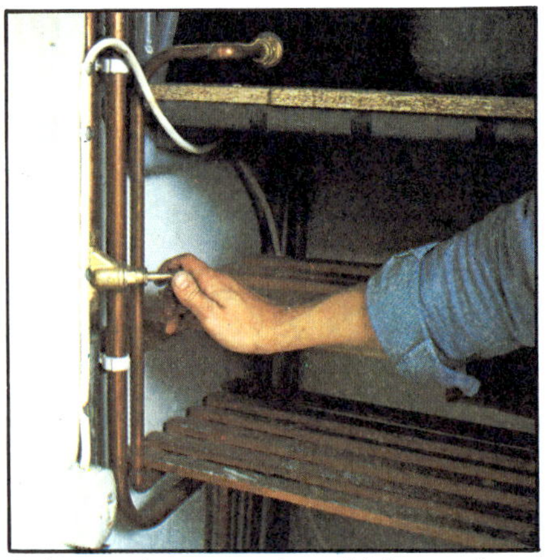

1 *Locate the water pipe which supplies the WC cistern and completely shut off the stop valve which controls it. If no valve exists, block the cistern outlet.*

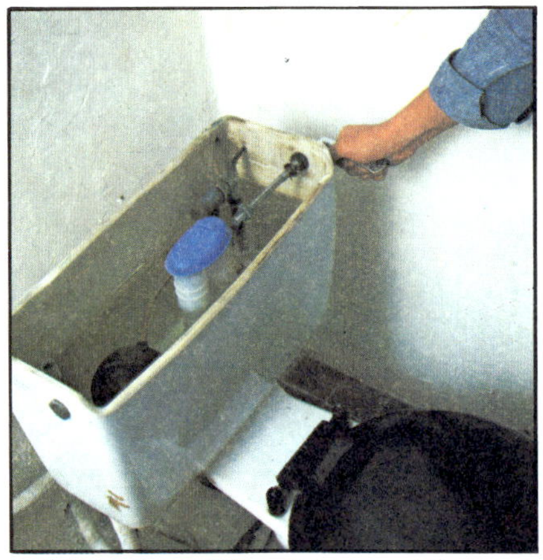

2 *Lift the top off the cistern and then press the flush handle to empty it. No more fresh water should flow in as the ball float falls.*

3 *Disconnect the overflow pipe. If it is made of lead you should replace it with a PVC pipe run. Saw it off if you are repositioning the WC elsewhere.*

4 *Disconnect the supply pipe in the same way as the overflow. If you are replacing the piping altogether, you can cut through it with a hacksaw.*

5 *Disconnect the cistern from the pan. A close-coupled one is lifted off; with other suites you may have to disconnect the flush pipe between cistern and pan.*

6 *Unscrew the pan from the floor, and then use a hammer and cold chisel to break the joint between the pan and the outlet, tapping gently but firmly.*

7 *When you have fractured the joint, ease the pan away from the pipe. Even if it is bedded on mortar it should come away easily. Chip away the old mortar.*

TIP

8 *Dispose of the pan and extract any loose bits of debris from the socket. Stuff newspaper into the opening to stop bits falling into the soil pipe.*

9 *If you are going to use the pipe again clean it out carefully, ready to be connected up to the new WC pan with a proprietary connector.*

INSTALLING THE NEW PAN

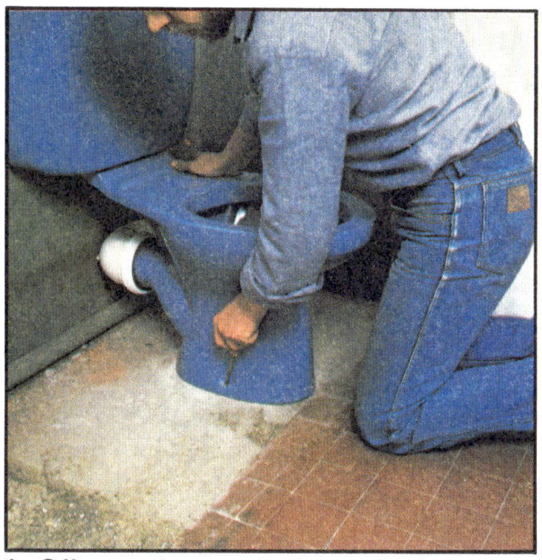

1 *Offer up the pan to the outlet (note that here a new PVC soil pipe has been installed). When it fits snugly, mark down the positions for the fixing screws.*

2 *Drill the holes and reposition the pan and cistern. Fit the pan outlet into the white push-fit adaptor so that it is firmly in position.*

3 *Secure the cistern to the wall with screws and plugs. Then attach the new overflow pipe, finally tightening up the lock-nut with an adjustable spanner.*

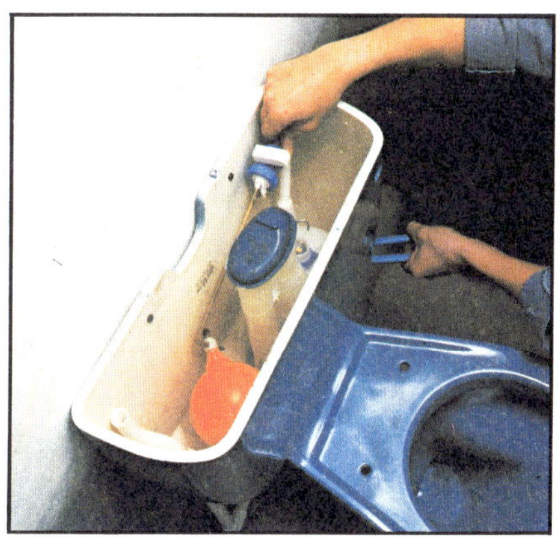

4 *Assemble the internal flushing mechanism, see* Ready Reference. *Attach the water supply pipe and the flushing handle.*

5 *Fit the seat assembly, making sure that the gaskets are correctly in place between the seat and the pan; screw up the nuts tightly.*

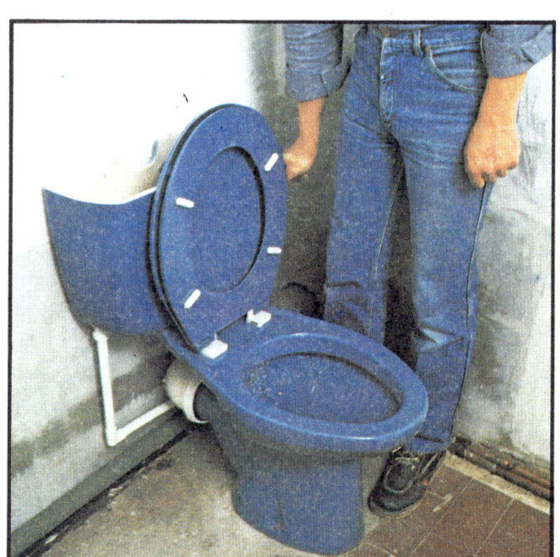

6 *Restore the water supply. Check that the cistern fills to the correct level and adjust the ball-valve if it does not. Finally flush to fill the pan trap.*

Ready Reference

CISTERN MECHANISMS

There are two sorts of flushing mechanism the bell type in well-bottom cisterns and the piston type found otherwise. The latter is by far the more popular today.

well-bottom cistern for replacement of high-level arrangements

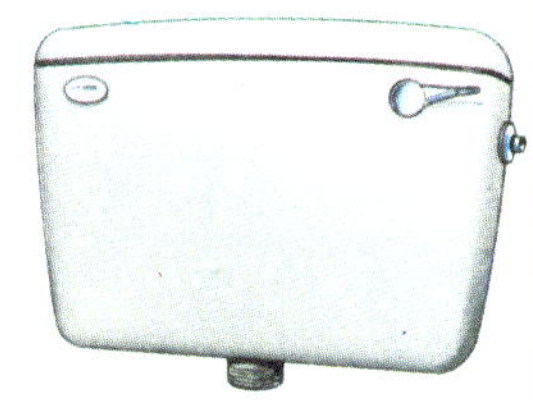

lever flush cistern for low-level suite

slim-line flush panel where depth is restricted – usually when a high-level arrangement is converted to a low-level one

THE FLUSH MECHANISM

You'll find you have to assemble the mechanism which is bagged up inside the new cistern. Lay out the components (A) and check them against the enclosed instruction leaflet before assembling them correctly (B).

A

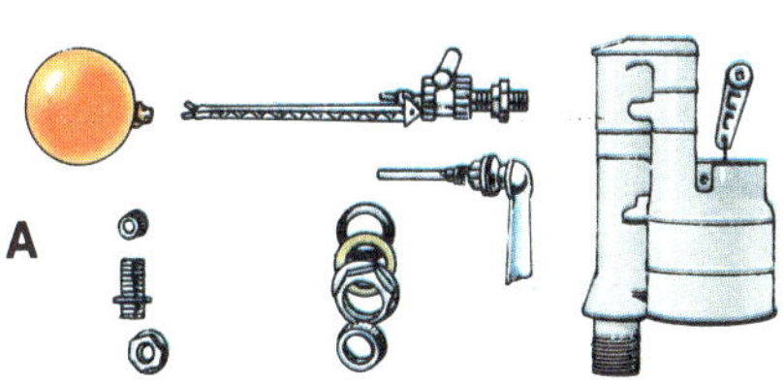

B

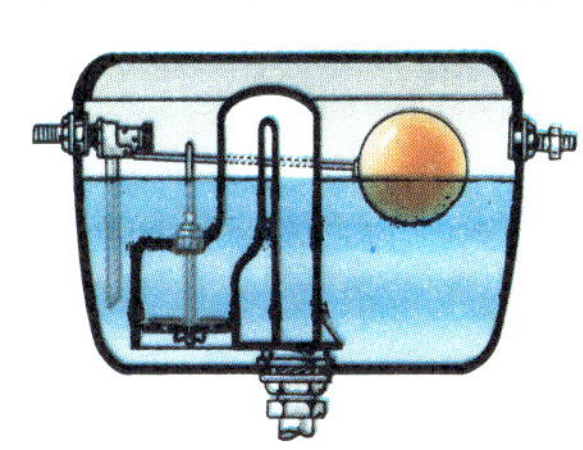

For more information on WCs see the following section.

THREE TYPES OF WC

Washdown WC

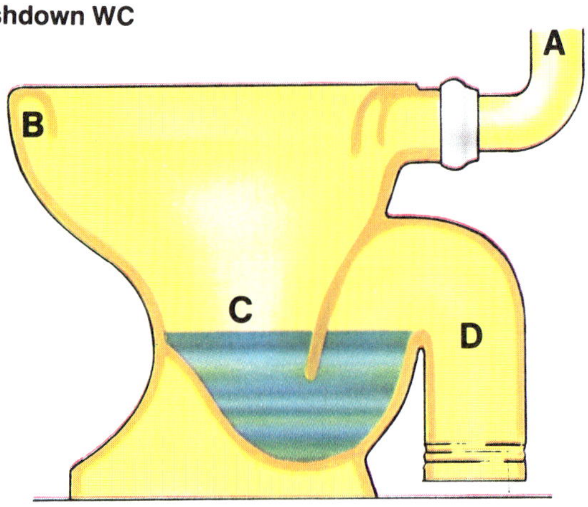

Left: Cross-section of a traditional WC pan showing the water supply inlet from the cistern (A), the open flush rim (B), the water seal (C) and the S-trap outlet (D).

Double-trap siphonic WC

Right: Cross-section of a double-trap siphonic WC suite – close-coupled. When water leaves the cistern it flows through a valve (A) which lowers the pressure in the chamber (B). This sets up a powerful siphon drawing the contents of the basin through the traps (C) and (D) into the soil pipe. At the same time the sides of the bowl are thoroughly washed by streams of water from the perforated rim (E). After flushing, the two traps are resealed by the after-flush chamber (F). The water only rises in the basin after the flush, not during it.

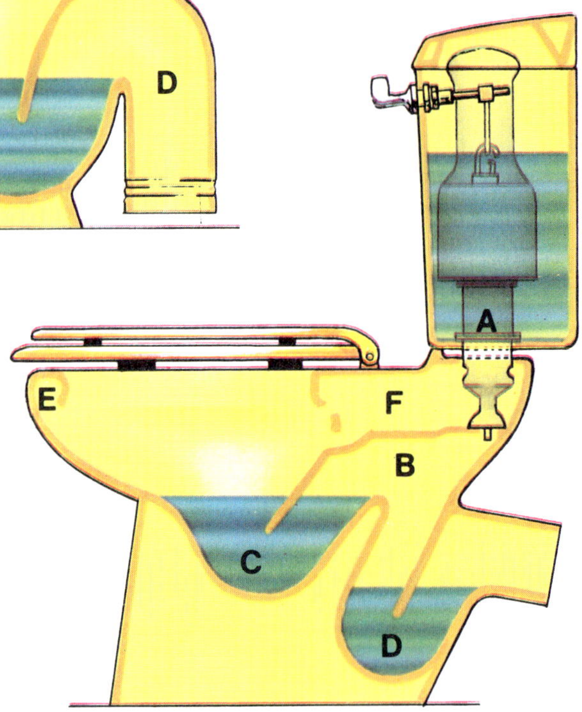

Single-trap siphonic WC

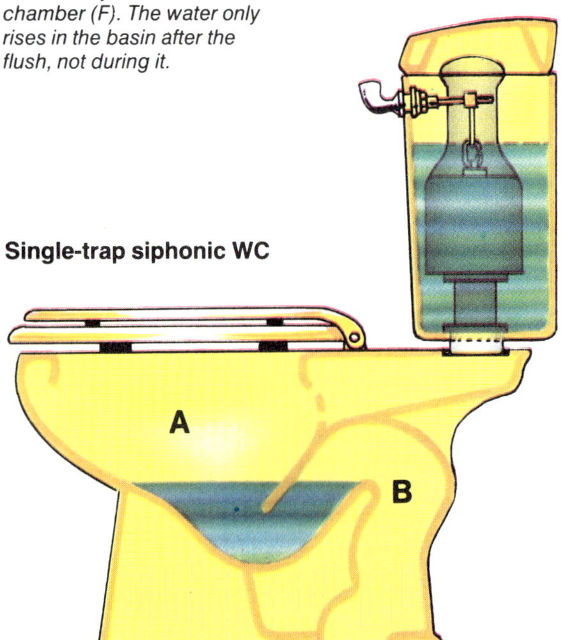

Left: Cross-section of a single-trap siphonic WC suite – close-coupled. When the flush mechanism is activated the water quickly rises in the bowl (A) and then rapidly discharges over the weir (B). This draws air through the top of the trap and creates the siphonic action which completely empties the contents of the pan. The trap is then refilled.

good idea to stuff a bundle of rags or screwed-up newspaper into the drain socket to prevent any debris getting into the soil pipe. Next attack the socket to remove the remains of the pan's outlet. For this, use a small cold chisel and hammer but do it carefully to avoid damaging the drain socket itself – this will be used again. It's best to keep the point of the chisel pointing towards the centre of the pipe. Try to break it right down to the shoulder of the socket at one point and the rest will then come out fairly easily. Repeat the chipping process to remove all the old jointing material. Remove the bundle of rags or newspaper with the fragments of pipe and jointing material. Then with your cold chisel, remove every trace of the cement base that secured the old pan to the floor.

Installing the new pan

Don't set the pan on a cement base – just use screws and plugs to fix it to the floor. But first you've got to get the connection to the pipe socket right. Start by positioning the patent push-fit joint in the pipe end. Then offer up the new pan to the patent push-fit socket and move the pan around until it fits snugly. To fix the pan, mark the screw positions on the floor by tapping a nail through the screw-holes, and draw round the base on the floor so that you can replace it in exactly the same position. Drill holes in the floor at the points marked and finally fit the screws. If it's a solid floor, of course, it's essential to use plastic or fibre plugs in the screw holes.

For fixing the pan, it's advisable to use brass non-corroding screws with a lead washer slipped over each one so you won't crack the pan as you tighten the screws. Screw the pan down, checking that it is exactly horizontal with the aid of a spirit level laid across the top of the bowl. If it is not dead-level, pack the lower side with thin wood or plastic strips. The latter are more suitable because thin wood rots too easily. Finally check that the outlet of the pan is firmly pushed into the connector and that you've followed any specific fitting instructions from the manufacturer.

Fitting the cistern

Fix the new cistern to the wall at the level above the pan recommended by the manufacturer. In the case of a separate cistern, secure the upper end of the flush pipe to the cistern, usually by means of a large nut, and the lower end to the pan's flushing horn with a rubber cone connector. With a close-coupled suite, follow the manufacturer's instructions. You will now quite likely have to extend or cut back the water supply pipe to connect it to the new cistern. Complete the job by cutting and fitting a new overflow.

REPOSITIONING YOUR WC

Often moving a WC is the only answer to bathroom planning problems. By using plastic soil pipes the job can be made fairly straightforward, and also presents the possibility of installing an extra WC.

You may want to move the position of your WC because you're redesigning your bathroom. You may even want to take it out of the bathroom altogether and create a separate toilet compartment by partitioning off part of an adjoining room. This would make more space in which to install a bidet or a shower compartment. Or you may want to provide a second WC to cope with an expanding family.

Rules and regulations

You will need to install a new WC pan and cistern as described previously. You will also have to adapt the water supply piping, provide an overflow for the new cistern and install a new soil pipe. In the case of the water supply and the soil pipe, this may mean either adapting the old pipes or putting in a new set of pipes and taking out the old redundant ones at the same time.

The adapted or replacement soil pipe must comply with the requirements of the Building Regulations as interpreted by your local authority. It's therefore essential to find out what you can and cannot do by discussing your proposals with the relevant official, who may be called the Building Inspector or Building Control Officer. The same officer must eventually approve the standard of the finished job.

If you want to put in a new WC in a separate compartment, the Regulations say that it must not have direct access to a living room or a kitchen. This may mean creating a lobby between the new compartment and the room it leads off, and installing a door in the lobby as well as one in the new compartment. However, you can have direct entry to a WC from a bedroom.

You have to think about ventilation as well. Any lavatory compartment must have an openable window in an outside wall or must be provided with an automatically-operating extractor fan (usually connected to the light switch) that is ducted to an outside wall.

Water supply and overflow

Putting in a water supply to a new cistern is straightforward. Make a T-joint with a convenient 15mm (½in) cold water pipe and run a branch pipe (using compression or soldered capillary joints) to the tail of the flushing cistern's ball-valve inlet. Don't forget that if the cistern is to be supplied with water from the main storage cistern it will need a low-pressure ball-valve, but if it's to be connected to the rising main it will need a high-pressure one.

You will also have to connect an overflow pipe to the cistern; this goes through the outside wall and should stick out far enough to take any overflow clear of the wall surface. If the WC compartment doesn't have an outside wall the overflow pipe is usually taken to a point over the bath. The end of the pipe must be open.

The soil pipe

If you are moving the pan a short distance, either a few feet along the bathroom wall or into the adjoining room, you can use the old connection to the outside soil pipe. You put on an angled socket and use a length of 100mm (4in) PVC soil pipe. You can do this as long as the whole length of pipe from the pan to the soil stack is not more than 6m (19ft 6in) and has a minimum gradient towards the stack of about 20mm per metre (¾in per yard). While this is a convenient and easy way of making a new soil run it means that you end up with an extended length of rather bulky pipe along the inside wall. This can be disguised by boxing it in, but it still takes up valuable space at floor level, and this might destroy the original purpose of installing it.

If you want to avoid a long inside soil pipe run or if you are installing a second WC on the same floor you can run the pipe straight through the wall and put the main pipe on the outside wall. This would mean that a new connection would have to be made to the soil stack. If the stack is made of cast iron you can't do this, and you would have to replace it with a new plastic stack.

An alternative is to connect the two WCs in series along one soil pipe run using swept junctions. In which case the maximum pipe run from the further WC to the soil stack can be as much as 15m (49ft) but you're not likely to need this much in an ordinary house. If the second WC is on a different floor you may be able to make a new soil pipe connection into a plastic stack, but a new groundfloor WC should be connected below ground to the underground drain via an S-trap (vertical) outlet. The operation requires considerable building work and a new entry to the underground drain, so you should employ the services of a professional builder.

How to move the WC

Remove the existing WC pan from its outlet pipe (covered in the previous section). If this pan connection is fairly modern and has been made using a rubber or plastic collar, then it may be possible to remove it intact and install it in the new position. But if its removal means breaking the pan itself in order to detach it from the outlet, then you'll obviously have to buy a new pan.

If you are going to use the existing outlet, clean it up and fit an adaptor bend to take the new pipe run. These bends are available in a number of designs to suit the angle you need. Then fix a length of 100mm (4in) PVC pipe to the adaptor (usually a push-fit type, but see the adaptor's instructions). If possible the length of pipe should run all the way to the new WC pan site in one length, but if you have to join it there are suitable connectors available.

In fixing the pipe run you may have to make a hole in an intervening wall. To do this, mark the position of the hole with circles on each side of the wall, using the end of the pipe as a template. Drill holes all round the marked out circles and carefully chop out the hole with a club hammer and chisel. If you're tackling a timber-framed stud partition wall obviously you must avoid the vertical studs, so drill small test holes first to ensure your planned pipe run passes between them. When you've made the hole, clean up the edges and ease the pipe through.

At the other end of the pipe, fix another adaptor bend of the type which will match the outlet from the WC pan. Your supplier will tell you which one is suitable. Before you fix the pan make sure it lines up with the adaptor. You should also check that the finished pipe position has a minimum fall towards the outlet of 20mm per metre (¾in per yard). It shouldn't be any more than 30mm per metre (1¼in per yard) on long runs or else you may find that the water trap in the new pan will siphon away (see pages 14 to 18). Don't forget that the total length of pipe from the pan to the stack should be no longer than 6m (19ft 6in).

Fix the pan to the adaptor and to the floor, and attach the cistern (described on pages 106–110). It's best to use a P-trap pan rather

MOVING A WC

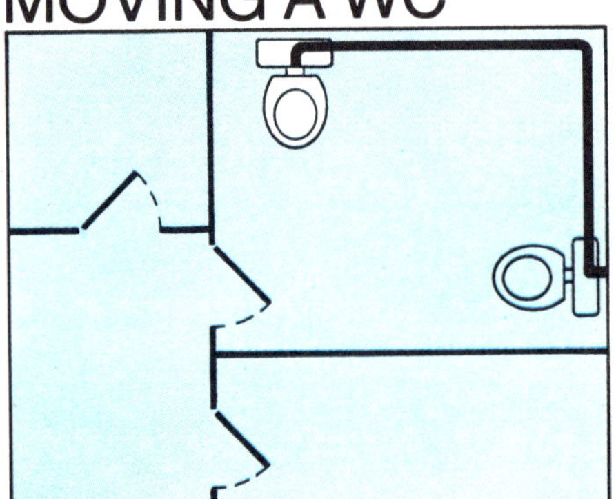

1 Altering the WC position in the bathroom

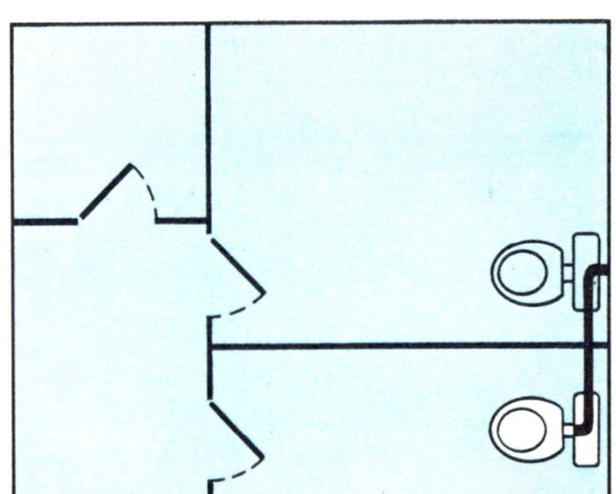

2 Moving the WC to an adjoining room

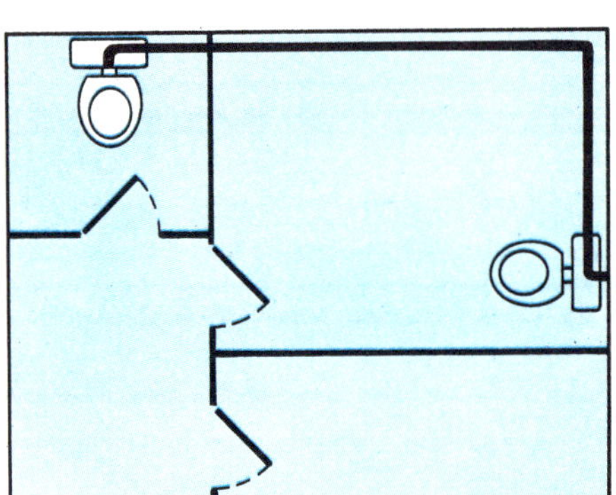

3 Moving the WC to an adjoining room using a longer soil pipe run

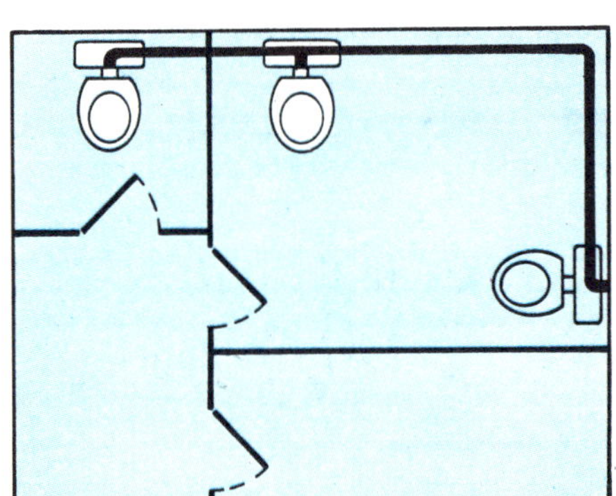

4 Moving inside the bathroom and installing another WC in series in an adjoining room

Ready Reference

CHECKING YOUR PLANS

Repositioning your WC or installing an extra one, means putting in new pipework for the water supply, the cistern overflow, and the soil pipe. Make sure that the design of the new soil pipe run conforms with the Building Regulations which include the relevant sections of the Public Health Acts. Discuss your plans with the local Building Officer before you start any installation. He must approve them and will want to inspect the finished work.

POSITIONING THE WC

Make sure that:

- there is no direct access to a WC from a living room or kitchen, though there can be from a bedroom
- any WC compartment has either an openable window in an outside wall or a duct to an outside wall which is controlled by an automatically operating extractor fan (usually connected to the light switch)
- the soil pipe run from the pan to the stack should be no more than 6m (19ft 6in) long with a minimum gradient of 20mm per metre (¾in per yard) and slopes towards the soil stack
- any new connection of the soil pipe to the stack must be swept, as must be the connection of WCs in series to the soil run
- any ground floor WCs which are connected directly to the underground drain must be situated so that the distance between the top of the WC trap and the bottom of the bend leading into the drain is not more than 1.5m (5ft).

Note: To avoid direct access from a living room to a new WC compartment you may have to construct a lobby of some sort. In the case of an existing windowless bathroom, a fan and duct should already be fitted.

Ground floor WCs

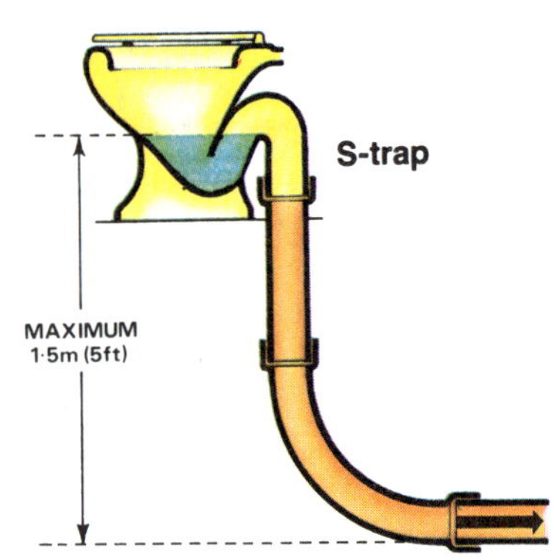

to underground drain

USING THE CONNECTION

You can connect the soil outlet of your repositioned WC to the existing soil outlet, (which is connected to the soil stack), by running new piping along the inside wall. A variety of fittings is available which makes this job comparatively easy as long as you stick to the regulations outlined in the Ready Reference *on the previous page. This can enable you either to move your WC to a different location in the bathroom, or move it to an adjoining room.*

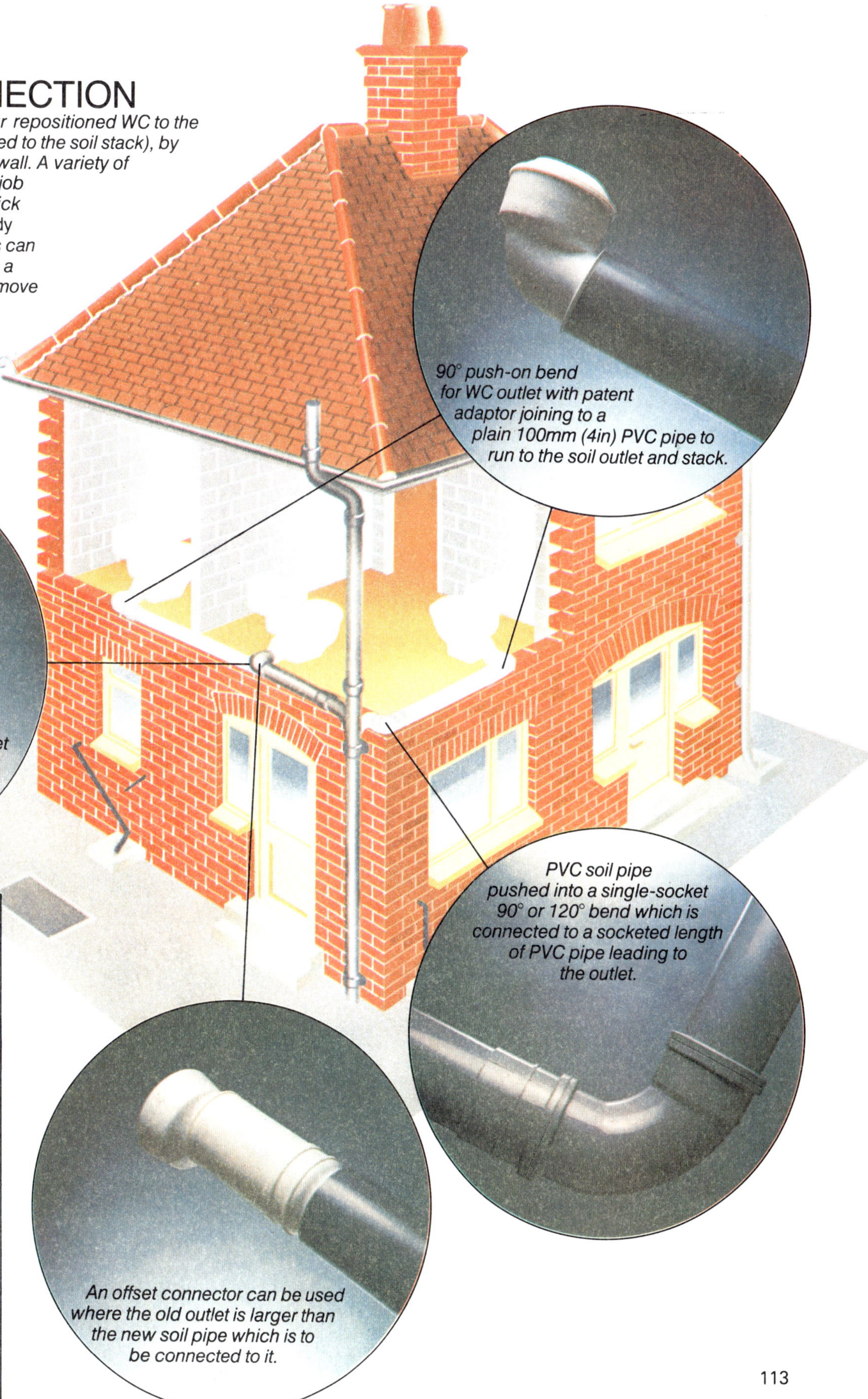

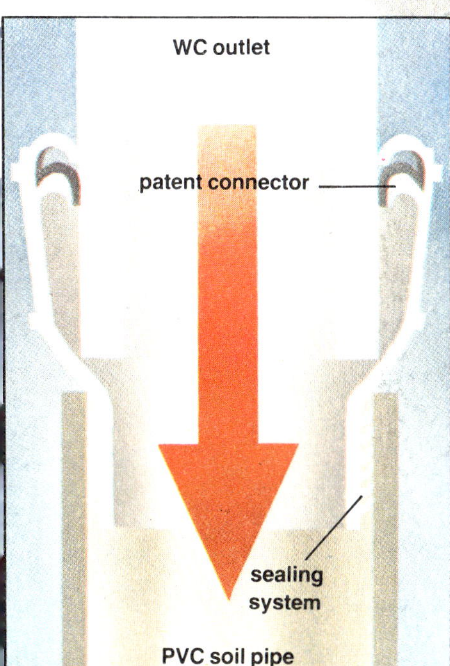

MAKING A NEW CONNECTION

If you want to avoid a long run of soil piping inside or want a second pan on the same floor you will have to make a new connection to the outside stack. If the stack is made of cast iron you'll need to install a new plastic stack.

than an S-trap as otherwise you'll need another adaptor bend, and the less bends you use on soil pipe runs the better. In any case if you're draining into a single-stack system you must have a P-trap pan.

When you've made all the connections and fitted the pan and cistern properly, flush the system and check for leaks.

Making a new stack connection

If it's not practical to use the old soil stack connection for your new WC site, you are faced with a rather larger task – making a new connection to the soil stack somewhere else along its length. A new connection can only be made to a plastic soil pipe; if you've got a cast-iron stack you will have to replace it.

When you have removed the pan from the old position, take out the old soil connection socket and make good the wall and floor. In the new WC site mark out the hole you will need to make in the outside wall. Do this using the pan outlet as a guide. Make the hole as described above and insert a short length of PVC pipe. This should be long enough to be inserted into the pan connector at one end and into a right-angle connector positioned as close to the surface of the outside wall as possible. Link up the pan, the connector and the pipe and make good the inside of the wall.

On the outside, fix the right-angle connector and add to it a length of pipe running all the way to the stack. This pipe should be fixed to the wall using brackets supplied by the soil pipe manufacturer. At the stack a connection can be made by cutting in and inserting a swept junction.

If you want to install two WCs in series using an inside or an outside pipe the connections for the one further from the stack are the same but the junction between that nearer to the stack and the outlet pipe must be via a swept joint.

TWO-PIPE WASTE SYSTEM

The traditional two pipe system takes all soil to the underground drain by one pipe, and all the waste from baths, basins etc down another. It is found in most pre-war houses, and is still used, particularly in bungalows where the installation is spread out.

Roof drainage may flow into the same underground drainage system; it may go into a separate storm drain (out in the street) in areas of high rainfall; or it may drain into a soakaway in the garden.

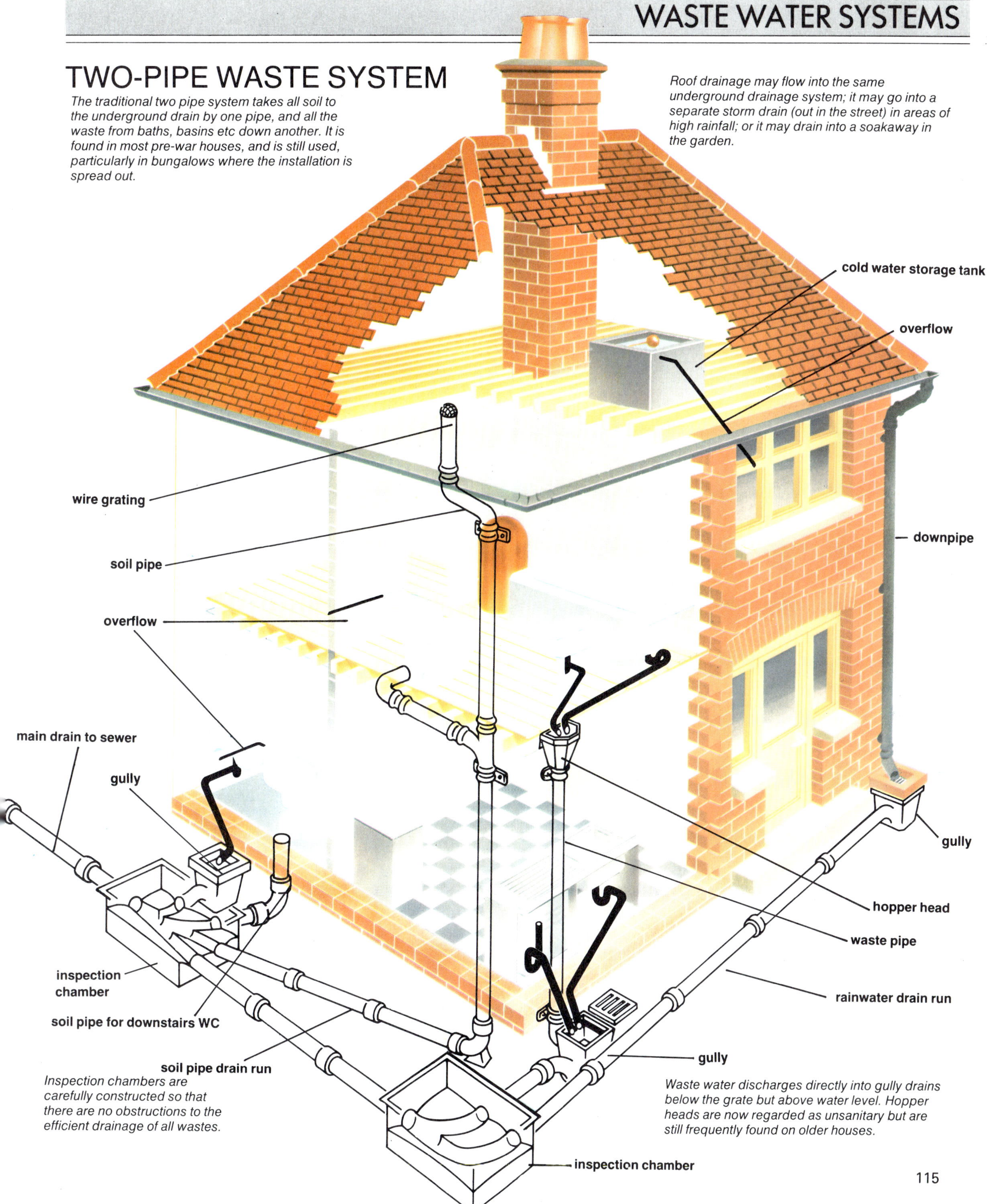

Inspection chambers are carefully constructed so that there are no obstructions to the efficient drainage of all wastes.

Waste water discharges directly into gully drains below the grate but above water level. Hopper heads are now regarded as unsanitary but are still frequently found on older houses.

REPLACING YOUR WC CISTERN

If you're modernising a bathroom or separate WC, one of the most common jobs you'll have to carry out is to replace a high-level cistern with a neater-looking low-level one. Here's how it's done.

Not very long ago every WC cistern was a high-level one set with its base about 2m (6ft) above floor-level. In better-off households there might have been a high level WC suite situated in an upstairs bathroom; but in most homes, until about 40 years ago, the WC was located in an outside cubicle.

Flushing cisterns in those days were all of the old-fashioned Burlington or 'pull-and-let-go' pattern. They were made of cast iron and had a well in the base. A stand-pipe, connected externally to the flush pipe, rose from the base of this well to terminate open-ended about 25mm (1in) or so above 'full water level'. A heavy iron bell, with lugs built onto its rim to permit water to pass freely underneath, stood over this stand-pipe with its base in the well.

The cistern was flushed by raising the bell, usually be means of a chain, and suddenly releasing it. Falling heavily into the well, the bell's 'wedge' shape forced the water contained within it up and over the rim of the stand-pipe. This water, falling through the stand-pipe and flush-pipe, carried air with it thus creating the partial vacuum that is necessary for siphonic action. Atmospheric pressure then pushed the water in the flushing cistern under the rim of the bell and down the flush-pipe to flush and cleanse the WC pan. The siphon was broken and the cistern started to refill when air passed under the bell lip.

High-level 'Burlington pattern' cisterns of this kind were efficient, tough and hard-wearing. Although they have been obsolete for years, many are still in use. Their disadvantages were, and are, a tendency to condensation, and thence to corrosion – though this could be treated by applications of anti-condensation paint – and their incurable noisiness. There was the heavy clank of the bell falling back into the cistern, the rush of the descending water and usually more rushing water as the cistern refilled.

The invention of the modern 'direct action' flushing cistern foreshadowed the end for the old high-level Burlington. These new cisterns are made of plastic or ceramic material and have a flat base. The stand-pipe does not terminate open-ended above water level, but bends over and opens out to form an open-based dome with its rim just above the base of the cistern. When the flushing mechanism is operated, a round plate is raised within this dome to throw water over the inverted U-bend into the stand-pipe and thus begin the siphonic action. The plate has a hole or holes in it to allow water to flow through freely once siphonic action has started. As the plate is raised these holes are closed by a plastic 'siphon washer' or 'flap valve'. Once it became the norm to build toilets within the house, silent operation became increasingly important and led to the almost universal provision of low-level WC suites.

Replacing at high level

However, it cannot be denied that the cleansing effect of a flushing cistern at high level is more positive than that of a low-level cistern. There are, too, situations – such as with a supplementary outside WC – where the noisiness of a high level cistern is acceptable. When an old Burlington cistern fails in such a situation (perhaps having rusted through and sprung a leak, or as a result of the lugs at the base of the bell having worn away), you may well decide to replace it with another high-level cistern.

Although direct-action cisterns are often referred to as 'low-level cisterns' there are models which can be chain-operated from high level. One difficulty that could arise when replacing an old Burlington cistern with a direct-action one is that the latter normally has a flat base while a well is an essential feature of a Burlington cistern. At least one manufacturer has simplified the task of conversion by producing a modern, plastic, direct-action cistern with a well in its

HOW A WC CISTERN WORKS

'Burlington pattern' cistern

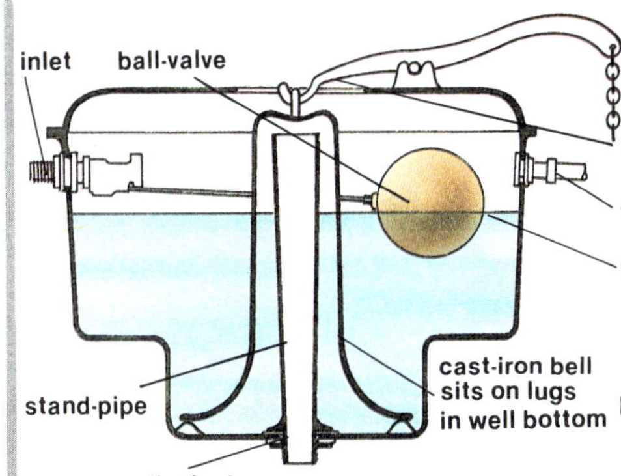

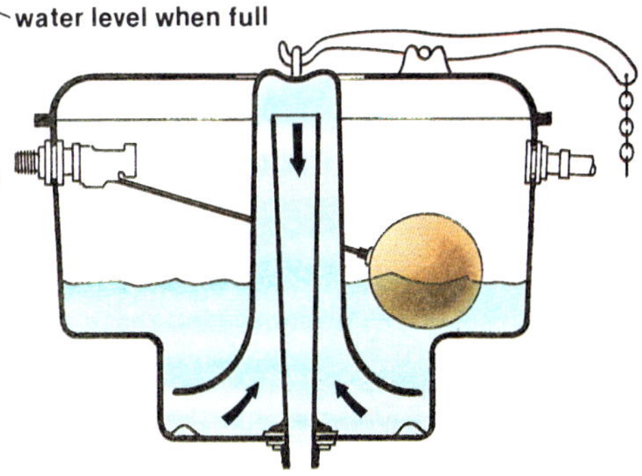

When the bell is raised (right), water is forced up and into the stand-pipe, which is connected to the flush pipe and pan.

'Direct action' cistern

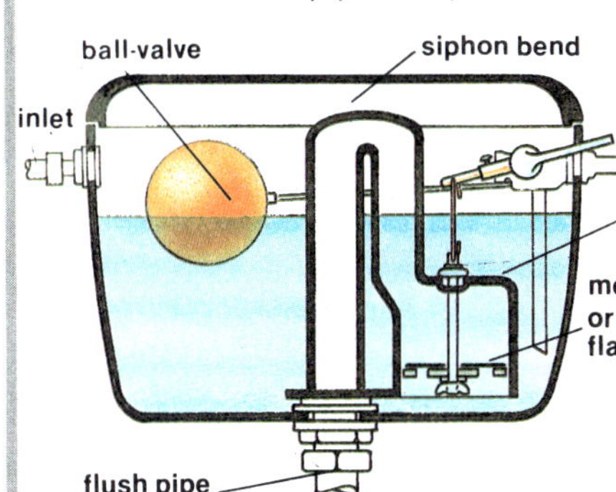

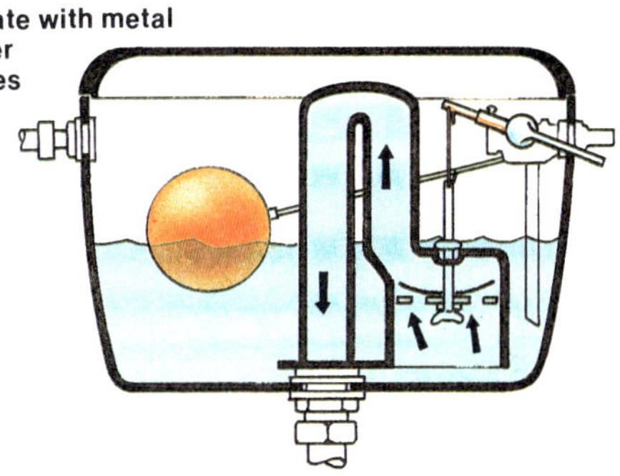

When the plate is raised (right), the flap-valves are closed and water is forced over the siphonic bend. Siphonic action maintains the flow through the open flaps on the plate.

base. A cistern of this kind can be used as a replacement without adjustment to the water supply pipe, overflow or flush pipe.

Replacing at low level

Usually, faced with the failure of an old Burlington cistern, you will decide to replace it with a more silent low-level one. This is a project that is easy enough to undertake but needs careful thought first. Many a home handyman has removed an old high-level cistern and flush-pipe and has replaced them with a low-level cistern and the slightly-larger-diameter 'flush bend' provided, only to find it impossible to raise the seat and hinged cover properly. For in order to accommodate the flushing cistern, the pan of a low-level lavatory suite is normally positioned 50 to 75mm (2 to 3in) further from the wall behind it than the pan of a high-level suite.

If the pan has a P-trap outlet and is connected to the socket of a branch soil-pipe by means of a mastic joint, an extension piece can be used without too much difficulty to bring it forward the required distance, but check that there is room to accommodate it. In some small bathrooms, moving the WC suite forward could mean having to alter the position of the washbasin and this, in turn, could make it impossible to open the door. If the pan has an S-trap outlet and is connected to a branch drain by means of a cement joint, bringing the pan forward is a daunting task.

However, it may well still be possible to convert the suite to a low-level operation without moving the pan. As an alternative to a conventional low-level flushing cistern, you could fit one of the new slim-line cisterns or 'flush panels' that have been developed in recent years to deal with this situation.

Ready Reference

CHECK THE PAN POSITION

You must check the position of the pan in relation to the old high-level cistern before you start work, as this may affect the sort of low-level cistern you install:

- if you intend to install an ordinary low-level cistern, check that the pan is far enough away from the wall to allow the seat to be raised freely. (With a high-level cistern, this problem will not arise as the cistern is well out of the way of the pan)
- if there's no room to move the pan forward, install a slim flush-panel cistern instead.

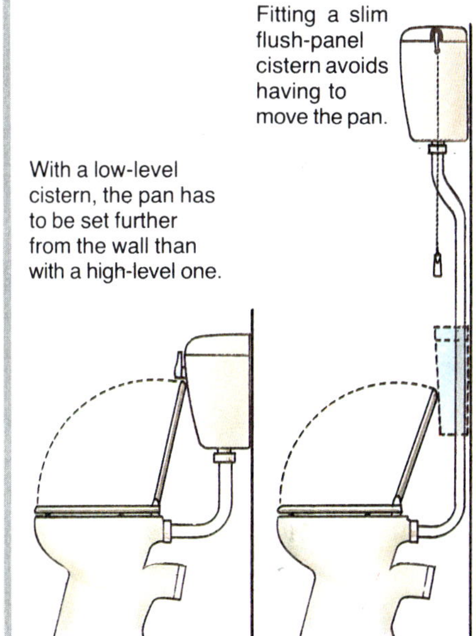

Fitting a slim flush-panel cistern avoids having to move the pan.

With a low-level cistern, the pan has to be set further from the wall than with a high-level one.

TIP: DON'T REMOVE THE BRACKETS

If your old high-level cistern is supported on cast-iron brackets, as it probably is, don't rip them out as this will make a mess of the wall. Paint them and construct a shelf using them as supports. This can be used for storing WC supplies or for displaying plants.

TAKING OUT THE OLD CISTERN

1 *Find out where you can turn off the water supply to the cistern, stop the flow and then flush the cistern to ensure that it is empty.*

2 *Cut the old supply pipe, catching any drips which may flow out, and insert a new stop-valve for later connection to the new cistern.*

3 *Disconnect the inlet pipe from the cistern using an adjustable spanner, and then pull the pipe right away from the cistern wall.*

4 *Detach the overflow in the same way, or simply cut it off with a hacksaw. It's likely to be made of lead and so will be easy to cut.*

5 *To break the seal on the nut connecting the downpipe to the cistern, use a blow-torch to heat it up, then a wrench to turn it.*

6 *When the cistern is completely detached from the pipework, lift off the heavy cast-iron cistern lid and place it to one side.*

7 *Next, carefully lift the cistern off its bracket supports and lower it; it will be very heavy and will still contain some water.*

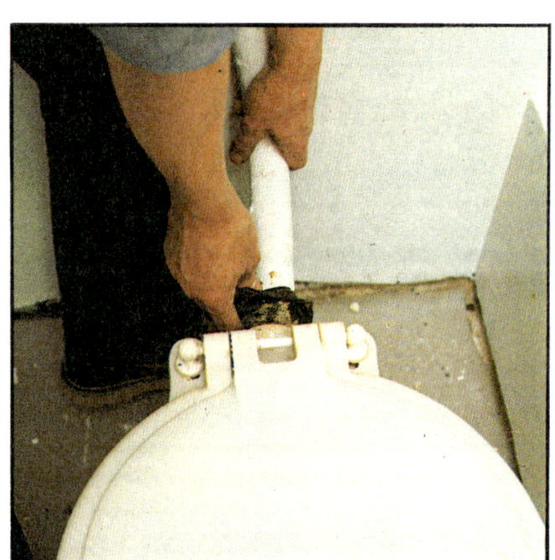

8 *Remove the downpipe from its connection with the pan – it should come free with some gentle wiggling – and dispose of it.*

9 *Detach any other redundant pipe-work as far as is practical; you'll probably have to find a new route for the overflow pipe.*

PUTTING IN THE NEW CISTERN

1 *Mark up the positions of the new cistern and support brackets; drill the holes, insert wallplugs and screw the brackets up.*

2 *Carefully rest the cistern on the brackets and check that they are holding it horizontally; if not, pack up one side or the other.*

3 *Drill and plug holes for the fixing screws, and fix the cistern in place. Pass the screwdriver through the holes in the cistern's front.*

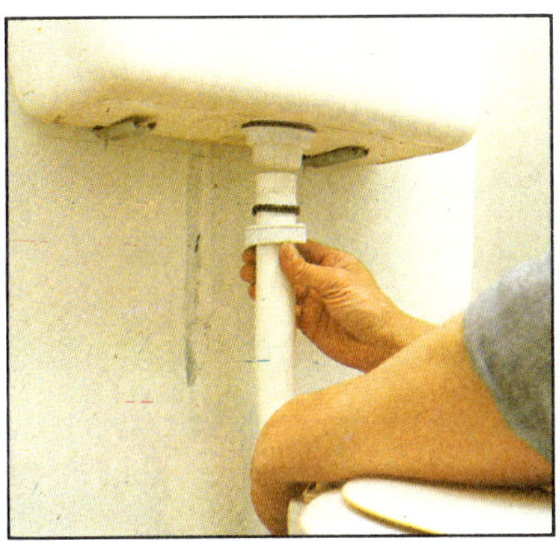

4 *Attach the new fall pipe to the pan with a rubber spigot. When connecting it to the cistern, make sure the rubber washer is in place.*

5 *With the central flushing assembly in position, you then have to screw up the inlet pipe connector to the ball-valve arm assembly.*

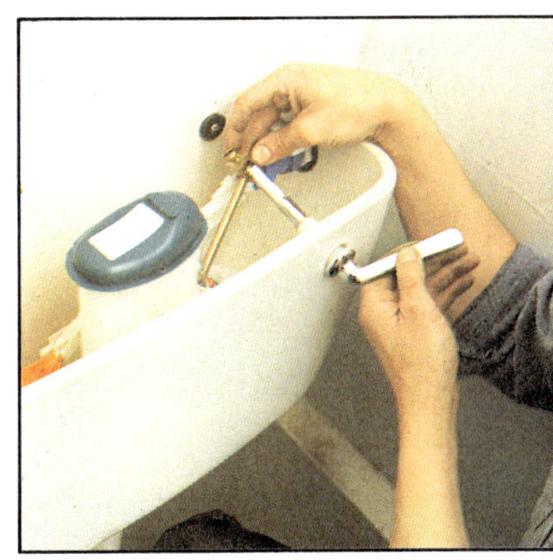

6 *Complete the internal cistern connections by making the flushing lever linkage attachments and checking that the ball arm is free.*

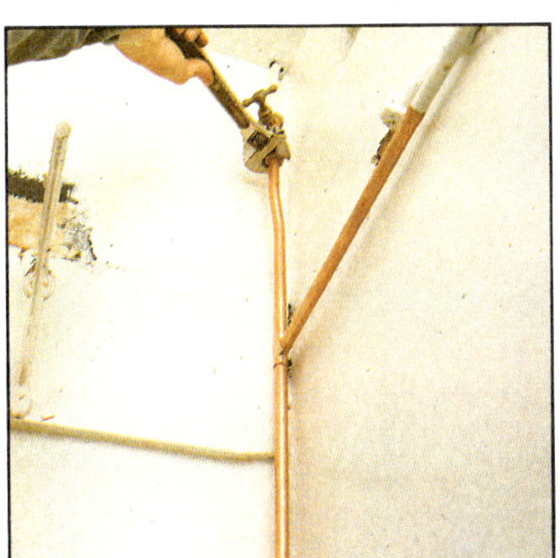

7 *Make up a new supply pipe run from the new stop-valve to the ball-valve inlet – plus a branch pipe, if needed, for a washbasin.*

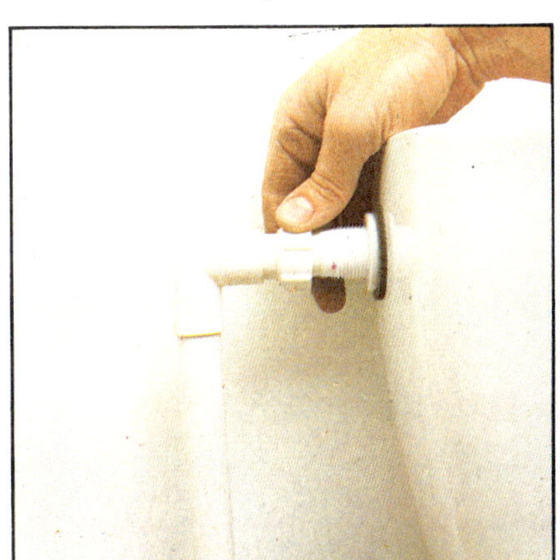

8 *Connect the overflow pipe to the cistern and either run it to a convenient outside wall or allow it to discharge to the floor waste.*

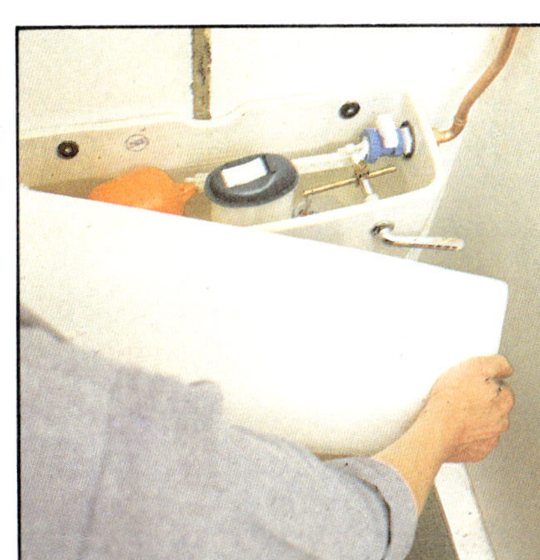

9 *Check all the connections, turn on the water, allow the cistern to fill and check that it flushes properly before putting on the lid.*

TANKS AND CISTERNS

Modern domestic hot and cold water supply systems rely on the storage of large quantities of water in the house to provide a ready supply at a constant pressure and to ensure a reserve of water should the mains supply be cut off for any reason.

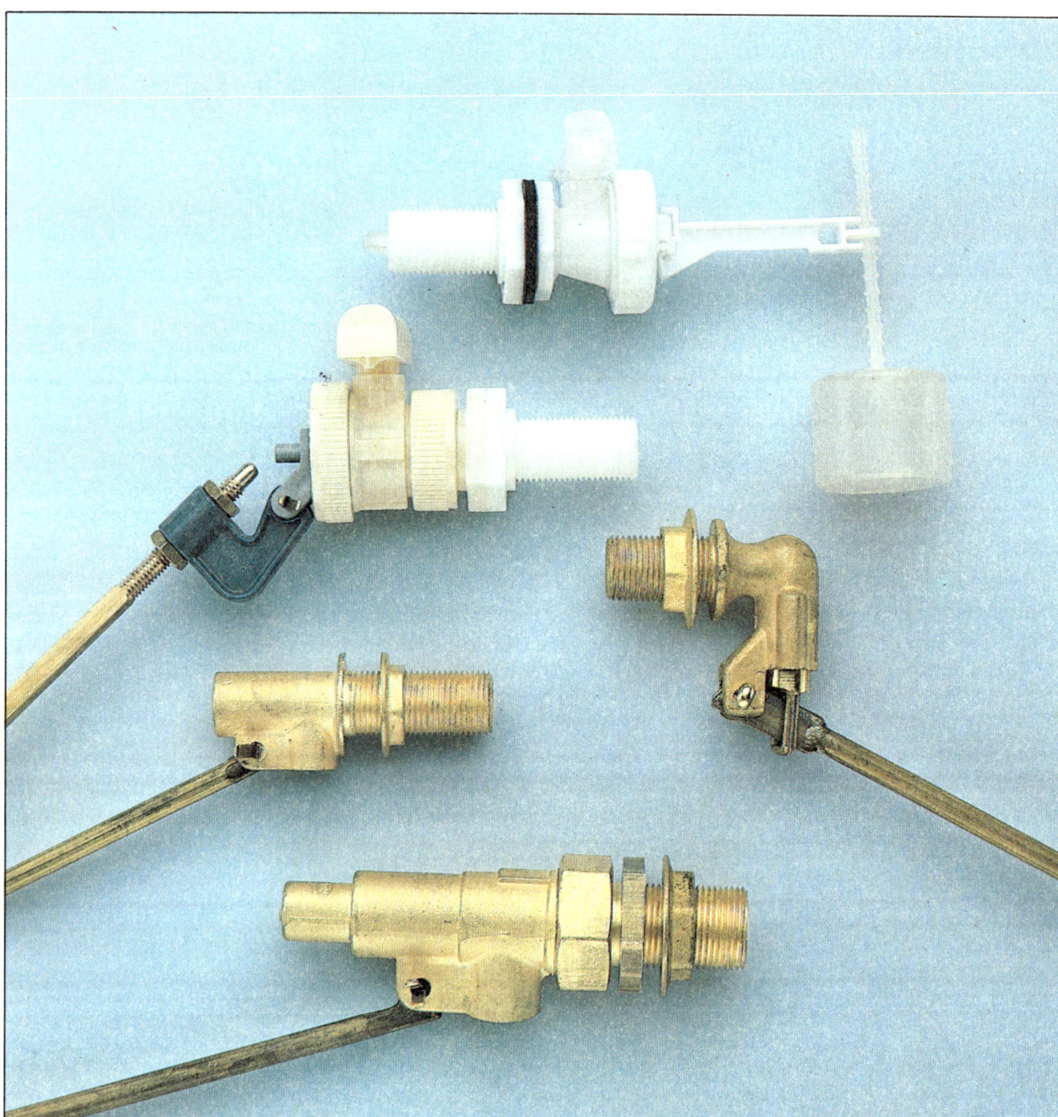

REPLACING A HOT CYLINDER

Copper hot water cylinders don't last for ever, and if they do spring a leak they need replacing quickly with the right type of new cylinder.

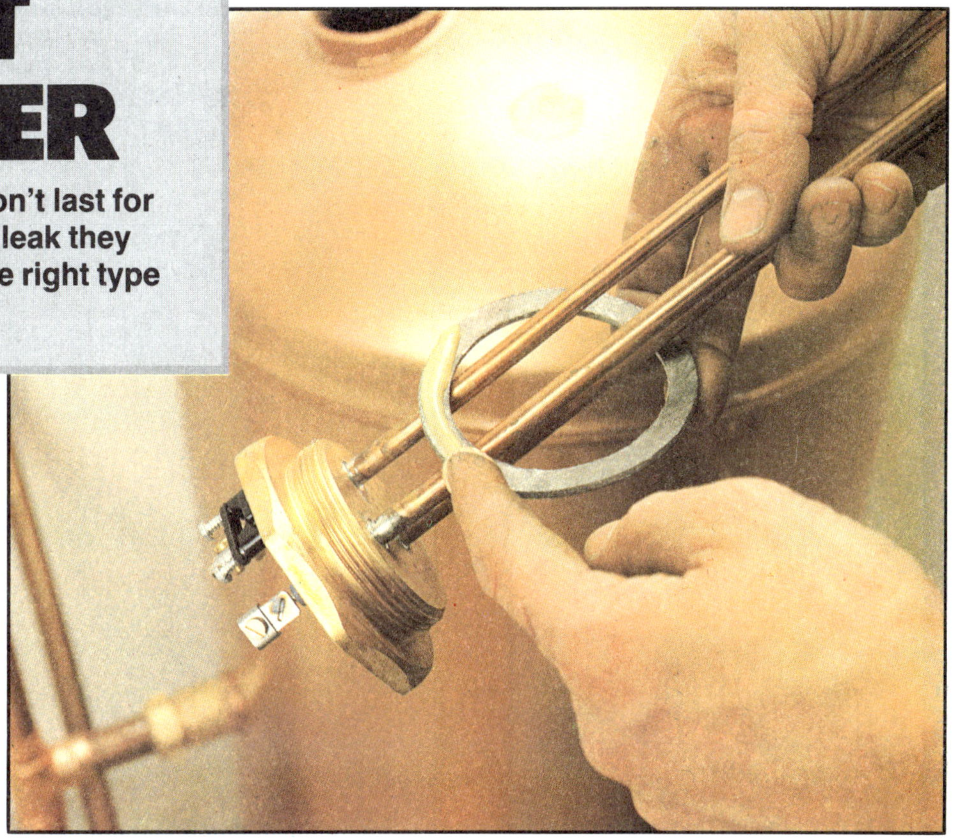

By far the most common means of hot water supply in British homes is a cylinder storage system of one kind or another. A copper cylinder of 115 to 160 litres (25 to 35 gal) capacity, usually situated in an airing cupboard, is supplied with cold water under controlled low pressure from the main cold water storage cistern, which is fitted at a higher level. The water supply enters the cylinder by a distribution pipe at least 22mm in diameter, at a tapping close to its base. A 22mm vent pipe rises from the top of the cylinder and is taken upwards and bent over to discharge, open-ended, over the cold water storage cistern. The distribution pipes supplying the kitchen and bathroom with hot water are taken from this vent pipe, via conections just above the level of the top of the cylinder.

Heating the water

Water in the storage cylinder may be heated solely by means of a thermostatically-controlled electric immersion heater, usually fitted vertically and screwed into a special boss provided in the dome of the cylinder. Alternatively, water may be heated by a solid fuel, gas-fired or oil-fired boiler. Quite often there is a combination of immersion heater and boiler. Where the water is heated by a boiler, 28mm circulating pipes connect the upper tapping of the boiler with a tapping in the upper part of the cylinder wall, and likewise connect the return tapping of the cylinder, in the lower part of the cylinder wall, with the lower tapping of the boiler. If the water is heated by immersion heater only, the cylinder's flow and return tappings, if they exist, are blanked off.

However the cylinder is heated, the hottest water will rise to the top to be available for drawing off from the bathroom or kitchen taps. As it is drawn off, it is replaced by cold water flowing into the lower part of the cylinder from the cold water storage cistern. Surprisingly the hot and cold water 'layers' do not intermingle much, and this layer effect, with the hottest water at the top and the coldest near the base, is an essential feature of a successful cylinder storage hot water system.

Direct and indirect systems

Where water in the cylinder is heated solely by means of an immersion heater, or where a boiler is provided only for the supply of domestic hot water, a simple direct cylinder is used. With a direct cylinder system all the water in the cylinder is heated by circulating it through the domestic boiler. As hot water is fractionally lighter than cold water, the water heated in the boiler will rise up the flow pipe to the upper part of the cylinder, while cooler water from the lower part of the cylinder flows down the return pipe and replaces it. A constant circulation will take place for as long as the boiler fire is alight.

But, where hot water supply is provided in conjunction with a central heating system, however small, an indirect cylinder system must be provided. There is also much to be said for providing an indirect system if hot water only is supplied, as it will protect the boiler, particularly in hard water areas.

With an indirect system the water stored in the cylinder does not circulate through the boiler. It is heated by means of a heat exchanger within the cylinder. Water from the boiler circulates in a closed circuit, giving up heat to the water stored in the cylinder through this heat exchanger. In this kind of system the flow and return pipes between the heat exchanger and the boiler are referred to as the primary circuit. In a conventional indirect system the primary circuit is supplied with water from its own small feed and expansion tank, usually situated in the roof space alongside the cistern, and it has its own separate vent pipe that terminates, open-ended, over this small open tank.

The water in the primary circuit cannot be drawn off from the taps. As the same water circulates over and over again there is a very small loss from evaporation, which is made up from the feed and expansion tank. Because of this, indirect systems are relatively immune to corrosion and scale formation, and this is why they must always be provided in connection with central heating installations.

Self-priming indirect cylinders don't need an expansion tank. They have a specially designed inner cylinder which serves as a heat exchanger and also has provision for the expansion of the water in the primary circuit when heated. In a conventional system this is an important function of the feed and expansion tank. When a self-priming cylinder is first filled with water from the main cold water storage system, water is able to overflow through the patent inner cylinder into the primary circuit. It is prevented from returning by an air bubble that forms an air lock within the inner cylinder.

A self-priming cylinder offers a simple and economical means of converting a cylinder hot water system from direct to indirect operation.

HOT WATER SYSTEMS

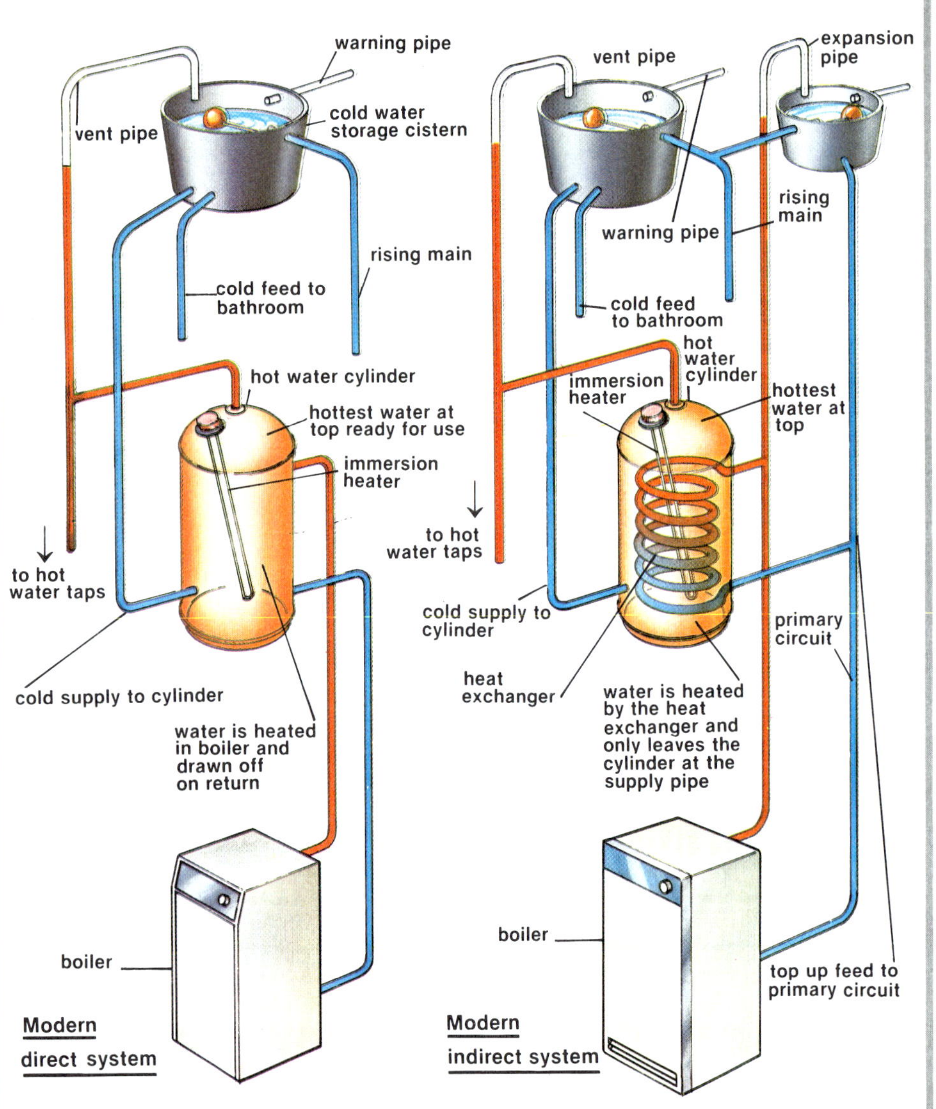

But many heating engineers are suspicious of these cylinders which they do not consider to give the same positive separation of the primary from the domestic hot water as would a conventional indirect system.

Choice of system

Before replacing a hot water cylinder it is essential to identify whether the existing cylinder is direct or indirect. You may think you can do this quite easily by checking whether or not there is, in addition to the main cold water storage cistern, a small feed and expansion tank in the roof space. The presence of a feed and expansion tank does indicate an indirect system, but of course self-priming indirect cylinders don't need them.

Another difficulty in identification is the 'two-in-one' or packaged plumbing system that has been developed in recent years to provide instant hot water systems in homes that had previously lacked this amenity. They are very often provided where a large house has been converted into a number of self-contained flats.

A packaged plumbing system is simply a hot water cylinder with a cold water storage cistern directly above it in the same unit. Some packaged plumbing units have a small cold water storage cistern – which is only adequate for the supply of the hot water cylinder. Others have a full sized 275 litre (50 gal) cistern that is capable of providing bathroom cold water supplies as well as supplying the hot water cylinder immediately beneath it.

Packaged plumbing systems may be direct, indirect, or self-priming indirect. The feed and expansion tank of a conventional indirect packaged plumbing system is usually contained within the walls of the main cold water storage cistern.

How then can you tell whether your hot water cylinder is direct or indirect? Well, if the water in it is heated by an electrical immersion heater only, you can be quite sure that it is direct. Indirect cylinders are never used in this situation.

If you have a boiler which, as well as supplying domestic hot water, serves a central heating system that has been giving trouble-free service, you can be pretty certain that you have an indirect cylinder of one kind or another. Look in the roof space, or within the main cold water storage cistern, if it is a packaged unit, for a small feed and expansion tank. If one exists then you definitely have a conventional indirect cylinder.

Self-priming indirect cylinders are normally marked as such but there is only one way to be absolutely certain whether your existing cylinder is indirect (though possibly self-priming) or direct.

The flow and return pipe connections for direct cylinders are always female screwed tappings, into which a male cylinder connector is screwed. The flow and return pipe connections for indirect cylinders (whether conventional or self-priming) are always male screwed connectors projecting from the heat exchanger within the cylinder, through the cylinder wall.

Armed with these clues you should find it possible to identify your cylinder; it's a good idea to do this for your own information before a leak or other emergency makes its replacement a matter of urgency.

Draining the system

The cylinder must, of course, be drained before it can be replaced. You can't do this simply by turning off the main stop-valve and opening up the hot taps. Since the distribution pipes to these taps are taken from the vent pipe above the cylinder, the cylinder will still be full of water when the taps cease to flow.

Boiler-heated systems, whether direct or indirect, will normally have a drain-cock fitted into the return pipe from cylinder to boiler, immediately beside the boiler. After letting out, or turning off, the boiler and switching off any immersion heater, drain off from this drain-cock by means of a length of hose, to an outside gully. You'll have to create a siphon by filling the pipe first. This will drain the primary circuit of an indirect system but it will not drain the domestic hot water in the outer part of the cylinder. To drain this use another drain-cock, usually fitted at the base of the cold water supply pipe just before it enters the cylinder. A drain-cock should also be provided in this position where a cylinder is heated by an immersion heater only as it could well prove to be useful.

REMOVING THE OLD CYLINDER

1 *Identify the cold water feed, and turn off the supply using the gate-valve. If there isn't one, turn off the mains and drain the cistern.*

2 *Drain the contents of the cylinder by attaching one end of a hose to the drain-cock and undoing the nut with a drain-cock spanner.*

3 *When the water stops flowing, pull the hose away from the drain-cock. A little more water may flow out, so have some mopping up cloths handy.*

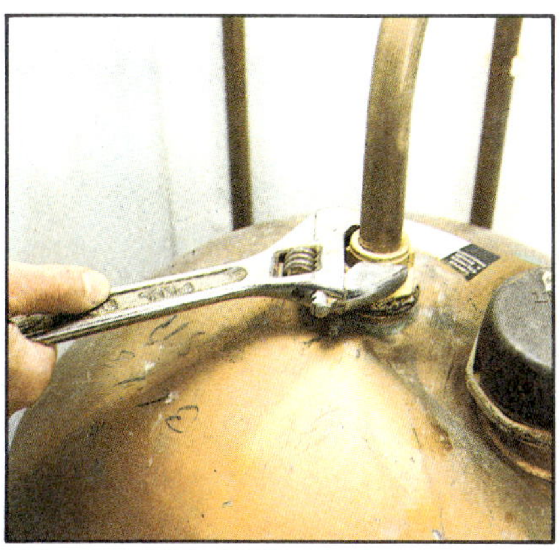

4 *Start to disconnect the pipework attached to the cylinder. It should be easy to unscrew the connections using an adjustable spanner.*

5 *As you disconnect the pipes make sure they will pull free from the cylinder; if not, gently bend them by hand, supporting them evenly.*

6 *The primary circuit connections are the trickiest to disconnect as the male iron cylinder connector may start to turn.*

7 *Disconnect the electrical supply to the immersion heater. If you want to reuse the immersion heater, hire a special spanner and unscrew it.*

TIP

8 *If the immersion heater will not unscrew, heat the cylinder boss with a blow-torch. Then allow it to cool and try the spanner again.*

9 *When you have disconnected the cylinder, pull it free from the pipework and dispose of it. It may be worth selling it for scrap.*

Renewing a hot water cylinder

After checking the type of your cylinder, you must also check its size before you can buy a new one.

Common cylinder capacities are 115 litres (25 gal), 140 litres (30 gal) and 160 litres (35 gal). Most cylinders are 900mm (36in) or 1050mm (42in) high, while common diameters are 400mm (16in) and 450mm (18in). When you are ready to begin, drain the cylinder. If the cylinder is not provided with adequate drain-cocks it can be emptied by siphonage. Unscrew the nut at the top of the cylinder, but be prepared for the water that will flow as you do so; it may be as much as a litre or so. Fill a hose with water and secure both ends. Thrust one end deeply into the cylinder through the tapping at its apex and allow the other to discharge over an outside gully. Siphonage will empty the cylinder.

To remove the immersion heater from the old cylinder, you'll have to hire a special extra-large immersion heater spanner. If you are installing a new one in the new cylinder, there's no need to take the old one out. The other tappings should be straightforward.

With the new cylinder in position you may find that the connections don't quite coincide with those of the old one. If not, lengthen or shorten the connecting pipes as appropriate using soldered capillary or compression fittings (see pages 14–18). You can alter the height of the new cylinder if necessary by raising it on stout strips of wood. The connections to the cylinder are made watertight by binding the male threads of the screwed joints in every case with PTFE thread sealing tape.

When you refill the system with water, check for leaks. When refilling a direct system, or the primary circuit of an indirect system, it is a good idea to use a length of hose to connect the cold tap over the kitchen sink with a drain-cock beside the boiler. Open up the tap and the drain-cock and the system will fill upwards; this will drive air in front of it and thus reduce the risk of air-locks forming. If the system is connected to a central heating circuit, the air vents on the radiators, and any other air vents, elsewhere, should be left open until water starts to flow through them.

When you are satisfied that the system is water-tight and leak-free you can switch on the immersion heater or boiler again. When the system heats up, check again for leaks. The cylinder and pipework will have expanded which may loosen some of your joints if you haven't tightened them properly, or used enough PTFE tape. Last of all, add an insulating jacket to the new cylinder. This is an extremely worthwhile investment as, without an efficient one, you'll lose a lot of the heat from your water which will add considerably to your bills.

PUTTING IN A NEW CYLINDER

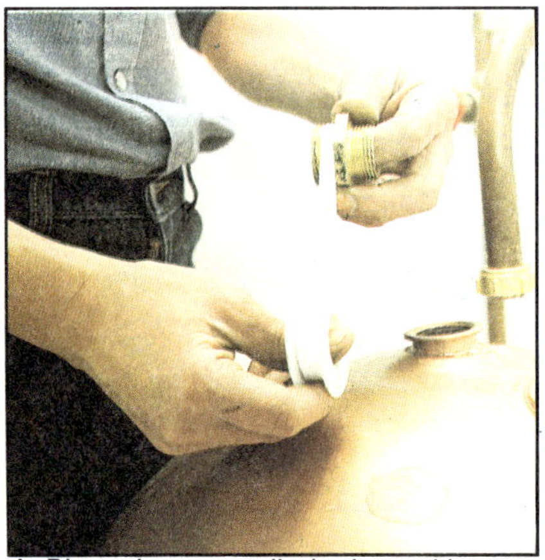

1 *Place the new cylinder in position and check that all the old connections are reusable. Wind new PTFE tape round the outlet male iron connector.*

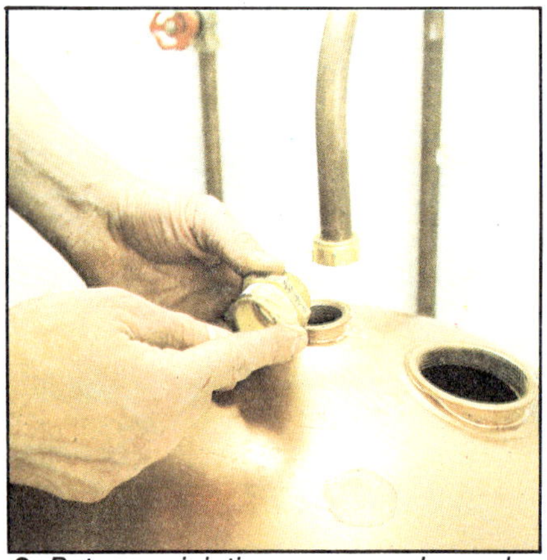

2 *Put some jointing compound round the thread; then screw the connector back into the outlet, making sure you don't cross the thread.*

5 *Connectors on the primary circuit are connected in exactly the same way, but you may have to adjust the pipe runs to match your new cylinder.*

TIP

6 *Check that the male to female iron connectors are tightly screwed into the cylinder; they may have come loose in transport.*

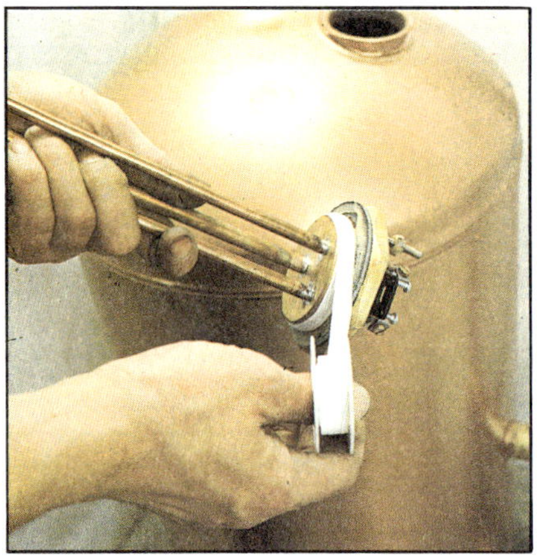

9 *Wind two layers of PTFE tape round the thread before inserting the immersion heater into the cylinder boss, and screwing it finger tight.*

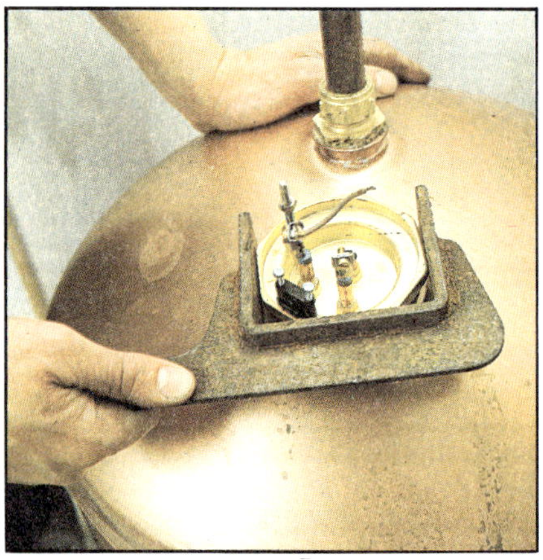

10 *Tighten the immersion heater carefully until it is completely home using the immersion heater spanner. Then check all the connections.*

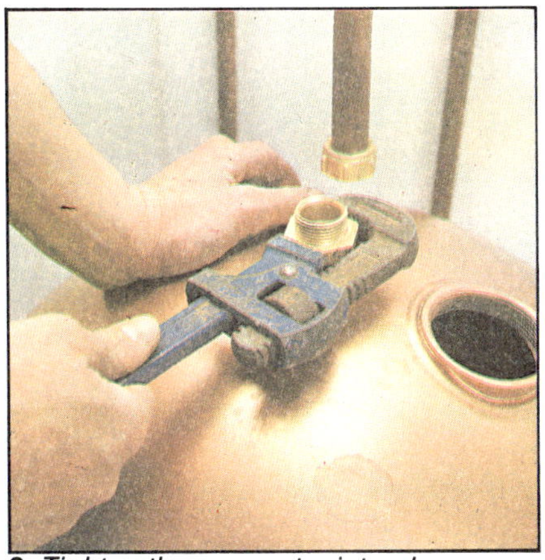

3 *Tighten the connector into place and screw up the cap-nut making sure that the olive is in position. If it's worn you should replace it.*

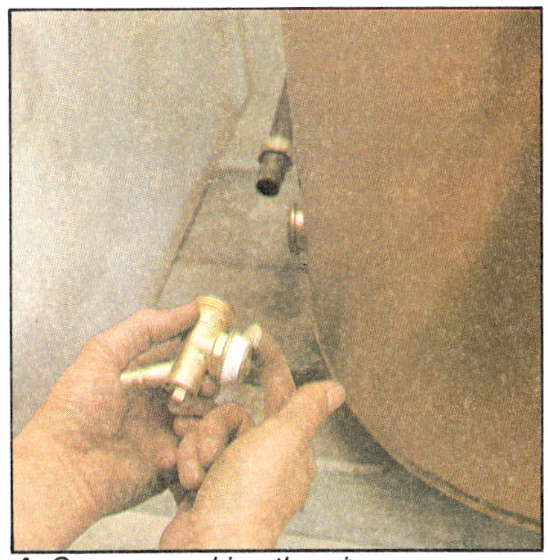

4 *Carry on making the pipe connections, using PTFE tape and pipe jointing compound each time to ensure that they are watertight.*

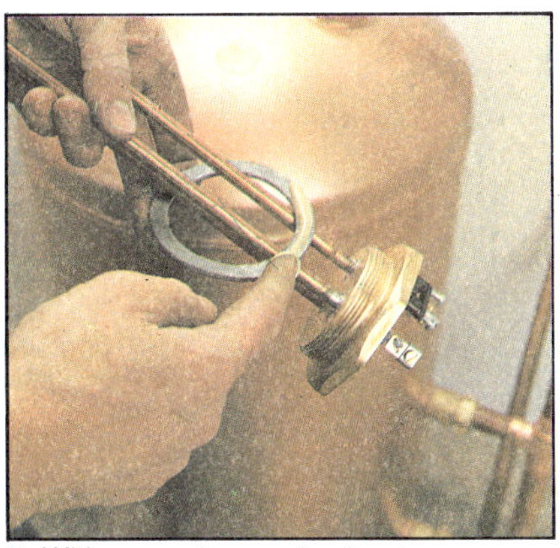

7 *With a new immersion heater, remove the protective cap, then take the larger washer supplied and coat the underside with jointing compound.*

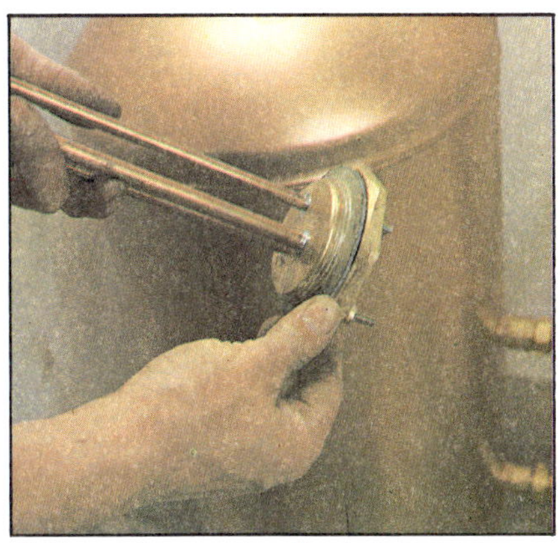

8 *Press the washer firmly into place against the underside of the head-nut. Try not to damage it when pushing it over the thread.*

11 *Place the immersion heater thermostat in its channel. Make sure it runs smoothly, and set it to the correct temperature.*

12 *Turn the water back on and check for leaks, then wire up the immersion heater and replace its cover. Finally fit a cylinder insulation jacket.*

Ready Reference

KNOW YOUR SYSTEM

Direct cylinders may be heated by an immersion heater; or by water which is heated by the boiler, and returned to the cylinder for use.

Indirect cylinders keep the water heated by the boiler separate from the water that you use, passing on the heat by means of a heat exchanger.
Indirect cylinders must have a small feed and expansion cistern, which is situated in the loft or inside the main cistern in a packaged system, or they may be self-priming with the unit inside the cylinder.

Female flow and return tappings for connection to the boiler mean a **direct system.**

Male flow and return tappings mean an **indirect system.**

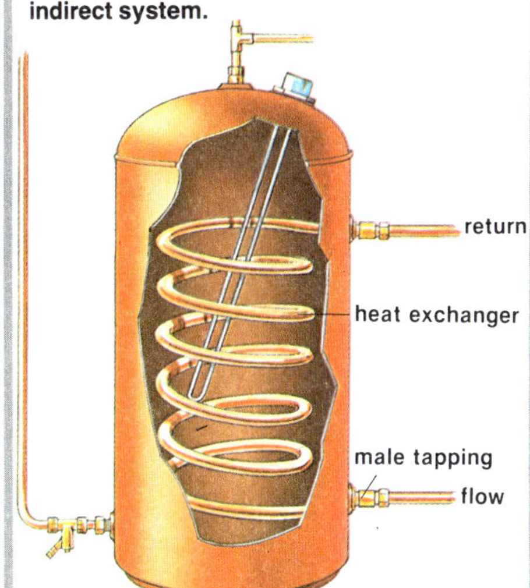

Indirect cylinder

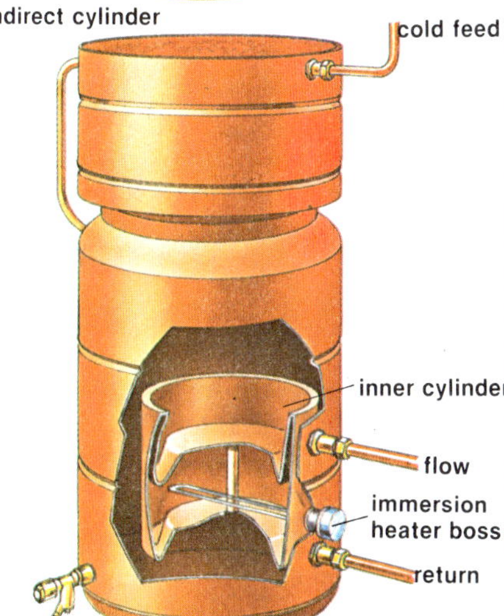

Self-priming packaged unit

REPLACING A CISTERN

Because a cold water storage cistern is out of sight does not mean it should be out of mind. It should be inspected at least twice a year: at the beginning and the end of winter. Otherwise a leak or overflow may have disastrous consequences.

You may well wonder why it's necessary to have a cold water cistern. After all it's possible to supply all cold water fittings direct from the rising main, using what is known as a direct supply system (as described on pages 8 – 12). However, in new or converted properties, most water authorities require homes to have an indirect cold water system, in which only the cold tap over the kitchen sink, and possibly a garden water tap, come direct from the main. The reason for this is that at times of peak demand the water mains may be incapable of supplying water as quickly as it is drawn off, so the storage cistern acts as a 'shock absorber' and evens out fluctuations in the flow. The cistern also provides a reserve of water which can be used for several hours, while the supply is cut off during repairs to the main, or when supply is reduced at times of water shortage. A leak from a pipe under pressure from a storage cistern is also likely to be less devasting than one from a pipe under mains pressure. However, one of the most important uses of a cold water cistern is to provide a source of water under constant, relatively low pressure for a cylinder storage hot water system.

If your home was built more than thirty years ago the chances are that it'll have a galvanised mild steel cold water storage cistern, unless it's already been replaced. Nowadays cisterns are usually built to a standard capacity of 227 litres (50 gal). In pre-metrication days it was common practice to install a cistern of 20 or 25 gal capacity if it supplied a hot water system only, and one of 40 gal capacity if it also supplied the WC cistern and the bathroom cold taps.

Why replace the cistern?

Galvanised steel cisterns are tough and hardwearing which is why there are still so many of them in use. But they are subject to corrosion and this failing has become much more common since the almost universal adoption of copper pipe for water supply and distribution. The mains water supply is never completely pure and contains minerals and salts which may make it slightly acid or alkaline. Where the mains water supply is very slightly acid, a galvanised steel cistern can be turned into a giant electric cell or battery. This won't give you any electric power, but it can be disastrous for the cistern. Current will flow between the zinc coating of the galvanised steel and the copper pipes connected to the cistern, and the thin zinc protective layer will dissolve away, leaving the steel beneath exposed to corrosive attack and rusting. This phenomenon is known as electrolytic corrosion. Never, therefore, connect copper pipes to a galvanised steel cistern without taking appropriate steps to protect the zinc coating (see below).

When you inspect your cistern you should look for rust. Once you've removed the cistern's cover, play a torch beam into the interior. Rust may appear as a light dusting on the cistern walls, in larger patches concentrated round pipe connections, or even as a cauliflower-like growth protruding inwards from the cistern walls.

A cistern that doesn't show evidence of corrosion can be protected by means of a 'sacrificial anode'. This consists of a lump of magnesium (the anode), placed in the cistern and connected to the outside metal wall. One well-known make is made up of a clamp which is attached to the magnesium anode by a length of copper wire. The clamp is fixed firmly to the cistern wall, which has to be rubbed down to the bare metal to ensure a good electrical contact. The magnesium is then hung over a batten placed across the cistern and suspended in the water below. The magnesium very slowly dissolves away – is 'sacrificed' – and the zinc coating of the galvanised steel is protected.

The presence of rust doesn't necessarily mean that the cistern must instantly be replaced. If the extent of corrosion is limited, the cistern can be reconditioned. After it has been drained and dried, every trace of rust has to be removed and the pit-holes filled with an epoxy resin filler. All the inside surfaces then have to be treated with two coats of a tasteless and odourless bituminous paint. It's best to disconnect the water supply and distribution pipes before doing this work.

THE OLD CISTERN

1 *Turn off the mains supply, drain the entire system and bail out the water that remains in the cistern below the outlet pipes.*

2 *Disconnect all pipes attached to the cistern, the supply at the ball-valve, the overflow, and any distribution pipes.*

3 *It's quicker to saw off the pipe connections if connections to the new cistern are going to be in a different position.*

Modern cisterns

Modern non-corroding cisterns may be made either of asbestos cement or a variety of plastics, perhaps reinforced with glass fibre. Although asbestos cement cisterns cannot corrode, they are rather heavy and tend to become heavier as they absorb water. They are also prone to accidental breakage. It's best to use a plastic cistern of one kind or another as they have a number of advantages. They are light in weight and easy to raise into the roof space, which means they can be installed by one person. And you won't need many tools as the walls are easy to drill and the pipe connections are simple to make. These cisterns are also quite flexible, which is handy if the opening to the loft is not very large, (see below). The smooth internal angles also make cleaning out easy.

Installing the cistern

It's likely that if you have an old galvanised steel cistern, it'll be resting directly across the joists in the roof space. But a plastic cistern must have a flat level base. Two or three pieces of floorboard or a square of chipboard will serve this purpose. However, you may decide to take the opportunity of raising the level of the cistern, particularly if you want to improve the pressure in the supply to a shower. This can be done by constructing a platform on a substantial wooden frame 600 or 900mm (2 or 3ft) above the joists. A shower works best if there is a vertical distance of 1500mm (5ft) or more between the shower rose and the base of the storage cistern: 900mm (3ft) is the minimum (see pages 79–81).

If you are raising the new cistern onto a platform of this kind you needn't worry too much about unscrewing the back-nuts securing the water pipes to the existing cistern. Just cut the pipes near the cistern. You'll have to extend them anyway.

Before purchasing your new cistern, make sure that it will go through the trap-door into your roof space. Round black polythene cisterns can often be flexed through a relatively small opening. If it is quite impossible to pass it through the existing trap door you can install two smaller cisterns, linked together by a short length of 28mm pipe connected 50mm (2in) above their bases. To avoid the risk of stagnating water, it's a good idea to take the distribution pipes from one cistern and to connect the ball-valve inlet to the other. This will ensure a through-flow from one cistern to the other one.

Installation instructions are usually supplied with a new cistern; read them carefully and follow them exactly. Usually, all pipes must be connected squarely to the plastic walls so as not to strain them. The

Ready Reference

CISTERN INSPECTION

Always check the cistern twice a year in spring and autumn:

- if there is any sign of rust then drain it out and look more closely
- if the rust is not extensive and thin consider cleaning if off and coating with special bitumen.
- if the rust is extensive or deep, replace the cistern as soon as possible.

CISTERN REPLACEMENT

First turn off the water supply at the rising main. Then:

- empty the cistern
- disconnect the cistern
- connect the new cistern to the existing pipework
- turn on the water and check for leaks.

CONNECTIONS TO THE CISTERN

WHAT YOU'LL NEED

Here is the equipment you may need:

- new plastic cistern
- new ball-valve if old one is not in good condition
- 15 and 22mm pipe for new connections to old pipework
- tank connectors
- drill with bit and hole saw of the same diameter as the connections
- wrenches for pipe connections
- PTFE tape
- hacksaw if you want to cut the old connections.

INSTALLING THE NEW CISTERN

1 *Place the new cistern in position, check that any expansion pipe fits over the edge, and cut the overflow pipe to the right length.*

2 *Mark the position of the outlet holes you need to cut out, then use a drill bit and hole saw to make the aperture to fit the tank connectors.*

3 *Clean up the hole with a fine file or glasspaper so that there is no swarf left round it. Check that the connector fits fairly tightly.*

5 *Push the connector into the hole from the inside of the cistern, place another plastic washer on the thread and screw up the connector nut.*

6 *Measure up the necessary linkage from the new cistern to the outlet pipework and make up suitable pipe lengths for the connections.*

7 *Fit stop-valves close to the outlet exits: these are useful if you have to make any repairs to some other part of the system.*

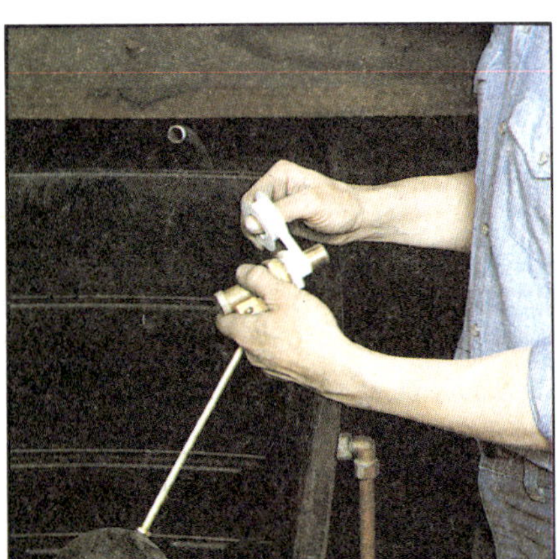

9 *Fit the plastic washer and nut on the ball-valve tail, then wind PTFE tape round the thread and push it through the hole.*

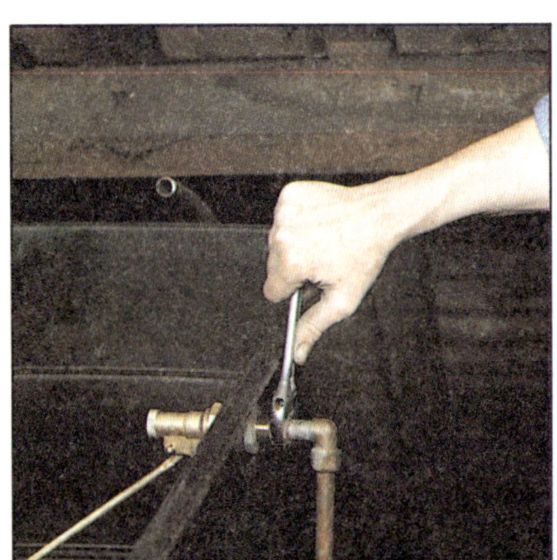

10 *Connect the inlet and support the pipe against the roof timbers to prevent any vibration. Finally, check that the ball arm lifts easily.*

11 *When you're sure the connections are firm and tight, turn the water back on, after you have turned off the outlet stop-valves.*

4 Place a plastic washer on the thread of the connector and run some PTFE tape around the thread right up to the end.

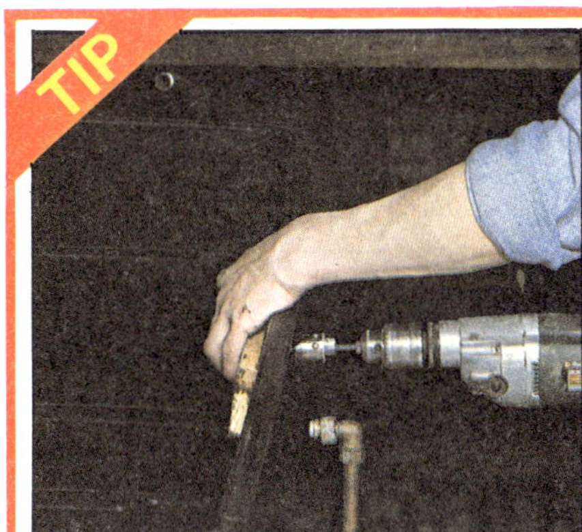

8 Next make a hole for the inlet using a hole saw. It's a good idea to support the wall of the cistern with a piece of scrap wood.

12 Check that the ball-valve works. Then place the cover on the cistern, having made a hole for an expansion pipe, and install the lagging.

connections should be made with one large plastic washer and one large metal washer on each side of the cistern wall, with the plastic washer in direct contact with the wall. No sealant or other jointing agent should be used in contact with the plastic.

Carrying out the work

Before you start the job, turn off the main stop-valve to prevent water flowing into the cistern and drain it by opening the bathroom cold taps. As long as you don't use the hot taps while carrying out the work there's no need to shut down the boiler if you have one. As the distribution pipes are taken from a point about 50mm (2in) above the base of the cistern, a certain amount of water will have to be bailed out.

When you've emptied the cistern you'll have to disconnect the ball-valve inlet, overflow (warning) pipe, and distribution pipes. Then you'll have to move it out of the way.

An old galvanised cistern will be quite heavy, so make sure you have strong helpers before attempting to lower it through the trap-door. If possible use a stout rope to support it. There's a good chance that it won't go through, as in many houses the cistern was installed before the roof was put on. You could cut it up with a hacksaw, but this is extremely arduous and if there is plenty of room in the roof space there's no great harm in simply leaving it there.

Before you make the connections to the new cistern you will have to mark and cut holes in the right places. You can use the fittings that will occupy these holes as templates to determine the correct size and position. In the case of the ball-valve this will be the ball-valve tail. The overflow and distribution pipes will be connected by a compression joint to the male screw tank connector, so use the threaded male end to determine the diameter.

A round polythene cistern will be supplied complete with a supporting plate for the ball-valve, which will determine the level at which the ball-valve is fitted. For other cisterns the ball-valve should be fitted about 25mm (1in) below the cistern rim. The hole for the overflow (warning) pipe should be cut about 50mm (2in) below the ball-valve inlet. The holes for the distribution pipes should be cut 50mm (2in) above the base of the cistern.

Water knocking

It sometimes happens that, after installing a new plastic cold water cistern, a plumbing system that has previously been quiet and unobtrusive, suddenly becomes intolerably noisy. This is because the old galvanised steel cistern, whatever its faults, did give very good support to the rising main. A plastic cistern does not. As water flows in through the ball-valve, a copper rising main

Ready Reference

TRAP DOOR PROBLEMS

If your loft entry is too small to get the old cistern out:

- just move it to one side and leave it in the roof space, or
- cut it into pieces – but this is hard work.

A modern plastic cistern will bend to a certain extent, but if it won't fit the loft entry. Buy two smaller ones that will give you the same capacity as a larger one. These should be connected together in series so there is no risk of the water stagnating:

- position the cisterns side-by-side
- connect them together 50mm (2in) from the bottom with 28mm pipe
- connect the mains supply to the side of one cistern
- connect the outlet and the overflow to the side of the other.

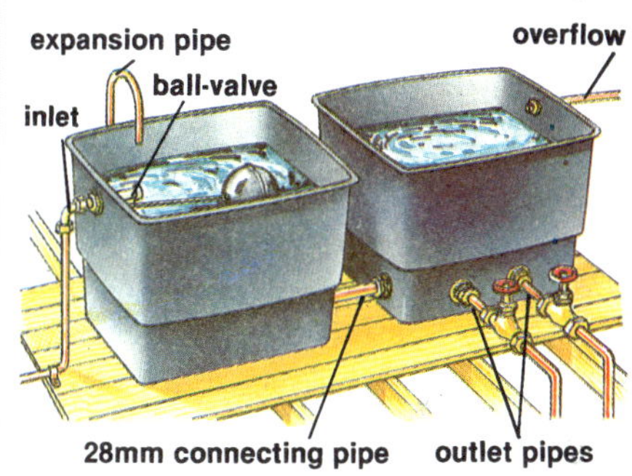

supported only by the cistern wall may vibrate uncontrollably. The remedy is to secure it firmly to the roof timbers. This is particularly important where the new cistern has been raised onto a platform in the roof space and the rising main lengthened. In these circumstances it should be secured to the platform.

Freezing

Plastic cisterns have a built-in frost resistance and, if the water in them should freeze, they are unlikely to be damaged. Insulation isn't therefore quite as important with a plastic cistern as with one of galvanised steel or asbestos. It is, however, well worth protecting it with glass fibre tank-wrap or similar lagging material. A dust-proof, but not air-tight, cover should always be fitted. Many manufacturers supply one as an optional extra, but it is quite easy to make one from a sheet of exterior grade plywood.

DRAINAGE AND OUTDOOR PLUMBING

Plumbing jobs need not necessarily be confined to indoors; there are many jobs that require plumbing skills outdoors as well. Foremost among these is the maintenance and repair of the rainwater system – the gutters and downpipes. Another problem area outdoors is the gullies into which rainwater downpipes and the waste pipes from downstairs sinks and appliances discharge.

REPAIRING AND REPLACING GUTTERING

The chances are you won't realise there is anything wrong with your home's guttering until it leaks. Note where the water is coming from, and, once the rain has stopped, get up a ladder and see what's wrong.

The gutters on your home are supposed to capture all the rain falling on the roof and channel it to one or more downpipes. In turn these downpipes take the water into the main drain, a storm drain, or to a soakaway in your garden. This efficient removal of rainwater is important to keep your outside walls sound. Any missing, damaged, or blocked guttering will result in water cascading down the face of your wall, leading to dampness, and eventually mortar and brick decay. You may be able to repair it; or you may be faced with having to replace whole sections or the complete system.

Until the mid-1940s most guttering was made of cast iron, although asbestos enjoyed a brief popularity. Cast iron had the disadvantage of being very heavy to work with – as you'll find if you take some of it down. It is also prone to rusting if not properly maintained. Asbestos was heavy, looked rather bulky in appearance and was easily damaged. When plastic piping and guttering was introduced, it became an obvious choice. It is light to work with, doesn't need painting and its smooth surface allows water to flow through it more effectively. In any case, cast iron is very expensive these days, and not particularly easy to obtain.

Blockages

You should check why a blockage has occurred in the first place. This may be due to sagging, or poor installation preventing a free run for the water. Or the blockage may be combined with a faulty joint which may be possible to repair. But if cast iron guttering is at all cracked it needs replacing.

If your gutter overflows during heavy rain, the chances are that it's blocked with leaves.

PREPARING FOR WORK

1 *Access is always a problem when working on guttering – a convenient garage roof made this job a lot easier. Scaffold towers are useful on high roofs.*

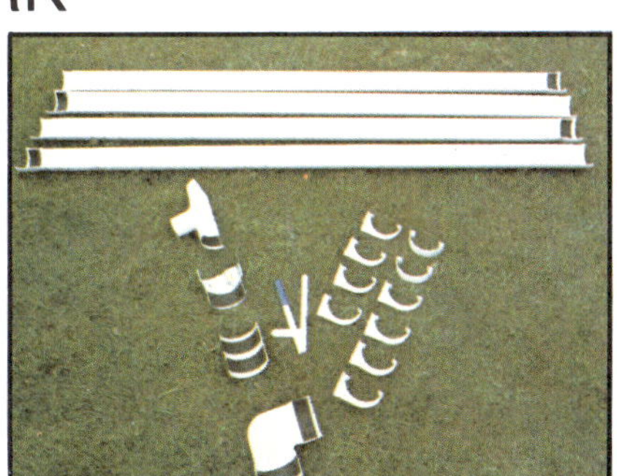

2 *Before you start work assemble all the components you will need. You can check them off against the existing guttering.*

Ready Reference

GUTTER SIZES

Plastic gutters come in three common sizes (measured as the width from lip to lip):

- 75mm (3in) – for extensions and outbuildings
- 100mm (4in) – for most house roofs
- 150mm (6in) – for house roofs of very large surface area

The 150mm size carries roughly seven times the volume of water that the 75mm size can take, and three times as much as the 100mm size.

A CAST IRON ALTERNATIVE

It is still possible to buy a new cast iron guttering in several 'classic' profiles as a match for existing gutters, but it's expensive and very awkward to install.

If you want the look of cast iron you could consider hiring a specialist firm to produce seamless extruded aluminium guttering for your house.

GUTTER PROFILES

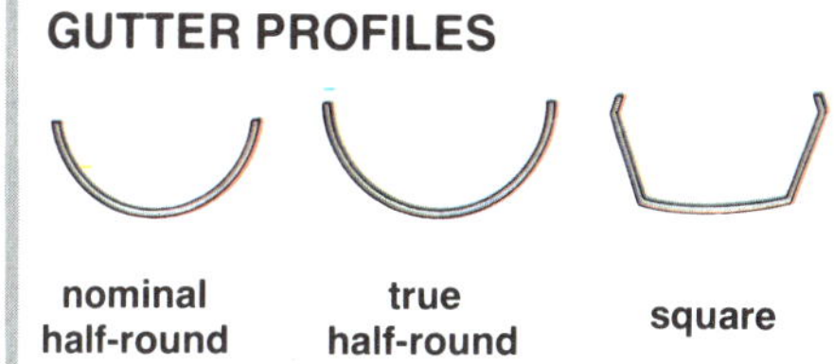

REMOVING OLD GUTTERING

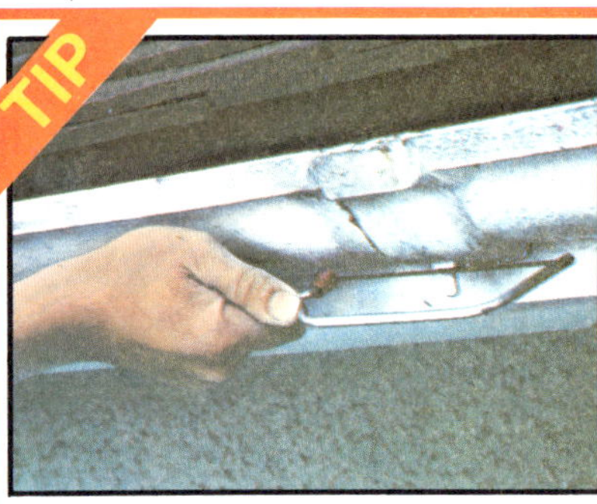

1 *Gutter sections are usually bolted together and these bolts won't come out easily. Saw through the nut.*

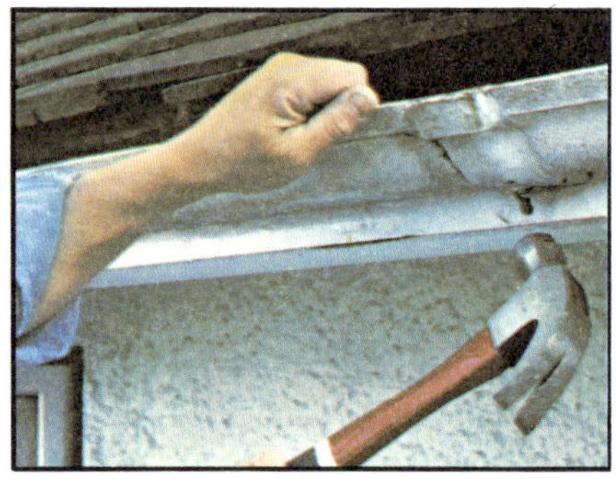

2 *When the nut has been detached try to hammer the bolt out but don't use too much force as the gutter itself may crack and collapse dangerously.*

3 *You may need to use a hammer and chisel to get the joints moving. Loosen the joints before unscrewing the gutter sections.*

4 *Cast iron guttering is supported by brackets or screws depending on its profile. You can lift it off brackets, or in this case unscrew it.*

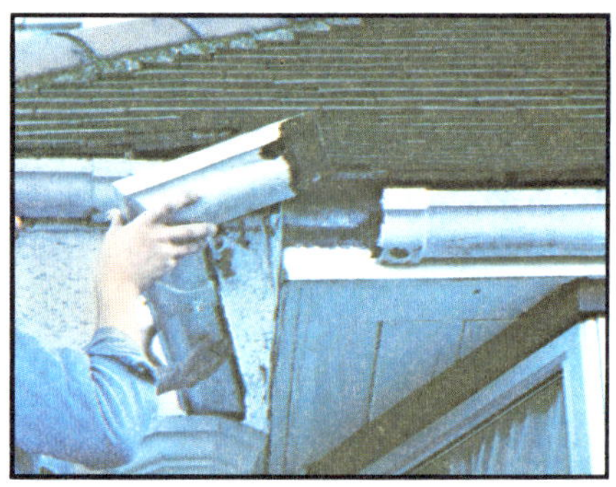

5 *Start to take down the guttering at the point closest to the down pipe – it should come free quite easily even if it's attached directly to the pipe.*

6 *Detach and lift off each succeeding section in turn – remember that cast iron is heavier than it looks. Be careful not to overbalance.*

7 *Always carry pieces of guttering down to the ground, never throw them down – you may cause the cast iron to splinter dangerously.*

8 *Thoroughly brush down the fascia board to remove dirt and cobwebs, then fill any holes using a filler suitable for outside work.*

9 *If the fascia board has not been painted, use this opportunity to do the work. Sand down first and then apply primer and topcoats.*

You can use an old dustpan brush to clean it out, scraping the debris into piles and scooping them out with gloved hands. But prevent any bits from getting into the downpipe or this may get blocked as well.

Coping with sags

If a section of guttering has sagged, making it lower than the top of the downpipe, the water will not drain away properly. And you will be able to see this from puddles of water collecting in the guttering itself. You must decide whether to raise the sagging section, or lower the mouth of the downpipe to bring everything back into line. If you flex cast iron guttering more than about 25mm (1in) you'll break the seal on the joints, causing a leak. So choose the option that involves moving the guttering least.

In order to reset the guttering to the correct gradient you'll need to fix a piece of string taut between two nails hammered into the fascia board. You can then use this as a guide as you reposition each gutter support in turn.

Leaking joints

Joints in cast iron gutters are made by overlapping the two lengths of gutter, and bolting them together with a layer of sealant in between to form a watertight seal. As this sealant begins to deteriorate with age, the joint starts to leak.

To make the repair, first remove the bolt holding the joint together. Often this is too rusty to undo, so hacksaw off the bolt between the nut and the guttering, or drill out the rest of the bolt. Lever the joint apart with an old chisel, and scrape away all the old sealant. Clean up the joint with a wire brush, then apply a finger-thick sausage of new sealant and bolt the sections back together using a new nut and bolt and a couple of washers. Scrape off any sealant that has oozed out before giving the repair a coat of bitumen-based paint on the inside of the gutter.

Dealing with rust

If one bit of guttering has rusted right through, it won't be long before the rest follows suit, so you may as well save yourself a lot of trouble and replace it all. If meanwhile you want a temporary repair, there are several suitable repair kits on the market. They consist of a sort of wide metal sticky tape which you apply inside the guttering and over the holes with bitumen adhesive.

Choosing a replacement

Assuming you won't be using cast iron again – you'll have a job getting hold of it and even more of a job putting it up, apart from the fact that it's expensive – your choice is between aluminium and plastic. Plastic guttering is made of UPVC (unplasticised polyvinyl chloride). It's probably the better choice for a do-it-yourself installation: it is far more widely available than aluminium, and has the edge in terms of cost and durability.

Two different cross-sections are commonly available – half-round and 'square'. The latter is often given a decoratively moulded face similar to the more ornate ogee cast iron guttering. In addition, a semi-elliptical guttering is available – it looks a bit like half-round but is deeper and more efficient. This, together with some brands of conventional profile, can be camouflaged by being boxed in with a clip-on fascia panel. Which type you choose is largely a matter of personal taste, but try to choose something that blends into the style of your home.

More important than looks is the size of the gutter. Too small, and it will be forever overflowing; too large, and you will have paid more for the installation than is necessary. It's all to do with relating the amount of water the guttering can carry to the amount of water likely to come off the roof during a heavy rainstorm. These calculations are complicated, but you can assume that they were done when the guttering was originally installed. Just measure the existing guttering at its widest point to find its size, and buy the same again. The most commonly available sizes are 75mm (3in), 100mm (4in), 112mm (4½in), 125mm (5in), and 150mm (6in). If in doubt, consult the manufacturer's literature.

The actual cross-section of the gutter may vary from brand to brand; this can make it difficult to join with existing guttering: for example, the guttering belonging to a neighbour on a semi-detached or terraced house. Most firms offer adaptors to link their product with cast iron guttering, or with a different size from within their range. However, they tend not to offer adaptors to tie in with the equivalent size from another brand, so if possible stick to one brand throughout the installation. If you have to link up with a neighbour's gutter, find out which brand was used, and try to use the same.

There are many different fittings as well as lengths of guttering available on the market. Before you start buying your new guttering get hold of a manufacturer's brochure from the stockist you use and carefully check to ensure you have all the fittings you will need. Make sure you understand how the particular system works before you buy anything.

Taking down old guttering

Cast iron guttering is heavy, and may also be rusted into place, so removing it can be tricky. But there is no need to be gentle with it: it doesn't matter if it breaks. The important thing is to work in safe conditions. If you are wrenching things apart, do it in a controlled way so you don't fall off the ladder, and so that great chunks of gutter don't fall down. Try not to drop cast iron guttering to the ground: it shatters easily, and, if it lands on a hard surface, dangerous fragments can fly off. If you toss the guttering clear of the house you might overbalance and fall off the ladder, so aim to lower larger sections gently to the ground with a rope.

Begin with the section linking gutter and downpipe. Cut through the old bolts holding the sections together. Then, if you lift the gutter slightly, you should be able to pull it free from the downpipe. Once it's out of the way, unmake the joints between the sections of gutter (as if you were repairing them), and lift the guttering off its supporting brackets. It may, of course, be screwed directly to the fascia board.

You can now turn your attention to the brackets themselves. These are usually screwed to the fascia board just beneath the eaves of the roof, and can either be unscrewed or levered off with a claw hammer. In older houses the brackets may be screwed to the tops or sides of the roof rafters, to support the weight of the iron guttering. If there is a fascia board to which

Ready Reference

HALF-ROUND GUTTER FITTINGS

This is the most common style of fitting available for gutter work. The means of joining varies according to manufacturer.

gutter with seal end

union

gutter strap

fascia bracket

ogee to half-round adaptor

An ogee/half-round adaptor will help you join up to your neighbour's gutter if it has an ogee profile. Other adaptors will connect new PVC guttering to half-round and square cast iron profiles.

90° gutter angle

120° gutter angle

Different gutter angles are available to get round corners which aren't square. Various fascia brackets make fixing possible under low eaves; measure up carefully so that you buy the right ones.

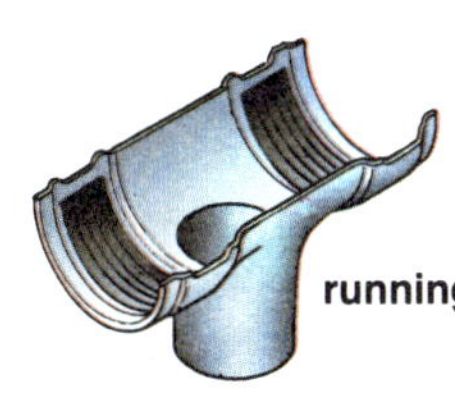
running outlet

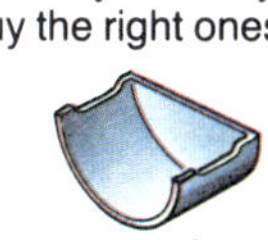
stop end

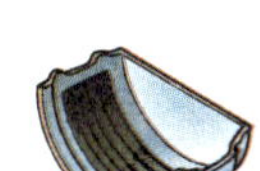
stop end with seal

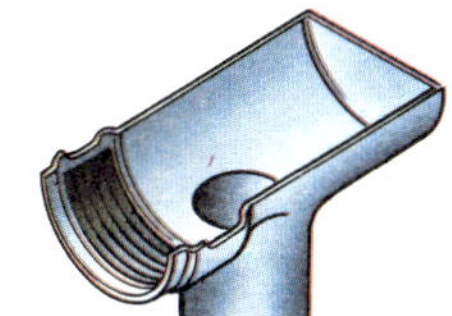
stop end outlet

The gutter outlet should fit *inside* the top of the downpipe. Measure the downpipe diameter before you buy a new outlet.

PUTTING UP PLASTIC GUTTERING

1 *If you are joining onto your neighbour's gutter you'll need a special adaptor. Line it with a lump of mastic and bolt it into place.*

2 *Fix a string at the level of the top of the adaptor or end furthest from the downpipe. Hammer a nail into position to hold it in place.*

3 *Pull the string taut and fix it with a nail at the other end of the gutter run. Make sure it is horizontal, then lower it enough for the correct fall.*

4 *Fix the brackets to the fascia board at intervals of about 1m (39in), making sure their tops are aligned with the string.*

5 *You can now put in the first section of guttering so that it is resting on the brackets, and connect it to the end piece or adaptor.*

6 *Each manufacturer has a different system for making joints. Here the next section rests in the previous one and is then firmly held with a clip.*

TIP

7 *You will very likely have to cut a section of guttering. Measure it exactly at roof level, then cut it squarely.*

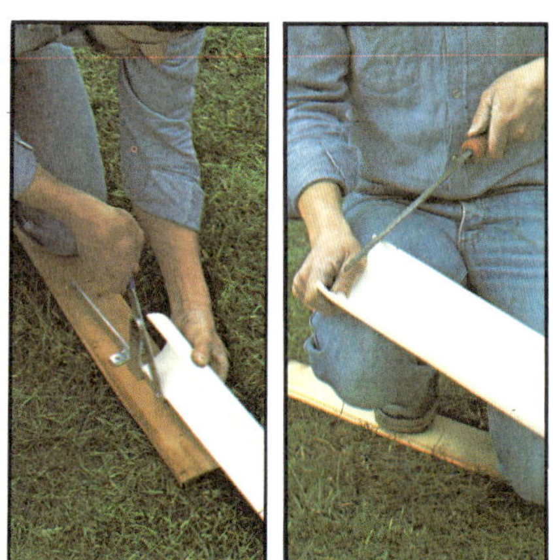

8 *In this system, once a section is cut, new notches must be made in the end for the clip. To do this you can use a proprietary notch cutter or a wood file.*

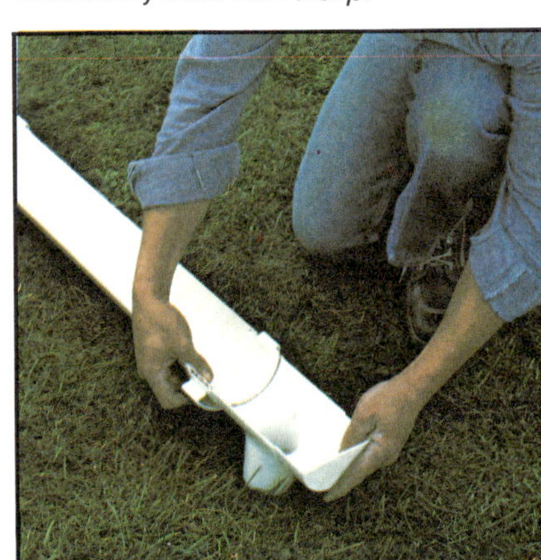

9 *The final corner piece and downpipe fitting is made up on the ground which is the easiest procedure when dealing with small sections.*

you can fit the new gutter, the ends of the brackets can be hacksawed off. Otherwise, you will have to lift off some of the roofing to remove them.

When all the old guttering has been removed, inspect the fascia board to make sure it is sound and securely fixed. If it is, fill the old screw holes and paint it before fixing the new guttering. If it isn't, it will have to be replaced.

Fixing new guttering

The obvious first step is to assemble the various bits and pieces you need, and you can use the old guttering system as a model to decide what's required. It's best to measure up the length of the guttering itself, allowing a little extra to be safe.

At the end of the run furthest from the downpipe, fix a gutter support bracket as high up the fascia as possible, and about 150mm (6in) from the end. The fixings here, and elsewhere, are made with 25mm (1in) screws. Choose ones that are galvanised to stop them rusting. Insert a nail into the fascia board level with the top of the bracket.

At the other end of the run, 150mm from the downpipe, fix another nail, tie a length of string tightly between the two, and use a spirit level to check that this string is level. When it is, lower the second nail by the amount needed to ensure that the guttering runs downhill towards the outlet. This 'fall', as it's called, varies according to the type of guttering, so check the manufacturer's recommendations. Usually, it is in the region of 5mm (¼in) for every metre (3ft) of gutter run. Once you've found the right line for the gutter, fix another bracket level with the lowest nail.

The next job is to fix the next bracket 1m (39in) from the one at the downpipe end of the run, using the string as a guide to set it at the correct level. Use these two brackets to support a length of gutter with the downpipe outlet attached.

Exactly how you join the gutter to the outlet – or indeed make any other joins in the guttering – will vary from brand to brand. With some, you slip the ends of the components into a special jointing piece called a union, and clip the whole lot together. With others, one of the components will have a union built into its end.

Now work your way along, building up the gutter run as you go and adding additional support brackets as required, again using the string as a guide. In most cases, you will need a bracket every metre, plus one on each side of every join – though some ranges contain combined unions and support brackets. Check the manufacturer's recommendations.

The only problem you may run into is when you have to cut the guttering to length, either to go round a corner, or to finish the run with a stop end. Do the cutting on the ground using a hacksaw, making sure that you cut the end square. Any roughness left by the saw should be cleaned up with a file. If you want to turn a corner, fix the corner piece before cutting the straight piece of gutter to length. You can then use it to work out exactly how long the straight gutter length needs to be. When cutting to finish at a stop end, it is usual to leave about 50mm (2in) of gutter projecting beyond the ends of the fascia.

When you've finished the job and checked to see that all the joints are properly connected, take a bucket of water to the highest point of the gutter and pour it down. If the gutter doesn't drain all the water then go back and check your work.

10 *The made-up section is fixed in place taking care to locate the downpipe end into the hopper head. Any pipe connection needs a sealant joint.*

11 *When the whole system is up, you should check that it will work by pouring water in at the point furthest from the downpipe.*

Ready Reference

SQUARE GUTTER FITTINGS

These fittings may be preferred to the half-round profile although they are slightly less efficient in discharging water.

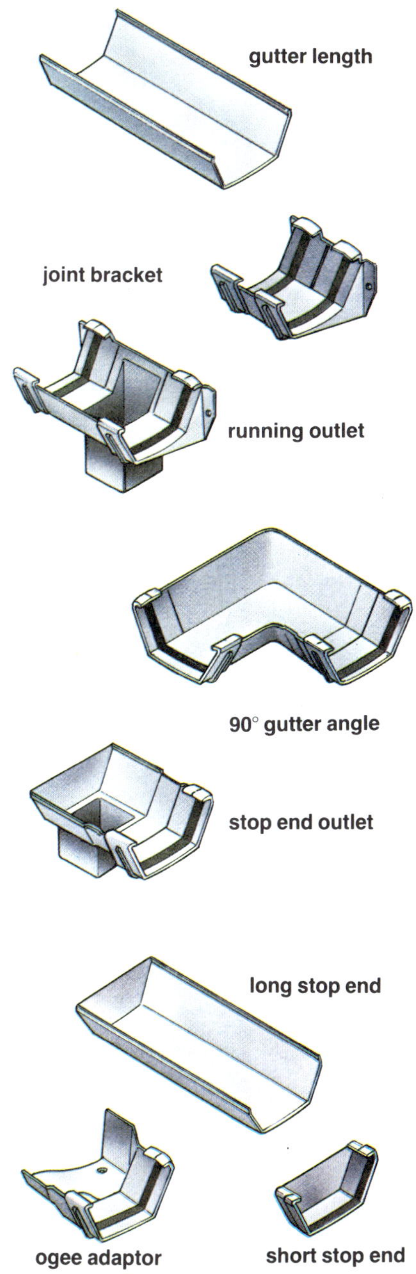

Remember that if you have old square or ogee profile cast iron guttering matched with round downpipes, you will have to replace the downpipes as well when you fit new square-profile guttering.

REPLACING DOWNPIPES

If your downpipes are blocked, damaged or badly fixed, the overflowing rainwater can damage your house (and soak passers-by). Routine maintenance is half the battle, but complete replacement may ultimately be the only solution.

The rainwater that falls on your house cannot be allowed to run off freely over the sides of the roof. If it were, it would soak the walls below, flood the ground all about, and drench anybody unlucky enough to be walking underneath. So it is taken away harmlessly by what is known as a rainwater disposal system. This consists of gutters that collect the water flowing off the roof, and convey it to downpipes which carry it to the drains. At one time most gutters and downpipes were made of cast iron. But although this is a tough material, gutters and downpipes made from it suffer from two big disadvantages: in use they are prone to attack by rust, a big drawback in something that comes into such close contact with water; they need to be kept well painted to ensure that corrosion is held at bay; and during installation (or removal) they are heavy and cumbersome to handle.

Because of this, alternative materials were sought for gutters and downpipes, and for a time they were made in asbestos. This was, however, a rather bulky material and is now recognised as a potential health hazard. So, when the full potential of plastics became apparent during the late 1940s, the opportunity was seized to manufacture rainwater systems in a plastic material – UPVC (unplasticised polyvinyl chloride). As a result, cast iron systems have just about disappeared from the scene and it's difficult to buy them at all. When a rainwater disposal system nowadays is being renewed in whole or in part, it is invariably plastic goods that are used.

UPVC gutters and downpipes have many bonuses. They seem to be everlasting (unless actually broken); they don't need painting, although they take paint if you don't like the colours in which they are available; they are also light to handle, and easy to cut with a sharp hacksaw. In fact, their only drawback is that they are not as rigid as cast iron, and so cannot support such things as ladders.

Simple maintenance

The faults that occur with downpipes are very much the sort of thing you get with gutters. For instance, you may occasionally get a blockage, caused by dirt, leaves or other debris being washed off the roof. You should clear this out as soon as possible, otherwise the surrounding wall of your house will get soaked with escaping water, and damp could find its way inside the house. You will see at a glance in which section of a downpipe the trouble has occurred because the joins between various lengths are not sealed. Thus when during a downpour water bubbles out of a join, you will know that the trouble lies in the section below.

The fact that the sections are just loosely joined also means that a blocked one can be taken down for clearance. You merely lift it up and pull it away, rather like a sliding door that operates in a groove.

On a straight run, you can usually push out the blockage with a long stick, although in stubborn cases you might have to tie a wad of rags to the end of the stick to make a sort of plunger. Bends will have to be poked clear with a length of wire or cane. Then clean them thoroughly by pulling through a piece of rope with a rag tied to the end of it.

Should the system have a hopper head, scoop debris out with a trowel. You should wear protective gloves as you do this. Take care not to push anything down the pipe; in fact, it's a wise precaution to push a rag bung into the top of the pipe as you work. When everything has been cleared up, fit netting to the top of the pipe so that the trouble will not occur again.

Another fault that sometimes develops is that one or more of the clips holding the pipe to the wall may become damaged or displaced in some way, and the pipe then becomes loose at the joint. The remedy is obvious: refix the clip securely (or replace it if it is badly damaged) and push the pipe back into place. Sections of pipe, too, may be badly damaged, or missing altogether. Again, you should replace them although minor damage on cast iron can be repaired with a glass fibre repair kit.

If you have cast iron downpipes, then a lot of these faults may arise because of rust, for unless you keep them well painted, they will eventually corrode. Even householders who are meticulous about regularly re-painting the exterior of the house tend to neglect the back of the downpipes because they cannot be seen, and it is difficult to treat them without getting paint all over the wall. There is one simple solution to this last problem: protect the wall with a scrap piece of card or hardboard as you work. Obviously, corrosion can take place just as readily at the back as at the front, so it is as well to be meticulous when you paint.

When one length of old downpipe becomes defective, you can replace it with a new one, and there is no problem about inserting a

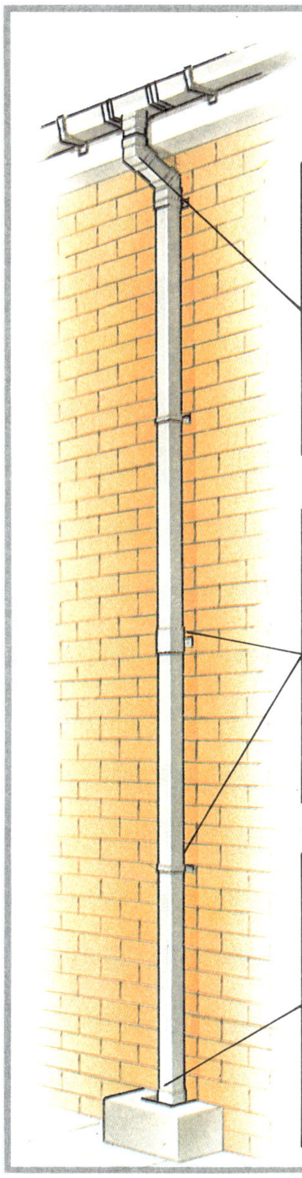

PARTS OF A DOWNPIPE

Select downpipe components carefully to ensure a well-designed and well-fitting installation.

1 Choose a long or short eaves offset.

2 Add pipe sockets or clips to wall brackets.

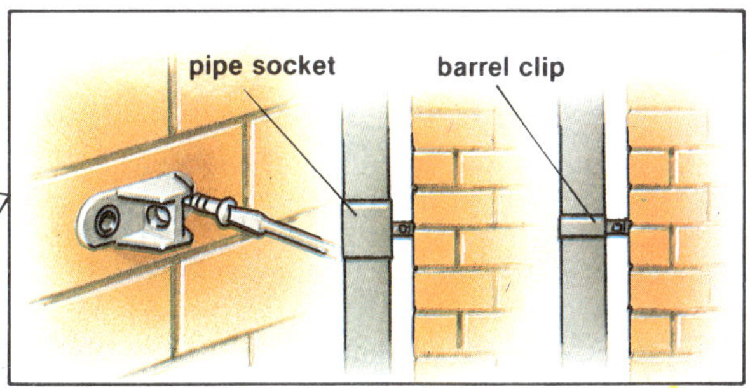

3 Fit a shoe, or connect direct to the drain.

length of plastic pipe in a cast iron system. It merely sits loosely in place, so you do not have to worry about sealing joints, as you do with gutters.

However, if one section of pipe corrodes, it is a good bet that all are coming to the end of their useful life. And, of course, if the whole system becomes ramshackle, it is time to replace the lot. This is especially true if you are fitting new gutters.

Putting in new pipes

There are a number of brands to select from, but little to choose between them, so settle for one which is available from a convenient store. If you are fitting new gutters, the pipes should be of the same brand to ensure that you can link the two at the eaves. With only a short length of guttering, consider replacing the whole gutter and downpipe system.

Begin by getting a manufacturer's catalogue. With this in one hand, inspect your existing downpipe system, and note down the exact replacements you will need. The pipes come in three common diameters – 75mm (3in) for extensions and the like, 100mm (4in) for most normal houses, and 150mm (6in) for very large roofs. Your pipes must, of course, match the gutters in size.

You have to begin the work by what is really the only troublesome part of the job, and that's taking down and getting rid of the old metal or asbestos pipes. Once you've freed each section you can lower it gently to the ground. Don't drop it as it may shatter. The clips holding the pipe to the wall can now be removed. If held by screws, there's a fair chance they will have rusted into place and will be virtually impossible to turn. However, there is a trick you can use to start the screw

Ready Reference

PIPE FITTINGS

Here are all the different sorts of downpipe fittings which you are likely to require. They are available in the square profile shown here or in the traditional round profile. Colours tend to be grey, white and black.

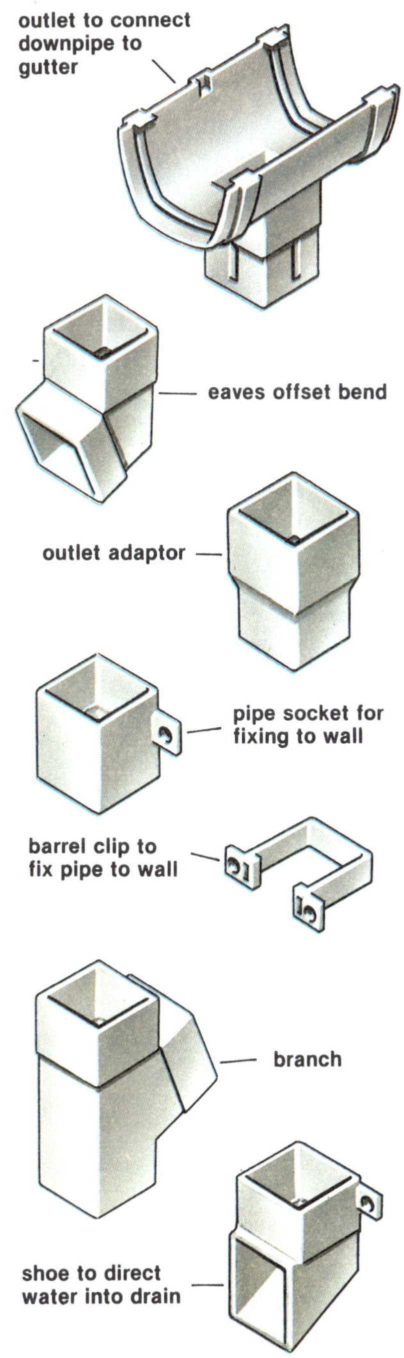

REMOVING AN ASBESTOS SYSTEM

1 *Try to unscrew the old downpipe brackets; if they won't move then lever them out of the wall with a hammer and cold chisel.*

2 *Ease the lowest pipe section away and remove it. Wear a mask and protective gloves when you're handling asbestos materials.*

3 *Work upwards, removing each section in turn. Once the brackets are off, the downpipe should come apart easily, so don't let any sections fall.*

4 *Once you've removed the downpipes, take down the guttering as well. Asbestos gutters are not usually screwed down, and should lift out.*

5 *When you've got the guttering down, remove the brackets. If they are old and rusted in, you may need a hacksaw to cut them off.*

6 *NEVER break up old asbestos pipe or guttering. Soak it thoroughly to avoid creating dust, and cut it up with a hacksaw.*

moving. Insert the screw-driver blade in the slot of the screw, then give the handle a short sharp blow with a mallet (if it's wooden). This should free the screw so you can turn it. Alternatively, the brackets may be held in place by large galvanised nails cemented into the mortar. These will have to be prised out. If all else fails, cut everything loose with a hacksaw.

The pipe itself comes in a series of standard lengths and you'll probably have to join two or more sections together with a special socket, or cut one down to size, to make up the required run. You should leave an expansion gap of 10mm (3/8in) at the end.

Plastic pipes are held to the wall by a series of small clips. These may come, according to the make, as one unit, or in two parts – a separate back-plate and clip. A clip should be placed at each joint socket, and at the manufacturer's recommended spacings in between – possibly every 2m (6ft 6in). Incidentally, there is no need to go to the trouble of drilling holes in brickwork to take the plugs for the screws that hold the clips in place. The pipes are so light that you will get a fixing by drilling the holes into the mortar.

On a simple structure, such as a garden shed, the gutter outlet may well be fitted directly into the top of the pipe without being sealed, and this makes it easier to locate and to deal with blockages. However, houses have eaves, which means the gutters won't be flush with the wall on which the downpipe is situated. So some form of fitting is needed to make the connection: this is known as an offset or 'swan neck'. You can make one of these yourself from an offset socket, an offset spigot, and a short length of pipe – perhaps an offcut from one of the main lengths – as shown in the diagram overleaf. The joins between the gutter outlet and the offset socket and spigot should be solvent-welded, for these do need to be watertight. The same is true of any section of the system that is not vertical.

Once you've made up the offset you can position it to work out where you can fix the downpipe. And this will also allow you to site the clip that holds the socket which connects the offset to the downpipe itself.

With this clip in place, you can plumb the drop of the pipe and mark the positions of the clips on the wall with chalk, so that they will all be directly underneath each other. Then fix these clips in place, and fit the pipe sections.

If your downpipes discharge into an open gully at the bottom, a curved or angled end, known as a shoe, is fitted. A clip will, of course, be needed here, as at every other joint. The shoe should be pointing away from the house wall, and should be only 50mm (2in) or so higher than the grating, so that splashes will not get onto the wall. Should the connection be direct to the drain, a special adaptor is required.

INSTALLING THE NEW SYSTEM

1 *Brush down the fascia and make good any damage to the wood. Fill the holes in the wall where the old pipe brackets were positioned.*

2 *Paint the fascia. If it's at all rotten you should replace it, as the new guttering is likely to last longer than an untreated wooden fascia.*

3 *Put up the new guttering brackets and use a taut line and a spirit level to make sure there is a slight fall along the run.*

4 *Assemble the guttering and clip it into the support brackets. Pour some water into it to make sure it flows away properly.*

5 *Attach the outlet to the gutter, using clips to make a watertight seal. Check that the outlet is vertically above the drain or gully below.*

6 *Measure the length of downpipe you need and cut it using a hacksaw. Remember to allow for an adaptor or a shoe at the bottom.*

7 *Attach the shoe to the last section of downpipe using solvent-weld cement. Check that the shoe will discharge directly over the gully.*

8 *Connect the downpipe to the outlet; this may mean inserting a 'swan neck' offset (see page 167) on buildings with overhanging eaves.*

9 *Attach the brackets to the wall using screws and wallplugs. When the system is complete, test it with water to make sure it doesn't leak.*

SOIL AND WASTE PIPE FITTINGS

The choice of modern plastic soil and waste pipes and fittings is quite bewildering. You will have to make a careful survey of the job to work out the individual components you will need. Try and get hold of a manufacturer's brochure which will show you the range available. Most soil fittings are made of unplasticised polyvinyl chloride (UPVC), but waste pipes may be of polypropylene (PP) and waste fittings of acrylonitrile butadiene styrene (ABS) or polyethylene. There are two systems for joining plastic pipes and fittings, push-fit and solvent welding (as described on pages 32–36). Push-fit fittings should be used where particularly hot water passes through the waste system, as they allow for expansion.

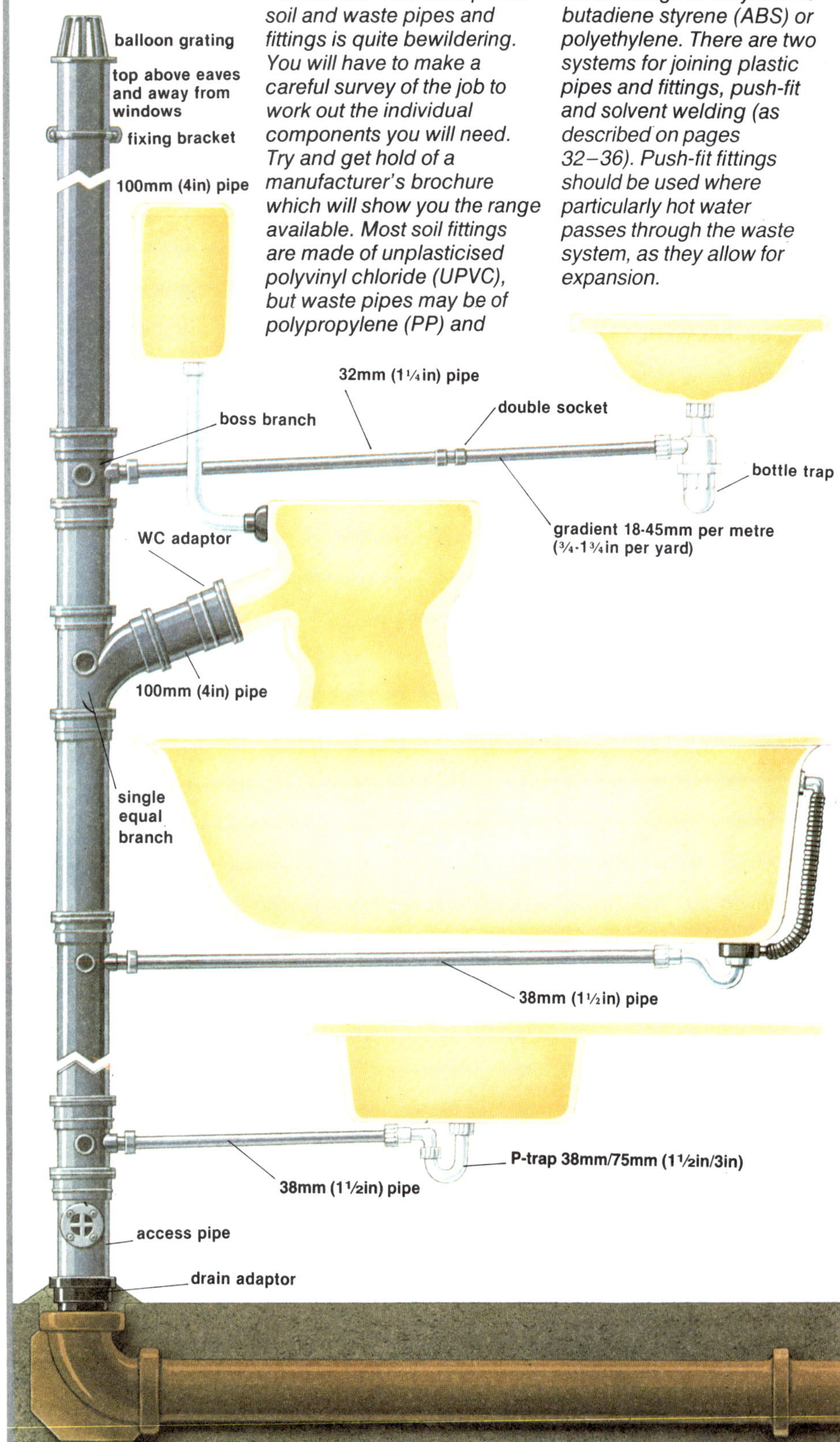

Ready Reference

CHECKING REGULATIONS

Before you install a single drainage stack you should consult your local Building Inspector to ensure that your plans are in compliance with the Building Regulations. He may also want to inspect the work after you have finished it. Remember:

- basins, baths, showers, washing machines and dishwashing machine outlets need P-traps. The depth of trap seal, except on baths and showers should always be 75mm (3in). The exception is WC pans which can have integral S-traps (see WASTE WATER SYSTEMS)
- wash basins and bidets need a 32mm (1¼in) diameter trap and branch pipe, if the branch is up to 1.7m (5ft 7in) long. If it is more – up to a maximum of 2.3m (7ft 6in) – use a 38mm (1½in) trap and pipe
- baths, sinks and showers need a 38mm (1½in) diameter trap and branch pipe
- washing machines should have a vertical standpipe (usually about 600mm/24in high) with a 32mm (1¼in) diameter trap, at the bottom of which should be a P- or running P-trap. You need an air gap where the hose enters the stack pipe
- WC branch pipes should be 100mm (4in) in diameter with a maximum length of 6m (20ft) from stack to pan, though a shorter run is preferable
- branch pipe gradients should have an angle of between 1° and 2½° (18-45mm per metre/¾-1¾in per yard)
- ground floor WCs can connect directly into the underground drain as long as the top of the trap is less than 1.5m (5ft) above the point of entry into the main drain
- there should be no connection nearer than 200mm (8in) below the WC branch connection from the opposite side of the stack
- the lowest connection to the stack must be at least 450mm (18in) above the bottom of the bend at the base of the stack
- the bend at the base of the stack where the pipe turns to flow into the underground drain must have a radius of at least 200mm (8in)
- stack pipes must be at least the same diameter as the WC outlet
- the top of the stack pipe, capped with a grille, must be above the eaves and at least 0.9m (35in) above any window which is within 3m (10ft) of the pipe.

GULLIES AND SOAKAWAYS

Gullies and soakaways are an integral part of the household drainage system, getting rid of waste water and rainwater quickly and efficiently. But things can go wrong, and prompt action is needed when they do.

The yard gully, over which the waste pipes from household sinks, baths and wash basins discharge, is a legacy of the Victorian conviction that 'drain air' was a primary cause of virtually all the ills to which the flesh is heir. It was provided to permit household waste to flow into the underground drainage system without the least risk of the supposedly noxious gases from the drain entering the house. This was achieved by discharging household wastes (other than those from 'soil fittings' such as WCs) in the open air over the gully grid. The gully had a trapped outlet, usually with a 50mm (2in) water seal, that was then connected to the underground drain. Drain gases couldn't pass that water seal and, even if they did, they would disperse inoffensively in the open air, not within the home. However, even this safeguard failed to satisfy all Victorian hygienists. The now-obsolete byelaws of some local authorities required that sink and other wastes must discharge, not directly over the gully, but into a glazed half-channel at a point at least 450mm (18in) away from it. The wastes then flowed down this half-channel into the gully itself. It is still possible to see this arrangement in some older properties, particularly in rural areas.

Stoneware gullies

Gullies provided up to World War II and for a decade or so afterwards (that is to say, the overwhelming majority of gullies still in use in this country) were usually made in one piece in glazed stoneware. The inlet was square in plan and was covered with a metal grid to prevent leaves and other debris washing into the drain to produce a blockage. The gully was set onto a 150mm (6in) thick concrete base and its spigot outlet was connected to the socket of a 100mm (4in) stoneware branch drain with a neat cement joint or, more likely perhaps, a joint made with a mix of two parts cement to one of sand. Very frequently, gullies were installed below the level of the adjacent yard surface in a purpose-made pit with cement-rendered sides, to drain surface water away from the yard. The yard surface might well be sloped to improve drainage into the gully.

This kind of gully, installed as described, often produced more problems than it solved. In this it resembled the rainwater hopper-head – another device intended to keep 'drain air' out of the home. For a start, it failed to meet what nowadays would be regarded as the very first requirement of any sanitary appliance: it was not self-cleansing. The self-cleansing flow of the waste water from a sink or bath was broken by discharging it over the gully grid, from which it descended into the water in the trap below in a gentle rain. Debris, if it was not retained by the grid, fell into the trap and stayed there, decomposing as water gently overflowed from the gully outlet above it into the drain. Much debris was, of course, retained by the grid and the scrubbing and cleansing of these grids was a revoltingly unpleasant regular household chore. Householders with a solid fuel open fire or boiler often solved the problem by extracting the grid with a poker and consigning it to the cleansing effect of the flames for half an hour or so. This, of course, could only be done with the old-fashioned metal grids, not the more modern plastic ones.

Then again, it needed only half a dozen fallen autumn leaves or a wind-blown paper bag to block the gully grid and so to produce a flooded yard. This was bad enough in bungalows or two-storey domestic premises, but if the gully took waste pipes from multi-storey buildings it was quite possible for people to continue to use sinks and basins on upper floors, totally oblivious of the havoc that they were creating at ground or basement level.

A flooded yard gully is one of the ways in which a blocked drain may manifest itself. But before getting out the drain rods and raising the drain manhole covers, it is always wise to raise the grid and probe into the flooding gully itself. The chances are that the water will instantly flow away. Sometimes, of course, the water will not flow away and raising the manhole covers may reveal no other evidence of drain blockage. In these circumstances the obstruction must be between the yard gully and the drain inspection chamber into which the branch drain from the gully discharges, and is most probably in the gully trap itself. It can usually be cleared quite quickly and easily by plunging, preferably with a purpose-made drain plunger (a 100mm/4in diameter rubber disc screwed onto the end of a drain clearing rod) but an old-fashioned long-handled domestic mop, or even a bundle or rags tied *securely* to the end of a broom handle, can be used in an emergency. Lower the disc or mop head into the gully and plunge it up and down sharply three or four times. If this doesn't do the trick, try passing a piece of flexible wire (expanding spring curtain wire, for instance) round the trap of the gully, or else rod back towards the gully from the drain inspection

TYPES OF GULLY

Yard gullies in older properties take waste water from kitchen sinks and rainwater from downpipes (1). Back-inlet gullies (2) often take waste water via a hopper from an upstairs bathroom too. Modern one-piece gullies (3) take waste pipes only; rainwater goes via separate gullies (right) to surface water drains.

Rainwater may be drained via separate gullies. The downpipe may discharge over a grid within a gully surround (4), into a back-inlet gully that also drains away surface water (5) or via a coupler direct to an underground drain or soakaway (6).

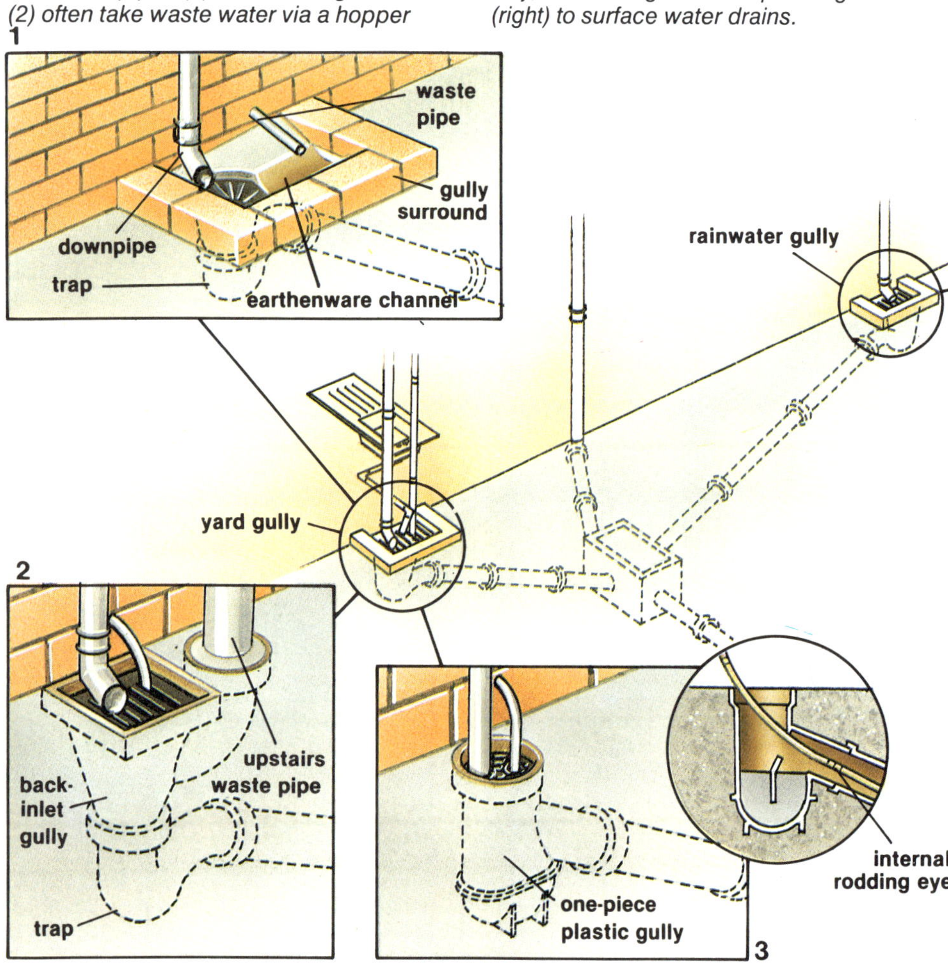

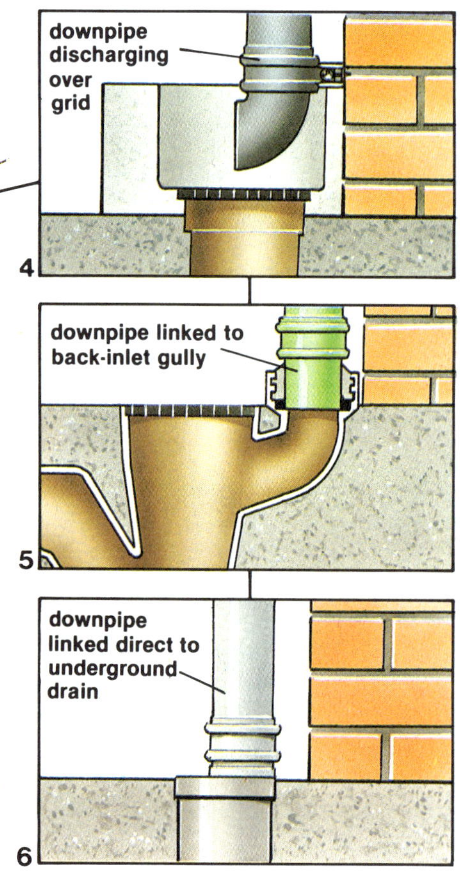

chamber into which its branch drain discharges, using a set of drain-cleaning rods – see pages 66–69.

Grid problems

Most of the troubles to which old-fashioned gullies are prone are caused by the grid which dissipates the force of waste discharges from sinks, baths and wash basins and thus prevents the gully from being self-cleansing. Debris trapped by the grid is a source of drain smells, and an obstructed grid is a common cause of yard flooding, as already described.

The remedy was an obvious one – to discharge the kitchen and bathroom wastes into the gully *above* water level but *below* the grid. To this end, back-inlet and side-inlet gullies were manufactured – often in two pieces – to be connected directly to the outlets of the branch waste pipes. They yielded an immediate benefit. The gully was thoroughly scoured out, and any silt and other debris that it contained was washed into the drain, every time a bath or sink was emptied into it. The gully grid no longer collected its evil smelling fragments; and anything obstructing the gully grid could no longer be the cause of a flood.

Back-inlet and side-inlet gullies were naturally more expensive than the older type. Furthermore, rather longer waste pipes were needed to connect to them and connection was a longer – and therefore slightly more expensive – job than simply discharging the waste over the grid in the traditional manner. Consequently, despite the fact that the advantages of the improved gullies were well-known to hygienists and sanitary engineers, they remained for many years the exception rather than the rule in the provision of domestic drainage systems.

Plastic gullies

The revolution, which produced the present generation of yard gullies and resulted in thousands of older gullies being converted to under-grid discharge, came with the widespread development of plastics in underground drainage, and (at about the same time) with the Building Regulations of the early 1960s which insisted upon under-grid discharge in all new drainage work.

A typical modern plastic gully assembly comprises three components – the gully inlet with two or more socket inlets for waste and rainwater pipes, the trap itself, and the outlet pipe. One-piece gullies are also available. Some manufacturers provide an access cap on the outlet pipe which eliminates the need for an inspection chamber at the point where the branch drain from the gully joins the main drain. Any blockage that occurs in this branch can be cleared by removing the cap and

REMOVING THE OLD GULLY

1 *Use a club hammer and cold chisel to break away the old gully surround. Don't worry at this stage about debris falling into the old gully trap.*

2 *Chop away surrounding concrete to expose the hopper, and then start to excavate carefully until you have exposed the nearby drain run.*

3 *Once you have exposed the joint between trap and drain, cut through it cleanly behind the socket with an angle grinder and cutting disc.*

4 *Use a club hammer to break up the trap outlet, taking care not to damage the cut drain pipe. Then lift out the old gully in one piece.*

inserting drain rods through the opening.

The three components are usually solvent-welded into one unit on the site, care being taken to ensure that the gully inlet is positioned so as best to accept the waste pipes to be connected to it and that the gully trap is positioned with its outlet pointing towards the main drain. To make solvent-weld joints, the surface of the spigot and the inside of the socket are roughened with medium-grade abrasive paper. Then an even coat of solvent cement is applied to the spigot and the interior of the socket, using a wooden spatula to stroke the cement along (rather than round) the surfaces to be joined together.

To assemble the joint the spigot is pushed into the socket with a slight twist, and is held in position for a few seconds. The joint can be handled within minutes, but the gully should not be used for at least 24 hours.

Ring-seal 'push-fit' joints may be used instead of solvent-welded ones to link the gully components. To make a joint of this kind, first clean the recess inside the socket and insert the sealing ring. You should then smear a small amount of petroleum jelly round the ring to lubricate it, and push the spigot firmly past the joint ring into the socket (or thrust the socket over the spigot if this is more convenient). Finally, you have to withdraw the spigot by 10mm (3⁄8in) to allow for expansion.

Gully repairs

An existing one-piece stoneware yard gully can be converted to under-grid discharge by discarding the existing metal grid and replacing it with a modern plastic one, provided with a slot through which the waste pipes can pass. All that is then necessary to convert the gully into a modern self-cleansing one is to lengthen the waste pipes so that they pass through this slot to terminate

Ready Reference

CLEARING BLOCKAGES

If a gully overflows, the likeliest site for a blockage is in the gully trap itself. To clean it:

- lift off the grating or cover
- scoop out solid debris with a gloved hand or an old tin
- mop out all the water
- scrub the gully and trap with hot water and soda
- flush it through with clean water from a garden hose.

If the blockage is between the gully and the next inspection chamber, rod the branch drain from the chamber to clear it – see CLEARING BLOCKAGES.

REPLACING A GULLY CHANNEL

The earthenware half-channel in an old gully may cause damp if it is cracked or the rendering in which it is set has become porous. To replace it:

- cover the gully grating with cardboard to catch debris
- break out the old channel, rendering and gully surround – usually bricks laid on edge
- buy a straight half-section of glazed earthenware pipe, lay it on a bed of sand and cut it carefully to the length required with a cold chisel and club hammer

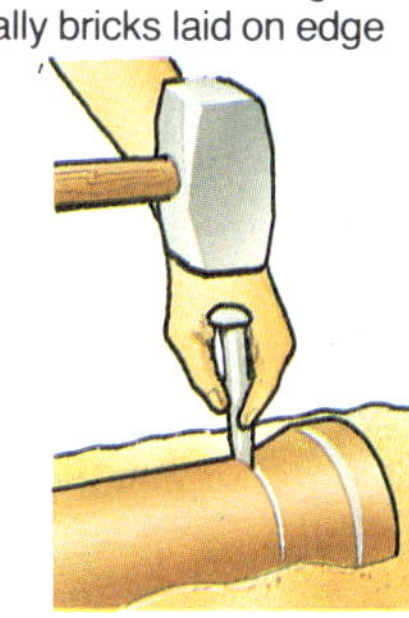

- bed the channel in mortar at a slight slope towards the gully
- build up the gully surround with new bricks, mortared into place
- slope mortar upwards from the half-channel to the gully surround and smooth it off.

TIP: COVER GULLIES

Provided that all the pipes entering a gully discharge below the gully grating, you can help to keep debris out of the trap by making a simple cover to fit over the grating and within the gully surround itself (so wind cannot lift it and blow it away). The simplest cover is a piece of exterior-grade plywood cut to the size required, with cut-outs to match the pipes passing through it.

INSTALLING THE NEW GULLY

1 *Use rapid-hardening cement to bed a PVC-to-clay adaptor on the cut end of the drain run. Hold the joint for a few minutes to ensure a sound bond.*

2 *Shovel a layer of almost-dry concrete mix into the hole, bed the gully trap in it and test the fit of the trap outlet to the adaptor.*

3 *Push the trap outlet firmly into the adaptor and check that the concrete bed supports the trap. Then hold the hopper in place to check its level.*

4 *If the hopper level is too low, you will have to insert a short length of pipe and another coupler. Lubricate the sealing rings with petroleum jelly.*

5 *Cut the extra pipe to length with a hacksaw, push it into place in the top of the trap and then add the coupler immediately above it.*

6 *Now you can position the gully hopper and press its outlet down firmly into the coupler. Make sure you align the hopper head with the wall.*

7 *With the hopper in place, use a spirit level to check that it is sitting flush with (or even fractionally below) the surrounding surface.*

8 *Back-fill round the gully with a fairly dry coarse concrete mix, treading it down well to ensure that all voids are filled. Fill to just below the surface level.*

9 *Finish off the surface round the gully with fine concrete, and check that the gully trap is clear of debris. Finally, add the gully grid.*

CREATING A SOAKAWAY

A soakaway is used to drain rainwater where no main surface water drain is provided. It's just a pit dug at least 1.2m (4ft) deep, filled with loosely-packed bricks and rubble and covered with heavy-duty polythene to prevent soil washing in and silting it up. The underground pipe should reach to its centre.

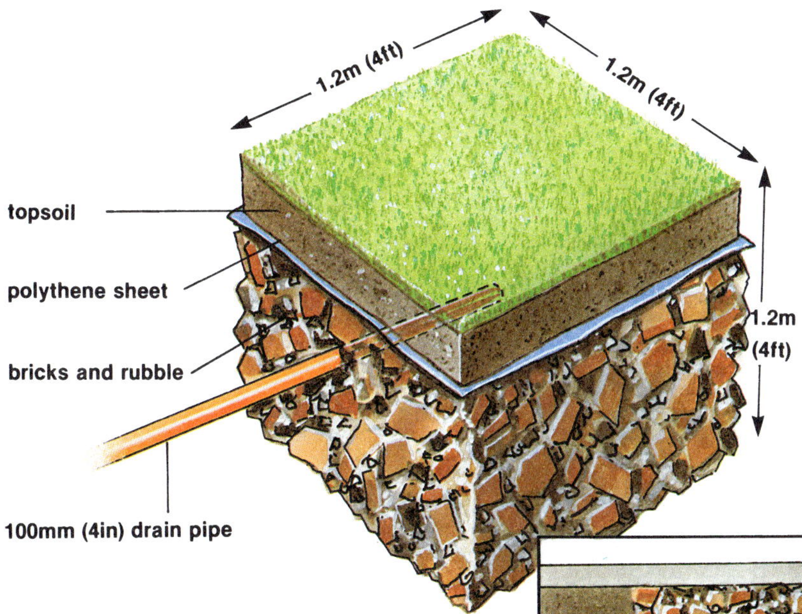

Right: Where the soakaway is underneath a drive or patio, the surface slab of concrete can be laid straight over the soakaway. No polythene is necessary.

below the grid but above water level.

Stoneware gullies, once installed, are virtually impervious to damage but the same cannot be said about the cement-rendered gully surround. The cement rendering is very liable to crack, chip or flake off, leaving cracks into which potentially smelly waste water can seep. Defects of this kind can be repaired using a pre-packed sand and cement rendering mix. It is wise to add a PVA bonding agent to the mix to ensure good adhesion of the new mortar to existing surfaces.

Replacing a gully

Occasionally it may be necessary (or at least desirable) to replace an existing glazed stoneware gully with a modern plastic one. As with so many other plumbing and drainage operations the most difficult part is likely to be the removal of the old fitting.

You will, of course, first have to excavate the surrounding surface to expose the old gully and its connection to the stoneware branch drain. Using a cold chisel and a club hammer, deliberately break the old gully so as to leave only the jagged end of its spigot outlet protruding from the drain socket. Remove the main part of the gully. Now attempt to remove the spigot and its jointing material from the drain socket *without* damaging the socket. Proceed carefully and with patience, using the cold chisel and a hammer. Keep the blade of the chisel pointing inwards towards the centre of the socket and try to break the spigot right down to the shoulder of the socket at one point. Having done this, the rest of the socket will probably come away fairly easily. Alternatively, cut through the drain pipe just beyond the socket using a cutting disc and an angle grinder.

Manufacturers of UPVC drainage systems provide various means of connecting plastic gully outlets (or other UPVC drainage components) to existing stoneware drains. Typically, a 'caulking bush' component is provided which is either solvent-welded or push-fit-jointed to the gully outlet. The other end of the caulking bush is then connected to the socket of the stoneware drain with a gasket (to centre the bush and to prevent mortar entering the drain) and the joint is completed with mortar.

Rainwater drainage

Yard gullies, as well as taking ground floor and (in older properties) upper floor wastes, may also take at least some rainwater from the roof and from the yard surface. Nowadays though, local authorities and water authorities usually require that rain water must be excluded from the main sewerage system and taken either to a separate surface water drain (where one is provided) or else to a soakaway. Surface water drains usually discharge their contents untreated into a ditch or stream. It is therefore vitally important, where a dual system of sewers is provided, to ensure that domestic waste cannot flow into the surface water drain.

Where there is such a system, trapped yard gullies should be used to collect the rainwater from roofs and yard surfaces. The trap serves a useful purpose in preventing the surface water drainage system from becoming an underground highway for rats and other vermin.

Building a soakaway

The alternative of a soakaway works best where the subsoil is light and the subsoil water level low. Typically it consists of a pit, dug up to 10m (11yds) from the walls of the house, some 1.2m (4ft) deep and perhaps 1.2m (4ft) square in plan. This is filled to within about 300mm (12in) of the surface with brick and other builders' rubble. In order to reduce the risk of the soakaway silting up, a sheet of heavy-duty polythene should then be laid over this rubble, before the soil is filled in and the surface made good. The pit can be capped with a 100mm (4in) concrete slab if desired. Rainwater pipes may be taken *untrapped* to a soakaway of this kind, though there is some advantage in providing a 'rainwater shoe with access plate' at the bottom of the rainwater downpipe to permit rodding if a blockage occurs. Pipes should enter the soakaway near the top of the rubble layer, and should reach approximately to the centre of the pit.

There are nowadays precast concrete ring soakaways on the market; these consist of concrete rings that are laid to the required depth and are perforated to permit soakage of water into the surrounding subsoil. These are provided with a concrete cover or with a manhole cover set into a frame, for access purposes.

It must be stressed that a soakaway should be used *only* for the disposal of rain and surface water; it should never be used for the waste from a sink, a bath, a washing machine or a dishwasher, and such use is contrary to the requirements of the Building Regulations.

DRAINING PATIOS & GARDENS

Poor drainage can ruin your enjoyment of your garden. Remedying this state of affairs is relatively straightforward, and the results will be well worth the effort involved.

You may be a keen gardener, growing a stunning array of plants and flowers each year, or you might simply enjoy sitting out of doors for meals and to relax. Whatever your pleasure, it is likely to be ruined if the drainage in your garden or on your patio is insufficient – a continually soggy lawn or patio covered in puddles will make life a misery. The answer is to provide adequate drainage for all parts of your garden.

How do the problems arise?

Unless your home is poorly sited or your garden has an exceptionally heavy clay soil, the chances are that the garden's soil will be able to cope perfectly adequately with the amount of water that falls as rain or snow throughout the year. Of course, you may occasionally get heavy storms that will cause standing pools on lawns, flower beds and vegetable plots, but this is nothing to worry about provided they all clear within a few hours. If the water can drain immediately into the subsoil the chances are that it'll disappear quite quickly.

However, where drainage is denied – by a patio, say, that incorporates no channelling or slope for the water to drain away – then there's likely to be a problem. The water will have nowhere to go and will disappear only gradually as it evaporates.

Flooding in the garden is unlikely to be caused merely by intense rainfall. More likely the cause will be the overflow of streams or rivers carrying away surface water from higher land, or the inability of the local storm drains to cope with a bout of particularly intense rainfall running off roofs, streets and pavements.

Dealing with small paved areas

A paved footpath in your garden is unlikely to create serious problems. The paved area involved is quite small compared to the length of the sides of the path along which rain can flow freely. The worst that can happen in a period of intense rainfall is the temporary flooding of the flower beds or grass on either side.

Most driveways slope from the garage or house towards the road, and the problems that are likely to arise from heavy rain are minimal. Water will flow down the drive and via the road gutter into a roadside gully and the local storm drain.

You may find you have problems if your drive slopes upwards from the garage to the road and in this case you may have to take action to ensure that surface water from the road can't use it as a route into your home. One solution is to install a low ramp just before the point at which the drive connects to the pavement crossing. Whether or not any other measures will be necessary will depend on the length and slope of the drive and whether or not a yard gully already exists into which run-off from the drive can flow. If there's a gully at the lowest point, then setting a channel across the entrance to the garage or carport so that surface water will run into the gully will prevent any flooding. For further information on installing a new gully see the previous section.

Patio drainage

If you're intending to lay a patio in your garden then you'll certainly have to have some kind of drainage for it. Patios are often surrounded by walls to provide privacy and a wind break, and after heavy rain a patio without a drainage system will become a paddling pool for a few days. Even where the patio is bordered directly by flower beds or shrubberies, the substantial paved area from which the rain water must flow will mean that these are regularly flooded or waterlogged.

When you're creating a patio, the simplest way of providing some sort of drainage is to ensure that its surface slopes imperceptibly to a shallow channel along one side. You'll have to make sure that the channel has a slight fall to a gully provided at one end so that the water can be disposed of.

A conventional glazed stoneware gully can be used, but you may find it easiest to fit

LAYING LAND DRAINS

1 *Dig a trench about 750mm (2ft 6in) deep away from the area you want to drain. Make sure there is a slight fall on the run. Then line the base with shingle.*

2 *Next set the drain in the trench. If you're using perforated pipes the holes should face downwards so silt can't enter and block the run.*

3 *At the start of the drain run, block up the exposed pipe end, for example, with a piece of slate, in order to prevent soil getting in.*

4 *Butt join the lengths of pipe together and prevent soil entering by covering the join with slate. You can then backfill the trench with soil.*

a one-piece bottle gully made of UPVC. This has a 'Q' outlet (halfway between the almost horizontal P outlet and the vertical S outlet) and so is particularly convenient for connection to a downward-sloping pipe run leading to a soakaway. The gully is also fitted with a polypropylene grating and baffle which can be conveniently removed to give access to the drain for rodding and the removal of washed-through leaves and other debris that could otherwise cause a blockage.

You'll have to set the gully on a 100mm (4in) thick concrete base for stability, and it's best to fix it with its inlet about 25mm (1in) below the level of the outlet of the drainage channel to ensure a smooth flow for the water.

It's important to realise that your local authority won't permit a gully draining a patio or any other paved area to be connected to an ordinary household drain. And even if a separate surface water drain is provided, the advantages of connecting the gully to this will probably be outweighed by the prohibitive cost and extra work. The problem of what to do with the water can be solved by discharging it by means of a short length of UPVC drain pipe into a garden soakaway.

Building a soakaway

Your soakaway should consist of a pit 1.2m (4ft) square and about 1.5m (5ft) deep. Fill it to within 300mm (1ft) of the surface with hardcore; before reinstating the topsoil lay a sheet of heavy-duty polythene over the rubble. This will lengthen the life of the soakaway by reducing the amount of silt that can be washed into it and so preventing it from clogging up.

Soakaways are most effective where the subsoil is light and crumbly. However, there is a chance that when digging one you could

Ready Reference

TEST NATURAL DRAINAGE

It's wise to test your garden's drainage before undertaking any work. You should:

- dig a hole about 600mm (2ft) deep
- fill it with water or wait for heavy rain.

If you have good drainage the hole will empty completely within 24 hours, but with poor drainage the water will still be there after 48 hours or more.

NATURAL DRAINAGE IMPROVEMENTS

Although your garden may have poor drainage there are a number of simple remedies you can make which do away with the necessity of laying special land drainage. You can:

- dig an impervious clay soil deeply to aerate it
- mix in organic matter such as peat or compost to make its texture more porous
- improve its texture by adding inorganic material such as sand
- introduce lime into a clay soil in order to break it up
- use a tining fork to make deep holes which should be then filled with fine gravel.

TIP: PERFORATED PIPES

When laying perforated pipes in a trench make sure the perforated side is laid on the bottom of the trench. That way water will seep up into the pipes, so preventing silt from getting into them and reducing their water-carrying capacity.

A LINED SOAKAWAY

An alternative to a hardcore-filled soakaway is a lined one. You should:

- dig the soakaway
- line it with dry brickwork, dry stone walling or perforated concrete liners
- top it with a 150mm (6in) thick concrete cover fitted 250mm (10in) below the top soil surface, so that grass and plants will have enough soil in which to grow.

A lined soakaway will have a greater capacity for water and will seldom need cleaning out.

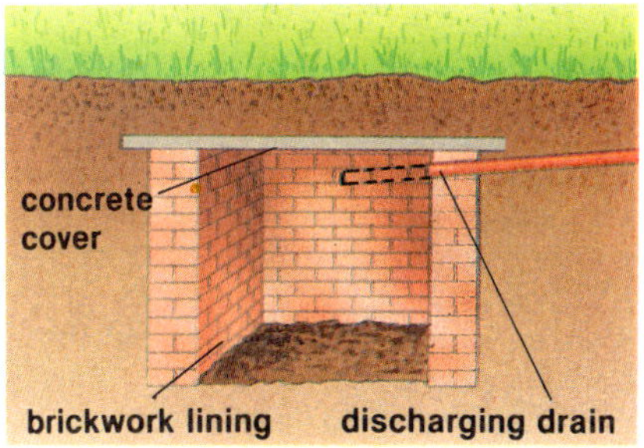

hit a layer of impervious clay at a depth of 600 to 900mm (2 to 3ft); in this case there's little point in digging any further. You should change your tactics and dig an extended soakaway – making up in length what it lacks in depth. Dig out a trench say 5 to 7m (15 to 20ft) long, 750mm (2ft 6in) deep and about 450mm (18in) wide across your lawn from the outlet of the gully. Lay a 150mm (6in) thick layer of pebbles or hardcore in the bottom of the trench and, after checking that it's level, lay land drain pipes along the trench.

Traditional unglazed agricultural drain pipes butt-jointed together will be perfectly adequate, but you'll probably find that UPVC drain pipes specially perforated for land drainage will be easier to lay.

Lay more pebbles and clinker in the trench so that you cover the pipes by at least 150mm (6in). Again, before filling in the last 150mm (6in) of the trench and reinstating the turf it's a good idea to lay a sheet of polythene over the clinker or pebbles in the trench to prevent silting.

Draining the garden

Land drainage, consisting of a series of pipes in trenches, can be used to prevent the continual waterlogging of a garden. This is often the result of subsoil water flowing from higher levels of land through the garden to a natural outlet. The remedy in this case is to intercept the water and divert it along a particular path. Dig a trench along the wettest part of the garden and a similar one connecting to it at right angles and leading down to an outlet at the front of the property. Lay the drains as before and make sure that those running across the property fall very slightly towards those laid down at the side. It's also a good idea to provide an inspection chamber at the point where the pipe run changes direction. This need not be watertight and can be just a simple square brick chamber covered by a concrete slab.

If your garden is consistently waterlogged and it's not just a question of subsoil water flowing through it, then you'll probably have to lay a different system of drainage. There are several to choose from. A natural system has the pipes following the contours of your garden and, like a grid system, takes the water to a main drain at one side of the property in much the same way as described above. A fan system will also direct the water to an outlet, while a herring-bone system consists of a main drain with a number of branch drains laid parallel with each other. With a herring-bone system the drains should be laid in at a gradient of no more than 1:250; otherwise there would be too little time for the water to soak in to the pipes. Once you've laid the pipes it's wise to protect their butt joints with a couple of pieces of slate to prevent soil entering them.

BUILDING A SOAKAWAY

1 *Dig a pit 1.2m (4ft) square and about 1.5m (5ft) deep. If you hit an impervious layer of clay extend the length of the soakaway to make up for the lack of depth.*

2 *Fill the bottom of the soakaway with a layer of hardcore. This will help to disperse the water quickly and so make the soakaway that much more efficient.*

3 *Extend the drainage pipe run to the middle of the soakaway, resting it on the hardcore. The water will then reach the optimum area of drainage of the soakaway.*

4 *Next, cover the drainage pipe and fill the rest of the soakaway to within 300mm (1ft) of the top with hardcore. Gently tamp it down to prevent later settling.*

TIP

5 *Lay a double sheet of heavy duty polythene over the hardcore. This will lengthen the life of the soakaway by stopping soil being washed into it.*

6 *Finally, reinstate the topsoil. Be careful if you dig over the ground in the future that you don't pierce the polythene sheet with a spade or fork.*

INSTALLING PATIO DRAINAGE

1 *To stop your patio from getting waterlogged install a gully and drainage system running into a soakaway. First lift the slabs where the water collects.*

2 *Dig a hole deep enough to accommodate a gully. Then excavate a trench directly to the site of your soakaway (see opposite).*

3 *Make the hole for the gully deep enough to allow you to lay a 100mm (4in) concrete base on which it is set. This will give the gully a stable foundation.*

4 *Use a one-piece UPVC gully fitted with a Q outlet. Alternatively, you can install a conventional stoneware gully fitted with a suitable adaptor.*

5 *Set the gully and outlet on the concrete base. Make sure the gully inlet is fixed about 25mm (1in) below the surface of the patio.*

6 *Secure the gully in position by packing round it with hardcore. Check several times as you do this that it remains completely level.*

7 *Fix a short length of pipe to the outlet and then fit an elbow to this pipe to reduce the 45° slope of the system, otherwise you'll have to dig much deeper.*

8 *After running the drainage pipes to the soakaway you can start backfilling. Make sure you tamp this down firmly to prevent settlement of the slabs.*

9 *Finally, replace the slabs and set a mortar fillet round the gully. Allow for the thickness of the grid, which should lay just below the patio surface.*

OUTSIDE TAPS AND PIPES

It's vital to know where your main water supply pipes are buried, so you don't damage them by accident and can trace a leak if one occurs. And it's useful to be able to install an outside tap.

Apart from any outside pipes you have, say, supplying a garden tap, the pipe you have to worry about is the service pipe which runs as a branch from the authority's main to supply your house's plumbing system. Usually it will run in a straight line from the authority's stop-valve to the point at which it enters the house and rises through the floor (usually in the kitchen) to become the rising main (see pages 8–12).

Because the service pipe is probably the most important water pipe in the home, it's vital that you know where the authority's stop-valve – which controls the flow of water in the pipe – is located. Often you'll find it under a small square or round hinged metal cover set in the pavement just outside the front gate, or in the concrete of your front garden path. It's quite likely that the valve will be protected in a guard pipe beyond the reach of a groping hand. It may have an ordinary crutch handle (the type found on old-fashioned taps) or a specially-shaped square head that can be turned only with one of the water authority's turnkeys.

Provided that you have another 'householder's stop-valve' where the service pipe enters your home, you will rarely have occasion to turn off the authority's stop-valve, but it's nice to be able to feel that you can do so should the need arise. Long-handled keys are available for turning crutch handles, or you may be able to improvise one by cutting a notch in the end of a piece of 75mm x 25mm (3in x 1in) timber and nailing another piece of wood across the other end to serve as a handle. You may have difficulty getting hold of a turnkey for the square-headed type of valve, as the water authority likes to feel that it can turn it off in the event of non-payment of the water rate, without the prospect of it being promptly turned on again, but they are usually entrusted to plumbers in whom the authority has confidence. It's really worth checking out what sort of tap you have, and if you find you haven't got a stop-valve on the rising main inside, you should definitely consider installing one. At the same time you can also make sure the guard pipe is clear of debris; having raised its cover, make sure you replace it securely. You could be liable to heavy damages if a pedestrian were injured as a result of tripping over a cover that you had left open.

The service pipe stop-valve

The service pipe will run underground directly to your home. It should rise slightly as it does so to prevent any air bubbles being trapped, but it should be at least 800mm (2ft 8in) below the surface of the ground throughout its length. This is an important frost precaution. Even in the most severe winters experienced in this country, frost is very unlikely to penetrate as deeply as this into the soil. Make sure that you don't reduce this protection by, for instance, digging a drainage channel or creating a sunken garden above the service pipe.

Where the service pipe passes under the foundations or 'footings' of the house wall, it should be threaded through a length of drainpipe to protect it against any settlement which could fracture it. Generally it will rise into the home through the solid floor of a kitchen. Where, however, it rises through the gap between the oversite concrete and a hollow boarded floor, it must be protected against the icy draughts that may whistle through the sub-floor space. This is best done by threading the pipe, when it is first installed, through the centre of a 150mm (6in) stoneware drainpipe placed vertically on the oversite concrete and filling the space between the service pipe and the inner walls of the drainpipe with vermiculite chips or other similar insulating material.

It isn't, of course, practical to do this with an existing installation. In such a case the length of pipe in the sub-floor area should be bound with a 100mm (4in) thickness of glass fibre tank wrap or glass fibre roof insulating blanket, which should then be covered with a polythene sheet to prevent it from becoming damp and so useless as insulation.

A leaking service pipe

An underground leak may go undetected for a long period, but there are some tell-tale signs which should raise your suspicions. The main ones include the sound of trickling water when no tap has been in use in the house for a long period, a persistent noise from the main pipework, a loss of pressure in the flow of water from the cold tap over the kitchen sink, or a persistently damp patch on the garden path or on the wall of a basement. If you suspect a leak, contact the water authority. They have listening apparatus with which they are supposed to be able to fix the position of a leak. At least they can advise you on how best to track down the leak.

It is generally best to get professional help to deal with a leak in the underground service pipe. In an older house – where a leak is most likely to occur – this pipe will be of lead or iron which is difficult to repair. If the pipe is a modern copper one it will probably be leaking at a joint. To reduce the risk of this happening, water authorities normally insist upon the use of special manipulative (Type B) compression joints in underground locations. With these the pipe ends have to be widened

PLANNING THE PIPE RUNS

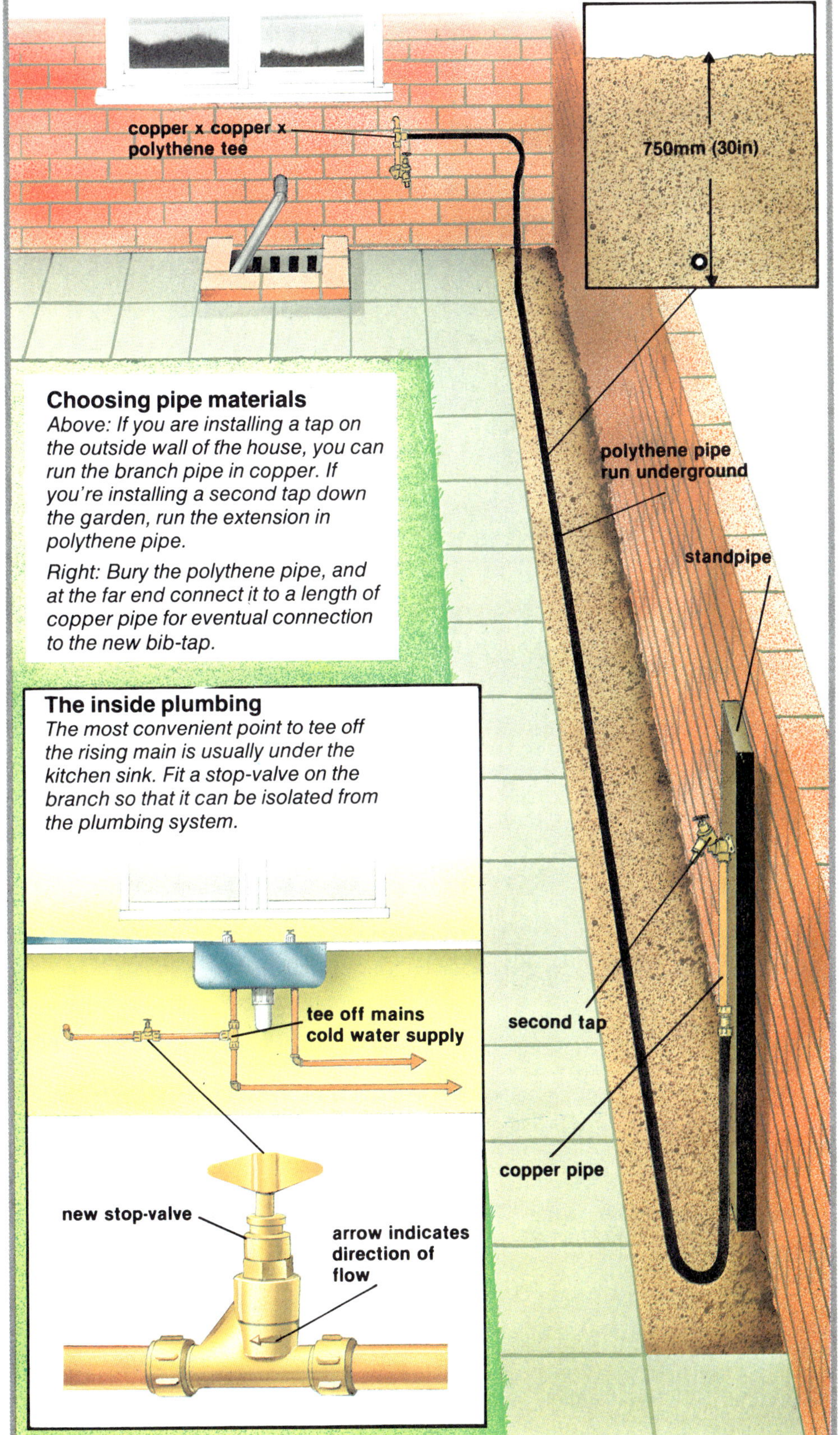

Choosing pipe materials
Above: If you are installing a tap on the outside wall of the house, you can run the branch pipe in copper. If you're installing a second tap down the garden, run the extension in polythene pipe.

Right: Bury the polythene pipe, and at the far end connect it to a length of copper pipe for eventual connection to the new bib-tap.

The inside plumbing
The most convenient point to tee off the rising main is usually under the kitchen sink. Fit a stop-valve on the branch so that it can be isolated from the plumbing system.

Ready Reference

TURNING OFF THE SUPPLY

You can control the flow of water in the service pipe supplying your home by turning off the stop-valve located
- under the kitchen sink
- under the stairs
- in the cellar
- in a guard pipe by the front fence
- just outside your front fence under the pavement.

TIP: CHECK THE STOP-VALVE

Occasionally turn all stop-valves off and on to check that they aren't jammed. You don't want to find in an emergency that they're not working.

A NEW OUTSIDE TAP

The most common outside taps are bib-taps. These have a plain brass finish and often there is no easy-clean cover to protect the headgear.

NEW PIPE RUNS

If a new outside tap is to be fitted to the house wall, use copper pipe. If the tap is to be situated away from the house use polythene pipe run underground.

TIP: FIT A STOP-VALVE

Fit a stop-valve on the new pipe run in the inside of the house. Turn the valve off in winter and leave the outside tap open to reduce the risk of freezing water causing damage to the pipe run.

INSTALLING AN OUTSIDE TAP

1 *After turning off the main stop-valve, cut out a small section of pipe and insert a compression tee in the rising main.*

2 *Insert a stop-valve in the branch supply as close to the tee as possible. Make sure that the arrow on the tap points in the direction of the flow.*

3 *Work out where you want the branch pipe to emerge from the inside. Then working from the outside (or the inside) drill a hole through the wall.*

4 *Feed the branch pipe through the wall, then screw a backplate elbow in place just below it; this will act as the fixing for a new bib-tap.*

5 *Slip a compression elbow over the branch pipe and measure the length of pipe needed to reach the backplate. Cut and fit it in place.*

6 *Wind PTFE tape several times round the thread of the bib-tap. Screw the tap into place, making sure it is upright when you finish.*

– 'manipulated' – with a special tool as the joint is assembled. You may consider it better to replace the existing pipe with a single length of soft-temper copper tubing. This is obtainable on reels in long lengths that eliminate the need for underground joints.

Many water authorities nowadays also permit the use of black polythene piping. This too is obtainable in long lengths and has the added advantage that its thick walls help to insulate the pipe against frost. And in the unlikely event of the water within the pipe freezing, polythene pipe is sufficiently resilient to accommodate the expansion of the freezing water without bursting.

Putting in an outside tap

The only occasion when you are likely to need a permanent supply of water out of doors is when you put in an outside garden or garage tap. Before doing this you should always seek the permission of the water authority. This is likely to be granted readily enough, but it will involve an additional charge on the water rate, particularly if you are going to use the tap for a hose pipe or sprinkler system. If you already have an outside tap you'll agree that the convenience of not having the garden hose snaking through the kitchen window, and putting the domestic water supply out of action while it is in use, makes this extra payment well worthwhile. Provided that your home has modern copper plumbing, fitting an outside tap is a straightforward job.

If the outside tap is to be fixed to the wall outside the kitchen, you will need a bib-tap with a horizontal inlet for outside water supply, with a threaded nozzle for a hose connector and an angled handle that you can turn without grazing your knuckles on the wall. You'll also need a 15mm wall-plate elbow with a compression elbow bend, one 15mm equal-ended compression tee joint, a screw-down stop-valve with 15mm compression inlet and outlet and a length of 15mm copper tubing – how much will depend on the distance between the rising main and the new outside tap.

As far as tools are concerned, you'll require a couple of wrenches, a hacksaw, a tin of jointing compound, a roll of PTFE thread-sealing tape and some means of cutting through the wall to take the pipe-run outside. It's best to hire a heavy duty electric drill with hole-cutting attachments; the job can be done with a hammer and cold chisel, but this takes longer and is not as neat.

Turn off the main stop-valve and drain the rising main from the cold tap above the kitchen sink and, if there is one, from the drain-cock above the stop-valve. Cut the rising main at a convenient point to take off a

ADDING A SECOND TAP

1 *Fit a 15x15x22mm compression tee into the existing branch. Use a piece of copper pipe to hold the fitting secure while it's tightened.*

2 *Fit the polythene pipe to the tee. Then clip it to the wall and take it down to a prepared trench at least 750mm (30in) deep.*

3 *At the other end of the trench, attach the second tap and a short length of pipe. Then run the polythene pipe up the foot of the post.*

4 *Link the polythene pipe to the copper using a 22x15mm compression coupling. Finally turn on the supply, check for leaks and back-fill the trench.*

feed branch pipe. If there isn't a drain-cock above the main stop-valve a little water will flow out as you do this, so be prepared for it. Make another cut 18mm (¾in) away from the first one and remove the 18mm segment of pipe.

Insert the 15mm compression tee into the cut pipe (described on pages 14–18) so that the branch outlet of the tee points along the kitchen wall in the direction of the position of the new tap. Cut a short length of copper pipe, say 150mm (6in), and fit it into the outlet of the tee. To the other end of this fit the screw-down stop-valve by means of its compression joint inlet.

There are two points to watch as you do this. Make sure that the arrow engraved on the body of the stop-valve points away from the rising main and towards the position of the new tap. Make sure, too, that the stop-valve handle is angled away from the wall so you have enough room to turn it with ease.

The first phase of the job is now complete. You can turn off the new stop-valve and turn on the main stop-valve to check for leaks. Because this will restore water to the rest of the house you can carry out the rest of the job in your own time.

Drill a hole – sufficiently large to take a 15mm copper pipe – through the wall above the position of the new tap. When deciding exactly where on the outside wall you want your tap to be positioned, remember that you'll want enough room to be able to put buckets and watering cans beneath it. Then cut two more lengths of copper pipe, one long enough to pass through the house wall and to protrude by 25mm (1in) at each end, and the other long enough to reach from the new stop-valve to the hole that you have made in the wall. Join these two lengths with a compression elbow and push the correct length through the hole in the wall. Connect the other end of the other length to the outlet of the new stop-valve.

Next you can go outside and cut the projecting pipe so that 25mm (1in) projects through the wall. Connect the other elbow to this so that its outlet points downward to the position of the new tap. Cut another short piece of pipe to reach the position of the new tap. Fit the wall-plate elbow to one end of this and connect the other end to the projecting elbow bend. Drill and plug the wall, and screw the wall-plate elbow into place. You'll then have to bind PTFE tape round the threaded tail of the tap and screw it into the outlet of the wall-plate elbow. If the tap doesn't point downwards when screwed fully home, you'll have to remove it and add washers to its tail until it does.

The job is now complete, apart from making good the hole through the wall with some mastic filler. With the onset of winter, turn off the new stop-valve and open the outside tap to drain the short branch to protect it from the risk of frost damage. There is no need to insulate the section of pipe on the outside wall.

Installing a garden standpipe

If you have a large garden, or a garage at some distance from the house, one tap fitted against the outside wall of the house may be insufficient, and you may need another standpipe to provide an adequate outside supply. This is an excellent opportunity to use polythene pipe for the water supply because of the long lengths in which it can be obtained. In fact, when new houses are built today this piping is usually chosen for all underground runs.

In order to install a second outside tap you have to carry out the preliminary work described above, but instead of fitting the tap into a backplate elbow, you can use a backplate tee. It is from the lower outlet of this tee that the additional garden supply is taken. You may not be able to get a tee of this kind to which polythene pipe can be directly connected. In this case fit a short length of 15mm copper pipe into the tee outlet and connect the end of the polythene pipe to it by means of a 15mm copper to ½in polythene compression coupling. However, probably the easiest method is to tee off the short section of supply pipe feeding the outside tap already installed.

Although polythene pipe will not be damaged by frost, it should still be laid in a trench about 750mm (30in) deep to avoid the risk of accidental damage from gardening operations. The pipe can be taken underground to any point required, and then connected to a tap fixed to a post or to the wall of an outbuilding by means of the usual backplate elbow.

PART 2

ELECTRICS

THE DOMESTIC ELECTRICAL SYSTEM

Prior to undertaking any work upon it, a thorough understanding of your domestic electrical supply is necessary, and certain rules must be observed.

Understanding ELECTRICS

In theory, you could do electrical jobs knowing nothing about electricity, given accurate step-by-step instructions. But you can't deal with any part of an electrical installation in isolation — everything is linked. And unless you understand how each part of the system works you have no way of knowing if you are making a mistake. With electricity, ignorance is dangerous.

We re all familiar with lights and power sockets, but how does the electricity reach them so we can use it? In fact, electricity enters your home along one thick cable (the service cable), passes through a large 'service fuse' and into a meter which records the amount you use. Everything up to and including that meter belongs to the electricity board, and is their responsibility. Everything beyond is the householder's property, which is perhaps why installations vary so much.

In a modern installation — one wired in the last 30 years — there are two wires carrying electric current that lead from the meter to what is called the consumer unit. These wires are known as the meter tails — one is termed live, the other neutral.

On the inlet side of the consumer unit there's a switch with which you can turn off the power altogether, but the unit's principal job is to divide up the power and send it round your home through a network of cables.

These cables are organized into circuits. There are circuits for lights, power sockets and so on, each with its own fuse in the consumer unit. The cables themselves run under the floor, above the ceiling and may even be visible on wall surfaces, although more often they are buried within them.

In older installations, instead of a consumer unit there may be individual fuse boxes protecting separate circuits. And each of these fuse boxes will have an isolating switch to cut off power to the circuit it controls. These fuse boxes are connected direct to the meter by live and neutral meter tails. Alternatively the fuse boxes may be supplied from a distribution board which in turn is connected to the meter.

Sometimes, even with a consumer unit you may find separate fuse boxes. This is normally the result of the system having been extended.

WARNING: *Electricity is dangerous. Before touching any part of the fixed wiring in your home, turn off the power at the main switch so you can be sure no current is flowing anywhere in the system.*

What are circuits?

If you take a battery, and connect a wire to the positive (+) terminal, and another to the negative (−), then bring the free ends of the wires together, electricity will flow from positive to negative along them. That's a circuit. You can build a torch bulb and holder into it to prove it works. Break the circuit by cutting one wire, and the light goes out (the flow of current has stopped), and it will stay out until the cut ends are rejoined. That's a simple switch.

Of course, the circuits in your home are a good deal more complex than that, and their design varies according to whether they supply lights, power sockets or whatever. Even the electricity is different. Instead of flowing in one direction, it goes back and forth 50 times a second — hence its name *alternating current*, or AC for short.

But the principle is the same., Think of 'live' as positive, 'neutral' as negative, and you will see that for any appliance such as an electric fire to work it must have wires connecting it to the live and neutral terminals in the consumer unit. Those wires may be contained in a single cable, but the link must always be there, with switches *en route* to make or break it, and for safety reasons, switches are on the live wire.

What are fuses?

The main service cable has its fuse; the various circuits have theirs in the consumer unit or fuse box and if you remove the back of a flat-pin plug you'll find a fuse in there.

Think of an electric light bulb. It gives out light because electricity passing through the filament (the fine wire just visible inside the bulb) makes it very hot. If you pass enough electricity through any wire, it will also heat up. If that wire happens to be a circuit cable, an appliance flex, or the service cable to the meter, then the consequences would be serious. So, to protect them, a weak link called a fuse is built into the circuit.

Most fuses are just thin pieces of wire. They can be fitted to rewirable fuse carriers, in which case you can replace them, or they may be in ceramic cartridges, in which case you throw them away and fit another. In any event, the fuse's thickness is described in terms of how much electricity — expressed in amps — is theoretically needed to melt it.

The word 'theoretically' is important because, in fact, fuses aren't particularly accurate or reliable. For this reason, a more sensitive device called a miniature circuit breaker (MCB) may be used instead. It's just a switch that turns off automatically when danger threatens. Once the fault responsible for the overload is put right, you switch on again.

Why cables?

It would be far too complicated to wire a house like a battery and bulb circuit using individual wires. Instead, the copper wires carrying the electricity are encased in PVC insulation to stop them touching and making their circuit in the wrong place — what's called a short circuit — and then bound together in PVC sheathing to form a cable. In this way, the live, neutral and earth wires can be run as one, even though each one is still connected up separately.

Different kinds of cable are used for different jobs. For full details of the most common types, see pages 164 and 165.

Earthing

The purpose of the earth wire within the cable is to make up the earth continuity conductor (ECC). This is an essential safety feature of any electrical installation. Its role is to act as a 'safety valve' in the event of a fault, causing a fuse to blow or an MCB to trip to isolate a faulty circuit or faulty appliance from the mains supply. In doing so it could prevent the risk of fire or someone being electrocuted.

Earth wires are connected to the metal parts of switches, socket outlets, fittings and appliances (and even plumbing) in a really up-to-date system. Electricity will flow along the line of least resistance, so that if by some mishap any of these parts became live (by coming into contact with a live conductor) the earth wire would offer a line of 'less' resistance. In effect the faulty current would travel along the earth wire rather than through a person touching the live metal part. And the extra current passing through one circuit would be sufficient to blow the fuse or activate the MCB.

Unfortunately this doesn't always happen – so, for added safety, a special device called a residual current circuit breaker (RCCB) can be fitted to detect the slightest leakage of current to earth. It shuts off the power within milliseconds – quickly enough to save a life – at the first sign of a fault.

RCCBs can be added to an existing system, or included within the consumer unit in a new installation. They usually protect all the circuits in the house and also act as a mains on/off switch.

Ring circuits

For getting electricity to the power points, the most common system of wiring is what's called a 'ring' circuit. Wired in 2.5mm² two-core and earth cable, most homes have one such circuit for each floor of the house.

The two-cores and the earth wire are connected to their terminals in the consumer unit (or fuse box) and then pass through each power socket in turn before returning to their respective terminals in the consumer unit (fuse box). The circuit is protected by a 30A

YOUR ELECTRICITY SUPPLY

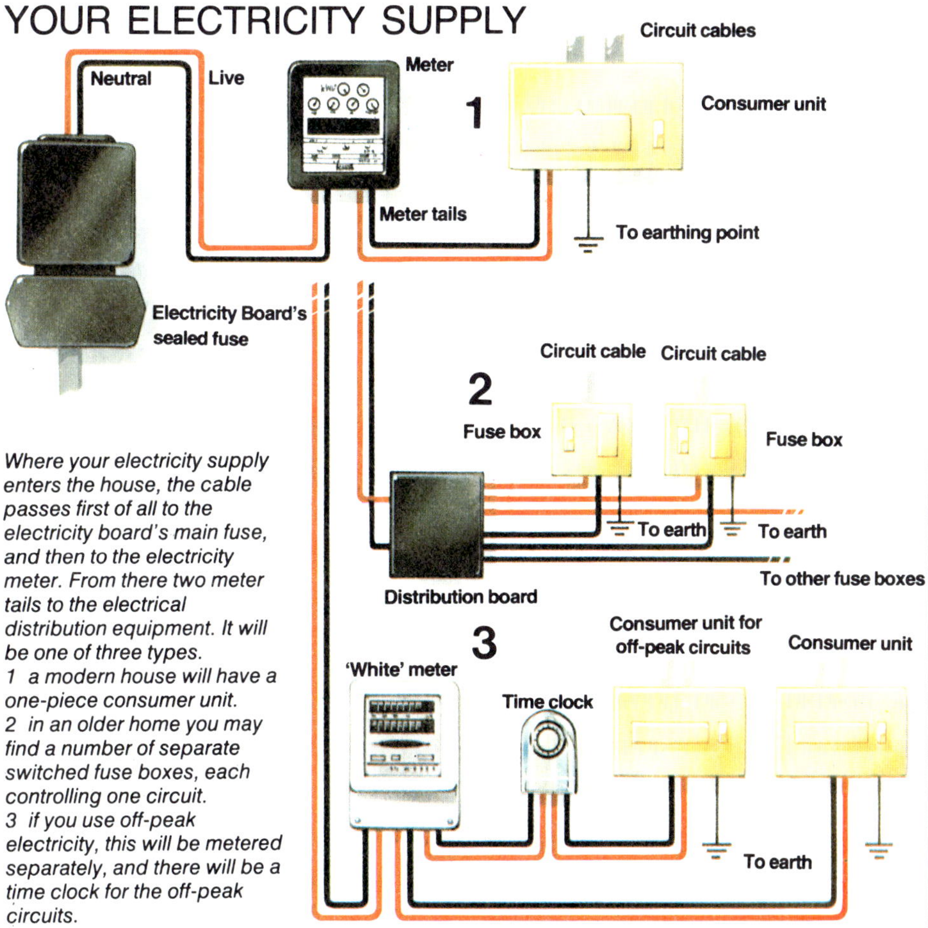

Where your electricity supply enters the house, the cable passes first of all to the electricity board's main fuse, and then to the electricity meter. From there two meter tails to the electrical distribution equipment. It will be one of three types.
1 a modern house will have a one-piece consumer unit.
2 in an older home you may find a number of separate switched fuse boxes, each controlling one circuit.
3 if you use off-peak electricity, this will be metered separately, and there will be a time clock for the off-peak circuits.

Trevor Lawrence

Ready Reference

USEFUL TERMS

Ampere (amp, or A for short) is the measure of the rate at which current flows through a circuit. The more powerful the appliance the more current it uses.
Volt (V) indicates the force driving the current between live and neutral. The mains voltage is usually 240 volts.
Watt (W) is the measure of electric power and is worked out by multiplying amps by volts. Also, 1,000W = 1kW (kiloWatt).

BATHROOMS

Special regulations apply for safety reasons:
- power sockets are not allowed
- lights should be operated by a pull-cord
- wall heaters should not be placed over a bath and must be operated by a pull-cord, or a switch outside the bathroom

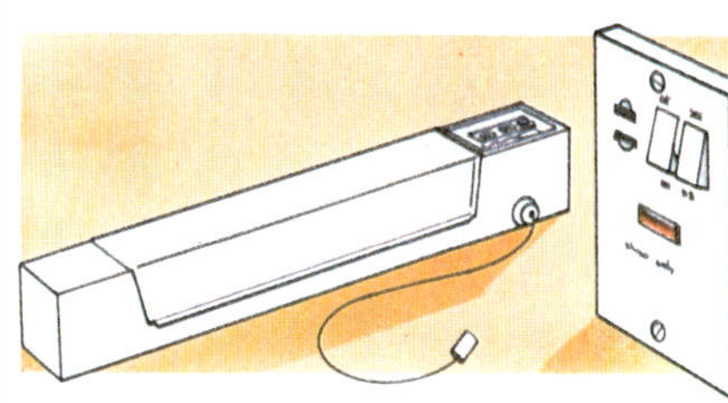

SHAVER UNITS

These have a special socket and plug connection and are safe to use in a bathroom because they isolate the razor from the earthed mains supply.

FOR SAFETY'S SAKE AVOID

- flexes under carpets
- too many adaptors

It's easier in the long run to have the system changed to meet your needs.

NEW ELECTRICAL WORK

If this involves installing a new consumer unit or fuse box, you must call in the electricity board to make the final connection between it and the meter.

TREATMENT FOR SHOCKS

- turn off the supply *or*
- pull person clear immediately but *don't touch* his/her body – grab the clothes or use a wooden stick, length of rubber or leather *(no metal, no moisture)*
- if breathing stops, give mouth-to-mouth resuscitation

Don't wrap the person in blankets or try to give him brandy. If severely shocked call the doctor.

fuse. The advantage of this system is it allows the cable to cope with more sockets than if it made a one-way trip (see Radial circuits -right). In fact, you are allowed as many sockets as you like on the ring, so long as the floor area served by the circuit doesn't exceed 100 sq metres (1,080 sq ft). What's more, you can increase the number of sockets by adding 'branch lines' off the ring. These are called 'spurs' and break into the ring via a junction box, a spur connection unit, or an existing socket. You are allowed as many spurs as there are sockets on the ring, and each spur can supply one single, double or triple socket, or one fixed appliance via a fused connection unit. Until a recent change in the IEE Wiring Regulations, a spur could feed two single sockets, and you may find such spurs on your existing circuits.

Of course, with all those sockets, there is a risk of overloading the circuit, but in the average family home it's unlikely that you'll have enough sockets in use at any one time. The circuit may carry up to 30 amps of current which is equivalent to having appliances and portable lamps using 7,200 watts of power all switched on together. It's doubtful that you would want all this on at the same time, but it's wise not to go above this level of power use. If the circuit does overload, the fuse will blow. or the MCB will switch off.

Radial circuits

Unlike ring circuits, radial circuits consist of a single cable that leaves the fuse box and runs to one or more sockets. In older homes in the UK, before ring circuits were introduced, all power circuits were wired as radials. Since homes had (and needed) only a few sockets, individual circuits were usually run to each one from the fuse box. The sockets themselves were rated at 2A, 5A or 15A, and had round holes to accept round-pin plugs. Such circuits will probably have been wired in rubber- or lead-sheathed cables, which deteriorate with age (see pages 14 and 15), and are not able to satisfy the far greater electrical demands of a modern household. It's wise to have such circuits examined by a qualified electrician, and best of all to have them replaced.

Radial circuits are, however, also used in modern wiring systems where a ring circuit could be inappropriate for some reason. There are two types, with different current-carrying capacity.

A 20A radial circuit uses 2.5mm² cable and

A ring circuit originates from a 30A fuseway in the consumer unit. Protection may be by an MCB rather than a rewirable or cartridge fuse.

Spurs are sometimes added when the ring circuit is installed to save on the wiring runs. They are usually connected at a three-terminal junction box.

Socket outlets on a ring circuit take the fused 13A flat-pin plug. They can have one, two or three outlets on the faceplate; the best have switches.

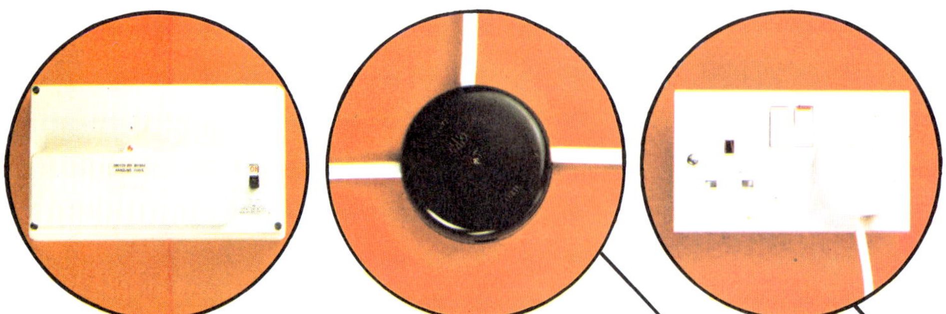

Jem Grischotti

THE RING CIRCUIT

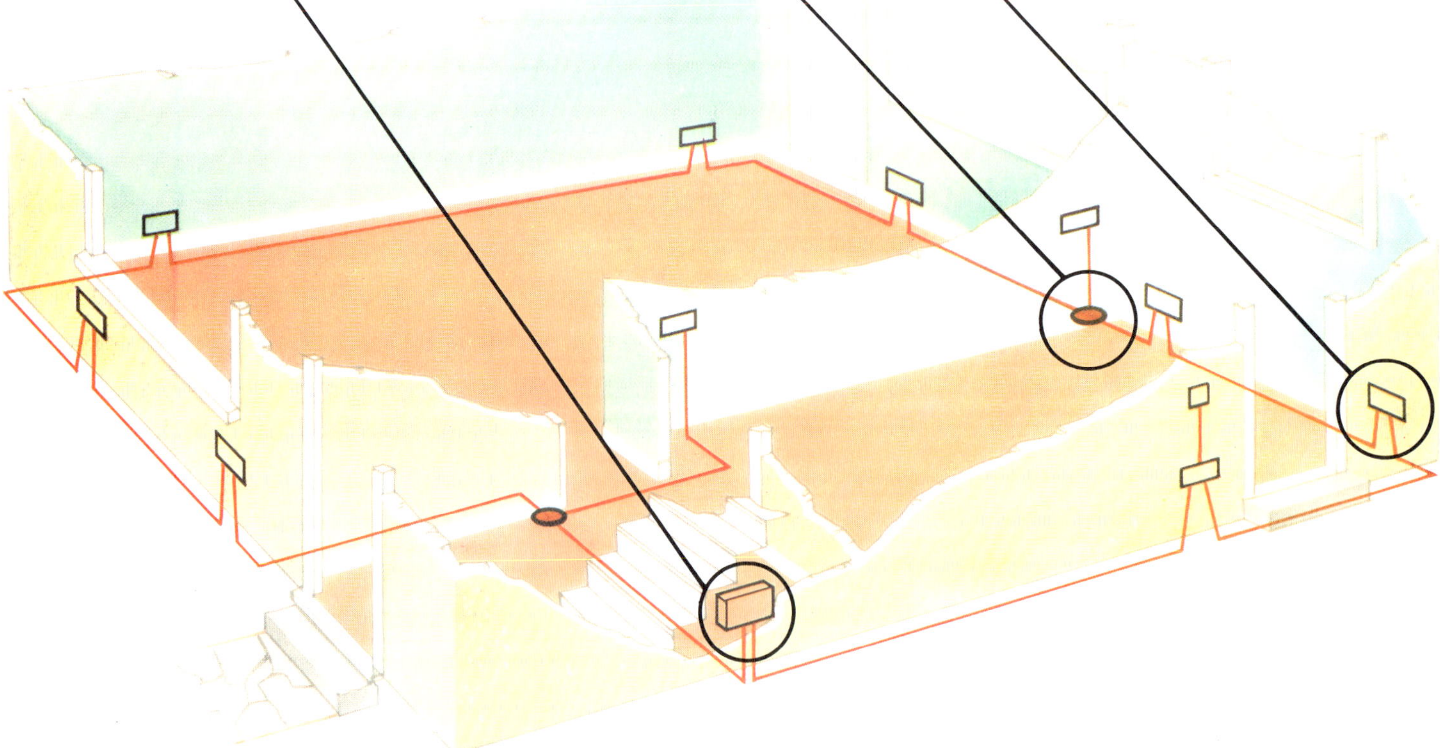

Trevor Lawrence

is protected by a 20A fuse (rewirable or cartridge) or an MCB in the consumer unit (or fuse box). It can supply an unlimited number of 13A socket outlets and fixed appliances using 3kW of power or less, providing they are within a floor area not exceeding 20 sq metres (about 215 sq ft).

The other type of circuit is the 30A radial which is wired in 4mm² cable and can feed a floor area of up to 50 sq m (540 sq ft). It can be protected by a 30A cartridge fuse or MCB, but not by a rewirable fuse.

These restrictions on floor area mean that several radial circuits would have to be installed to cover the same area as a ring circuit. This is one of the reasons why the 'ring' is now the most common method of wiring in the UK, but radial circuits can supplement an overworked ring circuit.

Special purpose circuits

In addition to rings and radials, your home may have special circuits which supply only one outlet or appliance. Cookers, immersion heaters, instantaneous showers and the like are wired in this way and each has its own individual fuse. In effect, these circuits are just radials that have had both the cable and fuse sizes 'beefed up' to cope with the often heavy demands of the appliances they supply — for example, a large family-size cooker might need a 45A fuse, and 6mm² or even 10mm² cable.

Because electric night storage heaters all come on together they could overload a ring circuit; consequently each one is supplied by

The various radial power circuits originate from fuseways in a consumer unit or from individual fuse boxes. They are protected by fuses or MCBs.

Modern radial circuits have sockets that take 13A flat-pin plugs. Older radials with lead or rubber-sheathed cable take round pin plugs.

Even if you have ring circuit wiring, radial circuits are used for special purposes, such as supplying a cooker. It may also contain a 13A socket outlet.

A fused connection unit sometimes supplies a fixed appliance on a radial circuit. This could be a wall mounted heater or an immersion heater.

RADIAL POWER CIRCUITS

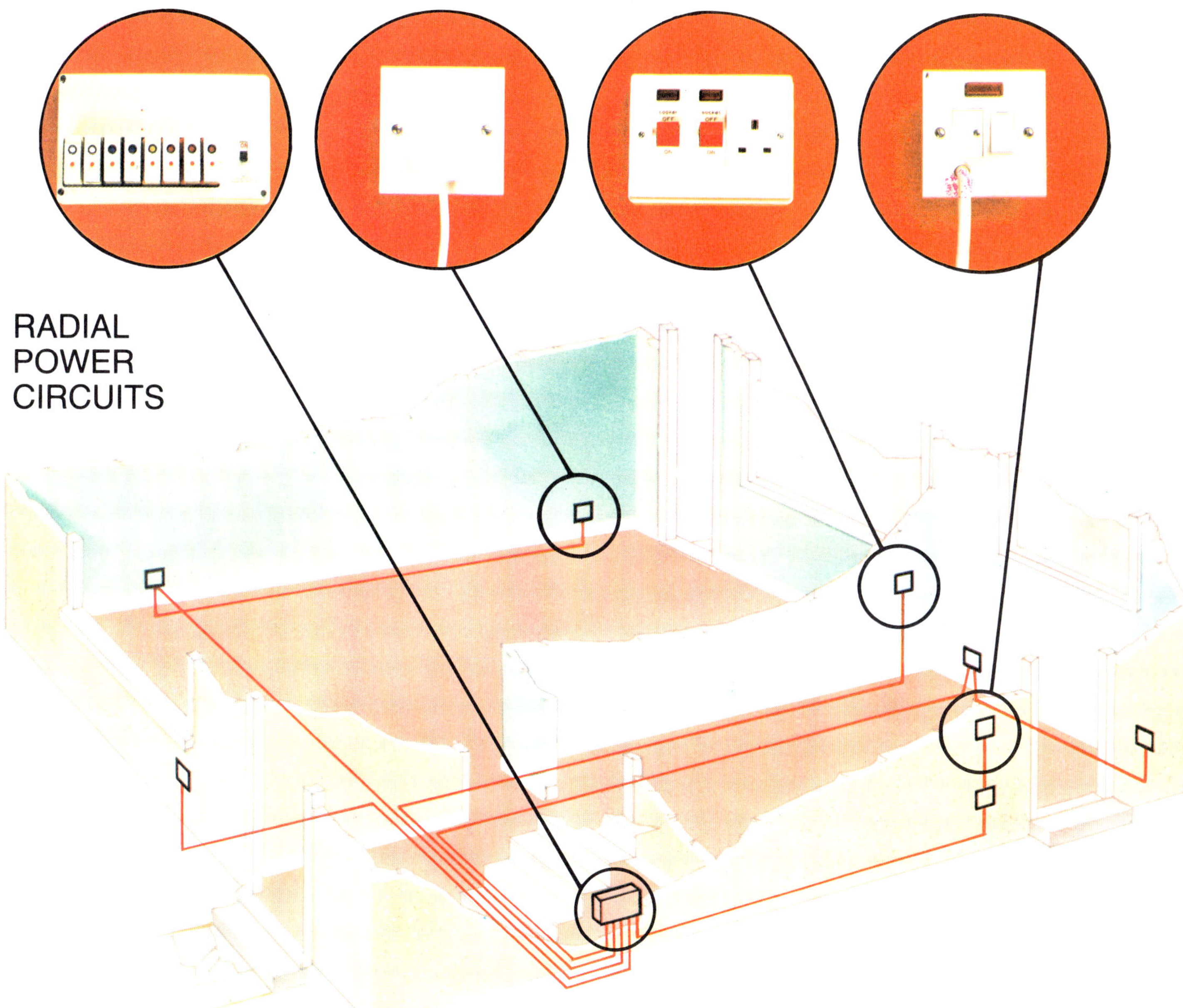

Jem Grischotti

Trevor Lawrence

LIGHTING CIRCUITS

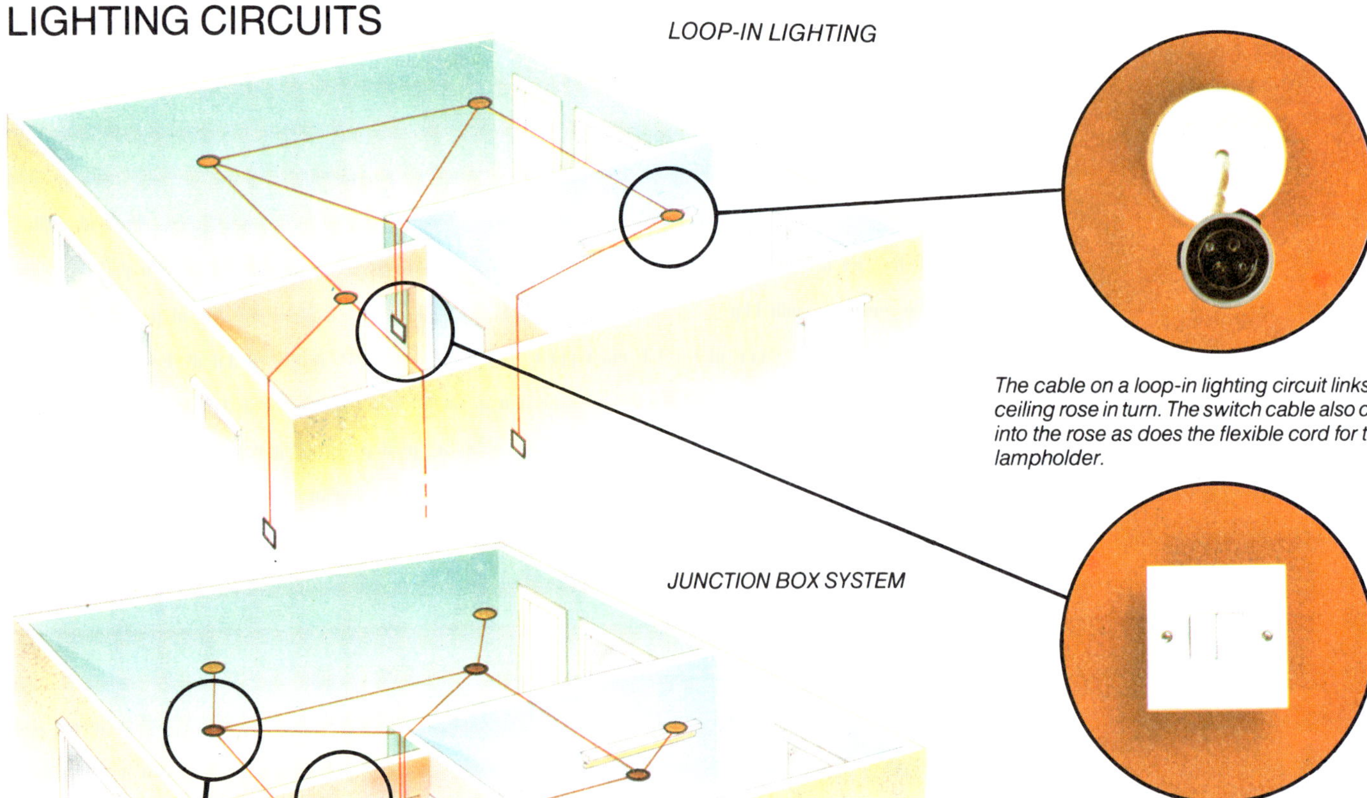

Trevor Lawrence

The cable on a loop-in lighting circuit links each ceiling rose in turn. The switch cable also connects into the rose as does the flexible cord for the lampholder.

A two-gang switch enables two lighting points to be controlled individually from the same point. Switches can be surface-mounted or flush.

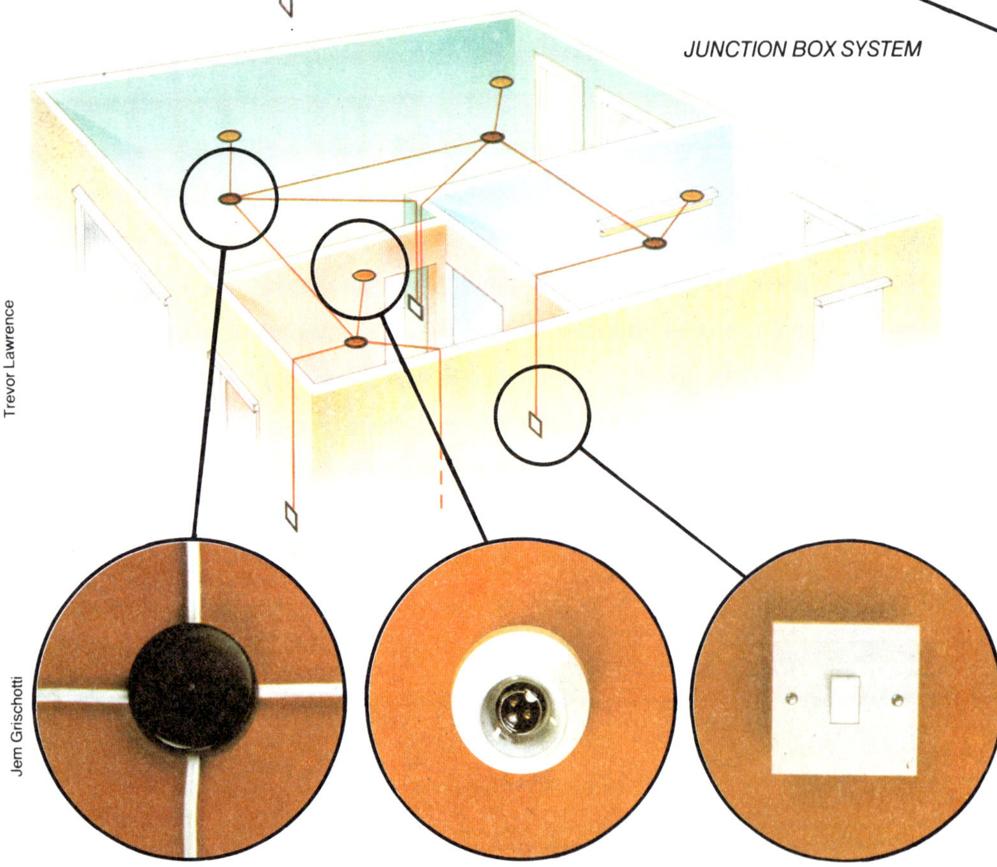

Trevor Lawrence

Jem Grischotti

With junction box wiring the main cable runs between four-terminal junction boxes. The other cables go to the lighting point and the switch.

Batten holders are used to fit a light close to the ceiling. In bathrooms, they must have a 'skirt' to prevent contact with metal on the fitting or bulb.

The simplest switch is a one-gang type mounted on a face-plate. They can be either surface mounted or recessed to be flush with the wall.

a separate radial circuit protected by a 20A fuse. The fuses are housed in a separate consumer unit which is linked to a sealed time clock and uses off-peak electricity.

Lighting circuits

Two systems of wiring lighting circuits are in common use, and it is not unusual for an installation to contain a little bit of each. One is called the loop-in system; the other the junction (or joint) box system.

With the loop-in system, a cable (normally 1.0mm² but sometimes 1.5mm²) leaves a 5A fuse in the consumer unit (or fuse box) and is connected to the first in a series of special loop-in ceiling roses. From this rose, one cable goes onto the next in the series, and another takes the power down to the switch controlling the light and back up through the light itself.

The junction box system uses the same idea but, instead of going from rose to rose, the cable from the consumer unit (or fuse box) passes through a series of junction boxes. From each box, one cable goes to the ceiling rose or light, and another to the switch that controls it. This system is particularly useful, for example, when fitting wall lights as there is little space at the back of a wall light fitting for looping-in.

Lighting circuits are rated at 5 amps, which means they can take a load of up to 1,200 watts. In effect, they could supply 12 lampholders containing bulbs of 100W each or smaller. But as you may want to fit bulbs with higher wattages, it is usual for a lighting circuit to supply up to eight outlet points, so separate circuits are required for each floor.

Strictly speaking it's better to arrange the circuits so that there is more than one on each floor — this means that you won't be in total darkness if a fuse in the consumer unit blows.

TOOLS & ACCESSORIES

Before you can contemplate carrying out any electrical work in your home, you must make sure you are familiar with all the components that go to make up the system.

PLUGS & FUSES

Fuses and plugs are the two parts of a home's electrical system that most closely concern the householder and it's important to know what they do and how to use them.

BE PREPARED

- Make a list of which circuit does what (eg, no 1: downstairs lighting) and keep it by the main fuse box or consumer unit
- Keep a fuse wire card containing adequate lengths of each rating, a small screwdriver and a torch near the fuse box or consumer unit ready for emergencies
- If the consumer unit contains cartridge fuses, always keep at least two spare fuses of each current rating in a plastic bag and hang it nearby.

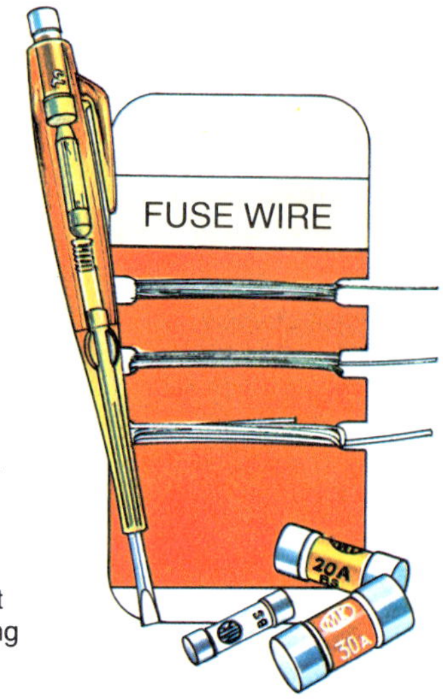

FUSES

A fuse is a safety device inserted into an electrical circuit to protect the mains wiring or any appliance from damage by overloading. This can be caused by anything from too many appliances overloading a particular circuit to a short circuit within an appliance, its plug or in some other part of the system. Basically the fuse is a thin wire that melts ('blows') and breaks the circuit if too much current flows through it. Circuit fuses are located in the house's main fuse box or consumer unit. Fuses are also fitted in modern plugs.

Circuit fuses

Circuit fuses protect the fixed wiring and apparatus, and if they 'blow' no equipment will operate on the circuit affected.

Every circuit fuse has a current rating in amps (A) appropriate to the rating of the circuit, and is colour-coded: white is for a 5A fuse (for lighting circuits), blue for a 15A, yellow for a 20A, red for a 30A (ring circuit) and green for a 45A (cooker circuit).

There are two types of circuit fuse – rewirable and cartridge. A rewirable fuse is the least sensitive method of protection, but it can be mended easily by connecting fuse wire of the correct rating between the terminals of the fuse carrier.

In a cartridge fuse, the fuse wire is enclosed in a clip-in ceramic cartridge filled with quartz powder (sand) and if it blows you simply replace the whole cartridge. Unlike the rewirable fuse where it's possible to fit the wrongly rated fuse wire, it's impossible to fit a larger amperage cartridge as the size of fuse holder usually depends on the rating of the circuit to which it is fitted. The only exception to this is with 15A and 20A fuses which are the same size, but as the cartridges are colour-coded, a mistake is avoidable.

Miniature circuit breaker (MCB)

MCBs can be fitted instead of circuit fuses in modern consumer units. An MCB is a switching device that is activated by the surge of current caused by overloading or a short circuit. It has the advantage that it can be reset at the push of a button or the flick of a switch – unless the fault that caused it to switch off in the first place is still present.

MCBs are more sensitive and faster reacting than circuit fuses. Some kinds have the same colour-coding as conventional circuit fuses; others are labelled with the circuit rating.

Residual Current Circuit Breaker (RCCB)

An RCCB may sometimes be fitted in conjunction with the house's earthing system, and usually protects all circuits in the house. It cuts off the power supply if it detects an electric current flowing to earth – this is what happens when someone receives an electric shock, or insulation fails on a mains cable. An RCCB is activated by far less current than is necessary to blow a fuse or trip an MCB, and operates within a fraction of a second.

THE CONSUMER UNIT

Miniature circuit breaker (MCB)

Cartridge fuse

Rewirable fuse

Warning

Electricity is dangerous. Before touching any part of the fixed wiring in your home, turn off the power at the main switch so you can be sure no current is flowing anywhere in the system

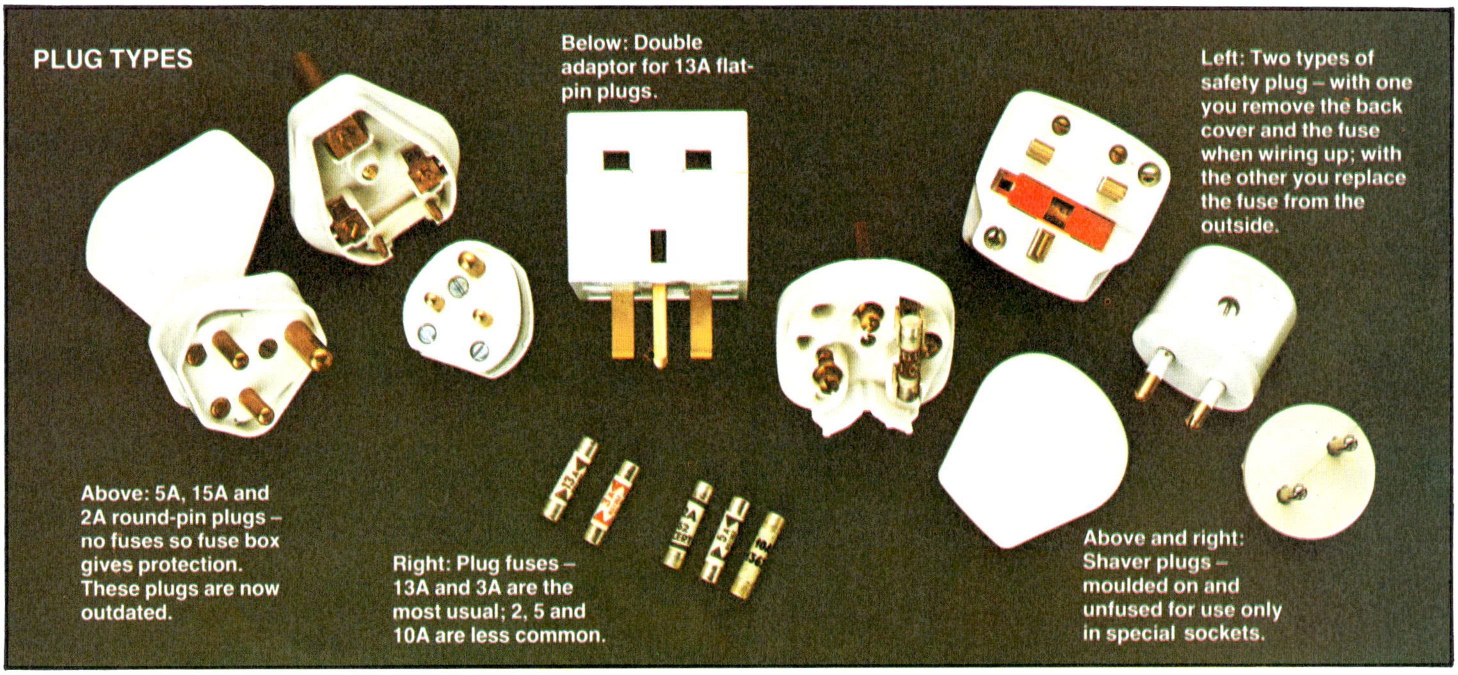

PLUG TYPES

Below: Double adaptor for 13A flat-pin plugs.

Left: Two types of safety plug – with one you remove the back cover and the fuse when wiring up; with the other you replace the fuse from the outside.

Above: 5A, 15A and 2A round-pin plugs – no fuses so fuse box gives protection. These plugs are now outdated.

Right: Plug fuses – 13A and 3A are the most usual; 2, 5 and 10A are less common.

Above and right: Shaver plugs – moulded on and unfused for use only in special sockets.

Jem Grischotti

Circuit fuses and faults
If a circuit fuse blows immediately after it has been mended, the cause could be a fault in an appliance, in the circuit wiring or in a socket outlet. A fixed appliance such as a shower unit or immersion heater (which has no plug or intermediate fuse) could also be to blame. Such faults should be investigated by a qualified electrician.

Continuous blowing of a lighting circuit fuse is probably caused by a short circuit in the flex or lampholder of a pendant light.

Plug fuses
Modern 13A flat-pin plugs contain fuses that protect the individual appliance and its flex in case a fault occurs. When they blow they only isolate the appliance concerned, so other appliances plugged into the main circuit will still function.

Plug fuses are of the cartridge type which fit neatly into a carrier in the plug, but are a different size to circuit cartridge fuses. The two standard ones have current ratings of 3A and 13A and are colour-coded red and brown respectively. Fit a 3A fuse for appliances rated at less than 700 watts, a 13A fuse otherwise (and always for colour TV sets). Plug fuses can also be fitted into connection units used to supply fixed appliances such as a night storage heater or a freezer.

When a plug fuse blows
If an appliance doesn't work, the most likely cause is a blown plug fuse. Replace it with a new one of the correct rating for the appliance (see above), then put the plug back in the socket and switch on. If nothing happens, check that the socket is live by plugging in an appliance that you know is working. Should this not work, check the circuit fuse.

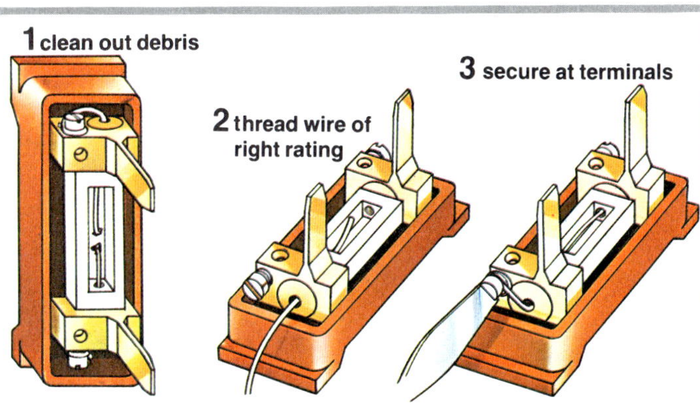

Craig Warwick

Replacing circuit fuses
Turn off the main on/off switch on the fuse box or consumer unit before tackling the repair. With a rewirable fuse, you may have to remove each in turn to locate the one that's blown. Always use fuse wire of the correct rating for the circuit when you make the repair – don't be tempted to use a higher rated one even if the fuse continues to blow. Don't make the wire taut between the terminals as this will reduce the current rating, resulting in overheating and premature failure of the fuse wire. NEVER fit any other metallic object into a fuse carrier.

If a cartridge fuse blows, and you've no list of the circuits (or it is not obvious which circuit has been affected), turn off the main switch and remove each cartridge in turn. Test it by holding it across the open end of a switched-on metal torch, with one end of the fuse on the casing and the other on the end of the battery. A sound fuse will light the torch. Alternatively, use a continuity tester (available from electrical stores). Replace the blown fuse with a new one of the correct rating.

PLUGS

The function of a plug is to connect a portable appliance (eg a lamp or power tool) to the fixed wiring via a socket outlet anywhere around the house.

The modern standard plug is a 13A fused three-pin plug, which has flat pins. There is also a moulded-on unfused two-pin plug used exclusively for electric shavers in conjunction with a special socket outlet. In older installations, instead of 13A plugs, round-pin plugs with current ratings of 2A, 5A and 15A are used. These are not fused.

A recent development is a 13A fused plug that is moulded onto the PVC sheathing of the flex and can't be dismantled. However, it's possible to change the fuse by lifting up a flap between the pins of the plug. It's also possible to change the fuse in some conventional plugs without removing the plug top. If you ever need to replace a moulded-on plug you have to cut off the flex as close to the plug as possible and replace it with a conventional 13A plug.

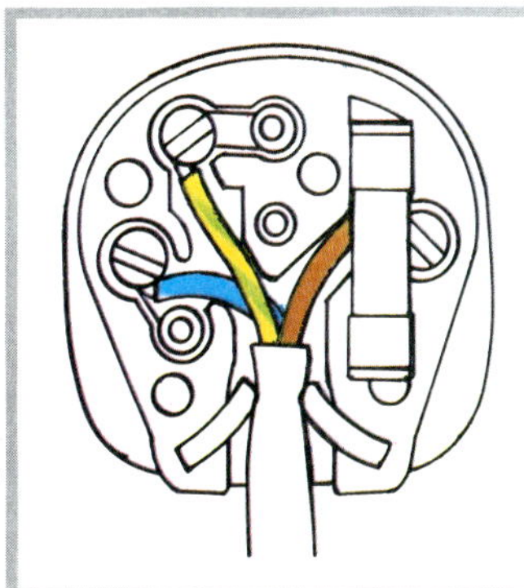

Craig Warwick

Plugs and earthing
Most electrical appliances are fitted with three-core flex (see pages 14-15). When plugged in, the earth wire (green/yellow) is linked to the house's earthing and ensures that the appliance is properly earthed. Two-core flex is for double-insulated appliances. Left: A correctly-wired 13A plug.
REMEMBER
BL (Bottom Left) = BLue
BR (Bottom Right) = BRown.

CABLE & FLEX

Two types of wiring are used in the domestic electrical circuits. Fixed cables are normally concealed, and carry electrical current to switches, ceiling lights, and socket outlets. Flexible cords (flexes) connect portable appliances and light fittings to the fixed wiring.

Fixed wiring

This consists mostly of PVC-sheathed cable containing three copper conductors (cores). The core insulated in red PVC is the 'live' and the one in black the 'neutral' though in lighting circuits in the cable to the switch both the black and red are live. (The black core is required to have a piece of red sleeving on it to indicate this, although this is often omitted by incompetent electricians. Cables having two red conductors are made for contract work, but rarely stocked and sold retail). The third core is the earth and this is uninsulated, but when exposed after the sheathing is removed ready for wiring up it must be sleeved in green/yellow striped PVC before being connected to the earth terminal. In some wiring circuits PVC-sheathed cables having one core only are used, for example, where a live core is looped out of a switch or a neutral core is looped out of a light, to supply an additional light or lights. Three-core and earth cable is used for two-way switching. The conductors are insulated in red, blue and yellow; the colour coding is for purposes of identification only.

Cables

PVC-sheathed and insulated, two-core and earth

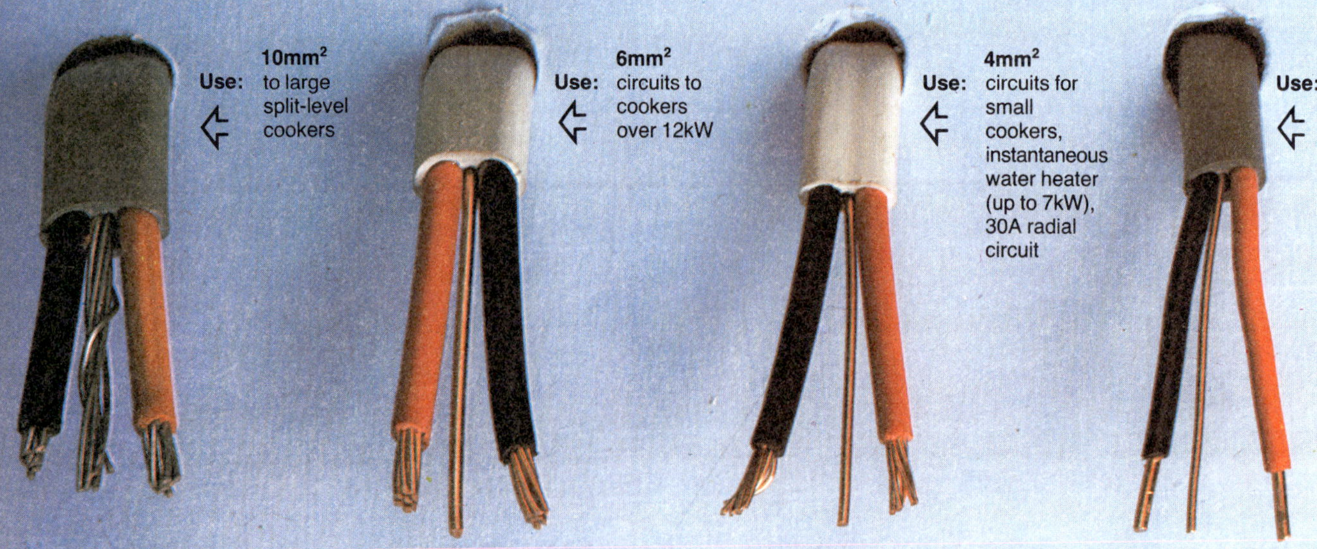

10mm² Use: to large split-level cookers

6mm² Use: circuits to cookers over 12kW

4mm² Use: circuits for small cookers, instantaneous water heater (up to 7kW), 30A radial circuit

2.5mm² Use: ring main, power circuit (eg, 20A radial circuit), immersion heater, instantaneous water heater (up to 5kW)

Jem Grimschotti

Flexible cords

Flexible cords are made in various sizes and current ratings and the types you'll most often come across are: *parallel twin unsheathed, circular PVC-sheathed, circular braided, unkinkable* and *heat-resisting*. Each conductor is made up of a number of strands of copper and it is this which gives the cord its flexibility.

The insulation used round the conductors now conforms to an international colour coding standard – brown denotes the live wire, blue the neutral, and green/yellow the earth, when it is part of the flex. Transparent or white insulation is used for a flex that carries a low current and where it doesn't matter which wire is connected to the live and neutral terminals of an appliance. It is used mainly for table lamps that need no earth.

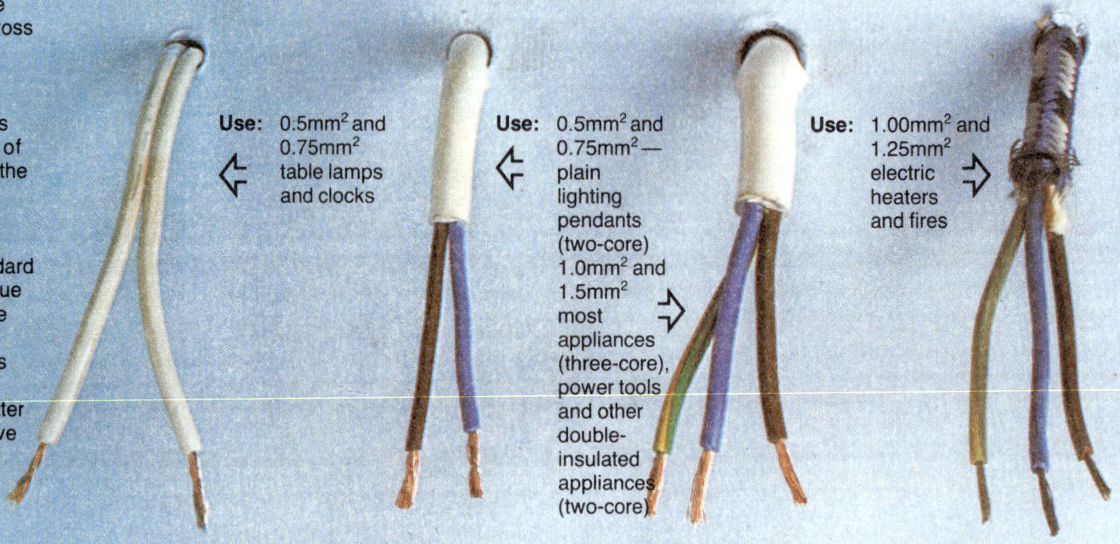

Parallel twin unsheathed

Use: 0.5mm² and 0.75mm² table lamps and clocks

Circular PVC sheathed two-core, and two-core and earth

Use: 0.5mm² and 0.75mm² — plain lighting pendants (two-core) 1.0mm² and 1.5mm² most appliances (three-core), power tools and other double-insulated appliances (two-core)

Circular braided (rubber insulated)

Use: 1.00mm² and 1.25mm² electric heaters and fires

Cables for fixed wiring

Most domestic wiring is now supplied in metric sizes which refer to the cross-sectional area of one of the conductors, whether it is composed of one or several strands of wire. Most common sizes of cable are $1.0mm^2$ and $1.5mm^2$ used for lighting, and $2.5mm^2$ used for power circuits.

Cable with grey sheathing is intended to be concealed in walls or under floors; white sheathing is meant for surface mounting.

PVC-sheathed and insulated, three-core and earth

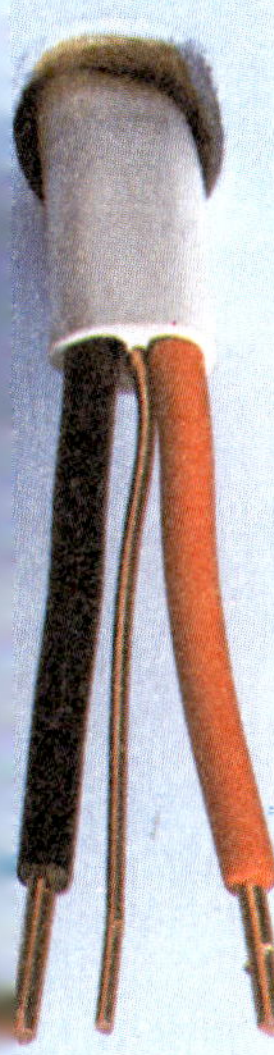

$1.5mm^2$
Use: lighting circuit, immersion heater ($1.0mm^2$ also used for lighting)

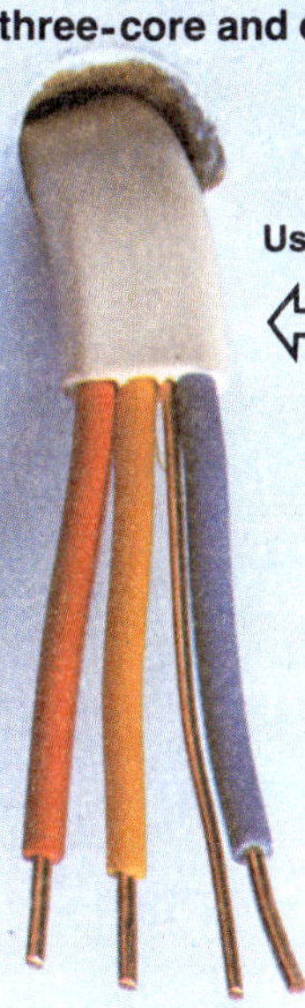

$1.0mm^2$
Use: two-way switching for lighting circuit ($1.5mm^2$ also available)

Unkinkable

Use: $1.25mm^2$ and $1.5mm^2$ electric irons, percolators and kettles

Heat-resisting

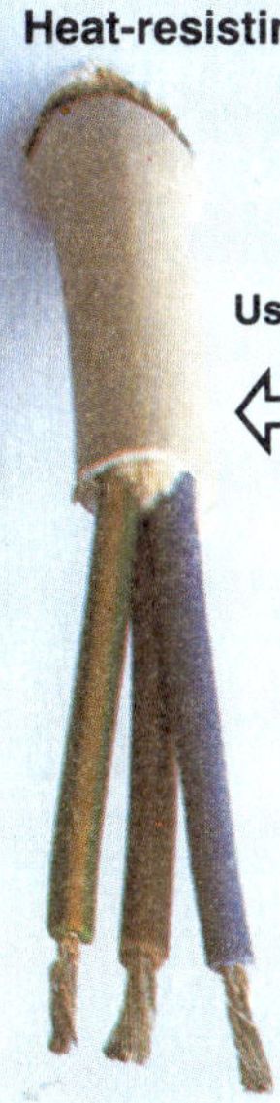

Use: $0.5mm^2$ and $0.75mm^2$ lighting pendants with 100W-200W bulbs
$1.25mm^2$ and $1.5mm^2$ immersion heater

hints

Safety with electricity

- never work on a circuit with current on. Turn off at mains and isolate circuit by removing relevant fuse. Keep this with you until you restore supply
- never touch plugs and sockets with wet hands
- remove plugs from socket when working on appliance
- always use the correct fuse wire when mending a fuse

The importance of earthing

Earthing is an essential safety feature of all wiring systems. To complete a circuit, electricity either flows down the neutral conductor of the supply cable or it flows to earth. That is why you get a shock if you touch a live wire. The idea of earthing is to connect all metal fittings and appliances in the house with a good conductor – the 'earth wire' in cables and flexes. If a fault occurs that makes this metal live, the presence of the earth wire prevents the voltage from rising much above earth voltage. At the same time, the fault greatly increases the current being drawn to the metal via the supply conductor, and this current surge is detected by the circuit fuse, which 'blows' and cuts off the current flow (see pages 162–163).

The earth conductor links socket outlets and appliances (via their plugs) and is connected to a main earthing terminal at the house fuse box or consumer unit. This is usually connected to the outer metal sheath of the underground supply cable.

All metal pipework in the house is also earthed by being connected to the earth terminal – this is called 'cross bonding'.

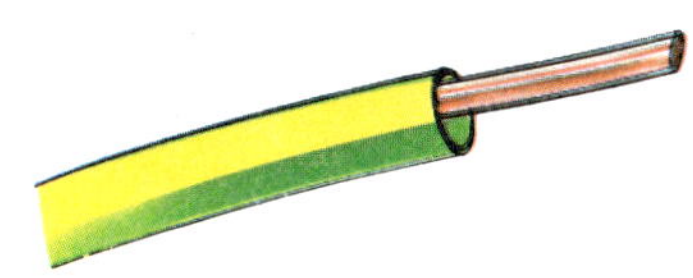

Old wiring

Some old installations may still be using lead-sheathed or tough rubber-sheathed (TRS) wiring, with the conducting wires insulated in vulcanized rubber, or vulcanized rubber insulated, taped and braided wire. These insulating materials deteriorate with age (about 25-30 years) so the wiring can become dangerous. Therefore it really does need to be replaced with modern PVC-sheathed and insulated cable.

The right connection

The plug is the vital link between any electrical appliance and the mains and must be connected up correctly if it is to do its job properly. With flex in the new colour codes, connect the BRown core to the Bottom Right terminal, the BLue core to the Bottom Left one and the green-and-yellow core (if present) to the top terminal. With cores in old colour codes, Red goes to the bottom Right terminal, BLack to Bottom Left and green to top.

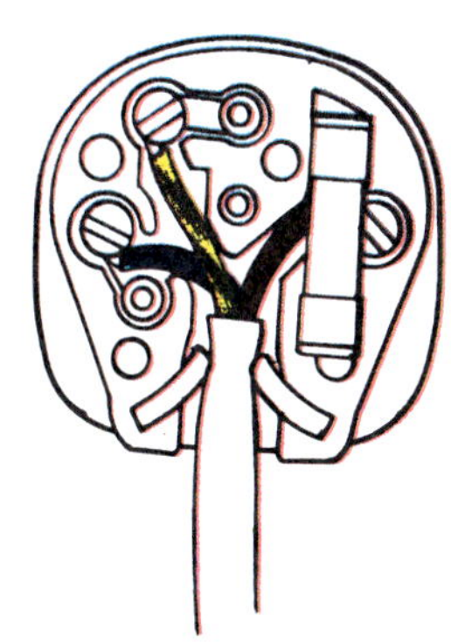

Old colour codes

Before the introduction of new international colour codes, flex used red insulation to denote the live conductor, black for the neutral and green for the earth.

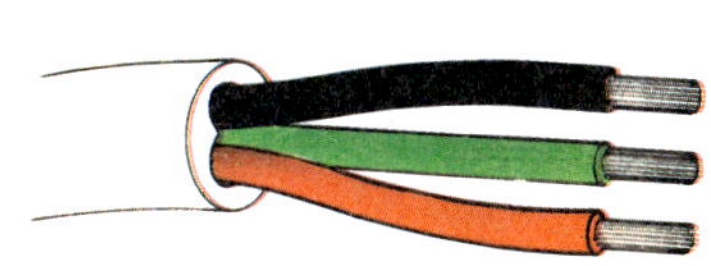

Warning: Electricity is dangerous

Before touching any part of the fixed wiring in your home, turn off the power at the main switch so you can be sure no current is flowing anywhere in the system.

ELECTRICAL WIRING ACCESSORIES

Without electrical wiring accessories you could never make use of the power carried round your home by the various circuit cables. These accessories include such things as power sockets, light switches and much more besides. Here are some of the most useful.

It's a good idea to have a thorough knowlege of the available accessories when you plan a wiring job. That way you'll know what to use, and both when and where to use it. If you're fairly new to the world of home electrics then the chances are that you'll have to follow to the letter any guide that you're using. But instructions, however good, cannot cover every eventuality and a wide knowledge of what accessories are available will help you to prepare for the job and also save you extra work. Once you know what the various types of accessories do, and the special features that they have, you'll be able to distinguish easily between those that will do a particular job and those that won't. Then you'll be able to work out exactly what you require before you go to the retailers and that way not risk making a fool of yourself. Before you go laying out a lot of money, it's important to understand a few technical terms that will help you to avoid making expensive mistakes.

Terms to know

Most accessories are rated at a certain number of amps, which indicates the amount of current the fitting can carry or control in complete safety. Under normal

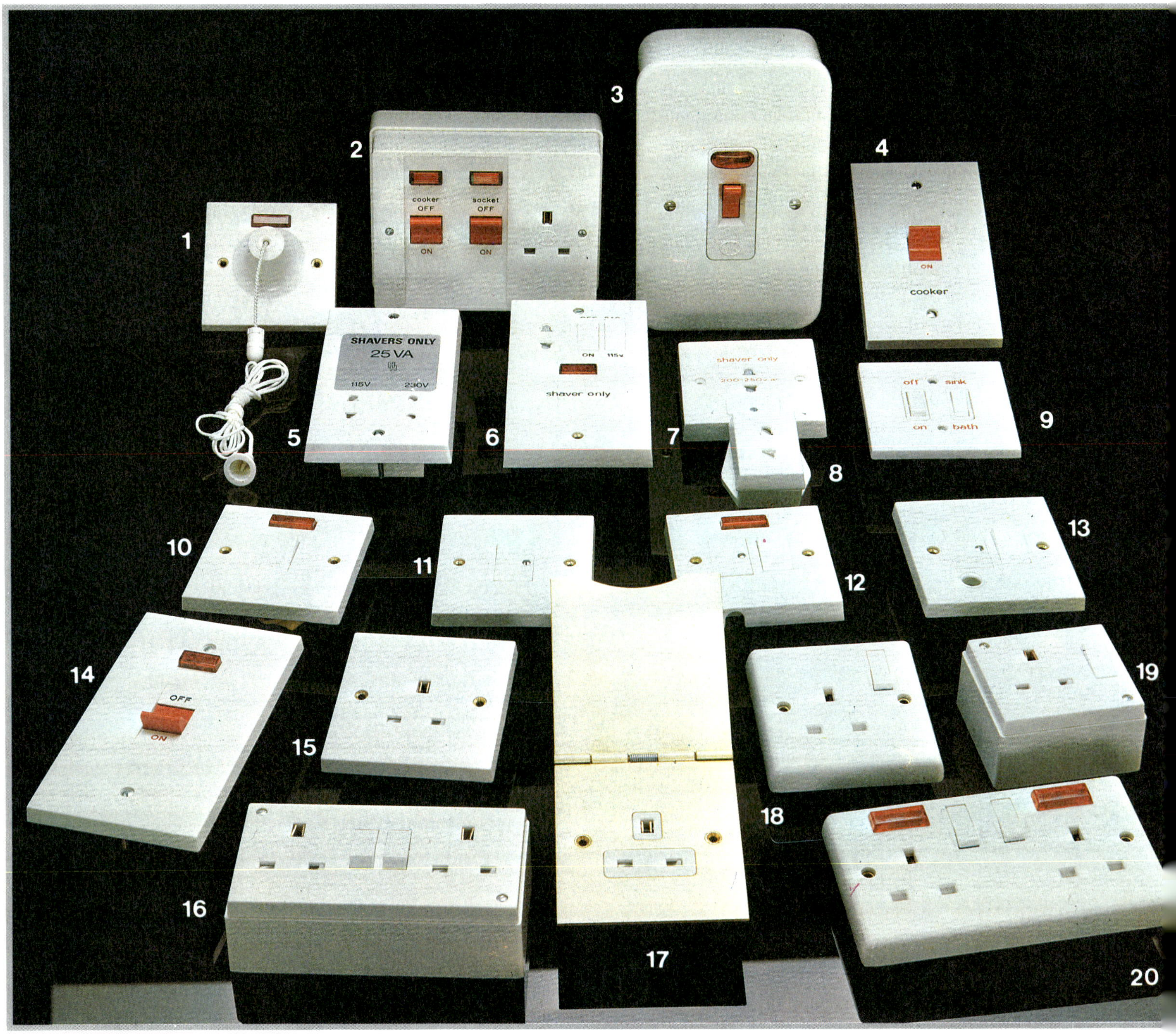

circumstances, a rating of 13A means that the accessory is for use on a ring circuit or its spurs, and any other rating means the fitting is designed to form part of a purpose-made radial circuit.

In the latter case, the current rating you need depends on what the circuit feeds and should therefore match the current rating of the fuse in the consumer unit controlling that circuit. But there are exceptions. A shaver socket, for example, may overload above 2A, yet is quite safe if connected to a 5A lighting circuit. And fused connection units won't be rated at all as you decide their rating when the fuse is put into the carrier.

Next, there are a number of terms that classify switches. You'll find some described as SP (single-pole) and others as DP (double-pole). When a switch is described as SP it means that when it is turned off, it breaks only the live side of the circuit. A DP switch, on the other hand, breaks both the live and neutral sides, and so ensures total disconnection.

SP switches are used mainly in lighting circuits (because they have a low current rating), while DP switches are used in most power circuits (because these have a higher current rating). It's all a question of safety; obviously the DP switch is the safer and is therefore used in most high rating circuits.

The other important expression you must understand is what is meant by a switch or socket having a certain number of gangs. This is, in fact, straightforward. Where switches are concerned, the number of gangs tells you how many separate switches you have built into a single face plate. With power sockets, the number of gangs refers to the number of plugs the socket will take without the need for an adaptor plug. An adaptor plug is not to be recommended as you can risk the danger of fire.

Decorative aspects

The days of all electrical accessories being finished in the same material are now, thankfully, long gone. The variety of different styles, colours and materials that are available make it possible for light switches, sockets and other accessories to be incorporated in the overall interior design.

That's really all you need to know if you're buying accessories for an electrics job in your home. You may well come across other odd expressions and terms but you'll find most of them explained satisfactorily in Chapter 1, pages 6-10.

POWER CIRCUIT ACCESSORIES

1 Ceiling switches with a higher current rating than a lighting ceiling switch are ideal for use in the bathroom to control appliances such as instantaneous electric showers.

2 Cooker control units are rated at 45A and incorporate a 13A power socket and two switches to control both cooker and socket.

3, 10, 14 DP switches are used to control permanently connected appliances such as water heaters and are rated at 20, 45, or 60A. Some 20A models have a flex outlet and many are fitted with pilot lamps.

4 Cooker switches are merely DP switches which control the power to the cooker. They are safer than a cooker control unit as you can't risk the danger of fire by trailing a kettle flex across a boiling ring.

5, 6 Shaver supply units are suitable only for electric shavers. A built-in transformer allows them to be connected to the power circuit, and an isolator provides complete safety for use in a bathroom. All have on/off switches and some a voltage selection switch for different models of shavers.

7 Shaver socket outlets don't have built-in transformers to lower the voltage which means that they must be wired into the lighting circuit and are not safe to be used in bathrooms.

8 Shaver adaptors will fit into any 13A plug and are protected by a fuse and a safety shuttered outlet.

9 Dual switches are used for controlling dual element immersion heaters – those with one element heating only the top part of the tank and another heating the entire tank. The unit has two switches, one controlling power, the other directing that power to one element or the other.

11-13 Fused connection units connect permanently the flex of an appliance, such as a freezer, to the power circuit. There is less risk of accidental disconnection than with a plug and socket, and a fused unit can be used to 'down-grade' the current for a spur off the ring circuit and so make it safe to use for a light. They are available with switches, lights and flex outlet holes.

15-20 13A socket outlets are for use with 13A square-pin plugs. One- and two-gang versions with switches and neon lights are available. They can be surface or flush-mounted or set in the floor – in which case they are fitted with a protective cover. There are versions fitted with earth leakage circuit breakers for extra protection and round-pin sockets are also available.

CABLE OUTLETS

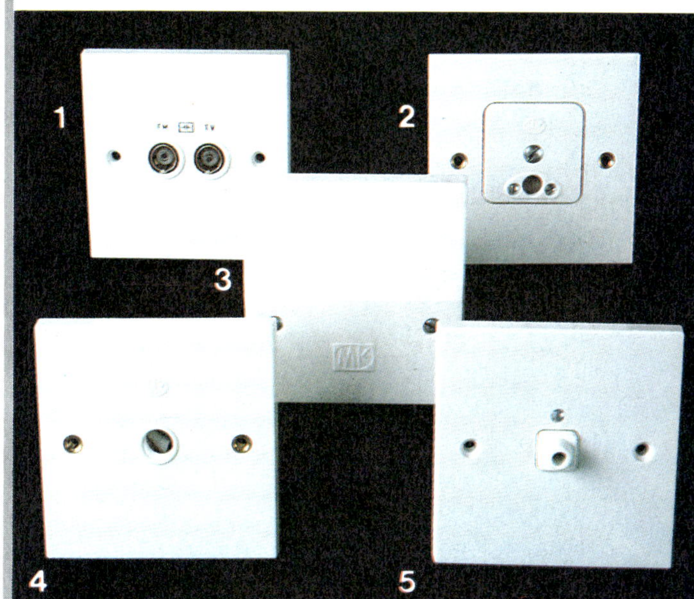

1 Aerial sockets can have either single or double outlets and allow you to use your outside aerial for both the television and the FM frequency of your radio.

2 Fused clock connectors are really specialised versions of the fused connection unit and were used to connect mains-operated clocks (now no longer made). They are also used in the installation of some extractor fans and can be flush or surface-mounted.

3 Cooker connection units are nothing more than purpose-built terminal blocks which allow you to connect the trailing cable of an electric cooker to a concealed, fixed cable run from the cooker control unit. They incorporate a clamp plate that protects the cable and connections in case the cooker is moved.

4 Flex outlet plates are similar to blank plates but a hole in the face plate allows the flex of an appliance directly into the DP cable run. This set-up should really only be used on radial circuits designed for a specific job, such as providing power for a bathroom towel rail in conjunction with a fused connection unit. So, they are used in much the same way as a cooker connector – where it is impractical to pass the flex of the appliance directly into the DP switch or fused connection unit.

5 Telephone cord outlets have a moulded outlet designed to carry standard telephone cable. Double outlet models are available.

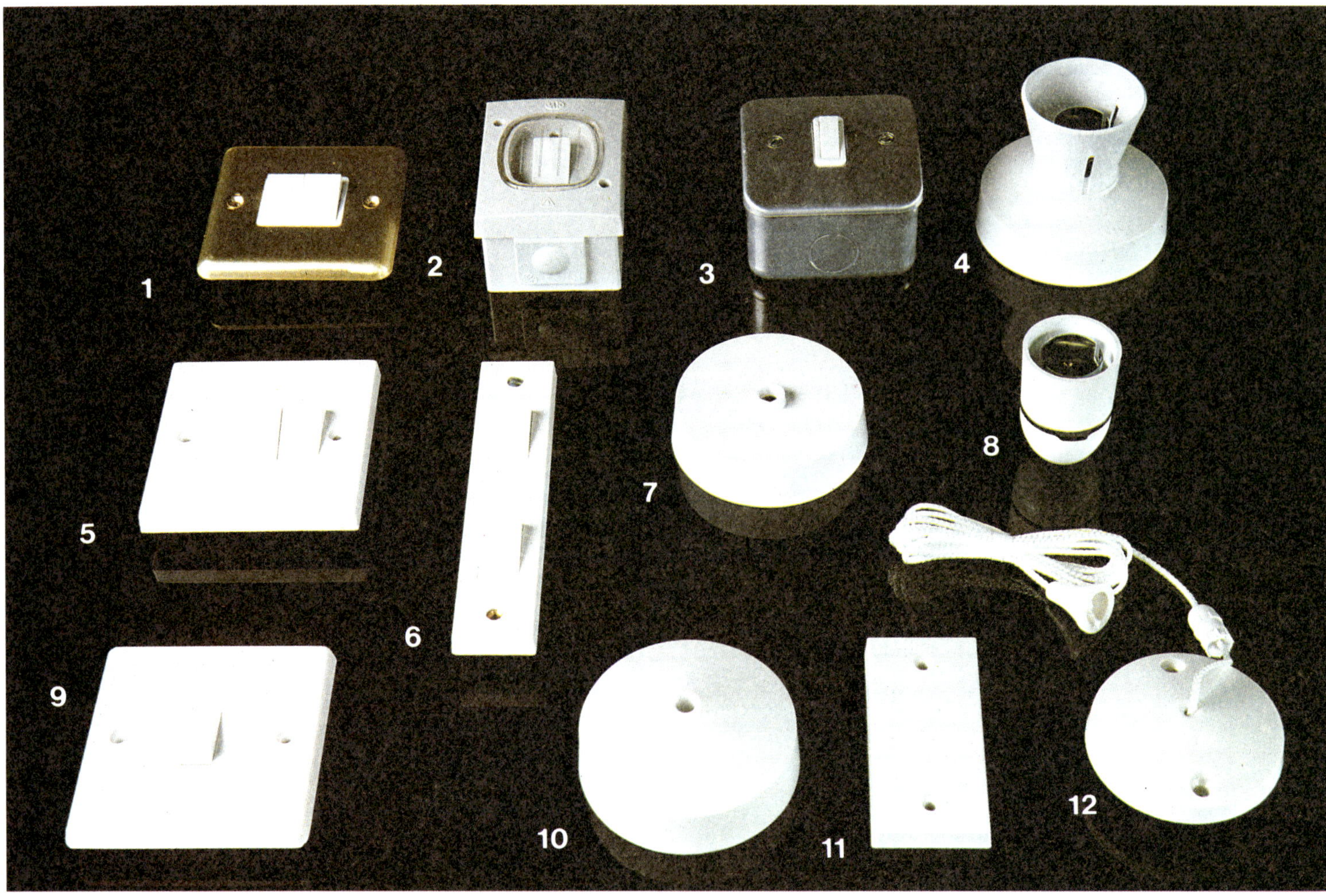

LIGHTING ACCESSORIES

1, 5, 9 *Plate switches are rated at 5A, and are used in ordinary lighting circuits. They have up to six gangs and most can be connected for two-way switching.*

2 *Sealed switches are used where the switch is likely to be exposed to water or the elements.*

3 *Metal clad switches are surface-mounted and are used when the switch needs extra protection – such as in a garage or else where it is likely to get knocked.*

4 *Battenholders are for lights that are surface-mounted on a wall or ceiling. They can be used in a junction box lighting circuit, at the end of a fused spur from a power circuit, or wired into a loop-in lighting circuit.*

6 *Architrave switches, so-named because they can fit into the decorative surround of a doorway, are about 32mm (1¼in) wide.*

7, 10 *Ceiling roses connect the lighting circuit's cables to the pendant light flex. Most have their terminals arranged for the loop-in system, but two terminal versions for use in a junction circuit are also available. When used with a heavy pendant light, the rose should have a strain wire clamp which takes the weight off the conductor cores in the light flex.*

8 *Lampholders fit on a pendant light's flex and hold the bulb and lamp shade in position. They should be heat resistant and in bathrooms it's essential to use one with a deep protective shield for extra safety.*

11 *Blank plates allow you to seal off a mounting box when it is no longer in use so saving you the extra work of removing it.*

12 *Ceiling switches are rated at 5A for the lighting circuit and are the only sort of light switch permitted in a bathroom where stringent safety regulations apply.*

MOUNTING BOXES

1 *Accessories of all types can be fitted in surface-mounted boxes.*

2 *Light switches can be flush-mounted in plaster-depth boxes.*

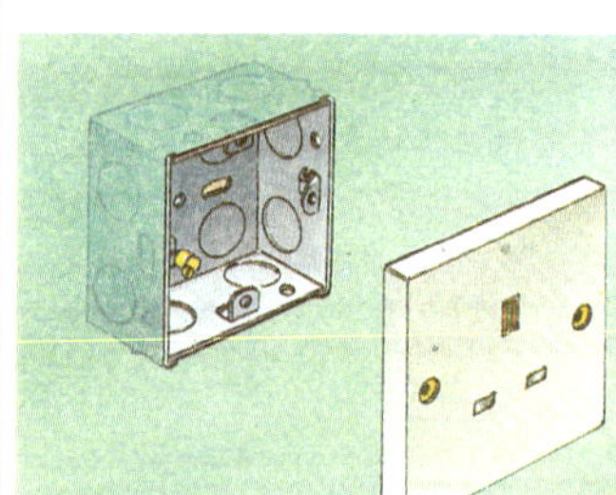

3 *Power circuit accessories need deeper boxes than light switches – 35mm (1⅜in) is the commonest.*

4 *Extra-deep boxes are needed for flush-mounting some accessories. Fit with care in single-brick walls.*

TOOLS FOR ELECTRICAL JOBS

Electrical work, like so many other jobs about the home, can be carried out more successfully and more quickly if you have the right tools to hand. Here is a selection of what you will need for installation work, and also to enable you to cope with emergencies.

To carry out electrical work properly without causing damage to cables and other household fittings, you'll need to have the right tools for the job. Most DIY enthusiasts will already have many of the tools needed for such heavy work as raising and replacing floorboards and chopping out chases in walls to bury cables. Very often the car tool kit will produce spanners for dismantling appliances when renewing flexible cords or heating elements.

Nevertheless, if you are contemplating carrying out your own electrical installation work, you should assemble a tool kit to cope with all the jobs you are likely to encounter. That way not only will you find the work much easier, but you'll also be able to ensure that the final result reaches a professional standard that will give you great satisfaction.

Screwdrivers

A minimum of three straight-tipped screwdrivers is required: a small, thin-bladed electrician's screwdriver for reaching shrouded grub screws in electrical fittings; and medium and large size normal screwdrivers. A selection of crosshead screwdrivers may also be helpful in dealing with Pozidriv and similar screws.

There are two other screwdriver types which you may find useful: a ratchet screwdriver with a chuck to accept a range of different driver bits, and an offset screwdriver. The latter is a simple steel bar, the ends of which are bent at right angles and terminate in a straight tip at one end and a crosshead tip at the other. It is ideal for reaching awkward screws, particularly when servicing electrical appliances.

Bradawls

A bradawl is needed for piercing holes in timber and plaster to mark the position of fixing screws for appliances and their mounting boxes or brackets.

Pliers

Pliers are among the essential tools for electrical work. They are used to grip and bend wire, and to hold small items such as nuts and washers in confined spaces.

Electrician's pliers are similar to engineer's pliers but have insulated handles suitable for working with voltages of 240 volts or above. However, remember you should never carry out any work on an installation unless the power has been turned off, so the presence of insulated handles is only an extra safeguard.

Complementing the standard electrician's pliers should be a pair of long-nosed pliers, which may also be obtained with insulated handles.

Cutters and strippers

Small side cutters are used for cutting the ends of fuse wires when rewiring circuit fuses, and for trimming cable and flex cores when making connections. The jaws are shaped to get close in to the work and still allow knuckle room to grip the handles.

A pair of wire strippers of the adjustable type to fit the various sizes of insulated conductor will permit the insulation to be removed efficiently without damaging the conductor itself. Also available is a cable stripper which will remove the outer sheathing of a cable without cutting into the insulation of the conductors inside. This is much safer than using a knife.

SPECIALIST TOOLS

GENERAL-PURPOSE TOOLS

Your tool box (above) should contain many general-purpose tools that will help you with your electrical jobs, as well as being useful for other repairs. Screwdrivers, chisels, drill bits and saws are all vital. In addition, it's a good idea to keep a number of spare electrical accessories in case of an emergency.

Handyman's knife

If you can't get hold of the type of cable stripper mentioned previously, a handyman's knife will do for trimming the insulation and cable sheathing, providing it is used carefully. Also, it it useful for trimming floor coverings when lifting and replacing floorboards.

Grips and wrenches

Where metal conduit, armoured and mineral-insulated cables are used, an adjustable spanner will be needed. A companion tool is the locking wrench which also has adjustable jaws, but they can be locked on to the workpiece to apply great pressure, leaving the hands free.

Hammers

Ideally, your tool kit should include three types of hammer, and you may already have some of them. A claw hammer is used for general work, a pin hammer for fixing cable clips and a club hammer for driving cold chisels.

Chisels

A selection of cold chisels will make installing cable runs and mounting boxes easier. A short, sharp, small-diameter chisel should be used for chopping out cable chases and recesses in plaster. Deeper recesses in brickwork and masonry can be cut with a thicker 150 to 200mm (6 to 8in) long chisel. A longer (at least 300mm/12in) thin chisel is ideal for cutting holes through brick walls.

The electrician's bolster chisel is useful for lifting floorboards; you drive it between the boards to split off the tongues and then lever them upwards. The wide blade spreads the load.

Since a certain amount of wood cutting is involved in laying cables beneath floors, a set of general-purpose wood chisels will also prove to be invaluable.

Saws

Various types of saw are needed in electrical work since metal, wood and plastic need to be cut.

For cutting plastic trunking, floorboards and other timber, you'll need a tenon saw.

Cutting down into floorboards and removing the tongues when lifting boarding can be done with a special floorboard saw. This has a curved blade, allowing the waste material to be cleared quickly from the groove the saw cuts, and so reducing the likelihood of damaging adjacent woodwork when cutting across a board. The tip of the back edge of the blade is set at an angle with cutting teeth to allow cuts to be made right up to a skirting board without the handle fouling the wall.

A padsaw is useful for cutting timber in confined spaces and for making holes in ceilings to accept mounting boxes for light fittings.

Metal fittings and large cables, including the armoured variety, may be cut with an adjustable hacksaw, which will take 200 to 300mm (8 to 12in) long blades. Finally, small sawing jobs and shortening fixing screws can be carried out with a junior hacksaw.

Drills

A hand drill should be available for light drilling of plastic or thin metal, and can also be used for drilling small holes in brickwork and masonry.

Alternatively, a power drill is a better bet providing, of course, that you already have a live circuit from which to operate it. Pick one with a large chuck capacity, and give serious consideration to buying a drill with an optional hammer action, which will be a great help when drilling into masonry.

Drill bits

A set of masonry drill bits is necessary for drilling brickwork. If you have a power drill with a hammer action make sure the drill bits are suitable for this; not all are.

For drilling holes in metal and plastic boxes, a selection of high-speed twist drills is a must.

SPECIALIST TOOLS

There are a number of specialist tools (below) which are essential for any electrical installation work. These will enable you to get perfect results with the minimum of effort.

KEY

1 *Torch*
2 *Flooring saw*
3 *Floorboard chisel*
4 *Adjustable wire strippers*
5 *Side cutters*
6 *Long-nosed pliers*
7 *Snub-nosed pliers*
8 *Joist brace*
9 *Continuity tester*
10 *Neon screwdriver*
11 *Ring-main tester*
12 *Screwdrivers*

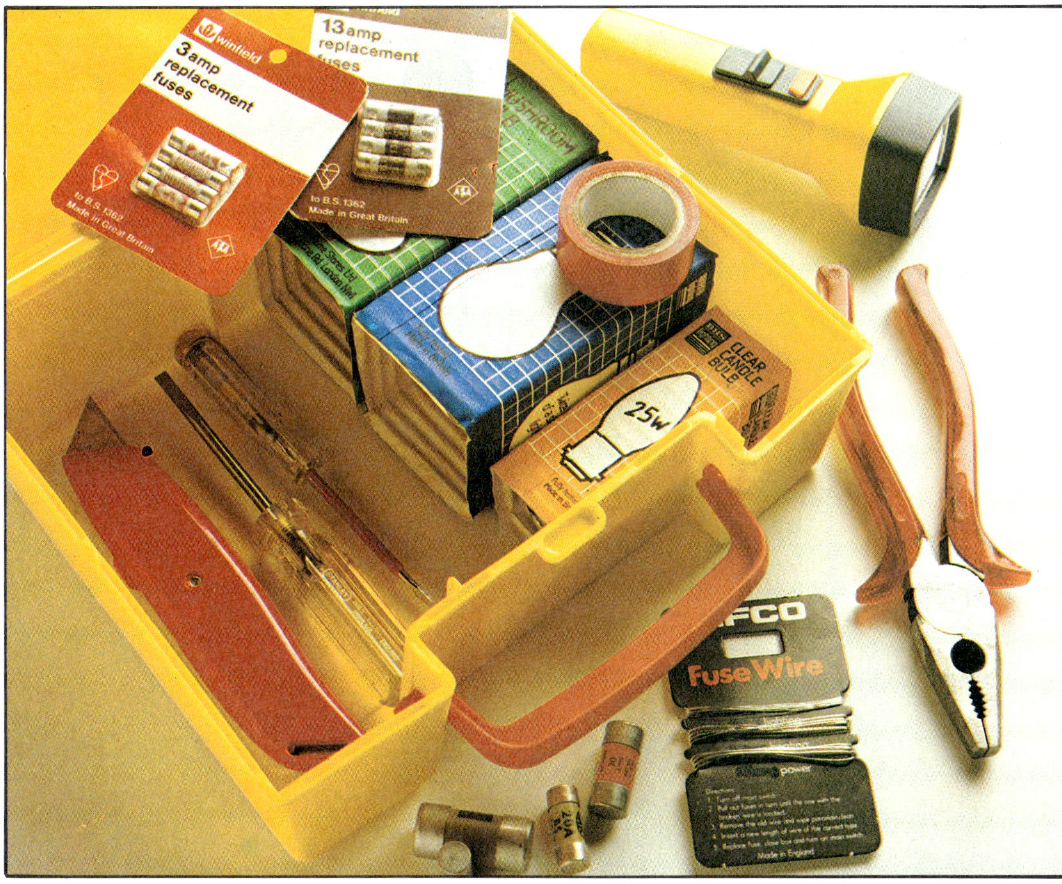

AN EMERGENCY TOOL KIT

Even if you're never likely to carry out any electrical installation work in your home, you're sure to have to cope with running repairs to your system when things go wrong. So you can find the tools and materials you will need when the lights go out, buy a small box and assemble an emergency tool kit you can keep near to the fuse board so you can always find it when you need it. Include a torch, a pair of pliers, a handyman's knife, a couple of screwdrivers, some PVC insulating tape and fuse wire or replacement fuses of appropriate types. It's also worth adding two or three spare light bulbs. Label the box, and always replace any components of the kit if they are used.

Emergency procedures

Before dealing with any repair, make sure that the circuit is safe to work on. If a fuse has blown, you should turn off the mainswitch and identify which circuit it is. Remove the fuse carrier and renew the wire or cartridge, or reset the MCB. Never undertake any work with wet hands and always make sure that you have sufficient light by which to see.

Hand brace and bits

Most general wood-drilling jobs can also be accomplished with a conventional carpenter's ratchet brace and a set of auger bits. However, drilling through joists often presents problems due to their close spacing. A special compact joist brace is made for this purpose and has a ratchet lever immediately behind the chuck.

Measuring tape

A retractable steel tape is essential for the accurate positioning of switches and other accessories. A 3m (10ft) one will do for installation work, but a longer one will be useful when estimating cable runs.

Plumb bob

The position of vertical runs of cable can be determined accurately with the aid of a plumb bob and line. It can also be used to carry a draw wire down into a hollow partition where it can be hooked out at the switch position.

Spirit level

Switch and accessory boxes need to be level, and a small spirit level is ideal for setting them correctly.

Soldering iron

For servicing and repairing electrical appliances, you will need a soldering iron to unsolder and remake connections. A range of sizes and wattages is available. You should keep a supply of flux and solder with it. FACTFINDER 57.

Testers

Two testers that every home electrician should have are a neon tester (usually in the form of a small screwdriver) and a continuity tester.

The neon tester is used to determine if a terminal is live. Place the tip of the tester blade on the terminal and a finger on the metal cap at the end of the tester's handle. This completes a circuit, causing a neon bulb in the handle to light if there is power. A built-in resistor prevents electric shocks.

Battery-powered testers are relatively cheap to buy. The most popular type has metal probes, and such a device will test cartridge fuses and other conductors of low resistance, continuity being indicated by a positive meter reading. Some models double as mains testers.

High resistance items, such as light bulbs and heating elements, should be checked with a special high-resistance tester.

Another useful tester takes the form of a 3-pin plug and is used for checking the cable connections at a socket. It has neon indicators to show whether the socket is wired correctly, has faulty earth, live or neutral connections, or reversed live and neutral connections.

hints

- *When lifting a floorboard, lever the end clear of the floor and lay a long cold chisel across the adjacent boards to support it in this raised position. Continue levering, moving the chisel as you go, until the board can be removed.*

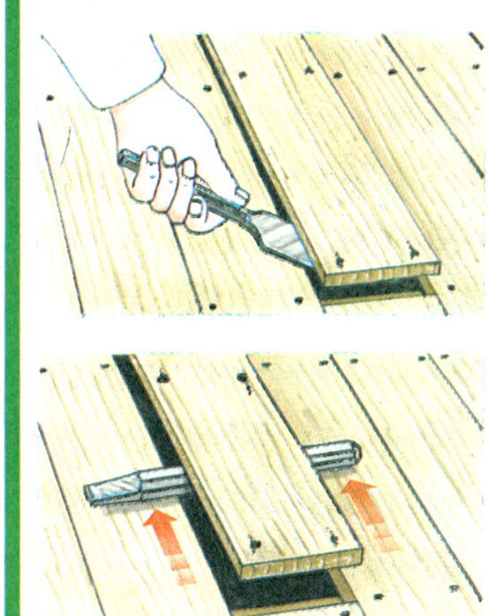

- *A flooring saw with its specially shaped blade will allow you to cut through floorboards right up to skirting boards without the handle touching the wall. It may also be used for cutting through the tongues of T & G boarding.*

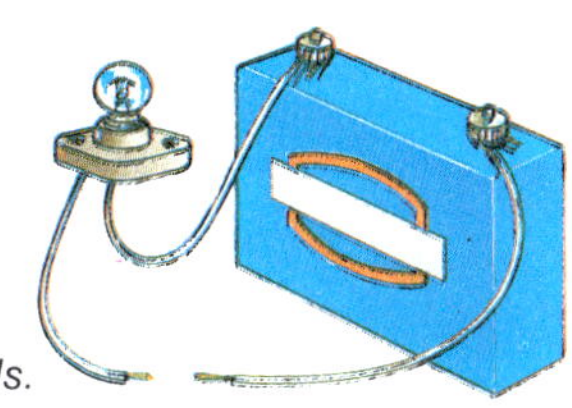

- *Right: A low-resistance continuity tester can be constructed using a 4.5V bell battery, a torch bulb, MES lampholder and insulated wire for leads.*

BASIC TECHNIQUES

There are a few basic tasks that you will be carrying out over and over again as you improve and extend your home's electrics, so it pays to learn some of the tricks employed by professional electricians.

CEILING LIGHTS AND SWITCHES

Most ceiling lights are positioned centrally in a room to give general lighting. But by adding another light, or changing the position of an existing fitting, you can highlight particular areas and enhance the decoration.

Keith Morris

Putting in a new pendant ceiling light and switch, or changing the position of an existing one, usually presents few problems – even if you have little or no experience of electrical work.

A pendant is the most common ceiling light and consists of a lampholder wired to a length of flexible cord which hangs from a ceiling rose. Another type can be plugged into the ceiling rose – in this case the flexible cord has to have a special fitting which slots into a batten holder.

Know your system

Installing a new ceiling light requires making a simple connection into a nearby lighting circuit either by inserting a junction box or at an existing loop-in rose and then running a cable to a switch. In order to connect into the circuit you'll first need to know how the lights in your house are wired and which lights belong to which circuit. Then you'll be able to work out whether you can actually add another light to the circuit that is nearest to the new light's position.

There are two principal methods of wiring a lighting circuit. In the loop-in method the cable runs from ceiling rose to ceiling rose, stopping at the last one on the circuit, and the switches are wired into the roses. With the junction box system the cable runs to a number of junction boxes each serving a switch and a light. You may well find that both methods have been used in the same circuit to simplify and reduce the cable runs.

It's possible to connect into a nearby rose provided it's a loop-in type. You can check this simply by turning off the power and unscrewing the rose cover. A loop-in rose will have more than one red insulated wire going into the central terminal bank of the three in-line terminal banks. However, it can be quite fiddly to fit another cable, given that the terminal banks are very small, so you might find it easier to insert a junction box in the main circuit. And if there isn't a loop-in rose you'll have to use this method anyway.

Earthing for lighting circuits

Modern lighting circuits are protected by an earth. But if you've got a fairly old system (it's likely to be based on junction boxes), you might find that it doesn't have one. So when you're extending such a circuit, you're now required to protect the new wiring, light fitting and switch by installing an earth. Consequently, you have to use two-core and earth cable for the extension, which will most probably connect into the existing circuit at a junction box. You then have to run a $1.5mm^2$ earth cable from this point to the main earthing point.

Circuit additions

Usually there's a lighting circuit for each floor of a house and in a single storey dwelling there are likely to be two or more. But it's easy to identify the individual circuits simply by switching on all the lights, turning off the power and taking out a 5A fuse from the consumer unit or switching off an MCB. When you restore the power you'll know that the lights that remain off all belong to the same circuit.

Generally speaking, a lighting circuit serves six to eight fixed lighting points. In fact it can serve up to 12 lampholders provided the total wattage of the bulbs on the circuit doesn't exceed 1,200 watts. This means that unless other lights have previously been added – wall lights for example – there shouldn't be a problem of connecting in another light.

Remember, when adding up the bulb wattages, a bulb of less than 100 watts counts as 100 watts and not its face value.

The place for lights

Apart from bathrooms, where special regulations apply, you can position lights and switches in any place you like inside the house. But bear in mind they are there to fulfil a function, so switches, for example, should be conveniently located – by a door is often the most satisfactory position. Usually they are set on the wall 1.4 metres (4ft 6in) above floor level. But they can be higher or lower to suit your needs.

You mustn't install pendant lights, especially plain pendants with exposed flexible cords, in a bathroom. This is for your safety. Flexes can become frayed, and if, say, you tried to change a bulb while standing in the bath and touched an exposed conductor you could electrocute yourself. Consequently, all light fittings here must be of the close-mounted type and preferably totally enclosed to keep out condensation. If instead you use an open batten lampholder it must be fitted with a protective shield or skirt which makes it impossible for anyone changing the bulb to touch the metal parts.

A wall-mounted switch must also be out of reach of a person using the bath or shower. In modern small bathrooms, however, this is often impossible. The alternative is to place the switch just outside the room by the door, or to fit a special ceiling switch operated by an insulating cord which doesn't have to be out of reach of the bath or the shower.

PREPARING THE CABLE RUN

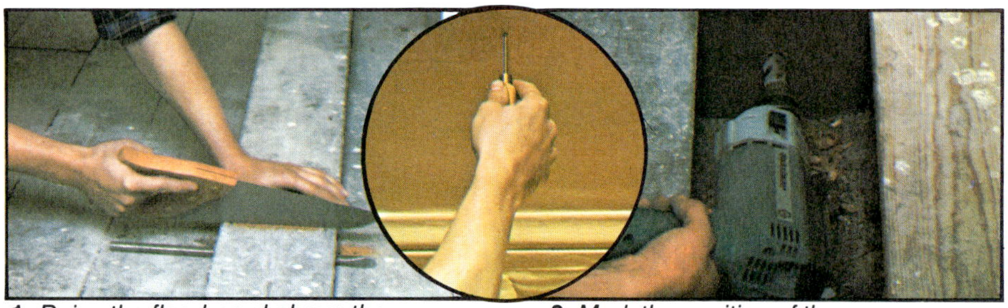

1 *Raise the floorboard above the proposed location of the new light and any others necessary for laying the power supply and switch cables.*

2 *Mark the position of the new rose, then bore a 12mm (1/2in) hole. Where the cable crosses a joist, drill a 16mm (5/8in) hole 50mm (2in) below the top.*

3 *If the new rose can't be screwed to a joist, drill a 12mm (1/2in) hole in a wooden batten to coincide with the hole in the ceiling and fix the batten in position.*

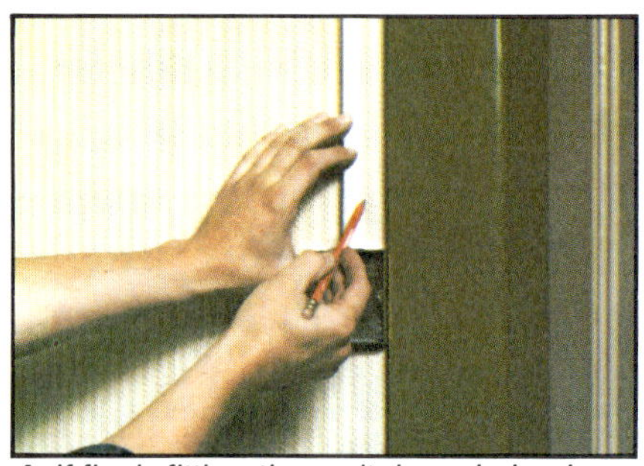

4 *If flush-fitting the switch and chasing in the cable, use a mounting box and a length of conduit to mark their positions on the wall.*

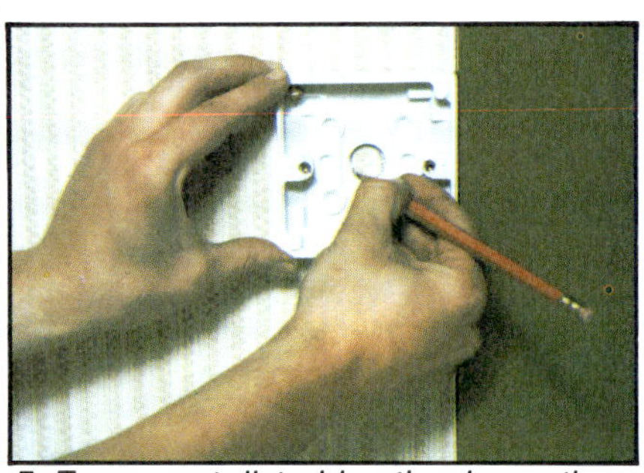

5 *To prevent disturbing the decoration in one room, you can bring the switch cable down the other side of the wall and surface-mount the switch.*

Mounting box: MK

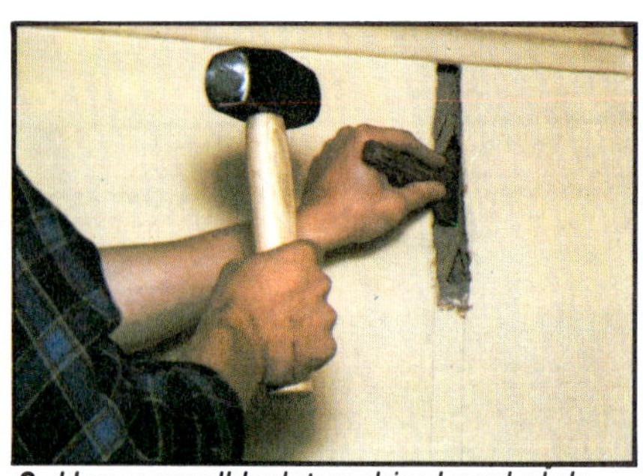

6 *Use a small bolster chisel and club hammer to channel out a groove in the wall to take the switch cable and to chop out the recess for the switch.*

TIP

7 *With cornices, make the channel in the wall first, then drive a long cold chisel gently up the back.*

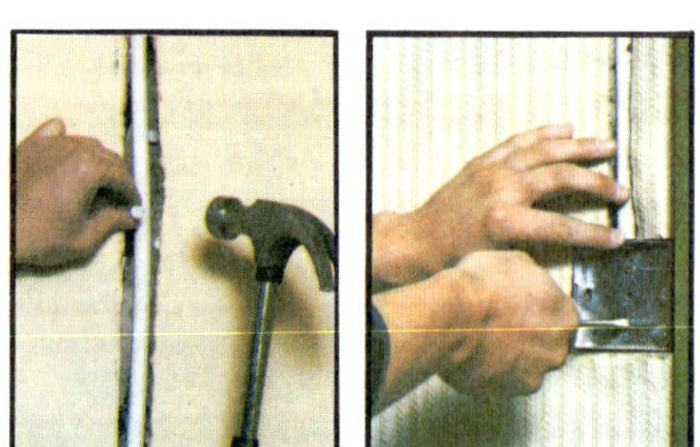

8 *Fix the conduit in place with old nails, although you can also use clout nails. Drill and plug the fixing holes for the box and screw it into place.*

Keith Morris

Ready Reference

LIGHTING BASICS

- Extensions to lighting circuits are usually wired in 1.00mm^2 two-core and earth PVC-sheathed and insulated cable.
- You can extend from an existing rose only if it is of the loop-in variety with three banks of terminals; such roses can accommodate up to four cables. If you have older roses, extensions must be made via a junction box.

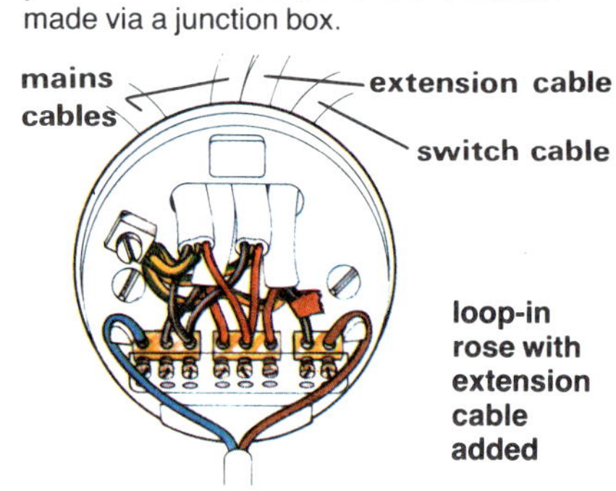

TOOLS FOR THE JOB

Electrician's pliers have cutting edges on the jaws and insulated handles.
Wire strippers can be adjusted to the diameter of the insulation to be stripped.
Handyman's knife – ideal for cutting back the sheathing of the cable.
Screwdrivers – a small one is best for the terminal fixing screws and a medium sized one for the fixing screws on the rose and switch.

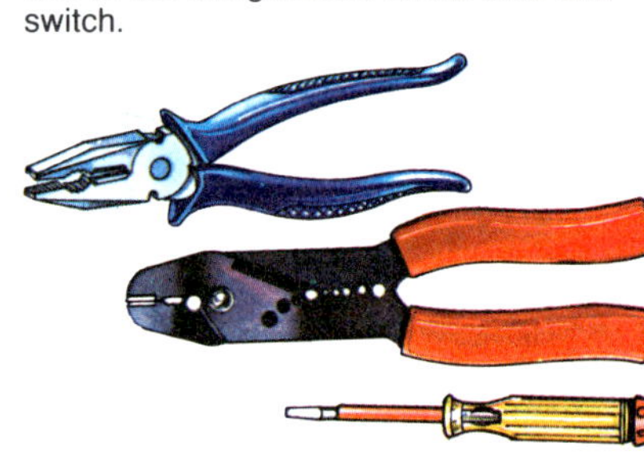

HOW TO STRIP CABLE

- Use handyman's knife to cut sheathing between neutral and earth cores.
- Use wire strippers to remove core insulation.

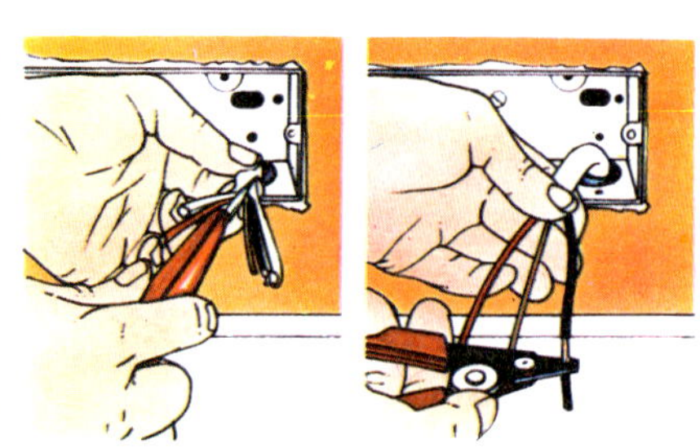

LAYING THE CABLE

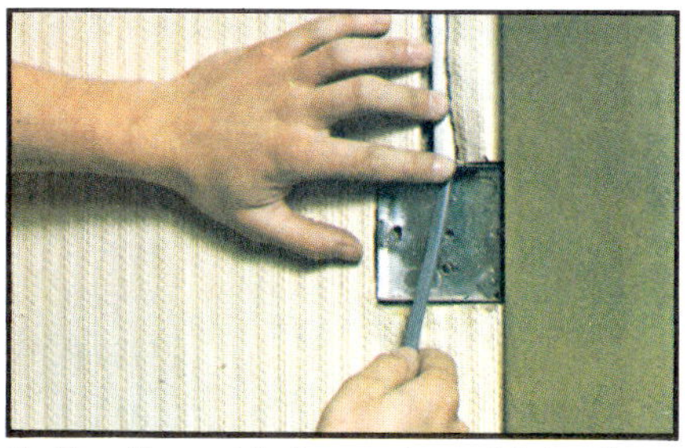

1 *Run the cable from where it joins the existing circuit to the new rose and lay in the switch cable. Allow 200mm (8in) for connections.*

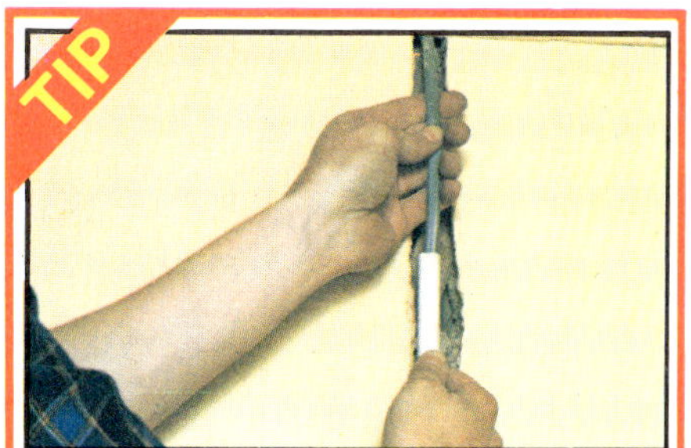

2 *With the switch cable, you might find it easier to pull down the required length and then slide on the conduit before fixing it in place.*

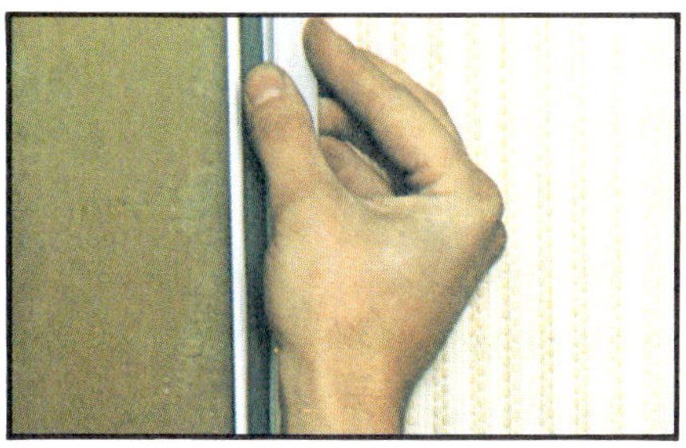

3 *It's not a good idea to leave cable exposed on a wall. When surface-mounting, the cable should be laid in PVC trunking with a clip-on cover.*

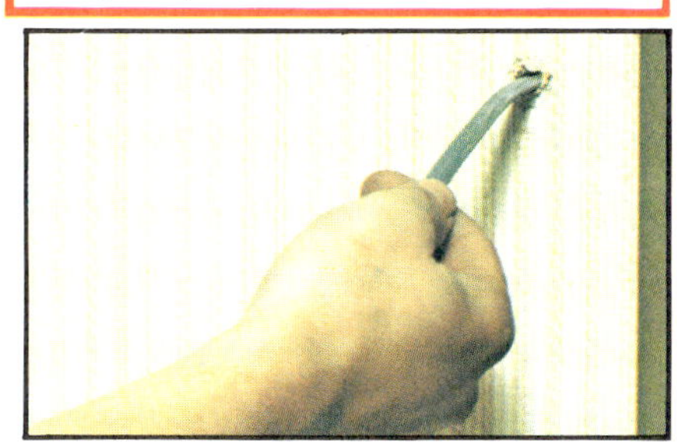

4 *If the cable is brought down on the other side of the wall to the switch, you'll need to drill a hole through so the cable enters the back of the box.*

Keith Morris

FIXING THE SWITCH

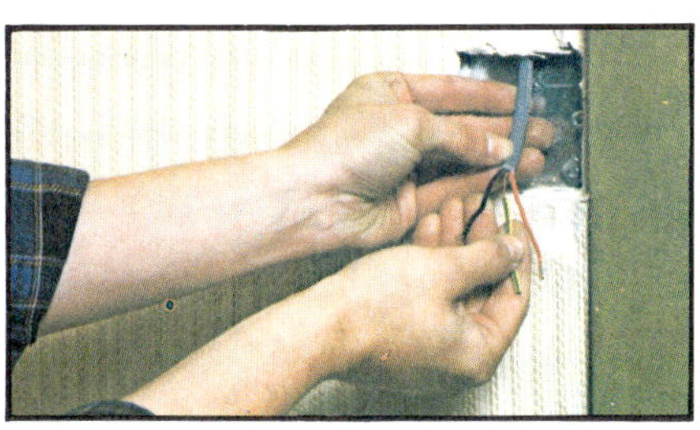

1 *After making good, strip back about 100mm (4in) of sheathing; take off 15mm (5/8in) of insulation and bend over the exposed wire; sleeve the earth wire.*

2 *Because the switch is wired into the 'live' of the circuit, the black wire is live and not neutral; mark it as such with red PVC tape.*

3 *Connect the earth wire to the earth terminal of the metal box and the two conductors to the terminals on the back of the faceplate.*

4 *Make sure a surface-mounted box is square before connecting the switch. With a flush fitting squareness can be adjusted when attaching the faceplate.*

Keith Morris

Switch: MK

Putting in switches

There is a great variety of switches available, but all perform the same function of breaking or completing an electrical circuit so you can turn the light off or on. Modern switches are of the rocker type; a one-gang switch has a single switch on the faceplate; a two-gang switch has two switches on the same faceplate, and so on. Dimmer switches are slightly different in that you can vary the power flowing to the bulb (so reducing or increasing its brightness) by rotating a control knob.

With a new light, you can either connect it into an existing switch position (fitting a two-gang switch in place of a one-gang one, for example) or a new switch. Depending on how you connect into the existing circuit, you'll have to run the switch cable above the ceiling from a rose or a junction box down the wall to where you are going to locate it. If you want to conceal the cable on the down drop you'll have to cut a shallow channel – which will damage the existing decoration – or you can surface-mount it in trunking.

Making the connection

Once you've decided where you want to put the light fitting and switch, you then have to decide where it's best to make the connection into the existing circuit.

Wiring runs may require some detective work to find out what each cable is doing – you don't want to connect into a switch cable by mistake. This may mean climbing into the roof space or raising a few floorboards. You'll need to do this anyway to run in the new cables to the required positions. As cable is expensive, it's best to plan your runs to use as little as possible. But when you measure along the proposed route, don't forget to allow about 200mm extra at the switch, rose and junction box for stripping back the conductors and joining in.

Changing the position of a ceiling light is even easier than adding a new one. If after you've turned off the power you undo the existing rose you'll see immediately the type of lighting circuit you are dealing with.

If there is only a black, a red and an earth wire going into it on the fixed wiring side then you have a junction box system. All you have to do is to disconnect the wires from the rose and reconnect them to the respective terminals of a new three-terminal junction box that you'll have to put in directly above the old fitting. You can then lead off another cable from this junction box to the repositioned ceiling rose. The switch remains unaffected.

If the rose is a loop-in type, you have to carry out a similar modification, but this time the switch wires have to be incorporated in the new junction box, which must be a four-terminal type.

FITTING THE NEW ROSE AND LAMPHOLDER

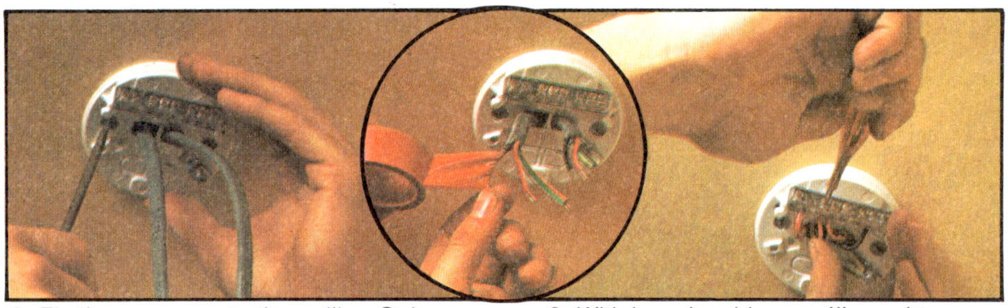

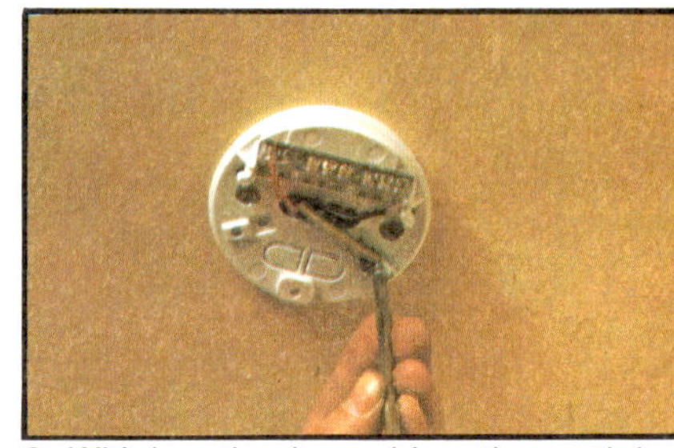

1 *Fix the new rose to the ceiling. Strip back 75mm (3in) of sheathing and 10mm (3/8in) of insulation from the conductors, and sleeve the earth wires.*

2 *With loop-in wiring you'll need to wrap red PVC tape round the black wire (inset) then make the connections to the terminals as illustrated.*

3 *With junction box wiring, the earth is connected to the earth terminal, the black conductor goes to the neutral bank and the red to the SW terminal.*

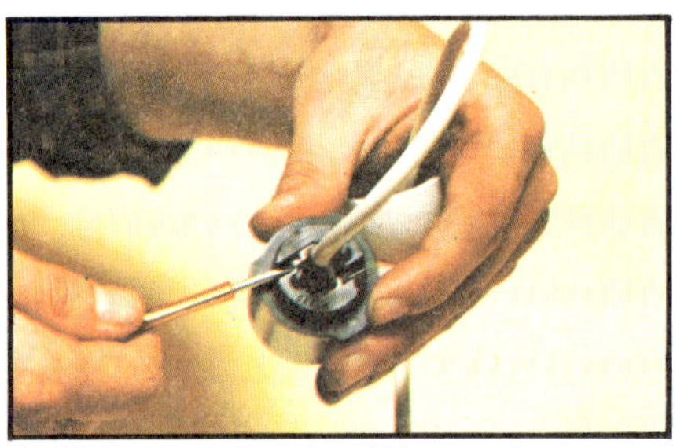

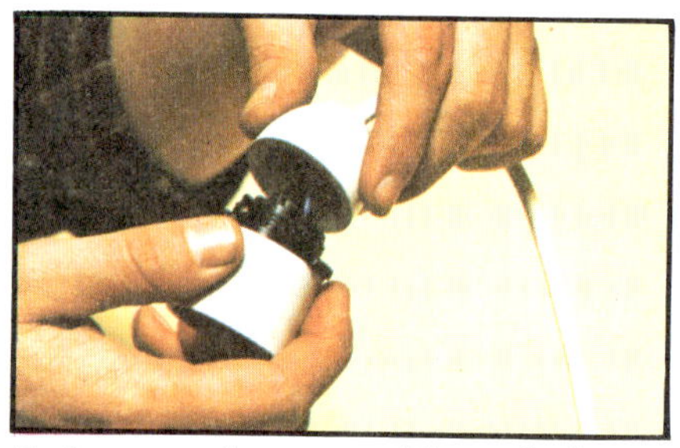

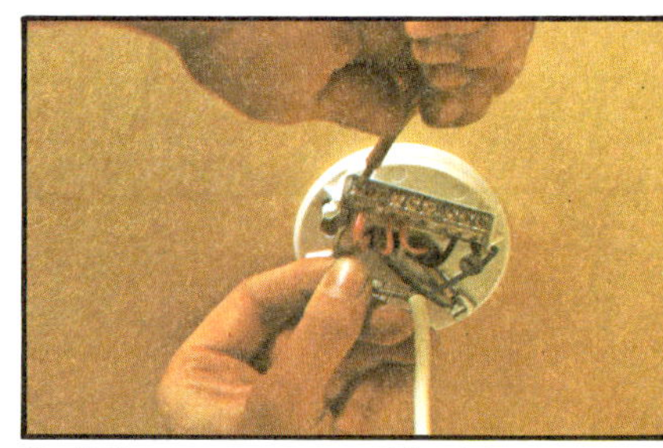

4 *Strip back the sheathing and insulation of one end of the flex and connect the blue and brown conductors to the two terminals of the lampholder.*

5 *Screw on the cap and then slip the rose cover over the flex. Cut the flex to length and prepare the free end for connecting to the rose.*

6 *At the rose, connect the blue conductor to the terminal on the neutral side and the brown to the SW side. Hook the wires over the cord grips.*

Ceiling rose: MK

Lampholder: MK

Keith Morris

CONNECTING INTO THE CIRCUIT

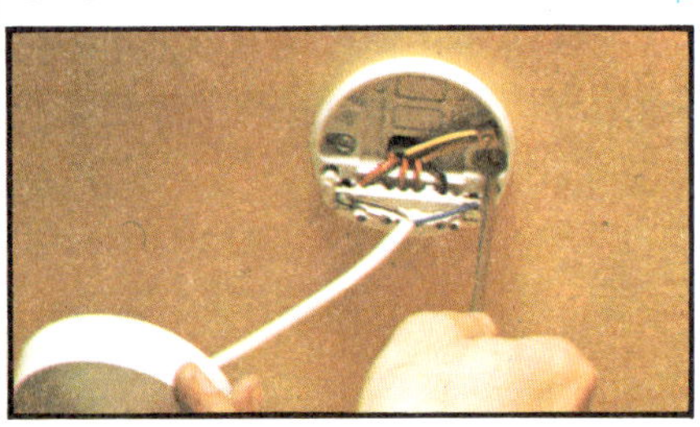

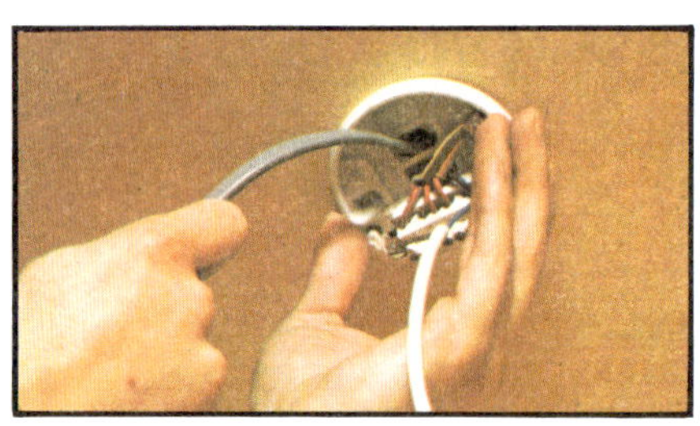

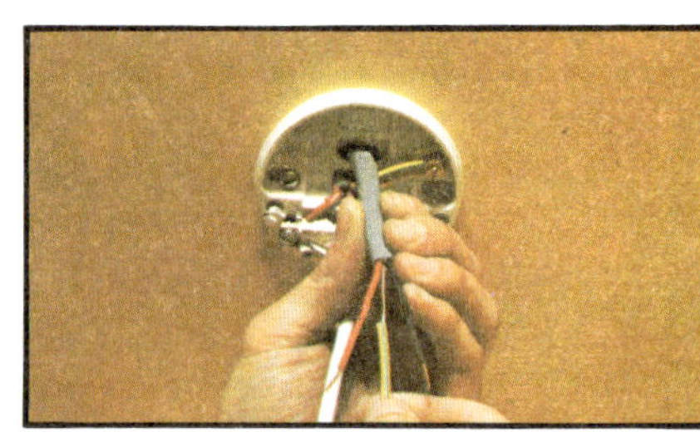

1 *When connecting into a loop-in rose, undo the fixing screws and pull the fitting a little way from the ceiling. But keep all the wires in place.*

2 *Tap out a knockout, then draw down through it about 200mm (8in) of the cable that leads to the new ceiling rose, or else feed the cable up from below.*

3 *Prepare the cable by stripping back about 75mm (3in) of sheathing and 10mm (3/8in) of insulation from the conductors. Sleeve the earth wire.*

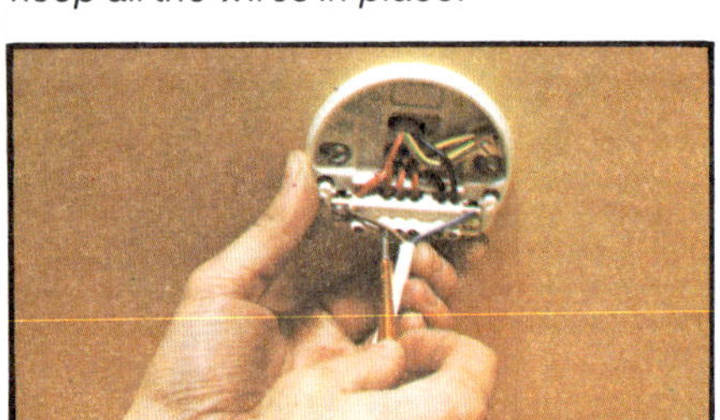

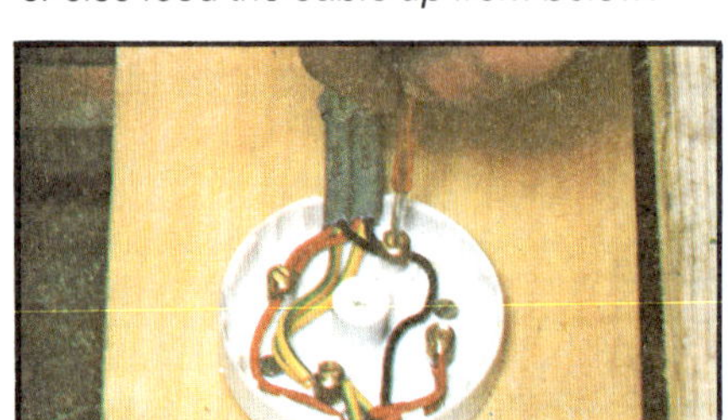

4 *Connect the earth to the earth terminal, the black to the neutral terminals and the red to the central in-line terminals.*

5 *When connecting in at a junction box, use a four-terminal type mounted on a batten. Connect the wires to the terminals as shown.*

6 *When taking out an old loop-in rose, disconnect the switch and feed cables and connect up the two feed cables as shown in a three-terminal junction box.*

Keith Morris

Junction box: MK

ADDING A POWER POINT

Electrical equipment is now used more and more in the home, so an extra power socket is always useful. Here's how to fit one.

Keith Morris

There's nothing really difficult about installing a new power point. It's easier than putting in a new light as you don't have to worry about a switch cable.

Ever since the early 1950s, the power supply to the sockets has almost always been wired as a ring circuit (see pages 156–160). And any house rewired since then will almost certainly have had this system installed. This means that once you've decided where you want the new outlet point – by a shelf in the living room for a hi-fi system, or over a worktop in the kitchen, for example – all you then have to do is to run a 'branch' or 'spur' to it from a convenient point on a nearby ring circuit.

The connection could be made at any socket on the ring (unless it already has a spur coming from it), or by using a three-terminal junction box inserted into the cable run. Each spur can have one single, double or triple socket fitted to it, or else a fused connection unit. Until a recent change in the Wiring Regulations, you were allowed two single sockets on a spur, but this is no longer permitted.

Checking your circuits

Although it's very likely that your house has ring circuits for the power supply, it's important to make sure. A ring circuit serves a number of 13A power outlets, and the sockets themselves take the familiar three-pin plugs with flat pins. But having this type of socket doesn't necessarily mean you've got a ring circuit – a new radial circuit may have been installed with these fittings, or an old radial circuit may simply have been modernised with new socket outlets. Pages 161–171 explain the distinction.

First you've got to check whether you've got a modern consumer unit or separate fuse boxes for each of the circuits. Having a consumer unit is a fair indication that you've got ring circuit wiring, and if two cables are connected to each individual 30A fuseway in the unit this will confirm it. Normally each floor of the house will have a separate ring circuit, protected by a 30A fuse or MCB.

If you have separate fuse boxes, look for the ones with 30A fuses. If they have one supply cable going into them and two circuit cables coming out, this indicates a ring circuit.

It's easy to identify the sockets on any particular circuit simply by plugging in electrical appliances, such as table lamps, turning off the power and then removing a 30A fuse from the fuse box or consumer unit, or switching off a 30A MCB. When you restore the supply, the equipment that remains off will indicate which sockets are on the circuit.

Dealing with radial circuits

Where a house hasn't got ring circuits, then the power sockets will be supplied by some form of radial circuit. Because there are different types of radial circuit, each governed by separate regulations controlling the number and location of sockets on the circuit, the size of cable to be used and the size and type of circuit fuse protecting it, you should only add a spur to an existing radial circuit if you can trace its run back to the fuse box or consumer unit and identify its type, and if it has been wired up in modern PVC-sheathed cable throughout.

If you've still got unfused 15A, 5A and 2A round-pin plugs, then this is a sure sign of very old radial circuits, which were installed more than 30 years ago. Rather than extending the system you should seriously consider taking these circuits out and replacing them with ring circuits, as the wiring will almost certainly be nearing the end of its life. You'll then be able to position the new sockets exactly where you want them. If you're in any doubt about the circuitry in your house you should contact your local electricity authority or a qualified electrician before carrying out any work.

Adding a spur to a ring

Once you've established you're dealing with a ring circuit and what sockets are on it, you'll need to find out if any spurs have already been added. You can't have more spurs than there are socket outlets on the ring itself. But unless the circuit has been heavily modified, it's unlikely that this situation will arise. You'll also need to know where any spurs are located – you don't want to overload an existing branch by mistake.

You can distinguish the sockets on the ring from those on a spur by a combination of inspecting the back of the sockets and tracing some cable runs (see *Ready Reference*, page 178). But remember to turn off the power first.

When you've got this information, you can work out whether it's feasible to add to the ring circuit. And you'll have a good idea where the cable runs.

Installing the socket

It's best to install the socket and lay in the cable before making the final join into the ring, since by doing this you reduce the amount of time that the power to the circuit is off.

You can either set the socket flush with the wall or mount it on the surface. The latter is the less messy method, but the fitting stands proud of the wall and so is more conspicuous.

FLUSH FITTING IN A BRICK WALL

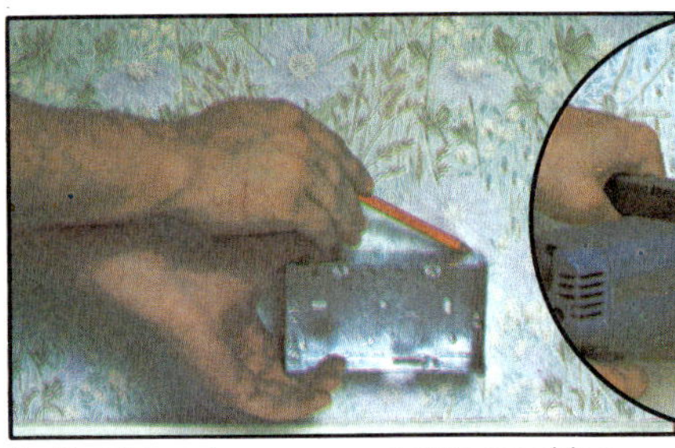

1 Decide where you want to position the socket, then pencil round the mounting box as a guide for where to chop out the wall.

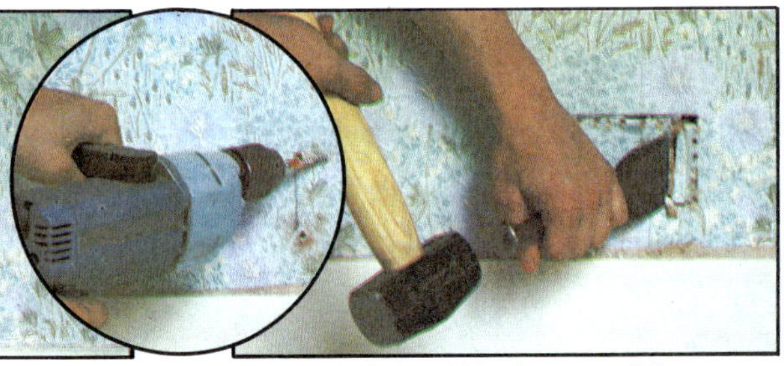

2 Drill slightly within the pencil lines to the depth of the mounting box, then work along the lines with a bolster chisel before chopping out the recess.

3 Channel a cable run down the back of the skirting using a long, thin cold chisel. Alternatively, use a long masonry bit and an electric drill.

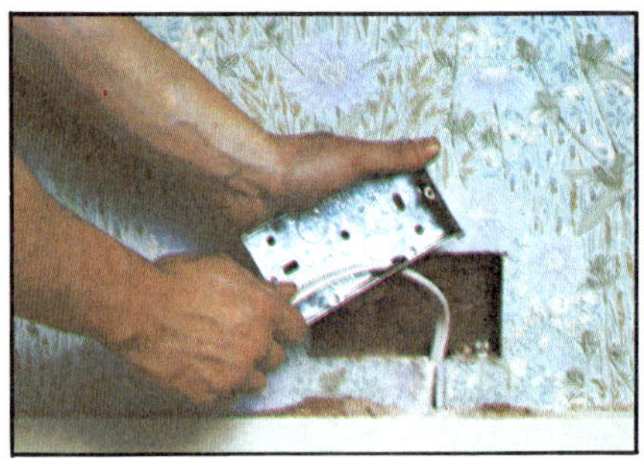

4 Thread the cable up from under the floor, through some PVC conduiting behind the skirting and into the mounting box.

5 Push the box into position, then use a bradawl to mark where the fixing holes are to go in the recess. Remove the box and drill and plug the holes.

6 Set the box back into place and screw it tightly into the recess. Check that it is level, and then make good if necessary with plaster or filler.

Keith Morris

Flush-fixing a socket on a plasterboard wall is a little more involved.

If you choose to surface-mount the socket, all you have to do is to fix a PVC or metal box directly to the wall after you've removed the knockout (and, if metal, use a grommet) where you want the cable to enter. The socket can then be screwed directly to this.

Laying in the cable

Because cable is expensive, it's best to plan the spur so that it uses as little cable as possible. When you channel cable into a wall you'll need to chase out a shallow run, fix the cable in position with clips, then plaster over it. But the best method of all is to run the cable in oval PVC conduiting. It won't give any more protection against an electric drill, but it'll prevent any possible reaction between the plaster making good and the cable sheathing. Always channel horizontally or vertically, and never diagonally, so it's easier to trace the wiring run when you've completed decorating. You can then avoid the cable when fixing something to the wall.

Normally the cable will drop down to below floor level to connect into the circuit. Rather than remove the skirting to get the cable down

Ready Reference

WARNING

The power supply to the sockets will probably be wired as a ring circuit. You can add a spur to this provided the number of spurs doesn't exceed the number of sockets on the ring.

CABLE SIZE

New spurs should be in $2.5mm^2$ cable

CHECKING OUT A RING CIRCUIT

These instructions assume that your installation conforms to the Wiring Regulations. If it seems to have been modified in an unauthorised way, get a qualified electrician to check it.

TURN OFF THE POWER SUPPLY. Start by undoing a socket near where you want to install the new socket.

AT A SINGLE SOCKET

One cable entering
Socket is on the end of a spur. There could be another single socket on the branch.
Action: trace cable. If it goes to another single socket and this socket has only two cables going to it, then you have found an intermediate socket on the spur. It goes to a double socket where there are three cables, then the single socket is the only socket on the spur. It's the same if the cable goes to a junction box.

Two cables entering
Socket is probably on the ring (see above). You can connect a spur into this.
Action: You'll need to trace the cable runs. If the cable is the only one going to another single socket, then the socket is on a spur. If the cable makes up one of two cables in another socket then it's on the ring.

Three cables entering
Socket is on the ring with a spur leading from it.
Action: to check which cable is which you'll need to trace the cable runs.

AT A DOUBLE SOCKET

One cable entering
Socket is on a spur. You can't connect a new socket from this.
Two cables entering
Socket is on the ring. You can connect a spur into this.
Three cables entering
Socket is on the ring with a spur leading from it. Checking to see which cable is which is the same as for a single socket with three cables. You can't connect a spur from this socket.

FLUSH FITTING IN A PLASTERBOARD WALL

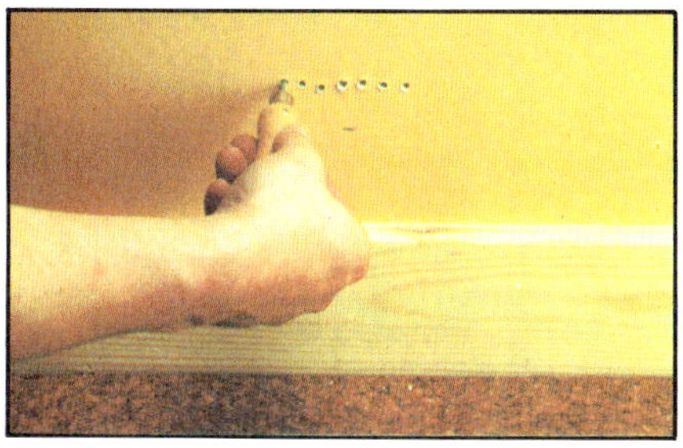

1 *Knock along the cavity wall to locate a stud near where you want the socket. Pierce the wall with a bradawl to locate the centre of the upright.*

2 *Position the box centrally over the stud and pencil round it. Be as accurate as you can because eventually the box should fit neatly in the opening.*

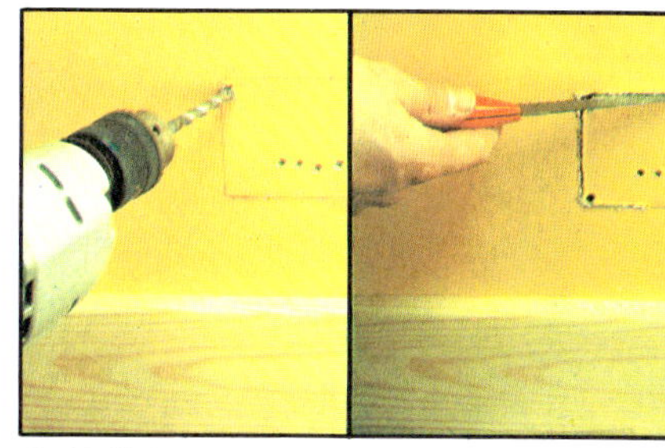

3 *Drill the corners of the guidelines. Push a pad saw (or keyhole saw) into one of them and cut along the lines. The plasterboard will come out in one piece.*

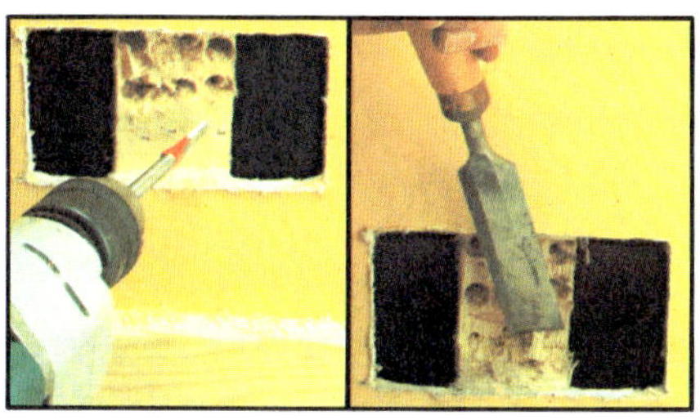

4 *Once you've exposed the stud, you'll need to remove some of the wood so the box can be fully recessed. You can do this with a drill and chisel.*

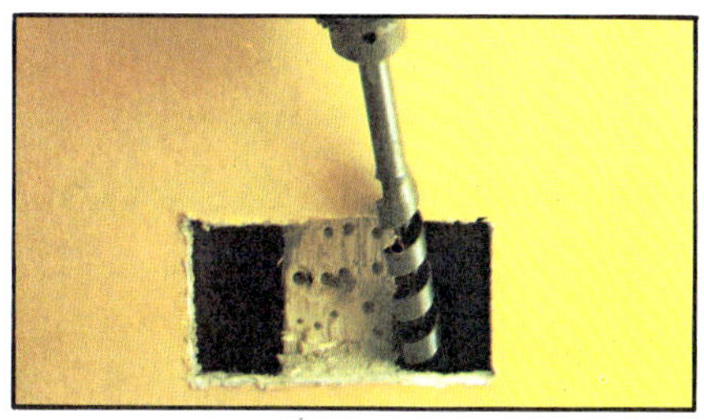

5 *Use a long drill bit to drill down through the baseplate of the stud partition. Try and keep the drill as upright as possible.*

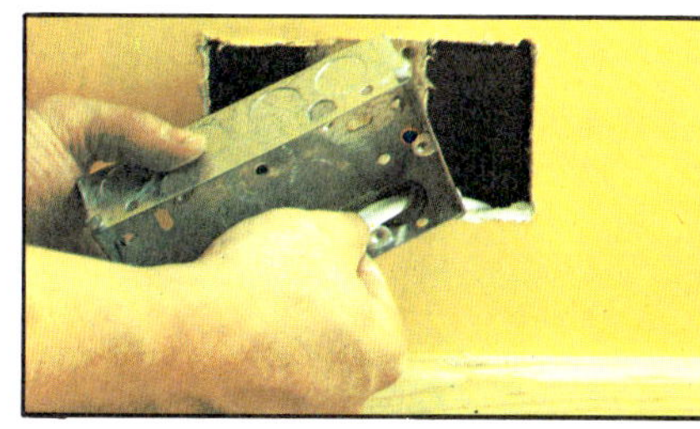

6 *Lay the cable from the point where it joins the main circuit and thread it up through the hole in the baseplate and into the box.*

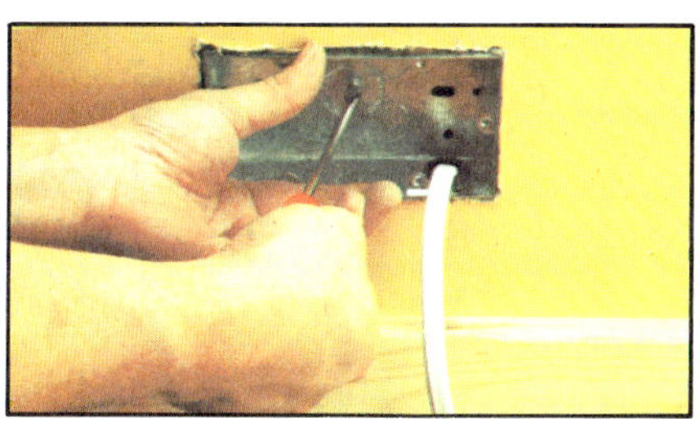

7 *Set the box in the recess and fix it in place by screwing to the stud. The cable end can now be prepared and connected to the socket terminals.*

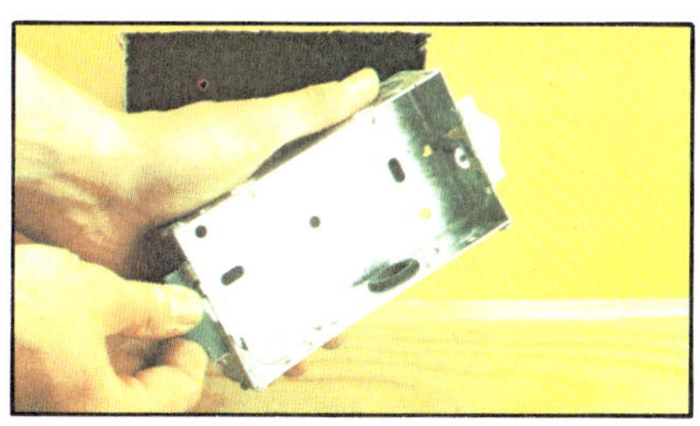

8 *Where there is no stud to fix to, fit special lugs to the box sides. These press against the plasterboard's inner face when the faceplate is attached.*

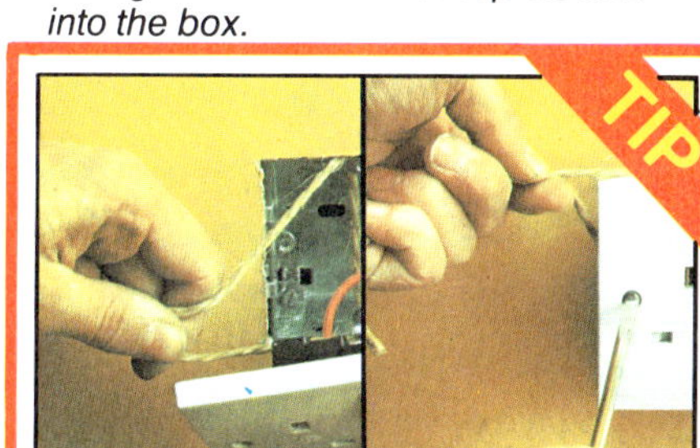

9 *Before manoeuvring the box into the recess, thread some string through the front so you can hold it in position.*

Jem Grischotti

CONNECTING THE NEW SOCKET

1 *Strip back the sheathing of the cable by running a sharp knife down the side of the uninsulated earth. Avoid damaging the other cores.*

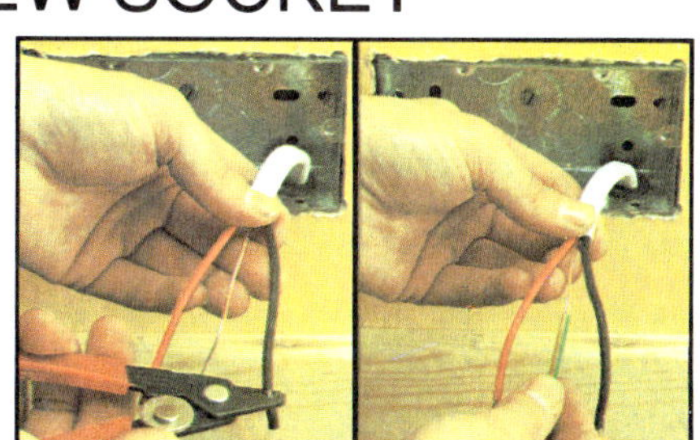

2 *Set the wire strippers to the correct gauge and remove about 9mm (3/8in) of insulation from the cores. Sleeve the earth core in green/yellow PVC.*

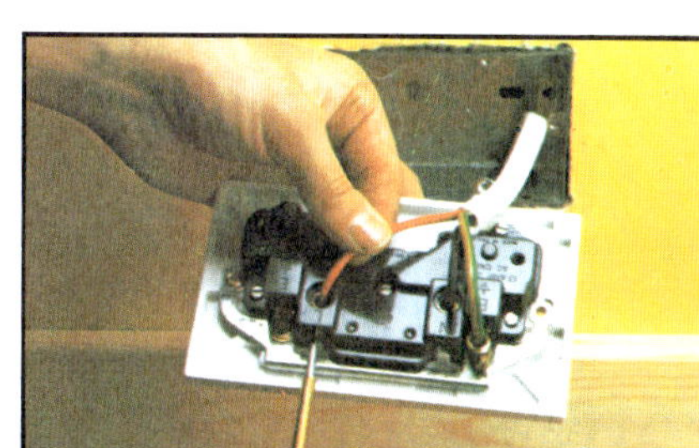

3 *Connect the three cores to the relevant terminals of the socket, making sure no exposed core is showing. Then screw the socket into position.*

Keith Morris

the back you can use a long steel cold chisel to chip out a groove. You'll then have to drill down through the end of the floorboard with a wood bit. Alternatively, you can use a long masonry bit with an electric drill to complete the task.

But if the floor is solid, the ring is usually in the ceiling void above, in which case the branch will drop down from the ceiling. And this will involve a considerable amount of channelling out if you want to install the new socket near floor level.

Stud partition walls also present a few problems. If the socket is near the floor, you should be able to get a long drill bit through the hole you cut for the socket to drill through the baseplate and floorboard. You can then thread the cable through. But if the socket is to be placed higher up the wall, noggings and sound insulation material may prevent the cable being drawn through the cavity. In this case you will probably have to surface-mount the cable.

In fact, surface-mounting is the easiest method of running the cable. All you do is fix special plastic conduit to the wall and lay the cable inside before clipping on the lid. But many people regard this as an ugly solution.

When laying cable under ground floor floorboards you should clip it to the sides of the joists about 50mm (2in) below the surface so that it doesn't droop on the ground. Cable in the ceiling void can rest on the surface.

When you have to cross joists, you'll need to drill 16mm (5/8in) holes about 50mm (2in) below the level of the floorboards. The cable is threaded through them and so is well clear of any floorboard fixing nails.

Connecting into the circuit

If you use a junction box, you'll need one with three terminals inside. You have to connect the live conductors (those with red insulation) of the circuit cable and the spur to one terminal, the neutral conductors (black insulation) to another, and the earth wires to the third. Sleeve the earth wires in green/yellow PVC first.

You might decide that it's easier to connect into the back of an existing socket rather than use a junction box, although this will probably mean some extra channelling on the wall. Space is limited at the back of a socket so it may be difficult to fit the conductors to the relevant terminals. However, this method is ideal if the new socket that you're fitting on one wall is back-to-back with an existing fitting. By carefully drilling through the wall a length of cable can be linked from the old socket into the new.

CONNECTING INTO THE CIRCUIT

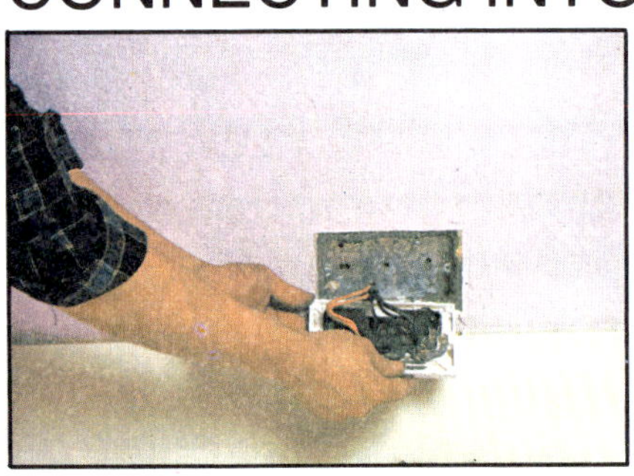

1 *Unscrew a nearby socket to check that it's on the ring – normally there'll be two red, two black and two earth wires. Sometimes the earths are in one sleeve.*

2 *Usually it's easier to push the new cable up into the mounting box from below the floor, although you might prefer to take it the other way.*

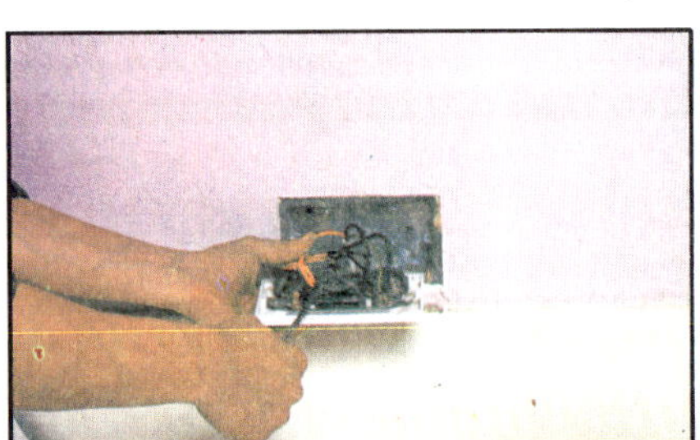

3 *Prepare the cores and sleeve the earth of the new cable, then connect them into the appropriate terminals on the back of the socket.*

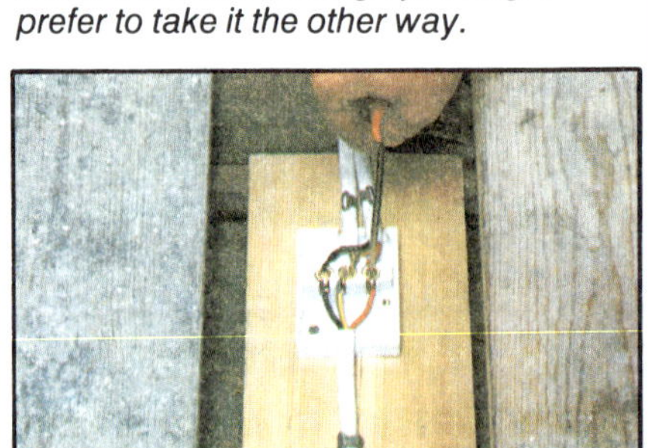

4 *If installing a junction box use a three-terminal type. Connect the red conductors to one terminal, the blacks to another and the earths to a third.*

Keith Morris

Ready Reference

SOCKET MOUNTINGS

Metal boxes are recessed into the wall and provide a fixing for the socket itself. Knockouts are provided in the back, sides and ends to allow the cable to enter the box. Rubber grommets are fitted round the hole so the cable doesn't chafe against the metal edges.

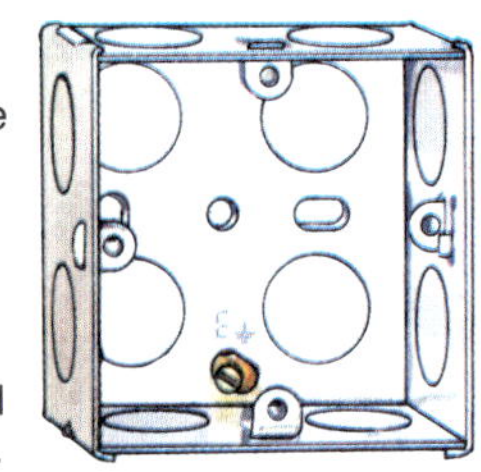

Elongated screw slots allow box to be levelled when fixed to wall.

Adjustable lugs enable final adjustments to level of faceplate on wall.

Boxes are usually 35mm deep, but with single-brick walls boxes 25mm deep should be used, along with accessories having deeper-than-usual faceplates.

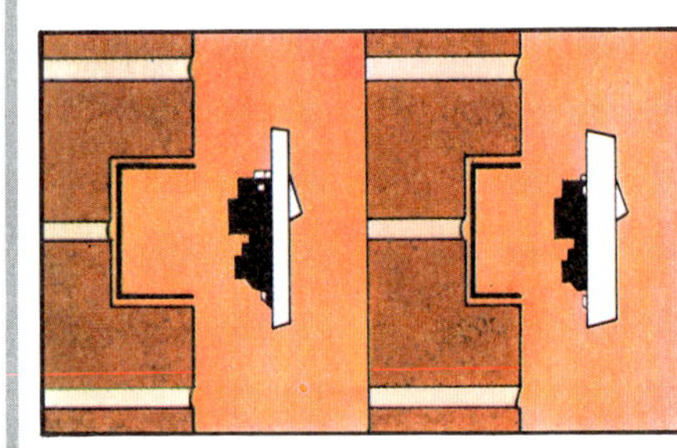

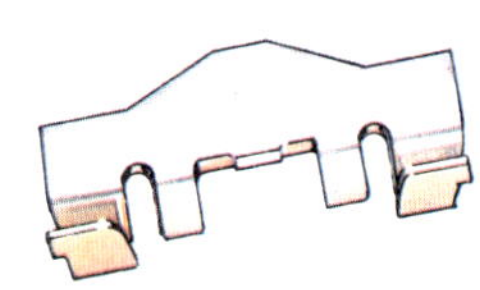

Lugs can be fitted to a metal box so that it can be fitted into stud partition walls.

Surface-mounted boxes (usually white plastic) are 35mm deep, and are simply screwed to the wall surface where required.

TIP: FIT SAFETY PLATES

Safety plates can be fitted to sockets to prevent young children playing with them.

PROBLEMS

- **Crumbly plaster** There's little that can be done other than cutting back to sound plaster. Position the box and socket as required then make good the surrounding area.
- **Poor bricks** Because of soft bricks you can quite easily chop out too big a recess for the box. Pack the recess with dabs of mortar or plaster.
- **Cavity walls** To prevent breaking through into the cavity only chop out a recess big enough to take a shallow box, about 25mm (1in) deep.

RUNNING CIRCUIT CABLES

The hardest part of the average electrical job is running the cables: it takes up a lot of time and a lot of effort. But there are certain techniques used by experts which can make it much easier.

Before you get involved in the details of how to install the wiring, there's one simple question you must answer. Does it matter if the cable runs show? This is because there are only two approaches to the job of running cable. Either you fix the cable to the surface of the wall, or you conceal it. The first option is far quicker and easier but doesn't look particularly attractive; it's good enough for use in, say, an understairs cupboard. For a neater finish, using this method, you can smarten up the cable runs by boxing them in with some trunking. Many people, however, prefer to conceal the wiring completely by taking it under the floor, over the ceiling, or in walls.

TYPICAL CABLE RUNS

More and more electrical equipment is now being used in the home. And the chances are that sooner or later you will want to install a new power point, wall or ceiling light, or another switch. In which case you will have to get power to your new accessory. To do that will involve running cable from an existing circuit or installing a completely new one. Running cable to a new appliance can be the hardest part of any job and, as the illustration on the right shows, you will be involved in trailing cable across the roof space or ceiling void, channelling it down walls and threading it behind partitions as well as taking it under floorboards. But it's much easier than it seems. There are a number of tricks of the trade that will make any electrical job simpler and less time consuming. For example, once you can 'fish' cable, the daunting task of running it under a floor is simple.

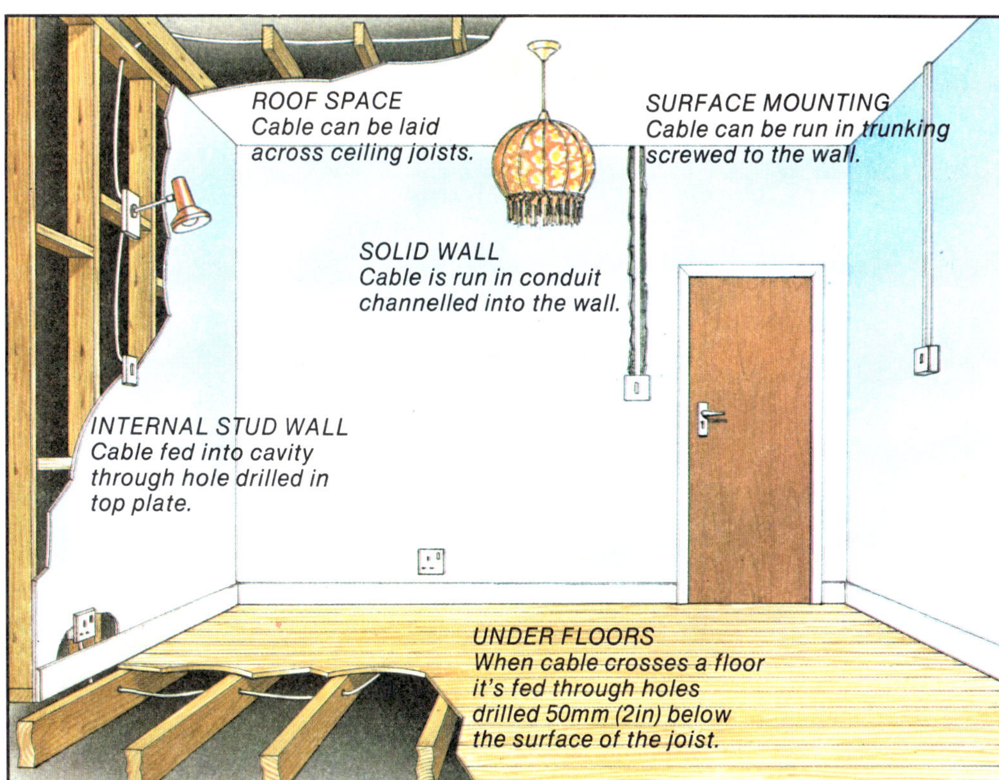

SURFACE MOUNTING CABLE

1 *To run cable in trunking, cut the trunking to length and fix the channel half to the wall with screws and wall plugs at 450mm (18in) centres.*

2 *Run the cable and press it firmly into the channel as far as it will go, carefully smoothing it out to avoid kinks and twists.*

3 *Next, snap the trunking's capping piece over the channelling, tapping it firmly along its length with your hand to lock it into place.*

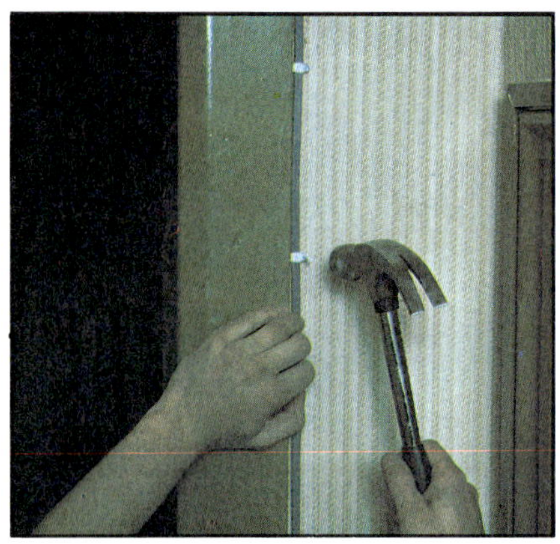

4 *If the cable is to be on show, merely secure it every 225mm (9in) with cable clips. Fit them over the cable and drive home the fixing pins.*

Planning the route

Having made your decision you must now work out a suitable route for the cable to follow.

If it is to be surface-mounted – with or without trunking – run the cable around window and door frames, just above skirting boards and picture rails, down the corners of the room, or along the angle between wall and ceiling. This not only helps conceal the cable's presence, but also protects it against accidental damage. This last point is most important, and is the reason why you must never run cable over a floor.

With concealed wiring, the position is more complicated. When running cable under a floor or above a ceiling, you must allow for the direction in which the joists run – normally at right angles to the floorboards – and use an indirect route, taking it parallel to the joists and/or at right angles to them.

When running cable within a wall, the cable should *always* run vertically or horizontally from whatever it supplies, *never* diagonally.

Surface-mounting techniques

If you are leaving the cable on show, all you need do is cut it to length, and fix it to the surface with a cable clip about every 225mm (9in), making sure it is free from kinks and twists. With modern cable clips, simply fit the groove in the plastic block over the cable and drive home the small pin provided.

Surface mounting cable within trunking involves a bit more work. Having obtained the right size of PVC trunking, build up the run a section at a time, cutting the trunking to length with a hacksaw. Once each piece is cut, separate it into its two parts – the

Ready Reference

RUNNING CABLE

You can mount cable:

- on the surface of a wall or ceiling
- concealed within the wall, above the ceiling or below the floor.

SURFACE-MOUNTED CABLE

This should be run above skirting boards, round window and door frames and in the corners of rooms to disguise the run and protect the cable. Never run cable across a floor.

Fix the cable in place every 225mm (9 in) with cable clips. Make sure the cable isn't kinked or twisted.

For a neater finish run the cable in PVC trunking, which you can cut to length using a hacksaw. Fix the channel part of the trunking to the wall first with screws and wall plugs at roughly 450mm (18in) centres. Then lay in the cable and clip the cover in position – tap it with your fist to ensure a tight fixing.

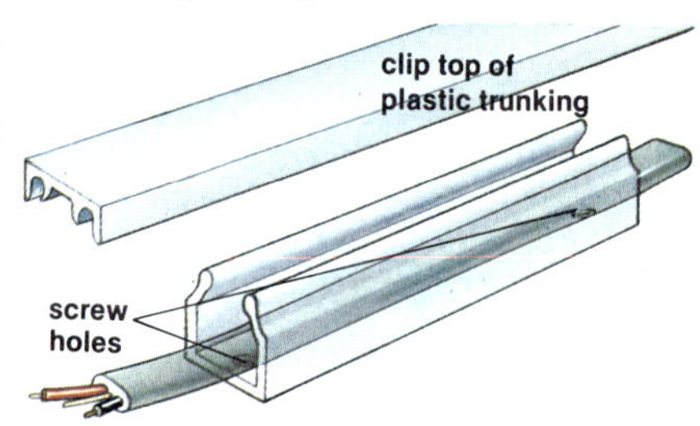

CONCEALED WIRING

To conceal a cable in a solid wall run it down a channel (chase) chopped in the surface and plaster over it. For added protection it's best to run the cable in PVC conduit and plaster this into the channel.

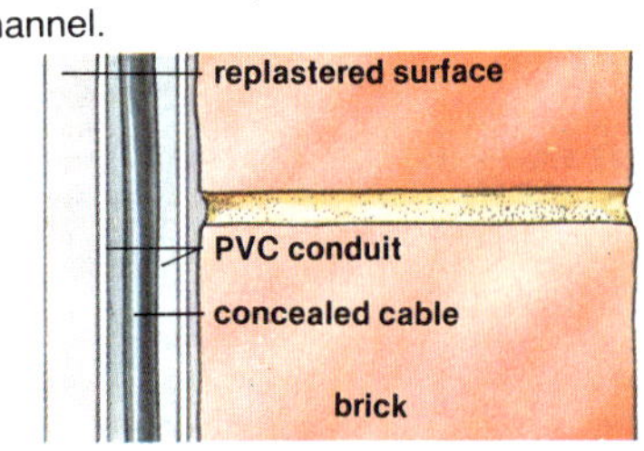

Concealed wiring should always be run vertically or horizontally from the fitting it supplies; never run it diagonally. This makes it easier to trace the runs in the future, when the wall has been decorated, and will prevent you drilling into the cable.

channelling and capping – and fix the channel to the wall with screws and wall plugs at roughly 450mm (18in) intervals (you may have to drill screw clearance holes in the channelling yourself).

Continue in this way until the run is complete. Turn corners by using proprietary fittings or by angling the ends of two pieces of trunking to form a neatly mitred joint, then run in the cable. Press this firmly into the channel and finish off by snapping the capping pieces firmly into place.

CHASING OUT SOLID WALLS

1 *Mark out the cable run using a length of conduit, and chop a channel ('chase') in the wall to receive it, using a club hammer and a bolster chisel.*

2 *Continue the chase behind any coving, skirting board, or picture rail by chipping out the plaster there with a long, narrow cold chisel.*

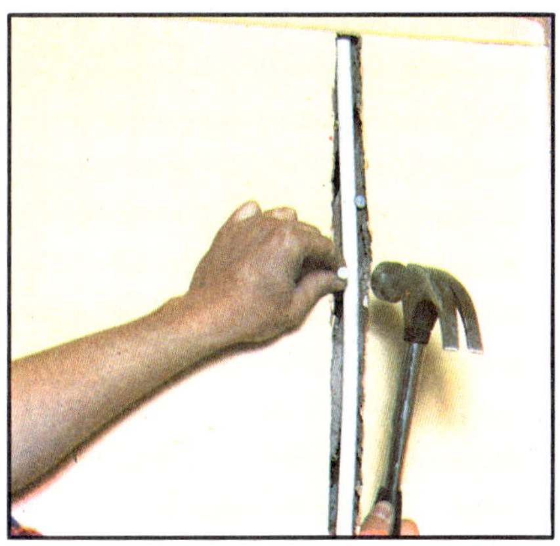

3 *Cut a length of PVC conduit to fit, and lay it in the chase, securing it temporarily with clout nails driven into the wall's mortar joints.*

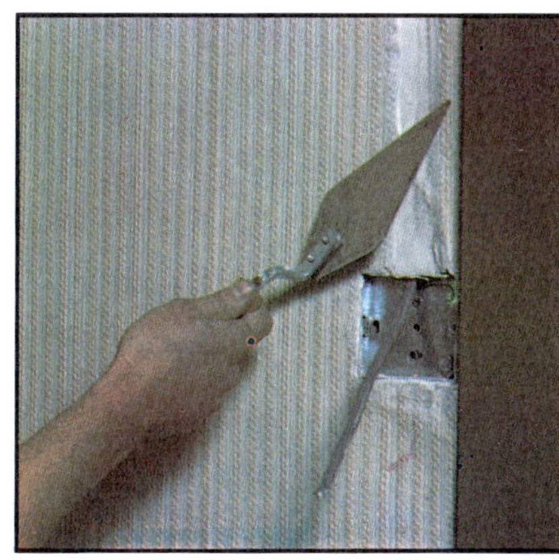

4 *Pull the cable through the conduit, then make good the wall by filling in over the conduit with plaster or cellulose filler.*

Concealing cables in walls

There are two ways to conceal cable in a wall. With a solid wall, chop a channel (called a 'chase') out of the plaster using a club hammer and bolster chisel, carefully continuing this behind any skirting boards, picture rails, and coverings. You could now run the cable in this chase and plaster over it. However, to give the cable some protection, it is better to fit a length of PVC conduit into the chase and run the cable through this before replastering.

To continue the run either above the ceiling or through the floor before you position the conduit, use a long drill bit so you can drill through the floor behind the skirting board. If a joist blocks the hole, angle the drill sufficiently to avoid it.

With a hollow internal partition wall, the job is rather easier, because you can run the cable within the cavity.

First drill a hole in the wall where the cable is to emerge, making sure you go right through into the cavity. Your next step is to gain access to the timber 'plate' at the very top of the wall, either by going up into the loft, or by lifting floorboards in the room above. Drill a 19mm (3/4in) hole through the plate, at a point vertically above the first hole, or as near vertically above it as possible.

All that remains is to tie the cable you wish to run to a length of stout 'draw' wire – single-core earth cable is often used – and then to tie the free end of this wire to a length of string. To the free end of the string, tie a small weight, and drop the weight through the hole at the top of the wall. Then all you do is make a hook in a piece of stout wire, insert it in the cavity, catch hold of the string and pull it (and in turn the draw wire and cable) through the hole in the room below.

What are the snags? There are two. You may find that, at some point between the two holes, the cavity is blocked by a horizontal timber called a noggin. If this happens, try to reach the noggin from above with a long auger bit (you should be able to hire one) and drill through it. Failing that, chisel through the wall surface, cut a notch in the side of the noggin, pass the cable through the notch, and then make good.

The second snag is that you may not be able to reach the top plate to drill it. In which case, either give up the idea of having concealed wiring, or try a variation on the second method used to run cable into the cavity from below the floor.

Here, it is sometimes possible to lift a couple of floorboards and drill up through the plate forming the bottom of the wall. Failing that you have to take a very long drill bit, drill through the wall into the cavity, then continue drilling through into the timber plate. You can now use the weighted string trick to feed the cable in through the hole in the wall, and out under the floor.

Running cable beneath a floor

The technique for running cable beneath a suspended timber floor depends on whether the floor is on an upper storey and so has a ceiling underneath, or is on a ground floor with empty space below. If it's a ground floor, it may be possible to crawl underneath and secure the cable to the sides of the joists with cable clips, or to pass it through 19mm (3/4in) diameter holes drilled in the joists at least 50mm (2in) below their top edge. This prevents anyone nailing into the floor and hitting the cable.

If you cannot crawl underneath, then the cable can be left loose in the void. But how do you run it without lifting the entire floor? The answer is you use another trick, called 'fishing'.

For this, you need a piece of stiff but reasonably flexible galvanised wire, say 14 standard wire gauge (swg), rather longer than the intended cable run, and a piece of thicker, more rigid wire, about 1m in length. Each piece should have one end bent to form a hook.

Lift a floorboard at each end of the

COPING WITH STUD WALLS

1 *Drill a hole in the wall where the cable is to emerge, then bore a second hole in the wooden plate forming the top of the wall.*

2 *Tie a weight to a length of string and lower this through the hole in the wall plate. Tie the free end of the string to a stout 'draw' wire.*

3 *If the weight gets blocked on its way to the hole in the wall, use a long auger bit to drill through the noggin obstructing it.*

4 *Fish out the weighted string through the hole in the wall, using a piece of wire bent to form a hook. Now, pull through the draw wire.*

5 *Tie the draw wire to the cable you wish to run, then return to the hole in the wall's top plate, and use the string to pull up the draw wire.*

6 *Then use the draw wire to pull the length of cable through. Remember, do this smoothly and don't use force if there's an obstruction.*

Ready Reference

TRICKS OF THE TRADE

Hollow internal partition wall

Drill a hole in the top or bottom plate, then drill another in the wall where the cable is to emerge. Drop a weighted piece of string through one of the holes and hook it out through the other. Use this to pull through a stout draw wire which is attached to the cable.

● if the weighted piece of string gets obstructed by a noggin or its way to the hole in the wall, use a long auger bit to drill through the noggin.

● don't pull the cable through with the weighted string – the string tends to snap

● never run cable down the cavity of an external wall– treat these as solid walls.

Under floors

Use a technique known as fishing:

● lift the floorboards at either end of the run

● thread stiff wire beneath the floor through one hole and hook it out of the other with another piece of wire

● use the longer piece of wire to pull the cable through.

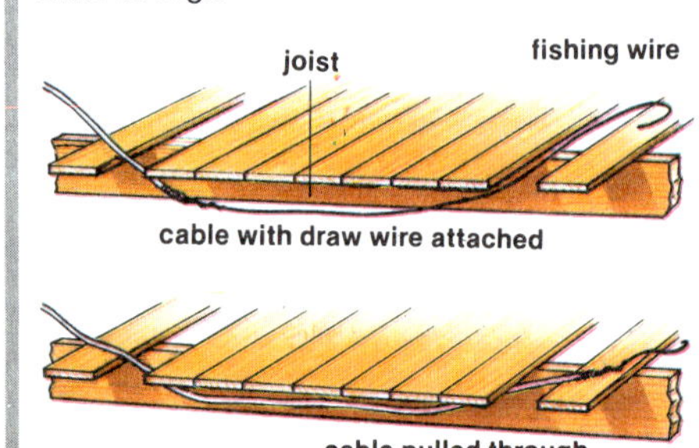

● if there's a gap beneath a ground floor you can 'fish' the cable diagonally across the room under the joist

● if the gap under the joists is large enough you can crawl in the space clipping the cable to the joists

● where the cable crosses the joists at right angles, run it through holes drilled 50mm (2in) below their top edges.

Over ceilings

If you can get above the ceiling into a loft, you can clip the cables to the joists. Otherwise you'll have to 'fish' the cable across (see above).

If you can't get above the ceiling and fishing doesn't work you'll have to surface-mount the cable.

proposed cable run and feed the longer piece of wire, hook end first, into the void through one of the resulting gaps in the floor. Hook it out through the second gap using the shorter piece of wire, and use it to pull through the cable in the same way as the draw wire used to pull cable through a hollow wall.

This technique is also used where there is a ceiling below the floor, and where you wish to run cable parallel to the joists, but in this case, check for any ribs and struts between the joists which might stop the fish wire getting through. Do this with the aid of a small mirror and a torch. If there is an obstruction, lift the floorboard above it, and drill a hole through which the cable can pass.

If the cable is to run at right angles to the joists, lift the floorboard above the line of the cable run, and feed the cable through holes drilled in the joists, 50mm (2in) below their top edge.

And what about solid floors? Obviously there is no way to run cable beneath these. Instead run the cable around the walls of the room, surface-mounting it just above the skirting board.

Running cable above a ceiling

Running cable above a ceiling is essentially the same as running it below a suspended timber floor. In fact, if there is a floor above the ceiling, it is generally easier to tackle the job from there, rather than from the room below.

If running the cable above the ceiling means taking it into the loft, then you can tackle it in much the same way as if you were running it below a suspended ground floor. If you cannot gain access to the loft, fish the cable through. If you can get into the loft, run the cable by hand, clipping it to the sides of the joists where it runs parallel to them.

You can run the cable at right angles to the joists by passing it through holes as already described, but this is frowned on by many electricians. Instead, they prefer to run it parallel to the joists as far as the 'binder' – the large timber cross-member linking the joists. They then clip the cable to the binder to traverse the ceiling, before running it to the desired position, again working parallel to the joists.

Unfortunately, there are situations in which running cable above a ceiling is almost impossible. The main ones are where the ceiling is solid concrete, as in many modern flats; where the ceiling is below a flat roof; and where, although there is a floor above the ceiling, you can't get at it (again this applies mainly to flats).

In the last two instances, if you intend the cable to run parallel to the joists, you may be able to fish it through. If not, you will have to treat the ceiling as if it were solid, and that means surface mounting the cable.

FISHING CABLE ABOVE CEILINGS

1 Take a piece of stiff wire and. check that it is just longer than is needed to reach between the cable's entry and exit holes in the ceiling.

2 Feed the wire into one hole, fish it out of the other with a second piece of wire, then tie the cable to the first wire and pull it through.

RUNNING CABLE UNDER FLOORS

1 When running cable parallel to the joists, fish it through in the same way as if fishing through cable above a ceiling.

2 If the cable or fish wire will not pull through, check under the floor for obstructions, using a small mirror and a reasonably powerful torch.

3 For cable runs at right angles to the joists, drill holes in the joists 50mm (2in) below their tops, angling these if the drill is too long to fit in.

4 Carefully thread the cable through the holes, without stretching it so that it chafes against the side of the hole and damages the insulation.

LIGHTING

Improving your home's lighting is one of the most dramatic moves you can make – the range of fittings and the switching systems available today virtually make it possible to decorate your home just by using lighting effects.

LIGHTING DESIGN 1: the basics

There is more to lighting your home than meets the eye, and well-designed lighting schemes can enhance every room in the house. To start with, you need to grasp some of the basic principles.

In most homes the standard of room lighting leaves something to be desired. Interior design generally has made immense strides in recent years, yet even new homes are built with a lighting specification left over from the dark ages – literally. Builders still follow what is known quaintly as the Builder's Norm – one pendant light in the centre of each room, switched by the entrance door – a standard that hasn't changed since the days of gas lighting, although in small rooms the gas light would often be a wall bracket fitting. You may be lucky enough to find the occasional wall light – in the lounge or bedroom, for example – but even homes that have been extensively modernised are unlikely to have anything much more adventurous.

This is a pity, because there is now a very wide range of attractive and versatile light fittings available, and a glance around many public buildings will show you some of the effects they can produce if used with a little flair. Installing fittings like these in your home isn't difficult, and the difference that well-designed lighting can make to every room in the house has to be seen to be believed.

How much light do you get?

Electric lamps – tungsten-filament bulbs and tubes and fluorescent fittings – are rated in watts (W). This tells you how much electricity the lamp uses when lit; it doesn't directly indicate how much light the lamp gives off (although it's obvious that a 100W lamp will be brighter than a 40W one), nor does it tell you how much useful light is provided or in what direction. The amount and quality of light needed for different tasks or effects varies widely; lighting to illuminate the dining table, the kitchen worktops or the family silver will differ from lighting for reading, sewing or lulling a child to sleep.

The actual amount of light emitted from a lamp is measured in units called lumens. Some lamps burn more efficiently that others, emitting more lumens per watt. Generally speaking, coiled-coil pear-shaped clear and pearl bulbs (see pages 190–192) have the highest efficiency in lumens/watt; next come mushroom-shaped bulbs, double-life bulbs and finally single-coil bulbs. What's more, the actual wattage of the bulb is also a factor; a 40W coiled-coil bulb has an output of 390 lumens (9.75 lumens/watt) while a 100W bulb of the same type emits 1260 lumens (12.6 lumens/watt).

Fluorescent tubes, as is widely known, are much more efficient light emitters than tungsten filament lamps. For example, a 40W warm white tube gives out 1950 lumens (48 lumens/watt) and an 80W tube of the same colour gives 3730 lumens (44 lumens) watt). On average, fluorescent tubes give about four times as much light as light bulbs of the same wattage.

How much light do you need?

When you're planning a lighting scheme these figures (see *Ready Reference* for a summary) will come in very useful. The other figure you need to know is how much light to provide in a given area. A rough and ready figure to work to for general lighting is 22 watts per sq m (2W/sq ft), and if seeing what you are doing was the only criterion for satisfactory illumination, it could be used without variation. However, several other factors have to be taken into account, including the type and position of the light fitting chosen, whether the lighting of a surface or object is direct or indirect, and the colour and reflectivity of the surface being lit. So as a general guideline it's a good idea to take the 22W/sq m figure as the minimum overall lighting required in each room, and to regard any additional local lighting as being supplementary to this. To

Ready Reference

LIGHT OUTPUT OF LAMPS

Fluorescent tubes are more efficient emitters of light (measured as lumens/watt) than coiled bulbs, which in turn are more efficient than single-coil ones. The outputs given below in lumens are for pearl bulbs and 'warm white' tubes.

Bulb wattage	Output	Lumens/W
15W single-coil	110	7.33
25W single-coil	200	8.00
40W coiled-coil	390	9.75
60W coiled-coil	665	11.08
75W coiled-coil	880	11.73
100W coiled-coil	1260	12.60
150W coiled-coil	2040	13.60

Tube wattage	Output	Lumens/W
15W (450mm/18in)	500	33.33
20W (600mm/2ft)	780	39.00
30W (900mm/3ft	1450	48.33
40W (1.2m/4ft)	1950	48.75
65W (1.5m/5ft)	3120	48.00
85W (1.8m/6ft)	3730	43.88

LIGHTING LEVELS

Aim to provide at least the following light levels in each room in the house:

- living room, dining room, bathroom, landing, hall, stairs – 100 lumens/sq m
- kitchen, reading area – 200 lumens/sq m
- bedrooms, garage – 50 lumens/sq m.

WHERE THE LIGHT GOES

Below: How light is emitted from various lamp types – GLS (A), ISL (B), CS (C), PAR (D), small spot (E) and fluorescent (F).

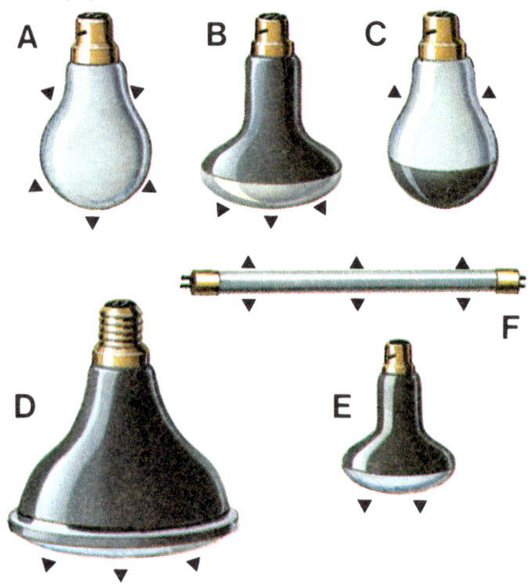

Below: The direction of light emitted may be modified by the type of fitting chosen. Shown here are a pendant (1), close-ceiling fitting (2), wall light (3), track spotlight (4), downlighter (5), wall washer (6), eyeball (7) and uplighter (8).

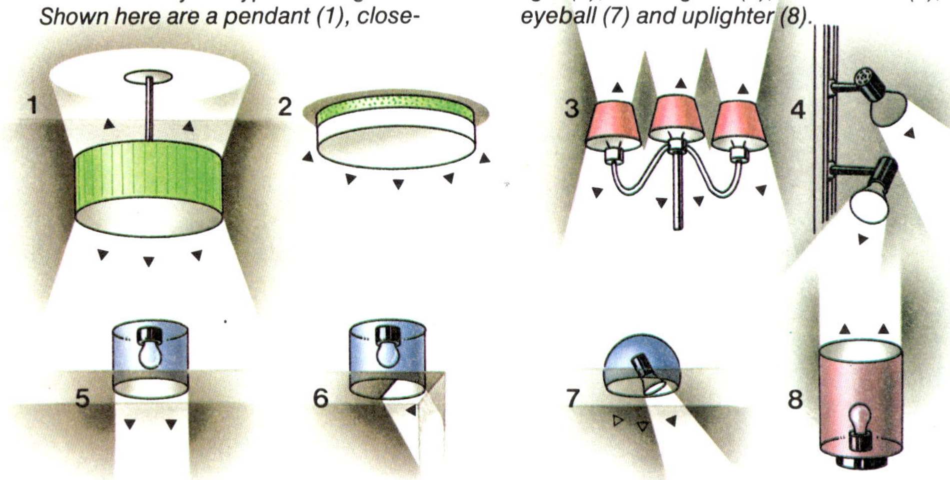

give a worked example, a living room measuring 6x4m (20x13ft) would need an overall lighting level of 6x4x22 = 528 watts.

The other point you need to take into account is that the amount of illumination you get – the amount of light falling on a surface – depends on how far it is from the light source. Double the distance and the level of illumination is halved.

Light bulbs and tubes

We tend to think of light bulbs and tubes as emitting light at random in all directions, and this is certainly true of the ordinary (GLS) bulb and the standard tungsten or fluorescent tube. But other types of lamp are available that emit light only in certain directions because the bulb or tube surface is coated with reflective or opaque material. For example, the internally-silvered (ISL) bulb has an internal reflector that covers the neck and sides of the bulb, resulting in a controlled beam that is ideal for projecting light onto walls and for spotlighting objects. The crown-silvered (CS) bulb has the reflector on the crown of the bulb, so that light is projected backwards into the fitting; when used with a parabolic reflector dish, the result is a parallel beam of light like that produced by a car headlamp. The PAR (parabolic aluminised reflector) lamp combines the CS optics into a single sealed unit that can provide spot or flood lighting.

Types of light fitting

There are four principal types of light fitting with which these various lamps can be used, and the type of fitting chosen may further modify the beam of light that the lamp itself emits, so giving you additional flexibility in the design of your lighting effects. The four types are: ceiling-mounted (pendant or close-fitting); wall-mounted; concealed (including 'downlighters' and 'wall-washers'), and free-standing (table, or standard lamps and 'uplighters').

Pendant fittings, the most familiar type, range from a plain lampholder carrying a decorative shade to multi-light fittings suspended from a ceiling plate by chains or a rod. Some give a general light output, others mainly direct downward and/or upward depending on the style of shade chosen. Rise-and-fall fittings are simply pendants with a spring-loaded flex extender concealed in the ceiling plate.

Close-ceiling fittings are mounted on the ceiling surface as an alternative to pendant fittings, and so by definition emit light in an overall downward direction only. They are usually fitted with a translucent glass or plastic cover, which may be coloured. Fluorescent fittings of various types also come into this category.

Wall-mounted fittings can range from simple brackets holding plain or decorative bulbs, with or without shades, to spot and flood fittings. Uplighters (see below under 'Free-standing fittings') can also be wall-mounted.

Concealed fittings include downlighters and wall-washers, both of which are usually recessed into the ceiling. Downlighters are cylindrical housings and usually contain an ISL bulb, so providing a fairly well-defined beam pointing to the floor. Wall-washers have either an adjustable aperture or an eyeball-type fitting that directs light downwards *and* to one side, allowing a ceiling-mounted fitting to 'wash' a nearby wall with light.

Free-standing fittings need little description – table and standard lamps come in a very wide range of models and offer general or local lighting according to type. The one comparatively unfamiliar member of this group is the uplighter, which bounces reflected light off ceilings and walls and is an excellent source of background or concealed light.

The effect of colour schemes

The colour scheme used in any room can have a profound effect on the level of lighting it requires. It goes without saying that dark wallcoverings and carpets will absorb a lot of light, so that a greater light wattage will have to be provided than if the room has white walls and pale furnishings.

The colour of walls and ceilings is particularly important when you plan to use a lot of indirect lighting, although this doesn't mean you have to have pale surfaces; you simply need more wattage. It's certainly true that you can achieve more dramatic lighting effects (at the expense of the general level of illumination) in rooms decorated in rich, deep colours.

Light and shadow

Before we begin to deal with the more detailed planning of lighting schemes, the last ground rule to remember – and one of the most important, too – concerns the problem of positioning lights to avoid glare and the creation of hard shadows. This is mainly solved by the correct choice of fitting for the job, and its careful positioning in the room. The illustrations opposite summarise some of the commonest problems and show how they can be overcome.

AVOIDING GLARE AND HARD SHADOWS

Living rooms *A central light is no good for reading as it casts shadows on the page.*

Position a reading lamp behind you, and provide indirect lighting near TV sets.

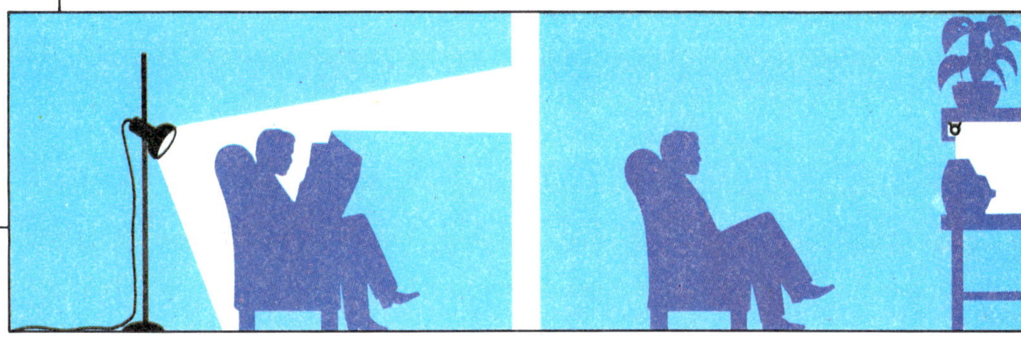

Dining rooms *Avoid fittings where the naked lamp is close to eye level and glares diners.*

Fit a rise-and-fall fitting, and provide two fittings above long tables.

Workrooms *A wrongly-positioned lamp means that you are working in your own shadow.*

Fit a concealed lamp above the work surface, adding an adjustable one for typing.

Bathrooms *Concealed lighting above mirrors leaves faces in shadow. Better illumination is provided by fittings at each side of the mirror.*

Bedrooms *Position reading lights on the wall above your head (and switch them at the bedside).*

Children's rooms *If night-time light is needed, provide it indirectly, or install a dimmer switch.*

LIGHT BULBS AND TUBES

You're always going to need artificial light, and so you should know what types of light bulbs and fluorescent tubes are available. Here's a brief summary.

There are two basic types of electric lamps in common use in the home. (We know them as light bulbs or tubes, but the professionals call them all lamps.) These are the filament lamp, a direct descendant of Thomas Edison's early bulbs, and the fluorescent tube, which has only come into widespread use in the past 30 years.

The filament lamp works on much the same principle as those early lamps that were produced over a hundred years ago. Electricity is passed through a wire which is suspended inside a glass envelope. Resistance to its passage produces heat, and when a certain temperature is reached, the conductor – called the filament – emits light. Today these filaments are made of tungsten that has been formed into coiled spirals, and the glass envelopes hold an inert gas such as argon that helps stop the filament from burning out. Previously the filament was suspended in a vacuum.

The range of filament lamps on the market is tremendous. They are available in different sizes, shapes and colours, and also come in a tube form that provides a more intense light and which is easily concealed above worktops and such like.

A fluorescent tube, on the other hand, has no filament; instead it has an electrode at each end and the tube is filled with a small amount of mercury vapour that glows when the lamp is switched on. This, in itself, doesn't produce much light, but it does produce quite a lot of invisible ultra-voilet light which causes the chemicals lining the inside of the tube to glow (or fluoresce) very brightly.

What about watts?

The power of a lamp is expressed in terms of wattage; so a 150W lamp will produce considerably more light that a 40W one. However, not all light fittings will accept the most powerful lamps, and as most are marked with their upper wattage limit, you should check beforehand – otherwise you risk damaging the fitting.

When deciding upon the actual level of light and the type of lamps you want, there are certain guidelines to bear in mind that may make things easier for you. As a rule, with general lighting from filament lights, you should be aiming at around 10 to 15 watts of lighting for every square metre of floor area in the room – although it obviously won't all be in use at any one time. With fluorescent lighting, the requirements are somewhat less; about 3 watts per square metre for general lighting, and between 8 and 10 watts per square metre for well-lit areas.

Light fittings

It's no good just buying a lamp without examining the light fitting in which it will be used. It's important to check the type of cap your fitting will accept.

Filaments lamps usually have either a bayonet cap, which comprises two small prongs that lock the lamp into the lampholder, or an Edison screw cap that is threaded like a large torch bulb and is screwed into the lampholder. There is also the single-centre contact usually found on filament tubes only. Fluorescent tubes nowadays almost always have bi-pin endcaps – two pin contacts that slot into the terminals of the fluorescent light fitting itself. Very old fittings may, however, need a tube with bayonet end caps like those on filament lamps.

Which types to choose

The type of light you want is also an important factor when deciding on the type of lamp to choose. In certain rooms, such as the kitchen, for example, the brighter the light the better. And, of course, you'll want a light that casts few shadows. In that case the answer is to use fluorescent lighting. However, this bright and sometimes slightly harsh light would hardly be suitable for a living area where you're more likely to want softer, warmer lighting that can be easily adjusted. Here, tungsten lamps will be a better bet.

Remember, the real secret to lighting a room successfully lies in giving it variety. In your living room, it's no good having just one high-wattage lamp in the centre of the ceiling, as you'll never be able to alter the mood and atmosphere successfully. You should really aim for a lamp that will provide satisfactory general light, and then supplement it with light over specific areas or for special decorative effects. So, in a kitchen although fluorescent lights will be adequate, you might well have filament reflector bulbs fitted into down-lighters above certain worktops.

Cost is another factor. As the majority of tubes require special fittings, fluorescent lighting can work out to be quite dear, whereas most filament lamps will fit into lampholders and can therefore be changed around quite frequently. A recent development is a two-contact fluorescent lamp that will fit into a standard fitting. But it is important to remember that most of the cost of lighting a room lies in the amount of electricity used; the actual lamp itself represents only about 10 per cent of the cost. So, using what is called a coiled coil filament bulb will cost more initially, but the light is brighter and actually costs less to run. Similarly, although fluorescent tubes cost more to buy than filament lamps, they do give between three and five times as much light for a given number of watts as a filament bulb and have a much longer life, usually lasting between 5000 and 7500 hours compared to the average of 1000 hours for an ordinary filament lamp.

REFLECTOR LAMPS

These lamps have a special silver coating to reflect the light in a particular way. There is a wide variety available and when looking for a replacement it's a good idea to take your old lamp to the shop with you.

1

GENERAL LIGHTING

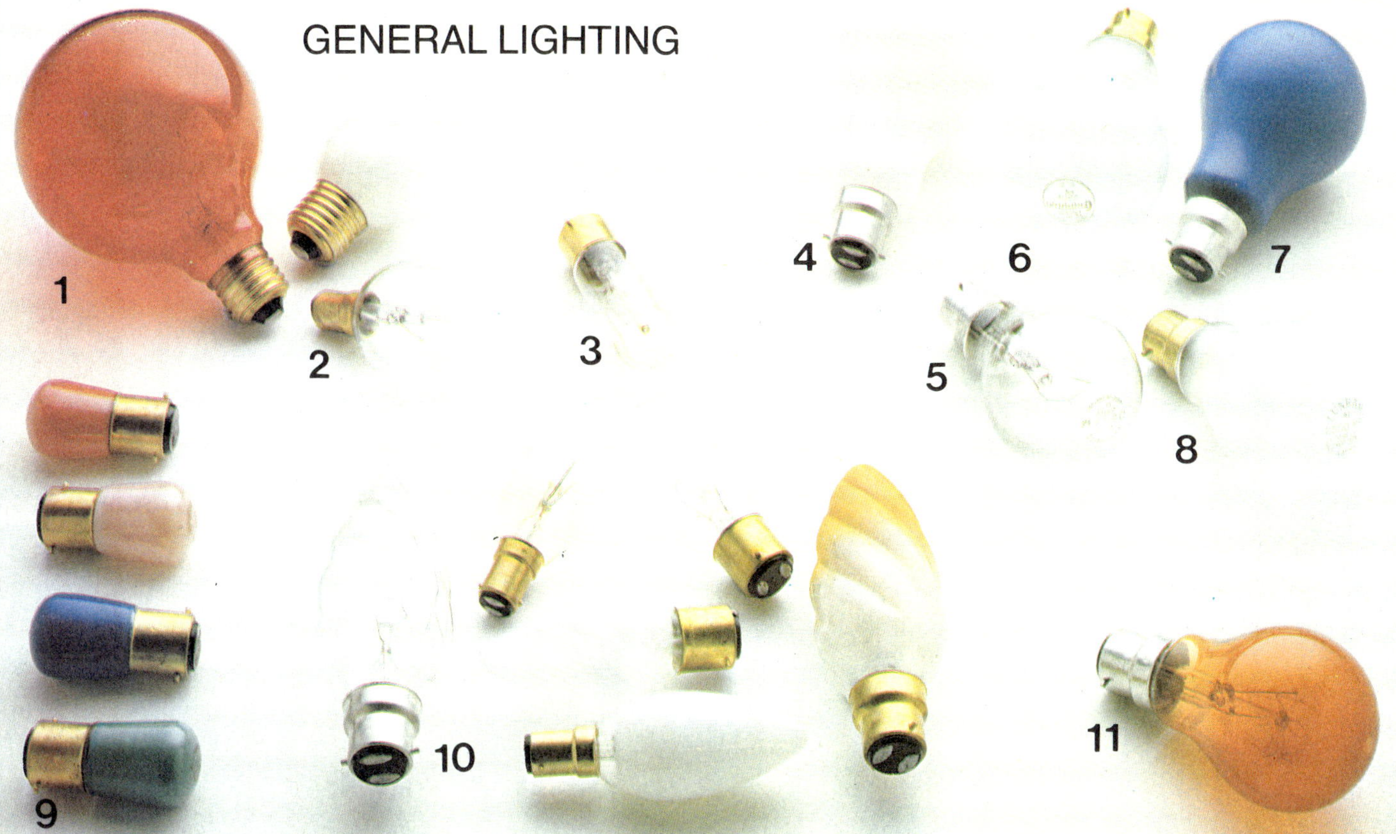

1 *Decor round lamps are designed for use with open type, ornamental shades where the lamp could be conspicuous. They give less light than other General Lighting Service (GLS) lamps.*
2 *Round (ball) lamps are normally used in small decorative fittings.*
3 *Single cap tubes are specially suited for bedside lights.*
4 *Mushroom lamps should be used in shallow fittings or where the lamp itself will be partly visible. Their silica coating gives them a softer and more diffuse light than pearl lamps.*
5 *Clear glass lamps are used in reflector fittings and chandeliers. The filament is visible and shadows sharp and hard.*
6 *Pearl lamps give a diffused light. The inside of the glass envelope is roughened by special treatment but there is no subsequent loss of light.*
7 *Coloured lamps usually have bayonet caps and range from 15 to 100W. Colours are amber, blue, green, pink, yellow and red. Low wattage lamps are safe outside without extra protection but others require special fittings.*
8 *Long-life bulbs give slightly less light than an equivalent standard lamp, but will have more than double the lifespan.*
9 *Pigmy lamps are 15W and are normally used for outdoor festoons, where they fit into special waterproof holders; good for wall lights too.*
10 *Candle lamps are used extensively in wall lights and chandeliers.*
11 *Fireglow lamps give the warm glow behind simulated log and coal electric fires. They're sometimes fitted with three-pin bayonet caps, so check your holder before buying one.*

1 *Internally silvered lamps (ISL lamps) are silvered round the base and sides. This throws the light forward and gives a broad beam.*

2 *Crown silvered lamps have the top of the envelope silvered to control the amount of glare and produce a narrow beam suitable for spotlights.*

3 *ISL lamps with the stem silvered.*

4 *Parabolic aluminized reflector (PAR) lamps have armoured glass for outside use.*

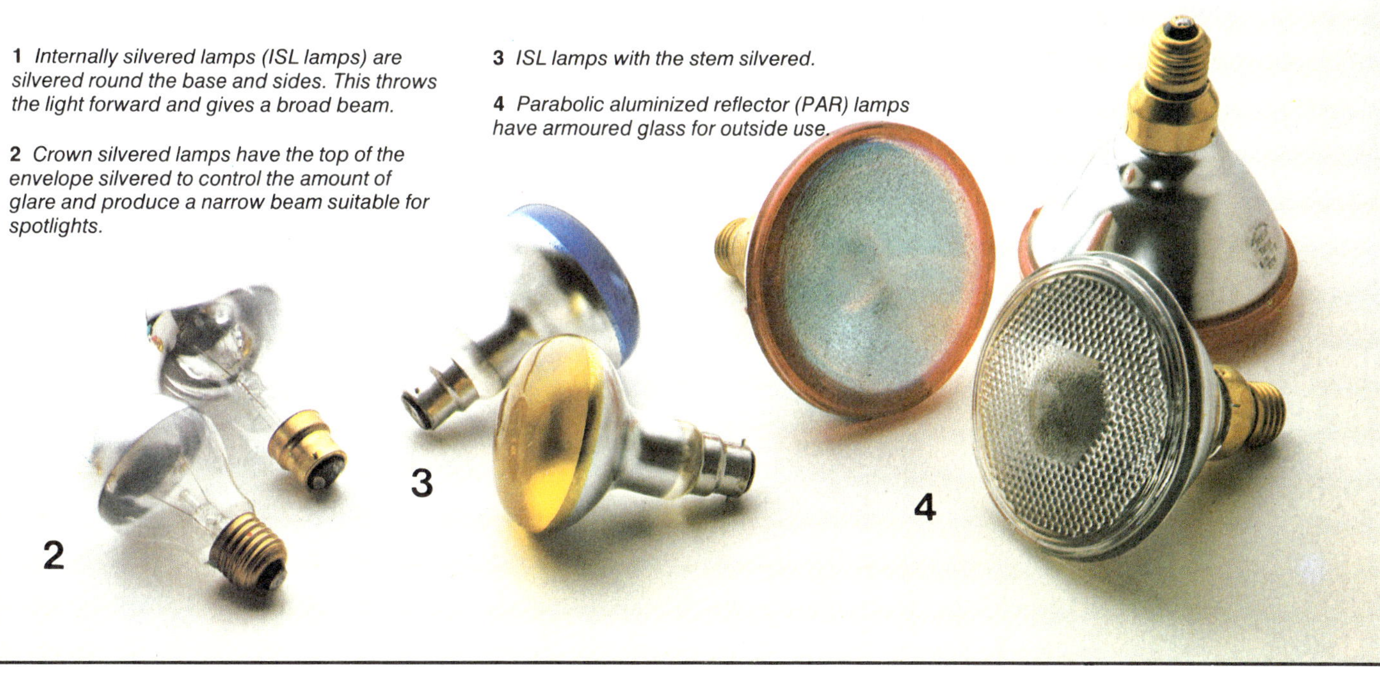

TUBES

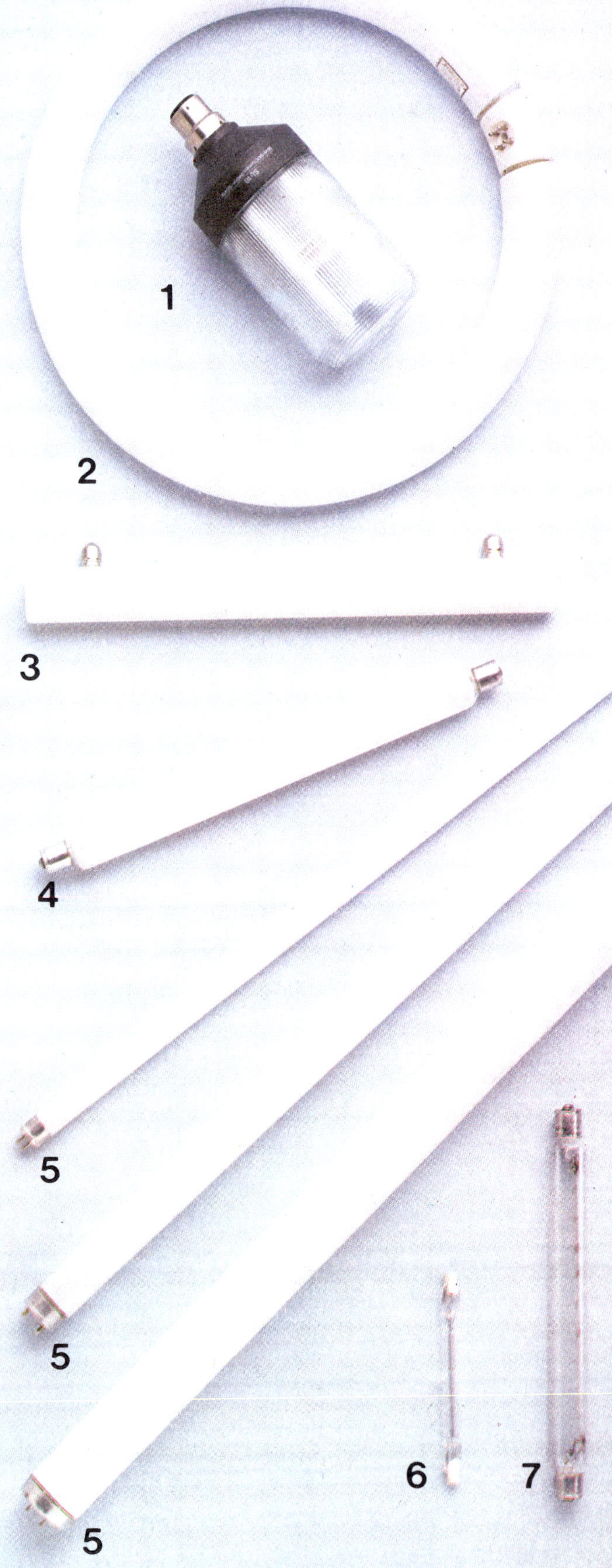

1 *SL lamps are a recent development and combine the efficiency and economy of the fluorescent tube with the convenience of an ordinary GLS lamp. They come with either Bayonet caps or Edison screws, and so can fit into any standard lampholders. As they are quite heavy you should check that your lampholder can take the extra weight.*

2 *Circular fluorescent tubes come in one of two diameters. There is the 300mm (12in) version which is 32W and the 400mm (16in) that can be either 40 or 60W. They are specially suited for use in bathrooms and come only in warm white.*

3 *Architectural tubes are often used to light paintings and pictures when a fluorescent tube would give too much light. They usually have special peg caps.*

4 *Double cap filament tubes are used in the same way as architectural tubes. They have single centre contacts.*

5 *Fluorescent tubes come in a number of different sizes and colours. The standard diameter is 38mm, while slimline tubes are only 26mm diameter. Miniature tubes, complete with miniature bi-pins, are perfect for installing above worksurfaces and are 15mm in diameter. Colours range from a bluish white to a warm pink white. If you want a fluorescent tube in a living area, it's best to aim for Deluxe warm white which will most closely match the yellow light given off by a filament lamp. Fluorescent tubes are particularly useful for lighting kitchens as they cast few shadows.*

6 *Tungsten Halogen lamps give an intense light from a small glass envelope. Special gas increases the efficacy of the filament and these lamps are being increasingly used in low voltage spotlamps in the home.*

7 *Linear filament tubes are used in the same way as other filament tubes and are specially useful for lighting a prominent painting or decorative feature.*

TYPES OF CAP

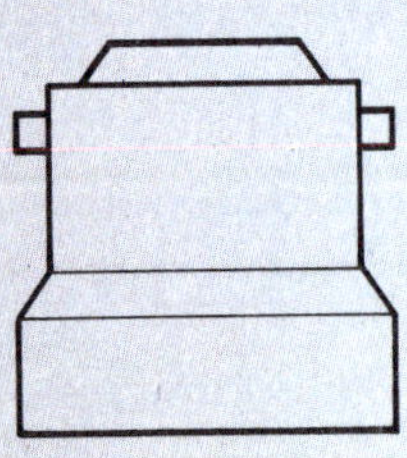

1 *Bayonet caps (BC) are fitted to most filament lamps. Usually 22mm in diameter, smaller lamps often have a 15mm version.*

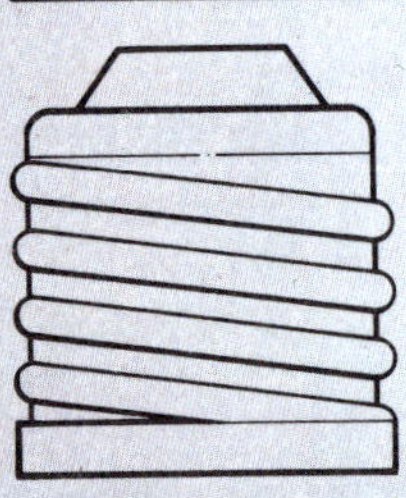

2 *Edison screw (ES) caps range from the miniature size on Christmas tree lamps to the giant that is seen on lamps over 300W.*

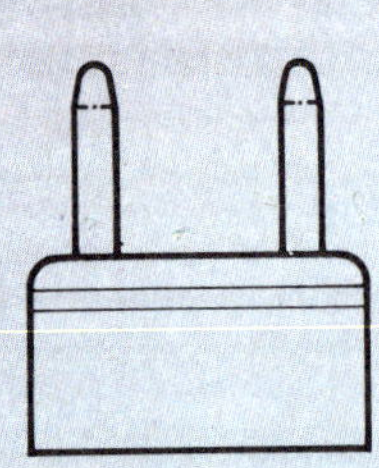

3 *Bi-pin end caps are fitted to most fluorescent tubes. The pins act as contacts and the caps are sized according to the tube diameter.*

4 *Single-centre contacts are normally fitted to filament tubes, although some tubes have peg caps.*

LIGHTING DESIGN: 2 the planning

Once you're familiar with the basic principles of lighting design, you can go on to some more detailed planning of your lighting and start to turn ideas into reality.

The lighting you choose for your home should meet two criteria: it should be functional, giving you light where you need it (and in the right quantity), and it should be decorative, enhancing the looks of the room concerned while conserving its character. The type of fitting chosen for each light source is of great importance (see pages 187–189) – certain fittings excel at particular jobs – but its positioning is ultimately responsible for helping to create exactly the effect you want.

Above all, the aim must be to provide a balanced mixture of light and shadow; uniformly bright lighting is stark and cheerless, while deep shadows are simply depressing. You can do this for the most part using fittings with tungsten light bulbs, or with fluorescent tubes concealed in some way and used for perimeter lighting. An unshielded fluorescent fitting, whether linear or circular, gives an overall flat lighting effect with no shadows, which robs a room of its character and makes it appear almost two-dimensional – satisfactory in a kitchen or garage, perhaps, but not for visual comfort in a living room.

LIGHT EFFECTS

You can create various effects by 'washing' walls with light. For perfect and graded washes, use wallwashers with reflector floods – all 150W for a perfect wash, in decreasing wattages for a graded one. For spill and scallop washes, use downlighters to graze the wall with light.

1 perfect wash

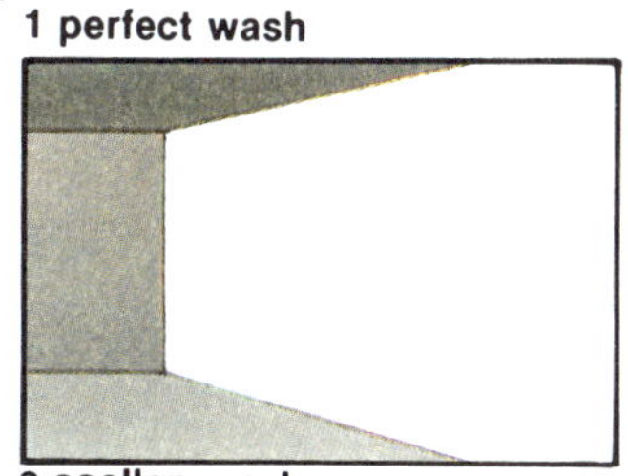

2 graded wash

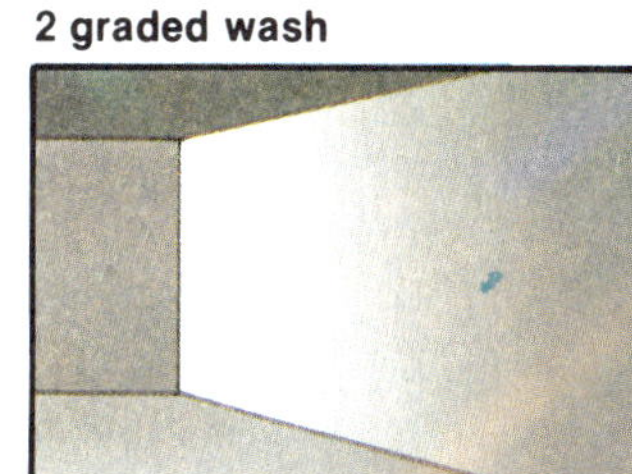

3 scallop wash

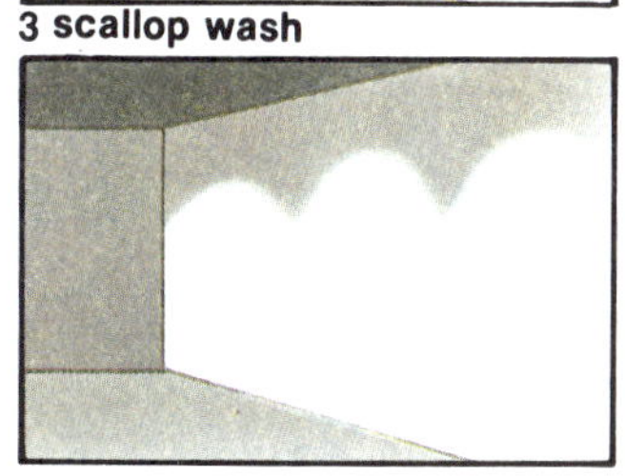

4 spill wash

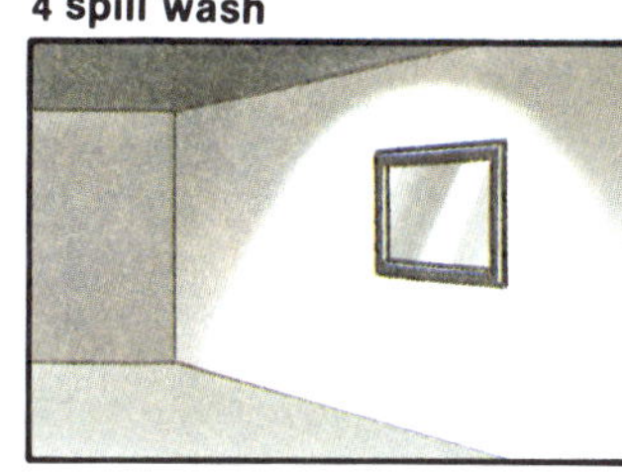

Lamp positions

There are a few simple guidelines to bear in mind when planning the positions of light fittings. The first golden rule is to ensure that naked bulbs cannot be seen by anyone in the room, whether standing, sitting or even lying (after all, you'll see most of your bedroom lighting effects from the bed). You can avoid this by judicious choice of fittings and shades, and also by thinking about the height of the fitting; examples are using a rise-and-fall fitting over a dining table, and setting wall lights low rather than high above bedheads.

Secondly, aim for an acceptable level of lighting throughout the room, even when local lights are providing extra illumination at individual points. This avoids creating pools of hard, dark shadows.

Thirdly, use lighting to highlight special features in the room; these can range from the obvious – an attractive fireplace or a group of pictures – to the sort of feature often ignored, such as a run of beautiful curtains that could be lit from above by perimeter lighting (behind pelmets) or wallwashers.

Lighting for special jobs

One activity needing good localised lighting is reading, and here a reflector lamp, table or standard lamp placed behind the chair gives the best illumination without glare. Where sewing is involved, even brighter illumination is needed, and a spotlight (wall-mounted or freestanding) is the best choice. For writing at a desk, a fluorescent or tungsten tube concealed behind a pelmet above the desk (or below its top shelf) will illuminate the whole desk surface and eliminate hand shadows; if a typewriter is being used, add an adjustable lamp to one side of the desk to illuminate the keyboard without creating glare. Lastly, amongst leisure pursuits, television watching comes fairly high, and here the aim should be to reduce contrast glare from the tube by providing low-level lighting behind the set – a dimmed wall light in an alcove, or a table lamp or standard lamp behind and to one side of the set.

In the kitchen, the first priority is good task lighting over work areas, and the best solutions are a ceiling-mounted fluorescent tube or track-light fitting over the sink and hob areas, and lighting above worktops concealed behind battens fixed to the underside of wall cupboards.

In the bedroom, the specific needs are bedhead lighting (two directional lights in shared bedrooms allow one person to read, the other to sleep) and good lighting at dressing tables, where the light should shine

LIGHTING FOR DOWNSTAIRS ROOMS

The best way to plan and co-ordinate your home lighting scheme is with a simple floor plan on which the position of fixtures and fittings are marked. This example is intended to show the scope you have for planning alternative lighting effects. In the living room the range of fittings allows general and task lighting, while wallwashers, track lighting and perimeter fittings allow a choice of lighting effects to be achieved. In the kitchen a central spotlight group back up the general and task lighting provided by fluorescent fittings on the ceiling and over the worktops.

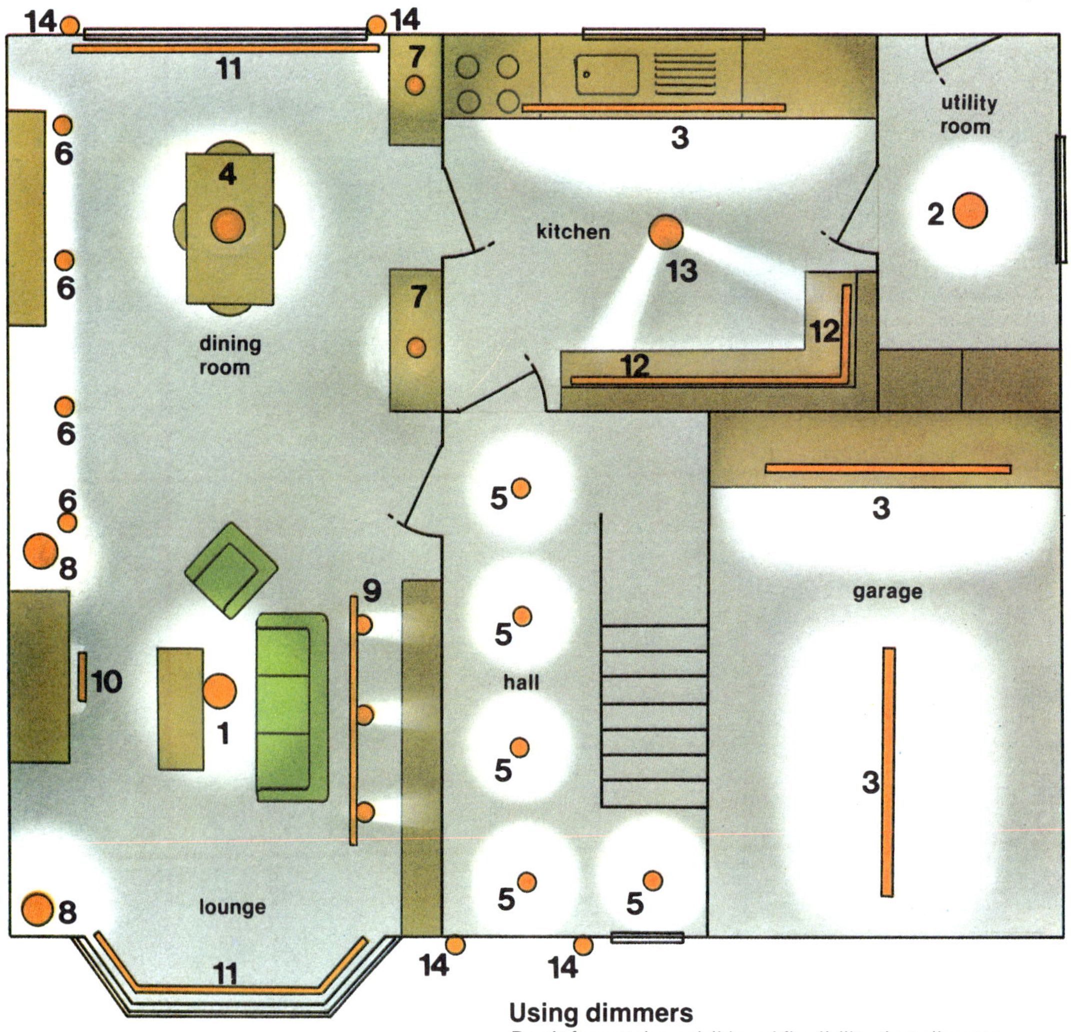

KEY

1 *Centre pendant fitting*
2 *Close-ceiling fitting*
3 *Fluorescent tube fitting*
4 *Rise-and-fall fitting*
5 *Recessed downlighters*
6 *Recessed wallwashers*
7 *Table lamps*
8 *Standard lamps*
9 *Track fitting with spotlights*
10 *Picture strip light*
11 *Perimeter lighting*
12 *Strip lighting over worktops*
13 *Ceiling-mounted spot group*
14 *Outside light*

Using dimmers
Don't forget the additional flexibility that dimmer controls can bring to lighting schemes of all types.

on the face, not the mirror. Table lamps or striplights at each side of the mirror offer the best lighting balance. The same point also applies to lighting next to mirrors in the bathroom, but make sure any lights chosen are switched from a point out of reach of bath, basin or shower.

One other specific form of task lighting is worth considering, and that is lighting in wardrobes and storage cupboards. Strip lighting positioned above the inner face of the door frame, or down each side if shelves would be in shadow, is the simplest answer, and control can be automatic if door switches are used. Remember that the circuit to such lights also requires an ordinary plateswitch, wired into the spur between the mains supply and the automatic switch/switches.

Room lighting

Apart from individual task lighting, every room needs more general illumination, and this can be provided in many different ways. Here are some of your options.

In the living room, the central pendant light (if fitted) should be an attractive feature unlit as well as lit. The same applies to wall lights, table and standard lamps too. Other forms of lighting tend to be more functional in their appearance – wallwashers and downlighters recessed into the ceiling, track lighting carrying spotlights above a display unit or a range of pictures, or perimeter fluorescent lighting hidden behind cornices or pelmets. Remember that an open-topped pelmet allows light to travel upwards and reflect off the ceiling. Where you are installing a run of downlighters or wallwashers, it's a good idea to have them individually switched so you can vary the areas of the room that are illuminated.

In the dining room the use of rise-and-fall fittings over dining tables has already been covered. What is needed in addition is some fairly subdued background lighting – say, wall lights or wallwashers illuminating the sideboard/serving area, or perimeter lighting throwing light downwards over curtains.

The landing, hall and stairs is one area of the home where good, bright lighting is essential; safety must take preference over 'mood', so that all parts of the stairwell are clearly lit without glare. Light should fall on the treads, with the risers in shadow. Suspended fittings must not be so low as to

LIGHTING FOR UPSTAIRS ROOMS

As with the downstairs, a simple floor plan makes it much easier to decide on what sort of lighting to provide for the various rooms. There is obviously less need for flexibility in bedrooms and bathrooms, but still plenty of scope for practical or restful effects to be achieved.
The most important points shown here include good lighting on landing and stairs (with the stair treads illuminated and the risers in shadow), adjustable light fittings at bedheads and over desks and dressing tables, and additional lighting in the bathroom for shaving, making up and showering.

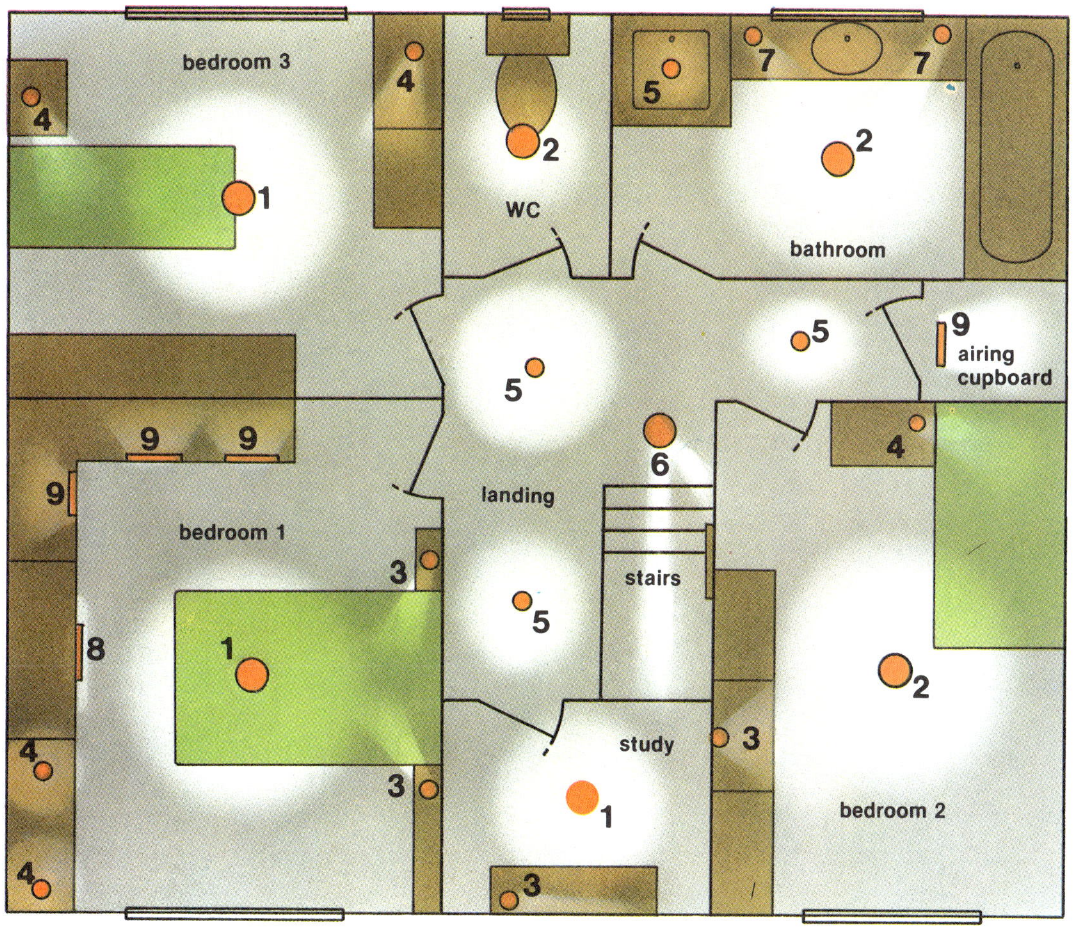

KEY
1 *Centre pendant fitting*
2 *Close-mounted ceiling fittings*
3 *Adjustable wall light*
4 *Adjustable table lamp*
5 *Recessed downlighters*
6 *Ceiling-mounted spot group*
7 *Wall-mounted strip light*
8 *Picture strip light*
9 *Strip lights for cupboard interiors (with door switches)*

For more information on choosing and installing lights and light fittings, see pages 187–192 and 196–220.

impede passage on the staircase. Downlighters can work extremely well if installed in the landing ceiling above an open flight; otherwise aim to light the flight from at least two positions so that it is evenly illuminated.

In kitchens you will need some sort of general lighting in addition to 'task' lighting over work surfaces. In a small kitchen this could be provided by the main ceiling-mounted fluorescent fitting, but you could experiment with either a close-ceiling fitting (easy to clean) or even track lighting carrying a number of spotlights directed towards the walls. If you eat in your kitchen too, add a rise-and-fall fitting over the table so you can turn off the fluorescent tube at meal-times and enjoy a softer light. Island bars are best illuminated with downlighters mounted directly above the bar surface.

Bedroom background lighting can be as simple or as sophisticated as you wish – ornate pendants, simple centre fittings, perimeter lighting or wall lights. However, do include two-way switching of whatever arrangements you choose, so that you aren't having to leap in and out of bed to turn lights on and off.

Lastly, in bathrooms a close-ceiling light, or even a fitting recessed into the ceiling itself, is the best way to provide even lighting over the whole room.

Drawing up your plans

The simplest way to plan your home lighting is to use sketch plans on which you can mark the positions of major pieces of furniture and the locations where task lighting will be required. The examples shown here illustrate the principle and help to give some idea of the scope and flexibility you have.

As you work out your requirements, don't hesitate to experiment with portable lamps and dummy fittings to see what effects you can achieve. For example, you can make up an extension cable carrying three or four lampholders with cardboard shades to try out the effect of a row of downlighters and wallwashers, or get a helper to hold spotlights in various positions in the room while you decide on the best angle and fitting height to choose. Light fittings and lamps are comparatively expensive, and a little time spent experimenting in this way will be worthwhile in the long run.

FLUORESCENT LIGHTING

Fluorescent lighting is glare-free and casts no hard, irritating shadows. It is therefore ideal for certain areas of the home, particularly the kitchen, bathroom, workroom and garage.

Many people have mixed feelings about fluorescent lights because of the nature or 'colour' of the light they emit. Admittedly they are not the best form of main lighting for living or dining areas as the light is harsh compared to ordinary tungsten filament light and doesn't give a relaxed atmosphere to the room. Nevertheless, they are ideal where good all-round lighting is required.

Fluorescent lighting can be fitted at any lighting point. However, an ordinary ceiling rose on a loop-in circuit will require some minor modification to the fixed wiring. This is not a difficult operation.

Types and uses

There are two basic types of fluorescent fitting – linear and circular – and both are made in a range of sizes. Circular tubes, in particular, are becoming more popular as they greatly improve the light output from a ceiling point and can be fitted flush to the ceiling and disguised with an attractive glass diffuser. The straight tubes likewise spread light evenly in a room, again often aided by a diffuser. In this case it's usually a corrugated or dimpled cover which is clipped over the fitting.

Fluorescent lights come in a variety of sizes; as a result they can be used for all sorts of purposes in kitchens, bathrooms, and in more specialised areas. For example, small tubes are ideal for concealed lighting in alcoves and can be hidden behind pelmets or baffles to highlight curtains drawn across a window. Sometimes they are used to feature cornices against the ceiling. There is also a type available which resembles a tungsten filament light bulb and can be used in an ordinary lampholder. And as the tubes last for 5,000 to 7,500 hours – about five year's average use – this more than compensates for the extra cost.

Installation and running costs

Fluorescent lights are more costly to install than a normal light, but because they are more efficient at turning electricity into light than a filament lamp they are cheaper to run. And they also have a longer life. In fact a 100W filament lamp will give light for ten hours for one unit of electricity (1 kilowatt/hour) while a 1500mm (5ft) tube will give four times as much light for the same cost over the same period.

The fluorescent fitting

There are two parts to a fluorescent fitting. The lamp itself is a long, thin glass tube, which is coated on the inside with a powder that fluoresces – gives off light – when the fitting is switched on. The tube contains argon gas, which is similar to neon, and a small amount of mercury, and at each end there is a tiny heater (electrode) which is coated in a special chemical. In some fittings there is more than one tube.

The other part of the fitting is the control gear. This is made up of several different components including a starter and 'choke' or 'ballast', and is responsible for starting up the light when it's switched on and controlling it when it's operating.

Most manufacturers sell an integral unit which incorporates both a tube and linear metal box designed to take the control gear. But they don't always have to be together. In fact, in some situations it's probably a good idea that they aren't. If you want to highlight some curtains, for example, you could conceal the tube behind a pelmet board or a baffle, holding it in place with spring clips about 150mm (6in) from the material. It should be connected to the control gear, which can be mounted on a solid surface nearby, using 0.5mm^2 (3 amp) or 0.75mm^2 (6 amp) flex. As the choke can

KNOW YOUR WIRING

If you are replacing a pendant fitting with a fluorescent light, you first need to check what type of wiring is at the ceiling rose. It doesn't matter whether you've got one of the neat, modern roses or an older style one mounted on a pattress or block as it will have to be removed before putting up the new fitting.

With loop-in wiring you might find two, three or four cables going into the rose. The black core of the switch cable going to the switch (SW) terminal should be wrapped with red PVC tape as it is live and not neutral, but in many cases you'll see this hasn't been done.

If you have junction box wiring there'll only be one cable going into the rose.

Don't be alarmed if there's no earth on

get rather warm, the control gear should have some ventilation.

Given the positions where most fluorescents are used, it's unlikely you'll want to be able to control their brilliance. If you do you'll need to use a special dimmer and modify the fitting.

How the light works

In an ordinary tungsten bulb electricity flowing through the filament causes it to heat up to a white heat and so emit visible light. In a fluorescent tube there's no filament, but the electricity flowing between the two heater elements at each end causes the mercury vapour in the tube to emit ultra-violet (invisible) light. This is converted to visible light by the fluorescent powder on the inside of the tube.

In order to get an electric current to flow in the tube a high voltage is needed initially when the light is switched on. And it's the function of the choke and starter to provide this. At the same time the starter also has to heat up the elements. Once the light is operating, the starter switches itself off while the choke and power factor correction capacitor (PFCC) regulate the current flowing through the tube.

There are two types of starter. The thermal type has a tiny heating element which acts like a thermostat and turns off the current in the starter circuit when the elements are hot enough and current is flowing in the tube. The more common starter is the two-pin 'glow' type which doesn't have its own internal heating element.

Quick-start fittings

Some fittings have 'quick start' ballasts that don't need a starter, but a special tube is required with a metal strip running along its length, which is earthed at the lampholders at either end. When the light is switched on the current passes down the tube immediately – so there is no flick-flick effect or delay in the tube lighting. This type of fitting needs to be earthed. The manufacturers' catalogues usually contain details and circuit diagrams.

Ready Reference

FLUORESCENT LIGHT SIZES

Linear tubes range in length from 150mm (6in) to 2400mm (8ft). Tube diameters are

- 15mm (5/8in) – miniature
- 25mm (1in) – slimline
- 38mm (1 1/2in) – standard

Light output varies from 4 to 125 watts.

Circular tubes are made in diameters of:

- 300mm (1ft) rated at 32 watts
- 400mm (1ft 4in) rated at 40 and 60 watts.

The most popular tube sizes for the home are 1200mm (4ft) with a light output of 40 watts and 1500mm (5ft) with light outputs of 65 and 80 watts. These are sold complete with their controls and usually a baffle or diffuser to disguise the tube. Apart from the tubes which give off 'white' light, others are available which give off pink, red, green, gold and blue light.

TYPES OF TUBE

Most fluorescent lights use the common bi-pin type of tube. There are two pins at each end which push into the sockets of the fitting to make the connection. The other type of tube is the bayonet type with a connection similar to that of an ordinary light bulb. It's now only found on 1500mm (5ft) 80W tubes.

A 40W tube 1200mm long will give adequate general lighting.

PARTS OF THE FITTING

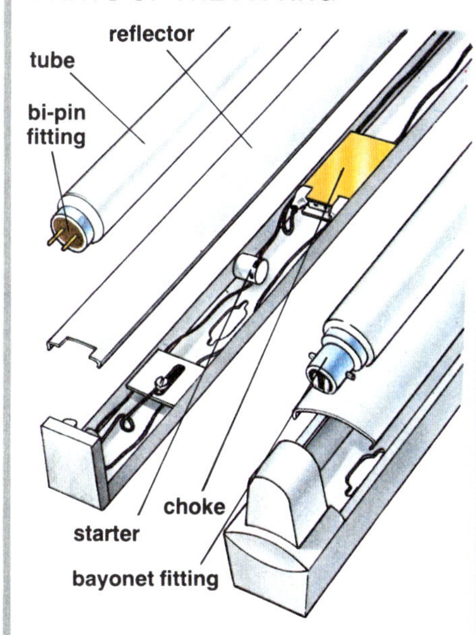

Loop-in wiring system

the lighting circuit, because two-core cable was once used for wiring. But when putting in the fluorescent light you'll have to make a separate connection to the main earthing

Rose on a junction box system

terminal. You'll have to run two-core and earth cable from the junction box to the fitting and then a single core 1.5mm² earth cable to the consumer unit.

MODIFYING LOOP-IN WIRING

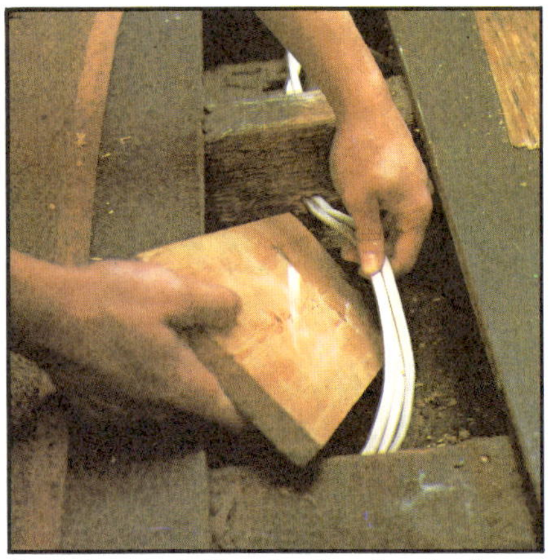

1 *Before installing the four-terminal junction box, you have to fix a wooden batten between the joists near the lighting point.*

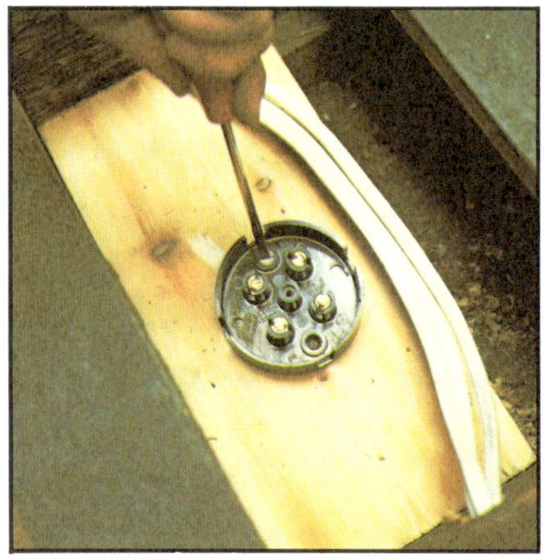

2 *Screw the junction box to the batten – it makes fixing the cores that much easier – and draw the cables into the ceiling void, then run them to the box.*

3 *Take earths to one terminal, red cores of the supply cables to another, black neutrals to a third and black switch core with red PVC to the fourth.*

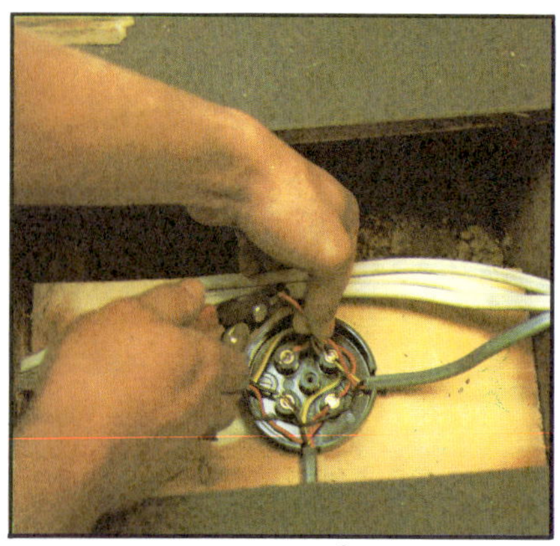

4 *Lay a length of 1.0mm^2 two-core and earth cable from the lighting point to the junction box, strip back the sheathing and prepare the cores.*

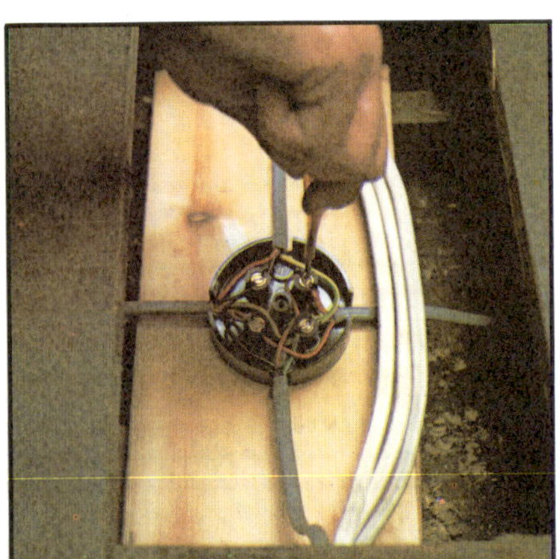

5 *After you've sleeved the earth core and connected it to the earth terminal, take the red to the switch terminal and the black to the neutrals.*

6 *Follow the same procedure if you have to extend the lighting cable on an existing junction box system, and don't forget to screw on the cover.*

Colour range

Fluorescent tubes are manufactured to give off different types of light. In all there are 13 different colours to choose from. These range from the very cold white 'northlight' to the warmer yellow colours. Most of the fittings sold in retail lighting shops are supplied with a tube marked 'warm white' – a colour that isn't really warm when compared with the yellow light given out by an ordinary filament lamp. The tubes giving a yellow light are listed as 'de luxe warm white'.

Some fittings such as the very useful circular fluorescents with their diffusers and some of the 25/26mm slimline tubes are available in 'warm white' or the colder 'natural'. The very neat 15/16mm miniature tubes are available in three or four colours, but not in 'de luxe warm white'. 'Warm white' tubes are ideal for the kitchen, but they're not really acceptable for living rooms except for lighting small areas displaying ornaments or paintings, for example. Here the colder colour of the fluorescent can be compensated by tungsten lighting elsewhere in the room. Colours such as 'daylight' and 'natural' are not really suitable for the home except for display cabinets.

Installing the fitting

You can install a fluorescent fitting almost anywhere instead of an existing tungsten filament lamp. If you want to connect the fitting to an existing lighting point, you'll first need to inspect the fitting or rose that's already there to see how the circuit is wired. If there is only one cable going into the rose or fitting on the fixed wiring side – ie, there's one black and one red insulated core and possibly an earth wire – then the circuit is wired on the junction box system. All you have to do when putting up the fluorescent light is to connect the cores to the relevant terminals in the fitting – black to the 'N' terminal, red to the 'L' terminal and the earth (which should be sleeved in green/yellow PVC) to the 'E' terminal.

However, if you've got loop-in wiring where there are two or more cables going into the fitting or rose, then some small modifications are necessary as there are no loop-in terminal facilities on a fluorescent fitting. All you have to do is to draw the cables back into the ceiling void or loft space and fit the cores to the relevant terminals of a four-terminal junction box. You then have to run a short piece of 1.0mm^2 two-core and earth flat PVC-sheathed cable from the junction box to the fluorescent light and connect it to the terminals.

If, as in many circuits, there is no earthing at the lighting point, it's necessary to run 1.5mm^2 green/yellow PVC-insulated cable from the fluorescent fitting back to the earthing terminal block in the consumer unit.

CONNECTING THE FITTING

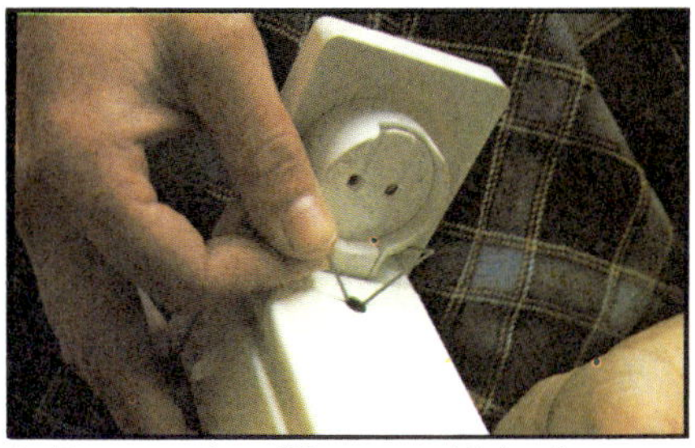

1 *Remove the diffuser and tube from the fitting and take off the backplate cover by undoing the retaining screws and prising out the spring clips.*

2 *Use the template supplied with the fitting – or the backplate itself – to test that the fixing holes are sound; then screw the fitting into position.*

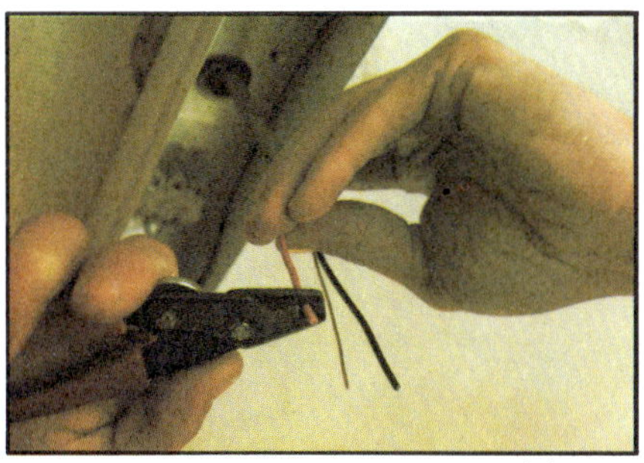

3 *If you've had to lay in a new cable, strip back the sheathing and prepare the cores. Don't forget, there should be a rubber grommet round the cable entry.*

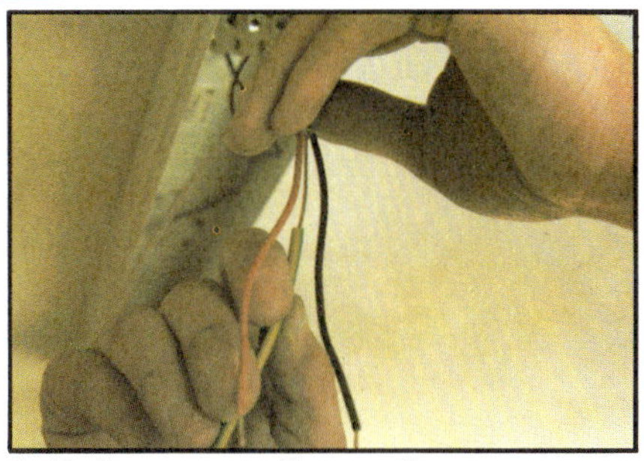

4 *Before connecting up the cores, you need to slip a length of greenlyellow PVC sleeving over the earth wire so there is no exposed wire in the fitting.*

5 *Push the cores well into their terminals and screw down the retaining screws. The back of the earth terminal is connected to the metal backplate.*

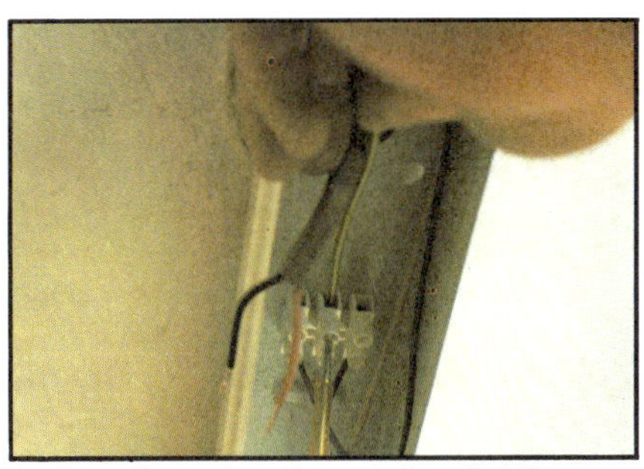

6 *If you're using the existing lighting cable and it's only two-core, you'll have to run a separate earth core from the fitting to the main earthing point.*

7 *Push the starter into its socket, which you'll find on the outside of the backplate. You have to twist it clockwise to secure it in position.*

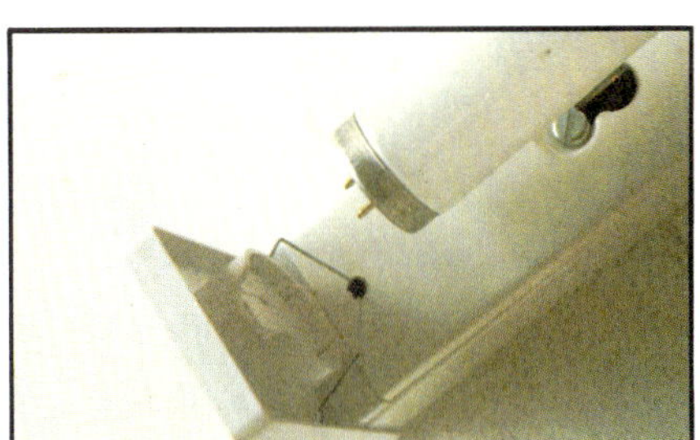

8 *Replace the cover of the backplate and refit the spring clips. The tube is inserted in the holders at each end, which spring outwards for easy fitting.*

Ready Reference

FAULTS AND REMEDIES

Turn off the power at mains when carrying out repairs other than changing the tube itself.

FAULT Tube flickers and is reluctant to light, or tube glows at each end but fails to start.

Solution Faults could be due to malfunctioning starter; if so fit new one. Or it could be an ageing tube. Look for tell-tale signs of blackening at ends of tube; if present fit new tube of same size and type.

FAULT Tube glows at one end and flashes.

Solution Check tube connections. If pin holders damaged or bent, fit new holder.

FAULT Strong oily smell.

Solution Check the choke for signs of burning and replace it making sure you use the correct type to match the wattage of tube.

REPLACING A STARTER

A simple operation – locate the starter, push in and twist anti-clockwise to remove. Replace with a new one of the same type.

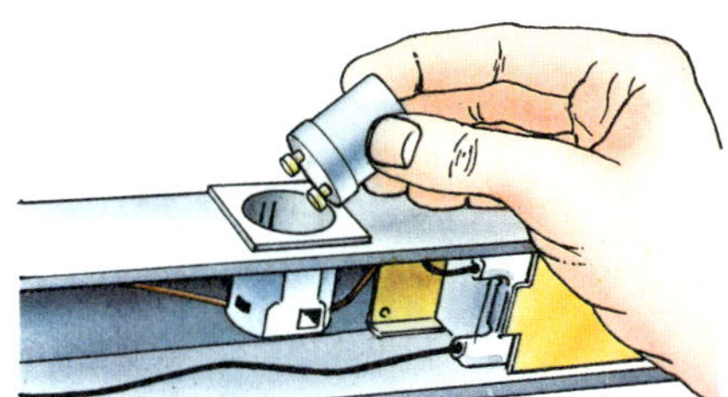

REPLACING A TUBE

With a bayonet-type fitting (1), push in and twist the tube against the spring-loaded lampholders. With a bi-pin tube (2), simply pull back one of the spring-loaded end brackets.

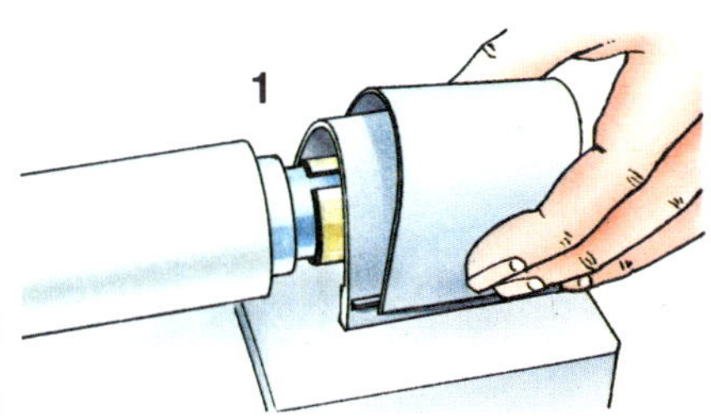

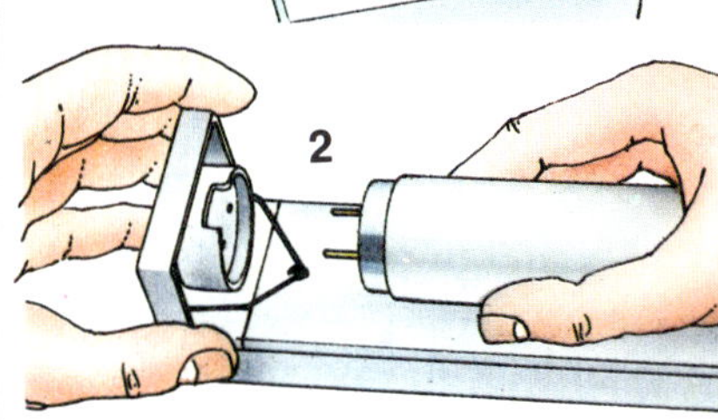

DECORATIVE LIGHTS

There is a tremendous range of decorative ceiling lights from which to choose. Normally they replace an existing rose and pendant fitting. They're not difficult to install but they may require some modification to the existing wiring.

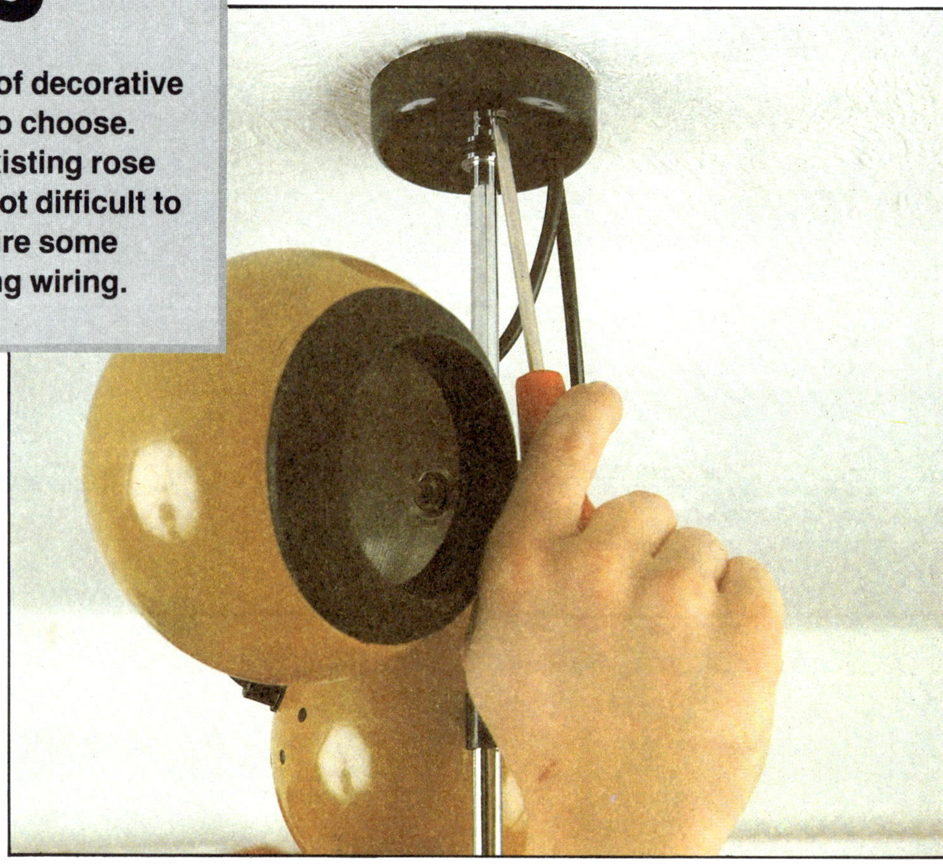

Lighting in a room has become more sophisticated. Whereas a central light was once the only form of lighting, giving uneven illumination and shadowy corners, you can now use spotlights, concealed lighting, wall-washers and downlighters, as well as table and standard lamps, to create more interesting lighting effects.

But the central light still has an important role to play. The tendency is for it to be more decorative and less functional; to be an attractive feature in a room even when turned off. You can, of course, always change lampshades to transform an ordinary pendant fitting, but there is now an ever-increasing number of decorative fittings which replace the pendant ceiling rose entirely. Whether they are ornate chandeliers, glass and brass lanterns or modern designs in multi-coloured acrylics, the choice is so large there is something to match the decoration in any room.

These fittings either hang down from the ceiling on a rod, chain or cord, or are close-mounted on the surface.

Close-mounted fittings are the answer to many lighting problems in smaller houses and flats, or in houses with low ceilings, because they give a good general spread of light and are unobtrusive.

As general room lights, ceiling-mounted spotlights can make a room look rather bare and cold. However, you can use other lights to supplement them. You can also use lighting track to enable more than one spotlight to be used from the same lighting point. Sometimes, particularly in smaller houses, bulky lighting track can look obtrusive. You can remedy this by recessing it into the ceiling, but you'll have to make sure that the track you buy is suitable.

Rise-and-fall pendants enable you to adjust the height of a light simply by pulling it down to the required level. They have particular uses other than over a dining table. Breakfast bars and through-room conversions from kitchen to dining room are becoming increasingly popular, and rise-and-fall pendants are ideal here because they can be pushed out of the way when the meal is finished.

Inspecting the fitting

Although the designs of decorative fittings vary enormously, there are only three ways in which they can be connected to the main lighting circuit. The method you adopt will depend on the type of fitting and the way the lighting circuit has been wired.

If you have a close-mounted fitting this will probably have a plastic or metal backing plate which you have to screw to the ceiling. You'll find three connectors attached to the plate and these take the cores of the circuit cable (red to live or 'L', black to neutral or 'N' and the earth to the earth terminal). If the lighting circuit isn't earthed (ie, if it's wired in two-core cable), and the fitting has a metal backing plate, then this needs to be earthed. You'll need to run a 1.5mm^2 green/yellow insulated earth wire from the terminal on the plate right back to the earthing terminal at the consumer unit or fuse box. If there's no earth terminal on the plate then you'll have to drill a small hole and insert a nut, bolt and washer set to which you can fix the earth wire. The glass or plastic cover of the fitting is screwed or clipped to the backing plate so that the bulb is totally enclosed.

If you've got a pendant-type fitting this will have either a two-core or three-core flex. Two-core flexes are used when a fitting is mainly made of plastic or a non-conductive material. If a fitting contains metal parts,

FITTING A BESA BOX

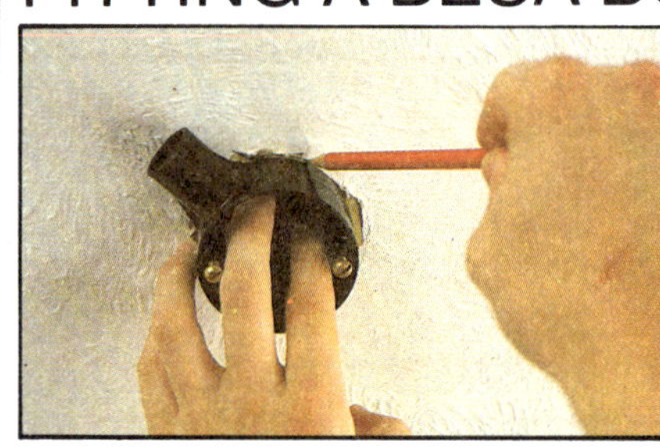

1 *Disconnect the rose and draw the cables back into the ceiling void. Then mark the position of a terminal BESA box on the ceiling surface.*

4 *Push the BESA box into the recess and screw it to the joist. Alternatively, fix a batten between the joists and screw the box in place to this.*

INSTALLING A JUNCTION BOX

1 *Mount a four-terminal junction box on a batten fixed between two joists. Disconnect the cables from the loop-in rose and draw them back to this position.*

2 *Connect the live cores to one terminal, the neutrals to a second and the earths to a third. The black of the switch cable goes to a fourth.*

3 *Lay a length of 1.0mm^2 two-core and earth cable from the lighting point to the junction box and prepare the ends, remembering to sleeve the earth core.*

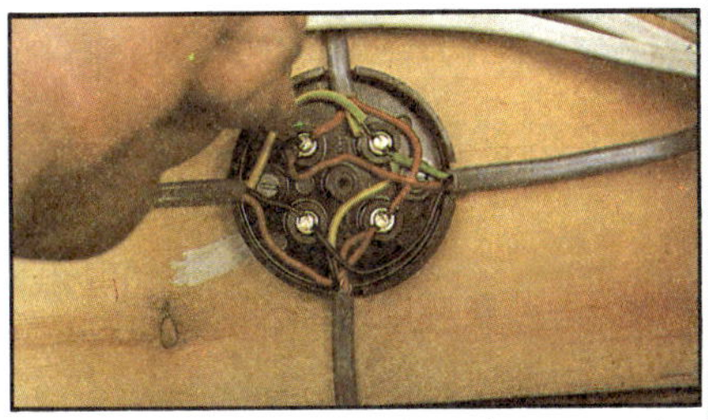

4 *Connect the sleeved earth core to the earth terminal, the black core to the neutral terminal and the red core to the switch terminal (top left).*

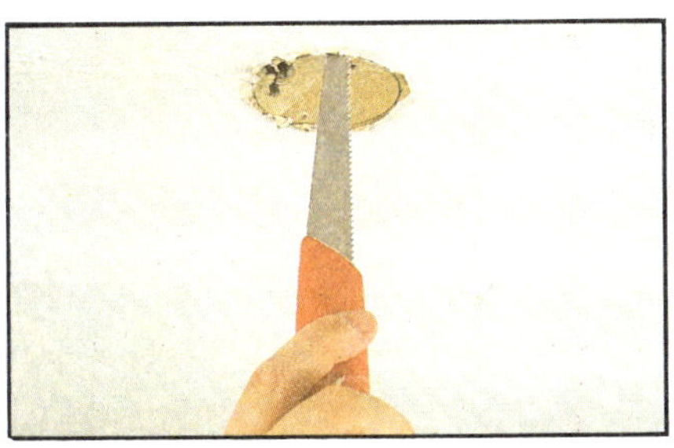

2 *Cut out the circular section of ceiling using a pad saw or keyhole saw. Make sure the cables are well out of the way to prevent damaging them.*

TIP

3 *If the lighting point is partly under a joist. use a wood bit in a power drill to cut away part of the joist to the depth of the BESA box.*

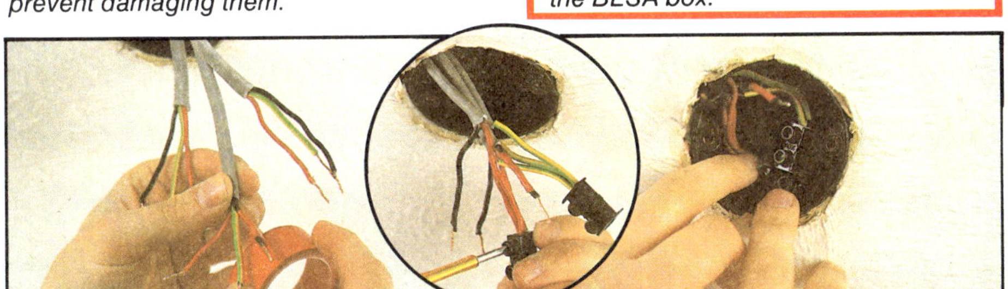

5 *With loop-in wiring, draw the feed and switch cables into the BESA box. Wrap red PVC insulating tape round the black core of the switch cable.*

6 *Connect the lives, neutrals and earths up to three separate connectors, and the taped switch core to a fourth (inset). Push all four up into the BESA box.*

Ready Reference

TYPES OF DECORATIVE LIGHT

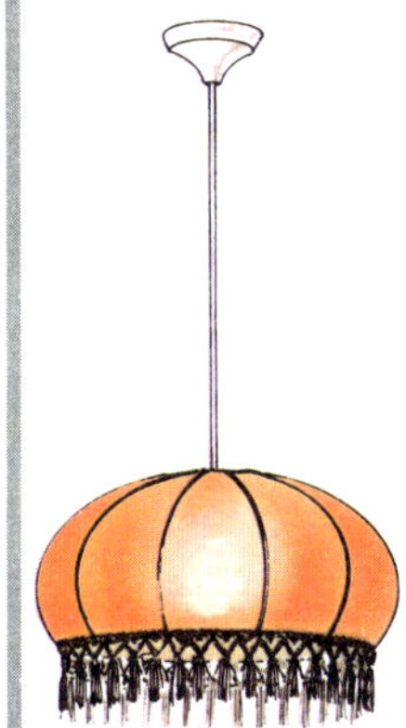

Pendant type

Chain fitting

Stem spotlight

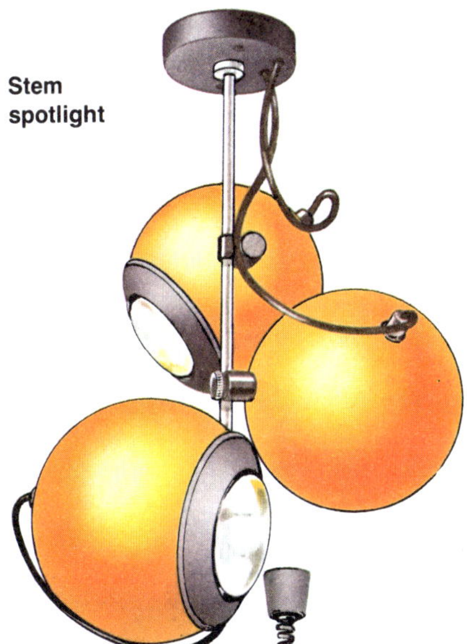

Rise-and-fall fitting

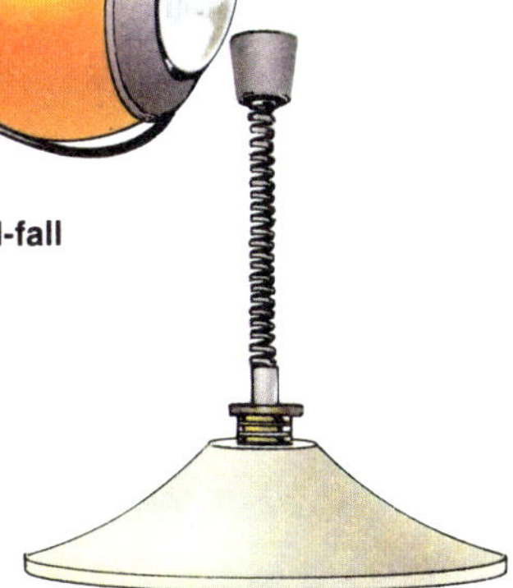

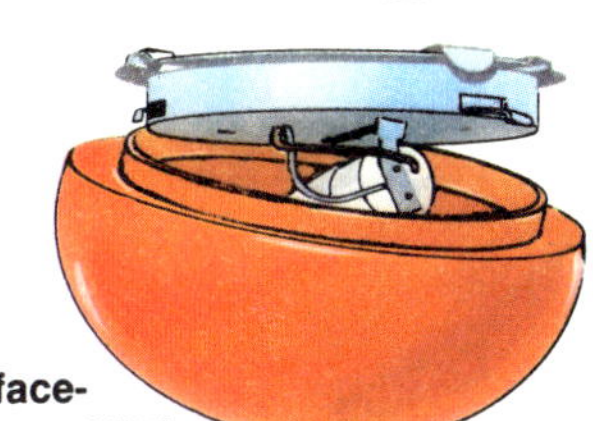

Surface-mounted fitting

SURFACE-MOUNTED FITTING

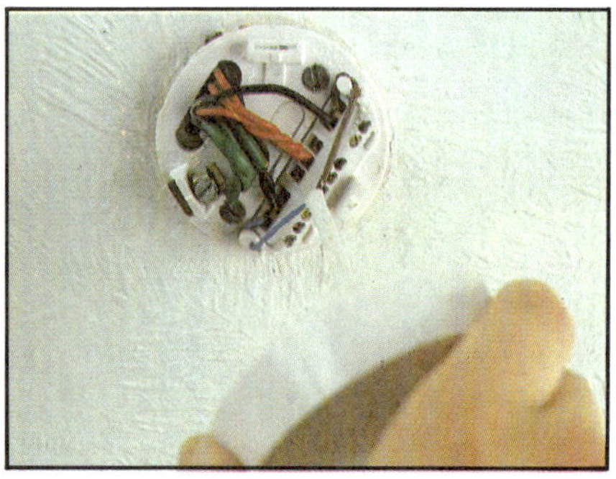

1 *Unscrew the ceiling rose to inspect the wiring. If it's the loop-in type you'll need to remove it and install a junction box (see page 51).*

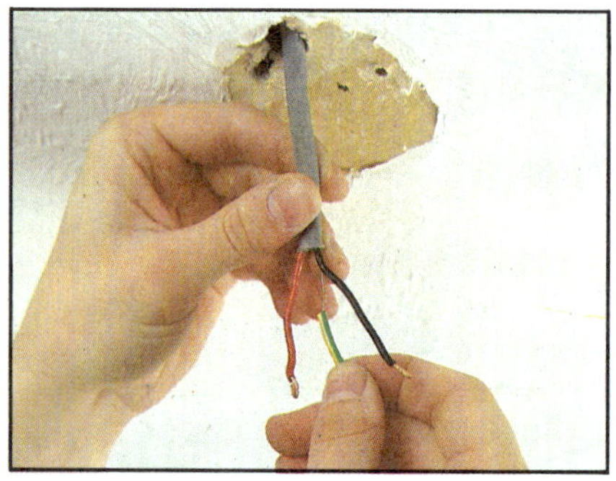

2 *Lay a cable from the junction box to the lighting point, prepare the cores and sleeve the earth in greenlyellow PVC sleeving.*

3 *Screw the fixing bar of the fitting into position. You should be able to use the same fixing holes that were used for the original rose.*

4 *It's a wise precaution to slip heat-resistant sleeving over the live and neutral cores before connecting the cores to the terminal block.*

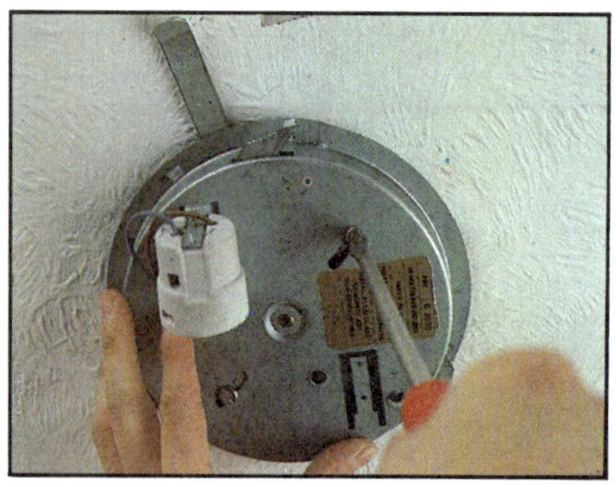

5 *The base plate can then be screwed to the fixing bracket. Pull out the lever and slide it round so that the fixing catches are fully recessed.*

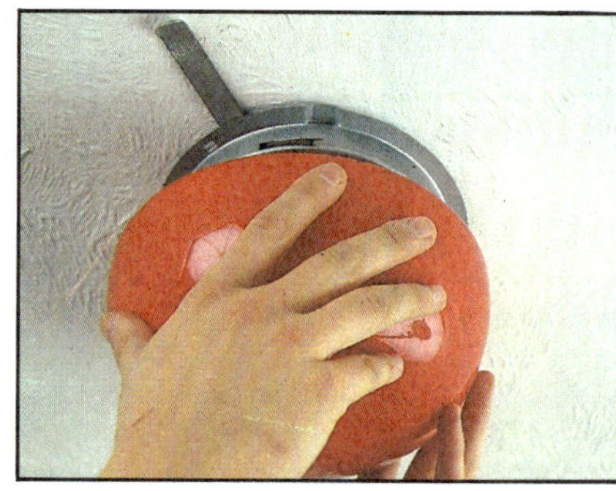

6 *Insert a bulb into the lampholder and position the cover. Rotate the lever so the catches slip under the rim to secure it, then push the lever out of sight.*

even a lampshade ring, then it must be earthed and so it should have a three-core flex. This is particularly necessary for pendants, which are suspended from a flat, metal ceiling-plate by a chain, and for the type where the flex runs down a hollow rod to the lights, as in some stem spotlights.

Making the connection

In all probability, your fitting will not connect directly to a ceiling rose and so you'll first have to remove the rose. But remember that before you carry out any electrical work you must turn off the power first. If you've got lighting track you can connect the flex from an existing ceiling rose into it, but this isn't a very neat method.

Once you've unscrewed the rose cover you'll be able to tell what type of wiring you've got – junction (joint) box or loop-in (see *Ready Reference*). However, it's not so obvious to see how the fitting connects to the wiring when the rose is removed. The fixing plates of, for example, pendants which you have to attach to the ceiling don't have a provision for connecting the flex of the fitting to the circuit wiring.

Close-mounted fittings

Probably the simplest combination is to have a close-mounted fitting with junction box wiring., You should be able to draw the mains cable through the fitting base plate, screw the plate to the ceiling and then connect the cable cores to the fitting terminal block. But if you've got loop-in wiring there's no facility for dealing with all the cores. The best thing to do is to draw all the cables back into the roof space or ceiling void and install a four-terminal junction box. You can then lead a single cable from this into the fitting.

Installing a pendant-type fitting

Despite the fact that there is a wide range of pendant-type fittings, they are connected up in basically the same way. Some are attached to the ceiling by a flat, metal plate which may have a decorative cover. With this type of fitting there is no provision for linking the flex to the lighting circuit, although some modern fittings have a base plate deep enough to take terminal connectors which allow the circuit wiring and the flex of the fitting to be joined together.

Where there is no space behind the base plate to fit connectors, you'll have to install a BESA box. This is now more commonly referred to as a terminal conduit box and it provides a protected recess in the ceiling for housing the connectors for joining the lighting circuit to the flex. Connectors have to be fitted regardless of whether you have loop-in or junction box wiring.

The boxes are made of metal or tough PVC and if you use the metal type you'll need to earth it. Sometimes, however, there is no earthing terminal, so you'll have to wrap the earths round one of the fixing screws – a fiddly job – or you can drill a hole and insert a nut, bolt and washer set to which you can attach the earth. PVC boxes don't need to be earthed.

To install the box, you'll need to cut out a small circle of ceiling so the box can be set flush to the surface. If your existing ceiling rose is screwed to a joist, you may need to drill out some of the joist to position the box. And if you can't do this you'll have to install a wooden batten between the joists and screw the box to this (see *Ready Reference* on facing page).

PENDANT-TYPE FITTINGS

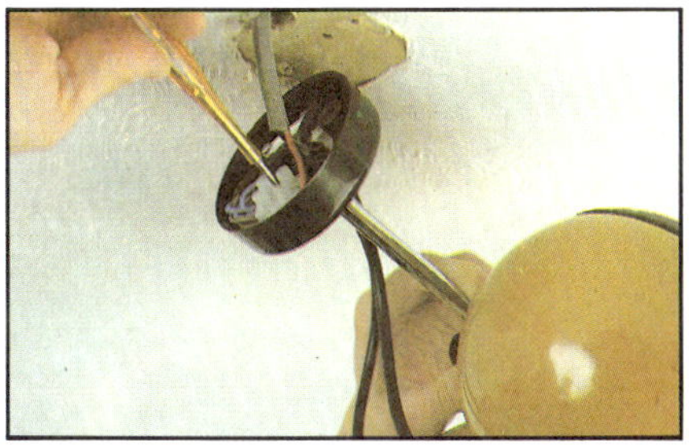

1 *With stem spotlights there may be room in the base plate for the terminal connectors, particularly if you have junction box wiring.*

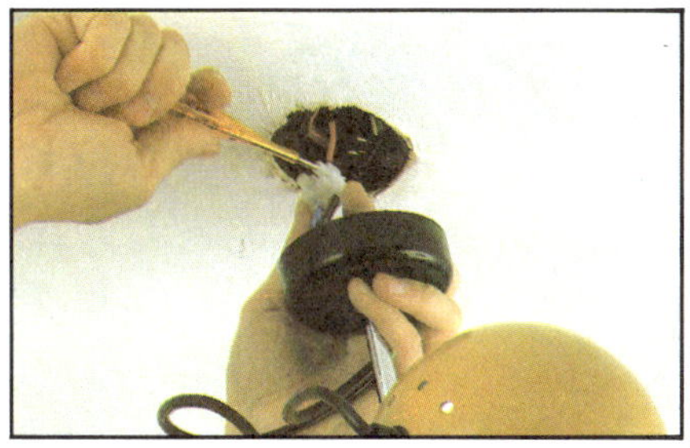

2 *If you install a BESA box to deal with loop-in wiring, attach the blue flex to the connector housing the neutrals and the brown to the taped switch core.*

3 *With a chain fitting there's usually no room behind the base plate to connect the wiring to the flex so you'll have to install a BESA box.*

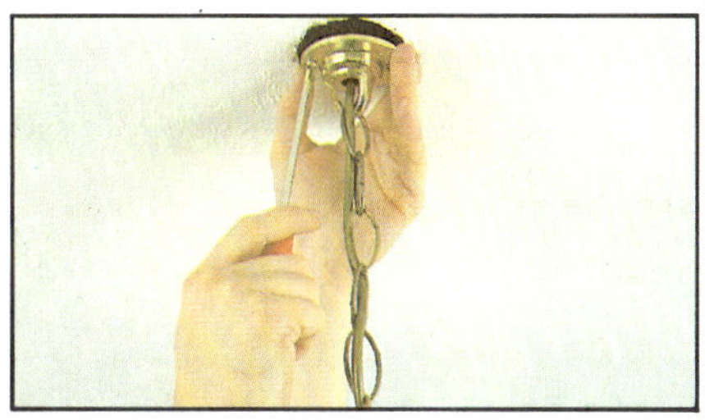

4 *The flex of the fitting is threaded through the chain which is suspended from a hook on the base plate to take the weight of the lampholder and shade.*

RISE-AND-FALL FITTING

1 *Install a BESA box in the ceiling and connect the cores of the circuit cables to the relevant connectors. Then screw the base plate and hook to the box.*

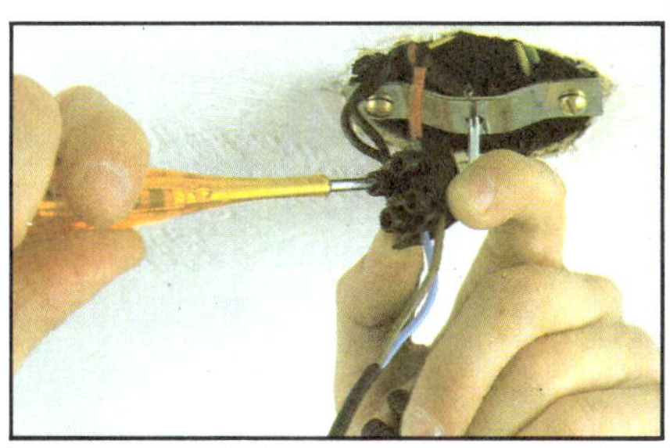

2 *The flex will probably be attached to a terminal block. Connect the neutral cores to the blue flex connector and the switch core to the brown one.*

3 *The rise-and-fall unit can now be slipped over the hook and the up-and-down movement adjusted by tightening or loosening the control screw.*

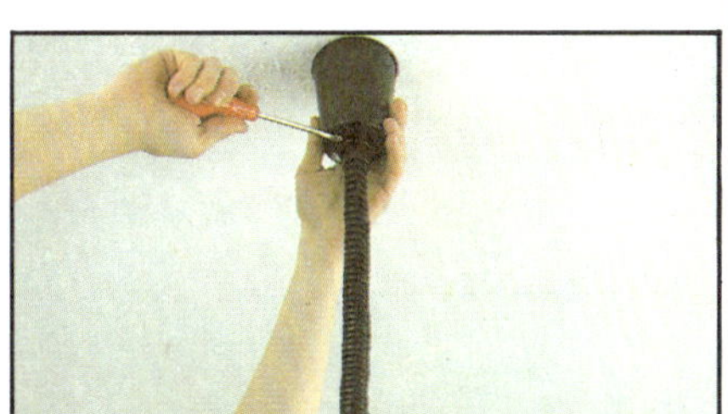

4 *Push the plastic cover up to the ceiling to conceal the rise-and-fall unit and secure it in position with a grub-screw. Then fit the shade and bulb.*

Ready Reference

BESA BOXES

Otherwise known as terminal conduit boxes. Install them where there is no room behind the base plate of the fitting to join the circuit cable to the flex. They are made of metal or tough PVC.

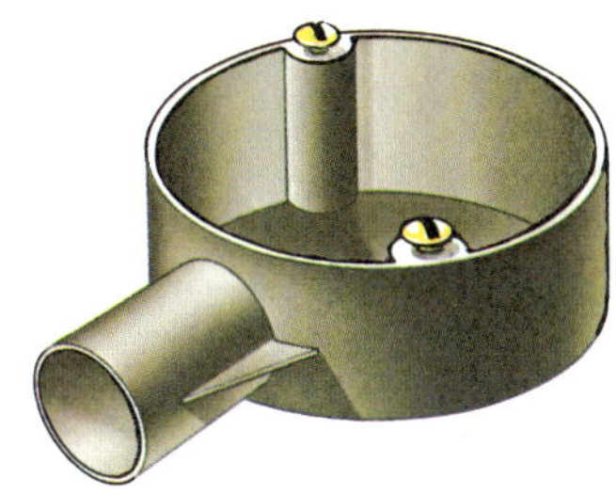

WAYS OF FIXING A BESA BOX

The box must be recessed into the ceiling and screwed to a joist or fixing batten.

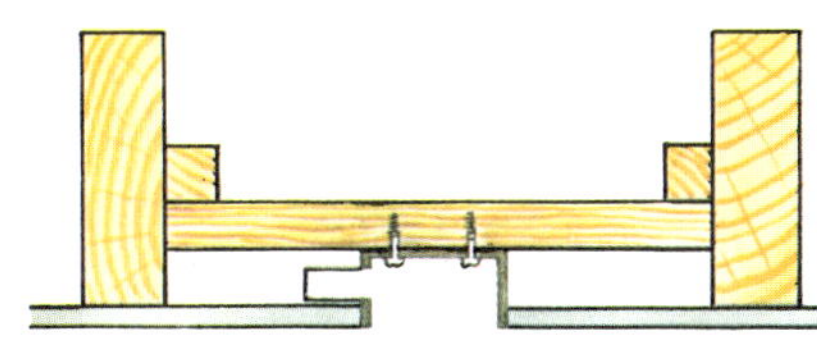

DEALING WITH THE WIRING

With loop-in wiring you will usually have to remove the loop-in rose and install a BESA box. Connect the mains and switch cables to the flex from the fitting using terminal connectors as shown (A). With junction-box wiring you may not need a BESA box unless the fitting is suspended from one; connect the single feed cable either directly to the terminals on the fitting, or use terminal connectors (B).

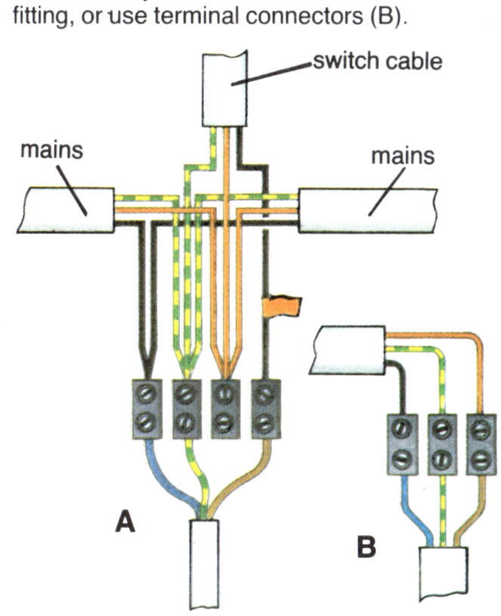

INSTALLING WALL LIGHTS

Ceiling lights are simple and effective, but if you want a lighting scheme that is a little more exciting, more decorative and more versatile, they are not enough. One solution is to fit wall lights. Here's how.

There are two keys to a really successful lighting scheme: variety and versatility. Variety, because having a uniform level of light throughout a room is just plain boring. And versatility because your lighting needs change from one part of the room to another. In a living room, for example, you may prefer the overall lighting level to be fairly low and restful, but you will still need pools of intense light for reading, or perhaps simply to show off decorative feature like pictures, plants or ornaments. That's where wall lights come in. They are very good at creating interesting pools of light.

Choosing a light

With so many wall lights to choose from where do you start? It really depends on what you want the light to do. Few provide a light you can put to practical use. Most are purely decorative.

The traditional wall light is a good example. It normally has a low wattage, candle-shaped lamp, mounted on a wooden base, and concealed behind a pretty parchment shade, so that it spreads a fan of soft light across the wall.

More recent versions take the imitation candelabra and gaslight theme still further, having ornate brass, copper, and aluminium stems, and, instead of shades, translucent bowls in plain, coloured, frosted, smoked, and sculpted glass or plastic. They tend to use more powerful bulbs, and can be made to light the top or bottom of the wall, but the net result is the same. They are for looking at, rather than seeing by.

This is also true of many modern wall light designs. There are, for example, cylindrical fittings open at top and bottom to spread a shaft of light in two directions, either vertically or horizontally.

Still attractive, but producing a more useful light, there are the fully enclosed fittings. 'Opals', for example, create a beautifully soft, even light, and look rather like round, square or rectangular blocks of milky glass or plastic. For those who prefer more ornate lights, sculpted glass versions (they look like cut crystal) are also available. Enclosed fittings are particularly handy where space is limited – in a hallway, perhaps – and since many are weatherproof, they are an excellent choice for the humid atmosphere of a bathroom or an outside porch.

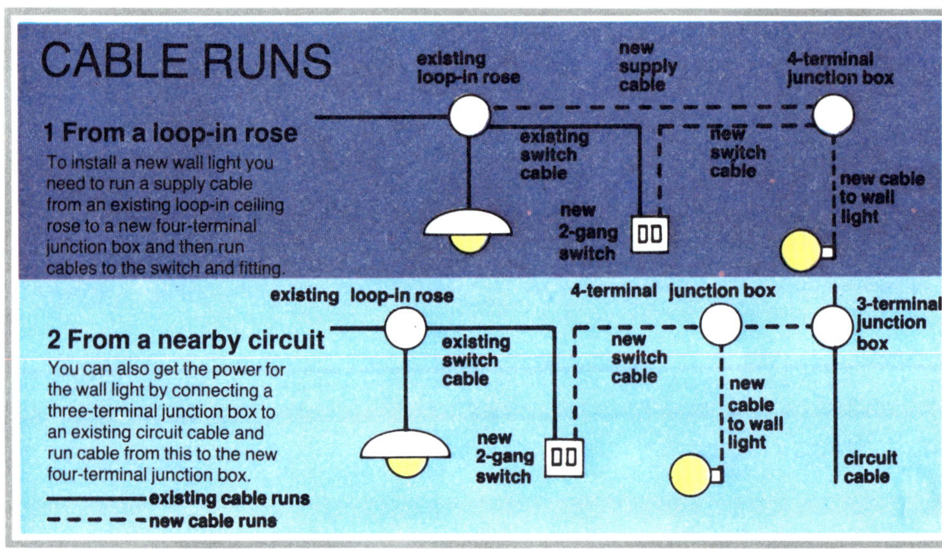

More useful still are the spotlights. Usually mounted on adjustable arms away from the wall, they can be used to send a strong beam of light almost anywhere – back onto the wall, say, to light a picture, or out into the room to illuminate a desk or sitting area. Their only real snag is that they need careful shading, if they are not to dazzle you. Mounting them on the ceiling may overcome this problem.

And finally, don't forget fluorescent lights. Slimline fluorescent tubes, though inhospitable looking, give off little heat and are easily concealed. Use them to spread a sheet of light over a wall. The light assembly can be mounted on a wooden batten and shaded by a pelmet or baffle. If you wish, the pelmet can be painted or papered to match the wall. Miniature fluorescents are also handy for lighting pictures and shelves, but whatever the size, be sure to use a 'de luxe' warm white' tube, or the light will look cold and harsh.

Positioning the fitting

Choosing a light is only half the battle. To give of its best it must be carefully positioned. With the exception of enclosed fittings, which stand very well on their own, most need to be arranged at least in pairs, and sometimes even in a group. Traditional wall lights and mock candelabra, for example, tend to look best when arranged symmetrically in pairs – say, on each side of a chimney breast. Spotlights, on the other hand, are often most effective in a cluster.

Of course, there are no hard and fast

INSTALLING THE FITTING

1 Mark the position of the BESA box on the wall where the light is to go. Use a through box if the light's switch is to be immediately below the BESA box.

2 With a club hammer and bolster chisel, chop out the hole to take the box, and channels to take cables up to the ceiling and down or across to the switch.

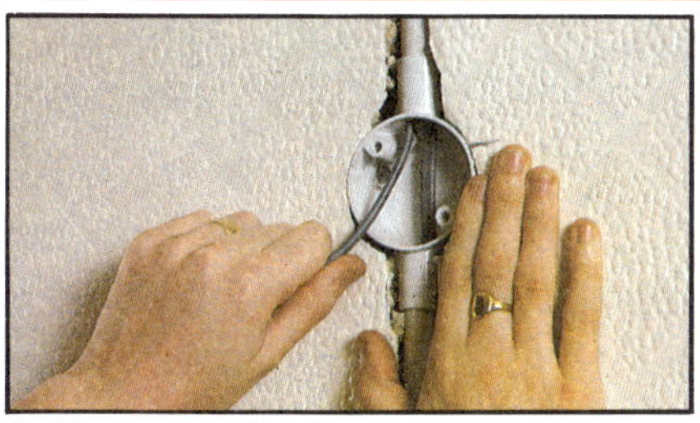

3 Fix the box in place with screws and wall plugs, then run in the cables for the light and switch. Note that the switch cable passes straight through the box.

4 Connect the light cable to the light with insulated cable connectors Tuck the earth wire out of the way if it is not needed.

INSTALLING A SWITCH

1 To install a new switch, mark out the position of the switch mounting box (a plaster-depth box) and chop out the hole to receive it.

2 Drill and plug the wall, then screw the mounting box in place, checking it is level. Next, feed in the cable coming from the new circuit's junction box.

3 Connect the cable to a one-gang one-way switch. Ensure the terminal marked 'TOP' is at the top. Connect the earth wire to the box terminal.

4 If using an existing switch position, insert a new two-gang plate switch. Connect existing cable to one set of terminals, new cable to the other.

Ready Reference

POSITIONING WALL LIGHTS

- fix ordinary wall lights about 1.5m (5ft) above floor level
- bedside lights are best set about 1.2m (4ft) above floor level.

WHAT SWITCH TO USE

Use a one-way plate switch for the wall light. Set it on a metal mounting box sunk into the wall or on a plastic box mounted on the surface.

- a separate switch is needed to isolate a wall light from the main circuit even if it has a built-in switch of its own

- alternatively you can use an existing switch position to control an extra wall light by replacing a one-gang switch unit with a two-gang unit.

FITTING THE WALL LIGHT

The wires of the fitting are linked to the circuit cable using insulated cable connectors. These are housed in a BESA box or an architrave box which is sunk into the wall and hidden by the light fitting.

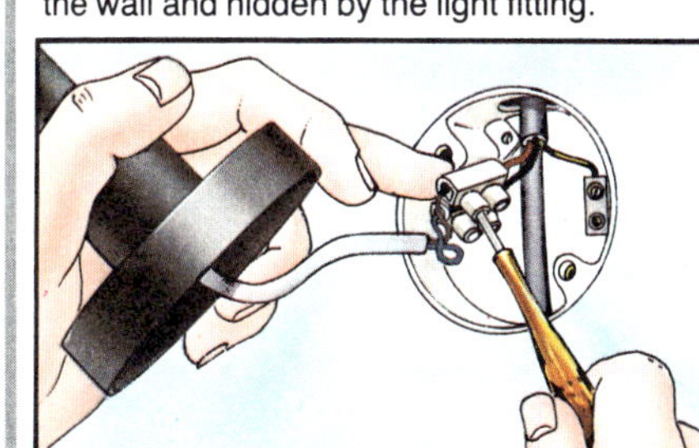

ALTERNATIVES

1 *If the light switch is not to be vertically below the light position, use a single entry BESA box instead of a through one, fitting it in the same way.*

2 *If the light cannot be mounted on a BESA box, connect the wires in an architrave mounting box. Knockouts let this act as a single entry or through box.*

LIGHTING CIRCUIT CONNECTIONS

1 *Turn off the power at the mains, unscrew the rose and ease it away from the ceiling so you can pull through new 1.0 or 1.5mm² cable.*

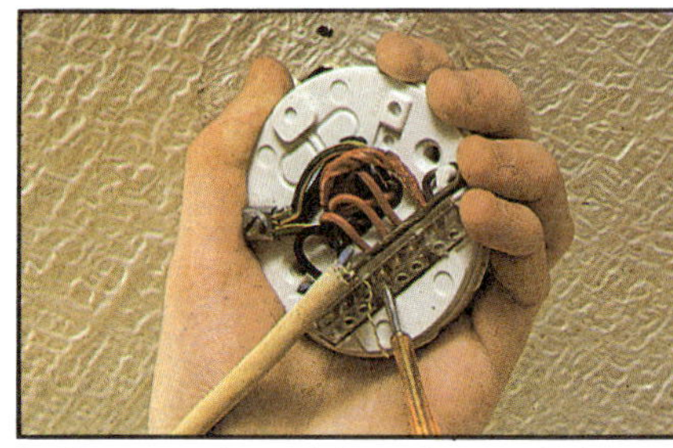

2 *Connect the cable to the rose's loop-in terminals; the red wire to the centre terminal block, the black to the neutral block, and the earth to the earth block.*

3 *Run the cable to a junction box between the switch and light. Then run one cable to the light, another to the switch position.*

4 *If you can't connect to the rose, insert a junction box at some point along one of the rose's feed cables. Run cables down to the light and switch as before.*

CONNECTING TO A RING CIRCUIT

1 *The easiest way to link a lighting spur to the ring circuit is to connect a 2.5mm² cable to the back of a socket. Ensure the socket isn't already on a spur.*

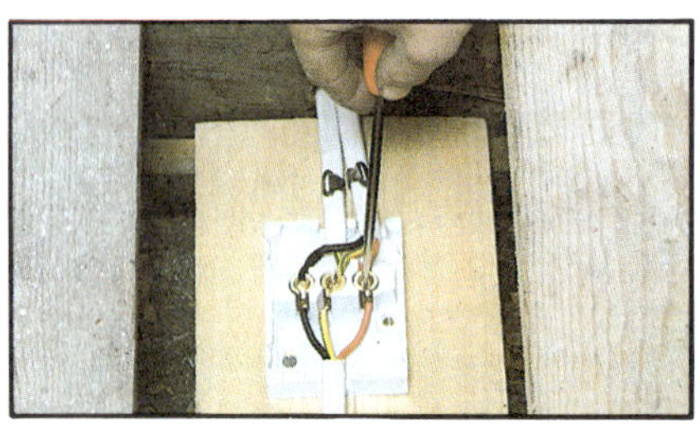

2 *Alternatively, cut the ring circuit cables and connect them to a three-terminal junction beneath the floor; then run the spur cable into that.*

3 *Mark the position of the fused connection unit. Cut through the wallpaper with a sharp knife before you chisel out the hole for the mounting box.*

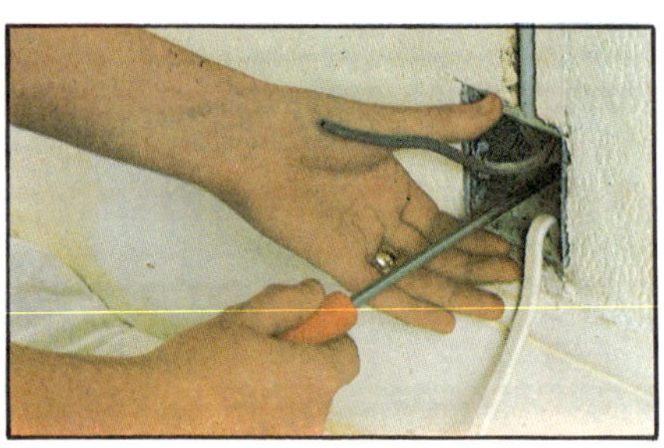

4 *Fix the mounting box for the connection unit into the whole, and then run the cable into it from the power socket or three-terminal junction box.*

5 *Having run the cable to the light position (or four-terminal junction box), fit the connection unit with a 5A fuse and connect it up.*

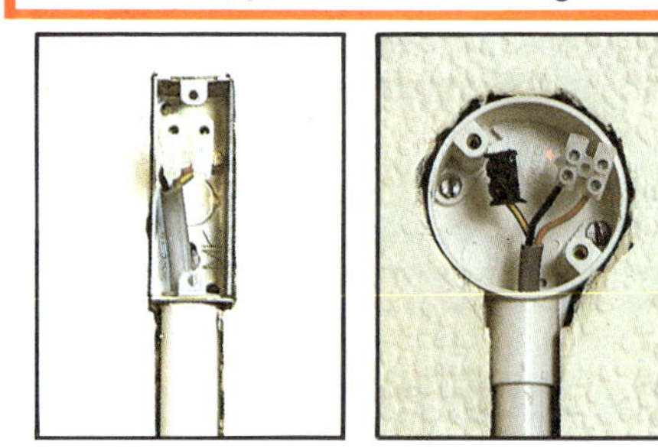

6 *Finally, fit an architrave box or a stopped BESA box at the light position and install the light as before. Note the cable will now enter from below.*

rules. In the end, it's all down to what looks and works best in your particular situation. Try to imagine how the lights will affect the room – not only the lights themselves and their position, but also the direction of the light they will give out.

You ought to pay particular attention to the light's height above the floor. The general rule is to place the light at just below eye level – about 1,500mm (5ft) – but you can vary this as necessary to stop the light getting in your eyes or to help direct it where it's needed. Wall lights used as bedside lamps, for example, should be about 1,220mm (4ft) above the floor and positioned so they can't get knocked as someone walks past them.

Installing the light

Having mastered the basic electrical techniques (see pages 173–176 and 181–185), you shouldn't find it difficult to fit the light. But remember electricity can be dangerous if abused, so follow the instructions to the letter. If they don't tie in with your home's existing wiring, or if you're unsure about what you're doing, don't take chances – get expert advice.

The first step is to find a power source, though it is best to leave the connections into the existing circuit until last. That way, you can do almost all the work with your home's electrics working normally; you'll have to turn off the power at the mains only for the few minutes needed to make the final connection.

In most cases, taking a spur off the existing lighting circuit is your best bet. Do check, though, that the wall light will not overload it. Isolate the circuit in question by removing the fuse carrier from the consumer unit, or by turning off its MCB, and add up the total wattage of the bulbs it feeds – those that are now dead, in other words. Bulbs rated at 100W or more count at face value; less powerful bulbs count as 100W. When you've done that, add on the wattage of the new light and make sure the grand total is less than 1,200 watts.

Assuming this is so, there are two ways to break into the circuit. In theory, the simplest is to connect a 1.0 or 1.5mm^2 two-core and earth cable to a loop-in ceiling rose, and run it to a four-terminal junction box above the ceiling. In practice, it's often hard to fit the extra wires in, so, as an alternative, trace a mains feed cable out of the rose, and connect the junction box into this cable.

Once you've got power to the junction box, wire up the wall light and its switch on the conventional junction box system (see pages 173–176 again) with one cable going to the light, and another to the switch. The switch can be anywhere convenient, either close to the light or away from it. You can use the switch position by the room's door if you wish. It's a simple matter to convert the existing one-gang switch there (for the ceiling light) to a two-gang (for ceiling light and wall light).

Many wall lights have a built-in switch, so you may wonder why a switch is necessary. Although these are fine for everyday use, you ought to be able to isolate the wall light completely so an additional ordinary plate switch is required.

Though fitting a wall light is not complicated there are two problems you may meet. The first is in fixing the light to the wall. Many can be screwed to the holes provided in the BESA box housing connections between light and cable. Failing that, you can fix the light to the wall using screws and wall plugs, and house the connections in a metal architrave mounting box sunk into the wall behind it.

The second problem is earthing. Even if the wall light doesn't need to be earthed, the earth wire in the new cables must be linked to your home's main earthing point at the fuse box or consumer unit. *(Never* connect earth wires to water or gas pipes.) You can, of course, do this by connecting it to the earth wire in the existing wiring, but, if the existing wiring is old, it may not have an earth wire. In this case, you should run a single sheathed earth core from the new junction box back to the earthing point.

Connecting to a ring circuit

If it's inconvenient or impossible to take power from the lighting circuit, you can connect the wall light to a ring circuit. Essentially, you run a spur to the wall light's junction box in the usual way. You then have to break into the ring either by connecting a 2.55mm^2 two-core and earth cable to the back of a power socket, or by joining it to a three-terminal junction box and connecting this to the ring circuit cable beneath the floor.

However, there is a snag. The ring circuit fuse has too high a rating for a lighting circuit (remember, these need a 5A fuse). To get round this, you have to run the 2.5mm^2 cable into a fused connection unit fitted with a 5A fuse, and continue the circuit to a four-terminal junction box and then on to the light and switch junction box with 1.0 or 1.5mm^2 cable.

Obviously, this will involve considerable extra work and expense; but there is a short cut. You can do away with the junction box and separate switch, and use a switched fused connection unit to control the wall light. It sounds appealing, but it too has its drawbacks. The connection unit will not match the other light switches in the room, and it needs to be as close as possible to the light – an unnecessarily complex cable run would be needed to control the light from the far side of the room.

Ready Reference

WIRING THE CIRCUIT

The easiest way to provide wall lights with power is to run a 1.0mm^2 two-core and earth, PVC-sheathed and insulated cable from a loop-in ceiling rose.

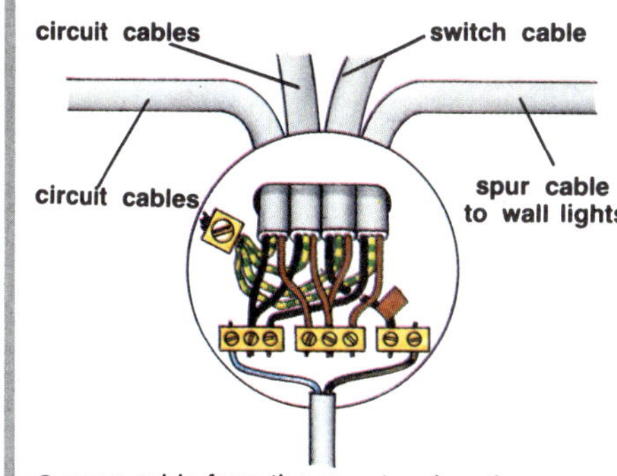

- run a cable from the rose to a junction box. Two cables then run from the box – one to the light and one to its switch (A)
- rather than connecting into the main lighting circuit at a rose, you can break into the main feed cable and install a junction box (B).

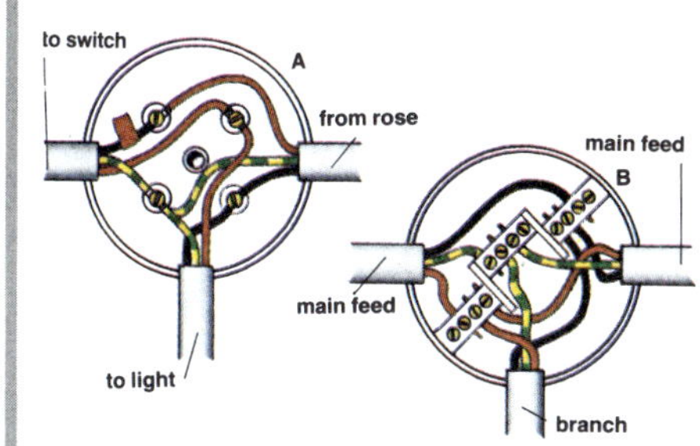

ALTERNATIVE WIRING

Wall lights can also take their power from a ring circuit.

- install a three-terminal junction box (A). Then run a 2.5mm^2 cable to a fused connection unit fitted with a 5A fuse (B). Continue the wiring to the light (C) and a switch (D) as if the power had been taken from the lighting circuit (ie, use 1.0mm^2 cable)

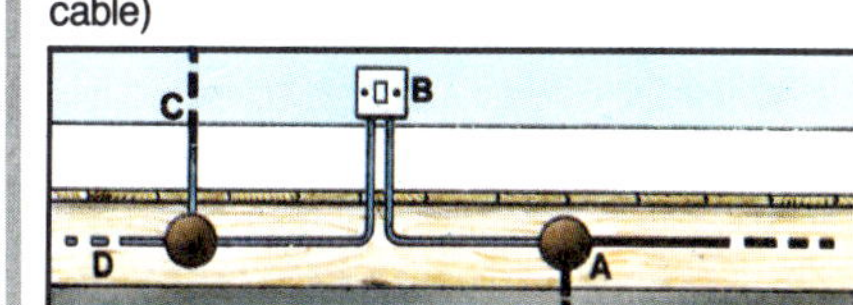

- alternatively use a switched fused connection unit (A), and run the 1.5mm^2 cable straight to the wall light. The unit then acts as an isolating light switch.

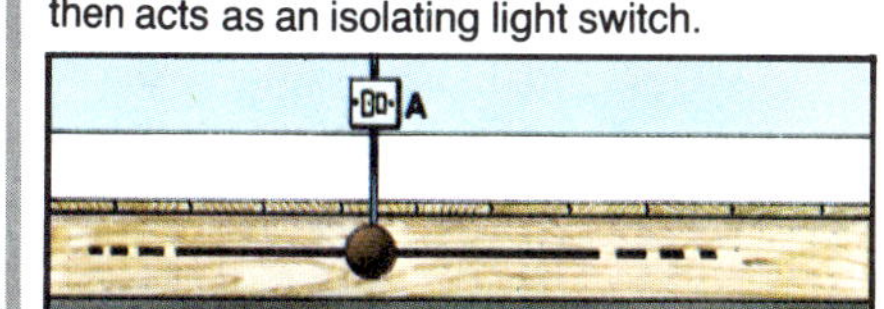

INSTALLING RECESSED LIGHTING

If you want an efficient lighting system that can provide both general and specific illumination without exposed fittings you should fit recessed lighting. It is stylish, practical and easy to install.

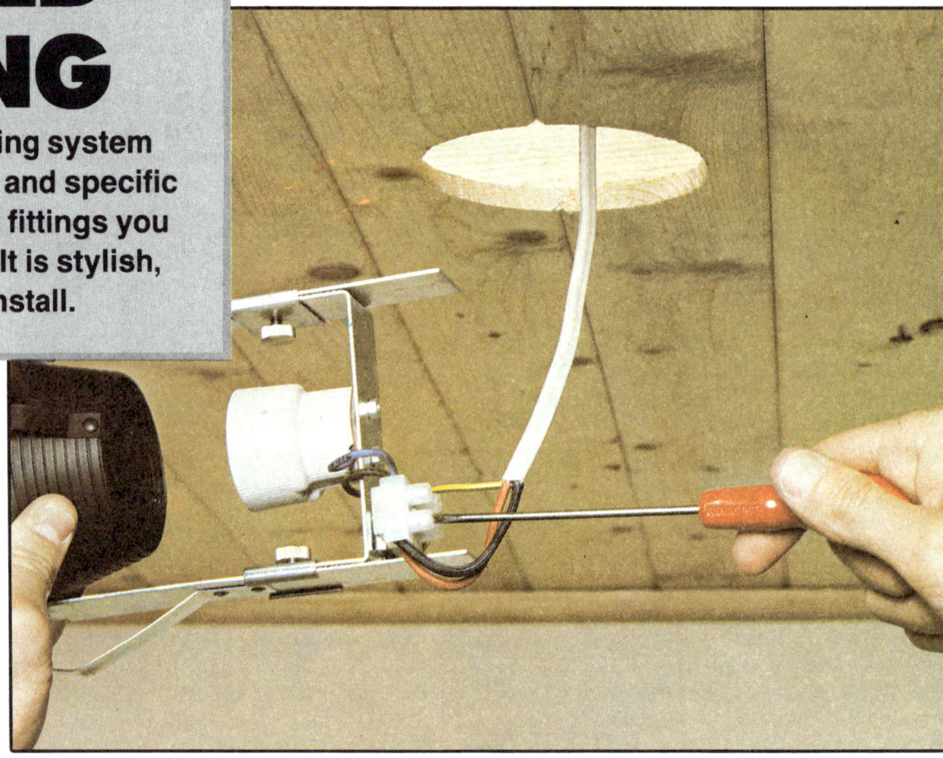

Choosing a lighting system that is both efficient and good looking is no easy task. You'll often find that lamps which provide perfectly adequate light have unattractive fittings out of style with the rest of your decor. Faced with this stark reality, people are beginning to realise that it's the light rather than the associated fittings which is important. For although there are numerous fittings which are attractive ornaments when unlit, their function is, after all, only as lampholders for the light source.

This is why recessed lighting has become so popular. It is the name for any type of light which has its fittings concealed above the ceiling surface, yet still adequately illuminates the room below.

Most homes are suitable for some form of recessed or hidden lighting, but which you install depends largely on the structure of your home. If, for example, you live in a flat where the ceilings are concrete, and therefore solid, you will be unable to fit lights recessed into the ceiling. Since, however, ceilings in flats are usually higher than those in a conventional house or bungalow, there is considerable scope for fitting a suspended ceiling and recessing the fittings into the void above it.

Similarly, the old country cottage with its oak beams and almost non-existent void between the ceiling and the floor above is hardly the ideal situation for recessed lighting. Here, the traditionally low ceiling rules out the addition of a false ceiling. However, even in situations like this there is some scope for hidden lighting or semi-recessed fittings as an alternative to fully recessed lighting.

THE CIRCUIT ARRANGEMENT

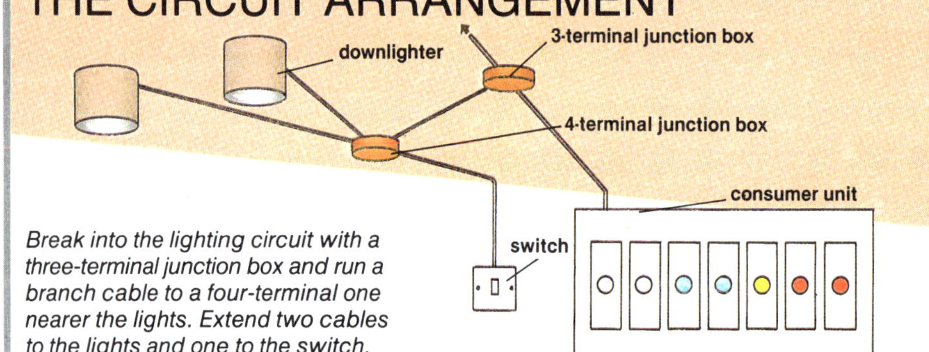

Break into the lighting circuit with a three-terminal junction box and run a branch cable to a four-terminal one nearer the lights. Extend two cables to the lights and one to the switch.

Types of recessed lighting

You'll probably find that you're familiar with recessed lighting in such places as restaurants, airports and reception rooms, where, no doubt, the lighting was planned at the design stage and incorporated into the original building. However, there is now a wide variety of recessed lighting which you can successfully install in your own home. Perhaps the most popular form is known as the downlighter or the highlighter. This consists of a tube-like fitting that's installed so that its edge sits flush with the ceiling surface. Other models can be installed so that they are, in effect, only semi-recessed, or, if you are stuck for space you could fit a model which has the lamp mounted on its side so the fitting takes up less vertical space. They usually house special light bulbs known as internal silvered lamps which reflect the light from the filament in a fairly wide beam. And different lamps can be fitted so you can select whichever type of beam you like. The particular advantage of the downlighter is that as all the light is directed downwards very little is wasted.

Another version of the downlighter is the wallwasher and, as its name implies, this fitting directs light an an angle of about 45° to illuminate a feature on the wall. However, its beam is usually somewhat less concentrated than that of a conventional spotlight. Similar to the wallwasher is the eyeball spotlight; but this can be adjusted through a full 360° to direct light onto a specific surface or feature.

Recessed fluorescent lighting

Fluorescent tubes are extensively used in recessed lighting and, in particular, in illuminated ceilings. This is a very popular way of concealing the tubes and their fittings, yet at the same time making use of their even light: a number of tubes are fixed to the existing ceiling and beneath them a grid of aluminium strips is used to support sheets of translucent diffusing panels (for further details, consult the manufacturers). In most homes, a completely illuminated ceiling is usually confined to the kitchen or bathroom. It is more usual in a reception room or living room to fit one or two panels of illumi-

OBTAINING THE POWER

1 *After lifting a floorboard to gain access to the lighting circuit, mount a three-terminal junction box on a batten between the joists.*

2 *With the mains switched off, cut the lighting circuit and connect the two sets of cores to the junction box. Sleeve the earth core in green/yellow PVC.*

3 *Run a branch cable in 1.0mm² two core and earth cable to take power to a four-terminal junction box that should be sited nearer the lights.*

4 *Fit the box to a batten and run a switch cable and one or two power cables to the lights. Clip them neatly to the batten.*

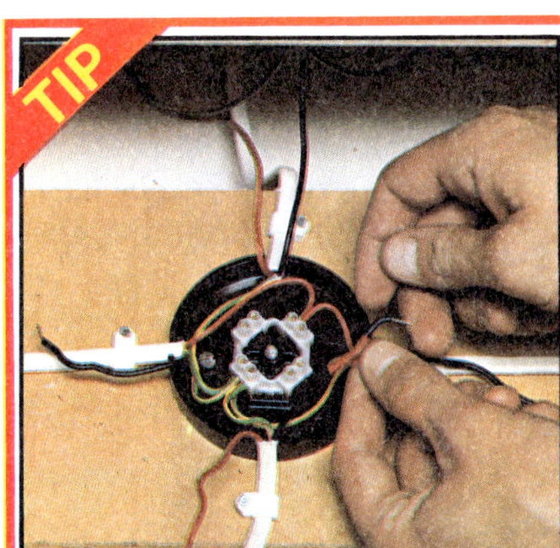

5 *After sleeving the earths in PVC, connect all the cores to their respective terminals. Remember to flag the black switch core with red tape as it's live.*

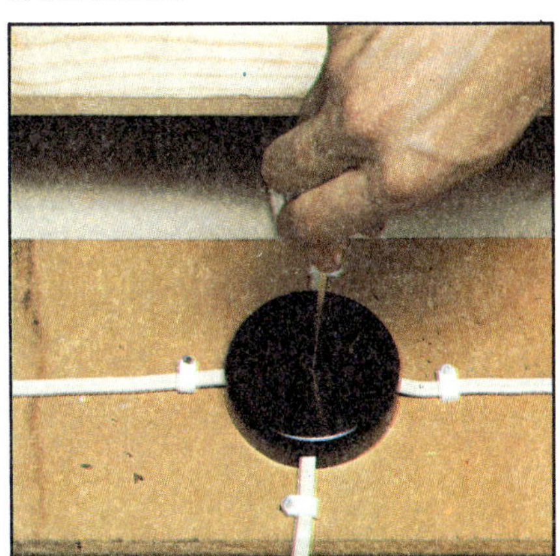

6 *Finally replace the lid on the junction box and tighten it up, making sure that the cable insulation reaches right into the box.*

Ready Reference

TYPES OF RECESSED LIGHTING

Downlighter

Eyeball

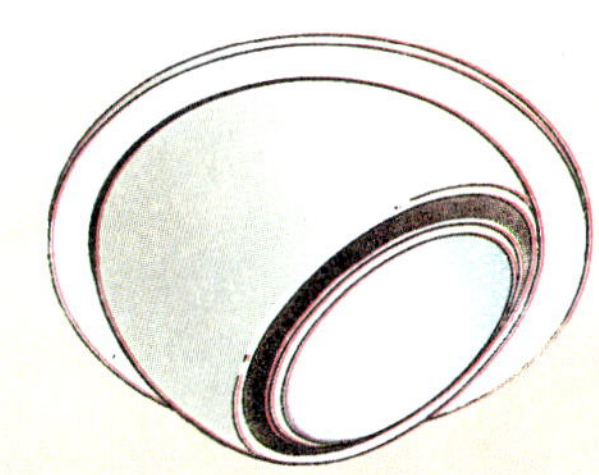

Wallwasher

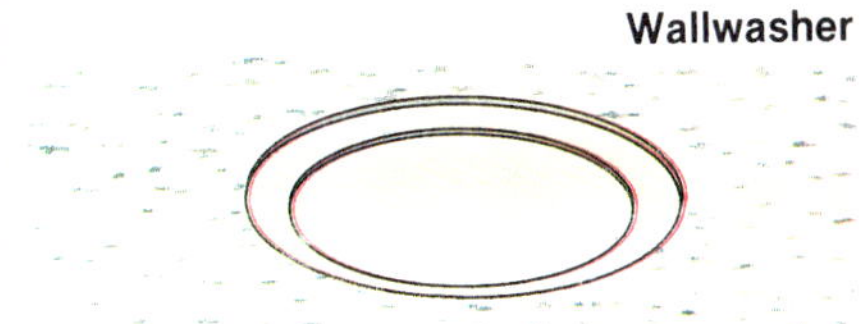

Fluorescent panel

Illuminated ceiling

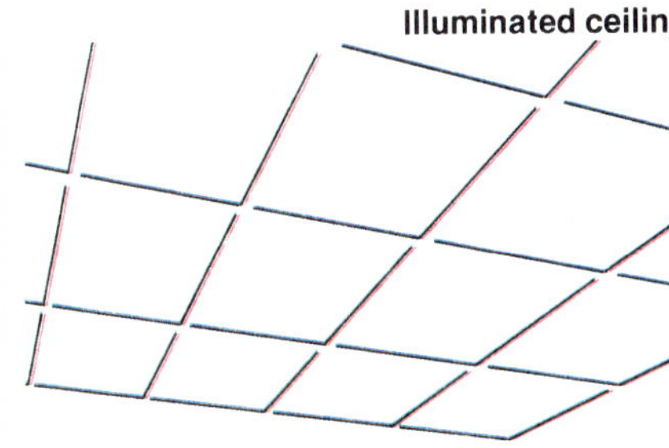

FITTING A DOWNLIGHTER IN A SUSPENDED CEILING

TIP

1 Fix a heat-resistant pad to your old ceiling before installing the new one. Use spacers to provide a gap so air can circulate.

2 You should drill a hole in the ceiling to check the new light won't be obstructed in any way. The whole section will eventually be cut out.

3 After checking with the manufacturer's instructions, you should mark on the ceiling the size of the hole required for the light.

4 Drill a small hole just inside the circle and use a pad saw to cut it out. Don't worry if the edges are rough as the light trim will cover them.

5 Pull the mains cable through the hole. If it isn't heat-resistant, you should sleeve the individual cores with special heat-resistant sleeving.

6 Make the connections before you recess the light. The earth can be sleeved in ordinary greenlyellow PVC and then connected.

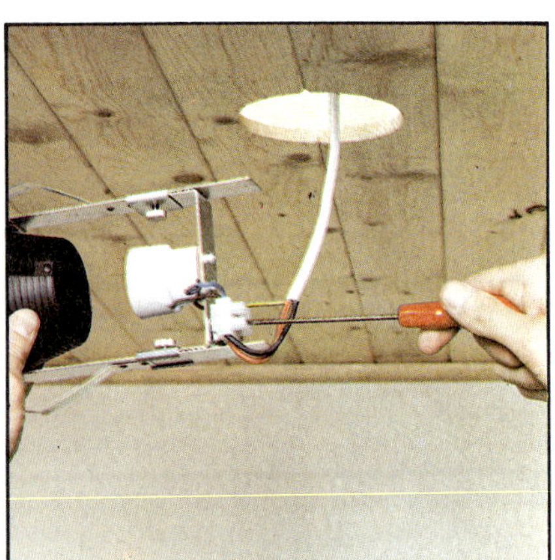

7 Connect the red core to the terminal that has brown flex linking it to the lampholder and the black to the one with blue flex.

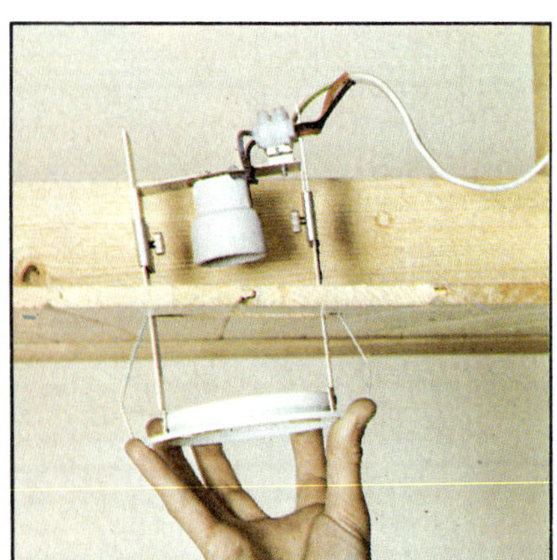

8 Remove the detachable trim and recess the light into the ceiling. Check that the butterfly clips are correctly positioned.

9 Finally adjust the cross piece so the lamp is at the correct level. Fit the detachable trim, screw in the lamp and test the light.

nated ceiling. This involves cutting away a small section of the existing ceiling and is an excellent way of supplementing a room lit by downlighters.

Installing a downlighter

Before buying downlighters to install in your home, it's a good idea to check the depth of the ceiling void where you want to fit them. A typical downlighter designed for domestic installation is about 170mm (6½in) deep and so can be readily accommodated in most ceiling voids. In fact, the depth of joist is not usually the limiting factor when you install a downlighter in the ceiling below the roof space; the real danger is the possibility of mechanical damage when the top of the fitting projects above the joists. There are two solutions to this problem: firstly, you could install a semi-recessed downlighter so the problem won't arise or, secondly, you could construct a box round the fitting to give it adequate protection (see *Ready Reference*). Having decided on the approximate position of your new downlighter, you should pierce a small hole in the ceiling to check that its position will be completely safe. Lift a floorboard in the room above, if you have access, so you can check that the light will clear the nearest joist and also that there are no cables or pipes obstructing it.

Once you've decided exactly where you want to fit your downlighter, you'll have to cut a hole in the ceiling to enable you to recess it. The size of hole needed varies between models, but it'll be made clear in the manufacturer's instructions.

Using a pair of compasses, mark the hole on the ceiling and then cut it out carefully with a pad saw. If your ceiling is merely plasterboard fixed to the joists, then you can simply cut through it and remove the section. However, if you've a lath-and-plaster ceiling then you should reinforce the ends of the lath after you've cut them. This is simply done, and requires you to fit a batten between the joists on either side of the hole and two battens between them to support the ends of the laths. You should then draw the power cable through the hole in the ceiling so you can make the connections before you actually recess the light itself. Because of the proximity of the lamp, it's a good idea to use heat-resistant cable, but if you can't obtain this at your local DIY or electrical shop, you can instead use heat-resistant sleeving round the individual cores.

Most downlighters have special terminal blocks which are connected to the lamp fitting at the time of manufacture, so the cable's red core should be connected to the terminal which has a brown flex leaving it and the black should go to the terminal with blue flex. You must remember to sleeve the earth core (ordinary green/yellow PVC will be adequate) before connecting it to the earth terminal. You should then push the downlighter through the hole and adjust the butterfly clips at either side so it sits flush with the ceiling. But before fitting the lamp it's wise to adjust the position of the cross piece so you can have the lamp at whichever level you like best.

Internally silvered lamps direct most of the light and heat downwards and, therefore, out of the ceiling void. However, it is still advisable to fit a pad of heat-resistant material – a mineral fibre ceiling tile, for example – to the underside of the floorboards above. If you're fitting a downlighter in a suspended ceiling, then this pad is often not necessary. However, if you're fitting your lights at the same time as a suspended ceiling you can fit pads onto the original ceiling surface.

Obtaining the power

Connecting your new recessed lighting to the existing lighting circuitry poses no extra problems. However, there are a couple of options open to you. Provided your lights are to be installed close to where the main lighting circuit runs, you can simply break into it at a convenient point using a four-terminal junction box. All you then have to do is add an extra cable to take power to the lights and one to act as a switch feed and return. The wiring is not complicated and it's all done in 1.0mm^2 two-core and earth cable. But do remember to flag the black switch neutral core with red tape as it's really live.

Alternatively, if your lights are going to be fitted some way from the circuit, you could interrupt it with just a three-terminal junction box and run a spur cable to a four-terminal junction box sited near the new lights; that way you save yourself money on the cable runs. If you are fitting two downlighters, run a cable to each from the junction box – see step-by-step pictures on page 209.

If you are installing several downlighters you can loop the mains cable into and out of each light. All can still be controlled by one switch connected to the four-terminal junction box. But, remember, if you have a suspended ceiling you'll have to drill a hole in the original ceiling to let through the mains cable.

Fitting other recessed lights

Most small recessed lights are fitted in much the same way as downlighters. Both eyeball and wallwasher lights do not require as much depth but nevertheless it's still wise to check your joist size beforehand. If you want to fit a fluorescent panel in your ceiling, you'll have to cut out a section of ceiling plaster and fit battens between the joists to hold the light fittings. You should then replace the section of ceiling with a sheet of diffusing material and finish off the edges with plastic beading.

Ready Reference

ELECTRICAL CONNECTIONS

Breaking into the lighting circuit to obtain power is simple. Use a three-terminal junction box and connect in a 1.0mm^2 two-core and earth branch cable.

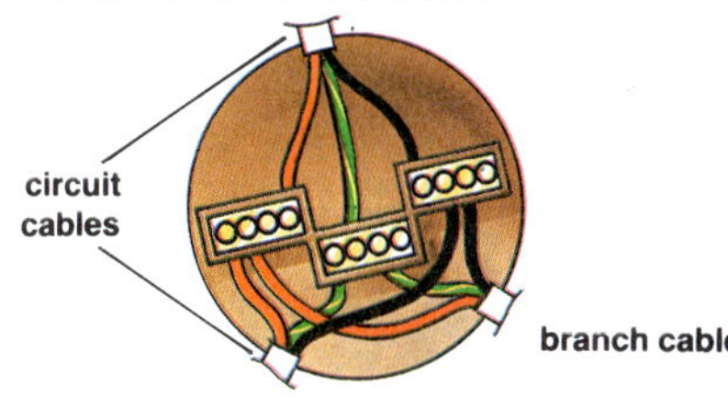

Take the branch cable to a four-terminal junction box situated near the light. Run a cable to each light (a maximum of two) and one to the switch. If you have more than two lights, you can loop-in and out of each one.

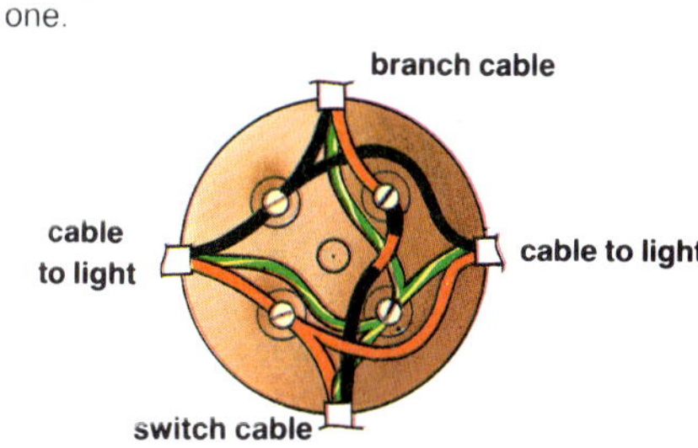

TIP: PROTECT YOUR FITTINGS

You can protect a downlighter that protrudes above joist level in the roof space by building a box. You should:

- use a 150 x 25mm (6 x 1in) timber
- leave a gap of 50mm (2in) between the box and downlighter
- fit a heat resistant pad.

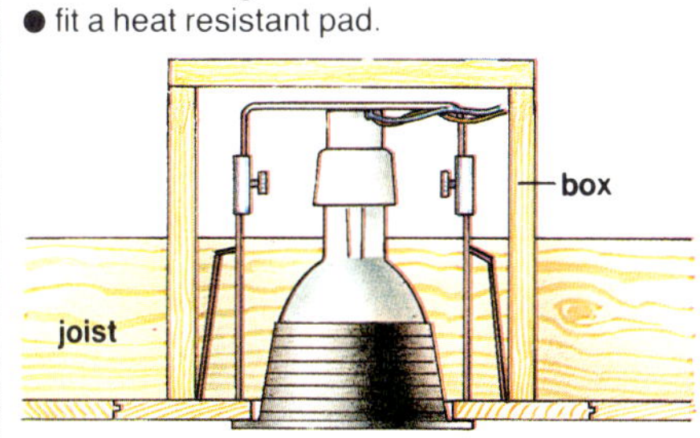

HEAT RESISTANT PADS

If you're fitting a heat-resistant pad such as a mineral fibre tile, you should leave a small gap between it and the underside of the floorboards above. That way air can circulate and help prevent too much heat building up. Use spacers to create the gap and fit the screws through them.

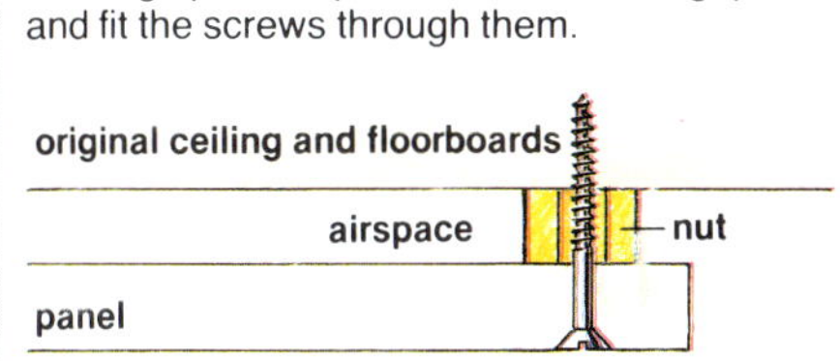

INSTALLING TRACK LIGHTING

Track lighting allows you plenty of scope in lighting your home. It's efficient, versatile and attractive and, what's more, extremely easy to install.

Track and fittings : Rotaflex

The time is bound to come when you want to alter the lighting in your home. You may want to highlight certain features, such as paintings, or merely provide yourself with extra light. You may want to change your wall lights or depart from the traditional concept of a ceiling rose and pendant light. In all these cases you should think about installing track lighting.

What is track lighting?

Track lighting consists of individual light fittings of various types that are mounted on special tracks fixed to ceilings or walls. This enables you to move the lights into whatever position you like and, in addition, to adjust them so their light is thrown in whichever direction you want.

The track itself is a metal casing, usually square or tubular in cross-section, that contains twin electrical conductors. These live and neutral conductors are bare and extend from one end of the track to the other. They function in much the same way as the conductor rails of an electric railway, with the light fittings instead of the trains picking up electric current from the live rails. The conductors are shielded from touch, while the lights are fitted with special adaptors for making contact with the conductors inside the track and which also serves to hold the lights in place.

Once the track has been fixed in position and the electrical connections made, then the adaptors are placed on to the track and the spotlights moved along to exactly where you want them. You can then lock them into position.

Obtaining the power supply for your track lighting is very simple. You're really faced with two options. On the one hand you can simply connect the 'live' end of the track to the existing ceiling rose, after removing the flex of the original lampholder, or you can run in an entirely new lighting circuit. For track lights mounted on the wall, power can be supplied either by an existing light circuit or the room's socket outlet circuit. The best method, however, is to wire the lights through a fused connection unit, as if it were a wall light linked to the power circuits.

Any number of lights can be fitted onto any one track, provided you don't exceed the track's current rating. With a 10A track, the most suitable for a domestic situation, this will be 2400W and with a 16A track, 4000W. In other words, with a 10A track you could, in theory, fit up to 24 100W spotlights. In practice the limiting factor is more likely to be the circuit wiring. Remember, lighting circuits are actually rated at 5A which means that each one can take a load of up to 1200W or, in effect, can supply twelve lampholders containing lamps of 100W each or smaller. So when you are adding track lighting to an existing circuit, check that the extra lights won't mean exceeding this figure. If they will, run a spur from a nearby power circuit (via a fused connection unit) instead – see page 64.

Choosing your lighting track

Lighting track for commercial purposes comes in various standard lengths. The domestic variety usually only comes in two lengths, 1000mm (39in) or 1500mm (59in). Once you've decided on the approximate lengths of track that you'll need, visit your local stockist to see exactly what is available. When making your choice of track, it's a good idea to check what type of light fittings are available with it and whether they'll meet your requirements. After all, the track itself is usually available in only a few finishes – white, brown, polished brass and polished silver are the commonest – while there are probably over a hundred different types of light fitting available. If you find that you can't get the exact length you require, don't worry; it can easily be cut to size with a hacksaw and if longer lengths are required, special connectors are available. And there are 90° angle connectors for when a track is required to turn a corner.

Choosing the lights

There are so many different types of fitting available that you're bound to find one that will suit the decor of your home and do the job you want it to. The number you fit on any one track will depend largely on what you want to light. As a rule, though, track lighting would prove expensive for just one or two fittings.

Installing the track

There are a number of ways of fixing the track to your ceiling or wall. It can be fixed almost flush to the surface with the help of small clips. Alternatively, you can use a special mounting canopy that will fit conveniently and neatly over an existing ceiling rose or

PREPARING THE CEILING

1 *Switch off the electricity supply at the mains and unscrew the existing ceiling rose cover. You can then remove the old pendant flex and lampholder.*

2 *Site the first surface clip so that the live end of the track will sit close to the power source. Make sure the clip has a secure fixing.*

3 *Measure the position of the second clip: with a 1m (39in) track it should be 600mm (2ft) away; with a 1.5m (5ft) track it should be 800mm (32in) away.*

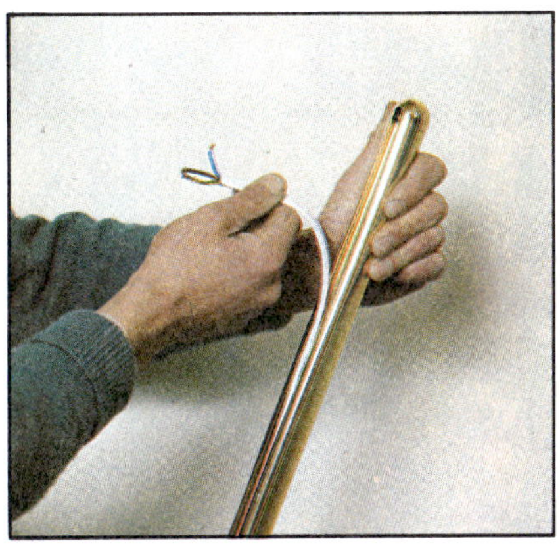

4 *Before fixing the track in place you'll have to free the flex. This is housed in a channel on the top side of the track and can be pulled clear.*

you can use mounting stems, which are merely short rods on backplates. You'll probably find that your lighting track will have a length of special flex already connected to its live end. This is likely to be the same length as the track. An advantage of these mounting methods is that in addition to providing a simple means for fitting the track itself, they help to conceal the track flex – so you won't have to cut it to length. The flex is fitted into a channel on the ceiling face of the track and you may well have to remove the shorter plastic end piece so you can free it. If you're going to use a mounting canopy and obtain power from an existing ceiling rose then the excess flex can be simply tucked into the canopy. Using surface clips will enable you to thread the flex up into the ceiling so that it can be neatly connected to a BESA box or a junction box. Only the mounting stems don't actually conceal the flex. But in their case all you do is run the flex in its channel and leave only a short section exposed where it runs up to the ceiling rose or BESA box.

Before installing the lighting you'll have to finalise the position for the track on the ceiling or the wall. Ideally you should make sure that the mains outlet of your existing light coincides with the live end of the track. This could mean altering the position of the outlet, or even installing some new wiring, and if this is the case it should be done before you fix up the track.

Mounting track on the ceiling is perfectly straightforward but it will require solid fixings. It's best to use the joists, but if these don't coincide with the fixing holes drilled in the square cross-sectioned track you can easily drill some new holes in it to match your joist spacings. Alternatively, secure a piece of chipboard between the revelant joists and fix the track to this. Most mounting canopies

Ready Reference

MOUNTING METHODS

There are three methods of fixing lighting track to a ceiling:

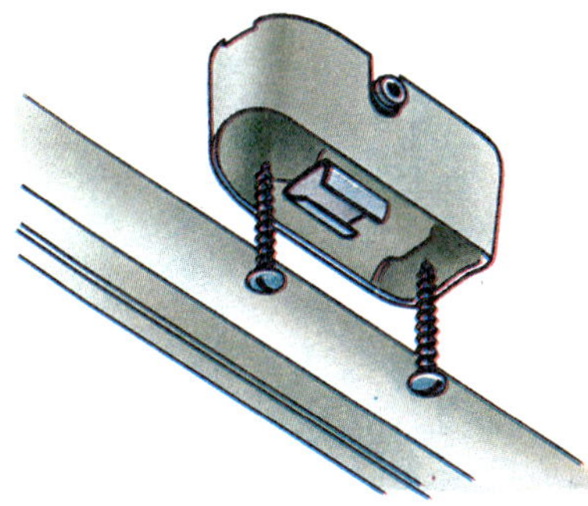

- surface clips – also suitable for use with wall-mounted track

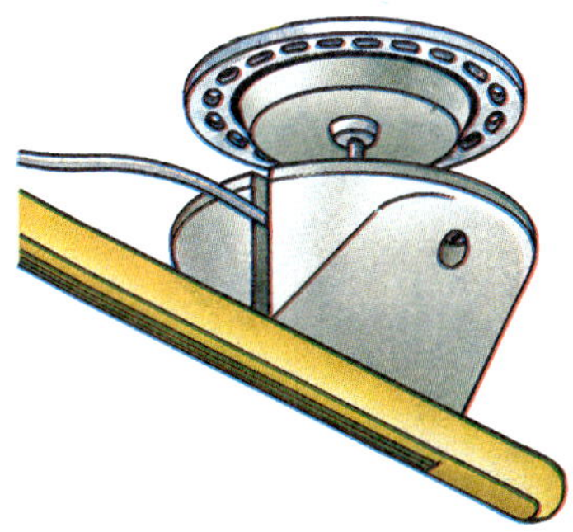

- mounting canopies – designed to fit neatly over an existing ceiling rose and to also conceal any excess flex

- mounting stems – also suitable for use with wall-mounted track.

TIP: USE A COVER PLATE

An existing BESA box and the connections within it can be neatly concealed by a cover plate with the surface clip fixed on top. You might well find that the mains outlet point is not immediately above where you want to position the lighting track. One solution is to use a cover plate and to run the connecting cable to the track in mini-trunking.

MAKING THE CONNECTIONS

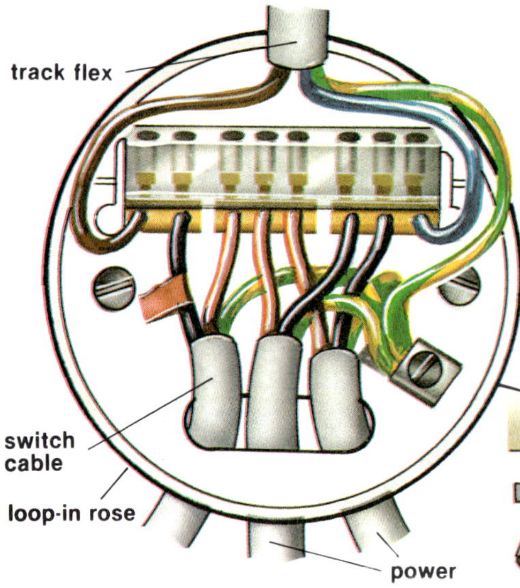

A mounting canopy will fit neatly and conveniently over an existing ceiling rose, shown left and right, concealing all the electrical connections. Begin by switching off at the mains and then disconnect the flex of your pendant light. Then thread the track lighting flex through the rose cover, make the connections and screw back the cover.

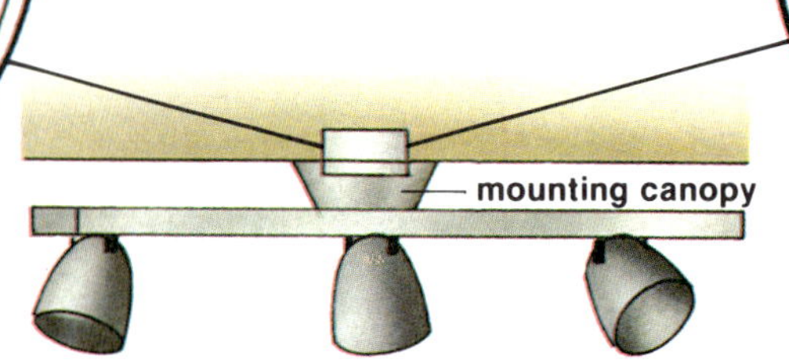

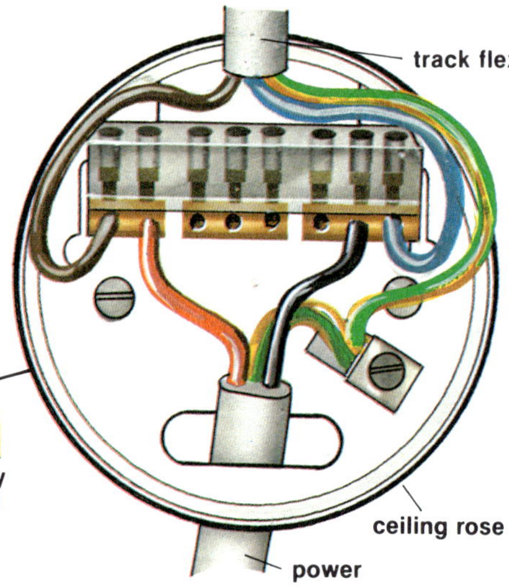

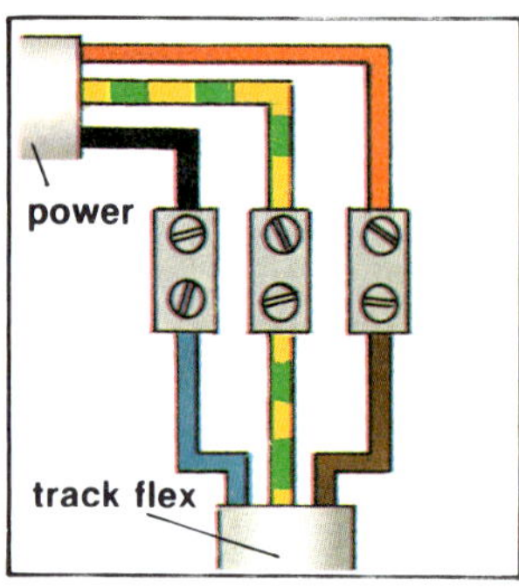

junction box system

If you're connecting to an existing BESA box use a cover plate to conceal it. You can then make the connections as shown, making sure that you flag the black core of the switch cable to indicate that it's really live.

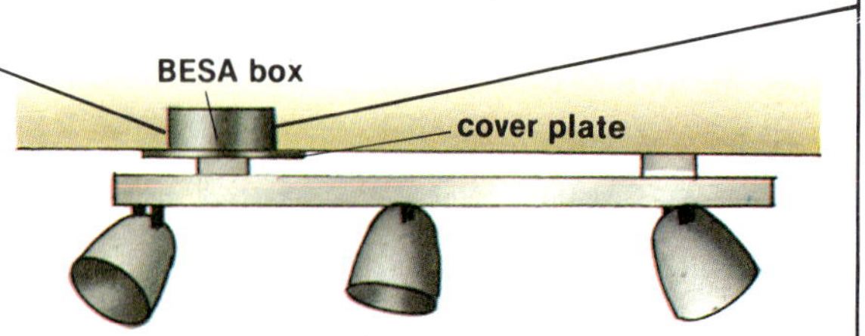

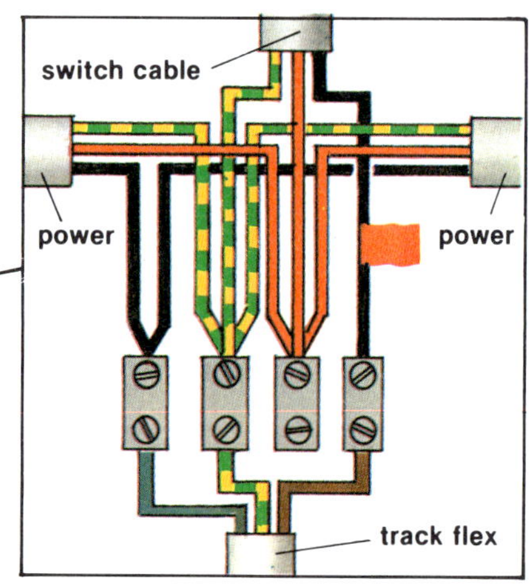

loop-in wiring

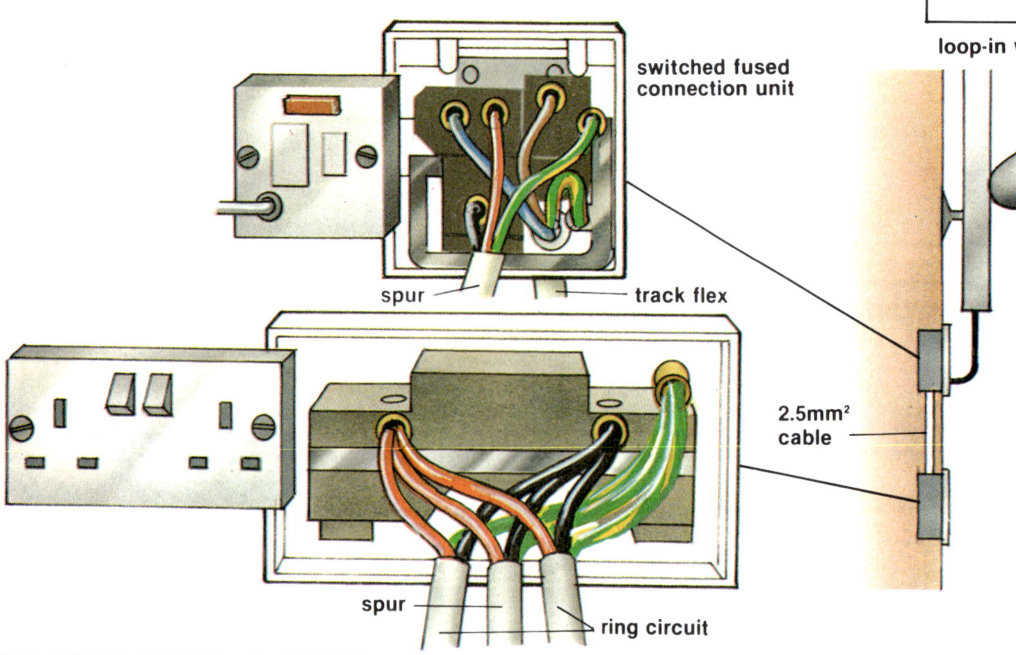

Providing power for wall-mounted track lighting is straightforward. The best method is to run a spur in 2.5mm² two-core and earth cable from a ring circuit to the feed side of a switched fused connection unit. This should be mounted close to the track position and will control the lights. You can then connect the flex of the track to the load side of the unit.

INSTALLING THE TRACK AND FITTINGS

1 Offer up the track to the surface clips, making sure that it will be centrally positioned and that the clip grub screws are slackened.

2 When you have the track precisely in position, secure it in place by tightening up the clip grub screws with the hexagonal key provided.

3 Before making the electrical connections, cut the flex to length. If you're using a mounting canopy, you can safely tuck the excess inside.

4 Next, make the connections. Link the brown core to the bank of live terminals, the blue core to the neutral bank and the green/yellow core to the earth terminal.

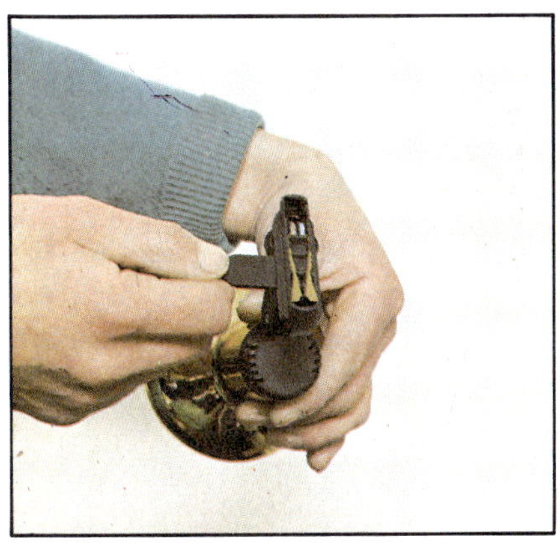

5 Most track lights are stepped on one side so you can't fit them incorrectly. Move the lever through 90° to retract the contacts and fixing levers.

6 Then fix the lights onto the track. Simply hold them in place, reposition the lever and lock the lights in the desired position on the track.

have fixing holes 51mm (2in) apart. In other words, the canopy will be able to fit over an existing rose, and the connection to the circuit can then be completely concealed. However, where the existing rose is old and has different spacings between its fixing holes you'll have to discard it and use an alternative method of connecting to the circuit.

This method involves fixing a BESA box flush with the surface of the ceiling. Inside the BESA box the flying leads of the lighting track are connected to the existing circuit wires with insulated cable connectors. The box itself has two screwed lugs that are spaced at 51mm (2in) centres, so the canopy will fit perfectly in place. If you're using stems, you'll find that the procedure is virtually the same although there could well be slight differences between the various systems currently on the market. Fixing track to walls is much the same as fixing it to the ceiling. However, you'll probably find that you have to drill and plug the wall to get a really secure fixing, and you'll also have to cut a channel in the plaster to run in the cable unless your track reaches right up to the ceiling and the cable can be concealed within it.

Obtaining power for track lighting

One of the major advantages of track lighting is that it can often be connected to an existing lighting point without any alteration of the circuitry. However, new wiring will be necessary when there is no convenient lighting which can be used to supply the track; where the addition of track lighting is likely to overload the lighting circuit, and where track lighting is to be used in addition to the existing lighting. If you're going to have to run in a new circuit for the track you should use $1.0mm^2$ two-core and earth cable rated at 5A. This will be able to supply power for up to 12 spotlights on three or four tracks. The circuit will be the same as an ordinary lighting circuit and you'll probably find it easiest to use junction boxes as each track will need to be controlled by a wall switch. That way you can use BESA boxes in which to make the connections to the track. For further details on running in a new circuit see pages 237–240.

Track lighting fixed to the wall will be able to obtain its power supply from the existing lighting point if it is replacing wall lights. However, if you're mounting new lights then you're faced with two options. You can either break into the lighting circuit in the ceiling void above and run cable down to the track or you can break into the socket outlet circuit. In the latter case you should take a spur to a switched fused connection and then run $1.0mm^2$ two-core and earth cable to the track itself.

TWO-WAY SWITCHING

In a room lit by a single pendant light, controlling that light from a single switch is no great hardship. But if the room contains wall lights it's useful to be able to control them from different parts of the room and that's exactly what two-way switching lets you do.

In most rooms, lights or groups of lights are controlled by just one switch. It's the standard set-up, and electricians call it one-way switching. However, there are situations where a one light, one switch arrangement isn't very convenient.

Take the light over a flight of stairs as an example. Having the light switch at the bottom of the flight is fine if you want to go upstairs. You can turn on the light before you go up without difficulty. But what happens when you reach the top? You can't turn the light off again. And suppose you want to come downstairs and the light is turned off? You can't switch it on without negotiating the stairs in the dark, which rather defeats the object of having a light there at all.

Obviously, what's needed is another switch at the top of the stairs and a system of wiring that allows either switch to turn the light on and off independently of the other. This system is called two-way switching.

Where it can be used

The example of the light above the stairs is such a common one that providing two-way switching for stair lights is now more or less standard procedure. There are, however, many other situations where two-way switching may be useful.

Think of the advantages of having a switch at both ends of a long hallway. And what about rooms with more than one entrance? It makes sense to have a switch beside each of the doors. The same applies to a garage with a side door in addition to the main one.

There are also situations where two-way switching is not vital but still worth considering. For example, where you have installed wall-mounted bedside reading lamps: it is a great advantage when you can control these from the door, as well as from a switch by the bed. You might also want to install a two-way switch for the main bedroom light so you can turn it on and off without getting out of bed.

And don't forget the hall light: in many homes this is one-way switched despite the fact that it often serves as a stair light by illuminating the bottom steps of the staircase as well as the hall itself. It's all too easy to go upstairs having forgotten to switch it off.

How it works

The key to two-way switching lies in using a special switch at both switching positions.

An ordinary one-way switch has two terminals and when you operate it you either make or break the electrical connection between them. For the current to reach the lightbulb and make it work, it must pass down one of the cores in the switch-drop cable, and back up the other. Making or breaking the link between terminals also makes or breaks the link between the two cores and therefore switches the light on or off.

A two-way switch works in a completely different way. It has three terminals, marked 'Common', L1, and L2, and when you operate it, flicking the switch one way provides a link between L1 and Common; flicking it the other way provides a link between Common and L2. If you link the terminals of two two-way switches in a certain way, then one switch can complete the circuit (and turn the light on) while the other can over-ride it and turn the light off again. The reverse also applies.

So, what is this remarkable wiring arrangement? Well, in its traditional form – the one normally illustrated in text-book wiring diagrams – the switches are linked with a pair of single-core cables called straps. Each joins the L1 terminal in one switch to the L2 terminal in the other. The switch drop from the light is

Ready Reference

SWITCHING SYSTEMS

A switch is able to turn a light on or off by completing or breaking a circuit. The one-way switching system, where the light is controlled by a single switch, is the usual system, but the two-way switching system, when two special switches are linked, allows you to control your light from two switches that are independent of each other.

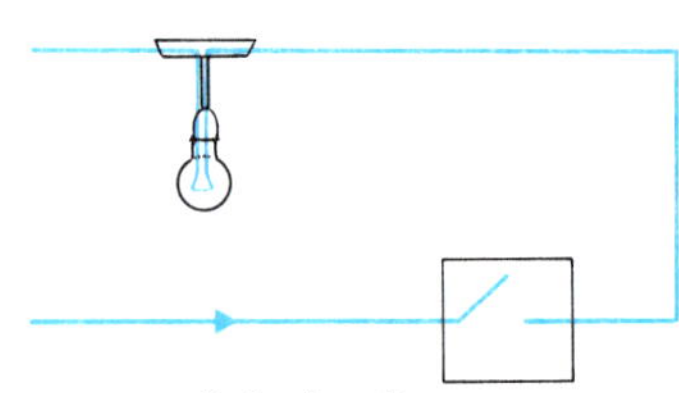

One-way switch circuit

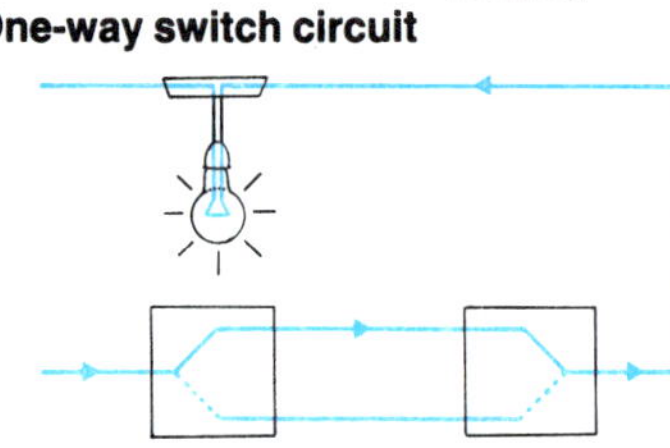

Two-way switch circuit

THE THEORY OF TWO-WAY SWITCHING

How a two-way switching circuit works can be seen in the way in which the switches are linked and how the power flows between them.

*In the traditional method of two-way switching, the two switches are linked by single-core cables called straps and the switch drop is divided with one core going to the Common terminal in switch **A** and the other to Common in switch **B**. The light is turned on when the power flows from the switch feed to Common and then **L1** in **A**, through the strap to **L2** and Common and the switch return in **B**. With either of the switches in a different position the circuit is broken and the light turned off.*

*In most homes three-core and earth cable is used in a two-way switching circuit. So, lights such as the hall light may be controlled from upstairs as well as downstairs. If the upstairs switch **A** links the Common and **L1** terminals, as shown in the diagram, then a circuit is completed and the light turned on. The power flows from **L1**, which is linked to the switch feed, via the Common to Common in switch **B** downstairs. The position of that switch allows the current to flow from Common to **L1** and back along the yellow core to **L2** in switch **A**, which is linked to the switch return, so completing the circuit.*

*If switch **B** is turned off, the power still flows from the **L1** to Common in switch **A**, but the link between Common and **L1** in switch **B** is broken. The power is directed to **L2** and then along the blue core to **L1** in switch **A**. This leaves the power 'shunting' between the switches but doesn't allow a circuit to be completed so the light is off.*

then divided in two: the first core goes to the Common terminal in one switch, the second to the Common terminal in the other. It's all run in single-core cable, and is designed for use where your home's wiring is run entirely in conduit – as it may well be if you live in a flat.

In most homes, though, the wiring takes the form of multi-cored PVC-sheathed cables, and in this case, a different two-way switching circuit is generally more convenient. What happens is that the switch drop, run in two-core and earth cable, is connected to only one of the two-way switches: one core to L1, the other to L2. This switch is then linked to its partner with three-core and earth cable, a cable which has rather oddly colour-coded wires – one red, one yellow, and one blue. However, this doesn't make the wiring up any more complicated. The yellow and blue cores are connected in the same way as the straps in the traditional system, and the red core is used to link the two Common terminals.

Converting an existing switch

That's the theory, but how does it work in practice? How do you convert an existing one-way switching circuit to two-way switching? You may be surprised at just how simple it is. Using a club hammer and cold chisel, make a hole in the wall to take a one-gang, plaster-depth mounting box at the spot where you want the new switch to go. This should be secured to the wall with a couple of screws and wallplugs.

Then, before running a length of 1.0 or $1.5mm^2$ three-core and earth PVC-sheathed cable to the original switch position, connect up the new switch in order to minimise the time the power has to be switched off at the mains. The red core should go to the Common terminal with the yellow and blue cores acting as strap wires. The running of the cable shouldn't pose any difficulty. The cable is taken up the wall, above the ceiling and back down the wall to the old switch.

Chop a channel in the plaster at the wall sections of the run, insert a length of PVC conduit and pass the cable through that. Above the ceiling, if the cable runs at right angles to the joists, feed it through holes drilled at least 50mm below their top edge.

If the cable runs parallel to the joists, simply rest it on top of the ceiling, unless it is likely to be disturbed – as in a loft, for example. In that case it must be secured to the sides of the joists with cable clips. Turn off the power at the mains before removing the fixing screws. Then, ease the original switch from the wall so you can pass the cable into the mounting box.

With the cable in position, all that remains to be done is connect it up to the new two-way switch at the original switch position. Finally, connect the two cores of the switch drop to terminals L1 and L2, screw the switch securely to its mounting box and restore the power.

CHANGING THE DOOR SWITCH

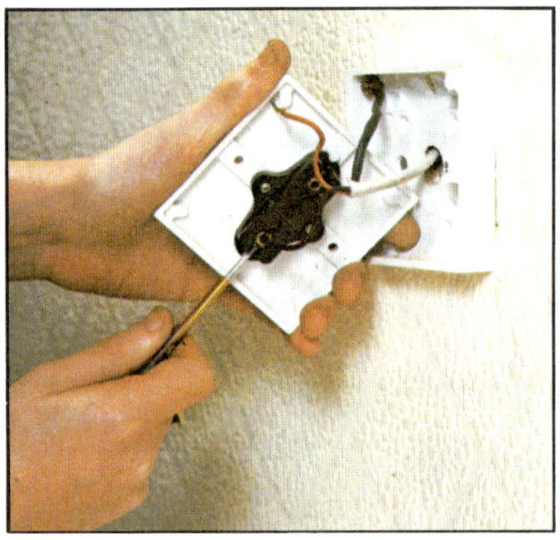

1 *Turn off the power at the mains and remove the screws in the old switch's faceplate. Ease the switch from the wall until you can disconnect it.*

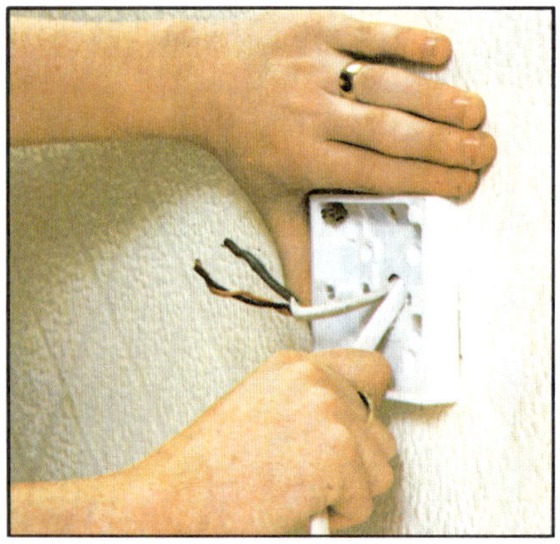

2 *Run one three-core and earth cable per light from the RB4 box to the switch mounting box, using an existing conduit to carry it down the wall.*

3 *For two wall lights, install a three-gang, two-way switch. Use two gangs to connect the three-core cables – yellow to L1, blue to L2 and red to Common.*

FITTING THE BEDSIDE SWITCHES

1 *Using a club hammer and bolster chisel, chop a channel in the wall from the ceiling down to the new switch position ready for the cable.*

2 *Mark the exact position of the switch on the wall, then chop out a recess, taking care to ensure that it is deep enough to take the metal mounting box.*

3 *Before running the cable, insert a length of PVC conduit into the channel; where possible poke it through into the void above the ceiling.*

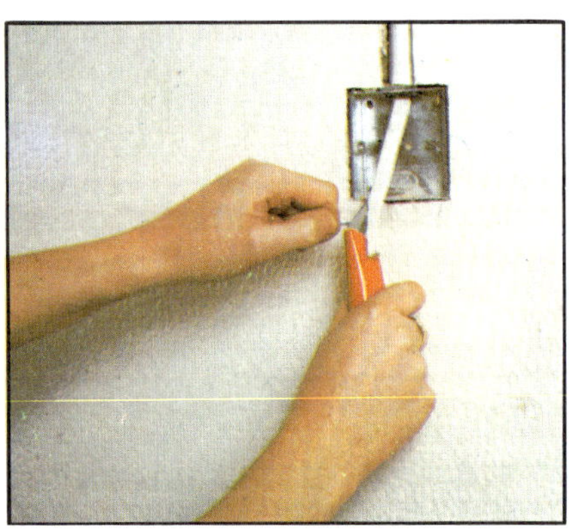

5 *Strip the ends of the three-core and earth cable from the RB4 ready for connection, remembering to fit the earth wires with green and yellow sleeving.*

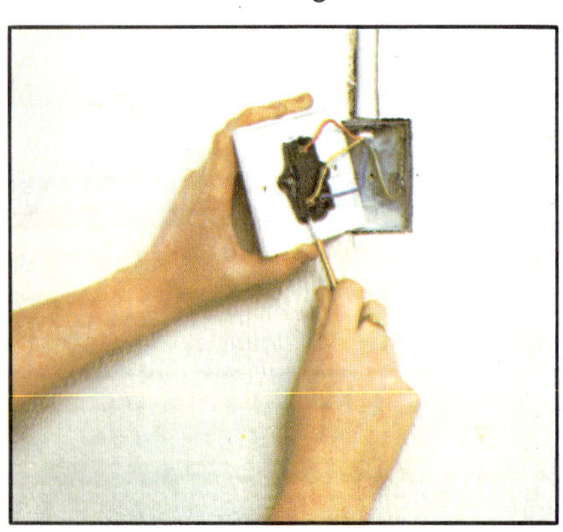

6 *Next connect the cable to a one-gang, two-way switch, linking the yellow core to the L1 terminal, the blue core to L2 and the red core to Common.*

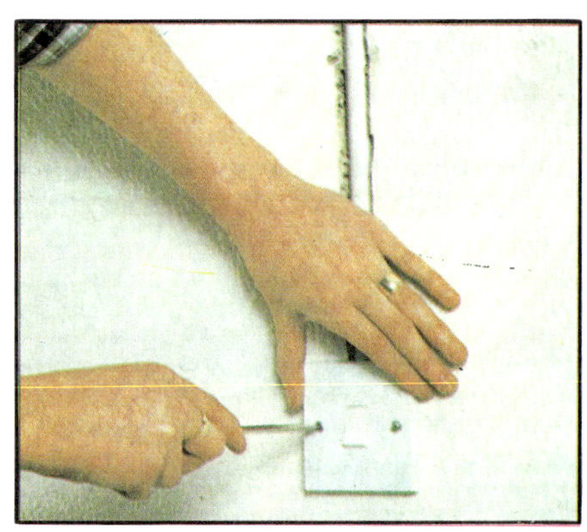

7 *Having connected the earth core to the terminal on the mounting box, screw the new switch securely into place and check that it is level.*

4 Connect the switch drop from the room's main light to the third gang to give one-way switching. One core goes to L2, the other to Common.

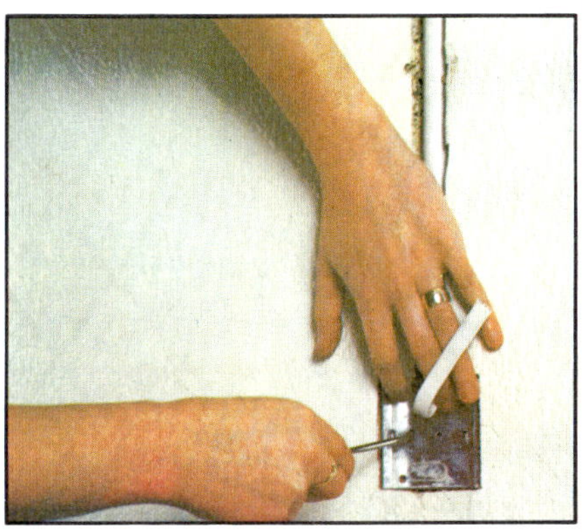

4 At the second switch position of each light, use screws and wallplugs to fix a one-gang, plaster-depth mounting box in a hole cut into the wall.

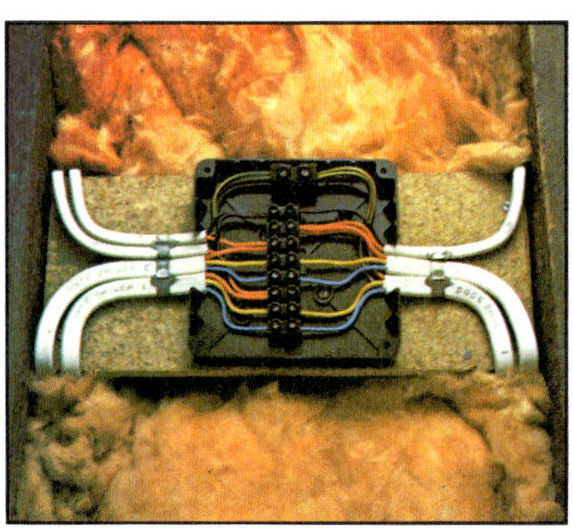

8 Finally, join up all the cables in the RB4 junction box. It's much easier than it looks and the connections can be seen in detail on page 70.

New circuits

The same system can also be employed in new work where you require two-way switching. For example, if you are installing a new wall light and want to be able to control it from a switch at the door of the room, as well as from a switch near the light itself, all you need to do is install the light and a new two-way switch in the normal way (see pages 173–176) and then run a length of three-core and earth cable from this switch to the switch by the door (the one controlling the room's main light). Here, you replace the old one-gang, one-way switch with a two-gang, two-way switch and connect the three-core and earth cable to one gang for two-way switching. Then connect the switch drop belonging to the room's main light to the other gang, this time connecting it up for one-way switching with one of the cores going to the L2 terminal and the other to the Common.

This method is quite straightforward, but it is not necessarily the most convenient way of setting about the job. Suppose you were installing not one new wall light, but two or more. If they are all to have two-way switches then you'll be involved in a great deal of cable running and, therefore, a great deal of work. After all, for each light you have to run a cable down to the new switch, back up above the ceiling, then back down the wall again to the second switch position.

This extra work can be avoided by using a junction box and a variation on the traditional two-way switching circuit. You run the circuit using three-core and earth PVC-sheathed and insulated cable. Doing this you are using the cable's red core as one half of the switch drop and the yellow and blue cores as straps. Then connect them up, together with the cables to the wall lights and the cable supplying the new circuit with power (taken from a loop-in ceiling rose, or from a junction box inserted into one of your home's main lighting circuits) in a large multi-terminal joint box called an RB4. The step-by-step photographs will explain what is happening but note that only one cable need be run to each wall-light.

Intermediate switching

There is one other kind of two-way switching that could be useful in your home. It's called an intermediate switching circuit and it means that a light or group of lights can be controlled by three or more separate switches. It's easy to install because all you do is introduce one or more additional switches into the circuit between the two two-way switches. This can, of course, be very convenient because you can then control a light from as many positions as you like. For example, you could control a hall light from a switch near the front door, from one near the living room door and from another switch on the landing upstairs.

Ready Reference

TWO-WAY SWITCHING

Two-way switching lets you control a light from two separate switches. The illustration shows the back of a two-way switch with its

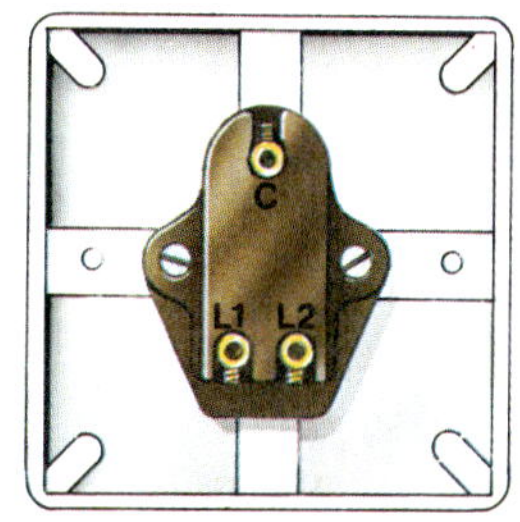

three terminals labelled Common, L1 and L2. In any two-way switching circuit, both switches are exactly the same and have equivalent terminals. But wiring up the switches is completely different from connecting up one-way switches.

This is because each two-way switch must be able to control the light independently of the other.

The traditional way of wiring two-way switches as used in flats or all-conduit installations is to use single core to make the connections:

- the L1 and L2 terminals of each switch are linked by single-core cables that are known as straps
- the switch drop cable that provides the power to the circuit is divided with the feed going to one Common terminal and the return going to the other.

More often PVC-sheathed three-core and earth cable, colour coded red, yellow and blue, is used:

- the Common terminals are linked by the red cores, with the yellow and blue cores acting as straps
- the switch drop is then connected to the L1 and L2 terminals of just one of the switches.

CONVERTING A CIRCUIT

To convert an existing one-way switching circuit to two-way switching:

- replace the existing switch with a two-way switch
- run 1.0 or 1.5mm² PVC-sheathed and insulated three-core and earth cable to the new switch position
- connect it to another two-way switch.

This method can also be used to create new two-way switching circuits.

There are two ways of carrying out the wiring but with both methods a special switch called an intermediate switch is needed. This has four terminals: two marked L1 and two marked L2. To install an intermediate switch in a two-way switching circuit all you do is use the switch to interrupt the three-core and earth cable – or the strap wires in a traditional circuit that has been installed in a flat or where the cables are all run in conduit.

The cores from the L1 terminals and L2 terminals in one two-way switch go to the L1 terminals on one side of the intermediate switch and the L1 and L2 cores from the second two-way switch go to the L2 terminals on the other side. However, with a three-core and earth circuit this leaves a break in the core linking the two-way switches' Common terminals. One way of solving this problem is to join the ends of the two cores with a cable connector. Once the two red cores have been joined the connector unit is then placed in the space behind the intermediate switch. However, it's better to interrupt the three-core and earth cable with a multi-terminal junction box above the ceiling near the intermediate switch position. You need six terminals in the junction box: one for the earth cores, one for both the red cores from the Common terminals and one each for the remaining yellow and blue cores.

At this stage you should introduce two lengths of two-core and earth cable which, by connecting up to the appropriate terminals, are used to extend the yellow and blue cores from each two-way switch. When that's done, run the two two-core and earth cables down to the intermediate switch and connect them up just as if they were the two pairs of yellow and blue cores in the three-core and earth cable. It is worth remembering that if one of the switches in an intermediate circuit is to be cord-operated then it should be one of the end switches. There are no cord-operated intermediate switches available.

INSTALLING A NEW TWO-WAY CIRCUIT

Using an RB4 multi-terminal junction box can save you running extra cable when you install a new two-way circuit with more than one light. Here it has been used to install a bedside lighting circuit, shown diagramatically. Page 68 shows how the circuit is wired up, step by step.

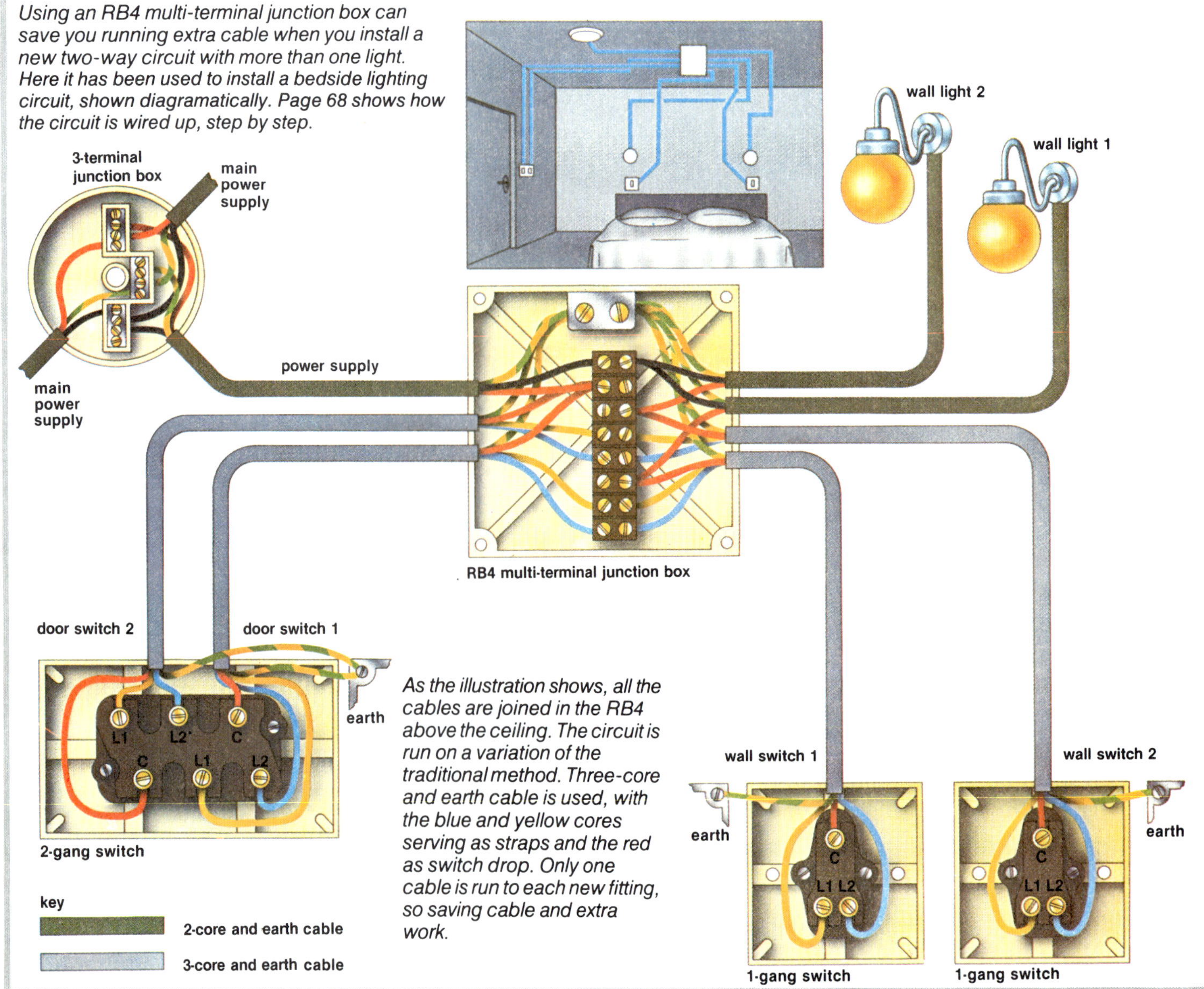

As the illustration shows, all the cables are joined in the RB4 above the ceiling. The circuit is run on a variation of the traditional method. Three-core and earth cable is used, with the blue and yellow cores serving as straps and the red as switch drop. Only one cable is run to each new fitting, so saving cable and extra work.

POWER CIRCUITS

With a never-ending stream of apparently indispensable electrical appliances reaching the high street, the demand on your home's power circuits seems set to grow and grow. Making provision for an adequate number of power points in every room makes it much easier – and safer – to use appliances wherever they are wanted.

WIRING FOR COOKERS

Installing the wiring for a new electric cooker is not such a daunting task as it seems. The mains circuitry is similar for freestanding and built-in cookers, and the final connection is simplicity itself to make.

cooker control unit from MK Electric

There are two main types of electric cooker which you will come across in the showrooms. The first is the traditional, freestanding electric cooker which consists of an oven, a hob with three or four boiling rings or hot plates, and a grill that is either at eye-level or else just above the oven. This type is self-contained and usually stands against a wall in the kitchen. The second type is the split-level cooker, and a separate hob and oven are normally built into the kitchen units. In addition to these two there are smaller, table-top models which have only two hot plates, and the increasingly popular micro-wave ovens.

Cooker circuits

Because cookers are heavy current consuming appliances, they require a radial circuit for their exclusive use. This will run from the consumer unit, provided there is a spare MCB or fuseway, or else from a separate switch fuse unit. A circuit like this may already exist, but it is more likely you will have to install it.

Small cookers that can rest on top of a kitchen unit, and micro-wave ovens, can be run without a special circuit. This is because they have an electrical loading of 3kW or less and when that is converted into current rating (see below) you will find that they can safely get their power supply from a 13A socket outlet. But before you install a new radial circuit (see pages 237–240 for further details) you will have to make sure that it is of the correct current rating.

Circuit current rating

A small electric cooker with, say two boiling rings, a grill and an oven, is likely to have an electrical loading of around 10kW, while a fully equipped cooker with a double oven will probably have a rating of 14kW or more. A cooker that rates up to 11kW is usually supplied by a circuit controlled by a 30A fuse, while one with a higher rating is supplied by a 45A circuit. The current rating of the circuit is determined by the maximum current demand from the cooker. To determine that, the total wattage is divided by the voltage of the mains electricity

CHOOSING CABLE RUNS

The cable and switching arrangements for cookers differ depending on whether you have a freestanding cooker or separate hob and oven sections.

1 Freestanding cooker

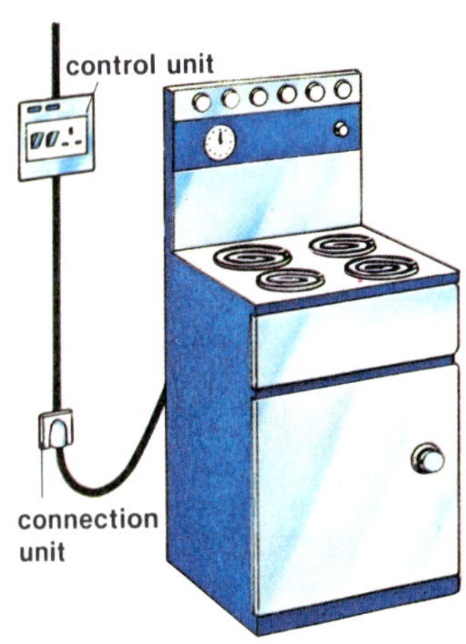

Above: A connection unit allows the trailing cable to join the chased cable, protects the connections and allows the cooker to be easily disconnected for repairs.

2 Separate hob and oven

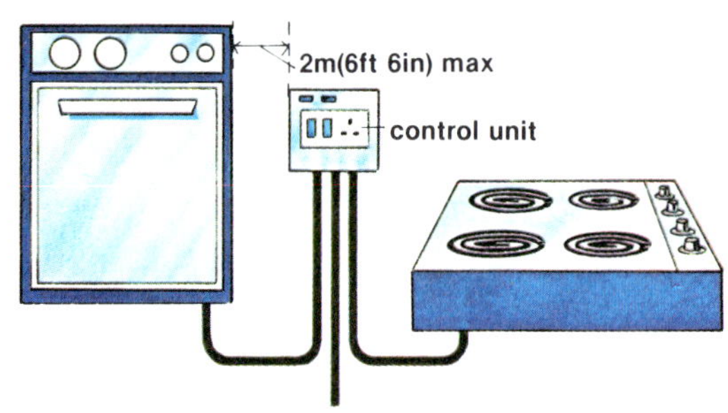

If you want the control unit centred between the sections, run two cables from the control unit, using 6mm^2 cable; the circuit must originate at a cartridge fuse or MCB.

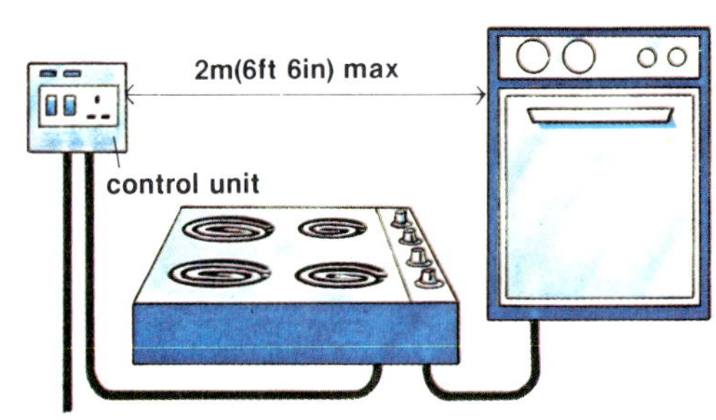

Another method is to run just one cable from the control unit and loop it in and out of one section and then run it onto the second section.

INSTALLING A COOKER CONTROL UNIT

1 *Using a club hammer and cold chisel, chop a recess for the mounting box and chases for the circuit cable and the cable to the connection unit.*

2 *Drill and plug holes in the wall before fitting the box. Remember to put grommets on the knockout holes and run the cable inside conduit.*

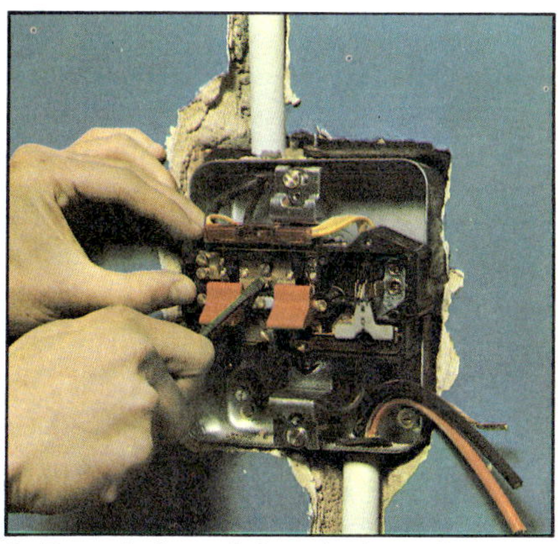

3 *Detach the unit from its faceplate to make the connections on the mains side. Earth the box by linking its earth screw with the earth terminal.*

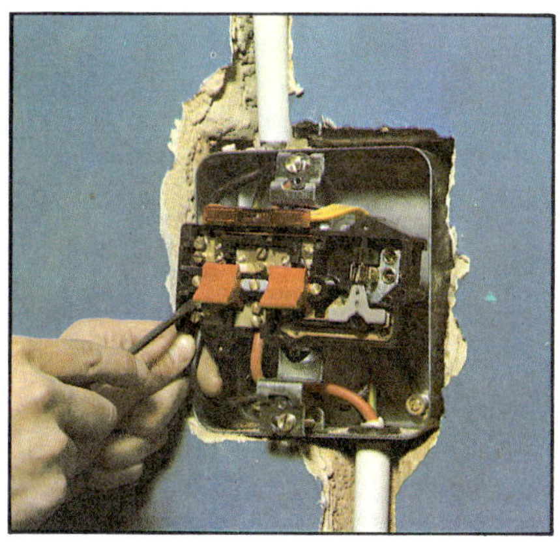

4 *Then make the connections on the cooker side. Remember to sleeve all the earth cores in green/yellow PVC before connecting them.*

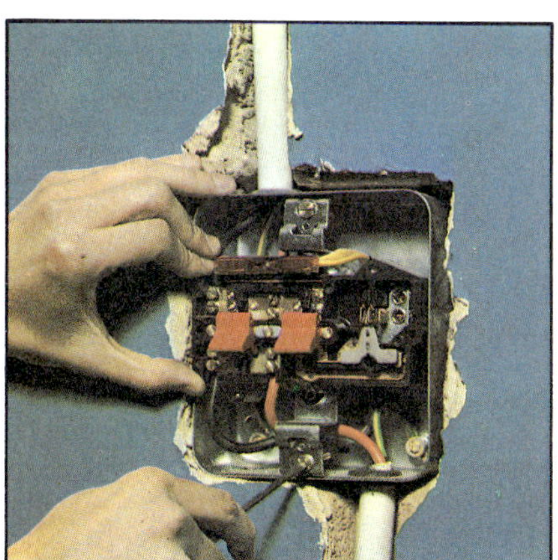

5 *When you've made all the connections, make sure the unit is square to the wall and then screw it securely onto the mounting box.*

TIP

6 *You can now fix the centre part of the face plate. Before fixing the rest, make good and redecorate the surface of the wall.*

Ready Reference

SIMPLE COOKER REPAIRS

You can carry out several simple repairs on most electric cookers. However, before starting work, isolate the cooker circuit at the main consumer unit by removing the circuit fuse or switching off the MCB.

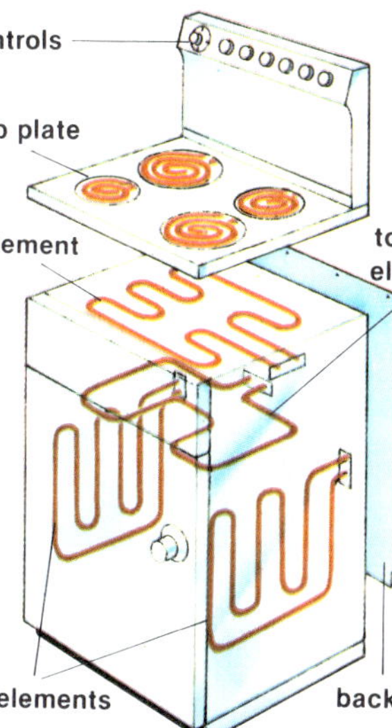

Replacing a boiling ring

Double check that you have bought the correct ring to install. Then:

- remove the faulty boiling ring
- lift off the hob or prop it up
- undo the fixing nuts and bolts in the correct channel
- lift out the faulty ring
- detach the wires, remembering to take note of their positions
- fit the new boiling ring.

Replacing a grill element

When replacing this:

- remove hob spillage tray and grill tray
- lift hob
- disconnect terminal leads to the grill
- disconnect cable leading to the earth
- remove screws holding element supports
- push supports inwards to free element
- replace new element in reverse order.

Replacing an oven element

This can usually be done from the front of the cooker. In some cases, the panels within the oven will have to be removed:

- disconnect the leads and earth to remove the old element or,
- to prevent them slipping back, immediately transfer the leads one by one to the new element with the old one only partially withdrawn
- make sure all parts are replaced in the same positions.

THE CONNECTION UNIT

1 *Chop the recess for the box and the chase for the cable. Then run in the cable and earth the box to give it extra protection.*

2 *Connect the earths to the centre terminals and other cores to the outer two. If you aren't connecting the cooker yet, fit the unit's cover.*

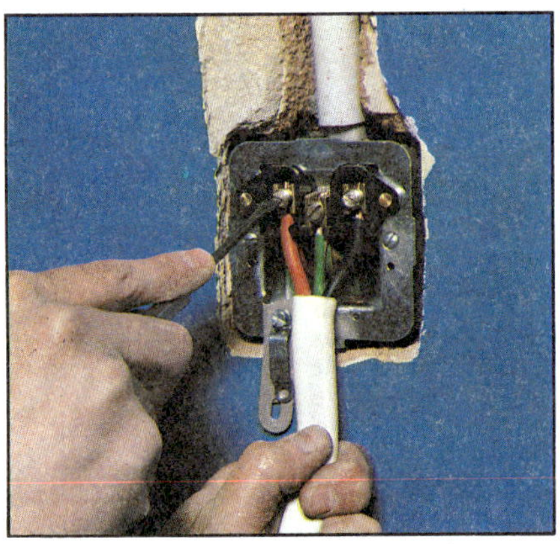

3 *Undo the clamp and hold in place the trailing cooker cable while you connect it. Remember, it should be the same size as the circuit cable.*

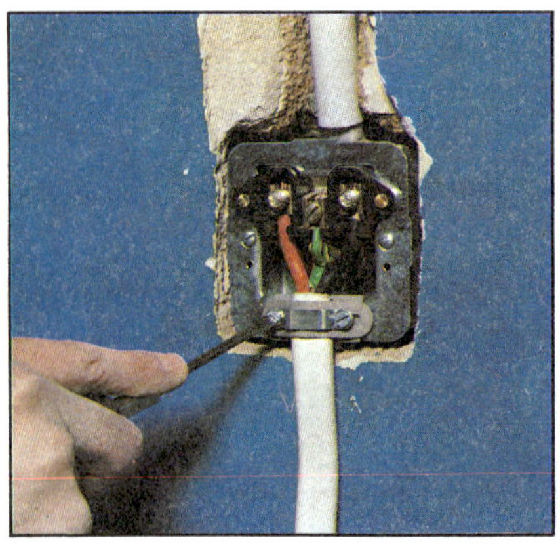

4 *Screw up the clamp plate to hold the cable and protect the connections. Make good before fitting the cover, which should cover any ragged edges.*

supply. So, if you have a 12kW cooker, dividing 12,000 by 240 indicates that, in theory at least, the cooker should be supplied by a 50A circuit. In addition, if the cooker control unit incorporates a 13A socket outlet, the total current demand reaches 63A. However, in practice allowance is made for the fact that the boiling rings, the oven, and the grill will rarely be used all at the same time. And, even if they are, the current demand will still be less than 63A because peak demand is reduced by thermostatic devices incorporated in the cooker.

In fact, when calculations are being made for the current demand of a domestic electric cooker, the wiring regulations take account of this. Therefore, the 12kW cooker, theoretically rated at 63A, is actually reckoned to have a current demand of 27A. That means it can be supplied safely by a circuit controlled by a 30A fuse or MCB.

The new circuit

Cooker circuits are normally run in two-core and earth PVC-sheathed cable. It's best to use 6mm^2 cable for a 30A circuit and 10mm^2 cable for a 45A one. The circuit cable runs from the consumer unit to a cooker control unit or control switch, taking the shortest possible route. This could be under the floorboards or in the ceiling void. You could either run the cable in a chase chopped in the wall or else surface mount it by using either mini-trunking or cable clips. Obviously it looks much neater to have your cable concealed within conduit beneath the surface of the wall. For more detailed information on running cable see pages 31-35.

Do remember that this larger size cable can be quite expensive and before buying it, it's a good idea to measure fairly precisely the length you will require, and to aim for the most economical cable run in your planning. However, you ought to allow a surplus for contingency purposes should you encounter obstacles when you run the circuit.

Cooker control units and switches

You will be able to control the power for your electric cooker from a cooker control unit or a cooker switch. A control unit has two switches, one of which controls the power to the cooker, while the other controls the power supply to a 13A socket outlet that is incorporated in the unit. A cooker control switch is an alternative to this sort of unit and is merely a double-pole switch marked 'cooker'. While it's more convenient to fit a control unit with an extra socket, there is the danger of having the kettle flex trailing across a switched on boiling ring and so risking fire. If you're planning to install a free-standing cooker, a special connector unit is fitted at the end of the chased cable run and from it cable is run on to the cooker. The advantage of this is that if you want to repair or replace your cooker all you have to do is disconnect it at the unit after switching off at the control unit or cooker switch. A connector like this also provides special clamps to prevent any unnecessary strain being put on the terminals when the cooker is moved out from the wall.

An alternative is to use a cable outlet unit which clamps the cable and allows it to run to the cooker without a break.

Position of the control unit

The traditional height for a cooker control unit is about 1.5m (5ft) above the floor so that it can be reached easily. It shouldn't be any closer than 300mm (1ft) to the cooker but mustn't be more than 2m (6ft) away from it. One control unit or switch may supply both sections of a split-level cooker, provided that both of them are within 2m (6ft) of the unit. As the control unit is usually sited midway between the two sections it means that they can be up to 4m (13ft) apart – which allows for considerable scope in kitchen planning. When the control unit is fixed between the two cooker sections, two cables can be run from the unit supplying the oven and hob sections respectively. But if the unit is fixed at the side of one of the sections then one cable is used to connect that and another links into it to provide power for the second section. However, the same size cable is used throughout. Another alternative is to install both a cooker control unit and a cooker switch. The main cooker circuit will still run from the consumer unit or switchfuse unit to the cooker control unit, and from there a cable of the same size will run to one of the sections. Another cable will loop out of the control unit and link the cooker switch into the circuit. Finally, a cable from the switch will then run to the second section. If you are installing an island hob unit, then this is

CONNECTING UP THE COOKER

1 *After removing the cooker's back plate, sleeve the earth core in green/yellow PVC and then connect the cores to their respective terminals.*

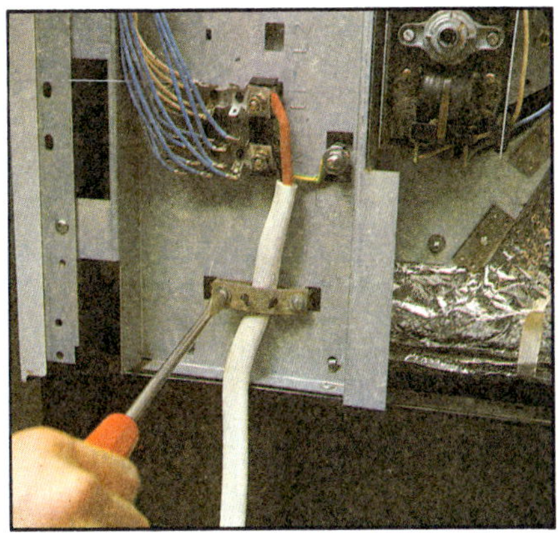

2 *Fix the cable under the clamp plate to give the connections extra protection. Then put on the back plate and switch on at the mains.*

obviously a more convenient circuit arrangement than running two new radial circuits to the units.

Connecting to the control unit

If you are fitting a flush-mounted unit you will have to sink a metal mounting box into a chase chopped into the plaster and masonry. Obviously the size and depth of the box depends on the type and model of unit you decide to use. Because the mounting boxes are quite deep, chop the recess out carefully on internal walls, or consider using a surface-mounted box instead. Before finally fixing the box into the wall, do remember to remove the necessary knockout blanks to allow in the various cables – usually two for a freestanding cooker and three for a split-level one – and to fix with plastic grommets into the holes to protect those cables.

For surface mounting a control unit, a plastic mounting box has to be fixed to the wall with wood screws. The circuit cable should run down from the ceiling or up from the floor and should be chased into the wall. Take it into the box and strip off the sheathing, leaving about 25mm (1in) within the box. If you're fitting a surface-mounted box unit it's easier to take the unit out of its box to make the connection. Trim the wires to about 18mm (3/4in) and strip 12mm (1/2in) of insulation from the end of each core. The earth cores should be enclosed in green/yellow PVC sleeving and connected to the earth terminal. The two insulated cores are connected to the terminals marked MAINS, with the red going to L and black to N. The cores of the cable, or cables, running to the cooker are connected to the equivalent terminals, marked COOKER, on the lower side of the control unit. These cables should be secured under the clamp (ie, incorporated in the unit). After you've connected the cables to the control unit, refit it in its box and fit the cover.

Wiring up the connector unit

The cable from the cooker control unit should be chased into the wall and run to the connector unit. Insert both the cable from the control unit and that leading to the cooker itself into the box. After preparing the ends, connect the sleeved earth cores to the centre terminal, the red insulated cores to one of the outer terminals, and the black insulated cores to the other. Then tighten the clamp screws that secure the trailing cable and replace the unit's cover. Double check this because if the clamp is on the individual cores and not the sheathing it could damage the connections.

Connecting to the cooker

At the back of a freestanding cooker there is a panel which must be removed to allow entry for the cable through the grommetted entry hole. Prepare the cable as you did when you connected to the cooker control unit, not forgetting to add an extra sleeve of green/yellow PVC to insulate the earth core. Then connect the red core to the terminal marked L, the black to the one marked N, and the earth core to the terminal marked E. Again, remember to secure the cable under the cable clamp before refitting the panel as this gives vital protection to the connections if the cooker is moved away from the wall at any time. If you are installing a split-level cooker the connections are basically the same as for a freestanding model, although the position of the terminal blocks may well vary from model to model.

Ready Reference

COOKER HOODS

There are two main types of cooker hood that you can fit easily above your electric cooker and so get rid of unpleasant cooking smells:

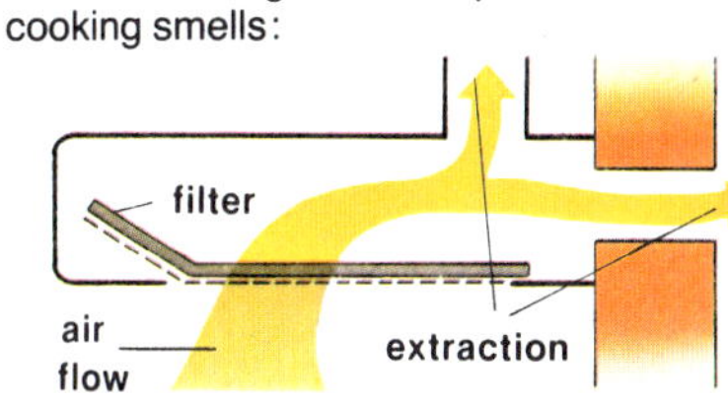

- re-circulating hoods, which contain a replaceable filter that purifies the air before returning it to the kitchen without heat loss

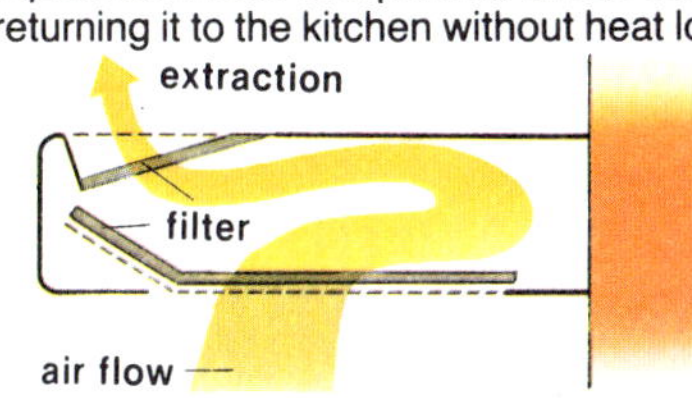

- ducted hoods, which carry the air to the outside. Ideally your cooker should stand against an outside wall, otherwise you'll have to use flexible ducting.

OBTAINING THE POWER

There are three sources of power for a cooker hood:

- from a 13A socket outlet in the cooker control unit
- from the lighting circuit, in which case you should use a 20A double-pole (DP) switch with a flex outlet
- from a spur on the ring circuit, in which case the outlet should be a 13A switched fuse connection unit with a 3A fuse.

TILED WALLS

To fit a cooker control unit or switch on a tiled wall you should centre the box at the join of four tiles for a neater finish.

For flush mounting:

- score the area of tiles to be removed with a tile cutter
- gently tap the scored lines with a bolster chisel, taking care not to crack the rest of the surface
- remove the pieces of tile, chop a hole for the box, then fit it in position.

For surface mounting:

- make a cross of masking tape and mark the point at which you want each hole
- drill through, being careful not to use too high a speed otherwise you risk crazing the tile
- fit the mounting box in the usual way.

FITTING A WASTE DISPOSAL UNIT

Unwanted food – everything from potato peelings to leftovers – usually ends up in a smelly kitchen bin. It can be got rid of more quickly and hygienically with a waste disposal unit.

Waste King disposal unit by Wilec Ltd

Waste disposal units are an excellent means of getting rid of waste food and the like. Potato and vegetable peelings, cabbage stalks and outer leaves, food scraps, apple cores, tea leaves, dead flowers and so on are simply washed down the kitchen sink, ground to a slurry and flushed into the drainage system. Disposal is instant and hygienic, so it removes the need for constantly emptying smelly bins of rotting food. Whether you live in a house, flat or apartment, one of these units can be a tremendous labour-saving device which makes keeping the kitchen clean that much easier.

Of course there are limitations to what a waste disposal unit can do: it can't deal with all household waste. Broken china, tin cans, bottle caps and large bones will only clog and possibly damage the appliance, so you must be careful not to put them in with other waste. Indeed, jamming is the most common problem with these units, and it usually occurs as a result of misuse. Many modern units have a reversible action motor which enables the jammed material to be cleared by flicking the reversing switch and restarting the motor. Jamming is likely to give rise to over-heating and may cause a thermal cut-out, automatically turning off the motor. In a case like this, it may take some five minutes for the motor to cool sufficiently for it to be restarted. Models without a reversible motor are usually supplied with a key to free the jammed unit. But remember, the electricity supply must be cut off before using it.

When waste disposal units were first introduced, the sewage authorities were concerned that the slurry produced by them could result in sewers becoming choked with silt. Although these fears have proved unfounded, you must make sure that any sediment produced is flushed safely through the household drainage system. It's therefore important to leave the cold tap running while the unit is in operation. This will also help to prevent jamming.

Installation requirements

Waste disposal units have to be plumbed permanently into the waste outlet of the kitchen sink. They are driven by a relatively powerful motor which turns a set of steel blades. It's these blades that grind the waste into the slurry that's washed into the drainage system.

In order to operate effectively the unit needs to be connected to an 89mm (3½in) diameter sink waste outlet instead of the usual 38mm (1½in) hole, although some models can be adapted to fit this size. You can usually buy a sink with this larger sized opening, but if you already have a stainless steel sink the outlet can be enlarged using a special cutting tool which is rather like a hacksaw with a saw file as a blade.

If you have a sink top made of ceramic or plastic material, or enamelled pressed steel, you can't fit a waste disposal unit unless you're prepared to renew the sink top at the same time.

The outlet from the unit itself is 38mm (1½in) diameter and, like any other waste outlet, must be connected to a trap to prevent smells from the yard gully or the main soil and waste stack entering the kitchen. It's best to use a simple tubular P-trap which will allow the waste and slurry to pass through without leaving any sediment behind. Bottle traps should not be used as they are more likely to block and they also discharge more slowly.

Where the waste pipe from a waste disposal unit situated on the ground floor of a house is taken to a yard gully, it is particularly important that the waste pipe should discharge into the gully above the water level but below the level of the gully grid. In this way the grid will not become fouled by the slurry and, more importantly, the full force of the water discharged from the sink waste will be available to ensure that the slurry will be flushed through the gully and then out into the sewer.

Back or side inlet gullies are available and these are to be preferred when a new drainage system is being installed. However, there are also slotted gully grids on the market and these are highly suitable for converting existing drainage systems. The branch waste pipe from the kitchen sink is simply extended to discharge just below the slot in the gully.

Fitting a waste disposal unit

An existing stainless steel sink can be adapted by using a special cutting tool, after removing the existing waste outlet. When you are trying to remove the outlet, use a pair of pliers to hold the waste grid while turning the back-nut with a wrench. If this proves difficult, try heating it with a blow-torch. If this still doesn't do the trick, try burning out the washer between the base of the sink and the back-nut with your blow-torch and cutting through the old waste with a hacksaw. When

MAKING A NEW WASTE OUTLET

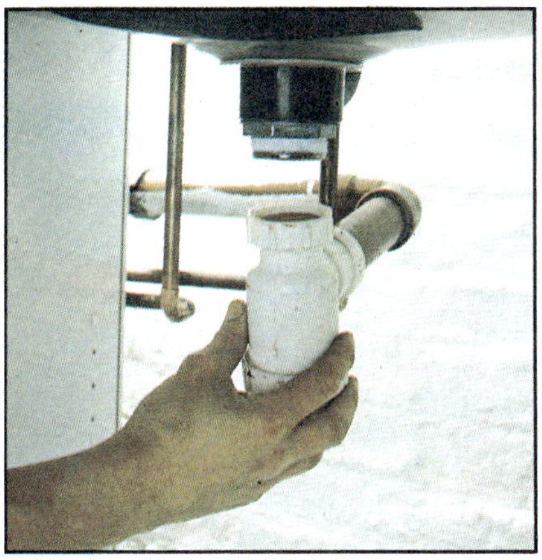

1 *Disconnect the waste trap from your waste outlet. If the trap is plastic this should be easy; for metal traps a little more effort may be required.*

2 *When you have detached the waste trap, use a wrench to unscrew the back-nut which holds the outlet in position. Remove it and the washer.*

3 *Pull out the outlet when you have detached the back-nut. If the mastic or putty holds it tightly in position, lever it out with a screwdriver.*

4 *When you have removed the waste outlet, measure the hole you need, mark it out in the sink and cut it with a saw file cutting tool.*

5 *Lift out the metal section carefully as it will be ragged and sharp where you have cut it. Check that the hole is the right size.*

6 *Take the new outlet flange supplied with the unit and put a bead of plumber's putty underneath it before placing it in the opening.*

Ready Reference

OPERATING A DISPOSAL UNIT

ALWAYS

- grind food waste with a strong flow of cold water
- grind all soft waste including paper napkins, paper towels, cigar and cigarette butts, tea bags provided they don't have strings, and also small bones such as chicken bones
- flush the unit regularly to aid thorough cleaning
- turn the power switch off before attempting to clear a jam or remove an object from the disposer
- use a long piece of wood to clear jams
- leave the outlet cover in place to reduce the risk of objects falling into it when not in use
- make sure the unit is earthed.

NEVER

- put your fingers or hands into the unit to clear a jam
- let children operate the unit
- use hot water when grinding waste – but you can drain it out between grinding periods
- feed in large quantities of fibrous waste at once – instead, this should be well mixed with other waste and fed in gradually
- grind cans, bottles, bottle caps, glass, china, leather, cloth, rubber, string, feathers, newsprint, or large bones
- pour any drain-cleaning chemicals through the unit
- turn off the motor or water until grinding is completed (ie, only when you can hear the motor running freely).

FAULT FINDING

Problems may occur with your unit:

- if there is a water leak round the sink flange: the seal will have to be remade
- if the water drains slowly when the unit is in operation and the waste is clogging up the outlet: keep on grinding and flushing through
- if the disposer won't start. There may be an electrical fault or the motor may have been overloaded: check the cut-out and reset if necessary
- if the unit doesn't function properly immediately after installation. It is likely that the drain line is blocked or can't cope with the outlet discharge – unless there is a problem with the unit itself
- if there are loud noises from the unit when it's in operation: switch off and check for foreign bodies
- if the unit jams: turn it off and follow the manufacturer's instructions for cleaning blockages.

INSTALLING THE WASTE DISPOSAL UNIT

1 Take the basic flange components supplied and check the assembly order. There will be a gasket ring, a spacer ring, and a protector ring.

2 Hold the sink flange down, slide the assembly into place, and tighten the screws evenly to make sure there is a watertight seal.

3 Lubricate the inner lip of the rubber flange on the top of the unit with a small amount of petroleum jelly or household oil.

4 Push the unit into place so that the rubber lip engages the sink flange and is held in place by it, leaving the unit hanging by itself.

5 Rotate the unit to align it with the waste outlet and tighten the screw clamp evenly all round to hold the whole assembly firmly in position.

6 Fix on the waste outlet elbow and attach a P-trap 38mm (1½in) in diameter. Check that the trap is tight and connect it to the waste pipe.

the outlet has been removed, check the size of the enlarged hole you need with the new outlet as a guide, then use the cutting tool to cut it out.

With your aperture cut, or with your new sink, bed down the new waste outlet with plumbers' putty, and screw up the back-nut and washer. Then attach the suspension plate for the unit, and finally the unit itself. The manufacturer should provide full instructions for the whole operation; follow them carefully.

A tubular P-trap should be attached to the unit via pipe connections which will be supplied. If there is no convenient way of attaching a sink overflow to a disposal unit, you can either seal it off or pipe it down to a socket fitted above the trap in the waste outlet.

PARTS OF A WASTE DISPOSAL UNIT

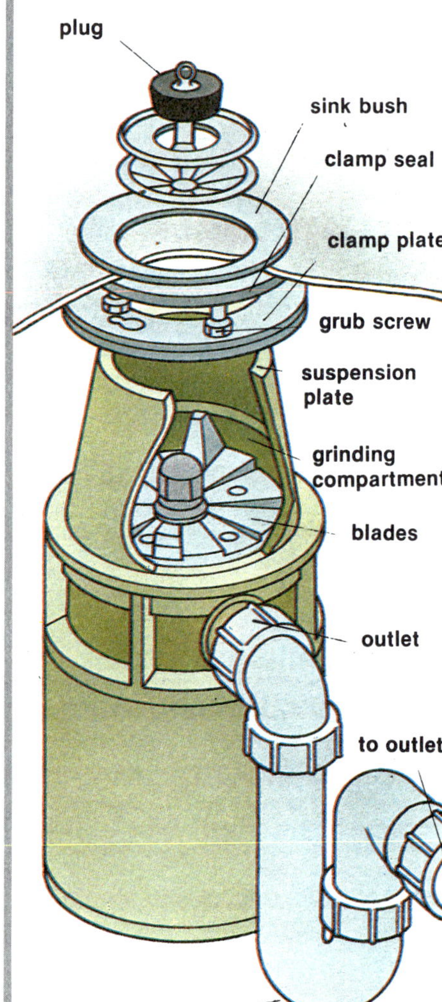

WIRING UP THE UNIT

Providing power for a waste disposal unit is simple. You can plug it directly into a 13A socket outlet, but it's better to run a spur and use a connection unit.

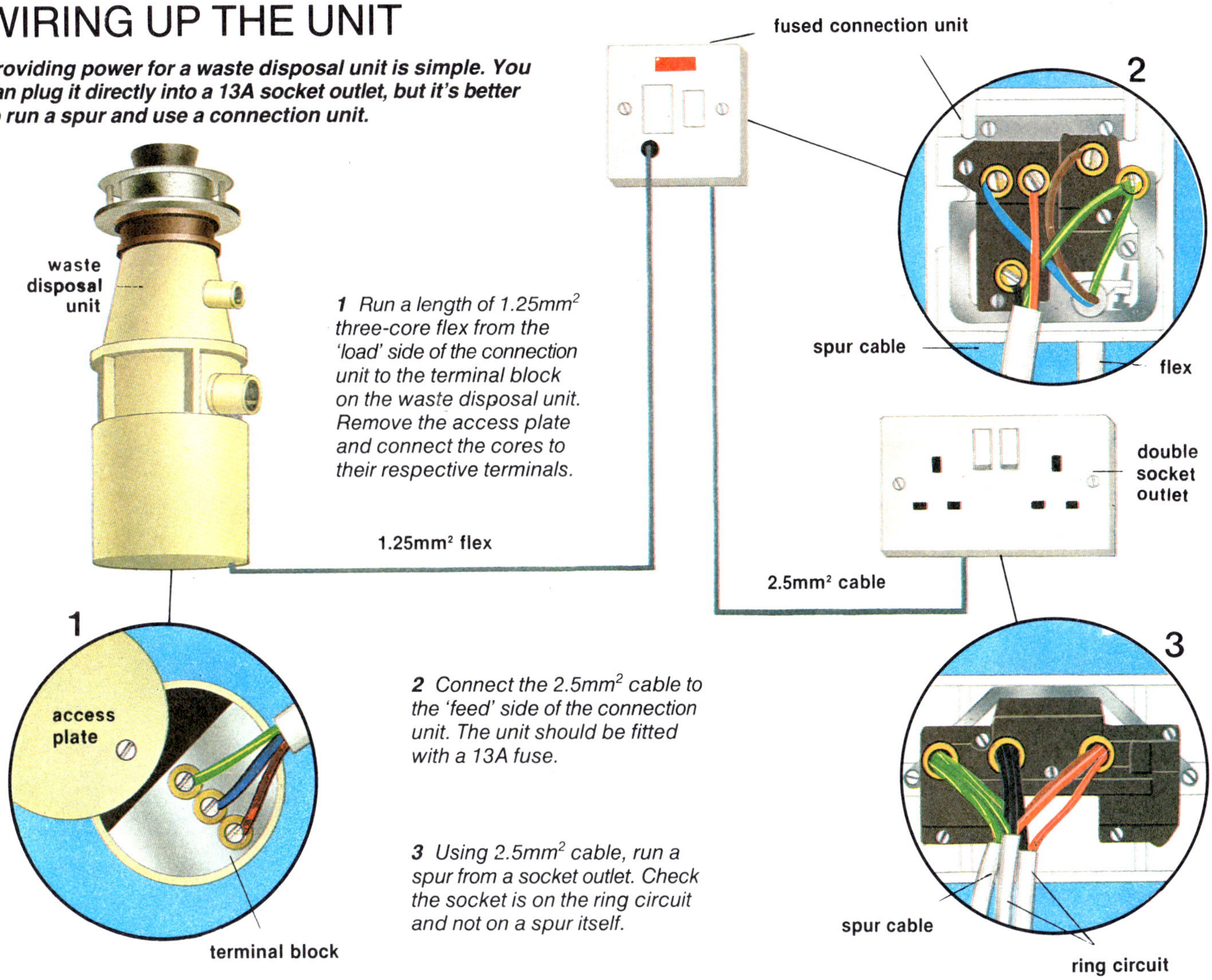

1 Run a length of 1.25mm² three-core flex from the 'load' side of the connection unit to the terminal block on the waste disposal unit. Remove the access plate and connect the cores to their respective terminals.

2 Connect the 2.5mm² cable to the 'feed' side of the connection unit. The unit should be fitted with a 13A fuse.

3 Using 2.5mm² cable, run a spur from a socket outlet. Check the socket is on the ring circuit and not on a spur itself.

Wiring up the unit

Most waste disposal units are powered by an electric induction motor. This sort of motor is constructed differently to the motor found in most other home electrical appliances. It starts immediately on full load, the starting current needed being much less than that of other types of electric motor. As a result a waste disposal unit needs only a 13A electricity supply, which can conveniently be provided from a nearby circuit.

There are a number of models on the market, and the differences between them can affect the electric wiring you have to provide. The principal difference is whether the unit has reversing facilities or not. The simplest type has no reversing facilities – it runs in one direction only. Should the unit become jammed the electricity supply must be switched off before a release key is inserted to engage the impeller and release the jam. Such one-way motors are protected from the overloading a jam causes by a thermal cut-out; after clearing the jam you will have to re-set this by depressing a button on the motor frame before the motor can be re-started.

Other versions have special switch-gear which reverses the direction of the electric motor every time it is switched on. With these types the reversing controller, which incorporates a double-pole switch and 13A fuse, is either mounted on the unit as an integral unit, or fixed to the wall in the kitchen some 300mm (12in) above the work surface.

A waste disposal unit should ideally be connected to a 13A switched fused connection unit (often called a fused spur unit). This unit has the required double-pole isolating switch and 13A cartridge fuse; it might be best to choose the version with a neon indicator light.

A possible alternative outlet is a 13A fused plug and switched socket outlet, but as the switch is only single-pole it is always necessary to remove the plug to isolate the unit and there is also a likelihood that the socket may be used temporarily for other appliances. The circuit wiring required to supply a waste disposal unit is simply a spur cable branching off the ring circuit cable. The connection at the ring circuit is usually more conveniently made at an existing 13A socket outlet than at a junction box inserted into the ring cable. You should use 2.5mm² two-core and earth cable and run it from the socket to the point where you intend to fix the switched fused connection unit or special reversing controller.

Connect a length of 1.25mm² three-core flex to the 'load' side of the connection unit and run it to the terminal block of the waste disposal unit. The brown core should then be connected to the 'L' terminal, the blue to the 'N' and finally the green/yellow to the 'E' terminal.

FITTING AN EXTRACTOR FAN

Stale air, poor ventilation and the build-up of condensation are potential problems in the modern home, particularly in the kitchen and bathroom. Extractor fans can help; they're easy to install, cheap to run and, most important, extremely efficient.

extractor fan from Xpelair

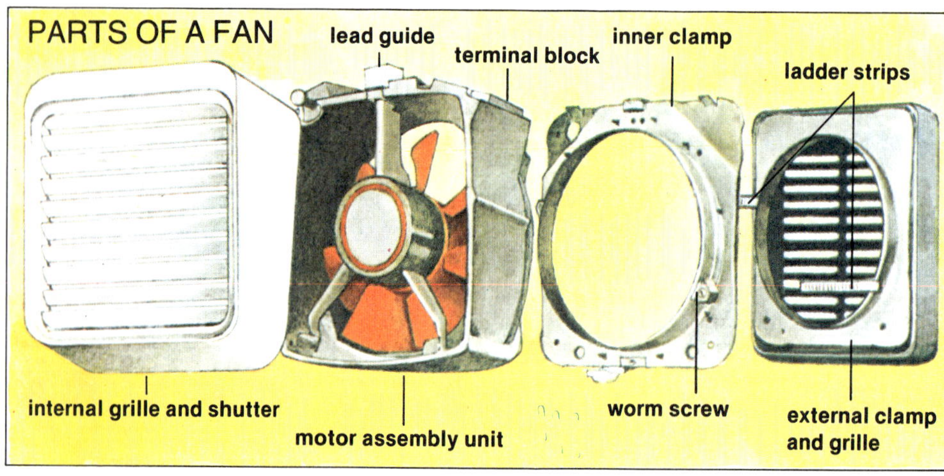

Every home experiences the unpleasantness of lingering cooking smells and poor ventilation. With draught-proofing, double glazing and central heating, the result, in the long term, is likely to be the constant presence of condensation which can eventually damage both the decor and the structure of the home. And in the kitchen persistent condensation is not only unsightly but also unhygienic.

There are a number of measures that can temporarily relieve the problem, but in the long run the only way to deal with it is to get rid of the stale air completely and replace it with fresh. To do this you need to install an extractor fan.

Types of fans

There are three types of extractor fan commonly used in the home and all are comparatively easy to install.

Perhaps the most common is the window fan which is fitted in a hole cut in a fixed pane of glass. These fans can be controlled by an integral switch, usually cord-operated, or else by a separate wall-mounted, rocker switch. The installation involves no structural work; just ask your glazier to replace the pane with one in which a hole has already been cut.

A wall fan, controlled by similar switches, is fitted in a hole made in an external wall or in an air brick vent. This sort of fan takes a little longer to install, as a hole has to be made in the external wall. However, by installing a wall fan in preference to a window-mounted fan you avoid restricting the view from a window and the inconvenience of having to have that window permanently closed.

There's one other common kind of extractor fan and that's the self-actuating, window-mounted plastic ventilator. But although the easiest to install and cheapest to run – no further expenses after installation – this type is also the least effective.

There are other, more specialised, types of extractor fans such as cooker hoods and timed fans for the bathroom or toilet which are variations on the three main types already described. Cooker hoods either recirculate the air in a kitchen after filtering it, or else extract it. Timed fans in the bathroom or toilet are activated by the lightswitch and are particularly useful when these rooms don't have external walls. Obviously, they will require ducting to enable the air to be expelled outside, but the timed switch poses no extra problems as it's connected up to the light switch when the fan is linked to the lighting circuit. Ceiling-fitted extractor fans are also available. They require an unobstructed space of 300mm (12in) between ceiling joists, and may also require ducting to an external wall if you have glass fibre roof insulation.

Calculating your needs

Which type of fan you install is obviously determined by the size of the room but also by whether there is an a accessible external wall available.

It's simple to work out the size of fan required for a particular room. All you do is work out the volume of the room in cubic metres or feet by multiplying the length by the breadth by the height. Then multiply that volume by the number of air changes (see *Ready Reference*).

Siting your fan

If your home has already been fitted with an extractor fan, and it has proved to be less than satisfactory, the chances are that it has been sited in the wrong place.

The most common sign of that is poor ventilation – the result of the short circuiting of air movements between the fan and the air inlet. The extractor fan should be sited as far away from and, if possible, opposite the main source of air replacement.

In a kitchen, fans should always be fitted as high up as possible on a wall or window,

CHOPPING THE HOLE

1 *Drill a hole through the wall and, using a length of string and the drill bit as a compass, accurately mark out the hole to be cut.*

2 *With a cold chisel and club hammer chop round the circle perimeter and then move inwards to dislodge the surface layer of plaster.*

3 *Once you've done this you can use the same chisel to chop away the bricks. Try to leave a brick in the middle of the hole for leverage.*

4 *The hole should be trued up outside. It doesn't matter if it's slightly inaccurate as the clamp plates will cover and seal any rough edges.*

but it is advisable not to install one immediately above a cooker or grill where temperatures are likely to exceed 40°C. So, the best place for it to be located would be on the wall or window adjacent to the cooker and opposite the door or main air inlet.

It is vital to make sure there is an adequate source of fresh air. If you have natural gas or smokeless fuel heating and your house is well sealed, but with no air inlet, an efficient extractor fan might cause a reversal of flow in the flue gases, which would prove extremely dangerous.

In addition, without an adequate inlet, the air pressure might drop and so impair the efficiency of your fan.

If you intend to fit a wall fan, it shouldn't be placed any closer than two brick lengths to a wall edge for fear of causing structural weakness. So, working out where to fit the fan is crucial to its ultimate success in ventilating your home. If you have any doubt about the supply of fresh air it might be an idea to fit an air brick.

Installing a wall fan

As only the very high capacity extractor fans rate over 100W, your fan can take its power from the lighting circuit. However, you should check that, including the wattage of the fan, the light circuit does not exceed the safety level of 1200 watts (counting each light as rated at 100 watts).

Before breaking into the lighting circuit for power a hole must be made in the wall to accommodate the fan. If you have to go through a cavity wall, it must be sealed with a special sleeve that can be obtained from the manufacturer. This will prevent unpleasant air leaking into the room from the cavity. The fan is connected to the circuit wiring by 1.0mm^2 two-core and earth PVC –

Ready Reference

TYPES OF FAN

There are three main types of extractor fan:

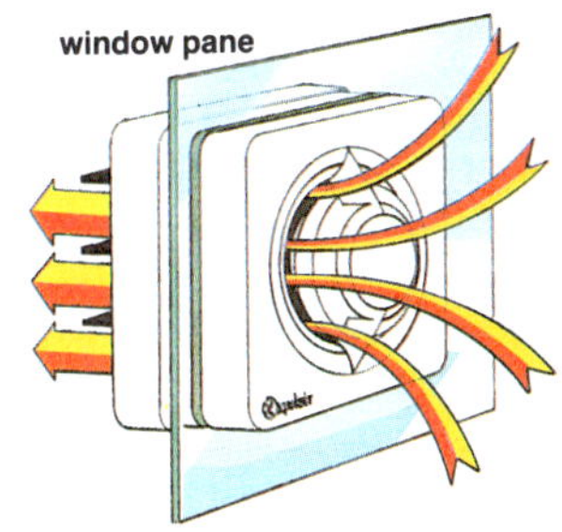

- the window fan fitted to a window with a hole cut in it

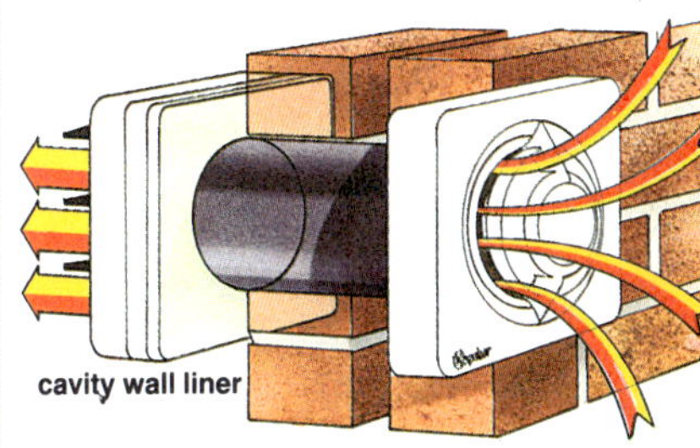

- the wall fan fitted in a similar way to a wall with a hole chopped through it

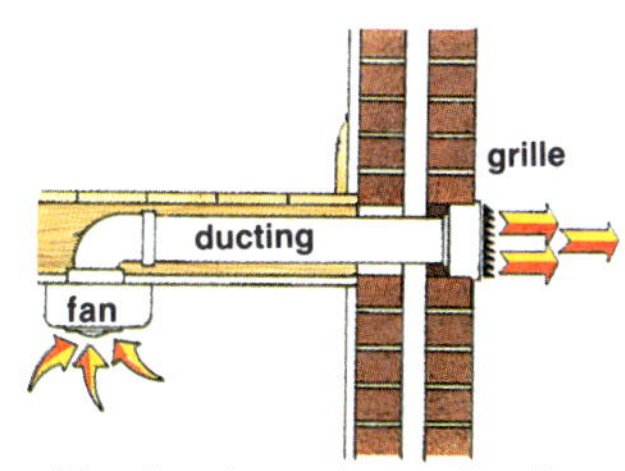

- the ducted fan fitted to an internal wall or ceiling, with ducting to carry the stale air outside.

CALCULATING YOUR NEEDS

To calculate the size of fan you require, multiply the volume of your room by the number of air changes needed per hour. Therefore, length x breadth x height x changes per hour = capacity.

Examples of air changes. Manufacturers recommend the following number of air changes per hour:
bathroom 15 – 20
kitchen 10 – 15
toilet 10 – 15
living room 4 – 6
Remember, always use the higher of these two figures to avoid any possibility of unsatisfactory ventilation.

INSTALLING THE FAN

1 *Attach the ladder strips to the outer clamp and position it in the hole. The ladder strips should run inside any cavity liner.*

2 *Slide the inner clamp plate over the ladder strips and tighten the worm screws to secure the two plates. Then trim the ladder strips to size.*

3 *Attach the motor assembly unit by screwing it to the inner clamp plate. Make sure that any exposed ladder strip is left outside the unit.*

4 *Thread the flex through the lead guide hole and connect it to the terminal block (see diagram), which can be temporarily removed for fitting.*

5 *Clip on and secure the external grille to the outer clamp plate making sure you tighten the holding screw on the underside.*

6 *Finally fit the inner clamp and connect the flex to the fuse unit of the clock connector, which is linked directly to the power supply.*

sheathed house wiring cable; the connecting point should be a fused clock connection unit. This makes isolating the fan for repairs easy: all you do is remove the fuse section.

There are three options for obtaining power for the new fan. You can connect into the circuit at an existing loop-in ceiling rose, run the cable to an existing junction box (always present if you have strip lighting in your kitchen), or install a new junction box in the lighting circuit feed cable and run the new cable to that.

At the fan end of the new cable connect it to the fixed section of the fused clock connector unit. With the main switch turned off connect the new cable to the appropriate terminals of the ceiling rose or junction box.

Then connect one end of a length of 1.0mm^2 three-core circular sheathed flex to the fan and the other end to the plug part of the connection unit. If your fan is double insulated, as in most cases, you need use only two-core flex.

A wall fan is fixed to the wall in almost exactly the same way as a window fan is fitted to a window, the assembly being straightforward and simply a matter of following the manufacturer's instructions. In some cases ladder strips are used to secure the inner and outer clamp plates, and these may need cutting to length to match the wall depth. Otherwise the two plates are mounted independently of each other on either the wall or a panel that must be at least 35mm (1½in) thick. The rubber gaskets on both inner and outer clamp plates are retained in both cases. All fans have shutters which close automatically when the fan is switched off and so prevent any draughts.

If your fan doesn't have an integral switch then a separate switch will have to be fitted. A mounting box should be fixed to the wall at a convenient height below the clock connector. From the connection unit run a length of the 1.0mm sq two-core and earth PVC flat-sheathed cable to the switch. Remember that as one of the wires is the live feed this must be joined at the connection unit end to the circuit live conductor with a plastic cable connector. The connector should be placed in the box behind the clock connector.

If you want to fit a speed controller in conjunction with a fan that has an integral cord-switch there is no essential difference in the wiring. It should be located at the same height as the new switch.

MAKING THE CONNECTIONS

Making the connections for a wall-mounted fan is the easiest part of the installation. Cable can be channelled in or run on the surface.

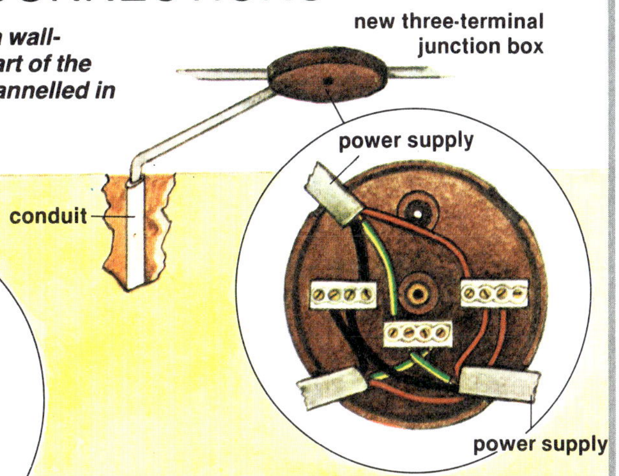

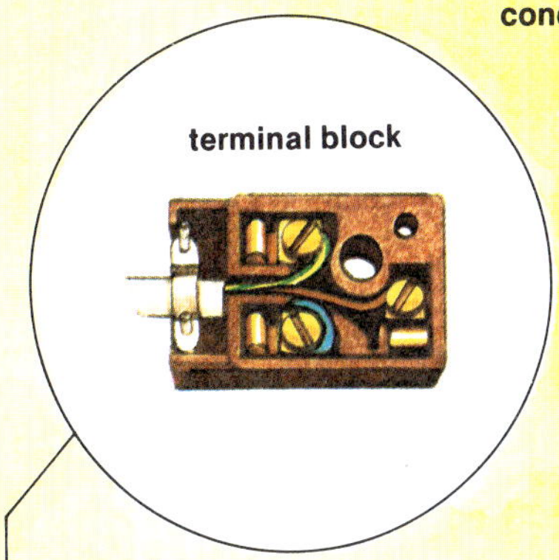

Power is obtained from a new three-terminal junction box (as above), an existing junction box, or a loop-in ceiling rose.

The connections at the fan terminal block are simple. It's easier to unscrew the block to connect the three-core flex and then re-attach the block, feeding the flex through the guide hole.

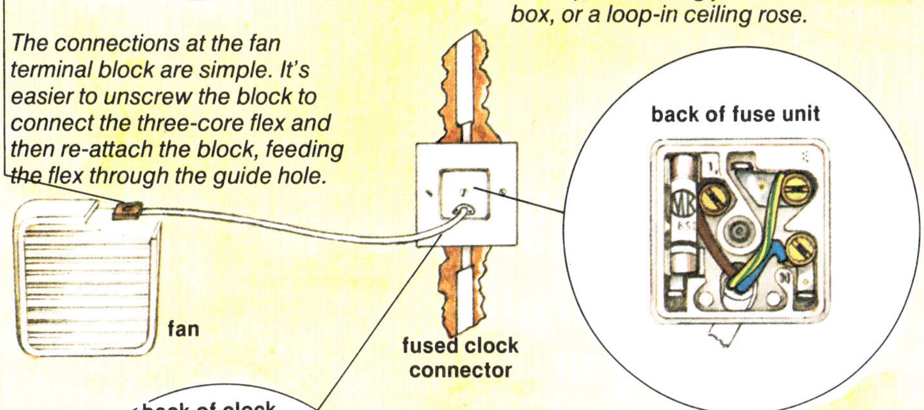

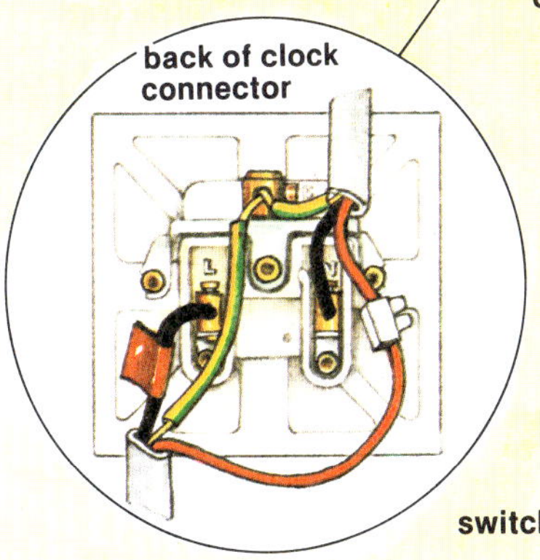

The fan gets its power at the plug-in fused section of the connector. The simple connections are shown above.

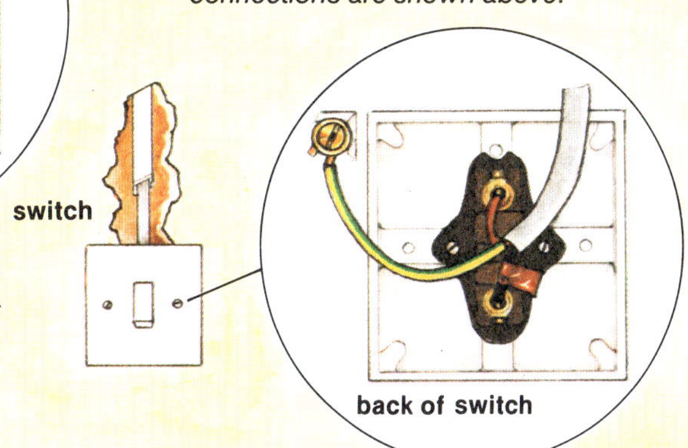

The cables from the junction box and switch meet at the fixed part of the clock connector unit. The two earth cores are joined at the earth terminal. The black core from the junction box goes to neutral and the two live cores are connected by a cable connector. The switch return, which is live, is flagged in red and goes to the live terminal.

At the one-gang switch remember to flag the black core in red, as it serves as the switch return and is therefore live.

Ready Reference

SITING YOUR FAN

Correct siting is crucial to a fan's efficiency. Fans should be installed in the window or wall furthest away from the door or source of fresh air.
In a kitchen, the fan should be located on the wall or window next to the cooker – the main source of smells – but not immediately above it.

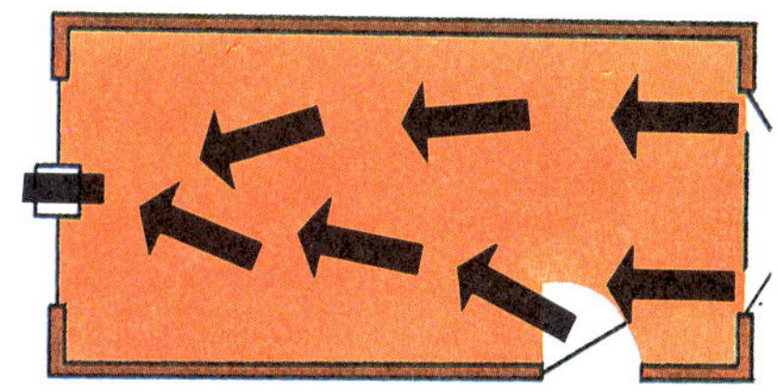

A SOURCE OF AIR

A good supply of fresh air is equally important. If you feel the supply is inadequate, fit an ventilator in the wall opposite the fan if possible.

For a cavity wall, you need a cavity liner or an air brick that will extend through the wall. You should:
- chop a hole with a cold chisel and club hammer
- insert the liner, or line the hole with mortar.
- fit the brick and repoint external wall.

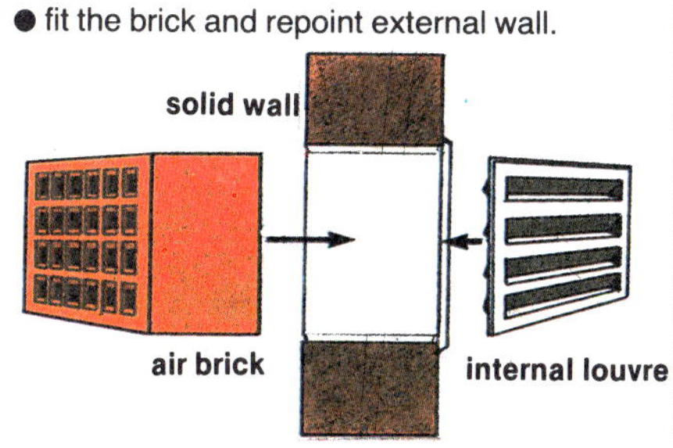

For a solid wall you should:
- cut the hole in a similar way and line it with mortar
- fit the brick as above
- plaster round the edges of the hole on the inside of the wall
- apply impact adhesive when the plaster is dry and hold the internal louvre in place until a good bond is established, or fit it with screws and wallplugs.

INSTALLING WALL HEATERS & TOWEL RAILS

Electric towel rails and wall-mounted heaters are straightforward to install, but you must obey the wiring regulations if you're fitting them in a bathroom.

A wall-mounted heater and heated towel rails are two electrical appliances guaranteed to make life in your bathroom that much more civilized. Everyone knows how unpleasant stepping out of a hot bath into a cold bathroom can be, and having to use a damp towel is just as bad. Installing both these appliances will not only increase your comfort, but will also provide help in cutting down on the amount of condensation in the bathroom. While mounting them and obtaining power for these appliances is quite straightforward, bathrooms require special consideration as they are potentially the most dangerous room in which to use electricity.

Bathroom regulations

There are a number of regulations that apply when you're doing any kind of electrical work in your bathroom and these must, of course, be strictly adhered to.

You are not allowed to install any kind of socket outlet other than a shaver supply unit in a bathroom. As a result this means that no portable appliance other than a shaver can be used there. Therefore all other electrical appliances, including both heaters and towel rails, have to be securely fixed and connected permanently to the mains. Switches must be cord-operated unless they are safely out of the reach of anyone in the bath or using the shower.

Installing a heated towel rail

There is a wide variety of towel rails available, so select one carefully to match your needs. As rails can be mounted against a wall they are not very obtrusive and you should really choose the largest one that can fit neatly into the space available in your bathroom. That way, of course, you'll be able to dry the whole family's towels at the same time. It's a good idea to get rails that incorporate a pilot light as this will help you not to leave them on when they're not being used – always an easy thing to do. If this is impossible make sure that the mains outlet point is fitted with a neon indicator. After deciding where you're going to mount the rails, make sure that they can be safely fixed to the walls. Check that they'll be level and mark their position before drilling and plugging the wall. You can then screw the rails in place. Floor-mounted models are also available, and will have to be screwed to the floor surface.

Towel rails obtain their power from a spur on the ring circuit via a switched fused connection unit fixed out of reach of bath or shower. Fix this as close as possible to the towel rail. However, as it's unlikely that the flex already attached to the rail will be long enough to reach the unit, you'll have run a length of 1.5mm^2 two-core and earth cable to a flex outlet plate mounted close to the rail, and connect in the flex at that point.

Installing a bathroom heater

There are plenty of different heaters that can be installed in the bathroom. Perhaps the most common is the reflector heater that consists of a rod element that glows while it's in use. Despite its wire guard, it's not difficult to touch the element in this type of heater so it must be fixed high up on a wall away from the bath or shower. Mounting the heater is a simple matter of drilling and plugging the wall before fixing it in place.

To obtain power you'll have to run a spur from the nearest socket outlet to a switched fused connection unit. This incorporates the required double-pole switch to isolate the heater completely when it's switched off. You'll find it more convenient if the model of heater you install has its own cord switch as well, so that you can switch it on and off in the bathroom. You'll probably then have to extend a cable from the switched fused connection unit to a flex outlet plate mounted close to the heater so that the heater's flex can be connected directly to the circuit. Alternatively, if the heater is not fitted with a length of flex, you'll have to run a cable directly into the heater. If your heater does not have its own cord switch and you want to be able to control it from within the bathroom then you'll have to run the cable from the connection unit up into the ceiling void and connect it to a cord-operated switch.

Other bathroom heaters

Oil-filled radiators that are thermostatically controlled and which include a pilot light can either be fixed to the bathroom floor or by brackets to the wall. If you're installing the radiator within reach of the bath or shower then, like a heated towel rail, it will have to be controlled by a switched fused connection unit outside the bathroom. Then all you'll have to do is run a cable to a flex outlet plate and connect in the radiator's flex. Waii panel heaters that consist of a metal panel containing an element to provide low radiant heat come in numerous sizes and obtain their power in the same way. Skirting panel heaters are very similar but as they're slimmer they can actually replace existing wood skirting or can be fixed above it.

Special heaters for airing cupboards are easy to install. They are basically a cylinder of perforated metal containing a wire element and can be fixed to either the wall or floor of the cupboard. Wall fixing is best as you mount the heater about 300mm (12in) above the floor and therefore away from any article that might fall down and become a fire risk.

MAKING THE CONNECTIONS

Towel rails and heaters installed in the bathroom must be controlled by a double-pole switch, so that they can be safely isolated from the mains.

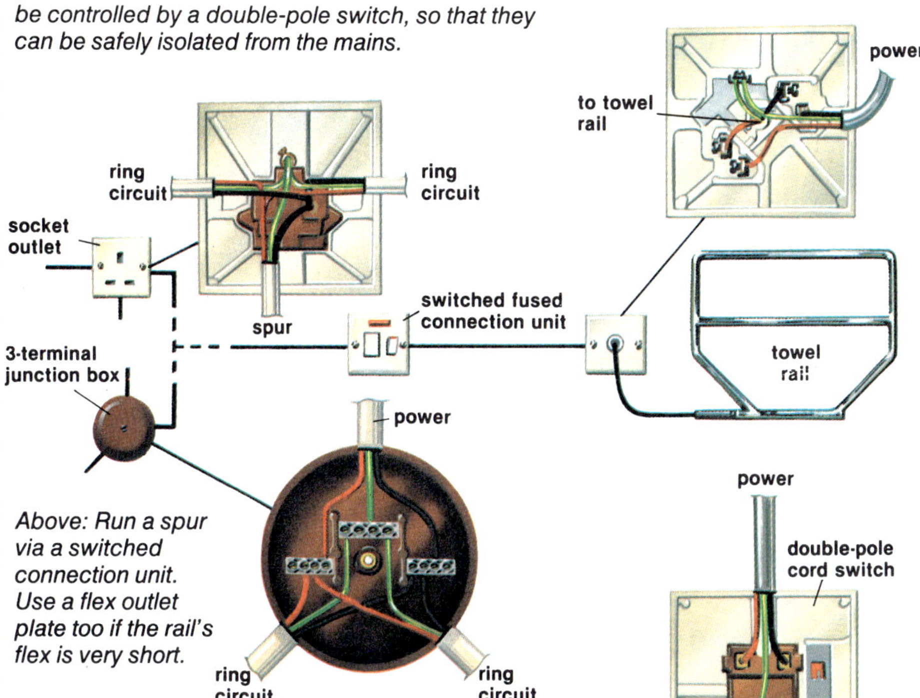

Above: Run a spur via a switched connection unit. Use a flex outlet plate too if the rail's flex is very short.

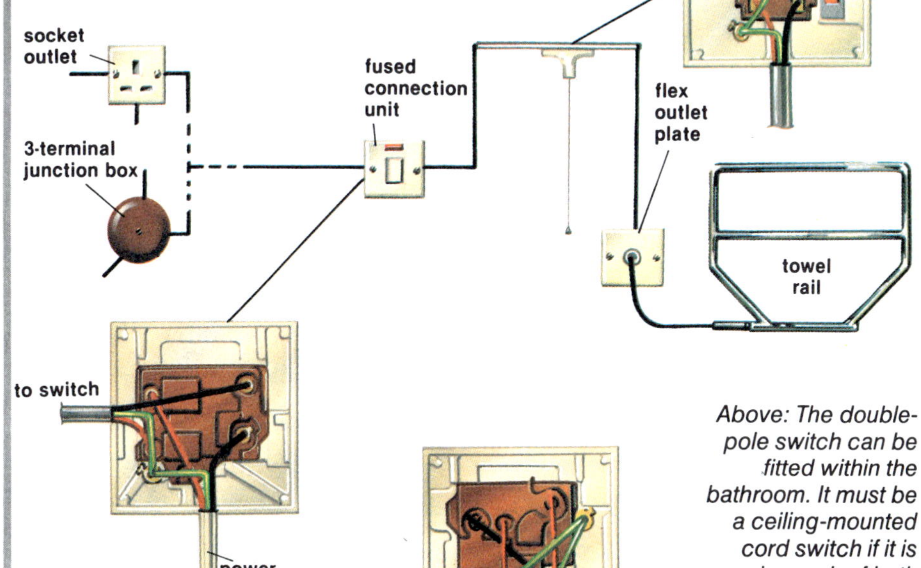

Above: The double-pole switch can be fitted within the bathroom. It must be a ceiling-mounted cord switch if it is in reach of bath or shower.

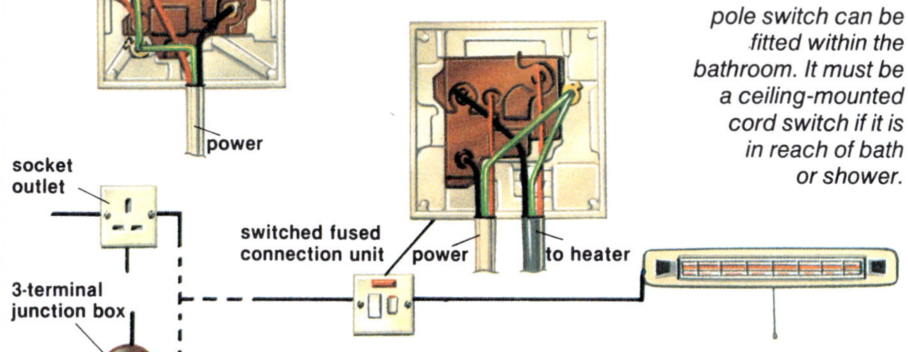

Above: Take the cable direct to the heater it it isn't fitted with a connecting flex.

Ready Reference

SAFETY IN THE BATHROOM

- Don't install any socket outlets. The only permissible type is a shaver supply unit
- don't use portable electrical appliances in the bathroom. The only permissible one is a shaver run from its own supply unit
- don't bring in portable appliances on extension cables plugged into a socket outside the bathroom
- don't fit lights with open lampholders. All lights must be totally enclosed
- don't fit ordinary rocker switches. For safety's sake all switches should be the ceiling-mounted cord-operated type fixed well away from the bath or shower.

INSTALLING A LIGHT/HEATER UNIT

If you're really short of space in your bathroom, installing a combined light and heater could be the answer. This consists of a ceiling-mounted light with a heating element round it. It incorporates a cord-operated switch to control the heater and you should also install a ceiling-mounted switch for overall control of the light. There are two ways of obtaining power. You can

- take a spur from the nearest socket outlet or break into the ring circuit with a three-terminal junction box. Run the cable to a switched fused connection unit outside the bathroom or,
- run in a completely new circuit from a 5A fuseway in your consumer unit, if you have a spare one available. In this case, make sure that the ceiling switch is a double-pole one.

TIP: USE NEON INDICATORS

When installing a ceiling-mounted cord-operated switch in the bathroom it's a good idea to fit one with a neon indicator as a reminder that your heater or towel rail may have been left on when not required. The indicator can be elsewhere in the house if this is handier.

INSTALLING A WALL HEATER

1 *When positioning the heater, make sure it's out of reach of anyone using the bath or shower and is at least 150mm (6in) below the ceiling.*

2 *Connect a length of $1.5mm^2$ two-core and earth cable to the heater terminals. If it's already fitted with flex, install a flex outlet plate close by.*

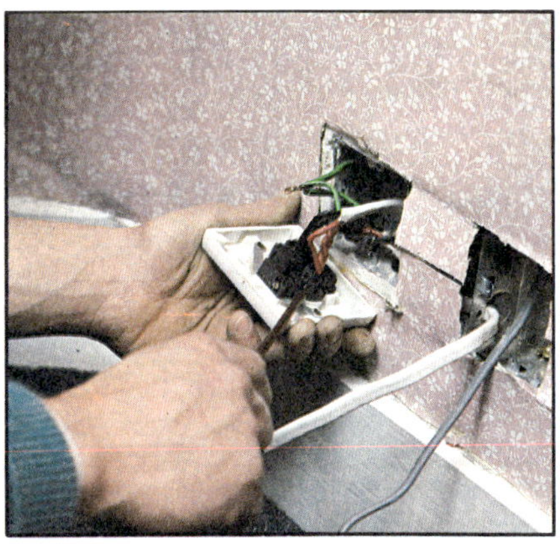

3 *Run a spur to the heater from the nearest socket outlet. Alternatively, break into the ring circuit with a three-terminal junction box.*

4 *Run the spur to the supply side of a switched fused connection unit mounted out of reach of the bath, or else to one outside the bathroom.*

5 *Connect the $1.5mm^2$ two-core and earth cable from the heater to the feed side of the connection unit, or to the terminals of the flex outlet plate.*

6 *Finally, drill and plug the wall and fit the heater securely in place. Link its flex to the terminals of the outlet plate if one is being used.*

A TOWEL RAIL

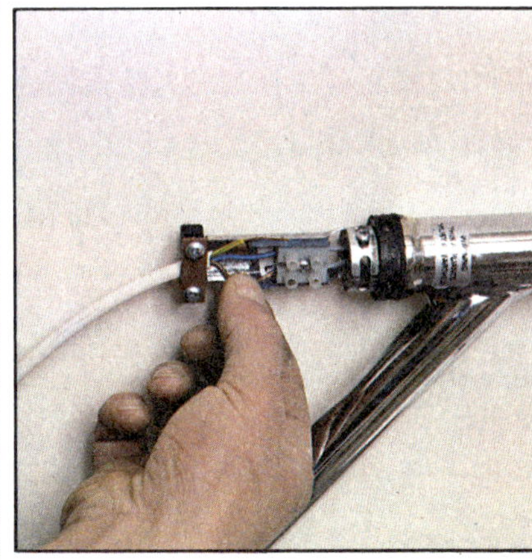

1 *Connect a length of three-core heat-resisting flex to the terminals of the towel rail. It will eventually get its power from a spur off a nearby power circuit.*

2 *Run the spur in $2.5mm^2$ two-core and earth cable to a fused connection unit. Then take a $1.5mm^2$ cable to a ceiling-mounted double-pole (DP) switch.*

3 *Finally, run the cable to a flex outlet plate mounted close to the rail. Fix the rail securely to the wall (or floor) and connect the flex to the terminals.*

ADDING NEW RADIAL CIRCUITS

A radial circuit can provide power for individual appliances such as cookers, immersion heaters and freezers, or can give you extra socket outlets for plug-in equipment. It's an easy job to install one.

switchfuse unit from Wholesale Fittings Co

Radial circuits have only one cable running from the consumer unit (fuse box) to the power outlet because the circuit terminates at the last outlet. In this way they differ from the more common ring circuit as their cable doesn't have to return to the consumer unit. Installing one can therefore save you both cable and extra work (see pages 161–171).

Before ring circuits were introduced the radial circuit was the standard domestic power circuit. There were fewer sockets and electrical appliances to be supplied than nowadays and a number of radial circuits each supplying an individual outlet usually proved adequate. As more and more electrical appliances came on the market, so the ring circuit was developed to cope with the greater current demands in the modern home. Nowadays, the ring circuit is the more common power circuit.

However, a new radial circuit is especially useful when you want to fit extra fixed electrical appliances such as a deep freeze or immersion heater, supply a couple of new sockets or else provide power for an extension to your home. That way you don't have to run spurs from an existing ring circuit and you avoid the possibility of overloading that circuit through heavy demand.

Types of radial circuits

There are two basic types of radial circuit. These are the 'solo' circuit, which provides power to one fixed appliance such as an immersion heater, cooker or freezer, and the power circuit which can help out a ring circuit or provide power to new sockets and appliances. The second type is itself divided into two kinds. The first is the 20A circuit. This uses 2.5mm^2 cable and can supply an unlimited number of 13A socket outlets (or fixed appliances using up to 3kW of power) – provided they are all within a floor area of 20 sq m (about 215 sq ft). The second type is the 30A radial circuit, which uses 4.0mm^2 cable and can carry power to a floor area up to 50 sq m (540 sq ft). If you look round your home you will see that these restrictions

POWER SUPPLY FOR RADIAL CIRCUITS.

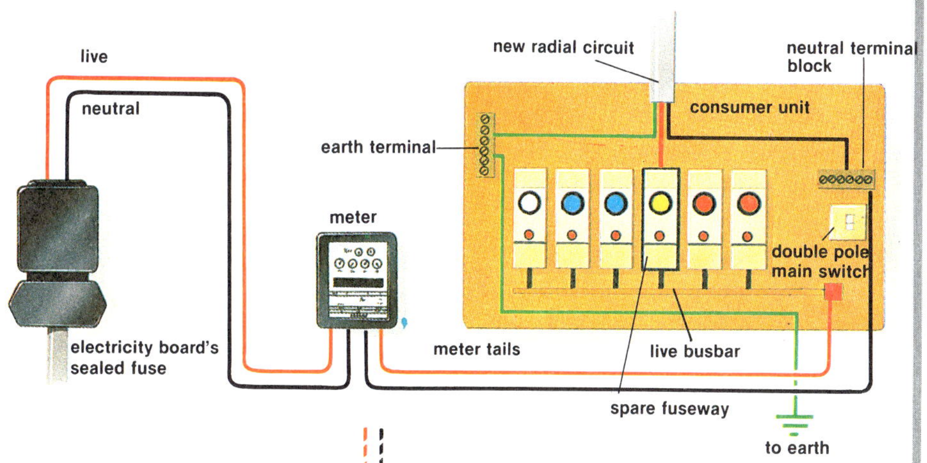

A new radial circuit can run directly from a consumer unit provided there is a spare fuseway. If this is not the case then it can originate from a new switch fuse unit installed near the electricity board's meter to which it is connected via a distribution board.

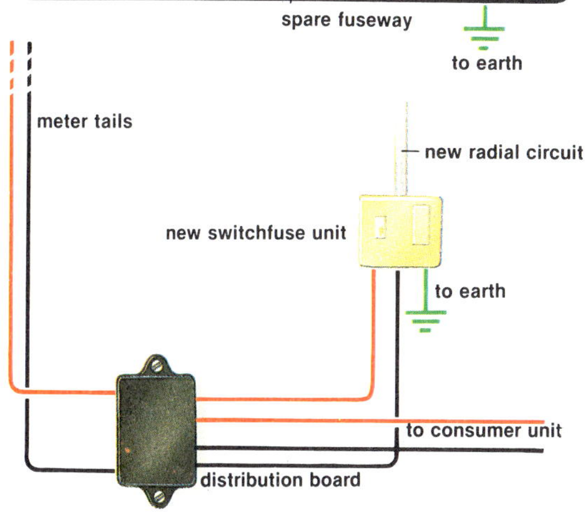

USING A SPARE FUSEWAY

1 After you've had the mains supply cut off, remove the consumer unit cover, lift the mounting plate forward and remove the live busbar.

2 Slide the units along the busbar to make space for the new MCB or fuse. Remember to arrange the units in the correct current rating sequence.

3 Fit the new MCB unit onto the mounting plate, making sure that it's in the right place. Then screw back the live busbar underneath the units.

4 Finally refit the mounting plate and connect the cable to the correct terminals. Get the electricity board to reconnect and test the circuit.

consumer unit and meter from MK

mean that several radial circuits would have to be installed to supply power to all the sockets and appliances supplied by a normal ring circuit. So radial circuits really come into their own when you want to supply power to fixed appliances. And radial circuits can be modified to cope with heavy demand. So, if you want to have a large cooker you will probably have to run a radial circuit that has been 'beefed' up and will use a 45A fuse and 6.0 or 10.0mm^2 cable.

Obtaining the power

If you want to install a new radial circuit you'll need a circuit fuseway. First check whether you have a spare (unconnected) one in the consumer unit. If so, check its current rating (see below). If not, you'll have to install a new main switch and fuse unit near the consumer unit and connect it separately. If you have to do this then it might be an idea to install one with two or more fuseways to save work if you are planning any future extension to your domestic wiring. If you decide to do this it is a good idea to blank off the fuseway you are not using or else fit another MCB or fuse unit without connecting it. Whatever you do, before inspecting or working on the consumer unit you must turn off the main switch.

If there is a spare fuseway it may well be sealed off with a blanking plate or else there might be a fuse unit or MCB without any circuit connections. If you use offpeak electricity for heating then you will have two consumer units and it's very important to make sure that you use the correct one. The unit supplying the night storage heaters will be on a restricted time switch and if you connect to that, you will only get power to your circuit at night (not a very good idea if it is supplying a freezer, for example).

Ready Reference

WHAT ARE RADIAL CIRCUITS?

Radial circuits were the original domestic power circuit, starting at the consumer unit (fuse box) and terminating at the last socket.

Nowadays ring circuits supply most domestic appliances. Radial circuits supply either fixed appliances, such as a cooker:

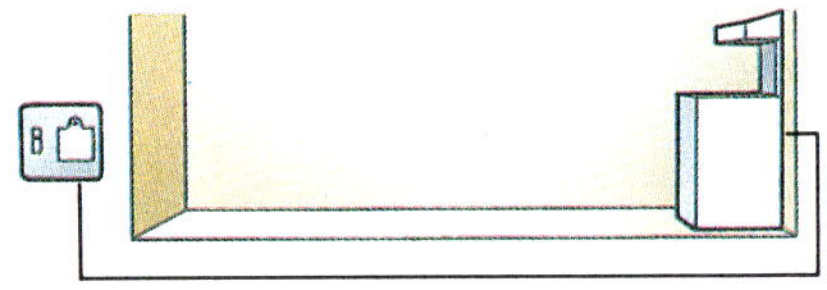

or a number of sockets.

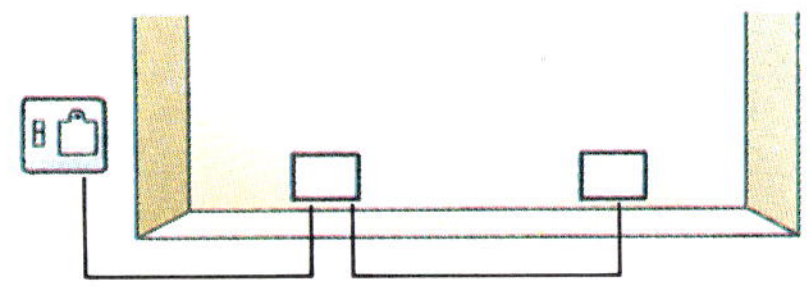

They are very useful for providing power to an extension to your home or supplementing a ring circuit.

CONNECTING THE MAINS

You can connect to a spare fuseway in the consumer unit or else fit a new switchfuse unit. Your fuse must have the same current rating as the new circuit. Modern fuses have a colour coding.

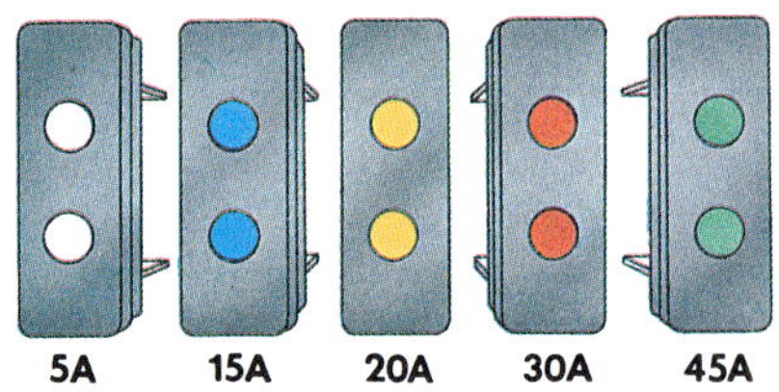

If you have to buy a new fuse, get a cartridge type. These are safer, more effective and it is impossible to fit the wrong sort.

USING A NEW SWITCHFUSE UNIT

1 *The new switchfuse unit should be mounted on a sheet of non-combustible material such as fire-resistant chipboard.*

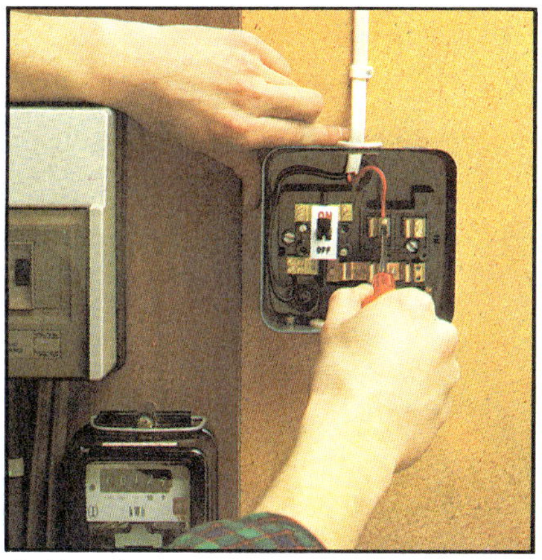

2 *Knock out a panel at the top of the new unit and fix a protective grommet before running in the new circuit cable and making the connections.*

3 *You will have to use extra single core cable (6.0mm^2) to connect the unit to the distribution board as you are allowed only two tails to the meter.*

4 *Screw on the colour-coded shields for the new MCBs. It's an idea to fit a new unit with a spare fuseway for an extra circuit in the future.*

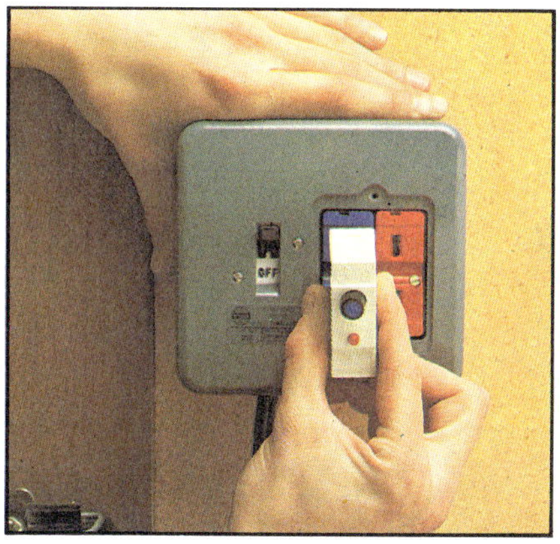

5 *Fit the cover over the unit and then slot in the new MCBs or fuse unit. You can fit a blanking plate until you decide to use the spare fuseway.*

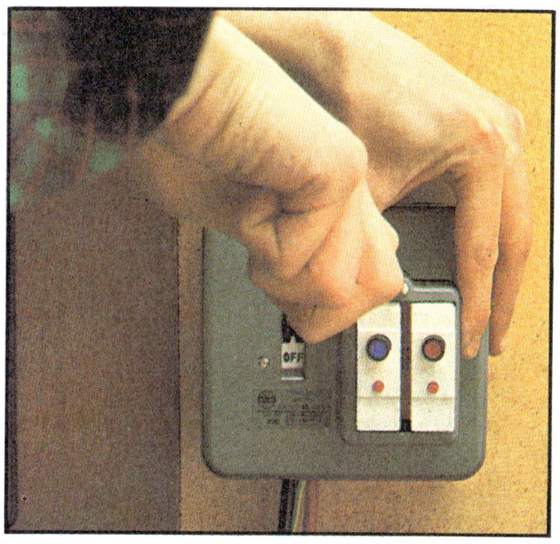

6 *Screw on the smaller shield to protect the new MCBs. Remember, you'll probably have to knock out its lid to allow access to the MCBs.*

7 *Fix the distribution board and then connect the live core from the switchfuse unit and the live meter tail to the live terminal block.*

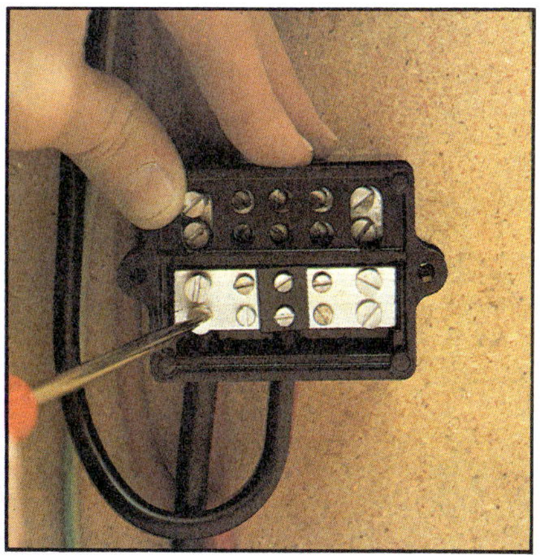

8 *Fit the neutral terminal block and base plate which hold the live block in place, and then connect the remaining neutral cores to the block.*

9 *Connect the earths and then get the electricity board to connect the old meter tails to the distribution board and the new tails to the meter.*

Using a spare fuseway

If you are connecting to a spare fuseway, you must check that it has the equivalent current rating to the circuit running from it. Most modern fuses have two spots on their cases to indicate their current rating: white indicates a 5A rating; blue 15A; yellow 20A; red 30A and green 45A. If it's not the correct rating for the circuit you're installing, you'll have to insert a new one. There is the chance that your consumer unit is so old that it could be obsolete. In that case, if you have a spare fuseway in it you will be able to use it only for a new circuit that has the equivalent current rating. Circuit fuses are either the rewirable type or the cartridge type and when buying a new one it is best to get the latter as they are safer and more effective.

The new radial circuit starts at the fuse unit and runs in two-core and earth PVC-sheathed cable, the size of which is determined by the circuit's current rating. A 5A circuit should be run in 1.0mm^2 cable, 15A in 1.5mm^2, 20A in 2.5mm^2 and 30A in 4.0mm^2 (the 30A circuit fuse must be a cartridge type or an MCB, not a rewirable one). Any circuit with a higher rating should be run in 6.0mm^2 or 10.0mm^2 cable.

For detailed advice on how to run cable under floors, in ceiling voids and down walls (see pages 181–185). Where you are using larger cable for a beefed up circuit, it might be a good idea to measure fairly precisely the length of the cable required as the larger the cable, the more expensive it is. Allow sufficient for connecting the cable within the consumer unit and in the mains outlet, plus extra for contingencies such as hidden obstructions. The choice of mains outlet depends upon its situation and the appliance supplied. For example, a 13A socket is fine for any appliance up to 3kW, but cannot be used in the bathroom where the only socket permitted is one for a shaver. An immersion heater with a dual element, say, should have a 20A dual switch as its outlet. More information on all these can be found in other sections.

Connecting to the spare fuseway

The spare fuseway in the consumer unit will usually be at the end of the row of units and furthest away from the main switch. Units should be placed in the correct rating sequence, with those of the largest current rating (45A) next to the mainswitch, and those of the lowest, (5A) at the other end. The new circuit should be located in sequence, and this might well entail moving the units. With some boxes the fuses slide along a 'top hat' bar after the screws have been released, and in others, the units are simply removed and refixed in their new positions. Turning off the main switch renders all live parts dead, but in some units, where the mains terminals (to which the meter leads connect) are not recessed, there is still a shock risk even if those main terminals are shrouded. So, in addition to turning off the main switch, it is sometimes advisable to get the electricity board to cut off the mains supply before you work on the consumer unit. Then, when they restore the power, you can ask them to test the new circuit. After you've rearranged the fuse units, thread in the circuit cable and strip off the outer sleeving, leaving about 25mm (1in) within the unit. Trim the cores by stripping off 10mm (3/8in) of insulation, and connect the red core to the fuseway terminal of the new unit and the black to the neutral terminal block. The earth should be sleeved in green and yellow PVC and connected to the earth terminal block. The cable can now be run to the circuit outlet, but remember, it is best to complete all the work at the outlet end of the circuit before connecting up. That way power is off for the shortest possible time and causes least inconvenience.

Unless there is plenty of room on your backing board you will have to fit a sheet of non-conbustible material, such as treated chipboard, to your wall to provide a base for the unit and prevent fire risk.

Installing a switchfuse unit

After choosing a switchfuse unit containing an MCB or cartridge fuse of the same current rating as the new circuit, fix it to the wall using No 8 wood screws with wall plugs. The unit should be sited close to the electricity board's meter so that the meter leads bringing power to the new unit are as short as possible. When the electricity board come to connect the new meter leads they might well require a distribution board to be fitted so that the power coming through the meter can be divided up and fed to both units. For the mains leads use 16mm^2 single core PVC-sheathed cable – one red and one black. They should be connected to the live and neutral terminals of the unit respectively, and you should use 6.0mm^2 green-and-yellow-sheathed cable for the connection to the earth terminal.

Sections of thin plastic will have to be knocked out to admit these cables and a blank will also have to removed at the top of the unit to allow for the entry of the circuit cable. It's a good idea to connect this cable before fitting the unit to the wall. Connect the red core of the circuit cable to the fuseway terminal, the black to the upper neutral terminal and the sleeved earth conductor to the earth terminal. If you are using a fuseway and an MCB, double-check that you have the correct one and then replace the cover. Finally, call the electricity board to connect the meter leads to the mains and test the circuit.

Ready Reference

TYPES OF CABLE

When installing a new radial circuit you must make sure that you run it in cable that corresponds to the current rating of the circuit.

Cable	Amps	Use
1.0mm^2	5	lighting
1.5mm^2	15	lighting circuit immersion heater
2.5mm^2	20	immersion heater instantaneous water heater (up to 5kW)
4.0mm^2	30	circuits for small cookers, instantaneous water heater (up to 7kW)
6.0mm^2 or 10.0mm^2	45	circuits for cookers over 12kW and large split-level cookers

MAINS DISCONNECTION

Even if you have turned off the power at the main switch you should get the electricity board to disconnect the mains supply.
To do this they require a minimum of 48 hours written notice.
If you want them to test your new radial circuit before they reconnect the supply, you must make a separate application.

BACKING BOARDS

If you are fitting a new consumer unit or switchfuse unit to a combustible surface, for added safety it is wise to fit a sheet of non-combustible material such as asbestos between the unit and the wall.

ALLOW A SPARE FUSEWAY

In your new consumer unit it is a good idea to allow more than one spare fuseway. That way you will save extra work should you want to run an extra circuit at a later date.

TREATMENT FOR SHOCKS

Here is what you should do:

- turn off the supply or
- pull person clear immediately but don't touch his/her body
- if breathing stops, give mouth-to-mouth resuscitation
- don't wrap the person in blankets or try to give him/her brandy
- if the person is severely shocked call a doctor.

INSTALLING AN RCCB

A residual-current circuit breaker (RCCB) will protect your home from the risk of electrical fires and its occupants from the danger of electric shocks. It's comparatively easy to add one to your existing installation, to protect some or all of the house's circuits.

A residual current circuit breaker is a form of double-pole on/off switch that automatically cuts out (switches itself off) when there is a leakage of electric current to earth from a circuit or from an appliance plugged into the mains. There are two types in use. The residual current circuit breaker (RCCB), formerly called a current-operated ELCB, is now the only type fitted in new installations. The other type is the voltage-operated ELCB, which is now obsolete but still found on older systems.

Voltage-operated ELCBs

With the voltage-operated type, earth-leakage current from the circuit or appliance flows through the earth conductor into a trip coil, and provided the coil is energised at about 40 volts it operates and cuts off the current. Before the cut-out operates, earth-leakage current flows to earth via an earth connection; this is normally a copper-sheathed steel rod driven into the ground outside the house. An earth conductor links the consumer unit to the ELCB and the ELCB to the rod – see *Ready Reference*.

In fact, the earth-leakage current does not necessarily all pass through the trip coil of the ELCB, but may follow a parallel path via the water or gas mains. Deprived of adequate energy to trip the coil, the ELCB does not operate and unearthed metalwork can remain 'live' and dangerous to touch.

What is more, a voltage-operated ELCB may trip for no obvious reason – a fault in a neighbour's installation has been known to cause tripping, usually because earth rods are too close together. So although voltage-operated ELCBs have been fitted extensively in home installations when an electricity board is unable to provide conventional methods of earthing, there has been a growing tendency to fit residual current types instead.

Residual current circuit breakers

Residual current circuit breakers work on the principle that there is normally a balance between the current flowing into the circuit on the live pole and the current returning to the system via the neutral pole. When an earth-leakage fault occurs, the earth-leakage current is lost to the system via the earth conductor and the amount of current returning via the neutral pole is that much less. The current flowing through the RCCB is therefore out of balance. This out-of-balance current causes a trip coil to be energised and cuts off the current to the circuit.

There are no direct connections of the earth conductors to the RCCB in this case; none are needed, as the circuit current operates the RCCB. The earth conductor from the consumer unit goes directly to the terminal clamp on the earth rod – see *Ready Reference* again.

A snag with residual current devices had been that early models were not very sensitive. If the earth resistance was high, the earth rod was unable to pass sufficient earth-leakage current to trip the RCCB. The standard 60 amp version needed an earth-leakage current of 0.5 amp to trip it and the 100 amp version required 1 amp. The usual practice was to fit a residual current circuit breaker where the soil resistance as measured by the electricity board was no more than 40 ohms, and to fit a voltage-operated ELCB where the electricity board's test showed the soil resistance to be 40 ohms or more. There are numerous voltage-operated ELCBs still in use, and also many of the old type current-operated ones, but the situation is now changing.

Modern current-operated devices

The modern current-operated residual current circuit breaker (RCCB) is of the high-sensitivity type. Some models are used to protect individual socket outlets or appliances and power tools, or circuits supplying socket outlets only. Those used to protect the whole installation usually have a trip current rating of 100mA (milliamps). Those used to protect individual socket outlets have a trip current rating of only 30mA. Some special versions designed for use in hospitals have a trip current rating as low as 10mA, which is too sensitive for general domestic use.

You can buy a consumer unit fitted with a residual current circuit breaker, or you can add one to your existing installation and retain the present consumer unit fitted with a double-pole isolating main switch.

Replacing the consumer unit

If you install a new consumer unit fitted with an RCCB you simply have it connected to the mains by the electricity board, using the appropriate size and type of meter leads and the correct earth conductor.

The RCCB fitted to a consumer unit is made in various current ratings up to 100 amps, and the trip ratings are from 30mA upwards. As the RCCB will trip whenever a live/earth fault occurs, it is wise to choose one having a trip current rating of 100mA. One of this rating is unlikely to be subjected

ADDING AN RCCB AT THE FUSEBOX

1 *If you're installing a new consumer unit, choose one that's big enough to incorporate an RCCB as well as enough fuseways for all your circuits.*

2 *Alternatively, you can install an RCCB near to the existing consumer unit, in its own enclosure. Screw the baseplate in place and clip on the RCCB itself.*

3 *Connect new live and neutral meter tails to one pair of terminals. They should be long enough to reach to the main terminals on the consumer unit.*

4 *Call in the electricity board to disconnect the existing meter tails, link them to the RCCB and reconnect the consumer unit. Then fit the cover.*

to 'nuisance' tripping that could cut off all lighting and power circuits.

Although the 100mA version does not give the same level of personal protection as does one of 30mA trip rating, the manufacturers have stated that no cases of electrocution have occurred where the 100mA version is fitted.

Adding an RCCB to an installation

Where the new RCCB is added to the installation and the existing consumer unit with its double-pole mainswitch is retained, the RCCB is connected into the meter leads between the consumer unit and the board's meter. To make the connection it is first necessary to ask the electricity board to remove its service fuse while the connections are made. Then the leads from the consumer unit are run into the RCCB and another pair are linked to the RCCB for the board to connect to its meter.

The meter leads are usually 16mm^2 single-core circular PVC-sheathed cable, colour-coded red for the live conductor, black for the neutral conductor, plus green/yellow striped cable for the earth conductor. The size required for the earth conductor is usually 6mm^2, but the board may require a larger size. The board may also require the meter leads to be 25mm^2 so it is best to check with them before starting the work.

Protecting socket outlets

One or more 13A socket outlets can be protected by an RCCB by inserting one into the appropriate circuit. The circuit can be a radial or ring circuit and the RCCB is connected to the appropriate fuseway of the consumer unit – see *Ready Reference*.

The new RCCB used should be of 40A current rating with a trip current rating of

Ready Reference

WIRING UP AN RCCB

When an RCCB is installed between the electricity meter and the consumer unit, the electricity board must be notified first so they can remove the main service fuse and disconnect the meter tails.

The actual connections are extremely simple, and are made using meter tails of the appropriate size – usually 16mm^2.

- with the older voltage-operated type, the connections look like this:

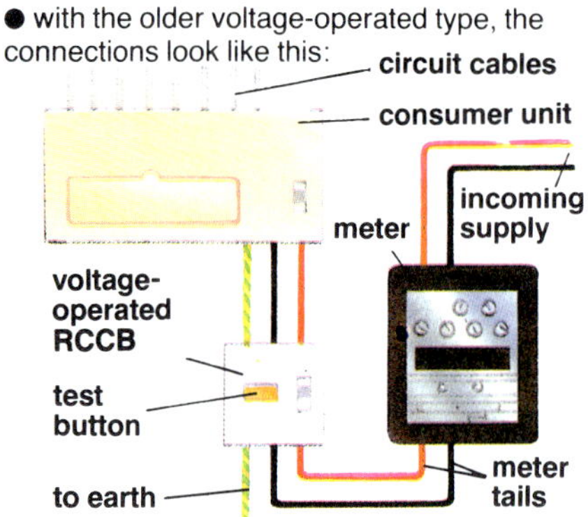

- with residual current circuit breakers, no earth connection is made with the unit itself; instead the consumer unit is linked directly to earth.

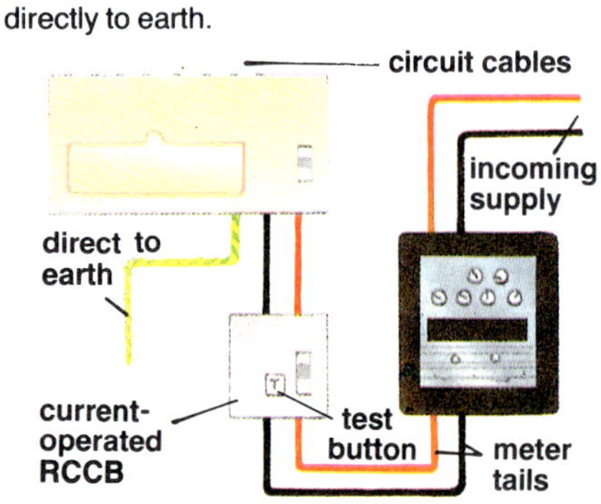

PROTECTING A CIRCUIT

If you want RCCB protection on just one circuit, the device is wired into the circuit cable close to the consumer unit. The earth conductors are linked via an external connector block to ensure earth continuity.

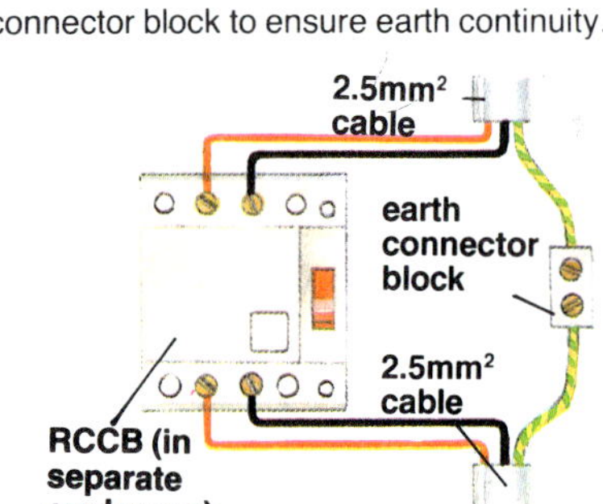

USING SOCKETS AND PLUG-IN RCCBS

1 You can fit a combined socket outlet and RCCB in place of an existing double socket outlet. Isolate the circuit, undo the faceplate and disconnect the cables.

2 Fit a deeper box if necessary to accept the unit. Then connect the cable cores to the three terminals on the back of the new RCCB socket faceplate.

3 Screw the unit back into place over the mounting box. Then plug in an appliance, switch on and test the unit, following the manufacturer's instructions.

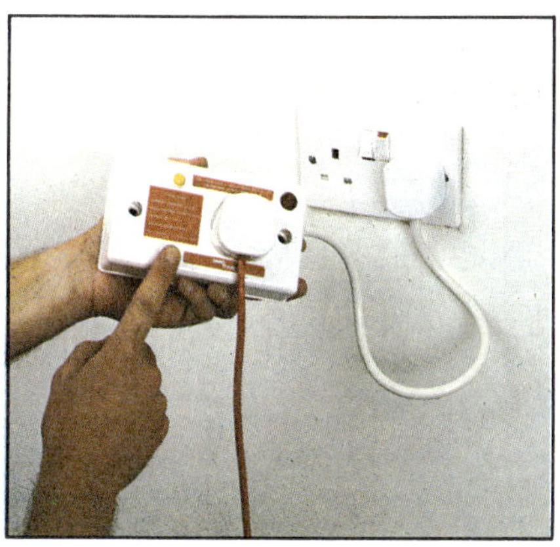

4 An alternative to the wired-in RCCB socket is this self-contained unit. Simply plug it in to any socket outlet, then plug in the appliance and test.

5 For high-risk appliances such as lawnmowers and hedgetrimmers, fit a plug-in RCCB. This is simply connected to the flex in place of the plug.

6 If this type of RCCB trips while the appliance is being used, it cannot be reset until the plug is removed from the socket, as the button is concealed.

30mA. All socket outlets on the circuit will be protected by the RCCB and users of any appliances and tools run off them will be protected from the risk of electrocution.

Socket-outlet RCCBs

One of the latest developments is a combined 13A socket outlet and RCCB. Its purpose is to meet the requirements of the 15th edition of the IEE Wiring Regulations; a new socket outlet (whether installed inside or outside the house) that will supply a power tool or appliance used out of doors must be RCCB-protected. The version having a tripping current rating of 30mA is chosen, for experience has shown that a current of 30mA passing through the human body for a period of up to 30 milli-seconds is unlikely to cause a fatal shock to the normally healthy person.

Some combined 13A socket outlets and RCCBs will fit a standard 2-gang socket box, flush or surface-mounted. The unit has an on/off switch, and a test button and neon indicator. The new socket can either replace an existing double 13A socket outlet or a spur of $2.5mm^2$ two-core and earth cable can be run from a ring circuit socket outlet to the new protected socket.

Plug-in RCCBs

There is also available an RCCB which plugs into any 13A socket outlet and has an integral 13A socket for plugging in a power tool or appliance, but the latest and most portable RCCB is one made in the form of a 13A fused plug that will fit any 13A socket outlet. The cover is removed and the appliance flex is connected to a readily accessible terminal block. On the outside face of the plug is a test button. If this is pressed, or if the RCCB trips due to a fault, it is necessary to remove the plug from its socket and press a reset button.

Many people believe that a double-insulated tool such as a lawnmower or hedge-trimmer fitted with two-core flex needs no RCCB, and that if one is fitted it will not operate since there is no means of current leaking to earth. This is not so, for the double-insulated tool needs RCCB protection at least as much as an earthed tool. Fatal accidents occur if the flex is cut and the unearthed (and now live) metalwork is being touched; the user will receive a severe electric shock if he is in contact with the ground. A 30mA RCCB will prevent such a shock.

Flex extension leads

Instead of connecting the fused-plug type RCCB direct to the flex of a power tool or appliance, it is better to connect it to a short three-core flex with a trailing 13A plug on the other end, into which a variety of power tools can be plugged in turn.

UPDATING & REWIRING

If you have an electrical installation that's sound but can't provide all the facilities you need, updating it could be a relatively inexpensive and simple way of bringing it up to scratch.

PLANNING TO UP-DATE YOUR ELECTRICS

Rewiring your home can be very straightforward but it still requires detailed planning and careful consideration. If you know exactly what you want from your home's circuits and where you want to site your power outlets and lights, then you're halfway to completing the job.

Completely rewiring your home is a job that sounds more difficult than it really is. If you've mastered such techniques as running cable, fitting new lights and installing new socket outlets then it certainly won't pose you any major problems.

Making the decision to rewire is perhaps the biggest step you'll have to take and, as with any electrical installation, you should never undertake the job without knowing exactly what you want and where you want it. Detailed planning is crucial to the final results and overlooking one important socket outlet or light can cause considerable inconvenience and, in the long run, extra work. Before making any decision about rewiring your home it's a good idea to examine the existing circuitry thoroughly to make sure that it really does need replacing.

When to rewire

There are two basic reasons for rewiring your home: first, because the existing fixed wiring is past its useful and safe life; and second, because the number of power outlets and lights no longer meets your requirements. There are certain tell-tale danger signs which you might come across when you inspect your circuitry. The use of rubber-sheathed cable ended in the early 1950s, so if you find this used in your circuits you'll know that they're quite old. If the insulation is worn and perished, then it's clear that the cable will have to be replaced to avoid the risk of fire or shocks. And, if you find that fuses in your consumer unit are blowing with alarming regularity, it's obvious something is seriously wrong.

You'll also have to consider whether the existing circuitry provides adequate lighting points and power outlets. Again there are a number of tell-tale signs. If you have to use adaptors to cope with all your appliances you'll know you don't have enough sockets; long trailing flexes will indicate that those existing outlets are not correctly sited. If you find you have to move lamps around to provide yourself with decent lighting, then it's clear that your lighting system is also inadequate.

Having examined your existing power and lighting systems, you're left with two alternatives. You can either adapt the existing circuitry (provided, of course, that the cable is in good enough condition) to give yourself extra power outlets and lighting points, or else you can completely rewire it. If you are in any doubt, then it's best to rewire; the chances are that it'll have to be done at some stage anyway and, by doing so immediately, it's likely to give you a safer and more efficient system cheaply and to increase the value of your home.

The circuitry

Before planning the number of sockets and lighting points you want, you'll have to decide exactly how you're going to run the circuits. Most modern homes are fitted with one ring circuit and one lighting circuit per floor. However, this is not necessarily the best arrangement. It's worth considering dividing your home up vertically, so that you have one ring circuit supplying one half of the house and another the second half. It'll mean a little more work, but, if one of the circuits blows at any time, you'll still have light and power left on each floor. It's a good idea to have your kitchen supplied by its own ring or radial circuit as, of all the rooms in the home, it uses most power.

Remember that certain electrical appliances, such as a cooker or immersion heater, should be connected exclusively to a separate radial circuit. Whatever you decide, you'll probably find that two ring circuits plus an extra radial or ring circuit for the kitchen, and additional radial circuits for certain fixed appliances, will suffice. Your next step will be the detailed siting of individual power outlets and lighting points in each room.

Living areas

The increase in electrical gadgetry and appliances over the past decade means that the average home now requires many more socket outlets. What with stereos, TVs, digital clocks and video games, as well as standard and table lamps, living rooms are going to need about ten sockets rather than the two or three usually fitted. Dining rooms are unlikely to need as many, unless you are in the habit of using toasters, coffee percolators, food warmers and so on at every meal, but remember that it's better to provide too many rather than too few.

For reasons of economy and convenience it's best to fit switched double sockets throughout, and you can, of course, re-use those from the previous circuits if they are in good condition. Flush-mounted ones are neatest, but require a bit of extra work to fit them.

Most living rooms and dining areas are

REWIRING YOUR LIVING AREAS

When rewiring your home you should carefully plan the wiring so that you have enough socket outlets for all your electrical appliances.

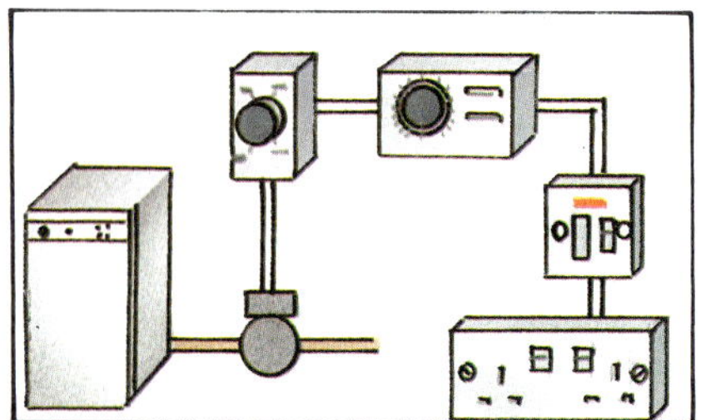

Boiler electrics (left) are linked up via a plug and socket or a switched fused connection unit. A safe alternative is to run them on their own circuit from a spare fuseway in the consumer unit.

An outside socket (below) gets its supply from the circuit supplying the garage. It should be completely weatherproof and the circuit must be protected by an RCCB (see pages 76-78).

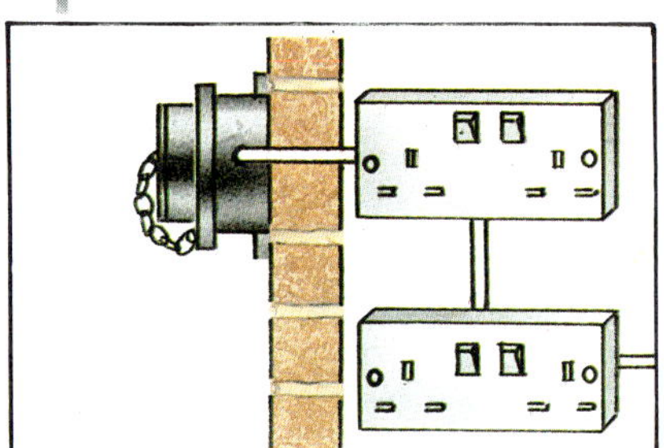

Wall lights (above) get their power either from a lighting circuit in the ceiling void above, or from a power circuit via a fused connection unit.

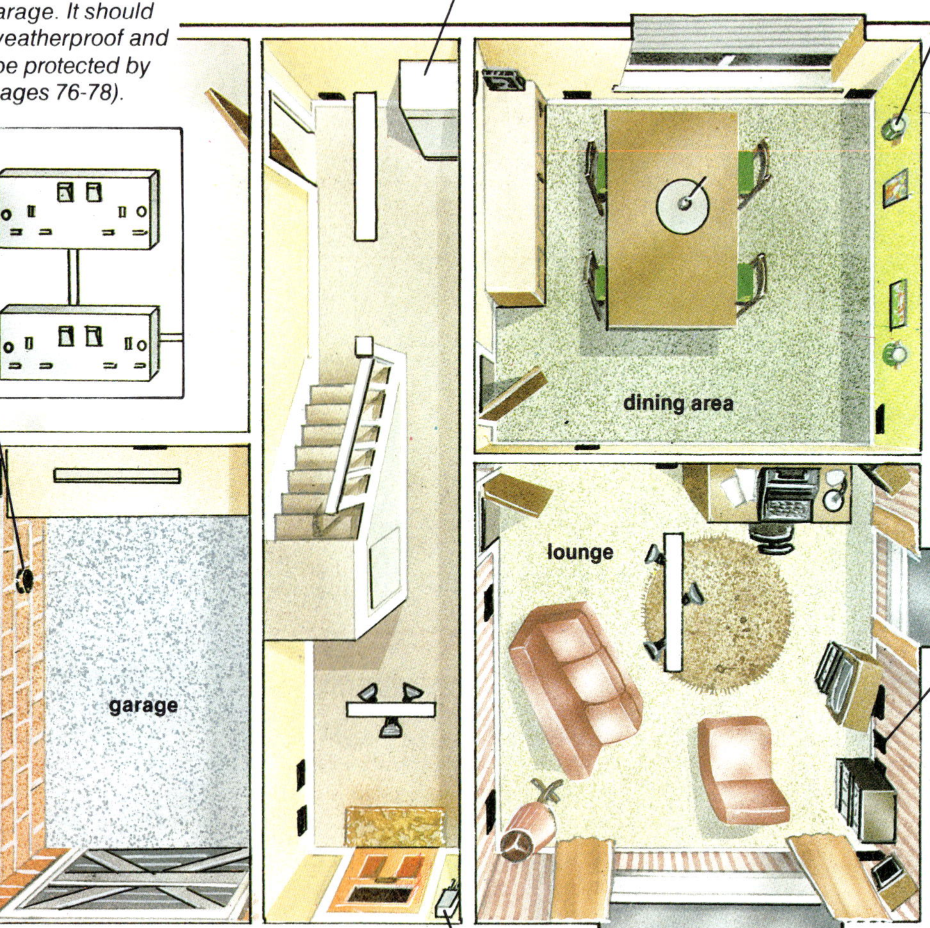

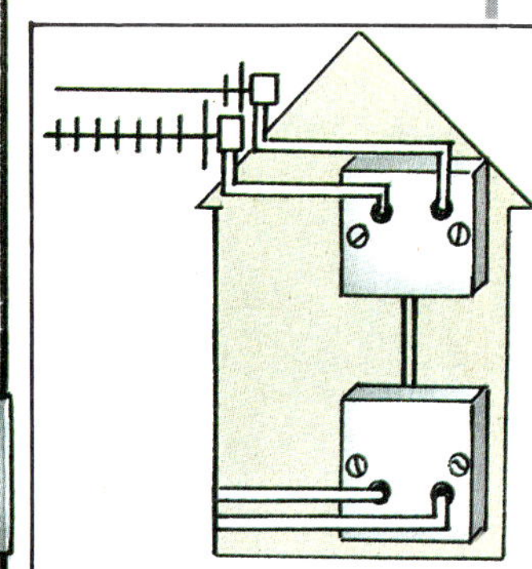

Aerial sockets (above) should be sited near the television. Co-axial cable can run outside the house direct to the aerial, or inside to another socket in the loft.

Porch lights (left) get their power via a spur from the existing light circuit. You have to install a new four-terminal junction box and then run cable outside to the lights and inside to a new switch.

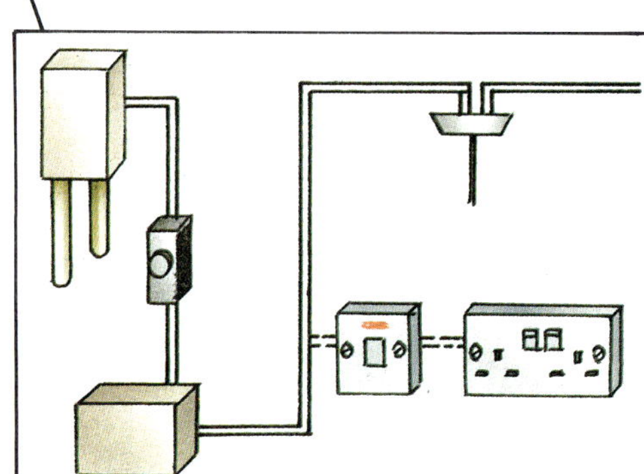

Door bells (left) with a low voltage transformer obtain their power from either the lighting circuit, via a ceiling rose, or the mains, via a fused connection unit. Alternatively, some can be powered by batteries.

REWIRING BEDROOMS AND BATHROOMS

Your bathroom and bedrooms can be made both warm and comfortable when you rewire. Extra care is needed in the bathroom where strict wiring regulations apply.

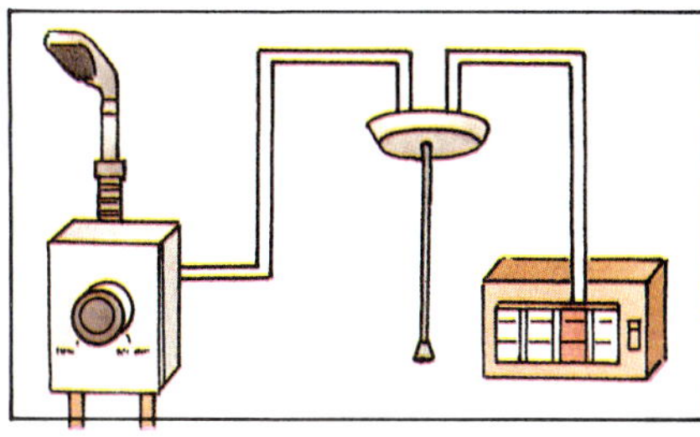

An instantaneous shower (left) should be run on its own 30A circuit in 6mm^2 two-core and earth cable. It should be controlled by a 30A double-pole cord switch mounted on the ceiling.

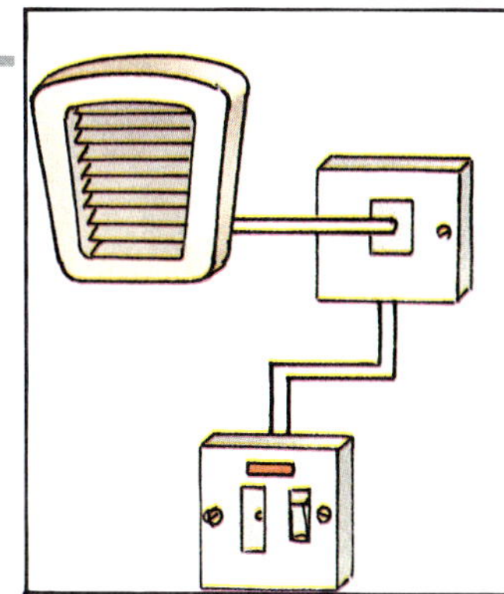

An extractor fan (above) should be connected to the mains via a clock connector and a switched fused connection unit.

A heated towel rail (below) should obtain its power from a flex outlet linked to a switched fused connection unit that is situated outside the bathroom.

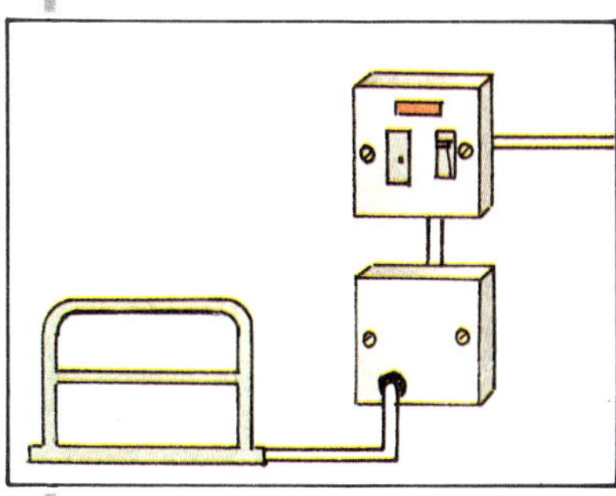

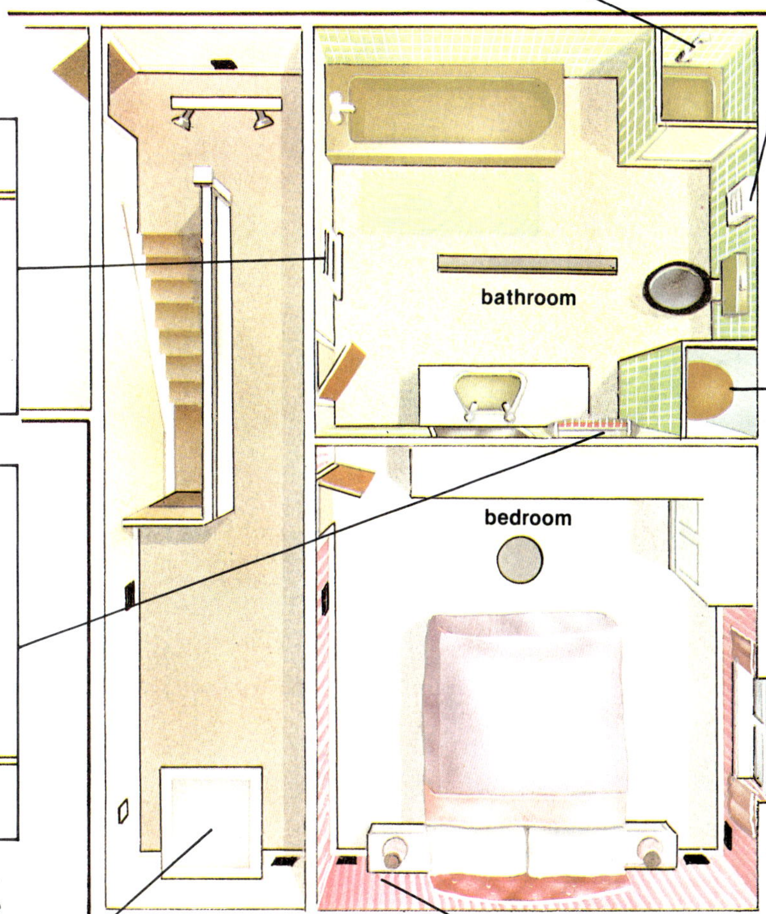

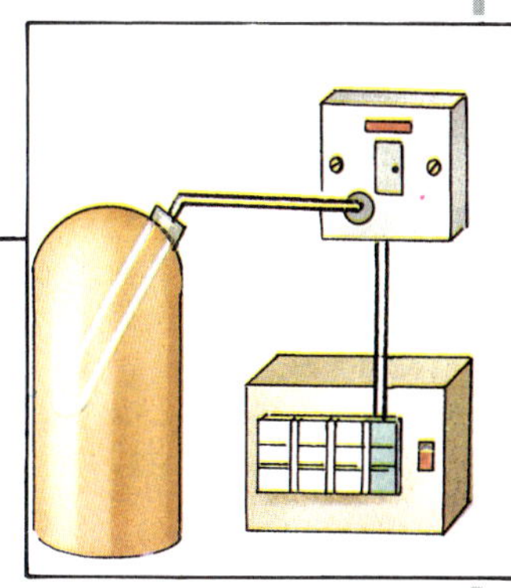

An immersion heater (above) of more than 3kW must be supplied by its own circuit. It should be controlled by a double-pole switch with flex outlet and neon indicator mounted close by.

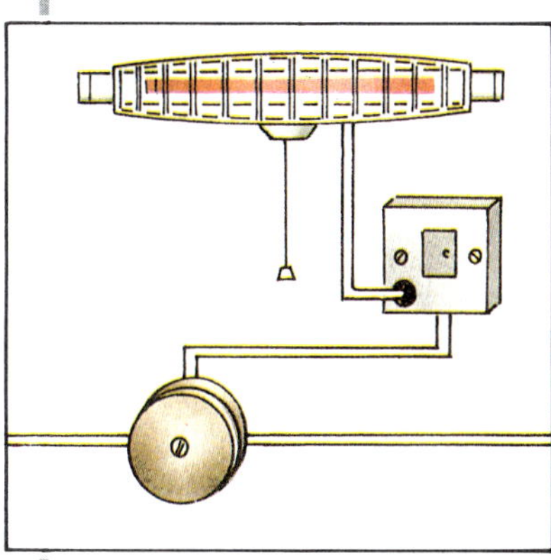

A wall heater (above) should be sited high up and away from the bath. It's controlled by a double-pole cord switch.

A loft light (left) can be extremely useful. Using a junction box, you have to break into the upstairs lighting circuit to provide the power. The switch should be sited on the landing and must be clearly labelled.

Two-way switching (left) is an ideal system for controlling bedroom lights. The two special switches, linked by three-core and earth cable, can control the lights independently of each other, so you don't have to stumble about in the dark.

fitted with a central light and if you decide to reposition this you must make sure that the new rose can be fitted securely to a joist or a wooden batten fitted between two joists. If you decide to install a fluorescent fitting instead, you'll have to alter the wiring only if you already have a loop-in system, in which case you'll have to install an extra junction box.

Spotlights or wall lights can provide a more specific light on particular areas of the room, or for special tasks such as reading or sewing. A point to remember, however, is that wall and table lights can be run from the power circuit to avoid the risk of overloading the lighting circuit. They should be connected to a fused connection unit or plug fitted with a 3A fuse.

Halls and passageways

Sockets for plugging in a vacuum cleaner are necessary in the hall or on the landing, but the lighting is likely to be your most important consideration. Adequate lighting over the stairs is vital as every year many people injure themselves by falling down badly-lit stairs. But, whilst lighting should be adequate, it shouldn't be so bright as to dazzle you as you're going up or down the stairs; so it's worth considering the use of downlighters or carefully directed spotlights. Incidentally, don't forget about two-way switching: it will prevent you ever having to use the stairs in the dark. If you have a cupboard under the stairs it's a good idea to run in power for a light there; it'll make a lot of difference when you're looking for things. Fit the light on its own circuit. As most consumer units are kept under the stairs, it will enable you to replace the fuse without having to work in the dark. At the same time as rewiring the hall, it's also worth installing a porch light. This will make your home that much more welcoming, deter burglars and can be connected to an ordinary lighting circuit. Also, as you'll be running cable in the roof space, it's a good idea to install a light in the loft.

Bathrooms

Bathrooms require special consideration as they are potentially the most dangerous room in which to use electricity. However, there are a number of regulations that apply to them and if you bear these in mind when planning the rewiring you shouldn't experience any difficulty.

The only socket outlets permitted in the bathroom are double-isolated shaver sockets so that means the only portable appliance you can use is an electrical shaver. Any other appliance plugged into this socket will trip the thermal overload device and cut off the current.

All switches must be cord-operated and any lights they control must either be completely enclosed, to prevent the use of the lampholder for any other appliance, or else be fitted with a protective skirt. They must, of course, be out of reach of anyone using the bath or shower.

Fixed appliances may be installed in the bathroom, but again you must proceed with caution. A towel rail, for example, can be connected to a fused connection unit, but the unit itself must be outside the bathroom and you'll have to use a simple flex outlet near the appliance. A wall heater or fire must be fixed high on the wall, away from the bath or shower, and must also be controlled by a cord switch, preferably with a neon indicator. An electric shower requires its own 30A radial circuit, and should be controlled by a double-pole cord switch to isolate it from the mains.

Bedrooms

Along with the living room and the kitchen, the bedroom is likely to be where you'll make most use of electric appliances – after all, you're going to want to make it as comfortable as possible. By the time you've plugged in the tea-maker, the radio/alarm, the electric blanket and two bedside lights you're already up to five sockets, and that's four more than most builders seem to think are necessary! When planning the siting of the socket outlets you should also bear in mind that the needs of a teenager are quite different from those of a young child, while those of an elderly parent staying permanently are different from those of an occasional guest. So you shouldn't necessarily install the same number of sockets in the same position in each room; but it's always better to install more than you immediately need. Once again, two-way switching is a useful way of avoiding stumbling around in the dark and is particularly suited to the bedroom. It's also important to have some kind of bright overall light so that you'll find it easier to look for something, should a small item, like jewellery, drop on the floor.

Outside the house

When you rewire your home you are advised to run a special circuit so you can have power and light in your garden, garage or shed. This will be classified as a sub-main cable and under new wiring regulations must be protected by a residual current circuit breaker (RCCB). This legislation also applies to simple extension cables which are only in use while the appliance they supply is being used. Special waterproof and hard-wearing accessories are available and these should be connected up with great care before being used.

Only after you've carefully considered the state of your home's electrics and determined exactly what your requirements are can you proceed with the actual re-wiring. This is covered in more detail on pages 249–262.

Ready Reference

A NEW CONSUMER UNIT

If you're rewiring your home it is advisable to install a new consumer unit at the same time, to cope with the extra circuits that will be needed. You should:

- choose a unit with enough fuseways to allow some to remain spare for future use
- install it where it can be easily and speedily located. You can always site it in a more convenient position, although extending the incoming mains cable can be costly
- include a residual current circuit breaker, and most importantly,
- get your electricity board to make the final connections to the meter.

A LIGHT UNDER THE STAIRS

If your consumer unit is under the stairs it's a good idea to fit a light there. You should:

- run it on its own circuit so you'll have light when other circuits are off
- use a loop-in battenholder
- fix the switch close to the door
- avoid fixing the lamp so it gets knocked by anyone entering the cupboard.

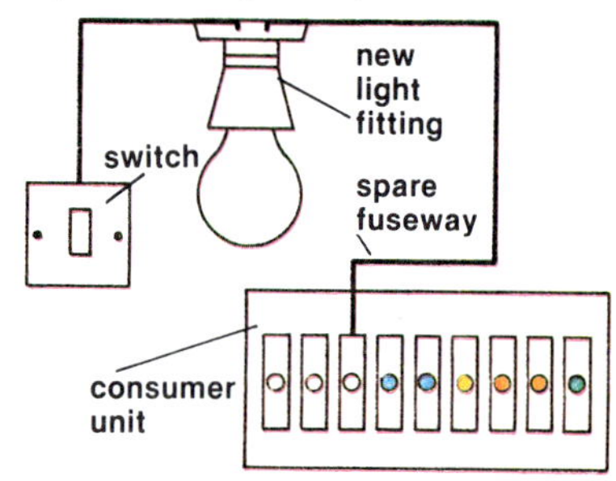

TIP: LABEL YOUR CIRCUITS

When you install your new consumer unit, make sure that you label all the fuseways. Then, in the event of a fuse blowing, you'll be able to identify which is affected almost immediately.

OTHER TECHNIQUES

Other techniques articles to which you can cross-refer include:

Adding ceiling lights and switches 173–176
Fitting extra power points 177–180
Fluorescent lights 196–199
Decorative lights 200–203
Porch lights 204–207
Two-way switching 216–220
Running cable 181–185
Connecting up a cooker 222–227
Instantaneous showers 83–87

REWIRING A HOUSE 1: inspection

Rewiring your home requires considerable preparation and planning. Before you actually decide to do the job, you'll have to give your circuitry a thorough inspection.

Electrical circuits, like most other things in the home, don't last for ever. If your circuits are run in rubber or lead-sheathed cable, then this indicates that they're probably about 30 years old and will have to be replaced. And if all your power circuits are wired as radials (see pages 156–160), then its clear these will have to be replaced with ring circuits to cater for the needs of the modern home. At the same time, it's best to renew completely all the various wiring accessories that allow you to make use of the power carried round your home by these circuits. This is what's meant by rewiring.

Accessories such as switches, socket outlets, ceiling roses, lampholders and plugs can, and do, get broken. As many of these items form an integral part of your home's decor, the chances are you'll want to replace them if they're old-fashioned, and especially if they're damaged. Similarly, the older sort of circuit cables will inevitably have deteriorated with age, or may, like the accessories, have been damaged and will also need renewing. Only if your circuits are run in PVC-sheathed cable will it be possible to leave them in situ and merely replace the accessories. If your cables do get damaged, then they become immediately dangerous and this is the most important reason for rewiring your home: as with any home electrical work safety is the keyword. Although they could still operate satisfactorily, old circuits may be a high shock and fire risk without this being immediately apparent. That's not to say more recent installations are completely safe; bad wiring, poor quality accessories and extensions that have resulted in overloading, can all render an installation or even just part of it, dangerous.

The first step before deciding what to do is to make a thorough examination of your home's existing circuitry.

Know your cables

Old installations are likely to have been wired in either tough rubber-sheathed (TRS) or lead alloy sheathed cable. Both types were insulated with vulcanised rubber and as this was expected to last about 30 years, many installations using these cables are still very much intact. However, the insulation tends to get brittle with age, and when handled can easily break away from the cores and so cause short circuits and current leakage. These faults are the principal causes of fires attributed to faulty electrical wiring. The insulation tends to deteriorate most at the ends of the cores where the cable is connected to whatever accessory it is supplying. This will become apparent when you remove the faceplate of a socket or light switch. Before replacing the faceplace of a socket or light switch. You should, as an interim measure, enclose any bare ends of cores where insulation has cracked or broken away in PVC sleeving and insulation tape. That way the circuit can be safely used until you actually rewire, without the risk of short circuits or earthing faults.

Lead-sheathed cable can prove extremely dangerous. With this type of installation, the sheathing itself was used as the earth and so if it's damaged or no longer intact it's essential to replace it. With age the sheathing often cracks and if this has happened you need look no further; you'll have to rewire as soon as possible.

Cable that is run in light gauge steel conduit is not often found these days, but was frequently used in large blocks of flats (and occasionally in houses). Usually single-core,

INSPECTING YOUR FUSEBOARD

1 *Double-pole fusing is potentially dangerous. With a fuse in both the live and neutral poles it means if the neutral fuse blows, the circuit is still live.*

2 *Switch off at the mainswitch before removing any of the fuseholders. This type of mainswitch is obsolete and should be renewed.*

3 *Carefully remove the fuseholders so you can inspect them. Look for cracked and damaged porcelain that will expose the fuse wire.*

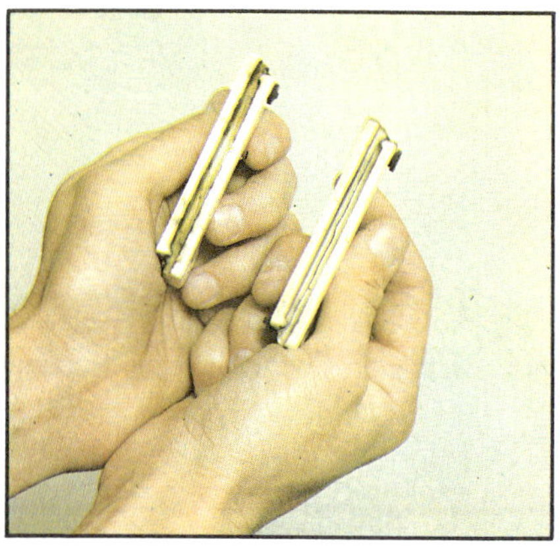

4 *Double-pole fusing should be replaced immediately with a safer system. Never use thicker fuse wire to prevent the fuses repeatedly blowing.*

taped and braided, rubber-insulated non-sheathed cable was used, and therefore had to be completely enclosed for safety. The conduit itself should terminate in a metal box at each accessory, not only to prevent cores from being in contact with combustible material, but also to provide efficient earthing, as without the box there will be no continuity. If there isn't a box you'll have to check that the conduit has been fitted with an earth clip and an earth tail at its outlet. If your home still uses this kind of cable and if the conduit is at all rusty or loose at the joints, there is likely to be no earth continuity anyway and it should all be replaced.

Inspecting the wiring

The best place to check the general condition of your circuitry is in the loft, where access to the cables is easy. At the same time you'll also get an impression of the condition of the remainder of the cable running round your home. Only if it is neatly run and properly fixed PVC-sheathed cable is it unlikely to need rewiring. In that case, however, you should still check that at all the accessories the sheathing ends within the mounting boxes. In addition, if there's PVC cable you must make sure that it's not merely a newer extension of an older circuit.

If you want to inspect the first floor wiring, you'll have to raise a floorboard or two. It's best to pick one that looks as if it's been raised before and you'll probably find that the one running down the centre of the landing usually has most cables concealed beneath it. To check the state of the cable at the outlets it's necessary to remove the faceplates from at least one switch, one lighting fitting and one socket outlet, but you should try not to disturb the existing cable otherwise you might damage the insulation.

Inspecting your fuseboards

If your home has a number of main switches and fuse units instead of one composite consumer unit then it's safe to assume that the installation is old and is likely to be in need of a rewire.

Old main switches and fuse units were usually an assortment of splitter units that each supplied several circuits. So, the chances are there would have been one for the light circuits, one for the power circuits and then single switchfuse units for individual circuits supplying such appliances as immersion heaters or cookers. But don't be taken in by the presence of a gleaming new consumer unit; this doesn't necessarily mean that your home has been recently rewired. It's possible that its presence is merely for cosmetic purposes and that it was installed by the previous owner prior to putting the house up for sale.

Whatever the superficial appearance of the existing units, it's best to carry out a more detailed check to see that the switches all work and, after switching off at the mains, whether any of the porcelain fuseways are broken, so exposing live wire. Watch out for two fuses per circuit which means you have what is termed double-pole fusing; this means there's a fuse in both the live and neutral poles in the unit. The big drawback of double-pole fusing is that in the event of a short circuit or overload it's possible for only the neutral fuse to blow, so leaving parts of the circuit live. With single pole fusing, which present-day regulations now require, the fuse is in the live pole of the circuit only and if it blows, the whole circuit is isolated from the live mains. If your circuits have double-pole fusing you should replace the fuse units without delay and resist the temptation merely to wire the neutral fuse with heavier fusewire to encourage the live to blow first.

Lighting circuit accessories

When inspecting the lighting circuit, it's best to start your inspection with the switches. If you have round switches with screw-on covers or ones that are secured by two screws they will have to be replaced as they are now totally obsolete. These types of switches, known as tumbler switches, are usually mounted on either hardwood blocks or plastic pattresses and either method is potentially dangerous. Standard practice during installation was to strip the cable sheathing behind the block, and that means non-sheathed ends of the insulated cores were frequently in contact with combustible material. Over the years, as the insulation grew brittle and thin, this will have turned into a potential fire risk.

Old pattern ceiling roses mounted on wooden pattress blocks and backless ceiling plates are risky for the same reason. Those

CHECKING SOCKET OUTLETS

1 *Socket outlets that have round holes and which make frequent use of adaptors are potentially dangerous and should be replaced.*

2 *To inspect the existing circuit cable, switch off at the mains. Then remove the cover of the switch, and check whether it is cracked or charred.*

3 *Remove the fixing screws holding the socket to the skirting. Then gently ease the socket away so that the circuit cable is exposed.*

4 *You should be able to pull a little extra cable out from the wall so that you can give each core and its sheathing a detailed inspection.*

5 *If you've damaged the insulation or sheathing during the removal of the socket, you should fit a length of PVC sleeving over any exposed core.*

6 *Finally, you must give those damaged cores extra protection by wrapping them securely in PVC insulating tape before reusing the circuits.*

Ready Reference

WHEN TO REWIRE

There are a number of tell-tale signs that will help you determine if your home needs rewiring. When you inspect your circuitry, look for

- old cable with brittle or cracked insulation
- cable with poor sheathing
- unsheathed cores that are touching combustible material
- loose, rusty or disconnected light gauge steel conduit
- poor earthing continuity
- damaged accessories
- obsolete accessories
- accessories that can't be earthed
- overloaded circuits
- frequent use of adaptors
- insufficient lighting points
- insufficient power points.

ALTERNATIVE ACTION

If you don't need to rewire, but want more sockets, you can divide an existing ring circuit to form two complete circuits.
You should

- break into the circuit at a convenient point
- extend each section so that it runs back to the consumer unit and so completes the new circuits (you need an extra fuseway).
- add new outlets on the way.

TIP: TESTING FOR EARTH CONTINUITY

It's a good idea to test your earthing continuity. For a really conclusive test you'll need an earth loop impedance tester, but these are very expensive. For a reasonable indication of the continuity you can make your own tester. You'll need a bell, a 9V battery and some cable. You'll have to

- switch off at the mains
- connect one core of the cable to the earth terminal on the consumer unit
- connect the other in turn to the main water pipe, other earthed metal and earth terminals in socket outlets.

If the bell rings it indicates earth continuity, but this is not conclusive of efficient earthing. Only professional testing can check that.

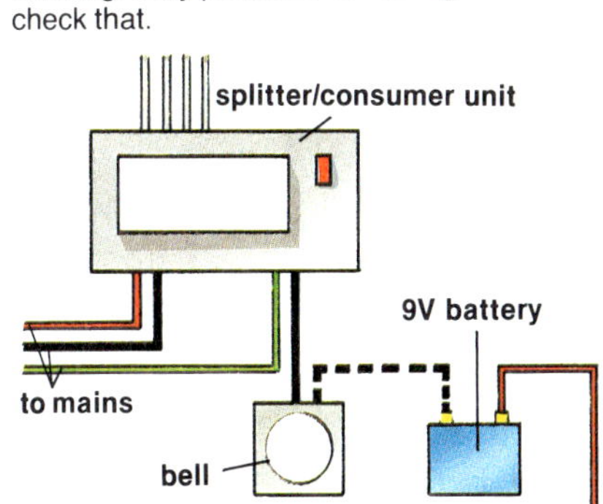

CHECKING PENDANT LIGHTS

1 *Before inspecting the lighting circuit, switch off at the mains. You can then remove the cover of a conveniently-located ceiling rose.*

2 *Unscrew the rose from its pattress block and ease it away so you can inspect the circuit cable. Look for any damaged or brittle sleeving.*

3 *It's also a good idea to inspect the flex at each lampholder. This can often be in poor condition and will pose a shock or fire risk.*

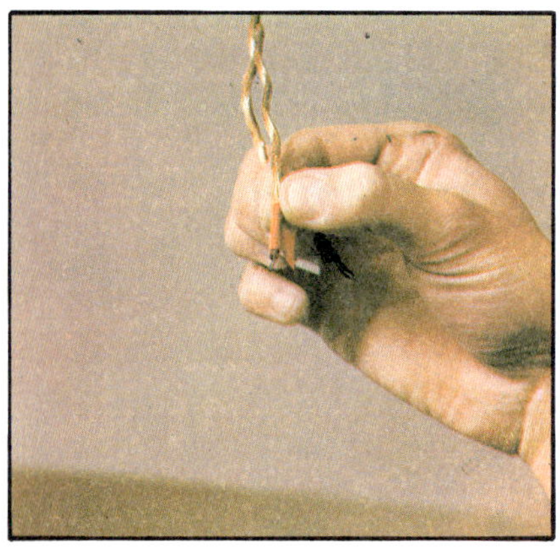

4 *All exposed cores must be sleeved in PVC and wrapped in insulating tape before the mainswitch is turned on and the lighting circuit used again.*

ceiling plates allowed circuit wires and flexes to be in contact with the ceiling which is especially dangerous if it's a lath and plaster one. Metal battenholders should also be replaced as, apart from the wooden pattress blocks, they weren't earthed and therefore presented a shock risk.

Socket outlets

Round pin plugs and sockets are now virtually obsolete, and as all new electrical appliances are fitted with square-pin plugs it makes sense that old sockets should be replaced in the course of rewiring. In addition, the two-pin version is dangerous as it doesn't allow the appliances to be earthed. You might well find that three-pin sockets have been fitted in place of old two-pin ones, but more often than not no extra earth core has been added. If that's the case, then you will certainly have to rewire. If the existing sockets are wired on a radial circuit there is no real advantage to be gained by inspecting the cable; you might just as well run in new cable and replace sockets when you put in a new ring circuit for the socket outlets.

But if you know that they are on a ring circuit then you should check whether the cable is in reasonable condition. If it is, you won't, of course, have to rewire it. Remember, if you do have to remove a socket you'll probably find it easier to remove one that is fixed to a wooden surface such as the skirting.

Checking the earthing

It is important that your electricity supply is connected to earth; that way if a fault develops in a circuit, current finds its way to earth and the fuse will blow to protect the circuit and its users. You can make some visual checks to get an idea of whether your circuit earthing is in order. If the electricity board's cable runs underground into your home then you should find an earth cable running from the fuseboard to a clip on the cable sheathing. It's important that all such clips and fixings are securely in place. Another method is for the earth cable to be connected to a clamp on the mains water pipe where it enters the house.

However, mains water pipes can no longer be used as the sole means of earthing. This is because of the now widespread use of plastic pipes, which interrupt earth continuity. Where the mains are run overhead, the earth cable can only be connected to a clamp on the mains water pipe or else an earth rod made of copper or wrought iron that is buried as deep as possible in the soil beneath the house. There are two important points to remember at this stage: first, even though rewiring is planned, poor connections of the main earth cable should be dealt with immediately and any corroded sections of cable replaced; and second, the presence of earthing at the mains does not mean that the earthing of individual circuits is effective.

You *can* test the earth continuity on your existing circuits using a home-made tester (see *Ready Reference*) or a proprietary plug-in tester. But such equipment will only give an indication of the efficiency of the earthing, and you should ideally call in a qualified electrician or your local Electricity Board to test the system with professional instruments. The Board must test your rewired installation anyway, and so it is as well to rely on professional expertise at the outset rather than to have a fundamental problem discovered later.

Planning the job

Once you've inspected your home's electrics and determined that they do, in fact, need rewiring, your next step is to start planning the work. This is an extremely important part of the job, as careful and thorough preparation will mean minimum disruption to your daily routine. If you are going to rewire your home before you move in, then it makes little or no difference where you start. However, if you are already living in the house you'll probably find it best to start the job in the loft and deal with the first floor lighting.

There is bound to be an element of disruption in your home when you do the rewiring – especially as you'll have to move furniture around, lift floorcovering such as fitted carpets and lino, and raise floorboards. Inevitably you're not going to be able to do the job as quickly as a professional electrician and you should make sure that you don't try and rush the work at the expense of doing a good job.

An obvious way of cutting down on the time spent rewiring is to have a helper, and it'll also make running cable that much easier.

CHECKING LIGHT SWITCHES

1 Round tumbler switches mounted on a block probably have worn and sparking contacts. To inspect one, isolate the circuit and remove its cover.

2 Loosen the terminal screws and remove the fixing screws that hold the switch in place. Then ease the switch away from the pattress.

3 Remove the switch, taking care not to damage any brittle insulation or sheathing. You can now examine the state of the circuit cable.

4 Any exposed cores present both a shock and fire risk. To lessen the danger, sleeve them temporarily in PVC and then wrap them in insulating tape.

With some assistance you'll be able to rewire the upper floor lighting and install a light in the loft in a couple of days; so you could set aside a weekend for this section of the job. For the rest of the house you should really allow about seven days.

Estimating your requirements

You'll have to cast a critical eye round your home and assess what your power and lighting needs really are before you buy any materials. The chances are that your current needs are going to be considerably greater than when the existing system was installed, and ideally you should aim to have one socket per electrical appliance. For further information on this, see the planning section on pages 245–248.

Your estimation of the cable you're going to need is likely to be less precise, and the amount you'll have to get depends on the size of your home, the number of circuits, the number of lights and the number of socket outlets you'll be installing. For the average three of four-bedroomed house that has one light and switch per room and two in the main living room and kitchen you'll probably need about ten metres of cable per light. So, as the chances are that you'll be running power to at least ten lighting points you might just as well buy a couple of 50 metres reels of cable for this part of the job. For socket outlets wired on, say, two ring circuits you'll probably need between 50 and 100 metres of 2.5mm^2 cable. It's a good idea to buy just one reel at first and then, if necessary, another – or else a specific extra length of the cable if you don't need another whole reel. But it's certainly worth taking accurate measurements of the circuit for cookers, showers and outside power because more expensive cable is used for these.

Ready Reference

INSPECTING CABLE

It's a good idea to inspect wiring that runs under floorboards, even though it is less likely to have been damaged since the cables are concealed. But the wiring may have been badly installed, particularly where extensions have been made to the original cable runs. You should

- look for a floorboard that has been lifted before
- lever up the end of the board with a bolster chisel
- saw through the tongue if the board still has one

- use a piece of timber as a lever to remove the board.

TIP: LABEL YOUR CABLES

After lifting the floorboards to inspect the wiring, label the cables as you identify which one feeds which circuit. That way, when you come to do the rewiring you won't have to trace all the cables again. And you won't risk removing or replacing the wrong circuits.

SHEATHING DAMAGED CORES

When you examine cables at switches, sockets and lighting points, it's very difficult not to cause further damage to already perished insulation. In that case you should

- check that the main switch is OFF
- cover each individual core in PVC sleeving
- wrap each sleeved core in PVC insulating tape
- finally, replace the accessory's face-plate.

REWIRING A HOUSE: 2 starting work

Once you've decided to rewire your home and have planned what you want to do, you'll have to start thinking about buying all your materials and beginning the actual job. Here's the way to proceed.

When buying the equipment for your rewiring, always choose good quality cable and fittings made by well-known and established firms. Obviously it's worth shopping around and it's a good idea to obtain a couple of catalogues so you can compare prices. However, beware of special bargains or similar offers of equipment from unknown sources. Make sure that the cable you buy has been produced to the relevant British Standard (see *Ready Reference*). This is likely to be stamped on the outside of the sheathing.

Itemising your requirements

Before you pay a visit to your local wholesalers, you should work out and itemise exactly what you need so that they'll be able to give you an accurate quote for all the materials. The quickest way to do this is to draw up a sketch floor plan of the house and mark on it the position of each socket outlet, light switch and light fitting, and then count up the numbers of each type of accessory you're going to need.

Work out the circuits next; an average two-storey house will probably have two lighting circuits, three ring circuits and a couple of exclusive circuits – for an immersion heater and cooker for example. That means you're likely tc need a new consumer unit with at least eight fuseways, and however many circuits you need it's worth choosing a unit that will leave one fuseway spare for future use. You'll have to decide whether to use rewirable or cartridge fuses, or else face the extra expense, but increased safety, by using MCBs and fitting an RCCB.

Decide whether you'll flush-mount or surface-mount switches and socket outlets, and note the number of each type of box you'll need. List how many ceiling roses, fused connection units, junction boxes and ceiling switches you'll need and also whether you're going to fit a shaver socket or supply unit. Finally, you should take a note of the number of switches and boxes you'll need for any special circuits you're going to run. When you've added cable, cable clips, PVC earth sleeving and other accessories to your list, you'll be ready to put it into some sort of order.

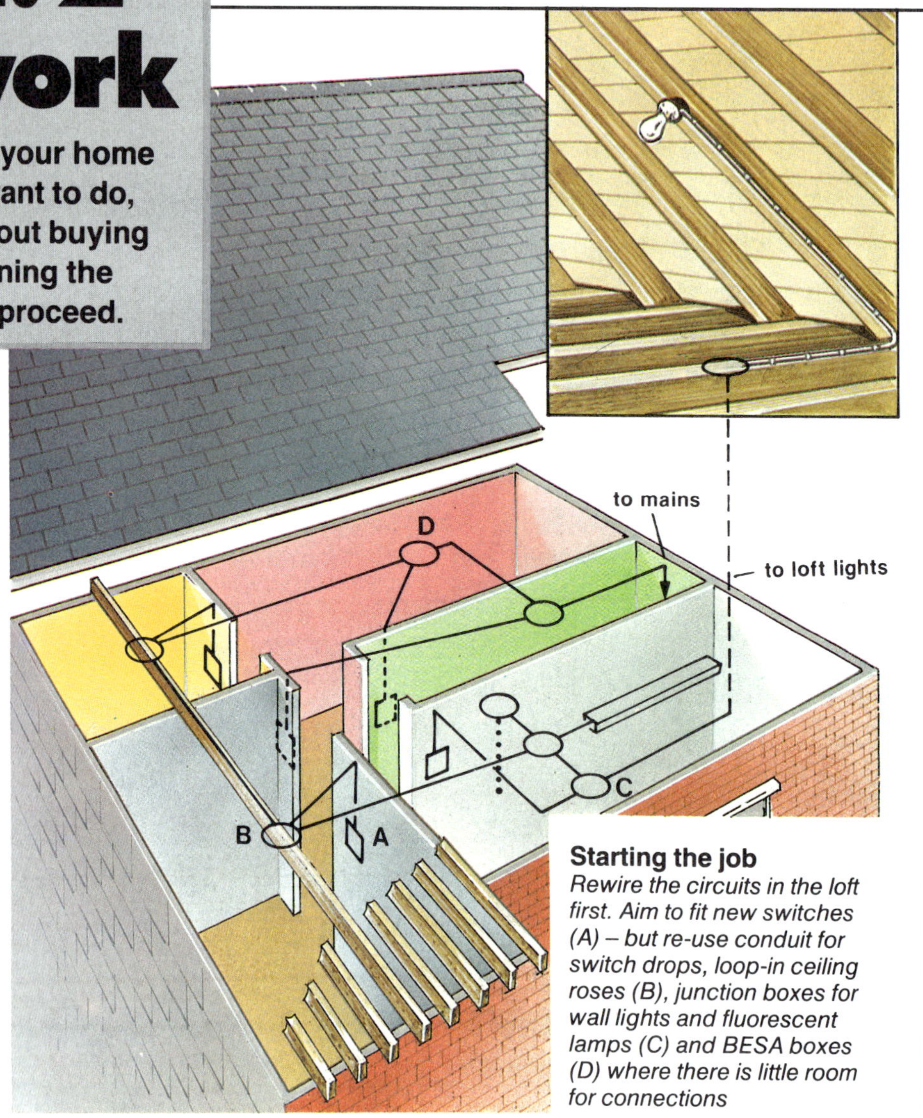

Starting the job
Rewire the circuits in the loft first. Aim to fit new switches (A) – but re-use conduit for switch drops, loop-in ceiling roses (B), junction boxes for wall lights and fluorescent lamps (C) and BESA boxes (D) where there is little room for connections

INSTALLING A NEW SWITCH

1 *Chase in the new switch cable or run it in an existing length of conduit. Strip back the sleeving on the cable and sleeve the earth core.*

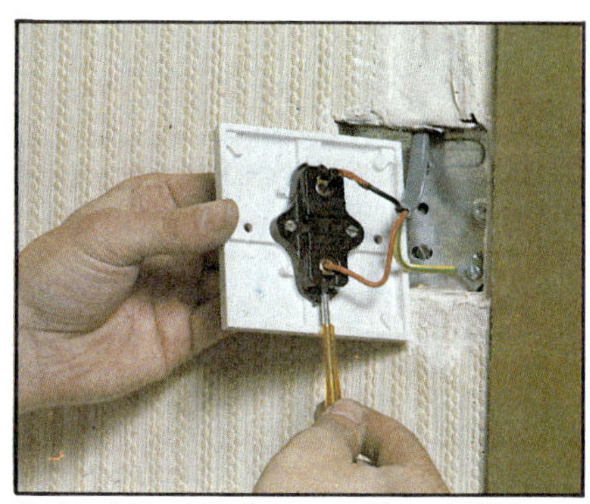

2 *Mark the black core with red PVC tape to indicate that it's live. Connect the conductors to the faceplate and the earth to the box.*

FITTING A ROSE AND LAMPHOLDER

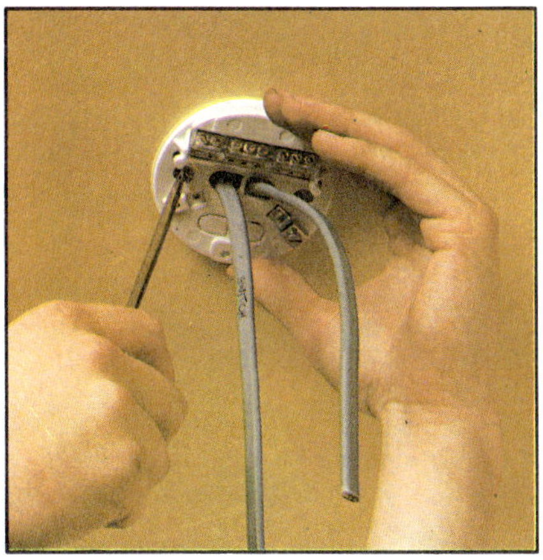

1 *Make a hole in the ceiling to let through the lighting circuit cable and the switch cable. Then fix the new rose to the ceiling.*

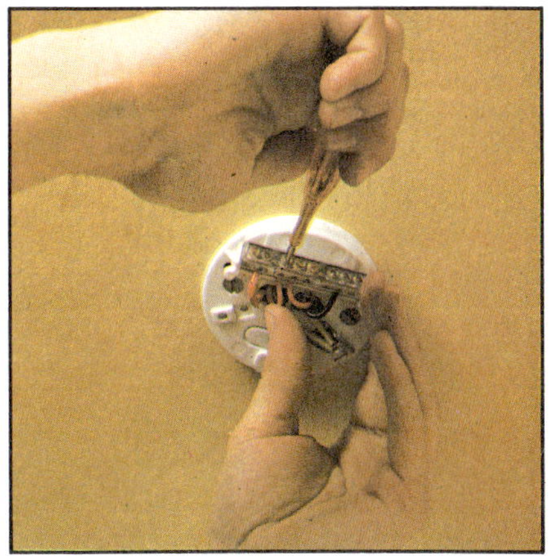

2 *With loop-in wiring, wrap the switch cable's black core in red PVC. Connect up the other cores as shown in the photograph.*

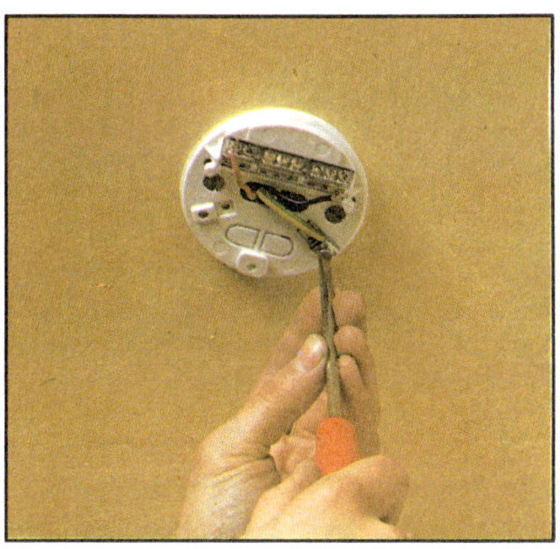

3 *With junction box wiring, the earth is connected to the earth terminal, the black conductor goes to the neutral bank and the red to the SW terminal.*

4 *To connect the flex, strip back the sheathing and insulation and connect the blue and brown conductors to the two terminals of the lampholder.*

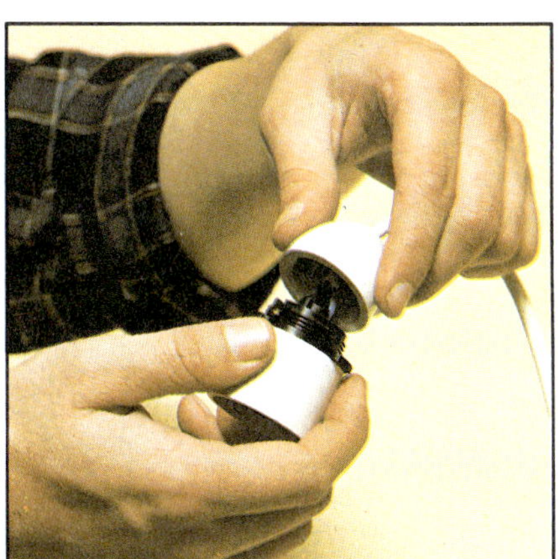

5 *Screw on the cap and then slip the rose cover over the flex. Cut the flex to length and prepare the free end for connecting to the rose.*

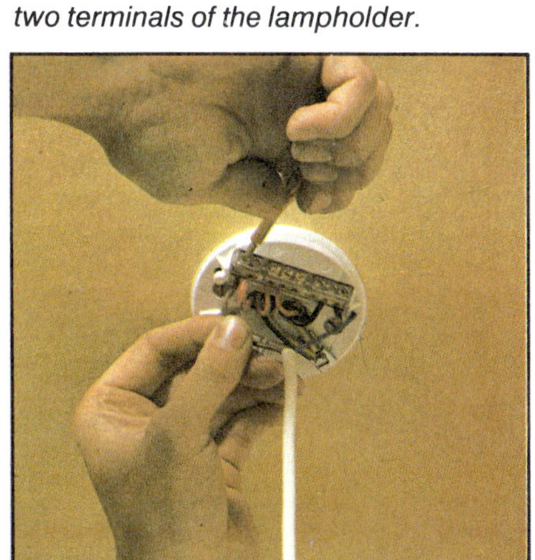

6 *At the rose, connect the blue core to the terminal on the neutral side and the red to the SW side. Remember to hook the wires over the cord grips.*

Ready Reference

BUYING THE MATERIALS

Before visiting your supplier, you should make a list of all your requirements. This should include both accessories and cable.

Accessories

For a typical three-bedroom house, with a loft and garage, your shopping list is likely to resemble the following:
25 double socket outlets plus flush/surface mounting boxes
3 single socket outlets plus boxes
14 one-gang plate-switches and boxes
3 cord-operated ceiling switches
2 two-way switches plus boxes
8 ceiling roses
8 lampholders
2 batten holders
1 close-ceiling light fitting
4 fluorescent fittings
1 shaver supply unit plus box
1 cooker switch plus box
junction boxes (optional)
1 eight-way consumer unit
8 MCBs plus an RCCB

Cable

Your cable requirements could include:
50 to 100m 1.5mm^2 two-core and earth
50 to 100m 2.5mm^2 two-core and earth
10m 1.0mm^2 three-core and earth cable
5 to 10m 1.0mm^2 flexible cord
Length of 6.0mm^2 two-core and earth cable
Length of 10mm^2 two-core and earth cable
Length of PVC-covered armoured cable
Approximately 5m 6.0mm^2 single core green/yellow PVC cable for main earthing lead
Approximately 5m 2.5mm^2 single green/yellow cable for bonding extraneous metal to earth
10m green/yellow PVC earth sleeving
Plastic cable clips

Other items you will need include wood screws, wall plugs, nails, fixing timber and PVC insulating tape.

CABLE CHECKLIST

The uses of cable varies according to its size:
1.0mm^2 and 1.5mm^2 – lighting
2.5mm^2 – power circuit, immersion heater and small water heater (up to 5kW)
4mm^2 – small cooker, 30A radial circuit, water heater (up to 7kW)
6mm^2 – cookers up to 12kW
10mm^2 – large cookers

STANDARDS

You must be sure that equipment you use corresponds to a British Standard of quality. Check that a BS number is stamped on all cable and accessories.

INSTALLING A JUNCTION BOX

1 To install a four-terminal junction box you'll have to fix a timber batten between two joists and screw the box in place onto this.

2 Connect the live cores to one terminal, the neutrals to a second and the earths to a third. The black of the switch cable (with red PVC) goes to a fourth.

3 Lay a length of $1.5mm^2$ two-core and earth cable from the lighting point to the junction box and prepare the ends. Remember to sleeve the earth core.

4 Connect the sleeved earth core to the earth terminal, the black core to the neutral terminal and the red core to the switch terminal (top left).

Once you've made a list, take it to at least a couple of suppliers so you'll be able to get the cheapest quote – and don't forget to ask for a discount for buying in bulk.

Working in the loft

As you'll be starting work in the loft, check which existing lights are on which circuits and label them accordingly. Inspect each circuit separately, with only its fuse in position in the fuseboard at the time. Then list which lights are on it. Before starting work you must turn off the mainswitch of the fuseboard that contains the fuses controlling those lighting circuits that run in the loft. Make a note of their positions so you know which is which, but in fact, it's probably better to keep all fuses out and mainswitches off when working on the old wiring itself. You should then remove all light fittings on the floor below, that are supplied by the wiring in the loft. That includes all switches as well, but not the two-way switch in the hall that controls the landing lighting as this is likely to get its power from a different circuit. You should then get up in the loft, taking with you a couple of battery-powered lights. This is extremely important. It's not worth working merely in torch light as you risk making errors in the wiring that could prove costly. It is possible to have electric lighting from an extension lead, but only if there is a socket outlet below that is supplied from a circuit controlled by a mainswitch independent of the lighting mainswitch. If you have a cooker control unit with a socket outlet that is supplied via a separate switch-fuse unit, then this would be perfectly suitable to use for makeshift extension lighting.

Once you're up in the loft you can pull out all the old wiring and any old conduit it's run in. Only if conduits are sunk into plaster and run down to switch positions should they be left in place and then reused for the new cable runs. Once you've removed the cables from fittings and switches you should find only one left. This will be the circuit feed cable that runs from the mains. It's likely to be in conduit and if you want to reuse this conduit then you can use the old feed cable to fish up the new through the wall. If, on the other hand, the new feed cable is to take a different route then you can just cut off the old feed cable where it emerges from the conduit in the loft and remove it when you tackle the rewiring on the floor below. But, of course, before you do anything else you must disconnect the feed cable at its fuse unit and pull it out so there is no danger of accidentally reconnecting it.

Lighting points

Before you start making the connections, you must decide whether to use a loop-in system, a junction box system or a mixture of the two. With the loop-in system, the lighting circuit cable leaves the consumer unit and is connected to the first in a series of special loop-in ceiling roses. From this first rose, one cable will then go on to the next in the series, while another takes the power down to the switch controlling the light and back up to the light itself. The junction box system is based on much the same idea but, rather than running from rose to rose, the lighting circuit feed cable passes through a series of four-terminal junction boxes that are fixed to battens between the joists. From each box, one cable runs to the ceiling rose or light, while another serves as a switch drop and goes to the switch that controls the new light. Using a junction box system can prove particularly convenient when fitting wall lights, for example. This is because not only is there little space at the back of the fitting for looping-in, but you'll also save on cable as you won't have to run two lengths down the wall. A mixture of the two systems is the likeliest compromise, using whichever method saves the most cable at any point. For further information see pages 156–160. Where your new light fittings are to be fixed in the same positions as the old, you must check that there are satisfactory fixing points above the ceiling. If not, fix a piece of 100 x 25mm (4 x 1in) timber between the joists and drill a 20mm (¾in) hole through that to coincide with the hole in the ceiling. Do the same if you are going to fit new lights, although it is possible, if slightly fiddly, to screw a ceiling rose to the underside of a joist and still leave enough room for the cables to enter. It's also advisable to fix a batten between a couple of joists at the position of any cord-operated switch in the bathroom and for any similar switch to be fitted in a bedroom at the bedhead.

FITTING A BESA BOX

1 Mark the position of the terminal block on the ceiling surface. Use either a pad saw or a keyhole saw to cut out the circular section.

2 Push the BESA box into the recess and screw it to the joist. Alternatively, fix a batten between the joists and screw the box in place to this.

3 With loop-in wiring, draw the feed and switch cables into the BESA box. Wrap red PVC insulating tape round the black core of the switch cable.

4 Connect the lives, neutral and earths up to separate connectors and the taped switch core to another. Push all four up into the box to await the light fitting.

Running in the cable

The next thing is to install the circuit feed cable. This should be 1.5mm^2 two-core and earth PVC cable and should originate at a 5A fuseway. If you're going to run it in an existing conduit you must make sure that each end of the conduit is fitted with a PVC bush to prevent the cable from getting damaged on any sharp edges. You'll probably find that you have to lift at least one other floorboard to gain access to the cable and run it to the mains. You should then start running the feed cable to the lighting points in the ceiling. Push the cable through the holes and make the connections to the roses but don't, at this stage, fix the fittings to the ceiling. It's a good idea to mark the feed cables 'feed' at each point where they emerge through the ceiling so there is no possibility of subsequent confusion. You then have to run the switch cables either from the rose itself (for loop-in wiring) or from the junction box where the feed to the light is taken (junction-box wiring) to the switch position. If there is no existing conduit just pierce a hole in the ceiling above the switch position and push the cable through. You can chase it into the plaster at a later date.

Once you've completed the wiring for the lights on the floor below, you can start wiring up a light in the loft itself. It's likely that the last light on the circuit will be close to both the first light and the trapdoor. From this last light you must extend the feed cable to a loop-in battenholder that is then screwed to one of the rafters. You then have to run a switch cable to a position on the landing below where the switch should be clearly labelled 'loft'. Alternatively, you might find it easier to break into the circuit with another four-terminal junction box and run one cable up to the battenholder on the rafters and take another down to the landing and to a conveniently located switch.

Whichever system you decide upon, it's worth making the extra effort to install this light as it will undoubtedly prove very useful in the future.

Fixing the cable

Before leaving the loft you must check that all the cables have been run neatly between the joists. It's probably best to run the cables parallel with the joists as far as possible as that way they can be neatly clipped to them with cable clips. It's generally frowned upon to drill holes in the joists in the loft as you risk weakening them, so run cables parallel to the joists as far as the binder – the large timber cross member linking the joists. You can then clip the cable to the binder to go across the joists before running it to the position of the next light or switch. For further information on running cables, see pages 181–185.

Installing the switches

When using an existing conduit for your switch drop you must make sure that it is fitted with a protective PVC bush at each end. If you want to fix surface-mounted switches, then this can be done neatly over the end of the conduit, but flush boxes have to be fixed below the conduit. If the conduit is too long it can, of course, be cut back, but you must pull back the cable first so as not to risk damaging it. If you don't have an existing conduit you'll have to cut a chase into the wall and, after fixing the switch in position and making the connections, make good with plaster filler.

Fixing the light fittings

Once you've connected up all the ceiling roses and switches, and fitted two-core PVC-sheathed flex and plastic lampholders to them, screw the light fittings to the ceiling with wood screws. Cord-operated switches should be fixed in much the same way, although some modern ones have detachable pattress blocks. Special pendant fittings that have backless ceiling plates have boxes called BESA boxes. These are fixed flush with the ceiling and secured to a timber batten fixed at the relevant height between two joists or actually to one of the joists. For further information on fitting new ceiling lights see pages 173–176 and 196–203.

Close-mounted ceiling fittings usually have a baseplate that allows them to be fixed directly to the ceiling. However, choose a totally enclosed fitting for the bathroom.

Finally, having installed all the lights and switches you can make the connections at the fuseboard/consumer unit end, insert the relevant fuse and test your new circuit.

REWIRING A HOUSE: 3 finishing off

With the new upstairs lighting cables in place, you'll be well into the job of rewiring. Here's how to tackle the next stage and finally complete the work by connecting all the cables to a consumer unit.

The remaining stages of the job involve tackling the light and power circuits in the ground floor ceiling void, and then the power circuits under the ground floor itself.

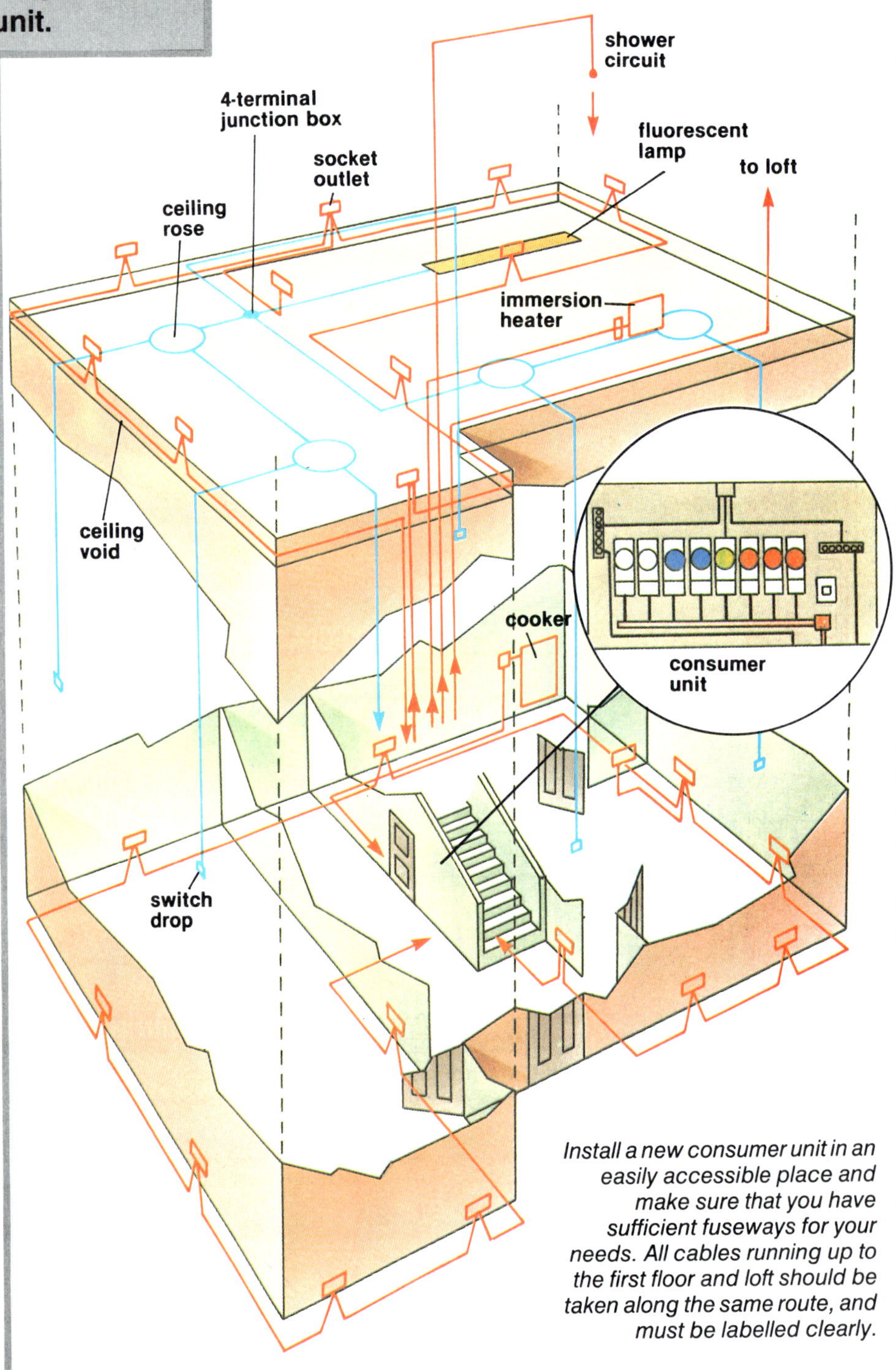

Install a new consumer unit in an easily accessible place and make sure that you have sufficient fuseways for your needs. All cables running up to the first floor and loft should be taken along the same route, and must be labelled clearly.

Once you've completed the rewiring in the loft, you'll have to turn your attention to the rest of your home. Normally in a two-storey house this will mean working in the void between the ground floor ceiling and the floorboards of the floor above. Here you'll find the circuits for the upstairs power outlets and the downstairs lighting. And, if your house has a solid concrete ground floor, you may also find the circuit for the downstairs power outlets and possibly the cooker as well. However, if the ground floor is made up of floorboards with a void underneath then this is where the power circuits will most likely be run because it means that cables don't have to be chased down the wall from the ceiling to reach a power socket at skirting board level – and saving on expensive cable is obvious.

There are two ways of approaching this part of the rewiring job. One is to turn off the power and then to rip out the existing circuitry in a fit of enthusiasm. But what happens when the work takes longer than you anticipated? Much of the house could be left without light and power. So a more cautious approach is what's needed. Deal with each circuit individually. That way if you come across a problem that delays you you'll still be able to have some supply of electricity at the end of the day. Furthermore there's less chance of getting the circuits confused.

Dealing with the downstairs lighting

It's a good idea to rewire the lighting circuit first, as that way you'll be able to have light when you do the rest of the wiring. The first thing to do is to switch off the mainswitch controlling the circuit and then remove the fuse and disconnect the circuit cable. Take down all fittings and switches and mark the position of the old fittings you're replacing and the new lights you plan to install. If you've got fitted carpets you'll have to lift them before you raise any floorboards to gain access to the circuitry. You should aim to lift a board above each lighting point and also one that runs the length of each room. It's quite likely that many of the circuits will run along the landing so it's wise to raise a floorboard that runs the length of the landing so

FITTING FLUSH SOCKETS

1 *Decide where you want to position the socket, then draw a pencil line round the mounting box as a guide for where to chop out the wall.*

2 *Drill slightly within the pencil lines to the depth of the mounting box, then work along the lines with a bolster chisel before chopping out the recess.*

3 *Channel a cable run down the back of the skirting using a long, thin cold chisel. Alternatively, use a long masonry bit and an electric drill.*

4 *Push a length of PVC conduit into the hole behind the skirting, then thread the cable through the conduit and into the mounting box.*

5 *Push the box into position, then use a bradawl to mark where the fixing holes are to go in the recess. Remove the box and drill and plug the holes.*

6 *Set the box back into place and screw it tightly into the recess. Check that it is level, and then make good if necessary with plaster or filler.*

Ready Reference

BONDING TO EARTH

The Wiring Regulations require all metal pipework, hot water radiators, metal baths, sink waste pipes and other metal work that could come in contact with electric cables to be connected to the earthing terminal.

CROSSBONDING OF SERVICES

It is also your responsibility to cross bond the gas and water mains to the earthing terminal. You should

- fix an earthing clamp to the mains water pipe on the street side of the stop-cock
- fix an earthing clamp to the mains gas pipe on the house side of the gas meter
- link the two together with $10mm^2$ earthing cable sleeved in green/yellow PVC
- without cutting it, continue the cable to the board's earthing terminal near the meter.

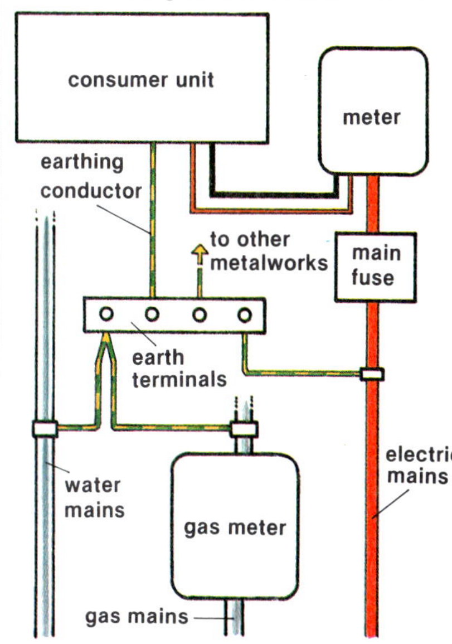

RUNNING CABLE UNDER FLOORS

Use a technique known as fishing:

- lift the floorboards at either end of the run
- thread stiff wire beneath the floor through one hole and hook it out of the other with another piece of wire
- use the longer piece of wire to pull the cable through
- if there's a gap underneath the ground floor you can 'fish' the cable diagonally across the room under the joists.

If the gap under the joists is large enough you can crawl in the space clipping the cable to the joists

- where the cable crosses the joists at right angles, run it through holes drilled 50mm (2in) below their top edges.

CONNECTING UP NEW SOCKETS

1 *Strip back the sheathing of the cable by running a sharp knife down the side, over the uninsulated earth core. Avoid damaging the other cores' insulation.*

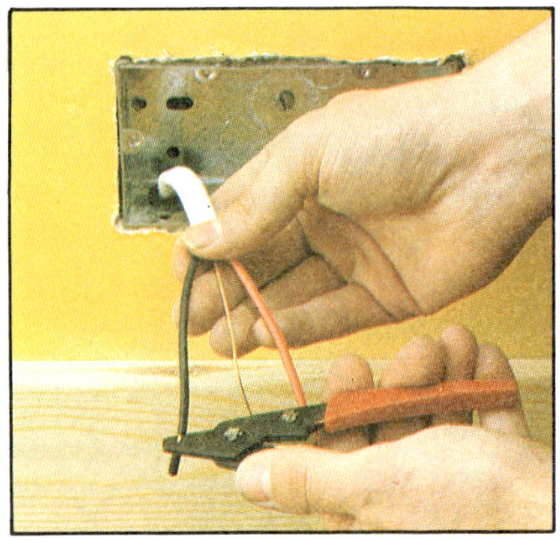

2 *To prepare the cable for connection you should set the wire strippers to the correct gauge and remove about 9mm (3/8in) of insulation from the cores.*

3 *Before connecting the cores you should sleeve the exposed earth core in green/yellow PVC. This is for purposes of insulation and identification.*

4 *Connect the three cores to the relevant terminals of the sockets, making sure no exposed core is showing. Then screw the socket into position.*

you can pull out the cables. If your floorboards run across the landing, then raise one at each end and fish the cable through. If switch drops aren't run in conduit then you'll have to just cut the cables at ceiling level and leave them chased in the wall. Work back towards the landing and then pull out the circuit feed cable running down to the fuseboard. If you find a cable that runs under numerous floorboards, it's a good idea to attach a length of stout wire to it before pulling it out. That way you'll have a draw wire in place for the new cable and so avoid having to lift further floorboards.

You should proceed in much the same way as for rewiring the loft. If you're going to install wall lights in any of the rooms on the ground floor you'll have to make a hole in the ceiling above each light and mark the position in the room above. If the wall runs parallel to the joints on the first floor you'll find that the cable can be 'fished' through from the raised board in the centre of the room. Otherwise you'll have to raise a floorboard directly over the lighting point. For further details on running cable see pages 181–185.

Wiring the circuit

Before running in the circuit cable, you must drill holes in the joists where the cable crosses them. These should be about 19mm (3/4in) in diameter and at least 50mm (2in) below the tops of the joists. Where you'll be running only one cable through them the holes can, of course, be slightly smaller in diameter. If you're using the loop-in system for the circuit then run a cable from the lighting point nearest the mains position down to the consumer unit and mark the end of this sheathing 'lighting circuit, ground floor'. As with the first floor lighting circuit, you must then link up the lighting points with 1.0mm^2 or 1.5mm^2 two-core and earth PVC-sheathed cable, and run in the switchdrops as well. At this stage, however, you needn't worry about taking cable to any wall lights. Remember, it's a good idea to label all cables so that there is no chance of any confusion at a later date.

From each wall light you should run a cable back up into the ceiling void to a four-terminal junction box fixed centrally above the lights. To obtain power you could break into the circuit with a three-terminal junction box and extend a branch cable to the four-terminal one or simply break into the mains with the four-terminal box. At this stage you should also run a cable to a porch light, a back door light or to any other light you want to fix outside the house. For further details see pages 204–207. It's also a good idea to take a length of three-core and earth cable from the landing two-way switch and link it to another in the hall to give yourself two-way control of the landing and hall lights. For further details see pages 216–220. Once you've made all the connections, you can fix the fittings to the ceiling and walls and temporarily connect the cable to the fuseway in your existing fuseboard so you can check that the circuit is working correctly.

Installing first-floor socket outlets

After again switching off at the mains and taking out the fuse carriers, you'll have to remove all socket outlets and lift a floorboard running to, or alongside, the skirting board or wall where each socket was fixed. Once you've done this, you can pull out all the cables and disconnect them at the fuseboard.

Start off by running two lengths of 2.5mm° two-core and earth cable down to the consumer unit position. One cable should run from the first socket outlet and the other from the last, but these two are likely to be in close proximity to each other. Link all sockets with the same sized cable, with the exception of remote sockets or fused connection units which can be supplied via spur cables wired into the nearest sockets to them. It used to be the custom to mount socket outlets on the skirting boards. However, you should position your new ones in the wall above the skirting boards and at least 150mm (6in) above the floor. Where possible it's best to install double sockets as this will cut down on the use of adaptors.

Having placed all the cables in position, and fixed all the socket outlets and fused connection units, connect the two cables to one of the existing 30A fuseways in your fuseboard. You should then replace the relevant fuse carrier and turn on the mains switch. To test the circuit, fit a 13A fused plug to a portable lamp and plug it into each socket outlet in turn.

FISHING CABLE ABOVE CEILINGS

1 Take a piece of stiff wire and check that it is just longer than is needed to reach between the cable's entry and exit holes in the ceiling.

2 Feed the wire into one hole, fish it out of the other with a second piece of wire, then tie the cable to the first wire and pull it through.

RUNNING CABLE UNDER FLOORS

1 When running cable parallel to the joists, fish it through in exactly the same way as if you were fishing through cable above a ceiling.

2 If the cable or fish wire will not pull through, check under the floor for obstructions using a small mirror and a reasonably powerful torch.

3 For cable runs at right angles to the joists, drill holes in the joists 50mm (2in) below their tops, angling these if the drill is too long to fit in.

4 Carefully thread the cable through the holes, without stretching it, so that it doesn't chafe against the side of the hole and damage the insulation.

Replacing other circuits

Working in the ground floor ceiling void will enable you to replace several other circuits at the same time. A new immersion heater circuit, for example, can be run along the same route as the old, but where the cable crosses joists, thread it through pre-drilled holes, whereas the old one was probably notched into the top.

A shower circuit is run in $6mm^2$ cable, so before running it you must again check the holes in the joists. If the holes are not large enough, drill another series which must be at least 75mm (3in) away from the old ones.

If your kitchen floor is of solid concrete, you may well find that the cooker circuit is also run under the floorboards on the first floor. If you find that you do have access to under the kitchen floor then you should really re-route the circuit so that it's run on the ground floor; otherwise it'll have to follow its original route. If you decide to run the cable up through the landing void then you should take it up in conjunction with all the other circuit cables which should be taken along the same, easily identifiable, route to the ceiling void.

With all the cables laid on the first floor, the remaining floorboards can be relaid permanently and cable chases made good. As there are likely to be many cables on the landing, it's a good idea to fix one floorboard back with woodscrews so that it can be readily lifted at any time you want.

Ground floor wiring

The chances are that the only wiring on the ground floor will be a ring circuit for the socket outlets and, possibly, the cooker circuit. The first thing to do is to check whether the floor is suspended or solid. If it is suspended, you'll have to lift a floorboard and check the depth of the void. With a pre-1914 house, it's possible that the void will be deep enough to allow someone to go down there, in which case you'll save a lot of extra work moving furniture and floorboards. A more modern home will probably have a void depth of about 355mm (14in) and the joists will be laid and fixed to cross beams. This allows the cable to be run underneath the joists, so doing away with the necessity of drilling them. If you can't get underneath the floorboards, then much of the cable laying can be done by fishing, so reducing the number of floorboards that have to be raised.

Start pulling out the cables, but leave them in place if there is any chance of using them as drawstrings for the new cable. This will save you a lot of trouble, especially when it comes to getting cable up behind the skirting boards. Where there is more than one socket on any one wall it might be just as well to raise an extra floorboard about 500mm (20in) from the skirting board. This will save you both work and cable.

Dealing with solid floors

If your home has a solid ground floor the old wiring, most likely in conduit, will have to be left in place; then the cables at sockets outlet and at the consumer unit are chopped off flush and, together with the conduit, abandoned. New cables should be run in mini-trunking fixed to the top of the skirting board and around the architraves of doorways. An alternative is to push the cables behind the skirting boards, having first cut away the plaster. Where the cable has to cross a doorway, the architrave can be removed and the cable placed in the gap between the door frame and the wall. However, when replacing architrave or skirting take extra care not to drive nails into the cables. You could, of course, run the power circuit in the ceiling void above the ground floor. Using this method, however, would involve extensive chasing and use of a lot of extra cable.

Installing a new consumer unit

Once you've rewired all the circuits, you'll have to install your new consumer unit. You'll probably find it easiest to site it in the same place as your old fuseboard and this must be in reach of the electricity board's service fuse which will serve as the installation's main fuse. This is because the modern consumer unit has only circuit fuses, not a main fuse. If, however, you want to fix the unit away from the board's apparatus you'll have to fit a new mainswitch and main fuse unit next to the meter and then run a submains cable to the consumer unit. This is likely to be 16mm^2 two-core and earth cable, while the switchfuse should have a rating of 80 to 100A.

Before the new consumer unit can be connected you'll have to ask your local electricity board to disconnect the leads of the existing mainswitch units so you can remove them. You must give them a minimum of 48 hours notice for this and it's best to apply for your wiring to be reconnected to the mains at the same time. That way if you've done the lion's share of the work beforehand you can get your home reconnected to the mains the same day it's disconnected.

Before removing the old switchgear, check that each circuit is working correctly. Then, after the meter tails have been disconnected, remove the circuit cables and the old units. You'll have to fix the new unit to the wall, run in the new cable, make the connections and fit the MCBs or fuses in the correct order. For further information on connecting up a new unit see pages 237–240. Finally refit the cover and await the electricity board official.

INSTALLING A COOKER CONTROL UNIT

1 Run both the circuit cable and the cable to the cooker in conduit and chase them into the wall. Then connect the circuit cable to the mains side of the unit.

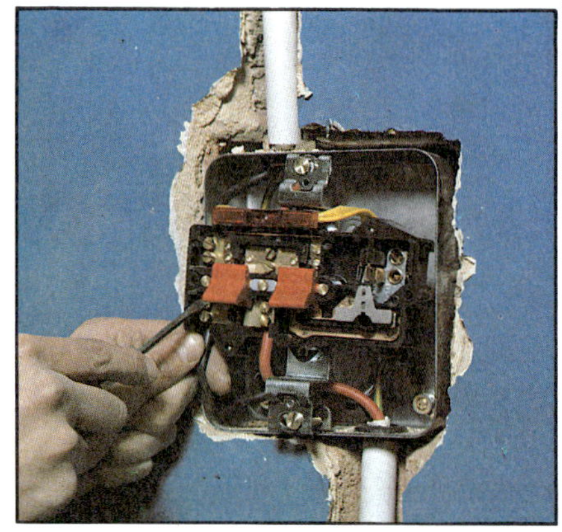

2 Next, make the connections on the cooker side. Remember to sleeve all the earth cores in greenlyellow PVC before connecting them to the earth terminal.

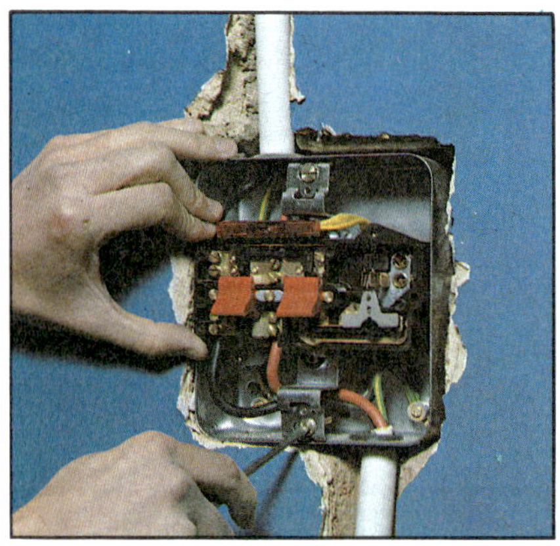

3 When you've made all the connections, make sure that the unit is positioned square to the wall and then screw it securely onto the mounting box.

4 You can now fix the centre part of the faceplate. Before fixing the rest, make good and redecorate the surface of the wall.

THE CONNECTION UNIT

1 Chase in the cable to the cooker and run it to the connection unit. Link the earths to the centre terminals and the other cores to the outer terminals.

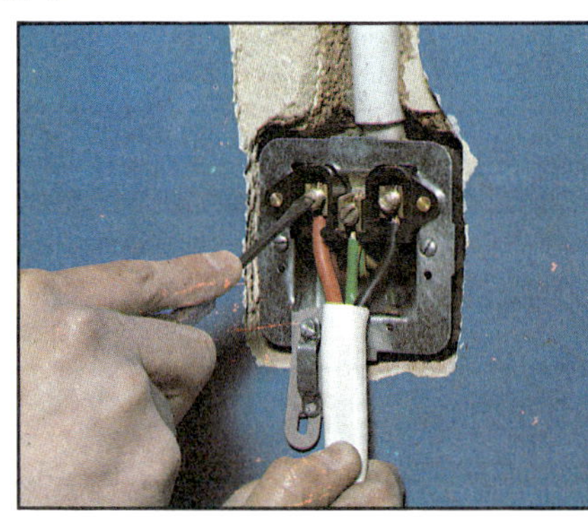

2 Undo the clamp and hold the trailing cooker cable in place while you connect it. Remember that it should be the same size as the circuit cable.

MAINTENANCE & REPAIRS

However well equipped and installed everything electrical may be in your home, there will still be occasional problems – faults, breakdowns, everyday wear and tear – that need to be solved properly and quickly if the system is to carry on functioning.

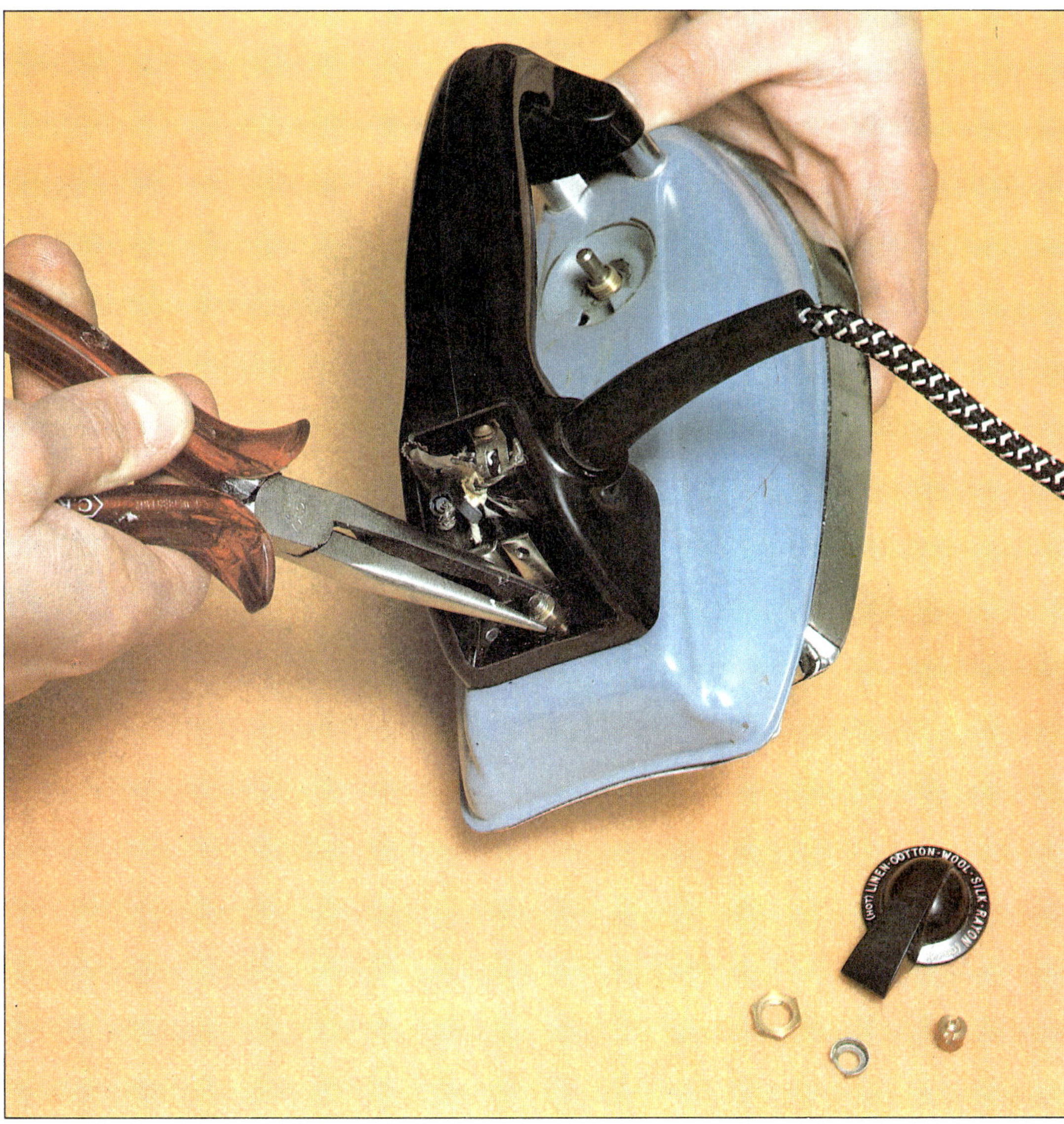

TRACING ELECTRICAL FAULTS

When the lights go out or an electrical appliance won't work, the reason is often obvious. But when it isn't, it helps to know how to locate the fault and put it right.

Most people's immediate reaction to something going wrong with their electricity supply is to head for the meter cupboard, muttering darkly about another blown fuse. Fuses do blow occasionally for no immediately obvious reason, but usually there is a problem that needs to be pin-pointed and put right before the power can be restored. It's no use mending a blown fuse, only to find that when the power is restored the fuse blows again because the fault is still present.

Tracing everyday electrical faults is not particularly difficult. You simply have to be methodical in checking the various possible causes, and eliminating options until you find the culprit. More serious faults on the house's fixed wiring system can be more difficult to track down, but again some careful investigation can often locate the source of the trouble, even if professional help has to be called in to put it right.

Safety first

Before you start investigating any electrical faults, remember the cardinal rule and switch off the power at the main switch. When fuses blow, it is all too easy to forget that other parts of the system may still be live and therefore dangerous, and even if you know precisely how your house has been wired up it is foolish to take risks. If the fault appears to be on an electrical appliance, the same rules apply: always switch off the appliance *and* pull out the plug before attempting to investigate. Don't rely on the switch to isolate it; the fault may be in the switch itself.

It's also important to be prepared for things to go wrong with your electrics; even new systems can develop faults, and in fact a modern installation using circuit breakers will detect faults more readily than one with rewireable or cartridge fuses, so giving more regular cause for investigation. Make sure that you keep a small emergency electrical tool kit in an accessible place where it won't get raided for other jobs; it should include one or two screwdrivers, a pair of pliers, a handyman's knife, spare fuses and fuse wire, and above all a *working* torch. For more details about tools for electrical work see pages 169–171.

Check the obvious

When something electrical fails to operate, always check the obvious first – replace the bulb when a light doesn't work, or glance outside to see if everyone in the street has been blacked out by a power cut before panicking that all your fuses have blown. Having satisfied yourself that you may have a genuine fault, start a methodical check of all the possibilities.

A fault can occur in a number of places. It may be on an appliance, within the flex or plug linking it to the mains, on the main circuitry itself or at the fuseboard. Let's start at the appliance end of things. If something went bang as you switched the appliance on, unplug it immediately; the fault is probably on the appliance itself. If it simply stopped working, try plugging it in at another socket; if it goes, there's a fault on the circuit feeding the original socket. If it doesn't go, either the second socket is on the same faulty circuit as the first one (which we'll come to later) or there may be a fault in the link between the appliance and the socket – loose connections where the cores are connected to either the plug or the appliance itself, damaged flex (both these problems are caused by abuse of the flex in use), or a blown fuse in the plug if one is fitted.

Plug and flex connections

The next step is to check the flex connections within the plug and the appliance. The connections at plug terminals are particularly prone to damage if the plug's cord grip or flex anchorage is not doing its job; a tug on the flex can then break the cores, cutting the power and possibly causing a short circuit. If the connections are weak or damaged, disconnect them, cut back the sheathing and insulation and remake the connections. Make sure that the flex is correctly anchored within the body of the plug before replacing the cover.

If the plug contains a fuse, test that it has not blown by using a continuity tester, or by holding it across the open end of a switched-on metal-cased torch – see *Ready Reference*. Replace a blown fuse with a new one of the correct current rating; 3A for appliances rated at 720W or below, 13A for higher-rated appliances (and all colour televisions).

Next, check the flex connections within the appliance itself. Always unplug an appliance before opening it up to gain access to the terminal block, and then remake any doubtful-looking connections by cutting off the end of the flex and stripping back the outer and inner insulation carefully to expose fresh conductor strands. If the flex itself is worn or

REWIRING A PLUG

1 *Strip the outer sheathing carefully, cut each core 12mm (1/2in) longer than is necessary to reach its correct terminal and then remove 12mm of core sheathing.*

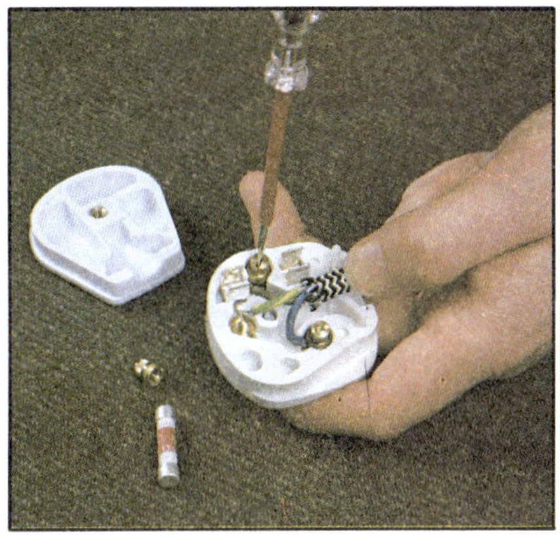

2 *Twist the strands of each core neatly and form a loop that will fit round the terminal screw. Connect the cores as shown here and screw down the studs.*

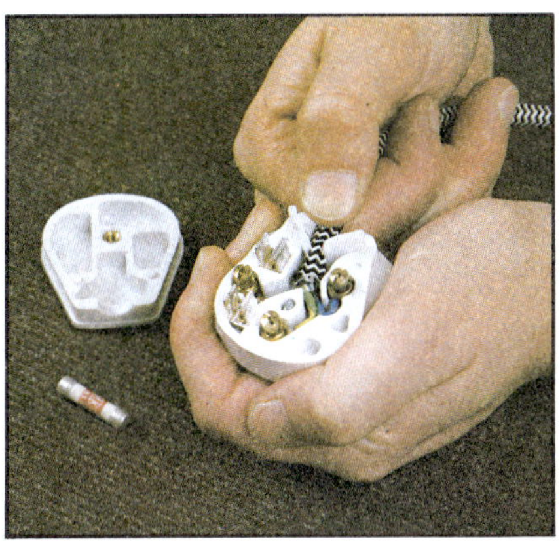

3 *Check that the core insulation reaches right to each terminal, and that there are no loose strands visible. Then fit the flex securely in the cord grip.*

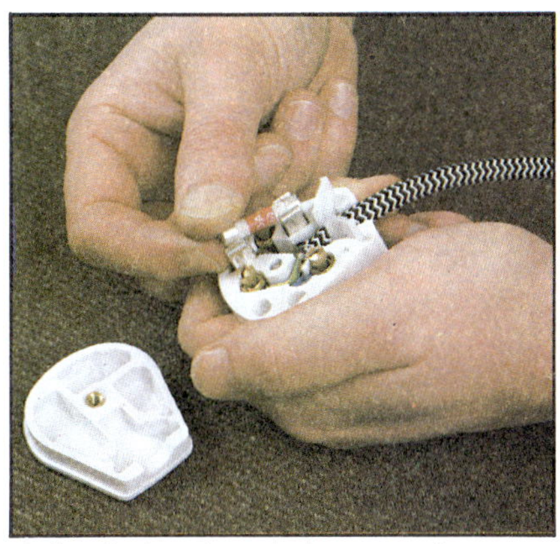

4 *Lastly, in a fused plug press in a cartridge fuse of the correct rating for the appliance concerned, and screw the plug top firmly on.*

damaged, take this opportunity to fit new flex of the correct type and current rating – see *Ready Reference*, step-by-step photographs and pages 164–165 for more details. Make sure you re-use any grommets, heat-resistant sleeving, special captive washers and the like that were fitted to the appliance.

Lastly, check the flex continuity; it is possible that damage to the flex itself has broken one of the cores within the outer sheathing. Again use a continuity tester for this, holding the two probes against opposite ends of each core in turn, or use your metal-cased torch again, touching one core to the case and the other to the battery. Replace the flex if *any* core fails the test; the appliance may still work if the earth core is damaged, but the earthing will be lost and the appliance could become live and dangerous to anyone using it in the event of another fault developing in the future.

Lighting problems

Similar problems to these can also occur on lighting circuits, where the pendant flex linking ceiling roses to lampholders can become disconnected or faulty through accidental damage or old age. If replacing the bulb doesn't work, switch off the power at the mains and examine the condition of the flex. Look especially for bad or broken connections at the ceiling rose and within the lampholder. Replace the flex if the core insulation has become brittle, and fit a new lampholder if the plastic is discoloured (both these problems are caused by heat from the light bulb). See step-by-step photographs on page 255 for details.

Mending blown fuses

A circuit fuse will blow for two main reasons, overloading and short circuits – see *Ready Reference*. Too many appliances connected

Ready Reference

COMMON FAULTS

Many electrical breakdowns in the home are caused by only a few common faults. These include:

- overloading of circuits, causing the circuit fuse to blow or the MCB to trip
- short circuits, where the current bypasses its proper route because of failed insulation or contact between cable or flex cores; the resulting high current flow creates heat and blows the plug fuse (if fitted) and circuit fuse
- earthing faults, where insulation breaks down and allows the metal body of an appliance to become live, causing a shock to the user if the appliance is not properly earthed and blowing a fuse or causing the RCCB to trip otherwise
- poor connections causing overheating that can lead to a fire and to short circuits and earthing faults.

TIP: TESTING FUSES

You can test suspect cartridge fuses (both circuit and plug types) by holding them across the open end of a switched-on metal-cased torch, with one end on the casing and the other on the battery. A sound fuse will light the torch.

CHOOSE THE RIGHT FLEX

When fitting new flex to an appliance, it's important to choose the correct type and current rating. The table below will help:

Size	**Rating**		**Use**
(mm^2)	amps	watts	
0.5	3	720	Light fittings
0.75	6	1440	Small appliances
1.0	10	2400	Larger appliances
1.5	15	3600	Larger appliances
2.5	20	4800	Larger appliances

If you are buying flex for pendant lights, remember that the maximum weight of fitting that each size of twin flex can support is

- 2kg (4 1/2lb) for 0.5mm^2 flex
- 3kg (6 1/2lb) for 0.75mm^2 flex
- 5kg (11lb) for larger sizes.

Select circular **three-core PVC-insulated flex** for most appliances, **unkinkable** or **braided flex** for irons, kettles and the like, **two-core flex** for non-metallic lamps and light fittings and for double-insulated appliances, and **heat-resisting flex** for powerful pendant lights and for heater connections. See pages 14-15.

to a circuit will demand too much current, and this will melt the fuse. Similarly, a short circuit – where, for example, bare live and neutral flex cores touch – causes a current surge that blows the fuse.

If overloading caused the fuse to blow, the remedy is simple: disconnect all the equipment on the circuit, mend the fuse and avoid using too many high-wattage appliances at the same time in future. If a short circuit was to blame, you will have to hunt for the cause and rectify it before mending the fuse – see photographs on the next page.

When a circuit fuse blows, turn off the main switch and remove fuseholders until you find the one that has blown. Then clean out the remains of the old fuse wire, and fit a new piece of the correct rating for the circuit – 5A for lighting circuits, 15A for circuits to immersion heaters and the like, and 30A for ring circuits. Cut the wire over-long, thread it loosely across or through the ceramic holder and connect it carefully to the terminals. Trim the ends off neatly, replace the fuseholder in the consumer unit and turn on the power again. If the fuse blows again, and you have already checked for possible causes on appliances, flexes and lighting pendants, suspect a circuit fault – see below.

If you have cartridge fuses, all you have to do is find which cartridge has blown by removing the fuseholder and testing the cartridge with a continuity tester or metal-cased torch. A blown cartridge fuse should be replaced by a new one of the same current rating. Again, if the new fuse blows immediately, suspect a circuit fault.

If you have miniature circuit breakers (MCBs) you will not be able to switch the MCB on again if the fault that tripped it off is still present. Otherwise, simply reset it by switching it to ON or pressing in the centre button.

REPLACING FLEX

1 *To replace damaged flex, remove the appropriate cover plate or panel from the appliance. Make a note of which core goes where before undoing it.*

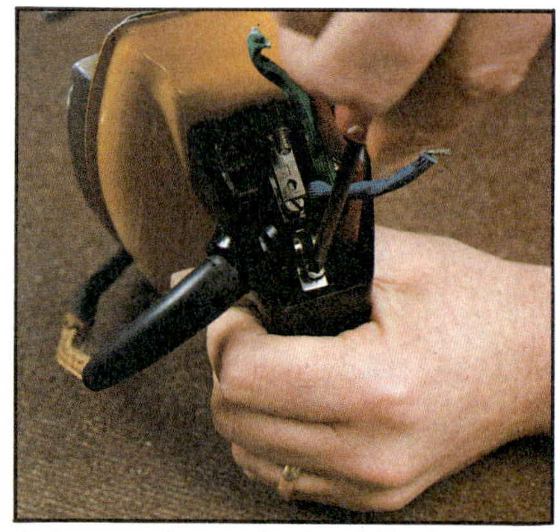

2 *Loosen the cord grip within the appliance and withdraw the old flex. Here heat-resisting sleeving has been fitted; save this for re-use.*

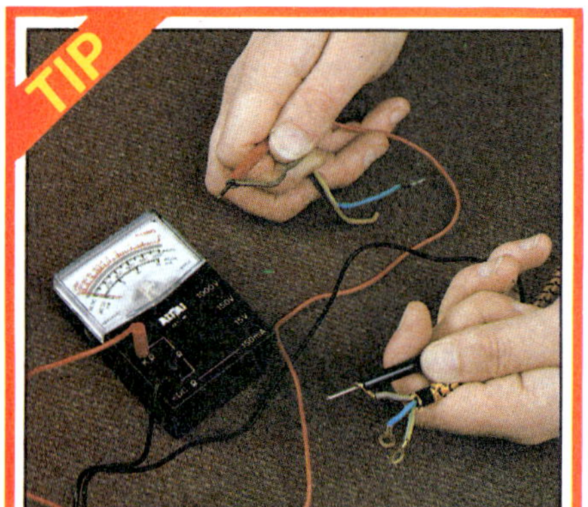

3 *If you suspect that the cores within apparently undamaged flex are broken, test each core in turn with a continuity tester.*

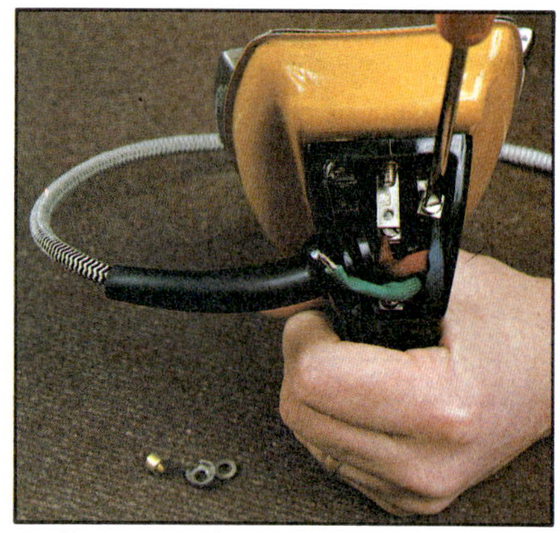

4 *Connect in the new flex by reversing the disconnection sequence, re-using grommets, sleeving and washers. Make sure each connection is secure.*

Residual current circuit breakers (RCCBs)

If your installation has an RCCB, it will trip off if an earthing fault occurs – for example, if a live wire or connection comes into contact with earthed metal. Like an MCB, it cannot be switched on again until the fault is rectified – a useful safety point. However, it will not trip off in the event of a short circuit between live and neutral, or when overloading occurs.

A modern high-sensitivity RCCB will, in addition to detecting earth faults, also protect against the danger of electric shocks by tripping off if it detects current flowing to earth through the human body. It can do this quickly enough to prevent the shock from causing death.

Tracing circuit faults

If you have checked appliances, flexes, plug connections and pendant lights, and a fault is still present, it is likely to be in the fixed wiring. Here, it is possible to track down one or two faults, but you may in the end have to call in a professional electrician.

The likeliest causes of circuit faults are damage to cables (perhaps caused by drilling holes in walls or by nailing down floorboards where cables run), ageing of cables (leading to insulation breakdown, and overheating) and faults at wiring accessories (light switches, socket outlets and so on). Let's look at the last one first, simply because such items are at least easily accessible.

If the cable cores are not properly stripped and connected within the accessory, short circuits or earth faults can develop. To check a suspect accessory such as a socket outlet, isolate the circuit, unscrew the faceplate and examine the terminal connections and the insulation. Ensure that each core is firmly held in its correct terminal, and that each core has insulation right up to the terminal, so that it cannot touch another core or any bare metal. There is usually enough slack on the mains cable to allow you to trim over-long cores back slightly. Check that the earth core is sleeved in green/yellow PVC, and try not to double over the cable as you ease the faceplate back into position; over-full boxes can lead to short circuits and damage to cable and core insulation ... and more trouble. You can carry out similar checks at light switches and ceiling roses. Any damaged accessories you find should be replaced immediately with new ones.

Damage to cables is relatively easy to cure provided that you can find where the damage is. If you drilled or nailed through a cable, you will of course be able to pin-point it immediately. Cable beneath floorboards can be repaired simply by isolating the circuit, cutting the cable completely at the point of damage and using a three-terminal junction

REPAIRING A CIRCUIT FUSE

1 *Switch off the mains and locate the blown fuse. Then remove the remains of the old fuse wire and clean off any charring that has occurred.*

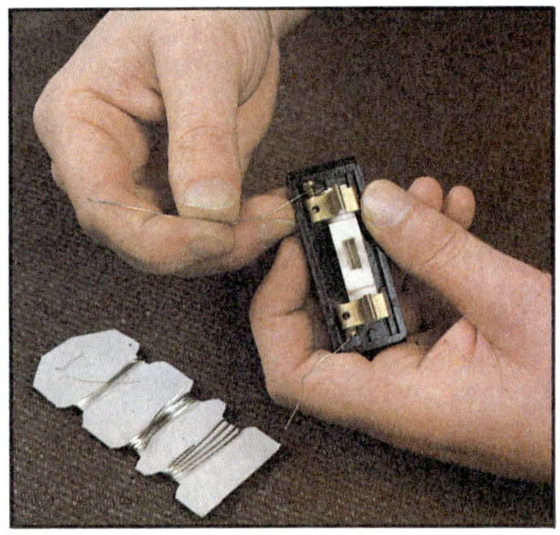

2 *Feed in a length of fuse wire of the correct rating and wind each end round the terminal before tightening up the screw. Don't pull the wire taut.*

3 *Trim off the unwanted ends of fuse wire neatly with wire strippers, then replace the fuse carrier in the fuse box and restore the power.*

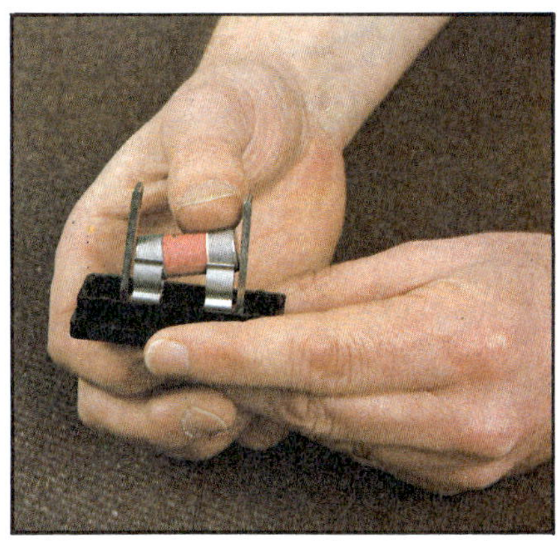

4 *Test a suspect cartridge fuse with a continuity tester or torch (see* Ready Reference*) and replace it by pressing in a new fuse of the correct rating.*

box to link the cut ends. Cable buried in plaster must be cut out and a new length of cable inserted between adjacent accessories to replace the damaged length. Where this would involve a long length of cable (on a run to a remote socket, for example) it is acceptable to use junction boxes in nearby floor or ceiling voids to connect in the new length of cable. You will then have to make good the cutting-out.

Tracking down a break in the cable elsewhere in the installation is a difficult job best left to a qualified electrician. If, however, you find that your house is wired in rubber-sheathed cable and faults are beginning to occur, don't waste time and effort trying to track them down; you need a rewire. For more information see pages 249–262.

If you are unable to trace an electrical fault after checking all the points already described, call in a professional electrician who will be able to use specialist test equipment to locate the fault. Do *not* attempt to bypass a fault with a makeshift wiring arrangement, and NEVER use any conducting foreign body such as a nail to restore power to a circuit whose fuse keeps blowing. Such tricks can kill.

Regular maintenance

You will find that a little common-sense maintenance work will help to prevent a lot of minor electrical faults from occurring at all. For example, it's well worth spending a couple of hours every so often checking the condition of the flex on portable appliances (especially those heavily used, such as kettles, irons, hair driers and the like) and the connections within plugs. Also, make a point of replacing immediately any electrical accessory that is in any way damaged.

Ready Reference

CHECKLIST FOR ACTION

When something goes wrong with your electrics, use this checklist to identify or eliminate the commonest potential causes of trouble.

Fault 1
Pendant light doesn't work
Action
- replace bulb
- check lighting circuit fuse/MCB
- check flex connections at lampholder and ceiling rose
- check flex continuity.

Fault 2
Electrical appliance doesn't work
Action
- try appliance at another socket
- check plug fuse (if fitted)
- check plug connections
- check connections at appliance's own terminal block
- check flex continuity
- check power circuit fuse/MCB
- isolate appliance if fuses blow again.

Fault 3
Whole circuit is dead
Action
- switch off all lights/disconnect all appliances on circuit
- replace circuit fuse or reset MCB
- switch on lights/plug in appliances one by one and note which blows fuse again
- isolate offending light/appliance, and see Faults 1 and 2 (above)
- check wiring accessories on circuit for causes of short circuits
- replace damaged cable if pierced by nail or drill
- call qualified electrician for help.

Fault 4
Whole system is dead
Action
- check for local power cut
- reset RCCB fitted to system (and see Faults 1, 2 and 3 if RCCB cannot be reset)
- call electricity board (main service fuse may have blown)

Fault 5
Electric shock received
Action
- try to turn off the power
- grab victim's clothing and pull away from power source, but DO NOT TOUCH WITH BARE HANDS
- if victim is conscious, keep warm and call a doctor; don't give brandy or food
- if breathing or heartbeat has stopped, CALL AN AMBULANCE and give artificial respiration or cardiac massage.

EXTENDING FLEX SAFELY

Ideally, electrical appliances should be linked to the mains via an unbroken length of flex. However, there are times when you may need a longer flex – which means extending the one that's fitted, or else using a separate extension lead with its own plug and socket.

If you've got enough socket outlets in your home, you should be able to plug in most of your appliances to a nearby socket without any problem. But there are often situations where the length of flex that's fitted just isn't long enough. For example, few vacuum cleaners have enough flex to allow uninterrupted cleaning without you having to keep unplugging the appliance and moving to another socket outlet to plug it in. And most power tools come with annoyingly short leads – fine if you always use them at your workbench, but not much use elsewhere.

There are two ways round the problem. The first is to fit a longer flex – the right answer for cases like the vacuum cleaner. The second is to use a separate extension lead into which appliances with short flexes can be plugged whenever the need arises.

Extension leads

An extension lead is just a length of flex with a plug on one end (to plug into the mains) and a socket on the other (into which you plug the tool or appliance you're using). You can buy one ready-made, complete with connectors and packed loose in a bag (in which case it will have what is called a trailing socket at the 'appliance' end of the lead), or complete with a drum onto which the flex is wound when the lead is not in use (here the socket is actually mounted on the drum). Alternatively, you can buy the various components and connect them up yourself.

Earthing and current rating

Any extension lead must serve the same purpose as the flex on the appliance whose reach it is extending, and this means that above all it must provide earth continuity. Many power tools (especially those intended for use out of doors, such as lawnmowers) are double-insulated, which means that they do not need an earth connection and are fitted with two-core flex. So, in theory, you could use an extension lead with just two cores as well.

However, the extension lead you intend to use with your lawnmower may end up being used with another appliance instead – one that *does* need earthing. So any extension lead you use should, for safety's sake, always have three-core flex. It will still work with any double-insulated appliance too, of course.

The other important thing about extension leads is the current rating of the flex used. You may have intended your lead to be used only for a power drill using, say, 400 watts – well within the capacity of a 3A 0.5mm^2 flex. But suppose someone unknowingly uses that same flex to power a fan heater rated at 3kW. The flex will then be heavily overloaded and unless a 3A fuse has been fitted in the lead's plug the flex will overheat and could start a fire. So play safe: always use 1.25mm^2 flex for an extension lead, whatever you intend to use it for.

If you're going to use the extension lead out of doors, it's best to choose an orange or white sheathed flex rather than a black one. Always use it in conjunction with an RCCB – see pages 241–243.

Safety with extension leads

There are two points to remember about using extension leads safely. The first is always to uncoil the lead from the drum before you use it, especially if it's powering a high-rated appliance. If you don't it may overheat and eventually melt. The second point is never to use a lead out of doors when it is raining, or after rain when foliage is wet and moisture could get into the socket.

Making up your own lead

The flex should, as already described, be 1.25mm^2 two-core and earth PVC-sheathed flex. The plug can be any conventional plug that suits your house sockets. However, a toughened plastic or moulded rubber one will stand up to knocks better.

The socket should also be toughened plastic or rubber. There's the same choice of pin type and colour as with moulded plugs, and you can have one, two or four outlets on the one socket.

It's best to keep your lead on a drum of some sort so it doesn't get kinked when coiled up. An empty cable reel is ideal, or you can make a simple drum from plywood and softwood offcuts – see *Ready Reference*.

Extending flex

On appliances like vacuum cleaners and lawnmowers, you may prefer to extend the appliance flex permanently instead of using an extension lead. The best way of doing this is to replace the existing flex completely, wiring the new flex into the appliance itself. But provided you use the right method, you can also extend the existing flex by adding on an extra length with a flex connector.

For most household appliances a one-piece connector is ideal – see the step-by-step photographs opposite. This simply links the old and new flex within a one-piece moulding. Make sure you use the right size – a 5A one for appliances rated at less than 1200 watts, a 13A one otherwise.

If you'll want to disconnect the flex extension for any reason, use a two-part connector instead. Fit a two-pin one to double-insulated appliances, a three-pin one otherwise. Remember always to connect the plug part to the appliance flex and the socket part to the extension flex. If you do it the other way round the plug pins will be live when the flex is plugged into the mains. For leads of this type being used out of doors, go for a weatherproof type with a shroud that locks the two parts together.

ASSEMBLING THE COMPONENTS

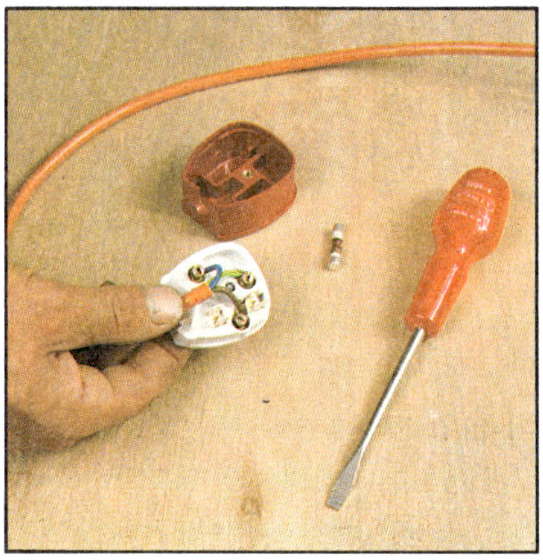

1 *If you're making up an extension lead, use orange or white 1.25mm² three-core flex and a toughened plug. Make sure the cord grip holds the flex securely.*

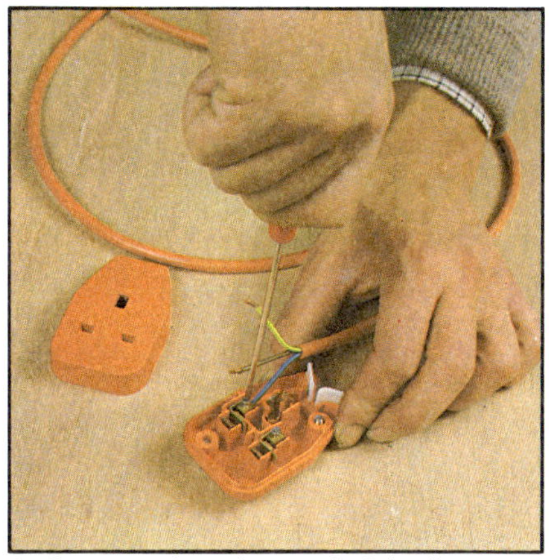

2 *Connect the other end of the flex to the correct terminals within the trailing socket. Again, make sure the cord grip is secure before fitting the cover.*

3 *With a two-part flex connector, prepare the cores. Thread the flex through the shrouds, connect up the cores and tighten the cord grips.*

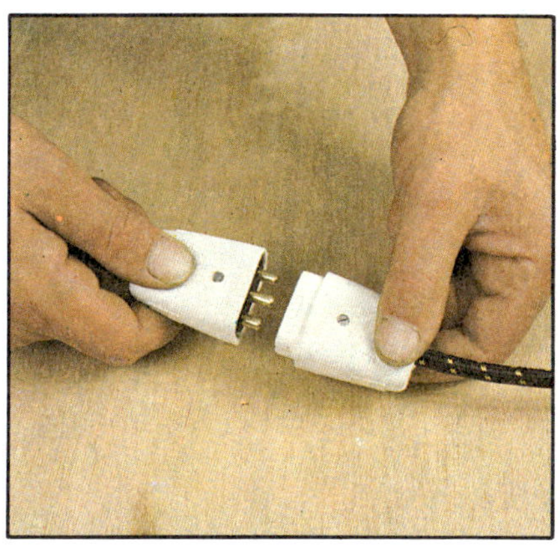

4 *Fit the shrouds over the terminal blocks. Check that you have connected the plug part to the appliance flex, the socket part to the mains flex.*

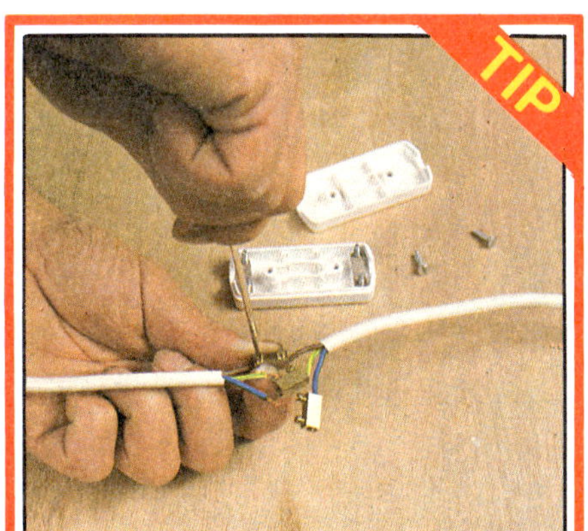

5 *With a one-piece connector it's easier to link the cores if you remove the terminals first. You may have to cut each core to a different length.*

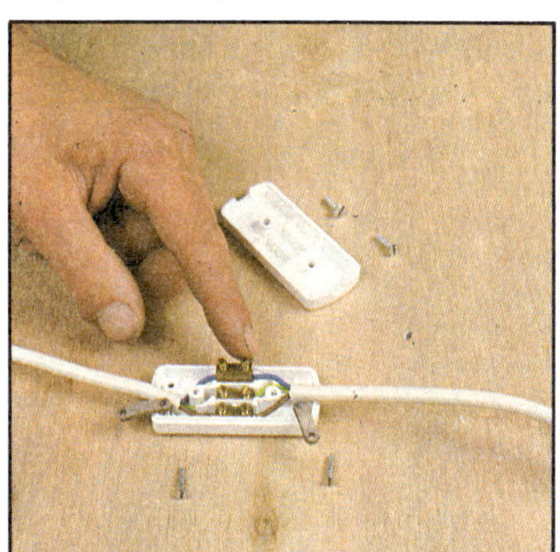

6 *Open up the cord grips and press the terminal blocks into place, laying the cores in their channels. Do up the two cord grips and fit the connector cover.*

Ready Reference

READY-MADE LEADS

You can buy extension leads ready-made and wound on plastic drums, complete with a carrying handle. Before you buy one

- check that the flex is rated at 13A rather than 5A
- check the flex length; it may be anything from 9 to 20m (30 to 66ft).

Look too for extra features like switched sockets with neons, hanging hooks and somewhere to stow the plug.

PICK THE RIGHT FLEX

For extension leads, always choose 1.25mm² two-core and earth PVC-sheathed cable – preferably orange or white rather than black. Fit a 13A fuse in the plug.

If you're extending an appliance flex via a flex connector, use the same type of flex and make sure you choose the right current rating, according to the wattage of the appliance.

Core size	current rating	max. wattage
0.5mm²	3A	720W
0.75mm²	6A	1440W
1.0mm²	10A	2000W
1.25mm²	13A	3000W

EXTENDING OLD FLEX

The flex you're extending may have the old colour codes on its core insulation. To make sure you connect the cores correctly, remember that

- live cores were colour-coded red, but are now coded brown
- neutral cores were black, are now blue
- earth cores were green, are now green/yellow striped.

TIP: UNCOIL DRUM FLEXES

If you're using a ready-made extension reel, it's safest to uncoil the flex fully before using it. Otherwise there is a risk of the flex overheating and melting, especially if a highly-rated appliance is being used.

MAKING A REEL

If you've made up your own extension lead, it's a good idea to store it on a makeshift or home-made drum so it doesn't become kinked or knotted. You can either use an empty cable reel (A), or make up a simple drum from plywood and softwood offcuts (B).

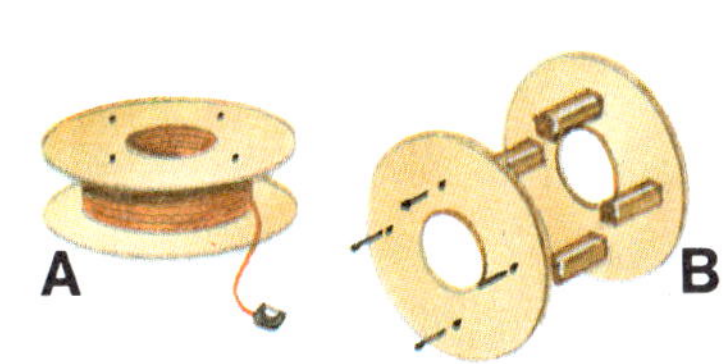

SERVICING ELECTRICAL APPLIANCES: 1

When electrical appliances go wrong getting them repaired can be a costly and time-consuming business. Here are the first steps that will enable you to undertake some simple repairs yourself.

From time to time electrical appliances will need servicing. You wouldn't dream of not looking after your car, so why your fridge or toaster? However, in spite of any servicing you might undertake, appliances do now and then go wrong, perhaps leaving you with an expensive repair bill. If an appliance packs up your first inclination may be to take it down to a local electrical repair shop, or, if it isn't portable, to call in a servicing engineer. But if you take the trouble to examine the appliance, its plug and flex, you may be able to locate the fault and make the necessary repairs so saving quite a lot of money. You could also save yourself the embarrassment of calling out an engineer only for him to discover that a fuse had blown in the plug.

However, before rushing for your screwdriver and taking your appliance to pieces, there are a number of checks you should make which may save you a lot of work.

Preliminary checks

Before examining any part of the appliance do make sure that it is unplugged. Then check that the socket, switched fused connection unit or double pole switch through which the appliance obtains its power was actually switched *on*. After all, if for some reason you're in a rush it's very easy to forget to do this. If your appliance has a thermal cut out device, or some other kind of cut out, check that this is closed otherwise it won't work. If it isn't, press the relevant button and switch on the appliance. If it trips within a minute or so you'll know that the appliance itself is faulty.

Then check that the fault isn't something as simple as a blown fuse in the plug. Remove the fuse and either test it (see Ready reference, page 265) or merely replace it with a new fuse that you know works.

If your appliance has a loading of more than 720W, and when you remove the plug fuse you discover that it has a current rating of 3 or 5A, then you can be almost certain that it has blown. Simply replace the fuse with a 13A one and your problem should be solved. Examine the flexible cord for damage or general wear and if there is evidence of any then there could be a short circuit. If possible you should check the flex connections at the appliance terminals as well as at the plug or fused connection unit terminals. Replace damaged or worn flex, and reconnect it if the cores at the terminals are loose or broken but it is otherwise in good condition. You should also check the flex continuity. A broken core within the outer sheathing will not be immediately apparent, for example. Use a continuity tester and if a core is damaged replace the flex immediately. For further information on how to do this see pages 264–267 again.

You should also make sure that you have power at the socket by plugging in another appliance that you know works. If there proves to be no power, you'll probably find that the circuit fuse has blown; check this and make the necessary repairs or adjustments and you'll find that your appliance works perfectly again.

If, however, after checking all these points you find that your appliance still doesn't work then it will certainly be in need of some attention.

Guarantees and service contracts

Don't immediately proceed with taking your faulty appliance to pieces in the hope that you'll spot the fault. Electrical appliances are delicate pieces of machinery and need careful treatment. And in any case you might still be able to avoid having to do the work yourself. Before dismantling anything check whether the maker's guarantee has expired. If not then don't attempt any work on the appliance; simply follow the terms of the guarantee and you'll probably be able to get it all done by qualified electricians completely free of charge. If the guarantee has run out then check that the appliance isn't covered by some other scheme for which an annual premium is paid. You'll often find that for large and complicated appliances such as automatic washing machines it'll prove cheaper, and in the long run more satisfactory, to take out a maintenance contract. To service such appliances special tools and equipment are often required and it's a good idea to have a servicing manual as well. However, these are not as easily obtainable as those for cars, and they're only available either to authorised dealers and servicing firms or at quite a high price. And, of course, you'll have to make sure that you can get any spares you might need. After all, it would be a complete waste of time to take something to pieces only to discover that spare parts

TYPES OF ELECTRIC MOTOR

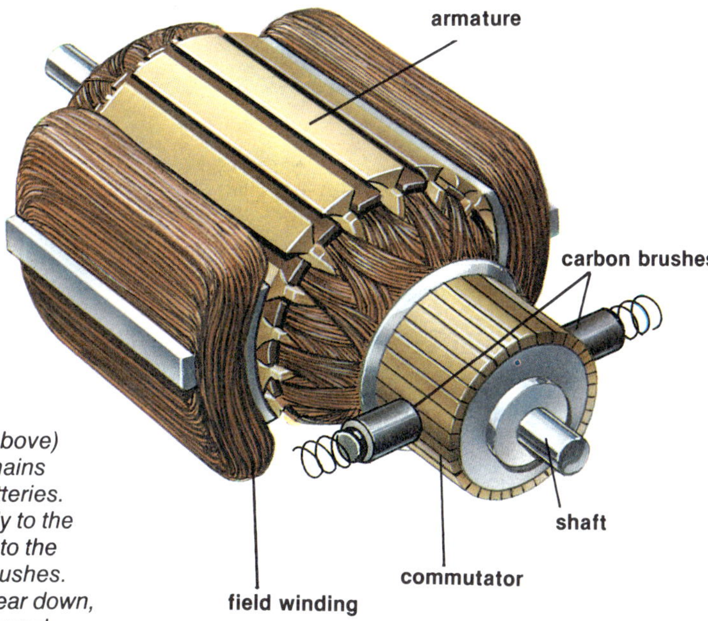

The brush motor (above) can be driven by mains electricity or by batteries. Power goes directly to the field windings and to the armature via the brushes. These can easily wear down, but are simply renewed.

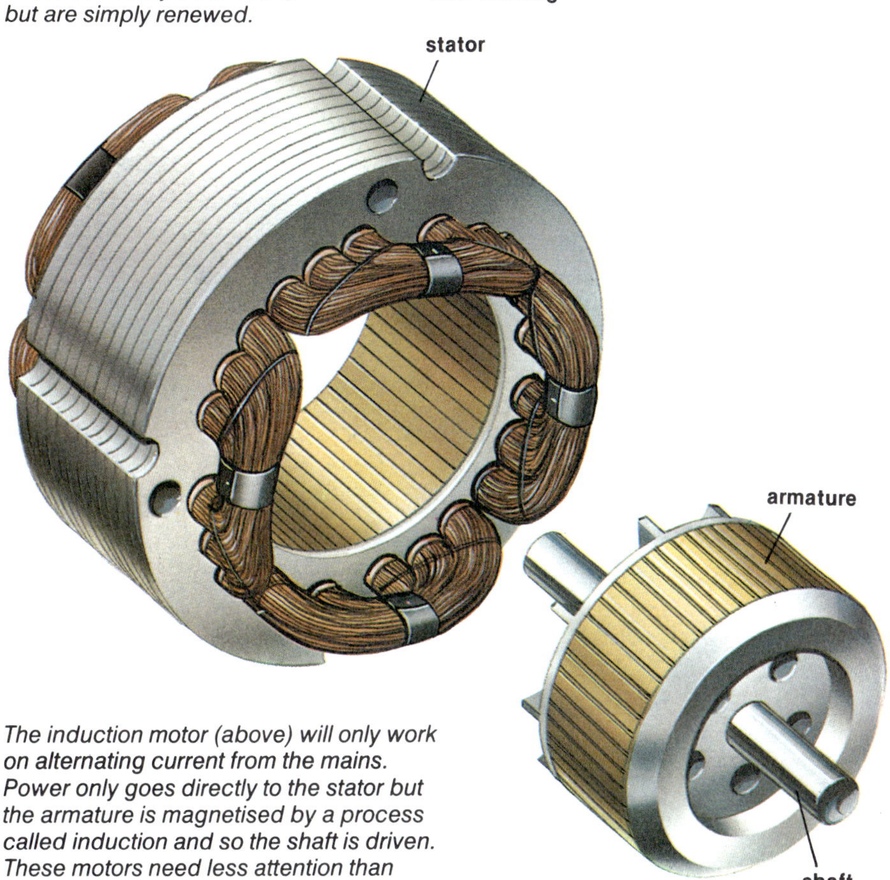

The induction motor (above) will only work on alternating current from the mains. Power only goes directly to the stator but the armature is magnetised by a process called induction and so the shaft is driven. These motors need less attention than brush motors, but occasionally the armature will get stuck. Repairs should be left to a servicing shop.

Ready Reference

USE THE CORRECT FLEX

When fitting new flex to an electrical appliance make sure you use the correct type. There are six available:

- parallel twin non sheathed PVC insulated flex that is used with clocks, shavers and small double insulated appliances

- flat twin sheathed flex for use on similar appliances
- circular sheathed flex. Two- and three-core versions of this general-purpose flex are available. If used outside use the flex with either orange or yellow sheathing

- unkinkable sheathed flex with three cores and rubber insulation. This flex is fitted to kettles, toasters and irons
- braided circular flex. Two- and three-core versions are available and are suitable for most appliances

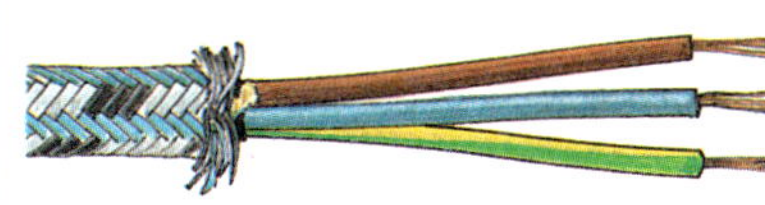

- heat resisting flex is similar to circular flex but with special sheathing.

For flex size details see pages 264–267.

FIT THE CORRECT PLUG FUSE

In order to fit the correct plug fuse you'll have to know the loading of the electrical appliance. Here's a brief guide:

electric blanket	50-100W
clock	negligible
coffee maker	380-1200W
dish washer	3000W
three-bar fire	1000-3000W
hair dryer	350-600W
automatic iron	750-1000W
kettle	1000-3000W
power operated tools	210-260W
fridge	80-175W
freezer	100-250W
sewing machine	75W
shaver	15W
spin dryer	100-320W
television	100-200W
toaster	400-600W
tumble dryer	2500-2750W
vacuum cleaner	220-300W
heated washing machine	3000W
waste disposal unit	200W

weren't available. Always check that replacement parts can be obtained and that you'll be able to buy them before you start work. In some cases parts might be made available only to trade repairers or simply not at all. Before trying to get any make sure you know the make and model of your appliance. If you're in any doubt, provided it's portable, take the appliance down to your local retailer for exact identification; that way you'll avoid making any mistakes.

How appliances work

Before undertaking any repairs to an electrical appliance it's important to understand just how it works. As a rule there are three basic types of electrical appliance. These are:

- those with heaters and which are not power driven such as cookers, toasters and kettles.
- those that have motors and which are power driven such as extractor fans, vacuum cleaners and lawn mowers.
- those that have both heaters and motors such as tumble dryers, hair dryers and washing machines.

The types of motor

While heaters in electrical appliances tend to vary a great deal, you'll probably find that your appliance is powered by one of two types of electric motor – a brush motor or an induction motor.

Both types of motor consist of two electromagnets. One is fixed and cannot move and is called the stator; the other is set so that it can revolve rapidly and is called the armature. The motor shaft is fixed to the armature, and when this spins it drives the equipment attached to it, a drill chuck, for example.

With a brush motor, power is directed straight to the stator, and also to the armature by a couple of carbon brushes which make a rubbing contact with the commutator. Both stator and armature are magnetised and so the latter is set spinning.

Brush motors can run on power from the mains or else on direct current from a battery, and are fitted to power tools, vacuum cleaners, polishers, food mixers, washing machines and lawn mowers.

Induction motors can only work on alternating current taken direct from the mains. Power goes only to the stator but by a process called induction the armature is magnetised as well. While its magnetism stays constant, the stator's magnetic field is reversed rapidly by the alternating current and so the armature and shaft are spun. This type of motor, or variations of it, are fitted to washing machines, refrigerators, fans, whisks and freezers.

Servicing brush motors

The most likely source of trouble will be the carbon brushes. These could be worn, sticking in their holders or simply in poor

SERVICING ELECTRIC DRILLS

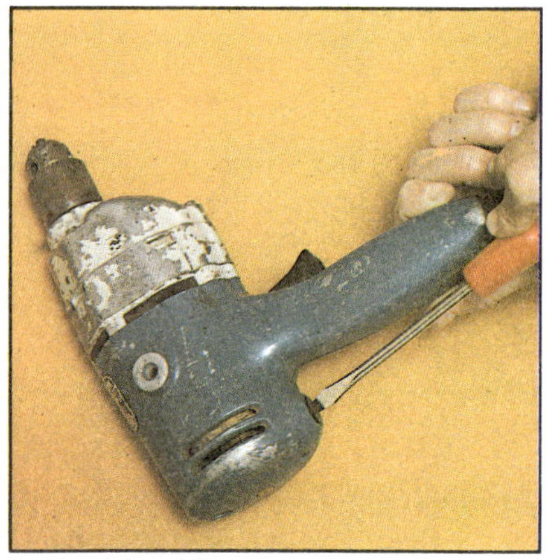

1 *On older drills, access to carbon brushes is often through insulated retaining caps on the motor casing. Don't damage the slot as you unscrew them.*

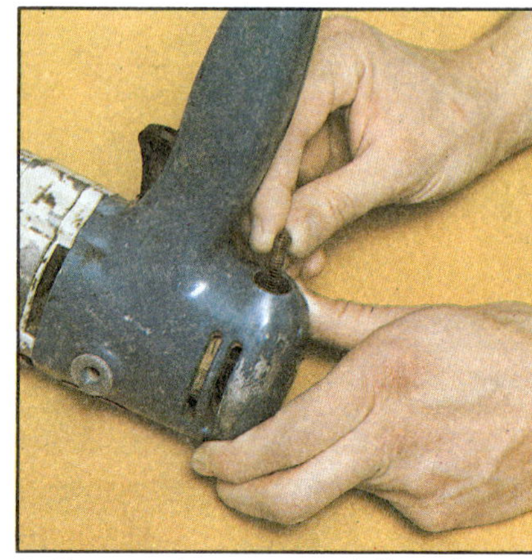

2 *Remove the caps carefully and you should be able to pull out the brushes; if not, hold the drill upside down and turn the chuck to loosen the brushes.*

5 *Finally, replace the retaining caps. If the motor sparks heavily when tested, ensure there is good contact between the brushes and commutator.*

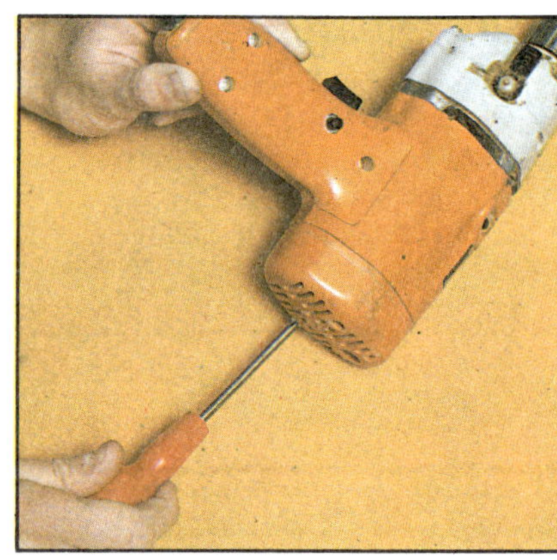

6 *With some drills, access to the brushes is from inside the casing. Take off the back section of the drill, first removing the fixing screws.*

9 *If the motor appears to be dirty now is the time to clean it. Use a brush or cloth previously dipped in petrol to clean the commutator.*

10 *It's quite easy for dust and other potentially damaging debris to find its way into the armature and field windings. Clear it away with a soft brush.*

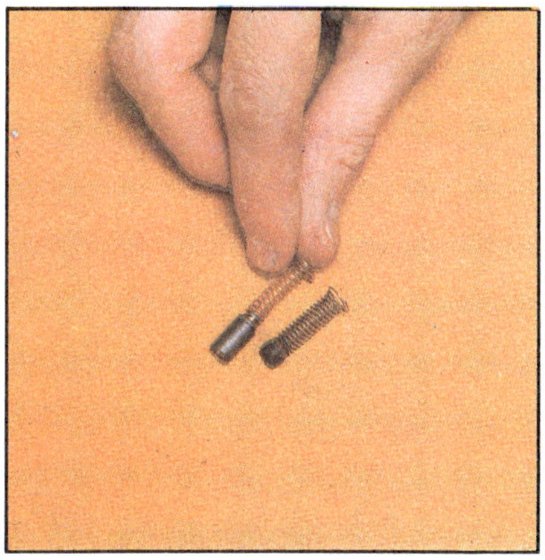

3 *If the brushes show signs of severe wear they should be replaced. Make sure you have identical brushes; otherwise they won't fit in the brush tubes.*

TIP

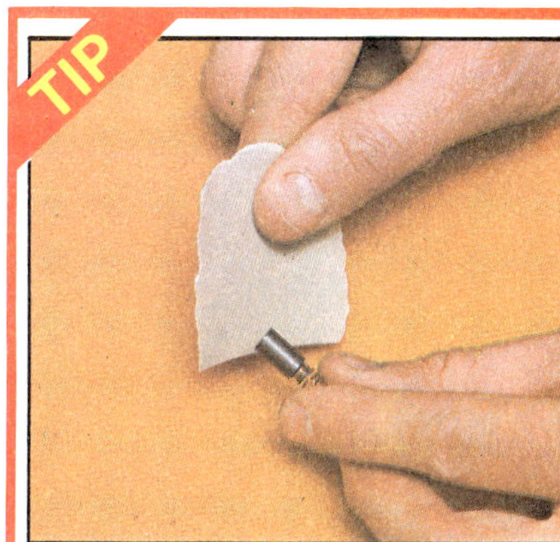

4 *New brushes can quite easily stick in the brush tubes. One solution is to rub down the brushes with fine glasspaper first.*

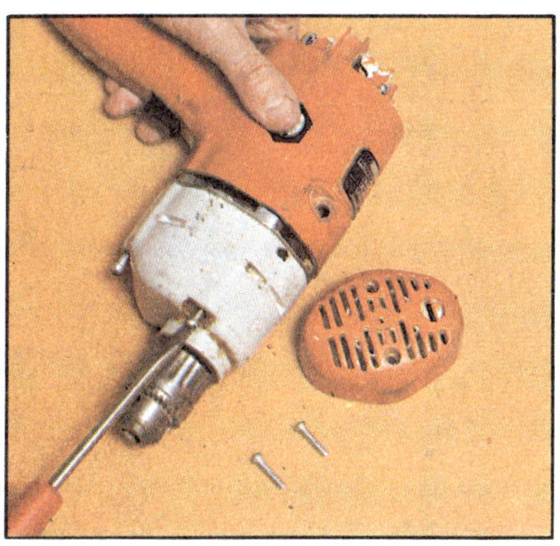

7 *If you want to service the motor at the same time, release the screws securing the chuck assembly and gear box to the main body of the drill.*

8 *Carefully pull away the front of the drill and end plate and ease the armature and commutator from the field windings. Inspect the motor's condition.*

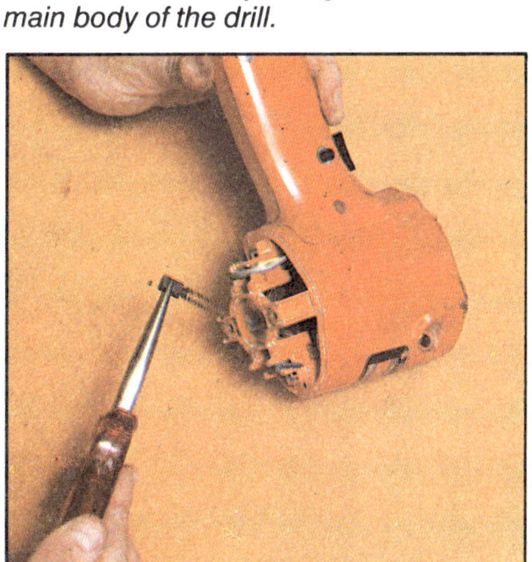

11 *As you reassemble the drill, replace the old worn brushes. When you come to refit the commutator, hold the brushes apart with a piece of card to admit it.*

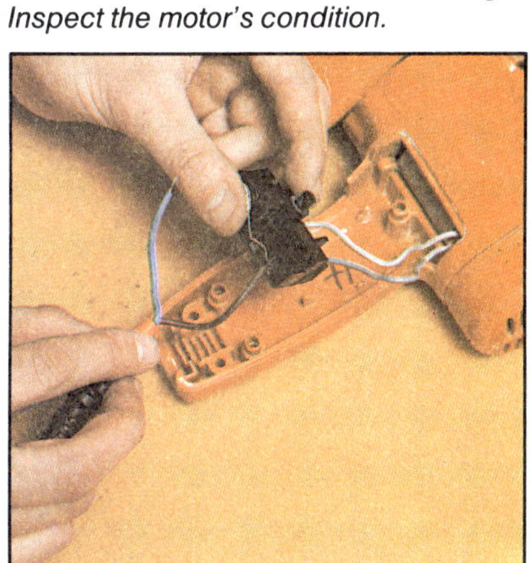

12 *Finally, if the flex is damaged fit a new one. Remove the handle piece and insert a paper clip to open the terminal clamps on the trigger switch.*

contact with the commutator. Occasionally the armature or field windings burn out but this is really only likely in power tools that are subject to considerable overloading.

Access to the brushes is usually via insulated retaining caps which are on the outside of the motor casing. However, with some motors, such as those in a horizontal vacuum cleaner, the power unit is inside the casing which means partly dismantling the machine. Remove the brushes by loosening the retaining caps or slips. Take care not to lose the springs that hold the brushes against the commutator: these are likely to pop out. You should also take note of the position of any guiding marks that will eventually help you to reset the brushes. Examine the condition of each brush and if either is worn down to as little as 5mm (⅕in) then it must be renewed. The replacement brushes must of course be identical to the old ones otherwise they won't fit into the brush tubes. If they do stick slightly then wipe them with fine glass paper before replacing the securing caps.

At the same time that you're replacing the brushes it's a good idea to examine the commutator; if it's blackened then wipe it carefully with a cloth previously dipped in petrol. You should then test the motor. If there's heavy sparking then you'll have to adjust the brushes to ensure good contact with the commutator surface. If you find that the sparking continues along with erratic running then the chances are that one of the armature coils will have burnt out. In this case you should stop the motor to avoid any further damage. Remove the motor end plate that's usually at the opposite end to the commutator and take out the armature for examination. It'll be obvious if one of the coils or a commutator segment has burnt out. You'll have to take the armature to an electrical servicing shop that offers a rewind service, although very often it's easier simply to buy a completely rewound armature. However, with some machines, such as lawn mowers, you'll probably find that in these cases you'll have to get a completely new power unit.

Servicing induction motors

Because there are no carbon brushes, a commutator and wound armature, an induction motor requires little attention during the life of the appliance. As with all motors, it should, of course, be kept clean and it's a good idea to check now and then that the armature can turn freely inside the stator. A voltage drop for some reason will mean that the induction motor won't be able to reach its correct running speed and this could result in a burnt out stator if it's not swiftly switched off. However, this and other damage that might occur is best left to a servicing shop to put right.

SERVICING ELECTRICAL APPLIANCES: 2

Kettles, irons, electric fires, cookers and vacuum cleaners are the sorts of electrical appliances that can sometimes go wrong. Here's a run through some of the repairs you can safely do yourself.

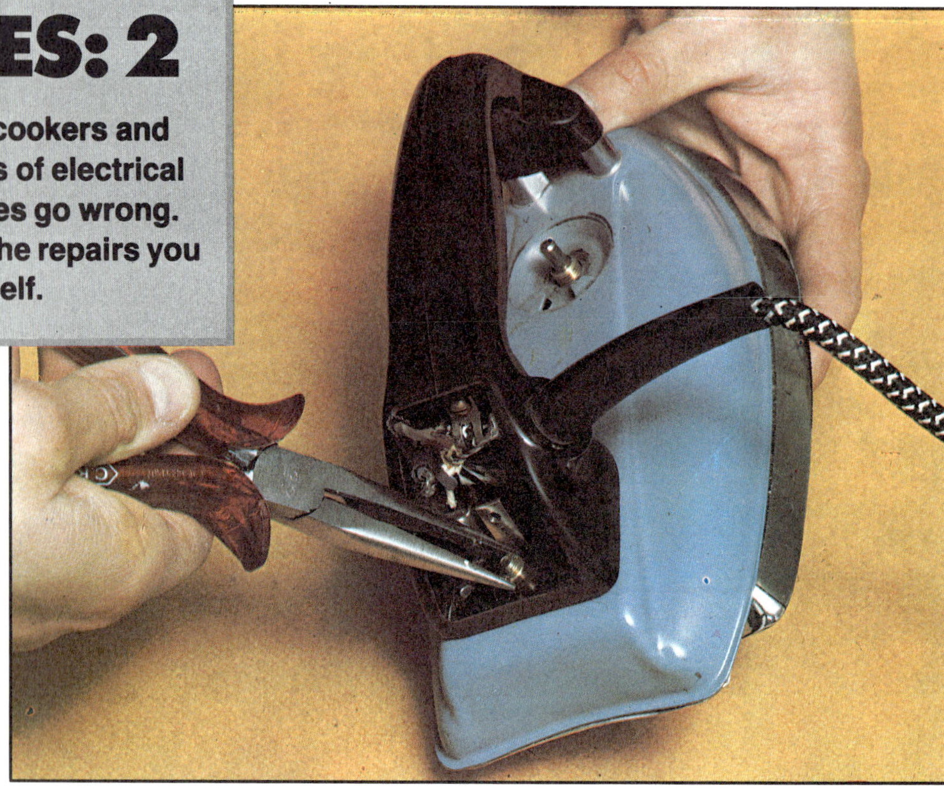

Once you've established that it's your electrical appliance that's gone wrong, and not just a blown plug fuse or damaged flex, you'll have to decide whether it's actually worth repairing. Always bear in mind the age of your appliance; after all, you might not be able to get spare parts. And, of course, you might just decide to buy a new model that is more efficient – and remember, electrical appliances are somewhat cheaper than they used to be.

Most electrical appliances differ between manufacturers so it's not possible to tell you exactly what to do if particular faults arise. However, there is a set procedure and a number of general steps you should follow for any electrical appliance repair.

Before doing anything, though, it's a good idea to contact the manufacturers or their agents and get hold of any relevant repair manuals they produce. These won't always be available to members of the public and there's bound to be a small charge. However, it is essential to know exactly what you're doing. Finally, you should make sure that all the correct spare parts are available and that you'll have all the tools required for the job. Only then should you start attempting any repairs.

Electric kettles

There are two main types of electric kettles, the non-automatic one which has to be turned off manually when the water boils, and the automatic type which switches itself off. Other than faults within the flex and plug, the most common problems are likely to be,

- a faulty element
- a burnt-out switch wiring or faulty cut-out
- leaks at the shroud.

To remove the faulty element and fit a new one (normally they are widely available) you should:

- remove the switch cover plate
- undo the screws securing the handle clamping and lift up the handle
- undo the screw fixing the switch assembly to the body of the kettle, then use long-nosed pliers or a specially shaped screwdriver to remove the earth connection screw and remove the switch assembly
- unscrew the nuts and washers securing the element, take out the old element and scrape off any rubber washer remains from the flange hole
- fit the new element by reversing the process, making sure you fit new sealing washers
- finally, check the kettle for earth continuity before using it.

Replacement switch assemblies are readily available for most makes and can be easily fitted. If you can't identify the fault on your kettle, most electrical servicing shops will test the element for you. Alternatively, test the element using an ohm meter to check the resistance level.

Electric irons

There are two types of iron – the steam iron and the dry iron. Both are thermostatically controlled and when the thermostat develops a fault – often indicated by the neon light being on but the soleplate, the shiny metal bottom of the iron, not heating up – you should take the iron to a servicing shop for repairs. Soleplates should always be regularly cleaned with a special non-abrasive solution that is readily available. On steam irons, outlets and valves should be regularly cleared with descaling liquid. You should then fill the tank only with distilled water – unless it is designed to take tap water – otherwise tap water will simply cause the iron to fur up.

An iron element will occasionally fail and will therefore have to be renewed. With some models the element is embedded in the soleplate, in which case a new soleplate is the only answer. To replace an ordinary element you'll have to:

- remove the iron cover and cast iron pressure plate that's normally bolted to the soleplate
- disconnect the element contact strips and remove the screw from the thermostat
- lift off the asbestos heat resisting pad and remove the element
- clean the soleplate and fit the new element by reversing the order of dismantling.

Vacuum cleaners

You're likely to have either an upright or cylinder vacuum cleaner. Both types can develop faults, most of which you'll probably be able to rectify. Keep your vacuum cleaner serviced to cut down on problems: never let dust bags get too full and inspect all hoses and tools regularly – an accumulation of dust and fluff will cause blockages.

Signs of a fault developing in your vacuum cleaner are likely to be:

- a motor not running, resulting from a faulty fuse, plug or flex connections, a damaged switch, or a burnt-out motor winding (see pages 270–273).
- erratic running resulting from worn or sticking carbon brushes (which may need replacing) or loose connections (which should be re-made)
- failure to pick up dust, resulting from a full bag or blockage in the inlet. Check also that

RENEWING A DRIVE BELT

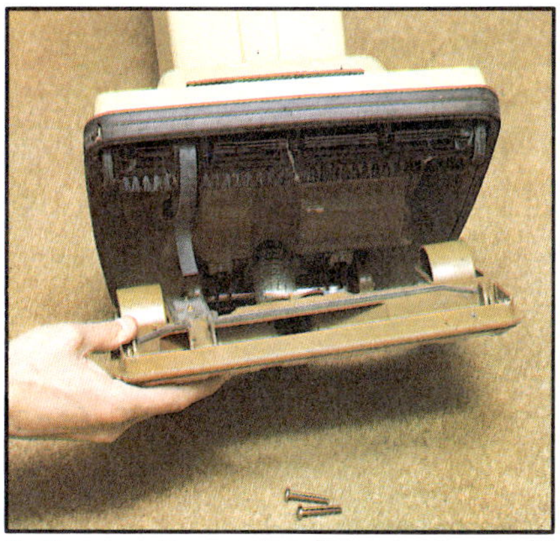

***1** Remove the casing fixing screws set in the bottom plate to gain access to the broken belt. On some vacuum cleaners you'll have to remove a front panel.*

***2** Lift out the roller brush and dispose of the broken drive belt. Also check the condition of the brushes at the same time and replace the roller if necessary.*

***3** Hook the correct-sized replacement drive belt over the drive shaft. At the same time you should also lubricate the wheels with a light machine oil.*

***4** Finally, fit the exposed section of the drive belt over the roller brushes and clip them back, making sure they are correctly located.*

Ready Reference

SAFETY FIRST

When attempting repairs to faulty electrical appliances you should:

- unplug all portable appliances at the socket outlet to which they're connected
- switch off all faulty fixed appliances at the circuit switch
- allow all heating elements and boiling rings to cool down before touching them
- make sure you have a service manual or detailed information about the faulty appliance
- make sure you have adequate tools for the job
- make sure you have the correct spare parts, if needed
- take note of all colour codes, disassembly order and screw position marks so that you'll be able to reassemble the appliance correctly.

For safety's sake some appliances should not be serviced or repaired by the do-it-yourselfer. These include microwave ovens and electric blankets.

KETTLE SWITCHES

A common fault on automatic kettles is a faulty switch. This means the kettle is slow or reluctant to switch itself off. There are several ways of dealing with this,

- simply adjust the thermostat screw found on the switch assembly of some models
- change the lid position so the steam outlet is close to the switch
- replace the switch assembly.

the drive belt hasn't slipped or broken; a sure sign of this is a fast-running motor on no load. On a cylinder model, check for badly-fitting joints

- excessive and unpleasant noise indicates that a metal object has been picked up and is making contact with the cooling fan, so check that the fan hasn't been damaged
- smell of burning caused by something hindering the belt operation; check that it is running properly
- smoke resulting from a burnt-out armature or field windings; this will probably mean a professional repair is needed.

Electric heaters

There are various types of electric heater, but the two main ones are radiant heaters, where elements operate at 'red' heat and heat up the air next to them, and convectors operating at 'black' heat and expelling warm air. Other types include fan heaters, panel heaters and radiators, and night storage heaters.

The most common fault with radiant heaters will be a faulty element or switch. To replace an element you should lift off the wire guard of the fire and undo the fixing nut at each end of the element. Connections vary between the different makes of fires, as do the lengths and types of element, so make sure the replacement element is identical to the old one.

Firebar elements comprising flat ceramic or fireclay bars with the element wires fixed in parabolic grooves can be removed from the back of the heater after first undoing the fixing screws and loosening the connecting wires. Reverse the process for fitting the new elements.

If the fan of a fan heater doesn't work then the heater must not be used; otherwise it will burn out, as no air can pass over the elements. Remember to keep all air grilles clear of dust and any blockages. The inbuilt thermostats of panel heaters and radiators rarely go wrong. If they do, or if anything goes wrong with your storage heaters, then you'll have to call in an electrician as the repairs are likely to prove too complicated for the average do-it-yourselfer.

Power tools

Faults with drills do develop and often you can repair some of these yourself. The most likely symptoms are:

- motor does not start, resulting from worn carbon brushes or burnt-out motor windings (see pages 270–273).
- motor runs erratically due to worn or sticking brushes, or loose connections in the switch gear
- overneating resulting from overloading or a burnt-out armature or field coil.

Cookers

The most likely repair you'll have to make to your electric cooker is to replace one of the boiling rings. Remember replacements must be identical to the originals. Grill and oven elements rarely fail, but if necessary they, too, can be replaced. The signs of a fault on your cooker will be,

- no power at the control switch, caused by a blown circuit fuse
- a ring or grill that fails to heat, resulting from a burnt-out element or faulty switch
- a double-heat boiling ring or grill element that produces only half heat, which indicates that half the element has failed
- a variable-heat element that doesn't respond to control, is a sign of a faulty control
- an oven that fails to heat up properly, again the result of faulty control
- automatic controls not working, suggesting they need adjusting or replacing.

You'll probably find that repairing the control panel or thermostat will be beyond you, in which case call in an electrician.

To replace a boiling ring, lift the hob on its hinges and support it. Most rings have individual fixed conections; some are connected in pairs to a terminal block, while with other models all four rings are connected to a central terminal block. Remove the cover screws and the terminal block and release the element-connecting nuts and washers. Take out the old element and fit and connect the new ring, making sure that the terminal screws are tight.

Grill elements are replaced in much the same way, although the terminal blocks are usually either reached from the back of the cooker or from under the hob.

If you need to replace the oven element then you'll have to take off the back panel.

Washing machines

There is a limit to the repairs and servicing which you can satisfactorily undertake. Washing machines usually incorporate elements for heating the water, a motor to agitate the water and clothes, as well as a pump. Failure of the agitator or impeller to operate while the motor is indicative of a broken or slipping belt. In some cases the belt might even have come off the pulley. Failure of the water to heat means either a burnt-out element or faulty heater switch. Water leakage can usually be traced to a split hose or a loose or broken hose clip. If water isn't pumped out when the pump is switched on, then the most likely cause will either be a blocked filter, a failed inlet valve or something fouling up the pump vane. Filters can be removed for cleaning, while inlet valves are usually quite straightforward to replace. In the case of a blocked pump, disconnect the pipe to the pump and remove the blockage.

1 *On a cooker lift the hob to get at the faulty ring. Most models are hinged and incorporate a special hob support; otherwise just prop it up.*

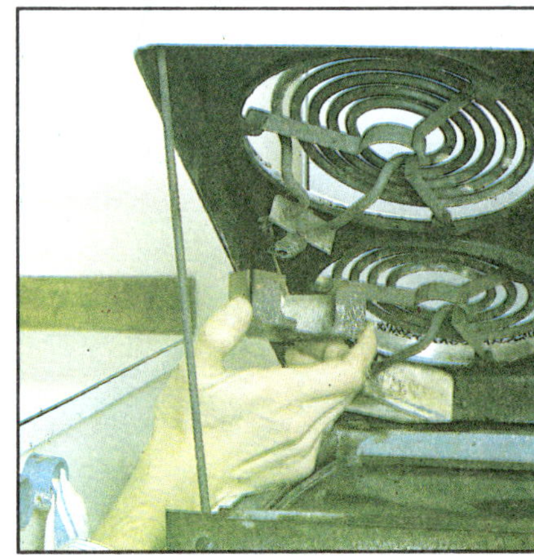

2 *The connections of most cooker rings are protected by a box-like cover. Undo the fixing screws and lower this cover to get at the terminals.*

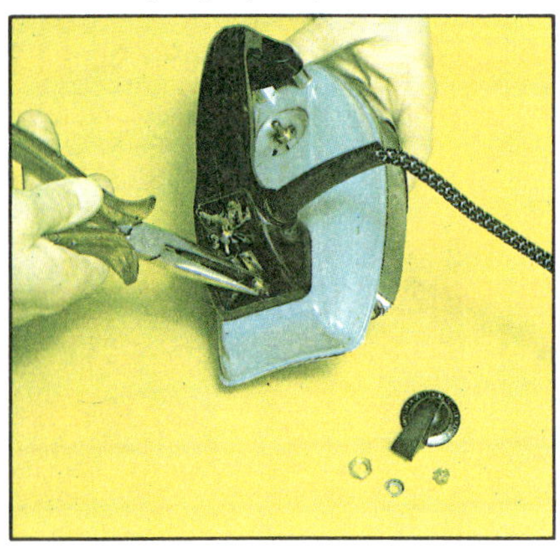

6 *On an iron you'll have to take off the cover by undoing the nut beneath the control dial and loosening the slotted nut under the earth terminal.*

7 *After disconnecting the flex completely you'll be able to lift off the cover to get inside the iron. If necessary, remove the terminal screws.*

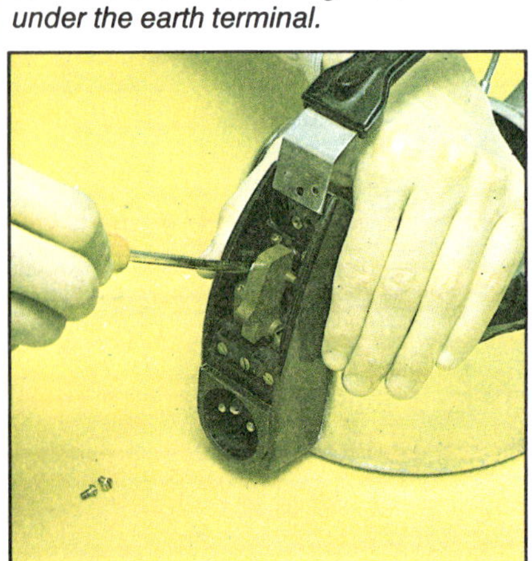

11 *On a kettle remove the switch cover plate and undo the handle screws. Then undo the screws securing the switch assembly to the body.*

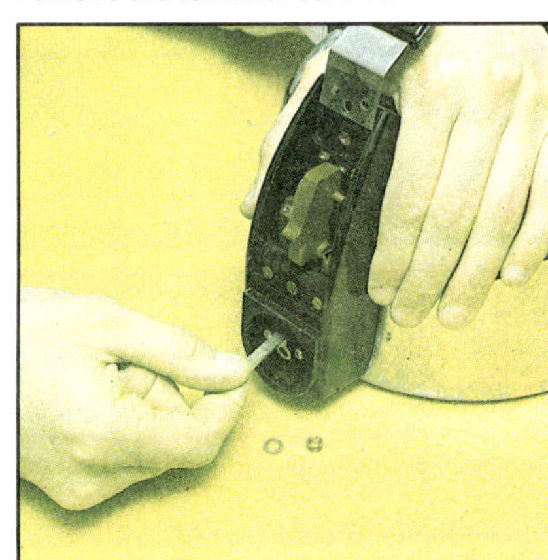

12 *Undo the slotted nuts securing the earth pin and remove the earth connection screw. Use long-nosed pliers or buy a special screwdriver.*

REPLACING ELEMENTS ON COOKERS, IRONS AND KETTLES

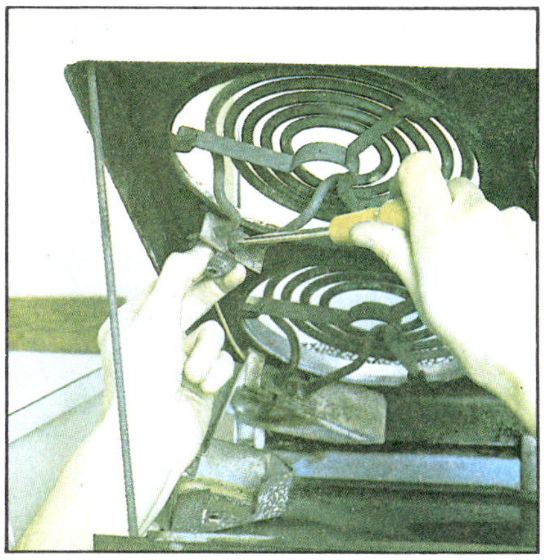

3 *In order to loosen the ring itself, you'll first have to remove the screw on the element fixing plate that secures it to the cooker frame.*

4 *You can then disconnect the faulty ring. The terminals will either be the screw or tab type. Ease the strain on the latter when disconnecting.*

5 *Finally, replace the old ring with an identical new one, connecting the terminals in the same way. Then simply reassemble the cooker in the reverse order.*

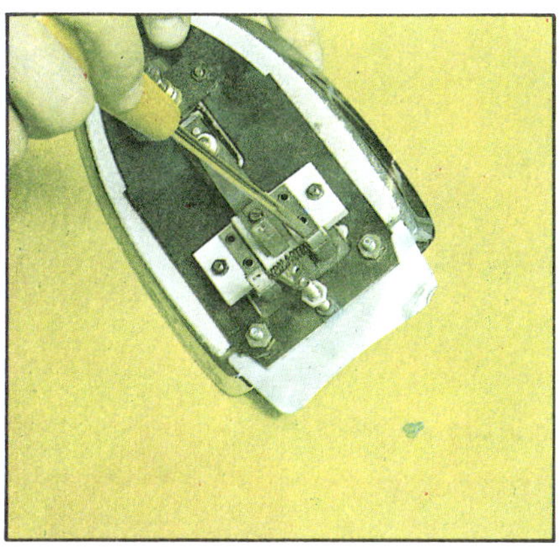

8 *Before removing the pressure plate, you must disconnect the contact strips of the faulty element. Use an ordinary screwdriver for this task.*

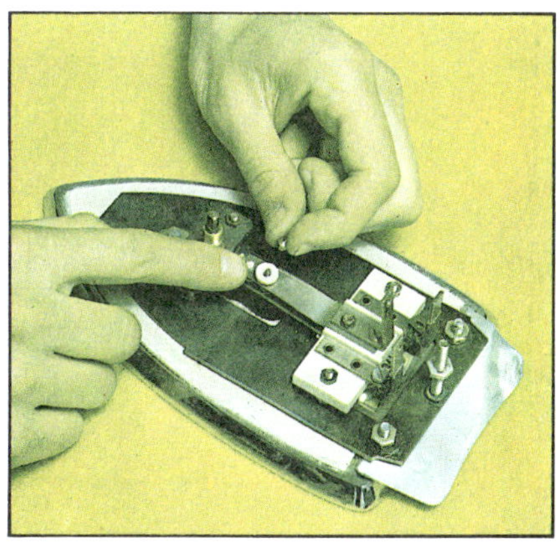

9 *You'll also have to remove the screw top of the temperature control rod, and undo the nuts at the back of the iron that fix the pressure plate in place.*

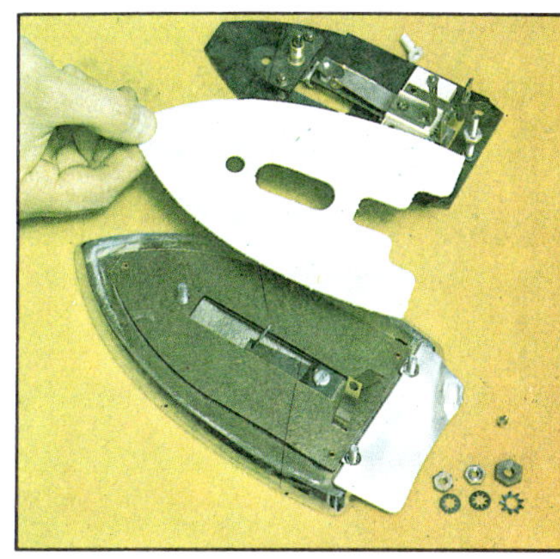

10 *Lift off the pressure plate and remove the old heat-resistant cover and element. Then fit the new element and reassemble the iron in reverse order.*

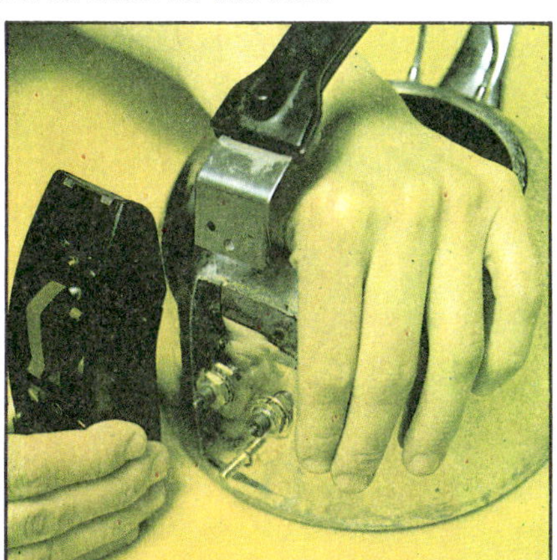

13 *In order to gain access to the element connections themselves, carefully pull away the complete switch assembly from the kettle.*

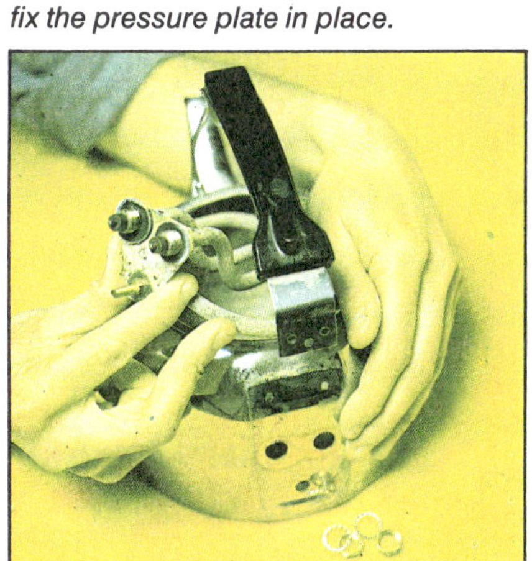

14 *Remove the nuts and washers securing the old element and lift it out. Scrape off any scale and the remains of old washers from the kettle surface.*

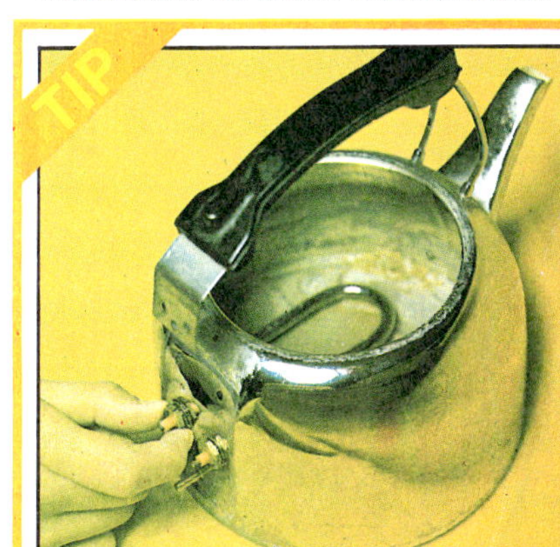

15 *Finally, fit the new element using the new nuts and washers supplied with it. Then reverse the dismantling process to reassemble the kettle.*

PART 3

BUILDING

PLASTERING WALLS AND CEILINGS

Of all the skills the home builder needs, apparently the most difficult to master is the art of plastering. Watching a plasterer at work seems like observing a conjuror, yet speed is not the essence of mastering the technique. Once the various operations involved in getting the plaster from hawk to wall are understood, it's simply a matter of practice and gaining confidence. It's a skill well worth getting to grips with, since it is probably the most labour-intensive of all building operations, and once you've mastered it you will be able to tackle solid walls, stud partitions, even ceilings with ease.

BASIC PLASTERING TECHNIQUES

Patching small areas of plasterwork is a fairly straightforward job, but sometimes you'll need to replaster a whole wall. Before you can start, you have to learn the basic techniques.

Plaster is used on internal walls to give a smooth, flat surface that you can decorate with paint, wallpaper or tiles. There are two basic types of plaster in common use. One is a mix based on a mineral called gypsum. The other, cement-based plaster, is used mostly as 'rendering' to weather-proof the exterior walls of a house. But it is also employed indoors, especially as part of the treatment of damp walls, or as an 'under-coat' for other plasters. Its disadvantages are a slow drying time and the possibility that mistakes in proportioning of the constituents could result in a weak mix.

Types of plaster

Gypsum-based plasters have largely superseded cement-based plasters. They are quicker-setting and usually available in pre-mixed form, which requires only the addition of clean water to make them workable. Another point in their favour is that they contain lightweight aggregates such as perlite and vermiculite instead of sand, so they're easier to use.

Ready-mixed plaster is usually spread onto the wall in two parts. The first is a backing or 'floating' coat, which is applied fairly thickly – up to 10mm (3/8in) – to take up any unevenness in the wall. The second is a finishing coat, which is spread on thinly – up to 3mm (1/8in) – and finished to give a smooth, matt surface.

Carlite is the most widely-used lightweight pre-mixed gypsum plaster and it's available in various grades for use on different wall surfaces, depending upon how absorbent they are: the plaster will crack if the wall to which it's applied draws moisture from it too quickly. Common brickwork and most types of lightweight building blocks, for instance, are described as having 'high suction', which means that their absorption rate is rapid. Concrete, engineering bricks, dense building blocks and plasterboard, on the other hand, have 'low suction'.

You can recognise which walls are high- or low-suction by splashing on a little clean water. If it's absorbed immediately, the wall is high-suction, but if it runs off the surface the wall is low-suction. If after this test you're still unsure, you can treat the wall with a coat of PVA bonding agent or adhesive, which, when brushed on, turns all backgrounds into low-suction, and both seals and stabilizes the surface.

For a high-suction background you'll need Carlite Browning plaster for the base coat; for low suction choose Carlite Bonding plaster. Use Bonding where the wall is of a composite nature (containing both high- and low-suction materials). Carlite Finish plaster is used as the final coat on Bonding and Browning plaster.

Preparing the surface

You'll achieve a smooth, flat and long-lasting plastered finish only if you've prepared the background properly If you're replastering an old wall of bricks or blocks, hack off all the old plaster using a club hammer and bolster chisel and examine the mortar joints. If they're soft and crumbly, rake them out and repoint them.

Lightly dampen the wall using an old paintbrush – this is essential if the new finish is to stick properly, and prevents the wall absorbing too much moisture from the plaster. New brick or block walls probably won't need any preparation before you plaster other than light wetting.

Smooth surfaces such as concrete and timber (used as lintels over doors and windows, for example), must be keyed to accept the plaster. You can do this either by nailing expanded metal laths (see *Ready Reference)* or plasterboard to them, applying PVA bonding agent, or by hacking a series of shallow criss-cross lines on the surface with a cold chisel.

Applying the plaster

Plaster is applied to the wall in a series of sections called 'bays'. These need to be marked out. One method is to use timber battens called 'grounds' lightly nailed vertically to the wall. Another method employs 'screeds', which are narrow strips of plaster. These are spread onto the wall

MIXING PLASTER

1 *Sprinkle handfuls of dry plaster onto clean water, breaking up any lumps between your fingers. Mix up equal volumes of plaster and water.*

2 *When the water has soaked into the dry plaster, stir thoroughly using a stout stick until the mix reaches a uniform consistency without any lumps.*

3 *Test the consistency of the plaster mix: Browning and Bonding plaster should resemble porridge and should be fairly stiff in texture.*

4 *When the plaster is mixed, tip it from the bucket onto your spot board, which should be positioned close to the wall you're about to work on.*

TIP

5 *Use the trowel to knead the mixed plaster on the spot board; if the mix is too sloppy sprinkle on more plaster.*

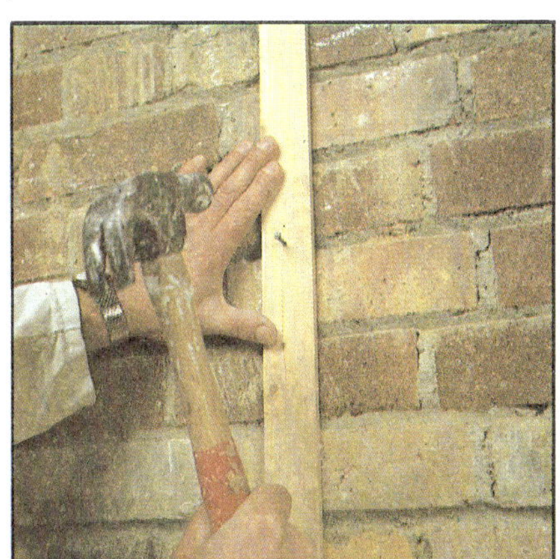

6 *Temporarily nail 10mm (3/8in) thick softwood battens vertically to the wall at 1m (3ft) spacings to act as grounds (thickness guides) during plastering.*

READY REFERENCE

TOOLS FOR PLASTERING

There are a number of specialist tools for plastering but the following are the basic requirements:

- hawk (A) – a 300mm (1ft) wood, aluminium or plastic square with a handle, used to carry plaster to your working area
- plasterer's trowel (B) – the basic tool for applying plaster to the wall; it has a thin rectangular steel blade measuring about 250 x 115mm (10 x 4½in) and a shaped wooden handle
- wood float (C) – generally used to give a flatter finish coat to plaster, it is rectangular in shape. It can be converted to a devilling float for keying surfaces by driving in two or three nails at one end so that their points just protrude
- rule – a planed softwood batten measuring about 75 x 25mm (3 x 1in) and about 1.5m (5ft) long, used to level off the floating coat when applied between screeds, grounds or beads
- water brush – used to dampen the wall and to sprinkle water on the trowel when finishing
- spirit level – for positioning the timber grounds accurately.

MAKING A SPOT BOARD

The spot board is used to hold the mixed plaster near the work area. Make one from a 1m (3ft) sq panel of exterior grade plywood mounted on an old table or tea chest so it's at a convenient height. Make sure it projects over the edge of the stand so you can place the hawk underneath when loading with plaster.

BUYING PLASTER

Large quantities of plaster are sold in 50kg (110lb) bags; smaller amounts for patching are sold in 2.5 to 10kg (5½ to 22lb) bags.

HOW FAR WILL IT GO?

- 10kg (22lb) of Carlite Browning laid 10mm (3/8in) thick will cover about 1.5sq m (1.8sq yd).
- 10kg (22lb) of Carlite Bonding laid 10mm (3/8in) thick will cover about 1.6sq m (1.9sq yd).
- 10kg (22lb) of Carlite Finish will cover about 5sq m (6sq yd).

USING A HAWK AND TROWEL

1 *Hold the hawk under the edge of the spot board and scoop a trowel-load of plaster onto it. Use the trowel to push the plaster into a neat mound.*

2 *With the hawk level, hold the edge of the trowel blade on it at right angles to the face. Push the trowel forward while tilting the hawk towards you.*

3 *When the hawk is vertical push up with the trowel, which should still be at right angles to the hawk face, and scoop off the plaster.*

4 *Return the hawk to the horizontal position and keep the trowel upright with the plaster on top. This whole sequence takes only a few seconds.*

5 *Without hesitating, tip the trowel forwards to return the plaster to the centre of the hawk. Don't drop it from too great a height or it will splash.*

6 *The mound of plaster should keep a roughly rounded shape, if it's of the right consistency. Practise this loading technique several times.*

from floor to ceiling, generally using wood blocks called 'dots' at the top and bottom as thickness guides.

The distance between these markers can vary according to your skill in applying the plaster, but 1m (3ft) is an easily manageable width for the beginner. Screeds and grounds are essentially guides that enable you to apply the backing coat to the correct thickness, and when the plaster's been applied to one bay it's smoothed off level with them using a timber straight edge called a 'rule'

Expanded metal screed beads for flat surfaces and angle beads for external corners (see *Ready Reference)* serve the same purpose as timber grounds.

Applying a plaster screed to the correct thickness takes some practice and it's much easier to use timber grounds or metal beads. When you've plastered one bay using timber grounds as guides, leave the plaster until it is partially set; then remove one of the battens, move it along the wall about another 1m (3ft) and refix it.

Plaster this second bay using the edge of the first one as a thickness guide, and rule off the surface carefully. Carry on in this way until you've covered the whole wall.

To ensure the finishing plaster will adhere to the backing coat the latter must be 'keyed' using a tool called a devilling float. This is a wooden or plastic block with nails driven in from the top so that their points just protrude through the base, and it's used to scratch the surface of the backing coat lightly.

Two thin coats of finishing plaster will give a smooth and flat surface. The first coat is applied from bottom to top, working left to right if you're right-handed, right to left otherwise, and is then ruled off. The second coat is applied straight away and then flattened off to produce a matt finish. When this has been done you return to the starting point and, with the addition of a little water splashed onto the wall, you trowel over the entire surface. When the plaster has hardened, trowel the surface again several times, applying water to the surface as a lubricant to create a smooth, flat finish.

Mixing the plaster

Cleanliness in mixing plaster is of prime importance because any dirt or debris that gets into the mix could affect the setting time and mar the finish. Keep a bucket of water nearby for cleaning the tools and don't use this water for mixing the plaster – use clean, fresh tap water. See the photographs on page 281 for how to mix the plaster.

PRACTISING ON THE WALL

1 *Place some plaster on your hawk and move over to the wall you're going to plaster. Repeat the process you've just practised (left, 2 to 6).*

2 *Take about half the plaster from the hawk. Keeping the trowel horizontal, position yourself near the right-hand timber ground.*

3 *With the right-hand edge of the trowel resting on the timber ground, tilt the blade up until its face is at about 30° to the wall surface.*

4 *Push the trowel upwards, keeping an even pressure on its heel, which rests on the timber ground. Decrease the angle of the blade as the plaster is spread.*

5 *When most of the plaster has been spread, the trowel blade should be parallel with the wall. Press in its lower edge to pinch in the plaster.*

6 *Spread a second trowel-full of plaster immediately to the left of the first one, taking care not to make the layer thinner by pressing in too hard.*

READY REFERENCE

MIXING PLASTER

When mixing plaster you'll need the following equipment:

- a trough about the size of a galvanized bath for large amounts, or a tea chest lined with polythene
- a 5 gallon (22 litre) bucket for small amounts
- a clean bucket containing clean water for adding to the mix
- a bucket to transfer mixed plaster to the spot board
- a clean shovel for stirring large mixes.

TIP: FIXING GROUNDS

It's important that the timber grounds are fixed truly vertical as they're guides to the thickness of the floating coat. On uneven walls, pad out gaps between the grounds and the wall with wood offcuts to make their faces vertical.

USING METAL BEADS

Expanded metal lath and plaster beads act as a thickness guide for applying plaster to the wall and levelling it off. They're bedded on plaster dabs and remain in the wall when plastering is complete.

- Screed beads are used instead of timber grounds or plaster screeds.

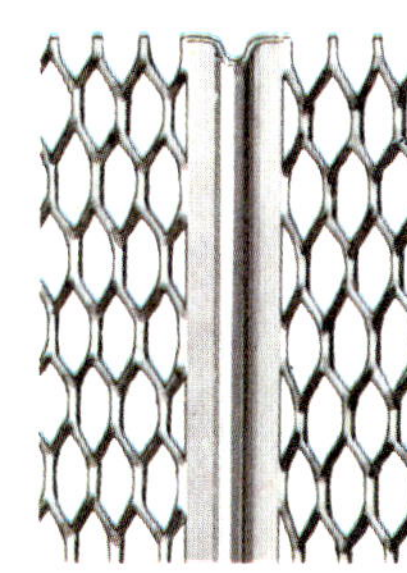

- Stop beads are used for plastering up to doorways or abutting skirtings

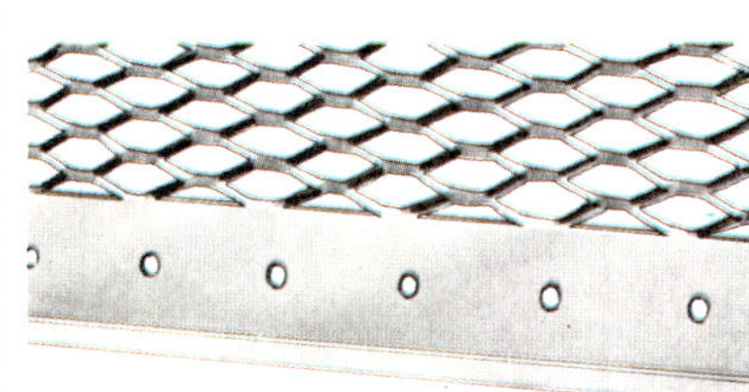

- Angle beads fit over external corners and protect the plaster from chipping.

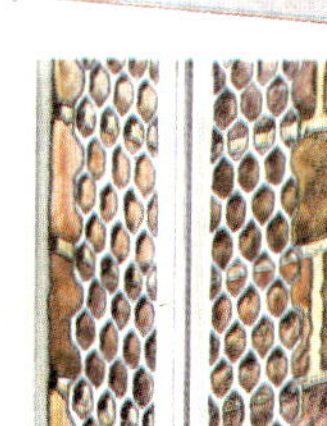

For plastering plasterboard see pages 294–298

APPLYING THE FLOATING COAT

1 *After your trial run, scrape the plaster from the wall, clean and dampen the surface, then start plastering at the bottom right of the bay.*

2 *Work your way up the bay, spreading on the plaster in rows. You'll have to rig up a trestle to reach the top of the bay.*

3 *Use a timber batten to rule off the plaster level with the face of the timber grounds. Draw the rule upwards with a side-to-side sawing action.*

TIP

4 *Look for any hollows in the surface and fill them in with more plaster. Then rule off again as before.*

5 *Key the floating coat before it sets with a devilling float. Wet its base and keep it flat to the wall so the nails score shallow marks in the plaster.*

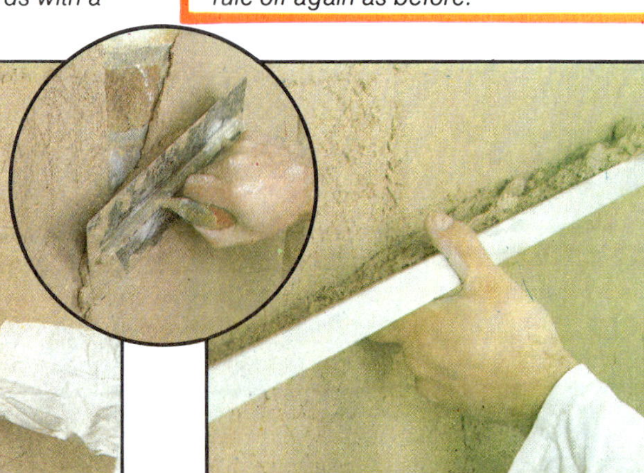

6 *When the first bay has set, refix the right-hand ground 1m (3ft) away. Plaster between this and the raw edge of the first bay (inset), then rule off carefully.*

APPLYING THE

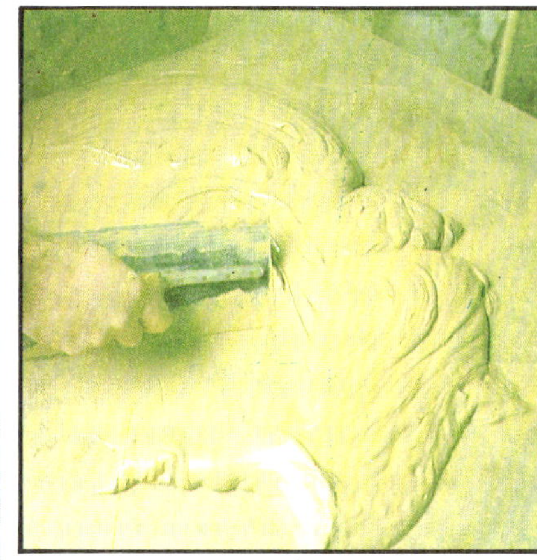

1 *Mix the finishing plaster in a bucket, then transfer it to the spot board and knead as before. It should have the consistency of melting ice-cream.*

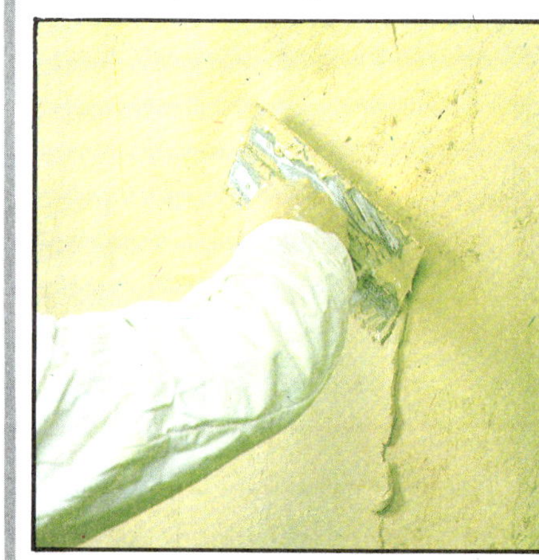

5 *Once you've applied the finishing coat of plaster to this area, return to the starting point and apply a second even thinner coat immediately.*

Basic techniques: Floating

Patching small areas of damaged plaster-work is fairly straightforward but plastering a whole wall calls for a degree of skill in using the various tools that can only be achieved by practice.

When you've mixed the plaster place it on the spot board. If you're right-handed, hold the hawk in your left hand and the trowel in your right (vice versa if left-handed). Grip the trowel so that your index finger is against the front shank, the toe of the trowel pointing left. The knuckles of your right hand should be uppermost. The hawk should rest in the left hand on your thumb and index finger.

To load the hawk, place it under the edge of the spot board, scoop a small amount of plaster onto the hawk and move it away.

Hold the hawk level and place the bottom

FINISHING COAT

2 *When the floating coat has hardened – after about two hours – scoop a trowel-load of finishing plaster onto your hawk and move over to the wall.*

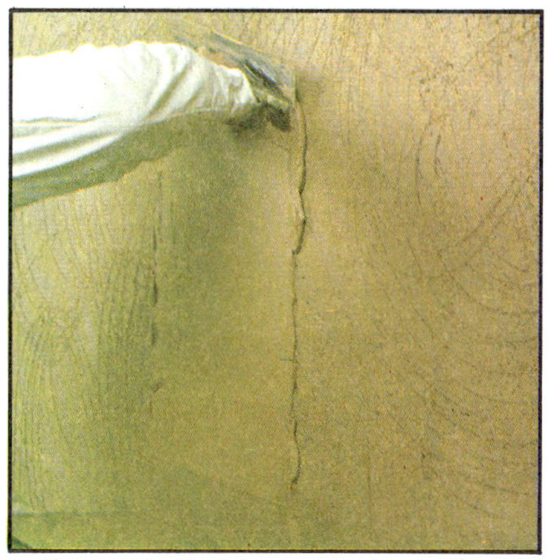

3 *Spread half of the amount onto the floating coat, working from bottom to top. Keep the coat very thin. Apply the other half, blending the two.*

4 *Work from bottom left to top right over an area about 2m (6ft 6in) wide, with broad, sweeping arm movements.*

6 *Trowel off any ridges or splashes on the finishing coat with light downward strokes; hold the wetted trowel blade at about 30° to the surface of the wall.*

7 *When the finishing coat has hardened, trowel again using water to lubricate the blade. This polishes the surface and gives a smooth, flat finish.*

TIP

8 *You probably won't be able to complete a whole wall in one go. If you do break off, scribe down the plaster and scrape off to form a neat edge.*

edge of the trowel on it, blade at right-angles to the hawk face. As you push the trowel forward against the plaster, tilt the hawk until it's almost vertical, keeping the trowel at right angles to the hawk face. Push the plaster off the hawk and gently slide it all back. Don't drop it from too great a height or too fast as it will splash. Repeat this several times before attempting to spread the plaster onto the wall.

When you're fairly confident, move to the wall and repeat the operation, but only remove half the plaster from the hawk. Keeping the trowel horizontal, place the lower edge hard against the wall at chest height. Open the gap between trowel and wall to about 5mm (¼in), tilt the trowel up until its face is at about 30° to the wall surface and then move the trowel upwards. The gap is similar to a valve and controls the thickness of plaster applied to the wall. As the material is spread evenly and disappears from under the trowel, decrease the angle between trowel and wall so that you apply the last of the plaster with a pinching movement between the trowel edge and the wall. This prevents the plaster from sliding down. Repeat this until you get the plaster to stay on the wall.

After your 'practice run', scrape the plaster from the wall, and apply a 'floating' coat of backing plaster between the grounds; don't worry about any ridges or hollows at this stage but aim to get coverage of an even thickness all over.

Rule over the plaster and fill in any hollow areas, then rule again. Before the plaster has set, lightly key it with a devilling float.

Basic techniques: Finishing

Carlite plaster sets in less than two hours, so you should apply the finish coat as soon as possible after the floating coat has hardened. Use the hawk and trowel as if applying the floating coat, but take less plaster onto the hawk and apply a very thin coat to the floating coat, working left to right and from bottom to top. Smooth out all ridges to leave the surface as flat as possible. Once you've covered the undercoat, repeat the operation. Lightly sprinkle water onto the face of the trowel using a brush. With the trowel blade at an angle of 25 to 30°, trowel over the finish coat with long straight sweeps to achieve a smooth, flat finish.

Leave the plaster until set, then trowel once more, aided by water and harder pressure, to polish the surface.

PLASTERING ANGLES AND REVEALS

When you're plastering large areas, you'll have to cope with corners sooner or later. Metal angle beads make it easy to get perfect corners every time.

Applying plaster to walls may seem like a daunting task, but you will have seen from other sections on pages 148 -153 and 162 -166 that, providing the right techniques are practised and used, professional-quality finishes can be quite easily obtained on both exposed brick and plasterboard surfaces.

In these earlier articles, plastering was confined to flat, uninterrupted surfaces, but in practice there will usually be a certain amount of finishing off needed at internal and external corners, and around door and window openings. You will need to learn a few more techniques to deal with these, although the method of applying the plaster, and the tools for doing so, are basically the same as those detailed previously with a few exceptions.

Internal angles

You are likely to meet two types of internal angle when plastering. The first is where your newly-plastered wall meets an existing hard plaster surface on the adjacent wall, and the second is where both adjacent walls are being plastered simultaneously.

Where you have a hard surface to work to, apply your floating coat to the wall in the normal manner. Then rule the plaster outwards from the corner, using the wooden rules vertically instead of horizontally. Key the plaster well with a devilling float and then cut out the internal angle. This is done by laying the trowel flat against the finished surface so that it is at an angle of 30 to 40° to the vertical and then moving it into the corner until the tip of the toe cuts into the fresh plaster. Move the trowel up and down the angle and then repeat the procedure with the trowel flat against the floated surface and its tip against the hard plaster. This will cut out the corner cleanly. Leave it to harden.

Next, apply the finishing plaster, ruling vertically away from the angle with a feather-edge rule and cut into the corner as before. The second coat of finishing plaster should be trowelled in to form a flat surface. Just before the plaster hardens fully, pass a wooden float up and down the angle.

When you are satisfied that the angle is straight, you can finish it off. To do this, hold your trowel so that its toe is flat against the finished wall with one corner just touching the new plaster at the angle. By moving the trowel down the entire length of the corner you should be able to produce a clean and sharp internal angle.

When plastering two adjacent walls at the same time, the procedure for dealing with the internal angle is basically the same, but extra care is required because there is no hard surface to work from. You can use a special internal angle trowel for finishing off the angle smoothly, but it is probably not worth buying one unless you will be doing a lot of plastering.

External angles

Although it is possible to finish off external corners freehand, considerable skill would be needed; for the do-it-yourselfer there are two simple methods which will produce successful results without too much trouble. Probably the easiest of these is to use a metal angle bead, which has the added advantages of allowing simultaneous plastering of both walls and providing an extremely durable corner. The other method is to use a timber rule to form first one side of the angle and then the other.

The metal angle bead will provide a true, straight arris (corner) that will not chip. It comprises a hollow bead, flanked by two bands of perforated or expanded metal lath. Two versions are available (see *Ready Reference*): one that will take the full thickness of a floating and finishing coat of plaster, and another that is shallower for use with plasterboard. The latter is called a 'thin coat' bead.

The first type of beading is fixed by means of 30mm (1¼in) thick dabs of backing plaster applied at 600mm (2ft) intervals to both sides of the angles. After pressing the bead into place on the dabs, it is trued up and straightened with the aid of a straightedge and plumb line. Then the plaster dabs are allowed to harden before the floating coat is applied. Alternatively, the bead can be bedded in a thin strip of plaster running the full height of the wall as this makes truing up easier. It can even be pinned in place with galvanised nails, trued up and then secured with plaster pressed through the lath on the

FITTING ANGLE BEAD

1 Cut a length of angle bead to fit the height of the corner to be plastered, then spread a screed of Carlite Browning plaster down the angle.

2 Position the length of angle bead on the corner and bed its mesh wings gently in the screed. Don't press hard until you've set the bead correctly.

3 Using a long, straight-edged length of timber and a spirit level, check the plumb of the angle bead, and adjust it if necessary before the plaster sets.

4 When you've accurately positioned the angle bead on the corner, spread plaster over the mesh wings to secure it, then check its alignment again.

READY REFERENCE

TOOLS AND EQUIPMENT

You'll need the following tools and equipment for plastering angles and reveals:

- metal angle bead of the appropriate type, plus tinsnips and hacksaw for cutting it to length
- a hawk to hold the plaster close to the work
- an angle trowel (A)
- a steel trowel (B) for spreading and smoothing the plaster
- a devilling float (C) for scoring the floating coat
- a floating rule – a planed softwood batten about 75 x 25mm (3 x 1in) and 1.5m (5ft) long, to level the floating coat up to the angle.
- a reveal gauge for gauging the plaster thickness within the reveal, plus a try-square
- a spirit level for positioning angle beads.

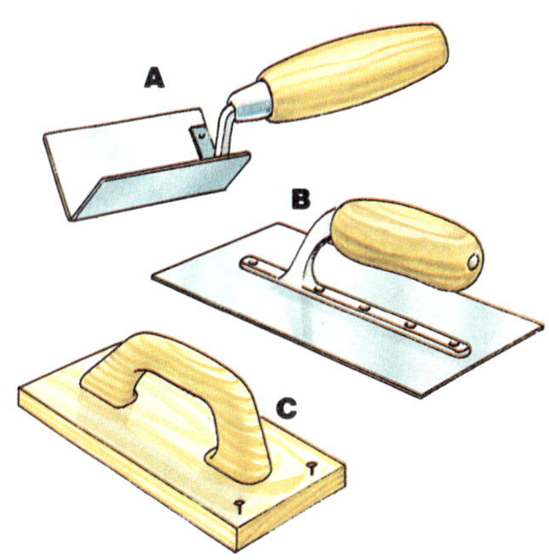

wall surface beneath. Thin coat bead is usually fitted by nailing (with galvanised nails) through the side wings into the wooden batten behind the plasterboard.

Whatever type is being used, the bead can easily be cut to length, using tinsnips to cut through the wings and a hacksaw to cut the nosing.

Once the bead is secure, it may be used as a screed for the floating coat. When this has become sufficiently hard, it should be cut back with a steel trowel to just below the level of the bead nose to allow room for the finishing coat. This coat is applied in the normal way, using the bead as a guide. When the finishing coat has been trowelled off to the angle bead, a sharp, clean and hard arris should be left exposed. The same method is used when applying the finishing coat to thin coat bead.

If you are using a wooden rule as a guide for plastering an external corner, you should nail it first to one of the walls so that it projects beyond the corner ready to act as a ground for floating the other wall. Once the floating coat has hardened on the first wall, the rule should be removed and nailed to the wall just floated to enable the second wall to be treated in the same way. Once again, you should wait until the floating coat has hardened and then remove the rule.

The next stage is to reposition the rule so that the wall floated in the first instance may be finish-coated. Wait until this coat has hardened, remove the rule once more and refix it to the second wall so you can complete the finishing coat. When this has hardened the rule may be removed.

When you remove the rule after applying the last finishing coat, you will probably find that a slight selvedge will have formed behind the rule. This should be removed by using the back edge of the laying trowel in a scything action, working away from the angle.

Sometimes you may find this tendency for a selvedge to form will allow you to finish the second wall without the aid of the rule. When you finish up to the rule on the first wall, a slight selvedge will form between the rule and the floating coat on the second wall

To finish off the plaster angle, a Surform block plane may be used lightly to produce a perfect slightly rounded corner. Alternatively, use a piece of fine abrasive paper. As with internal angles, there is a special trowel for finishing off external angles. Using angle beads or rules means you simply will not need one, however.

Door and window reveals

The narrow strips of wall at door and window openings, which are normally at right angles to the main wall surfaces, are known as

APPLYING A FLOATING COAT

1 *When the plaster retaining the bead has set, apply a floating coat between the bead nosing and the original, hard plaster at both sides of the angle.*

2 *Use a short wooden floating rule to level the backing plaster at each side of the corner. Draw the rule up the angle from bottom to top.*

3 *Place the trowel flat on the plaster, with one corner against the nosing; draw the trowel down the wall to cut in a margin for the finishing coat.*

4 *To plaster an area of wall between two corners, set a 'dot' of plaster at the base of the wall; press a small strip of wood in its centre as a thickness guide.*

5 *Lay one end of your floating rule and spirit level on the dot and the other end on the original plaster surface so that they're truly vertical.*

6 *Spread on a screed of backing plaster between the dot and the original hard plaster and level it off with your long floating rule to an even thickness.*

7 *Make another dot and screed at the other side of the area to be plastered. Spread on a floating coat between the two screeds and then rule off the surface.*

8 *Score the hardening plaster lightly with a 'devilling float', then draw the float down the angle between the original plaster and the freshly-applied coat.*

9 *Trim off the excess plaster from the angle by running the trowel down the original, hard plaster, with one corner cutting into the fresh plaster.*

FINISHING

1 *When the backing coat of plaster has set sufficiently, apply the first coat of finishing plaster, spreading it between the nosing and the hard plaster.*

2 *Apply a second coat of finishing plaster immediately after the first and smooth the surface. Use an angle trowel with a little plaster to smooth internal corners.*

3 *Trim off the excess ridge of plaster left by the sides of the angle trowel using your steel trowel. Be careful not to disturb the corner itself.*

reveals. They may also be found at the sides of a chimney breast or on a plain pier.

Actually forming the corner in this is straightforward, using the methods described previously. However, there are two points which require special attention. These are the depth of the reveals (ie, the distance from the face of the main wall to the window or door frame, or back wall) and the thickness of plaster, or 'margin', at the frame or back wall. It is essential that the depth of the reveal is the same all the way round the opening and that the plaster is the same thickness across the reveal. This will ensure that a uniform amount of frame remains visible.

Setting the depth of the reveal is simple providing the metal angle bead or fixed wooden rule for the arris is the same distance from the top of the door or window frame as it is from the bottom. Make sure, too, that it is vertical when viewed from the front.

When applying the plaster you will need a reveal gauge (see *Ready Reference*) to make sure the plaster is the same thickness all the way round. This may be simply constructed from a piece of wood which should be at least 50mm (2in) longer than the width of the reveal. After installing the metal angle bead (or fixed rule) as for external angles, lay a wooden or plastic set square (which should be long enough to reach from the back of the opening to beyond the main wall) on to the sill or floor. Push one side of its right angle against the horizontal window frame member, or bottom of the door frame, with the adjacent side against the front edge of the metal angle bead or rule. Now lay your reveal gauge on top of the square so that its long edge is in line with the set square edge that runs from the frame to the rule or bead. Using a pencil, mark the window frame end of the gauge opposite the inner edge of the window frame. Drive a nail into the end of the gauge at the pencil mark, leaving approximately 25mm (1in) protruding.

The nail acts as a shoulder when using the gauge as a horizontal rule for the plaster, supporting the inner end of the wood as you run it around the inside of the frame and maintaining an equal distance from the wall. Thus the thickness of the plaster where it meets the frame will be exactly the same all round. Or cut a right-angled notch out of the gauge to form a shoulder.

The gauge is also used to complete the underside of the reveal, although you may need to adjust the nail position if the frame is deeper at the top than down the sides. This is plastered last, after the reveal sides have been floated, and the same technique is used (with the obvious difference that you are working on a horizontal 'ceiling'). Lay on the floating coat firmly, working to the angle bead or batten, and rule off with the reveal gauge before adding the finish coat.

READY REFERENCE

TYPES OF ANGLE BEAD

There are two basic types of metal angle bead. These are:

- ordinary bead, fixed to masonry walls with dabs of plaster, which takes a floating and finishing coat of plaster (A)
- thin coat bead, nailed over the angle, which takes only a thin plaster finish on plasterboard (B).

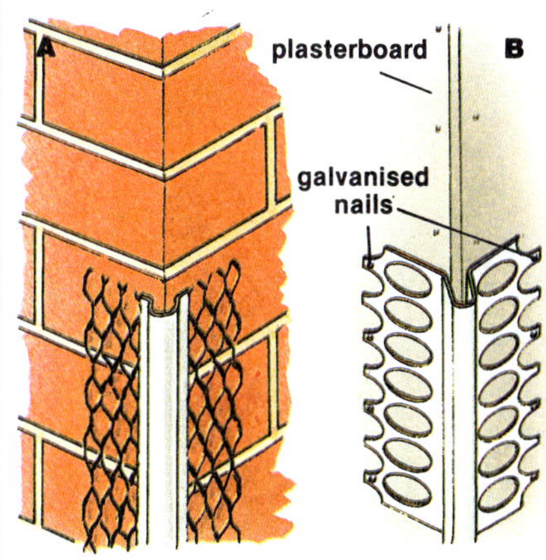

TIP: JOINING BEADS

Where you have to join two lengths of angle bead, fix the first length to the angle and insert a dowel – a short length of stout wire or a headless galvanised nail – into the nose of the bead. Then position the second length over the dowel and bed it into place.

MAKING A REVEAL GAUGE

To ensure that reveals are plastered squarely and with a uniform thickness of plaster, use a piece of softwood about 75mm (3in) larger than the reveal depth. Lay it in the reveal, against the angle rule or bead, and parallel to the blade of the square, and mark one end to match the margin on the frame. Cut out a notch and use the gauge as a short rule to level the plaster within the reveal.

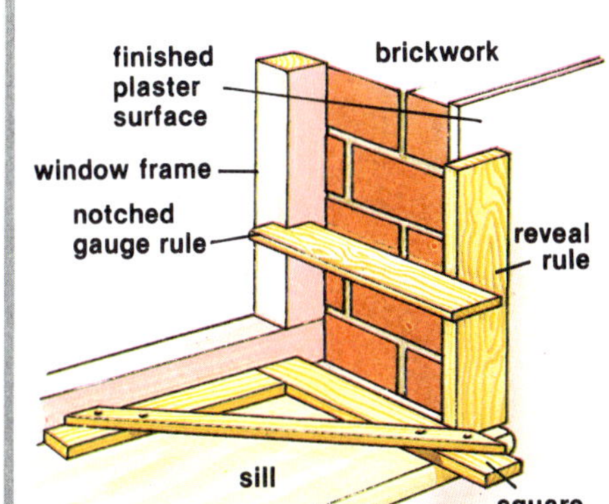

PATCHING PLASTER CEILINGS

Accidents in the loft, plumbing leaks, or simply old age can be responsible for cracks, sagging areas – or even holes – in a lath-and-plaster ceiling. But defects can often be repaired with a simple patch.

Ceilings may well be out of reach but they are, nevertheless, susceptible to damage. Accidents in the loft – a foot slipping off a joist, for instance – are a notorious cause of holes or cracks appearing. Plumbing leaks are another common source of damage, but the reason for the failure of your ceiling may simply be old age.

Types of ceiling

Modern ceilings are usually made from sheets of plasterboard nailed directly to the joists and skimmed with plaster. Accidents apart, it's unlikely that small areas of this type of ceiling will become damaged. If they do, however, you'll probably be able to remove part or all of the damaged sheet and replace it.

The ceilings of older houses, however, were usually constructed by a far more complicated method – narrow strips of timber called laths, usually measuring about 25 x 6mm (1 x 1/4in), were nailed to the joists with 10mm (3/8in) spaces between them, and the entire surface was coated with lime plaster, often mixed with animal hair fibres. The wet plaster, forced up between the laths, set to form ridges called 'nibs'. These anchored the ceiling surface in place.

Lath-and-plaster ceilings are prone to deterioration with age, and as a result of slight movement in the structure of the house. The usual signs of failure are cracks in the surface, sagging, or localised areas where the plaster has fallen away.

Whereas overall failure of your lath-and-plaster ceiling can really only be remedied by complete removal and replacement with a new one of plasterboard, minor damage can often simply be made good with an inconspicuous patch, using only basic plastering skills and tools (see pages 280–285). First of all, examine the entire ceiling to identify the type of damage and its extent; if the defects are widespread you may decide that replacement is the best bet in the long run.

Reaching the ceiling

So that you can work safely and in comfort close to the patch, you may need to hire slot-together platform tower sections or trestle stands fitted with sturdy scaffold boards – a ladder won't provide stable enough support. Your head should be about 150mm (6in) from the ceiling to enable you to work smoothly.

Covering a drab ceiling

If, on examination, you're sure that the ceiling isn't dangerously weak, and there are only minor damages to be made good, you could even conceal the poor finish by nailing up sheets of plasterboard to the joists, seal the joins, then plaster the surface.

Curing a sagging ceiling

The type of repair you make depends largely upon the extent of the damage to your ceiling. If the problem is sagging of the plaster in localised areas, for instance, this could be due to some of the nibs working loose, or even breaking off, separating the finished surface from the framework of laths.

You may be able to refix the plaster by forming new nibs. To do this you'll need to gain access to the top of the ceiling where the nibs are located – either in the loft or beneath the first floor floorboards. You will also need some assistance.

First of all, clean up the area where the nibs have come loose using a vacuum cleaner with a nozzle attachment. Then dampen the surface with water to prepare it for the new plaster: this prevents the plaster from drying out too rapidly, when it could crack.

Get your helper to push up the sagged area of ceiling gently against the underside of the joists using a home-made timber support (see *Ready Reference*). When the sagged area is back in place you can pour quick-setting plaster over the un-fixed area. Keep the ceiling propped until the new plaster has set fully, then remove the support carefully. Unless the ceiling is especially weak, the plaster should be sufficient to make a firm anchor.

There are basically two methods of repairing small sections of a damaged ceiling: the first applies where only the plaster has fallen

REPLASTERING SOUND LATHS

1 *Where the laths are sound, prepare the hole for replastering by scoring around the rough-edged perimeter with a trimming knife and metal straightedge.*

2 *Lever out the lumps of plaster within the scored lines using a trowel. Make the hole as regular in shape as you can and undercut the edges of the plaster.*

3 *Use the trowel to clear out the remains of the original nibs from between the laths, then brush away any dust. Dampen the laths with water.*

4 *Spread on a thin 'scratch' coat of Bonding plaster across the laths. Work away from obstructions such as electric cables, which should be insulated.*

5 *Use a tool called a 'comb scratcher' to key the surface. Scratch across the laths – not parallel to them – to avoid knocking out any plaster. Leave to set.*

6 *Apply a, thicker, floating coat of Carlite Bonding plaster to the patch, working onto the hard edges of the original plaster to make a firm bond.*

7 *Use an aluminium darby to rule off the floating coat. This will show up any hollows in the surface and will flatten any high spots.*

8 *Key and flatten the plaster with a devilling float, then spread on a coat of Finish plaster. Leave to set for 20 minutes, then apply a second coat.*

9 *When the finishing coat of plaster has begun to set, polish the surface with a dry trowel, paying particular attention to the join with the original plasterwork.*

REPAIRING A HOLE

1 *To repair a hole in the ceiling pull out the broken laths but leave any whole ones that aren't too bowed. Cut back the laths to the nearest joists.*

2 *Cut back the plaster to the centres of the joists, then measure the hole and cut out a piece of plasterboard to fit snugly inside.*

3 *Nail the plasterboard panel to the joists, grey side down, using 30mm (1¼in) long galvanised plasterboard nails at about 75mm (3in) centres.*

6 *Spread a coat of Carlite Bonding plaster over the entire patch, making sure it's pressed well into the edges of the hole for a better bond.*

7 *Flatten off the surface of the fresh plaster using a short wooden rule or a darby, then allow the plaster to stiffen slightly for about half an hour.*

8 *Use a devilling float to flatten the plaster to just below the finished level of the ceiling and to provide a key for the second coat of finish plaster.*

away from otherwise soundly fixed laths; the second where the laths themselves are loose, broken or even completely missing.

Plastering exposed laths

If the laths are intact and only areas of plaster have crumbled and broken away you may be able to replaster the framework as it was originally. One of the most important points to note is that the edges of the hole are sound. For this reason the first step is to cut back any loose plaster to firm fixings, making a regular-shaped hole.

Use a sharp trimming knife held against a metal straightedge to cut back the plaster It's also a wise precaution to undercut the edges of the hole to form a better bond for the new plaster.

There'll undoubtedly be some hard plaster wedged between the laths – the remains of the original nibs – and you can remove this by running the blade of your plasterer's trowel along the spaces. Brush away all dirt and dust from the laths, then dampen them with clean water to aid adhesion of the new plaster. When you apply the new plaster, the water in the mix will tend to be absorbed by the old plasterwork. This can cause serious staining to the original surface, so you can also treat the laths and the edges of the hole with a coat of PVA adhesive to improve adhesion of the plaster and minimise the suction of the background.

Spread on a fairly thin 'scratch' coat of Carlite Bonding plaster with a plasterer's trowel, working across the laths to force the plaster up between them. Use a tool called a 'comb scratcher' (see *Ready Reference*) to key the surface to accept the floating coat of plaster. Work across the laths – not along them – to prevent knocking out any of the fresh plaster, and don't criss-cross the scratches or you'll weaken the plaster key.

When the scratch coat has set, spread on the floating coat of plaster and rule it off using a darby (see *Ready Reference*). Again key the surface, this time using a devilling float and apply a coat of Carlite Finish plaster. After about half an hour you can spread on a final coat of finish plaster. When this has set, trowel the surface to a smooth, polished finish.

Always spread on the plaster away from any obstructions and towards the hard plaster edge of the hole to prevent an ugly ridge forming. Pay particular attention to this join between the patch and the original ceiling, cutting back the edges with your trowel when the plaster has started to set.

Using 'haired' plaster

When you're plastering an area of lathwork you can use a mix of sand and plaster with some fibrous material added – chopped sisal

4 *Dampen the surrounding paper and the edges of the original plasterwork with an old paintbrush, to ease stripping the paper and to prepare the plaster.*

5 *When the paper is soft scrape back a 50mm (2in) margin around the hole so that the new plaster can be spread on to the correct level.*

9 *Trim up the patch using your steel laying trowel. Make sure the new plaster is recessed a little to allow for the thickness of the finishing coat.*

10 *Spread two coats of Carlite Finish plaster onto the patch and then polish the surface when it has begun to set, using a clean trowel lubricated with water.*

is commonly used – to help bind it to the lathwork, only for the first coat. Or you can obtain special 'haired' Browning plaster, which has a fibrous content, for the first coat. For most small areas, however, this may not be an economical proposition.

Patching broken laths

Where any of the laths have worked loose you may just be able to refix them to the joists with nails, and then replaster as previously described. But if any of the laths are broken or bowed you must remove them as far as sound fixings at the joists. Cut back the plaster at the perimeter of the hole to the nearest joists, using a trimming knife. Then measure up for and cut a panel of plasterboard to fit snugly within the resultant hole.

Nail the plasterboard to the joists using 30mm (1 1/4in) long galvanised plasterboard nails at 150mm (6in) centres; then dampen the surrounding ceiling paper and existing plaster edges with clean water, both to soften the paper for removal and to prepare the plasterwork for the new coat. Scrape off the paper so you've a margin of bare plaster to blend the new finish into at the correct level.

Apply a coat of Carlite Bonding plaster to the patch and rule off the surface using a wooden feather-edged rule or a darby. Use a devilling float to flatten the new plaster to just below the level of the surrounding hard plaster, to accommodate the thickness of the finishing coat, and provide a key for it.

Finally, apply two coats of Carlite Finish plaster, working onto the hard edge; then polish the surface when it's set, lubricating your trowel with water splashed on from a brush.

Leave the patch to dry out thoroughly for about two or three days, before decorating with paint or paper.

READY REFERENCE

PATCHING HOLES

There are basically two ways to patch a hole in a ceiling. These are:

- to replaster existing soundly-fixed laths or
- to nail a panel of plasterboard, grey side down, to the joists where the laths are missing, and to plaster the surface.

TOOLS FOR PLASTERING

To plaster a defective area of ceiling you'll need few specialist tools. These are:

- a steel laying trowel
- a wooden feather-edged rule
- a devilling float
- a comb scratcher (A)
- an aluminium darby (B).

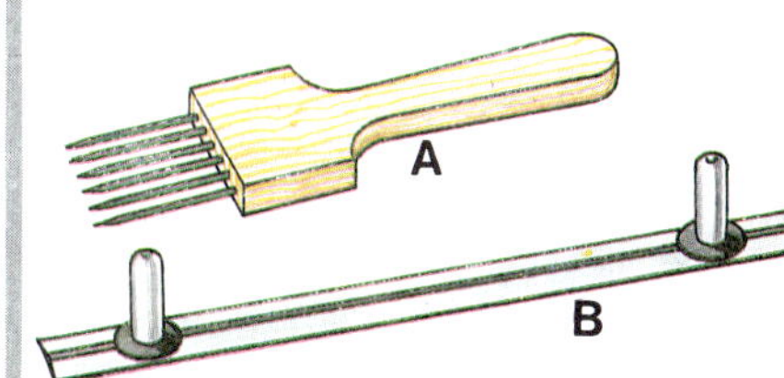

TIP: PREVENT STAINING

When you patch an area of ceiling, moisture absorbed from the fresh plaster by the existing plaster can cause serious staining. To avoid this, and greatly improve the adhesion of the new plaster, treat the laths and the plaster at the perimeter of the hole with a coat of PVA adhesive.

PROPPING SAGGING AREAS

You may be able to push back an area of ceiling that's sagged and then form new nibs. To do this:

- make a prop from 50 x 50mm (2 x 2in) softwood with a panel of chipboard screwed on top
- use the support to gently push the sagged plaster against the joists and wedge it between floor and ceiling (A)
- pour quick-setting plaster onto the laths at the top of the ceiling to form new nibs
- remove the prop when the plaster has set.

For more information on plastering see Working with plaster.
For more information on making a new ceiling see Replacing an old ceiling.

PLASTERING PLASTERBOARD

A timber stud partition makes a sturdy wall dividing up a room. You can clad it with sheets of plasterboard and finish the surface with a skim coat of plaster so it looks like an integral part of the house's structure.

You can build a timber-frame partition to divide a room into two separate areas using only basic carpentry techniques. In doing so you'll not only add areas of interest to the room but gain some extra space for putting up shelves and storing items.

Your partition can be built from floor to ceiling and wall to wall, or else simply project into the room; you can also incorporate a doorway, serving hatch or glazed areas. Timber studs form the frame of the wall and you can clad it with one of a variety of sheet materials to give a finish which can be easily decorated to match adjacent walls.

Insulating wallboards, which are made of lightweight fibre, can be used to give a surface you can paint or paper. They give good thermal and sound insulation but they're fairly soft and therefore susceptible to knocks.

You can also fix sheets of plywood and hardboard with a natural wood veneer or a plastic coating printed on one side to simulate natural wood; some even come with a decorative finish of imitation ceramic tiles. You might, however, prefer the look of real timber cladding on lengths of tongued and grooved knotty pine, for example.

Asbestos boards can also be used to clad your partition where you need some resistance to fire. They're normally used underneath other wallboards.

These materials are adequate if you want a ready-made decorative finish or a surface that you can paint or paper, but if you'd like your partition to look like a solid, integral part of the house, the best treatment is to plaster it to match adjacent walls.

To give your partition a suitable surface for plastering you'll have to nail sheets of plasterboard (see *Ready Reference*) to the studs. This is a sheet material that consists of a core of gypsum plaster sandwiched between two sheets of heavy-duty paper. There are various grades for use on ceilings or on walls that require insulation but the ones to use for a stud partition are called 'dry lining boards'.

They have a grey side intended for plastering and an ivory-coloured side specially prepared for decorating directly with paint or wallpaper.

Cladding the partition

Plasterboard cladding is nailed to the wooden framework of the partition wall so you'll have to take into account the dimensions of the sheets when spacing out the studs.

The commonest sheet size is 2440 × 1220mm (8 × 4ft), but a number of other sizes are available. Remember to space studs accurately so their centres coincide with joins between adjacent sheets; with 1220mm (4ft) wide sheets the studs should be at 610mm (2ft) centres.

If your house has very high ceilings a 2440mm (8ft) long sheet might not fit exactly from floor to ceiling height so you'll have to add a smaller panel above it. Fix extra noggins (see *Ready Reference*) to coincide with the horizontal joints in the cladding, so you can nail the boards in place.

It's best to stagger these horizontal joints in the cladding, to prevent the likelihood of the surface plaster cracking across the wall, and to stiffen the partition The way to do this is to fix the first whole sheet at the top of the partition and fill in the gap below with a cut piece, then to fit the second whole sheet at the bottom and clad the gap at the top (see *Ready Reference*). It's a good idea to use the waste piece from the first cut sheet to fill the gap in the second row, to avoid wastage.

Leave cladding around any doorways or

READY REFERENCE

WHAT IS PLASTERBOARD?

Plasterboard is a layer of gypsum plaster sandwiched between two layers of heavy paper. There are various types available for different uses:

- dry lining boards have a grey side for plastering and an ivory-coloured side for decorating with paint, wallpaper or a textured finish

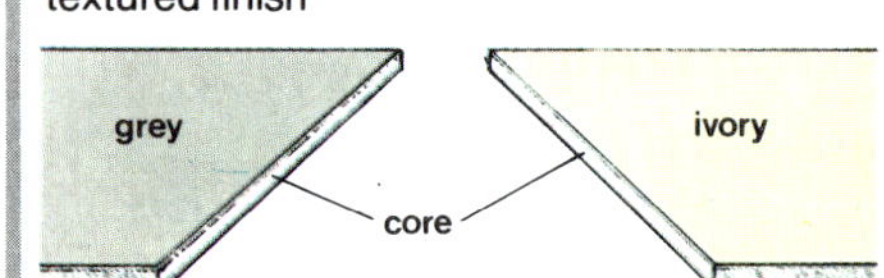

- baseboards have grey paper for plastering on both sides; they're generally used for ceilings
- insulating plasterboards have a layer of aluminium foil on one side to reflect heat back into the room and to stop moisture penetrating the partition.

PLASTER COVERAGE

One 50kg (1cwt) sack of Thistle Board Finish will make about three bucketfuls of plaster, enough to cover about 8 sq m (85 sq ft). It'll set in about 1½ hours and can be decorated after about 24 hours.

hatch openings until you've fixed all the full-width sheets you can. The best place to start fixing the boards to a half-partition is at the free end. Make sure the first sheet is flush with the end of the partition, parallel with the studs, and that the inner edge runs up the centre of an intermediate stud.

If you're cladding a wall-to-wall partition, however, you can start nailing on the boards at either end. You'll probably have to scribe and cut one edge of the first sheet to butt up with the adjacent wall accurately: few walls are truly vertical (see *Ready Reference*).

Fixing the plasterboard

You'll find that sheets of plasterboard are fairly heavy and cumbersome for one person to lift and the corners are likely to break off if knocked or dropped. When you're carrying a sheet you should grip it at each side at about shoulder height and tilt back the top so that you can walk without kicking it; if you allow it to tilt forward it'll tend to pull you over. You'll probably find it easiest to walk sideways with the board. When you reach the partition, set it down first then lean it against the wall.

To fit your first sheet of plasterboard measure the height of the partition and if it's less than the length of the board, transfer this dimension to one face and subtract about 12mm (½in). Scribe a line against a straight edge across the board using a sharp trimming knife and 'snap' back the waste piece. Run the knife up the opposite side to cut through the paper and free the waste piece.

It's important that the sheet is fixed tightly at the ceiling, so offer it up to the wall, pushing it up with a 12mm (½in) gap at the floor. There's a simple device you can use to lever the plasterboard into position. It's called a 'foot-lifter' and you can make it yourself from a small block of softwood and a thinner strip, which fits on top. It works like a seesaw, levering up the board from the floor so you can make the first fixings at both sides. When you've hammered in a few nails at each side you can remove the footlifter and hammer in the remaining nails.

Use only galvanised plasterboard nails 30mm (1¼in) long, evenly spaced about 150mm (6in) apart and no closer to the edge of the board than 12mm (½in) or there's a danger that the edge might tear away. Don't use ordinary nails that aren't galvanised or they'll rust and stain the plaster finish.

Hammer in the nail so that the head just grips the surface of the paper without tearing or punching its way through. If you don't hammer it in this far the projecting head will be visible on the finished plaster surface; if you knock it in too far so that it punctures the paper any subsequent vibrations will work the plasterboard loose.

Continue along the partition, nailing up whole sheets of plasterboard. If you find that they don't overlap the studs half-way you've made an error in the initial setting-out. This will have a cumulative effect across the wall but you won't have to remove all the boards to remedy the fault: simply cut one sheet to the required width.

Your last sheet of plasterboard will probably be narrower than a full sheet so you'll have to cut it to size. If the adjoining wall is fairly straight and vertical (test this with a spirit level) you can just measure the width of the gap, transfer this to the board and cut off the waste. Fit the board in the same way as the others. But if the wall's untrue you'll have to cut the cladding to fit the profile.

Hold the sheet against the partition, using your footlifter, and butt its edge up to the wall. Make sure that the opposite edge is parallel with the edge of the last fixed sheet or stud. There's a simple trick you can use to scribe the profile of the wall onto the face of the plasterboard: hold a small block of wood and a pencil against the wall and draw it along to mark the profile of the wall on the face of the board (see *Ready Reference*). Lie the board flat on the floor and carefully cut along the guideline with a sharp knife. Return the board to the wall and butt the cut edge up to the wall. Mark the opposite side where it falls halfway between the last stud. Cut off the waste and nail the sheet in place.

When you've covered one side of the partition you can move to the opposite side and clad that in the same way. Now's the time to add some form of thermal or sound insulation to the cavity between the two skins. You can cut strips of insulating fibreboard or sheets of expanded polystyrene to fit between the studs before you fix the second skin.

Don't forget that now is also the time to lay in any electric wiring or pipe runs that traverse the wall.

Plastering the plasterboard

You can apply a finishing coat of plaster to the partition as soon as you've nailed all the

CUTTING PLASTERBOARD

1 *Mark the height of the partition on the plasterboard, less 12mm (½in) for fitting, and scribe across the sheet with a trimming knife.*

2 *Hold the board against your side and grip the top end. Slap your other hand sharply on the waste piece, pulling it back gently as you do so.*

3 *The plaster core within the board should snap cleanly along the line of your cut, but the waste piece will be held by the paper lining at the back.*

4 *Go around to the other side of the sheet and, with the waste piece bent back, run your knife up the fold in the paper backing to remove it.*

5 You'll probably have to cut a sheet to width at the end of the partition. Measure the space at the top, centre and bottom of the partition.

6 If the wall is fairly even, simply transfer your measurements to the board, scribe along the side of a timber straight edge and cut off the waste.

TIP

7 To fit the board tightly into the ceiling angle you'll need a 'footlifter', made from two offcuts of wood, which you use to lever up the sheet.

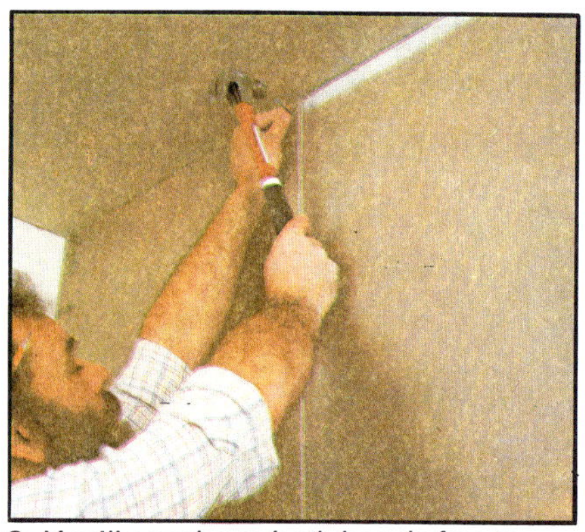

8 You'll now have both hands free to nail the plasterboard to the studs, using 30mm (1¼in) galvanised plasterboard nails 12mm (½in) in from the edge.

plasterboard sheets in place. When the plaster is set you can then decorate the surface with wallcovering, tiles, or just emulsion paint, to match adjacent walls.

You'll probably find plastering dry lining boards much easier than plastering a wall made of bricks or blocks because you don't need to worry about how absorbent the surface is (see Working with plaster, pages 280–285): the heavy grey paper that lines the board does away with the need to apply a backing coat of plaster.

The correct plaster to use on an internal stud partition is a ready-mixed gypsum plaster called Thistle Board Finish. It's usually spread on to the wall in two parts; the first is intended to cover the joints between the boards and the second is a flat, finishing coat.

Using the plasterer's tools

Plastering a large area of wall requires some skill in handling the various tools (see *Ready Reference*) and the only way to acquire this is to practise. First mix the plaster; you can do this in a 14 litre (3 gallon) bucket. Half-fill the bucket with perfectly clean water – any dirt that gets into the mix could affect the setting time and mar the finish – and add handfuls of plaster until you've almost filled the bucket. Leave the mix to soak until all of the dry plaster has been absorbed by the water, then stir vigorously with a stout stick. The plaster should have a smooth, creamy consistency – like melting ice cream.

The main tools you'll need are a steel trowel to apply the plaster and a hawk to hold the plaster close to the wall. If you're right-handed, hold the hawk in your left hand (resting on your thumb and index finger) and the trowel in your right. Your index finger should be against the shank of the trowel, with the toe of the trowel pointing left. Your knuckles should be uppermost.

It's a good idea to practise loading the trowel and spreading the plaster (see photographs on pages 282–283) on a spare

READY REFERENCE

TOOLS AND EQUIPMENT

You'll need the following tools for plastering your stud partition:

- steel trowel for spreading on and smoothing the plaster (A)
- hawk of wood or aluminium to hold small amounts of plaster (B)
- spot board to hold large amounts of plaster

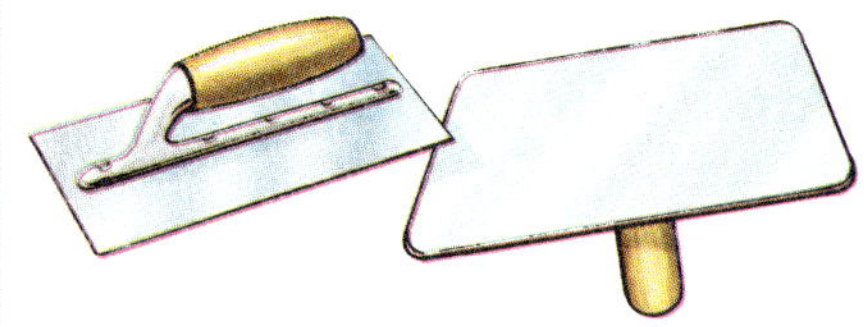

- two 14 litre (3 gallon) plastic buckets – one for mixing plaster, the other to hold clean water for mixing.

WHAT IS A STUD PARTITION?

A timber stud partition consists of:

- a timber sole plate, which runs the length of the partition at floor level
- a timber top plate, which runs the length of the partition at ceiling level
- vertical timber studs at intervals along the partition, their centres coinciding with joins in the plasterboard
- horizontal timber noggins nailed between the studs to strengthen the structure and provide support for the plasterboard cladding.

CLADDING A TALL ROOM

If your house has tall rooms a standard-sized sheet of plasterboard might not fit from floor to ceiling. You'll have to cut a piece to fill the gap. Avoid a continuous line across the partition, which could cause the plaster surface to crack, by staggering the joins. Proceed as follows:

- nail the first full sheet at floor level to the studs and noggins and fill the gap above with a cut piece
- fix the second full sheet at ceiling level and fill the gap below with a cut piece; use the waste from your first cut sheet
- continue across the partition alternating full sheets and cut sheets.

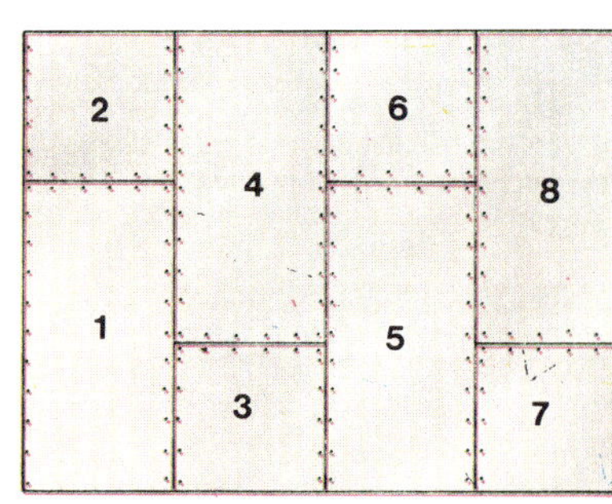

SCRIMMING THE JOINTS

1 *When you've nailed up all of the cladding, cut lengths of narrow tape (called 'scrim') to cover each joint from floor to ceiling.*

2 *Mix up some plaster and take a small amount on your hawk to the partition. Spread a thin 50mm (2in) wide layer along the joint from floor to ceiling.*

3 *Drape a length of scrim over your trowel and press it into the strip of wet plaster at the top of the partition. Then draw the trowel down the joint.*

4 *When you've laid the first length of scrim, trowel lightly over the surface from the bottom to the top to bed the tape completely in plaster.*

5 *You'll also have to seal any horizontal joints with scrim. Spread on the plaster as before, with your trowel blade held at 30° to the wall.*

6 *Press the scrim into the plaster and trowel it smooth. You mustn't allow an overlap of scrim where a horizontal joint meets a vertical joint.*

sheet of plasterboard until you're confident you can get the plaster to stick before attempting to plaster the partition.

Sealing the joints

Before you can apply the plaster you must seal the joints between the sheets so they won't show through on the finished surface. This is done by embedding a strip of hessian called 'scrim' in a thin layer of plaster covering each joint. Next you apply a thin coat of plaster to the board between the scrimmed joints to make the surface level again. The finishing coat is applied after this to conceal the joints, and you can polish it to a smooth, matt surface.

Scrim is sold by builder's merchants in rolls 100m (330ft) long × 75mm (3in) wide. It's best to cut your scrim to the length of the joints before you mix your plaster. If there are any horizontal joints in your wall you'll have to scrim these also. You mustn't fold or overlap the scrim as double thicknesses will prevent the plaster from sticking properly and will cause unsightly bulges on the finished surface. Where a horizontal joint meets a vertical joint you'll have to butt up the strips.

To stick the scrim to the wall, spread a thin 100mm (4in) wide strip of Thistle Board Finish along the first joint with a steel trowel. Drape one end of the scrim over the top of your trowel and position it on the screed at the top of the wall: you might need a stepladder to reach the top. Keep the trowel blade at about 30° to the surface of the wall and draw it down the joint, feeding the scrim on to the plaster strip with your free hand. Don't press too hard or you'll drag the scrim down the wall and might even tear it. When you've positioned the first strip, pass the trowel lightly over the joint from the bottom upwards to embed it in the plaster. Scrim the second joint in the same way, forming a 'bay' between the two joints. When the plaster has begun to set it'll turn from dark pink to light pink in colour and when this happens you should spread a thin layer of plaster over the bay, working from the bottom left hand side of the wall. This will bring the whole plastered surface to the level of the scrimmed joints. Scrim the remaining joints and plaster the bays between them.

By the time you've applied the first coat of plaster to the entire wall the surface will be set hard enough to acept the second, finishing coat. Apply an even layer of plaster 4mm (just over ⅛in) thick to the entire surface of the wall, again working from the bottom left, but this time make your strokes long, light, and sweeping to avoid ridges in the plaster.

When the finishing coat has almost set, go back over the area with your trowel – without any plaster – to give a smooth finish. When it's completely set, trowel again but splash a little clean water onto the wall from a brush to lubricate the trowel and create a polished and perfectly smooth surface.

PLASTERING THE PARTITION

1 Spread on the plaster in the bays between the scrimmed joints. Work from the bottom left, spreading a very thin layer of plaster.

2 You'll have to spread the plaster from the ceiling angle downwards to make a clean, neat edge and to avoid smearing the ceiling with plaster.

3 Complete the bay, applying a very thin coat of plaster, if required, from bottom to top. Try to avoid creating a build-up of plaster over the scrim.

4 Plaster the subsequent bays with a thin coat; by the time you've finished the plaster will have set enough to accept the finishing coat.

5 Spread on the finishing coat over the entire surface of the wall, working with long, sweeping strokes to remove any ridges in the plaster.

6 When the plaster has set trowel over it to polish and flatten the surface. Repeat this several times, lubricating the wall with a little water.

READY REFERENCE

FITTING TO AN UNEVEN WALL

If the wall which your timber stud partition meets is uneven or not truly vertical you'll have to cut the sheet of plasterboard to fit its profile. To do this:

- lightly tack the plasterboard against the partition, one edge butted up to the uneven wall, the other vertical
- place a small block of wood and a pencil against the wall, resting on the plasterboard
- draw the block and pencil up the angle to mark the profile of the uneven wall on the face of the plasterboard
- lie the board on the floor and cut along the guideline using your trimming knife
- return the board to the partition and butt up the cut edge to the uneven wall
- mark on the other edge of the board the position of the stud centre
- cut off the waste and nail up the board.

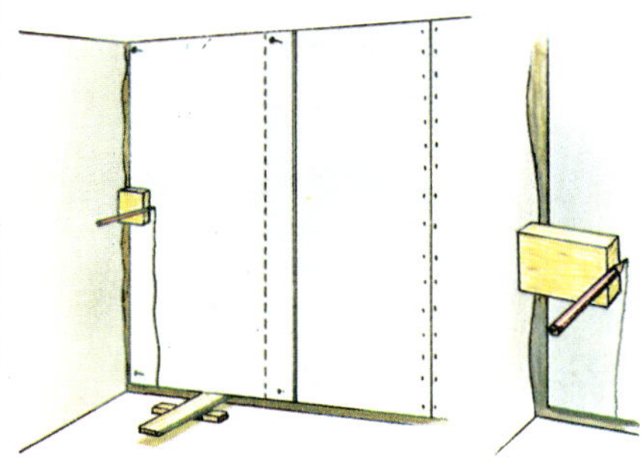

FINISHING HALF-PARTITIONS

To plaster the end of a half-partition:

- nail a plasterboard strip to the end stud
- scrim the external corners
- tack thin battens to the end, projecting over the corners by 3mm (1/8in)
- plaster both faces of the partition using the battens as thickness guides
- remove the battens when the plaster's set. Refix them to the faces of the wall, projecting 3mm (1/8in) over the end
- plaster the end (A)
- or bed 'thin coat metal angle bead' in plaster on each corner and use its 'nose' as a thickness guide (B).

A

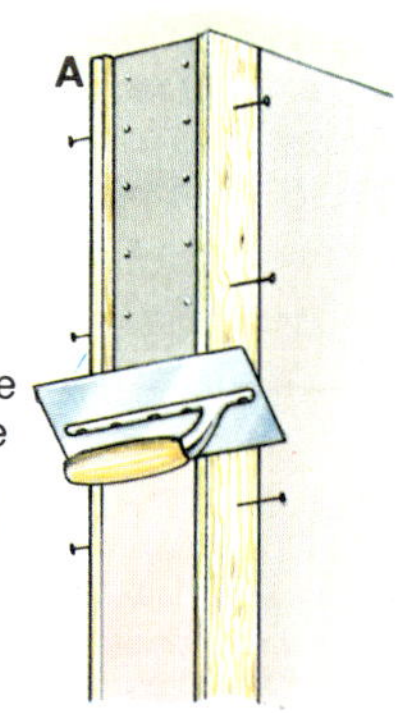

B

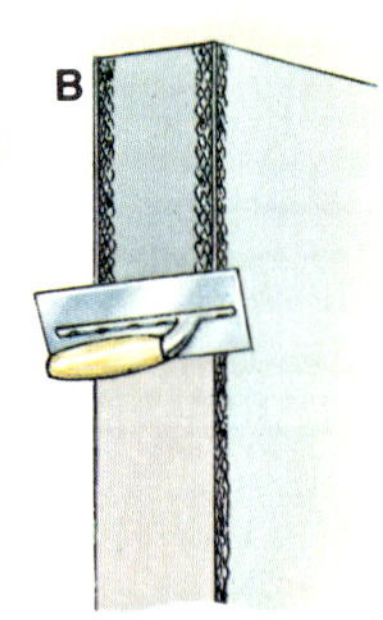

WALLS AND WALLING

Using the basic techniques of bricklaying, it's a short step to tackling simple garden walls – freestanding, or to retain earth and create split-level effects in sloping gardens. Perhaps the simplest type to build is the screen block wall, using square blocks available in a range of attractive pierced designs. If you want earth-retaining walls, you must build more sturdily and remember to allow water to drain from behind the wall.

BUILDING RETAINING WALLS

Regardless of whether your garden is flat or sloping, earth-retaining walls are an ideal way of remodelling it to create interesting features such as a raised lawn, a sunken patio or terraced flower beds.

A sloping garden, although it may be an attractive, natural-looking feature of your property, can be hard work to keep in good order. You'll probably find it tiresome to work on, especially if you have to carry heavy tools and equipment such as the lawnmower to the top.

You can, however, landscape the shape of the bank into a series of flat terraces, connected by steps which not only offer easier access when gardening but also give you greater flexibility in planning your planting arrangements.

But you needn't only alter the shape of a sloping plot; it's also possible to re-style a flat, featureless site by building a raised flower-bed, lawn or patio. By digging out areas of your garden you can even create sunken features.

However you design your new scheme you'll have to incorporate in it a solid, load-bearing barrier called a retaining wall, which must be strong enough to support your remodelled earth and prevent the soil from spilling onto the lower level.

Planning a retaining wall

The scale of your wall largely depends on the amount of earth it's to retain and the steepness of the bank. But if it's to be over about 1.2m (4ft) high, you should consult your local authority. They may demand that you include some form of safety measures for the structure or that you adhere to certain building standards, especially if it's part of a boundary wall, where it could affect public access.

Start planning by sketching out your landscaping ideas, and try to keep your terraced or sunken features in scale with the rest of the garden. If you simply want to border a shallow sunken patio or path, for instance, or create a raised lawn or flower-bed in a level garden, you could build a fairly low wall, 300 or 600mm (1 or 2ft) high, and lay flat coping stones on top to use as informal seating, or as a display for garden ornaments or plants in containers.

A gradual sloping site with two or more terraces will allow you more scope for varied planing than a single, high 'platform' would, and also forms a much stronger structure because there's less weight bearing on the individual walls.

Where you're building a flight of steps in a bank to connect your terraces, you may need to include 'stepped' retaining walls at each side to stop the earth from spilling onto the treads.

When you're remodelling your ground don't forget to set aside any topsoil and re-use it for any new planting beds. The remaining areas that you excavate for foundations must be well consolidated or compacted, then levelled, on a layer or hardcore, so that they're firm enough for normal traffic without danger of subsiding.

Laying the foundations

The prime requirement for your wall, whatever building material you use, is to build it on adequate foundations set below the frost line (see *Ready Reference*).

In effect, your foundations should be a cast concrete strip or 'raft' foundation the length of the wall and about twice its width. For example, for a typical 225mm (9in) thick brick wall 1.2m (4ft) high, built on clay soil, you'll have to lay your concrete 500mm (20in) wide and 150mm (6in) thick. Set the entire foundation in a trench about 500mm (20in) below soil level. In very loose soil you'll have to increase the width of the strip, or build a 'key', which projects down at the toe, or outer edge of the

READY REFERENCE

PARTS OF THE WALL

A retaining wall must have enough mass and sufficiently solid foundations to resist the lateral, or sideways, pressure of piled earth and the water that builds up within it. A typical retaining wall up to 1.2m (4ft) high should consist of:

- cast concrete strip foundations (A) the length of the wall, 500mm (20in) wide, 150mm (6in) thick, and set in a trench 500mm (20in) below soil level
- rigid construction using bricks (B), blocks or stone
- adequate drainage from the back of the wall (C).

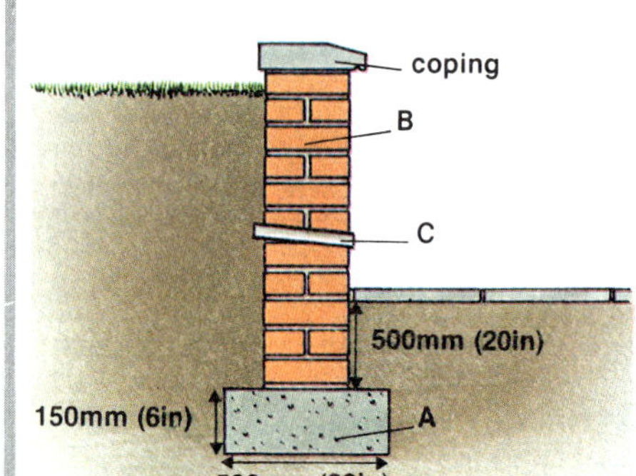

BUILDING UP TO GROUND LEVEL

1 *Start laying the first bricks at a corner if one is planned, at one end of the wall otherwise. Bed down the bricks in the outer 'skin' first.*

2 *Having laid several bricks on each side of the corner, lay the first course of the inner 'skin' alongside them. Note how the bond is arranged.*

3 *With the first course complete at the corner, check with a builders' square that there is a perfect right angle inside and outside the corner.*

4 *Return to the corner, and start to lay the second course of brickwork in the outer skin, scraping off excess mortar with the side of the trowel.*

5 *After laying two or three courses of stretchers, lay the next course as headers – a bonding pattern known as English Garden Wall bond.*

6 *As you add each course to the wall, check that it is level, that the faces of the wall are truly vertical and that the corner is a true right angle.*

7 *When the footings reach ground level, form drainage holes in the wall by bedding short lengths of plastic waste pipe in a generous mortar bed.*

8 *Check that the pipe slopes down towards the outer face of the wall at a slight angle so that it will drain water away efficiently.*

9 *With the piece of pipe in place, you will have to cut the bricks in the inner and outer skin of the wall to maintain the bonding pattern.*

10 *Continue building up the wall above ground level, alternating three to five courses of stretchers with a course of headers.*

11 *As an alternative to building in short lengths of pipe to provide drainage, you can form weep holes – simple gaps left between the bricks.*

12 *Where you have left weep holes in the ground-level course, lay the next course as stretchers to bridge them and maintain the wall's strength.*

foundation, to help prevent the wall sliding forwards under pressure from the retained earth (see *Ready Reference*).

Choosing walling materials

Your earth-retaining wall must have enough mass, as well as sufficiently solid foundations, to resist the lateral, or sideways, pressure of the retained soil and the rainwater that collects in it (see *Ready Reference*). So long as you provide this strength, you can build your wall from most common building materials – bricks, concrete or stone blocks, cast concrete, and even timber. Which you choose depends on the visual effect you want to achieve and on the conditions you're building in.

Bricks must be dense and durable to withstand the damp conditions to which your wall will be exposed, and can give a neat, formal appearance in a garden that has rigidly defined areas, such as lawn, patio and rockery. Choose 'special quality' or engineering bricks which are quite impervious and ideal in wet surroundings. Ordinary quality or common bricks are far too porous and susceptible to frost damage, although if your wall's going to be fairly small and in a sheltered situation you can use the more attractive second-hand ordinaries in conjunction with a water-proofing treatment (see below).

The strength of a brick wall is in its bonding and the mortar mix used. A brick retaining wall, therefore, must be built a minimum of 225mm (9in) – or one whole brick – thick in a tough bond such as Flemish, English, or English Garden Wall bond for strength.

Concrete blocks, which are much larger than bricks and much lighter to handle enable you to build a high wall relatively quickly. They're available either solid or with hollow cavities to take reinforcement (see *Ready Reference*, page 304). Make sure you choose dense quality blocks that are suitable for use underground.

If you don't like the plain, functional look of concrete blocks you can clad the completed wall with a cement render, or coat it with a textured masonry paint. A rendered finish, though, is likely to crack eventually in damp conditions. Alternatively you can just use the blocks underground and continue the wall above ground with bricks. Concrete blocks should be laid in stretcher bond to give the strongest structure.

Decorative concrete walling blocks are suitable for low retaining walls; they're available both in brick size and in the larger 215x440mm (9x18in) size, and usually have a split-stone or riven face for a more natural, softer look. They also come in a range of reds, greens, and buff tones for a more attractive finish. You should only use this

READY REFERENCE

DRAINING THE BANK

To prevent a build-up of rainwater behind the retaining wall:

- leave vertical joints free of mortar every 1m (3ft) just above lower ground level to act as weep holes, or
- bed 75mm (3in) diameter drainage pipes in the wall every 1m (3ft) just above lower ground level
- additionally, bury lengths of pipe in pockets of gravel behind the wall to drain water to the sides of the wall
- include a trench 200mm (8in) wide, filled with layers of compacted bricks, pebbles or gravel for rapid drainage.

TIP: WATERPROOF THE WALL

Although it's impossible to waterproof an earth-retaining wall totally, you can reduce the risk of serious damp penetration by:

- painting the back face of the wall with two coats of bituminous paint, or
- tacking a 250-gauge thick polythene sheet to the back face of the wall.

PREVENTING LANDSLIDES

In loose soils your wall may tend to be pushed forward by the weight of the retained earth. To prevent this:

- form a 'key' at the toe of your strip foundation
- set your wall and foundation at an angle or 'batter' – no more than 1 in 5 – into the bank
- build the bank side of the wall in steps, becoming narrower at the top.

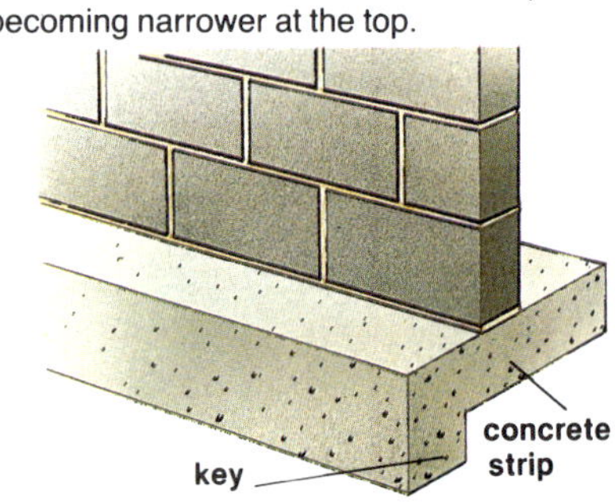

INSTALL MOVEMENT JOINTS

A long retaining wall will need a break in the bond, called a movement joint, which allows for seasonal expansion or contraction and prevents the masonry from cracking. Joints should be:

- the height of the wall
- filled with strips of expanded polystyrene
- pointed with a weak mortar mix to conceal the polystyrene filling.

In a brick wall:

- leave joints every 3.6m (12ft)

In a block wall:

- leave joints every 1.8m (6ft).

COMPLETING THE WALL

1 Instead of English Garden Wall bond, you can use Flemish bond; each course has alternate stretchers and headers laid as shown.

TIP

2 When your wall has reached the height you want, finish it off with a soldier course – a course of bricks laid on edge to form a coping.

3 Since the top of the wall is the most exposed, ensure that a complete layer of mortar is 'chopped' down between each of the soldiers.

4 Complete the soldier course by pointing neatly between the bricks. Rounded joints, formed with a piece of metal or hosepipe, look neatest.

5 Finish the job by brushing down all the wall surfaces with a soft brush to remove any excess mortar that could stain the brickwork.

6 Leave the wall to stand for a few days, then start to back-fill behind it, tamping the soil down gently but firmly as the level rises.

type of block above ground. Use the same bonding patterns as bricks for a stronger structure.

A cast concrete retaining wall is tough and durable, but it has a drab, slab-like appearance and calls for the construction of sturdy timber formwork to mould the mix while it hardens. If you think you'll need such a robust structure you can make it look a little more attractive by adding a pigment to the mix.

You can even build a dry stone retaining wall for an unobtrusive cottage-style garden wall, although it's not suitable for holding high banks or heavy soil weights. The irregular soil-filled gaps between each stone make ideal places for introducing creeping plants to mellow the overall look of the wall. In this type of wall, each stone must be tilted downwards into the bank, forming a slanted or 'battered' wall. This will increase the strength of the structure, and will also give it a much less formal appearance.

Naturally rot-resistant hardwoods or preservative-treated timber can be used to make a wooden earth retaining wall, or you can use it as cladding for a concrete or blockwork wall. Railway sleepers, for instance, which you can often buy from specialist suppliers, can be used to make sturdy retaining walls if you pile them on top of each other, or stick them in the ground vertically, and support them with steel rods or stout fence posts set in concrete foundations. You could even stack concrete or wooden fence posts in this fashion, or in a dove-tailed design, to leave small soil-filled gaps between each post for planting.

Reinforcing the wall

Brick walls and walls made of small-scale block materials are susceptible to bulging outwards under pressure. You can reinforce them by setting hooked metal rods in their mortar joints, which project through the back of the wall into the bank where they're 'tied' to blocks of cast concrete called 'deadmen', which act as stabilisers. Timber retaining walls can be reinforced with a similar arrangement of sturdy timber braces set in the bank.

In a hollow concrete block wall you can lay a wider strip foundation on the downhill or outer side of the wall and set in it L-shaped steel rods on which you can slot the blocks for extra reinforcement (see *Ready Reference*), then fill in the block cavities with concrete.

A tall wall over about 1.2m (4ft) high must incorporate supporting columns called 'piers' (see *Ready Reference*) at each end, and also at intermediate positions along its length if it's very long. You may, though, just want to include piers in a smaller wall purely for visual effect, where the wall breaks at each side of a flight of steps, or where the wall must support a heavy gate.

In a brickwork wall you should bond the piers into the structure for strength but in solid block walls you can simply tie a stack-bonded pier to the wall by setting galvanised expanded metal mesh in the horizontal mortar joints.

A wall of hollow concrete blocks can be similarly tied to a matching pier with special metal cramps, and the hollow cavities can then be filled with concrete for extra rigidity.

Another means of reinforcing an earth-retaining wall is to build it thicker at its base, stepping back the courses from the earth side to the final thickness at the top (see *Ready Reference*, page 302).

Long walls must also incorporate breaks in the bond called 'movement joints', which allow for seasonal expansion and contraction. Joints should run the full height of the wall and can be packed with a compressible material such as expanded polystyrene which can then be pointed with a weak mortar mix to conceal the gap. You should leave movement joints at every 3.6m (12ft) in brick walls and at every 1.8m (6ft) in block walls.

Drainage and damp-proofing

Because of their location, buried in the ground and holding back a large amount of earth, retaining walls are susceptible to dampness. It's vital, therefore, that you include adequate drainage in the structure so that the earth behind doesn't become waterlogged and heavy. In the long run this would weaken the wall and could even cause it to collapse. Freezing water trapped behind the wall could also cause the masonry to crack.

You can provide drainage in two areas: at the back of the wall and actually through its face. To drain the back you can set pipes of porous, unglazed terracotta or plastic – slightly sloping and surrounded by gravel to quicken the rate of drainage – behind the wall, just above the foundation. Take the pipe run along the wall to each end, where the rain-water can drain into a soakaway or other suitable drainage point.

To drain the retained bank through the wall you can simply leave 'weep holes' – open mortarless joints – every one metre (3ft) just above ground level, or set short lengths of 75mm (3in) diameter drainage pipe in the wall at these intervals, tilted slightly downwards to the outside.

In very wet areas, or where you're building a high wall, you'd be wise to dig out the earth behind the wall and make an infill trench of well-rammed broken bricks topped with gravel. This will help to relieve the pressure on the wall from expansion as the soil soaks up water in winter.

Where there's an excessive amount of water draining from your wall you should make a shallow gutter or gully at its base to carry the water to a suitable drainage point.

In addition to providing drainage for the bank you can further protect your wall from damp by applying two coats of bituminous paint to the back face, or by tacking on a sheet of thick 250 gauge polythene. Take care not to damage this membrane when you back-fill behind the wall.

It's not usual to incorporate a damp-proof course (dpc) in a garden wall, but for greater protection from rising damp you can bed a layer of slate between courses, or lay a course of water-resistant engineering bricks at this point instead. If the wall adjoins the house, and rises above the house damp course level for any reason, a vertical dpc must be included between house and wall to prevent any moisture from rising into the house structure.

Finally, you should bed sound copings of concrete or brick on top of your wall, to keep water out of the mortar joints. Precast concrete copings usually have a bevelled top for drainage, project beyond the face of the wall, and have channels called 'drip grooves' under the front edge to prevent water trickling back onto the surface of the wall. You can also buy a variety of special coping bricks with shaped edges for a softer, decorative effect.

Supporting the excavated earth

Where you're building your earth retaining wall in a steep bank, or in loosely-packed earth, you might have to construct a type of 'dam' from temporary timber struts and braces to shore up a series of vertical boards or planks called shuttering. This should be laid directly against the face of the soil to hold it in place while you can dig and lay your concrete strip foundations and build your wall.

On very high walls you might find it easiest to build the shuttering in stages as you excavate the site. You should leave about 300 to 600mm (1 to 2ft) between your proposed retaining wall and the face of the shuttering to allow you plenty of access when laying foundations and building the wall.

Once the foundations have been laid and you've completed the lower courses of bricks or blocks you should start to lay your drainage pipes. Set some actually in the wall, draining to the front, and lay others at the back of the wall, set in gravel or hardcore, to drain the sides.

Continue to build the wall in the normal way and, when it's completed, and you've pointed the joints, you should leave the structure for at least 24 hours to set before removing the shuttering.

Back-fill the wall with well-compacted soil or a porous filling (see *Ready Reference*) and top the wall with concrete or brick copings to complete the structure.

READY REFERENCE

BUILDING PIERS

Retaining walls over about 1.2m (4ft) high need supporting columns called 'piers' at each end, and at intermediate positions if they're very long. Piers should be:

- a brick or decorative block column bonded into a brickwork or blockwork wall (A)

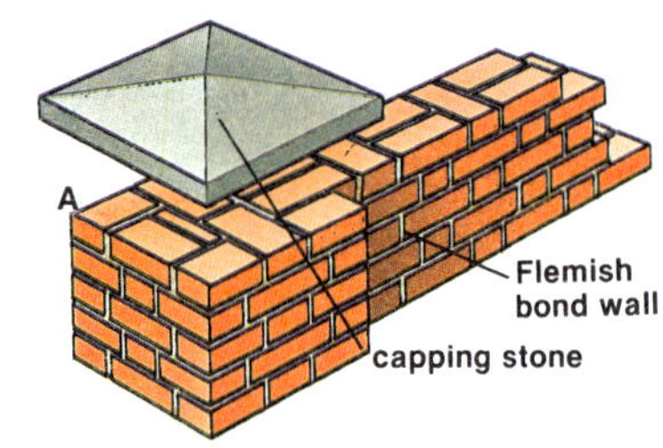

- a hollow concrete-filled blockwork column tied alongside a hollow block wall with metal cramps (B)
- a column of blocks tied to a solid block wall with galvanised expanded metal mesh (C).

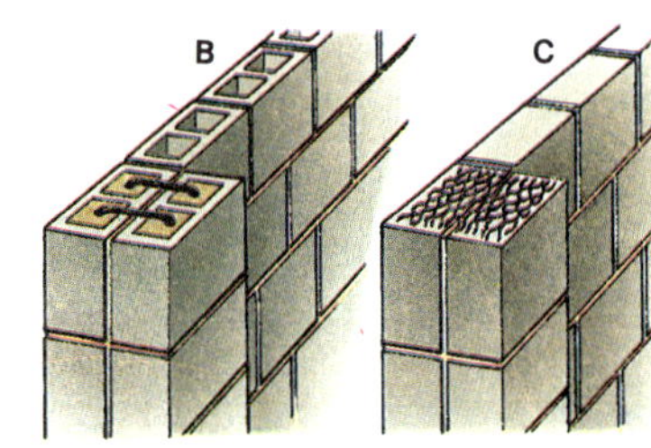

REINFORCING A LARGE WALL

High, heavy-duty walls will require reinforcement to hold back the weight of the earth. Hollow concrete blocks are the simplest to reinforce. To do this:

- set L-shaped steel rods (A) the height of the wall in a wide concrete strip foundation (B)
- slot hollow concrete blocks (C) onto the rods as you build the wall
- fill the cavities in the blocks with concrete (D).

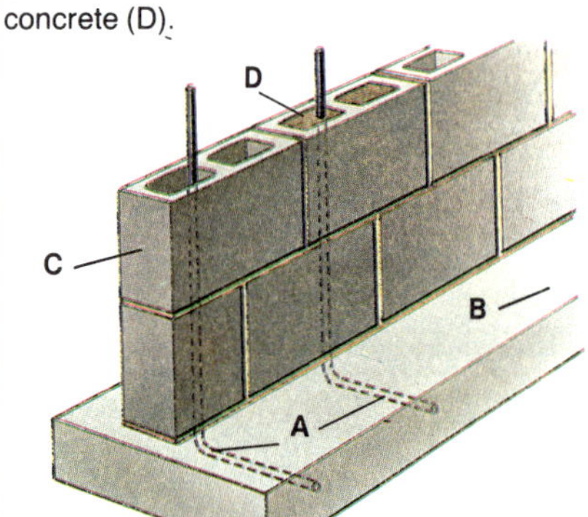

BUILDING A SCREEN BLOCK WALL

If you want privacy in your garden but don't like the idea of looking at a blank brick wall or a solid timber fence, then a wall made from pierced screen blocks could be the answer.

A garden wall made from pierced screen blocks offers a measure of privacy, yet doesn't shut out light and welcome cooling breezes. The blocks are quick and easy to lay, and give you a wall that's equally attractive from both sides. This makes them extremely good for marking out areas within the garden, without forming a heavy-looking solid barrier.

Screen blocks can also be used for boundary walls, though obviously they cannot provide total privacy. And while they're not intended to be load-bearing, they are able to support, say, the corrugated plastic roof of a carport, or the beams of a pergola or awning of light-weight construction.

Choosing the blocks

It's best to write off for manufacturers' brochures, or to visit a local builder's merchant, to find out exactly what's available in your area. You'll find several geometric patterns available (see *Ready Reference*): some are self-contained within each block, others need a set of blocks to complete the design. Solid patterned blocks are also sold, and can be set at intervals throughout the wall for added interest.

Most blocks are made from white concrete (to enhance their light appearance) and measure 300mm (1ft) square by 100mm (4in) thick. Because of the nature of their design, there are no half blocks, nor can blocks be cut.

To strengthen the wall, you have to install supporting columns called 'piers' at regular intervals along its length; while these can be built using bricks it's more common to construct them from special 'pilaster blocks'. These are basically hollow 200mm (8in) cubes, which incorporate slots to take the screen blocks. Four types of pilaster are available: those forming intermediate piers have a slot on two opposite sides; end pilasters have a single slot; corner pilasters have a slot on two adjacent sides; finally, there are pilasters with a slot on three sides, which are used at T-junctions. In addition, you'll find half-pilaster blocks to leave the tops of the piers level with the tops of the screen blocks, and to complete the wall there are pilaster capping pieces, and bevelled coping to protect the wall from the weather.

Designing the wall

Before you buy any materials, plan your wall carefully, making a scale drawing on squared paper to enable you to calculate what you need.

Start by deciding what happens at the base of the wall. The simplest option is to lay a concrete strip foundation finished off at ground level. However, here the foundation will be left on show, so you may prefer to stop the foundation below ground level. But this in its turn presents a problem: part of the first course of blocks will be buried in the ground, which makes the wall look sunken. It's therefore best to build a low wall in bricks or solid concrete blocks, and to surmount this with a flat coping to form a sort of plinth on which the screen wall proper can be built.

The next step is to work out the arrangement of the blocks. Screen walls are always laid with what's called a 'stack bond': that is without staggering the vertical joins, as in conventional brick and blockwork. This makes the wall quick and easy to build, but does mean that its dimensions are restricted. The wall must be a whole number of blocks high, and the length must be an exact number of blocks plus pilasters (remember, there are no half blocks and blocks cannot be cut). What's more, stack bond gives the wall little intrinsic strength, and so it's vital that you incorporate piers at the intervals recommended by the manufacturer of the blocks.

Unfortunately, even then the wall may not be strong enough for some situations. High walls, walls subject to strong winds, boundary walls (especially those next to a public highway) and the like, require additional reinforcement, and here, once again, it's best to follow the manufacturer's recommendations. In general, though, if the wall is inside the garden, has piers at no more than 3m (9ft) intervals, and is over 1.8m (6ft) high, the pilasters must be reinforced using 50x50mm (2x2in) angle iron of the sort used as fence posts. All boundary walls should have the pilasters reinforced in this way, and if the wall is over 1.8m (6ft) high, then 60mm (2½in) wide welded steel mesh made for the purpose and available from a builder's merchant should be bedded into the horizontal mortar joins to stop the vertical joins 'zipping' open. This mesh should also be used to tie the blocks into piers made of brick.

Storage and handling

Working from your scale drawing, you can order the necessary materials. First, though, there are a few points to bear in mind about handling and storage.

BUILDING A PIER

1 *When you've prepared your wall's foundations, stack your blocks nearby, mix some mortar and trowel on a bed where the first pier is to go.*

2 *Position your first pilaster block squarely on its mortar bed and use your trowel to scoop off any excess mortar that's squeezed out.*

3 *When you're satisfied that the first block is bedded evenly, trowel a mortar bed around its top rim, on which to lay the second block.*

4 *Lay the second block on top of the first and bed it down. Scrape off excess mortar but don't smear any on the face of the blocks or it will stain.*

5 *Continue to build up the blocks until you reach the height you want for the pier. If it's higher than about seven blocks, include reinforcement.*

6 *Check at intervals that the pier is built level and square by holding your spirit level against and on top of the blocks; adjust if necessary.*

READY REFERENCE

SCREEN BLOCK FORMAT

Screen walling blocks are made from white concrete and can be used for garden and boundary walls or semi-load-bearing walls. To make a wall you'll need:

- standard blocks (1) measuring 300mm (12in) sq x 100mm (4in) thick, with a variety of cut-out geometric patterns and some solid patterned blocks
- hollow 200mm (8in) cubes called 'pilasters', with slots in one side (2) or in two opposite sides (3), to make end and intermediate piers
- pilasters with slots in two adjacent sides (4) for corners
- pilasters with slots in three sides (5) for T-junctions.

To finish off the wall you'll need:

- capping pieces (6) to complete the pier tops
- coping stones (7) to protect the top of the wall from the weather.

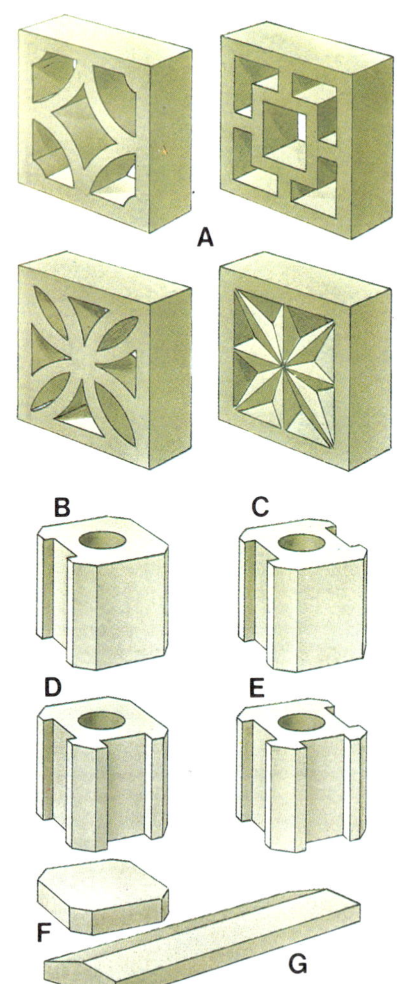

BUILDING THE WALL

1 *Once you've built the first pier you can build your wall out from it. Lay a bed of mortar about three blocks wide on the foundations.*

2 *Butter one edge of your first block with mortar and trowel furrows in the surface to aid positioning of the block and adhesion of the mortar.*

3 *Position the buttered edge of the block in the slot in the side of the lowest pilaster block; then trowel mortar onto the opposite side.*

6 *Continue to build up the wall, checking constantly with your level that it isn't bulging or crooked; then stack up the second pier.*

7 *Fill the cavity down the centre of the piers with mortar for extra strength, then bed capping stones in mortar on top.*

8 *Finish off the top of the wall with coping stones bedded in mortar. These have bevelled tops so that rainwater is thrown clear.*

The edges and corners of the blocks are particularly vulnerable to damage, so handle them with care. Any chipping will result in unsightly joins in the finished wall. As for storing the blocks until they're needed, stack them on edge with alternate rows at right angles to each other to stop them toppling over, then cover them with a tarpaulin or plastic sheeting to protect them from the rain so they're not soaking wet when you come to lay them.

Finally, remember that concrete is rough on the hands, and that the edges of the blocks can be sharp. It's therefore best to wear thick gloves when handling them.

Laying the foundations

The first step in building your wall is to lay the foundations. These should be twice the width of the wall; that is 200mm (8in) with wider sections for the pilasters. Their depth depends on the height of the wall and on the condition of the ground, but in general a 125mm (5in) layer of well-rammed hardcore topped with 125mm (5in) of concrete is sufficient. Reduce this to 200mm (8in) overall – 100mm (4in) of concrete – if the wall is less than 900mm (3ft) high.

The concrete used is a 1:2½:4 mix of Portland cement, sharp sand, and coarse aggregate. Alternatively, if you prefer to use mixed aggregate, you'll need five parts of this to one part of cement.

Where you're going to reinforce the pilasters, rather than set the reinforcing bars into the foundations, set in what are called 'starter bars'. These are short lengths of 10mm (⅜in) diameter mild steel rod, bent at right angles to hold them fast in the concrete. About 300mm (1ft) of rod should protrude above the surface of the foundations, and it's important that these stubs are vertical.

Once you've completed the foundations, leave the concrete to harden for three or four days before proceeding to build the wall.

Mortar and pointing

Screen blocks are best laid using a mortar made from one part masonry cement (this contains a plasticiser to make the mix more workable) and five parts builder's sand. Alternatively, you can use a 1:1:6 mix of Portland cement, lime, and builder's sand. For small jobs, however, it's often more convenient to use a dry-mixed bricklaying mortar.

Using any of these mortars, you can obtain a neat finish by scraping off the excess as each block is laid, then, having built a reasonable amount of wall, run a piece of plastic tubing along the joins to give them a half-round profile.

For a more attractive finish to the mortar joins it's better to rake them out after the

4 *Butt the second block up to the first and scrape off any excess mortar that's squeezed out of the vertical joint or out of the mortar bed.*

5 *Continue to lay more of the first course until you reach a point where you need another pier. Check that the wall is level across its top.*

9 *If you're building a second wall from one of your piers but won't finish it in one day, 'rack back' the corner to leave a stronger bond.*

10 *When your screen wall is complete, point the mortar joints between each block with a length of plastic tube to give a neat, half-round profile.*

mortar has stiffened then point the joins with a coloured mortar.

Building up the piers

Begin your wall construction by building up at least one pair of pilasters to a minimum of three courses high. If you're including any reinforcement, tie lengths of angle iron firmly to the starter bars using stout wire, having cut it to finish about 50mm (2in) below the tops of the pilasters.

You now just thread the pilaster blocks over the reinforcing bars, and bed them in mortar, ensuring that they're accurately centred, as well as vertical and level. Make sure, too, that the spacing between pilasters is correct. Check this by dry-laying the first course of screen blocks.

With each pilaster block in place, fill the pier with a slightly runny concrete mix of one part cement to three parts sharp sand.

Laying the blocks

You can now start to lay the screen blocks, each course being laid working inwards from the pilasters. It's just like ordinary blocklaying but without the bonding. With the two end blocks in position, stretch a string line between them and use this as a guide to laying the rest of the course.

Continue in this way building up one course after another and extending the pilasters as necessary. Check frequently with a spirit level that the blocks are correctly aligned, laid to a horizontal and standing truly vertical. As the wall rises, check, too, that it's not 'bellying out' by laying a long, straight-edged batten diagonally across its face.

Lastly, once the wall has reached its final height, top the pilasters with the special capping pieces, and lay coping stones on top of the screen blocks, bedding both in mortar in the normal way.

READY REFERENCE

FOUNDATIONS FOR SCREEN WALLS

For walls over 900mm (3ft) high, foundations should be 200mm (8in) wide – and wider where there are piers – and should consist of 125mm (5in) of well-rammed hardcore topped with 125mm (5in) of concrete.

For lower walls, foundations should consist of 100mm (4in) of well-rammed hardcore topped with 100mm (4in) of concrete.

REINFORCING THE WALL

Walls over 1.8m (6ft) high subject to strong winds, and boundary walls, especially if they're close to a public highway, need extra reinforcement. This should consist of:

- starter bars consisting of lengths of 10mm (3/8in) diameter mild steel rod bent at right angles and set in the foundations so that about 300mm (1ft) of metal protrudes
- lengths of 50mm (2in) sq mild steel angle iron tied to the starter bars with stout wire (A)
- the hollow pilasters slot onto the bars and lengths of 50mm (2in) wide steel mesh are bedded into the horizontal mortar joins to stop the vertical joins opening (B).

A

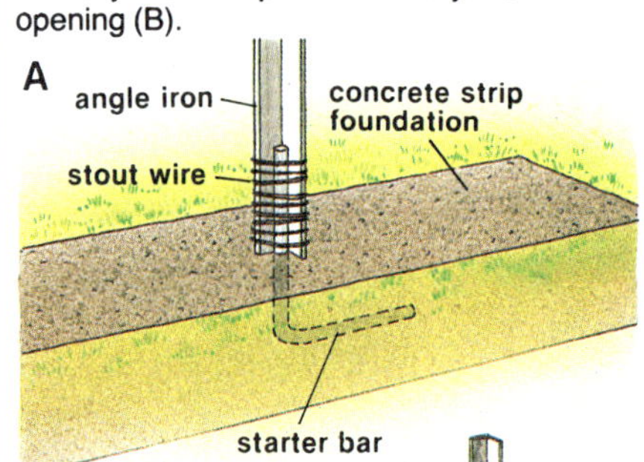

B

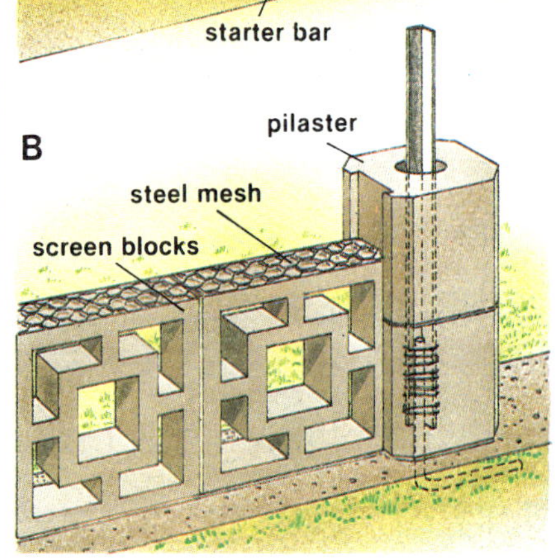

CONCRETE MIXES

For the foundations, use a concrete mix consisting of 1 part Portland cement to 2½ parts sharp sand and 4 parts coarse aggregate, or 5 parts mixed aggregate to 1 part of cement.

PATHS AND PATIOS

One of the best areas to practise your building skills is in the garden. Absolute perfection won't matter so much, it doesn't matter if you make a mess and to begin with you only have to work in two dimensions. Garden paths and patios can be laid extremely quickly using prefabricated slabs or bricks, once you've mastered the art of laying them level.

BUILDING A PAVED PATIO

Building a patio close to the house is one way of transforming a dull and featureless garden into a durable paved area that's geared especially for outdoor living.

A patio makes a versatile summertime extension to the house, providing space for dining, entertaining, or merely for relaxing and soaking-up the sun. You must plan your patio to take advantage of the best aspect and construct it from materials that are both in keeping with the house and garden and durable enough to withstand harsh weather conditions.

Siting the patio

Patios are usually sited as close to the house as possible – ideally adjoining it – or at least nearby for easy access. The best aspect is south-facing, but whichever way your garden faces, you should examine the proposed site at different times of the day during the summer to see how shadows fall. Neighbouring buildings, or your own house, might obscure the sun and this will severely limit the use of the patio. Unfortunately there's nothing you can do about this, but if the obstruction is just a tree or tall hedge you might be able to prune it.

Some shadows can be used to your advantage: although you might want to lie sun-bathing at certain times of the day, you'll appreciate the shade while you eat. If there's no natural shade, you could attach an awning to the house wall, which can be folded away when not needed. A pergola or trellis on which you can train climbing plants will also provide shade where you need it. Or you might prefer simply to allow enough space for a table with an umbrella or a swing seat with a canopy.

What size patio?

In theory a patio may be as large or small as you wish, but in practice you'll be limited by available space. Try to relate the dimensions of the patio to the needs – and size – of your household. Measure your garden furniture and allow enough space around it so that you won't be cramped: the patio must measure at least 2.4m (8ft) from front to back to enable you to position furniture and allow free passage. In general a patio measuring about 3.7m sq (12ft sq) is big enough to take a four-seater table or four loungers.

To work out the size and position of the patio make some preliminary sketches of the garden with the proposed patio in various locations. When you've decided upon a suitable scheme transfer your ideas to a scale plan on graph paper. Cut out a paper template of the patio and use it in conjunction with the plan to help you decide upon the best position.

What type of surface?

There is a wide range of paving materials available in various shapes, sizes and colours and you should choose those which blend with materials used around the house exterior and garden for a sense of unity. The main requisites are that the surface is reasonably smooth, level and free-draining. Whatever your choice of paving, avoid too great a mix – two types are usually sufficient to add interest without making the surface look cluttered. You can, however, include confined areas of small-scale materials such as cobblestones and granite setts to add a textural change to an otherwise flat scheme composed of larger slabs.

Cobblestones – oval pebbles – can be laid in three ways: on a continuous mortar bed over hardcore foundations; on a bed of dry mortar 'watered in' by watering can; or loosely piled on top of each other on compacted earth. Granite setts are durable square-shaped blocks with an uneven

PREPARING THE BASE

1 *Set a long prime datum peg in a hole 300mm (1ft) deep at one side of the patio. Its top should be 150mm (6in) below the house dpc.*

2 *Set a second peg at the other side, level with the first. For a very wide patio use intermediate datum pegs set 1.5m (5ft) apart.*

3 *Use a string line to set timber pegs accurately in line with each other so that they outline the proposed perimeter of the patio.*

4 *Check with a builder's square to make sure that the corners of the patio are perfectly square. Adjust the peg positions if they are not.*

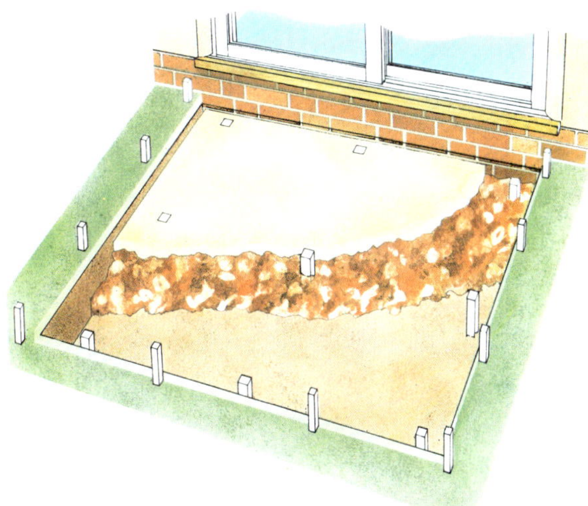

5 *Dig out the site to a depth of about 230mm (9in), saving the top-soil and turf. Then compact the earth with a garden roller.*

6 *Drive in pegs 1.5m (5ft) apart over the entire area. Check that they are level with the datum peg and each other using a spirit level.*

7 *Fill the hole with hardcore, then compact it thoroughly to a depth of about 125mm (5in) using a tamper. Don't disturb the pegs.*

8 *Rake out and roll a 50mm (2in) layer of sand over the hardcore. The peg tops should be level with the sand surface.*

LAYING THE SLABS

1 *Start to lay the slabs at the corner marked by the prime datum peg. You can lay them dry on the sand bed, without using any mortar.*

2 *As you progress across the patio you should check frequently with a builder's level that the slabs are bedded evenly on the sand.*

3 *Lift up any slabs that are unevenly bedded and trowel in some more sand until the bed is filled out and the slabs are flush with their neighbours.*

4 *Alternatively you can lay the slabs on dabs of fairly stiff mortar, one placed under each corner of the slab and one under the centre.*

5 *Position the slab carefully on top of the mortar dabs. Space out the slabs using offcuts of timber 9mm (3/8in) thick for pointing later.*

6 *Bed down the slabs using the handle of your club hammer. If any of the slabs are too low, remove them and add more mortar to the dabs.*

TIP

7 *Stretch the string lines across the patio every second course to help you align the slabs accurately.*

8 *When all the slabs are laid, brush a dry mortar mix between the joins and remove any excess from their faces. This will form a bond when watered in.*

9 *Water in the dry mortar mix with clean water from a watering can fitted with a fine rose. Avoid over-watering or you'll wash away the mortar.*

surface texture, and can be laid on sand or mortar.

Other small-scale paving materials that can be used in large or small areas include concrete blocks, brick pavers and paving-quality bricks. They're available in various colours and the blocks also come in a range of interlocking shapes. Lay these materials in patterns for best effect and use coloured mortar joints as a contrast.

You can also use special frost-proof ceramic tiles for a patio surface but they are very expensive and need a perfectly flat base if they are to be laid correctly. Consequently, they're really only suitable for very small patios.

Probably the simplest of surfaces is one made of a solid slab of cast concrete. Although the concrete can be coloured with pigments, many people find its surface appearance unattractive.

Concrete paving slabs are probably the best materials for a simple rectangular patio. Made with reconstituted stone, they're available in a range of reds, greens, yellows and buff tones with smooth, riven or patterned faces. Square, rectangular, hexagonal and half-hexagonal shapes are also made and they're easy to lay on a sand bed. Broken concrete slabs, known as crazy paving (see pages 61 -63 for details), can also be used as a patio surface, laid on a mortar bed.

Link the patio to the rest of the garden by building walls, paths and steps in matching or complementary materials.

Marking out patterns

Whatever paving materials you choose you have enormous flexibility in the design of your patio. There's no reason why, for instance, it should be square or rectangular – most of the materials previously described can be laid in curves or can be cut to fit other shapes and angles.

Sketch out some patterns and dry-lay the paving in both width and length to test how the designs work in practice. Adjust the pattern or the dimensions of the patio to minimise the number of cut pieces you use. This will ensure the surface looks 'balanced'.

Concrete slabs can be laid in various grid and stretcher bond patterns but, for a more informal effect, whole and half slabs can be used together in a random fashion. Crazy paving should be laid with larger, straight-edged pieces at the borders and smaller fragments inside. You can lay bricks in herringbone or basket-weave designs.

Setting the levels

Draw your plan on graph paper, then use it to transfer the shape of the patio onto the site. Use strings stretched between pegs to mark out the perimeter of the patio. You must also drive pegs in to represent the surface level of the patio, so to ensure they're accurately placed you have to drive a 'prime datum' peg into the ground against the house wall (if the patio is to abut the house). The peg should indicate one corner of the patio and should be set in a hole about 300mm (1ft) deep with its top 150mm (6in) below the level of the house damp-proof course. If the soil is spongy you may have to dig deeper in order to obtain a firm enough surface on which to lay the foundations.

Set a second peg in the ground against the wall to mark the other side of the patio, and check that the level corresponds to that of the prime datum peg by holding a long timber straight-edge between the two and checking with a spirit level.

All other marking-out strings and pegs should be taken from the base line formed between these two datum pegs. Indicate squares and rectangles by stretching strings from the two pegs and checking the angle with a builder's square. Plot out curves by measuring from the base line at intervals and driving in pegs at the perimeter, or use lengths of string or a long hosepipe to mark the curves. Circles and half-circles can be marked out by taking a string from a peg placed as the centre of the circle: you place the first slabs or other paving along the string, then move it around the radius and set the next row.

If size permits, you could incorporate planting areas in your patio by leaving sections un-paved, or simply place tubs of plants on the perimeter.

Laying the paving

When you've marked out the shape of your patio, remove the topsoil (which you should save for use elsewhere in the garden) from within your guidelines and set intermediate datum pegs at 1.5m (5ft) intervals over the entire area of the excavation. These pegs have to be sunk to the level of the prime datum peg, using a spirit level on a batten between the pegs. Now is the time to set the drainage fall away from the house.

When you've set the levels, fill the hole with hardcore, which you must compact thoroughly by rolling and tamping. Then a layer of sand rolled out flat over the hardcore brings the level of the foundation up to that of the peg tops, and provides a flat base for the paving.

On a site that slopes away from the house you'll have to build a low retaining wall of bricks or blocks; the ground behind it can be filled with hardcore and then paved. However, where the ground slopes towards the house you must excavate the patio site in the bank (forming a drainage fall away from the house), and build a retaining wall.

READY REFERENCE

PREPARING THE FOUNDATIONS

Patio paving requires foundations of compacted hardcore covered with a blinding layer of sand. The excavation should be:

- about 150 to 200mm (6 to 8in) deep to allow for 75 to 125mm (3 to 5in) of hardcore plus the sand and paving
- about 230mm (9in) deep if the patio is to be built up to a house wall, so the paving can be set 150mm (6in) below the dpc.

ALLOWING FOR DRAINAGE

To ensure run-off of rainwater the patio surface must slope by about 25mm in 3m (1in in 10ft) towards a suitable drainage point, which might be an existing drain or soakaway.

On ground sloping away from the house: construct perimeter walls for the patio from brick, block or stone, to form a 'stage'. Infill with hardcore and a blinding layer of sand and gravel, then pave. The walls must be set on 100mm (4in) deep concrete footings.

On ground sloping towards the house: excavate the site for the patio in the bank, forming a fall away from the house. Build a retaining wall to hold back the earth.

INSPECTION CHAMBERS

The patio must not interfere with access to drainage inspection chambers. If drain covers are within the patio area:

- build it up to the level of the new surface
- cover it with loose-laid slabs for access.

TIP: PAVING ROUND TREES

If you're paving around a tree or shrub to make a garden feature, keep the paving at least 300mm (1ft) from the trunk to allow rainwater to reach its roots.

LAYING BLOCK PAVING

Concrete block pavers can be used to make a durable and decorative surface for a drive, path or patio. They're quick and easy to lay in an interlocking pattern on a sand bed – and no mortar is needed.

A path or patio must be durable enough to withstand fairly heavy traffic – from people, wheelbarrows, other garden equipment and furniture; and a drive has the additional weight of a car to contend with. So the surface must be tough and long-lasting.

But traditional surfacing materials – commonly cast concrete, asphalt and paving slabs – tend to give a plain, slab-like appearance, which often detracts from other features. 'Flexible' paving, however, is a method of making a hard surface that's both attractive and easy to lay.

Using concrete pavers

This type of surface uses concrete paving blocks, small-scale units that are very tough and can be laid in numerous patterns. Each block interlocks with its neighbours to form a solid, firm and decorative surface capable of supporting fairly heavy loads.

Concrete paving blocks are made in a variety of shapes (see 'Types of block') some with a rough texture for a more natural effect, others with smooth faces for a formal setting. They're also made in a choice of reds, blues, greys, charcoal and buff tones, and some have a mottled effect that resembles old brick. The simplest types of blocks are rectangular – usually about 200 x 100mm (8 x 4in) and about 65mm (2½in) thick. Some have a bevel or 'mock joint' on their top edge so that the shape of each block – and the bonding pattern – is accentuated when laid in a large area.

Other types – approximately the same size overall as the rectangular ones – incorporate zig-zag edges, some sharp, some gently rounded, which mate together when laid. There are basically three bonds in which you can lay concrete blocks: herringbone, stretcher and parquet (see 'Forming patterns with blocks').

By using the irregular-shaped blocks you can also create a rippling effect across the area of paving.

Herringbone is the strongest bond and ideal for drives, where the wearing and load from cars is considerable; stretcher and parquet bonds aren't as tough and so they're better for areas that will receive lighter traffic.

It's also possible to create variations on standard bonds, by laying blocks in pairs, for example, or mixing two bonds in an area of paving.

Laying the blocks is straightforward: they're simply positioned on a layer of sand between permanent edge restraints (see 'Site preparation') and are bedded down by vibration, using a special machine which you can hire. Suitable edge restraints are: existing paving, kerbstones set in concrete, a house or garden wall, pegged boards or a row of bricks. In most types of flexible paving no mortar is needed, either to bed the blocks or to point the joints between them. For this reason it's quite simple to remove the blocks whenever you like and reposition them on a new sand bed in a new bonding pattern.

Preparing the base

The base for your paving must be firm and level. Firstly, clear all weeds, and loose materials from the area. Dig out any soft spots and fill the holes with firmer soil – or even broken rubble – then compact the surface thoroughly using a garden roller.

If you're making a drive or other area that's to be used for vehicular traffic you should excavate the site and lay a firm base of at least 100mm (4in) of clean, fine hardcore, which you should also compact thoroughly.

Areas that are only to be used for foot traffic, such as paths and patios, will probably only need a base of compacted soil, unless the surface is clay or soft, peat soil; here, the base should be the same as for drives.

The base must be at least 115mm (4½in)

TYPES OF BLOCK

Block paving may be fired clay (A) or concrete (B, C and D – like small paving slabs). The clay ones are usually rectangular, but the concrete types come in a range of interlocking shapes as well. The surface texture is fairly coarse, and most have chamfered top edges to give the effect of a mock joint when laid.

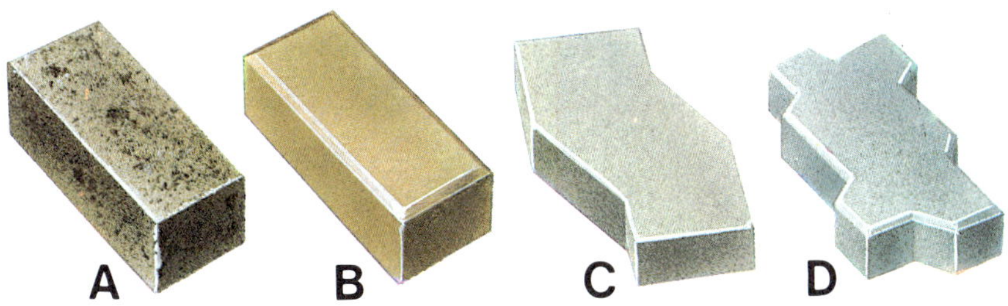

Forming patterns with blocks

1 *Interlocking blocks such as type D above look highly attractive when laid in a parquet bond of alternating pairs. They can also be laid in a herringbone pattern.*

2 *So-called 'fishtail' blocks (type C above) look best when laid in stretcher bond. The effect is of undulating lines in one direction, aligning joints in the other.*

3 *The simplest way of laying rectangular blocks is in stretcher bond, with successive rows having their joints staggered by half the length of a block.*

4 *An alternative to stretcher bond that looks very attractive with the rectangular block format is a simple herringbone pattern. Half-blocks form the edging.*

READY REFERENCE

CONCRETE BLOCK FORMAT

Concrete block pavers are available in a variety of shapes, colours and textures (see 'Types of block'). They measure:

- 200 x 100mm (8 x 4in) overall
- 50, 60 or 65mm (2, 2¼ or 2½in) thick.

FOUNDATIONS FOR BLOCK PAVING

Concrete block paving must have firm, level foundations. These should consist of:

- a well-compacted sub-base of soil for light use
- 110mm (4½in) of well-compacted hardcore for heavy traffic
- plus 50mm (2in) of sharp sand levelled and smoothed over the sub-base
- suitable edge restraints.

EDGE RESTRAINTS

To retain the edges of your paved area:

- fix creosoted timber formwork at the perimeter
- bed kerb stones or bricks in concrete
- or lay the paving against an existing wall or fence.

DRAINAGE FALLS

Your paved area must slope away from house walls. To allow for this:

- fix timber 'datum' pegs into the sub-base at 1.5mm (5ft) intervals so their tops are level with the sand bed
- check across the pegs with a spirit level on a straightedge
- incorporate a fall of about 1 in 50 with a 25mm (1in) thick wedge of timber (shim) under one end of the level.

TIP: LAYING BY HAND

For small, decorative, non-loadbearing areas of paving it's not really worth hiring a plate vibrator. Instead:

- lay the blocks as normal on sand
- bed each in place using an offcut of wood just larger than the block and a wooden mallet.

TIP: CUTTING BLOCKS

To cut paving blocks:

- chop along the cutting line with a club hammer and bolster chisel, or
- use a hydraulic stone splitter or guillotine.

SITE PREPARATION

Bed the blocks on sand over a levelled hardcore base. The area can be bounded by a wall (A), kerbstones set in concrete (B), pegged boards (C) or bricks (D).

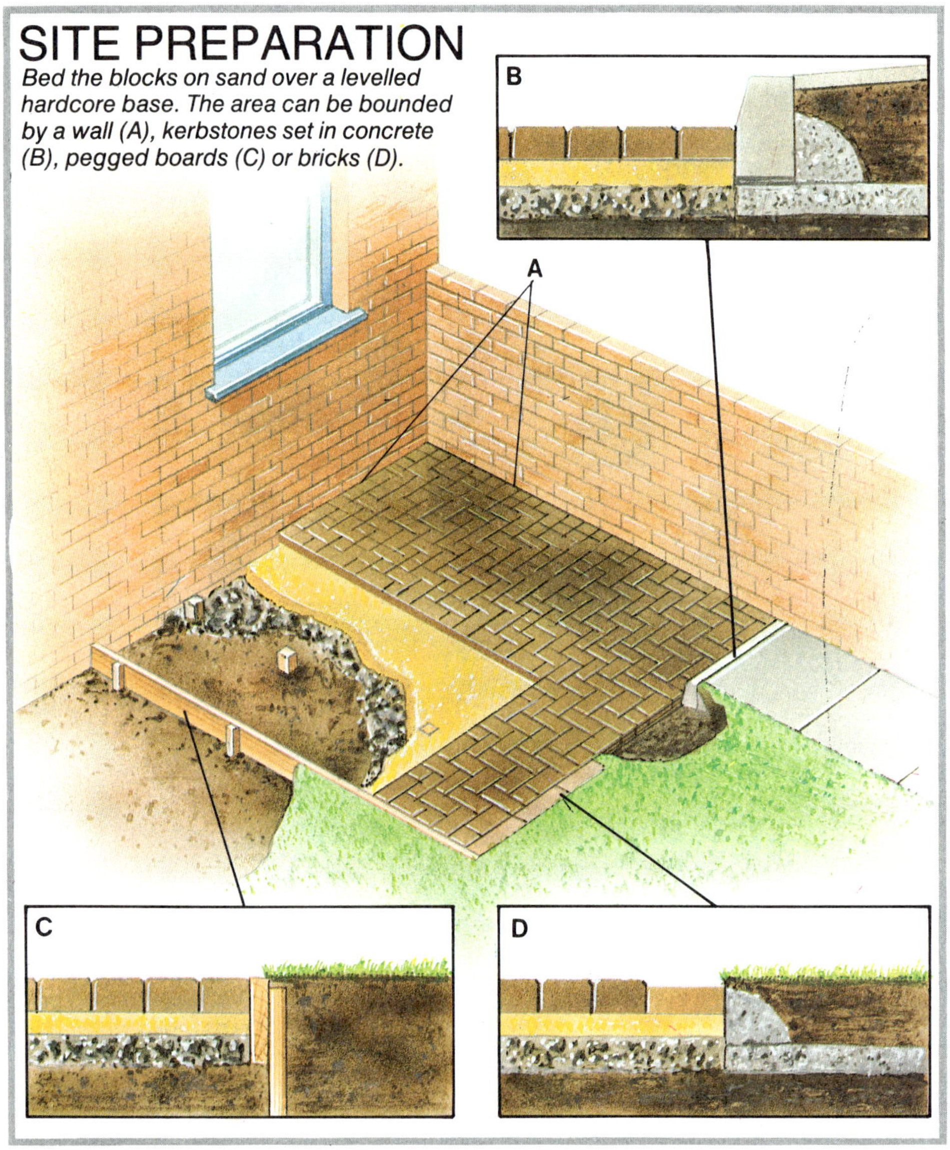

below the level of the completed paved surface. The top surface, in turn, must be at least 150mm (6in) below the house damp-proof course (dpc) to prevent moisture rising in the walls or rain splashing up above the dpc.

Setting levels

Unless there's a natural slope to the site you'll have to excavate the base so that the finished surface will slope to one side – or at least away from the house walls – with a fall of about 1 in 40, to ensure efficient drainage of rainwater.

To set the levels over the area of the base drive 300mm (1ft) long timber pegs into the ground at about 1.5m (5ft) intervals and set them at the correct level, taken from a 'prime datum', or fixed point of reference: two bricks below the dpc is adequate, for example. Use a long timber straightedge with a spirit level on the top edge to check that the pegs are set at the correct depth. Place a small wedge or 'shim' of timber under one end of the spirit level to incorporate an adequate drainage fall (see 'Site preparation').

Edge restraints

The edges of your concrete block paving are best retained, by the walls of your house, garden walls or existing paving: simply setting them against earth won't prevent eventual spreading of the blocks. If your dpc is lower than 150mm (6in), however, you must leave a 75mm (3in) wide channel between the wall and the paved surface to stop rainwater from splashing up and soaking the wall above the dpc. In this case you'd need to fit an edge restraint.

If there isn't a natural or existing edge restraint you'll have to install permanent formwork. Precast concrete, concrete path edging stones or a row of bricks on edge can be used, bedded in a strip of concrete, or you could use creosoted lengths of 38mm (1½in) thick softwood screwed or nailed to stout 50 x 50mm (2 x 2in) pegs driven into the ground outside the area you're going to pave. The depth of these battens should equal the thickness of the blocks plus the sand bed.

The sand bed

When you've levelled and compacted the sub-base and have set up the formwork you can lay the bedding sand directly on top. For this you'll need sharp (concreting) sand. As a rough guide to amounts, 1 tonne of sand is ample for 10 sq metres (110sq ft) of paving.

Although the final thickness of the sand bed should be 50mm (2in) you'll have to add more to allow for compaction of the paving.

You'll find it more convenient to work if you divide the load of sand into separate piles and position them at intervals along the site, away from the point at which you want to start laying the blocks.

Spread out the sand evenly over the sub-base, between the edge restraints, using a garden rake, then 'screed' or smooth the surface to the correct level with a straight-edged length of timber that spans the width of the area you're paving. The top of the sand bed should be levelled to about 50mm (2in) below the finished paving (and therefore the level of the edge restraint) when you're using 65mm (2½in) thick blocks, and about 45mm (1¾in) below when using 60mm (2¼in) thick blocks. To allow for this depth you can cut notches in the straightedge to form 'arms' that rest on the formwork; the body of this 'spreader' should be the thickness of the blocks plus about 15mm (½in) for compaction of sand (see 'Site preparation' for more details).

Where you're using an existing wall or fence as an edge restraint you'll have to set a temporary screeding batten on the sub-base, which you can remove after levelling. Fill the groove left by the batten with more sand and level the surface.

Screed the sand in areas only about 2m (6ft) ahead of the blocklaying for convenience and avoid walking on the sand during or after you've levelled the surface.

Laying the blocks

Start to lay the blocks in your chosen pattern against the edge restraint nearest to your pile of blocks. Bed each block up to its neighbours, without any gaps. The blocks can be fairly rough, so you'd be wise to wear thick gloves.

As your area of paving enlarges you should work from a plank laid across the blocks as a kneeling board, to spread the load. Lay plank runs also for transporting barrowloads of blocks from the main pile to the laying edge

LAYING THE BLOCKS

1 *Unless the blocks abut a wall, you'll need some sort of edge restraint. Here preservative-treated boards are nailed to stout timber pegs.*

2 *Start placing the blocks by hand in the pattern you want (here, a herringbone pattern). Leave gaps at the edges to be filled later with cut blocks.*

3 *As laying proceeds, kneel on a board to spread your weight. This avoids pressure on individual blocks, which could bed them too deep in the sand.*

4 *If you find that occasional blocks are obviously sitting proud of their neighbours, lift them and scrape away some of the sand beneath before replacing them.*

5 *Then tap the offending block back into place using the heel of a trowel or club hammer. Similarly, if a block is sitting too low, lift it and add more sand.*

6 *To avoid having to traipse to and fro for more blocks, fill a barrow with blocks and park it nearby. Use boards to spread the barrow's weight.*

7 *With stretcher and herringbone patterns, you will have to cut blocks to fill the edge gaps. Hold a block over the gap and score the cutting line on its surface.*

8 *You can cut paving blocks by hand with a brick bolster and club hammer, but if you have many to cut a hired hydraulic splitter will make light work of the job.*

9 *Finish off the laying sequence by placing the half blocks in position round the edges of the area as you cut them. Set them level with their neighbours.*

to avoid disturbing the blocks you've already laid but haven't compacted.

Cutting the blocks

Although you should use whole blocks wherever possible for maximum strength, you'll certainly need to cut some to size and shape where the paved area contains obstacles such as drains or inspection covers, and where it meets the edge restraints.

It's possible to mark the individual blocks to size and cut them using a club hammer and bolster chisel but you can hire a hydraulic stone splitter or guillotine, which will make the job much easier. Keep the guillotine close to the edge of the paving for convenience. If you must stand it on the paving, rest it on a board so you don't mark or upset any of the blocks. If you use a hammer and chisel be sure to wear gloves and goggles to protect your eyes from flying fragments.

Compacting the blocks

When you've laid a large enough area of blocks bed them firmly into the sand using a plate vibrator fitted with a rubber sole plate. This will settle the blocks into place and force sand up into the joints, without damaging them.

The plate vibrator should have a plate area of 0.2 to 0.3sq metres (2 to 3sq ft), a frequency of 75 to 100 Hz and a centrifugal force of 7 to 20kN, to ensure the blocks will be bedded correctly. Most machines of this type will fit easily into the boot of a car.

Make two or three passes over the paving with the plate vibrator in order to bed the blocks to the correct level, but avoid lingering in one place or you might sink them too low. Also, don't take the machine closer than 1m (3ft) to the unrestrained edge you're laying or you're likely to form a dip in the surface.

Finishing the paving

Finally, simply brush sand onto the paved surface and make a few more passes with the plate vibrator to force the sand down between the blocks.

If you're laying a very small, mainly decorative, area of blocks that won't be used for vehicles – a narrow border around a flower bed, for instance – it's acceptable to lay them without using the vibrator, although the job is more laborious and the results won't be as durable

Instead lay a thinner sand bed, moistened with water from a watering can fitted with a fine rose, and level and compact this with a straight-edged tamping board. Lay the blocks as previously described but bed each as level as possible using a wooden mallet with an offcut of timber just larger than the block (see *Ready Reference*). Water more sand into the joint, again using your watering can, to complete the area of paving.

COMPLETING THE JOB

TIP

1 *Vibrate the blocks into the sand bed with a hired plate vibrator. You can avoid marking the blocks by running the machine over some old carpet.*

2 *After the first passes with the plate vibrator, scatter sand over the surface and brush it well into the gaps between the individual blocks.*

3 *Run the plate vibrator over the surface again, making two or three passes over each area, to compact the sand between the blocks thoroughly.*

4 *Finish off the paving by brushing off excess sand with a soft-bristled broom, taking care not to brush out the joints. The paving is ready for immediate use.*

Immediately you've laid the blocks and vibrated them into place, your paved area is ready for use. Inspect the surface after a few months to make sure there aren't any areas that have subsided fractionally. If there are uneven areas you may simply be able to lever out the relevant blocks and rebed them on more sand.

Paving irregular areas

Because of the small size of the blocks, you can use them to good effect to pave irregularly-shaped areas. Where necessary the blocks can be cut at an angle to form neat edges, and circles can be formed by laying the blocks with wedge-shaped joints instead of parallel-sided ones – rather like forming a brick arch. To achieve perfect curves, lay the blocks using a string line attached to a peg at the centre of the curve, so that by holding the string taut you can align them accurately.

Coping with steps

If you have used blocks for a path or patio, you may want to link these areas with steps paved in the same way. Because of the small size of the blocks it is vital to bed them on mortar rather than on sand, particularly at the edges of the treads. You can still use sand to fill the joints between the blocks and so maintain the overall sense of unity.

Building with blocks

Similarly, you may want to build dwarf walls at the edges of your paved area, and while you could use any garden walling blocks for this there is nothing to stop you using two or three courses of paving blocks instead. The rectangular ones are laid just like bricks with pointed mortar joints between, but the interlocking and fishtail types can also be built up into walls if they are overlapped by half a block and aligned carefully.

ALTERATIONS

Once you've mastered the basic builder's skills, you can turn your attention to some more ambitious internal alterations. Fireplaces that have been gutted may need to be reinstated if you want to join the rush back to open fires; conversely, unwanted fire openings can be removed and blocked up to create much-needed living space.

CUTTING AND DRILLING TOOLS

1: masonry saw *with tungsten carbide-tipped teeth*
2: angle grinder *with masonry cutting discs*
3: interchangeable cutters *for jumping bit (4); diameters match screw gauges*
4: star drill; *diameters match masonry bolt sizes*
5: jumping bit *holder and cutter*
6: hammer-action drill *with depth stop, plus masonry drill bits*
7: circular saw *with masonry cutting disc.*

FITTING A NEW FIREBACK

If you're renovating an open fireplace one of the jobs you're likely to come across is replacing an old, cracked fireback. This is essential if you want your fire to be safe, and although it is rather a messy job it is not at all difficult to do.

Until quite recently, all houses were built with an open fireplace in at least one room, and houses built in the 19th century are likely to have one in every room. Few people nowadays actually rely on open fires to heat their homes or their water and many fireplaces were removed or covered up, especially in the '60s and '70s. Gas fires and central heating were obviously cleaner and more convenient. However, it is becoming more and more popular to open up a fireplace again, especially in the living room.

When you uncover the old fireplace, you may be lucky to find both the surround and fire opening in good condition. But often the surround was removed before the opening was concealed, and the fireback may be damaged or partly missing. You'll probably have to have the chimney swept and clean up all the accumulated soot and dust before you can check what condition it's in.

Of course, you may have been using your fireplace for many years. But after so much intense heat from the fire as well as occasional knocks from the poker, the fireback will start to deteriorate and may need replacing.

The fireback is the part most likely to need attention in any case. Most firebacks are made of refractory concrete or fireclay, and their function is to provide a safe and convenient enclosure for the fire, helping to direct the heat into the room and the smoke up the chimney. But with age, cracks will start to form and will eventually open up so the fireplace becomes unsafe to use.

Repairing small cracks

If there are just a few cracks in the fireback it is relatively easy to repair them and there'll be no need to replace it entirely. You'll need some fire cement and a small trowel.

If the fire has been used recently you should leave it for two days to cool down completely. Then brush off all the soot and dust and rake out the cracks with the point of the trowel, undercutting them slightly. Brush out all the debris from the cracks and soak the area with plenty of clean water. The water helps the fire cement to adhere to the cracks by stopping it drying out too quickly. Fill in the cracks, using the trowel to work the fire cement well in. Then smooth off the surface by drawing a wet brush over the crack.

If the cracks are large, or part of the fireback has come loose, then a repair like this will not be safe and you'll have to replace the whole fireback.

Removing the old fireback

Although this is a heavy and dirty job, it doesn't require any great skills and you shouldn't have any problems with it. Before you start work, lay down dust sheets around the fire and, if you've a tiled hearth, lay some sheets of cardboard over the tiles first to protect them from accidental damage.

Now you can remove the fire grate. If this is an old-fashioned one it will be free-standing and can merely be lifted clear. A modern appliance will be fixed by screws driven through its base into plugs inserted in the back hearth; the gap at its sides and base will be pointed with fire cement. Withdraw the screws in the normal way (leaving the plugs intact) and break the concrete pointing by tapping it with a hammer and cold chisel.

Under the fire cement at the sides you will come across short lengths of rope. These are made of asbestos and you should keep them as they will be needed when the fire is re-installed. Remember always to treat asbestos with respect, for if you create and inhale any asbestos dust there is a possible health hazard.

You can now take out the old fireback. As it fits behind the fire surround you must break it up to remove it – use a club hammer and cold chisel, or even a crowbar. If the fire surround is missing then you can probably wrench the fireback forwards without needing to break it up. Behind the fireback you will find a mass of solid rubble – packed in to help dissipate the heat from the fireback – and most of this should be cleared out. It is not very hard and will break up easily with a cold chisel and hammer. When this is all removed you'll be left with a brick-lined recess known as the builders' opening.

Ordering a new fireback

New firebacks are available from builders' merchants and fireplace specialists. Measure the size of the old one and order a new one of the same size. The part you need to measure is shown in *Ready Reference*.

A fireback for a normal-sized fire opening has to be installed in two pieces so that it can expand under heat without cracking. However, it will normally be delivered to you in one piece. About halfway up you will see a break line. Tap gently along this line with a

REMOVING THE OLD FIREBACK

1 *Start to knock out the old fireback at one of the top rear corners using a club hammer and cold chisel. It should break up quite easily.*

2 *If a large crack forms, follow along it with the hammer and chisel – you'll often be able to remove quite large pieces of fireback in one go.*

3 *There may be a line of fire cement along the front edges of the fireback. Break this off carefully without damaging the fire surround.*

4 *Often the rubble behind the fireback will be loose and can easily be removed. If it's solid you'll have to break it up first with a club hammer and bolster.*

hammer and bolster until it splits in two. Some suppliers call this a one-piece fireback while others call it a two-piece fireback, so be sure to describe exactly what you want when you're ordering. Large fire openings may need a four-piece or six-piece fireback.

Installing the fireback

The heat thrown out by an ordinary domestic fire is intense and you must take steps to counteract this. Obviously, you must use non-combustible materials throughout, but that's not all. The heat will also cause the materials to expand. As different materials expand at different rates they could cause a lot of strain if they were allowed to press against each other. So various 'buffers' are installed in a fireplace to prevent the expansion causing any damage.

The first step is to fit lengths of asbestos rope behind the top and sides of the fire opening. If the original rope is in a good enough condition you can use that. The lower half of the fireback is then manoeuvred into position and pulled forward so it lightly compresses the rope at the front of the opening. The area behind the fireback will be filled in, but first you need to fit another sort of buffer. This one is made from two sheets of corrugated cardboard which should be cut to the shape of the fireback and then tucked in place behind it. The idea is that once the fire is lit this cardboard will char away under the intense heat, leaving a gap for expansion of the infill and fireback. Often the paper stays intact – you might have come across some when you took out the old fireback – but that doesn't matter.

The whole area around the rear of the fireback – both the back and sides – must be filled in with a weak mortar mix. A suitable mix can be made from four parts vermiculite

READY REFERENCE

PARTS OF A FIREPLACE

Here are some of the specialist terms used to describe a fireplace:

- the decorative part fixed to the wall, made of wood, marble, metal or tiled concrete, is called the **fire surround**
- the opening at the centre where the fire burns is the **fire opening**
- the floor in front of the fire – often tiled – is the **superimposed hearth**
- below the superimposed hearth is the **constructional hearth**
- the concrete under the fire is the **back hearth**
- behind the opening is the **fireback.**

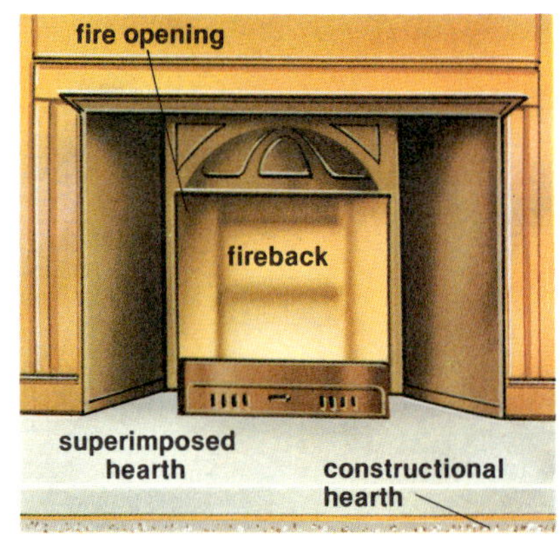

MEASURING UP FOR A NEW FIREBACK

You need to measure the old fireback to find out what size to order. Standard sizes are 16 and 18in (406 and 457mm), but larger sizes are available. The part you need to measure is the inside front opening (A).

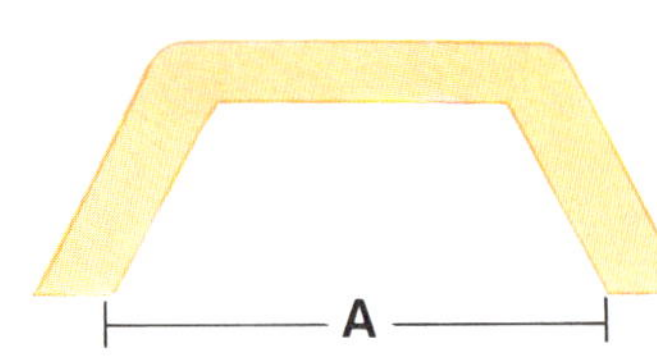

TIP: FIT A THROAT RESTRICTOR

A throat restrictor will help cut down on the amount of fuel used by reducing the air flow up the chimney. It comes in the same sizes as the fireback and is quite easily fitted at the same time.

CONSTRUCTION OF A FIREBACK

This illustration shows what goes on behind the fireback. The corrugated cardboard and asbestos rope act as buffers to protect the fireback against expansion. Then the whole area behind the fireback is filled with vermiculite mortar and rubble. Extra mortar is used to form the flaunching at the back and sides.

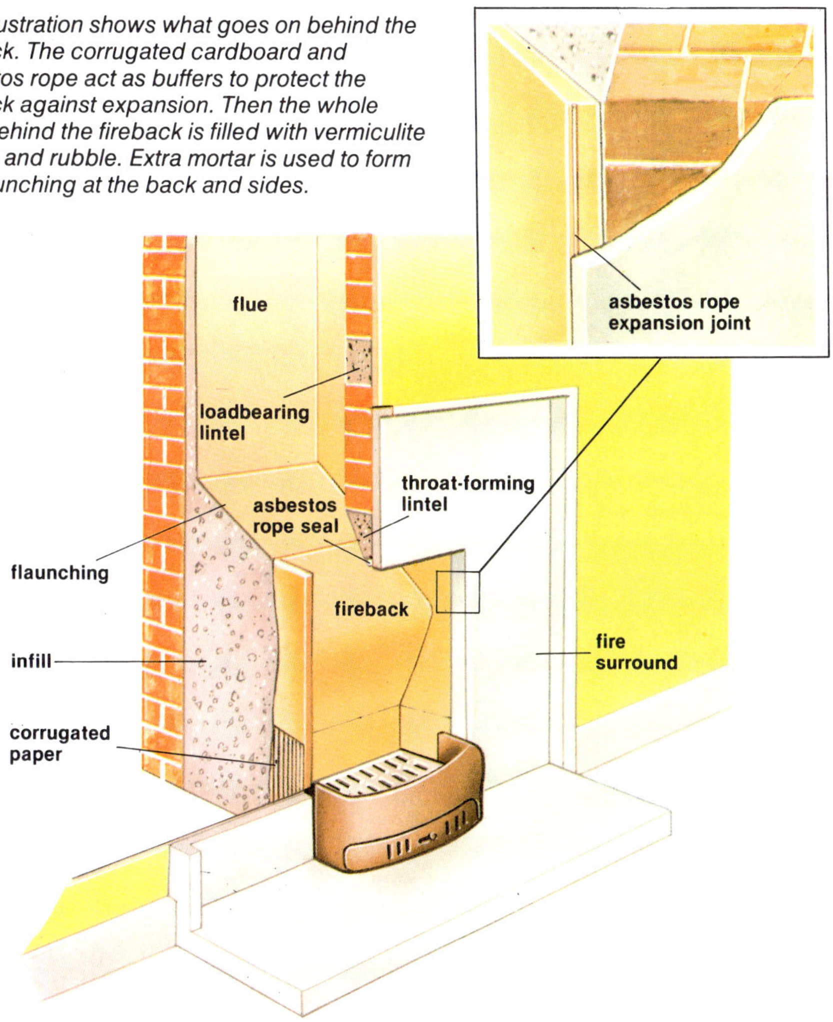

(an inert filler available from builders' merchants) to one part lime or cement; or nine parts sand to one part lime and one part cement. Do not make the mix too wet; it should be damp rather than soggy. The infill should be brought to the top of the fireback and tamped down so it is truly solid. You can, if you wish, put old bricks or bits of the old fire-back in the middle of the infill to save you mixing too much material. This type of mortar mix is ideal, as it has good heat insulation qualities and will not expand too much.

You can now fit the top half of the fireback. Sit it squarely on top of the lower half, bedding it onto a layer of fine cement and levering it into place if necessary with a bolster. Using the same mix, fill in behind this section – there's no need for any corrugated card-board – and tamp it down until the filling is level with the top of the fireback.

Just behind the surround (and over the front of the fire opening) is a lintel, called the throat-forming lintel. If you peer inside you should be able to see that the centre section of the lintel slopes upwards. You must now add extra infill mortar to the top of the fireback so that its slope is parallel to the slope of the lintel. Together, these two slopes form an opening known as the throat, which conducts the combustion gases and smoke up to the flue. It will normally be about 110mm (4½in) wide. The flaunching, as the sloping section is called, should be trowelled smooth as a rough surface can cause friction that would impede the flow of gases. Fill in the sides too to avoid any ledges where soot could accumulate. Finally fill in the join between the sides of the fireback and the fire surround with some fire cement and smooth off with a damp brush.

Replacing the grate

With the fireback in place you can now put back the grate. If it's a free-standing one you simply stand it in place. If it's an old-fashioned one, this is the time to think of replacing it with a modern fitted one which will perform much more economically and be easier to control.

Whether it's a new or existing modern fire the installation procedure is much the same – except that a new fire will need new plugs in the back hearth to take the fixing screws. Note that the plugs should be made of some non-combustible material – metal for instance. To fix the grate in place, drive the fixing screws into the plugs. Then push asbestos rope into the gap between the sides of the appliance and the fire opening. You can hold the rope in place with a smear of fire cement; then make the fixing permanent by pointing lightly with more fire cement.

Leave the installation for a few days to allow the various mortars to dry out and set properly before lighting a fire, and make only small fires for the first few days.

Fitting a throat restrictor

While you are fitting a new fireback it's worth considering adding a throat restrictor to the fireplace. This is a device for reducing the size of the throat, and it has several ad-vantages. As smoke and gases rise up the chimney, they draw with them air from the room, and this air has to be replaced with air from outside the room. This is a cause of the notorious draughts that used to be associated with open fires. However, modern appliances with their restricted air intake have largely overcome this problem. In fact, the air changes they do cause are often beneficial in that they give good ventilation to the room and help to overcome condensation. Even so, the new air that is drawn into the room has to be warmed up, and that means extra work for the fire – and extra fuel burned. A throat restrictor, by reducing the amount of air flowing up the chimney, cuts down on the number of air changes, and this means the fire doesn't have to work so hard.

The restrictor is a metal device that is placed on top of the fireback and held in place by the flaunching. Once the flaunching has set and the fire has been fitted you can adjust the restrictor. Light the fire and get it going properly, then slowly close the restrictor until you reach the point when puffs of smoke start to billow into the room. You have then closed it just too far, so open it up slightly until the smoke flows properly upwards; that is the correct setting. You will probably find that you have reduced the throat aperture from something like 110mm (4½in) to about 20mm (¾in). From time to time the gap will need to be adjusted to suit varying weather conditions and your heating needs.

FITTING A NEW FIREBACK

1 *In most cases a one-piece fireback will be supplied, but if this is difficult to fit in the opening it can be split along the break line.*

TIP

2 *You need to tap along the line very gently for quite some time before the two halves will separate. If you try to hurry it will crack in the wrong place.*

3 *Make up sufficient mortar for the infill and use some of this along the bottom of the opening to bed in the bottom section of the fireback.*

4 *Position the fireback on the mortar, tapping it into place until it is central in the opening. The sides must be vertical and the top horizontal.*

5 *Push one or two layers of corrugated cardboard behind the fireback. This chars away when the fire is lit, leaving a gap for expansion.*

6 *Using a weak mortar mix fill in behind the fireback, tamping it down until it is level with the top. You can fill up part of the space with rubble.*

7 *Trowel a layer of fire cement along the break line and bed the top half of the fireback in place. Make sure the two halves are lined up.*

TIP

8 *Trowel off the fire cement, then go over the surface again with a wet brush for a really smooth finish. Point the sides at the same time.*

9 *Finally, fill in behind the top section and, using the same mortar, build up the flaunching at the back so its slope matches that of the throat-forming lintel.*

REMOVING A FIREPLACE

If you've a drab, old fire surround that detracts from your decor, or a fireplace made redundant by central heating, you can remove it and block off the opening, as long as you ventilate the flue.

Although natural fire with a decorative surround can be an attractive focal point in a room, if you live in a centrally heated house you may feel that obsolete fireplace takes up valuable wall space and detracts from the rest of your decor; it can also create difficulties in placing furniture exactly where you'd like it.

Many modern homes are designed and built without chimney breasts or fires, so the problem doesn't arise, but if you live in an older house with fireplaces in every room you may want to remove one (or more) of them. It's possible to completely remove the chimney breast. But, although this can give you a considerable amount of extra space, it'll tend to make your room look 'boxy'; and you'll also lose the useful alcove space at each side of the chimney breast, which is ideal for fixing shelves.

The best solution is to remove the fireplace and its surround and block up the hole. It isn't a difficult job but it can be rather messy, and you'll probably need some help to lift the heavy hearth and surround.

Surrounds and hearths

There are many types of modern and older-style fireplaces, although they're usually fixed to the wall in a similar way. The opening, known as the 'builder's recess', might have been converted to take a gas or an electric fire but once this and its wiring or pipework is removed, blocking it off is just the same as for a 'real' fire.

Your fire surround may be one of the decorative cast-iron types and will have four of six integral 'lugs' at the sides through which are inserted the screws that fix it to the wall. You may also find a separate cast-iron section framing the opening and secured to the main surround by nuts and bolts.

This type of surround is very heavy, so you'd be wise to dismantle the separate section before you try to remove it from the room.

Surrounds are also made of brickwork or stonework; they're built like a wall flat against the chimney breast, and sometimes they're bonded to the wall. You can remove either type by dismantling them piece by piece.

Timber surrounds, whether elaborately moulded, carved, or simple hardwood frames, are usually screwed to timber battens fixed to the wall, sometimes as a separate mantelshelf and side pieces. They often have a central tiled area, which may be fixed directly to the wall or stuck on a slab and secured to the wall with metal lugs and screws. Cast-iron and wooden surrounds can be valuable and some types are much sought-after, so you may think yours is worth selling. You'll have to take great care when removing it so you don't damage it.

Concrete slab surrounds are usually clad with ceramic tiles and have wire mesh or steel rod reinforcement, and fixing lugs set in the concrete at the sides.

Most decorative or 'superimposed' hearths are made of reinforced concrete, often clad with tiles, or stonework. The decorative hearth is set in mortar on a concrete slab called the 'constructional' hearth, which is set flush with the floor surface. It forms the base of the fireplace opening and also extends into the room – often with an asbestos tape or rope expansion joint where it protrudes from the cavity – to provide a barrier between the heat of the fire and the combustible material of the floor.

Inset tiled hearths are mostly found in upstairs rooms. You probably won't need to remove the tiles if your floorcovering conceals them, but you may have to lay a concrete screed over them or glue hardboard on top to bring the surface level with the floor.

Firebacks and lintels

There will be a fireclay fireback cemented inside the cavity, which protects the brickwork of the chimney breast from the heat of the fire. You can remove this by chopping out the mortar which secures it, but if on the other hand you think you may want to restore the fire to working order later, leave it in place.

The builder's recess itself is formed in the chimney breast and has a concrete lintel or iron bar and brick arch above to support the walling above the opening.

Removing your fireplace can be a messy job, so before you start, it's wise to have the chimney swept: any vibrations could bring

HOW FIREPLACES ARE BUILT

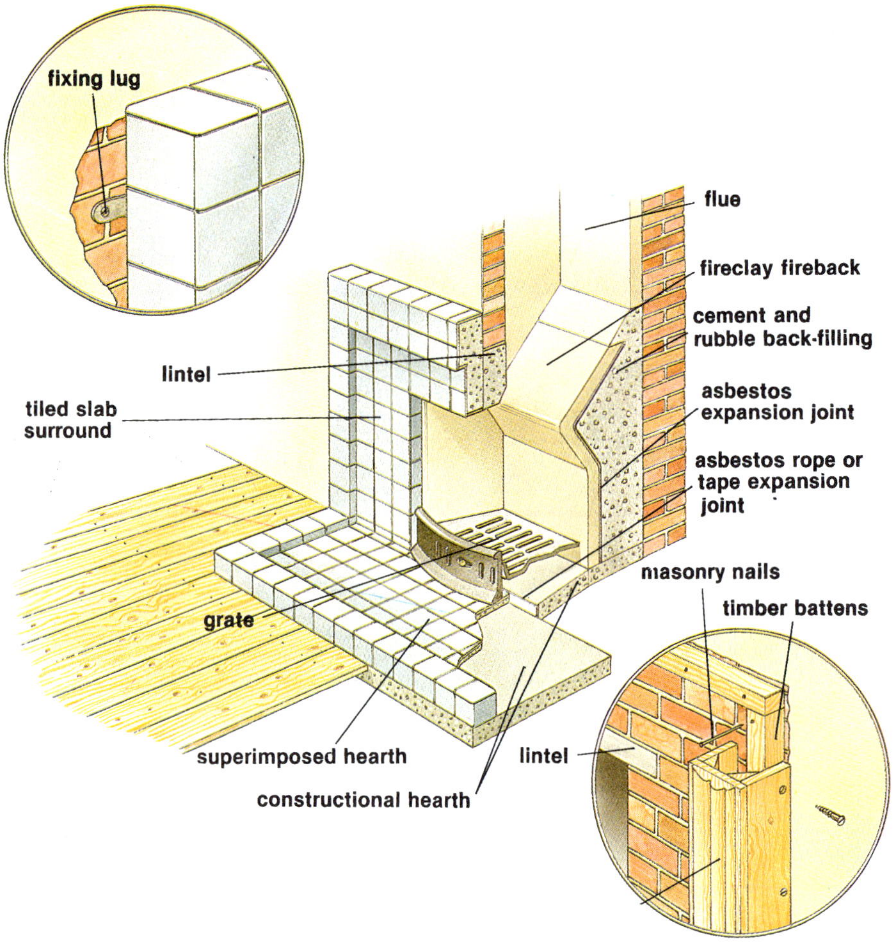

Most fireplaces are constructed along similar lines: this diagram shows a typical type of construction for a tiled slab surround and hearth.

soot down. Clear the room of as much furniture as you can, or group it in the centre of the room and cover it with dust sheets. Roll back the floorcovering from around the hearth and lay a large sheet of heavy gauge polythene on the floor as protection against dust and debris: don't use newspaper as it tears too easily. You'll also need something in which to collect the debris, such as a large metal bucket or even a wheelbarrow.

Removing the hearth

The decorative hearth is usually laid after the surround has been fixed to the wall, so this is the first thing you should remove. If, on the other hand, the surround has been laid on top of the hearth you'll have to remove this first. A little investigation will show you what the first move should be.

Use a club hammer and bolster chisel to loosen the mortar bond between the two hearths and ram a crowbar or garden spade underneath to prise them apart. It's a good idea to wedge offcuts of wood under the hearth to give you more leverage. If you find the hearth too heavy to lift – or if it's firmly bedded in mortar – you may be able to smash it into smaller, more manageable, pieces with a sledge hammer, although you'll have to cut the metal reinforcement with a hacksaw. Don't forget to wear goggles as protection against flying fragments. A stonework hearth can be removed in the same way.

When you've lifted the hearth clear you can make good the surface of the constructional hearth by filling any cracks or voids with ready-mix mortar. If your floor's solid you can simply level off the hearth area to floor level by laying a screed of concrete, but if the floor's timber, and you want to continue the floorboards up to the wall, you'll have to chisel away the constructional hearth to just below the floor level with your club hammer and bolster chisel, then fit a

READY REFERENCE

CAPPING THE CHIMNEY

To prevent moisture forming in the disused flue, where it could cause dampness on the face of the chimney breast:

- fit a metal cowl (**A**) to the chimney pot (**B**) to ventilate the flue and prevent rain getting in or
- remove the chimney pot and bed a half-round tile (**C**) over the opening to the flue.

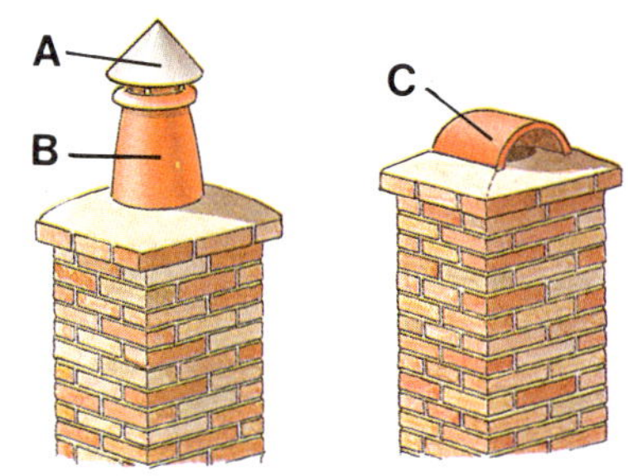

CONTINUING THE FLOOR

If you've got a timber floor you want to feature, you'll have to continue the floorboards over the hearth area. To do this:

- chisel the constructional hearth (**A**) to just below floor level
- nail a new joist (**B**) across the hearth
- lay short lengths of floorboard
- fit new skirting across the chimney breast.

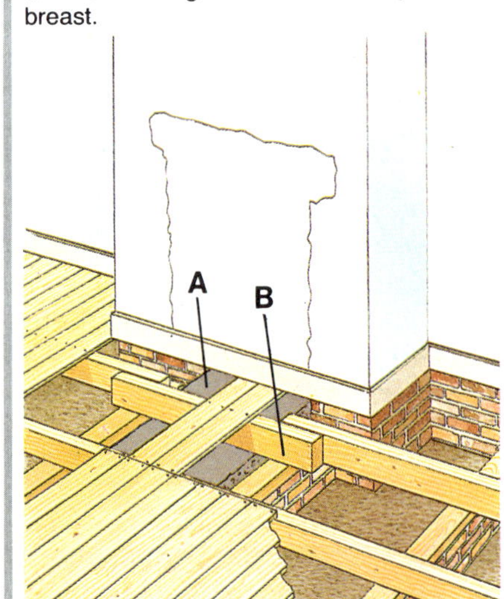

MAKING A FEATURE

If you want to make a feature of your fireplace opening:

- remove the fireback and rubble behind it by breaking it with a hammer and chisel
- fit a ventilated chipboard roof just above the opening within the chimney
- mount shelves on battens inside the opening for books, ornaments or the TV.

REMOVING THE HEARTH

1 *Not all fireplaces have slab hearths and tiled surrounds. Some of the older types have a recessed hearth, and a decorative inner surround.*

2 *If your tiled hearth is set flush with the floorboards you needn't completely remove it; lift the tiles using a club hammer and bolster chisel.*

3 *Your surround might have a separate mantelshelf simply bedded in mortar; break the bond by lifting the front edge.*

4 *If the mantelshelf is marble or metal it'll be very heavy. Get someone to help you lift it off the columns and carry it from the room.*

5 *If the side columns are fixed to the wall by lugs, unscrew these first and pull the columns free; they may simply rest against the wall.*

6 *When you've removed both columns you should be able to pull away the heavy cast iron centrepiece, which may have tiled panels.*

new joist on which you can lay new floorboards.

Removing the surround

Your cast-iron or tiled slab surround will probably be fixed to the brickwork with screws inserted through its side lugs into wall plugs. Small surrounds usually have only two lugs, one at each side, about 75mm (3in) down from the top; large ones may have two at each side and maybe two at the back of the mantelshelf.

The lugs are usually screwed directly to the brickwork and buried in the plaster surface, unless your surround is a later addition. To avoid having to remove too much plaster, strip off a margin of your wallcovering from the perimeter of the surround; if it's not apparent where the lugs are located, tap the surface with your knuckles until you hear a change of sound. When you've located all the lugs, chip away about 50mm (2in) of plaster at each point to reveal them, using your club hammer and cold chisel.

Undo the fixing screws using a screwdriver: it's a good idea to squirt a little penetrating oil on them first, and leave it to soak in. If they're still difficult to remove you can drill out their heads using a drill bit the size of the screw shank, or saw them off with a hacksaw.

Wedge a crowbar behind the edge of the surround near the top lugs and insert an offcut of timber behind it to protect the wall and give better leverage. Lever the surround away from the wall slowly and lower it gently to the floor: you may need someone to help you at this stage.

If the surround is too heavy to remove in one piece – and you don't intend to sell it – you can break it up with a sledge hammer, even if it's made of cast iron. Cover it with sacking first to contain any flying fragments, and wear goggles as a precaution.

You can dismantle a stone or brick surround piece by piece, and if you're careful to keep the bricks intact you may be able to use them elsewhere. In which case it's useful to number each piece in relation to its position on the wall.

As you remove the bricks or stone blocks you may find metal 'ties' enbedded in the mortar joints, which hold the surround against the wall, and a steel plate supporting the walling above the opening.

Timber surrounds are screwed at the sides to a timber frame fixed to the chimney breast. The screws are usually countersunk about 6mm (¼in) and concealed with filler or dowels, glued in and smoothed flush with the surround. If you can't locate the screws by tapping you'll have to scrape off the paint or varnish to reveal them. To reach the screws you can either drill down to their heads or cut out the filler or dowels with a small firmer chisel. Use penetrating oil to loosen the screws, then withdraw them using a screwdriver. Lift the surround clear of the wall and remove the battens.

Blocking the opening

Once you've removed the fire surround and hearth you can block off the opening in a number of ways. You may, for instance, be able to use the opening as a display recess for hi-fi or ornaments by fitting shelves inside. You'll have to fit a ventilated roof to the opening, strong enough to contain any soot or debris that might fall down the flue.

But if you want to block off the opening completly you can fit a panel of plasterboard over the cavity, or fill it with bricks or blocks. You can then plaster over the panel and decorate it with paint or wallpaper to match adjacent walls.

If, on the other hand, you want to fit a gas fire against the chimney breast, you can block off the opening with a sheet of asbestos-free insulating board with a hole cut in to take the vent outlet from the fire.

Whichever method you use, you'll have to fit a ventilator – which can be a simple metal, plastic or plaster grille – to prevent moisture collecting inside the flue and forming damp patches on the face of the chimney breast. The easiest place to put the grille is in your panel, although you could fit it in the wall higher up, or even at the side of the chimney breast. You'll also have to 'cap' the chimney pot with a proprietary ventilator or a half-round roof tile to provide a flow of air and to keep rain out (see *Ready Reference*).

Boarding up the opening

The advantage of fitting a panel to the opening is that you, or a future owner of the house, can easily restore the fireplace to working order.

To fit the panel first make up a simple frame of 50 x 50mm (2 x 2in) sawn timber to fit snugly inside the opening. On very wide openings you'll have to fit a central vertical batten to support the panel. If you want to plaster the surface flush with the wall you'll have to recess the frame about 12mm (½in) from the face of the chimney breast to allow for the thickness of the plasterboard and the skim of plaster.

If you simply want to decorate the panel with wallcovering you can recess the frame about 9mm (⅜in) from the finished suface of the chimney breast so that the plasterboard is at the same level.

Secure the frame – which can be simply butt-jointed – to the wall with masonry nails about 50mm (2in) apart; if the top of the

BOARDING UP THE OPENING

1 *If you want to cover the recess with plasterboard, you'll have to fix a stout frame of 50x50mm (2x2in) timber within the opening.*

2 *Where the sides of the opening are damaged you won't be able to fix the studs securely; nail short supporting battens at each corner of the frame.*

3 *Cut a panel of plasterboard to fit over the opening and nail it to the frame using 25mm (1in) plasterboard nails. Recess to allow for plastering.*

4 *If you're fitting a plastic ventilator, mark out the shape of the grille on the panel, just above skirting level, and cut it out using a pad saw.*

5 *Screw the first part of your plastic grille to the panel, locating the screw in a stud, and clip on the top piece. Remove the grille before plastering.*

6 *To finish the panel to match the adjoining plastered walls, spread on a thin layer of Thistle Board finish; refix the ventilator when set.*

opening is curved you can wedge offcuts of timber between its lower edge and the top.

Cut a piece of 9mm (3/8in) thick plasterboard to fit tightly inside the opening using a sharp trimming knife held against a steel straight edge. Nail the panel to the framework using 25mm (1in) galvanised plasterboard nails. Don't forget to fit it ivory side out if it's to be decorated directly with paint or wallpaper, and grey side out if it's to be plastered.

Measure the size of your ventilator and transfer its dimensions to the board. It's best to position the ventilator near the bottom of the opening. Drill a row of holes along the guideline to form a slot so you can insert a pad saw to cut out the waste.

If you're going to plaster the surface, fit a length of expanded metal lath over the joint between the brickwork and the panel to prevent the plaster surface from cracking along this line.

Plaster the surface or decorate it with wallcovering, then fit the grille.

Bricking up the opening

If you want to make a permanent job of blocking off your fireplace you should fill the opening with bricks or blocks and plaster the surface to match adjacent walls.

Your new brickwork should ideally be 'toothed' into the sides of the opening, by removing the half bricks around the perimeter at alternate courses and inserting new whole bricks to continue the bond. Install an air brick in the centre of the opening just above the skirting level. If you don't tooth in the new brickwork, you'll have to fix strips of expanded metal lath over the joint between old and new brickwork with dabs of plaster or masonry nails to prevent the plaster finish cracking.

When the mortar has set, rake back the joints to about 13mm (1/2in) deep to key the surface for plastering. Apply one coat of Carlite Browning plaster (see Working with plaster) to the brickwork – except for the airbrick – followed by a skim coat of Carlite Finish plaster to bring it flush with the wall. When the plaster has set, trowel over it (without any plaster) to polish the surface. Lubricate the trowel with water splashed on from a brush so that you don't score the smooth finish with the edge of the blade. Use light strokes of the trowel.

Fit a plastic or metal grille over the air brick. If you use concrete blocks to fill in the opening, you'll have to cut some to size to maintain the bond; you can fill in small gaps around the air brick with bricks. Don't forget to fix metal lath over the joint with the brickwork.

Fit a new length of skirting across the chimney breast.

BRICKING UP THE OPENING

A more durable method of blocking off your fireplace opening is to brick up the recess and then to plaster the surface to ensure that it matches the rest of the chimney breast and the adjacent walls of the room.

The first steps in bricking up your opening are to remove the hearth and surround, make good the floor and chop away the plaster from around the opening to reveal the old brickwork.

Chop out the half bricks at the sides of the opening so that you can 'tooth-in' the new brickwork to make a firm, bonded joint. Lay an air brick just above skirting level to allow for ventilation in the flue.

Continue bricking up the opening, toothing-in the bricks at alternate courses; then plaster the surface when complete to match the rest of the chimney breast. Don't plaster over the air brick. Fit a plaster grille on the finished surface.

USING BUILDING BLOCKS

If your fireplace opening is especially large you can use building blocks instead of bricks, which will enable you to span the distance much more easily. Where the size of the opening is less than a whole block you can fill in with half blocks or with bricks. Leave a gap for the ventilator when plastering the surface and fit a plaster grille on top. It's best to fix strips of expanded metal lath over the join between the brick- and blockwork.

PART 4

CARPENTRY

CARPENTRY MATERIALS

The raw material of any carpentry project is wood – either one of the many species of natural timber, or man-made board, but you will also need fixings to help you assemble whatever you are making, and some means of giving your workmanship an attractive and durable finish.

SOFTWOODS

The do-it-yourselfer uses enormous quantities of wood every year for projects of all sorts, and the bulk of it is properly termed softwood. But what is softwood, and what do you need to know about it to be able to buy and use it successfully?

Softwoods come from coniferous (cone-bearing) trees such as pine, spruce, fir and larch – evergreens with needle-like leaves. These grow in a well-defined belt running round the northern hemisphere, with the greatest reserves being found in Canada, Scandinavia and Siberia. Some species of softwood also grow at high altitude in tropical regions, but in nothing like the same quantities.

The name 'softwood' is generally rather misleading: yew, for example, is technically a softwood, yet is dense and quite difficult to cut, while balsa is one of the softest woods there is and is classified as a hardwood (see pages 334 and 335).

How they're grouped

Softwoods are divided fairly arbitrarily into two groups.

The first group is commonly called redwood, pine, red deal or yellow deal. There is actually no such thing as a deal tree; deal originally meant a piece of sawn wood 9 inches wide, not more than 3 inches thick and at least 6 feet long. Red deal comes from the Scotch Pine, yellow deal from the Yellow Pine. The second group is called whitewood or white deal (Norway spruce – the traditional Christmas tree).

Both generally have a very pale colour and weak grain pattern, and these properties are more pronounced in timber grown recently, with the accent on fast-growing species. You can see this clearly by comparing a plank of recently-cut softwood with the timber used in, say, a Victorian house, which will have a deeper colour and a closer, more noticeable grain.

Softwood is comparatively strong in the direction of the grain, weak across it. It is easy to saw, plane, chisel and sand, and holds screws well (nails can cause the wood to split along the grain). The wood is fairly porous, and is generally not durable enough to be used out of doors unless protected by paint, varnish or preservative. Western Red Cedar is the one commonly-available exception to this rule, its red colour weathering to a pleasant grey if exposed to wind, rain and sunlight. Most softwoods are easy to treat with preservatives, however, since their porous nature means that the preservative penetrates deep into the wood to protect it by keeping rot and wood-boring insects at bay.

How softwoods are used

By far the greatest use for softwoods is in building houses – for floor and ceiling joists, roofs, doors and windows, wall cladding, staircases, floorboards, skirtings and a whole range of other smaller features. For the do-it-yourselfer softwood is the perfect material for jobs large and small, from building extensions and outbuildings to making free-standing or built-in furniture.

Sawn or planed?

Softwood is converted (sawn) into a vast range of sizes – see overleaf. The most important thing to remember is that these are nominal sizes, not actual ones. The wood is sawn to the nominal size, but then shrinks during seasoning. It may then also be planed, which reduces the wood's actual size still further – by about 3mm ($^1/_8$in) on each dimension with smaller sizes, more on larger timbers. Such wood is known as planed all round (PAR) or dressed all round (DAR), but is still described by its nominal size.

Use sawn timber (which is cheaper) where the wood will be hidden – in partition walls, for wall battening and so on. You should also buy sawn timber to plane down yourself if you want to produce wood of a particular cross-sectional size that is not available PAR (DAR). Alternatively, you can order it planed to 'finished' size from the next available sawn size – more expensive than PAR wood.

Softwood is also machined into an enormous range of mouldings, rounds ('broomsticks') and matchings (profiled tongued-and-grooved boards for decorative wall cladding).

1 Parana pine *is whitish yellow with occasional red streaks, straight-grained and usually has few knots, so is easy to cut and plane. Don't use it outdoors, and, since it tends to twist, for open shelving.*

2 European redwood *(deal) is a type of pine varying from dusty red to pale yellow. It can be used outside when preservative-treated. It's strong, hard and easy to work unless there's a lot of resin or knots.*

The metric foot

Timber now leaves the sawmill in metric lengths, and so to save wastage many timber merchants sell wood measured in a contrived unit of 300mm – the so-called metric foot, actually measuring $11\frac{3}{4}$in. So if you order '6 feet' of wood, you may be sold a piece 6 metric feet – 1800mm or 5ft $10\frac{1}{2}$in – long. If you actually need a full 6ft (1830mm) of wood, you may have to pay for 7 metric feet (2,100mm/6ft 10in) and waste the off-cut.

The sawing processes

It is much easier to understand wood as a natural material if you know how it is 'converted' – turned from logs into usable rectangular planks. The secret of the sawmill lies in producing the largest quantity of good-quality wood from each log, with the minimum of wastage. Three methods are commonly used.

Plain sawing means cutting the log into parallel planks. It yields pieces with two different grain patterns, depending on their position in the log, and those cut from the edge tend to curl and warp badly. This can be avoided

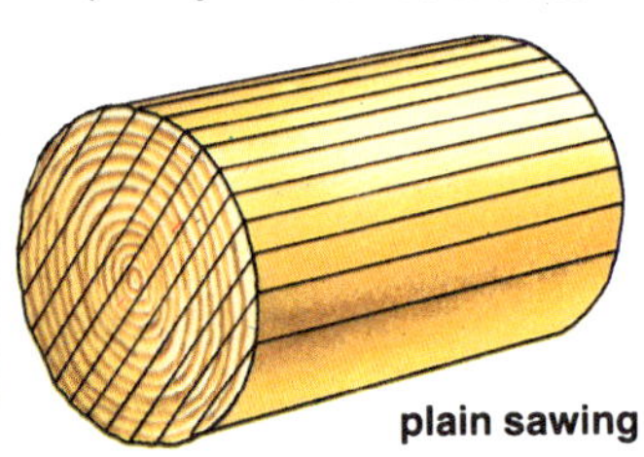

Brian Watson

plain sawing

by *quarter* sawing – cutting the log along radial lines – and this also yields wood with a similar grain pattern throughout; it is,

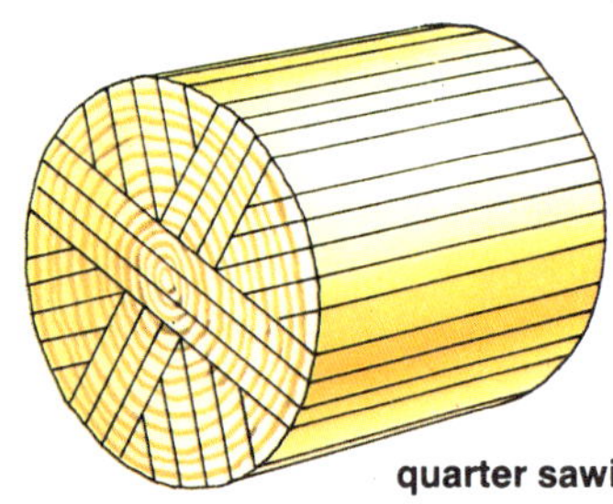

quarter sawing

however, more wasteful. The third method is *tangential* sawing, used to produce more wide planks from relatively small logs; wood sawn tangentially also has a plainer, more open grain pattern.

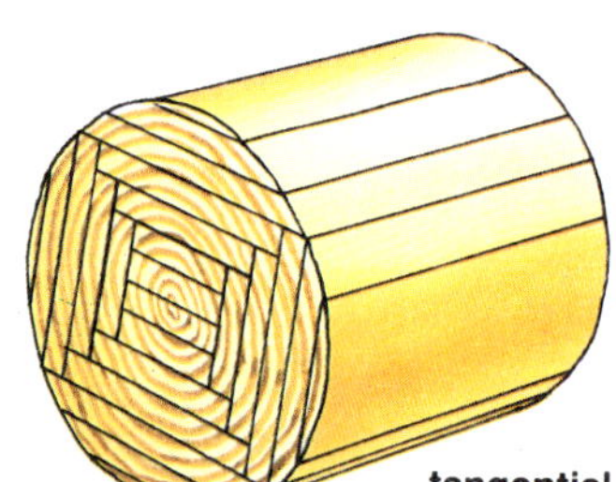

tangential sawing

Seasoning wood

Once wood is sawn, it has to be 'seasoned' at a controlled rate to dry out the sap and reduce the moisture content of the wood to around 10 or 12% – when felled wood can contain as much as twice its own weight of water. Seasoning makes the wood easier to work (anyone who has cut down a tree knows how difficult 'green' wood is to saw), lighter to handle and more

Brian Watson

3 Western Red Cedar *is rather oily, fragrant and pinkish-red to reddish brown. It's the most common type of cedar available. It can be used outdoors untreated – the weather will turn it silver grey.*

4 Spruce, *also known as whitewood, is cream in colour. It's light and strong, physically easy to work and finishes well. It does not take preservatives well and so is restricted to interior use.*

---

resistant to attack by rot and insects. Carefully seasoned wood is also less prone to shrinkage and warping than unseasoned wood.

Faults in wood

Because wood is a natural material, it has its normal share of faults. One of the commonest is the knot, the cross-section of a branch exposed at the point where its starts growing from the trunk. Knots may be fresh (live) and tight-fitting, perhaps even oozing resin, or they may be dead, dark-coloured and loose – a sign that the branch was damaged before the tree was felled.

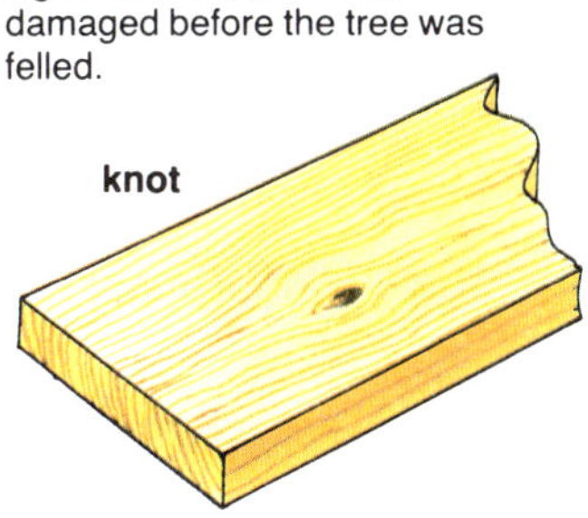

Another common fault is the shake. Star shakes are caused by

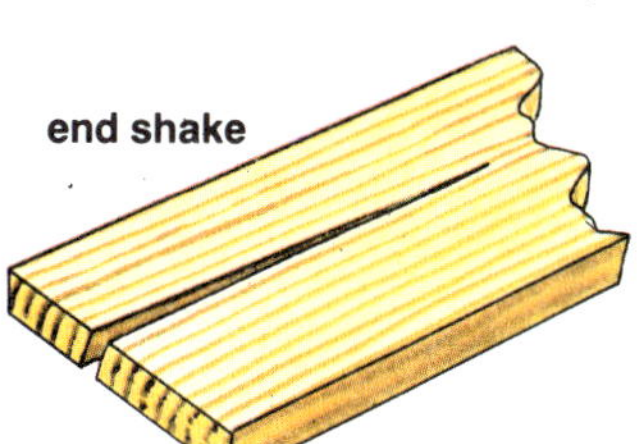

the outside of the log drying and shrinking more quickly than the rest, resulting in splits running from the centre to the outside of the log. Cup shakes occur when the inner part of the log dries

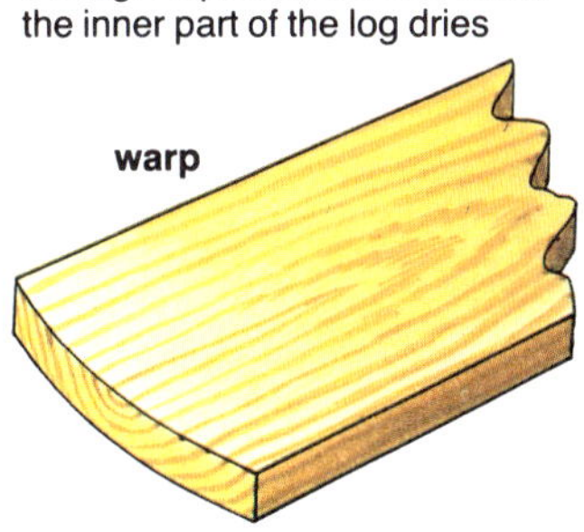

more quickly than the outside, causing the wood to split between the annual rings. End shakes are caused by too speedy drying during seasoning.

Warping is caused by uneven drying during seasoning, and may

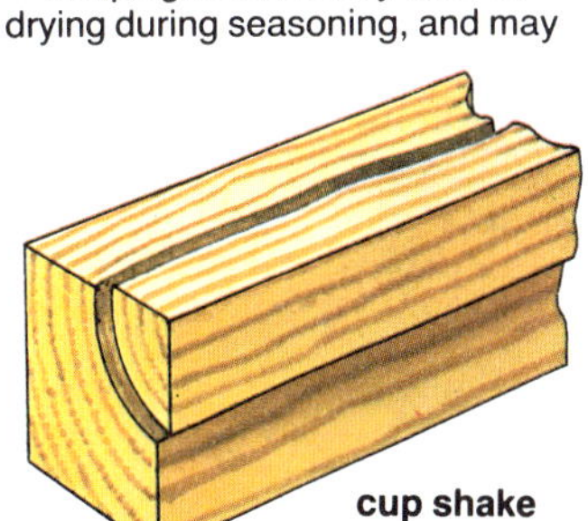

occur across the grain (giving the wood a cupped cross-section) or along it as well (a twist, visible if you sight along the length).

You should look out for these faults when buying wood (except in the case of wood you want to be deliberately 'knotty') and reject any that is not sound and straight.

Quality control

Softwood is graded according to its quality when it leaves the sawmill in its country of origin. Wood from Scandinavia and Russia is divided into two broad categories called 'unsorted' (the better quality) and 'fifths'. Wood from Canada is usually sorted into 'clears' and 'merchantable' grades, with clears being somewhat better in quality than Russian or Scandinavian unsorted grade. Parana pine is often graded into 'No 1' and 'No 2', both as good as the best Canadian wood.

Softwood may be further sorted by timber merchants into three grades – 'best joinery', 'joinery' and 'carcassing' (or building) grade. Best joinery grade is top-quality wood, virtually free of knots and suitable for use where the wood grain will be visible. Joinery grade is used for most general woodwork, carcassing grade for rough structural work where the wood will eventually be hidden from view.

Do-it-yourself shops usually sell only joinery grade wood. For other grades you will have to go to a timber merchant.

hints

Most softwoods bruise and mark easily; take care when using your woodworking tools to avoid damage. In particular, always protect the wood surface with an offcut of scrap wood when tapping joints together or when pulling out nails with a claw hammer.

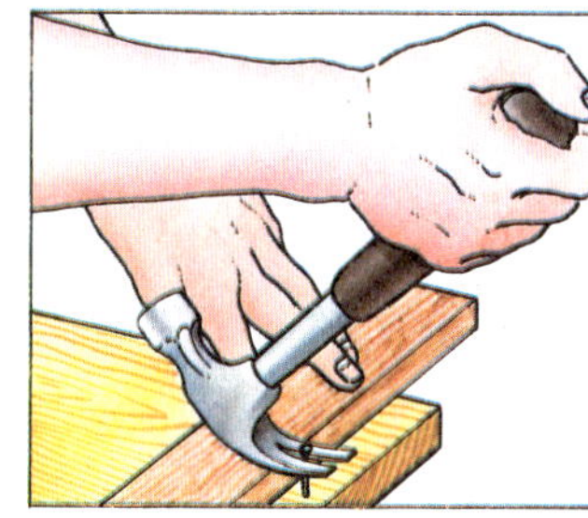

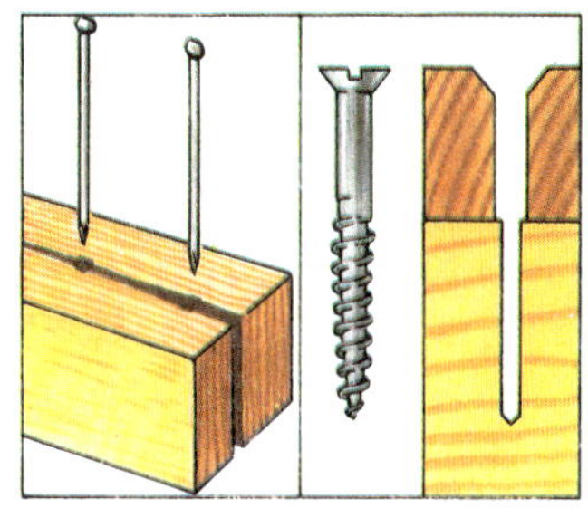

Splitting is likely to occur if you drive several nails in a row along the line of the grain – it's best to stagger them. Ideally you should use oval nails driven in with their flatter sides parallel to the wood grain. Drill clearance holes if using screws, countersinking if necessary to accommodate the screw heads.

When you are using a plane you should work with the grain to get a clean finish; you will find that the plane cuts much more easily in one direction than in the opposite one. Always sand wood along the grain too, never across it.

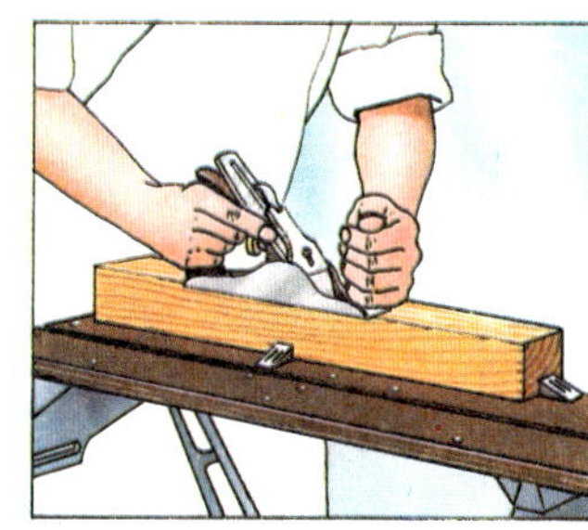

Some softwoods have a high resin content and this may show up in sticky pockets. You can seal small pockets by drawing out the resin with a blow-torch, then brushing on knotting. If pockets are large, they are best cut out – so always choose timber with care at the start.

HARDWOODS

There's no mystery about hardwoods. Oak, walnut, mahogany, teak and many more well-loved timbers are readily available if you want to use their rich, varied shades and patterns in your home.

Most hardwoods really are harder than softwoods – but not quite all; the two classifications are named for botanical, not practical reasons, and hardwoods themselves vary widely in strength, toughness and weather-resistance. Their denseness can make accurate work easier, but it can also blunt tools faster; and you'll need to keep a sharp eye out for variable grain directions which make it hard to get an even surface with the plane.

Hardwoods do cost more, which is why softwoods are used for all rough house-carpentry. But your money buys a fascinating, inexhaustible variety of beautiful colours and grains. Once you have the confidence to work without paint to cover up your mistakes, and preferably with proper concealed joints rather than just screws and nails, you'll want to use hardwoods for all their subtle decorative possibilities, varnishing or polishing them to bring these out.

There are thousands of hardwoods, many strangely named and hard to get. Here we show only those you're most likely to find. But they give an idea of the tremendous range available. If your timber merchant shows you a piece of afzelia or jelutong, don't turn your nose up: it may be just what you want.

Many hardwoods are often used as thin sheets of veneer, to give the appearance without the cost. Sticking veneer down by hand is a fairly specialised operation, unless you buy the 'iron-on' real-wood veneers which are available in some of the more common timbers. Ready-veneered chipboard, or plywood with a decorative top layer, is another option.

Hardwood sizes

You can't buy hardwoods in standard sizes like nails, screws or even softwoods. Dimensions available depend on the supplier – and the wood. No-one can cut wide planks from narrow trees, or long straight pieces from short, twisted trees.

However, two groups of basic cross-sections are generally obtainable. Squarish pieces, for table and chair legs, panel edges, etc, can usually be found in sizes between 25 x 25mm (1 x 1in) and 50 x 50mm (2 x 2in); and wider, flatter boards, eg, for wall cladding or joining edge-to-edge to make tabletops, from 6mm (1/4in) to 25mm (1in) thick, and 150-300mm (6-12in) wide.

But visit your timber merchant, discuss your requirements and see what he's got. Although you may have to consider alternative woods, he'll often be willing to cut wood specifically to suit your measurements. In fact, since hardwoods come in so many different types and sizes, he may well have to. Be prepared, however, to modify your design if he suggests a more economical way of cutting the timber. His advice will save you money.

1

Beech, *while not particularly decorative, is strong, and easy to work and finish because of its straight, close grain. Not durable enough for outdoor use, it is used in furniture, especially for chair-frames, and is sometimes given a pinkish colour by steaming.*

2

Mahogany *is either American (the Honduras variety is on the right; Brazilian is also common) or African, left – not the same species, but closely related and just as good. Mahogany is widely used for reproduction furniture. Its attraction lies in its rich colour and lustre.* **Utile** *(on top), another fine African wood, is very similar.*

Oak *can be red or, more commonly, white. Varieties of white oak come from Europe, America (underneath in the picture) and Japan. English oak (on top), the hardest, strongest and most durable, was universally used for hundreds of years. Imported European oak is now commoner, while Japanese oak is the lightest in weight of the three. Oak is not richly coloured, but it can have an attractive figure.*

6

3

Ramin *is a plain wood whose straight grain and even texture, like those of beech, make it very useful, though it is lighter and less sturdy. It splits quite easily. Mouldings are often cut from it, and it is used in furniture. Like beech, it is easily stained to match its surroundings.*

4

Afrormosia *is just one of many African hardwoods which are unfamiliar to most people but nevertheless widely used. (Iroko is another.) Dense, richly coloured and durable, it is more than just a substitute for teak, with which it is often compared: it is even stronger, and not greasy.*

5

Elm *resembles ash except for its rather darker colour and often crooked grain – qualities which make it more ornamental but rather less generally useful. Devastation by Dutch elm disease has made it temporarily abundant in Britain, and varieties from Europe and Japan and also available.*

Teak *has long been celebrated for its great strength and extraordinary weather-resistance: it is ideal for all outdoor work. Its rich colour has been in demand for furniture in recent years, though it is not cheap. Its greasiness presents difficulties in glueing and for some finishing processes.*

7

Ash *is another strong, pale wood like beech, but with the coarse, open texture of oak. Its exceptional toughness and straight grain suit it for bending and for such things as tool handles. However, it is not a good outdoor timber.*

8

Walnut *was widely used in English furniture of the Queen Anne period. True walnut really comes from England (like the top piece in the picture) and other parts of Europe, as well as North America, but other similar woods are African (underneath), Queensland and New Guinea walnut. Its value lies in its depth and variety of colour and its nicely varied grain.*

9

Sycamore *is one of the most attractive types of maple, and has a lustrous creamy colour, sometimes nearly white. This, plus its compact grain and frequent rippling figure, give it a beauty of its own.*

10

COMMON SIZES FOR SOFTWOODS

Planed or dressed timber is sold in the same nominal dimensions as sawn timber but it is in fact roughly 3mm (1/8in) smaller all round (the exact amount varies according to the cross-section). Thus the pieces of timber shown below are in fact slightly less in size than the dimensions by which they are sold. Not all planed timber sizes you can buy are shown here but the picture should give you some idea of the different sizes relative to each other.

The large sizes, eg 100 x 75mm (4 x 3in) or 150 x 75mm (6 x 3in) are used for structural work whereas the slim battens, eg 25mm x 12.5mm (1 x 1/2in) are used for decorative work or situations where strength is not a necessary requirement. You can also see how timber may be offered for sale split, warped, bowed or with knots and you should look out for these faults when buying.

The table below lists the range of sizes in which sawn and planed softwoods are sold and which you should find relatively easy to obtain. Softwoods are sold in other sizes by some stockists depending on the source of supply and the sawmill which processes the timber. You can also, of course, ask your stockist to plane a piece of timber for you from the next size up, though this is an expensive way of buying timber. All the PAR or DAR sizes listed here are available sawn but the reverse does not apply. A solid symbol means the size is available sawn or planed, an open one denotes a sawn size only.

Sawn and planed (dressed) sizes

thickness mm	width mm 12.5	16	19	25	32	38	50	75	100	125	150	175	200	225	300	thickness in
12.5	●			●		●	●	●	●		●					1/2
16		●		●		●	●									5/8
19			●	●		●	●	●	●		●	●		●	●	3/4
25				●		●	●	●	●	●	●	●	●	●	●	1
32					●		●	●	●		●	●		●	●	1 1/4
38						●	●	●	●		●			●	●	1 1/2
50							●	●	●		●	○	○	●	○	2
75								●	●		●	○	○	●		3
100									●				○	●	●	4
width (in)		5/8	3/4	1	1 1/4	1 1/2	2	3	4	5	6	7	8	9	12	

CHOOSING HARDWOODS

To help you select hardwoods for particular jobs, their properties are summarized in this table. All the woods listed will make fine interior furniture and fittings, and can be finished with oil, polish or varnish (teak is an exception, for it is too oily to varnish successfully). Woods in **bold type** are those you're most likely to find.

	Walnut	**Walnut (Afr)**	**Utile**	**Teak**	**Sycamore**	Sapele	Rosewood	**Ramin**	Obeche	**Oak**	Meranti	Maple	**Mahogany**	Iroko	Idigbo	**Elm**	Cherry	**Beech**	**Ash**	Agba	**Afrormosia**
Shade Woods range from light to dark. 1 = palest	2	2	1	1	2	2	2	2	2	1	★	2	1	1	3	2	1	2	2	2	3
Richness Some timbers look bland, while others glow with a deep lustre when sealed. 1 = plainest	3	2	2	1	2	2	2	2	3	2	2	2	3	1	3	2	2	3	2	3	3
Figure Grain patterns vary from straight to swirling (sometimes depending on how the wood is cut). 1 = plainest	2	1	2	1	1	3	1	2	3	2	2	2	1	1	3	2	2	2	1	2	3
Durability Some timbers need preservative treatment for outdoors. 1 = most perishable	3	3	1	1	1	1	2	3	2	1	3	3	1	1	3	3	1	3	3	2	1
Density Timbers vary greatly in heaviness and hardness. 1 = lightest/softest	3	2	2	3	2	2	2	3	2	3	★	3	1	2	3	3	2	2	3	2	3
Cost Timber prices change constantly, and rarity value has to be taken into account. 1 = cheapest	3	1	1	1	2	★	1	1	★	2	1	★	1	1	3	1	3	3	2	2	3

★ *depends on variety*

hints

Hardwoods have an outer layer of 'sapwood', usually removed because it's paler and less insect-resistant than the inner 'heartwood'. A 'waney-edged' or 'unedged' (UE) piece still has both sapwood and bark. However, hardwoods also come square-edged (SE) and planed on one or more edges. As with softwoods, look out for distortions in shape – and for knots, though these are sometimes desirable on the grounds of appearance.

Remember that different and even unrelated species may have the same name – 'walnut' can mean English, European (French or Italian), American, African, New Guinea or Queensland walnut. Also the same species may have several names.

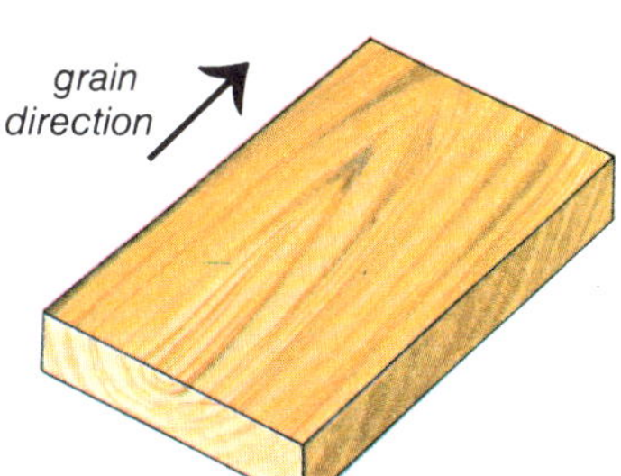

Since hardwoods are hard and dense, you must know the grain direction of your piece, and if possible plane 'with' it. Planing against the grain is difficult and at worst tears out the wood. Some species have 'interlocked' grain, which goes both ways at once! In such cases you just have to go carefully.

Hardwood must be conditioned for at least 72 hours in the environment where it will eventually be used – indoors if you're making fine furniture – to prevent shrinkage or swelling from marring the finished work.

With hardwoods the finish is all-important. Ensure it's perfect by using a cabinet scraper (right). This is a metal rectangle whose edge is squared on the oilstone, then turned over with a burr so that it will remove shavings far finer than any plane. Use it with a pushing or pulling action (below). Finally clean off dust and grease with turps.

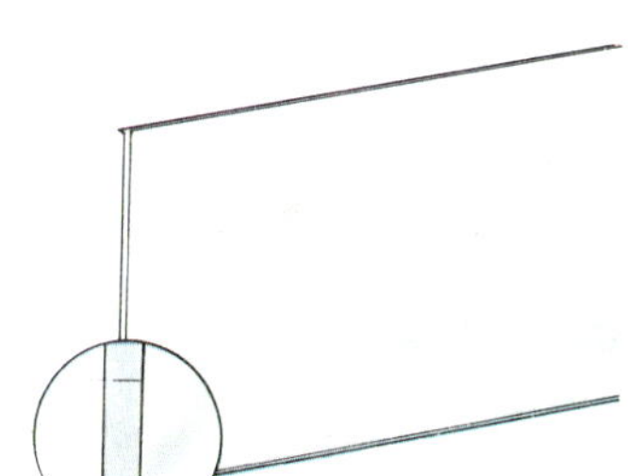

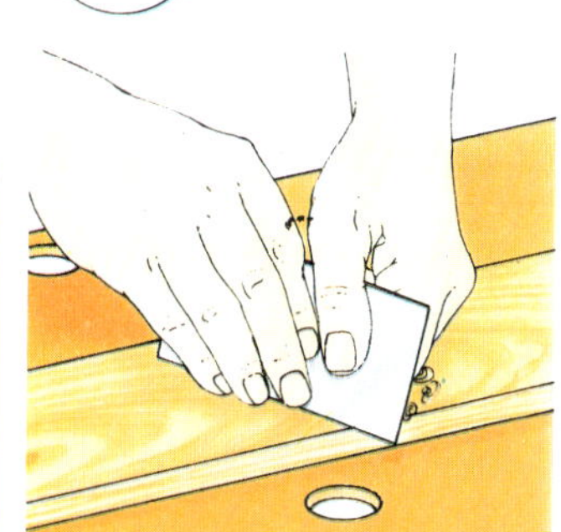

MAN-MADE BOARDS

Versatile, cheap and manufactured for uniform quality, man-made boards have become indispensable to all kinds of projects around the house. Here's a guide to the differences between them and what each is suitable for.

You only have to make some simple furniture or a few shelves from natural timber to realise just how expensive wood is. Man-made boards are the cheap alternatives. But they're not just substitutes for the real thing. In many situations, they have much more to offer than a low price. Most resist shrinking, swelling and warping better than natural woods. And because all are carefully manufactured for consistency in use, it's worth knowing exactly what each board can and can't do.

Fibreboards

Standard hardboard is the cheapest of all man-made boards and is produced by compressing wood fibre into hard, brown sheets. It is smooth on one side with a rough, mesh pattern on the other. Because it contains no adhesive, it's relatively weak, and if it gets wet it'll break up. But it's worth considering as a cladding, especially if you want something you can easily bend round curves.

● Thicknesses 2mm (5/64in) to 13mm (½in); 3, 5 and 6mm (⅛, 3/16 and ¼in) are by far the most common.

Tempered hardboard is standard hardboard which has been treated to improve its strength and resistance to moisture, and is therefore suitable for use outdoors. It shouldn't be confused with oil-treated hardboard, which has only a short-lived and superficial moisture-resistance.

Decorative hardboards may be covered with PVC or melamine. They may also be factory-painted in a process known as 'enamelling'. Both types are easy to clean, but only their surfaces resist water. You can also get standard hardboard ready-primed for painting.

Moulded hardboards are often used as wall claddings. Some even have a paint or plastic finish. You can buy them with embossed and textured designs – woodgrain, tile and brick being among the most popular. But you'll probably have to order the less common types.

Perforated hardboard has holes or slots in it. It comes in a range of designs, including plain 'pegboard' (with regular rows of small holes).

Duo-faced hardboard is smooth on both sides.

Medium board is softer and weaker than the others, and this is the main reason why it's used in thicker sheets – 6-13mm (¼-½in). The denser type HM, also called 'panelboard', is used for cladding partitions in much the same way as plasterboard. The velvety grey/brown type LM is used for pinboards, etc. Both are available in versions made to withstand high humidity, and may also be flame-retardant, oil-treated, duo-faced or lacquered.

Softboard ('insulating board'), also made from fibres, is not compressed and is therefore even lighter and less dense than medium board. Apart from insulation, it too is used for pinboards.

MDF (medium-density fibreboard), although expensive and hard to obtain, is an extremely versatile material and can often be used instead of solid timber. It's far stronger than other fibreboards because it includes adhesive (like chipboard), and is highly compressed so that it's far denser than medium board. This means it not only does everything other man-made boards do, but also overcomes their two main problems – it doesn't flake or splinter, and when sawn it gives a smooth, hard edge which doesn't need disguising (it can even be stained to match a face veneer).

● Thicknesses 16mm (⅝in) to 35mm (1⅜in).

Chipboard

Chipboard is made by bonding wood chips with plastic resin. It's quite strong, and one grade is tough enough to be used for flooring. However, it's difficult to work it neatly or to screw into it effectively: the thread breaks up the chips so the screw pulls out under load. Few chipboards can withstand moisture, though grades for external use are available.

● In the simplest type of chipboard, all the chips are approximately the same size – but usually those nearer the surface are finer. The surfaces mostly come filled and sanded, ready for decoration, and some are even primed for painting. Much chipboard is sold with a wood or PVC veneer, or a melamine laminate. Plastic-faced boards come in a limited range of colours and wood effects.

● Thicknesses range from 4mm (3/16in) to 40mm (1½in); 12, 18, 22 and 25mm (½, ¾, ⅞ and 1in) are commonest.

Plywood

Plywood is made by glueing wood veneers in layers. The grain of each veneer is laid at right angles to the ones on either side, the aim being to stop the sheet warping (though this isn't always completely successful). The sheet has an odd number of layers – hence the names, 'three-ply', 'five-ply' and so on. This ensures that the grains of the outside veneers always run in the same direction.

● Birch and gaboon are two of the main woods used for plywood.

Ideally, the veneers should be of the same wood and the same thickness. In fact, the outermost ones are always thin, and you'll often find thick veneers made of less dense timber in the centre.

● 'Stoutheart' plywood is the name given to a sheet where there is only one central thick veneer. This makes the edges of the sheet harder to work.

● Some plywoods have a decorative finish, which can range from a factory-applied paint or a plastic laminate to a particularly attractive wood veneer. Others are grooved to resemble match-board cladding.

● Two grading systems are used for plywood. The first indicates the number of knots, joins and other blemishes in the surface veneers. Its three grades are A (perfect), B, and BB for rough work. Where a board appears to have two grades (eg, B/BB), the first refers to one veneer the second to the other. The other system grades the

1 4mm (3/16in) 3-ply
2 6mm (1/4in) stoutheart 3-ply
3 9mm (3/8in) 5-ply
4 12mm (1/2in) 5-ply including oak veneer
5 12mm (1/2in) 7-ply, melamine-faced
6 18mm (3/4in) multi-ply (13-ply)
7 12mm (1/2in) duo-faced blockboard
8 18mm (3/4in) duo-faced blockboard
9 18mm (3/4in) duo-faced blockboard including teak veneer

adhesive between the veneers. WBP (weather-and-boil-proof) will withstand severe weathering for at least 25 years; then, in order of durability, come BR, MR and INT, the last of which is only for dry internal use. The adhesive may outlast the veneers; but especially durable types of plywood (eg, marine plywood, used in boatbuilding) are also available.

● Thicknesses range from 3 to 6, 12 and 19mm (1/8, 1/4, 1/2 and 3/4in), but thinner and thicker types are made.

Blockboard

Blockboard is a bit like stoutheart plywood. It has a thick core of softwood slats glued side by side, and two outer hardwood veneers, one of which may be decorative. The veneer grain runs at right angles to the core grain. In more expensive (double-faced or five-ply) boards, two outer veneers are used on each face, which makes the core joins less likely to show through.

● Blockboard is very useful where you need a relatively light, inexpensive slab, eg, for a tabletop or door. However, it's hard to get the edges neat, especially those where the core endgrain shows: there are often unsightly gaps between the slats, too. Fixing into these edges can be a problem for the same reasons.

● Surface veneers and adhesives are graded as for plywood, but no blockboard is really suitable for external use. There's no WBP grade (see above), and anyway the board contains too much softwood to be truly durable.

Laminboard is a superior blockboard. Its core is made from thinner, more uniform slats with no gaps between them. But it's hard to get.

● Thicknesses range from 12mm (1/2in) to 32mm (1 1/4in); occasionally up to 50mm (2in).

hints

EDGINGS FOR MAN-MADE BOARDS

For the best finish, edge man-made boards with a timber 'lipping'. Often this can be bought or planed to the same width as the board thickness so it fits flush on both the face and the underside. Use panel pins and PVA adhesive to fix it in place, and mitre the ends at the corners for a clean edge all round.

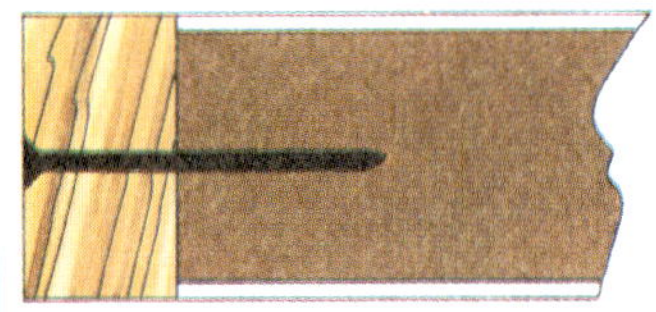

Rectangular-section strip, pinned and glued in place

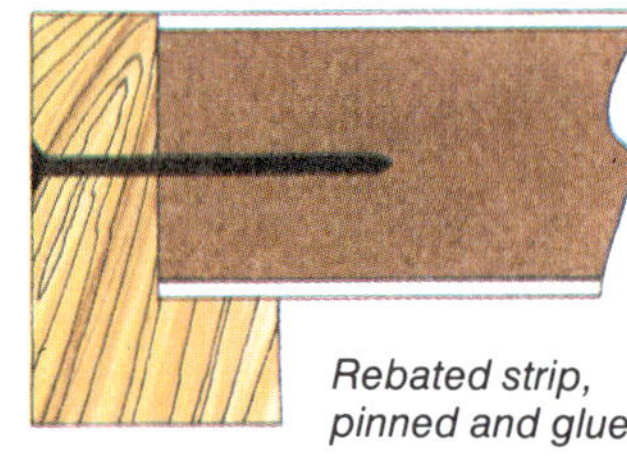

Rebated strip, pinned and glued

Half-round beading, pinned and glued in place

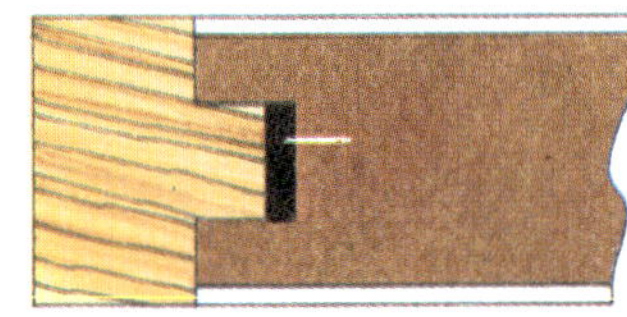

Tongue and groove – can be cut easily with power tools

Reeded moulding, pinned and glued

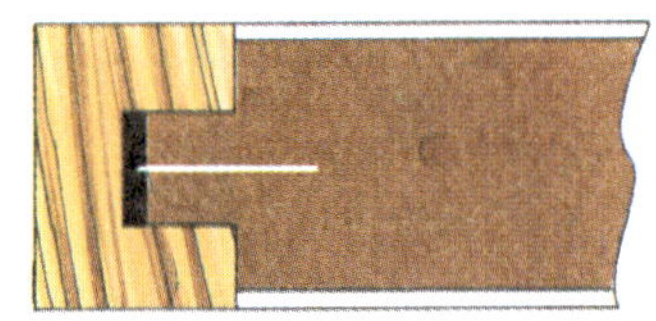

Another type of tongue and groove, slightly weaker

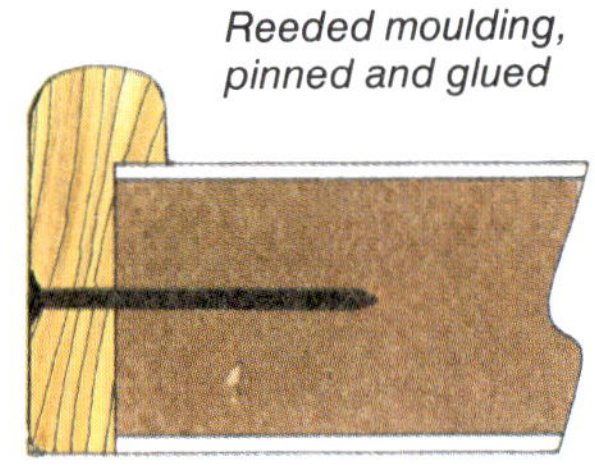

Hockey stick moulding, pinned and glued

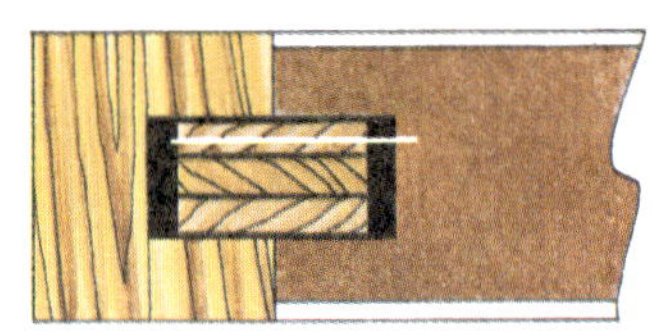

Loose tongue of thin plywood in two matching grooves

Plastic edging strip

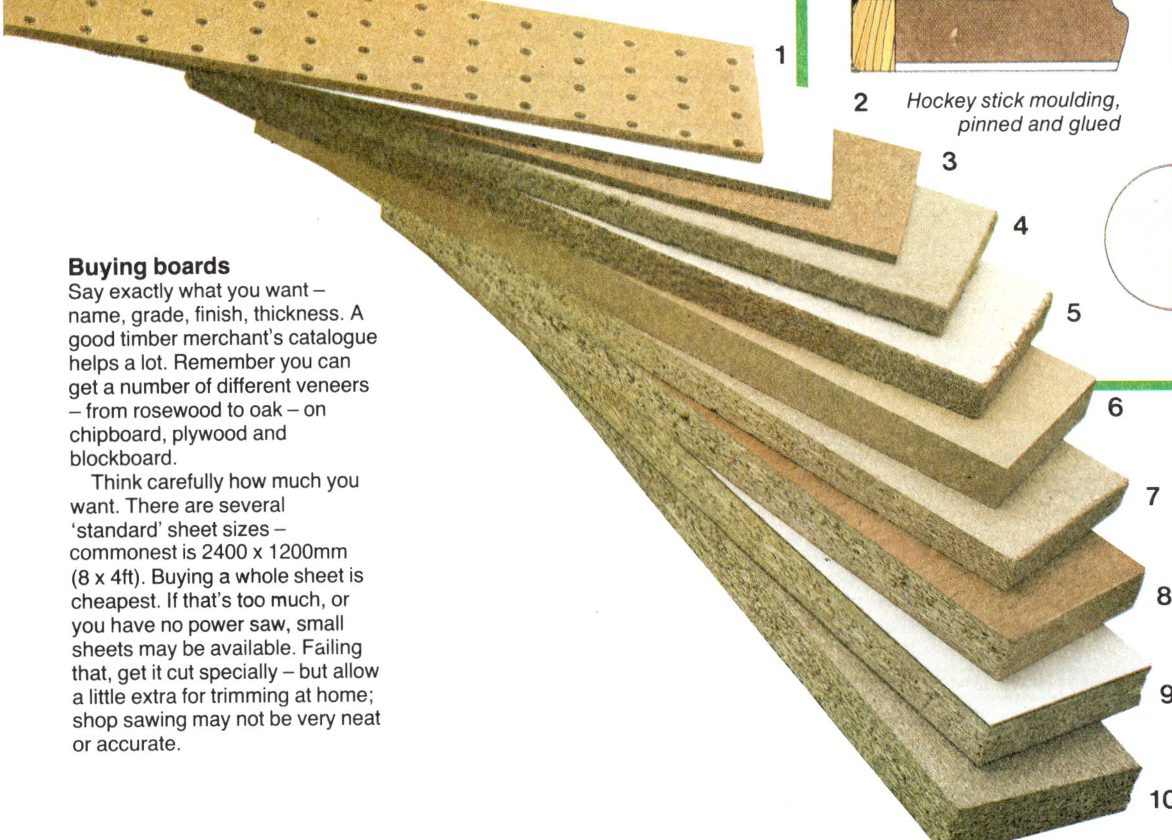

1 4mm (3/16in) pegboard
2 3mm (1/8in) hardboard, melamine-faced one side
3 3mm (1/8in) standard hardboard
4 9mm (3/8in) medium board, type LM
5 12mm (1/2in) canite board, painted one side
6 15mm (5/8in) MDF
7 12mm (1/2in) chipboard
8 15mm (5/8in) chipboard, wood-veneered and edged
9 15mm (5/8in) chipboard, melamine-faced
10 18mm (3/4in) chipboard

Buying boards

Say exactly what you want – name, grade, finish, thickness. A good timber merchant's catalogue helps a lot. Remember you can get a number of different veneers – from rosewood to oak – on chipboard, plywood and blockboard.

Think carefully how much you want. There are several 'standard' sheet sizes – commonest is 2400 x 1200mm (8 x 4ft). Buying a whole sheet is cheapest. If that's too much, or you have no power saw, small sheets may be available. Failing that, get it cut specially – but allow a little extra for trimming at home; shop sawing may not be very neat or accurate.

FINISHES FOR FURNITURE

There are many products you can use to give your furniture and fittings a fine finish. The range includes polishes, waxes and oils as well as lacquers or varnishes of various types.

Once furniture has been assembled it must be finished to seal its pores, protect its surface against heat, liquid and scratches, and to give it an attractive appearance. Before doing so, however, you might have to give it some preparatory treatment.

Preparing the wood

Restorer and cleaner contains refined alcohol and gum spirit of turpentine to dissolve old finishes. It should be applied gently using fine steel wool. A further application will probably be necessary, but don't overclean as you could mark the wood. To remove just oil or wax, apply restorer with a clean rag.

Wood bleach literally turns wood lighter in colour and also removes stains. It can only be used on bare wood and comes in two parts. You can make up to four applications, but after that many you'll have to accept any remaining stains.

Reviver contains pure boiled linseed oil that sinks into wood that has had its finish removed and appears dry and unattractive. It will prevent further drying and cracking and give some surface protection. Allow it to soak in for 24 hours.

Finishing the wood

The finish you select will depend on two factors. Firstly, the amount of protection the surface requires from water, heat and so on, and secondly, the degree of shine you want it to have.

French polish will give a superb finish with a mirror-like gloss provided it is correctly applied. However, the finish won't provide any real protection. It is made from the finest quality shellac and industrial alcohol, and you can use white or transparent polish to keep the wood a light colour, or flake orange or garnet for a darker finish. The secret of success lies in the application and the building up of several layers to get a beautiful, reflective surface.

White polish is french polish with bleached white shellac added. It is designed for use on light-coloured woods where the true natural appearance is to be maintained. It can also be used for sealing wood before waxing.

Button polish is applied like french polish but produces a harder, more orange-coloured finish.

Wax polish can be applied on its own, but it also makes an excellent surface covering for other finishes. It is not resistant to heat or scratches and needs frequent re-application. It is available in traditional wax blocks or as a liquid or spray.

Varnish (often called synthetic lacquer) provides a durable matt, eggshell or gloss finish that is highly water-resistant and can also cope well with spills and heat. It cannot be applied to wood that has been waxed or oiled unless all trace of the previous finish has been removed.

It comes in both one and two-part forms and can be sprayed, brushed or rubbed on. Follow the manufacturer's instructions closely as some lacquers require rapid application of coats to give amalgamation between layers, while others need 24 hours between each coat.

Plastic coating is a modern alternative to french polish that provides resistance to heat, liquids and scratches. It is available in clear, black or white, while other shades can be obtained by adding a small amount of wood stain. It requires a two-part treatment and can be given a matt finish by gentle rubbing down with wax polish and 0 or 1 grade steel wool. For a mirror finish, rub down with glass paper and apply a burnishing cream.

Using oil

Wood can also be sealed with oil but the treatment is best used only on hardwoods – softwoods become dirty and discoloured very quickly. The finish gives good resistance to moisture, but not to spills or heat. Rub the oil well in to the grain and repeat the application. Allow drying time between the coats and finish with fine grade steel wool, wax polish and a clean cloth.

Teak oil contains 'drying agents' to speed up the drying process, and gives an attractive seal to most hardwoods. It gives a minimal sheen.

Danish oil will not dry to a gloss if used on wood that has been already oiled. It gives a natural, open-grained lustrous finish, and can be lacquered over (unlike the other oils).

Linseed oil is slow-drying and forms a poor film. Heat-treated linseed oil, called boiled oil, is a better bet, and is easier to apply if mixed first with equal parts of turpentine.

Olive oil should be used to seal wooden articles, such as a chopping board, that will be used in food preparation.

KEY
1 *Preparatory treatments*
2 *Finishing in various forms*
3 *Oils for sealing hardwoods*
4 *French polish in liquid and solid form; shellac flakes are the main ingredient. Plastic coating is a modern alternative*
5 *Varnishes and synthetic lacquers.*

NAILS & SCREWS

To ensure the success of all your carpentry projects, be sure to choose the right nails and screws for the task.

Nails come in many guises for all sorts of different jobs, though some are easier to find than others. Before looking at them all, a few general points are worth considering.

The first is strength. Friction is what makes a nail grip, so long thick nails provide a better grip than short thin ones. Another factor is the shape of the nail's shank; on the whole, nails with specially shaped shanks are strongest, and cut nails are stronger than wire nails.

Cut nails cause fewer splits than wire nails because, being blunt, they break the wood fibres and create their own holes, while wire nails merely force the fibres apart.

Nails aren't very attractive. The standard method of hiding them is to punch their heads below the surface of the wood and fill the resulting hollows with stopping. But if you're securing such things as carpet, fabric or roofing felt, the large head found on most tacks and roofing nails is essential to hold the material in place.

Finally, think about rust. In most indoor work ordinary mild steel nails are fine but outdoors, you need a nail with more rust resistance. Normally this means a galvanised nail, but other rust-resisting finishes are available – and you can also get nails made entirely from metals that don't rust at all, such as brass, copper and even bronze.

Buying nails

When buying nails, remember they're described by length rather than diameter. Also, though it may be sensible (if more expensive) to buy small amounts in packets and boxes, it's more economical to buy loose nails sold by weight, not quantity.

General-purpose nails

Round wire nails (12) are used only for rough carpentry. They're available plain (12) or galvanised (15), in lengths from 20 to 150 mm (¾ to 6in).

Oval wire nails (14) are used in all types of general woodwork. Lengths are as for round wire nails; galvanised types are also available.

Lost head nails (16) are often used instead of ovals. Lengths range from 12mm (½in) to 150mm; you'll find plain or galvanised finishes.

Cut floor brads (11) are traditional fixings for floorboards. Lengths range from 20 to 150mm; they have a plain finish.

Cut clasp nails (17) are used for rough fixings in wood, and in masonry if it's not too hard. Lengths range from 25mm to 100mm (1 to 4in).

Masonry Nails (4) are specially hardened to make a reasonably strong fixing in brickwork and the like. Twisted shanks grip better than plain ones. They come in various gauges (thicknesses) and in lengths from about 12 to 100mm (½ to 4in).

Plasterboard nails used for fixing plasterboard to ceilings and stud walls, are similar but have a jagged shank for extra grip.

Panel pins (6) are slim versions of the lost-head nail, used in fine work for fixing mouldings and the like. Lengths range from 12 to 50mm (½ to 2in).

Moulding pins (9) and **veneer pins** (7) are still thinner lost-head nails and are used for fixing thin lippings and mouldings. Lengths range from 12 to 25mm (½ to 1in).

Specialised nails

Hardboard pins (8) are for fixing hardboard. Their diamond-shaped heads burrow into the surface as the pin is driven home. Most have a coppered finish; lengths are from 10 to 38mm (⅜ to 1½in).

Sprigs (5), also called cut brads, are mainly used for holding glass in window frames. Normally plain, lengths range from 12 to 19mm (½ to ¾in).

Cut tacks (2) have large flat heads for holding fabric and carpet in place. Finishes are blued, coppered or galvanised; lengths range from 6 to 30mm (¼ to 1¼in).

Roofing nails are used for fixing corrugated roofing sheets. One (1) is used with curved washers; the other has a special sprung head. Both are usually galvanised. Lengths range from 63 to 112mm (2½ to 4½in).

Staples (3) are used to fix wire fencing, upholstery springs and the like, and are either galvanised or plain. Lengths range from 12 to 40mm (1½ to 1⅝in).

Annular nails (10) have ribs along the shank to prevent them pulling out, and are used for fixing sheet materials. Lengths range between 25 and 75mm (1 to 3in); finishes are plain steel or coppered.

Clout nails (13) have extra-large heads which make them ideal for fixing roofing felt, slates, sash window cords and so on. Lengths range from 12 to 50mm (½ to 2in); most are galvanised.

To be able to pick exactly the screw you need for a particular purpose, it helps to know what each part of the screw does.

The thread is the spiral that actually pulls the screw into the wood and holds it there. Most have the same profile, but chipboard screws combat the material's crumbly quality with their shallower spiral; some screws have a double thread, which means the screw won't wander off-centre and can be driven more quickly. Most wood screws have about two-fifths of their length unthreaded, forming the shank, but chipboard screws are threaded all the way up to head for better grip.

Screw heads come in three main shapes. Countersunk is the commonest. The name describes how the screw head fits into the surface of what you're fixing – into a hole with sloping sides. This hole is made in wood with a special countersink bit; many metal fittings such as hinges have their screw holes already countersunk.

The raised countersunk head looks more handsome, and is often used with exposed metal fittings. The round head is used for fixing metal fittings without a countersink to wood.

On wood screws the Pozidriv recess has now given way to the similar-looking Supadriv type. Each has its own screwdriver shape, but you can use a Pozidriver for both.

Screws for special purposes include the clutch-head screw, which can't be undone once driven. The coach screw, used for heavy framing work, has a square head and is tightened with a spanner. The mirror screw is inserted in the usual way; then a chrome-plated dome is screwed into the head, making it a decorative feature.

Sizes and materials

How big is a screw? Its length ranges from 6 to 150mm (¼ to 6in). The gauge – the diameter of the shank – has a number from 0 (the smallest) to 32; 4, 6, 8, 10 and 12 are the commonest. Remember that you can have the same screw length in different gauges and the same gauge in different lengths.

And what are screws made of? Steel is the commonest and cheapest material, but isn't very good-looking and rusts easily. Luckily there are several alternatives. Steel itself comes with various coatings, from nickel plate to black japanning. Of other metals, brass (available plain or chromium-plated) is fairly corrosion proof but weak. Aluminium (also weak), stainless steel and silicon bronze are virtually corrosion-free. Stainless steel is the strongest of the three, but is expensive.

Remember when buying screws to give all the relevant details – length, gauge number, head type, material, recess type and finish.

HEADS AND THREADS

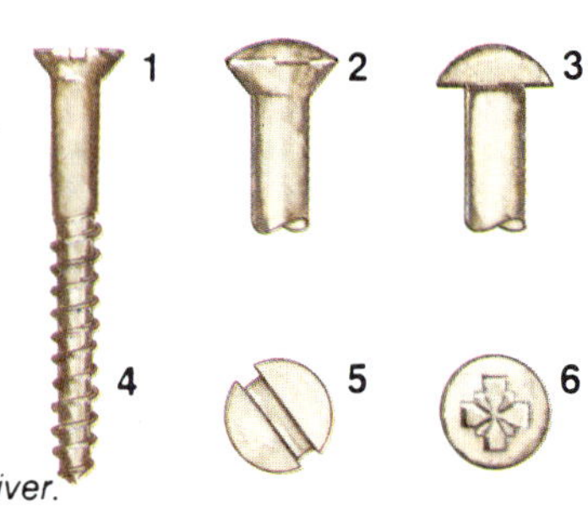

1 The commonest head profile is countersunk, with a flat top and sloping sides.
2 Raised countersunk heads have a slightly domed top, and are used with metal fittings.
3 Round-head screws are used to fix metal fittings without countersunk screw holes.
4 The screw thread usually extends to about three-fifths of the screw length, but chipboard screws are threaded all the way up.
5 Most screws have a slot in the head.
6 Supadriv recesses need a special screwdriver.

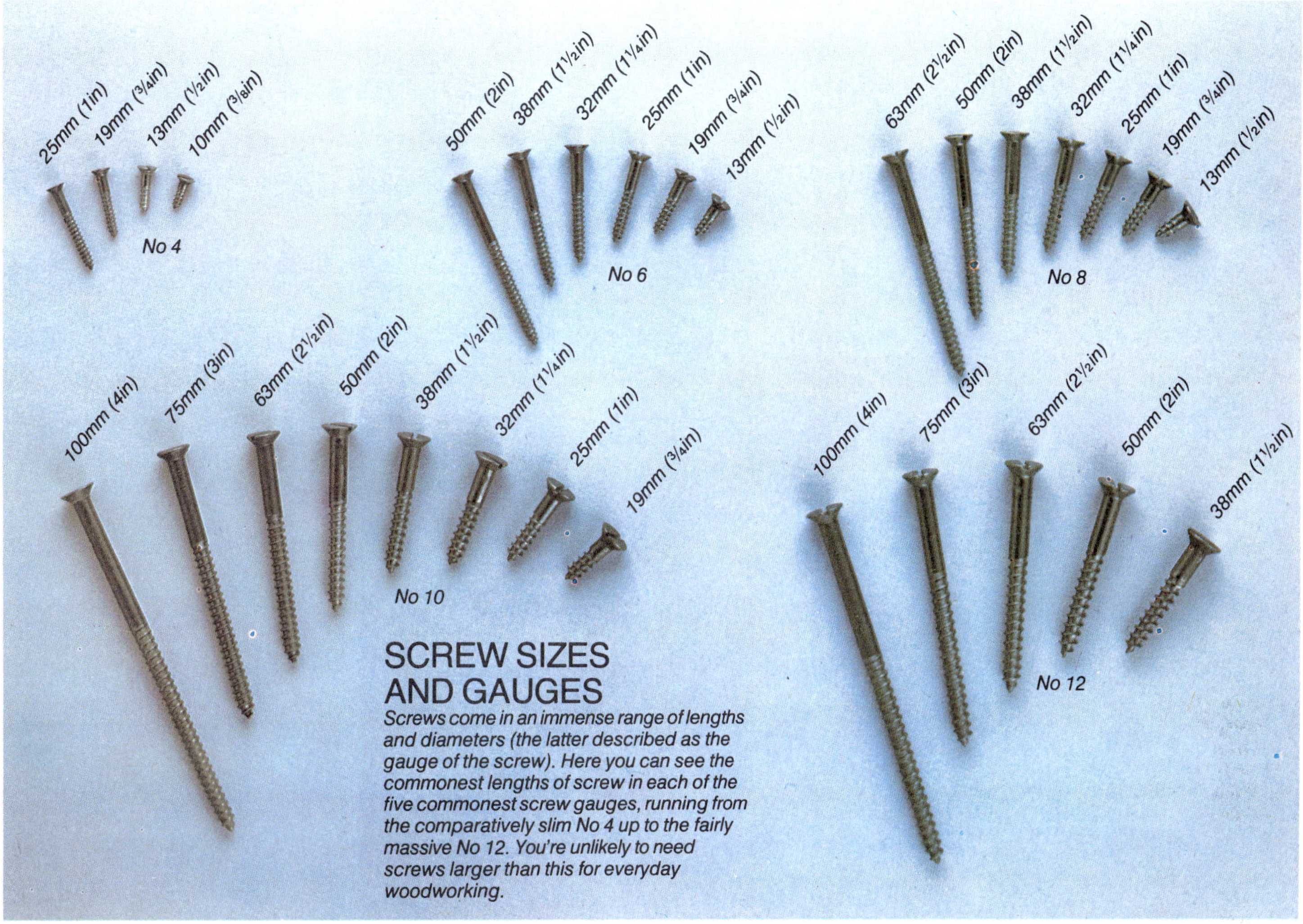

SCREW SIZES AND GAUGES

Screws come in an immense range of lengths and diameters (the latter described as the gauge of the screw). Here you can see the commonest lengths of screw in each of the five commonest screw gauges, running from the comparatively slim No 4 up to the fairly massive No 12. You're unlikely to need screws larger than this for everyday woodworking.

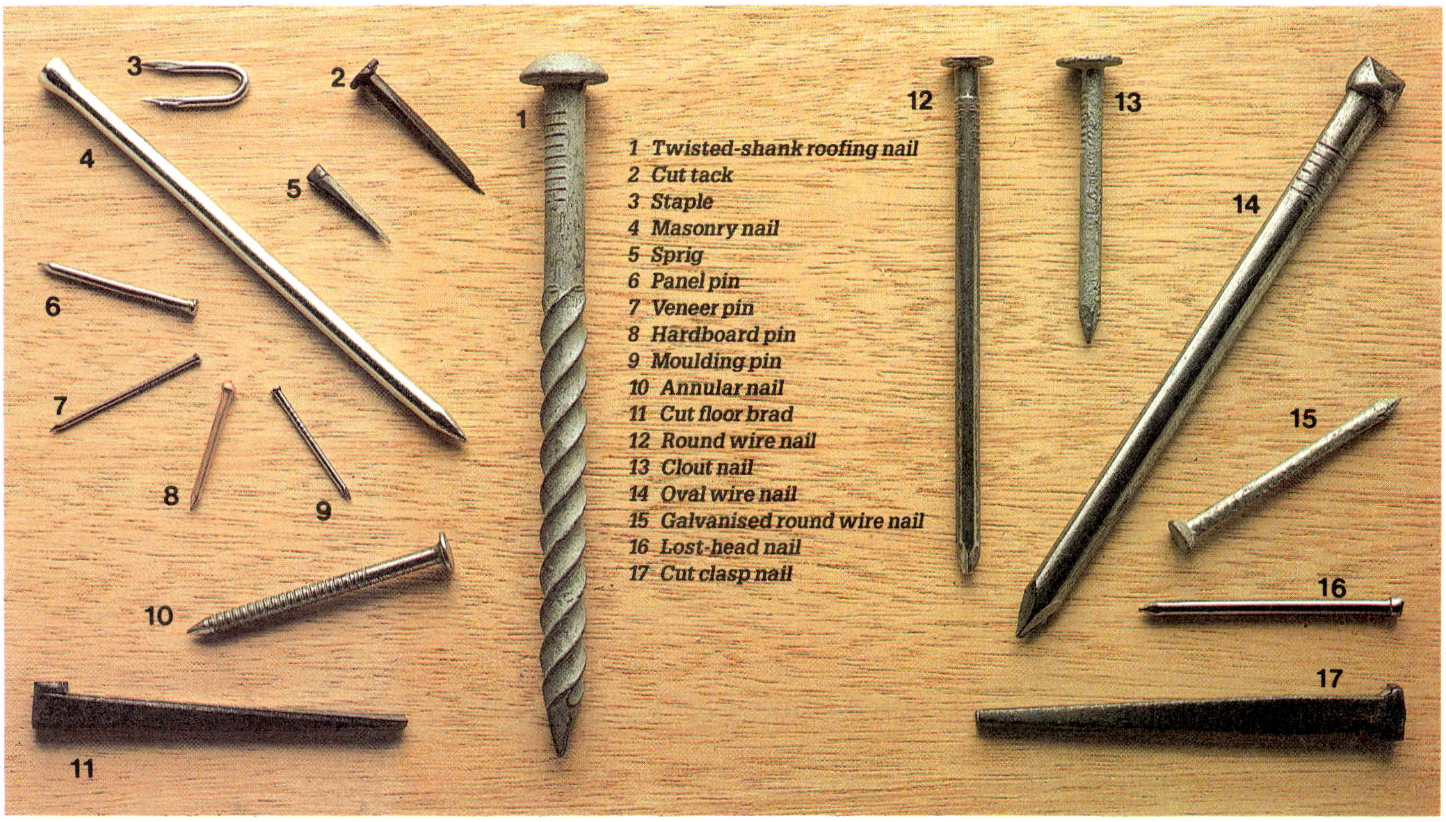

1 Twisted-shank roofing nail
2 Cut tack
3 Staple
4 Masonry nail
5 Sprig
6 Panel pin
7 Veneer pin
8 Hardboard pin
9 Moulding pin
10 Annular nail
11 Cut floor brad
12 Round wire nail
13 Clout nail
14 Oval wire nail
15 Galvanised round wire nail
16 Lost-head nail
17 Cut clasp nail

HINGES

There's a very wide range of hinges available, in all sorts of sizes and materials. Some are general-purpose types, while others are designed to do just one specific job, so it's important that you select the correct one.

When choosing a hinge, the first essential is to know what kind of door or flap you're fitting – what it's made of, and whether it's lay-on or inset (see Adding doors to basic boxes).

The second is to know how wide a choice you have. For most applications there are three or four suitable hinges. In all, there are scores of variations: here we show the main types you're likely to use.

Most hinges are made of steel, brass and white nylon, singly or in combination. Chromium and nickel plate, and brown plastic, are also used.

Butt hinges

Butt hinges, the traditional type, are still used constantly. They consist of two rectangular *leaves* (except on a flush hinge, these are the same shape), joined by a *knuckle* with a pin through it. Butt hinges come in sizes from 25mm (1in), for use on furniture, to in excess of 100mm (4in) long for hanging room doors. Materials include steel, brass and nylon.

- Some butt hinges (usually brass) have ornamental *finials* at each end of the knuckle; on some of these, such as the **loose-pin** type (4), the finials unscrew so you can tap out the pin. This makes fitting them a lot easier, because you can fasten one leaf each to door and frame separately before hanging the door by assembling the two.
- A **piano hinge** (8) is simply a narrow butt hinge sold as a continuous length of up to 1800mm (6ft), and originally designed to hinge the keyboard cover on a piano. You can easily cut it with a hacksaw to any length you need.
- The **back flap hinge**'s wide leaves (5) equip it for the task of holding table and desk flaps.
- **Rising butts** (6) are widely used on room doors. They enable the door to be lifted off at any time – and the spiral in the knuckle pulls the door closed automatically. You may have to remove the inner top corner of the door to prevent it catching on the doorstop as the door swings home.
- The **flush hinge** (7) isn't strictly a butt hinge, because one leaf closes within, rather than against, the other. It's unsuitable for heavy doors, but – unlike ordinary butt hinges – it doesn't need to be recessed. Instead, its leaves are simply screwed onto the meeting surfaces – the smaller one to the door. The thickness of the leaves equals the clearance around the door.

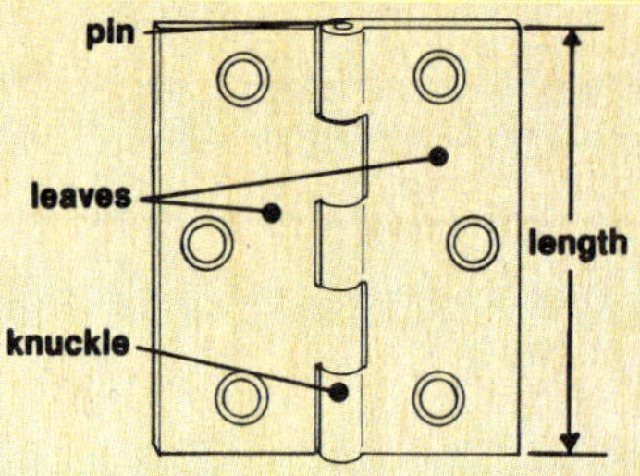

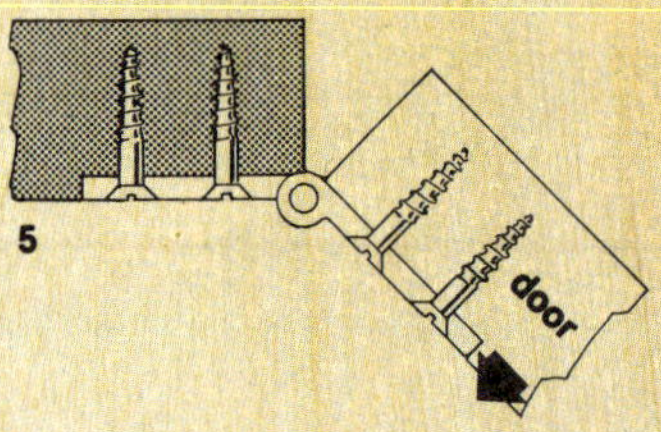

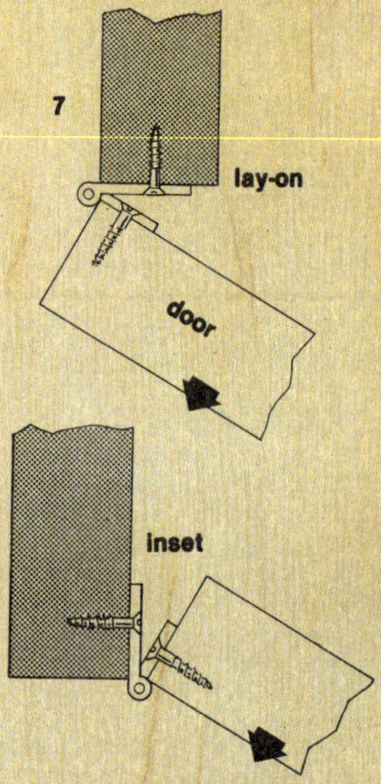

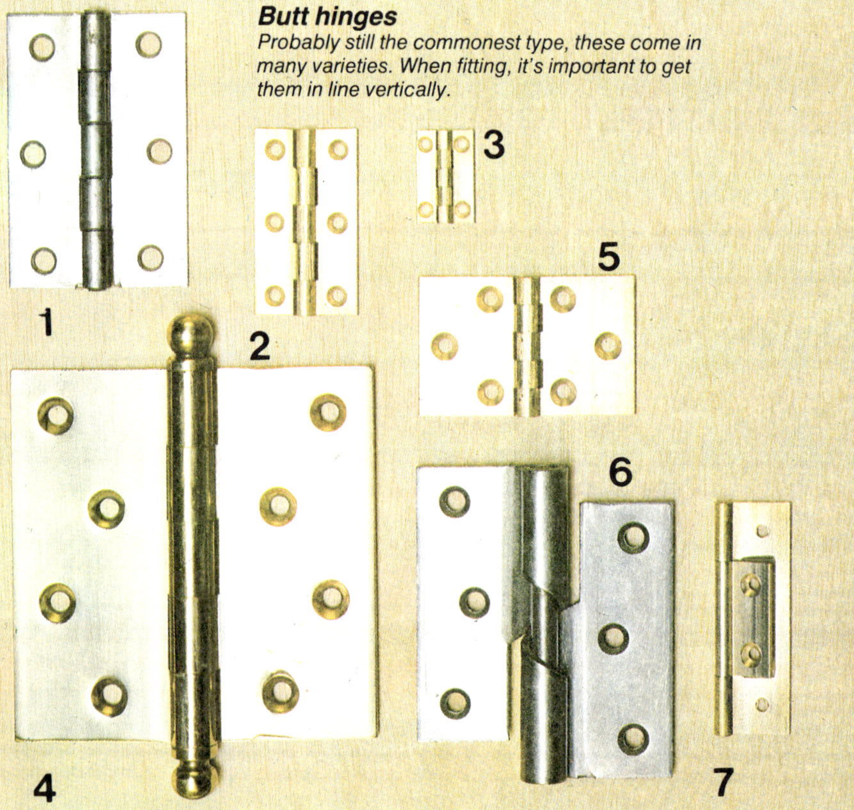

Butt hinges

Probably still the commonest type, these come in many varieties. When fitting, it's important to get them in line vertically.

Fitting butt hinges

Butt hinges usually fit in pairs of chiselled rectangular recesses. They work on both lay-on and inset doors.

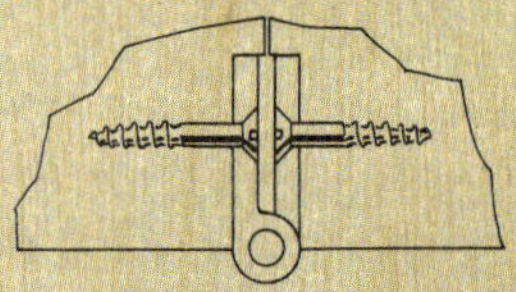

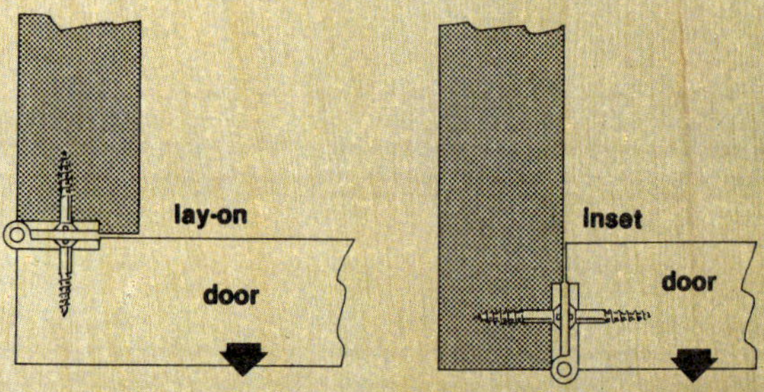

Decorative hinges

These hinges, also surface-fixing (9, 10 and 11), are of course used for their ornamental effect. Note that the front frame or edges of the cabinet must be fairly wide to accommodate them.

There's also a much smaller and less ornamental type of surface-fixing hinge which looks rather like (14) and is suitable for light doors.

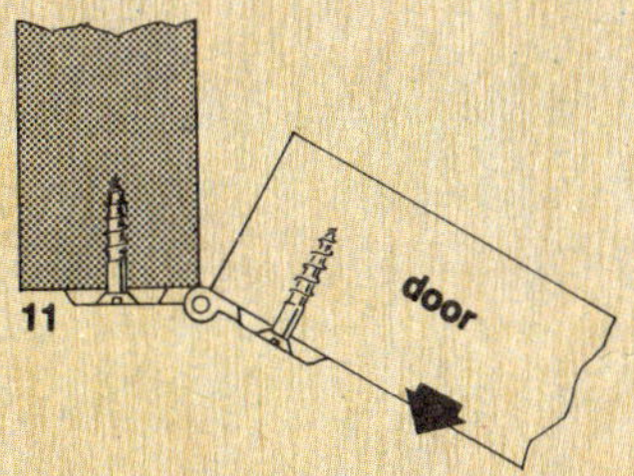

Pivot hinges

Pivot hinges are so called because all or part of each leaf lies in a horizontal plane and so needs only a small pivot, rather than a long knuckle, to connect it to the other.

- **Centre hinges,** the traditional type (12), can only be used on inset doors. A door hung with these has one hinge on its top edge, and one at the bottom; one leaf of each hinge is recessed into the door, one into the cabinet.

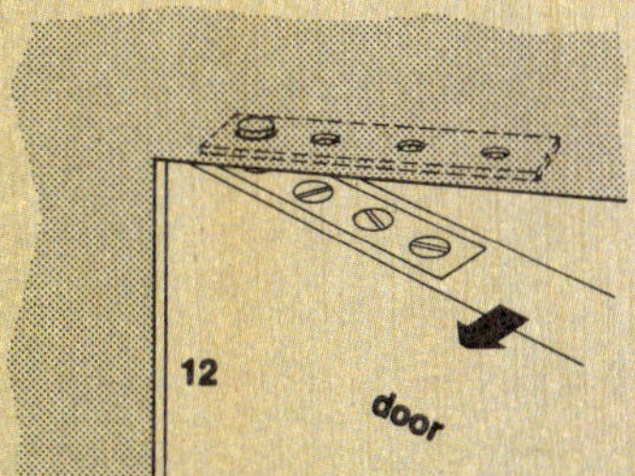

This hinge is hidden when the door is closed – and it's handy if for any reason you can't attach butt hinges to the door or cabinet or both.

- The more modern type (sometimes confusingly called 'semi-concealed') is *double-cranked.* On a cranked hinge, one leaf is bent into a right angle. On a double-cranked hinge this is true of both leaves.

Either way, the door swings from a different point to that on a non-cranked hinge – ideal for a lay-on door, because it will open fully (ie, to 90°) without passing beyond the cabinet side. If the cabinet is beside a wall, or next to another cabinet of the same or greater depth, this is essential.

The other good point about cranked hinges is that they're easier to fit accurately, because their angles locate over the edges of timber or board.

The cranked pivot hinge shown here (13) and on page 106 requires a small saw cut to be made in the edges of the door and cabinet to take its neck. Other types are simply fitted to the top and bottom edges of the door, without the need for cuts. All can be bought for left- or right-hand opening doors.

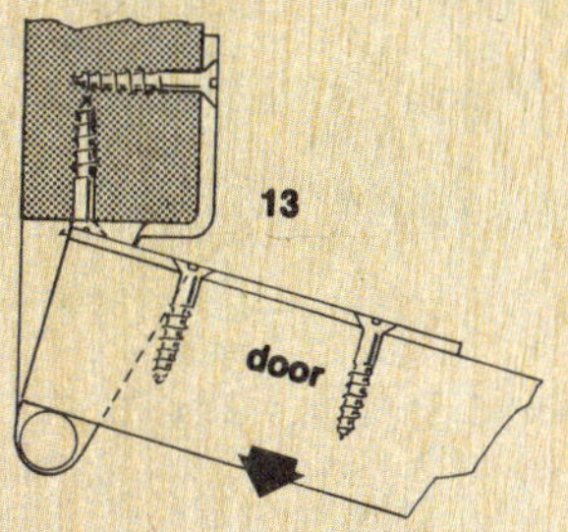

- Not shown is the **lift-off pivot hinge,** for lightweight lay-on doors, half of which screws bodily into the door and half into the cabinet. One half incorporates a pin and the other a socket, so you can hang the door after fitting them, as with a loose-pin hinge. (Lift-off butt hinges are also available.)

Cranked hinges

The main family of cranked hinges have knuckles rather than pivots. They give you several further options for fitting lay-on doors. Their main disadvantage is that they're highly visible on the edge of the door.

- The **cranked surface-fixing hinge** (14) will only take light weight doors because it isn't recessed. The one shown accommodates 6mm (¼in) thick plywood.

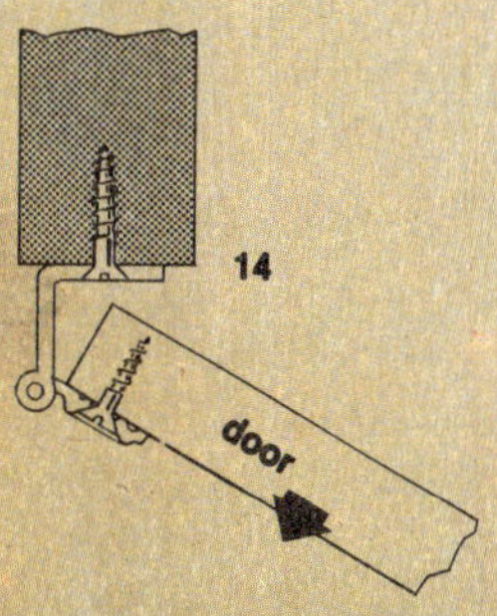

Decorative hinges
Because they're surface-fixing, and the knuckle is short compared to the leaves, these are useful where the meeting edges of door and cabinet aren't straight.

- The **lift-off cranked hinge** (15) combines the advantages of a cranked hinge with the ease of fitting given by separable leaves (see page 585). It is recessed like a butt hinge.
- 16 is similar except that it lacks the lift-off facility. This particular model is very solidly made in brass.

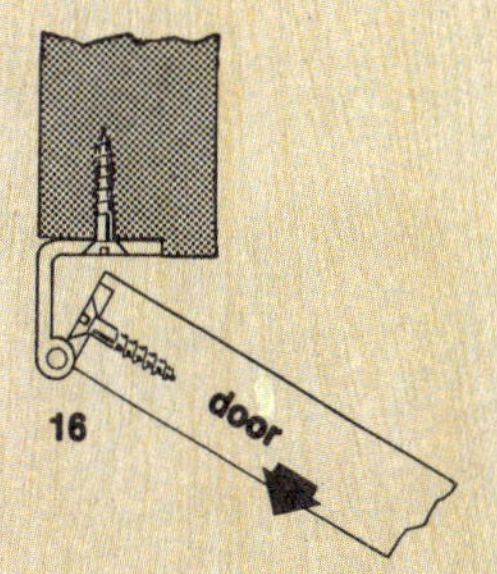

Cranked hinges
Always try these out (like pivot and concealed hinges) on scraps of timber or board before buying, to see how they work.

Pivot hinges
Traditional pivot hinges have two flat leaves. Modern types, which are cranked, differ in being especially easy to fit.

Invisible hinges

Invisible hinges are especially neat little devices. Although completely hidden when the door is closed, they have intricate mechanisms which allow it to open to 180°. They work on both inset and lay-on doors.

- The **cylinder hinge** (17) simply fits into a pair of drilled holes.
- The mechanism of the **Soss** or **invisible mortise hinge** (18) fits into a mortise, while its face plate sits in a shallow recess like the leaf of a butt hinge.

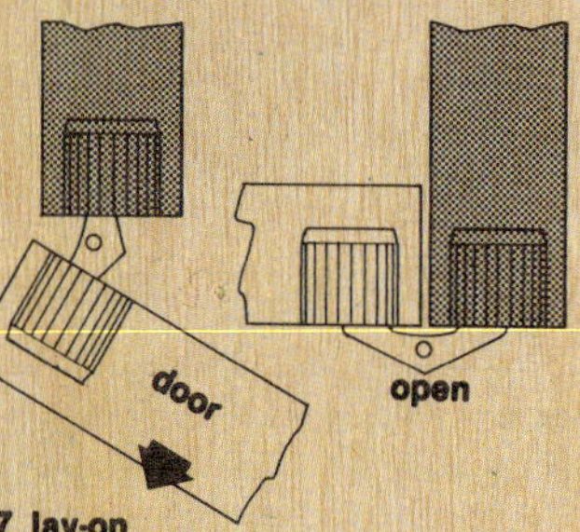

17 lay-on

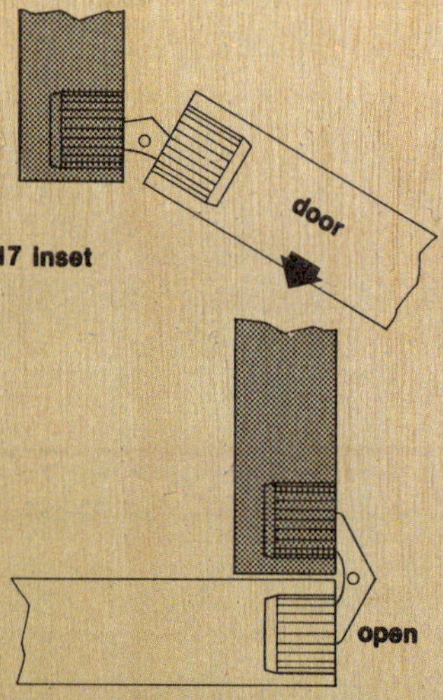

17 inset

Concealed hinges

An enormous amount of work has gone into the development of concealed hinges, and many different models are available.

While most are designed, like cranked hinges, to allow lay-on doors to open within the overall width of the cabinet, some will fit inset doors, and some both – those for lay-on doors varying according to the amount of overlap they give. Often the thickness of timber or board is important. You'll also find variations in how far the hinges open. And some concealed hinges, such as the two shown here, have a positive spring action which serves instead of a catch to keep the door closed.

The concealed hinge can't be seen, because it's fixed entirely inside the door and cabinet. As a rule, the part fixed to the door includes a threaded cylindrical section which fits into a wide, shallow circular recess bored in the surface, where it's held in position by screws.

- This recess is readily and accurately milled out by industrial machines, but less so by the home woodworker. That may lead you to choose a surface-fixing type like (19), which fixes in the easiest possible way – by screwing onto both surfaces.

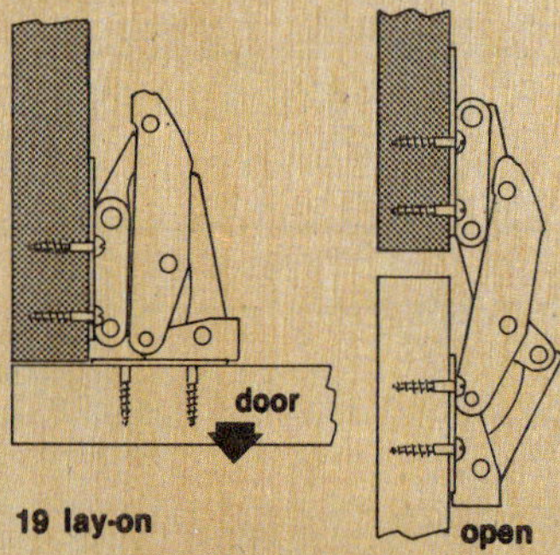

19 lay-on

17

18

Invisible hinges

Invisible and concealed hinges both have clever mechanisms which pull the door clear of the cabinet instead of letting it swing. With invisible hinges this is completely hidden.

19

20

21

Concealed hinges

The great attraction of these is their adjustability and variety. Many models, too, don't require a separate catch to be fitted.

19 inset

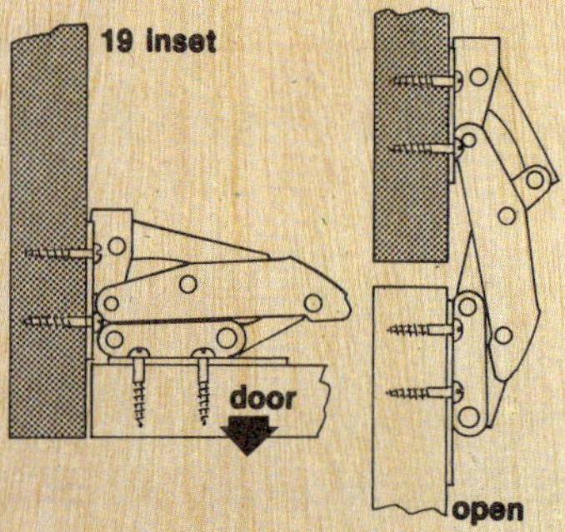

This model also has a spring to keep the door firmly open, as well as closed. The action is so sure that it will even hold up a light flap without the need for a stay

- (20) is the **recessed** type, (21) is its **mounting plate**, which is screwed inside the cabinet; the thin end of the hinge is screwed, in its turn, to the plate. This arrangement, like that of a lift-off or loose-pin hinge, makes for easy door hanging; but it's also unique in allowing easy adjustment of the door's position after it's been fitted.

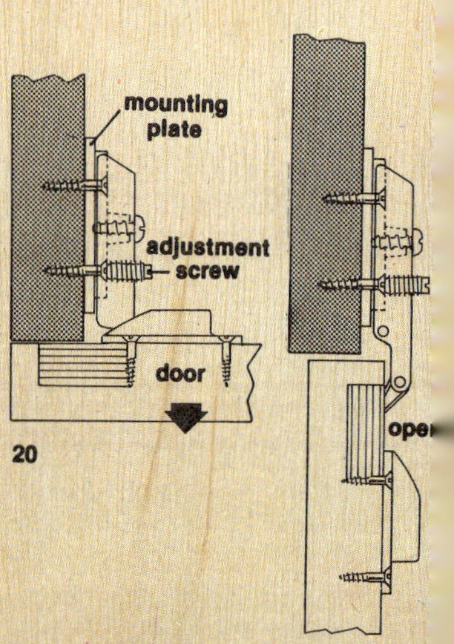

20

FITTING HINGES

In essence, the fitting procedure is the same for all hinges.

1 Make sure the door fits.
2 Work out exactly how the hinges will be positioned, including the dimensions of any recesses.
3 Mark out the hinge positions on the door, plus recesses if any.
4 Fix the hinges to the door.
5 Position the door accurately, and fix the hinges to the cabinet.

All doors need at least two hinges, unless you're using a piano hinge. The very tallest and heaviest need four; intermediate ones need three.

There are no rules about the spacing of hinges. However, with butt and similar types, the top hinge is often placed a distance equal to its own length down from the top of the door and the bottom one up from the bottom by the same or twice the distance. On framed doors, the upper end of the top hinge is often lined up with the lower edge of the top rail in the frame, and the lower end of the bottom hinge with the upper edge of the bottom rail.

All hinges will work in any material. But they have to take a lot of stress, so you need to make sure they're secure. Don't use small, light hinges for a large, heavy door. Recesses usually make for greater strength than surface fixing, provided the hinges fit into them tightly.

But surface fixing is stronger in veneered or plastic-faced chipboard, because breaking through the facing weakens the material. If using butt hinges in this type of board, get round the problem by recessing them to twice the depth in the other material.

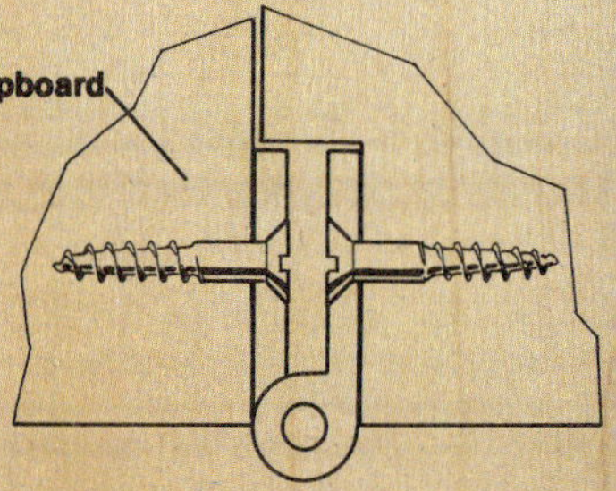

In chipboard, too, you should use chipboard screws. Fixing into its edges is not, however, to be recommended.

ADVANCED TECHNIQUES

Once your confidence has grown, you can begin to extend your repertoire by acquiring some of the more advanced woodworking skills.

USING A ROUTER : 1

The router is the ultimate portable power tool. Almost all the jobs it tackles are difficult or impossible with any other machine. We begin with one of the simpler tasks – making grooves.

The power router is both beautifully simple and outstandingly versatile. As on all power tools, its heart is an electric motor which turns a spindle. Its most important feature, however, is the motor's very high speed – between 18,000 and 27,000 rpm, compared with the maximum of 4000 rpm given by power drills. This is what allows it to handle such an enormous variety of grooving, rebating, shaping and other cutting jobs in wood, plastic and even soft metals.

A router's power is from 300 to 2000W. Naturally, the more powerful models are meant for professionals and are more expensive. The power sets strict limits on the amount of material you can cut away without overloading the motor. A 300W model will make a groove 6mm (1/4in) square in one go, whereas a 600W motor allows a 10x6mm (3/8x1/4in) groove.

This means that some jobs take a bit longer with a low-powered machine, because you need to make two or three passes (adjusting it for a deeper cut each time) instead of just one or two.

At the end of the spindle is a 'collet chuck', into which you fit the bit (also called a cutter), very much as you fit a drill bit into a drill chuck. A collet chuck, however, is tightened with a spanner – while you hold the spindle steady with a tommy bar, another spanner, or a locking switch. Collets are made in three main sizes, to accept bits whose shank diameter is 1/4, 3/8 or 1/2in.

The 'overhead router' used in industry is a fixed machine, suspended in a large stand – like an enormous drill stand, but fastened to the floor – and lowered onto the workpiece with a lever. On the portable router, however, the motor (complete with spindle) is mounted in a frame or 'carriage' with handles, in which it moves up and down as you adjust it. This frame has a flat base, through which the bit projects to make the cut. In operation you generally rest the base on the workpiece, and move the machine along bodily – though you can fix the machine and move the workpiece instead.

The general principle is the same as when using shaping cutters in a power drill to form profiled edges on timber and man-made boards. But the router is far easier to handle (though larger models can be quite heavy), and it's capable of harder and more efficient work because it's purpose-built.

The plunging router

Portable routers are either fixed-base or plunging models. A fixed-base router is lowered into the material with the bit already protruding from the base, after you've got it to project the required amount by adjusting the height of the motor in the carriage.

With a plunging router, on the other hand, the motor is on sprung mountings, and this means you set the projection (ie, the depth of cut) in two stages. First you lower the motor until the bit just touches the workpiece, and you rotate one of the handles to lock it in position. Then, on most models, you simply adjust the height of the depth bar – a sliding or threaded vertical rod fixed to the side of the motor – so that, when you 'plunge' the motor right down to cut, the lower end of the rod will meet the base of the carriage and prevent your going any deeper than you want. Lastly, you turn the handle the other way to release the motor so that it springs right up, back to its original position.

That done, you're ready to start cutting. This is a straightforward matter of positioning the router where you want it, switching on, and pressing down fully on the handles to plunge the rotating bit into the workpiece.

Ready Reference

WHICH MACHINE?

A **fixed-base** router must be inserted into the workpiece bodily, with the bit protruding and the motor already running.

This requires great care when starting the cut if you're to avoid inaccuracy – especially with a heavy machine.

A **plunging** router is placed on the workpiece before you switch it on and 'plunge' the bit down to cut.

On the whole this gives greater precision, because you can position the machine correctly from the start. It's also safer, because you let the bit spring up out of the way again once you've finished the cut.

WHICH TYPE OF BIT?

High-speed steel (HSS) router bits are only for use on softwoods, and soft plastics such as PVC and clear acrylic (Perspex).

Tungsten carbide (TC) bits – tipped or solid – are needed for hardwoods, hardboard, plywood, chipboard, blockboard, plastic laminates, glass-reinforced plastics, tinted acrylics, and soft metals such as aluminium.

Then you turn the handle again to lock it there, before running the tool along to do the actual job. When you've finished, you just use the handle to unlock it, allow it to spring back up, and switch off.

The plunging router's sprung action makes it safer than the fixed-base type, and also ensures that the bit always enters the work at exactly 90°.

Using a router

If the sound of a router motor drops from a high-pitched whine during a cut, you're probably trying to work too fast – or cut too deeply. The harder the material and the wider the bit, the slower and shallower each cut will have to be to avoid straining the motor. The general rule is to cut no deeper than the diameter of the bit.

A smell of burning, on the other hand, may mean you're cutting too slowly. The important thing is to acquire a feeling for the tool's natural cutting rate. It shouldn't take long.

But either of these symptoms may denote a blunt bit instead. So may a 'furry' finish (although that's common on moist wood anyway), or difficulty in pushing the router along. And remember that, as with any other tool, the texture of your material matters. In solid timber, the grain may dictate the direction in which you have to move the machine for a clean cut.

As for safety, remember that a power router runs at a tremendous speed. Treat it with respect. Wear goggles to protect your eyes from whirling dust. On a plunging router, always release the lock after a cut to let the bit spring up out of the way. Unplug the machine whenever you're not using it – and keep it in a cupboard. If stored on a shelf, it could fall off; and, if you leave it on the floor, wood chips and other debris may get into the air intake.

Router bits

Router bits come in an extremely wide range of shapes – from straight bits, which are for grooving, to angled and curved patterns, plus a number of others. Not only knowledge but also imagination is required to exploit them to the full, for just about all can be used in several different ways; and of course you can use more than one in succession for creating compound shapes – see below.

It's also important to know what they're made from. Although special drilling bits have been designed for use with plunging routers, no bit or cutter of ordinary steel should ever be used in a power router, because the high speed will very likely smash it to pieces. Proper router bits are made, instead, of high-speed steel (HSS) and tungsten carbide (TC).

HSS bits are cheaper, and fine for working softwoods and fairly soft plastics. Their draw-

SETTING UP FOR A CUT

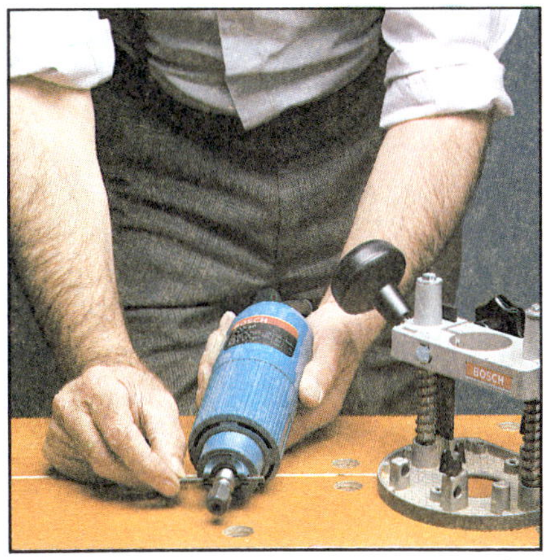

1 *With the machine unplugged and the motor removed from its carriage if possible, steady the spindle with the tommy bar.*

2 *Insert the shank of the bit into the collet, tighten the nut as far as you can by hand, and then finish securing it with a spanner.*

3 *If you've removed the motor, fit it back into the carriage now, and tighten it up firmly with the knob or other fastening provided.*

4 *'Plunge' the motor down in its carriage till the bit meets the surface on which the machine is standing, and lock it there with the handle.*

5 *Adjust the depth bar until the gap below it roughly equals the depth of cut you want – ie, the amount the bit should project. Release the lock.*

6 *Plunge the bit below the surface through a convenient hole, use the gauge to check the depth, and let the motor spring back up.*

ROUTING GROOVES

1 *Set the fence attachment so that, with the fence against the edge, the groove will be in the position you want. Mark the groove out first if you like.*

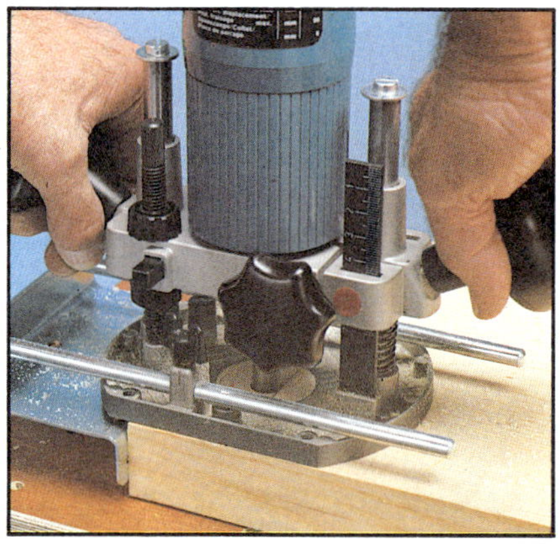

2 *Switch on, plunge into the workpiece some way along the groove, and lock the handle when you've reached the full pre-set depth.*

3 *Move the router along, still holding the fence firmly against the edge – especially at the end. Then return across the piece to complete the groove.*

5 *If grooving across the middle of a piece, you may have to abandon the fence attachment and instead cramp on a straight batten as a guide.*

6 *A router will cut through knots and other blemishes without difficulty – provided you keep its cutting speed up, without dawdling.*

7 *Grooves needn't have square bottoms. Different-shaped bits produce a whole variety of profiles, many of which are extremely decorative.*

back is a tendency to blunt quickly, which is greatly accelerated if they're used on harder and/or more abrasive materials. However, by the same token, they're soft enough to sharpen at home – if you know how. Not only must the front of each cutting edge be dead flat and smooth; there must also be a 'clearance angle' of at least 15° between its back and the circle made by the bit as it rotates.

For chipboard, plywood and blockboard (all of which contain synthetic resins), as well as for plastic laminates and glass-reinforced plastics, you need TC bits. They're even a good idea for use on hardboard and hardwoods. Their higher initial cost – and they can be very expensive – is often outweighed by their much longer life. Usually they consist of TC tips (cutting edges) brazed onto steel bits – but you can get bits made from solid TC. For eventual sharpening, TC and TC-tipped (TCT) bits must go back to the manufacturer or another specialist firm.

Remember that a router is only as good as its bit. If you find you have a blunt one, don't just go on using it and hoping for the best – see that it's sharpened. What's more, bit shanks should be kept smooth and undamaged to avoid damaging the collet when you insert them.

Routing grooves

Cutting grooves across the face of timber or boards is a fine example of a task which is as trouble-free with a router as it's demanding by hand.

Even the marking-out process is simpler, because you need only indicate where one side of the groove is to go. In some cases you can even omit marking-out altogether, because the essential thing in all routing work (except for a very few truly freehand applications) is to make sure the tool is properly guided anyway: refer to *Ready Reference*.

The simplest method of doing this is to use a fence attachment. This is very similar to the rip fence on a circular saw: in other words, it's a removable metal fitting which locates against the edge of the workpiece, and thus keeps the router on a parallel course. It's important that the edge should be reasonably straight in the first place – in other words, that there should be no bumps or hollows which are pronounced, and/or which run for any distance. However, if there are only small unevennesses, the fence attachment will actually bridge the defects and allow a straight groove despite a less-than-perfect edge.

You can extend the fence attachment, too, by screwing to it a piece of timber or board about double its length. This is very useful when the groove runs right out at one side of the material, because you can 'follow through' with it, still keeping it pressed against the edge as the cut finishes – thereby preventing

4 *Repeat the procedure after doubling the depth of cut. Sometimes a cut takes three passes, depending on the machine, the material and the bit.*

8 *Grooving with a shaped bit can produce a panelled effect. Sharp corners will always occur where the grooves cross each other.*

the tool from suddenly slipping, as it can easily do with an ordinary fence.

Better still, you can also cramp a straight-edged piece of scrap material (an 'overcut board') beyond the workpiece and level with it, and simply continue the cut into that. This will not only prevent a ragged end to the cut, especially when working across the grain, but also provide additional support for the fence and so help to ensure an absolutely parallel groove.

Some manufacturers supply a special guide roller or extra fence plates, to enable the router to follow edges which have fairly gentle curves. These are screwed to the main fence attachment. However, edges which have sharp concave curves, or are otherwise too elaborate, will rule out such devices.

Even if you want a straight groove, the fence attachment itself will be no use if the edge is curved or angled, or if you're working too far in from the nearest parallel straight edge. In either of these cases your best plan is to cramp on a straight, solid guide batten parallel to your intended groove, and run the machine against that. The batten must, of course, be at such a distance that the bit will run along your mark. That means the distance from the edge of the router base to the centre of the bit, minus half the bit diameter.

It also helps if the batten overhangs at both ends, so you can keep the router pressed against it when entering and leaving the cut. The idea is, once again, to avoid swinging off course.

If you're cutting a whole set of housings, you can even add a T-piece to the end of the batten. Apart from forming an overcut board, this will enable you, without effort, to locate the batten squarely every time. Moreover, when you've continued a groove through into the T-piece, you'll be able to use it as a guide mark for aligning subsequent cuts (see *Ready Reference*).

If possible, fit your router with a straight bit whose diameter equals the width of the groove you want. In the case of a housing, this will be the thickness of the piece being housed (usually a shelf).

With a light-duty router, start by setting the depth of cut at about 2 to 3mm (1/16 to 1/8in), and remove that much again with each subsequent pass; in other words, double the setting for the second pass and treble it for the third. That way, three passes will cut a housing 6 to 9mm (1/4 to 3/8in) deep. In chipboard, don't go deeper than half the board's thickness, in case you weaken it too much.

Some routers have a 'rotary turret stop', which is simply a means of pre-setting the depth bar for three different heights. This allows you to change the depth of cut for the second and third passes merely by rotating the device to the next setting, without having to stop and adjust the tool.

Rotating bits mean that all routed internal corners will be rounded, however slightly (the radius depends, of course, on the bit diameter). The ends of stopped housings are no exception; you'll either have to chisel them square, or round the edges of the housed pieces to match. The latter operation, however (see pages 353–357), is simply another straightforward cut in the router's repertoire.

Shaped grooves

A groove needn't be square-bottomed. There are a number of graceful shapes for decorative work. You can create panelled effects, too (although grooving in man-made boards will, of course, expose the core).

Moreover, even simple combined cuts – for example, a rounded groove 15mm (5/8in) wide superimposed on a deeper square groove 10mm (3/8in) wide – can look very good.

Ready Reference

GUIDING THE GROOVE

A long strip of timber or plywood screwed to the fence attachment (A) makes it easier to keep the router steady as you finish a cut.

A

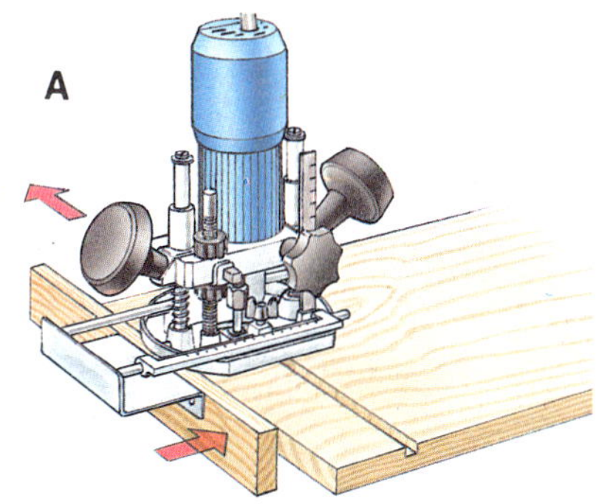

An **overcut board** (B) achieves the same result by supporting the fence (short or long), and also prevents splintering at the end of cross-grain cuts.

B

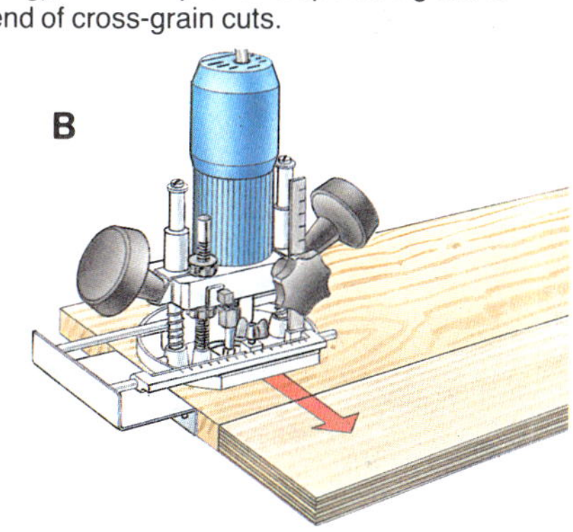

A **T-square guide** (C) is ideal for repeated grooves which are too far from a parallel edge for a fence attachment to be useful. After each cut, you un-clamp it and reposition it for the next groove. The T-piece, if accurately fitted, ensures instant squareness, and acts as an overcut board; the groove routed in it aids alignment with your marked groove position.

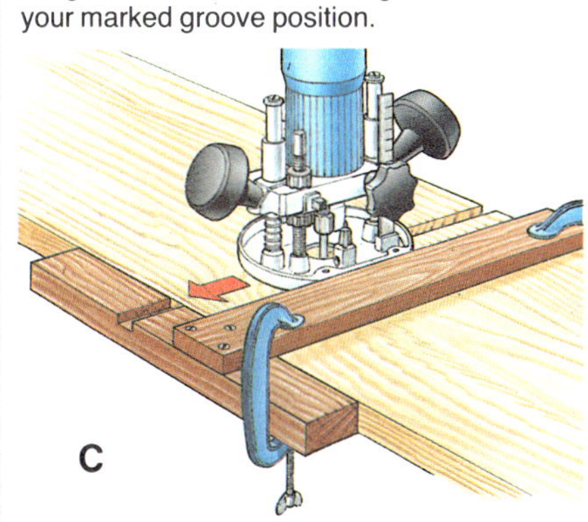

C

KNOW YOUR ROUTER

To get the best from a power router, you need to know how to set it up for the cut you want. This is a typical 'plunge' model – so called because of the sprung mountings, which make for safety and accuracy. You position the router before pushing down to start the cut – and let the motor spring up again as soon as you've finished.

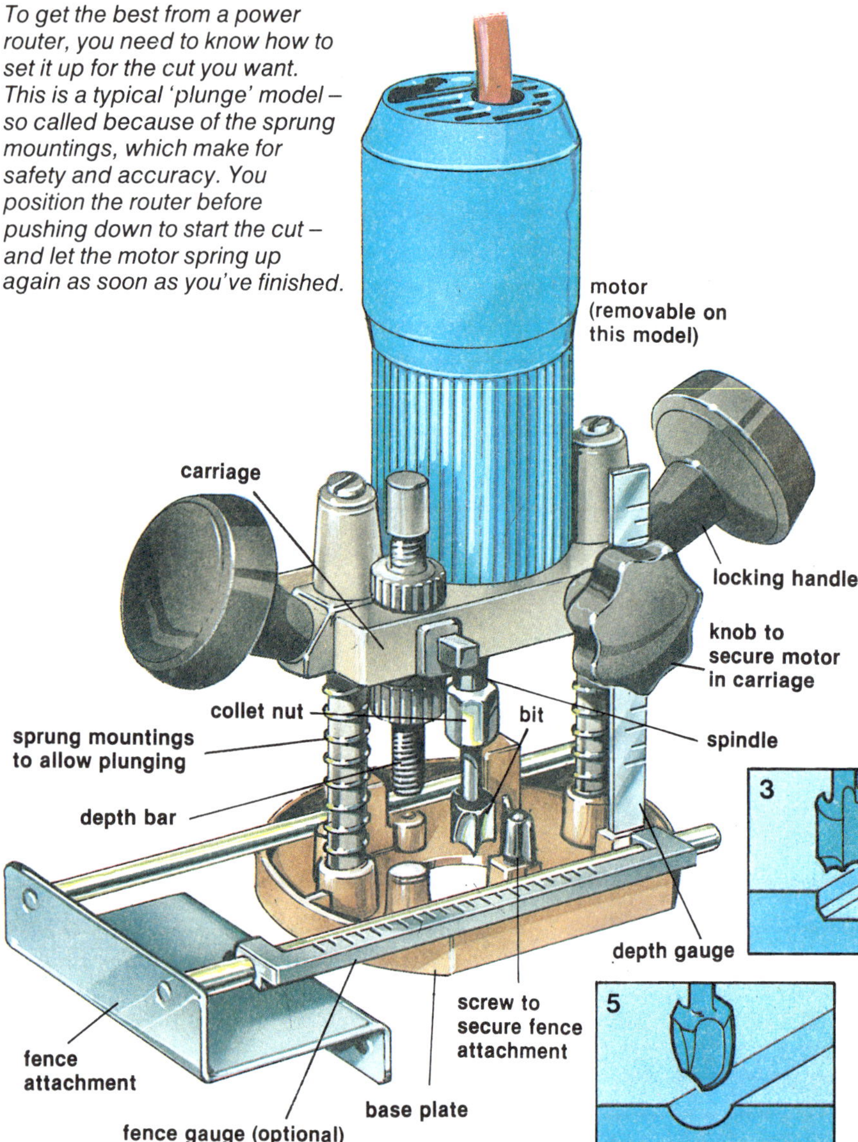

All these router bits (cutters) will make grooves – and shape edges (see pages 353–357). Some, like 10, give varied profiles.

KEY

1 *Straight: one-flute (veining)*
2 *Straight: two-flute*
3 *Groove and chamfer*
4 *Radius (veining)*
5 *Core box, radius or half-round*
6 *V-carving or V-groove (veining)*
7 *V-groove and chamfer*
8 *Panel raising*
9 *Chamfer*
10 *Ovolo*
11 *Pointed round or quarter-round*
12 *Pointed ogee*
13 *Ogee (end cutting)*
14 *Panelling*
15 *Classic*

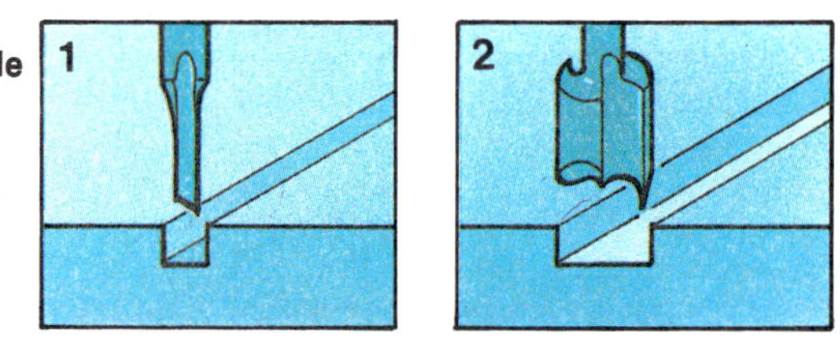

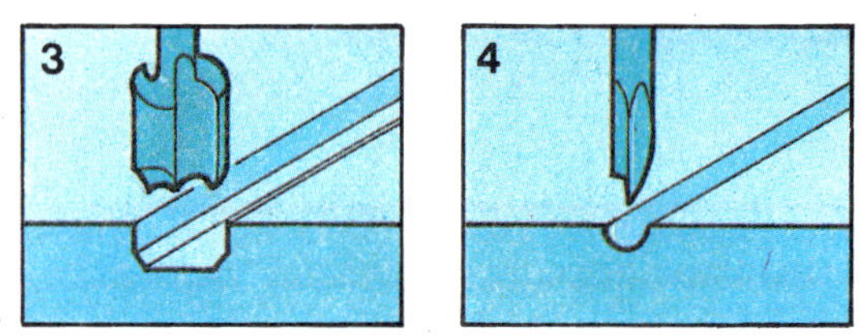

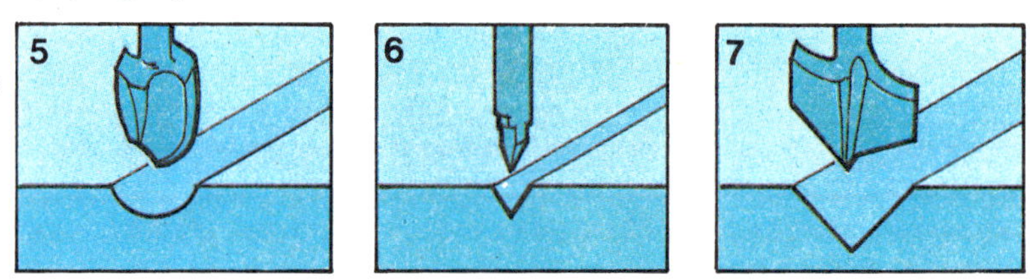

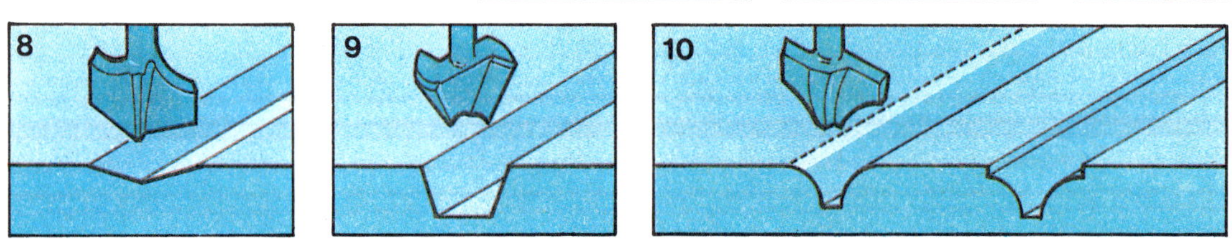

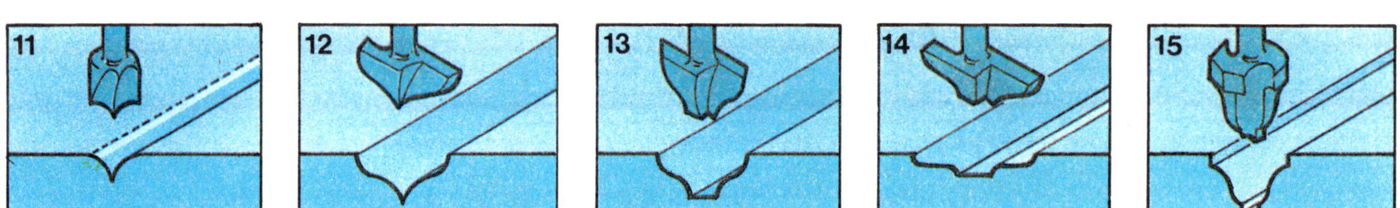

USING A ROUTER : 2

Once you've grasped the power router's basic workings, you can move on from making simple grooving cuts to the vast possibilities of edge profiling, box jointing and other techniques.

After cutting housings and other square or shaped grooves (see pages 348–352), the use of the router that next springs to mind is usually shaping edges.

That may sound unimportant, but it covers a tremendous range of jobs, both functional and decorative. The router will cut any number of ornamental mouldings (eg, ovolo, ogee) along the edges of tabletops, shelves, skirting-boards and the like – and indeed make lengths of moulding, such as architrave or staff bead, to your own design from the timber of your choice, as an alternative to buying them off the shelf. It will also produce straightforward rebates, plus bevels and chamfers at various angles; trim off overhanging edges of plastic laminate after it's been glued down; and, very importantly, make a whole variety of joints which involve grooved, tongued and rebated edges.

Bits for edging

The first step, of course, is to choose the right shape from the range of bits available. All grooving bits (see opposite) can be used for edging, and there are also several for edging alone. Rebates, for example, can be cut either with an ordinary two-flute bit, or a special wide rebating bit. Other edging bits include rounding-over, coving, ogee and a number of others. Any router supplier should be able to give you further details, or tell you where to find them.

Each individual router bit will produce cuts of different shapes, depending not only on its profile and size but also on your depth setting. In the case of edging, you can also vary the shape according to the width of cut – ie, whether the bit just skims the edge or bites deeply into it.

Guiding the cut

There are two main ways of profiling edges with a router. One is to use the fence attachment – if necessary with accessories for following curves. The other is to fit a 'self-guiding' bit.

As when grooving, working with the fence attachment is a simple matter of keeping it pressed firmly against the edge of the material. In this case, that's the self-same edge in which you're making the cut – therefore the fence must be right underneath the router base, on or near its centre line.

A self-guiding bit has its own built-in guide, in the form of a pin – like a small extra shank, but at the opposite end – or else a roller bearing. This guide is in addition to the cutting edges and almost always below them. You keep it pressed against the workpiece (whether straight or curved) in exactly the same manner as a fence attachment, thus ensuring a uniform cut all the way.

Self-guiding bits involve no cumbersome setting up, unlike the various types of fence. They will also follow the tightest curves, and even go round corners. Their corresponding snag is that they reproduce any bumps or hollows in the original edge, to a greater extent than fence attachments do. On blockboard, for instance, the guide will wander into any exposed voids between the core battens. So, if you can't get your edge absolutely true and smooth, it's best to stick with the fence attachment – or, still better, a guide batten clamped across the work. A template which the router can follow is another possibility.

A guide batten (or template) is also needed if for any reason you have to cut away the whole of an edge, rather than just part of it, since there will be nothing for a guide pin or bearing to run against when using less than the bit's maximum width of cut.

Ready Reference

GROOVING EDGES

If you use an ordinary one- or two-flute bit for edge grooving (A), the router must run along the edge. So you'll need extra material on each side to prevent the machine tilting over.

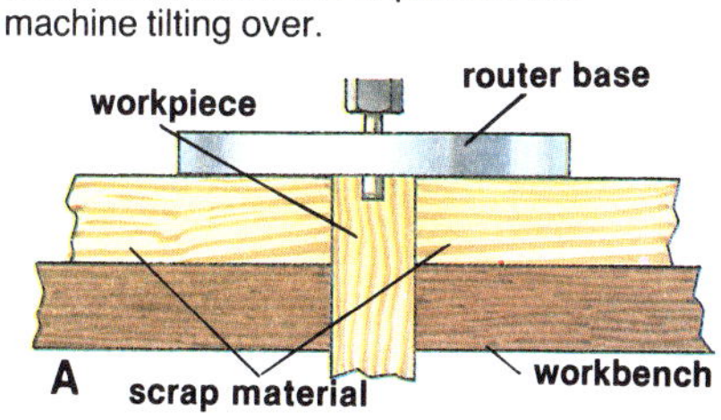

If you use an arbor and groover (B), the router runs over the face, so it will be steadier. This method also lets you position the cut more accurately, since you use the depth adjustment.

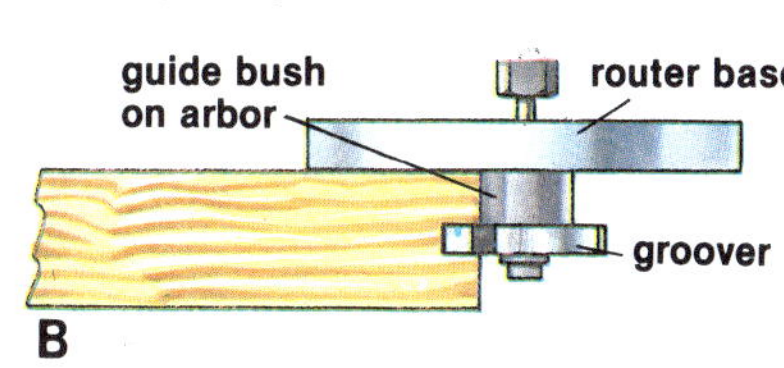

ROUTER BITS FOR EDGING

Some bits (1-5) must be used with a fence attachment, guide batten or template.

1 *Dovetailing*
2 *Edge-rounding*
3 *Double edge-rounding*
4 *Staff bead*
5 *Tongueing for staff bead*

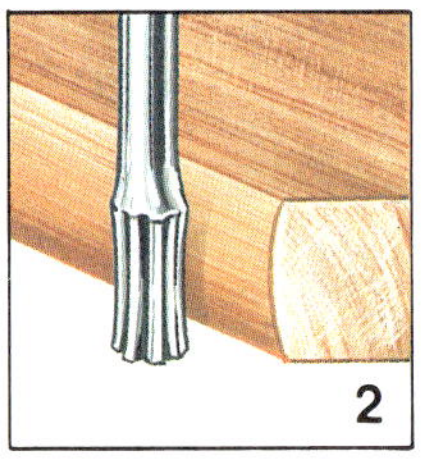

Others have a guide pin or bearing, whose size (6-9) varies the cut.

6 *Rounding-over (large pin)*
7 *Ovolo or corner round (small pin)*
8 *Ovolo or corner round (small bearing)*
9 *Rounding-over (large bearing)*
10 *Rebating (pin)*
11 *Chamfering (pin)*
12 *Coving (pin)*
13 *Roman ogee (pin)*

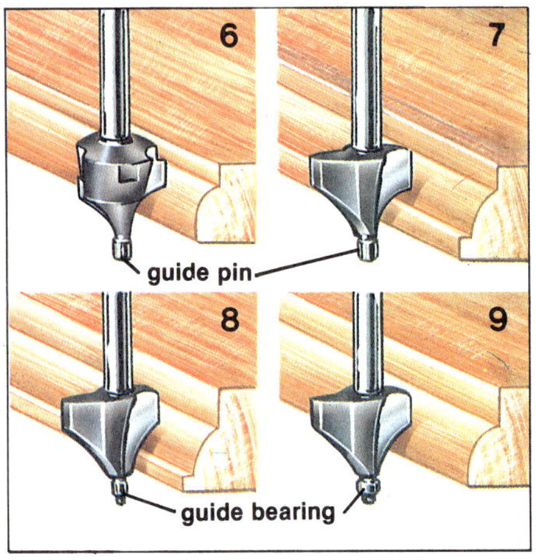

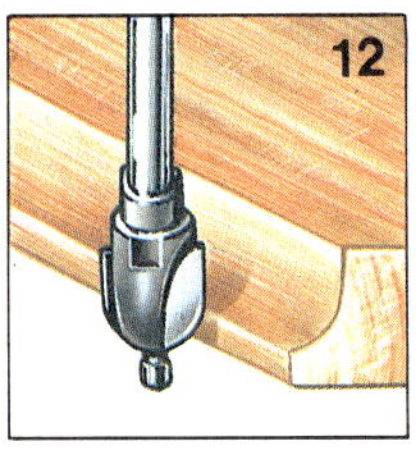

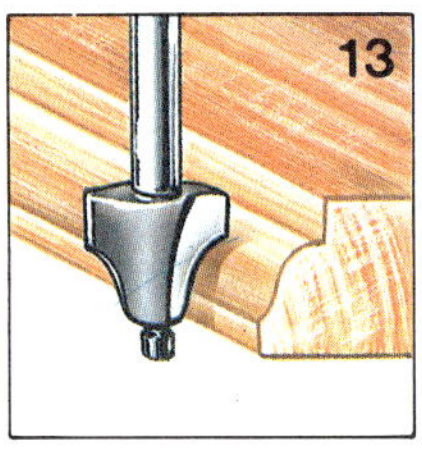

There are also special bits for trimming plastic laminates.

14 *Pierce and trim*
15 *90° trimmer (self-guiding)*
16 *90° trimmer*
17 *90° trimmer with guide bearing*
18 *Bevel trimmer*

The pierce and trim bit (14) drills through the laminate, then cuts it away cleanly. This is useful if you've laminated over an internal cut-out, for a sink in a kitchen worktop, for example.

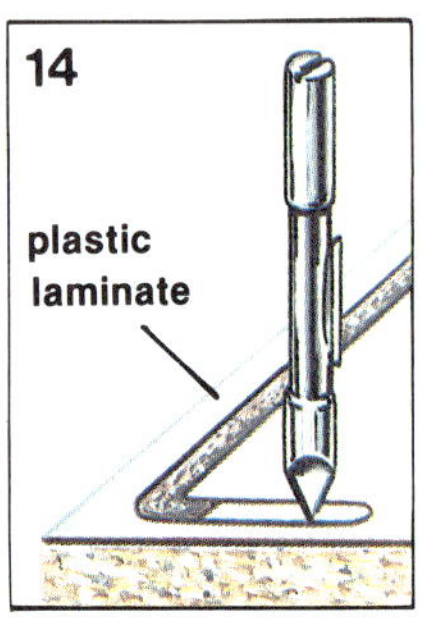

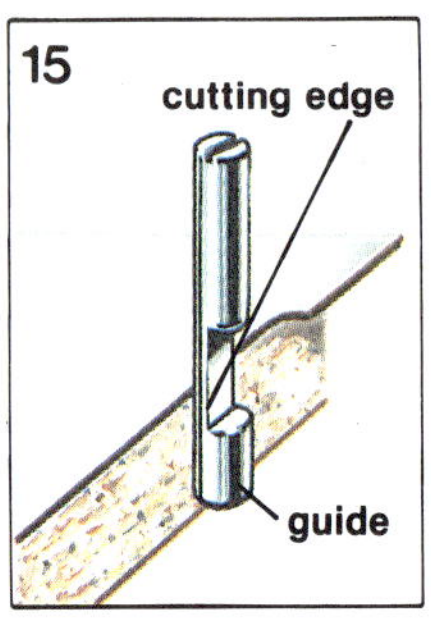

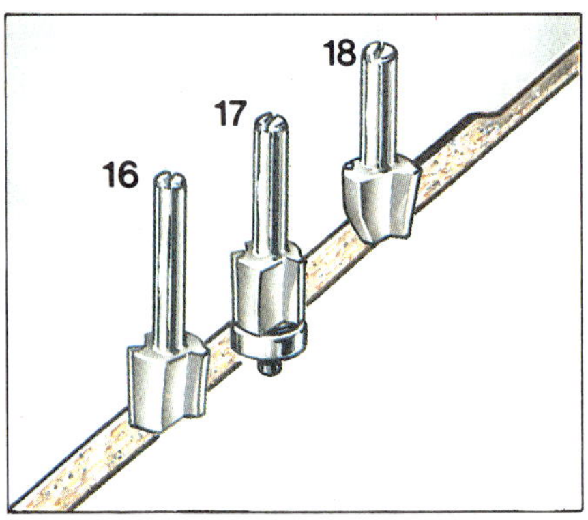

PROFILING EDGES

1 *Set the depth for the exact edge profile you require (see page 71). The bit shown inserted here is known as a staff bead cutter.*

5 *When cutting, keep the guide pin pressed against the edge. That way, the bit will follow the edge even if it's curved or has corners.*

Bits with roller bearings, as opposed to pins, are very expensive, and so only worth getting if you'll be using them a great deal. Their advantages are that the bearing, unlike a pin, won't burn or mark the edge, and that you have only to change the bearing in order to vary the width of the cut (and thus its shape).

In all edging work it's important to remember that routers can usually only do their job properly if they're fed (moved along the workpiece) against the rotation of the bit – ie, so that the bit's cutting edges are always travelling into the cut rather than away from it. Remember that the bit rotates clockwise if you're looking from above at a router pointing downwards. The same principle applies if the router is fixed in position to a router table.

You can in fact work the other way, eg, for a clean cut in difficult grain. But care is needed in order to prevent the bit from 'snatching' uncontrollably.

2 If you're not using a self-guiding bit – see below – slide the fence attachment in and adjust it for the precise width of cut.

3 With the router plunged and locked at the pre-set depth, switch it on and make the cut. Always 'feed' it so the bit rotates into the work.

4 A self-guiding bit lets you do without a fence, because it has its own guide pin (like the one shown here) or roller-bearing guide.

6 A rounding-over bit like this will also give a 'stepped' moulding: you just have to set it for a deeper cut (see no. 10, page 74).

7 A coving bit gives yet another edge profile. Simply stopping a cut short always produces a nicely rounded end like the one shown here.

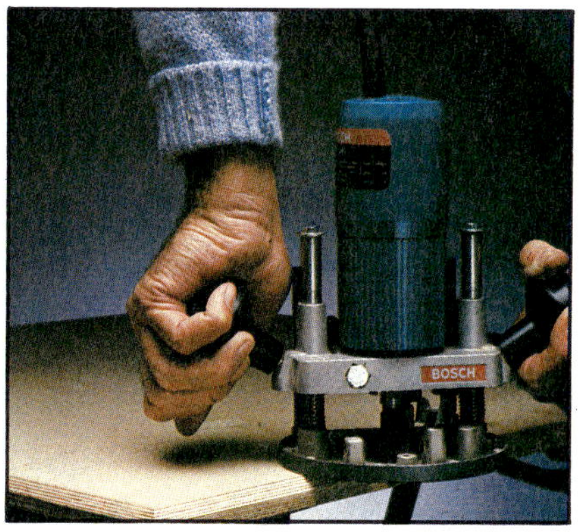

8 A chamfer bit puts a neat angle on the edge. A guide pin, like a guide bearing, enables you to follow corners as well as curved edges.

Routing joints

When you make box furniture one of your prime considerations must naturally be how to joint it. In the ordinary way, this isn't an easy decision. Butt joints are weak, and almost any form of strengthening (nails, screws, timber strips or even assembly fittings) is bound to show – inside the cabinet, if not outside.

The professional answer is to use a joint which doesn't need reinforcement, and it's here that power tools come into their own. The router, in particular, is ideal when you want a rebate in one or both pieces. You can match a rebate in one piece with a groove in the other, to form a barefaced housing joint. And one of the strongest joints available (though it's not for corners, and not for chipboard) is the dovetail housing. This is very easily made by using a dovetail bit – set to a uniform depth – to cut both the groove and the sides of the matching tongue. You'll need the fence attachment, and maybe a guide batten for the groove. For a tongue of exactly the right width to fit the groove, careful alignment is required. Remember, to, that the 'undercut' dovetail shape means you can't plunge into the work.

Any kind of tongue-and-groove joint, in fact, is a natural for the router. If you're grooving an edge, make sure that the machine is properly supported so it can't tilt while cutting. This may mean clamping additional pieces on either side of the work. It's better, however, if you're doing a lot of edge grooving, to use an arbor with a groover fixed over it. An arbor is a separate shank, often with a guide bush or bearing, that fits into the collet. A groover is like a circular-saw blade but smaller, and with fewer and thicker teeth. The advantage of this arrangement is that you can run the router base over the face of the work, as with most edging jobs, and thereby gain stability.

A matching tongue can usually best be formed by cutting two rebates.

Trimming plastic laminates

Before fixing a sheet of plastic laminate to a timber or board base, you'll naturally try to cut it to approximately the right size, aiming to trim the slight overhang once the sheet is stuck down in position.

Laminates are exceptionally hard, and therefore not really suitable for shaving with a hand plane. A router, however, makes light work of the job. You'll need a tungsten carbide (TC) bit, solid or tipped, to avoid rapid blunting. Special trimming bits are available; some make right-angled cuts, some make bevelled cuts at various slopes, and some provide a choice between the two. Several are self-guiding – and, to make the work even easier, there are bits which will trim

ROUTING BOX JOINTS

1 For a dovetail housing, start by cutting the groove. Use a dovetail bit – and don't plunge into the material, or you'll spoil the job.

2 Clamp the other piece on end, with scrap wood either side. Without changing the depth of cut, set the fence and mould one side of the tongue.

3 Re-adjust the fence to cut the other side. Keep the scrap edge on your left – ie, against the direction in which the bit rotates.

6 Clamp the other piece on end and make an identical cut; if using a fence, don't change the setting. Use scrap timber to steady the router as you work.

7 When you fit the pieces together, the cuts should match exactly. You may need to fix lipping to conceal the exposed core of a man-made board.

8 For edge grooving, a slotter on an arbor makes it easier to keep the tool steady, since it still rests on the face. The guide bearing follows the edge.

laminate from both faces of a panel at once.

Even when using a TC bit, make sure the laminate doesn't overhang by more than about one-third of the bit diameter, otherwise you'll cause unnecessary wear. Varying the depth setting, too, will spread the wear more evenly along the cutting edges.

Unless you're using a self-guiding bit, you'll need to set up the fence attachment for the job. What's known as a 'fine screw feed' – available on some machines – is very useful here, as for many other tasks. It's a mechanism that adjusts the fence attachment more precisely than you can manage when you just slide it over and tighten the screws.

If the panel's edge is lipped with laminate too, it's best to trim that before laminating the top surface – so that any marks left by the bit will only mar the top of the base board, to which the laminate has still to be fixed, rather than the plastic finish itself. Marks on the edge lipping will be much less obvious.

You needn't turn the router on its side for this, as long as you're using a bit with a 'bottom cut' – namely cutting edges at the bottom as well as on each side. At least one router manufacturer supplies a special 'sub-base' accessory to act as a guide for this particular operation

Occasionally, you may have already cut holes in the base board (eg, for an inset sink and taps) before laminating it. If you fit a 'pierce and trim' bit, you can then drill through the laminate – and trim it exactly to follow the shape of the cut-out, because the bit is self-guiding, with the pin being aligned for this purpose.

Cutting circles

A unique feature of the router is the ease with which it will make a perfect circle. Most models come with an accessory which acts like the point of a pair of compasses. You use it as a pivot while you swing the machine round.

This way you can employ the various grooving bits to make any number of patterns which depend on circles or parts of circles. If you take enough passes at successively greater depths, you can even cut right through the material – producing, for example, a perfectly circular table-top or bread-board. Such a job is almost impossible with hand tools alone.

Freehand routing

It's also possible to use a router completely freehand, without any sort of fence or other guide at all. This happens mainly when you're 'carving' or 'engraving' lettering or other patterns on a flat surface, and it needs a bit of practice. A light machine is easiest to handle on this type of job. The usual bits for the purpose are 'veining' bits (see USING A ROUTER 1, page 348), which have very small diameters and square, V-shaped or rounded ends.

4 *The tongue should be a tight push-fit in the groove. Cut it too thick, if anything: you can always re-set the fence and make it thinner.*

5 *For a double rebate joint, set a two-flute or rebating bit to a depth of half the board thickness before cutting. The bit used here is self-guiding.*

9 *A loose tongue, usually of thin plywood, is often useful. If necessary, widen the groove by making a second cut, slightly higher or lower.*

10 *When grooving the second piece, be sure to keep it the same way up, for perfect alignment when you glue the tongue into position.*

As with all other routing techniques, your best plan is simply to make a few test runs on scrap timber and board to see what effects you can obtain, before applying your ideas to an actual project.

Setting up a job

As a matter of fact, the use of a 'test piece' is absolutely standard practice in professional woodworking shops. In general, power tools are capable of very fine adjustment, and among do-it-yourself models this is especially true of the router. An alteration of even a millimetre or so in the setting – up, down or sideways – will usually have a noticeable effect when you come to do the actual machining.

Indeed, in the timber trades 'setting up' a tool quite often takes longer than the job itself. This preparation time isn't wasted; on the contrary, it's essential for a trouble-free result. The care you invest in choosing the right bit, setting the depth, adjusting the fence, and so on, will always be repaid with better finished work.

Router safety

Despite its extremely high speed, the portable router in normal use is probably less dangerous than a circular saw. Plunge routers score in this respect because the bit retracts.

However, you need to get into the habit of only plunging immediately before cutting, and always letting the motor spring back immediately afterwards. Don't lay the machine down, either upright or on its side, while it's still plunged – and certainly never, ever, if it's switched on too. That would mean either a hole in your workbench, or a horribly dangerous exposed bit.

While cutting, keep both hands on the tool, and feed it in the right direction when doing edging jobs. Lastly, when changing bits, pull the plug out.

Ready Reference

ROUTED JOINTS

Because a router cuts grooves and rebates very easily, it lets you make several strong yet inconspicuous board joints. The plain housing (A) requires no edge work – just a groove. The barefaced housing (B) needs a rebate as well. Rebate (C) and double rebate joints (D) are also simple; while the dovetail housing (E, and see photographs) repays in strength what it demands in precision. Tongued-and-grooved joints can have a moulded tongue (F) or a loose tongue in paired grooves (G).

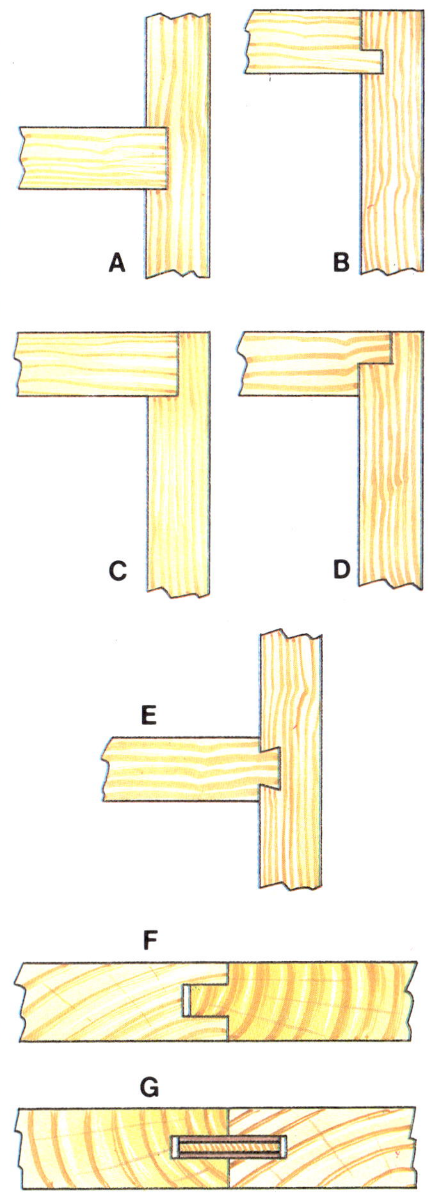

USING A ROUTER : 3

Earlier articles on using a router have dealt with basic techniques. To exploit your machine to the full, it's also well worth knowing some of the methods professionals use for speed and accuracy.

The advanced uses of the router fall under three main headings. You can use special jigs and templates; you can mount it for use as a 'spindle'; and you can mount it in a stand.

Using a jig

What marks out a good wood machinist is largely his inventiveness in using jigs and templates – devices for guiding the cutter or blade accurately through, into, along or round the workpiece and vice versa. The clamped-on batten, which guides the router to cut a straight groove (see pages 348–352) is a very simple jig, but the same principle is used for all others.

Suppose, for a start, that you want a wide groove, but have no bit large enough. You merely clamp battens on both sides, instead of just one, and move the router from side to side as well as forwards.

You can extend the batten principle to cut joints, too. If you want a number of identical halvings, it's usually a simple matter to clamp all the pieces side by side, fix battens across them, and move the router between these as if making a groove – cutting all the halvings at once. This ensures speed, plus (if you've set the job up correctly) total accuracy.

Similarly, suppose you want a recess – eg, for a flush handle in a sliding door. Trying to make this freehand is most unwise, because you're unlikely to cut accurately all the way round. Even if you manage it once, you'll never repeat the trick – as you might need to if you were fitting a pair of handles.

The solution is, of course, a jig: in this case, a 'box guide', the equivalent of four straight battens to guide the tool round the four sides of the recess. These pieces should be positioned and joined so that, when the router base is run against them, the bit will cut round the line you require. The box guide must therefore be bigger than the recess you want, so the base fits inside with room to manoeuvre.

You'll also need a means of locating any jig firmly and accurately. For small jobs, cramps are probably most efficient. In general, too, jigs and templates should be fairly heavy and substantial. That way there's less risk of slipping and harming the work or yourself.

A BEDSIDE CABINET

Almost all the joints in this unit are cut with the router, like the shapes at the bottom – see photographs. The groove in each front leg stops above the mortise.

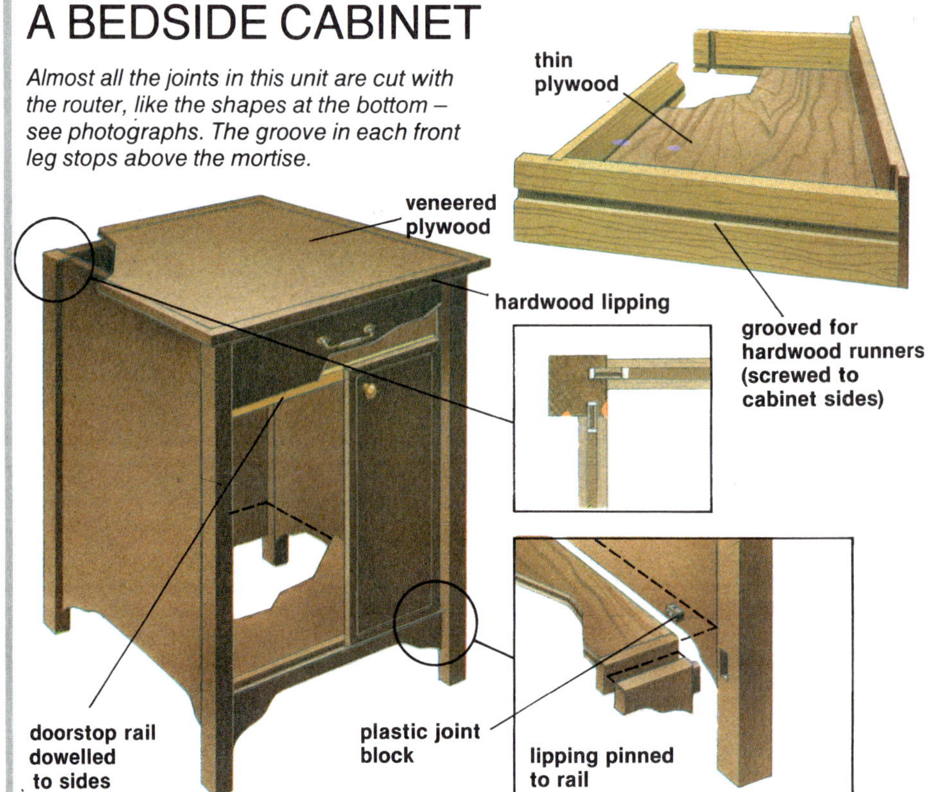

A ROUTER TABLE

Made of chipboard, plywood or blockboard, and jointed with screws and/or plastic blocks, this table serves for a spindle (below) or for an 'overarm router' set-up (see Ready Reference*).*

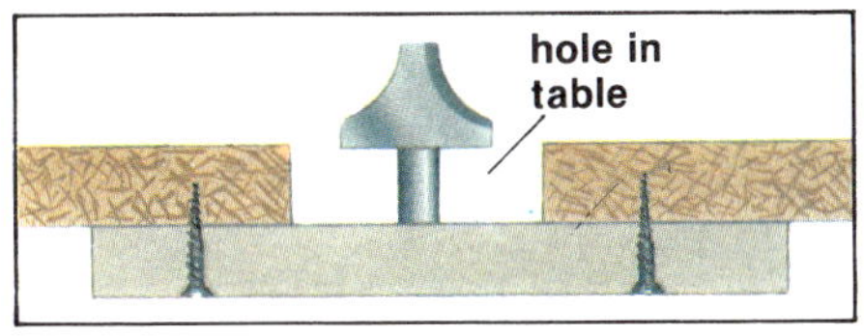

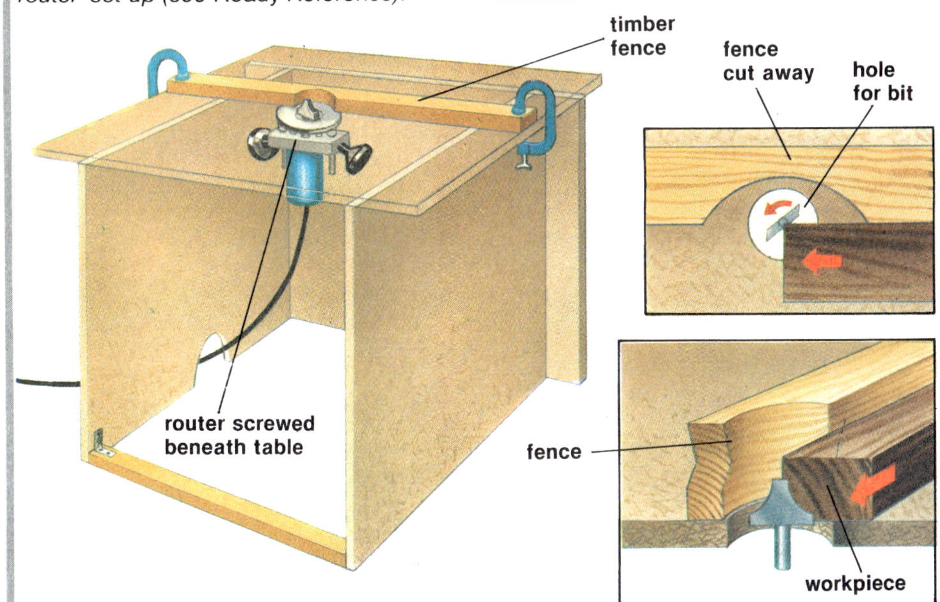

The template guide

When the router is guided by its base, you have to allow for as much as half the base diameter when making the jig or positioning your guide battens. This is no good for fine work, especially where curves are involved. The answer there is a 'template guide'. This is a small metal plate with a sort of funnel in the middle. The plate is screwed across the hole in the router base, so that the funnel fits over the bit like a sleeve and projects in the same way as the bit does.

You can then guide the router by running the side of the funnel along the edge of a jig, which is often a flat pattern or 'template' of plywood (or a harder material) cut to the desired profile. The workpiece – often cut roughly to shape already – is fixed under the template with cramps, pins or double-sided adhesive tape, so that the bit cuts into or through it as the router is guided along. The template must be thicker than the funnel is long, so the guide will slide easily.

When making a template (see *Ready Reference*) for use with the hand-held router, you have to allow for the difference between the diameter of the bit and the outside diameter of the funnel. If you subtract the former from the latter and divide by two, you'll know how much smaller (or larger) the template should be than the piece you want to end up with.

Templates are useful whenever you want to repeat a special shape. You'll get perfect copies – provided the template doesn't include any concave curves whose radius is smaller than that of the funnel, because the template guide won't follow them. The results, of course, depend on the accuracy of the template. To make it, use shaping tools to cut out and create exactly the profile you require for the job.

Self-guiding trimming bits (shown on pages 353–357 are also useful for template work. While the ball-bearing guide runs along the template, the cutter cuts the workpiece. The template goes on top of or underneath the piece, depending on the position of the bearing.

Such bits do away with the template guide, and – provided the bearing is the same size as the cutter – they let you make the template the same size as the final shape. In fact, you don't need a template as such. You just make the first piece the right shape by hand, and use that instead.

The template guide itself has other uses than for making repeated shapes. It can be used for recessing, if you make a jig on the lines described, and for mortising, because a mortise is simply a deep, narrow recess.

Lastly, it can be used for dovetailing – in conjunction with a dovetail bit, plus a dovetailing jig which you clamp over the

Ready Reference

THE OVERARM ROUTER

One way of making a router table is to fit the machine into a drill stand. Lower it, and push the work under the bit – usually against a fence.

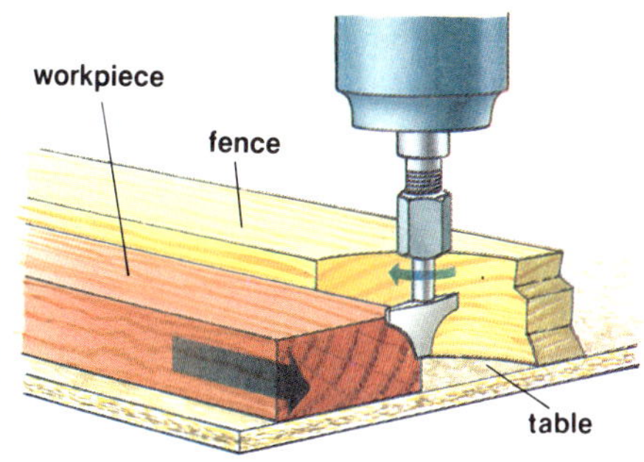

USING TEMPLATES

With a hand-held router, you fit a template guide to follow a jig or template which will produce the required shape. The template needs to be a different size from the workpiece. To find out by how much (A), subtract the bit diameter (B) from the outside diameter of the guide (C). Make the template thicker than the amount the guide protrudes from the router base to allow the guide to slide easily.

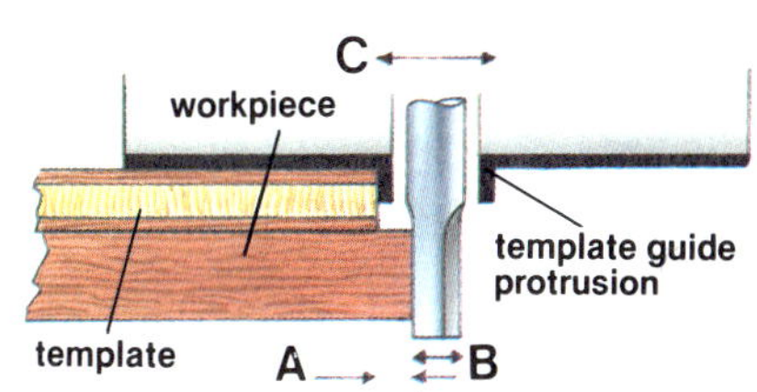

On the overarm router, templates are used with a guide pin, centred under the bit. A pin and bit of the same diameter (1) let you make the template the same size as the workpiece. Otherwise make the template smaller (2) or larger. The pin can be made of hardwood or steel. A hardwood pin lets you do without a packing piece, allowing the bit right down to meet the pin.

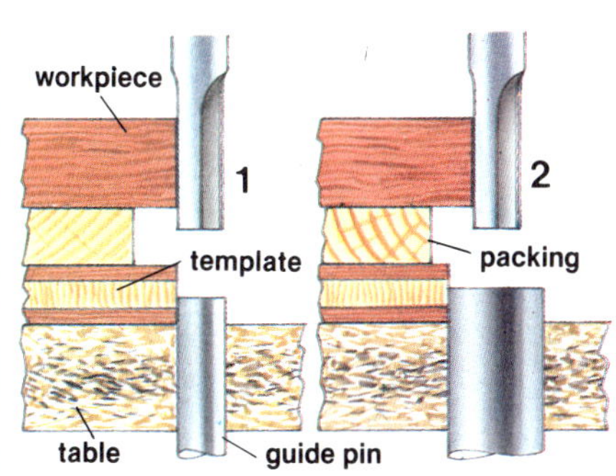

USING A SPINDLE

1 With the bit poking up through the table, move the cutaway fence over it, and cramp it tightly in position to give the width of cut you need for the job.

2 Switch on and push a test piece into the bit, holding it against the fence. Then check the depth and width of cut, adjusting either or both if necessary.

3 For stopped cuts (those which don't continue right along the piece) cramp a block of timber to the fence as a buffer in the position you want.

4 When you're sure the setting is right, switch the router on again and push each workpiece carefully past the bit with both hands to make the cut.

5 Good design may let you re-use a setting for several cuts. This is a drawer side. When ending a cut, it's often safest to use a push stick.

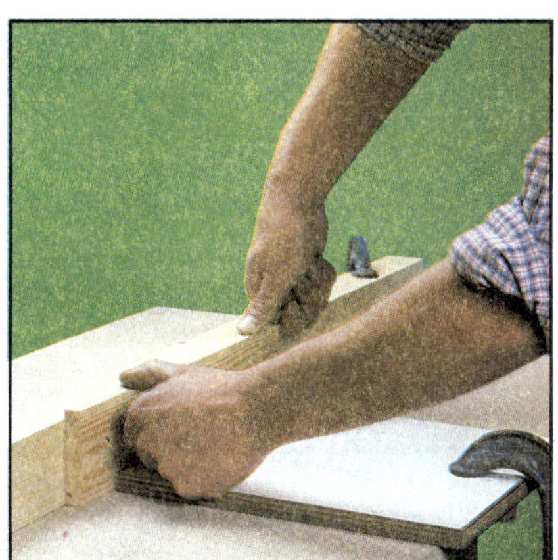

6 Another way of holding thin workpieces safely against the bit is with a straight board, cramped to the table so the pieces can just be pushed past it.

workpieces. The procedure is very like dovetailing with a power drill.
And you can use the same jig with a straight bit (in a router or drill) to cut finger joints.

The spindle

As already hinted, you can turn the portable router into a fixed machine. This is especially convenient for small workpieces – or long, narrow ones such as lengths of moulding – where it's hard to support the tool properly.

In a 'router table', as the fixed set-up is called, the machine may point upwards or downwards. Some manufacturers supply mountings in which it points sideways. The first arrangement is known as a spindle. You can buy a ready-made table for this, or make one from timber and boards – see illustration on page 359. The essentials are solid construction, and a flat top. The router is secured to the underside of the top, with its bit sticking up through a hole. Use wood or chipboard screws – or, better still, machine screws in threaded bushes.

You'll also require a timber or plywood 'fence' along which to slide the work past the bit. Ideally this should itself be mounted to slide back and forwards, so you can vary the width of cut more easily, but it can be clamped on. It should be cut away, in width or thickness, at the point where the bit emerges through the table. You can adjust the depth of cut (ie, the amount the bit protrudes) on the machine as usual.

When using a spindle, safety should never leave your mind. Don't switch the router on until you're sure that both it and the fence are firmly fixed in position. Make sure you feed the workpiece against the rotation of the bit – ie, from right to left – or it may kick back at you. Always hold it firmly on course; this is important for accuracy as well as safety. And **keep your hands clear of the rotating bit at all times.** At the end of a cut, it's often better to push the workpiece through with a stick, while still holding the already machined end with your other hand.

The 'overarm' router

The alternative to a spindle is to mount the router in a stand, just like a power drill (removing it from the carriage first if necessary). This makes an 'overarm' router. Here too you'll need a table; the photographs show a ready-made pattern, but again, you can improvise if you prefer. You'll also require a removable fence.

Apart from all everyday jobs, the overarm router will tackle mortising, like a drill mounted in a shaping table. Tenoning is possible on either type of table (though it's usually more accurate on a spindle). You just fit a large straight bit and run the workpiece over (or under) it, end-on to the fence; then

MORTISING AND TENONING

1 *For mortising with a hand-held router, first screw the metal 'template guide' into position in the router base. Its 'bush' projects below the base plate.*

2 *Allowing for the size of the guide, make a jig for it to follow when cutting. This should locate over the workpiece to give the cut you want.*

3 *Cramp the workpiece and jig together. Fit a straight bit (ideally one which is the same width as the mortise) and place the router on the jig.*

4 *With the template guide against the side of the jig, switch on, plunge and cut – still keeping the guide pressed against the jig's side and ends.*

5 *You'll end up with a round-ended mortise. A bit which was smaller than the mortise width would need a jig with four sides for an accurate groove.*

TIP

6 *Use a spindle for routing tenons. Fit a wide straight bit, adjust it for the tenon shoulder depth and push the timber fence gently over it.*

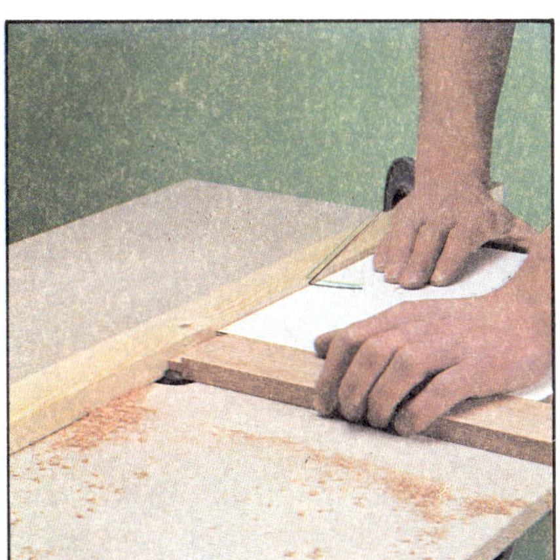

7 *Clamp the fence at the right width of cut. Short tenons need only one cut on each side. Use a broad push block to keep the piece square to the fence.*

8 *Re-adjust the depth of cut (but not the fence). Then turn the piece on edge and cut each of the edge shoulders in turn in the same way.*

9 *Round the corners of the tenon with a chisel, and try it in the mortise for fit. If necessary, re-adjust the spindle slightly and re-cut the tenon.*

turn the piece over to cut the other side – plus any edge shoulders. If the diameter of your bit is smaller than the length of the tenon, you'll need two or more passes. Set the fence so that you'll have cut the full length of the tenon by the time you're holding the piece up against it.

On any router table, you can make repeat shapes by removing the fence and using a template (you don't need a template guide). Again, you can use a self-guiding trimming bit. On the overarm router, however, there's an alternative – namely, to fit a guide pin. The guide pin is simply a cylindrical length of steel or even hardwood – or maybe a round-headed screw – driven into the table top with its centre exactly beneath the cutter's centre. It sticks up so you can run the template against it, lowering the router to cut the workpiece at the same time. A packing piece between workpiece and template helps ensure that the bit doesn't meet the guide pin.

In all template work (except on the spindle), you can cut internal as well as external shapes. You can shape, for example, the inside of a frame as well as the outside. The guide pin will do nicely for this. What's more, you can use the pin for recessing. Suppose you want to make a small box from a piece of solid hardwood, by recessing out the inside. You just make a template to the same size and shape as the recess, fasten the wood on top of it, and place it over the pin. Then you switch on, lower the router into the piece, and move the template and workpiece to and fro until the recess is hollowed out. The sides of the template will come up against the pin and stop you cutting too far.

If the template matches the shape you want, and the guide pin's diameter matches that of the bit, you'll get exact copies. If you vary the size of the pin (see *Ready Reference*) or bit, you'll get a shape that's larger or smaller – just as if you vary the size of the template instead.

The possibilities don't end there. For example, if you nail a board to the table and rotate it, you can cut a circle whose radius is the distance between the nail and the outside edge of the bit. It's simple enough – if you've got the imagination!

The router lathe

Perhaps the most ingenious appliance for routing is the router lathe. A do-it-yourself version of the automatic lathes now used in industry, this lets you make and shape cylindrical pieces.

You secure your length of timber – initially square in section – between the 'stocks' at each end, and fit your router to the carriage which slides on rails above it. You turn the work with a hand crank while the bit, often shaped, makes the cut. The router can also move along simultaneously at a pre-set rate, giving spiral cuts.

USING TEMPLATES

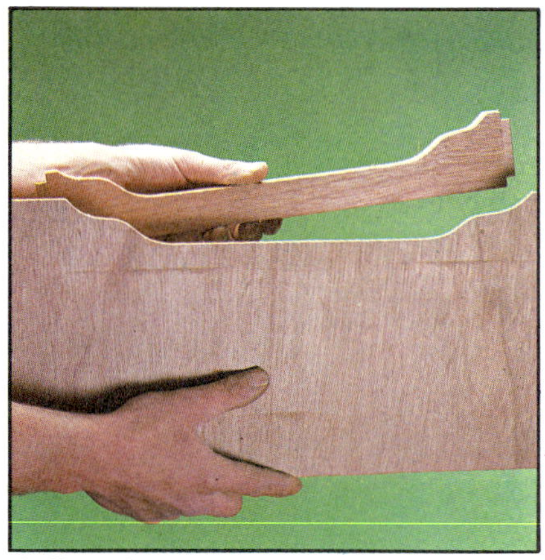

1 *Template work is one use of the overarm router. Shape the workpiece roughly, then fix it over the template – eg, with double-sided adhesive tape.*

2 *When cutting, hold the template against the guide pin. If the pin is wooden, lower the bit into it – you need no packing between template and workpiece.*

3 *Hold the work firmly and feed it against the bit's rotation. Note that a larger guide pin means a smaller template (and vice versa).*

4 *With larger pieces, it's easier to fix the template on top, and cut with a hand-held router – plus a template guide with which to follow the shape.*

5 *The cabinet's legs are joined to the sides and back with plywood tongues in routed grooves. The shaped template is used for sides, back and lower rail.*

6 *Routed grooves also take the drawer runners and bottom, and join its sides and back. Rebates are routed in the front to accept the sides.*

USING CIRCULAR SAWS

The circular saw cuts natural timber and man-made boards accurately. It's an indispensable tool for all types of woodwork – as long as you know how to get the most out of it.

Circular saws do nothing that hand tools can't do, but they do the job much more quickly. This eliminates much tiring work – which in many cases also means greater accuracy, especially for the beginner. They're particularly useful for cutting man-made boards, because of the long cuts involved.

The one thing of which you must be constantly aware is the need to work safely. But that, of course, is a matter of developing good habits.

Choosing a saw

Circular saws are available either as integral units on their own, or as attachments for power drills; each type has its advantages. There's also a range of sizes and power outputs which demands careful consideration before buying. And there's a special blade for every purpose from coarse to fine cutting, in timber or man-made boards.

Circular saw drill attachments are often satisfactory for general use, and fairly cheap. Naturally, however, this depends on the power of the drill itself – and that's unlikely to be enough if you do a great deal of sawing, or if you frequently use hardwoods. There's also the fact that the attachment has to be removed if you want to do any drilling, and must then be replaced afterwards.

If you do get a saw attachment for your drill, remember one thing. Unlike integral circular saws, most drills can be locked in the 'on' position so that the drill is rotating even if it is unattended – in a saw bench, for example. Never do this while the saw attachment is fitted. You *must* always be able to stop a saw in an emergency by simply lifting your finger from the trigger.

Integral saws (those with their own motors) are rated according to size and power in a quite complex way. The lowest-powered, with a motor of 300-450W, will generally accept blades 125mm (5in) in diameter and will be capable of making cuts up to 30mm (1$\frac{3}{16}$in) deep. The highest-powered saws have motors around 1000W, use 180mm (7in) blades, and can make cuts to a depth of 60mm (2$\frac{3}{8}$in).

What you should check before you choose a saw is whether its vital statistics suit your likely use of it. Saws vary considerably in their maximum and minimum cutting depths – and these will be reduced if you're cutting with the blade at an angle.

The larger and more powerful the saw, the faster it will cut. This may not be all that important unless you make constant use of it. You may get good value from a cheaper saw, and some people find the larger ones daunting. But there's always the risk of burning out the motor on a low-powered saw by overloading it (ie, trying to cut too fast, or through material that's too tough).

The anatomy of a saw

On almost all types of circular saw, the blade cuts on the up-stroke. It's attached to the drive shaft or 'arbor' with a bolt fitted with a washer.

The top of the blade is protected by a permanent safety guard; the bottom (protruding) part has a spring-loaded guard which recedes automatically as the cut progresses, and springs back as you finish. This sprung guard may be made of either metal or plastic. If at any time you intend to cut metal or masonry, choose a saw with metal guards, which can't come to any harm from flying fragments, etc; plastic ones may crack or chip.

The depth of cut (ie, the amount by which the blade protrudes through the bottom of the saw) is adjusted by a calibrated knob on the side of the machine, raising and lowering

Ready Reference

SAFETY WITH POWER SAWS

Circular power saws are entirely safe to use provided you follow a few commonsense rules:

- never wear loose fitting clothing that could get caught in the revolving blade. It's a good idea to keep your sleeves rolled up as an added precaution
- keep children and pets out of the room
- always follow the correct working procedures
- clamp the work piece and support the ends of long runs
- always hold the saw firmly, particularly at the end of the cut. Don't rest it on the waste wood which will fall away
- wear eye protectors and possibly earplugs
- always switch off the mains power when checking or adjusting the saw – ideally take the plug out of the socket
- don't overstretch yourself: walk parallel to long workpieces
- let the blade stop before lifting it away
- never carry a saw that's switched on at the mains – you could start it by accident if you tripped.

KNOW YOUR SAW

A circular saw is an indispensable tool, especially for cutting up man-made boards quickly and easily. You'll find it's not at all complicated to use, once you know your way round it. Very useful features are the depth adjustment, which regulates how far the blade protrudes downwards, and the angle adjustment, which enables you to cut with the blade at a slope (eg, for mitres).

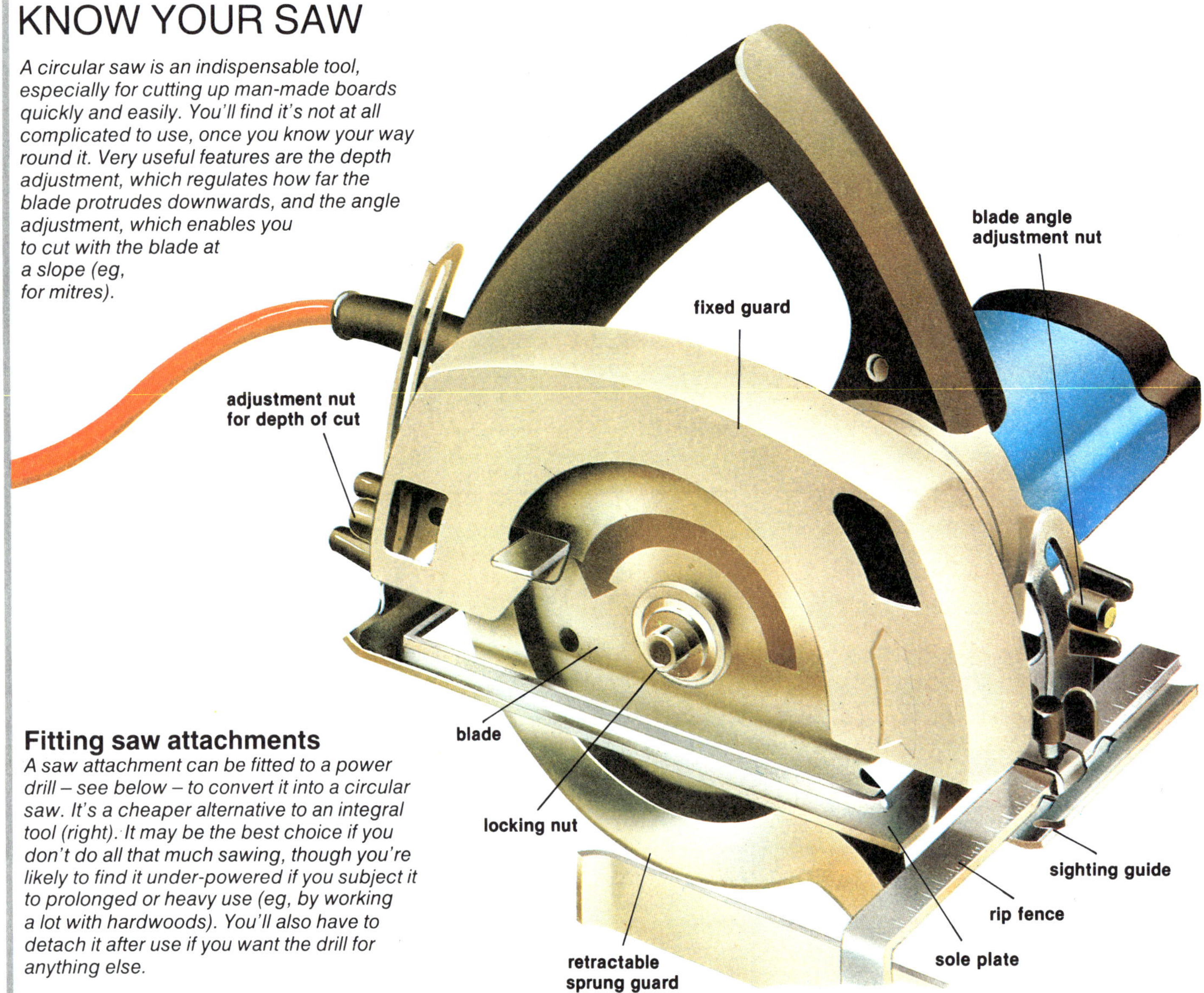

Fitting saw attachments

A saw attachment can be fitted to a power drill – see below – to convert it into a circular saw. It's a cheaper alternative to an integral tool (right). It may be the best choice if you don't do all that much sawing, though you're likely to find it under-powered if you subject it to prolonged or heavy use (eg, by working a lot with hardwoods). You'll also have to detach it after use if you want the drill for anything else.

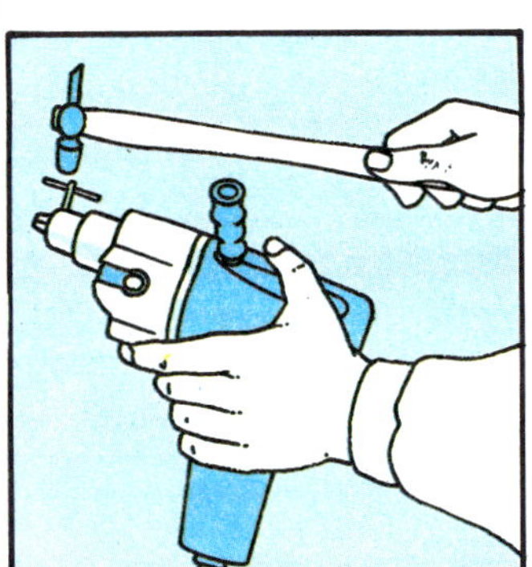

1 *Remove the chuck from the front of the drill, inserting the chuck key and tapping it with a hammer if necessary.*

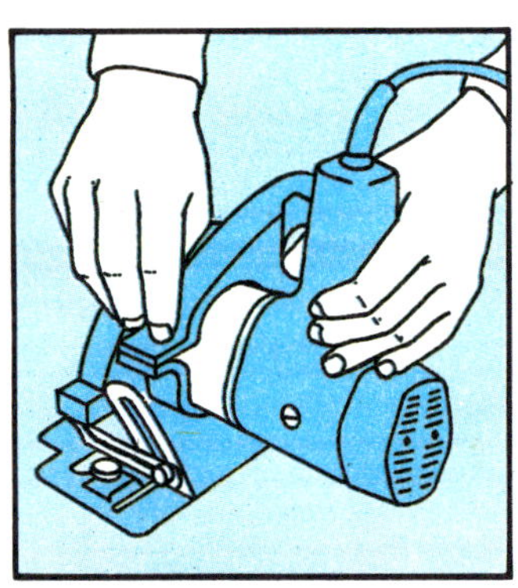

2 *Locate the saw attachment over the front of the drill, and tighten any fixing nuts which are provided.*

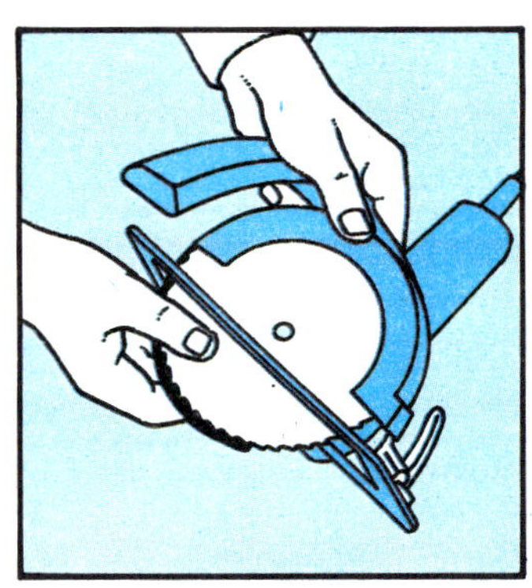

3 *Fit the blade, together with the retractable lower guard, into position over the shaft of the drill.*

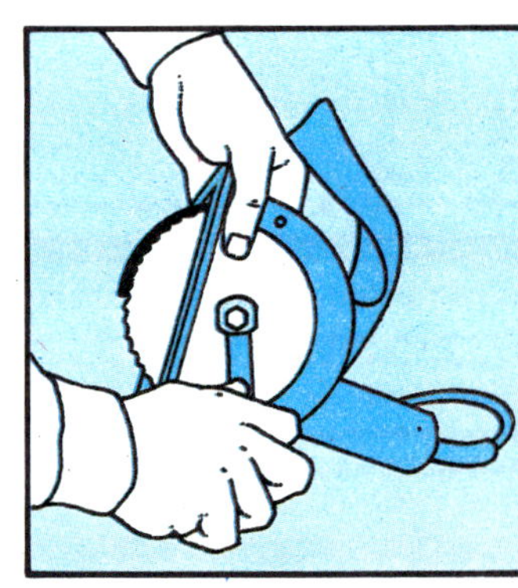

4 *Add the nut which holds the blade in place, get it finger-tight by hand, and finish tightening it up with a spanner.*

the body of the saw in relation to the sole plate (the saw's flat base). This depth should be slightly greater, by a millimetre or two, than the thickness of the material to be cut; if the blade protrudes too much, it will cause splintering.

There's also a second knob for angling the blade, usually adjustable in 5° steps – but you'll need to double-check with a protractor to guarantee accuracy, and make test cuts in scrap wood. Bear in mind that you'll also need to increase the cutting depth to allow for the cut being at an angle.

Circular saws use a detachable rip fence to guide the saw when making long, straight cuts parallel to the edge of the workpiece (eg, when 'ripping' – that is, cutting solid timber lengthwise). This is a T-shaped piece of metal; the 'leg' is fitted to the sole plate so that it sticks out to one side, while the cross of the T locates over the edge of the material you're cutting.

Some saws are also fitted with a 'riving knife' behind the blade, which keeps the cut open to prevent the saw from sticking.

Fitting the blade

Using a circular saw is extremely simple once you know your way around it and have practised a bit and gained confidence.

Fit the blade with the power off and the saw resting safely on the workbench. Be sure that the blade is the right way round and is properly centred on the spindle. Then jam it in place. Most blades have holes in them through which you can put a screwdriver blade for this purpose; otherwise, insert a piece of wood between the teeth. Start the fixing bolt on the thread with the utmost care – you want it to be a tight accurate fit to avoid accidents. Don't forget the washer, either.

Making a cut

Before you switch the mains power on, check that the retractable safety guard is working smoothly.

Always make sure, too, that the piece of wood you're cutting is securely clamped, either in a vice or with G-cramps. Don't work along long unsupported runs of material; clamp the other end as well, if necessary, to stop the piece wobbling about. And check that there's nothing beneath the work to get in the way of the saw. In a situation like this, it's all too easy to cut through your workbench by mistake, so beware.

Don't start the saw and then present it to the workpiece. It could jump back at you. Instead, rest the sole plate of the saw flat on the work and line the blade up, but keep it just a few millimetres back from the actual start of the cut. Then press the trigger and wait for a moment for the saw to reach full speed. Holding it firmly, advance it to the start of the cut.

SETTING UP AND BASIC CUTTING

TIP

1 Fit the blade and jam a piece of wood between the teeth to stop it moving. Some blades have holes for you to insert a screwdriver instead.

2 Tighten the blade nut very firmly indeed with a spanner. It's absolutely vital that it shouldn't come loose while you're cutting.

3 Adjust the height of the saw's body in relation to its sole plate, so the blade just protrudes through what you're cutting.

4 Line the saw up so the blade is on the waste side of your cutting line. A mark or cut-out on the front of the sole plate will guide you.

5 Draw the saw back, still keeping its sole plate flat on the surface. Press the trigger and let it reach full speed before starting to cut.

6 As you move the saw forward, the guard is pushed up from the back. It springs back down to cover the blade when the cut is finished.

USING A RIP FENCE

1 *To cut timber lengthwise, or remove any narrow strip parallel to an edge, fit the fence the required distance from the blade and tighten the screw.*

2 *While cutting, make sure the fence stays flat against the edge of the material so you end up with a straight, parallel cut.*

3 *Where a rip fence is too short, use a batten instead. First measure from the side of the saw teeth to the edge of the sole plate.*

The motion of the blade itself will help to draw the saw forward: don't force it, because that will strain the motor and may snag the blade, causing kickback – though most modern saws do have a slip clutch to prevent this kind of trouble.

At the end of the cut, switch off the saw and let the blade stop before removing it. Otherwise you'll cause splintering (always a problem with circular saws).

Using a guide batten

There will often be times when you want more accuracy than you can get from cutting freehand, yet the rip fence is no use, because your intended cut is either too far from the edge or not parallel to it.

In such cases the answer is to cramp a batten across the surface of the material you're cutting, so that you can keep the sole plate of the saw against it while sawing, thus maintaining a straight line. If you fix it to the part you want to keep, rather than on the waste side, you'll make it impossible for the saw to wander into the wrong area; the worst than can happen is for it to deviate onto the waste side, so that the workpiece will require trimming afterwards.

The batten needs to be thin enough for the body of the saw to pass over it. Also ensure that you position it accurately so that the blade cuts exactly down the waste side of the cutting line you've marked otherwise you'll simply be making more work for yourself.

Cutting joints

Jointing boards (for example, when you're making box furniture) always demands thought and care. The circular saw is a great help here, because it can cut three types of joint: mitre, rebate and housing.

Cutting a mitre (ie, a mitre in the thickness of a board, rather than across it – see photograph 2 on page 367) is simply a matter of setting the blade accurately to an angle of 45° from the vertical. The great thing about the mitre is that it hides the end grain of both pieces, and this makes it very usefui in furniture construction, especially where man-made boards are used. However, in freestanding structures it needs some reinforcement, such as plastic jointing blocks.

CUTTING REBATES AND HOUSINGS

1 *Using the rip fence, cut along the inside of the marked rebate first. Set the depth of cut to less than the material's thickness.*

2 *Make parallel cuts to remove the rest, moving the fence in each time, and clean up the finished rebate with a chisel if necessary.*

3 *Make a housing in a similar way. Cut its sides first, then remove waste from the middle of the housing with successive parallel cuts.*

4 *Align a straight piece of timber or plywood parallel to the cutting line, distancing it from the line by the amount you've just measured.*

5 *Cramp the batten on and hold the saw against it as you cut. If it's fixed to the workpiece, not the waste, you can't cut too much off.*

A rebate can be cut by using the rip fence, set very close in and adjusted for successive parallel cuts until you've made the required 'ledge' across the edge of the piece.

Parallel saw cuts also make housings and grooves (for example, to take the ends of shelves). The rip fence may be too short for use here, so you may need a batten instead; re-locate it for each individual cut.

Using a saw table

So far we've dealt with using a portable circular saw freehand. However, professional woodworking shops possess larger circular saws ('bench saws') which are mounted in fixed units. The advantage of fixed saws is that you have both hands free to guide the work into the blade. That, plus a flat surface on which to rest the work, means greater convenience and accuracy.

While full-scale purpose-built home bench saws for the keen do-it-yourselfer are available, there's a cheaper alternative. You can mount your portable circular saw in a bench – basically a table with a hole in it. The saw is fixed underneath the bench so that the blade sticks up through the hole. The bench can be either bought or home-made from timber and man-made boards.

All saw benches are fitted with adjustable fences for accurate cutting, whether parallel to an edge or at an angle. Perhaps their only drawback is that the exposed blade makes them more dangerous than portable saws.

MAKING ANGLED CUTS

1 *To cut at other than 90°, adjust the angle of the sole plate in relation to the blade. Degree markings are calibrated on the fitting.*

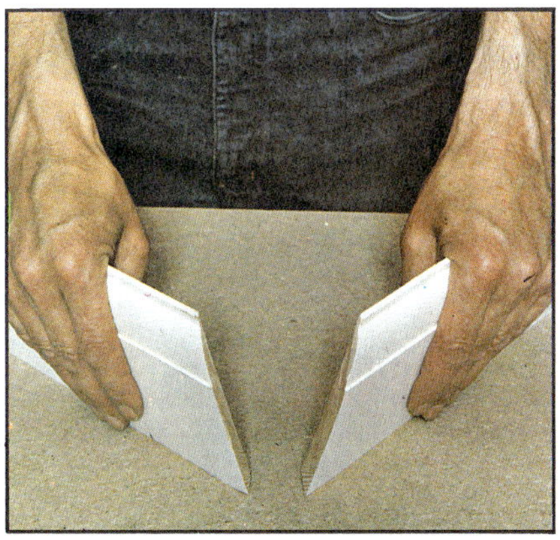

2 *A circular saw with the blade set at 45° is ideal for cutting mitres in skirting boards where they join at external corners.*

Ready Reference

WHAT BLADE TO USE

There are a number of blades available for cutting a variety of materials. These are some of the more common:

General purpose blade
Sometimes known as a **combination blade** (A). This is good for softwood and chipboard. You can buy blades for rip (B) or cross-cuts (C).

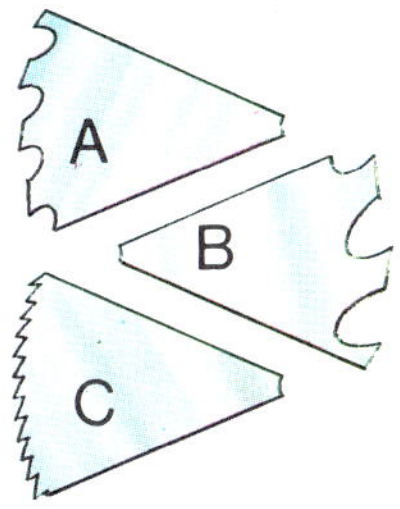

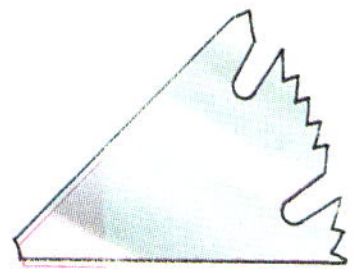

Planer blade
This gives a neat cut in timber hardboard and plywood.

Compo or wallboard blade
Used for cutting wallboards. It has fine teeth to prevent fraying.

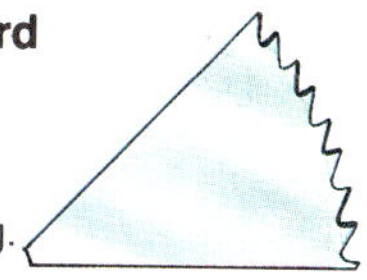

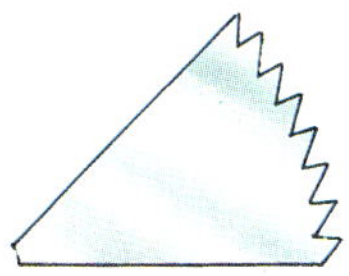

Flooring blade
You should use this blade for old wood that might conceal nails.

Masonry cutting disc
Cuts ceramics and other tough materials. It's hard going using one of these without a powerful saw.

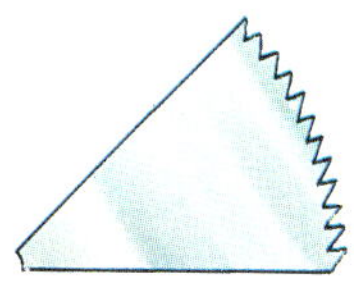

Metal cutting blade
This is used for soft metals.

Metal cutting wheel
You'll have to use one of these when cutting hard metal or plastics.

CUTTING LAMINATES

Circular saws are not ideal for cutting laminates, but you can cut them with a tungsten carbide blade. For coated boarding cut with the decorative side down. Otherwise use a hand tenon saw or a fine toothed jig saw.

BASIC VENEERING

Veneering offers effects of spectacular beauty which you can't obtain in any other way. It's a specialised procedure, but you can soon master the basic techniques and produce highly acceptable results on almost every kind of furniture.

The word 'veneering' smacks slightly of deceit and camouflage. This is unfair. For centuries, sticking down a thin sheet or veneer of especially attractive and often exotic timber to a 'ground' of cheaper and commoner material has been a means of displaying its beauty where cost, rarity (and often available sizes) would prevent its use in any other way.

Veneering was extensively used throughout the golden age of cabinet-making, and nowadays veneers of even the highest quality are mass-produced. The invention of artificial boards has been another stage of progress – closely related, in that plywood is made entirely of veneers, and blockboard includes them on both faces. The two developments have combined in the veneered boards which go into a huge proportion of all modern furniture.

A companion skill is that of marquetry – the creating of patterns, often incredibly beautiful and complex, from small pieces of veneer arranged side-by-side. Though within the scope of the skilled do-it-yourselfer, this demands a lot of time and practice, so consult a specialist book first.

Types of veneer

Veneers are produced in three main ways:

- sawing, the traditional method, which is now only used for hard and difficult woods
- rotary cutting, which has revolutionised veneer production and made plywood possible. It involves steaming the log and rotating it against a knife to peel the veneer off in a continuous sheet. This is why a large piece of plywood often displays a repeated pattern. Such veneers are usually cut from cheap, plentiful and featureless timbers, eg birch, pine, gaboon and lauan. They can be anything from 0.25mm (1/100in) to 10mm (3/8in) thick
- knife cutting, which has solved the problem of mass-producing veneers that display fine timbers at their best, unlike most examples of rotary cutting. In this process, standard for decorative face veneers, the log (again usually steamed) is slid repeatedly against a fixed knife. The resulting thickness is generally 0.7mm.

Basic considerations

Although even the nearest equivalent to industrial veneering gear would require a huge outlay, you still have at your disposal two time-honoured if much less sophisticated methods – hot veneering and caul veneering.

But what advantage is there in veneering? It enables you to make furniture and fittings with natural decorative effects which are exactly tailored to your own requirements. You can put the uniformity of factory pieces behind you. Even simple white-painted units, if they incorporate your own veneered doors and drawers, give an air of quality to any room.

How do you obtain veneers? If you don't live within easy reach of a veneer merchant, you can order them by post. Addresses can be found in woodworking magazines, and a wide range of timber species is on sale.

Veneer merchants are helpful people who will give you advice on comparative costs, size, availability, quality, matching, suitability, etc. As a general guide, remember that there's little point in using common African hardwoods which are widely available already laid on boards, nor in taking a lot of trouble with bland, characterless veneers such as beech. But don't go to the other extreme. Exotic and expensive veneers such as Rio rosewood and macassar ebony should be left alone until you've had some experience; they can be difficult to work with, and you don't want to waste your money.

You need not only the decorative facing

Ready Reference

USING ANIMAL GLUE

Animal glue comes as jelly and liquid, but more often in 'pearls' or slabs which you soak 2:1 with water in a plastic container (breakable if the contents solidify) and heated over a gas or electric ring. It must be used hot, but never boiled or it won't stick. Dried scraps and crusts can be put back in the pot and melted down.

USING LIPPING

Lipping is often best applied (A) before flushing off and veneering over (B). On doors, it's not needed below eye level – but make it thicker to take hinges.

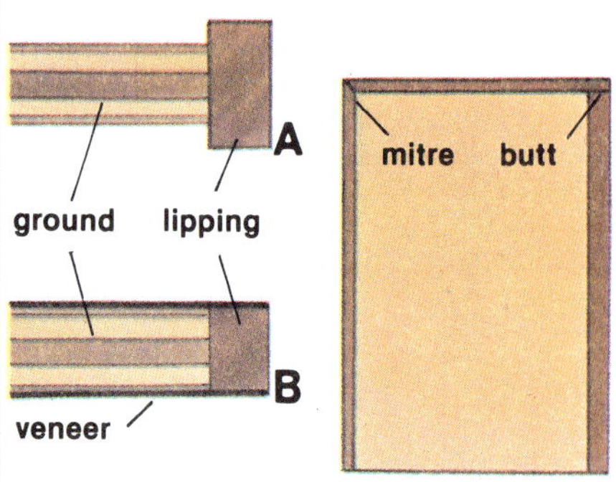

HOT VENEERING

TIP

1 *Clear your work area, and make ready a fresh pot of glue, a warm iron, hot water and rags. Put your veneer hammer in the water to warm.*

2 *Check the glue is very hot and free of lumps, then quickly spread it all over your 'ground' (the board on which you're laying the veneer).*

3 *Slightly dampen the veneer (trimmed just oversize), lay it on the ground, spread a little glue on top as a lubricant, and push hard with the hammer.*

4 *Squeeze out as much of the glue as you can. When it gels as it cools, fold a wet cloth and iron the veneer through it. Don't let it steam too much.*

5 *Then use your hammer again to force out the rest of the glue and ensure suction all over. You can hold it by the handle instead of the head.*

TIP

6 *Trim edges by placing a scrap block on top and tilting it to press the overhang downwards; then cut through the underside with a sharp knife.*

veneer but also a 'balancer' veneer for the reverse side – even if, for example, it's the underside of a table top that will never be seen. If only one side of a board is veneered, it will quickly bow. A balancer equalises the stresses and thus removes this tendency. Naturally, a cheaper wood – commonly African mahogany – is used for this purpose.

You can veneer on solid timber or man-made board. However, chipboard is too porous for hot veneering. If used for caul work, it must have a 'furniture finish' – a surface of small particles.

Whatever ground you use will require edge treatment ('lipping') if the edges are to be visible. This can be a strip of veneer, but the way edge veneers chip and come unstuck gives veneering a bad name. Instead, use a solid wood lipping (see page 320) – especially if the edges are likely to come in for a lot of wear. This will never chip, and bruises can eventually be planed off.

If you first lip and then veneer the board, the veneer covers the edges of the lipping. It will never be seen, and the result will look like solid timber. Use the same wood for the lipping as for the face veneer.

Make your lipping about 4mm wider than the board is thick, because it's impossible to cramp in position with absolute accuracy: plane off the excess afterwards. Tongued-and-grooved lipping should locate more precisely. Thin lippings are best cramped with 'softening' battens to distribute the pressure evenly right along them.

Hot veneering

Success in all veneering depends on leaving nothing to chance. Begin by giving your panel a good sanding, for smoothness and so the adhesive will stick. Don't use glasspaper in case you cause scratches or leave lumps of glass in it: both may show through the veneer.

The adhesive must be animal ('Scotch') glue – not an impact type. This has the tremendous advantage of quick setting coupled with equally fast melting under heat. It's prepared by soaking or heating; it mustn't be burnt or boiled.

First 'size' your prepared panel with thin glue from a fresh pot and leave it to dry. Meanwhile, trim your veneer to size by making repeated gentle cuts with a very sharp knife. Leave about a 12mm (½in) overhang on all sides in case the veneer slips; don't leave too much or you'll find it tends to lift from the edges.

Before going any further make sure you have at hand a veneer hammer (see *Ready Reference*), a supply of clean rags and clean hot water, a hot iron and some more fresh glue. Your bench top should be cleared of all other tools and equipment, and free of dirt and shavings. When you're hot veneering,

POSITIONING VENEERS

Decorative veneers, if not bought singly, come in bundles or 'packs' sliced from the log and stacked like rashers of bacon. These leaves can be cut and arranged in numerous patterns (A).

On solid wood, the veneer grain should run parallel to that of the ground (B), to allow shrinkage and swelling in tandem. If veneering only one side, make it the 'heart' side, to equalise natural bowing or 'cupping' (C). On artificial boards, the grain of the decorative veneer you're laying should be at right angles to that of the existing face veneer (D).

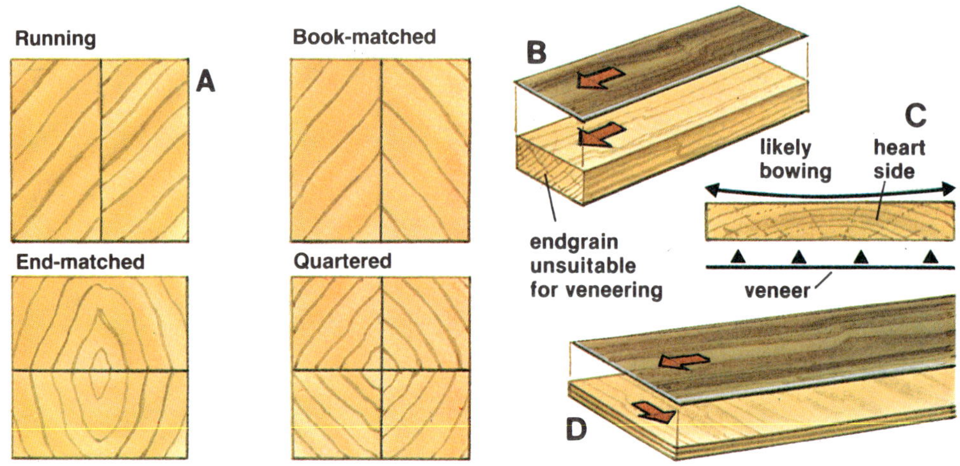

CROSSBANDING AND JOINTING

1 *A crossband is a strip of veneer cut across the grain, glued along the margin next to the main veneer, hammered towards it and trimmed.*

2 *To join two sheets when hot veneering, first lay one in the usual way, ensuring it overlaps a centre line marked on the edge of the ground.*

3 *Lay the second piece likewise, again overlapping the centre line. If you're matching the grain (see illustration above), the overlaps must be equal.*

4 *Position (and ideally cramp) a straight edge along the line, and cut through both pieces at once. Avoid rust by taping its underside.*

5 *Remove the offcut of the second piece; then prise that up to remove the offcut of the first. Add more glue and/or iron the joint if needed, then hammer it.*

6 *Tape across and then along the joint to counteract shrinkage as the veneers dry out. As the surface is damp, gummed paper tape will stick best.*

the glue gets everywhere, so you may want to cover the whole surface with newspaper – but you may also find that its tendency to get stuck to the work makes this more trouble than it's worth. Animal glue is water-soluble; you can wipe any surplus off with a damp cloth when you've finished.

Damp (without soaking) both surfaces of the veneer to stop them curling up with the glue. Spread it quickly and evenly on the ground and position the veneer. Some craftsmen advocate gluing the veneer too (perhaps temporarily securing it to the bench with four dabs of glue first); but this may not be necessary. Still working very fast, press the veneer down with your hammer. You may well find it helpful to spread glue on top of the veneer first as a lubricant, because you'll be applying a lot of pressure. Start from the middle and make zig-zag strokes to squeeze out every bit of excess glue; it should ripple ahead of the hammer. Always push along the grain, never across it.

However quickly you work, you're unlikely to finish before the glue has cooled enough to form intractable jellified lumps under the veneer. Fold a piece of cloth and iron the veneer through it. Keep the iron moving, and ensure that it's not so hot as to make steam: like soaking, this will expand the veneer, causing trouble when it shrinks as it dries after laying. An aluminium-soled iron, incidentally, avoids rust and consequent stains.

Use your hammer again as before. When you think the veneer is well and truly down (held by suction as well as by the glue), tap the surface to detect any unglued parts.

Correct these by either of two methods. One is to slit the veneer with the grain, ease it up, add a little more glue, squeeze the surplus out and then cover the slit with adhesive paper – to be removed with water when the glue is properly set. It won't show. The other is to push some glue towards the loose patch, let it cool, force it away again, and then iron the veneer to get rid of the glue with a hammer before bursting the blister with a pin and finally sticking it down.

A sharp-edged piece of wood makes a safe and effective scraper for excess glue. Lay the balancer veneer in exactly the same way, and leave the board to dry for a day or two before sanding.

Many exotic veneers are only available in narrow widths (because they come from thin trees) and will require jointing – a technique also used to form decorative patterns. You do this by laying the pieces so they overlap, and cutting through both.

Traditionally, veneered work was cleaned up with a cabinet scraper and fine glass-paper or garnet paper. Nowadays these have been largely replaced by the orbital sander. Don't use a coarse abrasive: you can soon go through a thin veneer.

Caul veneering

Hot veneering, though fascinating, may sound too risky and too much like hard work. Caul veneering is a different story. It's a straightforward technique which produces excellent results even for beginners. And it lets you do a dry run first.

You need a board at least 18mm (¾in) and preferably 25 to 32mm (1 to 1¼in) thick – slightly larger than the panel to be veneered. This 'caul' is laid on top of the veneer, which in turn is laid on top of the glued panel, and pressure is applied to it – usually by means of cramps.

Obviously, even large G-cramps don't reach to the middle of a wide panel, so battens are enlisted to help. These need to be strong – at least 50x25mm (2x1in) and, for larger jobs, preferably 75x50mm (3x2in). Both caul and battens can be used for any number of jobs.

Prepare and lip the ground just as for hot veneering, and select your veneers likewise. If using more than one leaf, match the pieces as necessary and cut them to length, adding about 6mm (¼in) at either end. Don't cut them to width, because your next job is to plane their edges to make a perfect joint – an apparently impossible task that is, in reality, quite easy. All you do is to cramp the veneers between two lengths of wood which act as a guide for the plane.

Now tape them together. A transparent adhesive tape is probably best, though some people still prefer sticky paper. Then trim the veneers to width on the outer edges, leaving an overhang here too.

Place your panel on the bench, or another suitable base if you don't want your bench out of action. Nearby, position your caul and battens, plus cramps which have been opened at the correct distance (base + panel + caul + battens + 12mm/½in).

Veneer both sides at once (in fact, you can even veneer several panels at once, stacking them up before cramping). A PVA adhesive is best here; cover the panel, and allow it to get just a little tacky (but only a little) to prevent slippage. Then position the panel on the backing veneer – itself laid on a sheet of plastic to prevent it sticking to the base. Position the face veneer (or veneers) on top, followed by the caul. Position the battens and tighten the cramps as shown in *Ready Reference*.

Leave the job until the adhesive has set. At that stage, remove the cramps, batten and caul, and trim the veneer – but resist the temptation to pull off the tape. The veneer may come with it. Instead, test a short length first. If the tape doesn't come away cleanly, gently sand it off.

Glue that's come through to the face interferes with some finishes, so a good final cleaning-up is essential.

Ready Reference

MAKING A VENEER HAMMER

The veneer hammer – not really a hammer at all – can't be bought. Make it from hardwood (not oak, because it stains), with the grain running as shown.

TIP: RIGHT SIDE UP

Knife-cut (sliced) veneers have slight raised areas on one side and hollows on the other. Lay the latter face down.

MAKE YOUR OWN GLUE POT

A cast-iron double boiler is traditional for hot veneering – but a glass jar will do.

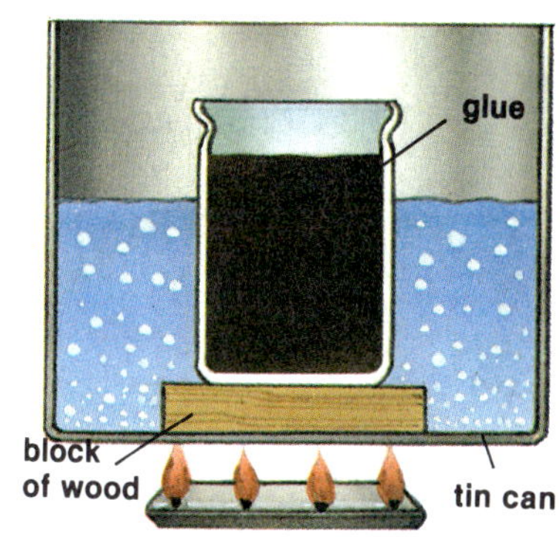

TIP: CRAMPING CAULS

To make sure adhesive isn't trapped in the middle, tighten the cramps on each batten in the order shown (A). Battens should be very slightly 'bellied' (B).

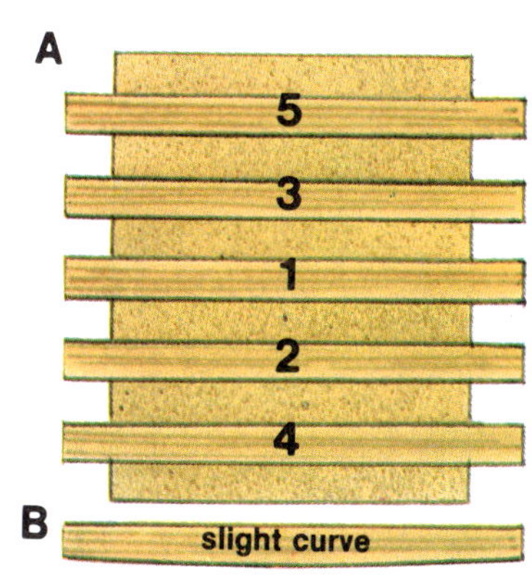

CAUL VENEERING

1 *To join two pieces for caul work, cut them roughly straight with a knife, then stack and cramp them between battens so 2-3mm (1/8in) protrudes.*

2 *Plane the twin edges flush with the battens. You may find it easiest to start by planing the far end, and then work back towards you.*

3 *Join these pieces – or the sections of any pattern – tightly across and along with transparent adhesive tape (which is also easy to remove).*

4 *Preferably on trestles, lay a stiff board larger than the panel to be veneered, followed by plastic (not newspaper) and backing veneer – also slightly oversize.*

5 *Mark on the panel edge where you want to position any joint between veneers (eg, on the centre line). This is the only way to align the pattern.*

6 *Spread PVA adhesive thinly but evenly and thoroughly over one side of the panel (especially edges), reverse it, and lay it on the backing veneer.*

7 *Spread PVA on top of the panel, and carefully position the face veneer. Be sure to align any joint with the appropriate mark on the panel edge.*

8 *Gently lay another sheet of plastic on the face veneer, and position a thick, oversized board (the caul) squarely on top of the stack.*

9 *Squeeze the 'sandwich' with stout battens (Ready Reference) and lots of cramps, hired if necessary. An extra-thick caul and weights might work too.*

MORTISE & TENON JOINTS

Mortise and tenon joints are indispensable if you're making furniture that's both strong and good-looking, and are particularly useful for making the most popular pieces of furniture – tables and chairs.

Jem Grischotti

Take a piece of wood, shape the end to form a 'tongue', then fit the tongue into a matching slot in the side of another piece, and you've made a mortise-and-tenon joint.

The tenon is the tongue and the mortise is the slot, and the joint has proved its usefulness over centuries in all kinds of wooden frameworks because of its strength and resistance to movement. It's the best joint for fixing horizontal pieces of wood – 'rails' – into uprights such as table and chair legs.

Once you've got the knack of cutting it cleanly, you've mastered a joint which will stand you in very good stead. Whenever you're joining two lengths of wood in a T or L shape, and you want something stronger and more elegant than a halving joint, go for a mortise and tenon joint. The only time it won't work is on thin, flat pieces – boards, planks and panels: use housing joints instead.

There are numerous types of mortise-and-tenon joint at your disposal. Think carefully about the job the joint has to do before deciding which to use.

Choosing the right joint

A *through tenon* passes right through the mortise piece (which makes it easier to cut the mortise). Because you can see its endgrain, it's used in rougher work or as a decorative feature. It can also be wedged from the outside for strength and/or visual effect.

A *stub tenon* is one which doesn't pass right through, but fits into a 'blind' mortise – a hole with a bottom. The most familiar kind, especially in furniture, has shoulders all round which conceal the joint.

A *barefaced tenon* has the tenon cut with only one side shoulder instead of two – useful if the tenon piece is already very thin; or the tenon may be reduced in width by having edge shoulders cut in it – see *Ready Reference*.

A *haunched tenon* is a compromise often used at the corner of a frame to keep it from twisting. The haunch – an extra step between the tenon and the piece it projects from – can be square or sloping. A sloping haunch is hidden and easier to cut – see *Ready Reference* again.

A *double tenon* is just a pair of tenons cut on one piece of wood – used if the piece is very wide and you don't want to cut a single enormous mortise to take one wide tenon.

An *offset tenon* is simply one which isn't in the centre of the tenon piece.

Making the joint

Let's assume you're making a basic stub tenon joint. It doesn't really matter whether you start by making your mortise or your tenon; the important thing is to get them to fit together. However, cutting the tenon first means you can mark off the mortise from it, possibly getting a better fit. This is easier than the other way round. Either way, play safe by making the tenon a little too large (or the mortise a little too small), rather than the reverse. You can always cut off a bit more.

Marking and cutting the tenon

Begin by scoring round the tenon piece with a knife and try-square to mark the length of the tenon, using the width of the mortise piece as a guide. A through tenon should be a little bit over-long to allow for planing it flush to give a neat finish; a stub tenon should go about halfway through, and be about 3mm (1/8in) shorter than the mortise to leave room for any excess adhesive.

A mortise gauge is very useful for the next stage. Choose a mortise chisel which has a blade about one third the thickness of the tenon piece (under rather than over, though you can use a wider one if the tenon piece is

Ready Reference

WHICH JOINT IS WHICH

A through tenon goes right through the mortise piece. A **stub tenon,** on the other hand, fits into a stopped mortise.
Either sort can have shoulders cut away on one, two or three sides to form a **barefaced tenon.**
The idea of a **haunched tenon** – with either a square or sloping haunch – is to help prevent the pieces from twisting in relation to each other.

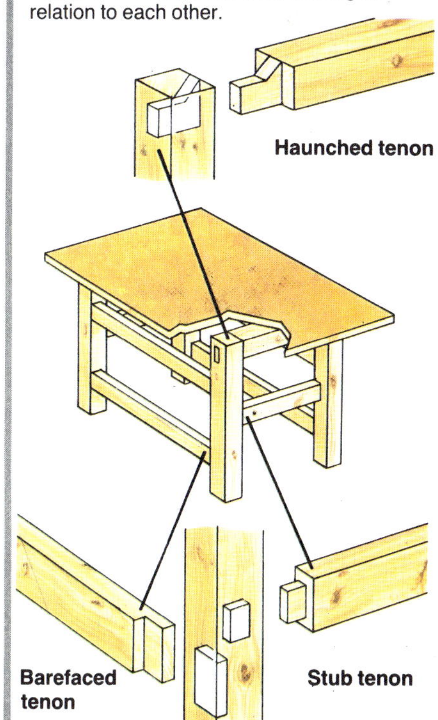

MARKING THE TENON

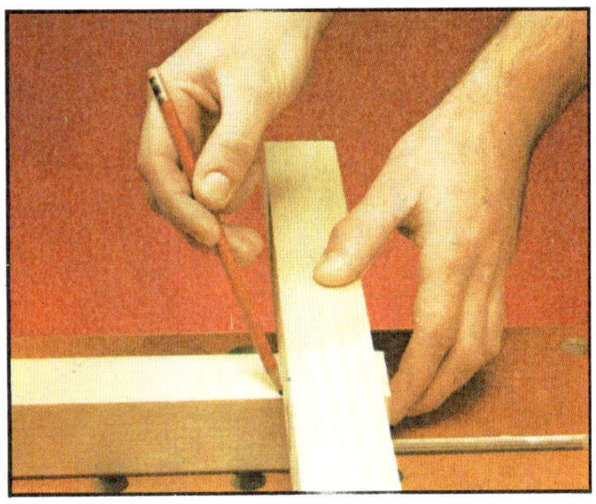

1 Lay the mortise piece on the tenon piece and mark where the tenon starts. Leave a through tenon over-long, as shown, for later trimming.

2 If you're making a stub tenon, it'll be easier to mark the tenon length if you lay the tenon piece on top of the mortise.

3 Square the mark round all four sides of the tenon piece by scoring across them with your marking knife against a try-square.

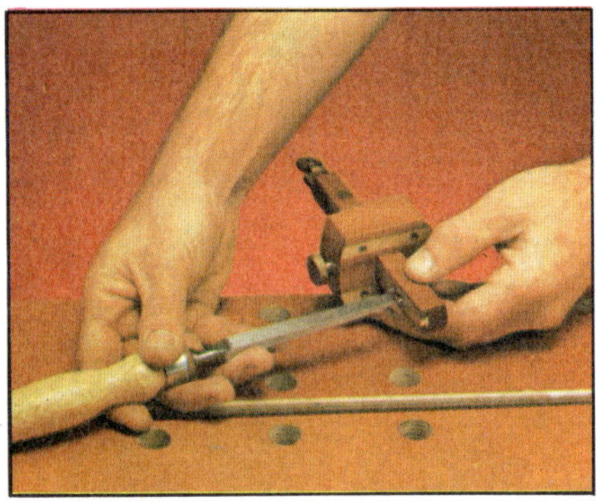

4 Set your mortise gauge to the exact blade width of your mortise chisel, or to the diameter of your drill auger bit if you have one available.

5 Use the gauge to score out the tenon width down the sides and across the end of the piece, stopping at the length marks you have already made.

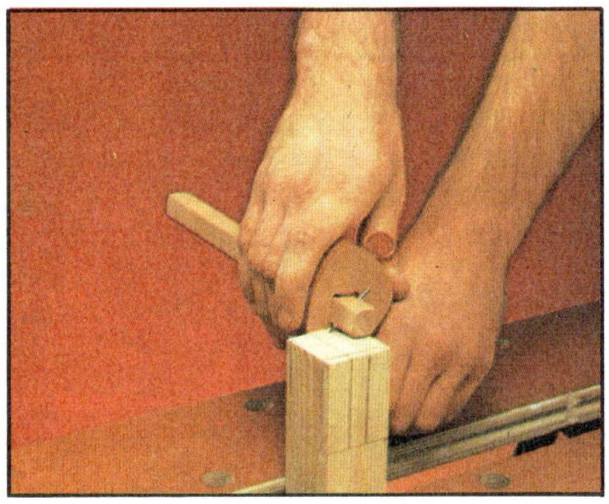

6 If you are cutting edge shoulders as well, use an ordinary marking gauge to score lines the other way for each of the shoulders in turn.

Jem Grischotti

much thinner than the mortise piece), and set the gauge's twin spurs that distance apart. Then set the stock so as to place the resulting 'tramlines' in the centre of the timber thickness – unless you're deliberately off-setting the tenon – and try it from both sides, adjusting the position of the stock till the two sets of tramlines coincide.

Now you can score the edges and end of the tenon piece to mark where the tenon will be cut. If you don't have a mortise gauge, use an ordinary single-spur marking gauge and mark the tramlines separately.

For a straight tenon, that's all the marking-up you need. If you're cutting shoulders in the width as well, set a marking gauge to one sixth the width of the tenon piece and mark down both faces and across the tramlines on the end.

If you're including a haunch, use the gauge to mark its width across the end and down the faces; then mark its depth with a knife and try-square. For maximum strength, the haunch should be not more than one third the tenon's width, and its depth not more than one quarter the length (or 12mm/½in long, whichever is smaller). We will be dealing with these joints in more detail in another section.

To cut a tenon you need, not surprisingly, a tenon saw. All you have to do is grip the piece upright in a vice and saw down each side of the tenon; then lay the wood flat and saw off the shoulders. The vital thing is always to keep your saw-cuts on the waste side of the lines.

Marking and cutting the mortise

At this stage, you can lay the tenon on the mortise piece and mark the mortise length on it. Then score its width with the gauge.

To cut the mortise, cramp the timber in position. If working near the end of a piece, leave extra length – a 'horn' which you saw off later – to prevent the wood from splitting as you chisel into it. If you have a carpenter's brace or a power drill, you can start by drilling holes close together along the length of the mortise. Make quite sure you keep the drill vertical – a drill stand will help.

Then chop and lever out the waste with the mortise chisel, and cut the recess for any haunch. Lastly, clean off the sides and ends with a bevel-edged chisel.

If you have no drill, use a mortise chisel by itself, keeping the bevel away from you and working from the centre of the mortise towards the ends – stopping just short of them so as not to bruise them when you lever out the waste before going deeper. On a through mortise, chisel halfway and then work from the other side. Clean up with a bevel-edged chisel.

Assembling the joint

Now you can fit the pieces together. Don't be tempted to force them, or you may split the wood; if the joint is impossibly tight, carefully shave the tenon with a chisel and glass-paper checking all the time. When it's a neat, close fit, glue it, cramp it and leave it to set.

Ideally, you need sash cramps – long steel bars with one fixed head and another which you tighten – plus some pieces of scrap wood to protect the work.

CUTTING THE TENON

1 After marking off the waste areas, clamp the piece upright and start to cut the tenon. Be sure to keep the saw on the waste side of the lines.

2 You may find it easier to work accurately if you clamp the piece in the vice at an angle of about 45° while you saw down for the next few strokes.

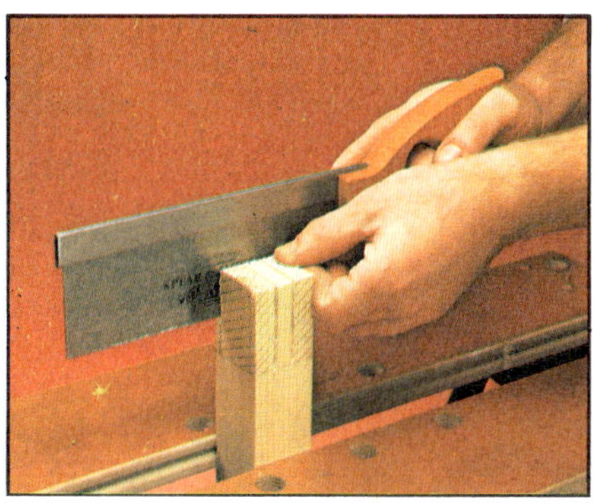

3 Finish off the cut with the piece upright again. It's easy to overshoot when sawing along the grain, so be careful as you approach the depth marks.

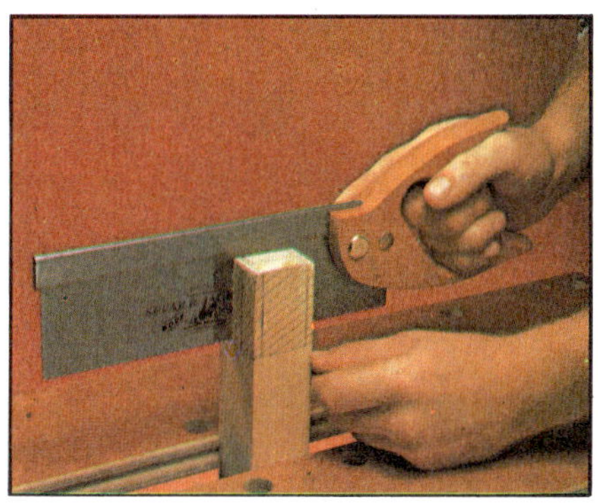

4 Make identical cuts along the grain, down to the same depth marks, for each of the edge shoulders if you have marked any.

5 Firmly hold or clamp the piece down flat on the workbench as you cut away each of the tenon's face shoulders by sawing across the grain.

6 Lastly, turn the piece over on to its side and make similar cross-cuts to remove the edge shoulders, if any are included. This completes the tenon.

Jem Grischotti

Ready Reference

STRENGTHENING THE JOINT

For extra strength and decorative possibilities, consider wedging or pegging the joint once it's fitted. Hardwood wedges go either into previously made saw-cuts in the end of a through tenon (A), or into the mortise above and below it (B). The mortise needs to be slightly tapered. Pegging is done with one or more dowels inserted into holes drilled sideways through the joint.

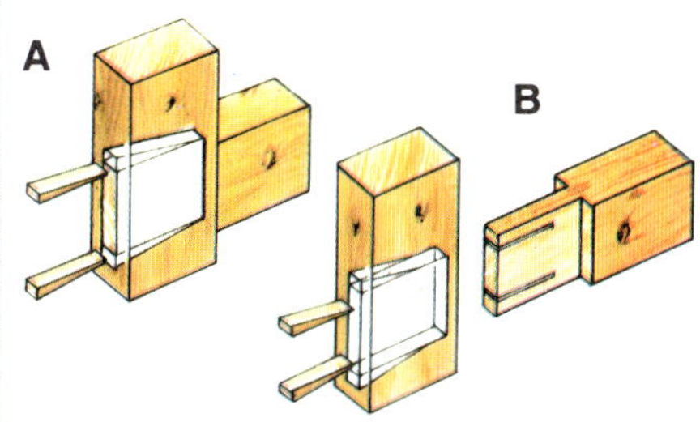

TIPS FOR BETTER JOINTS

- a through tenon should be cut too long, and made flush once the joint is assembled
- some people find it easier to start cutting the tenon while holding the piece upright, then to re-position the wood and saw at 45°, and to finish off with it upright again
- set your mortise gauge from the exact width of your mortise chisel
- if mortising near the end of your timber, leave it over-long to prevent splitting, and cut off the extra bit later
- to keep drill or chisel vertical, stand a try-square on end beside the tool as you're working

- leave it till last to pare down the mortise ends, so as not to risk bruising them while levering out the bulk of the waste
- to stop yourself drilling too deep when starting a mortise, fit a depth stop (an item you can buy) or wrap masking tape round the bit as a depth indicator.

MARKING AND DRILLING THE MORTISE

1 *If you're working near the end of the mortise piece, mark off a short length or 'horn' as waste, for removal once the joint is assembled.*

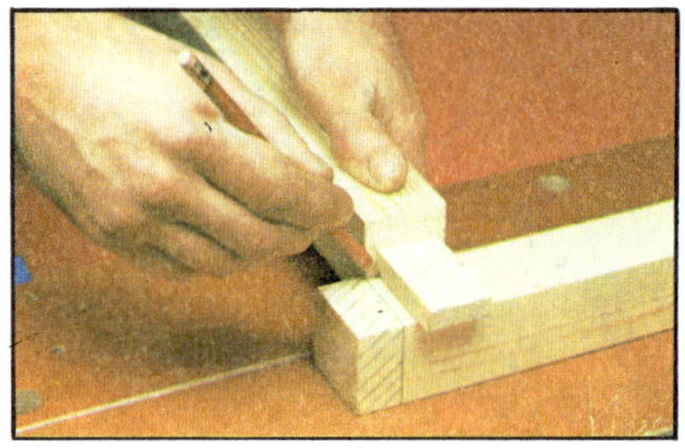

2 *Lay the tenon on the mortise piece, allowing for any horn, and mark there the tenon's width.*

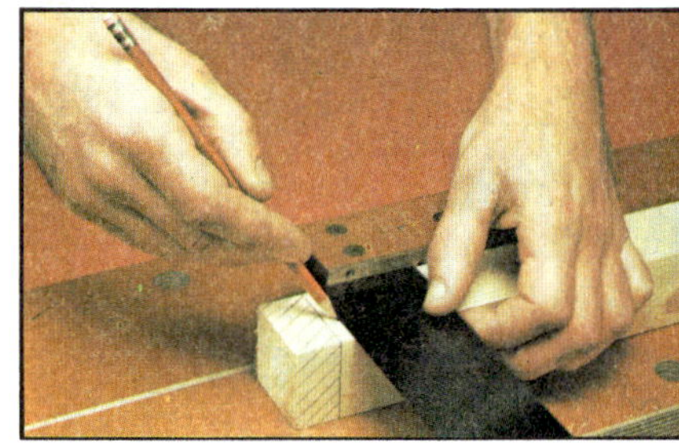

3 *Square these two length marks across the inner side of the mortise piece.*

4 *With the gauge at its existing setting, score down the mortise piece, between the last two marks, to give the mortise's width.*

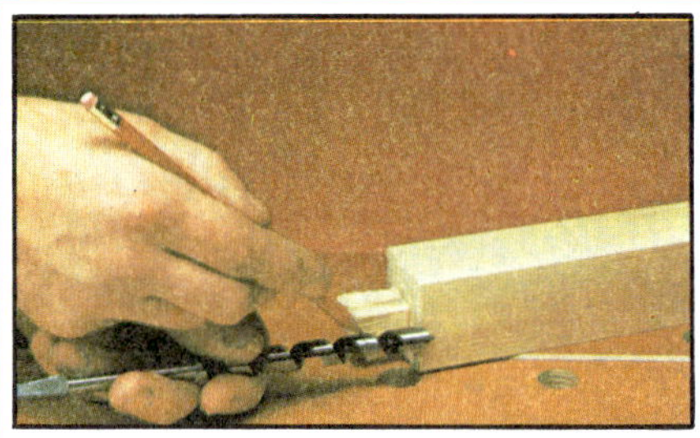

5 *For a stub mortise-and-tenon joint, mark out the tenon length on your drill bit, if you have a bit of the right diameter.*

6 *Drill holes to remove the bulk of the mortise. For a stub joint the tape at the mark on the bit warns of the depth.*

CHISELLING OUT THE MORTISE

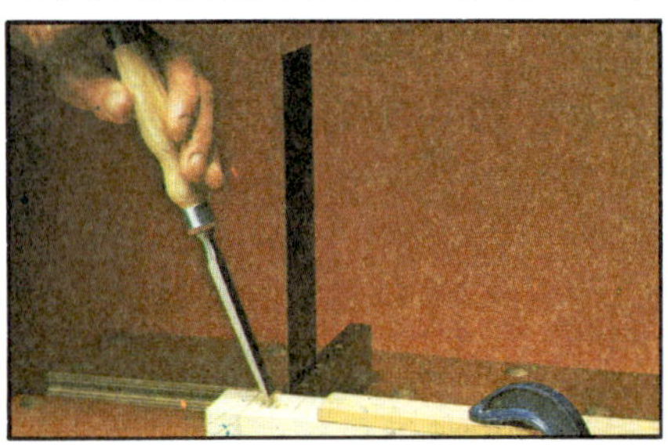

1 *Instead of drilling, you can chop and lever out the waste with a mortise chisel, starting halfway down the length of the mortise.*

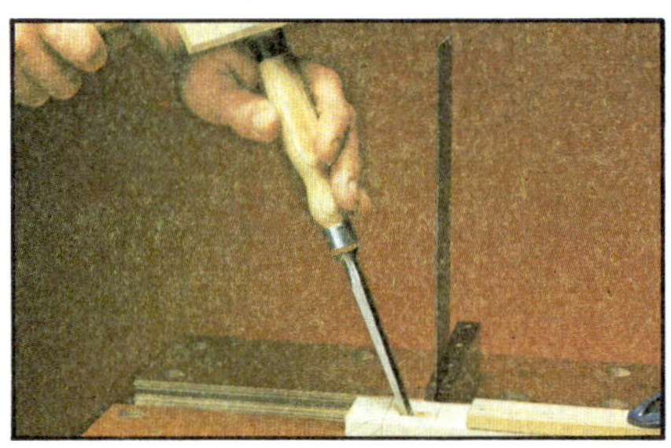

2 *Work along to its ends as you chisel deeper. For a through mortise, chop halfway through, then work from the other side of the piece.*

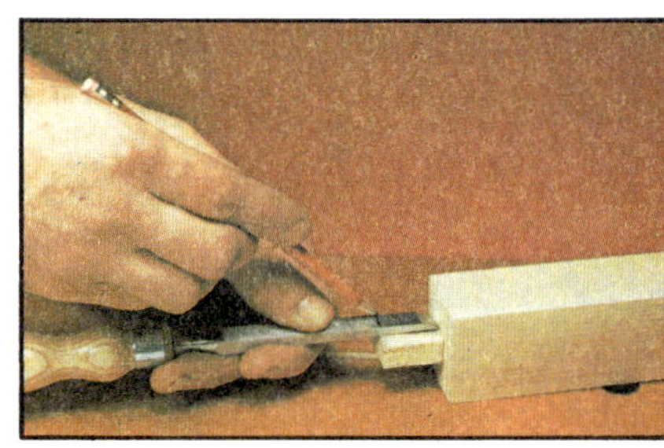

3 *For a stub mortise and tenon joint it pays to mark off the length of the tenon on the chisel as a depth guide, just as you would for a drill bit.*

4 *Then you can wind sticky tape round it next to the mark, again as a depth indicator, for use when you chisel out the bottom of the mortise.*

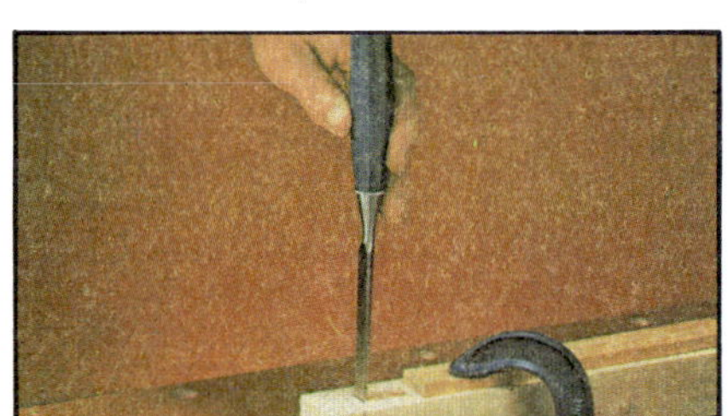

5 *After removing most of the waste, use a bevel-edged chisel to pare down each end of the mortise, shaving off any irregularities.*

6 *Work on the sides likewise. As you're cutting along the grain, you'll need greater care, to avoid splitting out more wood than you want.*

Jem Grischotti

MAKING DOVETAIL JOINTS

Dovetail joints are not only beautiful, they're very strong. Once you know the right way to cut them, it only takes practice to get a good fit every time.

Most pieces of wooden furniture are built as either frames or boxes. The mortise and tenon, as the principal framing joint, is common in chairs and tables. But in box construction the dovetail has traditionally reigned supreme.

True, modern storage furniture often uses screws, dowels, assembly fittings, and edge joints cut with power tools. But you only have to look at a set of dovetails to see that they make the perfect corner joint between flat timbers such as box sides – including the top and side panels of furniture 'carcases'.

In fact, dovetails are impossible to pull apart. That's why they're found joining drawer sides to drawer fronts and sometimes backs. Every time you open a drawer, you're trying to pull the front off – and the dovetail joint withstands this tendency as no other joint can. Note, however, that it only locks in one direction. If you use it the wrong way round where its strength matters, its unique properties are wasted.

There's one other major point to remember. Chipboard is far too weak a material in which to cut dovetails – although, at a pinch, they'll work in plywood and good-quality blockboard.

The dovetail joint is always admired and even respected. But there's really no mystery about it. While no one could pretend that well-fitting dovetails are easy for a beginner to cut, the only secret of success is practice; and you'll find things go a lot more smoothly if you stick closely to the time-tested procedure described here.

Anatomy of a dovetail joint

Dovetails themselves are fan-shaped cutouts in the end of one of the pieces being joined – fan-shaped, that is, when you look at the face of the piece.

The sides of each tail slope along the grain at an angle of between 1 in 5 (for a 'coarse' but strong joint, suitable for softwood and man-made boards) and 1 in 8 (generally considered the best-looking, and usually used with hardwoods). If you make them any coarser, they may break; any finer, and they may tend to slip out under strain.

Between the tails, when the joint is assembled, you can see the 'pins' cut in the other piece. These, of course, follow exactly the same slope or 'rake' as the tails – but across the endgrain, so you can only see their true shape when looking at them end-on. Note that there's always a pin at either end; this helps to secure both pieces against curling up.

The spacing of the tails is another factor in the joint's appearance. In general, the wider they are (and therefore the further apart the pins are) the better – but this too affects the strength if you overdo it.

Marking out the tails

The first step in making a dovetail joint is to get the ends of both pieces square (they needn't be the same thickness). Particularly if it's your first attempt, you may find it wise to leave a little extra length as well – say a millimetre or two.

After that, it's customary to start with the tail piece (which is the side, not the front, in the case of a drawer). First decide on the slope of your dovetails – say 1 in 6 – and mark it out on a scrap of wood or paper. That's just a matter of drawing two lines at right angles to each other, then making a mark six units along one, and another mark one unit up the other. Join up the marks with a diagonal, and set a sliding bevel to the same slope.

Now you need to work out where each tail should come. However, there's no need for fiddly calculations. First decide the width of

Ready Reference

WHAT IS A DOVETAIL JOINT?

A dovetail joint consists of 'tails' on one piece and 'pins' on the other. When they're fitted together, the joint is completely inseparable in one direction (shown by an arrow). It's very strong the other way too.

The contrast between endgrain and face grain (especially if the two pieces are of different woods) can also make an attractive decorative feature.

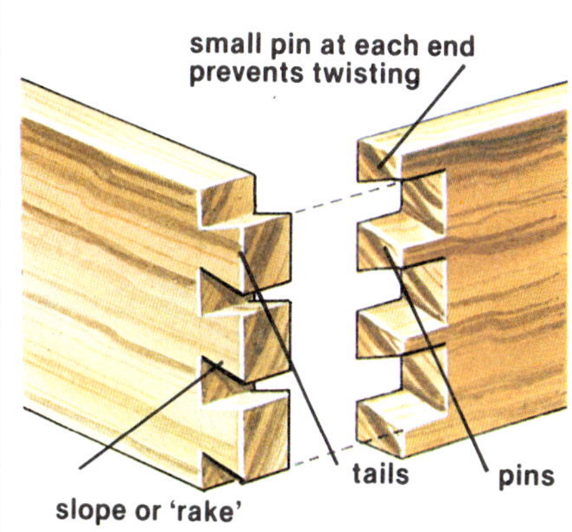

MARKING OUT THE TAILS

1 *Plane both pieces to exactly the same width, and check that the ends are dead square. Correct with a block plane if necessary.*

2 *Square the end pins' width along the tail piece, then slant a measure between the lines to give handy divisions for the pin centres.*

3 *Use a gauge to extend these centre marks from the slanting line down to the end of the piece, where the tails will be cut.*

4 *Make another mark 3mm ($^{1}/_{8}$in) either side of each centre mark. This will give you the widths of the tails at their widest.*

5 *Set a sharp marking gauge, or preferably a cutting gauge, to the exact thickness of the pin piece or a bit more – but no less.*

6 *Score a neat line all round the end of the tail piece with the gauge. It's usual to leave this visible in the finished joint.*

7 *Set a sliding bevel (or make a card template) to a slope of 1 in 6 – ie, six units in one direction and one unit in the other direction.*

8 *Use the bevel or template to mark out the slope of the tails, working inwards from the marks which denote the tail widths.*

9 *Square the width marks across the end of the piece, then mark the slope again on the far side with the bevel or template.*

TYPES OF DOVETAIL JOINT

Coarse and fine dovetails
For general work, tails and pins are equally spaced and steeply raked (below left) – unlike fine work (below right).

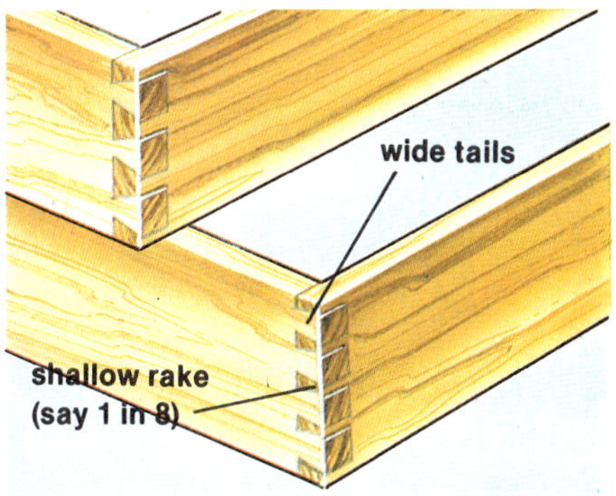

Carcase dovetails
A coarse dovetail joint traditionally joins sides to top on solid timber cabinets. An added top panel hides it.

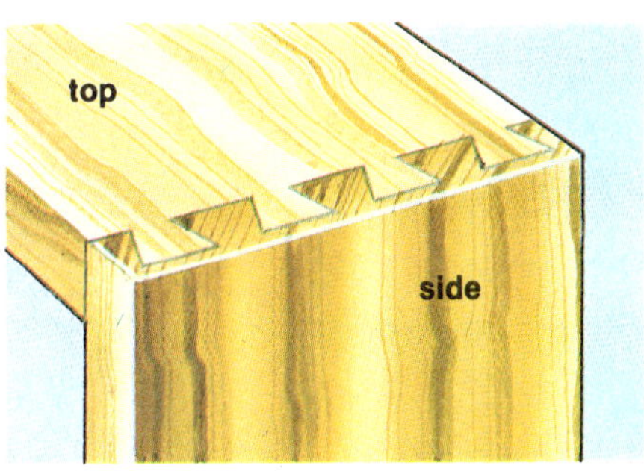

Lap dovetails
Concealed by an overlap, unlike through dovetails (shown in Ready Reference*), these are traditional in drawers.*

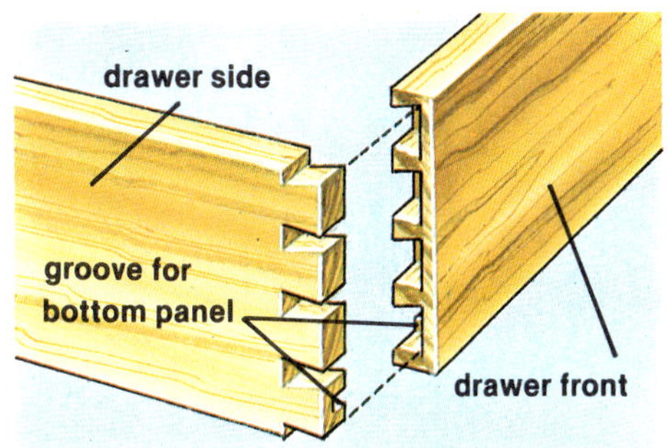

Framing dovetails
A large dovetail can provide useful strength in a frame where its locking properties are especially vital.

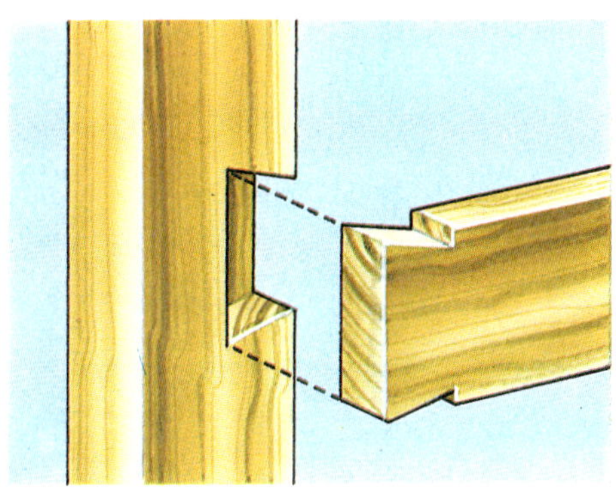

Dovetail housings
The dovetail housing is the odd man out – it's not a corner joint. The tail runs across the width.

Cut like other housing joints (see pages 40-43), it can be plain (above) or barefaced (below). The latter will usually do.

the pin at each end, and square that along the grain. Then place a tape measure diagonally between the squared lines, and swing it round to give a figure easily divisible into equal parts. Mark off these equal divisions, and square them along to the end of the piece. These are the centres of the gaps between your tails.

Then make a mark 3mm ($\frac{1}{8}$in) either side of each centre mark, and draw a line sloping inwards from it along the face – using the sliding bevel as your guide. Square these marks across the end, and then repeat them on the other face.

Lastly, set a marking or cutting gauge to the exact thickness of the pin piece, and scribe a line all round the end of the tail piece. If you've been allowing for extra length, add that to the scribed thickness. This will make the tails slightly too long; when the joint is complete, trim them flush with a block plane.

At this stage, a very wise precaution is to hatch in – or mark with an X – all the bits you're going to cut out.

Cutting the tails and pins

The next essential is to have the right saw. An ordinary tenon saw is too heavy; you need the lighter version actually known as a dovetail saw, or the still finer gent's saw. But even one of these, especially if new, will have too much 'set' – the teeth will project too far sideways, giving too wide and inaccurate a cut. You can remedy this by placing the blade on an oilstone, flat on its side, and very lightly rubbing it along. Do this once or twice for each side.

To make your cuts, cramp the tail piece in a vice. (If making, say, two identical sides for a box, you can cut more than one piece at the same time.) Align the timber so that one set of sloping marked lines is vertical. Cut along all these, one after the other, before tilting the piece the other way and cutting those on the opposite slope.

Saw immediately on the outside of each marked line, and begin each cut with the saw angled backwards, steadying its blade with your thumbnail. Once you've got the cut established, tilt the saw forwards to make sure you're keeping to the line on the other side. Lastly, level the saw up as you finish the cut. Whatever you do, don't cut down past the gauged line!

The next step is to use your gauge to mark the thickness of the tail piece in turn on the pin piece.

A neat trick follows. Hold the pin piece in a vice, and cramp the tail piece over its end in exactly the intended position. Then, inserting the saw in the cuts you've just made, use it to score corresponding marks on the endgrain of the pin piece. Square these across its faces.

At this point you can remove the waste from between the tails. Begin by sawing out the little piece next to each of the two outer tails; then use a chisel. (Some people like to get the bulk of the waste out with a coping saw first.) Drive the chisel down into the face each time, keeping well in front of the gauge line, then tap the blade into the endgrain to get the chips up and out. Turn the piece over and do the same on the other side.

COMPLETING THE JOINT

1 *With your gauge at the exact thickness of the tail piece or a little more, scribe a line all round the end of the pin piece.*

2 *Square along from this gauged line, on each side, to the ends of the slanting lines you've scored across the endgrain with the saw.*

3 *Make all the saw cuts at one angle first, then those at the other – their edges exactly on the outsides of the lines, as before.*

TIP

4 *After chiselling out the waste between the pins as for the tails, pare down the inside edge of each tail a little, for a smooth fit.*

5 *Fit the joint together halfway (but no further), keeping the pieces square to each other. Note any places where it sticks.*

6 *Holding the chisel blade, carefully shave where needed. Glue and cramp the joint, and plane the endgrain flush if necessary.*

Lastly, place the chisel against (not over) the gauge line and pare away the rest. It's sensible to angle the tool inwards from each side, so that you actually 'undercut' – ie, cut beyond the line, but only inside the timber where it won't be seen. This helps to ensure the joint goes all the way home.

Saw out the pins as you did the tails. Again, the crucial thing is to cut immediately on the waste side – so that the outer edge of the saw teeth touches the line. If anything this is even more important now, at the pin stage, because you won't be able to make any further adjustments if the pins are loose between the tails.

Lastly, chisel out the gaps between the pins. Here too the procedure is similar to that for the tails.

Putting it together

Before you try assembling the joint, pare away any remaining unevenness which might make things difficult – being quite sure not to overdo it. You can even carefully shave the inside edge off both sides of each tail (especially the outer ones). This will be hidden after assembly.

Now comes the nerve-racking part: fitting the pieces together. At first, don't attempt to force them more than halfway, because dovetails fitted more than once become slack. See how well they go home, separate them, and make further adjustments with a chisel.

Then put some adhesive between the pins, and tap the tails right in. That's it. If it's a good joint, congratulations. If not, your next will be better, and the one after that better still – as long as you rely on sharp tools and gentle, accurate cutting. Hurry and force will only cause imprecision and heartbreak.

Lap dovetails

'Through dovetails', described above, can be seen from both sides. They look fine in most circumstances – especially since the modern tendency is to make a feature of them, using them in preference to hidden versions.

However, there is one variant worth knowing. In 'lap dovetails', only part of the endgrain on the pin piece is cut away to form pins; the rest (say one-third of the thickness) is left to overlap and thus hide the endgrain of the tails. For this reason, lap dovetails are traditional in fitting drawer-fronts.

When marking them out, you have to remember not to score a gauge line round the outside of the pin piece, and to allow for the lap thickness when gauging for the tails and pins. Cutting the pins is likewise a bit more difficult. However, mastery of through dovetails will give you the confidence to tackle lap dovetails, and thus expand your range of techniques still further.

ADVANCED PROJECTS

For the really skilled woodworker, complicated framing-up jobs and even structural work such as fitting a complete new door and door frame or laying a new timber floor hold no terrors.

BUILDING BEDS: the basics

Building your own bed – single or double – isn't difficult. You'll save a lot of money and get something which is not only attractive but custom-built to suit your needs exactly.

Constructing a bed may sound a big task, but there are occasions when it can definitely be worth tackling yourself.

Your home-made bed may not be as luxuriously comfortable, or give you quite so many years of service as the ones you buy in the shops (remember that a bed is usually occupied for at least eight hours a day – much longer than any other piece of furniture). But it will be a lot less expensive; and often this consideration can be of prime importance.

For example a home-made bed might be the ideal solution for a young couple setting up their first home on a tight budget, or for a guest room that's not often used. Likewise, when a child grows out of sleeping in a cot, its first bed could easily be one you make yourself. Children don't demand the same standards of comfort as adults and, since they weigh much less, they impose less strain on a bed.

The basic box

There's more than one way of building a bed, but this one is straightforward and economical.

Although you can do the initial carpentry anywhere that's convenient, the final assembly should be carried out in the room the bed will occupy. Hauling it up or downstairs and through doorways is no joke.

But your first job is to buy the mattress, so you can be sure it will fit on the bed. Even if you're making your own mattress by buying foam and covering it, you should still do that first. When completed, the bed should be slightly wider and longer than the mattress, so that there's enough room to tuck the bedclothes in properly. An extra 25mm (1in) all round should be ample.

The basic principle is to take four lengths of wood or man-made board and make up a big, shallow, rectangular box without a bottom. Veneered or plastic-faced chipboard is a good material, combining cheapness with an attractive range of finishes. It comes in standard lengths of 2440mm (8ft) and 1830mm (6ft). You could make a single bed from three pieces of 2440mm (8ft) – cutting one in half to form the head and foot – and a double bed from two pieces of 2440mm (8ft) and two of 1830mm (6ft). There's a good range of widths, so you'd be able to make the box any depth you wanted.

Chipboard of this kind is veneered or plastic-faced on both sides and on the two long edges. The raw ends and other cut edges can be disguised with iron-on edging strip or timber lipping (see pages 338–340).

Just as convenient to use, yet even stronger, is 25mm (1in) thick natural timber. And of course you don't have to hide its edges. However, it's difficult to obtain in widths over 225mm (9in), which somewhat restricts your design possibilities.

You could also use 12mm (½in) thick plywood – with or without a decorative wood veneer or plastic facing. This will involve you in extra work if you have to cut the pieces to size (it doesn't usually come in sheets less than 1220mm/4ft wide), but it gives a strong, attractive result, without any restriction on width. Many people find bare plywood edges quite acceptable. If you have a circular saw, it might be economical to buy a standard 2440x1220mm (8x4ft) sheet, and cut it into four pieces yourself

Putting it together

When joining the corners of the box, you must carefully consider whether you are going to have legs on the bed.

You can, of course, do without them, and simply put your basic box directly onto the floor. But most people prefer to fit beds with legs as it looks better, and gives a more convenient height for bedmaking. A good overall height from the floor to the top of the box is 450mm (18in). For a single bed, two legs on each side is enough, but three is safer on a double.

A good method of adding legs is to cut four pieces of 50mm (2in) square planed timber, and fix them to the inside of the box so that they project below it. In this way you can also form corner joints for the box – tackling both details in one go. If you use screws, they should enter from the outside, for a secure hold. Brass screws in brass cups will turn this into a decorative feature.

Adding glue on only one side of each leg (while screwing into two sides) ensures that all the joints can be dismantled at least once by simply removing the screws through the unglued parts. Bolts here will make an even stronger fixing, and enable you to take the bed apart any number of times without loss of strength.

Other options are dowels, with or without the ends on view from the outside, and nails. These, of course, can't be removed; but you could use nails or dowels through one piece, and screws or bolts through the other.

Another idea is to make up legs which are L-shaped in section. (These cannot of course number more than four). Each one consists of two lengths of planed softwood 38mm (1½in) thick, fixed to the outside of the box at each corner – one to the side, the

PUTTING THE BED TOGETHER

These details show all the parts of the bed, including the joints you'll need to cut in the bearers – plus two other ways of making legs: one L-shaped and one notched.

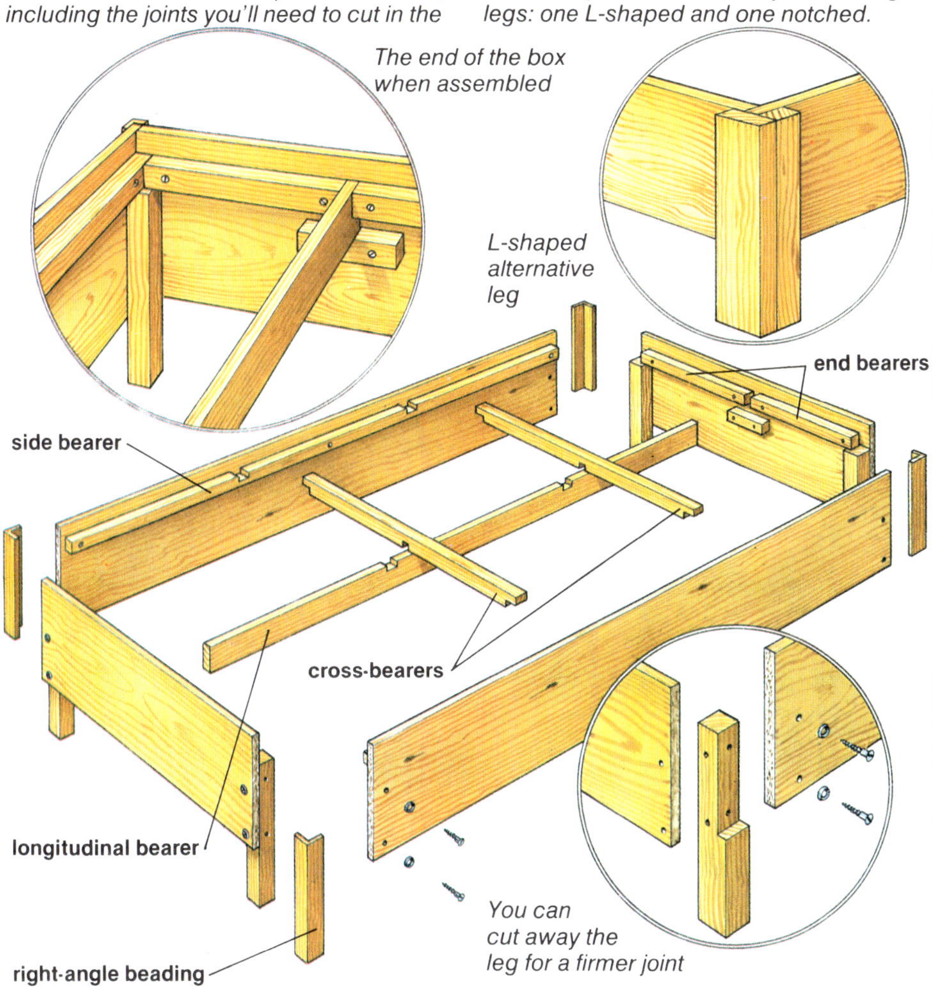

other to the foot or head – so that they overlap. To get both sides of the L of equal width, you'll need to buy one piece 75mm (3in) wide and one 100mm (4in) wide, and plane down the narrower one.

The two pieces can then be glued, and screwed or nailed in place, while the corner joint itself is made with a reinforced butt joint. If a screwed-on reinforcement is used, the whole thing can still be taken apart, that is provided you haven't glued the halves of the L where they overlap.

It's a good idea to fit castors to the legs, so you can move the bed around easily. But this is difficult with L-shaped legs, which may make you decide on plain ones. Use a socket-fixing type castor – for which you bore a hole in the legs, then insert a metal or plastic sleeve before pushing home the spindle of the castor. The other kind, mounted on a plate, isn't suitable for legs, because to fix it you'd need to drive screws into end grain – something to avoid wherever possible. However, it is the one to use if you're omitting legs; just mount it on a triangular block screwed inside each corner of the box.

Supporting the mattress

The next consideration is how to support the mattress. Any mattress, but especially a foam one, must be able to 'breathe'. So a good material is perforated hardboard, or pegboard, as it's more commonly called. This is strong enough, provided that it's well supported in its turn.

The pegboard rests on pieces of 38mm (1½in) square planed softwood, screwed horizontally inside the head, foot and sides of the box. Position them with their upper faces 38 to 50mm (1½ to 2in) below the top of the box. This will ensure not only that the top of the mattress stands well clear of the

Ready Reference

BED DIMENSIONS

Height: it's best to choose a height at which you can sit down comfortably – that is, unless you prefer an 'on-the-floor' bed. Usual heights are

- 100-300mm (4-12in) without legs
- 300-450mm (12-18in) including legs.

Width: standard widths are

- narrow single bed 750mm (2ft 6in)
- standard single 900mm (3ft)
- twin 975mm (3ft 3in)
- double 1350mm (4ft 6in)
- large double 1500mm (5ft)
- extra large double 1900mm (6ft 4in).

Length: ideally a bed should be 75mm (3in) longer than its occupant's standing height. The common lengths are:

- standard 1875mm (6ft 3in)
- large 2100mm (7ft).

FITTING CASTORS

The socket-fixing castor has a spindle which fits into a metal or plastic sleeve. You drill a hole in the timber, insert the sleeve and then push in the spindle. Provided you drill the hole accurately, this makes a secure mounting even in end grain, eg on the bottom of a leg.

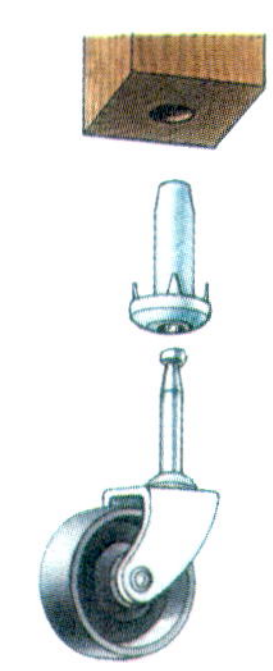

The plate castor is screwed directly onto the timber. Often a special block will be needed to mount it. For a box-type bed, your best plan is to cut out a triangular block from timber which is at least 25mm (1in) thick, and screw it inside the corner of the box at the appropriate height. Then just screw the plate to that. You cannot do this, however, if your bed has legs.

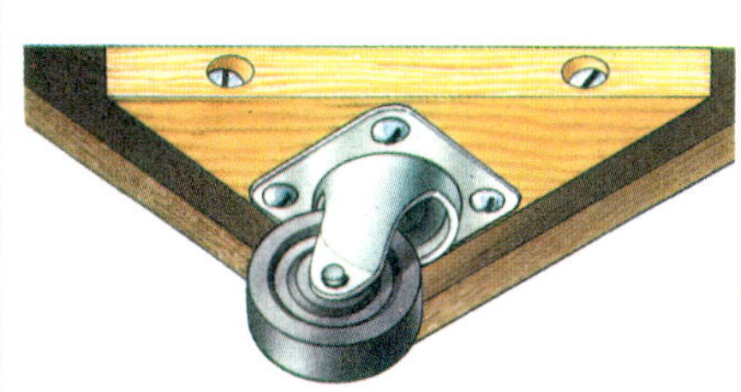

THE BASIC BOX

1 *Square a mark across the legs to indicate how much will protrude below the main box. For speed and accuracy, mark them all out at once.*

2 *Align the mark on each leg carefully with the lower edge of the box head or foot, cramp both pieces together and drill them.*

3 *Spread PVA glue on one piece, then fix the joint with 50mm (2in) No 10 screws. Keep a wet rag handy to wipe off excess adhesive.*

4 *Cramp the box side over the joint, drill it and screw it to the leg. Then repeat the same procedure for the other three corners of the box.*

bed – so you don't bang yourself on the sides when you sit down on the bed or get in and out of it – but also that you can tuck the bedclothes in without bruising your knuckles on the box. These bearers, as they are called, can fit at each end on top of the legs.

You'll also need two cross-bearers, which should be fitted over the side bearers with some halving joints, plus a longitudinal bearer (two or three on a double bed). The latter should be made of 75x25mm (3x1in) planed timber, used on edge; it can be slotted into gaps between the pairs of bearers screwed to head and foot, and rest on another short piece of 38mm (1½in) square timber also screwed in place. None of these pieces needs to be glued, or even screwed or nailed. This too makes for easy dismantling if you ever want to move the bed.

An alternative to pegboard is a series of slats running across the width. They should be of 50x25mm (2x1in) or 75x19mm (3x¾in) planed timber, spaced at most 75mm (3in) apart, and screwed on top of the bearers at either side. To protect the bedclothes, countersink the screw heads. In this instance, there's no need for cross-bearers, and the longitudinal bearer can fit at each end between three short pieces of 38mm (1½in) square timber which are screwed vertically to the head and foot, forming a U-shaped bracket.

Finishing the bed

For a smooth finish on veneer or solid timber, your first step is to sand it down with a fine-grade glass- or garnet-paper. Then you can stain it to a different colour and apply varnish or wax finish. Alternatively paint it.

1 *Mark out and cut two halvings in each of the bearers which will be screwed to the sides of the box. Work on both pieces at once.*

5 *Cut two pieces from each end bearer, cramp them against this pencil line and screw them on, leaving a gap for the longitudinal bearer.*

9 *Position the longitudinal bearer, re-position each cross-bearer over it, and mark out on both pieces the halving joint where they overlap.*

SUPPORTING THE MATTRESS

2 *Screw a bearer to each side with 50mm (2in) No 8 chipboard screws, making sure it's quite straight and doesn't rise or dip along its length.*

3 *Mark and cut all the other bearers to length. Position one at each end. Halfway along mark the thickness of the longitudinal bearer.*

4 *Still resting the end bearer in position, use it as a straight edge to mark where its upper edge comes on the inside face of the box.*

6 *With the box on its side, position the longitudinal bearer (its top edge flush with the side bearers) and mark its bottom edge.*

7 *Screw a short length of wood, the same size as the bearers, centrally to each end of the box, with its upper face against the mark you've made.*

8 *Position each cross-bearer in the halvings you've cut in the side bearers, and mark out on it the other half of the joint.*

10 *Once all the halvings are cut, you can fit the longitudinal and cross-bearers into place without glue or any other fixing.*

11 *If the box sides are made of chipboard or blockboard, hide their cut ends with right-angle beading, glued and fixed with moulding pins.*

12 *Lastly, cut the pegboard to size and simply lay it on top of the bearers. The bed is now ready for finishing, and to receive its mattress.*

REPAIRING HANDRAILS & BALUSTERS

Replacing old spindles, or even installing a completely new balustrade, requires great care and attention, but it can add a really impressive feature to your home.

The staircase is probably the most complicated piece of joinery in the average home, so don't tamper with it unnecessarily.

However, maintenance work is sometimes essential for safety. This could involve simple jobs such as securing and repairing the 'guts' of the staircase: the treads you walk on, the risers (if any) between them, and the strings which support them.

But that's only half the story. The balustrade which stops you falling off the side is equally important. If broken or shaky, it should be attended to quickly. What's more, renovating it can make a big difference in terms of looks as well. Ranges of attractive components for it are available in both softwood and hardwood from many suppliers.

Newels and handrails

The basic items are the newel posts. These are fixed very firmly to the joists, often with coach screws or bolts. Any new fixings should be to the same standard: rock-solid.

You can't be too thorough here, because the newels not only carry the handrail between them – and thus the balustrade as a whole, which comes under great stress – but also at least partly support the outer string. This is usually either housed into them, or fitted via a large double haunched tenon, pegged with dowels which run through it sideways.

In addition, at least one tread and riser are usually housed into the newel where it meets the ends of the steps. You'll need to re-cut these grooves in any new post.

A newel post is either a single piece, or made up in sections – a square base, plus a more ornamental upper part which has a projecting peg to fit a hole in the base.

Even before fixing a newel, you must get all your measurements sorted out. Regulations dictate the heights of handrails – see *Ready Reference*. A rail must also be at exactly the same slope as the stairs: on a closed-string staircase, that means parallel to the string. Ouite apart from considerations of safety and looks, a handrail that's out of true will give you problems when you come to fit the balusters.

So your first job is to cut the newel post, or its base, to exactly the right height for the handrail or rails which meet it. This measurement is especially important with a turned (partly cylindrical) newel whose top end has only a short length of square section with suitable flat surfaces; and the situation is further complicated where more than one handrail meets the same newel. Other newels must be in line with each other, too.

Traditionally, the handrail is mortised into the newel – either bodily, or via a tenon pegged with a dowel. Dowels on their own form a strong enough alternative. Nailing is another possibility: crude, but often adequate, provided you punch the heads and fill the resulting holes.

Lastly, you can screw through the rail at an angle. At the lower end, screw from underneath. If using screws at the upper end, you'll need to counterbore them and plug the holes with wooden pellets, finished flush.

At the bottom of a staircase, the handrail may start with an 'opening rise' instead. This is a graceful curve, made up separately, which terminates in a 'newel cap' fitting over a peg in the top of the newel post. It requires extra length in the newel – another thing to allow for when cutting.

An opening rise is joined to the main handrail with a 'handrail screw'. This is easy to fit (see illustrations) as long as you work carefully and use the right spanners and drill bits. It makes a secure joint between any two lengths of handrail; dowels are the only effective alternative.

Where a handrail meets a landing wall, it may be mortared into the brickwork, or sometimes fixed to a 'half newel' – like a newel cut in half lengthwise – lying flat against the wall.

Fitting balusters

In theory, fitting the balusters (or spindles, as the turned variety are called) should be a simple, repetitive job. But you must still work carefully if they're all to be tight and vertical.

First of all, check that the handrail doesn't sag in the middle. If it does, it will throw your measurements out, so fit a temporary support. Then, as you cut the balusters, measure for each one individually, in case there are variations. Position a sliding bevel in the angle between the newel and the handrail or string capping (see below) to gauge the exact slope for angled cuts.

When marking the balusters, double-check that angled cuts at both ends slope the same way. And, unless the balusters are absolutely plain, make sure you leave the same amount of the plain section at the bottom of every baluster which is cut to the same length; likewise at the top. If you're using an opening rise,

PREPARING THE NEWELS AND STRING

1 *Each newel post must be the right height for the handrail, and securely fixed to a joist. Here the upper newel base has been cut away for a snug fit.*

2 *Position the newel base accurately, checking it for plumb in both directions, and carefully mark on it the housing or mortise for each string.*

3 *Cut out the stopped housing as precisely as you can. First work along the sides of the groove with a tenon saw or broad-bladed chisel.*

4 *Then work along the housing, if possible with a chisel the same width as the groove. Use it with the bevel downwards if necessary.*

5 *Lastly, make a cut that slopes inwards at the end to house the projecting end of the string, if any. This adds some extra strength.*

6 *Fit the housing over the string, and screw or bolt the newel base very firmly to the nearest joist or joists. Pack it out if necessary.*

7 *House the lower newel over the string and secure it to a floor joist like the upper one. Make sure the posts are exactly in line with each other.*

8 *With a two-part newel, you simply tap the upper part into the lower – being very careful that you don't force it and thus split the timber.*

9 *Before fixing a new capping to take the balusters, you may have to pack out the string with planed timber of a suitable thickness.*

FITTING A HANDRAIL SCREW

1 *This is the usual way of joining lengths of handrail. Drill an access hole in one piece, and mark the endgrain centre with a template.*

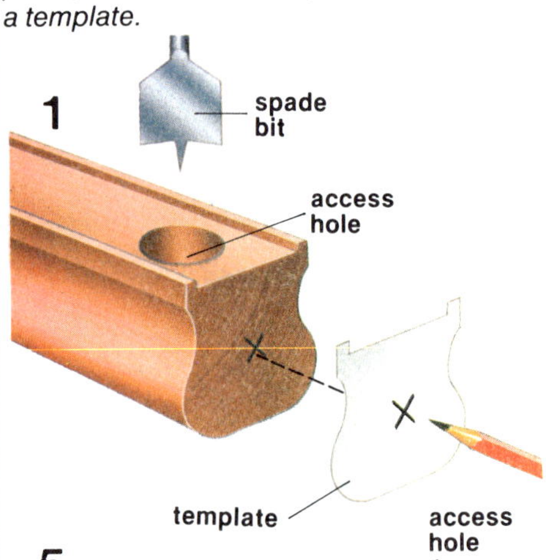

2 *At your marked centre, drill a clearance hole for the bolt-threaded end of the fitting, through to the access hole. Make sure it's perpendicular to the wood.*

3 *Using a slightly smaller bit, drill a pilot hole in the other piece for the screw-threaded end of the fitting. Make it the same length as the screw.*

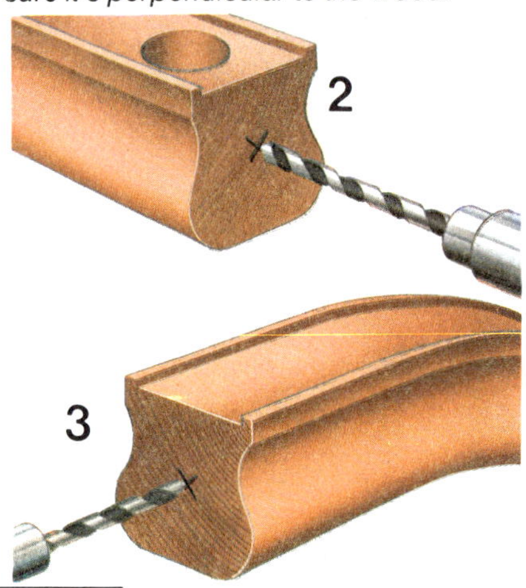

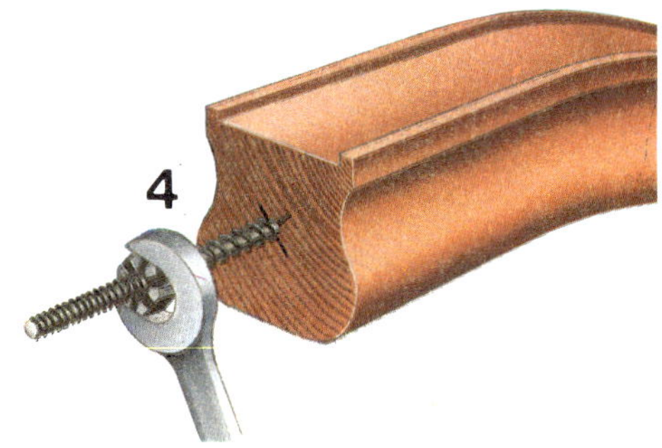

4 *Thread the special nut temporarily onto the bolt end so that you can use a spanner to drive the screw firmly into the second piece of wood.*

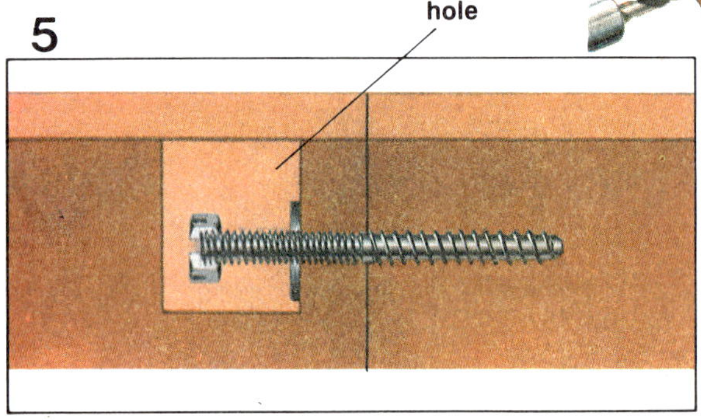

5 *Remove the nut and push the bolt end through the clearance hole. Use the access hole to fit the washer and replace the nut.*

6 *Tighten the nut with a ring spanner, ensuring the pieces are aligned.*

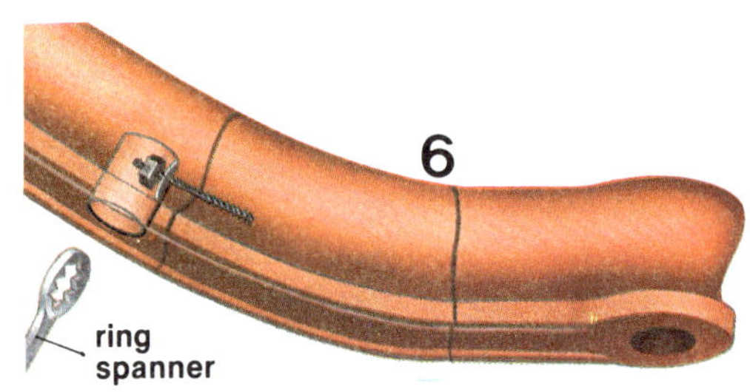

don't forget that any balusters below it must be longer than the rest.

There's also a rule that the spacing of balusters must be close enough to prevent a sphere 100mm (4in) in diameter from passing between them. Before you buy a set of new balusters, you'll have to measure the total distance between newels and divide it by that spacing (minus the baluster thickness) to find how many balusters you need. On a closed-string staircase, mark all their positions before fitting them.

There are several different ways of fixing balusters – see *Ready Reference*.

A common arrangement nowadays, and a very neat one, uses a factory-cut channel in the underside of the handrail. A corresponding 'capping', channelled in its upper surface, fits on top of the string – which may need to be packed out in thickness to receive it. The square or rectangular ends of the balusters fit into these channels, and are held in place by nailed 'spacer fillets' – cut off at an angle from timber supplied with the capping and rail, and ready-planed to fit the channels.

Cut strings present a different picture. The baluster at the front of each tread is a different length from the one at the back (though you'll still want to leave the same length of plain section at the top all the way up the stairs). The balusters fit into notches, sometimes dovetail-shaped, in the end of each tread, and are held there by lengths of pinned moulding.

Staircase shapes

There are quite a few variations in the way staircases rise from one level to the next.

The simplest shape is the straight flight. However, stairs can also turn a corner – and very often they double back on themselves completely, making either a 'dog-leg' or an 'open-well' staircase.

In a dog-leg staircase, the newel post at the turn supports both the upper and the lower flights, because it's mortised to receive the outer strings of both. The handrail and balusters of the lower flight terminate against the underside of the upper string.

In an open well (or 'open-newel') staircase, the flights are separate. There's a gap between them, and each one has its own newel at the level where the stairs turn. A short length of balustrade joins these two posts.

The turns in the steps may take the form of a half-landing – in effect, a platform made of joists (supported against the walls) covered with floorboards. The joist called the 'trimmer' along the edge of the landing has the newel or newels fixed to and often notched over it. The floorboard immediately on top of it has a rounded edge so it can act as the uppermost tread of the lower flight.

Instead of pausing at a half-landing, the stairs may continue to rise round the turn. On a dog-leg staircase, that means a half-turn of 'winders' – tapered steps. An open-newel staircase may have two quarter-turns of winders, one in each corner, separated by either a small landing or another short flight.

The balustrade in an open-well staircase may not always run between newels as described. The handrail may curl right round, with a continuous row of balusters beneath.

Apart from the opening rise, other handrail components are available for special situations. These include horizontal turns on landings, and places where the handrail has to change levels. In the latter case, a 'goose neck' made with a 'vertical turn' will meet the discrepancy.

BALUSTRADE FIXINGS

*All sorts of details make up a balustrade. They vary a lot, but it's worth knowing the probabilities if you're considering renovation. The main drawing shows an **open-well** or open-newel staircase – so called because of the gap between flights.*

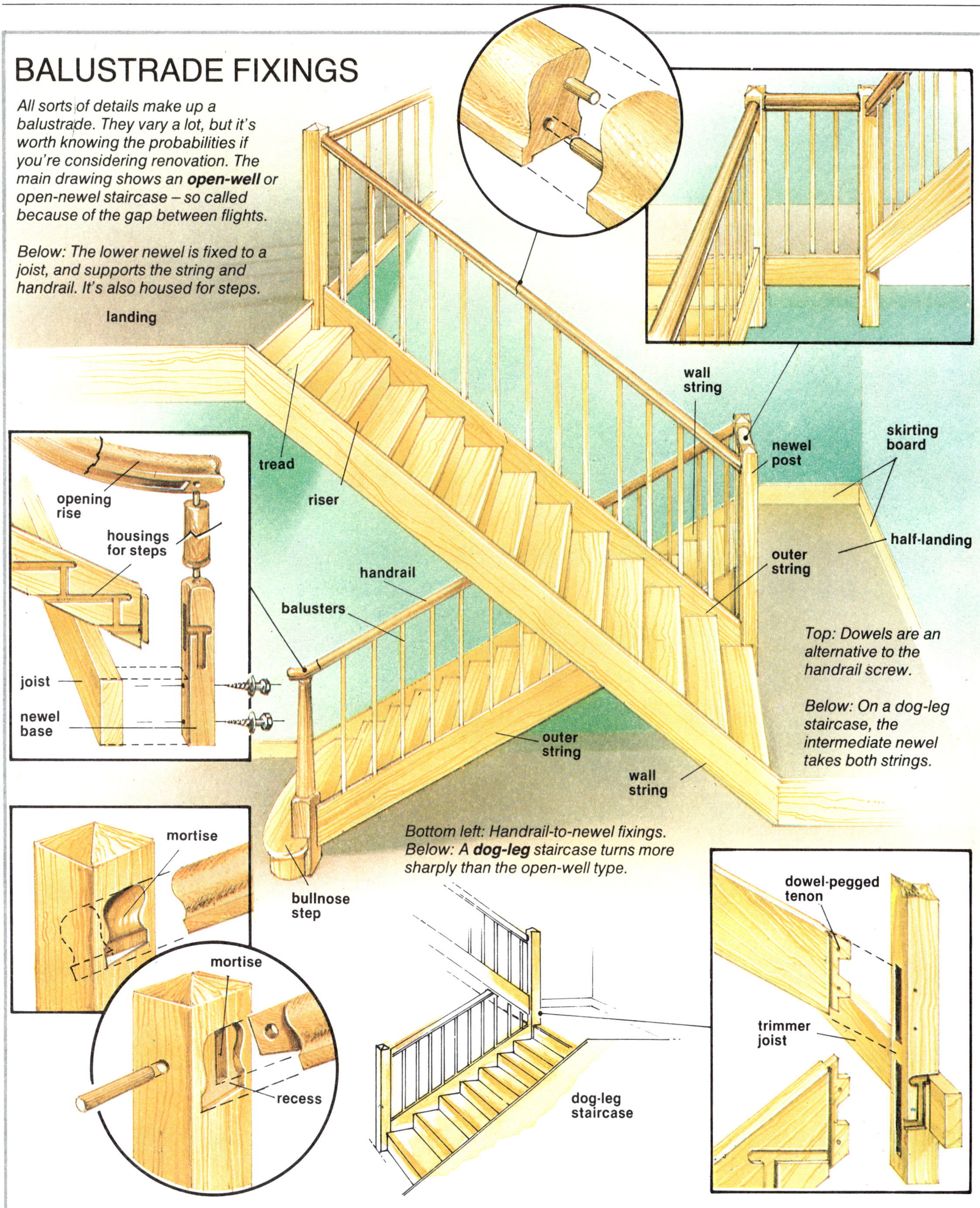

Below: The lower newel is fixed to a joist, and supports the string and handrail. It's also housed for steps.

Top: Dowels are an alternative to the handrail screw.

Below: On a dog-leg staircase, the intermediate newel takes both strings.

Bottom left: Handrail-to-newel fixings.
*Below: A **dog-leg** staircase turns more sharply than the open-well type.*

FITTING THE HANDRAIL AND SPINDLES

1 *If you're using an opening rise, fit it to the rail with a handrail screw (see illustrations) and then to the newel post as shown here.*

2 *Nails form the easiest handrail fixing. Punch them in and fill the holes with wood stopping. Alternatively, use tenons or dowels or both.*

3 *Cut the capping and nail it to the string. It's vital that this should be exactly parallel to the handrail, so the spindles will all be the same length.*

4 *Provided the newel is plumb, a sliding bevel will give the exact slope of the handrail and string. Use it to mark the cuts on the spindles.*

5 *Cut the spindles at your marked angles. In theory they should all be the same length when vertical – but check before cutting each one.*

6 *Fit each spindle against the handrail and capping. If you're using spacer fillets, cut them to length at an angle and nail them in place.*

Ready Reference

SAFETY RULES

A run of stairs more than 600mm (2ft) long must have a handrail on at least one side (though not necessarily beside the bottom two steps). This rail must normally be no

On a landing, the minimum height is 900mm (35in). The space between the balusters should be less than 100mm (4in).

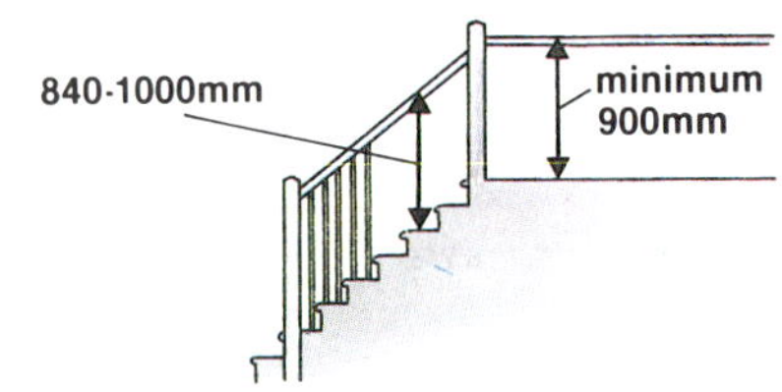

FIXING BALUSTERS

There are several ways of fixing balusters in place – although, if you're only replacing old ones, you'll probably want to keep the existing arrangements.

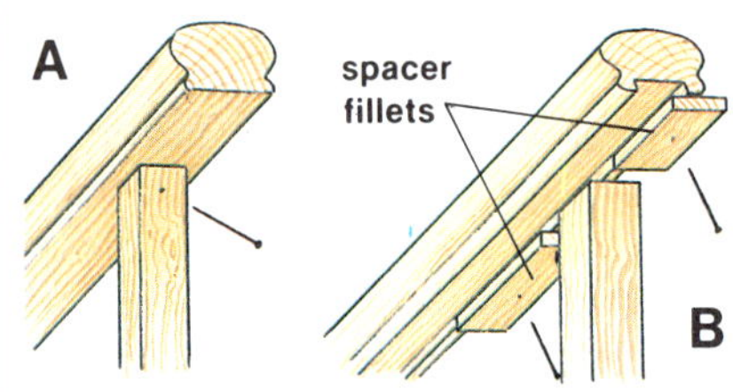

Balusters may be just nailed to the handrail (A), or held by spacers (B).

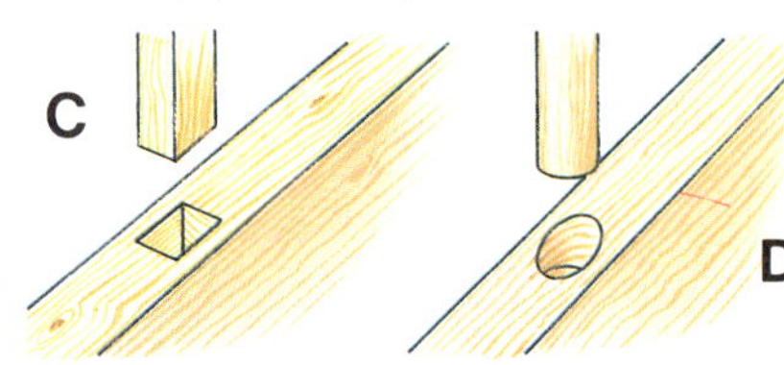

Fixing to a closed string may be via nails, mortises (C), or bored holes (D).

Spacer fillets are also used in a capping (E), fitted over the string. This may or may not have a channel cut in its underside.

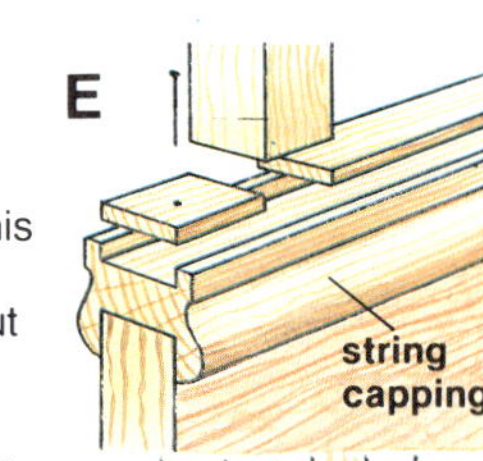

With a cut string (F), each tread will have its own notches for the balusters. Lengths of moulding hold them in position.

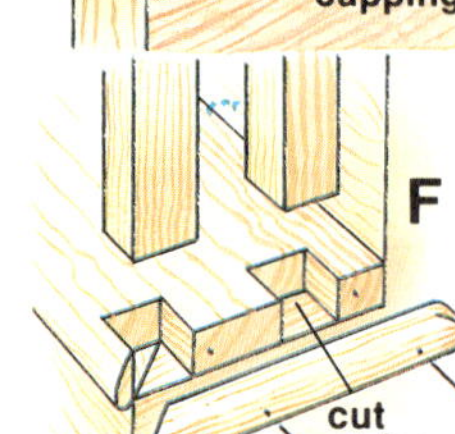

LAYING A NEW TIMBER FLOOR

Suspended timber floors, consisting of floorboards nailed to joists, can last for years without giving trouble. But there may eventually come a time when they need replacing.

Timber floors are durable and long-suffering. But eventually they can become loose, worn, damaged by woodworm and sometimes cracked. This means annoying creaks, an uneven surface (which in turn causes worn patches on your floor-coverings) and, in extreme cases, actual hazards. All these are signs that it's time to think about laying a new floor.

Even the joists on which the floorboards rest can become distorted, and may sag towards the middle of the room. A bonus of laying new floorboards is that you can compensate for this sagging into the bargain, so that you end up with a floor that's newly flat and level as well as sound.

Timber or chipboard

Before detailing how to use floorboards, it's worth pointing out that there is an alternative to them, namely chipboard. This will be dealt with more fully in another section. Special flooring grade chipboard is usually 18mm (3⁄4in) thick, although it's also available in greater thicknesses for added rigidity where the joists are spaced more widely than usual. It can even be bought with tongued-and-grooved edges.

Chipboard is a fair bit cheaper than solid timber floorboards, and it doesn't shrink. Moreover, because it comes in bigger pieces you have to hammer in fewer nails when you're fixing it. But by the same token it takes more work to fit, because you may have to cut out large sections to accommodate chimney breasts and similar obstacles; and removing it, if that should ever become necessary, is harder, especially if you're trying to keep the pieces intact. Lastly, it should never be used where it's likely to get in the least bit wet – in bathrooms, for example – because if moisture penetrates the edges they'll soon swell and break up.

Buying floorboards

Floorboards are made of planed softwood, and come in two varieties: square-edged, and tongued-and-grooved (T & G). In the latter type each board has a tongue down one edge and a matching groove down the other. T & G boards take a little more effort to lay (the tongues fit the grooves very tightly), but they repay that in being draughtproof, and in their greater strength: once laid, they form what is in effect a solid sheet.

The tongues and grooves aren't centred in their respective edges. Boards should be laid with the tongues towards the bottom, not the top; this allows more wear before the tongues become exposed. Standard widths for floorboards (ie, across the face, excluding the width of the tongue) are 100mm (4in) and 150mm (6in), though these vary slightly with the supplier. The standard nominal thickness is 25mm (1in), planed down from sawn timber to 20mm (3⁄4in) or so.

Boards planed down from 32mm (1 1⁄4in) to a finished thickness of about 25mm (1in) are also available, and they make a fine substantial floor; but they cost more. Remember, too, that if they're thicker than the old boards they probably won't fit under the existing skirting. You'll either have to butt them up against it (which may create problems when it comes to supporting their ends, since the last joist may be flush with the wall surface) or replace the skirting too.

Floorboards must, of course, be laid across the joists, not parallel to them. To work out how much timber you'll need, make careful calculations, dividing the length of the room by the width of board to find how many lengths to buy. A good tip is to visit your timber merchant even before this, to find out the exact width of the boards he stocks.

If possible, buy boards which will just span the width of the room with a little to spare. In any case, make sure you get enough to cover the total length you need (found by multiplying the number of board widths by the width of the room).

Buy the boards a week or two before doing the job, and stack them flat inside the house. This will give them time to dry out and therefore shrink a bit before you lay them. The precaution is important because, if they shrink appreciably afterwards, you'll be left with unsightly gaps, no matter how tightly you fit them during the job.

HOW THE JOISTS RUN

Right: The way the joists run in your house will depend on a number of structural factors. Where the joists meet a chimney breast at right angles, trimming and trimmer joists will surround the hearth as shown here.

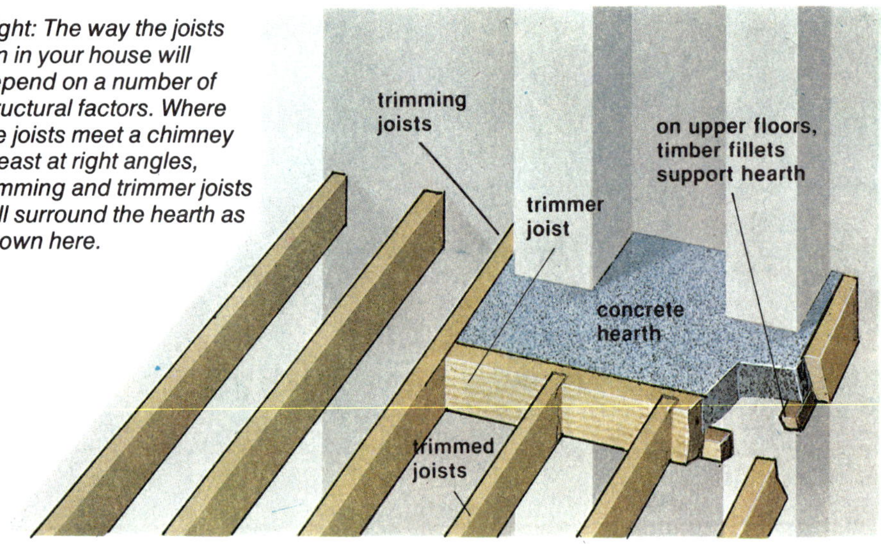

Right: Where the joists run across the face of the chimney breast, the arrangement will look like this. Again, the hearth will be supported on timber fillets, while a hardwood surround may frame the hearth itself.

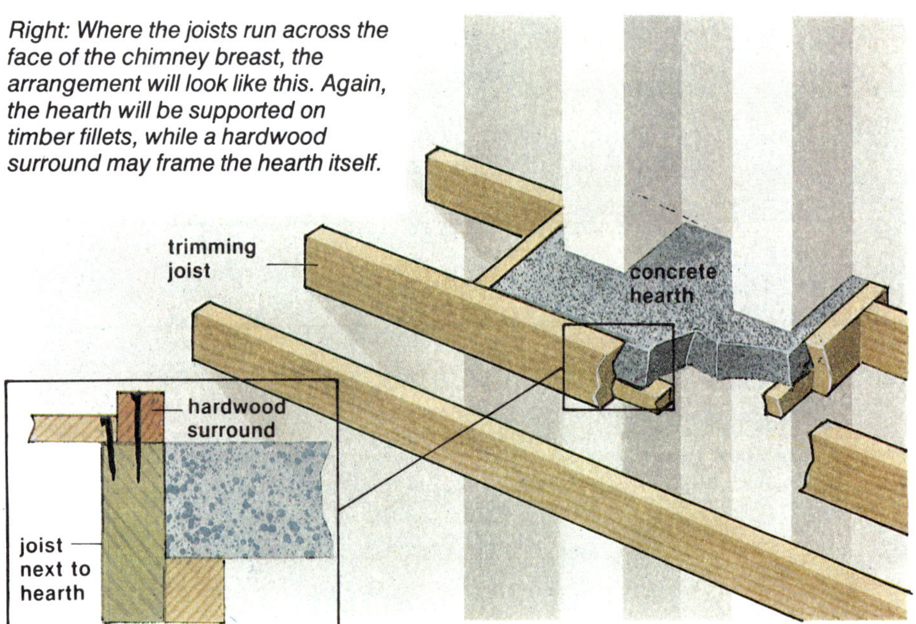

Skirting details

Normally, the floorboards are tucked in under the skirting board (top left), but if thicker boards are used you can conceal the gap with quadrant moulding (centre). Where a joist is right alongside the wall, add a strip of timber to it to support the board ends at the required height.

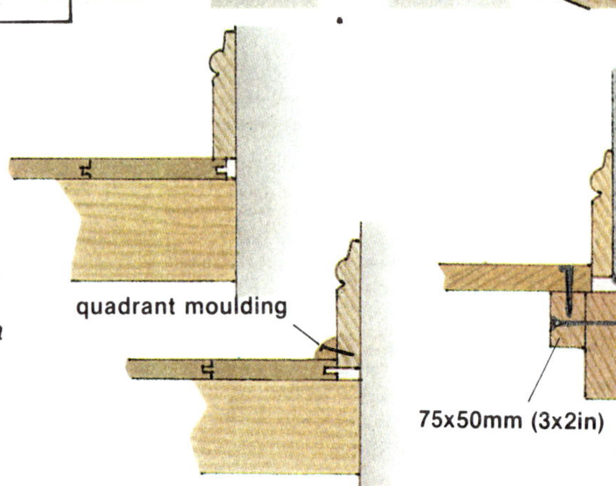

You may have to cut the boards to length straightaway in order to get them into a convenient indoor spot for stacking.

Removing old floorboards

Your first job is to take up the old boards. Decide where you're going to start (probably near a wall but not right up against it) and lever up the first board with a bolster and, if necessary, a claw-hammer. If it's tongued-and-grooved, you'll need to cut through its tongue first with a pad saw, a floorboard saw, a tenon saw, or a circular saw whose depth of cut is set to the floorboard thickness. Be very careful not to cut into the joists.

After you have lifted one end, by far the quickest way to continue (and to lift all the other boards) is to use a long piece of substantial timber – say 75x50mm (3x2in) – as a lever, and a shorter piece as a fulcrum. With stubborn boards, you can put your feet on the lever.

Make sure none of the boards are screwed down. If they are, don't try to lever them up before undoing the screws!

In a wide room, you'll probably be able to wiggle and release from under the skirting even those boards which span the room's full width. In a narrow room, you may have to saw across them first.

You'd do well to extract the nails from the old boards as you put them aside, to avoid injury if you tread on one – especially if you mean to keep some of the boards for re-use. And you'll need to extract any nails left in the joists. If they won't come out, drive them in flush.

Note that, if gaps between boards are the only problem with your old floor, you can give it a new lease of life by carefully lifting them up, removing the nails, scraping down the boards' edges to clean them up for a snug fit, and then re-laying them all tightly against one another in just the same way as you lay new boards (see below). The odd damaged board can be replaced by a new one of the same thickness. You'll need to add a strip of board along the wall after re-laying the last board, to make up for the gaps.

Laying new boards

Before starting to lay the floor, place a straight-edged piece of timber (a floorboard will do) across the joists to check whether their top edges are in line. If not, cut packing pieces (planing them to the right thickness, or using hardboard) and pin them in position.

Then measure for the first four or five boards, and cut them to length. For economy, aim to use up any short pieces that you may be left with. If making up a length from two or more of these, make sure they meet in the centre of a joist each time, so that it supports the ends of both. See that the ends are cut squarely and butt tightly against one another – and stagger such joints, so that they don't occur one after the other on the same joist.

Lay the first board in position with the groove facing out into the room, and scribe it to fit against the wall. Then cut it to shape, removing the waste from the tongue side, and nail it down to each joist through its face.

After that, the basic procedure is to lay the boards on the floor in sequences of four or five (inserting the tongues, if any, into the grooves); cramp them tight and nail them down.

There are two ways to cramp floorboards. You can use pairs of wedges, cut from 75x50mm (3x2in) planed softwood, tapped together between the last board and another piece of timber nailed across the joists. Or you can hire flooring cramps, which clamp themselves onto the joists while being tightened against the floorboards. They exert tremendous pressure, and you'll have to use offcuts of floorboard (including their tongues) as 'softening' to prevent the cramps from damaging the edges of the boards you're laying.

The right nails to use for fixing are cut floorbrads about two and a half times as long as the floorboards are thick. These are blunt and thus won't split the timber. Drive two through each board wherever it crosses a joist. Make quite sure at all times that you know where pipework and electrical wiring runs. A nail through a gas pipe or mains cable is no joke.

Remember, when laying a timber floor at ground level, it's vital not to leave any wood debris under the boards after laying them, since it can encourage the spread of rot.

Making boards fit

No room is without various irregularities in, and protrusions from, the walls at floor level, and you'll have to cut the boards to fit round them. The first and last boards must be scribed to fit along the walls, and you'll also need to cope with the chimney breast (if any) in a similar way. A combination square is ideal for scribing round small obstacles.

A fitted cupboard can create problems if the floorboards run into rather than parallel with it, but these aren't insurmountable (see *Ready Reference*). You can remove the bottom cross piece in its frame, and replace it after laying the floorboards. Or you can leave the cross piece there, saw through the old floorboards immediately in front of it, and butt the ends of the new ones up against them. In the latter case, the remaining old boards (those under the cupboard) may no longer be supported; if not, you'll have to screw down through the cross piece to hold them in position.

In places where you need access to pipes and wiring, you can include a trap-door in the form of a short board such as an off-cut (or a full-length board, cut into two), held down by countersunk screws instead of nails. In the case of T & G flooring, you'll have to plane or chisel the tongue off the adjacent board first.

PREPARING THE JOISTS

1 *Lever up the end of a convenient board with a bolster. If the board has a tongue, you'll have to saw through that beforehand.*

2 *Use a piece of timber as a lever to finish removing the first board and then to tackle the rest, taking one board at a time.*

3 *If necessary, saw the old boards in two so that you can get them out with ease from under the skirting at either side of the room.*

4 *Pull the old nails out of the joists with a claw hammer, using a piece of wood under its head to provide you with more leverage.*

5 *Lay a straight piece of timber across the joists, and measure the gaps below it to see how far the joists have sagged out of level.*

6 *Cut packing pieces, plane them to a thickness which will fill the various gaps, and nail them to the tops of the joists.*

LAYING THE FLOORBOARDS

1 *Boards will have to be scribed to fit round obstacles. Cut out the waste portions with a coping saw, or use a tenon saw and chisel.*

2 *Scribe and cut the first board to fit along the wall if necessary, then use a chisel to wedge it in place as you nail it to the joists.*

3 *Where two boards make up a length, nail one down, then push the other against the far wall and square its length across from the first board.*

5 *With the cramps still tight, nail the nearest board down onto the joists. Always check for pipes and cables before nailing.*

6 *You can remove the cramps before nailing the other boards down. Note that pairs of boards should always meet in the centres of joists.*

7 *Pairs of wedges, tapped together, are an alternative to flooring cramps. Again you'll need 'softening' blocks between them and the boards.*

9 *At the end wall, plane the tongues off two boards and wedge one up against the last board which you have nailed in position.*

10 *Use the other board, or a piece the same width, to scribe a line on the first board so that you can cut it down to the right width.*

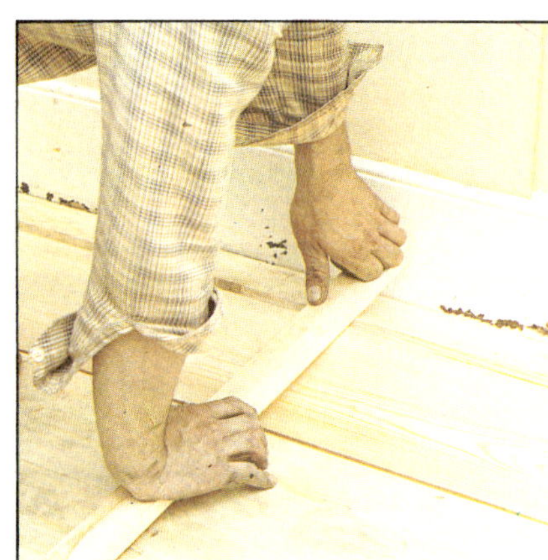

11 *Cut to the scribed line, swap the boards round, and press them both into position with a piece of wood before nailing them down.*

4 *After nailing the first length, lay the next three or four in position and cramp them together tightly. Flooring cramps are ideal for this.*

8 *When you come to a chimney breast, mark out on the floorboard how much you'll need to cut away from it for a snug fit around the obstacle.*

12 *Finish the job by systematically going over the whole floor and punching all the nail heads below its surface for safety's sake.*

Finishing the job

You can't, of course, use wedges or cramps to get the last couple of boards tight, because there's no room for them. An alternative procedure is as follows.

After cutting the last two boards to length and planing the tongues off both, place one of them next to the last board already nailed (see *Ready Reference*). Wedge it tightly against the board by using a chisel as a lever (see photograph 9, left). Then scribe the profile of the wall on it, using a block of wood the same width as the boards. Even if the wall were dead straight and parallel to the board edges, you'd still need to do this in order to find out the width to which you need to cut the last board down: it would be quite a coincidence if a full-width board fitted exactly into the final gap.

Then cut the board along the scribed line, lay the whole board next to the last board nailed, and place the cut board next to the wall.

Now you can spring them both into place at once – using a piece of timber to press them flat – and nail them down.

When you've laid all the boards, punch all the nail heads below the surface. Then look at how neatly the boards fit under or butt against the skirting. If the effect is ragged, you can improve it enormously by nailing quadrant moulding into the angle (fixing it to the skirting, not the floor).

The choice of finishing treatment is of course yours. You may be going to lay carpet; but brand-new floorboards do give you the opportunity to make a feature of them. They'll provide a pleasant texture if painted – but you might well want to give them a clear varnish finish, perhaps even staining them first in another timber colour. Whatever happens, you must treat them in some way, otherwise they'll soon become very grubby (in fact they'll probably need a lot of cleaning up after they're laid, because of the mess the job creates).

And do make sure the paint or varnish will stand up to the wear it receives. Use only full gloss paint, complete with appropriate primer and undercoat, or three coats of heavy-duty floor sealer (furniture varnish is not really hard-wearing enough).

Replacing skirtings

If your old timber floor was in bad enough condition to need replacement, it's possible that the skirting boards are in pretty poor shape too. If that is the case, now is the time to consider replacing them. The job will be dealt with in detail in another section, but briefly all you have to do is to prise off the old boards carefully with a bolster chisel or crowbar (they are usually nailed to the wall through wooden packing pieces with cut nails) and nail up new boards with new packing pieces when you have laid new floorboards.

Ready Reference

TONGUED-AND-GROOVED BOARDS

Note that the boards are cut with the tongue and groove off centre. Lay them as shown here.

DEALING WITH FITTED CUPBOARDS

If the floorboards run parallel to the cupboard, saw through them at the front and run the new ones up against them.

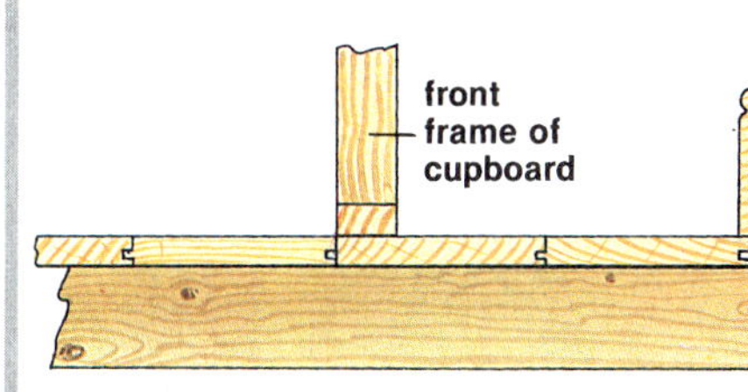

If they run into the cupboard, you can do the same, but support the ends of the old boards with screws driven down through the frame.

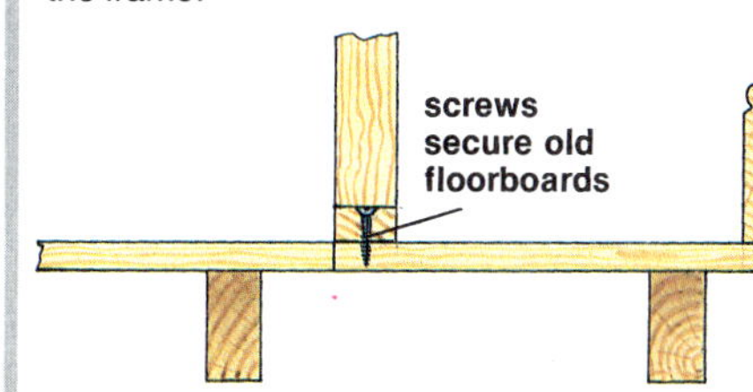

TIP: FITTING THE LAST TWO BOARDS

1 After planing the tongues off two lengths (A & B), place A against the last nailed board, and scribe it to fit the wall – using a piece the same width as B.

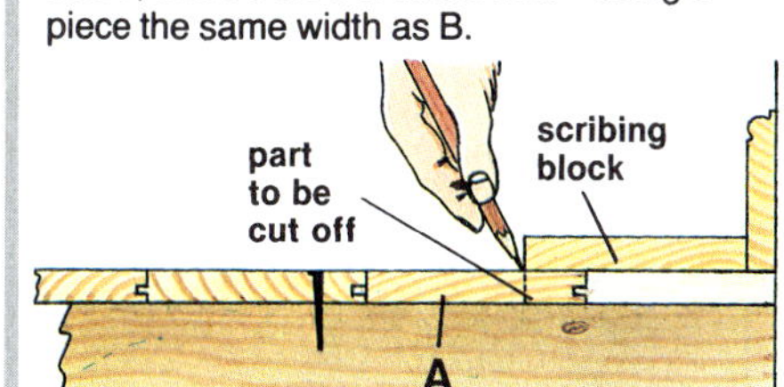

2 Remove A, replace it with B, cut A as scribed, and put A next to the wall. Then press them both in place and nail down.

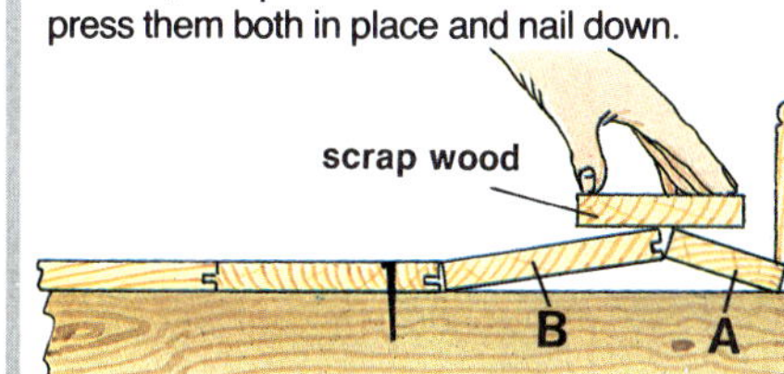

FITTING DOORS AND FRAMES

The finest external door is only as good as its frame. A sound and sturdy frame is vital to keep out intruders and the weather; what's more, it needs to match the door in size and style.

Not all doors have frames. Internal doors are generally fitted into 'linings', also known as 'casings'. A lining differs from a frame in being made from wider pieces of timber. These are usually flat, cut at the time of installation to the lengths required, and fitted together in the opening with simple housing or rebate joints.

A frame, on the other hand, is a fairly sophisticated piece of joinery, often in hardwood, which comes ready-made. It's heavier and stronger than a lining, and it's always used for external doorways; as a result, it's specially designed to keep out the weather. Lighter frames are sometimes also found in internal doorways – especially those in thin walls, because the pieces in a frame are narrow and squarish in section, not flat. Rebates are moulded in them to receive the door, and they're usually machined in other ways as well.

Joints, usually mortise-and-tenon, are already cut in the frame components, so that you can't choose your own length and width. In other words, the opening in the wall has to fit the frame you've bought, because you can't make the frame fit the opening. So you need to make sure you buy the right size of frame for the door in the first place.

A door frame may consist of only three pieces – the head, which goes at the top, and the two jambs which go on either side. In that case, for an external doorway you'll have to buy a separate threshold or sill (the part you step on). However, four-piece door frames, which include thresholds, are also available.

Why install a frame?

Strong though it is, an existing door frame isn't invulnerable. Often fully exposed to the elements, it may eventually rot, usually in the bottoms of the jambs. Hard knocks (and even an attack by vandals or burglars) may necessitate replacement, too.

Alternative reasons for installing a new frame may be to improve security, fire protection, weather resistance or appearance. Ask your timber merchant or other joinery supplier about frames with the particular characteristics you're looking for. Yet another reason for fitting a new frame may be because you want a new door, and the old frame is the wrong size or is otherwise unsuitable.

Lastly, you might want to make a new doorway where none existed before (eg, for access to a back yard). This might mean enlarging an existing window opening by removing the brickwork beneath the sill. But if you're making a completely new opening, remember you'll need a lintel to support the wall above, and flashing to stop moisture from penetrating and causing rot and damp within the structure.

Removing an old frame

Before putting in your new frame, you may well have to take out an old one. It's worth knowing the quickest way of doing this (see *Ready Reference*).

First, saw through the head in two places, making the cuts slope upwards and inwards, towards the centre of the frame. The middle portion of the head will then come away easily.

Next, saw through the jambs – again at an angle – downwards and outwards. This enables you to pull the lower part of each jamb up and out. Then you have plenty of freedom to work the top corners of the frame away from the brickwork.

Lastly, clean up the opening, removing any loose timber plugs to which the frame

Ready Reference

DOOR LININGS

Door linings differ from door frames in being made up from broader pieces of wood. In addition, these are cut to length and jointed on site, whereas door frames are ready-made to standard sizes. Linings are used only for internal doorways

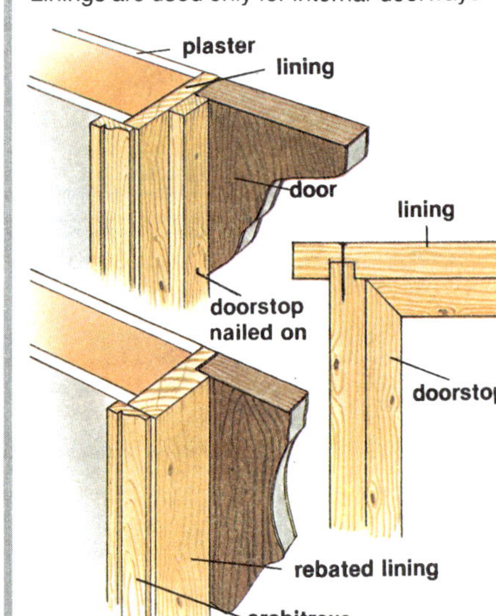

FITTING THE DOORS

1 *Decide and mark the hinge positions along the inner edge of each door. Heavier doors need three hinges, but two usually suffice.*

2 *Mark the hinge recesses' depth with a marking gauge, and use a hammer and chisel to cut them. Begin by chopping round the edges.*

3 *Cut across the grain, then finish the recesses by carefully removing the waste. You need a sharp chisel; don't split the timber.*

4 *Position the hinge, making sure it's absolutely straight. Use a bradawl to make starting holes for the screws; then drive them home.*

5 *Position each door in the frame, and prop it up at the right height. Then use the loose leaf of each hinge to mark its recess in the frame.*

6 *Screw the hinges to the jambs, after chiselling out the recesses as in the door. Half the knuckle's thickness projects beyond the edge.*

7 *A neat way of fixing glass into a door is to start by laying putty or other suitable sealant in the rebates before you insert the glass.*

8 *Then lay the panes of glass (ready cut to size) into position, making sure that they are bedded carefully into the putty or sealant.*

9 *Finally, pin mitred lengths of glass bead all round. Don't glue them, in case you need to remove the glass (eg, after a breakage).*

may have been fixed plus, of course, any rubble which may be lying at the bottom.

Removing a doorframe while keeping it intact for subsequent re-use is a trickier business, since at the top corners frames often have 'horns' (these are projections where the head overhangs the jambs at either side; they are built into the brickwork for maximum stability). You'll have to extract these by carefully cutting out the mortar joints from between the bricks around the horns.

To remove the fixings at either side of the frame, carefully cut away any plastering or rendering that conceals the frame edges and run a pad saw fitted with a hacksaw blade down between the jamb and the wall on either side; saw through any obstacles you meet. This will be easy enough if the fixings are nails or screws, but quite hard if they're metal anchors.

Occasionally, steel dowels are also used to fasten a door frame to the floor, projecting down into it from the ends of the jambs. They prevent the jambs from working loose with heavy use. Although they can often be omitted when fitting a new frame, their presence makes it very difficult to remove an old frame in one piece. But it may be possible to chip the floor away round them.

Lastly, place a large flat piece of timber against the edge of the frame, in various positions all round it in turn, and hit it so as to knock the frame out of the opening.

Fixing a new frame

There are three ways of fixing the jambs to the walls on either side. Firstly, you can screw them into plastic or fibre wallplugs; in external doorways, use screws which are rust-proof (eg, stainless steel) or rust-resistant (eg, zinc-plated), not plain steel ones.

Secondly, you can attach the jambs to metal anchors or fixing cramps, cemented into the brick joints. And thirdly, you can nail them to wooden plugs wedged between the bricks.

The first of these methods is probably the simplest, but the second is the strongest, and the last means you can get a secure fixing in brick or blockwork even if there are gaps between the frame and the wall, because you can cut the plugs off to exactly the length you need. The method works as follows.

Assemble the frame and see how it fits the opening. If it's too big, your best plan is to enlarge the opening slightly, by chopping away up to one third of a brick's length from either side of the opening. Then insert the timber plugs, opposite each other, firmly in the brickwork joints – at least three on each side. Drop a plumbline from the top of the opening on one side, and mark its position on each plug there.

Measure the width of the frame (from outside edge to outside edge) and, working from the mark you've already made on one of the plugs, mark that width on the plug opposite. Then drop the plumbline past this and mark its position on the other plugs that side. Lastly, cut off all the plugs at the marks. The plug ends should now give an opening which is exactly the right width for the frame, with its sides vertical and parallel, even if the wall itself has ragged edges.

After that you can insert the frame for final fixing. Although most frames are made of preservative-treated timber, the new frame should also be primed first – and ideally given a complete paint finish of undercoat and top coat on all surfaces which will adjoin brickwork or concrete, to keep out any damp which finds its way through and so prevent rot. However, few people bother with this.

Once the frame is in position, check that the head is level and that one jamb is more or less plumb (vertical). Nail through that jamb into the top plug. Adjust the jamb further till it's exactly plumb, and nail it into the bottom plug. Then repeat the procedure for the other jamb; in addition, before you nail through its bottom end, sight across both jambs to ensure that the frame isn't twisted.

Finish off by nailing into all the intermediate plugs, and punching all the nail heads below the surface of the timber.

This is also the time to mortar the horns, if any, into the brickwork.

Finishing the job

The final stage is to pack timber into any remaining gaps between the frame and the wall. On an internal door frame, you'll need to finish the whole thing with architrave mouldings, which may need to be fixed to timber grounds (see page 399). In an external doorway, a mastic seal between frame and wall on the outside is also essential to keep out the damp.

For protection against driving rain, the threshold of an external door frame will either be rebated (ie, stepped), or will have a metal 'water bar', if not both. The latter rests in a groove along the top of the threshold, into which it needs to be set on a bed of non-setting mastic. The bottom of the door will have to be rebated to fit over it.

If you've bought wisely, the door should fit the frame exactly – but you can always saw and plane off small amounts from the top, bottom or sides if necessary.

Hanging the door is a straightforward matter of marking out and chiselling hinge recesses on the door, screwing the hinges into them, and repeating the procedure on the frame.

Remember, however, that a door must hang quite vertically. The hinges should be exactly above one another; you may have to enlarge or pack out the recesses.

Ready Reference

REMOVING A DOOR FRAME

This procedure is especially appropriate when you're removing a frame from a solid wall:

- start by sawing through the head at an angle in two places; the piece in the middle should then come away easily

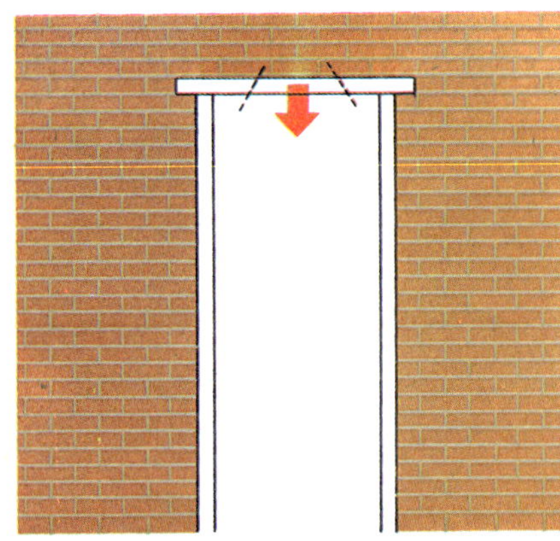

- next, saw through the jambs at an angle, and remove the lower part of each; you may have screws or nails to contend with here. And, if the jambs are fixed to the ground with metal dowels inserted into the end grain, you'll have to pull these free at the same time

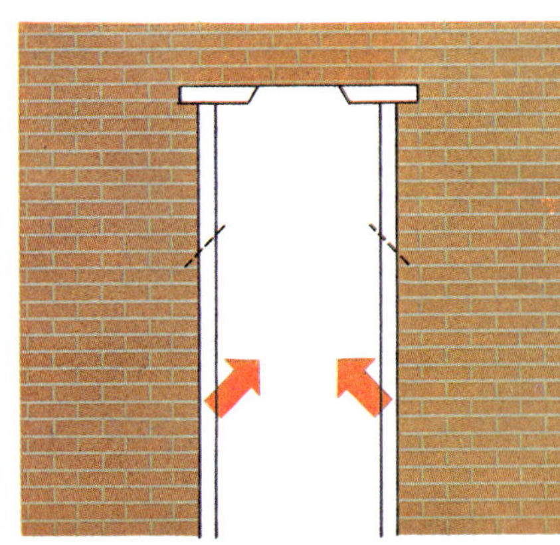

- lastly you can remove each of the top corners from the brickwork or blockwork. Having cut away the rest of the frame first means that you now have freedom to work any 'horns' (projecting ends of the head) loose from the wall.

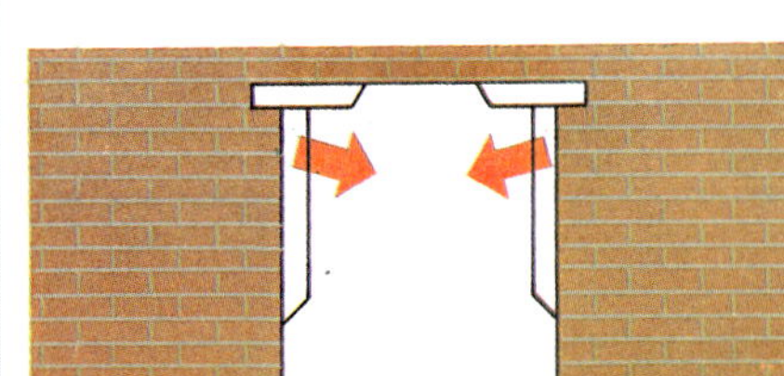

WAYS OF FITTING DOOR FRAMES

External doorways

Here are two ways of fitting a frame into an outside wall. Note that mastic and a dpc are both used to prevent moisture from penetrating.

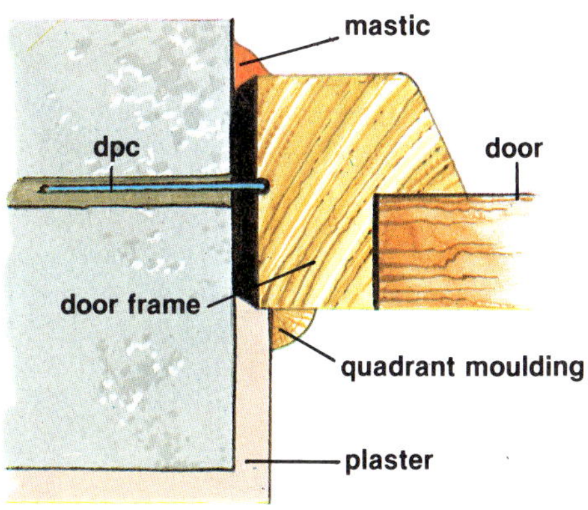

Internal doorways

A is a common arrangement, B a specially shaped frame, and C a frame narrower than the wall is thick: lengths of wood make up the width.

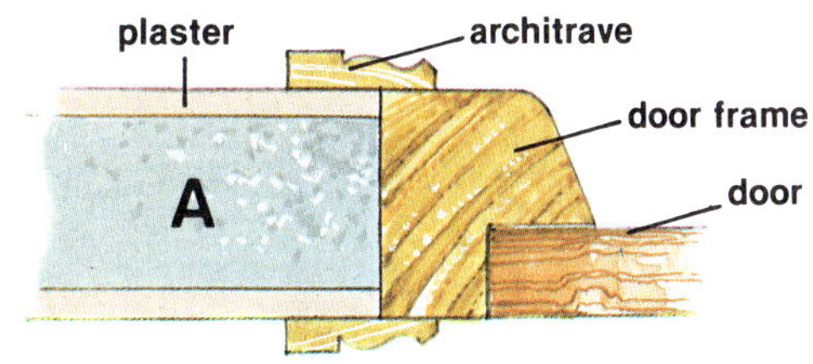

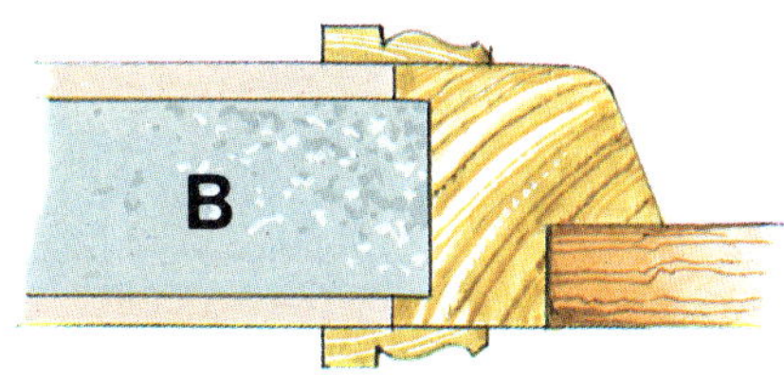

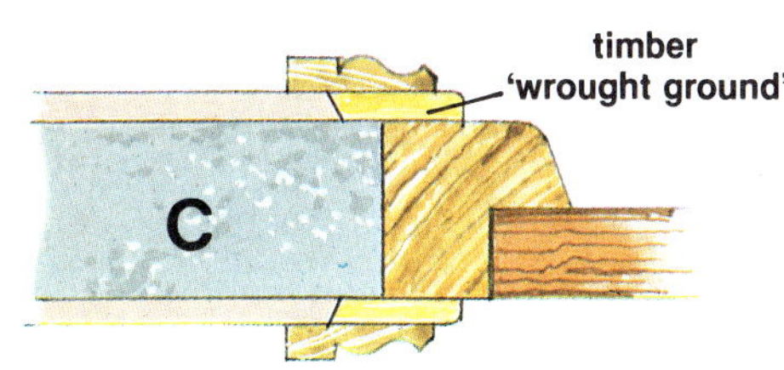

Fixing frames to walls

Apart from screwing into wall plugs, you can use metal anchors (A), or timber plugs (B), cut as shown and driven into the joints between bricks.

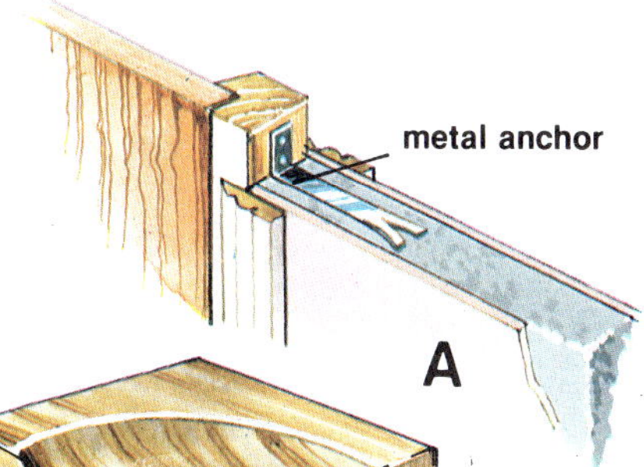

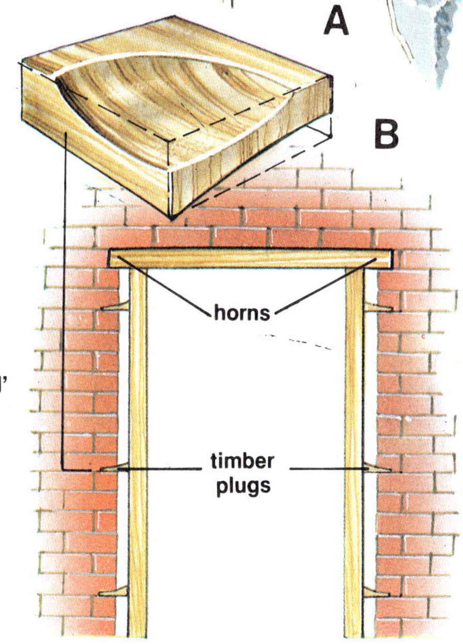

Joins between frame and skirting

Usually skirting (nailed to battens fixed to the wall) is butted against the back of the architrave (A).

If the skirting is too thick (B), add a 'plinth block' below the architrave. Chamfer its edges for neatness.

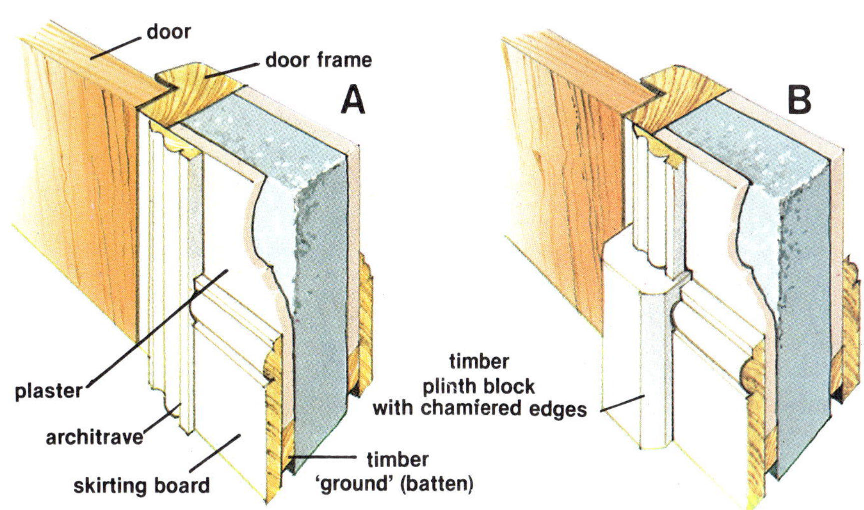

Threshold design

A ready-made hardwood threshold has either a metal water bar, which you bed in mastic as shown, or a rebate which does the same job.

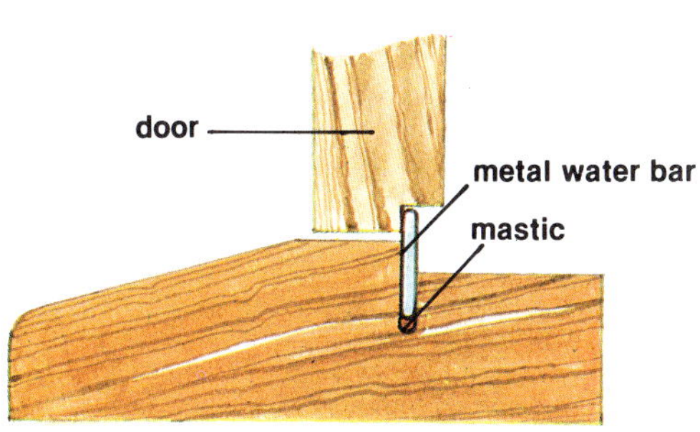

PART 5

DECORATING

USING PAINT AND VARNISH

Whether you're painting your woodwork or using varnish and stain to enhance its natural grain pattern, thorough preparation is as important as careful application. There's skill involved in painting walls and ceilings too – and you can create attractive three-dimensional effects using the latest textured paints.

PAINTING WALLS AND CEILINGS

The quickest and cheapest way to transform a room is to paint the walls and ceiling. But, for a successful result, you have to prepare the surfaces properly and use the correct painting techniques.

Dulux Russet over Dulux Cameo

Paint is the most popular material used to protect and decorate walls and ceilings in the home. Whereas many people hesitate before hanging wallpaper or sticking more permanent wall and ceiling coverings in place, few would worry about wielding a paint brush for the first time.

One of the chief advantages of painting a room is that it doesn't take much time; large areas can be given two or even three coats of emulsion paint in a day. The paints now available are hardwearing and totally unlike earlier distemper and water paints. They are easy to apply by brush, roller or pad and can be safely washed at frequent intervals to keep them looking fresh.

Any drawbacks are usually caused by faults in the wall or ceiling surface, rather than by the paints. A standard paint alone cannot cover up defects in the same way that some other wallcoverings can, so a surface which is to be painted usually needs more careful preparation than one which is to be papered.

The majority of walls and ceilings are plastered and this type of surface, when in sound condition, is ideal as a base for emulsion and other paints. But it is not the only surface finish you are likely to come across.

Previous occupiers of the house may well have covered the walls with a decorative paper and even painted on top of that. At the very worst there may be several layers of paper and paint, making it very difficult to achieve a smooth paint surface. In this situation it is invariably better to strip the surface completely down to the plaster and to start again from scratch.

This does not mean that no paper should be overpainted. Certain types such as plain white relief wallcoverings and woodchips are intended to be so treated, and actually look 'softer' after one or two redecorations. In short, most wall or ceiling surfaces you are likely to encounter will be paintable. All you have to do is select the right paint for the job and get the surface into as good a condition as possible.

Choosing paints

Vinyl emulsion paints are the most commonly used types of paint for painting walls and ceilings. They are easy to apply and come in a wide range of colours. You will usually have a choice of three finishes: matt, silk, or gloss.

There are also textured paints which are increasing in popularity, particularly for ceiling use. These are vinyl emulsion paints with added 'body' so they can be applied more thickly and then given a decorative textured finish.

Oil-based eggshell paints can be used where a more durable surface is needed or where you want to use the same colour on both walls and woodwork. Resin-based gloss paint is used occasionally also on walls and ceilings, particularly in humid rooms like kitchens and bathrooms.

You should choose paint carefully. The fact that one make is half the price of another may indicate that it has only half the covering power and you would therefore need to apply two coats of the cheaper paint. Also, if you're using white paint, you may find that one brand is noticeably 'whiter' than another.

Tools and equipment

Few specialised tools are needed for wall and ceiling paintwork. If you are content to work with only a brush you will require two sizes: one larger one for the bulk of the work, and a smaller brush for working into corners. It is worth decanting quantities of paint into a paint kettle which is easier to carry around than large heavy cans.

Rollers make the job of painting large areas of wall or ceiling much quicker and also help to achieve a better finish. But you will still need a small brush for working into corners and for dealing with coving, cornices etc.

To prepare a new fibre roller for painting, soak it in soapy water for 2 to 3 hours to get rid of any loose bits of fibre, then roll it out on the wall to dry it off. One point to remember: if you intend using silk vinyl emulsion paint, it's best not to use a roller as this tends to show up as a stippled effect on the silk surface.

Large paint pads will also enable you to cover big expanses of wall or ceiling very quickly. You can use a brush or a small paint pad for work in corners.

Apart from these paint application tools you'll need a variety of other items for preparing the surfaces so they're ready for the paint. The walls must be cleaned, so you'll need washing-down equipment: sponges, cloths, detergent, and a bucket or two of water.

You'll need filler for cracks and a filling knife about 75mm (3in) wide. When any filler is dry it will need to be sanded down, so have some glasspaper ready for wrapping round a cork sanding block. A scraper will also be needed if old wallpaper has to be stripped from the walls.

Finally, because of the height of the walls and ceiling, you'll need access equipment, such as a stepladder, to enable you to reach them safely and comfortably.

Preparing the surface

No painting will be successful until the

PAINTING THE CEILING WITH A ROLLER

1 *Use a brush to paint a strip about 50mm wide round the outside edge of the ceiling; a roller cannot reach right into angles or corners.*

2 *Pour paint into the roller tray; don't put in too much at a time or you risk overloading the roller and splashing paint out of the tray.*

3 *Dip the roller in and pull it back so there is paint at the shallow end of the tray. Push the roller back and forth in the paint at the shallow end.*

4 *Run the roller over the ceiling so there is a band of paint next to the strip of paint you have brushed along the edge of the ceiling.*

5 *Reverse the roller's direction so you join up the two strips of paint into one band. Then finish off by running the roller over the band.*

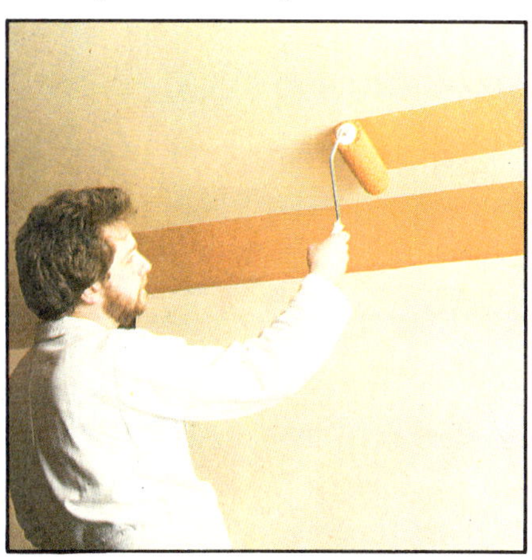

6 *Now start the next section by running the roller alongside the completed band. Work your way round the ceiling in bands.*

Ready Reference

LINING WALL SURFACES

You can use lining paper to do the same job for paint as it does for wallpapers, covering minor cracks and defects on the wall or ceiling and providing a smooth surface for painting.

TIP: SEAL STRONG COLOURS

Wallcoverings with strong colourings, and particularly those tinted with metallic inks, will almost certainly show through the new paint. To prevent this they should be stripped off, or sealed with special aluminium spirit-based sealer.

FILLING HAIRLINE CRACKS

You may not be able to push enough filler into hairline cracks to ensure a good bond:
- it is often better to open the crack up further with the edge of an old chisel or screwdriver so the filler can penetrate more deeply and key better to both sides of the crack
- when using a textured vinyl paint there is no need to fill hairline cracks, but cracks wider than 1mm ($^1/_{32}$in) should be filled.

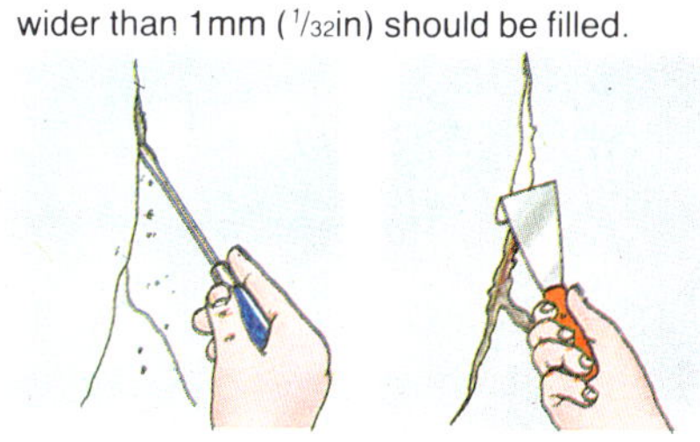

DEALING WITH FITTINGS

Protect electrical fittings so paint or water can't enter them during cleaning and decorating:
- ideally, power to these fittings should be cut off and the fittings removed
- if items cannot be removed, use masking tape to protect them.

SELECTING PAINTS

When choosing paints, remember that:
- emulsion paints are quicker to apply, dry more quickly and lack the smell of resin- or oil-based paints. They are also cheaper and can be easily cleaned off painting equipment with water
- non-drip paints are best for ceilings and cover more thickly than runny ones, cutting down on the number of coats
- a silk or gloss finish will tend to highlight surface irregularities more than a matt finish
- textured paints are suitable for use on surfaces which are in poor condition since they will cover defects which a standard emulsion paint cannot.

PAINTING THE WALL WITH A BRUSH

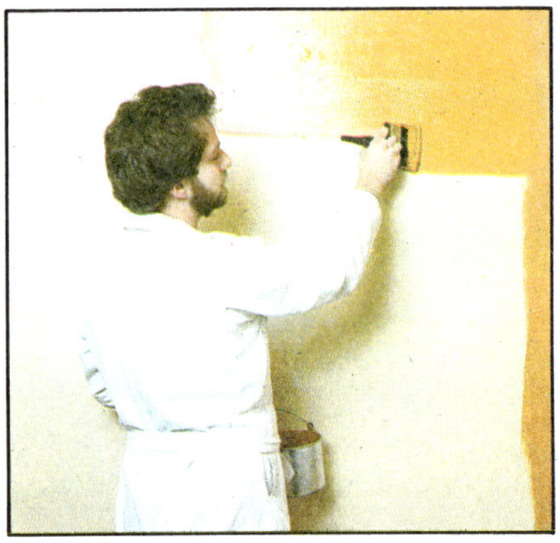

1 Use a small brush to cut in at the wall and ceiling join and in corners. With a larger brush paint the wall in bands. First, brush across the wall.

2 Move the brush across the wall in the opposite direction. The bands of paint should be about 1m wide and you should be working downwards.

3 When you are working at the top of the wall your next strokes should be downwards to complete the area you have covered with crossways strokes.

4 At the bottom two-thirds of the wall continue working in crossways strokes, but this time finish off each section by brushing upwards.

USING PAINT PADS

1 Thin the paint a little (with water for emulsions, turps for oil-based ones). Cut in with a small brush or pad and use a larger pad to paint in bands.

2 For precise work you can use a small pad like this. Ensure that you cover areas you don't want painted with masking tape.

surface beneath has been properly prepared. Unless wallpaper is of a type intended for painting it is usually better to strip it off, and walls which have been stripped of their previous wallcoverings need a thorough washing to remove all traces of old paste. Make sure the floor is protected against debris by covering it with a dust sheet or sheets of old newspaper. Emulsion-painted walls also need washing to remove surface dirt. In both cases, use warm water with a little household detergent added. Then rinse with clean water.

If you decide to leave the wallpaper on the walls you will have to wash it down before you paint. Take care to avoid overwetting the paper, particularly at joins. When the surface is dry, check the seams; if any have lifted, stick them down with a ready-mixed paste.

Ceilings should be washed in small areas at a time and rinsed thoroughly before you move onto another section systematically.

If the surfaces are left in perfect condition, they can be painted as soon as they are dry.

It's possible that walls or ceilings may have been painted with distemper, which may only become apparent after you have removed the existing wallcovering. Unless it is the washable type, you will have to remove it completely since emulsion paint will not adhere well to it. Use hot water, detergent and a scrubbing brush to soften and get rid of the coating; this is hard work, but you could use a steam stripper to speed up the process.

With all the surface cleaned, the next job is to fill any cracks and repair defects such a as indentations caused perhaps by knocks or the blade of a carelessly handled wallpaper scraper (see *Ready Reference*).

Whenever a filler has been used it should be sanded down flush with the wall surface, once dry, and the resulting dust should be brushed away.

If the plaster is in bad condition and obviously covered in cracks you should consider covering it completely with liningpaper, woodchip or other relief wallcovering before painting it. The paper will provide a good base for redecoration, and will save a great deal of preparation time. However, this can only be done if the plaster itself is still bonded securely to the wall. If it is coming away in chunks or sounds hollow behind the cracks, then the wall should be replastered.

Cracks which have developed round door and window frames are best filled with a flexible sealant, which will be unaffected by movement of the frames. Acrylic-based sealants are available for this purpose and they can be easily overpainted.

After all the preparation work has been

PAINTING PROCEDURE

Paint the ceiling first in 1m-wide bands (1 & 2). Paint round a ceiling rose (3), then complete the rest of that band (4). On walls work downwards (1). At a window, paint along the top band (2) and repeat the process at the bottom (3). Work from right to left unless you are left-handed.

completed, have a good clear-up in the room so that when you begin painting you do not stir up dust and have to work around numerous bits and pieces scattered over the floor space.

Re-lay dust sheets and set up your access equipment before even opening the first can of paint. Make sure your brushes or rollers are clean and ready for use.

Painting sequences

If possible, do all your painting in daylight hours. Artificial light is less easy to work by and can lead to small areas being missed.

Painting is always done from the highest point downwards, so ceilings are the first areas to be tackled. The whole ceiling will be painted in bands across the room no wider than you can easily reach without stretching on your stepladder or platform. This generally means that at any one time you will probably be painting a band no wider than 1m and less than 2m long unless you are using scaffolding boards to support you.

You start at the edges first and then work into the main body of the room.

Linking one section to another is seldom difficult with emulsion paint and is simply a matter of blending the paint from the new section back into the previous one.

Walls are treated similarly, starting at the top and working downwards in sections about 1m wide, cutting in at the ceiling and at return walls.

Painting tips

The number of coats required will depend on the previous colour and condition of the surface and the type of paint. If another coat has to be applied, be sure that the previous one is fully dry first. With modern vinyl emulsion paint it may be that because the paint is water-based it will cause the paper underneath to swell and bubble; however, you shouldn't worry about this because as the water in the paint dries out the paper and paste behind the paint surface will begin to flatten again.

If the paper is badly hung with a lack of adhesive at the edge, seams may lift as the paint dries. They will have to be stuck down in the same way as if they had lifted during washing. Careful preparation would prevent this problem anyway.

Ready Reference

HOW MUCH PAINT?

Coverage per litre depends on the wood's porosity and roughness and the painter's technique but an approximate guide is:
Runny gloss 17 sq m (183 sq ft)
Non-drip gloss 13 sq m (140 sq ft)
Satin gloss (eggshell) 12 sq m (130 sq ft)
Runny matt emulsion 15 sq m (161 sq ft)
Non-drip matt emulsion 12 sq m (130 sq ft)
Silk emulsion 14 sq m (150 sq ft)
Gloss emulsion 14 sq m (150 sq ft)

TIP:PAINTING POLYSTYRENE

Paint polystyrene tiles only with emulsion paint. Don't use a solvent or oil-based paint since this will cause a fire risk.

BRUSH SIZES

If you are using brushes only, you will need:

- a brush about 100mm (4in) wide; brushes wider than this tend to be unwieldy and very tiring to use
- a brush about 25mm (1in) wide for cutting in at edges and in corners.

THE RIGHT ROLLER

For emulsion, use a foam or short-pile synthetic fibre sleeve along with a roller tray. Remember that:

- emulsion paints make natural fibre sleeves go soggy
- a sleeve with long fibres will leave an 'orange peel' effect finish.

PAD SIZE

For painting walls and ceilings, choose a pad measuring around 190 x 100mm (7½ x 4in) for the main area, and a smaller pad (or a paint brush) for touching-in work.

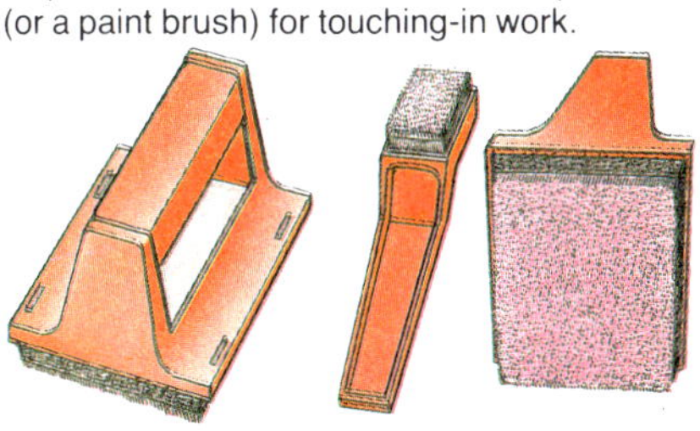

MAKING ACCESS EASIER

Use scaffold boards as well as stepladders so you can work over large areas at a time without having to keep moving the ladders. You can hire scaffold boards or mobile scaffold platforms.

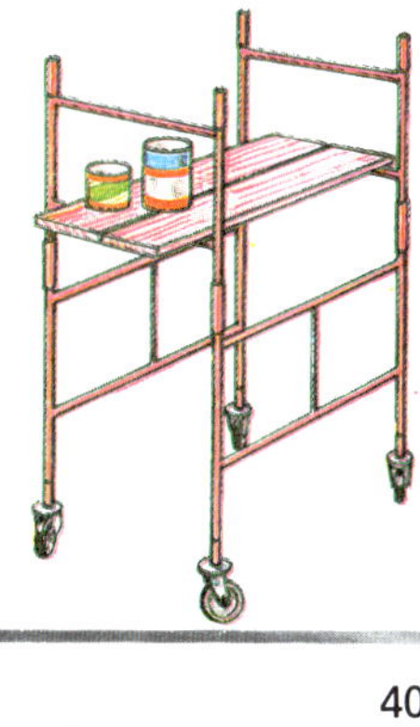

APPLYING TEXTURED FINISHES

Textured finishes which you can paint on walls or ceilings are an inexpensive way of covering up poor surfaces. They also give you the chance to exercise your ingenuity in creating relief patterns on them.

Textured wall and ceiling finishes can provide a relatively quick form of decoration. You don't, for example, need to apply more than one coat. And, unlike relief wallcoverings (another type of product commonly used to obtain a textured wall or ceiling surface), you don't have to go through the process of pasting, soaking, cutting, hanging and trimming; you simply spread the finishes on the surface with a paint brush or roller.

One of the advantages of using a 'texture' on walls is that it will tend to mask the effect of any general unevenness in the surface. Similarly, ready-mixed textures are often marketed specifically as a solution to the problem of improving the appearance of old ceilings. They are very suitable for this and can save a lot of tedious repair work.

However, there is no need to think of textures just as a cover-up. You may simply prefer a textured surface to a flat, smooth one. If you use patterning tools, the range of textured effects you can achieve is practically endless, depending only on your skill and imagination.

Choosing textured finishes

One of the factors which will influence your choice of finish is, obviously, how much you are prepared to pay. The traditional compound which you buy in powder form to mix with water is the cheapest type, but, like ordinary plaster, is rather porous and needs to be painted over. Even so, the cost of coverage, including over-painting, is very reasonable. Ready-mixed types are rather more expensive but you don't normally need to paint over them, and some brands offer a reasonable range of colours.

The traditional powder type, thickly painted on a wall or ceiling, has a slow setting time, which makes it ideal for creating a decorative impression with a patterning tool. Ready-mixed products can also be given a textured finish in the same way as the powdery type, but doing so will tend to vary the thickness of the finish so that overpainting might be necessary. (If you just paint them on without carrying out any follow-up patterning treatment, you will be left with a random textured effect.) Some of the textured products suitable for exterior use can also be patterned with tools; check the manufacturer's instructions for guidance here.

Tools and equipment

Apart from the texture finish itself, and paint if you're going to overpaint, you will need a brush or roller to apply the finish. The most suitable type of brush is a 200mm (8in) distemper brush. The type of roller you use will affect the pattern created and special rollers are available to create certain effects (see step-by-step photographs). Sometimes you paint the material on first with an ordinary roller (or a brush) and then work it over with a patterning roller; follow the manufacturer's instructions for the type of roller you will need.

If you are dealing with a ceiling you will need some form of access equipment; two stepladders with a plank resting between them will usually suffice. Textured finishes, especially when applied with a roller tend to spray and spatter about, so it's best to have goggles and a mask to protect your eyes and mouth when you are looking up; also, don't forget to protect your hair. In addition, whether you're painting walls or ceiling, you'll need a dust sheet or some other form of protective covering for the floor.

You may also require a plumb bob and line (see *Ready Reference*) and any equipment required for filling cracks or joints such as a caulking tool, jointing tape knife, filling knife, filler and so on.

Where you intend to texture the surface after painting on the finish you will also need your patterning tool(s). These can be proprietary or home-made; you can even use equipment which was chiefly designed for other purposes which you may decide will create the pattern you want. Apart from patterning rollers, the proprietary tools available include combs (some of which can give special effects within the combed patterns such as 'rose' and 'flower'), stipple brushes and pads and special 'swirl' brushes. You can also buy a tool called a 'lacer' to dull any sharp ridges; however a plastic straight edge or the blade of a filling knife is a suitable alternative.

Preparing the surface

Textured finishes can be applied to bare or painted surfaces but the surface must be sound and, in some cases, treated. You should not, for example, think of textured finishes as a means of covering up walls which really need replastering or a ceiling which should be replaced.

All porous surfaces should first be treated

SEALING JOINTS

1 To seal a joint between boards, first use a caulking tool to apply cellulose filler (or a thicker mix of texture compound) along it.

2 Use a special taping knife to press a length of jointing tape into the filler so it's securely embedded and free of air bubbles.

3 Spread on another layer of filling material, again using the caulking tool, but this time so the filler covers the jointing tape.

4 Use a damp sponge to wipe away surplus filler and to feather the edges so the joint surface becomes flush with the plasterboard.

with a stabilising primer recommended by the manufacturer of the finish so that the setting of the texture material is not spoilt by suction. Surfaces requiring such treatment include brick, render, concrete, plaster and some types of wallboards.

Texture finishes can be used to hide very fine hairline cracks and are usually marketed for their flexible ability to cope with normal movement so cracks don't reopen. However, none of them can cover cracks or joints of more than 1.5mm (1/16in) with any guarantee that these will remain covered up. You will have to caulk the cracks or joints with texture compound (perhaps thickened with a little ordinary filler). Ideally, joints between boards of any kind should also have a layer of jointing tape over them between layers of whatever types of filler you are using (see step-by-step photographs). Make sure you feather the edges of the filling material so there is no noticeable ridge when the texture covers it.

Painted surfaces should be clean, sound and sanded lightly to provide a key for the finish. Distemper and low-quality emulsion paint may not hold the texture; test by pressing adhesive tape on a small area first and remove any painted surface that has a tendency to delaminate when the tape is peeled off. If the surface has been painted in a dark colour it's best to paint over it in a light colour first before you apply the texture.

You will have to remove wallpaper or light tiles such as polystyrene tiles. You can, however, safely apply a textured finish over ceramic tiles provided they are clean, the gaps are filled and they are primed with a coat of PVA adhesive, diluted according to the manufacturer's instructions.

Do check that lath-and-plaster ceilings are strong enough to support the extra weight of the textured coating. If they are

Ready Reference

PROPRIETARY TOOLS TO USE

You can buy various tools designed for patterning textured finishes. They include combs, patterned rollers, various types of brushes and a 'lacing' tool for smoothing high points.

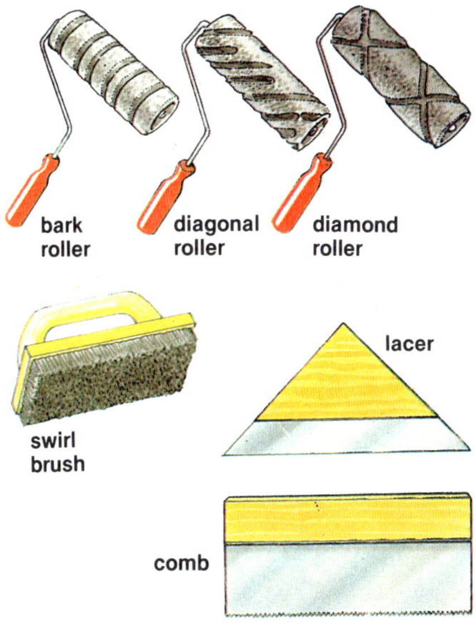

MAKE YOUR OWN COMB

You can make a comb with a wooden handle and a rigid plastic blade (cut, for example, from an old ice-cream carton). Cut your own designs out of the plastic.

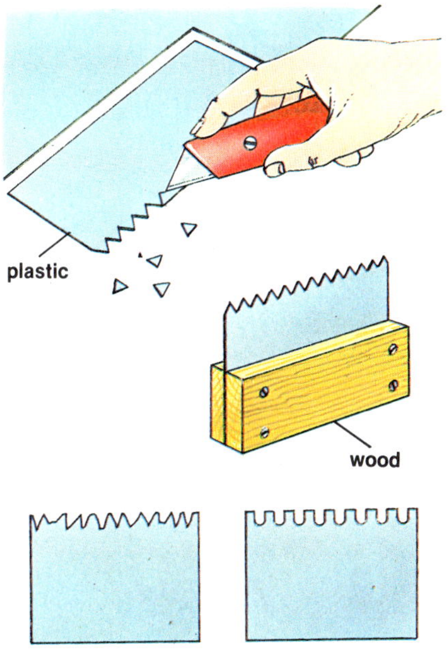

MAKING TEXTURED PATTERNS

Textured materials can be applied by brush or roller. If you are applying this type of finish to walls it's best, if possible, to work in an upwards direction to minimise the amount of material which gets sprayed over you and the floor. Apply the finish to the wall in bands and apply it thickly so the texture will stand out. You can roll it on with an ordinary foam roller (see left) which will give a stipple effect and then leave the surface to dry as it is. Alternatively, you may prefer to go ahead and use other tools to create other kinds of textured effects.

showing any signs of sagging, lift a floorboard in the room or loft above and check that the laths are still nailed firmly to the joists, and the plaster is well keyed to the laths.

Where there are fixing nails or screws which will be embedded in the texture material, you should paint them over with gloss paint to prevent them from rusting.

You will have to prime wood-faced wallboards if they are absorbent and it's best to treat wood-effect plastic boards with PVA adhesive in the same way as ceramic tiles. In the case of thin wallboards there is a risk that movement will cause the texture material to crack, so test them for flexibility and remove them if necessary.

Applying textured finishes

It's best to apply a textured finish thickly; remember you will only be applying one coat and the thicker the coat the more protection it will provide for the wall or ceiling surface. Also, if you intend using a patterning tool, working on a deep, even coat of texture will give the best results. Apply the finish in bands across the room until the entire wall or ceiling is covered.

Exterior textures are normally applied with a natural bristle brush, though on smooth surfaces where you want a coarser texture you can use a foam roller. Whenever possible, you should work in the shade. If you are painting near drainpipes, you should tape newspaper round the pipes to protect the area you wish to avoid painting. Similarly, use masking tape to protect window frames (outdoors and inside) and also window reveals, light fittings, ventilator grilles and so on. If it does get on any of the areas, wipe it off with a damp rag immediately

Using patterning tools

The drying time for textured finishes varies from 12 to 24 hours, though the working time for patterning can be much lower, depending on atmospheric conditions. You will normally have at least 4 hours to complete your patterning, but it would make sense to complete one wall or ceiling at a time as far as possible. If in doubt, study the manufacturer's instructions for the particular product you are using.

A random pattern will usually be quicker to achieve than a regular one where you will have to take care in matching up the pattern. In the latter case, it may be better to spread the texture on in strips and pattern each strip as you go rather than covering the whole wall or ceiling and then patterning it.

Finishing off

After patterning, it is normal practice to 'lace' the pattern (to dull any sharp ridges) just as the material begins to dry. Even after it has dried you may still need to remove sharp points; use the blade of a filling knife to knock them back, or, if you want to go to the trouble, wrap fine glasspaper round a sanding block and sand them down. If you don't remove sharp ridges and points, the surface may cut someone who leans against it or brittle parts may break off.

Textured finishes can usually be covered with either an emulsion or oil-based paint but check the manufacturer's recommendations.

Cleaning and maintenance

Most texture finishes are designed to last, which is just as well as it's a messy, time-consuming and difficult job to remove them. Maintenance will normally consist of re-decorating them with a coat of paint when they show signs of wear or hard-to-remove dirt or stains. Surfaces should be kept clean: to do so, apply warm soapy water with a paint brush to loosen dirt and dust.

3 *A specially designed, grooved 'bark' effect roller is being run over the textured material to produce a bark pattern on a wall surface.*

6 *This diamond pattern was formed by a purpose-designed roller. With a regular pattern like this you should check that the pattern rows match.*

1 *A straightforward and at the same time striking effect can be produced by running a purpose-designed diagonal roller up and down across the surface.*

2 *A wide variety of tools, proprietary or otherwise, can be used to form patterns on texture materials; here a coarse nylon mitt produced a swirled effect.*

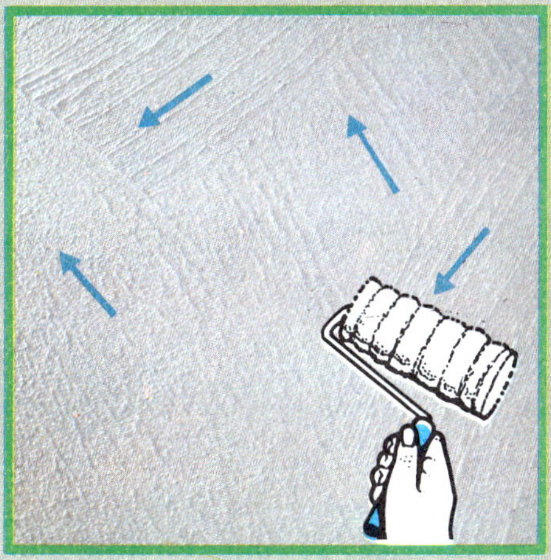

4 *Here a 'bark' effect roller was again used but this time in a random sweeping motion to create a curved criss-cross variation of the basic pattern.*

5 *The fine stipple effect (left) was made using an ordinary foam roller; the coarser stipple (right) by dabbing with a sponge wrapped in plastic.*

7 *Another design: the background pattern was produced by running a 'bark' roller over the surface; a sponge was then used to make circles on this.*

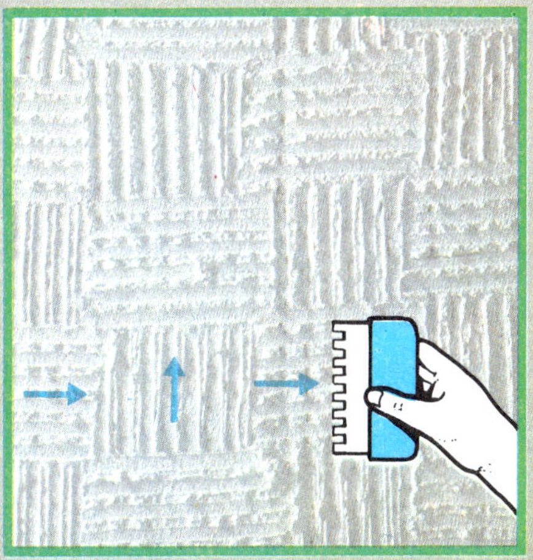

8 *This criss-cross pattern of alternate facing 'squares' could be created using a comb but here a serrated scraper was used instead.*

Ready Reference

TYPES OF FINISH

There are various types of textured finishes available. They include:

- the traditional type, which is a powder compound, generally available only in white, which you mix with water; it needs to be painted afterwards
- textured 'paints', which are ready-mixed products containing similar light aggregates and binders to the traditional type but also plasticised like modern paints; they come in a range of colours and usually don't have to be painted over (though you can if you wish)
- textured paints and coverings suitable for exterior use.

HOW FAR WILL THEY GO?

Powder compounds will cover about 2.5sq m per kg (12sq ft per lb) of unmixed powder and are available in 5, 10, 12½ and 25kg bags. Ready-mix materials will cover 2 to 2.5sq m (22 to 27sq ft) per litre and are supplied in 5, 10 and 12½ litre tubs.

BEWARE ASBESTOS

Traditional compound powder textures sometimes contain asbestos (check the manufacturer's instructions); such types should be mixed in well-ventilated conditions to protect you against a potential health risk.

THE RIGHT TEMPERATURE

Texture finishes can be affected by extremes in temperature so:

- don't apply ready-mix products to a ceiling which incorporates a heating system
- don't carry out application when the temperature is below 5°C or above 40°C or when the temperature is likely to exceed these limits before the material is dry.

You can apply a traditional compound type of texture over 'hot' surfaces such as heated ceilings and chimney breasts, but you should first seal the surface with a good quality alkali-resisting primer.

Don't apply either type in freezing conditions.

CREATING REGULAR PATTERNS

If you are creating a regular pattern which requires matching, use a plumb bob and line to mark guidelines on the walls (or to snap chalked lines on the ceiling); paint and pattern in bands between the straight lines.

TIP: REMOVE MASKING QUICKLY

If you have used tape or newspaper to protect window frames, pipes or fittings, remove it before the texture dries; it may be difficult to remove later when the texture has set.

STRIPPING WOOD

Wood has a natural beauty, but it's often a beauty concealed by layers and layers of paint. Doors, window frames, even skirting boards and architraves can all become attractive features in themselves when stripped back to reveal the wood. Even if you prefer to repaint, using the right techniques to strip off the old will give the best possible surface on which to work.

Stripping wood of old paint or layers of ancient varnish isn't the easiest of jobs. It's usually only done because you're after a natural finish, or because the painted surface has degenerated to such an extent that further coats of paint simply can't produce a smooth finish. Either way, once wood has been stripped back to its natural state, it then has to be sealed again – to protect it from moisture which can cause cracking, warping and ultimately decay. Both varnishes and paints act as sealants, giving a durable finish. But which one you choose might depend on the wood itself – and you won't know what that's like until you've stripped it. If you're unsure of its quality, it's advisable to strip a test area first.

Some of the timber used in houses is of a grade that was never intended for a clear finish – large ugly knots, cracks, splits or even an unattractive grain are some of the signs. In cases like this it is probably better to treat the problems (eg, applying 'knotting' – a special liquid sealer – to make the knots tight and prevent them 'bleeding', filling cracks and splits to give a flush surface) and then paint to seal.

If you are set on having the wood on show and don't want to paint it – because it wouldn't fit in with a colour scheme or make the feature you want – you can give it a better appearance and extra protection with stain or coloured varnish.

Stripping with abrasives

For dry stripping there are several different kinds of powered sanders available, all of which use abrasive papers of some kind to strip the surface off wood. On large areas such as floors it is best to use a purpose-made power sander which you can hire. A drill with a sanding attachment, however, is useful for getting small areas smooth after paint has been removed by other methods.

One such attachment is a 'disc sander' and is quite tricky to use effectively without scoring the wood surface. Hold it at a slight angle to the wood and present only half the disc to the surface. Work in short bursts and keep the disc moving over the surface – if it stays too long in one place it can damage the wood.

A 'drum sander' attachment has a belt of abrasive paper stuck round the edge of a cylinder of foam, and if used along the grain only is rather easier to handle than a disc

USING SCRAPERS

1 *A triangular shavehook needs two hands when paint is thick. Hold the blade at an angle to the wood so it doesn't cause gouges.*

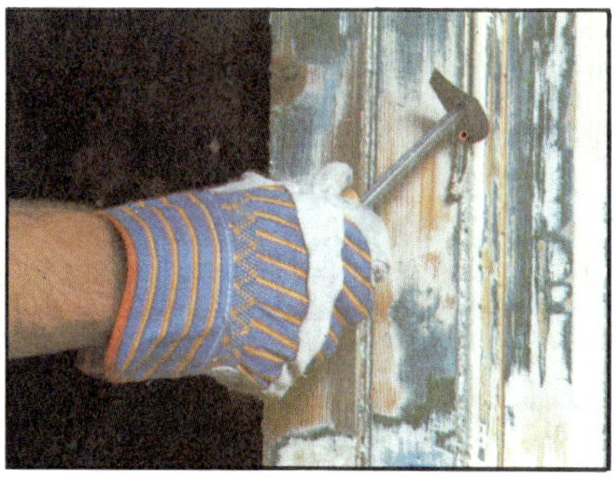

2 *A combination shavehook has round, straight and pointed edges to help remove paint and varnish from mouldings round windows and doors.*

3 *A special hook scraper has a sharp replaceable blade suitable both for scraping paint off flat surfaces and for getting into awkward crevices.*

sander. Whichever type is chosen, a fine grade abrasive should be used for finishing stripped wood.

Orbital sanders (which are also known as finishing sanders) usually come as self-powered tools – although attachments are available for some drills. These have a much milder action and as long as the spread of wood isn't interrupted by mouldings they smooth well and are useful for rubbing down between coats. These sanders are rectangular and should be moved over the surface in line with the grain. Make sure you choose the right type of sander, depending on the work in hand.

For sanding by hand – hard work, but much better for finishing – there are many grades of glasspaper from the coarse to the very fine. On flat surfaces it's best to wrap the paper round a small block of wood. As an alternative to glasspaper, there's also steel wool, which is most useful when you're trying to smooth down an intricate moulding. Always sand backwards and forwards *with the grain of the wood,* not across it. Scratches across the grain will always be highlighted by a clear finish. To remove remaining bits of paint use medium grade glasspaper; for finishing, a fine grade is better. Renew the glasspaper frequently as the paint will clog the surface, although a useful tip is to try cleaning clogged paper with a wire brush. It'll work once or twice, but after that the abrasive surface is usually lost. Alternatively pull the sheet backwards and forwards, abrasive side uppermost, over a table edge to dislodge paint particles.

A useful tool for cleaning paint from corners and mouldings is a hand scraper with replaceable blades. These 'hook' scrapers are also used for 'smoothing' and often need two-hands – they slightly raise the surface of a clear run of wood, giving an attractive finish under a clear seal. Use with the grain.

Heat stripping

Heat stripping is the quickest way to remove paint or varnish, but it needs a lot of expertise if you are to avoid charring the wood. So it is best reserved for stripping out of doors where a less-than-perfect surface will be less noticeable. A gas blow-torch is used along with metal scrapers to lift the finish off the wood while it's still warm. Blow-torches with gas canister attachments are light to use and a flame spreader nozzle makes the job easier (it can be bought separately).

Where there's no glass, it's a two-handed operation. Light the blow-torch and hold it a

HEAT STRIPPING

1 *Play the blow-torch onto the paint and when it begins to bubble, start to scrape. Protect floor and sills with a sheet of non-flammable material.*

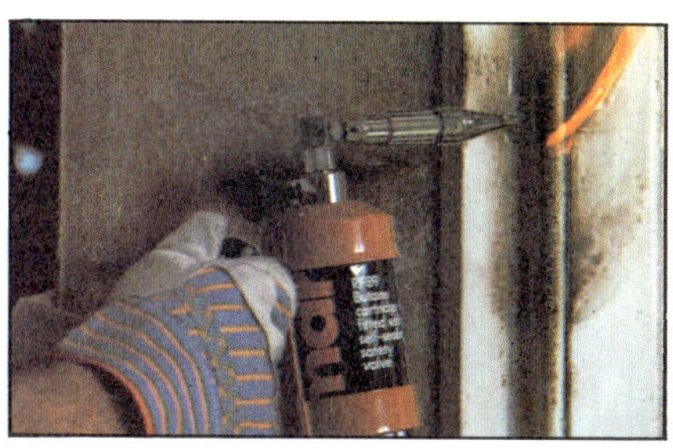

2 *When stripping paint near windows one hand must hold protection for glass. When paint hardens again, return the flame to the area.*

3 *Working overhead can be tricky if using a blow-torch. Protect your hands with gloves, your eyes with safety goggles and cover surfaces below.*

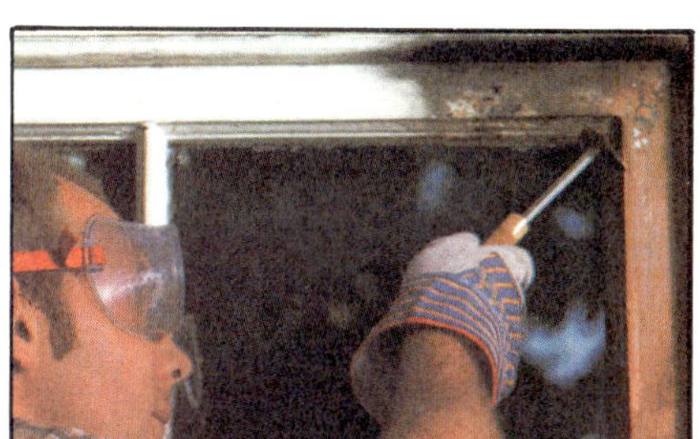

4 *To strip paint overhead, remove torch (be careful where it points), blow out flames and scrape quickly. As the paint loses heat it hardens.*

Ready Reference

WHICH TOOLS?

Wide bladed scraper: useful for scraping off large areas of old paint loosened with a blow-torch or chemical strippers.

Triangular shavehook: useful for both flat surfaces and crevices. Take care not to gouge surface of wood.

Combination shavehook: because it has both straight and rounded blades, as well as a point, this is the most versatile scraper for awkward areas.

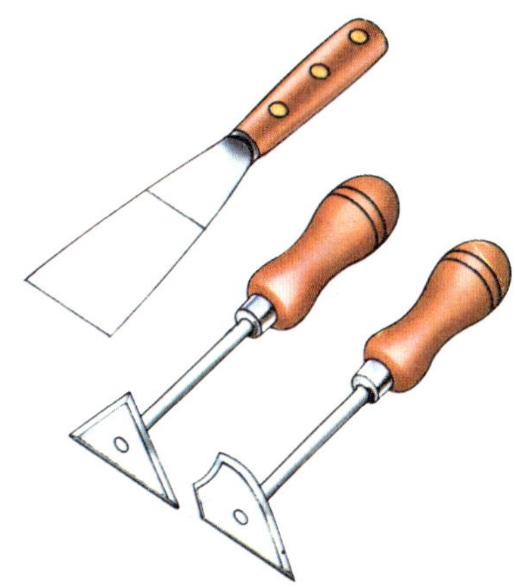

Steel wool: especially useful for tricky corners. Use medium grade (no 2) wool, and keep turning it inside out so all the cutting surfaces of the steel are used.

TIP: PICK THE RIGHT ABRASIVE

- Silicon carbide abrasive papers are less likely to clog up than glasspaper. They can also be used wet or dry.

DIFFICULT SURFACES

Where old paintwork is very thick, stripping may require repeated efforts.

- with a blow-torch, heat the paint until it bubbles up and scrape off as much as possible before softening and scraping the next layer
- when the wood is exposed and only stubborn bits of paint remain, use chemical stripper or sand by hand
- with chemical strippers, allow the first application to bubble up and then stipple on fresh stripper with a brush – working it well into the unstripped surface – before scraping off. If necessary repeat until the wood is fairly clean
- to remove stubborn bits, use wire wool and a small dab of stripper.

little way from the surface. Move it back and forth, going nearer and withdrawing, till the paint starts to wrinkle and blister. Now begin to scrape – be careful where you point the flame at this stage or you may damage other surfaces. As soon as the paint is hard to move return the flame to the area. Wear gloves to save your hands from being burnt by the falling paint, and cover areas below where you are working with a sheet of non-flammable material to catch the scrapings. In awkward areas, especially overhead, you should wear protective goggles for safety's sake.

Chemical stripping
Chemical strippers are probably the easiest way to strip wood. Available in liquid, gel and paste forms, their methods of application and removal vary, so always remember to read the manufacturer's instructions before you begin. Though all of them will remove paint and varnish, if you are dealing with a large area of wood they can work out to be very expensive – they're also very messy.

Liquid and gel strippers, decanted if necessary into a more convenient-sized container (read the instructions as to whether it can be heavy gauge plastic or should be glass or metal), are stippled onto the surface with a brush and left till the paint bubbles before scraping. Usually these strippers will work through only 1 layer of paint at a time so several applications can be necessary. If stripping a chair or table, stand the legs in old paint cans or jam jars so that any stripper which runs down the legs can be recycled. Artists brushes rather than paint brushes are useful when applying these strippers to mouldings or beading in windows and No 2 steel wool is useful for removing it.

After liquids or gels have been used, the surface must be cleaned down with white spirit or water (it depends on the stripper used) to remove any trace of chemical and must be left till completely dry before any stain or seal is applied.

Pastes are mostly water soluble and manufacturers stress important conditions for using them safely (eg, not in direct sun, in well ventilated rooms, the wearing of protective gloves, etc). Bought in tubs ready-mixed or in powder form to be made up, they are spread in thick (3-6mm) layers over the wood which must then be covered with strips of polythene (good way of using up plastic carrier bags) or a special 'blanket' (supplied with the tub) which adheres – when you press it – to the paste. They have to be left for between 2 and 8 hours after which the paste can be scrubbed off (with a firm brush) or washed down. Frequent changes of water are needed; follow manufacturer's advice about additives (eg, vinegar). Pastes are particularly effective with extraordinarily stubborn paint or varnish in very awkward places (eg, windows, bannisters etc); or where using a scraper might damage old wood. Some pastes are unsuitable for certain types of wood and can stain it – so read instructions carefully. Washing down should not be done, for example, with valuable furniture for this can raise the grain of the wood.

Bleaching
If the wood is discoloured once stripped (either from the stripper used or from some other source) you can try and achieve an overall colour with bleach – the household type, used diluted 1:3 with water to begin with and more concentrated if necessary, or better still a proprietary wood bleach.

Clean the surface of the stripped wood with paint thinner and steel wool and leave for 15 minutes to dry. Cover areas you don't want bleached with polythene, then brush bleach on generously. Work it into the wood *with the grain* using medium steel wool.

Leave for 2-4 minutes, then wipe off with rags. Leave to dry (up to 5 hours) before sanding after which you can finish the surface as desired.

CHEMICAL STRIPPING

1 *Liquid strippers are stippled onto wood with a brush. First pour the liquid into a smaller container — but remember it will dissolve light plastic.*

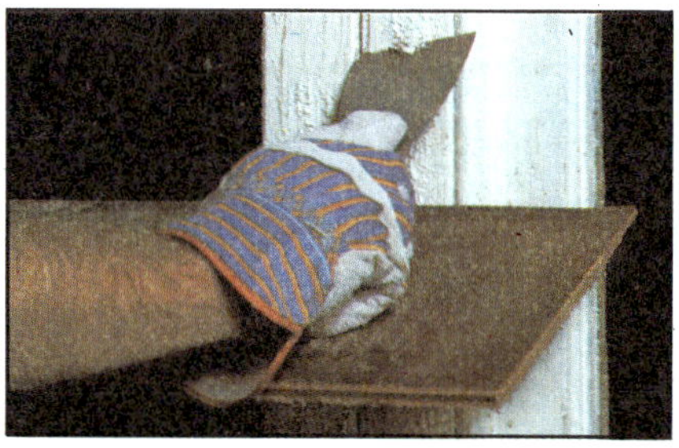

2 *When paint is bubbling use a scraper to remove it. Work upwards and be careful not to gouge the wood with the blade.*

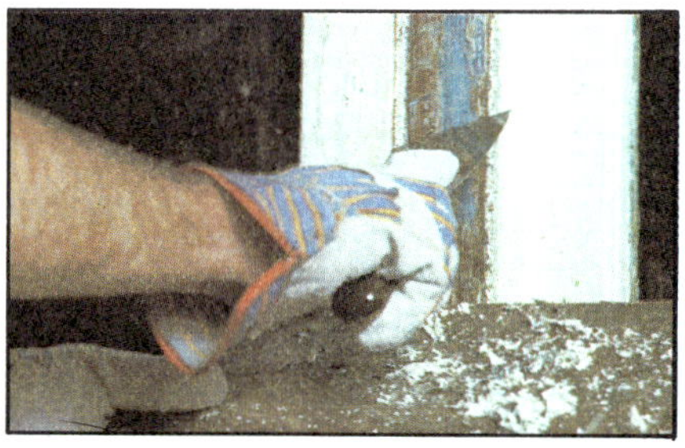

3 *Several applications of liquid may be needed as chemicals often only eat through one layer at a time. Use gloves to protect your hands.*

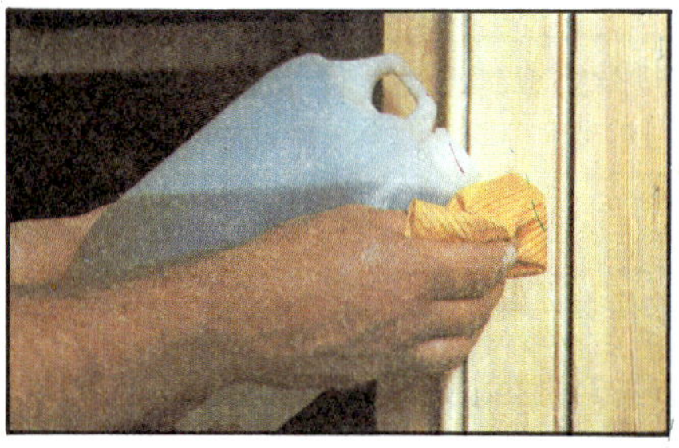

4 *After all paint has been stripped off, wipe the wood down with white spirit or water so that the chemicals are neutralised.*

5 *A good way to deal with mouldings is to apply a thick layer of stripping paste. This needs to be covered while it works, but is very effective.*

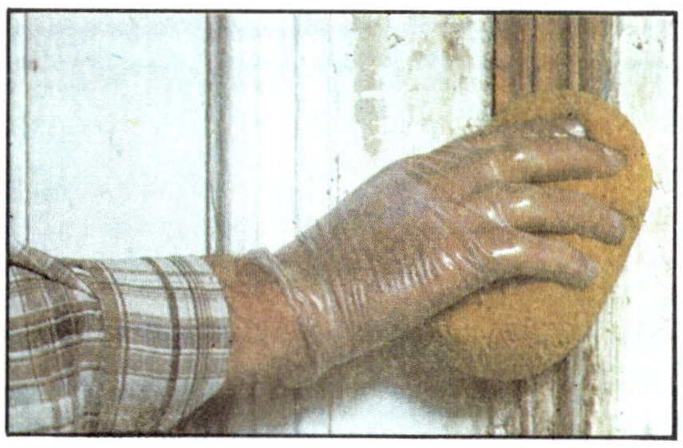

6 *After leaving for the specified time (can be several hours) wash the paste off with sponge or a scrubbing brush, changing the water often.*

COLOURING WOOD

On a plank of freshly planed wood the colours of different stains highlight the grain attractively (results will differ according to the age and condition of the wood). Stains don't seal and so they need a finishing coat of clear varnish — either gloss, satin or matt.

There are several different ways of altering the look of stripped wood.

● *Wood stains* are based on water, white spirit, alcohol, lacquer thinner or oil. Named after the wood whose colour they resemble, these penetrate the wood permanently. To give an even staining, the trick is to apply several thin coats — work from top to bottom on vertical surfaces to prevent drips and overlap marks. Use a pad (not a brush) made with cotton wool wrapped in a lint-free cloth and work backwards and forwards along the grain. When completely dry, seal with a clear varnish that is compatible with the stain. If applying more than one sealing coat, rub down the surface each time with fine glasspaper.

● *Coloured varnishes* both seal and 'stain' the wood surface and are removeable. They are also named after natural timber and are applied like ordinary clear varnish to sanded-smooth wood. You just go on applying the coats till you get the colour you want — rubbing down between each. Varnishes are oil (interior and exterior grades), spirit (not suitable for outdoors) or polyurethane based. Polyurethane varnishes can also be non-wood colours (such as red and green) and are especially useful if you want inexpensive wooden furniture to fit in with a colour scheme.

When using varnishes remember:

○ Never use a cellulose filler for it will always remain as a white mark. Choose a wood filler of similar colour to the stripped wood.

○ They have to be applied to perfectly smooth surfaces with all dust, grit and paint particles removed — wipe down with white spirit first, then leave to dry.

○ Don't attempt to apply them in dusty or windy conditions — the merest speck will spoil the finish and to be truly effective, stripped and sealed wood has to be beautifully smooth to the touch. A spray will give a more even finish than a brush.

● *Stained oils* both colour and seal. They are particularly suited to wood exposed to the elements (eg, outside doors and window sills) or wood that isn't in very good condition. Choose from a range of natural timber colours and apply several coats to give the wood 'depth'.

Ready Reference

WHAT TO USE WHERE

For large flat areas such as flush doors and skirting boards, use a
- blow-torch for speedy stripping if you're going to repaint it
- powered sander if you're going to varnish.

For **intricate mouldings** and **awkward areas** such as staircases, panelled doors and window frames, use
- a blow-torch and a shavehook if you're repainting
- chemical strippers if varnishing (remember they're relatively expensive).

For **fine finishing** use
- glasspaper and sanding block or an orbital (powered) sander.

Caustic soda

This is used for 'immersion' stripping of doors and other fairly durable pieces of furniture. If you have a suitable old galvanised iron tub or water tank, remember to put the water in first then add the crystals. BUT remember that
- caustic soda is a powerful chemical: handle with care
- immersion stripping can loosen old joints and peel off veneers
- you must wash down the wood with water after stripping
- you'll have to finish the wood with glasspaper or a powered sander.

DOS AND DON'TS

- DO leave a freshly lit blow-torch to stand for a few minutes or it may flare dangerously when moved
- DO wear gloves if you're using a blow torch OR chemical strippers
- DO wash splashes of chemical strippers off your skin immediately
- DON'T use a blow-torch to strip wood you intend to varnish – scorch marks are almost impossible to avoid
- DON'T work in a very confined space with chemical strippers.

STAINING AND VARNISHING WOOD

If you want to decorate and protect the woodwork around your home without obliterating its grain pattern with paint, wood stains and varnishes offer a wide choice of finishes. Here's how to get the best results.

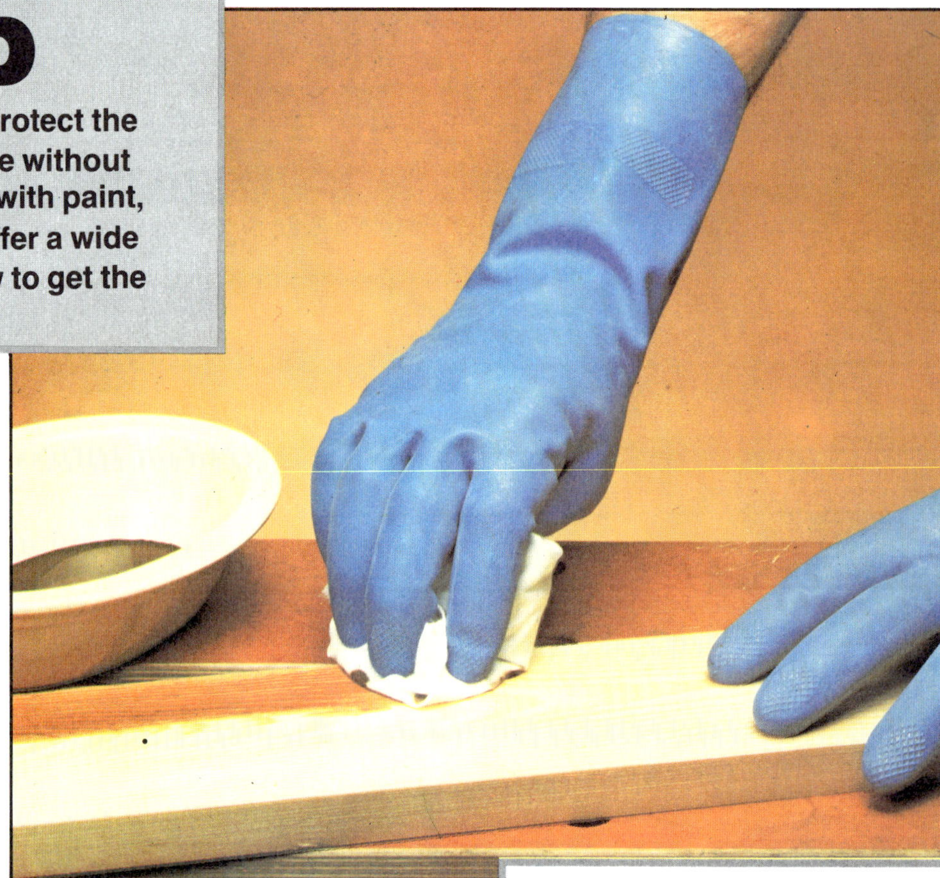

When it comes to giving wood a clear finish, you can choose from a variety of traditional and modern materials, including oils, wax, French polish and different types of varnish. Some are suitable for exterior use, others for interior use only. The degree of skill you need to apply them varies; some are quite simple to use, whereas others, like French polish, require special techniques acquired only by patient practice. The type of wood may affect your choice of finish; for example, open-textured woods like teak, iroko and afrormosia are best treated with an oil finish – they don't take varnishes well.

You may decide to change the colour of the wood before you finish it. You can use a varnish which incorporates a colour or apply a wood stain and then coat the wood with clear varnish or another clear finish.

If you don't wish to change the colour of the wood, but want to restore it to its natural colour – for example, where the wood has been slightly darkened by the action of a paint stripper – you can use a proprietary colour restorer.

Types of varnish and stains

Clear varnishes are like paint without the pigment. They contain a resin carried in a drying oil or spirit and it is the resin which gives a hard protective finish to wood. Traditionally, the resins used were like copal, natural and obtained from various tropical trees, but in modern varnishes they are synthetic, for example alkyd or polyurethane.

While other varnishes are available, by far the easiest to obtain and most widely used are those containing polyurethane resin. Polyurethane varnish is available in gloss, satin or matt finishes and for interior or exterior use. A non-drip variety is particularly suitable for vertical surfaces, ceilings and hard-to-get-at areas.

There are polyurethane varnishes which have added pigments and are known as coloured sealers. It's quicker to use one of these rather than to apply a wood-stain followed by a clear finish but you won't get the same depth of colour, and if the coloured varnish chips in use, timber of a different colour will show through.

Wood stains are colouring pigments suspended in water, oil or spirits. Some come ready-mixed; others in powder form to be mixed up. Oil-based stains tend to be more difficult to obtain and are not as widely used as the other two types.

Preparing the surface

Before staining, bleaching, varnishing or using other types of finish you should ensure that the surface is clean, dry, smooth and free from any old paint or varnish.

To smooth down a flat surface you can use glasspaper wrapped around a sanding block. On small curves and fiddly bits wrap small strips of abrasive round a pencil. For larger curves use a sanding glove which you can make yourself (see *Ready Reference*).

A powered sander is a boon on large surfaces; use an orbital sander rather than the disc type which is tricky to use without causing scratches across the grain.

Besides getting rid of shallow scratches, sanding will also get rid of cigarette burns and similar marks on the wood surface. However, make sure you don't sand for too long in one place or you will leave a depression that will show up after finishing.

Large cracks and dents can be filled with wax (from a crayon of a suitable colour, for instance) or with a proprietary wood

Ready Reference

KNOW YOUR STAINS

- water-based stains penetrate the wood more deeply than other types and are therefore suitable for use on wood which will be subject to hard wear
- oil stains are easier to apply without blotching than water-based ones and, since they dry quite slowly, any overlaps are less likely to show
- spirit stains are available in a wide range of colours. They dry quickly so you have to work at speed; but this also means you can apply the varnish sooner
- don't use a polyurethane varnish over oil stains or a chemical reaction will spoil the finish.

CHECKING COMPATIBILITY

Always check that the stain and finish you intend using are compatible. Buying both from the same manufacturer should ensure this. If you are in any doubt, stain and varnish a small test area first.

filler. But since stains don't hide fillers in the same way as paint would, you may decide not to carry out such treatment and to leave the blemishes for an authentic 'old wood' look. If you do decide to use a filler, don't try to smooth it flat as you apply it with the knife or you'll risk spreading it round – it tends to show up in the nearby grain if it is rubbed in when wet.

Finally, you should make sure the surface is dust-free by wiping it with a clean, dry cloth or a fine brush. It's a good idea, too, to wipe it with a cloth soaked in turpentine to remove any greasy fingermarks you may have left while preparing the surface.

Bleaching wood

One of the snags with staining wood is that you cannot make the surface lighter; you can only make it darker. A light-coloured stain on a darkish piece of wood just won't work. The way round this problem is to bleach the wood before you start sealing it – and for this proprietary wood bleaches are available at most hardware stores.

Some bleaches are applied in one stage and others in two stages. The wood is washed with a neutralizing agent afterwards so the bleach doesn't carry on working when the finish is applied. Follow the manufacturer's instructions when applying the bleach, particularly concerning the time you should allow for each stage of the treatment. Usually, bleach is applied with a sponge or brush; make sure you use a white fibre brush or the dye in the brush may come out onto the wood.

Staining wood

You can apply the stain with a brush or a folded lint-free rag. Aim to get the colour you want in one coat; a second coat can be applied if needed to get a darker finish, but too many coats will result in the stain lying on the surface, lengthening the time it takes for the subsequent coat of varnish to dry and even preventing it from bonding properly to the surface. With water-based types, if overlaps show when the first coat dries you can add about 20 per cent more water to a mixed-up solution of stain and apply a second coat over the whole surface, brushing it out well.

After the stain has dried (usually about 24 hours after application), you should rub the surface thoroughly with a dry cloth to remove excess stain.

Filling the grain

It's not necessary to fill the grain of softwoods, but for a good finish on open-grained hardwoods like oak, mahogany and walnut you will have to apply a grain filler

BLEACHING WOOD

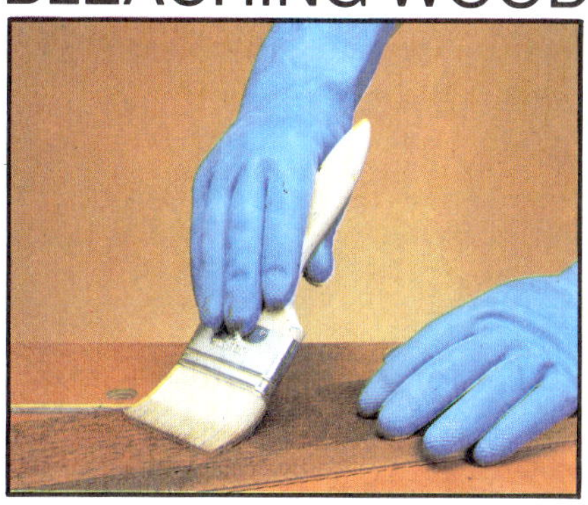

1 *In a two-stage bleaching process, apply the first solution liberally and leave it to work for the recommended time – usually 10 to 20 minutes.*

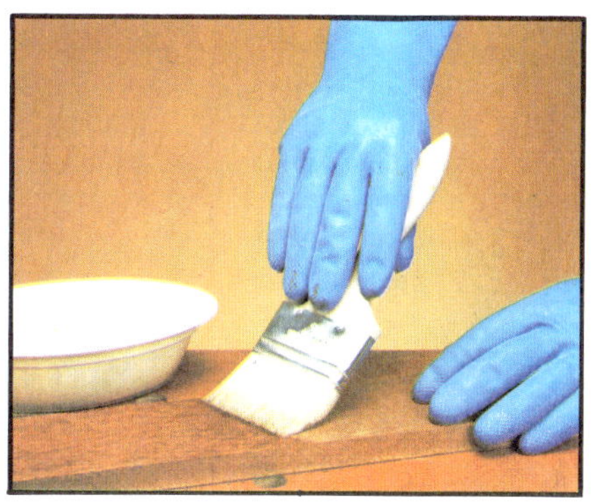

2 *Brush on the second solution, leaving it to work. If the wood is very dark or stained, reapply both solutions. If a crust forms, wipe it off with a damp rag.*

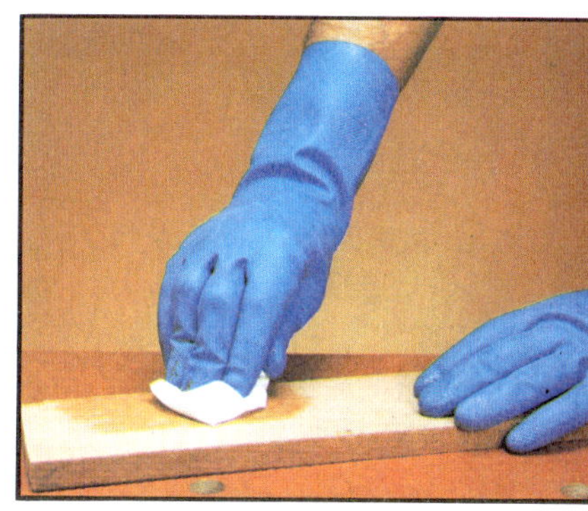

3 *Wash the wood with a solution of acetic acid (white vinegar) and water to neutralise the bleach. Allow it to dry completely before staining it.*

STAINING WOOD

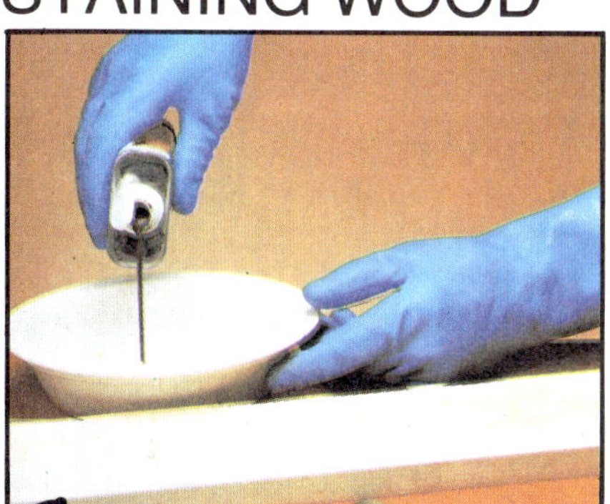

1 *Shake the can well and then pour the stain into a dish wide enough for you to dip in a cloth pad. Avoid plastic dishes; some stains may attack them.*

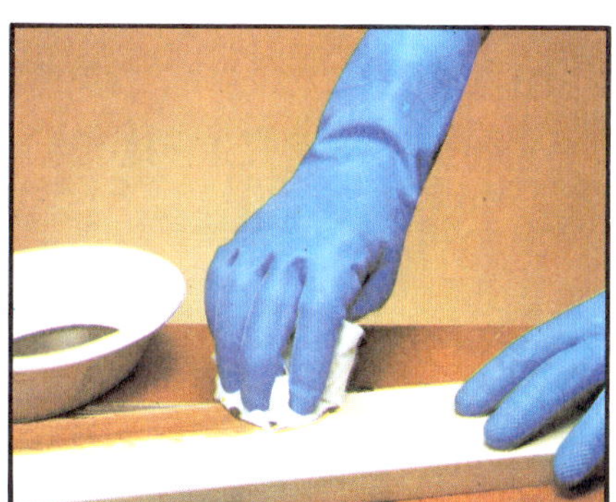

2 *Apply the stain liberally using a cloth pad. If you apply it too sparingly you run the risk of getting light and dark areas instead of even coverage.*

TIP

3 *For greater grain contrast, wipe over each strip with a rag after allowing a minute or so for penetration. Leave to dry for 24 hours before varnishing.*

VARNISHING WOOD

1 *After you've made sure the surface is clean and dry, use a clean cloth pad to apply the first coat. Rub it well into the wood along the grain.*

2 *Leave the first coat to dry and then brush on the next coat. Make sure the brush is really clean, with no paint particles or loose bristles to mar the finish.*

3 *When brushing, it is important to work with the grain and brush out fully. On a narrow surface like a shelf upright, first apply the varnish in one stroke.*

4 *Then work the brush out towards the edges of the upright, working first to one edge and then to the other, using gentle but firm strokes.*

5 *To complete coating the upright, again move the brush in one upward stroke. This technique will ensure that there are no ugly 'runs' at the edges.*

6 *Leave each coat to dry for the recommended time (approx 12 hours) before re-coating. Rub down between coats with flour-grade glass paper.*

to the wood surface before using varnish.

There are various proprietary fillers available in either a paste or liquid form; choose one to match the wood or stain you are using. Follow the manufacturer's instructions for applying it; normally, you work the filler over the wood with a brush or cloth, wipe off the excess and then sand the surface lightly down with fine glasspaper.

Varnishing wood

Polyurethane varnish is easy to apply; you simply brush it on, taking care to work with the grain of the wood. Follow the manufacturer's instructions as to the number of coats you should apply and the time allowed between each coat – at least 12 hours. You should sand down the surface lightly with flour-grade glasspaper between coats to provide a key for the next coat, and remove any dust that's accumulated during application with a damp cloth.

As with paints, it's advisable to stir the contents of any can of varnish that's been stored for a while. This ensures an even distribution of the solvents so that the varnish dries evenly when it is applied. Although the varnish will be touch-dry in about 4 hours, it may take as long as 7 days before the surface reaches full hardness – so avoid standing anything on the newly-decorated surface for a week or so.

Ready Reference

SAFETY FIRST

Varnishes, bleaches and stains can be flammable. Always work in a ventilated area away from the naked flames and don't smoke when applying them.

PROTECT YOUR SKIN

Bleach can burn skin and clothing so you should wear rubber gloves and an apron or old clothes when applying it.

AVOID SCRATCHES

When sanding take care not to leave scratches on the wood which will be highlighted by the finish. Always work in the direction of the grain, not across it, and finish off with the finest grade of glasspaper. If you are using power tools, never press too hard.

MAKING A SANDING GLOVE

For sanding large curves, staple two ends of a sheet of glasspaper together so it forms a 'glove' when you put your hand through the middle.

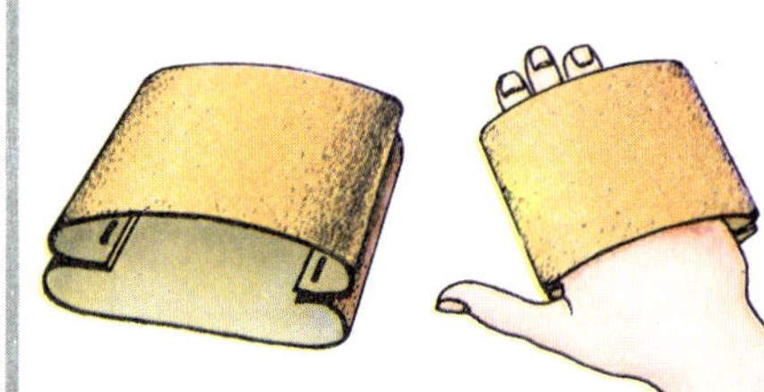

TIP: HOW TO REMOVE STAINS

Place a damp cloth over the dent, then apply a warm iron on top of the cloth so the wood swells up and fills out the hollow.

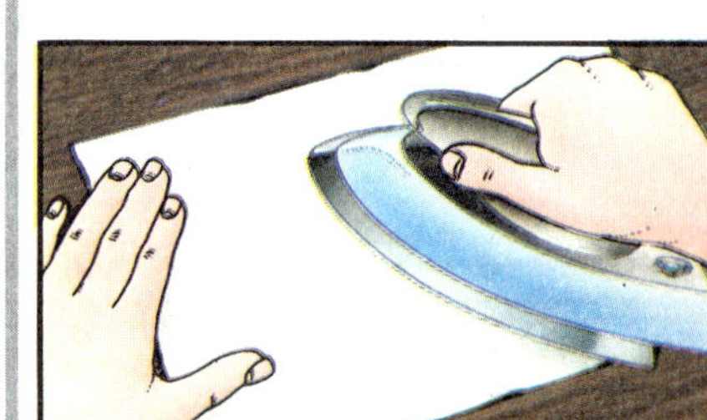

WORKING WITH VENEERS

- never use a bleach on a wood veneer; the bleach has to be washed off and water can loosen the veneer and cause it to swell
- take special care when sanding a veneer; it's easy to go right through it, especially at the edges, and expose the timber underneath. Such damage is very difficult to repair.

PAINTING WOOD

Painting is the most popular way of decorating and protecting much of the wood in our homes. As with so many do-it-yourself jobs, getting a good finish depends on your skill. Here's how to paint wood perfectly.

Wood is used extensively in every part of our homes — from roof trusses to skirting boards. Structural timber is usually left rough and unfinished, while joinery — windows, doors, staircases, architraves and so on — is usually decorated in some way. Wood has just one drawback; as a natural material it's prone to deterioration and even decay unless it's protected. Painting wood is one way of combining decoration and protection, and the popularity of paint is a testimony to its effectiveness. Properly applied and well looked after, it gives wood a highly attractive appearance and also provides excellent protection against dampness, dirt, mould, insect attack, and general wear and tear.

Of course, paint isn't the only finish you can choose for wood. If its colour and grain pattern are worth displaying, you can use

PREPARING WOOD FOR PAINT

1 *Before you can apply the paint you must fill any cracks or holes with wood filler (applied with a filling knife) and leave to dry.*

2 *Sand down the filled areas using medium-grade glasspaper. Wrap the abrasive around a sanding block or wood offcut so it's easier to use.*

3 *Where paint has been chipped off, sand down the area and apply an ordinary wood primer to the bare wood using a small paintbrush.*

4 *When the surface of the wood is smooth, apply undercoat (as the maker recommends) and leave to dry before you put on the top coat.*

Ready Reference

PAINT TYPES

Paints for wood can be:

- **solvent-based gloss** (the 'oil' paints of the days before the advent of synthetic resins), which can be used indoors or outdoors
- **solvent-based satin** (also called eggshell or silk), intended for indoor use.

Both are fairly slow-drying, have a strong smell and have to be cleaned from equipment with white spirit, paraffin (kerosene) or proprietary solvent.

- **water-based satin and gloss** (emulsions) don't give a finish as hardwearing as that of a solvent-based paint but are quicker drying and have less smell. Clean equipment with hot or cold water and soap or washing-up liquid.

Non-drip paints (thixotropic or jelly paints, as they're also known) are available in both solvent-based and emulsion forms.

PREPARING PAINT

1 *Remove the lid from the paint can using the edge of a knife as a lever – don't use a screwdriver or you'll damage the lip of the lid.*

2 *Stir the paint (if recommended by the maker) using an offcut of wood, with a turning, lifting motion, or use an electric drill attachment.*

3 *Decant some paint into a paint kettle, which you'll find easier to carry than a heavy can. Top up the kettle from the can as you work.*

4 *To load the brush, dip the bristles into the paint to one-third of their length and wipe off excess on a string tied across the kettle rim.*

oils, stains or varnishes to enhance the overall effect and protect the surface. But as most of the wood used in our houses is chosen more for performance and price rather than looks, bland and uninteresting softwoods are generally the order of the day for everything from windows and door frames to staircases, skirting boards and door architraves. And painting them offers a number of distinct advantages.

Firstly, paint covers a multitude of sins — knots and other blemishes in the wood surface, poorly-made joints patched up with filler, dents and scratches caused by the rough and tumble of everyday life — and does it in almost every colour of the spectrum. Secondly, paint provides a surface that's hard-wearing and easy to keep clean — an important point for many interior surfaces in the home. And thirdly, paint is easy to apply ... and to keep on applying. In fact, redecorating existing paintwork accounts for the greater part of all paint bought.

What woods can be painted?

In theory you can paint any wood under the sun. In practice, paint (solvent-based or emulsion, see *Ready Reference*), is usually applied only to softwoods — spruce (whitewood), European redwood (deal), pine and the like — and to man-made boards such as plywood, blockboard, hardboard and chipboard. Hardwoods and boards finished with hardwood veneers can be painted, but are usually given a clear or tinted finish to enhance their attractive colour and grain pattern.

Paint systems

If you're decorating new wood, there's more to it than putting on a coat of your chosen paint. It would just soak in where the wood was porous and give a very uneven colour — certainly without the smooth gloss finish expected. It wouldn't stick to the wood very well, nor would it form the continuous surface film needed for full protection. All in all, not very satisfactory. So what is needed is a paint system which consists of built-up layers, each one designed to serve a particular purpose.

The first in the system is a primer (sometimes called a primer/sealer) which stops the paint soaking into porous areas and provides a good key between the bare wood and the paint film. Next, you want another 'layer' — the undercoat — to help build up the paint film and at the same time to obliterate the colour of the primer, so that the top coat which you apply last of all is perfectly smooth and uniform in colour. With some paints — emulsions and non-drip glosses — an undercoat is not always used and instead several coats of primer or two top coats are applied with the same result.

The general rule to obey when choosing primer, undercoat and top coat is to stick with the same base types in one paint system, particularly out of doors and on surfaces subjected to heavy wear and tear (staircases and skirting boards, for example). On other indoor woodwork you can combine primers and top coats of different types.

If the wood you are painting has been treated with a preservative to prevent decay (likely only on exterior woodwork) an ordinary primer won't take well. Instead use an aluminium wood primer — not to be confused with aluminium paint — which is recommended for use on all hardwoods too. Oily woods such as teak must be degreased with white spirit and allowed to dry before the primer is applied.

As far as man-made boards are concerned, chipboard is best primed with a solvent-based wood primer to seal its comparatively porous surface. Hardboard is even more porous, and here a stabilising primer (a product more usually used on absorbent or powdery masonry surfaces) is the best product to use. Plywood and blockboard should be primed as for softwood. There's one other

HOW TO APPLY PAIN

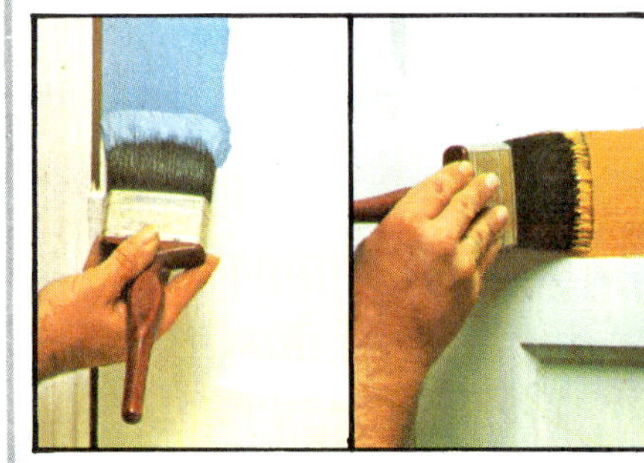

1 *Apply the paint along the grain; with non-drip paint (left) you can apply a thicker coat in one go without further spreading (brushing out).*

4 *Now you must 'lay off' the paint with very light brush strokes along the grain to give a smooth finish that's free from brush marks.*

2 *Still working with the grain and without reloading the brush, paint another strip alongside the first one and blend the two together.*

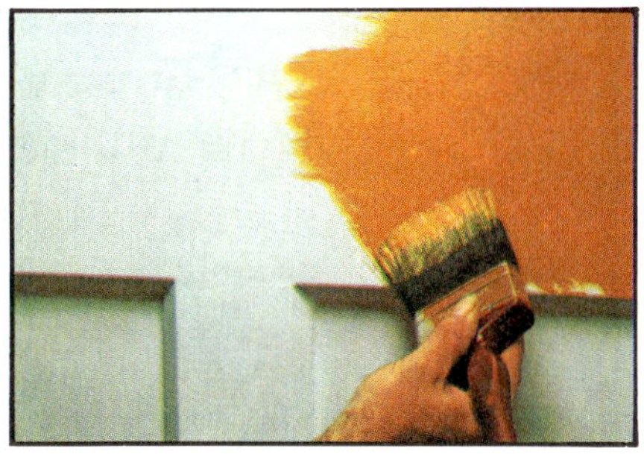

3 *Reload the brush and apply strokes back and forth across the grain over the area you've just painted to ensure full, even coverage.*

5 *Paint an area adjoining the first in the same way, blending the two sections together by about 50mm (2in) and laying off as before.*

6 *Brush towards edges, not parallel with them or onto them, as the paint will be scraped onto the adjacent face, forming a ridge.*

WHAT CAN GO WRONG WITH PAINT

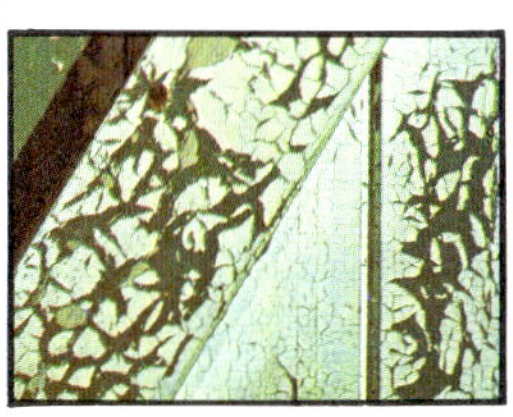

Left: Lifting and flaking occurs if paint is applied over a surface that is damp or powdery.

Right: Crazing is caused when paint is applied over a previous coat that was not completely dry.

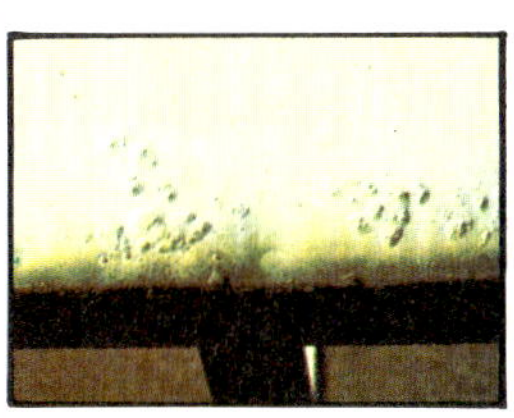

Left: Blistering.occurs when damp or resin is trapped beneath the paint film and is drawn out by heat.

Right: Cratering results from rain or condensation droplets falling onto the wet paint surface.

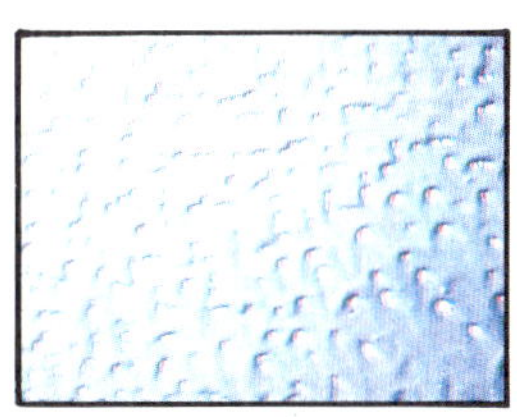

Left: Running, sagging or 'curtaining' happens when paint is applied too thickly on vertical surfaces.

Right: Wrinkling or shrivelling can occur on horizontal surfaces if paint is applied too thickly.

Ready Reference

HOW MUCH PAINT?

Large areas – in all cases coverage per litre depends on the wood's porosity and the painter's technique:
Wood primer 9-15 sq metres (95-160 sq ft)
Aluminium primer 16 sq metres (170 sq ft)
Primer/undercoat 11 sq metres (120 sq ft)
Undercoat 11 sq metres (120 sq ft)
Runny gloss or satin 17 sq metres (180 sq ft)
Non-drip gloss or satin 13 sq metres (140 sq ft)
Runny emulsions 15 sq metres (160 sq ft)
Non-drip emulsions 12 sq metres (130 sq ft)

Small areas – add up all the lengths of wood to be painted. One sq metre is equivalent to:

- 16m (52 ft) of glazing bars
- 10-13m (33-43 ft) of window frame
- 6m (20 ft) of sill
- 10m (33 ft) of narrow skirting
- 3-6m (10-20 ft) of deep skirting

CHOOSING BRUSHES

The best brushes have a generous filling of long bristles and are an even, tapered shape. Cheaper brushes have short, thin bristles and big wooden filler strips to pack them out. The ideal sizes for wood are:

- 25mm (1in) or 50mm (2in) for panel doors, skirtings
- 50mm (2in) or 75mm (3in) for flush doors, skirting, large areas
- 25mm (1in) cutting-in brush for window glazing bars
- 12mm (½in), 25mm (1in) or cheap paintbox brush for spot priming, applying knotting

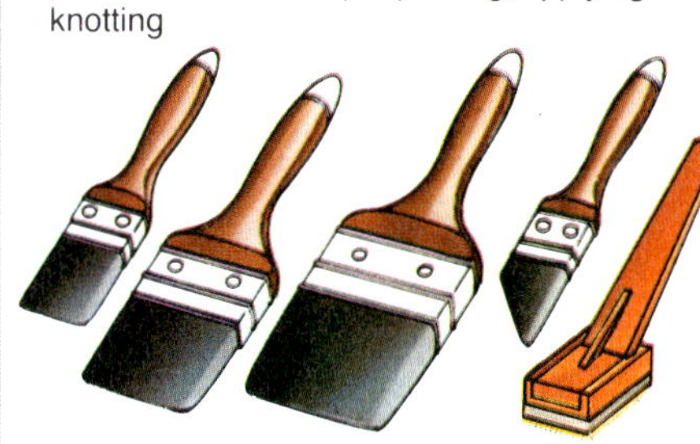

Alternative to brushes
Paint pads are more widely used on walls than on woodwork, but the crevice or sash paint pad will do the same job as a cutting-in brush. It should be cleaned with white spirit or hot water and washing-up liquid (paint solvents might dissolve the adhesive between the mohair pile and foam).

TIP: PREPARING A BRUSH

Before using a new (or stored) brush work the bristles against the palm of your hand to remove dust and loose hairs.

thing you need to know. If the wood you want to paint has knots in it you should brush a special sealer called knotting over them to stop the resin oozing up through the paint film and spoiling its looks. If the knots are 'live' — exuding sticky yellowish resin — use a blow-torch to draw out the resin and scrape it off before applying knotting.

Paint on paint

You'll often want to paint wood that has already been painted. How you tackle this depends on the state of the existing paintwork. If it's flaking off and is in generally poor condition, you will have to remove the entire paint system — primer, undercoat and top coat — by burning off with a blow-torch, applying a chemical paint stripper or rubbing with an abrasive. You then treat the stripped wood as already described for new wood.

Where the paintwork is in good condition, you simply have to clean it and sand it down lightly to provide a key for the new paint and to remove any small bits that got stuck in the surface when it was last painted. Then you can apply fresh top coat over the surface; the paint system is already there. You may, of course, need two top coats if you add a light colour to a dark one to stop the colour beneath from showing through.

If the paintwork is basically sound but needs localised attention, you can scrape or sand these damaged areas back to bare wood and 'spot-treat' them with primer and undercoat to bring the patch up to the level of the surrounding paintwork, ready for a final top coat over the entire surface.

Painting large areas

Though the same principle applies to wood as it does to any other large surface area — ie, you divide it into manageable sections and complete one before moving on to another — if you're using an oil-based gloss paint you have to make sure that the completed area hasn't dried to such an extent that you cannot blend in the new. On the rare occasion that you might want to paint a whole wall of wood you should make the section no wider than a couple of brush widths and work from ceiling to floor.

With emulsions there isn't the same problem for although they are quick drying the nature of the paint is such that brush marks don't show.

You might think that a wide brush is the best for a large area but the constant flexing action of the wrist in moving the brush up and down will tire you out fast. Holding a brush is an art in itself and aches are the first indication that you're doing it wrongly. A thin brush should be held by the handle like a pencil, while a wider brush should be held with the fingers and thumb gripping the brush just above the bristles.

You'll find a variety of paint brushes on sale — some are designed to be 'throwaway' (good if you only have one or two jobs to do), others will stand you in good stead for years. But remember before using a new brush to brush the bristles back and forth against the palm of your hand — this is called 'flirting' and will dislodge any dust or loose hairs that could spoil your paintwork.

It is wise to decant the paint to save you moving a heavy can from place to place — a paint kettle which resembles a small bucket is made for the purpose. Plastic ones are easier to keep clean than metal ones.

Never be tempted to dip the bristles too far into the paint and always scrape off excess from both sides. Paint has the habit of building up inside the brush and if this happens on overhead work, you risk it running down the handle and onto your arm.

Painting small areas

These tend to be the fiddly woodwork on windows, around doors and lengths of stairs or skirting boards — and the hardest bit about all of them is working out how much paint you'll need (see *Ready Reference*).

Special shaped or narrow brushes can make painting these areas easier — for example, they prevent you 'straddling' angles in wood (like you find on mouldings) which damages the bristles in the middle of the brush. With windows and panelled doors you should also follow an order of working to

ORDER OF PAINTING

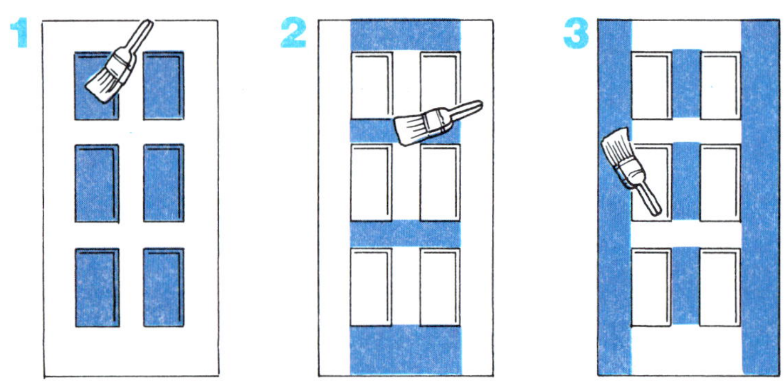

Panel doors: *tackle any mouldings first, then the recessed panels, horizontal members, vertical members and lastly the edges.*

Casement windows: *start with any glazing bars, then paint the opening casement itself (the hinge edge is the only one which should match the inside); lastly paint the frame.*

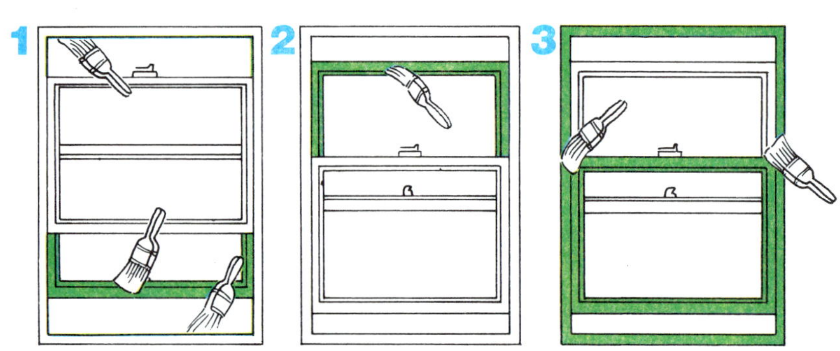

Sash windows: *paint the inside top and bottom and a little way up and down the sides of the frame first. Then paint the bottom of the outer sash. Move the sashes and do the rest of the outer sash, the inner sash and finally the frame.*

avoid causing overlap marks on the parts you've already painted.

Fiddly or not, they are the jobs you have to do first if you are putting up wallcoverings (if you're painting a room, the walls should be done before the woodwork) so that the drops can be placed against finished edges. If you want to touch up the paint without changing the wallpaper, it's best to use a paint shield.

Getting ready to paint

Ideally, before painting doors and windows you should remove all the 'furniture' — handles, fingerplates, keyholes, hooks etc — so you can move the brush freely without interruption. You should also take time to read the manufacturer's instructions on the can. If, for example, they tell you to stir the paint, then stir it for this is the only way of distributing the particles which have settled.

If you open a can of non-drip paint and find a layer of solvent on the top, you should stir it in, then leave it to become jelly-like again before painting.

All your brushes should be dry — this is something to remember if you are painting over several days and have put them to soak overnight in white spirit or a proprietary brush cleaner. If you don't get rid of all the traces of the liquid it will mess up your paintwork. They should be rinsed, then brushed on newspaper till the strokes leave no sign.

Cleaning up

When you've finished painting clean your brushes thoroughly, concentrating on the roots where paint accumulates and will harden. They should be hung up, bristles down, till dry, then wrapped in aluminium foil for storage. Don't ever store them damp for they can be ruined by mildew.

If there's only a small amount of paint left, you can either decant it for storage into a dark glass screw-topped jar so you can use it to touch up damaged spots — it's important to choose a suitable sized jar so there's very little air space. Air and dust are both potential paint spoilers and there are two ways to keep them out if you're storing the can. Either put a circle of aluminium foil over the paint surface before putting the lid on securely, or — and this is the best way if the lid is distorted — put on the lid and then invert the can to spread the paint round the inner rim to form an airtight seal. Set it back the right way for storage.

If despite these safeguards a skin forms on the paint (usually over months of storage) you have to cut round the edge of it with a sharp knife and carefully lift it off.

PAINTING WINDOWS

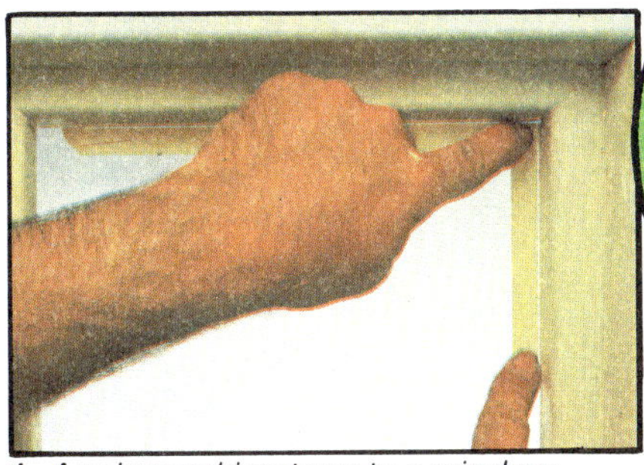

1 Apply masking tape to a window pane to prevent paint getting onto the glass – leave 3mm (1/8in) of glass exposed so the paint forms a seal.

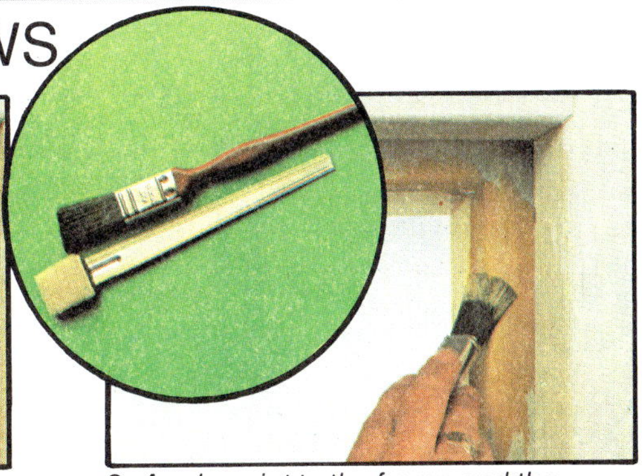

2 Apply paint to the frame and the glazing bars using a small brush, or (inset) a cutting-in brush or a sash paint pad.

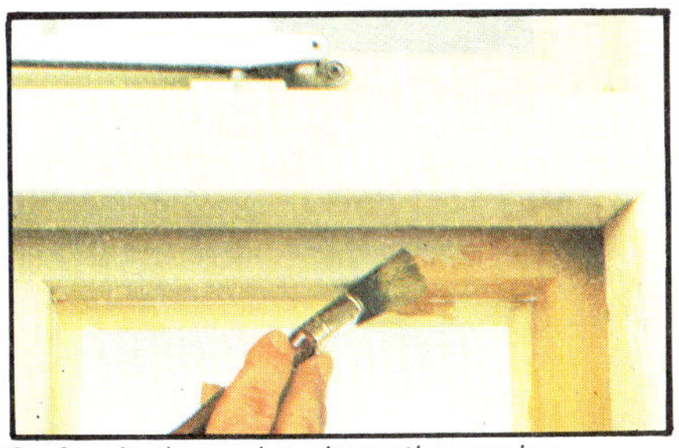

3 Apply the paint along the grain; remove the tape when the paint is almost dry – if it dries completely you might peel it off with the tape.

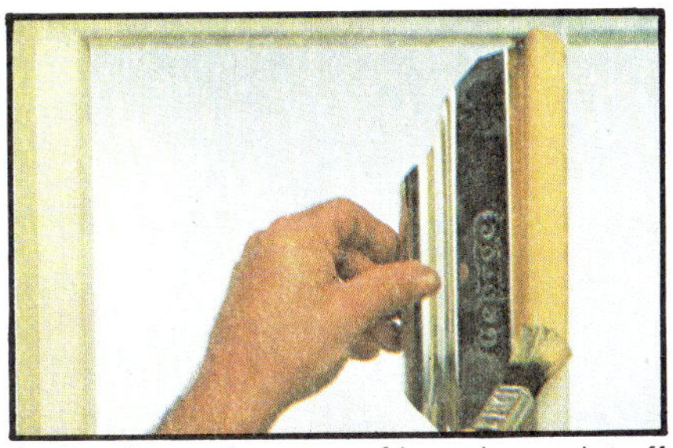

4 An alternative way of keeping paint off the glass is to use a paint shield or offcut of plywood but, again, leave a paint margin on the glass.

Ready Reference

PRIMING WOOD

Primers can be solvent- or water-based. Outdoors, use the former (plus a solvent-based undercoat); indoors, you can use either, but water-based primer dries more quickly. If in any doubt as to which primer goes with which undercoat, consult your local supplier.

Other primers include:

- stabilising primer, for hardboard which is very porous
- wood primer, for wood that's been treated with a preservative, and for hardwoods.

TIP: STRAINING PAINT

Paint that has been stored badly can become bitty, and should be strained into a paint kettle before use. Secure nylon stocking over the kettle rim with string or an elastic band, and pour the paint through into the kettle.

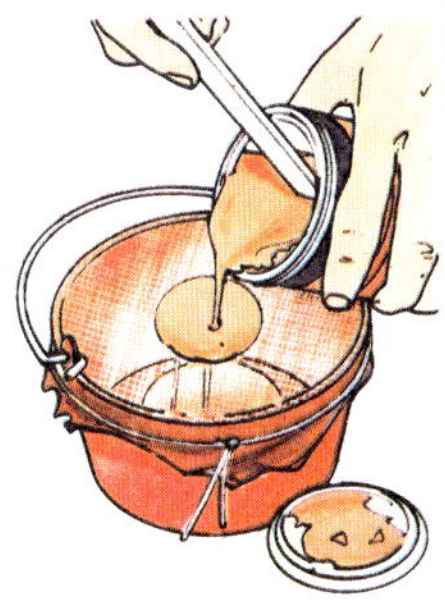

CLEANING BRUSHES

To ensure the long life of brushes:

- remove excess paint from the bristles with the back of a knife
- wash out solvent-based paint in white spirit followed by soapy, then clean water – the soap restores flexibility and softens the brush
- wash out non-drip paint in a hot water/washing-up liquid solution then rinse in clean cold water
- hang up brushes, bristles down, to dry (drill a hole in the handle to take a nail)
- at the end of a job a build-up of paint can be difficult to remove; soak the brush in a proprietary brush cleaner
- if leaving brushes overnight before continuing a paint job, suspend them in a jam-jar containing white spirit (drill a hole near the ferrule to take a nail) but remove all traces of spirit next day

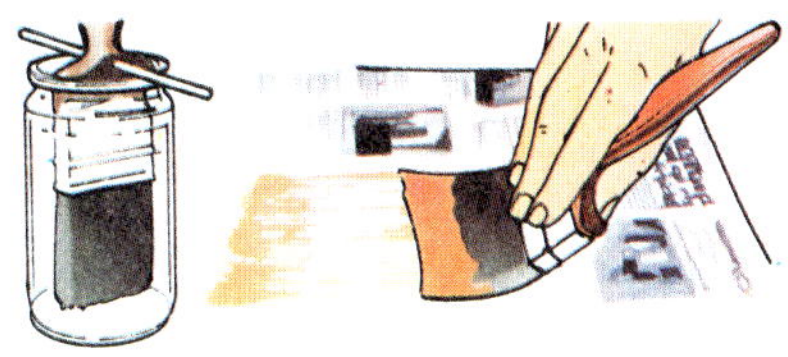

TIP: STORING BRUSHES

During a short break wrap brushes in plastic cling-film to keep air off and the paint in the brush wet.

EXTERIOR DECORATING

Painting the outside of your house can seem more of a chore than a pleasure, simply because of the size of the job. By breaking it down into separate, manageable areas and using time-saving tools and techniques, you can keep the weather at bay and complete the task more quickly than ever before.

EXTERIOR PAINTING 1: the basics

The main reason for decorating the outside of your house is to protect it from the elements. But paint can also transform the appearance of your house and increase its value, so it's a job worth doing well.

The outside of your house is under continuous attack from rain, frost, heat and light from the sun, dirt and pollution. Properly applied paint or varnish is the best way of protecting the fabric of the house, and it should last for about five or six years before it needs renewing. If the outside hasn't been touched for several years it's probably looking rather shabby by now and you should start to think about repainting.

Modern paints come in a very wide range of colours and are very easy to apply. A little time spent preparing and painting your house now can transform a drab old building into a desirable residence; and increase the value of the house with very little outlay.

The main parts of the house that have to be painted are the woodwork, metalwork, and possibly the walls. Plastic gutters and pipes do not need to be painted. It's up to you whether you paint the walls or not. Brick, pebbledash, stone and rendering can all be left in their natural state, but if the walls are in need of repair or are porous, stained and dirty, a good coat of paint will both protect the surface and brighten up the house.

The first thing to do is to take a long, critical look at your house to assess what needs to be done. Search for any defects that may affect the final paintwork. A common fault on older houses is leaking gutters. These can leave unsightly stains on the wall or cause woodwork to rot. They can be easily sealed or even completely replaced with new gutters. Other common faults are flaking and peeling paint, rotten window sills and cracked rendering. The illustrations on the next page show many different defects that need repairing. It's unlikely you'll find all of these faults on one house, but you'll probably find a few. It is very important that you remedy every fault you find before you begin to paint or the paint won't be able to do its job and your house will only deteriorate further. This preparation will usually be the most time consuming part of the decoration and will often be quite hard work. But it has to be done if you want your new paintwork to last. Details on how to prepare each different type of surface – wood, metal, brick, render etc – will appear in a later article.

When to paint

Outside painting should only be done in dry weather and after at least two days without rain, fog or frost. The ideal time is late summer when the wood has had a good time to dry out and the weather is usually quite settled. Even a small amount of moisture trapped under a new paint film will vaporise, causing blisters and peeling. For the same reason you should wait an hour after sunrise to let the dew dry out, and stop work an hour before sunset. On the other hand, don't paint under the full glare of a hot sun as this will dry out the surface too quickly, leaving relatively soft paint underneath which may cause wrinkling as it dries in turn. The ideal practice is to follow the sun, and only paint when it has dried one part of the house and passed on to another. Unfortunately this advice is often difficult to follow in practice as some walls may never see the sun, so you'll have to look for the best compromise.

What to paint first

There is a logical sequence of painting which holds for nearly all houses. In general it's best to start at the top and do larger areas before smaller ones. So if you're going to paint the whole of your house try to follow this order: do the fascia boards and barge boards first, followed by the gutters. The rendering (if any) comes next, then the windows and doors and finally the downpipes. The reason for doing it in this order is that splashes of paint dropped onto a wall beneath a fascia or gutter, even if wiped off immediately, will leave a mark; but subsequent painting of the wall will cover them up. Also, since windows and doors are smaller in area than the rendering, it will be easier to 'cut in' (that is, leave a finer edge) when painting them, so giving a much neater finish.

You will need to follow this sequence three times in all, first to do the preparation, then to apply primers or under coats, and finally to paint on the top coat. If this sounds like far too much work to do all at once there's no reason why you shouldn't split it up and do just a part each year. You could, for instance, do the walls this year, the woodwork next year and the gutters and downpipes the year after. It may even be better to do it this way, spread over several years, as you'll be more aware of the condition of the paintwork and will be able to touch up bits and make small repairs as you go along, when the first signs of wear show. (But remember that this will restrict you to using the same colour as you have at present. It's going to look odd if you change the colour only gradually.)

COMMON SURFACE DEFECTS

Before painting your house, give it a thorough going over to find out where any faults and defects may lie. You're certainly not likely to find all the faults shown here, but the drawings do point out the problem areas. All faults must be put right before you start to paint, otherwise you are likely to achieve a poor result and will waste much time and money in the effort.

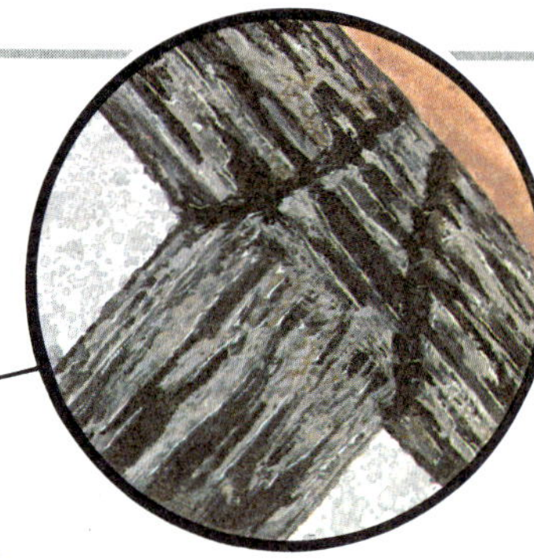

Decorative woodwork like this, as well as fascias and barge boards, are very exposed. Scrape off loose paint and fill holes.

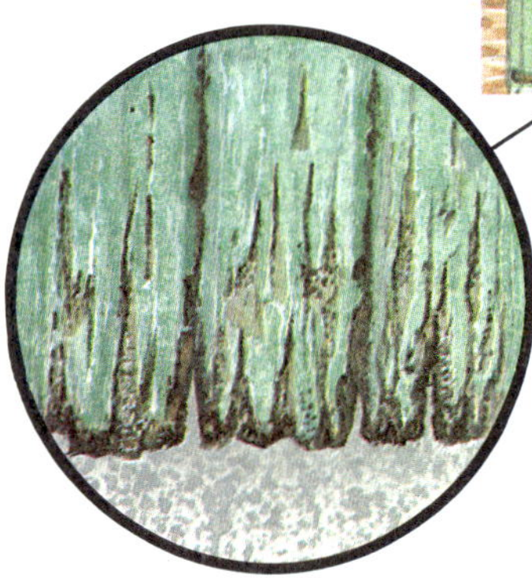

The bottom edge of a garage door may start to rot and break up. You'll have to replace it with new pieces or a whole new rail.

Small holes in asbestos or iron roofs can be repaired, but extensive damage may mean replacing parts of the roof.

Over the years, rendering can crack and come loose. Clean and fill all holes and sterilise mould and algae growth.

Old flashing can crack and tiles can come loose, letting damp inside. Renew flashing and replace tiles.

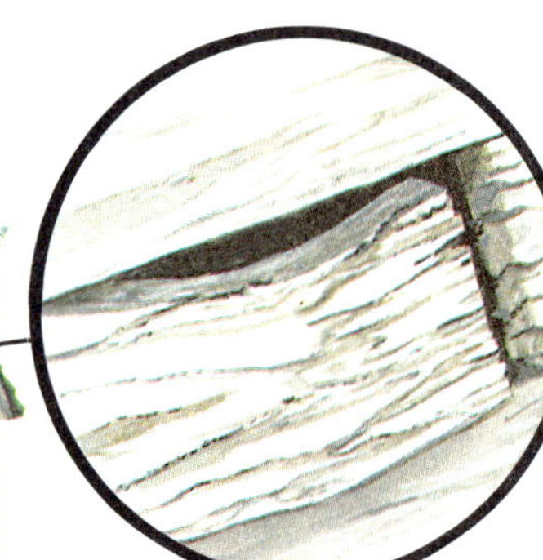

Weatherboards are sometimes painted only on the surface and if rain gets in they will warp and rot, and paint will flake off.

Any cracks and blisters in paint will let in water, and metal will start to rust. All rust must be removed and the metal primed.

TESTING A PAINTED SURFACE

1 *Try this easy way of testing your paint surface to see if it's suitable for repainting. First, score a double cross in the paint with a sharp knife.*

2 *Stick a piece of adhesive tape over the length of the cross cuts and press it down firmly. Then pull the tape away from the surface slowly.*

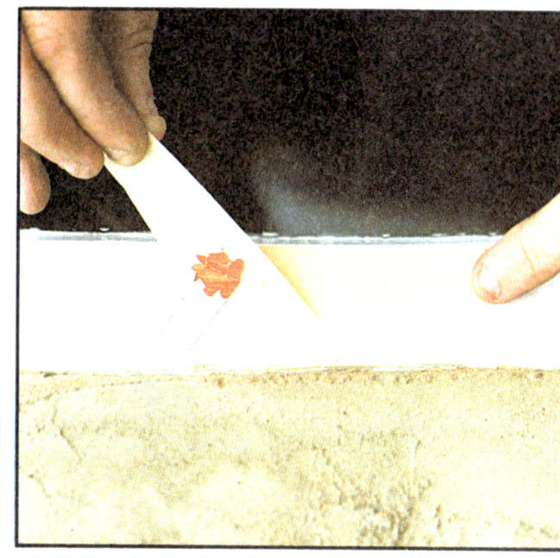

3 *If the tape is clean, the paint surface is sound and safe for painting. If flakes of paint are pulled off you must strip off the old paint first.*

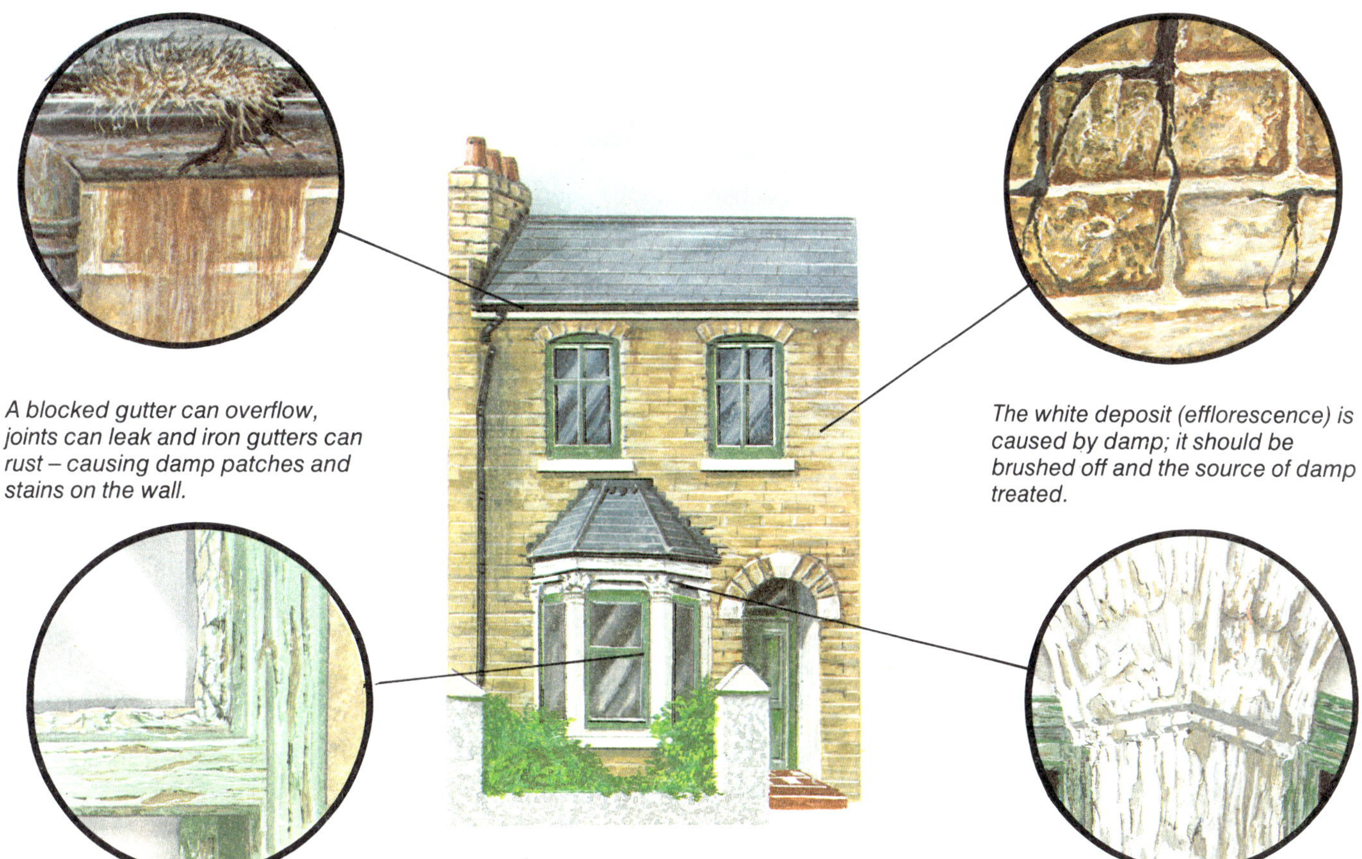

A blocked gutter can overflow, joints can leak and iron gutters can rust – causing damp patches and stains on the wall.

The white deposit (efflorescence) is caused by damp; it should be brushed off and the source of damp treated.

Old, dry putty can fall out and must be replaced; knots should be stripped and treated; rotten wood must be cut out and holes filled.

Flaking paint on render should be scraped off and the render brushed down. Fill holes and, if the surface is powdery, apply a stabiliser.

WORKING SAFELY AT HEIGHT

Ladders are an easy and convenient way of reaching heights, but since most domestic accidents involve ladders, it's worth taking time to secure them safely.

Always lean the ladder at a safe angle so that for every 4m of height, the base is 1m from the wall. Always tie it securely at the top or bottom to stop it slipping, and overlap an extension ladder by at least three rungs.

You'll need a roof ladder if you want to paint or repair the chimney or the dividing wall between two roofs. If your house has overhanging eaves, use a ladder stay to hold the ladder away from the wall.

Right: if you have a wide clear area round your house a tower platform is the safest way of getting up high. Make sure it stands perfectly level.

Left: often the gap between two houses is too narrow to put up a ladder at the correct angle. The only answer is to use a special narrow tower.

Special brackets fit on a pair of ladders to provide a long working platform which is useful for reaching the area over a bay window. A third ladder is needed to gain access to the platform.

Tower platforms can be assembled in a cantilevered structure to bridge an outbuilding or a bay window. Protect the roof with sacking and blocks of wood, or use sandbags if the roof is very steep.

Working in safety

To paint the outside of your house in comfort and safety you need the right tools and equipment. There's nothing worse than balancing dangerously on a makeshift working platform with a paint pot in one hand, trying to reach into an awkward corner with the other. But as long as you follow a few simple rules you should be able to work easily and safely. Always work from a step-ladder or an extension ladder and make sure it stands on a firm and level surface. If the ground is uneven, push wedges under a board until the board is level then stand the ladder on this. You'll have to put down a board on soft ground too. If you're working on grass there's a danger of the board slipping, so drive in two stakes on either side of the ladder and rope the ladder to these. On a slippery surface put down some canvas or sacking, and put a board on soft ground. Don't use plastic sheeting as a dust sheet, because the ladder could slip on it.

If you're working high up it's best to tie the ladder to something solid at the top. Don't tie it to the gutter or downpipe as these are not designed to take the extra weight and wouldn't support a ladder if it started to slip. The best way is to fix big screw eyes into sound woodwork such as a window sill, fascia or barge boards and tie the ladder to these. Or, if convenient, you can tie the ladder to the centre mullion of an open window. If there's no sound woodwork, it's advisable to drill and plug the wall to take the screw eyes. Fix them at intervals of about 2m (6ft) and leave them in place when you've finished so they're ready the next time you have to decorate.

Be sure to position the ladder square against the wall so it won't wobble, and lean it at the correct safe angle of 4 to 1, that is, for every 4m of height the bottom should be 1m out from the wall.

When you're working on a ladder don't lean out too far as it's all too easy to loose your balance. Never work from the very top of a step ladder as you'll have nothing to hold on to. A paint kettle, to hold your paint, is an essential piece of equipment as you can hook it on to a rung of the ladder, leaving both hands free.

A safer alternative to a ladder or step-ladder is a tower platform which you can hire from most hire shops. The tower comes as a set of interlocking sections which you build up to the required height; you then lay boards across to provide the platform. A handrail fits around the top and there is plenty of room for tools and paint. The towers can be extended over bay windows or round chimneys so you can reach all parts of the house in safety. If you have a wide, flat area around your house, choose a tower with locking castors so you can move it along more easily. Always lock the castors before using the tower, and always climb up on the inside, NEVER on the outside.

THE TOOLS YOU'LL NEED

It saves a lot of time and trouble to have the right tools to hand before you start any job. The tools shown here are the ones you'll need to prepare and paint the outside of your house – the walls, metalwork and the woodwork. Some large items (not shown here) which you'll also need are a dust sheet, a large bucket and a ladder or tower platform.

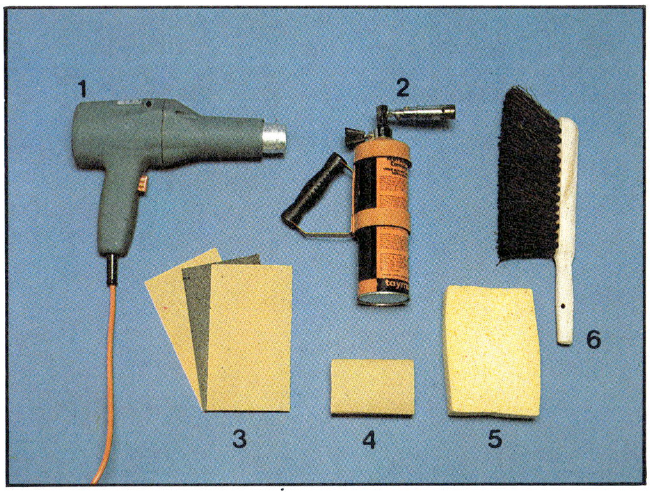

1 Hot air electric stripper for stripping unsound paintwork.
2 Gas blow lamp may be preferred as it saves trailing wires about.
3 A selection of fine, medium and coarse grades of sandpaper for woodwork, and emery paper for metal.
4 Sanding block to hold sandpaper.
5 Sponge for washing down woodwork.
6 Stiff brush for removing dust from masonry.

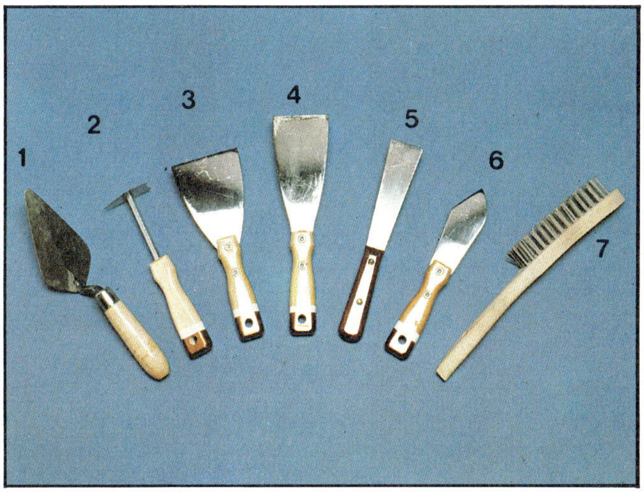

1 Small trowel for repointing brickwork and repairing holes.
2 Combination shavehook for scraping paint from mouldings.
3 Scraper for flat areas of woodwork.
4 Filling knife for filling holes and cracks.
5 Narrow filling knife for tricky areas round window frames.
6 Putty knife for re-puttying windows.
7 Wire brush for removing rust and paint from metal.

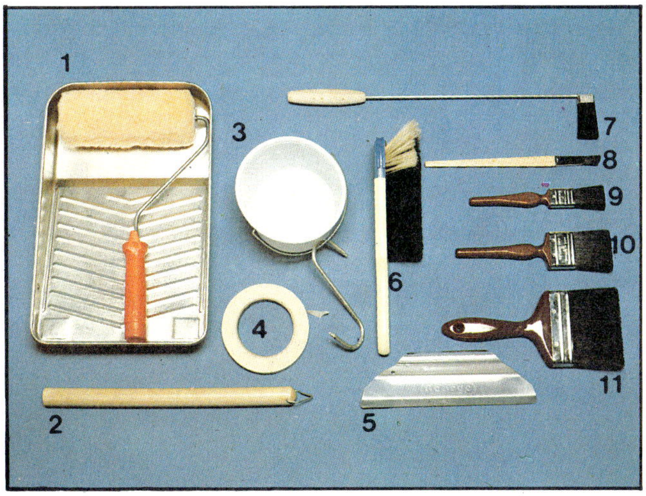

1,2 Long pile roller with extension handle and tray for large areas of masonry.
3 Paint kettle and hook to hold the paint when working on a ladder.
4,5 Masking tape and shield protect areas you want unpainted.
6 Banister brush for painting rough textured surfaces.
7,8,9,10 A selection of brushes for wood and metalwork.
11 Wide brush for smooth surfaces.

EXTERIOR PAINTING preparation

Whether you like it or not, preparing the outside of your house before painting it is a job that has to be done. If you provide a sound surface the paint will last much longer.

If your house is in good order and has been decorated regularly, then the paintwork may need no more than a quick wash down and a light sanding before it's ready for re-painting. But if your house is in a rather worse state than this, take some time now to make a really good job of the preparation and you'll have a much easier time in the future. The preparation may seem rather time-consuming, but don't be tempted to miss out any of the steps. Properly applied, paint will protect your house for several years, but it won't stick to an unsound surface.

The most convenient order of working is to start at the top of the house and work down, and to do all the preparation before you start to paint so that dust and grit won't fall on wet paint. When working at a height, make sure the ladder or platform is firm and secure.

Gutters and downpipes

Gutters manage to trap a surprising quantity of dirt and old leaves, so clear this out first. It's a good idea to check that the gutter is at a regular slope towards the nearest downpipe. You can easily check this by pouring a bucket of water into one end and seeing if it all drains away. If puddles form, you'll need to unscrew some of the gutter brackets and adjust the level of the gutter until the water flows away freely. Check all the joints for leaks and if you do find any, seal them with a mastic compound applied with a gun.

Plastic gutters need little maintenance, and they don't need painting. But if you want to change their colour, simply clean them thoroughly and wipe them over with a rag dipped in white spirit or turps to remove any grease spots before starting to paint. There's no need for a primer or undercoat, but you may need two top coats for even coverge.

Metal gutters and pipes need more attention as all rust has to be removed. Scrape off flaking paint first, then use a wire brush and emery paper to remove the rust. A wire brush attachment on an electric drill would make the cleaning easier (but wear a mask and goggles while using one). You can buy an anti-rust chemical from paint shops which is useful for badly rusted metalwork. It works by turning iron oxide (rust) into phosphate of iron which is inert and can be painted over. In any case, prime all bare metal immediately with either a red lead primer or a zinc chromate metal primer. Metal primers contain a rust-inhibitor which protects the metal against further corrosion, so don't miss them out. If the gutters and pipes are in good condition with no sign of rust, simply wash them down and sand the surface lightly to key it ready for repainting.

Fascias and barge boards

Fascias and barge boards run along the top of a wall just below the roof. Fascias support the guttering below pitched roofs and edge flat ones, while barge boards are fitted beneath the roof tiles on gable ends. Because they are so high up, don't worry too much about their appearance; the main consideration is protection as they are in such an exposed position. Clean out well behind the gutters as damp leaves or even bird's nests can be lodged there. Then, using a wide scraper, remove all loose flaking paint, sand down the whole board surface and prime the bare patches. Fill holes and cracks with an exterior-grade filler or waterproof stopping and smooth it level while still damp using a filler knife. You can prime the filler when it's dry.

Walls

The main surface materials and finishes used on the outside of your house are brick, stone, wood and render.

Walls of brick and stone, especially when weathered, have a beauty all of their own and don't really need painting. But the surface can become cracked and dirty and a coat of paint will cover up repairs that don't match the original surface, and protect the wall from further damage. Examine the pointing and, if it has deteriorated, rake out the damaged parts and re-point with fresh mortar. Use a mixture of about 1 part cement to 4 parts of fine sand, or buy a bag of ready-mixed mortar. Use a small trowel and try to match the original pointing in the surrounding brickwork. Don't worry about hairline cracks as these will easily be covered by the paint. The white crystalline deposit which sometimes appears on brickwork is known as efflorescence. It is caused by water-soluble salts in the brick being brought to the surface, and should be brushed off with a dry brush. Don't try to wash it off as this will only make it worse.

The main types of render are plain, roughcast and pebbledash. Plain render can be applied to give a smooth finish or a textured 'Tyrolean' finish, for example. Roughcast consists of pebbles mixed with mortar before application, and with pebbledash the pebbles are thrown on while the mortar is still wet. Pebbledash deteriorates more quickly than the other types of render as, over the years, differences in rates of expansion between each pebble and the surrounding mortar may result in small surface cracks causing the pebbles to become loose and fall out. Paint will bind in the pebbles and protect small cracks.

PREPARING THE WALLS

1 *Before painting an exterior wall, brush it down well to remove any loose material. Start at the top and use a fairly stiff brush.*

2 *Kill mould and algae with a solution of 1 part bleach to 4 parts water. Leave for two days, then wash down and brush off.*

3 *Rusty metal and leaky gutters can easily cause stains, so cure the leaks and clean and prime all metal first. Sterilise the stain and brush down.*

4 *Holes in the wall are often created when old downpipe brackets are removed. Brush them out well and damp the surface with a little water.*

5 *Fill the hole with a sand and cement mixture using a small trowel. Small bags of ready-mixed mortar are ideal for jobs of this size.*

6 *If the wall is powdery or highly porous, or if a cement-based paint has been used previously, seal the surface with a stabilising primer.*

Ready Reference

CHOOSE THE RIGHT PRIMER

Different materials require different primers; be sure to choose the right type.

Wood

softwood & hardwood	wood primer or acrylic primer
resinous wood	aluminium wood primer

Metal

iron and steel	calcium plumbate primer, zinc chromate primer or red lead primer
galvanised iron	
(new)	calcium plumbate primer
(old)	calcium plumbate or zinc chromate primer
aluminium	zinc chromate primer
brass, copper and lead	none necessary: allow new lead to weather

Masonry etc

brick, stone,	stabilising primer
concrete & render	alkali-resisting primer, acrylic primer

Other materials

asbestos	stabilising primer, alkali-resisting primer or acrylic primer
bitumen-coated wood	aluminium wood primer
bitumen-coated metal	aluminium spirit-based sealer

PROPERTIES AND COVERAGE

Where there is a choice of suitable primers, it's often helpful to know something more about each type. For instance, many primers are toxic and you should choose a non-toxic one if you're painting anything in a child's room.

- Acrylic primer – white or pastel shades, water-based, quick drying, non-toxic, 13-18m² (140-190sq ft) per litre.
- Alkali-resisting primer – needs two coats on very porous surfaces, non-toxic, 3-10m² (30-110sq ft) per litre.
- Aluminium wood primer – dull metallic grey, self-knotting, non-toxic, 16m² (170sq ft) per litre.
- Calcium plumbate primer – off-white, rust inhibiting, toxic, 8-12m² (90-130sq ft) per litre.
- Lead-free wood primer – white or pink, non-toxic, 10-12m² (110-130sq ft) per litre.
- Red lead primer – bright red, rust inhibiting, only for exterior use, toxic, 12-17m² (130-180sq ft) per litre.
- Lead-based wood primer – white or pink, only for exterior use, toxic, 12-14m² (130-150sq ft) per litre.
- Zinc chromate primer – yellow, rust inhibiting, non-toxic, 11m² (120sq ft) per litre.

PREPARING THE WOODWORK

1 *Start preparing the woodwork by scraping off all the loose flaking paint. Large areas of unsound paint are better if stripped completely.*

2 *Sand and prime all the bare wood, taking care to work the primer well into cracks and any exposed end grain, then leave the surface to dry.*

3 *Where joints have opened up, scrape off the paint and rake out the gap with a knife or shavehook. Clean out all the loose debris.*

TIP

4 *Small cracks can be filled with putty, but use exterior-grade filler or waterproof stopping for larger cracks and holes.*

5 *Gaps often appear between the window frame and the wall. Fill these with a mastic compound to provide a continuous water-tight seal.*

6 *Make sure the drip groove underneath the window sill is clear of paint, then thoroughly sand down the whole of the window frame.*

REPLACING OLD PUTTY

1 *Old, damaged putty must be raked out. Scrape old paint from the glass, and clean the glass with methylated spirit to remove any grease spots.*

2 *Work the putty in your hands until it has an even consistency. If it's too oily, roll it on newspaper first. Press it firmly into the gap.*

3 *Smooth the new putty level with the old using a putty knife, then run a soft brush over it to make a water-tight seal with the glass.*

TREATING KNOTS

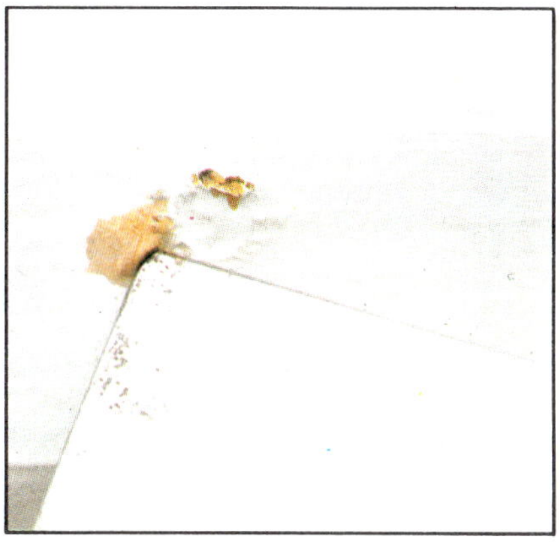

1 Active knots like this ooze out a sticky resin which quickly breaks through the paint surface, leaving a sticky and unsightly mess.

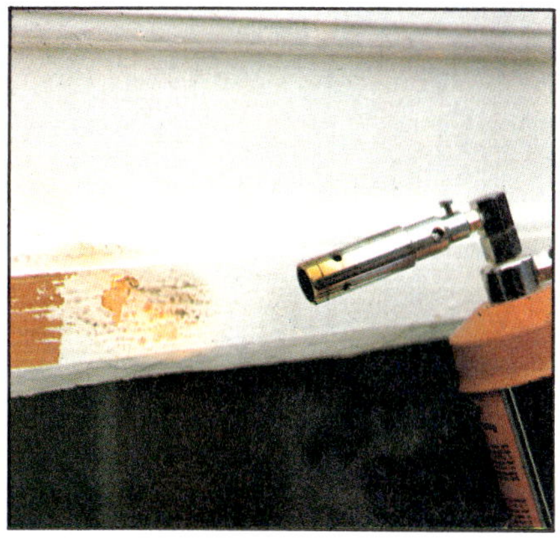

2 The paint must first be stripped off to expose the knot. Use any method of stripping, and scrape the paint off with a shavehook or scraper.

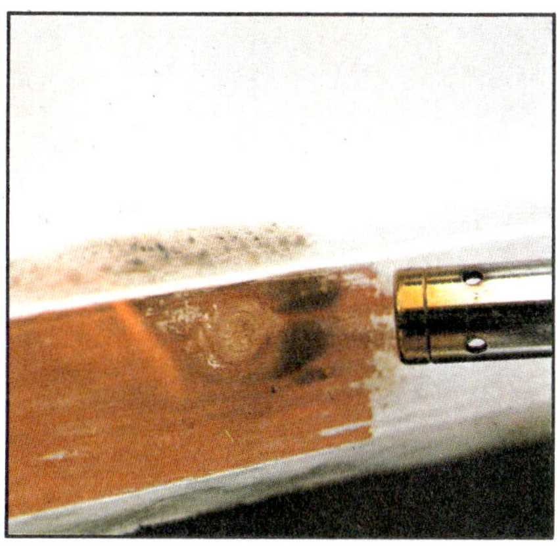

3 Use a blow-torch to heat the knot until the resin bubbles out. Scrape off the resin and repeat until no more of it appears.

4 Sand the knot with fine glasspaper, then wipe over the area with knotting applied with a soft cloth. Prime the wood when it has dried.

When repairing any of these surfaces, try and achieve the same finish as the original, or as near as you can, so that when it's repainted the repair won't be too noticeable. Stop up cracks with mortar, using a mix of 1 part cement to 5 parts sand. Chip away very wide cracks until you reach a firm edge, then undercut this to provide a good key for the new mortar. Dampen the surface, then stop up with a trowel. Use a float if the surface is plain, or texture the surface to match the surrounding area. Where the rendering is pebble-dash, throw on pebbles with a small trowel while the mortar is still wet, then press them into the mortar lightly with a flat piece of wood.

Mould and stains

If there's any sign of mould or algae on the wall, treat this next. Mix up a solution of 1 part household bleach to 4 parts water and paint this on the affected area. Be generous with the solution and cover the area well. Leave for 48 hours for the bleach to kill off all the growth, then wash off thoroughly and brush down with a stiff brush.

Rusty gutters, pipes and metal fittings can all cause stains if rusty water drips down the wall. So cure any leaks first and clean and prime all metal to ensure there's no trace of rust. Mould and algae thrive on damp walls; even if you can't actually see any growth on a damp patch, there may be some spores lurking there, so you should make absolutely sure that you sterilise all stains with the bleach solution just to make sure.

Dusty or chalky walls

All walls, whether dusty or not, should be brushed down thoroughly to remove any loose material. But if, after brushing, the wall is still dusty or chalky, if a cement-based paint was used previously to decorate it, or if the wall is porous, you'll have to brush on a stabilising solution. This will bind together loose particles to allow the paint to stick, and it will seal a porous surface and stop paint from being sucked in too much. The stabiliser also helps to waterproof the wall and you can paint it on as an extra layer of protection whether it's really necessary or not. Most stabilisers are colourless, but off-white stabiliser/primers are available and this would be a good choice if you were planning to paint your house in a light colour, as it could save one coat of the finishing colour. These off-white stabilisers, however, are not recommended for use on surfaces painted with a cement-based paint.

Stabilisers must be painted on a dry wall and should be left to dry for 24 hours before painting on the top coat. Don't paint if rain is expected. Clean your brush in white spirit or turps as soon as you stop work.

Timber cladding

If the cladding or weatherboarding is bare and you want to leave the natural wood surface showing, it should be treated with a water-repellent wood preservative to give protection against damp penetration and decay. The preservative is available clear or pigmented with various colours.

If the wood has been varnished, scrape off the old varnish and sand down well, following the grain of the wood. Fill cracks and holes with plastic wood or a tinted stopper to match the colour of the wood.

If you wish to paint the surface you'll have to wait a year or so for the water-repellent agents in the preservative to disperse before priming with an aluminium wood primer.

Woodwork

If the paintwork on the windows is in good condition all you need do is give them a wash and a light sanding. If the paint is cracked and flaking, a little more preparation is needed. To check if the paint surface needs stripping, lay on a piece of sticky tape and see if it lifts off any paint. Occasional chipped or blistered portions can be scraped off and cut back to a firm edge. As long as the edge is feathered smooth with glasspaper, it shouldn't show too much. If previous coatings are too thick for this treatment, build up the surface with outdoor grade hard stopping until it is just proud of the surrounding paint, then sand level when it's dry. Don't allow the stopping to extend too far over the edge of the damage or it'll be difficult to sand it smooth.

There comes a time, however, when the condition of the old coating has become so bad that complete stripping is advisable.

A blow-torch or an electric hot air stripper are the quickest tools to use. Start at the bottom softening the paint, and follow up immediately with a scraper. Hold the scraper at an angle so the hot paint doesn't fall on your hand, and don't hold it above the flame or it may become too hot to hold. Try not to concentrate the flame too long on one part or you're likely to scorch the wood.

PREPARING METAL

1 *Metal pipes and gutters are often in a very bad state of repair and need a lot of preparation. Scrape off all the old flaking paint first.*

2 *Brush well with a wire brush to remove all traces of rust. Badly rusted pipes should be treated with an anti-rust chemical.*

3 *Hold a board or a piece of card behind the pipe to keep paint off the wall, and paint on a metal primer, covering every bit of bare metal.*

4 *A small paint pad on a long handle is a useful tool for painting behind pipes, especially when they are very close to the wall.*

though this rarely matters on exterior woodwork which will be over-painted again. Always be extremely careful when using a blow-torch, and keep a bucket of water or sand nearby in case something does catch fire. A chemical paint stripper is the best method to use near glass in case the glass cracks under the heat of a blow-torch.

Knots, putty and holes

Check the woodwork for any live knots which are oozing out resin. If you find any, strip off the paint over them and then play a blow-torch or electric hot air stripper over them to burn out the resin. Sand lightly and treat with knotting, then prime when dry.

You should also check the putty fillet round each pane of glass, and if any has disintegrated, rake it out with an old knife. Then sand and prime the wood and bed in new putty using a putty knife. Use linseed oil putty on wood and metal glazing or all purpose putty on metal-framed windows. Smooth the putty with a damp cloth and leave it for about a week before painting.

Rake out any cracks in the wood and cut back wood which is starting to rot. If a large amount of wood is rotten – usually along the bottom edge of a sash window – a larger repair is needed. This could involve replacing a section or all of the window. Prime the bare wood, working the primer well into cracks and end grain as this is where the weather gets in. Small cracks can be filled with putty, but larger ones should be filled with exterior grade hard stopping or filler. Sand level when dry and spot-prime. Gaps between the window frame and wall should be filled with a flexible, waterproof, mastic compound applied with a special gun.

Finally, sand down the whole of the woodwork to make it ready for repainting.

New doors and windows

New wooden windows and doors may already have a coat of pink primer applied at the factory, but it's best not to rely on this for complete protection. Knots, for instance, will rarely have been properly treated, and the primer film will have been damaged here and there in transit. So sand down the whole surface, treat any knots with knotting compound and apply another coat of wood primer overall. It may be advisable to paint doors while they're lying flat; certainly it's vital to paint the top and bottom edges before you hang them in place. It's very important to paint the bottom as rain and snow can easily penetrate unpainted wood causing it to swell and rot. Paint also protects the wood against attack from woodworm.

Metal and plastic windows

Metal doors and windows should be treated in the same way as metal pipes and gutters. So sand them down and make sure all rust is removed before priming. Aluminium frames can be left unpainted, but if you do want to paint them you must first remove any surface oxidation which shows as a fine white deposit. Use a scraper or wire brush, but go very gently and try not to scratch the surface. Prime with a zinc chromate primer. Plastic window frames should not be painted.

Galvanised iron and asbestos

You're likely to find galvanised iron used as corrugated iron roofing, gutters and down-pipes. The zinc coating on galvanised iron is to some extent 'sacrificial', so that if a small patch becomes damaged, the surrounding zinc will, in time, spread over to cover the damage. But this weakens the coating and an application of paint will prolong its life. If the galvanising is new and bright, simply clean it with a rag dipped in white spirit or turps to remove any grease, and apply a calcium plumbate primer. If it's old and grey-looking, first remove any existing paint by rubbing lightly with a wire brush, trying not to scratch the surface. Then clean with white spirit or turps and apply zinc chromate primer.

Asbestos is often used for guttering, fascia boards, as walls on out-houses and as corrugated sheeting for roofs. Asbestos is a very dangerous material and for this reason great care should be taken when dealing with it. It'll probably need cleaning before painting and the only safe way is to wet it thoroughly first and scrub it down with a scrubbing brush. Be sure to wear rubber gloves and a face mask. Leave it to dry, then prime it with a stabilizing primer, an alkali-resisting primer, or simply a coat of thinned-down emulsion paint. Asbestos is very porous, so always paint both sides of any asbestos sheet to prevent damp penetrating from the back.

EXTERIOR PAINTING
completing the job

The first two parts of this article described how to prepare the outside of your house to make it ready for repainting. This last part shows you the best way to paint the walls, pipes, windows and doors to give a professional look to your home.

If you have completed all the cleaning, repairs and preparation on the outside of your house, and if the weather has been dry for the past couple of days and looks settled for a while, you are now ready to start painting. Tackle the painting in more or less the same order as the preparation, starting at the top and working downwards.

Gutters, fascias and barge boards

If you have plastic gutters and want to paint them, simply apply a thin coat of gloss paint to the outside surface. This is the only case outside where paint is used purely for decoration rather than protection. Iron gutters can be painted on the inside with a bituminous paint as this will provide a waterproof coating and protect the iron. Paint the outside of gutters and downpipes with the usual gloss paint system. You'll need a small paint pad or crevice brush to get into the narrow gaps at the back of gutters and pipes. Protect the fascia with a piece of board held behind the guttering. Don't miss out these awkward bits as this is where the rust will start up again. You can use bitumen paint on the inside of asbestos gutters too, but it's best to use

TEXTURED WALLS

1 *Use a 'banister' brush or 'dust pan' brush for painting rough-textured finishes such as pebbledash or a randomly-textured finish.*

2 *Paint brickwork with a well-loaded old brush. Small cracks are bridged by the paint, but larger cracks have to be filled first with exterior filler.*

3 *Alternatively, use a roller on brick to give a thicker coat of paint and a slightly textured finish. Special rollers give even deeper textures.*

emulsion paint rather than solvent-based gloss ones on the outside. Asbestos is porous and needs to be able to 'breathe'. Gloss paint would trap moisture within the asbestos, and this would eventually cause the paint to blister.

Fascias and barge boards are so exposed that it's best to give them an extra coat of gloss. You'll need your crevice brush or paint pad again to paint behind the gutters.

Walls

There is a wide range of paints available for exterior walls, and full information is usually available from suppliers. As for tools, a 100mm (4in) brush is the easiest size to handle; anything larger would put too much strain on the wrist. An alternative is a long-pile roller which has the advantage of being much quicker to use – about three times quicker than a brush. An extra long-pile roller is needed for roughcast or pebbledash; choose one with a pile 32mm (1¼in) deep, or use a banister brush instead. Use a cheap disposable brush or roller for cement paints as they are almost impossible to clean afterwards.

A large plastic bucket or paint kettle is essential when working up a ladder. Stir the paint thoroughly first, then pour some into the bucket until it's about one third full. If you're using a roller, use a special roller tray with a large paint reservoir, or else stand a short plank in the bucket (see step-by-step photographs, page 435) to allow you to load the roller evenly.

Hook the bucket or tray onto a rung of the ladder with an S-hook to leave both hands free. Lay a dust sheet below to catch any drips and you're ready to start.

Application

Start at the top of the wall and paint a strip across the house. Work from right to left if you're right-handed, and left to right if you're left-handed. Be sure to secure the ladder to prevent it slipping and allow a three-rung overlap at the top.

Use a brush to cut in under the eaves or fascia boards and to paint round obstacles, then fill in the larger areas with a brush or roller. Paint an area only as large as you can comfortably manage and don't lean out too far, your hips should remain between the ladder's stiles at all times.

If you have an awkward area which is too far away to reach, push a broom handle intc the hollow handle of the roller, or buy a special extension handle. Protect pipes by wrapping them in newspaper, and mask any other items you don't want to paint. Leave an uneven edge at the bottom of each patch so the join won't be too noticeable, then move the ladder to the left (or right) and paint another strip alongside the first. The principle is always to keep working to the longest wet edge so the joins won't show. When you've done the top series of strips, lower the ladder and paint another series across the middle. Lower the ladder again or work from the ground to do another series along the bottom. Working across the house like this means you have to alter the ladder height the least number of times.

Woodwork

You can choose either a non-drip gloss or a runny gloss for the exterior woodwork. The non-drip jelly paints combine the properties of undercoat and finishing coat so a separate undercoat is not required. But this single coat won't be as long-lasting as the undercoat-plus-runny-gloss system and you'll have to apply two or three coats to build up a thick enough paint film to give adequate outside protection. Inside, however, one coat of non-drip paint would be quite sufficient.

The sequence of painting all jointed woodwork – windows, doors and frames – is determined by the method of construction. In nearly all cases the rails (horizontal bars) are tenoned into mortises cut into the stiles (uprights). Therefore, you should paint the rails and cross bars first, then deal with the stiles. By painting in this way, any overlaps of paint from the rails and bars are covered up and leave a neater finish. An even edge on the glass is best achieved freehand, but if you doubt the steadiness of your touch, use a paint guard or masking tape. Bring the paint onto the glass for up to 3mm (⅛in) to protect the edge of the putty. If you are using masking tape, remove it shortly after painting round each pane; the paint may be peeled off if it is left to harden completely before the tape is removed.

When a visitor calls at your house, he'll stand face to face with your front door and have nothing to do but examine it while he awaits your answer. So it's here you should put in your best work. Remove all the door furniture such as knobs, knockers, locks, keyhole covers and letterbox. Prepare the woodwork carefully and wipe it down with a tackrag (a soft cloth impregnated with a sticky varnish) to collect any remaining dust. Tack-rags are obtainable from any good paint shop. Use a perfectly clean brush, preferably one that has been used before so that no loose bristles will come adrift. Wedge the door ajar and cover the floor with a dust cloth or old newspapers. Use paint which doesn't need straining, and pour about 50mm (2in) into a small container or paint kettle.

All coats of paint should follow the grain of the wood. Don't attempt to cross-hatch – that is, apply a primer in one direction, undercoat at right angles and finishing coat in the direction of the primer. If you do, you'll get a criss-cross effect when the paint dries which produces a poor finish.

Ready Reference

HOW MUCH MASONRY PAINT?

The spreading power of masonry paints varies according to the porosity and texture of the surface. Roughcast, for instance could take twice as much paint as smooth render. These spreading rates are usually given on the side of the paint tin but in general the coverage is:

- smooth surfaces – 6 to 10m² (65 to 110sq ft) per litre
- lightly textured surfaces – 4 to 6m² (44 to 65sq ft) per litre
- pebbledash, roughcast and Tyrolean – 3 to 4m² (33 to 44sq ft) per litre.

CALCULATING THE AREA

To estimate the area of a house wall, simply measure out its length and multiply by the eaves height. Only allow for window area if this is over one fifth of total wall area.

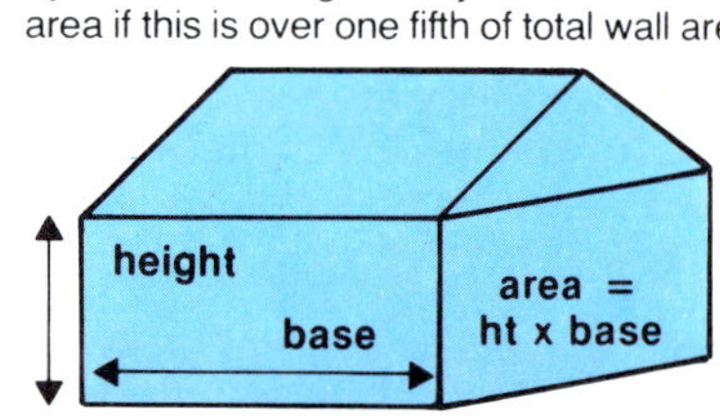

- if you don't know the height, measure the length of the lowest whole section of a downpipe and multiply this by the number of sections making up the complete pipe drop
- for triangular areas, measure the base of the triangle, multiply by the height and divide the answer by two.

$$\text{area} = \frac{\text{ht x base}}{2}$$

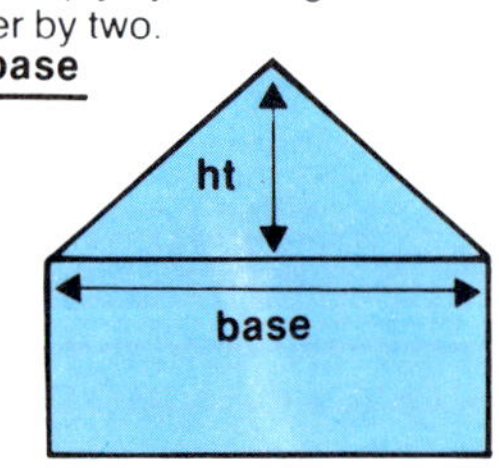

TIP: CLEANING BRICKWORK

Paint splashes from previous careless work can be removed with a chemical paint remover. The paste type is best as it won't run down the wall. This will only strip off the surface paint, however, and some will have soaked into the brick. You may be able to remove this with a wire brush, but if not, apply a poultice of whiting and ammonia kept in position with a piece of polythene taped down at the edges. This will leave a light patch which can be disguised by rubbing with a piece of old, dirty, broken brick. By the time the brick dust has been washed out by rain, natural weathering will have evened out the tone.

PAINTING WALLS

1 *A roller is much quicker to use than a brush, but make sure you have a large enough bucket to dip the roller in. Fill this about ⅓ full.*

TIP

2 *Cut a short plank of wood to the same width as the roller and put it in the bucket so you can load the roller evenly by pressing against it.*

3 *When painting the house wall, start at the top right hand corner (if you are right-handed) and use a brush to cut in round the edges.*

4 *Using the roller, cover a strip on your right-hand side. Don't lean over too far and only make the strip as long as you can easily manage.*

5 *Move the ladder to the left and paint another strip by the first, without overlapping too much. Touch in round obstacles with a brush.*

6 *Using the brush again, carefully paint round the window. Try to leave a neat edge with the woodwork and wipe off any splashes with a damp cloth.*

7 *Continue painting a strip at a time from right to left, then lower the ladder and paint a further series of strips until the wall is covered.*

TIP

8 *Protect pipes by wrapping old newspaper round them and securing it with adhesive tape. Use a brush to paint the wall behind the pipes.*

9 *Be very careful when painting the bottom edge of the wall, and don't load the brush too thickly or paint will run onto the path.*

Ready Reference

HOW MUCH GLOSS PAINT?

The coverage of a litre of gloss paint depends on several factors, including the smoothness of the surface and whether it is interrupted by edges and mouldings. Also, a lot depends on the painter's technique. However, as a general guide, for one litre of paint:

- runny gloss covers $17m^2$ (180sq ft)
- non-drip gloss covers $13m^2$ (140sq ft).

CALCULATING AREAS

It would be very difficult to calculate the area of every bit of wood and metal you wanted to paint. But you need to make a rough estimate so you'll know how much paint to buy. The following examples are intended as a rough guide and they should give you an idea of how much paint you'll need, assuming you're using **runny gloss** and you give everything **two coats of paint.** If you're using non-drip gloss you'll have to buy about 25% more paint:

- a panelled front door will take ⅓ litre (½ pint)
- a flush door will take about ⅕ litre (⅓ pint)

3 doors/litre
5 doors/litre

- a sash window, about 2x1m (6ft 6in x 3ft 3in) with an ornate frame will take about ⅙ litre (¼ pint)
- a modern picture window of the same size with a plain frame will take only ⅛ litre (⅕ pint)

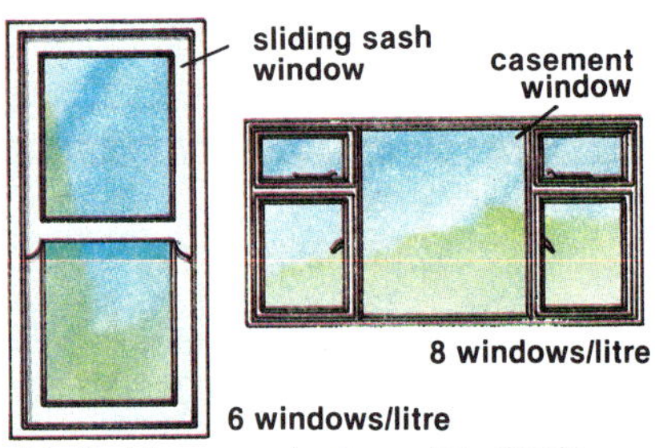

8 windows/litre
6 windows/litre

- to find the area of a downpipe, simply measure round the pipe and multiply by the height, then add a little for clips and brackets. For two coats of paint, one litre will cover 18m (60ft) of 150mm (6in) diameter pipe and 27m (90ft) of 100mm (4in) pipe.

PAINTING WINDOWS

1 *Start to apply undercoat at the top of the window. Prop the window open, tape up the stay and paint the frame rebates first.*

2 *Paint the rebates on open casements next. If you get paint on the inside surface, wipe it off immediately with a cloth dipped in white spirit or turps.*

3 *Close the window slightly and paint the area along the hinged edge. You may need to use a narrow brush (called a fitch) to reach this part.*

4 *A neat paint line on the glass is best achieved free-hand, but if you find this too difficult, use a paint shield or apply masking tape.*

5 *The general order of painting is to do the cross bars (rails) first, followed by the uprights (stiles) and then the window sill.*

6 *When the undercoat is dry, sand it down with a fine grade glasspaper, then apply the top coat in the same order as the undercoat.*

PAINTING SEQUENCES

Windows and panelled doors are tricky areas to paint properly but you shouldn't have any trouble if you follow the correct sequence of painting shown here.

Start with the rebate on the frame (1), then paint the outside edge of the window (2). Do the putty (3) next, followed by the glazing bars (4) and the rails and stiles (5 to 8). Paint the frame (9 to 13) last.

Wedge the door ajar and paint the frame (1 to 3), the hinged edge of the frame and door. Do mouldings and panels next (4 to 13) followed by the muntins (14,15), the rails (16 to 19) and finally the stiles (20, 21).

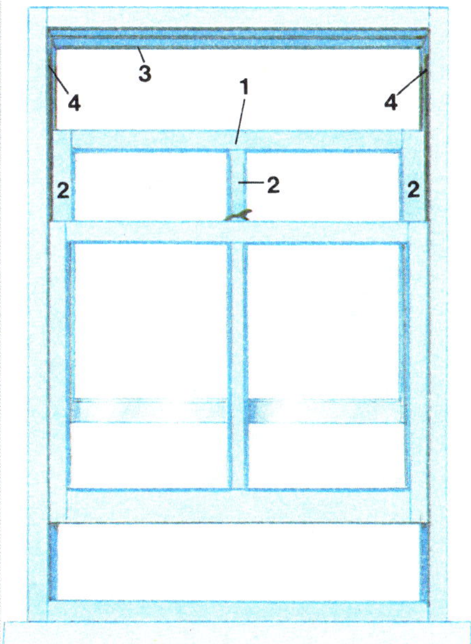

Sliding sash windows need to be painted in two stages. Pull down the top sash and paint the top rail of the inside sash (1) and the sides as far as you can go (2). Do the runners at the top of the frame (3) and a short way down the outer runner(4). Almost close the windows, then paint the bottom runners (5,6), and the remainder

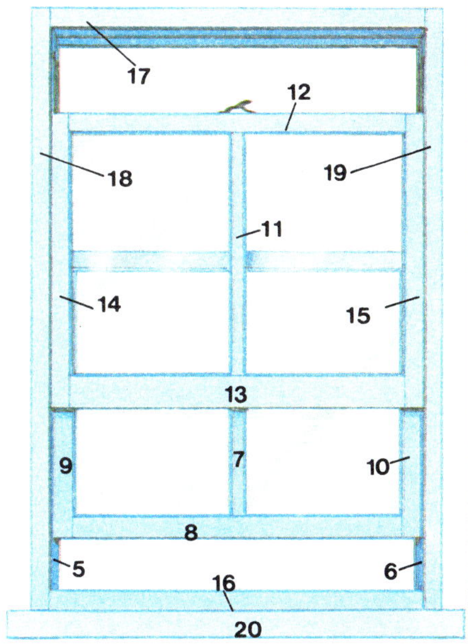

of the bottom sash to meet the other paint (7 to 10). Paint the whole of the top sash including the bottom edge (11 to 15) and finally the window frame (16 to 20). This view shows the interior of the window: for the exterior the sequence is identical except of course, that you start with the top sash.

Deal with the door frame first (the top, then the sides) so that any splashes can be wiped off an unpainted surface immediately. Then do the door itself, following the sequence of painting shown on this page. Don't put too thick a coat on the inner edge of the door frame because although gloss paint dries fairly quickly, it won't oxidise (ie, thoroughly harden) for about a week. So in that period, when you close the door, paint may 'set-off' from the frame onto the door, producing a vertical streak an inch or so from the door's edge. A good idea to prevent this is to insert a thin strip of polythene sheeting round the door's edge after the paint has become touch dry, and leave it until the paint has thoroughly hardened.

If you want to apply two finishing coats, wait at least 12 hours but not more than a week between coats. There's no need to sand down between coats because the solvent used in modern gloss paints is strong enough to dissolve the surface of the previous coat and so to ensure a firm bond between the two layers.

Weatherboards

Weatherboards and timber cladding can be left in their natural state as long as you treat them with a wood preservative, and you can use wood stains to enhance or change their colour. If you prefer a glossy finish, use a suitable external varnish such as an oil-resin varnish (marine varnish), rather than a one-pack polyurethane varnish which can prove brittle and difficult to over-coat in future. If you wish to paint the wood you'll have to apply one coat of wood primer, followed by an undercoat and two finishing coats of gloss.

Galvanised iron and asbestos

Because it is waterproof, bituminous paint is best for galvanised or asbestos roofs. In addition to the customary black it can be obtained in shades of red, green or brown to simulate or match tiles. These colours are more expensive than black and may have to be ordered specially from a builders' merchant. Bitumen soon loses its gloss and its surface tends to craze under a hot sun. But that doesn't matter as roofs are not usually visible.

Paint the walls of asbestos outhouses with outdoor-grade emulsion in a colour to match the rest of the house. Thin the first coat to allow for the porosity of the asbestos and follow this with a normal second coat. Apply emulsion on the interior surface as well to minimise moisture absorption. Galvanised iron on vertical surfaces should be painted with gloss paint.

When painting corrugated surfaces, give the high parts a preliminary touch-up with paint, leave it to dry and then paint the whole lot. If you apply paint all over in one go it will tend to flow from high to low parts, giving an uneven coating.

SPRAYING EXTERIOR WALLS

Painting the exterior walls of your home with a brush or roller can be a fairly time-consuming job. But with a properly-used spray gun you can soon finish the job.

Painting the exterior walls of your house with a brush is hard and tedious work; even if you switch to a roller, things will not be a lot simpler. To avoid this drudgery, you can use an alternative method: you can spray the paint onto the walls. It's quicker, easier and, because it tends to give a more even coverage, should give more durable results, particularly on rough surfaces where brushes and rollers tend to leave tiny gaps through which moisture can penetrate to undermine the paint film.

If the only experience you have had of spray painting is retouching scratches on a car with an aerosol, then spraying houses may seem very novel. But it isn't a new idea. Specialist contractors have been doing it for years, though their advertising has tended to concentrate on the fact that they use special, very durable paints. In fact you'll find that you don't need special paint; so long as it's of a type suitable for exterior use.

Types of spray gun

Although you don't need special paint, you do need costly special equipment: you need a spray gun. Fortunately, these are widely available at a modest rental from good local tool hire shops. The important thing is that you choose the right kind of spraying equipment for the paint you wish to use. Choosing the gun can, in fact, be rather complicated – there are so many different kinds available – so you could tell the hire shop what you want to spray and leave the decision to them.

The simplest type of spraying equipment you are likely to be offered is called an airless spray unit. It is a straightforward pump which takes paint from a container (any container will do) and then squirts it out through a spray nozzle. It is very efficient in terms of labour and use of materials and very fast. It is capable of delivering up to 2.25 litres (4 pints) of paint per minute (a practised operator would normally cover about 240sq m/262sq yd in an hour). This type of gun does, however, have a few drawbacks. To begin with the paint must be thinned before it can be sprayed, which may mean applying an extra coat in order to achieve the required coverage and colour density. Also, with the pump at ground level, problems may arise when you are working on buildings higher than about two storeys. The machine may not be powerful enough to pump the paint that distance. In addition, this type of unit will not handle paints containing fillers.

An alternative is a machine that works a bit like an old-fashioned scent spray: the air flow is provided by a compressor which may or may not be rented out as a separate item (if you do have to hire the compressor separately, make sure it is sufficiently powerful for the application you have in mind). Reaching heights with a machine of this type should not be a problem. The only limitation is the length of the hose between the compressor and the spray gun, but many hire shops supply 10m (30ft) hoses. A point here: not all compressor-operated units are the same and you should check that you are using a suitable type. At the bottom end of the scale, you'll find small portable units primarily designed for spraying cars and the like. So long as you use a paint that does not contain fillers, these can be used to spray walls, but since the integral paint container normally has a capacity of less than a litre (1½ pints), you will spend a lot of time running up and down to refill. Larger 'industrial' versions using more powerful compressors are available and these are faster and have feed cups of around 1 litre (1½ pints). They too will only handle ordinary resin- and water-based paints.

If you want to spray on a reinforced paint there are a number of options, with different suppliers calling them by different names. Those able to cope with most ordinary filled exterior paints may have a shoulder-carried, or back-pack style, paint container. Those capable of spraying anything from reinforced paint to very heavy, plaster consistency materials tend to be fed from a gravity feed hopper on top of the spray gun, or from a separate pressurised tank – see step-by-step photographs.

Whatever you decide on, do double-check that the gun is suitable for the material you wish to spray; even if the basic equipment is right for the job a different nozzle may be required. Also make sure you get adequate instructions on using and cleaning the equipment before you take it home. If you damage it or return it dirty, you may lose some or all of your deposit. Again, bear in mind that some compressors are electric and some petrol-driven, but the smaller units are almost always electrically operated (check that you get a 240V model, not a 110V one).

Choosing access equipment

Since the main virtue of spray painting walls is speed, it's only sensible to choose a means of reaching the heights that allows you to get up, down and along with the minimum of fuss. This means that a scaffold tower, even one on castors, although excellent when you are preparing the surface, is not a particularly

PREPARING THE WALLS

1 *Most exterior wall paints will fill hairline cracks when sprayed on. Rake out and fill larger cracks and holes with mortar or exterior-grade filler.*

2 *The paint will not adhere properly to a dusty, crumbly surface. Go over areas like these with a stiff brush to remove dirt and any loose material.*

3 *Where old paint has begun to crack and flake off, use a scraper to remove it from affected areas of the wall. Prime bare areas with paint before spraying.*

4 *Look out for green spots, which are a sign of mould growth. To prevent any further outbreaks, brush on a solution of bleach or apply a proprietary fungicide.*

good choice for spraying unless you have a suitable flat, hard 'road' running right round the area you wish to paint. A step ladder (or possibly two, spanned by a scaffold board) for the lower levels, and a lightweight, aluminium extension ladder for the rest is generally a better bet.

Having said that, you should not, of course, allow speed to take precedence over safety. It's probably true that as there is no physical contact with the wall, you are less likely to push yourself off balance than you would be if using a brush or roller and that as spraying is quick and easy you are less likely to overstretch in order to reach that extra little bit before climbing down and moving the ladder along. But don't take any chances. Always make sure that the ladder is set at the correct angle on a firm, level footing and that it is roped in place at the top. If necessary, spend an hour or two fixing stout hooks at intervals into the top of the wall to make roping off easier. You'll find they come in handy wherever you need to scale a ladder.

Preparing the site

You should thoroughly prepare the surface so it is clean, dry and sound. In particular, fill any cracks which are wider than about a millimetre with mortar, and check that all rendering is securely adhering to the surface underneath. Also, you should treat dusty surfaces with stabilising primer and kill off any mould or algae using a proprietary fungicide or algicide.

Masking off will normally be your next step (see *Ready Reference*). This can take time and you may feel it rather cancels out the benefits of spraying. This is true to some extent, but wielding a heavy brush can hardly be compared with snipping away at a length of sticky tape. However, it is possible to do

Ready Reference

SUITABLE TYPES OF PAINT

Most paints which are suitable for use on exterior walls can be used for spraying. Water-based paint like exterior emulsion does, however, have the advantage that you use water for thinning and cleaning the equipment and this is obviously cheaper than using white spirit (turps) with other types of paint.

CHOOSING A SPRAY GUN

When you are choosing a spray gun you should check that the gun is suitable for use with the type of paint you will be applying. Some guns are not suitable for use with paint containing filler.

TIP: PROTECT YOURSELF

There will always be some fall-out from a spray gun so you should wear a face mask and protective goggles.

MASKING OFF

You'll normally need to cover up areas you don't want painted like drainpipes, guttering, window frames, glass panes and doors. To protect these surfaces

- cover them with masking tape and polythene sheeting (you could use newspaper but only if you can be sure to paint that section on the same day or early morning dew or overnight rain could ruin your work); also
- don't forget to cover the ground as well, not only to catch the falling spray but also to pick up any drips and spillages when you fill the gun's paint container. Use canvas dust sheets in areas where you will be walking or standing ladders as they are less slippery and, if carefully laid out and weighted down, less of a trip hazard than polythene sheeting. Lightweight polythene, again well weighted down with bricks or other weights, is better when it comes to covering up plants.

CLEAN EQUIPMENT

You may find that the spray equipment, especially the spray nozzle, clogs up with drying paint. You can reduce this nuisance when you are working by

- cleaning up the nozzle from time to time with water or white spirit, depending on the type of paint, picking out any bits that have begun to harden (a safety pin is ideal for this); also
- if you want to take a break, you should clean the equipment as thoroughly as you would when finishing for the day (before you start work again make sure the system is clear of white spirit or water to ensure the spraying will be up to standard).

MASKING OFF

1 *Masking off takes some time, but it's essential that you do it properly. Cover drainpipes with newspapers, working from the bottom up.*

2 *For larger areas such as windows it's easier to use larger sheets (paper is cheaper than polythene). Tape all edges and joins carefully for the best results.*

TIP

3 *To prevent the spray from falling over surrounding areas, it's a good idea to protect the ground at the bottom of the wall with dust sheets.*

SETTING UP THE EQUIPMENT

1 *Make sure you've got all the equipment you need. Then assemble the components; here, start with the gun and paint hose.*

2 *Link the other end of the paint hose to the pressurised paint tank. Then connect the air hose to the turbine and the gun. Tighten all connections fully.*

3 *Fill up the paint tank to the level recommended by the hire company. If thinning is necessary, do it now and then stir the paint thoroughly.*

4 *Fit the lid of the tank back on. When you are sure it's correctly placed, screw it down so the tank is properly sealed and can be pressurised.*

5 *Next, pressurise the container by pumping with the integral pump. Don't exceed the recommended pressure level shown on the gauge.*

TIP

6 *Test the gun by spraying paint onto an old board, and adjust the nozzle on the front of the gun as necessary to give a uniform spray pattern.*

SPRAYING THE WALLS

1 *If you are right-handed, begin at the top right-hand corner (or the top left if you are left-handed). Spray towards a natural break such as a downpipe.*

2 *As soon as you've completed one band of paint you can begin work on the next. Here, the two windows neatly define the next area to be tackled.*

3 *Keep the gun at right angles to the wall surface when you are spraying. Spray over the edges of the masked-off areas; the paper will protect them.*

4 *Before you reach the end of the wall, make sure that you have covered up any adjacent areas which you don't want to be splotched with paint.*

TIP

5 *Remove the masking tape before the paint dries. Otherwise it would be more difficult to remove and you also risk peeling off the paint.*

6 *If your masking-off has been effective there should only be small areas left for you to fill in by hand. A small brush is best for cutting-in work.*

away with masking; though you will still need to protect the ground. All you do is stop spraying when you get too close to whatever it is you don't want painted; normally within 300-600mm (1-2ft). These 'safety zones' can then be painted in using a brush or roller. Do be warned though: a sudden puff of wind or a momentary loss of concentration could have disastrous consequences. If you intend using this technique you should be prepared to have to paint the woodwork and metalwork soon after and to keep some white spirit (turps) or water (according to the type of paint) handy to wipe off any spray that strays onto the window panes.

Spraying technique

The basic technique for spraying walls is to aim to cover the surface with a series of barely overlapping stripes. You should keep the gun moving a constant distance from the surface at a constant speed: slow enough to ensure good coverage and fast enough to avoid the runs that result from applying too much paint. If you don't get a perfect result at the first attempt you can put things right by applying another coat.

Keep on working as blockages may occur if you stop spraying. When you have to stop clean the equipment thoroughly.

Order of work

As when you are brushing on paint, you should follow the sun round the house so your new paintwork won't be exposed to the full blistering heat of the sun until the next day.

It's certainly worth dividing the area into manageable sections using features such as drainpipes and window bays to provide sensible boundaries. This not only gives natural cues for rest breaks but also helps boost morale. Having completed a section, you'll feel you're really getting somewhere.

Similarly, for the sake of comfort and efficiency, tackle each section working down and across, starting at the top right if you are right-handed, top left otherwise. Overstretching is dangerous so climb down and move the ladder.

You'll have to take the weather into account. Don't work in the rain, or if rain is likely within the next few hours, and don't start work if the surface is wet with rain or dew; give it time to dry out. The heat of the sun can damage new paint and will exacerbate the problem of paint drying in the gun so avoid working when the weather is really scorching.

And don't forget the wind. The stiller the day the easier it will be to spray accurately and the less paint you will waste. With a reasonably powerful modern gun, you should be alright working in anything up to a gentle summer breeze, possibly a bit more. But if you have trouble when you first start work, take a rest and try again later.

INDEX

ACKNOWLEDGEMENTS

Photographers: Jon Bouchier, Simon Butcher, Paul Forrester, Simon Gear, Jem Grischotti, Barry Jell, Keith Morris, Karen Norquay, Ian O'Leary, Roger Tuff
Artists: Roger Courthold Associates, Bernard Fallon, Nick Farmer, Val Hill, Trevor Lawrence, Linden Artists, David Pope, Peter Robinson, Mike Saunders, Ian Stephen, Ralph Stobart, Ed Stuart, Craig Warwick, Brian Watson, David Webb, Universal Studios